1996

HISTORIC

DOCUMENTS

OF

1996

1996

HISTORIC
DOCUMENTS
OF
1996

Cumulative Index, 1992–1996

Congressional Quarterly Inc.

Historic Documents of 1996

Editors: Marty Gottron, John Felton, Bruce Maxwell
Production and Associate Editor: Kerry V. Kern
Indexer: Victoria Agee

The Library of Congress cataloged the first issue of this title as follows:

Historic documents. 1972–
    Washington. Congressional Quarterly Inc.

    1. United States — Politics and government — 1945– — Yearbooks.
2. World politics — 1945– — Yearbooks. I. Congressional Quarterly Inc.

E839.5H57   917.3'03'9205   72-97888

ISBN 1-56802-294-8
ISSN 0892-080X

PREFACE

The U.S. presidential election played a significant role in many events during 1996, and not just those in the United States. American policymakers at all levels of government had a keen interest in the outcome of the November elections, and overseas governments were just as interested in knowing who would be at the helm of U.S. foreign policy.

As the year opened, the American political scene was contentious. Congressional Republicans, who had dominated Washington after their dramatic victories in the 1994 elections, miscalculated the extent of their electoral mandate and by early 1996 appeared vulnerable. On the flip side of the coin, President Bill Clinton, who appeared imperiled after the 1994 elections, was making a remarkable political recovery in 1996.

Clinton grew stronger politically as the year progressed, particularly in comparison with the field of Republican candidates. Experienced and highly respected Republican leaders, such as Gov. Pete Wilson of California, Sen. Richard Lugar of Indiana, and former governor Lamar Alexander of Tennessee, failed to catch on with voters in the early Republican primaries and caucuses and dropped out of the running.

By February only two serious contenders remained: Bob Dole, the Senate majority leader, and Patrick Buchanan, a television commentator and former speechwriter. Dole always had been considered the front-runner because of his standing within the Republican party. Buchanan's deeply conservative stands on such issues as abortion and affirmative action won him intense loyalty within the far-right wing of the party but also made him too controversial a candidate to win the nomination. Dole had the nomination locked up by March—the earliest end to a contested race in recent memory. Clinton faced no serious opposition for the Democratic nomination.

In the remaining seven months of the election season Dole constantly lagged behind Clinton in the public opinion polls. Despite his record as a war hero and his decades of service in Washington politics, Dole was unable to make a convincing case to voters why he should take Clinton's place in the White House. Ross Perot, the Texas billionaire, made a second run at the presidency in 1996, this time as the nominee of his newly created Reform party. When the votes were counted, Perot won only 8 percent, far below the 19 percent he pulled in 1992.

How to Use This Book

The documents are arranged in chronological order. If you know the approximate date of the report, speech, statement, court decision, or other document you are looking for, glance through the titles for that month in the table of contents.

If the table of contents does not lead you directly to the document you want, turn to the index at the end of the book. There you may find references not only to the particular document you seek but also to other entries on the same or a related subject. The index in this volume is a five-year cumulative index of *Historic Documents* covering the years 1992–1996. There is a separate volume, *Historic Documents Index, 1972–1995*, which may also be useful.

The introduction to each document is printed in italic type. The document itself, printed in roman type, follows the spelling, capitalization, and punctuation of the original or official copy. Where the full text is not given, omissions of material are indicated by the customary ellipsis points.

During the closing days of the campaign, it seemed possible that Clinton's coattails might enable Democrats to recapture the House of Representatives, but the voters endorsed the continuation of divided government. Republicans managed to hold their majority in the House, although the margin of control was narrowed, and they even picked up two seats in the Senate.

Before members headed out on the campaign trail, Congress enacted several pieces of important legislation with the potential to affect the lives of millions of Americans. Perhaps the most controversial measure was a top-to-bottom overhaul of federal welfare policy. Conservative Republicans drafted and pushed through Congress a bill ending the government's decades-old commitment to provide income support for low-income families and their children. The welfare overhaul also denied federal benefits to immigrants, even those in the country legally. Despite his misgivings about some of the key provisions, President Clinton signed the bill into law.

Democrats won a major legislative victory when Congress voted to raise the minimum wage from $4.25 an hour, the level it had been at since 1991, to $5.15 an hour by October 1997. Passage of the measure was a big political victory for Democrats and their union allies; it was an embarrassment for the Republican congressional leadership, including Bob Dole, who opposed the increase. Democrats initially had thought to use the issue to paint

Republicans as insensitive to the needs of working men and women, but when several House Republicans said they would support the politically popular increase, the Democrats, backed by Clinton, pressed the issue and won handily in both chambers.

Congress also swept aside decades of federal agriculture policy by enacting a Republican-drafted bill replacing crop subsidies with a system of fixed but declining payments to farmers. On a related issue, Congress overcame years of disagreement and inertia and enacted legislation setting new regulations on the use of agricultural pesticides.

For the most part, differences over difficult social issues such as abortion were muted during the 1996 election campaign. One issue that attracted a lot of attention was an initiative on the California ballot that effectively would end most of the state's affirmative action programs. Among the initiative's supporters were Wilson and Dole, who had promised to end federal affirmative action programs if elected president. Similar initiatives had been proposed in several other states, but none had advanced as far as California's Proposition 209. The initiative passed with the support of 54 percent of the state's voters, but it was immediately challenged in court, where a federal district judge issued an injunction against enforcing it. Most observers thought the matter would eventually go to the U.S. Supreme Court.

In several recent cases, the Supreme Court had made clear its distaste for antidiscrimination programs based on race, but so far it had neither ruled all such programs unconstitutional nor set out clear guidelines delineating the circumstances under which consideration of race would be permissible. In its third decision in four years concerning racial gerrymandering, the Court was unable to muster a clear majority for a decisive ruling, leaving open to continued legal challenge those districts deliberately drawn to give majority status to blacks and other minorities.

Families were a main theme of the presidential campaign. The Clinton administration undoubtedly won some votes from parents when it issued regulations making it difficult for teenagers and children to buy cigarettes and sharply curbing cigarette advertising directed at youthful smokers. The number of teenagers who smoke had been increasing for some years, even as the number of adults who smoke decreased. Among other things, the regulations provided that cigarette ads on billboards and in publications with a significant teenage readership be in black-and-white text, with no accompanying images. Cigarette makers were also barred from using the brand name of their cigarettes when sponsoring sporting, cultural, and other events. The major manufacturers immediately challenged the new regulations in federal court as a violation of their right to free speech.

Republicans charged that the administration's campaign against teenage smoking was designed to distract attention from a disturbing set of statistics on teenage drug abuse. According to an annual government survey, the number of adolescents using drugs had more than doubled since 1992, to nearly 11 percent. Most teens and younger children who used illegal drugs used marijuana, but the number using cocaine and hallucinogens was also rising.

Republicans pinned responsibility for the increase on the Clinton administration, which they said had a permissive attitude toward drugs.

Even as the government was taking action to curb cigarette advertising, the liquor industry announced that it was giving up its voluntary ban on advertising its products on television and radio. It said that any ads aired on radio or television would be targeted to adults.

For the fourth year in a row, the incidence of crime in the United States fell, and the crime rate—the number of crimes committed per 100,000 people—dropped to its lowest level since 1985. The government also announced that the rate of deaths caused by cancer had declined in the early 1990s—the first decline in the cancer death rate ever recorded. A decrease in the number of people who smoke was considered the biggest factor in lowering the death rate, but lower alcohol consumption levels, less exposure to the sun, and better diets also contributed to the decline.

Internationally, Russia was the focus of attention for much of the year, as the biggest and most important of the emerging democracies continued to stumble its way through major challenges. At the outset of 1996 it appeared likely that President Boris Yeltsin, who led Russia into a new era of democracy and free markets, had spent his last remaining political capital and would be ousted from office by a resurgent—if somewhat reformed—Communist party. Yeltsin proved to have more resiliency than most people imagined, and in June he handily won the first presidential elections that Russia held as an independent country after the collapse of the Soviet Union. Even so, Yeltsin's health was precarious, and by the end of 1996 the future of Russian democracy was again uncertain.

In a similar vein, peacemaking survived serious challenges during the year in Bosnia and the Middle East. Bosnia was at peace in 1996—no one died in conflict there for the first time since 1992. The process of rebuilding the war-torn and still bitterly divided country was kept on track, if only through constant pressure from outside powers and the unwillingness of any one party to be held responsible for the collapse of the peace agreement.

The United States and its European allies applied pressure to force Radavon Karadicz, the leader of the Bosnian Serbs who had been indicted by the United Nations war crimes tribunal, out of office. That step enabled an election to proceed as planned in September. Bosnians once again gave political power to the same nationalist parties that dragged Bosnia into war in 1992. Despite numerous charges of electoral fraud, UN-appointed monitors certified the validity of the outcome, allowing the peace process to continue.

The fragile peace process between Israel and its Palestinian foes also survived a political challenge when Israeli voters narrowly ousted the Labor party, which negotiated the peace, and installed a right-wing coalition opposed to the concepts underlying that peace. Benjamin Netanyahu, who denounced the Oslo peace accord negotiated in 1993, in June became the first Israeli prime minister elected directly by the voters. Once in office, Netanyahu discovered that it was easier to criticize the peace process than to undo it. Within weeks, many of his political allies were angered by his willingness to meet with Palestinian leader Yasir Arafat and his refusal to back-track on Israel's commitment to give Palestinians control over daily affairs in much of the West Bank.

A sticking point for much of the year was the question of how Israel would keep its promise to give the Palestinians control over most of the West Bank city of Hebron. Several hundred Israeli settlers had moved into Hebron and were demanding that the Israeli government protect them against the Palestinian majority by retaining military control of the city. U.S. envoy Dennis Ross mediated the Hebron dispute for months and at year's end was still trying to bridge the gap.

Negotiations were more successful during 1996 on another long-term proposition: an international treaty banning the testing of nuclear weapons. President Dwight Eisenhower had first proposed the concept in the 1950s, and several limited nuclear testing treaties had gone into effect in the inter-vening four decades. It took the end of the cold war to give life to the idea of a comprehensive ban on nuclear tests. India, which exploded a nuclear device in 1974, tried to block international agreement on such a treaty, but proponents took the measure to the UN General Assembly, which adopted it overwhelmingly in September.

Meanwhile, Senate Republicans derailed, at least for 1996, U.S. ratification of another treaty banning the manufacture, possession, or use of chemical weapons. Concluded in 1993 and signed by President George Bush as one of his last official acts, the treaty had been pending in the Senate and seemed close to approval. Responding to concerns by conservatives about the treaty, Republican presidential nominee Bob Dole used his leverage to block Senate action. As a result, the treaty was to go into effect without the involvement of either the United States or Russia, which had the world's largest arsenals of chemical weapons.

These are but some of the topics of national and international interest chosen by the editors of *Historic Documents of 1996*. This edition marks the twenty-fifth volume of a Congressional Quarterly project that began with *Historic Documents of 1972*. The purpose of this series is to give students, librarians, journalists, scholars, and others convenient access to documents on a wide range of topics that set forth some of the most important issues of the year. In our judgment, the official statements, news conferences, speeches, special studies, and court decisions presented here will be of last-ing interest.

Each document is preceded by an introduction that provides background information and, when relevant, an account of continuing developments dur-ing the year. We believe these introductions will become increasingly useful as memories of current times fade.

John Felton and Marty Gottron

CONTENTS

January

February

March

May

June

CONTENTS

August

September

October

November

Financial Crisis in the Schools of the District of Columbia

National Cancer Institute on the Decline in Cancer Deaths

CIA-FBI Statement on Nicholson Espionage Case

Proposed Regulations for Air Bags

December

State Department on Refugee Crisis in Central Africa

London Conference Report on Progress in Bosnia

Clinton and Boutros-Ghali on New UN Secretary General

Broadcasters on New Television Rating System

January

FEDERAL DIETARY GUIDELINES
January 2, 1996

In new dietary guidelines released on January 2, the federal government reaffirmed its long-standing recommendation that Americans eat a varied diet high in fruits, vegetables, and whole grains and low in sugar, salt, fat, and cholesterol. For the first time, the government urged Americans to maintain their ideal body weight into old age and stressed the importance of exercise. "The scales are not lying," Donna Shalala, secretary of health and human services, said at a news conference. "When at least one-third of all adults and one-quarter of all children are overweight, we have a weight problem in America." Also for the first time, the guidelines acknowledged that a vegetarian diet could be consistent with good health and that drinking alcohol in moderation could have health benefits.

The guidelines, issued jointly by the Agriculture Department and the Health and Human Services Department, form the basis of federal nutrition policy, including the school lunch program. The food industry also uses the guidelines in its consumer information on the nutritional content of various foods. First issued in 1980, the Dietary Guidelines for Americans *are reviewed and revised every five years in light of new scientific findings on health and nutrition.*

Two health organizations issued their own dietary guidelines in 1996. In September the American Cancer Society warned that eating red meat and drinking alcohol could contribute to certain kinds of cancer, while the American Heart Association urged Americans to meet weekly, rather than daily, nutritional goals.

Moderation in All Things

The government's statement on the health benefits of drinking in moderation might have been the most controversial aspect of the new guidelines. The statement did not recommend that adults drink alcoholic beverages, pointing out that too much alcohol can raise a person's risk of high blood pressure, stroke, heart disease, and certain cancers, as well as contribute to accidents, violence, and suicide. But, the report noted, current evidence indicates that "moderate drinking is associated with a lower risk for coronary disease in some individuals."

If adults drink, the guidelines said, they should do so in moderation— no more than one drink a day for women, two a day for men. A drink is defined as 12 ounces of regular beer, 5 ounces of wine, or 1.5 ounces of 80-proof distilled spirits. The report also listed those who should not drink: children and adolescents, individuals who cannot control the amount they drink, women who are trying to conceive or who are pregnant, people who are planning to drive within the next few hours, and people on medication.

The statement on drinking was a significant departure from the 1990 guidelines, which said that "drinking has no net health benefit." At a news conference releasing the guidelines, Assistant Secretary of Health Dr. Philip Lee noted that in 1990 there was no scientific evidence on the health benefits of drinking. "There was a significant bias in the past against drinking. To move from antialcohol to health benefits is a big change," he said. Dr. Marion Nestle, a member of the advisory committee that revised the guidelines, said the recommendation was "a triumph of science and reason over politics."

If the statement on drinking was the most controversial aspect of the revised guidelines, the statements on weight might be the most difficult for many Americans to follow. Because excess weight can lead to certain cancers, heart disease, stroke, diabetes, and other illnesses, the guidelines said, "most adults should not gain weight" but should try to maintain their ideal body weight throughout life. To do that, people must not only eat a balanced diet, but also increase their physical activity. Shalala said that physical activity did not mean "mandatory marathons" or "Cal Ripken-style workouts," but normal activities that can be fitted easily into most people's daily routine—gardening, brisk walking, using stairs instead of elevators, walking the golf course. The guidelines recommended that Americans engage in at least thirty minutes of moderate physical activity every day.

The Food Guide Pyramid

The guidelines repeated the broad recommendations of earlier reports. Americans should eat a variety of foods, using the Food Guide Pyramid as a guide. The pyramid, issued in 1992, advises people to eat nine to eleven daily servings of grains, such as breads, rice, pasta, and cereal; three to five servings of vegetables; two to three servings of fruit; two to three servings of dairy products; two to three servings of meat, poultry, fish, dry beans, eggs, and nuts; and to consume fats, oils, and sweets "sparingly." (Food Guide Pyramid, Historic Documents of 1992, p. 397)

The guidelines do not recommend that people stop eating meat, but they repeatedly emphasize that beans and bean products are a good source of protein and thus a good substitute for meat. For the first time, the guidelines warned Americans to be cautious of partially hydrogenated vegetable oils, used in many margarines and shortenings. These oils contain trans-fatty acids, a form of saturated fat that may raise blood cholesterol.

The guidelines also said that vegetarians could obtain enough protein "as long as the variety and amounts of foods consumed are adequate." Vegetarians must pay special attention to ensuring that their diets contain enough iron, zinc, and B vitamins, which in most American diets are supplied by meat, fish, and poultry. Vegans, who do not eat any animal products, must supplement their diets with vitamin B12, which is naturally present only in meat products. Certain other situations may also warrant supplements—pregnant women might take an iron supplement, for example. "However," the guidelines said, "because foods contain many nutrients and other substances that promote health, the use of supplements cannot substitute for proper food choices."

Cancer Society, Heart Association Guidelines

Although the government's dietary guidelines were more specific and more direct than earlier iterations, some critics nonetheless said they did not go far enough. "The guidelines should motivate the public to choose a better diet. I don't see any motivational language in these guidelines," said Michael Jacobson, director of the Center for Science in the Public Interest. "They should have urged diets much lower in saturated fat, . . . cholesterol, sodium, and sugar."

In dietary guidelines issued on September 16, the American Cancer Society also urged Americans to eat more grains, vegetables, and fruits. Where the federal guidelines allowed up to two or three servings of lean meat, fish, and poultry daily, the society recommended that people "limit" their consumption of meat and that they avoid processed meats. Where the federal guidelines condoned drinking in moderation, the society warned that the risk of cancer begins to rise with as few as two drinks a day. It has been estimated that nearly one-third of all cancer in the United States could be avoided if all Americans adopted healthy diets.

In the first revision of its guidelines since 1988, the American Heart Association sought to reduce the guilt many feel when they stray from the recommended diet. The association did not change its recommended maximum levels of calories, fat, and cholesterol in the American diet, but instead of urging people to meet those levels daily as it had once recommended, the association said Americans could eat a few more calories one day, a few less the next, so long as the daily average over a week met the recommended levels.

"It's fairly clear now that the changes we associate with heart disease risk do represent more of a long-term trend than changes that occur with any given meal," said Dr. Ronald Krauss, chairman of the committee that developed the new standards. "This fits the theme of consuming a variety of foods and reducing guilt from eating something 'bad' now and then."

Following are excerpts from Dietary Guidelines for Americans, *released jointly on January 2, 1996, by the Agriculture Department and the Health and Human Services Department:*

Nutrition and Your Health

What should Americans eat to stay healthy?

These guidelines are designed to help answer this question. They provide advice for healthy Americans age 2 years and over about food choices that promote health and prevent disease. To meet the *Dietary Guidelines for Americans*, choose a diet with most of the calories from grain products, vegetables, fruits, lowfat milk products, lean meats, fish, poultry, and dry beans. Choose fewer calories from fats and sweets.

Eating is one of life's greatest pleasures

Food choices depend on history, culture, and environment, as well as on energy and nutrient needs. People also eat foods for enjoyment. Family, friends, and beliefs play a major role in the ways people select foods and plan meals. This booklet describes some of the many different and pleasurable ways to combine foods to make healthful diets.

Diet is important to health at all stages of life

Many genetic, environmental, behavioral, and cultural factors can affect health. Understanding family history of disease or risk factors—body weight and fat distribution, blood pressure, and blood cholesterol, for example—can help people make more informed decisions about actions that can improve health prospects. Food choices are among the most pleasurable and effective of these actions.

Healthful diets help children grow, develop, and do well in school. They enable people of all ages to work productively and feel their best. Food choices also can help to reduce the risk for chronic diseases, such as heart disease, certain cancers, diabetes, stroke, and osteoporosis, that are leading causes of death and disability among Americans. Good diets can reduce major risk factors for chronic diseases—factors such as obesity, high blood pressure, and high blood cholesterol.

Foods contain energy, nutrients, and other components that affect health

People require energy and certain other essential nutrients. These nutrients are essential because the body cannot make them and must obtain them from food. Essential nutrients include vitamins, minerals, certain amino acids, and certain fatty acids. Foods also contain other components such as fiber that are important for health. Although each of these food components has a specific function in the body, all of them together are required for overall health. People need calcium to build and maintain strong bones, for example, but many other nutrients also are involved.

The carbohydrates, fats, and proteins in food supply energy, which is measured in calories. Carbohydrates and proteins provide about 4 calories per gram. Fat contributes more than twice as much—about 9 calories per gram. Alcohol, although not a nutrient, also supplies energy—about 7 calories per gram. Foods that are high in fat are also high in calories. However, many low-fat or nonfat foods can also be high in calories.

Physical activity fosters a healthful diet

Calorie needs vary by age and level of activity. Many older adults need less food, in part due to decreased activity, relative to younger, more active individuals. People who are trying to lose weight and eating little food may need to select more nutrient-dense foods in order to meet their nutrient needs in a satisfying diet. Nearly all Americans need to be more active, because a sedentary lifestyle is unhealthful. Increasing the calories spent in daily activities helps to maintain health and allows people to eat a nutritious and enjoyable diet.

What is a healthful diet?

Healthful diets contain the amounts of essential nutrients and calories needed to prevent nutritional deficiencies and excesses. Healthful diets also provide the right balance of carbohydrate, fat, and protein to reduce risks for chronic diseases, and are a part of a full and productive lifestyle. Such diets are obtained from a variety of foods that are available, affordable, and enjoyable.

The Recommended Dietary Allowances refer to nutrients

Recommended Dietary Allowances (RDAs) represent the amounts of nutrients that are adequate to meet the needs of most healthy people. Although people with average nutrient requirements likely eat adequately at levels below the RDAs, diets that meet RDAs are almost certain to ensure intake of enough essential nutrients by most healthy people. The Dietary Guidelines describe food choices that will help you meet these recommendations. Like the RDAs, the Dietary Guidelines apply to diets consumed over several days and not to single meals or foods.

The Dietary Guidelines describe food choices that promote good health

The *Dietary Guidelines* are designed to help Americans choose diets that will meet nutrient requirements, promote health, support active lives, and reduce chronic disease risks. Research has shown that certain diets raise risks for chronic diseases. Such diets are high in fat, saturated fat, cholesterol, and salt and they contain more calories than the body uses. They are also low in grain products, vegetables, fruit, and fiber. This bulletin helps you choose foods, meals, and diets that can reduce chronic disease risks. . . .

Eat a Variety of Foods

To obtain the nutrients and other substances needed for good health, vary the foods you eat

Foods contain combinations of nutrients and other healthful substances. No single food can supply all nutrients in the amounts you need. For example, oranges provide vitamin C but no vitamin B_{12}; cheese provides vitamin B_{12} but no vitamin C. To make sure you get all of the nutrients and other substances needed for health, choose the recommended number of daily servings from each of the five major food groups . . . .

Choose different foods within each food group

You can achieve a healthful, nutritious eating pattern with many combinations of foods from the five major food groups. Choosing a variety of foods within and across food groups improves dietary patterns because foods within the same group have different combinations of nutrients and other beneficial substances. For example, some vegetables and fruits are good sources of vitamin C or vitamin A, while others are high in folate; still others are good sources of calcium or iron. Choosing a variety of foods within each group also helps to make your meals more interesting from day to day.

What about vegetarian diets?

Some Americans eat vegetarian diets for reasons of culture, belief, or health. Most vegetarians eat milk products and eggs, and as a group, these lacto-ovo-vegetarians enjoy excellent health. Vegetarian diets are consistent with the *Dietary Guidelines for Americans* and can meet Recommended Dietary Allowances for nutrients. You can get enough protein from a vegetarian diet as long as the variety and amounts of foods consumed are adequate. Meat, fish, and poultry are major contributors of iron, zinc, and B vitamins in most American diets, and vegetarians should pay special attention to these nutrients.

Vegans eat only food of plant origin. Because animal products are the only food sources of vitamin B_{12}, vegans must supplement their diets with a source of this vitamin. In addition, vegan diets, particularly those of children, require care to ensure adequacy of vitamin D and calcium, which most Americans obtain from milk products. . . .

Where do vitamin, mineral, and fiber supplements fit in?

Supplements of vitamins, minerals, or fiber also may help to meet special nutritional needs. However, supplements do not supply all of the nutrients and other substances present in foods that are important to health. Supplements of some nutrients taken regularly in large amounts are harmful. Daily vitamin and mineral supplements at or below the Recommended Dietary Allowances are considered safe, but are usually not needed by people who eat the variety of foods depicted in the Food Guide Pyramid.

Sometimes supplements are needed to meet specific nutrient requirements. For example, older people and others with little exposure to sunlight may need a vitamin D supplement. Women of childbearing age may reduce the risk of certain birth defects by consuming folate-rich foods or folic acid supplements. Iron supplements are recommended for pregnant women. However, because foods contain many nutrients and other substances that promote health, the use of supplements cannot substitute for proper food choices. . . .

Balance the Food You Eat with Physical Activity— Maintain or Improve Your Weight

Many Americans gain weight in adulthood, increasing their risk for high blood pressure, heart disease, stroke, diabetes, certain types of cancer, arthritis, breathing problems, and other illness. Therefore, most adults should not gain weight. If you are overweight and have one of these problems, you should try to lose weight, or at the very least, not gain weight. If you are uncertain about your risk of developing a problem associated with overweight, you should consult a health professional.

How to maintain your weight

In order to stay at the same body weight, people must balance the amount of calories in the foods and drinks they consume with the amount of calories the body uses. Physical activity is an important way to use food energy. Most Americans spend much of their working day in activities that require little energy. In addition, many Americans of all ages now spend a lot of leisure time each day being inactive, for example, watching television or working at a computer. To burn calories, devote less time to sedentary activities like sitting. Spend more time in activities like walking to the store or around the block. Use stairs rather than elevators. Less sedentary activity and more vigorous activity may help you reduce body fat and disease risk. Try to do 30 minutes or more of moderate physical activity on most—preferably all—days of the week. . . .

The kinds and amounts of food people eat affect their ability to maintain weight. High-fat foods contain more calories per serving than other foods and may increase the likelihood of weight gain. However, even when people eat less high-fat food, they still can gain weight from eating too much of foods high in starch, sugars, or protein. Eat a variety of foods, emphasizing pasta, rice, bread, and other whole-grain foods as well as fruits and vegetables. These foods are filling, but lower in calories than foods rich in fats or oils.

The pattern of eating may also be important. Snacks provide a large percentage of daily calories for many Americans. Unless nutritious snacks are part of the daily meal plan, snacking may lead to weight gain. A pattern of frequent binge-eating, with or without alternating periods of food restriction, may also contribute to weight problems.

Maintaining weight is equally important for older people who begin to lose weight as they age. Some of the weight that is lost is muscle. Maintaining muscle through regular activity helps to keep older people feeling well and helps to reduce the risk of falls and fractures. . . .

Location of body fat

Research suggests that the location of body fat also is an important factor in health risks for adults. Excess fat in the abdomen (stomach area) is a greater health risk than excess fat in the hips and thighs. Extra fat in the abdomen is linked to high blood pressure, diabetes, early heart disease, and certain types of cancer. Smoking and too much alcohol increase abdominal fat and the risk for diseases related to obesity. Vigorous exercise helps to reduce abdominal fat and decrease the risk for these diseases. The easiest way to check your body fat distribution is to measure around your waistline with a tape measure and compare this with the measure around your hips or buttocks to see if your abdomen is larger. If you are in doubt, you may wish to seek advice from a health professional.

Problems with excessive thinness

Being too thin can occur with anorexia nervosa, other eating disorders, or loss of appetite, and is linked to menstrual irregularity and osteoporosis in women, and greater risk of early death in both women and men. Many people—especially women—are concerned about body weight, even when their weight is normal. Excessive concern about weight may cause or lead to such unhealthy behaviors as excessive exercise, self-induced vomiting, and the abuse of laxatives or other medications. These practices may only worsen the concern about weight. If you lose weight suddenly or for unknown reasons, see a physician. Unexplained weight loss may be an early clue to a health problem.

If you need to lose weight

You do not need to lose weight if your weight is already within the healthy range in the figure, if you have gained less than 10 pounds since you reached your adult height, and if you are otherwise healthy. If you are overweight and have excess abdominal fat, a weight-related medical problem, or a family history of such problems, you need to lose weight. Healthy diets and exercise can help people maintain a healthy weight, and may also help them lose weight. It is important to recognize that overweight is a chronic condition which can only be controlled with long-term changes. To reduce caloric intake, eat less fat and control portion sizes. . . . If you are not physically active, spend less time in sedentary activities such as watching television, and be more active throughout the day. As people lose weight, the body becomes more efficient at using energy and the rate of weight loss may decrease. Increased physical activity will help you to continue losing weight and to avoid gaining it back. . . .

Many people are not sure how much weight they should lose. Weight loss of only 5–10 percent of body weight may improve many of the problems associated with overweight, such as high blood pressure and diabetes. Even a smaller weight loss can make a difference. If you are trying to lose weight, do so slowly and steadily. A generally safe rate is ½–1 pound a week until you reach your goal. Avoid crash weight-loss diets that severely restrict calories or the variety of foods. Extreme approaches to weight loss, such as self-induced vomiting or the use of laxatives, amphetamines, or diuretics, are not appropriate and can be dangerous to your health.

Weight regulation in children

Children need enough food for proper growth. To promote growth and development and prevent overweight, teach children to eat grain products; vegetables and fruits; lowfat milk products or other calcium-rich foods; beans, lean meat, poultry, fish, or other protein-rich foods; and to participate in vigorous activity. Limiting television time and encouraging children to play actively in a safe environment are helpful steps. Although limiting fat intake may help to prevent excess weight gain in children, fat should not be restricted for children younger than 2 years of age. Helping overweight children to achieve a healthy weight along with normal growth requires more caution. Modest reductions in dietary fat, such as the use of lowfat milk rather than whole milk, are not hazardous. However, major efforts to change a child's diet should be accompanied by monitoring of growth by a health professional at regular intervals. . . .

Choose a Diet with Plenty of Grain Products, Vegetables, and Fruits

Grain products, vegetables, and fruits are key parts of a varied diet. They are emphasized in this guideline because they provide vitamins, minerals, complex carbohydrates (starch and dietary fiber), and other substances that are important for good health. They are also generally low in fat, depending on how they are prepared and what is added to them at the table. Most Americans of all ages eat fewer than the recommended number of servings of grain products, vegetables, and fruits, even though consumption of these foods is associated with a substantially lower risk for many chronic diseases, including certain types of cancer.

Most of the calories in your diet should come from grain products, vegetables, and fruits

These include grain products high in complex carbohydrates—breads, cereals, pasta, rice—found at the base of the Food Guide Pyramid, as well as vegetables such as potatoes and corn. Dry beans (like pinto, navy, kidney, and black beans) are included in the meat and beans group of the Pyramid, but they can count as servings of vegetables instead of meat alternatives.

Plant foods provide fiber

Fiber is found only in plant foods like whole-grain breads and cereals, beans and peas, and other vegetables and fruits. Because there are different types of fiber in foods, choose a variety of foods daily. Eating a variety of fiber-containing plant foods is important for proper bowel function, can reduce symptoms of chronic constipation, diverticular disease, and hemorrhoids, and may lower the risk for heart disease and some cancers. However, some of the health benefits associated with a high-fiber diet may come from other components present in these foods, not just from fiber itself. For this reason, fiber is best obtained from foods rather than supplements.

Plant foods provide a variety of vitamins and minerals essential for health

Most fruits and vegetables are naturally low in fat and provide many essential nutrients and other food components important for health. These foods are excellent sources of vitamin C, vitamin B6, carotenoids, including those which form vitamin A ... and folate.... The antioxidant nutrients found in plant foods (e.g., vitamin C, carotenoids, vitamin E, and certain minerals) are presently of great interest to scientists and the public because of their potentially beneficial role in reducing the risk for cancer and certain other chronic diseases. Scientists are also trying to determine if other substances in plant foods protect against cancer.

Folate, also called folic acid, is a B vitamin that, among its many functions, reduces the risk of a serious type of birth defect.... Minerals such as potassium, found in a wide variety of vegetables and fruits, and calcium, found in certain vegetables, may help reduce the risk for high blood pressure....

The availability of fresh fruits and vegetables varies by season and region of the country, but frozen and canned fruits and vegetables ensure a plentiful supply of these healthful foods throughout the year. Read the Nutrition Facts Label to help choose foods that are rich in carbohydrates, fiber, and nutrients, and low in fat and sodium....

Choose a Diet Low in Fat, Saturated Fat, and Cholesterol

Some dietary fat is needed for good health. Fats supply energy and essential fatty acids and promote absorption of the fat-soluble vitamins A, D, E, and K. Most people are aware that high levels of saturated fat and cholesterol in the diet are linked to increased blood cholesterol levels and a greater risk for heart disease. More Americans are now eating less fat, saturated fat, and cholesterol-rich foods than in the recent past, and fewer people are dying from the most common form of heart disease. Still, many people continue to eat high-fat diets, the number of overweight people has increased, and the risk of heart disease and certain cancers (also linked to fat intake) remains high. This guideline emphasizes the continued importance of choosing a diet with less total fat, saturated fat, and cholesterol.

Foods high in fat should be used sparingly

Some foods and food groups in the Food Guide Pyramid are higher in fat than others. Fats and oils, and some types of desserts and snack foods that contain fat, provide calories but few nutrients. Many foods in the milk group and in the meat and beans group (which includes eggs and nuts, as well as meat, poultry, and fish) are also high in fat, as are some processed foods in the grain group. Choosing lower fat options among these foods allows you to eat the recommended servings from these groups and increase the amount and variety of grain products, fruits, and vegetables in your diet without going over your calorie needs.

Choose a diet low in fat

Fat, whether from plant or animal sources, contains more than twice the number of calories of an equal amount of carbohydrate or protein. Choose a diet that provides no more than 30 percent of total calories from fat. The upper limit on the grams of fat in your diet will depend on the calories you need. . . . Cutting back on fat can help you consume fewer calories. For example, at 2,000 calories per day, the suggested upper limit of calories from fat is about 600 calories. Sixty-five grams of fat contribute about 600 calories (65 grams of fat $\times$ 9 calories per gram = about 600 calories). . . .

Choose a diet low in saturated fat

Fats contain both saturated and unsaturated (monounsaturated and polyunsaturated) fatty acids. Saturated fat raises blood cholesterol more than other forms of fat. Reducing saturated fat to less than 10 percent of calories will help you lower your blood cholesterol level. The fats from meat, milk, and milk products are the main sources of saturated fats in most diets. Many bakery products are also sources of saturated fats. Vegetable oils supply smaller amounts of saturated fat. . . .

Monounsaturated and polyunsaturated fat. Olive and canola oils are particularly high in monounsaturated fats; most other vegetable oils, nuts, and high-fat fish are good sources of polyunsaturated fats. Both kinds of unsaturated fats reduce blood cholesterol when they replace saturated fats in the diet. The fats in most fish are low in saturated fatty acids and contain a certain type of polyunsaturated fatty acid (omega-3) that is under study because of a possible association with a decreased risk for heart disease in certain people. Remember that the total fat in the diet should be consumed at a moderate level—that is, no more than 30 percent of calories. Mono- and polyunsaturated fat sources should replace saturated fats within this limit.

Partially hydrogenated vegetable oils, such as those used in many margarines and shortenings, contain a particular form of unsaturated fat known as trans-fatty acids. Current research shows that trans-fatty acids may raise blood cholesterol.

Choose a diet low in cholesterol

The body makes the cholesterol it requires. In addition, cholesterol is obtained from food. Dietary cholesterol comes from animal sources such as egg yolks, meat (especially organ meats such as liver), poultry, fish, and higher fat milk products. Many of these foods are also high in saturated fats. Choosing foods with less cholesterol and saturated fat will help lower your blood cholesterol levels. . . .

Advice for children

Advice in the previous sections does not apply to infants and toddlers below the age of 2 years. After that age, children should gradually adopt a diet that, by about 5 years of age, contains no more than 30 percent of calories from fat. As they begin to consume fewer calories from fat, children should replace these calories by eating more grain products, fruits, vegetables, and lowfat milk products or other calcium-rich foods, and beans, lean meat, poultry, fish, or other protein-rich foods. . . .

Choose a Diet Moderate in Sugars

Sugars come in many forms

Sugars are carbohydrates. Dietary carbohydrates also include the complex carbohydrates starch and fiber. During digestion all carbohydrates except fiber break down into sugars. Sugars and starches occur naturally in many foods that also supply other nutrients. Examples of these foods include milk, fruits, some vegetables, breads, cereals, and grains. Americans eat sugars in many forms, and most people like their taste. Some sugars are used as natural preservatives, thickeners, and baking aids in foods; they are often added to foods during processing and preparation or when they are eaten. The body cannot tell the difference between naturally occurring and added sugars because they are identical chemically.

Sugars, health, and weight maintenance

Scientific evidence indicates that diets high in sugars do not cause hyperactivity or diabetes. The most common type of diabetes occurs in overweight adults. Avoiding sugars alone will not correct overweight. To lose weight reduce the total amount of calories from the food you eat and increase your level of physical activity. . . .

If you wish to maintain your weight when you eat less fat, replace the lost calories from fat with equal calories from fruits, vegetables, and grain products, found in the lower half of the Food Guide Pyramid. Some foods that contain a lot of sugars supply calories but few or no nutrients. . . . These foods are located at the top of the Pyramid. For very active people with high calorie needs, sugars can be an additional source of energy. However, because maintaining a nutritious diet and a healthy weight is very important, sugars should be used in moderation by most healthy people and sparingly by people with low calorie needs. This guideline cautions about eating sugars in large amounts and about frequent snacks of foods and beverages containing sugars that supply unnecessary calories and few nutrients.

Sugar substitutes

Sugar substitutes such as sorbitol, saccharin, and aspartame are ingredients in many foods. Most sugar substitutes do not provide significant calories and therefore may be useful in the diets of people concerned about calorie

14

intake. Foods containing sugar substitutes, however, may not always be lower in calories than similar products that contain sugars. Unless you reduce the total calories you eat, the use of sugar substitutes will not cause you to lose weight. . . .

Choose a Diet Moderate in Salt and Sodium

Sodium and salt are found mainly in processed and prepared foods

Sodium and sodium chloride—known commonly as salt—occur naturally in foods, usually in small amounts. Salt and other sodium-containing ingredients are often used in food processing. Some people add salt and salty sauces, such as soy sauce, to their food at the table, but most dietary sodium or salt comes from foods to which salt has already been added during processing or preparation. Although many people add salt to enhance the taste of foods, their preference may weaken with eating less salt.

Sodium is associated with high blood pressure

In the body, sodium plays an essential role in regulation of fluids and blood pressure. Many studies in diverse populations have shown that a high sodium intake is associated with higher blood pressure. Most evidence suggests that many people at risk for high blood pressure reduce their chances of developing this condition by consuming less salt or sodium. Some questions remain, partly because other factors may interact with sodium to affect blood pressure.

Other factors affect blood pressure

Following other guidelines in the Dietary Guidelines for Americans may also help prevent high blood pressure. An important example is the guideline on weight and physical activity. The role of body weight in blood pressure control is well documented. Blood pressure increases with weight and decreases when weight is reduced. The guideline to consume a diet with plenty of fruits and vegetables is relevant because fruits and vegetables are naturally lower in sodium and fat and may help with weight reduction and control. Consuming more fruits and vegetables also increases potassium intakes which may help to reduce blood pressure. . . . Increased physical activity helps lower blood pressure and control weight. Alcohol consumption has also been associated with high blood pressure. Another reason to reduce salt intake is the fact that high salt intakes may increase the amount of calcium excreted in the urine and, therefore, increase the body's need for calcium.

Most Americans consume more salt than is needed

Sodium has an important role in the body. However, most Americans consume more sodium than is needed. . . . In household measures, one level teaspoon of salt provides about 2,300 milligrams of sodium. [The recommended daily maximum is 2,400 milligrams.] Most people consume more than this amount.

There is no way at present to tell who might develop high blood pressure from eating too much sodium. However, consuming less salt or sodium is not harmful and can be recommended for the healthy normal adult. . . .

If You Drink Alcoholic Beverages, Do So in Moderation

Alcoholic beverages supply calories but few or no nutrients. The alcohol in these beverages has effects that are harmful when consumed in excess. These effects of alcohol may alter judgment and can lead to dependency and a great many other serious health problems. Alcoholic beverages have been used to enhance the enjoyment of meals by many societies throughout human history. If adults choose to drink alcoholic beverages, they should consume them only in moderation. . . .

Current evidence suggests that moderate drinking is associated with a lower risk for coronary heart disease in some individuals. However, higher levels of alcohol intake raise the risk for high blood pressure, stroke, heart disease, certain cancers, accidents, violence, suicides, birth defects, and overall mortality (deaths). Too much alcohol may cause cirrhosis of the liver, inflammation of the pancreas, and damage to the brain and heart. Heavy drinkers also are at risk of malnutrition because alcohol contains calories that may substitute for those in more nutritious foods.

Who should not drink?

Some people should not drink alcoholic beverages at all. These include:

- Children and adolescents.
- Individuals of any age who cannot restrict their drinking to moderate levels. This is a special concern for recovering alcoholics and people whose family members have alcohol problems.
- Women who are trying to conceive or who are pregnant. Major birth defects, including fetal alcohol syndrome, have been attributed to heavy drinking by the mother while pregnant. While there is no conclusive evidence that an occasional drink is harmful to the fetus or to the pregnant woman, a safe level of alcohol intake during pregnancy has not been established.
- Individuals who plan to drive or take part in activities that require attention or skill. Most people retain some alcohol in the blood up to 2–3 hours after a single drink.
- Individuals using prescription and over-the-counter medications. Alcohol may alter the effectiveness or toxicity of medicines. Also, some medications may increase blood alcohol levels or increase the adverse effect of alcohol on the brain.

GENERAL MOTORS ON PLANS
TO SELL ELECTRIC AUTOMOBILES
January 4, 1996

General Motors (GM) in 1996 became the first major automaker in modern times to market in the United States an automobile powered by electricity, rather than by an internal combustion engine. GM in early December began leasing the EV1 (for Electric Vehicle One) at Saturn dealerships in southern California and Arizona. GM was planning to introduce an electric-powered pickup truck in 1997, and other U.S. and Japanese automakers were planning to follow the GM lead starting in 1997.

These tentative steps by automakers were not expected to transform modern transportation, at least not yet. GM and other companies anticipated that early sales or leases of electric-powered models would represent a tiny fraction of the American auto market.

The move toward electricity did represent a major concession by the automakers, which for years had resisted demands by environmentalists and some government regulators to produce nonpolluting vehicles. Independent auto researchers had taken the lead in developing technology for electric-driven vehicles, and only in recent years had the larger companies reluctantly followed suit.

For at least the immediate future, it appeared likely that electric vehicles would find their greatest use as part of fleets. For example, the German postal service was considering buying thousands of vans powered by an Israeli-developed battery.

In a November 3 review of the new EV1, the New York Times *said the car "is unlikely to be anyone's primary transportation" because its driving range, before a battery recharge, was only seventy to ninety miles. But, the newspaper added, "for weekend jaunts or urban errands, the eerily quiet and nonpolluting EV1 behaves well and attracts considerable attention."*

Some experts noted that the first generation of modern electric vehicles would have little impact on cleaning up the environment, if only because there would be so few of them. Environmental advocates said it was still important to produce cleaner cars for the future.

Pressures for an Electric Car

The apparent sudden interest in developing electric cars actually was long in coming. The major U.S. and overseas automakers for decades had resisted investing large sums of money in researching electric technology, arguing that the cost of electric-powered cars would be too high and consumer interest would be too low.

Two factors came together in the late 1980s and early 1990s that increased interest. Independent researchers and entrepreneurs developed increasingly sophisticated technology for electric-powered automobiles, thus undermining claims by the big automakers that such vehicles were not feasible. Tough new environmental laws and regulations, especially in California, threatened the automakers with a loss of market share if they failed to produce automobiles that could meet new emissions standards.

The California regulations were especially important in encouraging action on electric vehicles. Over the vigorous objections of automakers and oil companies, the state's Air Resources Board adopted a standard requiring that 2 percent of all new cars sold in California in 1998 be electrically powered, with the requirement reaching 10 percent by 2003. Political pressure by the automakers and other businesses eventually succeeded in getting the California board to repeal its 1998 requirement, but the longer-term requirement for electric vehicles remained in place.

Even while working on electric vehicles, most automakers were trying to meet the new emissions standards by developing cleaner internal combustion engines. Honda was among the companies taking the lead in producing what was called an Ultra Low-Emitting Vehicle. Some researchers were advocating a hybrid as the ultimate solution to the demand for cleaner-running cars. A hybrid would get most of its power from electricity, with a separate internal combustion engine providing a boost for acceleration or for operation in cold weather, when electric-only cars tended to falter.

Development of the EV1

General Motors had been among the automakers most resistant to exploring electric car technology. Company spokesmen and lobbyists repeatedly told government regulators that electric autos were technically and economically unworkable. Even so, in the late 1980s GM quietly began work on a vehicle known as the "Impact," a sporty, two-seat coupe. GM spent nearly $300 million on the Impact before halting work in 1993. GM officials argued at the time that the car was proving to be an unmarketable money-loser.

With California's tougher emission standards still looming and other automakers working on low-polluting cars, GM in early 1995 resurrected the Impact, with a new goal of getting it to test markets by 1997. Apparently conceding that a car named "Impact" might become the butt of jokes, GM renamed its new product the EV1, for Electric Vehicle One.

The "one" designation clearly was important to America's largest car manufacturer. On January 4, 1996, GM proudly announced that it would

be "the first major automaker in modern times" to market a car specifi-
cally designed to be powered by electricity. Chairman John F. Smith Jr.
said one of GM's goals was to "recapture our leadership in the public's
mind as an innovative technology company."

The EV1 was marketed initially in four areas: Los Angeles, San Diego,
Tucson, and Phoenix. Saturn president Donald W. Hudler said those areas
"afford the topographical and climatic conditions found to be most favor-
able to electric vehicle operation." In other words, the first generation of
electric cars performed best in relatively flat terrain and in warm climates.

GM planned to lease the EV1 at an initial price of $34,000 through twen-
ty-six Saturn dealerships. The company said it would expand the market,
and possibly reduce the EV1 price, if consumer demand proved adequate.

More electric vehicles were to reach U.S. consumers in 1997, including
a light pickup truck by Chevrolet and passenger models from Chrysler and
Honda. Toyota was testing in Japan an electric version of a sport utility
vehicle.

Following is the text of a January 4 announcement by General
Motors Corporation of its plan to begin marketing an electric
automobile:

General Motors will be the first major automaker in modern times to market specifically designed electric vehicles to the public when its new EV1
passenger car goes on sale later this year, GM Chairman John F. Smith, Jr.
said today.

"It's time to get electric vehicles out of the lab, into the showroom and
onto the road," Mr. Smith said in making the announcement.

The two-seat EV1—first vehicle in the company's history to carry a General
Motors designation—will be marketed this fall by Saturn retailers in four western markets: Los Angeles, San Diego, Phoenix and Tucson. "While the EV1's
market initially may be limited in scope, we are expansive in what we believe
this car says about the kind of company GM is going to be," Mr. Smith said.

Saturn's dedication to customer care and the total ownership experience
made it the right team to market the car, Mr. Smith said.

Pointing to the EV1 as a symbol of GM's commitment to technological and
environmental leadership, Mr. Smith described the car as "the first product in
a portfolio of high-technology products that we will be bringing to market in
the years ahead."

"These products will define the GM of the future," he added.

Mr. Smith said the EV1 is equipped with dual airbags, anti-lock brakes, a
CD player and cruise control. "Most important, it's a car designed for people—to commute, to shop, to run around town. And it's a car for people who
never want to go to the gas station again," he said.

Mr. Smith said GM tests showed consumers were overwhelmingly
impressed with the car. "It's quiet, peppy and fun to drive," he said. It is the

world's most aerodynamic production vehicle and it carries 23 new patents in a variety of new technologies, he said.

"When auto industry historians look back, they will see this car as the first in the new generation of vehicles," Mr. Smith said. "And they will note that GM made it."

In referring to the GM badge carried by the car, Mr. Smith said EV1 represents the design, engineering and manufacturing work of many partnerships within the company. "We have the resources no one else can match," he said. "And they were all brought to bear in developing this car. Delphi Automotive Systems, Delco Electronics and our North American Operations all contributed their technology and creativity in bringing the car to the consumer."

Mr. Smith said GM will also market an electric pick-up truck nationwide in 1997 for use in commercial fleets. The truck—the Chevrolet S-10—will be built in Shreveport, La. and will use the same technologies as the EV1. "These pick-ups will be especially appropriate for predetermined routes where the truck comes back to the garage every night," Mr. Smith said.

Robert C. Purcell, executive director of GM Electric Vehicles, said his main objective was to "make a business" of electric vehicle technology. "And in this business, it all comes down to the hardware," he said.

He called the EV1 "the world's most energy-efficient vehicle platform. If you look at virtually every system in this vehicle, there are innovations in design, processing and materials that create an entirely new class of automotive transportation product focused on energy efficiency and environmental compatibility," he said.

Mr. Purcell said both the EV1 and the Chevrolet electric pick-up truck will use the Delco Electronics Magne-Charge inductive charging system. "We believe this system will set the standard for convenient, efficient and safe electric vehicle charging," he added.

The Magne-Charge System has already been tested and well received by over 500 consumers nationwide in GM's PrEView Drive electric vehicle test drive program.

Mr. Purcell said the EV1 will be built at GM's Lansing (Mich.) Craft Centre, an assembly operation that will "set a new benchmark for manufacturing efficiency in a low-volume build." He cited UAW [United Auto Workers] Local 1618 for "an outstanding job in working with the EV platform to develop the processes and systems necessary to put this vehicle into production."

Donald W. Hudler, president of Saturn, noted the EV1 will be launched much the same way as the first Saturn models back in 1990, with the first introductions coming in southwestern states.

"Another reason we're launching in the southern California and Arizona markets is because they afford the topographical and climatic conditions found to be most favorable to electric vehicle operation," Mr. Hudler said.

He said Saturn retailers who will sell the EV1 are "truly excited about this new opportunity, not only for themselves but for what this vehicle's success can do for the image of Saturn as a 'different kind of company.'"

STATE OF THE UNION ADDRESS AND REPUBLICAN RESPONSE
January 23, 1996

The American public was given a taste of the likely 1996 presidential race on January 23 when President Bill Clinton delivered his third State of the Union address to Congress and was answered by his Republican challenger, Senate Majority Leader Bob Dole of Kansas. Most pundits awarded this unofficial first-round victory to the president, who was gracious and conciliatory to congressional Republicans even as he preempted themes, such as family values and crime control, more closely identified with the GOP. Dole, in contrast, drew sharper philosophical distinctions between Democrats and Republicans. But the majority leader appeared tired and wooden, reinforcing sentiments among some Republicans and others that he would be unable to match Clinton's personal appeal on the campaign trail.

Clinton strove to sound "presidential," above the acrimonious partisanship that was blocking action on the budget and that had twice forced the federal government to shut down. The president called on Congress to "never—ever—shut the federal government down again," even as he complimented Republicans for bringing the issue of balancing the budget to the forefront of national debate. He praised Democrats for enacting a deficit reduction bill in 1993, which the president said had already cut the federal deficit almost in half. While acknowledging that significant differences remained between the White House and Congress concerning the 1996 budget measure, he urged Congress to enact a budget based on "the combined total of the proposed savings common" to both the Republican and Democratic budget plans. That total, Clinton said, was enough to balance the budget in seven years and still provide a modest tax cut.

The following day, January 24, House Speaker Newt Gingrich signaled that the Republicans were ready to abandon their confrontational budget strategy, which they had hoped would force the president to give in to their demands. In short order, Congress passed a stopgap funding bill to keep the government operating past the January 26 deadline. The GOP leadership also withdrew its threats to hold up action on a measure to raise the debt ceiling, which might have forced the U.S. Treasury to default on its obligations. (Budget debate, p. 147)

Clinton's 'Age of Possibility'

For most of his speech, the president focused on the opportunities and challenges the nation was facing as it moved from an industrial economy to one driven by "technology, information, and global competition." This "age of possibility," Clinton said, has "opened vast new opportunities for our people, but [it has] also presented them with stiff challenges." These challenges can be met, the president said, not with big government programs—"The era of big government is over"—but with a smaller government working together with "all of our citizens . . . to enable all our people to make the most of their own lives with stronger families, more educational opportunity, economic security, safer streets, a cleaner environment, and a safer world."

Declaring that much of the responsibility for meeting these challenges rested with individual citizens, Clinton outlined several measures to help. These included welfare reform that provided child care along with work requirements, time limits on receiving welfare, and strict enforcement of child support payments; legislation to bar health insurance companies from dropping people when they changed jobs and from denying coverage for pre-existing conditions; and an increase in the minimum wage. He urged Congress to help the working poor by retaining the Earned Income Tax Credit at its current levels, to promote academic excellence by retaining the Goals 2000 initiative, to protect the environment by restoring funds for enforcing environmental protection laws, and to reduce violent crime by retaining the Brady handgun control bill and the ban on nineteen kinds of assault weapons. Republicans had or wanted to cut back all these programs. (Welfare reform, p. 450; minimum wage hike, p. 563)

Clinton also called for congressional approval of a tax deduction of up to $10,000 a year for college tuition and a requirement to install "v-chips" in TV sets; the chips would allow parents to screen out violent and sexually explicit programs.

The president also took the opportunity to praise his wife, Hillary Rodham Clinton, who was seated in a gallery with their daughter, Chelsea. Mrs. Clinton had been under scrutiny by a Senate panel investigating Whitewater, an Arkansas land development deal, and had been subpoenaed to testify before a federal grand jury investigating possible obstruction of justice in the White House's handling of related legal billing records. Clinton called her "a wonderful wife, a magnificent mother, and a great first lady."

Dole's Response

In his response, Dole, who officially became the Republican presidential nominee in August, sought to portray Clinton as a liberal Democrat in favor of big government who "claims to embrace the future while clinging to the policies of the past." Clinton might talk of change, Dole said, but his vetoes of the Republican welfare reform, defense, and balanced budget bills showed that the president "shares a view of America held by our country's elites: A nation of special interest groups, united only by a dependence on government, competing with each other for handouts and held back by outdated values."

In addition to trying to assert his political differences with the president, Dole also sought to show himself as a key Republican leader, on a plane above his Republican rivals, none of whom could claim a similar leadership position. Ironically, in May, when it was clear that he would win the Republican presidential nomination, Dole gave up that leadership position—and his Senate seat—to concentrate his energies on his presidential campaign. (Dole resignation, p. 270)

Following are the texts of President Bill Clinton's State of the Union address, as delivered January 23, 1996, and the Republican response by Senate Majority Leader Bob Dole of Kansas:

STATE OF THE UNION ADDRESS

Mr. Speaker [Newt Gingrich], Mr. Vice President [Al Gore], members of the 104th Congress, distinguished guests, my fellow Americans all across our land.

Let me begin by saying to our men and women in uniform around the world, and especially those helping peace take root in Bosnia, and to their families. I thank you. America is very, very proud of you.

My duty tonight is to report on the state of the union, not the state of our government, but of our American community, and to set forth our responsibilities—in the words of our founders—to form a "more perfect union."

The state of the union is strong.

Our economy is the healthiest it has been in three decades. We have the lowest combined rate of unemployment and inflation in 27 years.

We have created nearly 8 million new jobs, over a million of them in basic industries like construction and automobiles. America is selling more cars than Japan for the first time since the 1970s, and for three years in a row we have had a record number of new businesses started in our country.

Our leadership in the world is also strong, bringing hope for new peace. And perhaps most important, we are gaining ground in restoring our fundamental values. The crime rate, the welfare and food stamp rolls, the poverty rate and the teen pregnancy rate are all down. And as they go down, prospects for America's future go up.

["An Age of Possibility"]

We live in an age of possibility. A hundred years ago we moved from farm to factory. Now we move to an age of technology, information and global competition. These changes have opened vast new opportunities for our people, but they have also presented them with stiff challenges. While more Americans are living better lives, too many of our fellow citizens are working harder to just keep up, in search of greater security for their families.

We must answer three fundamental questions: First, how do we make the American dream of opportunity a reality for all Americans who are willing to work for it? Second, how do we preserve our old and enduring values as we move into the future? And third, how do we meet these challenges together, as one America?

We know big government does not have all the answers. We know there's not a program for every problem. We know and we have worked to give the American people a smaller, less bureaucratic government in Washington. And we have to give the American people one that lives within its means. The era of big government is over.

But we cannot go back to the time when our citizens were left to fend for themselves. We must go forward as one America—one nation working together, to meet the challenges we face together. Self-reliance and teamwork are not opposing virtues—we must have both.

I believe our new, smaller government must work in an old-fashioned American way—together with all of our citizens, through state and local governments, in the workplace, in religious, charitable and civic associations. Our goal must be to enable all our people to make the most of their own lives with stronger families, more educational opportunity, economic security, safer streets, a cleaner environment, and a safer world.

To improve the state of our union, we must all ask more of ourselves; we must expect more of each other; and we must face our challenges together.

Here, in this place, our responsibility begins with balancing the budget in a way that is fair to all Americans. There is now broad bipartisan agreement that permanent deficit spending must come to an end.

I compliment the Republican leadership and the membership for the energy and determination you have brought to this task of balancing the budget. And I thank the Democrats for passing the largest deficit-reduction plan in history in 1993, which has already cut the deficit nearly in half in three years.

Since 1993, we have all seen the benefits of deficit reduction: Lower interest rates have made it easier for business to borrow and to invest and create new jobs. Lower interest rates have brought down the cost of home mortgages, car payments and credit card rates to ordinary citizens. Now it is time to finish the job and balance the budget.

Though differences remain among us that are significant, the combined total of the proposed savings common to both plans is more than enough, using the numbers from your Congressional Budget Office, to balance the budget in seven years and to provide a modest tax cut. These cuts are real, they will require sacrifice from everyone. But these cuts do not undermine our obligations to our parents, our children and our future by endangering Medicare, Medicaid, education or the environment, or by raising taxes on working families.

I have said before and I'll say again that many good ideas have come out of our negotiations. I have learned a lot about the way both Republicans and Democrats view the debate before us. I have learned a lot about the good ideas that each side has that we could all embrace. We ought to resolve our remaining differences. I am willing to work to resolve them. I am ready to meet tomorrow. But I ask you to consider that we should at least enact these savings that both plans have in common and give the American people their balanced budget, a tax cut, lower interest rates and a brighter future. We should do that now and make permanent deficits yesterday's legacy.

[Children and Families]

Now is the time to look to the challenges of today and tomorrow, beyond the burdens of yesterday. The challenges are significant, but our nation was built on challenges. America was built on challenges, not promises. And when we work together, we never fail. That is the key to a more perfect union: Our individual dreams must be realized by our common efforts.

Tonight, I want to speak about the challenges we all face as a people.

Our first challenge is to cherish our children and strengthen American families.

Families are the foundation of American life. If we have stronger families, we will have a stronger America. Before I go on, I'd like to take just a moment to thank my own family, and to thank the person who taught me more than anyone else over 25 years about the importance of families and children. A wonderful wife, a magnificent mother and a great first lady. Thank you Hillary.

All strong families begin with taking more responsibility for our children. I've heard Mrs. Gore say that it's hard to be a parent today, but it's even harder to be a child. So all of us, not just as parents but all of us in our other roles—our media, our schools, our teachers, our communities, our churches and synagogues, our businesses, governments—all of us have a responsibility to help children make it, and to make the most of their lives and their God-given capacities.

To the media: I say you should create movies, CDs and television shows you would want your own children and grandchildren to enjoy. I call on Congress to pass the requirement for a "v-chip" in TV sets, so parents can screen out programs they believe are inappropriate for their children.

When parents control what their children see, that's not censorship. That's enabling parents to assume more responsibility for their young children's upbringing. And I urge them to do it. The v-chip requirement is part of the telecommunications bill now pending in this Congress. It has bipartisan support, and I urge you to pass it now.

To make the v-chip work, I challenge the broadcast industry to do what movies have done to identify your programs in ways that help parents protect their children. And I invite the leaders of major media corporations and the entertainment industry to come to the White House next month to work with us in a positive way on concrete ways to improve what our children see on television. I am ready to work with you.

I say to those who produce and market cigarettes: Every year, a million children take up smoking, even though it's against the law; 300,000 of them will have their lives shortened as a result.

Our administration has taken steps to stop the massive marketing campaigns that appeal to our children. We are simply saying: Market your products to adults, if you wish—but draw the line on children.

I say to those on welfare, and especially to those who have been trapped on welfare for a long time: For too long our welfare system has undermined the values of family and work instead of supporting them. The Congress and I are near agreement on sweeping welfare reform. We agree on time limits, tough work requirements and the toughest possible child-support reinforcement. But I believe we must also provide child care so mothers can go to work without worrying about what is happening to their children. I challenge this Congress to send me a bipartisan welfare reform that will really move people from welfare to work and do right by our children. I will sign it immediately.

But let us be candid about this difficult problem. Passing a law, even the best possible law, is only the first step. The next step is to make it work. I challenge people on welfare to make the most of this opportunity for independence. I challenge American business to give people on welfare the chance to move into the workforce. I applaud the work of religious groups and others who care for the poor. More than anything else, they know the true difficulty of this task, and they are in a position to help. Every one of us should join with them. That is the only way we can make welfare reform a reality in the lives of the American people.

To strengthen the family, we must do everything we can to keep the teen pregnancy rate going down. I am gratified, as I'm sure all Americans are, that it has dropped for two years in a row. But we all know it is still far too high. Tonight I am pleased to announce that a group of prominent Americans is responding to that challenge by forming an organization that will support grassroots community efforts all across our country in a national campaign against teen pregnancy. And I challenge all of us and every American to join their efforts.

I call on American men and women in families to respect one another. We must end the deadly scourge of domestic violence in our country. And I challenge America's families to work harder to stay together. For families that stay together not only do better economically, their children do better as well.

In particular, I challenge fathers to love and care for their children. If your family has separated, you must pay your child support. We are doing more than ever to make sure you do, and we are going to do more. But let's admit something about that too: A check will never be a substitute for a father's love and guidance, and only you, only you can make the decision to help raise your children, no matter who you are, how low or high your station in life, it is your most basic human duty of every American to do that job to the best of his or her ability.

[Educational Opportunities]

Our second challenge is to provide Americans with the educational opportunities we need for this new century.

In our schools, every classroom in America must be connected to the information superhighway, with computers, good software and well-trained teachers. We are working with the telecommunications industry, educators and parents to connect 20 percent of California's classrooms by this spring, and every classroom and library in the entire United States by the year 2000. I ask Congress to support our education technology initiative so we make sure this national partnership succeeds.

Every diploma ought to mean something. I challenge every community, every school and every state to adopt national standards of excellence to measure whether schools are meeting those standards, to cut bureaucratic red tape so that schools and teachers have more flexibility for grassroots reforms, and hold them accountable for results. That's what our Goals 2000 initiative is all about.

I challenge every state to give all parents the right to choose which public school their children attend and let teachers form new schools with a charter they can keep only if they do a good job.

I challenge all schools to teach character education: to teach good values, and good citizenship. And if it means teen-agers will stop killing each other over designer jackets, then our public schools should be able to require their students to wear school uniforms.

I challenge parents to be their children's first teachers. Turn off the TV. See that the homework is done. And visit your children's classroom. No program, no teacher, no one else can do that for you.

My fellow Americans, higher education is more important today than ever before. We have created a new student loan program that has made it easier to borrow and repay loans; and we have dramatically cut the student loan default rate. That's something we should all be proud of, because it was unconscionably high just a few years ago. Through AmeriCorps, our national service program, this year 25,000 young people will earn college money by serving in their communities to improve the lives of their friends and neighbors. These initiatives are right for America, and we should keep them going.

And we should work hard to open the doors to college even wider. I challenge Congress to expand work study and help 1 million young Americans work their way through college by the year 2000; to provide a $1,000 merit scholarship for the top 5 percent of graduates in every high school in the U.S.; to expand Pell Grant scholarships for deserving and needy students; and to make up to $10,000 a year of college tuition tax deductible. It's a good idea for America.

[Economic Security]

Our third challenge is to help every American who is willing to work for it achieve economic security in this new age.

People who work hard still need support to get ahead in the new economy. They need education and training for a lifetime, they need more support for families raising children, they need retirement security, they need access to health care.

More and more Americans are finding that the education of their childhood simply doesn't last a lifetime. So I challenge Congress to consolidate 70 overlapping, antiquated job training programs into a simple voucher worth $2,600 for unemployed or underemployed workers to use as they please for community college tuition or other training. This is a GI Bill for America's Workers we should all be able to agree on.

More and more Americans are working hard without a raise. Congress sets the minimum wage. Within a year, the minimum wage will fall to a 40-year low in purchasing power. $4.25 an hour is no longer a minimum wage. But millions of Americans and their children are trying to live on it. I challenge you to raise their minimum wage.

In 1993, Congress cut the taxes of 15 million hard-pressed working families, to make sure no parents who worked full time would have to raise their children in poverty, and to encourage people to move from welfare to work. This expanded Earned Income Tax Credit is now worth about $1,800 a year to a family of four living on $20,000. The budget bill I vetoed would have reversed this achievement, and raised taxes on nearly 8 million of those people. We should not do that. We should not do that.

But I also agree that the people who are helped under this initiative are not all those in our country who are working hard to do a good job raising their children and at work. I agree that we need a tax credit for working families with children. That's one thing most of us in this chamber, I hope, can agree on. I know it is strongly supported by the Republican majority and it should be a part of any final budget agreement.

I want to challenge every business that can possibly afford it to provide pensions for your employees, and I challenge Congress to pass a proposal recommended by the White House Conference on Small Business that would make it easier for small businesses and farmers to establish their own pension plans. That is something we should all agree on.

We should also protect existing pension plans. Two years ago, with bipartisan support, it was almost unanimous on both sides of the aisle. We moved to protect the pensions of 8 million working people and to stabilize the pensions of 32 million more. Congress should not now let companies endanger those workers' pension funds. I know the proposal to liberalize the ability of employers to take money out of pension funds for other purposes would raise money for the treasury, but I believe it is false economy. I vetoed that proposal last year, and I would have to do so again.

Finally, if our working families are going to succeed in the new economy, they must be able to buy health insurance policies that they do not lose when they change jobs or when someone in their family gets sick. Over the past two years, over 1 million Americans in working families have lost their health insurance. We have to do more to make health care available to every American. And Congress should start by passing the bipartisan bill sponsored by Senator [Edward M.] Kennedy [D-Mass.] and Senator [Nancy Landon] Kassebaum [R-Kan.] that would require insurance companies to stop dropping people when they switch jobs, and stop denying coverage for pre-existing conditions. Let's all do that.

And even as we enact savings in these programs we must have a common commitment to preserve the basic protections Medicare and Medicaid give, not just to the poor, but people in working families, including children, people with disabilities, people with AIDS, senior citizens in nursing homes. In the past three years we have saved $15 billion just by fighting health care fraud and abuse. We have all agreed to save much more. We have all agreed to stabilize the Medicare trust fund. But we must not abandon our fundamental obligations to the people who need Medicare and Medicaid. America cannot become stronger if they become weaker.

The GI Bill for Workers, tax relief for education and child-rearing, pension availability and protection, access to health care, preservation of Medicare and Medicaid, these things—along with the Family and Medical Leave Act passed in 1993—these things will help responsible hard-working American families to make the most of their own lives.

But employers and employees must do their part as well, as they are in so many of our finest companies, working together, putting long-term prosperity ahead of short-term gain. As workers increase their hours and their productivity, employers should make sure they get the skills they need and share the benefits of the good years as well as the burdens of the bad ones. When companies and workers work as a team, they do better. And so does America.

[Take Back the Streets]

Our fourth great challenge is to take our streets back from crime, gangs and drugs.

At last, we have begun to find the way to reduce crime—forming community partnerships with local police forces to catch criminals and to prevent crime. This strategy, called community policing, is clearly working. Violent crime is coming down all across America.

In New York City, murders are down 25 percent, in St. Louis 18 percent, in Seattle 32 percent. But we still have a long way to go before our streets are safe and our people are free from fear.

The Crime Bill of 1994 is critical to the success of community policing. It provides funds for 100,000 new police in communities of all sizes. We are already a third of the way there. And I challenge the Congress to finish the job. Let us stick with a strategy that's working and keep the crime rate coming down.

Community policing also requires bonds of trust between citizens and our police. I ask all Americans to respect and support our law enforcement officers. And to our police I say: Our children need you as role models and heroes. Don't let them down.

The Brady Bill has stopped 44,000 people with criminal records from buying guns. The assault weapons ban is keeping 19 kinds of assault weapons out of the hands of violent gangs. I challenge the Congress to keep those laws on the books.

Our next step in the fight against crime is to take on gangs the way we once took on the mob. I am directing the FBI and other investigative agencies to target gangs that involve juveniles in violent crime and to seek authority to prosecute as adults teen-agers who maim and kill like adults.

And I challenge local housing authorities and tenant associations: Criminal gang members and drug dealers are destroying the lives of decent tenants. From now on, the rule for residents who commit crimes and peddle drugs should be: One strike and you're out.

I challenge every state to match federal policy: to assure that serious violent criminals serve at least 85 percent of their sentence.

More police and punishment are important, but they're not enough. We have got to keep more of our young people out of trouble, with prevention strategies not dictated by Washington, but developed in communities. I challenge all of our communities, all of our adults, to give our children futures to say yes to. And I challenge Congress not to abandon the crime bill's support of these grassroots prevention efforts.

Finally, to reduce crime and violence, we have to reduce the drug problem. The challenge begins at home, with parents talking to their children openly and firmly. It embraces our churches and synagogues, our youth groups and our schools. I challenge Congress not to cut our support for drug-free schools. People like these DARE [Drug Abuse Resistance Education] officers are making a real impression on grade school children that will give them the strength to say no when the time comes.

Meanwhile, we continue our efforts to cut the flow of drugs into America. For the last two years, one man in particular has been on the front lines of that effort. Tonight I am nominating a hero of the Persian Gulf and the commander in chief of the U.S. Military's Southern Command, Gen. Barry McCaffrey, as America's new drug czar.

Gen. McCaffrey has earned three Purple Hearts and two Silver Stars fighting for this country. Tonight I ask that he lead our nation's battle against drugs at home and abroad. To succeed, he needs a force far larger than he has ever commanded. He needs all of us. Every one of us [has] a role to play on this team. Thank you, Gen. McCaffrey, for agreeing to serve your country one more time.

[Commitment to the Environment]

Our fifth challenge: to leave our environment safe and clean for the next generation.

Because of a generation of bipartisan effort, we do have cleaner water and air. Lead levels in children's blood have been cut by 70 percent and toxic emissions from factories cut in half. Lake Erie was dead. Now it is a thriving resource.

But 10 million children under 12 still live within four miles of a toxic waste dump. A third of us breathe air that endangers our health. And in too many communities, water is not safe to drink. We still have much to do.

Yet Congress has voted to cut environmental enforcement by 25 percent. That means more toxic chemicals in our water, more smog in our air, more pesticides in our food. Lobbyists for the polluters have been allowed to write their own loopholes into bills to weaken laws that protect the health and safety of our children. Some say that the taxpayers should pick up the tab for toxic waste and let polluters who can afford to fix it off the hook.

I challenge Congress to re-examine those policies and to reverse them. I believe . . . This issue has not been a partisan issue. The most significant environmental gains in the last 30 years were made under a Democratic Congress and President Richard Nixon. We can work together. We have to believe some basic things. Do you believe we can expand the economy without hurting the environment? I do. Do you believe we can create more jobs over the long run by cleaning the environment up? I know we can. That should be our commitment.

We must challenge businesses and communities to take more initiative in protecting the environment, and we have to make it easier for them to do it. To businesses, this administration is saying: If you can find a cheaper, more efficient way than government regulations required to meet tough pollution standards, do it—as long as you do it right.

To communities we say: We must strengthen community right-to-know laws requiring polluters to disclose their emissions, but you have to use the information to work with business to cut pollution. People do have a right to know that their air and water are safe.

[American World Leadership]

Our sixth challenge is to maintain America's leadership in the fight for freedom and peace throughout the world.

Because of American leadership, more people than ever before live free and at peace and Americans have known 50 years of prosperity and security. We owe thanks especially to our veterans of World War II. I would like to say to Senator Bob Dole [R-Kan.] and to all others in this chamber who fought in World War II and to all others on both sides of the aisle who have fought bravely in all our conflicts since, I salute your service and so do the American people.

All over the world, even after the Cold War people still look to us, and trust us to help them seek the blessings of peace and freedom.

But as the Cold War fades into memory, voices of isolation say America should retreat from its responsibilities. I say they are wrong.

The threats we face today as Americans respect no nation's borders— think of them: terrorism, the spread of weapons of mass destruction, organized crime, drug trafficking, ethnic and religious hatred, aggression by rogue states, environmental degradation. If we fail to address these threats today, we will suffer the consequences in all our tomorrows.

Of course we can't be everywhere. Of course we can't do everything. But where our interests and our values are at stake—and where we can make a difference—America must lead. We must not be isolationist; we must not be the world's policeman. But we can and should be the world's very best peacemaker.

By keeping our military strong, by using diplomacy where we can and force where we must, by working with others to share the risk and the cost of our efforts, America is making a difference for people here and around the world.

For the first time since the dawn of the nuclear age, for the first time since the dawn of the nuclear age, there is not a single Russian missile pointed at America's children. North Korea has now frozen its dangerous nuclear weapons program. In Haiti, the dictators are gone, democracy has a new day, the flow of desperate refugees to our shores [has] subsided.

Through tougher trade deals for America, over 80 of them, we have opened markets abroad, and now exports are at an all-time high, growing faster than imports and creating good American jobs.

We stood with those taking risks for peace—in Northern Ireland, where Catholic and Protestant children now tell their parents violence must never return, and in the Middle East, where Arabs and Jews, who once seemed destined to fight forever, now share knowledge and resources and even dreams.

And we stood up for peace in Bosnia. Remember the skeletal prisoners, the mass graves, the campaigns of rape and torture, the endless lines of refugees, the threat of a spreading war—all these threats, all these horrors have now begun to give way to the promise of peace.

Now our troops and a strong NATO, together with our new partners from Central Europe and elsewhere, are helping that peace take hold.

As all of you know, I was just there with a bipartisan Congressional group and I was so proud not only of what our troops were doing but at the pride they evidenced in what they were doing. They knew what America's mission in this world is and they were proud to be carrying it out.

Through these efforts, we have enhanced the security of the American people. But make no mistake about it, important challenges remain. The START II treaty with Russia will cut our nuclear stockpiles by another 25 percent; I urge the Senate to ratify it—now. We must end the race to create new nuclear weapons by signing a truly comprehensive nuclear test ban treaty—this year. As we remember what happened in the Japanese subway, we can outlaw poison gas forever, if the Senate ratifies the Chemical Weapons Convention—this year. We can intensify the fight against terrorists and organized criminals at home and abroad, if Congress passes the anti-terrorism legislation I proposed after the Oklahoma City bombing—now. We can help more people move from hatred to hope all across the world in our own interest—if Congress gives us the means to remain the world's leader for peace.

[Reinventing Government]

My fellow Americans, the six challenges I have just discussed are for all of us. Our seventh challenge is really America's challenge to those of us in this hallowed hall tonight—to reinvent our government and make our democracy work for them.

Last year, this Congress applied to itself the laws it applies to everyone else. This Congress banned gifts and meals from lobbyists. This Congress forced lobbyists to disclose who pays them and what legislation they are trying to pass or kill. This Congress did that, and I applaud you for it.

Now I challenge Congress to go further, to curb special interest influence in politics by passing the first truly bipartisan campaign finance reform bill in a generation. You Republicans and Democrats alike can show the American people that we can limit spending and we can open the airwaves to all candidates.

And I also appeal to Congress to pass the line item veto you promised the American people. Our administration is working hard to give the American people a government that works better and costs less. Thanks to the work of Vice President [Al] Gore, we are eliminating 16,000 pages of unnecessary rules and regulations and shifting more decision-making out of Washington back to states and communities.

As we move into an era of balanced budgets and smaller government, we must work in new ways to enable people to make the most of their own lives. We are helping America's communities, not with more bureaucracy, but with more opportunities. Through our successful empowerment zones and community development banks we're helping people to find jobs, to start businesses.

And with tax incentives for companies that clean up abandoned industrial property, we can bring jobs back to the places that desperately, desperately need them.

But there are some areas that the federal government should not leave and should address and address strongly. One of these areas is the problem of illegal immigration. After years and years of neglect, this administration has taken a strong stand to stiffen the protection on our borders. We are increasing border patrols by 50 percent. We are increasing inspections to prevent the hiring of illegal immigrants.

And tonight, I announce I will sign an executive order to deny federal contracts to businesses that hire illegal immigrants. Let me be very clear about this: We are still a nation of immigrants, we should be proud of it. We should honor every legal immigrant here working hard to be a good citizen, working hard to become a new citizen. But we are also a nation of laws.

I want to say a special word to those who work for the federal government. Today, the federal work force is 200,000 employees smaller than it was the day I took office as president—our federal government today is the smallest it has been in 30 years, and it's getting smaller every day. Most of our fellow Americans probably don't know that, and there's a good reason, a good reason. The remaining federal work force is composed of Americans who are working harder and working smarter than ever before to make sure that the quality of our services does not decline.

I'd like to give you one example. His name is Richard Dean. He's a 49-year-old Vietnam veteran who's worked for the Social Security Administration for

22 years now. Last year, he was hard at work in the federal building in Oklahoma City when the blast killed 169 people and brought the rubble around him. He re-entered the building four times. He saved the lives of three women. He is here with us this evening, and I want to recognize Richard and applaud both his public service and his extraordinary personal heroism.

But Richard Dean's story doesn't end there. This last November, he was forced out of his office when the government shut down. And the second time the government shut down, he continued helping Social Security recipients, but he was working without pay. On behalf of Richard Dean and his family, and all the other people who are out there working every day doing a good job for the American people I challenge all of you in this chamber: Never—ever—shut the federal government down again. On behalf of all Americans, especially those who need their social security payments at the beginning of March, I also challenge Congress to preserve the full faith and credit of the United States, to honor the obligations of this great nation as we have for 220 years, to rise above partisanship and pass a straightforward extension of the debt limit and show the people America keeps its word.

I know that this evening I have asked a lot of Congress and even more from America. But I am confident. When Americans work together in their homes, their schools, their churches, their synagogues, their civic groups or their workplace, they can meet any challenge.

[Torch of Citizenship]

I say again: The era of big government is over. But we can't go back to the era of fending for yourself. We have to go forward, to the era of working together—as a community, as a team, as one America—with all of us reaching across these lines that divide us. The division, the discrimination, the rancor, we have to reach across it to find common ground. We have got to work together if we want America to work.

I want you to meet two more people tonight who do just that. Lucius Wright is a teacher in the Jackson, Miss., public school system. A Vietnam veteran, he has created groups to help inner city children turn away from gangs and build futures they can believe in. And Sgt. Jennifer Rodgers is a police officer in Oklahoma City. Like Richard Dean, she helped to pull her fellow citizens out of the rubble and deal with that awful tragedy. She reminds us that, in their response to that atrocity, the people of Oklahoma City lifted all of us with their basic sense of decency and community.

Lucius Wright and Jennifer Rodgers are special Americans, and I have the honor to announce tonight that they are the very first of several thousand Americans who will be chosen to carry the Olympic torch on its long journey from Los Angeles to the centennial of the modern Olympics in Atlanta this summer—not because they are star athletes, but because they are star citizens, community heroes meeting America's challenges. They are our real champions. Please stand up.

Now each of us must hold high the torch of citizenship in our own lives. None of us can finish the race alone. We can only achieve our destiny together—one hand, one generation, one American connecting to another. There have always been things we could do together, dreams we could make real which we could never have done on our own. We Americans have forged our identity, our very union from the very point of view that we can accommodate every point on the planet, every different opinion, but we must be bound together by a faith more powerful than any doctrine that divides us, by our belief in progress, our love of liberty, and our relentless search for common ground.

America has always sought and always risen to every challenge. Who would say that having come so far together we will not go forward from here? Who would say that this age of possibility is not for all Americans? Our country is and always has been a great and good nation, but the best is yet to come if we all do our part.

Thank you, God bless you, and God bless the United States of America. Thank you.

DOLE'S REPUBLICAN RESPONSE

Good evening. I'm Bob Dole, and I'm here to briefly reply to the president's message on the state of the union. But a reply need not be an argument. Instead, I want to present another view. Another way of thinking about the problems we face.

A few years back I met with a group of 100 high school seniors—one young man and a woman from every state. During the meeting, one young man stood up and said, "Senator, everybody has somebody who speaks for them. But who speaks for us?" he asked me. "Who speaks for the future?"

That's what I want to talk with you about tonight—the future and the values that will shape it. Those values are at the heart of our disagreements with the president. President Clinton says our differences are few, the budget numbers are close and that we should try to find common ground. We have tried and tried, again and again. But such a place appears to be elusive.

For while we share an abiding love of country, we have been unable to agree. Why? Because we have starkly different philosophies of government and profoundly different visions of America. So all the talk and fighting in Washington can seem very remote. And we political figures can seem detached and petty and far removed from the everyday struggle of American citizens and families.

But the truth is we cannot ignore the future. The point of our lives, after all, is to raise children who are smarter and healthier and nobler than we are; to contribute to a country that is better than today's America; to make a world that is better and finer for all of God's creation.

America's greatness—all that we take such justified pride in today—America's greatness was built by men and women who sacrificed ease and comfort and the joys of today, to build a better future for those who came after. How many pioneers faced a hostile and threatening frontier? How many immigrants gave their bodies to the mines? And how many soldiers lost their lives on the distant battlefields to secure a better future for their children and their children's children?

In every generation Americans have made these sacrifices and found in their making a purpose and a direction to life. Now we have to do that in this generation. And thanks to God and fortune and those who went before, we don't have to conquer a dangerous frontier. We don't have to fight another great war. What we do have to do is face the fact that we cannot give in to all of our own desires. As we have just heard, President Clinton and those who share his vision of America have chosen their ground.

The president has chosen to defend, with his veto, a welfare system that no one can defend—for it is a daily assault on the values of self-reliance and family. He has chosen to defend an education establishment run by liberals whose goal is to operate every school in America by remote control from Washington. He has chosen to veto a defense bill because it provided for defending America against weapons of mass destruction.

He has chosen to defend the status quo in Medicare—a system on which lives depend and a program in urgent need of rescue. President Clinton has chosen to defend and increase a tax burden that has pushed countless families into their own personal recessions. And unfortunately, he has chosen to veto the first balanced budget in a generation, offering only a fantasy in its place.

Now if you have a child asleep in your home tonight, you will probably check on him or her before you go to bed. As you bend over to tuck your child in, think about this: If we continue down this path we will place a tremendous burden of debt on every child in America. How can we betray them and their parents and grandparents? How can we fail to act? We cannot, and we will not.

Every political movement and every public official must locate a place in his heart where compromise ends—a core of conviction where we keep our conscience. There comes a time when even practical leaders must refuse to bend or to yield. And for Republicans and countless Democrats and independents, we have arrived at that time.

America's troubles are real, but our choices are clear and our will is strong. We must rein in our runaway government, return power to the people, reduce the tax burden. Put parents back in charge of our schools. Untie the hands of our police. Restore justice to our courts and put our faith once again in the basic goodness, wisdom and self-reliance of our people.

The president spoke with great eloquence about a future with unlimited possibilities. It is a vision we all share, for it is the story of America.

But while the president's words speak of change, his deeds are a contradiction. The president claims to embrace the future while clinging to the policies of the past.

For three years this administration has valued dependence on government over self-reliance. Federal power over community, federal planning over individual enterprise. It has tried to place government experts in charge of our economy and our health and our lives.

It has put liberal judges on the bench to war with our values and it questions the participation of religious people in public life, treating them as fanatics out of step with America.

President Clinton shares a view of America held by our country's elites:

A nation of special interest groups, united only by a dependence on government, competing with each other for handouts and held back by outdated values. Now, for those who hold this view, there is only one answer for our problems:

More government.

Bigger government.

More meddlesome government.

And if you listened closely tonight, that's what President Clinton talked about. President Clinton may well be the rear guard of the welfare state. He is the chief obstacle to a balanced budget and the balanced-budget amendment. He is almost the last public defender of a discredited status quo. We Republicans will not give up the struggle because America will round the corner to a brighter future if we prevail.

I come from Russell, Kansas—there's not much money there, but the people are rich in many other ways. Life isn't always easy, but the values are durable—love of God and country and family, commitment to honesty, decency and personal responsibility, and self-reliance tempered by a sense of community.

Those values made America the greatest nation on earth, and there is no doubt in my mind that we can get our country back on track if we reassert them again as a people, and if our government returns to them as a matter of national policy.

Now just like the debate over the budget this winter, our arguments this spring will seem a maze of conflicting numbers, assertions and high-sounding words. But what we're really arguing about are the values that will shape our nation, our government, and the future of that child sleeping down the hall.

Now some people try to make these matters complicated, but they're simple in my hometown—and probably where you are, as well. Americans know that handouts without responsibility destroy human dignity.

We know that the help of a neighbor is preferable to that of a bureaucrat. And we know that wealth is created by free individuals with their smarts and their sweat. Government programs can only spend it.

Now I'm a very practical man, but I believe in the miracle of America and I've never gone in for dramatics, but I do believe we have reached the defining moment. It is as if we went to sleep in one America and woke up in another.

It is as though our government and our institutions and our culture have been hijacked by liberals and are careening dangerously off course. Oh but we know the way back, but we must act now. And my promise tonight is that we can, and we will.

If there is no agreement, we will send President Clinton another balanced budget with tax relief for American families, regulatory relief for small businesses, farmers and ranchers and real welfare reform.

We will always be mindful of the poor and disadvantaged, education and the environment. But we will begin the defunding of Big Brother by unfunding wasteful programs and meddlesome departments. We will send the president bill after bill, returning power and programs to the states and to the people.

We will challenge President Clinton again and again to walk the talk he talks so well. As we do, remember this: Our battles will not be about numbers. They'll be about the character of our nation. Yes, our country has problems. But we can handle them.

Whether it's deficit spending or the welfare bureaucracy or our liberal courts or the trouble in our schools, what's wrong is that the elites in charge don't believe in what the people believe in. That we can fix. We know what made America great. All we need now is the resolve to lead our country back to her place in the sun and the courage to speak for the future.

So when you close the door to your child's room tonight, remember, it's not too late. This is a great country. Our strength has always come from the truth, and from sacrifice and honor, and from the bottomless reservoir of hope and work and courage that is the American people. Always, we have built for the future with a half-silent consciousness that we were doing the work of the Lord.

Today, we feel ourselves beset by many difficulties: by violence and resentment, by racial and partisan divisions, by economic storms, by dizzying changes of every kind.

Yet, the blood of greatness, of noble forebears, of men and women of incredible achievement still runs through us all. That birthright is what it means to bear the name "American."

In this time, in this generation, in this year, we—like they—can and will overcome. We need only to rededicate ourselves to earning the name we have inherited.

Thank you very much. God bless America and good night. Thank you.

February

LABOR SECRETARY REICH ON CORPORATE RESPONSIBILITY
February 6, 1996

Dismayed by a pervasive sense of job insecurity among American work-ers despite steady economic growth, low inflation, high employment, and record profits, the Clinton administration throughout the year prodded American companies to assume more responsibility for their employees. "It is a time for companies to focus beyond the bottom line," Labor Secre-tary Robert B. Reich declared in a speech delivered February 6 at George Washington University in Washington, D.C.

Three months later President Bill Clinton presided over a day-long Con-ference on Corporate Citizenship in which business executives offered what Clinton called proof that corporations "can do the right thing and make money." In August the Democratic Party platform called on "corpo-rate leaders to invest in the long-term, by providing workers with good wages and benefits, education and training, and opportunities for greater investment in company decision making and ownership." (Democratic platform, p. 623)

Job anxiety spread among both blue- and white-collar workers through-out the 1990s, as wages for many stagnated and as companies laid off tens of thousands of workers in an effort to make themselves more competitive in a world economy. This restructuring was a consequence of an economy that was shifting from a manufacturing base to a service base, from one in which workers could rely on mass production jobs and job ladders to advance their wages and careers to one that favored workers skilled in high technology and problem solving. Many also saw the downsizing as a con-sequence of shareholders demanding maximum returns on their invest-ments at the expense of long-term investments in the employees, such as job training.

Workers were also expressing anger at companies that laid off employ-ees at the same time that their executives were receiving pay increases and bonuses. One prominent example was AT&T, which announced it was lay-ing off 40,000 workers even as the value of the pay package for its chair-

man, Robert E. Allen, went up by 143 percent in 1995 to nearly $16 million. "There's a lot of rage out there," Warren Bennis, management professor at the University of Southern California, told Business Week. "Unless the private sector finds a way both to make money and reestablish a sense of trust in the workplace, we'll continue to be in trouble. Worried workers do not engage in the kind of creative problem-solving that contemporary business requires."

Reich Speech

Reich voiced similar sentiments in his speech. "In too many instances, top executives are not creating values. They are merely redistributing income from employees and their communities to shareholders," he said. "Top executives, talented entrepreneurs, Wall Street intermediaries have done very, very well. . . . Workers without adequate education and skills or with outmoded skills are in free fall. This situation is not sustainable."

Reich suggested that the corporate income tax might be reduced or eliminated for those companies that met certain minimum standards, such as upgrading their employees' skills and ensuring adequate pensions and health care coverage. He offered no other concrete proposals but urged corporations to engage in a national dialogue to exchange ideas about how corporations "can best respond" to the growing insecurities and inequalities in the American workforce.

Conference on Corporate Citizenship

That national dialogue began on May 16 when President Clinton hosted a Conference on Corporate Citizenship at Georgetown University, attended by prominent business leaders from around the country. Like Reich, Clinton made few specific proposals; he urged that tax incentives for employee education be restored and expanded to small businesses, and he announced the creation of an annual award for outstanding corporate citizenship to "celebrate business for the quality of their relationship to their workers and their communities." The award, which was to be financed and operated by the private sector, was named the Ron Brown Corporate Citizenship Award, after the late secretary of commerce who died in April. Clinton's primary focus at the conference was to highlight by example "the good practices that are going on, show how they are consistent with making money and succeeding in the free enterprise system."

Among the businesses showcased at the conference were:

- *Fel-Pro, Inc., of Skokie, Illinois. Half of the workers at this automotive supply manufacturer are minorities. Over the years Fel-Pro has provided a 220–acre employee recreation area, a summer camp for employees' children, and a wellness center and a day-care center at its factory. Legal counseling is available on site one day a week for employees. The company also offers a counseling program to help employees resolve personal problems, an elder care program, tuition* *assistance for employees, and scholarship and tutoring programs for their children. It also sponsors the Better Neighborhood Fund, which gives grants of up to $1,500 to grassroots organizations in employees' neighborhoods.*

All these services cost the company $.70 an hour per employee, less than 10 percent of total benefits. According to Fel-Pro executive Kenneth Lehman, a University of Chicago study found that "employees who utilized and appreciated our benefits most extensively, participated most regularly in productivity cost and quality improving programs. They were the employees who had the best performance evaluations and the ones that had the fewest disciplinary notices. And they were the employees who embraced change most willingly."

- *In addition to earmarking 1 percent of its sales for environmental projects, Patagonia, a manufacturer and seller of outdoor clothing, provides a day care center on site, gives two months' paid parental leave to both mothers and fathers, and is flexible in allowing workers to fulfill other family obligations. Founder Yvon Chouinard said he wanted "employees who feel secure enough at home that they can be creative while at work. I want them to bond with their children. I want them focused. And if they're distracted by guilt, they can't focus. We don't provide these benefits because we're nice. We provide them because it's good for our company."*

- *Starbucks Coffee, a nationwide chain of coffeehouses, gives all its employees, including part-timers who make up a majority of the work force, full medical benefits. It also offers equity shares to all employees.*

- *The Cin-Made Company, a manufacturer of paper packaging products in Cincinnati, has not paid a raise since Robert Frey bought the failing company in 1984. Instead, the company sets aside 35 percent of its pretax profits in a profit-sharing plan; "the company makes more money, you make more money," Frey said to his workers. In return, workers schedule their own production and their own work hours, purchase their own materials, approve all managers and office workers coming into the company, and "hire" their fellow workers. In return they are given the financial information and the training to make informed decisions. Cin-Made is now a profitable company that averages more than $4,000 a year in profit-sharing bonuses. "Courage and tenacity" are the two elements a company's leaders need to make this sort of management change, Frey said—"the courage to let go, the courage to take risk, the courage to manage by the force of your ideas and not by your position power, and the tenacity to see it all through."*

Whether these examples and the president's exhortations were likely to have much effect remained to be seen. A spokesman for Republican presidential candidate Bob Dole called the conference election-year gimmickry: "Bill Clinton proffering business advice while companies are laying employees off makes about as much sense as throwing a drowning man a brick. Bob Dole understands job creation is key to economic growth."

Companies were still laying off large numbers of workers in efforts to make their companies more competitive and profitable. In November Albert J. Dunlap, the chairman and chief executive of Sunbeam Corp., announced that the appliance manufacturer was letting go 6,000 employees—50 percent of its workforce—either through layoffs or by selling off divisions. Dunlap is perhaps best known for the sale of Scott Paper Co., which boosted shareholder returns, but Dunlap laid off more than 11,000 workers during his two years as Scott chairman and CEO.

> *Following are excerpts from the text of a speech delivered February 6, 1996, by Labor Secretary Robert B. Reich to the George Washington University School of Business and Public Management:*

. . . [B]usiness issues cannot be separated from public policy issues, and public issues cannot be separated from what the private sector does or does not do. . . . Because if the government is going to do less, then the private sector will have to do more. The stunning announcement that we heard on the first business day of 1996 that a major American corporation, enjoying record profits, would downsize, laying off tens of thousands of workers, raises serious questions about the private sector's capacity or willingness or ability to take on these new responsibilities.

What may feel like a nightmare for affected workers is in fact hailed as a dream come true on Wall Street, suggesting that the company may have done exactly the right thing by its shareholders. But that is precisely the question I want to raise with you this morning.

Does a company have obligations, responsibilities beyond the bottom line? Does a company owe anything to its workers, its workers' families, the communities in which it does business? . . .

In fact, I think that we have embarked in this country on a little bit of a false debate between family values on the one side, and economics on the other. Family values are intimately intertwined with what might be called home economics.

The necessity to work longer hours in order to make ends meet may mean that a parent isn't home when a child is in most need of parenting.

The urgency of finding a new job may mean that one spouse has to move to another city, meaning long commutes. Again, you can't be there with a family. Or it may require that an entire family uproot itself from its support system of family and friends and extended relatives. The financial pressures resulting from a declining pay check or the loss of a job can disrupt and sometimes destroy families.

Now, whether we like it or not, whether we recognize it or not, corporate decision-makers in our society have significant influence over the future strength of America's families and our communities. Yet many business executives protest, with some justification, that they have no choice. They argue that they must do what is in the interest of shareholders, even sometimes at the expense of employees and communities. If wages and benefits can be cut without imperiling production, then they must be cut. If employees' efforts do not generate a sufficient return, then the jobs have to go. And if an entire community loses its economic base because the company can do its work more efficiently elsewhere, then so be it.

Managers who balk at executing the judgments of the market may fear, with some reason, that they will quickly face their own day of reckoning.

And yet I want to suggest to you that this restricted vision of stewardship may be ultimately disastrous for this country, and it may ultimately harm American business. Corporate leaders need to reconsider.

This era of government downsizing is also a time for corporations to size up their responsibilities in general to America. As the President noted in his State of the Union address, employers must do their part along with employees, sharing with workers the benefits of the good years, not just the burdens of the bad. It is a time for companies to focus beyond the bottom line. It's time for a new corporate citizenship, or at least a vision of a new corporate citizenship. . . .

[Demise of an Implicit Social Contract]

. . . Why do we find very highly profitable companies now turning their backs on employees and communities?

Well, for one thing, competition. American businesses have been transformed in the intervening years from very comfortable and stable rivals into bloodletting gladiators. Information technologies have radically reduced the transaction time between suppliers, wholesalers and customers.

Airlines, telephone companies, utilities, common carriers, Wall Street itself have all been de-regulated. Global competitors threaten the very survival of many American businesses. Entry barriers, such as preferential access to capital markets, have dropped, allowing small companies to grab market share from big ones.

Now, today what all that means is that vast amounts of capital can be moved from place to place almost at the speed of an electronic impulse. Investors face an ever wider array of choices of where to put their money, and again they can move it at extraordinary speed. You might call it electronic capitalism, and this electronic capitalism has replaced the rather gentlemanly investment system that [once gave CEOs] the discretion to balance the interests of shareholders against the interests of employees and communities.

Nowadays, any chief executive officer who hesitates to subordinate all else to maximize shareholder returns risks trouble, and by the same token, chief executives who ruthlessly subordinate all else to maximizing shareholder returns can reap very handsome rewards. . . .

Now this transformation of the corporation into the agent of the shareholder alone and the consequent stranding of so many working people and their communities is occurring at a particularly unfortunate time in American history.

Much of the American workforce is facing a stark challenge of adapting to a very, very different economy, just as sources of support in meeting that challenge are quickly eroding. Precisely the same explosion of technological change and global integration that I mentioned before has intensified competition among companies and expanded investors' options, but it is also changing the nature of work.

The mass production jobs that once characterized most of the American economy, and certainly which were the gateway into the middle class as high volume standardized mass production jobs, particularly of the post-Second World War, are being replaced by jobs requiring technical or problem-solving skills, and also the capacity to continuously upgrade skills, continuously learn and re-learn.

The earnings of people who are poorly educated to begin with or who have outmoded skills are declining. The earnings of those with good educations, good connections, the right skills, they are rising. The gap is widening rapidly. . . .

[A Problem for Everyone]

Now, this is a problem for all of us. It is not just a problem for the bottom half of the American workforce trapped in the old economy. . . . If a significant portion of our people in this country lack the skills to succeed in the new economy, the standard of living of all Americans is imperiled.

The corporation's relentless focus on one goal, the exclusive goal of maximizing shareholder returns, makes it less willing, less able, gives it less capacity to ease the transition of the American work force to this new economy. And that is one of the ironies we are dealing with. . . .

The narrow economic calculus discourages investments that the country needs so badly. The nation as a whole may be better off when employers provide adequate pensions and decent health care coverage.

And when they teach their workers basic or industry wide skills beyond what is required to function on the specific job, the economy, as a whole, may be more productive and flexible. . . .

And yet, because the employers' shareholders don't reap the full benefits of these kinds of investments, investments in skills, investments in transforming the work place, there is no incentive on the part of the corporation to make these kinds of investments.

Even the most enlightened chief executive officer will be loath to make them to the extent that society needs them to be made. Now, to be sure, some companies do take the high road to higher profits bringing employees along, while improving and enlarging their businesses and thus expanding their payrolls. Rather than taking the low road of merely paring back payrolls, or suppressing wages.

And shareholders of these companies do perfectly well. In fact, the long term payoff to shareholders from taking the high road may be in many cases higher than the payoff from taking the low road. Because you are left with a more loyal and dedicated and skilled work force. That may be the most important sustainable competitive advantage a business can possibly have in the long term. . . .

Unfortunately, the high road is the exception rather than the rule. In too many instances, top executives are not creating values. They are merely redistributing income from employees and their communities to shareholders. As corporations have focused more and more exclusively on increasing shareholders' returns, the consequences for society have become very obvious.

The stock market has soared. Last year, [the] Dow Jones industrial average [went] up 33 percent while pink slips have proliferated. Health care and pensions have been cut and the pay checks of most employees have gone nowhere.

Top executives, talented entrepreneurs, Wall Street intermediaries have done very, very well. Some of them have never done as well. Workers without adequate education and skills, or with outmoded skills, are in free fall. This situation is not sustainable.

You do not want your children to live in a society divided radically between the have mores, and the have [lesses]. You do not want to live in a society becoming a two tiered society. But, what can be done about it? . . .

Exhortation, what about exhortation, speeches? Exhortation can have some effect, I believe. After all, most companies are understandably concerned about their public image. Good corporate citizenship is often a wise business strategy. . . .

Now earlier I listed several companies that have distinguished themselves as fine employers. Many companies are also taking an active role in improving their communities, actively participating in local training programs, contributing to public schools. And that is all to be commended. But unfortunately, these efforts are too often canceled out by companies that conduct bidding wars among states and localities. Threatening to leave one place or offering to go to another depending on how much their taxes are cut, or how much of a cash subsidy they can elicit from the public sector.

Such tactics result in a giant zero sum gain that does not create a single new job, but merely moves jobs from place to place. And it also puts those competitors, those businesses that are not engaging in this kind of zero sum tactic, at a competitive disadvantage because they are not getting the tax break, they are not getting the subsidy. But worst of all, these giant zero sum gains started by companies rob and drain local tax jurisdictions, local cities and towns of resources that could otherwise be put into education, or roads, or playgrounds, or libraries or other public services so critical to that community.

These kinds of activities, starting bidding wars for tax breaks or subsidies, these are the opposites of good corporate citizenship and they deserve condemnation. Now assume, for the sake of the argument, that we've gone as far as we can in exhorting companies to be more responsible and in quelling their appetite for political favors.

[Possible Incentives for Change]

. . . What else can we be doing, what else can be done? Let's look at the basics. The corporation is, remember, a creature of law. Corporations do not exist in a state of nature. The corporate form of business carries with it several special advantages. Investors are not personally liable for damages or debts. A corporation has the same rights of free speech and legal action that an individual has but a corporation can live forever.

Now there are marked disadvantages in incorporation as well. The most notable, corporations must pay taxes on their incomes as do investors who receive dividends. The result is a double taxation on dividends. If we want businesses to take more responsibility for the American work force and the work force's transformation in the global economy, we will have to alter this mix of advantages and disadvantages to provide the proper incentives.

For example, if we want companies to do things which do not necessarily improve their shareholders' returns but do help society as a whole, actions such as upgrading the general skills of employees, providing them with decent pension and health care protections. Sharing more of the profits with them. And when laying them off, retraining them and placing them in new jobs. . . . If we want companies to do this then presumably we've got to give companies an economic reason to do this. One possibility would be to reduce or eliminate the corporate income tax. But only for companies that achieve certain minimum standards, certain minimum requirements along these dimensions.

Now this is admittedly just one proposal and it is a very modest proposal. The tax code already treats different types of organizations differently. Charitable organizations meeting certain minimum requirements of structure and behavior are treated quite differently from the standard corporation as are partnerships and proprietorships.

These differences, let me remind you, reflect judgments about the societal benefits and responsibilities stemming from these various forms of organization. Now similarly there are societal advantages in improving the quality and the flexibility of the work force. And there are societal costs in failing to do so. Certain enterprises may be well positioned to maximize these advantages and minimize these costs. Let us as a society encourage them to do so and reward them accordingly. . . .

Now, others are going to have different ideas for how corporations can best respond to the growing inequalities and insecurities of our workforce. Let us, at the very least, have a national discussion about this, about the role of corporations at this unique moment in American history.

Surely, this discussion is no less urgent, no less important than the one we're having about the role of government. Chief executives should contribute to this discussion—not in order to defend the status quo, but in recognition that the trends we're observing, the trends with regard to wider and wider disparities of income in this country, the trends with regard to wages . . . cannot be allowed to continue.

In this era of smaller government, at a time when so many Americans are foundering in the face of record profits and a soaring stock market, the failure of the private sector to respond imperils this nation's continued prosperity and stability.

Will the end of the era of big government signal the beginning of a new era of corporate citizenship? Nobody can yet say for sure, but I am certain that unless checked, the resentments of stranded workers will eventually undermine the political conditions, the political preconditions for continued prosperity.

. . . If too many of our people feel excluded from . . . a dynamic economy, if they don't feel that they are reaping the benefits of economic growth but they feel instead that they are disproportionately burdened by the downside risks and costs of economic growth, they will support policies that ultimately sacrifice growth for the sake of economic security. They may support policies like trade protection or capital controls or inflexible labor market rules.

Now, I sincerely hope we don't ever get to that point. You in this room have an enormous interest in sustaining the culture of openness and economic dynamism that has served this country so well. . . . I urge you, for the sake of not only our economy, but our society, to help create and sustain a new era of corporate citizenship.

PRESIDENT'S ECONOMIC REPORT, ECONOMIC ADVISERS' REPORT
February 14, 1996

President Bill Clinton was able to bolster his reelection prospects Febru-ary 14, when he announced in his third annual economic report that the American economy is "healthy and strong." As evidence Clinton pointed to the creation of 8 million new jobs during the first three years of his presi-dency, a decline in the "misery index"—the sum of the inflation and unem-ployment rates—to its lowest level since 1968, a declining federal budget deficit, and soaring private investment. Even some of the more worrisome, long-term economic trends—poverty and stagnating wages—were showing signs of ameliorating, Clinton reported.

In its accompanying report, the Council of Economic Advisers (CEA) also lauded the economy, and by implication the president, saying the economy had "performed exceptionally well" since Clinton had taken office. Nonetheless, it noted, "pressing challenges remain."

The CEA celebrated its fiftieth anniversary in 1996. Congress estab-lished the council in the Employment Act of 1946 to advise the president on economic matters. In addition to an annual report, the CEA monitors key macroeconomic indicators for the president and provides advice and analysis on domestic and international economic issues and policy.

The President's Report

In his brief report, the president outlined his administration's eco-nomic agenda: to balance the federal budget, to prepare Americans for the world of work, to increase economic security for all Americans, to create high-wage jobs through technology and exports, and to make government smaller but more efficient. Noting that the federal budget deficit had already been cut nearly in half during his tenure, Clinton said that he had proposed a plan to balance the budget within seven years "without under-cutting Medicare, Medicaid, education, or the environment and without raising taxes on working families." The president also repeated earlier calls for programs that would achieve other elements of his economic *agenda—among them, making the first $10,000 of college tuition tax deductible, giving the top 5 percent of students in every high school a $1,000 merit scholarship, replacing the current worker training system with a voucher system that would allow workers to tailor training to their needs, raising the minimum wage, ensuring that workers can obtain health insurance coverage when they change jobs, and extending pension coverage. "Our strategy of deficit reduction and investment in our people has begun to work," Clinton said. "It would be a grave error to turn back."*

The CEA Report

In the report's opening chapter, the CEA said that despite good economic performance, "pressing challenges remain." In the short run the challenge was to maintain full employment with low inflation. In the long run the challenges were to increase productivity growth and to "ensure that all Americans share in the benefits of a stronger economy."

Reduction of the federal budget deficit was a key to solving all these challenges. Since Clinton took office, the advisers said, the deficit had been cut nearly in half, and the fiscal 1995 deficit was the lowest since fiscal 1979. The "major macroeconomic policy event" of 1995, according to the CEA, was the bipartisan commitment to balance the budget by the year 2002. Continued deficit reduction should increase private investment and thus raise living standards, the advisers said.

The advisers noted some evidence that the negative effects of slow productivity growth were beginning to turn around. Real median family income rose in 1994 for the first time since 1989; it was, however, still just 2.5 percent above its level in 1973. The poverty rate fell in 1994 for the first time in five years. Nonetheless, income inequality was continuing to grow. Between 1979 and 1993, real incomes for the wealthiest 20 percent of American families rose by 18 percent, while real incomes for the poorest fifth fell by 15 percent.

In its 250-page report, the CEA predicted that the impressive gains made in 1994 and 1995 would continue. For 1996 the advisers predicted that the economy would grow at an annual rate of 2.2 percent; that inflation would increase somewhat, from 2.7 percent in 1995 to 3.1 percent; and that unemployment would hold relatively steady at about 5.7 percent. The advisers also expected both long- and short-term interest rates to edge lower as reductions in the federal budget deficit continued to ease demand in the capital markets.

"Perhaps the best news" of 1995 "was that inflation remained low and stable despite an unemployment rate that in the past was associated with rising inflation," the CEA report said. At a news conference, CEA chairman Joseph E. Stiglitz told reporters that "it is possible that the economy of the mid-1990s will be reminiscent of the economy of the 1950s and 1960s," a halcyon period in American economics of growth, rising incomes, low unemployment, and low inflation.

Following is the text of the Economic Report of the President and excerpts from chapters 1 and 2 of the Annual Report of the Council of Economic Advisers, both issued by the White House February 14, 1996:

ECONOMIC REPORT OF THE PRESIDENT

To the Congress of the United States:

FIFTY YEARS AGO, the CONGRESS passed and President Truman signed the Employment Act of 1946, which committed the U.S. Government to promote policies designed to create employment opportunities for all Americans. I am proud that my Administration has made President Truman's commitment a reality. Over the past 3 years, we have created a sound economic foundation to face the challenges of the 21st century.

Strong Economic Performance

Overall, the American economy is healthy and strong. In the first 3 years of this Administration nearly 8 million jobs were created, 93 percent of them in the private sector. The so-called "misery index"—the sum of the inflation and unemployment rates—fell last year to its lowest level since 1968. Investment has soared, laying the basis for future higher economic growth. New business incorporations have set a record, and exports of American-made goods have grown rapidly. Ours is the strongest and most competitive economy in the world—and its fundamentals are as sound as they have been in three decades.

This turnaround occurred because of the hard work and ingenuity of the American people. Many of the new jobs are high-wage service sector jobs—reflecting the changing structure of the economy. The telecommunications, biotechnology, and software industries have led the high-tech revolution world-wide. Traditional industries, such as manufacturing and construction, have restructured and now use technology and workplace innovation to thrive and once again create jobs. For example, in 1994 and 1995, America was once again the world's largest automobile maker.

Our 1993 economic plan set the stage for this economic expansion and resurgence, by enacting historic deficit reduction while continuing to invest in technology and education. For over a decade, growing Federal budget deficits kept interest rates high and dampened investment and productivity growth. Now, our deficit is proportionately the lowest of any major economy.

Today, our challenge is to ensure that all Americans can become winners in economic change—that our people have the skills and the security to make the most of their own lives. The very explosion of technology and trade that creates such extraordinary opportunity also places new pressures on working people. Over the past two decades, middle-class earnings have stagnated, and our poorest families saw their incomes fall. These are long-run trends, and 3 years of sound economic policies cannot correct for a decade of neglect. Even so, we are beginning to make some progress: real median family income increased by 2.3 percent in 1994, and the poverty rate fell in 1994 for the first time in 5 years.

Addressing Our Economic Challenges

I am firmly committed to addressing our economic challenges and enhancing economic security for all Americans. People who work hard need to know that they can and will have a chance to win in our new and changing economy. Our economic agenda seeks both to promote growth and to bring the fruits of that growth within reach of all Americans. Our overall strategy is straightforward:

- *Balancing the budget.* In the 12 years before I took office the budget deficit skyrocketed and the national debt quadrupled. My Administration has already cut the budget deficit nearly in half. I am determined to finish the job of putting our fiscal house in order. I have proposed a plan that balances the budget in 7 years, without violating our fundamental values—without undercutting Medicare, Medicaid, education, or the environment and without raising taxes on working families. The plans put forth by my Administration and by the Republicans in the Congress contain enough spending cuts in common to balance the budget and still provide a modest tax cut. I am committed to giving the American people a balanced budget.
- *Preparing workers through education and training.* In the new economy, education is the key to opportunity—and the education obtained as a child in school will no longer last a lifetime. My Administration has put in place the elements of a lifetime-learning system to enable Americans to attend schools with high standards; get help going to college, or from school into the workplace; and receive training and education throughout their careers. We expanded Head Start for preschoolers; enacted Goals 2000, establishing high standards for schools; created a new direct student loan program that makes it easier for young people to borrow and repay college loans; gave 50,000 young people the opportunity to earn college tuition through community service; and enacted the School-to-Work Opportunities Act. Now we must continue to give our people the skills they need, by enacting my proposals to make the first $10,000 of college tuition tax deductible; to give the top 5 percent of students in each high school a $1,000 merit scholarship; and to enact the GI Bill for Workers, which would replace the existing worker training system with a flexible voucher that workers could use at community colleges or other training facilities.
- *Increasing economic security.* We must give Americans the security they need to thrive in the new economy. We can do this through health insurance reforms that will give Americans a chance to buy insurance when they change jobs or when someone in their family is sick. We can do this by encouraging firms to provide more extensive pension cover-

age, as I have done through my proposals for pension simplification. In addition, we should make work pay by increasing the minimum wage and preserving the full Earned Income Tax Credit (EITC), which cuts taxes for hard-pressed working families to make sure that no parents who work full-time have to raise their children in poverty.

- *Creating high-wage jobs through technology and exports.* We must continue to encourage the growth of high-wage industries, which will create the high-wage jobs of the future. We have reformed the decades-old telecommunications laws, to help spur the digital revolution that will continue to transform the way we live. We must continue to encourage exports, since jobs supported by goods exports pay on average 13 percent more than other jobs. My Administration has concluded over 200 trade agreements, including the North American Free Trade Agreement and the Uruguay Round of the General Agreement on Tariffs and Trade, seeking an open world marketplace and fair rules for exporters of American goods and services. As a result, merchandise exports have increased by 31 percent.

- *A government that is smaller, works better, and costs less.* A new economy demands a new kind of government. The era of big, centralized, one-size-fits-all government is over. But the answer is not the wholesale dismantling of government. Rather, we must strive to meet our problems using flexible, nonbureaucratic means—and working with businesses, religious groups, civic organizations, schools, and State and local governments. My Administration has reduced the size of government: as a percentage of civilian nonfarm employment, the Federal workforce is the smallest it has been since 1933, before the New Deal. We have conducted a top-to-bottom overhaul of Federal regulations, and are eliminating 16,000 pages of outdated or burdensome rules altogether. We have reformed environmental, workplace safety, and pharmaceutical regulation to cut red tape without hurting public protection. And we will continue to find new, market-based ways to protect the public.

The Need to Continue with What Works

As *The Annual Report of the Council of Economic Advisers* makes clear, this is a moment of great possibility for our country. Ours is the healthiest of any major economy. No nation on earth is better positioned to reap the rewards of the new era. Our strategy of deficit reduction and investment in our people has begun to work. It would be a grave error to turn back.

Our Nation must reject the temptation to shrink from its responsibilities or to turn to narrow, shortsighted solutions for long-term problems. If we continue to invest for the long term, we will pass on to the next generation a Nation in which opportunity is even more plentiful than it is today.

William J. Clinton
The White House
February 14, 1996

THE ANNUAL REPORT OF THE COUNCIL OF ECONOMIC ADVISERS

Economic Policy for the 21st Century

The American economy has performed exceptionally well over the past 3 years. The combined rate of unemployment and inflation fell to its lowest level since 1968. Productivity in the manufacturing sector has increased by an average of 4 percent per year. Investment has soared, laying the basis for increased productivity in the future, while exports have boomed: equipment investment and merchandise exports both have climbed more than 25 percent since the beginning of 1993. Yet despite these encouraging developments, many Americans remain concerned about the state of their own economic affairs. Their dissatisfaction reminds us of the many challenges that remain.

In 1992, more than 9 million Americans were unemployed, and the unemployment rate was above 7 percent. In parts of the country, such as California, nearly one-tenth of the labor force was without a job. By late 1995, however, the unemployment rate had dropped to 5.6 percent, and the economy was poised to reach the target the Administration had set for it: 8 million new jobs in 4 years.

Before the Administration could move ahead with its own positive economic agenda (which this Report describes), it had to address some of the economic problems it had inherited. The economy suffered from multiple infirmities—a weakened banking system, increasing poverty, and lackluster overall performance—but the most visible problem was the soaring budget deficit. The first step required to set the economy on the right course was to reduce the Federal budget deficit. By cutting the Federal Government's borrowing needs, deficit reduction has contributed to lower interest rates for businesses and consumers, thereby spurring investment and growth.

The Omnibus Budget Reconciliation Act of 1993 (OBRA93), which embodied the President's deficit reduction plan, put the country solidly on the road to fiscal responsibility. For over three decades the country had been gradually reducing the burden of the debt that had financed victory in World War II: the ratio of debt to gross domestic product (GDP) fell from 82 percent in 1950 to 27 percent in 1980. Within 12 years much of this progress was lost, and the debt to GDP ratio soared to 50 percent by 1992. . . . Following passage of OBRA93, the debt to GDP ratio has stabilized.

Since OBRA93, the deficit has been cut nearly in half, from $290 billion in fiscal 1992 to $164 billion in fiscal 1995. . . . The deficit has been reduced in dollar terms for 3 consecutive years for the first time since the Truman Administration. The decline in the deficit as a percentage of national output has been particularly striking: at 2.3 percent of GDP, the fiscal 1995 deficit is the lowest since fiscal 1979 and less than half the fiscal 1992 level of 4.9 percent. The Federal Government is now running a primary budget surplus: in other words, were it not for the interest payments on the inherited debt, there would be no deficit. And the general government deficit is now a smaller percentage of GDP than in any of the other major industrial economies. . . .

This restoration of fiscal responsibility, achieved without sacrificing crucial investments in our Nation's human, physical, and natural resources, provided the background for the current bipartisan resolve to eliminate the deficit within 7 years. . . .

Economic Challenges

The economy's recent performance notwithstanding, pressing challenges remain. In the short run, . . . the principal economic challenge is to maintain full employment with low inflation. In the long run, the two paramount challenges are to increase productivity growth and to ensure that all Americans share in the benefits of a stronger economy. Since 1973, productivity growth has been relatively sluggish: its pace in the economy as a whole is significantly slower than it was during the two and a half decades immediately following World War II. Output per hour grew by an average of 2.9 percent per year between 1960 and 1973, but has grown by only 1.1 percent per year since then. The cumulative impact of this productivity shortfall, compounded over decades, is dramatic: output per hour would be over 40 percent higher today if the pre-1973 rate of productivity growth had been maintained. Slower productivity growth since 1973 has resulted in stagnating real wages. Because of the difficulties in measurement, the extent of the weakness in wages may be overstated, but concern over slow wage growth is genuine and cannot be ignored. Some evidence suggests that the tide may now be turning. In 1994 real median family income rose for the first time since 1989. But a 20-year trend cannot be corrected in one year. Indeed, even with the 1994 improvement, real median family income was just 2.5 percent above its 1973 level. More needs to be done. The Administration's economic policies are intended to boost growth and living standards well into the 21st century.

The negative effects of slower productivity growth have been sharpened for low-income Americans by a marked increase in income inequality. Between 1966 and 1979 Americans all across the income distribution enjoyed the benefits of economy-wide growth in real incomes: families in the poorest fifth of the population saw their real incomes grow by 20 percent, while families in the top fifth experienced real income growth of 28 percent. But since 1979 family incomes have grown apart. Between 1979 and 1993 real family incomes in the bottom fifth *fell* by 15 percent, while the incomes of the top fifth rose by 18 percent. . . .

It is too soon to tell for sure, but we may be beginning to succeed in sharing the benefits of growth and reducing poverty. The poverty rate, for example, fell in 1994 for the first time in 5 years. But we must do more to reduce inequality and poverty: despite an improvement in 1994, over one-fifth of American children still live in poverty.

Principles for Raising Living Standards

The Administration's economic policies address the twin problems of slow productivity growth and rising income inequality. Three principles guide the Administration's efforts to solve these long-run problems: *embracing change, creating opportunity*, and *promoting personal responsibility*. These principles reflect core American values, and as such they provide the basis for a national consensus for addressing our economic challenges.

Putting this consensus into practice requires a variety of partnerships—between workers and firms, between the public and the private sector, between individuals and their communities, and between the Federal Government and State and local governments. Competition is the driving force of a market economy, but companies compete more effectively when workers and managers cooperate. The public and private sectors can cooperate in solving environmental problems and in meeting skill shortages. And the Federal Government can work with the States to meet the need for infrastructure investment and a social safety net.

Much of the current debate over the economy and the budget stems from different conceptions of the roles that markets, governments, and individuals should play in improving our society. Private enterprise lies at the very heart of our modern economy. Individuals and corporations provide the initiative and innovation that have enabled the market economy to bring unrivaled prosperity to our Nation, and the underlying dynamism of markets is fundamental to continued improvements in living standards.

Yet unfettered markets occasionally fail to yield desirable outcomes or to meet important national objectives. For example, in a completely unregulated marketplace, firms may produce too much of some "goods," such as pollution, and too little of others, such as basic research and development. This failure to produce the "right" amounts of certain goods and services is due to the presence of *externalities*. Externalities arise when the actions of one firm or individual produce costs or benefits for others without that firm or individual being charged for the costs or compensated for the benefits. In such cases the government has a special role. The government has an obligation to perform that role as efficiently as possible, minimizing the burden on the economy and the intrusions in the lives of its citizens. Not every market "problem" calls for government action. In order to raise living standards, government actions therefore must meet two criteria: they must address some serious imperfection in the private marketplace, and they must be designed so that their benefits outweigh their costs.

A variety of government programs have proved extremely successful in raising living standards. We take for granted many of the government services—such as retirement and disability benefits (Social Security), health insurance for the aged (Medicare), and unemployment insurance—that the market had failed to provide. . . . Before Medicare was enacted in the 1960s, for example, many elderly Americans lacked health insurance, whereas today almost all have it. . . .

In sum, government has a place, but government must know its place. We now turn to exploring what government's place should be with regard to the three principles enunciated above: embracing change, creating opportunity, and promoting personal responsibility.

Embracing Change

Our continued prosperity and well-being depend on our embracing, not retreating from, the constant succession of new opportunities and challenges of an ever-changing world. During the past few years American firms have been through a technological revolution. They have taken a hard look at what they do, how they do it, and what they must do differently. The result: in many sectors American firms are the most competitive in the world. U.S. computer firms continue to lead the industry at a breakneck pace of technical innovation, of which the explosive growth of the Internet and the increasing popularity of the World Wide Web are merely the newest manifestations. When firms and workers embrace change as these industries have done, the economy as a whole benefits in the form of higher real incomes, lower prices for goods, a wider variety of products, and enhanced opportunities.

But while embracing change raises growth and average living standards, not everyone is made better off. In a rapidly changing economy some will find themselves without the skills required for the new jobs being created. When workers with outdated skills lose their jobs, they face the threat of prolonged unemployment or reemployment at much lower wages. Estimates suggest that about one-third of full-time workers who lose their jobs and are subsequently rehired at another full-time job take a pay cut of 20 percent or more. By providing retraining, and by establishing one-stop career development centers where workers can find out about both training and job opportunities, the government can increase the efficiency of the economy even as it reduces the burden on those who otherwise would be harmed by economic change.

This Administration has actively promoted change, by opening up markets here and abroad, by sponsoring research and development, by devising tax policies to stimulate the growth of new enterprises, and by easing the burden of government regulation. Critics sometimes claim that open trade and investment harm the economy. But . . . outward-looking trade and investment policies remain the best choice for America. They boost living standards by encouraging firms to innovate and become more competitive, by stimulating the flow of ideas across national borders, and by providing a wider variety of goods—at lower prices—to consumers and firms.

This Administration has not only promoted change for others—the workers and firms affected by its policies—but has embraced it in its own practices. The Administration recognizes that what the Federal Government does, and how it does it, is sometimes the result of a seemingly haphazard accumulation of functions rather than a coherent, concerted response to a present need. Programs inaugurated yesterday with great optimism in response to yesterday's exigencies too often survive long after their usefulness has passed. In an era of difficult budget choices, those programs that have outlived their purpose, or whose benefits no longer justify their costs, have to be cut back or eliminated to make room for programs that may be needed for success in the 21st century. Efforts to reinvent government over the past 3 years are explored in more detail below.

Creating Opportunity

The Administration is committed to extending opportunity to all Americans. Opportunity means allowing each individual to live up to his or her full potential, and ensuring that those who suffer temporary setbacks have a chance to bounce back. The commitment to opportunity is not only a fundamental American value; it is also necessary for achieving faster growth rates and higher standards of living.

Education and training are essential tools for expanding opportunity. Educational opportunities must be available at all stages of a person's life: from the preschool years through high school or college, and continuing through one's career. But these opportunities are not universally available. Children from low-income families, for example, do not enter formal schooling with the same readiness as their more economically advantaged peers—a disparity that Head Start (a government program that provides a range of preschool services to young children and their families) helps redress. And the difficulties involved in borrowing against future income highlight the importance of government student loan programs. Although college is an investment that usually pays high returns to the student and to society, private lenders view these loans without collateral as simply too risky. . . .

Opportunity entails more than just education and training: having learned the requisite skills, Americans should have the opportunity to obtain jobs. During the Great Depression, when the unemployment rate soared to over 25 percent, our economy failed to offer the opportunity to work to millions of Americans, unemployed through no fault of their own. The Employment Act of 1946 committed the government to combating unemployment. The act declared that "it is the continuing policy and responsibility of the Federal Government to use all practicable means . . . to foster and promote . . . conditions under which there will be afforded useful employment opportunities, including self-employment, for those able, willing, and seeking to work. . . ." The Administration's macroeconomic policies . . . have provided opportunity to millions of Americans by fostering job growth and reducing unemployment.

Opportunity in the labor market requires much more than active education, training, and macroeconomic policies. It also requires policies that make work pay for low-skilled workers and eliminate labor market discrimination for all. Today a full-time, year-round minimum wage worker with a family does not earn enough to stay out of poverty. To help these low-income working Americans and their families, in 1993 the President and the Congress expanded the Earned Income Tax Credit (EITC), and the President has since proposed an increase in the minimum wage from $4.25 to $5.15 an hour.

All forms of discrimination contradict a fundamental tenet of American society: that every American should have a fair chance to succeed. Our Nation has made tremendous strides in reducing discrimination, but the job is not finished. "Audit" studies, in which white and minority job seekers are given similar resumes and sent to the same sets of firms for interviews, indicate that discrimination remains a problem in the labor market. Our civil rights statutes and affirmative action programs combat such discrimination and seek to ensure equal opportunity, and the Administration is fully committed to promoting opportunities in employment, education, and government contracting for Americans subject to discrimination or its lingering effects.

Finally, opportunity also means that those who suffer temporary setbacks have the ability to put themselves back on the right track. The EITC can help, and it does more than help those who directly benefit: it also provides an enhanced sense of security to the millions of other Americans who know they might need assistance at some time in their careers.

Promoting Personal Responsibility

It is each individual's responsibility to make use of the opportunities that society offers, and not to abuse the protections that society affords. The Administration is firmly committed to designing policies and programs to bolster personal responsibility. But ultimately it is up to each and every American to assume responsibility for his or her own life.

Policies must encourage people to assume responsibility for their own lives, not discourage them from it. And policies intended to address other challenges—for example, ensuring equity—must be carefully designed to minimize any adverse impact on individual incentives. A number of government programs provide, or can be thought of as providing, insurance. Yet a problem common to all types of insurance is *moral hazard*: having the insurance makes the insured-against event more likely to occur. For example, fire insurance reduces the incentives for homeowners to take precautions against fire, and thus may make fires more likely. In the policies they write, private insurance companies include mechanisms, such as deductibles and copayment provisions, aimed at minimizing moral hazard. Similarly, government programs that compensate for misfortune—such as employment and disability insurance, and welfare programs—must be designed so as to promote responsibility, minimize adverse incentive effects, and diminish moral hazard, including dependence on government programs.

In summary, an appropriate role for policy—an effective partnership between the public and the private sector—is crucial to raising living standards. Markets are the engine of prosperity, but sometimes government must help markets to work more efficiently.

The Administration's Economic Policies

Embracing change, creating opportunity, and promoting personal responsibility—these principles are a common thread running through the Administration's economic policies. Those policies are intended to bolster, not replace, the underlying strength of markets in building a better society and raising living standards. Raising living standards entails more than just raising incomes; it also includes providing educational opportunities for our children, protecting the environment, and supplying security against devastating adversity. The Administration's economic policies include expanding markets; investing in human, physical, and technological capital; making government more efficient; and reducing the budget deficit.

Expanding Markets

Promoting Competition

Competition is the driving force of efficiency and innovation. But as we all know, life is often more comfortable with less rather than more competition. Over 200 years ago, Adam Smith recognized that, "People of the same trade seldom meet together, even for merriment and diversion, but the conversation ends in a conspiracy against the public, or in some contrivance to raise prices." It is all too easy to advocate competition for others while seeking protection from competition for oneself. Such protection is often rationalized by claims of "unfair" competition. Economists have long criticized such self-serving arguments and have advocated strong antitrust laws to secure the advantages of effective competition: lower prices, greater efficiency, increased output, more rapid growth, and enhanced innovation. Under the leadership of the Justice Department's Antitrust Division, the Administration has implemented an aggressive policy to prevent unhealthy concentrations of market power and promote competition. . . .

Promoting Exports

Both theory and evidence demonstrate that outward-looking trade and investment policies raise wages and living standards: jobs supported by merchandise exports pay 13 percent more than the national average. . . .

The Administration's trade policy record includes several historic trade agreements that have opened foreign markets. Over the past 3 years the Administration has brought the Uruguay Round to a successful close; created the North American Free Trade Area with our largest and third-largest trading partners; reached agreement with 33 other countries to seek a Free Trade Area of the Americas by 2005; set the vision for achieving free trade and investment in the Asia-Pacific by 2020; concluded 20 bilateral trade agreements with Japan; and promoted macroeconomic and trade policies that have contributed to strong export growth. . . . The Administration's aggressive support of intellectual property rights has benefited not only American firms, which lead the world in research and innovation, but also other innovative firms throughout the world, providing a spur to innovation everywhere. U.S. living standards have benefited and will continue to benefit from the Administration's efforts to promote trade.

Investing in Physical, Human, and Technological Capital

Increases in productivity are largely the consequence of investment: in physical capital (plant, equipment, and infrastructure), human capital, and in the development of new technology. Government can promote all three. Through the sound macroeconomic policies of the kind pursued during the past 3 years, the government can create an economic climate conducive to physical capital investment. But the government must play an even more direct role in making investments in people and in technology.

Investing in People

Preserving and extending lifelong investments in people has been central to the Administration's economic strategy. Investments in people are estimated to account for approximately a fifth of the annual increase in productivity achieved over the past three decades, and economic studies have demonstrated the high returns of *public* investments in this area. As Benjamin Franklin once put it, "An investment in knowledge pays the best interest." Early childhood programs, such as Head Start, seem to produce fewer repeated grades, a lower likelihood of being assigned to special education classes, and a higher likelihood of graduating from high school.

The Administration has expanded investments in education and training not only as a pro-growth policy, but also as an essential ingredient in breaking the vicious cycle of poverty. . . . [P]ast cutbacks in public support for education have aggravated trends in inequality. Between 1980 and 1994 the average tuition at public 2-year colleges increased by 70 percent, and that at public 4-year colleges by 86 percent, while the value of the maximum Pell Grant—the primary Federal program for low-income students—fell by more than 25 percent in real terms. The results of these changes are not unexpected. Returns to education have risen sharply in the past 15 years, but the expected response—increased enrollments—has occurred disproportionately among the children of the better off: over the same time period, the gap in enrollment rates between high-income and low-income children has actually increased.

This Administration is working to revitalize the Federal role in education and training. It has supported rigorous academic standards and comprehensive school reform through the Goals 2000: Educate America Act, which provides funding for the implementation of voluntary content standards and local educational innovation; created a new direct lending program for college tuition, to reduce costs and inefficiencies and make the terms of repayment less onerous; and encouraged a smooth transition from school to the workplace through the School-to-Work Opportunities Act. That piece of legislation is especially important because it funds programs to prepare high school students for today's careers. The Administration has also begun to transform the Nation's unemployment system into a reemployment system, by creating one-stop career centers and proposing a system of skill grants (job training vouchers) for low-income and dislocated workers. . . .

Investing in Research and Development

The Federal role in research and development and technology—both in conducting research and in disseminating the ideas that research generates—dates back to the 19th century. That investment has produced impressive returns: from a more productive agricultural sector to the underpinnings of what is today one of America's largest export sectors, aeronautics, and to the basic science that has given rise to one of America's most prominent high-technology sectors, biotechnology. Recent studies suggest that half or more of all increases in productivity are due to improvements in technology, and these studies have verified the high total returns to such investments—returns far in excess of those from investments in plant and equipment. As the 21st century approaches, our technology programs must be both strengthened and reoriented to emerging sectors. The Administration has promoted public sector investments in technology through programs such as the Advanced Technology Program and the Manufacturing Extension Partnerships (at the Department of Commerce's National Institute of Standards and Technology) and the Technology Reinvestment Project (at the Department of Defense's Advanced Research Project Agency).

Making the Government More Efficient

The Administration recognizes the need for change not only in *what* the government does, but also in *how* it does it.

Reinventing Government

The reinventing government initiative was undertaken to improve the efficiency of government, learning from the private sector wherever possible, while acknowledging the differences between public and private sector activities. The National Performance Review, headed by the Vice President, has focused on making government agencies more performance- and customer-oriented, developing performance measures, and ensuring that those measures are used for evaluation. These efforts are already beginning to bear fruit, in the form of better customer service and greater efficiency.

The Administration is committed to continuing the reinvention of the Federal Government, eliminating outmoded programs designed for the 19th and 20th centuries, and promoting new ones designed for the 21st. For example, the Department of Agriculture has reduced the number of its agencies from 43 to 29 and is in the process of closing or consolidating 1,200 field offices. It has also plowed under a bumper crop of paperwork: America's farmers this year will fill out 3 million pages fewer of government forms than in years past. Meanwhile the Administration has cut the overall Federal workforce by 200,000 positions. As a percentage of total employment in the United States, Federal employment is smaller today than at any time since the early 1930s.

In its efforts to reinvent regulation, the Administration has attempted to ensure that each regulation it reviews is consistent with its identified objectives, and that the benefits from the regulation justify its costs. Many of the proposals for reinventing government are intended to reduce those costs by fundamentally changing our regulatory philosophy. In its regulatory role, government should seek to facilitate compliance, not to act as a disciplinarian. And regulations should be as market-friendly and performance-oriented as possible. They should encourage innovation and cost-effective ways of achieving the objectives of the regulation. They should take advantage of incentives and market mechanisms, rather than try to suppress them. . . .

Protecting the Environment

Americans want to know that the air they breathe, the water they drink, and the rivers and lakes in which they swim and fish are safe. They want to be sure that the places where they live and work do not harbor threats to their health from contamination by dangerous chemicals, and that the Nation's natural resources are properly protected and managed. Protecting the environment is one of the best investments we can make on behalf of our children. Preserving and improving our environmental heritage is an essential part of maintaining and raising overall living standards.

The country has made enormous progress in this area. The air we breathe today is cleaner than before the Clean Air Act was passed. Substances that pose real dangers to human health and the environment, such as lead and DDT, have been eliminated or their use sharply reduced. Rivers and lakes have been restored to health: 25 years ago Lake Erie was all but dead; today life thrives in it again. With U.S. leadership, the international community has made considerable progress in phasing out substances that damage the earth's stratospheric ozone layer, which shields us from dangerous radiation.

But the battle is far from over. Air quality in some locations remains unacceptably poor. The outbreak of water poisoning in Milwaukee in 1993, and other episodes in which drinking water in our major cities has failed to meet quality standards, do more than just raise anxiety. Chemical runoff from cities, subdivisions, and farms into our rivers and lakes is a constant challenge. Pressures from economic development and increased demand still threaten the Nation's wetlands, fisheries, and other natural resources.

Although we all enjoy the benefits of cleaner air and cleaner water, as individuals—whether managers of steel companies or of oil refineries, or the producers or the drivers of automobiles—we have little incentive to spend our own money to make these things happen. Few are willing to shoulder all the costs of something for which all share the benefits. Acceptable environmental quality cannot be achieved without collective action. With appropriate policies—including cooperation with States and localities, partnerships with the private sector that engender creative solutions as well as set standards, and careful assessment of the advantages and disadvantages of alternative government action—environmental protection can be secured at an affordable cost.

The Administration is improving the way in which we protect the environment, making government a partner rather than an overseer. The Environmental Protection Agency is eliminating 1,400 pages of obsolete regulations and revising 9,400 more. In the process it is cutting paperwork requirements by 25 percent, saving private industry about 20 million hours of labor per year. . . .

Redesigning Welfare Policies

The government has a crucial role to play in increasing economic independence, rewarding work, and ensuring that children are not trapped in poverty. This is important not only for social cohesion; it is an economic imperative as well. Each year that a child spends in poverty raises the probability of that child later dropping out of school. And dropouts tend to contribute less to national income: in 1994, mean annual earnings for a full-time, year-round worker aged 25 to 34 who had dropped out of high school were $18,679. Mean earnings for high school graduates in that age range were $23,778.

Although individuals must ultimately be responsible for their own actions, opportunities at least partially affect our behavior. The limited economic opportunities available to dropouts make recourse to antisocial behavior all the more likely. On any given day in 1992, 25 percent of men aged 18 to 34 who lacked a high school diploma were in prison, on probation, or on parole, compared to only 4 percent of high school graduates. This is not merely a tragic outcome for those young men: increased crime imposes a wider social cost, in the form both of greater expenditure by the criminal justice system and of reduced personal security for all of us.

The policies adopted in the past to reduce income inequality and poverty are in need of reform. Everyone agrees that the current welfare system is broken. Welfare dependency does enormous harm to individuals and families, by discouraging work and undermining personal responsibility. Welfare recipients are robbed of their dignity, and administrators spend too much time determining eligibility and too little time helping families get back on their feet.

Figuring out how to fix the welfare system, however, is a great challenge. With no easy answers, the Administration has worked to give States the flexibility they need to experiment with new approaches to welfare. As of February 1996, 37 States have received waivers allowing them to pursue a wide range of reforms. For example, Wisconsin has received a waiver to impose stringent work requirements and time-limited benefits.

In order to help move parents from welfare to work, the Administration has proposed to impose a time limit nationwide. Within 2 years, parents would be required to work. Within 5 years, they would lose their benefits. Children would receive vouchers for support if their parents' benefits were terminated. . . .

Reducing the Deficit

Before it could pursue the rest of its economic agenda, the Administration had to bring the Federal budget deficit under control. One of the most detrimental legacies left by previous Administrations was the perilous state of public finances. The large budget deficits run up during the 1980s and early 1990s, and the associated increase in public debt, were restricting the private investment that is so crucial to growth and were deepening our indebtedness to foreigners.

Borrowing to finance the deficit absorbs funds that could otherwise be used to finance investment in plant and equipment—investment that would increase the productivity of the American economy. Combined with a low rate of private saving, government borrowing forces America to borrow more abroad, increasing our indebtedness to foreign countries. . . .

Deficit reduction can right many of these wrongs and provide the springboard for faster economic growth. But throughout the recent debate over the budget, the Administration has stressed that there is a right way and a wrong way to reduce the deficit. Deficit reduction is not an end in itself, but a means to the end of higher living standards for all Americans. How the deficit is cut may determine whether or not those ends are accomplished.

Deficit reduction done the wrong way will reduce living standards and worsen inequality. Cutting spending to reduce the deficit requires hard choices. In making these hard choices, we must assess what the government does now and what it should do in the 21st century. The Federal budget is not just a bland accounting statement—it is an expression of the Nation's priorities and values and should reflect a vision of where the country is going and the problems it faces. Some proposed budget cuts, such as those that would reduce equality of educational opportunity, represent attacks on fundamental American values. Others, such as in programs that protect the environment and Americans' health and safety, would have adverse effects on living standards in the future, and thus undermine the very purpose of deficit reduction.

Deficit Reduction and Public Investment

Investment is a key factor in stimulating growth. Reducing the deficit should lower interest rates and stimulate private investment. Cutting the deficit by cutting high-return *public* investments makes little sense: it merely substitutes one worthwhile investment for another. Indeed, deficit reduction that reduces high-return public investments—like those in research and development, technology, education, and training—may compromise long-term economic growth. Deficit reduction should not be achieved by running down our public infrastructure, by failing to invest in research and development, or by neglecting education and training.

Deficit Reduction and the Social Safety Net

Deficit reduction financed through ill-conceived and excessive cutbacks in social programs is also counterproductive. Reducing inequality not only is essential to keep from shredding the common fabric of our Nation, but may also be important in the more limited objective of promoting economic growth.

Economic growth would suffer if opportunities were reduced for those Americans—and especially the children—at the bottom of the income distribution. We would only worsen the inequality in our society by reducing support for the most vulnerable members of society while handing out large tax benefits to the richest. The better course is to ensure that all Americans who work hard and play by the rules have a chance to escape poverty. To do so would increase national output at the same time that it reduces inequality.

Deficit Reduction and Health Care

As the President has long emphasized, growth in health care expenditures must be contained. Failing to do so would not only pose the renewed threat of large budget deficits; it could also force unacceptable cuts in other programs that are vital to the country. It would be wrong, however, for the richest country in the world to abandon its commitment to increase access to basic health care.

Ongoing changes in our health care system not only allow us to take advantage of structural reforms (such as more extensive use of managed care), but also offer the hope that market forces will help contain rising health care costs. The restraint exercised by health maintenance organizations, for example, should serve to increase the relative supply of health care services in other segments of the market and, through the usual workings of supply and demand, help bring down costs. But more is needed, and experiments could provide the information required to implement effective reforms in the coming decade—reforms that would protect the elderly even as they reduce the growth rate of public expenditures. Possible demonstration initiatives include reforming the reimbursement system, developing a system of regional hospitals specializing in certain high-cost treatments, and cutting administrative costs at hospitals.

Deficit Reduction and Taxes

Fifteen years ago, marginal tax rates and the progressivity of the tax system were dramatically reduced. Some suggested that these policies would so spur economic growth that tax revenue would actually increase. The outcome of that experiment is now a matter of record: not only did this response not occur, but the national debt quadrupled in the span of a dozen years. . . .

In developing its tax proposals, this Administration has emphasized fairness. The Administration has proposed tax cuts for the middle class and argued forcefully against increasing taxes on low-income families through a reduction in the EITC. And the Administration objects to proposals that would give a disproportionate share of tax relief to upper income individuals.

At the same time, the Administration has argued that existing expenditure and tax provisions that benefit particular sectors of the economy, and that cannot be justified in terms of some market failure, should be reduced. Although the Administration succeeded in persuading the Congress to eliminate some of the most obvious examples—the subsidies for mohair and honey, for example, and the tax deductions for lobbying expenses—billions of dollars in corporate subsidies and other loopholes remain.

Approaching the 21st Century

The U.S. economy has changed profoundly in this century. It will continue to change as we enter the 21st century. Advances in technology will continue at a rapid pace. The globalization of economies will also continue. American firms will face competition from abroad, and all the evidence indicates that they can and will rise to the challenge. Lower priced imports and increased export sales will play a role in increasing living standards, as the United States is able to exploit its comparative advantage on an increasingly global scale.

Some sectors of the economy, such as the services sector, will expand, while others will contract. In 1850, the majority of Americans worked on farms; by 1950 only 12 percent did. In 1900, 20 percent of the workforce was employed in manufacturing; by 1950 this had increased to 24 percent. The manufacturing share has since declined and now stands at 16 percent. Today, the main growth sectors of the economy include service industries such as telecommunications services. Service industries in the private sector accounted for 46 percent of employment in 1950; today they account for 63 percent.

People naturally tend to recall the past in a softened light that obscures its blemishes, and to see in the future adversities that may never materialize. For some, the prospect of a future in which the service economy dominates even more than it does today is one that raises anxieties. To be sure, some of the service sector jobs that are being created are not good jobs. On the other hand, many new service sector jobs—in computer programming and management consulting, for example—are high-tech, high-wage jobs.

Markets and government will need to respond to ongoing changes in the economy. For government, change will require rebalancing: more emphasis on new problems, less emphasis on those of the past. The best combination of policies to address the problems of 2030 will be markedly different from those that got us through the problems of 1930 or 1830. Ideological and extremist solutions reflect neither the realities of today nor the tradition of American pragmatism. Rather, the problems of the 21st century need to be addressed with a balanced perspective. Markets are at the core of our economy, but they do not always operate fully efficiently and do not adequately meet all the needs—even all the economic needs—of Americans. It is then that the government can often help. In the face of increased income inequality, for example, it can make greater efforts to enhance educational opportunity so that the vicious cycle of poverty is not perpetuated.

Government cannot solve all of society's problems, and it certainly cannot solve the more persistent problems overnight. But even if the benefits do not manifest themselves immediately, government must continue to invest in the future. Only by making such investments can the long-term problems of slow productivity growth and increasing inequality be addressed. This Administration firmly believes that government—through selective, focused, and well-designed policies—can help American workers and families achieve higher living standards and develop a more humane, more just society. . . .

Forecast and Outlook

The economic expansion is forecast to continue throughout 1996, as the effects of recent declines in long-term rates boost spending. Over the 7-year forecast horizon, output is projected to track potential output and the rate of inflation is expected to remain roughly constant. . . .

Real GDP is projected to grow at its potential rate of 2.2 percent during 1996 (on a fourth-quarter-over-fourth-quarter basis), as investment in both the housing and the business sectors responds to lower interest rates and as consumption spending is supported by recent gains in stock market prices. Inflation, as measured by the CPI, is expected to increase to 3.1 percent in 1996 from 2.7 percent in 1995, as food and energy prices, which had held down the overall rate of price increase last year, are expected to rise in line with overall inflation this year. The core rate of inflation is expected to remain roughly unchanged during 1996, consistent with our forecast that unemployment is likely to remain relatively unchanged, and that at current unemployment rates, pressures for increasing inflation are weak or nonexistent.

Although true inflation is expected to remain constant from 1996 onward, inflation as measured by the CPI is expected to edge lower as revised procedures gradually remove part of the upward biases in current CPI inflation figures. CPI inflation is likely to slow by 0.2 percentage point in 1997, when the Bureau of Labor Statistics (BLS) will implement procedures to correct for problems associated with bringing new stores into the survey sample. CPI inflation is expected to slow by another 0.1 percentage point in 1998, when the BLS updates the CPI market basket to reflect more recent data on expenditure patterns. As a result of these adjustments, CPI inflation is expected to fall from 3.1 percent in 1996 to 2.8 percent in 1998 and thereafter. Some of these CPI adjustments pass through to the GDP price index and, given the growth rate of nominal GDP, raise estimates of real GDP growth. Consequently, real GDP growth is projected to rise to 2.3 percent from 1997 onward.

The impetus from the decline in interest rates in the second half of 1995 is expected to keep aggregate demand growing at the economy's potential rate for 1996. Over the medium term, interest rates are expected to edge lower as projected reductions in the Federal deficit reduce demands on capital markets. The projected decline in interest rates is expected to sustain growth at its potential rate as deficit reduction further restrains Federal spending.

The unemployment rate is projected at 5.7 percent in the near term and is expected to remain at that level throughout the forecast period. Economic growth of 2.3 percent over the forecast horizon is expected to generate enough jobs to employ all the new entrants implied by the expected 1.1 percent annual growth rate of the labor force. This unemployment rate is also expected to be consistent with long-term stability of the inflation rate.

As always, the forecast has risks. A basic assumption is that monetary policy will be calibrated to offset the ongoing effects of fiscal contraction. Obviously, monetary policy may not achieve this goal. Monetary policy has long lags, and so the course of fiscal policy must be properly anticipated. But fiscal policy depends on budgetary and other policy decisions of the Congress, and at present future Congressional action remains uncertain, despite bipartisan consensus toward achieving a balanced budget.

In the short term, the economy may hit a pothole in the first quarter of 1996, resulting at least in part from the effects of the government shutdown and bad weather in the eastern United States during January. But even if this should come to pass, the economy is expected to rebound, and the growth rate over the four quarters of 1996 is likely to be unaffected. The economy also faces the risk that foreign economic growth may stall, reducing foreign demand for U.S. exports. Still, the U.S. economy's export performance in 1995, in the face of economic weakening in three of our major trading partners, was impressive. Increased exports to strengthening economies in Canada, Japan, and Mexico would help offset any losses elsewhere.

Conclusion

As the year 1995 ended, the economy was fundamentally sound. None of the imbalances that typically precede a recession were evident. All signs pointed to continued economic expansion at a sustainable pace. Unemployment was expected to stay low, the inflation rate was expected to remain low and stable, and business investment was expected to continue powering the economy as interest rates declined.

The economy during 1995 made the transition from economic recovery, during which growth was driven by removing slack from labor and capital markets, to a period where growth is and will continue to be determined by expansion of the economy's capacity. Although the transition to sustained growth was not entirely smooth, the economy rebounded smartly during the second half of 1995 from the earlier bump in the road and should continue to expand during 1996.

Perhaps the best news during the year was that inflation remained low and stable despite an unemployment rate that in the past was associated with rising inflation. The stability of inflation even as the unemployment rate was essentially unchanged at about 5.6 percent appears to signal a shift in the economic environment. The improved economic environment also was apparent in bond and stock markets, as long-term interest rates fell and stock prices soared, reflecting in part an outlook for inflation reminiscent of the early 1960s.

The bipartisan commitment to balance the budget over the next 7 years was the major macroeconomic policy event of the year, and represents a continuation of Administration efforts to redress the fiscal imbalance inherited from the past. As the deficit is further reduced, private investment should increase, helping to raise living standards. And, deficit reduction that is credible means that the decline in interest rates needed to sustain growth in the short run is likely to be forthcoming with only modest accommodation from monetary policy. A significant portion of the decline in long-term interest rates during 1995, particularly over the second half of the year, probably reflected investors' perception that credible further deficit reduction was on the horizon. The Administration's success in reducing the deficit over the last 3 years certainly demonstrates the firmness of its commitment to restoring balance to the Federal budget.

NATIONAL RESEARCH COUNCIL ON CARCINOGENS IN THE DIET
February 15, 1996

The fat, calories, and alcohol in the American diet pose a far greater threat of causing cancer than do the natural and synthetic carcinogens found in food, a panel of scientists concluded in a report released February 15. Cancer-causing agents that occur naturally in food or that are introduced by humans through pesticides, preservatives, or flavoring and coloring additives are present at such low levels that they appear to pose little threat to human health, a committee of the National Research Council said.

In its report, "Carcinogens and Anticarcinogens in the Human Diet," the National Research Council cautioned that although the present risks from cancer-causing agents in the food supply were low, more research was needed before the role that dietary chemicals play in causing cancer was fully understood. Many of the chemicals in food have never been tested for their effects, and scientists do not have an extensive understanding of how chemicals in food might interact.

Report Findings

Cancer is the second leading cause of death (after coronary disease) in the United States, responsible for some 500,000 deaths each year. About one-third of these are attributed to diet, but few, if any, are thought to be caused by individual carcinogens in food. About 6,000 synthetic chemicals are found in the food supply; many that have been shown to cause cancer have been regulated out of the food supply. An example is the artificial sweetener cyclamate, which the Food and Drug Administration (FDA) has prohibited from being added to food since 1969, after laboratory tests linked it with bladder cancer.

The committee said that natural chemicals could eventually prove to "be of greater concern" than synthetic agents but that additional evidence was needed before conclusions could be drawn. Perhaps as many as one million chemicals occur in food naturally, and some of these are recognized carcinogens. For example, caffeic acid, which is found in apples, lettuce, peaches, pears, potatoes, tomatoes, citrus fruits, and coffee, has been shown to cause cancer in laboratory animals. No link between caffeic acid and cancer in humans has been established, however.

Another example is the group of naturally occurring chemicals known as mycotoxins; these chemicals are produced by fungi that often contaminate grain and nuts. Mycotoxins have been shown to cause cancer in laboratory animals, and epidemiological studies link the chemicals to human liver cancer.

At the same time, the American diet contains many anticarcinogens, such as the vitamins A, C, and E, that can reduce the risk of cancer. Many common foods, including broccoli and beef, contain both carcinogens and anticarcinogens. Studies indicate that the anticarcinogens in diets rich in vegetables and fruits appear to be more influential than the carcinogens, while in beef the carcinogens and other cancer-promoting agents such as fat appear to be more influential. The committee observed that the mechanisms through which these carcinogens and anticarcinogens worked were not fully understood, but urged Americans to eat more fruit and vegetables. "The varied and balanced diet needed for good nutrition also provides significant protection from natural toxicants," the report said. "Increasing dietary fruit and vegetable intake may actually protect against cancer."

The committee recommended improved testing for carcinogens and anticarcinogens and that more natural food chemicals be tested to determine whether they were carcinogenic. High priority should be given to nonnutritive chemicals that occur in relatively high concentrations in commonly consumed foods and in foods whose consumption is associated with diets and lifestyles known to be deleterious to good health, the panel said. Additional data were needed on concentrations of chemicals in food and human exposure to them. As advances were made in identifying dietary chemicals that enhance or inhibit cancer, the committee said, it might be possible to modify the food supply, through genetic engineering and other techniques, to minimize the risk of cancer. To achieve those goals, the committee concluded, "a major effort will be needed to educate the American public regarding appropriate life-style modifications."

Representatives of the food industry applauded the report. "No responsible scientist in the food system would deny there are substances in the food supply that in theory could be nasty if consumed in excessive amounts, but bodies aren't piling up because of lethal substances in food," Joyce A. Nettleton *of the Institute of Food Technologists told the* Washington Post. *"Diet-related health conditions are related to our overall habits, not to specific food chemicals present in minuscule amounts."*

Al Meyerhoff of the Natural Resources Defense Council acknowledged that carcinogenic chemicals in the food supply are much less important than overall diet, but, he said, "they can still cause thousands of cancers in consumers, and they should be avoided whenever possible."

The National Research Council committee was headed by Ronald Estabrook, chairman of the department of biochemistry at the University of Texas Southwestern Medical Center at Dallas. The council, a congressionally chartered, private nonprofit institution, is the principal operating agency of the National Academy of Sciences and the National Academy of Engineering. The study was funded by the National Institute for Environmental Health Sciences, the U.S. Environmental Protection Agency (EPA), the National Cancer Institute, the FDA, the American Industrial Health Council, and Nabisco Food Groups.

Delaney Clause Revised

In a related development, Congress in July replaced a long-standing law as it applied to pesticides. Enacted in 1958, the Delaney Clause had barred even minute traces of cancer-causing chemicals in processed foods. The new safety standard set tolerances for pesticide residues in both raw and processed foods at levels that would ensure a "reasonable certainty of no harm."

The Delaney Clause, named after its principal sponsor, Rep. James J. Delaney, D-N.Y., was added to the Federal Food, Drug and Cosmetic Act in 1958. It prohibited the use of any processed food that contained any trace of a carcinogenic substance. Over the years, as scientific testing became able to detect ever smaller amounts of carcinogens, farmers, food processors, and pesticide manufacturers feared that the Delaney Clause would eventually lead to a ban on pesticide use. Those fears intensified after federal courts in 1992 and 1995 ordered strict enforcement of the Delaney Clause, and the EPA began to prohibit use of some common pesticides that left residues in processed foods.

The new standard—ensuring a "reasonable certainty" of no harm—is generally interpreted to mean that there may be no more than a one-in-a-million chance that the residue will cause cancer. The EPA has applied that standard to most raw fruits and vegetables; the new law would ensure that the standard be observed.

The law (PL 104–170) also required the EPA to take into account the susceptibility of infants and children to pesticide poisoning. When setting tolerance levels, the agency was directed to consider which foods children eat in large quantities (such as apples) and which pesticides are known to have a severe effect on children.

Following are excerpts from the executive summary of the National Research Council report, "Carcinogens and Anticarcinogens in the Human Diet," released by the National Academy of Sciences on February 15, 1996:

From earliest times people have been aware that some plants are poisonous and should be avoided as food. Other plants contain chemicals that have medicinal, stimulatory, hallucinatory, or narcotic effects. The Romans were among the first to enact laws that, over time, have been developed to protect the public from food adulteration, contamination, false labeling, spoilage, and the harmful effects of chemicals added to foods and beverages.

In the past 50 years, great strides have been made in understanding nutrition and the role it plays in human health. This same period has seen vast improvements in the safety and diversity of the diet in the United States, with technological advances in preservation and shipment of foods, and the ability to identify and reduce various food hazards. U.S. laws regulate the safety of the food we eat and the water we drink. Federal agencies, such as the Food and Drug Administration, Department of Agriculture, and Environmental Protection Agency, as well as many state and local agencies, are charged with interpreting and enforcing these laws. As a result, the food supply in the United States is widely recognized as safe, economical, and of high quality, variety, and abundance.

Despite these efforts, concerns remain that some dietary components may contribute to the burden of cancer in humans. For example, the use of pesticides continues to be watched closely, because of indirect exposures of the general public through trace amounts in the food supply (as well as direct exposures of agricultural workers). Yet, by controlling insect vectors, pesticides have profoundly decreased the spread of human diseases, and pesticide usage has increased agricultural yields.

Plants have evolved chemicals that serve as defensive agents against predators. These chemicals may be present in the diet in amounts exceeding the residues of synthetic pesticides used to enhance agricultural productivity. Ames et al. contend that the percentage of naturally occurring chemicals testing positive for carcinogenicity in rodent bioassays does not differ significantly from the percentage of synthetic chemicals testing positive, and that these proportions are likely to hold for untested agents, leading to their conclusion that the cancer risk from natural chemicals in the diet might be greater than that from synthetics. There are, after all, many more naturally occurring chemicals than synthetic. In fact, although the number of naturally occurring compounds in the human diet is certainly far greater than synthetic compounds, the implications concerning health risks—particularly impact on cancer in humans—remain controversial. In addition, it should be noted that synthetic chemicals are highly regulated while natural chemicals are not. This report addresses several elements of this controversy, including the relevance of animal bioassays (including those using the maximum tolerated dose) for identifying human dietary carcinogens, the adequacy and availability of human exposure data, and the complexity of the human diet.

Since the 1930s, scientists have recognized that the occurrence of certain cancers may be related to substances in the diet or to patterns of food consumption. They have also recognized that some chemical constituents of food—either initially present in the food, formed during preparation (especially cooking), or added for preservation or presentation—are capable of inducing tumors in high-dose rodent tests. Many of the early studies on chemicals that cause cancer were carried out to determine what levels of exposure to specific chemicals, such as polycyclic aromatic hydrocarbons

(PAHs), and certain food colors, such as butter yellow (N,N-dimethyl-4-amino-azobenzene), resulted in the formation of cancers in the liver and gastrointestinal tract of rodents. Later it was recognized that a number of naturally occurring chemicals present in some foods, such as mycotoxins (chemicals produced by fungi that often contaminate grains and nuts) and plant alkaloids, could also cause cancer in experimental animals. These findings have stimulated research to better understand the health consequences of naturally occurring chemicals found in our diet.

Doll and Peto, in their 1981 review, concluded that 10% to 70% of human cancer mortality in the U.S. is attributable to the diet, with the most likely figure being about 35%. Epidemiologic studies linking the aforementioned mycotoxins to human liver cancer provide convincing evidence that some constituents of foods can cause cancer. Less firmly established, however, is the contribution to human cancer of other naturally occurring chemicals present at low levels in the food we eat. In addition, the diet is a source of calories derived from fats, carbohydrates, and proteins. Calories and macronutrients (principally fat and oxidation products of fatty acids) in excess of body needs serve as an important risk factor that can contribute to the processes of tumor formation and growth. The observations of Doll and Peto are based on statistical and epidemiologic data which many regard as inconclusive. It is important to note that diet also plays a role in protecting against cancer, since diets rich in fruits and vegetables have been associated with reduced rates of cancer. Although dietary factors are certainly involved in carcinogenesis, the percent of cancer attributable to diet has remained uncertain. . . .

Conclusions

Several broad perspectives emerged from the committee's deliberations. First, the committee concluded that based upon existing exposure data, the great majority of individual naturally occurring and synthetic chemicals in the diet appears to be present at levels below which any significant adverse biologic effect is likely, and so low that they are unlikely to pose an appreciable cancer risk. Much human experience suggests that the potential effects of dietary carcinogens are more likely to be realized when the specific foods in which they occur form too large a part of the diet. The varied and balanced diet needed for good nutrition also provides significant protection from natural toxicants. Increasing dietary fruit and vegetable intake may actually protect against cancer. The NRC report Diet and Health concluded that macronutrients and excess calories are likely the greatest contributors to dietary cancer risk in the United States.

Second, the committee concluded that natural components of the diet may prove to be of greater concern than synthetic components with respect to cancer risk, although additional evidence is required before definitive conclusions can be drawn. Existing concentration and exposure data and current cancer risk assessment methods are insufficient to definitively address the aggregate roles of naturally occurring and/or synthetic dietary chemicals in human cancer causation and prevention. Much of the information on the carcinogenic potential of these substances derives from animal bioassays conducted at high doses (up to the maximum tolerated dose, or MTD), which is difficult to translate directly to humans because these tests do not mimic human exposure conditions, i.e., we are exposed to an enormous complex of chemicals, many at exceedingly low quantities, in our diet. Furthermore, the committee concluded upon analyzing existing dietary exposure databases, that exposure data are either inadequate due to analytical or collection deficiencies, or simply nonexistent. In addition, through regulation, synthetic chemicals identified as carcinogens have largely been removed from or prevented from entering the human diet.

Third, the committee concluded that it is difficult to assess human cancer risk from individual natural or synthetic compounds in our diet because the diet is a complex mixture, and interactions between the components are largely unknown. . . .

Complexity of the Diet

• The human diet is a highly complex and variable mixture of naturally occurring and synthetic chemicals. Of these, the naturally occurring far exceed the synthetic in both number and quantity. The naturally occurring chemicals include macronutrients (fat, carbohydrate, and protein), micronutrients (vitamins and trace metals), and non-nutrient constituents. Only a small number of specific carcinogens and anticarcinogens in the human diet have been identified (e.g., aflatoxin). However, it seems unlikely that important carcinogens are yet to be identified. In part, this may reflect the limited number of studies performed.

• Human epidemiologic data indicate that diet contributes to a significant portion of cancer, but the precise components of diet responsible for increased cancer risk are generally not well understood.

Carcinogenicity and Anticarcinogenicity

• Current epidemiologic evidence suggests the importance of protective factors in the diet, such as those present in fruits and vegetables.

• Current evidence suggests that the contribution of excess macronutrients and excess calories to cancer causation in the United States outweighs that of individual food microchemicals, both natural and synthetic. This is not necessarily the case in other parts of the world.

• Epidemiologic data indicate that alcoholic beverages consumed in excess are associated with increased risk for specific types of cancer.

• Given the greater abundance of naturally occurring substances in the diet, the total exposure to naturally occurring carcinogens (in addition to excess calories and fat) exceeds the exposure to synthetic carcinogens. . . . However, data are insufficient to determine whether the dietary cancer risks from naturally occurring substances exceeds that for synthetic substances. . . . Indeed, at the present, quantitative statements cannot be made about cancer risks for humans from specific dietary chemicals, either naturally occurring or synthetic.

• Current regulatory practices have applied far greater stringency to the regulation of synthetic chemicals in the diet than to naturally occurring chemicals. . . . Only a very small fraction of naturally occurring chemicals has been tested for carcinogenicity. Naturally occurring dietary chemicals known to be potent carcinogens in rodents include agents derived through food preparation, such as certain heterocyclicamines generated during cooking, and the nitrosamines and other agents acquired during food preservation and storage, such as aflatoxins and some other fungal toxins.

• The human diet also contains anticarcinogens that can reduce cancer risk. For example, the committee evaluated relevant literature on antioxidant micronutrients, including vitamins A, C, E, folic acid, and selenium, and their suggested contributions to cancer prevention. Human diets that have a high content of fruits and vegetables are associated with a reduced risk of cancer, but the specific constituents responsible for this protective effect and their mechanisms of action are not known with certainty. The vitamin and mineral content of fruits and vegetables might be important factors in this relationship. In addition, fruits and vegetables are dietary sources of many non-nutritive constituents, such as isoflavonoids, isothiocyanates and other sulfur-containing compounds, some of which have inhibited the carcinogenic process in experimental animal studies. Foods high in fiber content are associated with a decreased risk of colon cancer in humans, but it is not yet clear that fiber per se is the component responsible for this protective effect.

• Carcinogens and anticarcinogens present in the diet can interact in a variety of ways that are not fully understood. This makes it difficult to predict overall dietary risks based on an assessment of the risks from individual components due to uncertainties associated with rodent-to-human extrapolation and high-dose to low-dose extrapolation. It is likely that there is also considerable interindividual variation in susceptibility to specific chemicals or mixtures due to either inherited or acquired factors.

Synthetic Versus Naturally Occurring Carcinogens

• Overall, the basic mechanisms involved in the entire process of carcinogenesis—from exposure of the organism to expression of tumors—are qualitatively similar, if not identical, for synthetic and naturally occurring carcinogens. The committee concluded that there is no notable mechanistic difference(s) between synthetic and naturally occurring carcinogens. . . . Of the selected agents tested, both types of chemicals have similar mechanisms of action, similar positivity rates in rodent bioassay tests for carcinogenicity, and encompass similar ranges of carcinogenic potencies. Consequently, both naturally occurring and synthetic chemicals can be evaluated by the same epidemiologic or experimental methods and procedures.

• Although there are differences between specific groups of synthetic and naturally occurring chemicals with respect to properties such as lipophilicity, degree of conjugation, resistance to metabolism, and persistence in the body and environment, it is unlikely that information on these properties alone will enable predictions to be made of the degree of carcinogenicity of a naturally occurring or synthetic chemical in the diet. Both categories of chemicals—naturally occurring and synthetic—are large and diverse. Predictions based on chemical or physical properties are problematic, due in part to the likely overlap of values between the categories.

Models for Identifying Carcinogens and Anticarcinogens

• The committee evaluated current methods for assessing carcinogenicity and concluded that current strategies for identifying and evaluating potential carcinogens and anticarcinogens are essentially the same. The methods can be grouped into epidemiologic studies, in vivo experimental animal models, and in vitro systems. The committee recognized the value and limitations of each approach for identifying dietary carcinogens and anticarcinogens.

• In its assessment of traditional epidemiologic approaches to identifying dietary carcinogens and anticarcinogens, the committee concluded that these can be beneficially expanded by incorporating into research designs more biochemical, immunologic, and molecular assays that use human tissues and biologic fluids. Furthermore, incorporating the identification of biologic markers into these approaches may provide early indicators of human carcinogenicity—long before the development of tumors.

• The committee analyzed the applicability of rodent bioassays—specifically the long-term bioassays conducted by the National Toxicology Program—for identifying dietary carcinogens and anticarcinogens. The committee concluded that, despite their limitations, rodent models (involving high-dose exposures) have served as useful screening tests for identifying chemicals as potential human carcinogens and anticarcinogens. Concerns about the use of data generated from these models for predicting the potential carcinogenicity and anticarcinogenicity of chemicals in food arise from the fact that they do not mimic human exposure conditions, i.e., we are exposed to an enormous complex of chemicals, many at exceedingly low quantities, in our diet.

Recommendations

Numerous and extensive gaps in the current knowledge base were apparent as the committee endeavored to examine the risk of human cancer from naturally occurring versus synthetic components of the diet. These gaps are so large—and resources are so limited—that careful prioritization of further research efforts is essential. The following recommendations emphasize the need for expanded epidemiologic studies, more human exposure data, improved and enhanced testing methods, more detailed data on dietary components, and further mechanistic studies, if these gaps are to be filled. These research endeavors may prove inadequate, however, when the complexity and variability of diets and food composition, as well as human behavior, are considered.

Epidemiologic Studies and Human Exposure

• Improved methods are needed to enable the incorporation of relevant cellular and molecular markers of exposure, susceptibility, and preneoplastic effects (DNA damage, etc.) into epidemiologic studies. . . .

• Additional data on the concentrations of naturally occurring and synthetic chemicals in foods and human exposures to them are needed. . . .

Testing

• Improved bioassay screening methods are needed to test for carcinogens and anticarcinogens in our diet. . . .

• Further testing of naturally occurring chemicals in the food supply for carcinogenic and anticarcinogenic potential should be conducted on a prioritized basis. . . .

• To help fill the data gaps on the cancer risk of dietary constituents, improved short-term screening tests for carcinogenic and anticarcinogenic activity should be developed, especially for detecting nongenotoxic effects that are relevant to carcinogenesis. . . .

Dietary Factors

• The risk of cancer from excess calories and fat should be further delineated vis-a-vis naturally occurring and synthetic substances in the diet. . . .

• The specific chemicals that provide the protective effects of vegetables and fruits should be identified and their protective mechanisms delineated. . . .

Closing Remarks

At the present time, cancers are the second leading cause of mortality in the United States, resulting in over 500,000 deaths per year. It is agreed that smoking-related lung cancer is a major contributor to this statistic. However, it appears that dietary factors play an important role in the causation of a major fraction of these cancers. Current knowledge indicates that calories in excess of dietary needs, and perhaps fat or certain components of fat, as well as inadequate dietary fruits and vegetables, have the greatest impact. Most naturally occurring minor dietary constituents occur at levels so low that any biologic effect, positive or negative, is unlikely. Nevertheless, a significant number of these chemicals have shown carcinogenic or anticarcinogenic activity in tests. Overall, they have been so inadequately studied that their effect is uncertain. The synthetic chemicals in our diet are far less numerous than the natural and have been more thoroughly studied, monitored, and regulated. Their potential biologic effect is lower. . . .

Finally, as advances are made in identifying with certainty specific naturally occurring dietary chemicals that either enhance or inhibit cancer risks in humans, it will be possible to formulate rational dietary guidelines for the American public. It may also be possible to use this information to modify the composition of our food sources through breeding methods, genetic engineering, and other advances in biotechnology, so as to optimize the quality of the diet with respect to cancer prevention. Above all, a major effort will be needed to educate the American public regarding appropriate life-style modifications if we are to achieve these goals.

VICE PRESIDENT GORE ON EVERGLADES RESTORATION
February 20, 1996

The Clinton administration on February 20 launched a major new effort to clean up the Florida Everglades—the nation's largest and most important wetlands. Vice President Al Gore announced an ambitious $1.5 billion, seven-year program to restore the Everglades, which he called "one of America's richest treasures."

Later in 1996 Congress enacted legislation carrying out some parts of the administration's Everglades plan, but a proposed state tax of one cent a pound on sugar grown in the Everglades area—a key financial element of the plan—was defeated by Florida voters in November.

Encompassing about 4,000 square miles in south Florida, the Everglades is an enormous ecosystem that drains billions of gallons of fresh water from giant Lake Okeechobee to Florida Bay and the Gulf of Mexico. For most of the last hundred years, the state and federal governments and private business saw the Everglades more as an obstacle to progress than as an essential part of the environment. The state began draining the Everglades in 1906 to create farmland, eventually creating the Everglades Agriculture Area for sugar growers, the cattle industry, and other farmers. After World War II the federal government sped up construction to divert fresh water from the Everglades, using dikes and canals to stem annual floods and to provide fresh water for south Florida's growing cities.

The draining created farmland but destroyed much of the marshlands that were the heart of the area's ecosystem. Runoff of agricultural chemicals, primarily phosphorous, from the fields also polluted much of the fresh water that reached the Everglades.

Environmentalists began warning in the 1940s and 1950s about the long-term dangers of destroying the Everglades. It was not until the 1960s and 1970s that scientists were able to demonstrate the damage to wildlife and to Florida's commercial and recreational fishing industries.

In 1993 the federal government and the sugar growers reached agreement on a plan to spend about $11 million annually over twenty years *building filtration marshes to reduce the pollution entering the Everglades. In 1994 Florida mandated a broader plan, called the Everglades Forever Act, which assessed sugar growers and other agricultural landowners $24.89 an acre for two years to reduce pollution and replace marshlands. The program was the result of a federal lawsuit against the state for failing to enforce clean water standards and was expected to generate $200 million to $300 million a year.*

The Administration Plan

The plan outlined by Vice President Gore on February 20 was the most sweeping federal proposal yet developed to reverse a century of policies and actions damaging to the Everglades. The announcement was made by the vice president, rather than the president, because the plan had been spearheaded by Gore, a prominent environmentalist. Gore called the proposal an "innovative, flexible, and fair plan" to revive the Everglades after decades of destruction.

The plan included all of the south Florida ecosystem related to the Everglades, including Everglades National Park at the southwest tip of the state and Big Cypress National Preserve just north of the park.

Gore estimated the total cost of the plan over seven years at $1.5 billion, about double the current level of spending on Everglades restoration and pollution control. He said the plan included two major elements: buying agricultural and other lands to "restore the heart of the Everglades," and instituting various federal programs and water projects to restore natural water flows in the south Florida ecosystem.

The plan called for creation of an Everglades Restoration Fund, which would purchase 100,000 acres of farmland in the Everglades Agriculture Area and return it to its previous marshy condition to help restore natural water flows. Gore proposed creating the fund with $100 million of federal tax money annually for four years, along with the penny-per-pound tax on sugar production, which was expected to generate $245 million over seven years.

Gore's plan was greeted enthusiastically by environmental organizations because it broadened the federal government's commitment to protect the Everglades. Sugar growers and other business interests were hostile; the day before Gore announced the plan, some 2,000 industry officials met in Miami to develop a strategy for opposing the sugar tax.

Several key Florida politicians reacted coolly to Gore's announcement, at least in part because the administration had failed to consult with them ahead of time. One of the administration's natural allies, Sen. Bob Graham, D-Fla., was among those who appeared ruffled by the lack of advance consultation.

Graham and Florida's other senator, Republican Connie Mack, succeeded in getting Congress to include in the 1996 farm bill a $200 million authorization for purchases of farmland in the Everglades area. The bill also authorized another $100 million for that purpose from the sale or trade of surplus federal land in Florida.

Florida Sugar Tax

The goals of the Everglades cleanup were overshadowed during 1996 by the high-volume fight over the sugar tax. Major sugar producers reportedly spent nearly $15 million to defeat the tax, which they claimed would have imposed too heavy a burden on their industry. The main proponent of the tax was Save Our Everglades, financed by Wall Street commodities broker Tudor Jones, who reportedly spent nearly $7 million of his own money on the issue.

The proposal rejected by Florida voters was a state constitutional amendment imposing a one-cent-per-pound fee on raw sugar grown in the Everglades Agriculture Area during the next twenty-five years. The tax would have generated about $36 million a year.

Proponents said the tax was a fair method of financing the Everglades cleanup because the sugar industry was almost entirely to blame for the runoff of agricultural chemicals that had polluted the fresh water entering the wetlands. They noted that the sugar industry benefited from an enormous amount of government assistance, starting with the draining of Everglades land to create the sugar farmland and continuing with federal sugar crop subsidies protecting them from foreign competition.

Sugar growers insisted they were already paying their fair share for Everglades cleanup under a 1994 state law requiring them to pay up to $322 million annually over twenty years. In their television advertising just before the voting, the sugar companies also charged that the government would waste the money raised by the tax.

Although technically a state issue, the tax question became embroiled in national politics, with Clinton favoring the tax and his Republican challenger, Bob Dole, opposing it. Echoing industry complaints, Dole said the tax was unfair because "you can't pick out a single industry" to pay for a government program.

> *Following is the text of the statement made February 20, 1996, by Vice President Al Gore at the Anhinga Trail in Everglades National Park announcing a new plan to restore the Florida Everglades:*

On behalf of President Clinton, I am proud to be here today to announce an innovative, flexible and fair plan to restore one of America's richest treasures—the Florida Everglades.

Today we are charting a course that will lead Florida's families, Florida's economy, and Florida's children into a future of limitless possibility. We are announcing more than a restoration plan. It is an investment in Florida's—and our nation's—future.

We know the Everglades can't survive on its own. Nor can it restore itself. We can save the Everglades—but only if we work as a community united by ideals that have bonded Americans for more than two centuries: taking responsibility and creating opportunity.

First, in partnership with the State of Florida, we will work to acquire the lands necessary to restore the heart of the Everglades. President Clinton will commit $100 million every year for the next four years for this purpose.

Second, we will increase funding for agency programs, sound science, land management, water projects, and other programs essential to restore the natural flow into the Kissimmee River, Lake Okeechobee and Florida Bay. Overall, President Clinton will double the federal investment in the Everglades, calling for a $1.5 billion commitment over the next seven years.

And finally, we believe the way to ensure the reliable long-term revenue needed to restore the Everglades and protect South Florida's economic future is through a balanced cost-share between the federal and state governments and those who have benefited so long from public investment.

That is why we are asking the sugar industry to contribute its fair share to this historic plan—specifically, by putting "a penny a pound" toward enhancing water quality and ensuring water quantity in South Florida. Through this investment we can build a sustainable sugar industry in a healthy Everglades.

We can—and we will—make the Everglades everlasting.

EDUCATION DEPARTMENT ON UNIFORMS IN PUBLIC SCHOOLS
February 23, 1996

Citing evidence that wearing school uniforms leads to less violence and greater discipline among students, the Clinton administration in February lent its support to public school systems and parents interested in instituting such policies. "If it means teenagers will stop killing each other over designer jackets, then our public schools should be able to require their students to wear school uniforms," the president said in his weekly radio address, broadcast February 24. "If it means that the school rooms will be more orderly, more disciplined and that our young people will learn to evaluate themselves by what they are on the inside instead of what they're wearing on the outside, then our public schools should be able to require their students to wear school uniforms."

President Clinton first endorsed uniforms in public schools in his January State of the Union address. On February 23 he formally instructed the Department of Education to circulate a "Manual on School Uniforms" to the nation's 16,000 public school districts. He followed that up the next day with the radio address and several public appearances lauding the potential benefits of uniforms in public schools. (State of the Union address, p. 21)

One of the February 24 stops was at the Jackie Robinson Academy in Long Beach, California, the first public school system to require all of its elementary and middle school students to wear uniforms. Each school determines what that uniform will be, and students may opt out of the program with parental consent. Fewer than 1 percent have done so. A year after the Long Beach program was instituted in 1994, school officials reported that overall school crime had decreased 36 percent, fights had decreased 51 percent, sex offenses had gone down 74 percent, weapons offenses had decreased by 50 percent, and vandalism was down 18 percent.

Schools in Baltimore, Cincinnati, Dayton, Detroit, Los Angeles, Miami, Memphis, Milwaukee, Nashville, New Orleans, Phoenix, Seattle, St. Louis, and Washington, D.C., have also adopted mandatory or voluntary uniform policies. All report improved discipline and a better learning environment in the schools.

Stressing that his administration had no intention of trying to make uniforms mandatory in public schools, Clinton said the adoption of a uniform policy was a question for each school district to decide in conjunction with parents. The Education Department manual was a road map for "schools that want to use the tool. It provides a central source of information about successful programs, yours, and those that have followed that are making a difference all across America," Clinton told the Long Beach audience.

In addition to decreasing violence and theft and instilling discipline in students, the manual said, school uniform policies could also help prevent gang members from wearing gang colors and insignia to school, help students and their parents resist peer pressure, help students concentrate on their school work, and help school officials recognize intruders in the schools.

The manual is similar in form to one the department issued in 1995 setting out guidelines for schools regarding permissible expressions of religion in public schools. As did the 1995 directive, the uniform guidelines spelled out the circumstances under which students may display religious messages. The manual said that schools generally could not bar students from wearing specific religious attire, such as yarmulkes. A uniform policy could not prohibit students from wearing or displaying other expressive items, such as a political campaign button, "so long as such items do not independently contribute to disruption by substantially interfering with discipline or with the rights of others" or "undermine the integrity of the uniform." That meant that schools could bar items displaying a gang insignia, for example, or a sweatshirt bearing a political message worn over the school uniform. (Directive on religion in public schools, Historic Documents of 1995, p. 546)

The manual stressed that parental support was critical to the success of any uniform policy, both in getting it adopted and in ensuring that students abide by it. It also emphasized that a uniform policy should be just one aspect of an overall safety program, which might also include truancy reduction programs, drug prevention efforts, and community efforts to limit gangs.

While many school officials, teachers, and parent organizations apparently believed that uniforms can help improve safety in public schools, not everyone agreed that uniforms should be required. Some critics see school uniforms as an infringement on the right of freedom of expression. Others add that uniforms will not solve underlying behavior problems. Uniforms are "just a Band-Aid on a much deeper wound," Kent Willis, director of the American Civil Liberties Union of Virginia, told the Washington Post. *"Problems with juvenile crime and behavior in school are not going to be solved by having uniforms. We're simply going to delay the problems or drive them deeper."*

Others voiced concerns about the cost of uniforms, which, according to one report, range between about $30 and $150. Most of the school districts that have instituted uniform policies have also developed programs to help needy families pay for them. Many schools solicit funds from the business community and local foundations to help defray the costs; graduating students often donate their uniforms to the school. The Education Department manual urges schools and school districts to provide uniforms to students who cannot otherwise afford them.

Following is the text of the "Manual on School Uniforms," prepared by the U.S. Department of Education in consultation with the U.S. Department of Justice and local communities and released to the public on February 23, 1996:

A safe and disciplined learning environment is the first requirement of a good school. Young people who are safe and secure, who learn basic American values and the essentials of good citizenship, are better students. In response to growing levels of violence in our schools, many parents, teachers, and school officials have come to see school uniforms as one positive and creative way to reduce discipline problems and increase school safety.

They observed that the adoption of school uniform policies can promote school safety, improve discipline, and enhance the learning environment. The potential benefits of school uniforms include:

- decreasing violence and theft—even life-threatening situations—among students over designer clothing or expensive sneakers;
- helping prevent gang members from wearing gang colors and insignia at school;
- instilling students with discipline;
- helping parents and students resist peer pressure;
- helping students concentrate on their school work; and
- helping school officials recognize intruders who come to the school.

As a result, many local communities are deciding to adopt school uniform policies as part of an overall program to improve school safety and discipline. California, Florida, Georgia, Indiana, Louisiana, Maryland, New York, Tennessee, Utah and Virginia have enacted school uniform regulations. Many large public school systems—including Baltimore, Cincinnati, Dayton, Detroit, Los Angeles, Long Beach, Miami, Memphis, Milwaukee, Nashville, New Orleans, Phoenix, Seattle and St. Louis—have schools with either voluntary or mandatory uniform policies, mostly in elementary and middle schools. In addition, many private and parochial schools have required uniforms for a number of years. Still other schools have implemented dress codes to encourage a safe environment by, for example, prohibiting clothes with certain language or gang colors.

Users' Guide to Adopting a School Uniform Policy

The decision whether to adopt a uniform policy is made by states, local school districts, and schools. For uniforms to be a success, as with all other school initiatives, parents must be involved. The following information is provided to assist parents, teachers, and school leaders in determining whether to adopt a school uniform policy.

1. Get parents involved from the beginning

Parental support of a uniform policy is critical for success. Indeed, the strongest push for school uniforms in recent years has come from parent groups who want better discipline in their children's schools. Parent groups have actively lobbied schools to create uniform policies and have often led school task forces that have drawn up uniform guidelines. Many schools that have successfully created a uniform policy survey parents first to gauge support for school uniform requirements and then seek parental input in designing the uniform. Parent support is also essential in encouraging students to wear the uniform.

2. Protect students' religious expression

A school uniform policy must accommodate students whose religious beliefs are substantially burdened by a uniform requirement. As U.S. Secretary of Education Richard W. Riley stated in "Religious Expression in Public Schools," a guide he sent to superintendents throughout the nation on August 10, 1995:

> Students may display religious messages on items of clothing to the same extent that they are permitted to display other comparable messages. Religious messages may not be singled out for suppression, but rather are subject to the same rules as generally apply to comparable messages. When wearing particular attire, such as yarmulkes and head scarves, during the school day is part of students' religious practice, under the Religious Freedom Restoration Act schools generally may not prohibit the wearing of such items.

3. Protect students' other rights of expression

A uniform policy may not prohibit students from wearing or displaying expressive items—for example, a button that supports a political candidate—so long as such items do not independently contribute to disruption by substantially interfering with discipline or with the rights of others. Thus, for example, a uniform policy may prohibit students from wearing a button bearing a gang insignia. A uniform policy may also prohibit items that undermine the integrity of the uniform, notwithstanding their expressive nature, such as a sweatshirt that bears a political message but also covers or replaces the type of shirt required by the uniform policy.

4. Determine whether to have a voluntary or mandatory school uniform policy

Some schools have adopted wholly voluntary school uniform policies which permit students freely to choose whether and under what circumstances they will wear the school uniform. Alternatively, some schools have determined that it is both warranted and more effective to adopt a mandatory uniform policy.

5. When a mandatory school uniform policy is adopted, determine whether to have an "opt out" provision

In most cases, school districts with mandatory policies allow students, normally with parental consent, to "opt out" of the school uniform requirements. Some schools have determined, however, that a mandatory policy with no "opt out" provision is necessary to address a disruptive atmosphere. A Phoenix, Arizona school, for example, adopted a mandatory policy requiring students to wear school uniforms, or in the alternative attend another public school. That Phoenix school uniform policy was recently upheld by a state trial court in Arizona. Note that in the absence of a finding that disruption of the learning environment has reached a point that other lesser measures have been or would be ineffective, a mandatory school uniform policy without an "opt out" provision could be vulnerable to legal challenge.

6. Do not require students to wear a message

Schools should not impose a form of expression on students by requiring them to wear uniforms bearing a substantive message, such as a political message.

7. Assist families that need financial help

In many cases, school uniforms are less expensive than the clothing that students typically wear to school. Nonetheless, the cost of purchasing a uniform may be a burden on some families. School districts with uniform policies should make provisions for students whose families are unable to afford uniforms. Many have done so. Examples of the types of assistance include: (a) the school district provides uniforms to students who cannot afford to purchase them; (b) community and business leaders provide uniforms or contribute financial support for uniforms; (c) school parents work together to make uniforms available for economically disadvantaged students; and (d) used uniforms from graduates are made available to incoming students.

8. Treat school uniforms as part of an overall safety program

Uniforms by themselves cannot solve all of the problems of school discipline, but they can be one positive contributing factor to discipline and safety. Other initiatives that many schools have used in conjunction with uniforms to address specific problems in their community include aggressive truancy reduction initiatives, drug prevention efforts, student-athlete drug testing, community efforts to limit gangs, a zero tolerance policy for weapons, character education classes, and conflict resolution programs. Working with parents, teachers, students, and principals can make a uniform policy part of a strong overall safety program, one that is broadly supported in the community.

Model School Uniform Policies

States and local school districts must decide how they will ensure a safe and disciplined learning environment. Below are some examples of school districts that have adopted school uniforms as part of their strategy.

Long Beach, California

Type: Uniforms are mandatory in all elementary and middle schools. Each school in the district determines the uniform its students will wear.

Opt-out: Yes, with parental consent

Size of program: 58,500 elementary and middle school students

Implementation date: 1994

Support for disadvantaged students: Each school must develop an assistance plan for families that cannot afford to buy uniforms. In most cases, graduating students either donate or sell used uniforms to needy families.

Results: District officials found that in the year following implementation of the school uniform policy, overall school crime decreased 36 percent, fights decreased 51 percent, sex offenses decreased 74 percent, weapons offenses decreased 50 percent, assault and battery offenses decreased 34 percent, and vandalism decreased 18 percent. Fewer than one percent of the students have elected to opt out of the uniform policy.

Dick Van Der Laan of the Long Beach Unified School District explained, "We can't attribute the improvement exclusively to school uniforms, but we think it's more than coincidental." According to Long Beach police chief William Ellis, "Schools have fewer reasons to call the police. There's less conflict among students. Students concentrate more on education, not on who's wearing $100 shoes or gang attire."

Seattle, Washington

Type: Mandatory uniform policy at South Shore Middle School

Opt-out: Yes, with parental consent. Students who opt out must attend another middle school in the district.

Size of program: 900 middle school students

Implementation date: 1995

Support for disadvantaged students: South Shore works with local businesses that contribute financial support to the uniform program. In addition, the administration at South Shore found that the average cost of clothing a child in a school with a prescribed wardrobe is less than in schools without such a program, sometimes 80 percent less. School officials believe that durability, reusability and year-to-year consistency also increase the economy of the school's plan.

Results: The principal of South Shore, Dr. John German, reports that "this year the demeanor in the school has improved 98 percent, truancy and tardies are down, and we have not had one reported incident of theft." Dr.

German explains that he began the uniform program because his students were "draggin', saggin' and laggin'. I needed to keep them on an academic focus. My kids were really into what others were wearing." Only five students have elected to attend another public school.

Richmond, Virginia

Type: Voluntary uniform policy at Maymont Elementary School for the Arts and Humanities

Opt-out: Uniforms are voluntary.

Size of program: 262 elementary school students

Implementation date: 1994

Support for disadvantaged students: Responding to parent concerns about the cost of uniforms, the school sought community financial support for the uniform program. Largely as a result of financial donations from businesses and other community leaders, the percentage of students wearing uniforms rose from 30 percent in 1994–95, the first year of the program, to 85 percent during the current year.

Results: Maymont principal Sylvia Richardson identifies many benefits of the uniform program, including improved behavior, an increase in attendance rates and higher student achievement.

Kansas City, Missouri

Type: Mandatory uniform policy at George Washington Carver Elementary School

Opt-out: None. Carver is a magnet school to which parents and students apply knowing about the uniform policy.

Size of program: 320 elementary school students

Implementation date: 1990

Support for disadvantaged students: Students receive their uniforms at no cost to them. The state and school district pay for the uniforms primarily with magnet school funding.

Results: Philomina Harshaw, the principal for all six years that Carver has had uniforms, observed a new sense of calmness throughout the school after students began wearing uniforms. "The children feel good about themselves as school uniforms build a sense of pride. It forces adults to know a child."

Memphis, Tennessee

Type: Voluntary uniform policy at Douglas Elementary School

Opt-out: Uniforms are voluntary.

Size of program: 532 elementary school students

Implementation date: 1993

Support for disadvantaged students: Douglas has business partners in Memphis that have contributed financial support to purchase uniforms for needy families.

Results: According to Guidance Counselor Sharon Carter, "The tone of the school is different. There's not the competitiveness, especially in grades 4, 5, and 6, about who's wearing what." Ninety percent of the students have elected to wear uniforms on school uniform days, Monday through Thursday. Fridays are "casual" days during which none of the students wear uniforms.

Baltimore, Maryland

Type: Voluntary uniform policy at Mt. Royal Elementary/Middle School

Opt-out: Uniforms are voluntary.

Size of program: 950 elementary and middle school students

Implementation date: 1989

Support for disadvantaged students: Mt. Royal Elementary/Middle School keeps a store of uniforms that are provided free to students who cannot afford the $35.00 to purchase them. Ninety-eight percent of graduating eighth graders donate their uniforms to the school.

Results: According to Mt. Royal's assistant principal, Rhonda Thompson, the uniform policy "has enhanced the tone and climate of our building. It brings about a sense of seriousness about work." All of the students have elected to participate in the uniform program.

Norfolk, Virginia

Type: Mandatory uniform policy at Ruffner Middle School

Opt-out: None. Students who come to school without a uniform are subject to in-school detention.

Size of program: 977 middle school students

Implementation date: 1995

Support for disadvantaged students: The school provides uniforms for students who cannot afford them.

Results: Using U.S. Department of Education software to track discipline data, Ruffner has noted improvements in students' behavior. Leaving class without permission is down 47 percent, throwing objects is down 68 percent and fighting has decreased by 38 percent. Staff attribute these changes in part to the uniform code.

Phoenix, Arizona

Type: Mandatory uniform policy at Phoenix Preparatory Academy

Opt-out: Yes, with parental consent. Students who opt out must attend another middle school in the district.

Size of program: 1,174 middle school students

Implementation date: 1995

Support for disadvantaged students: A grant from a local foundation covers the $25 to $30 cost of uniforms for families that cannot afford to buy them.

Results: According to the principal, Ramon Leyba, "The main result is an overall improvement in the school climate and a greater focus on positive behavior. A big portion of that is from uniforms."

CLINTON ON CUBAN ATTACK
ON CIVILIAN AIRPLANES
February 26, 1996

On February 24 a Cuban jet fighter fired antiaircraft missiles at two civilian airplanes, apparently killing four crew members belonging to Brothers to the Rescue, a Florida-based group opposed to Cuban leader Fidel Castro. President Bill Clinton on February 26 denounced the attack as "a flagrant violation of international law" and moved to reverse his policy of gradually easing relations between the United States and Cuba.

Three weeks later, Clinton signed into law a bill toughening U.S. economic sanctions against Cuba. Clinton had previously opposed the bill, but Cuba's attack on the planes during an American election year intensified political pressures on the president. Cuban Americans had become a potent political force in several states, especially Florida and New Jersey—both of which were seen as crucial to Clinton's reelection bid.

The president's policy reversal won little praise from leading Cuban-American groups, conservative organizations, and Republican opponents in Congress. Most of these factions argued that Clinton still was not tough enough on Castro. At the other end of the spectrum, the new sanctions dismayed some U.S. companies hoping to do business in Cuba, as well as key U.S. allies (especially Canada) that did not share the American eagerness to force Castro out of power.

The incident set back the Clinton administration's carefully staged policy of using carrots and sticks to win concessions from Castro's government. Trying to balance domestic politics and international concerns, the administration for two years had been gradually easing some U.S. restrictions against Cuba, particularly limits on contacts with Cuba by Cuban Americans, business people, journalists, academics, and others. The goal was to make Cuba more open to outside influence. (U.S.-Cuban agreement on refugees, Historic Documents of 1995, p. 203)

The United Nations Security Council on July 26 adopted a mild resolution criticizing the shooting down of the airplanes as unlawful and a violation of the principle that military weapons should not be used against

civilian aircraft. The United States failed to obtain a harsher UN condem-
nation of Cuban action, largely because few countries supported Washing-
ton's hard-line stance toward the Castro regime. Russia and China
abstained from voting on the UN resolution.

Details of the Incident

U.S. officials said that the Brothers to the Rescue organization flew three
Cessna Skymaster planes toward Cuba early on the afternoon of February
24, taking off from Opa Locka airfield near Miami. The first plane, pilot-
ed by Jose Basulto, a cofounder of the group, contacted the Cuban air traffic control tower and was told that proceeding south of the 24th parallel
would be dangerous. Basulto's plane reportedly acknowledged the danger
but continued south, actually entering three miles into Cuban air space.

In the meantime two Cuban MiG jet fighters were ordered into the air.
According to transcripts of radio messages intercepted by U.S. intelligence
services, the lead MiG pilot requested and received permission to shoot
down the second Cessna. After destroying that craft with an air-to-air missile, the MiG pilot sighted the third Cessna, requested and received permission to shoot it down, and did so. U.S. officials said neither of the
downed aircraft had entered Cuban air space; the first was north of Cuban
air space by about five nautical miles and the second by about sixteen
miles. Basulto's lead Cessna, which apparently was not targeted by the
Cubans even though it had entered Cuban air space, headed back north and
returned to Opa Locka airfield.

U.S. officials said the shooting down of the two aircraft constituted a
violation of the Chicago Convention on international air travel because the
Cuban MiGs made no attempt to warn the Cessnas. Customarily under
such circumstances, aircraft of a nation defending its air space are supposed to try to establish radio contact with a civilian aircraft, or at the
least conduct warning maneuvers, such as tipping their wings.

While condemning the Cuban action, U.S. officials noted that they had
repeatedly warned leaders of the Brothers to the Rescue group that they
were endangering themselves with repeated flights near or into Cuban air
space. The group had been founded in 1989 to help rescue Cubans fleeing
their homeland on rafts. By 1994 the group was spending much of its time
harassing the Cuban government, engaging in such actions as dropping
anti-Castro leaflets in Cuba.

In August 1994 the Federal Aviation Administration (FAA) announced
that it was suspending Basulto's license because he had flown into Cuban
air space. The FAA case was still pending at the time the planes were shot
down. The Cuban government had repeatedly sent the United States diplomatic messages protesting the group's activities.

Cuba rejected the U.S. version of how the shoot-down occurred, charging
instead that Washington was to blame for allowing exile groups to violate
Cuban sovereignty. At a news conference in Havana on February 25,
Ricardo Alarcon, head of the Cuban parliament, insisted that the downed

planes were over Cuban air space and said that U.S. officials deliberately lied about the facts. Alarcon called Brothers to the Rescue a "terrorist" organization and charged that the Clinton administration was catering to the "Miami mafia" of Cuban exile groups in hopes of securing their support during an election year.

The shoot-down came as Castro was taking a harder-line stance on dissidents; just a week earlier his government had arrested about fifty members of a group called Concilio Cubano when it announced plans for a public meeting. Most of those arrested were later released.

Clinton's Response

Clinton condemned the attack just a few hours after it occurred and ordered the U.S. military to support and protect search-and-rescue operations.

A more formal and complete response came from the president two days later, when he said in a statement at the White House that Cuba had shot down the planes "without justification." The civilian planes "posed no credible threat" to Cuba, he said. "This shooting of civilian aircraft out of the air was a flagrant violation of international law," he added. "It is wrong and the United States will not tolerate it."

The president said he was taking several steps in response to the attack, the most significant of which was his new willingness to negotiate with Congress on the sanctions bill he had previously opposed. Other steps the president announced on February 26 included:

- Asking Congress to authorize compensation for the families of the four missing men, to be paid out of Cuban government assets that the United States had previously seized.
- Ordering an expansion of broadcasts by Radio Marti, the U.S. government radio station directed at Cuba.
- Placing additional restrictions on travel within the United States by resident Cuban officials (such as diplomats at the United Nations) and limiting visits to the United States by other Cuban officials.
- Suspending indefinitely all charter air travel from the United States to Cuba. The main effect of this was to make it more difficult for Cuban Americans, journalists, and others to travel to Cuba.

The Sanctions Bill

Before the planes were shot down, the Clinton administration had effectively blocked congressional approval of a bill tightening the unilateral U.S. sanctions against Cuba. President Kennedy had imposed the original sanctions in 1962, and later presidents had strengthened or weakened them in response to Cuban behavior. The new legislation was authored by Sen. Jesse Helms, R-N.C., and Rep. Dan Burton, R-Ind. Each chamber had passed a version of the Helms-Burton legislation in 1995, but administration opposition had stymied agreement on a unified version.

Just four days after the attack, administration officials and House and Senate conferees settled their differences. Each chamber passed the compromise version early in March, and Clinton signed it into law on March 12.

The key sticking point between the administration and the bill's sponsors had been a provision allowing Cuban Americans to file suit in U.S. courts against companies or individuals that acquire or "traffic" in properties those Cuban Americans had once owned but had been confiscated by the Cuban government.

The administration had raised a host of legal and practical objections against that provision but ultimately agreed to it, with the stipulation that the president could suspend implementation for six-month periods. Officials said that provision, even if implemented, would affect few companies because the Cuban government had turned only a handful of confiscated properties over to private entities.

Over the long term, the most important provision of the Helms-Burton bill might prove to be one that had no immediate impact: a codification of existing U.S. sanctions against Cuba. In the past, all sanctions had been in the form of presidential executive orders, which any president could suspend, revoke, or modify at will. The Helms-Burton bill put those sanctions into law, in effect requiring congressional action before any of them could be changed.

Once law, the sanctions could be lifted only after the president found that a "democratic transition" was under way in Cuba, as evidenced by twelve criteria. Among the criteria were a commitment to hold free elections and the absence of Fidel Castro or his brother Raul from any transitional government in Cuba. Another section of the bill would reduce U.S. foreign aid to other countries—principally Russia—that supported Cuban intelligence or nuclear facilities.

Following is the text of President Bill Clinton's statement on February 26, 1996, denouncing the shooting down of two civilian airplanes by Cuban jet fighters and explaining his response:

Good afternoon. Two days ago, in broad daylight and without justification, Cuban military aircraft shot down two civilian planes in international airspace. Search and rescue efforts by the Coast Guard, which began immediately after we received word of the incident, have failed to find any of the four individuals who were aboard the airplanes.

These small airplanes were unarmed and clearly so. Cuban authorities knew that. The planes posed no credible threat to Cuba's security. Although the group that operated the planes had entered Cuban airspace in the past on other flights, this is no excuse for the attack, and provides—let me emphasize—no legal basis under international law for the attack. We must be clear:

This shooting of civilian aircraft out of the air was a flagrant violation of international law. It is wrong and the United States will not tolerate it.

Saturday's attack is further evidence that Havana has become more desperate in its efforts to deny freedom to the people of Cuba. Also on Saturday the Cuban Council, a broad group that wants to bring democracy to Cuba, had planned a day of peaceful discussion and debate. Instead, in the days leading up to this gathering, scores of activists were arrested and detained. Two have already been sentenced to long prison terms. They join about 1,000 others in Cuba who were in jail solely because of their desire for freedom. Now the downing of these planes demands a firm response from both the United States and the international community. I am pleased that the European Union today strongly condemned the action.

Last night, on my instructions, Ambassador [Madeleine] Albright convened an emergency session of the United Nations Security Council to condemn the Cuban action and to present the case for sanctions on Cuba until it agrees to abide by its obligation to respect civilian aircraft and until it compensates the families of the victims.

Today, I am also ordering the following unilateral actions. First, I am asking that Congress pass legislation that will provide immediate compensation to the families, something to which they are entitled under international law, out of Cuba's blocked assets here in the United States. If Congress passes this legislation, we can provide the compensation immediately.

Second, I will move promptly to reach agreement with the Congress on the pending Helms-Burton Cuba legislation so that it will enhance the effectiveness of the embargo in a way that advances the cause of democracy in Cuba.

Third, I have ordered that Radio Marti expand its reach. All the people of Cuba must be able to learn the truth about the regime in Havana—the isolation it has earned for itself through its contempt for basic human rights and international law.

Fourth, I am ordering that additional restrictions be put on travel in the United States by Cuban officials who reside here, and that visits by Cuban officials to our country be further limited.

Finally, all charter air travel from the United States to Cuba will be suspended indefinitely.

These deliberate actions are the right ones at this time. They respond to Havana in a way that serves our goals of accelerating the arrival of democracy in Cuba. But I am not ruling out any further steps in the future, should they be required.

Saturday's attack was an appalling reminder of the nature of the Cuban regime—repressive, violent, scornful of international law. In our time, democracy has swept the globe, from the Philippines exactly 10 years ago, to Central and Eastern Europe, to South Africa, to Haiti, to all but one nation in our hemisphere. I will do everything in my power to see that this historic tide reaches the shores of Cuba.

And let me close by extending on behalf of our family and our country our deepest condolences to those in the families of those who lost their lives.

GAO ON THE COUNTERFEITING OF U.S. CURRENCY
February 26, 1996

Counterfeiting of U.S. currency—including the widely publicized fake $100 bill known as the "superdollar"—was a serious issue but posed little immediate threat to the U.S. economy, according to a report issued February 26, 1996, by the General Accounting Office (GAO). The GAO, the investigative arm of Congress, quoted government figures showing that detected counterfeit funds represented less than one one-thousandth of the approximately $380 billion in U.S. currency in circulation.

Nevertheless, the GAO warned that procedures to detect counterfeiting were inadequate, especially overseas, and suggested a more intense effort to protect U.S. currency. The agency said U.S. government figures on counterfeiting did not give a complete picture of the extent of the problem.

The GAO report to Congress, entitled "Counterfeit U.S. Currency Abroad: Issues and U.S. Deterrence Efforts," came less than a month before the Treasury Department and Federal Reserve System introduced a new $100 note intended to thwart counterfeiters. The note, which had been in the planning stages for nearly a decade, was the first of several currency denominations to be substantially redesigned using technical advances to make illegal duplication difficult. U.S. currency had been unchanged—except for two technical improvements made in 1990—since 1929.

The Extent of Counterfeiting

At the request of Rep. John M. Spratt Jr., D-S.C., a GAO team spent nearly nine months in late 1994 and early 1995 assessing the question of counterfeiting. The GAO focused in particular on counterfeiting overseas, in part because an estimated 60 percent of U.S. currency was circulating outside the nation's borders.

The report was an unusual one for the GAO in that it contained no definitive conclusions or recommendations for legislative action. The GAO said it faced several limitations in conducting its study, including securi-

ty constraints imposed by U.S. agencies because of ongoing investigations into the superdollar and other issues. Even so, the report contained substantially more information about the extent of counterfeiting than was easily available to the public, and it suggested several areas for improvement in government policy.

The GAO said its first problem was in finding how widespread counterfeiting was. The report cited only one readily available figure: the Secret Service's annual report on how much counterfeit currency had been detected. That figure was nearly $209 million for fiscal year 1994, the most recent year available at the time of the GAO report.

The GAO concluded that the actual extent of counterfeiting could not be measured because it was a secret and illegal activity. While it was the best estimate available, the Secret Service figure left open the question of how much counterfeiting was not detected, the GAO said. The Secret Service estimates, the GAO said, were "incomplete and present only a partial picture of counterfeiting."

The Secret Service estimates also appeared to be unreliable, the GAO said, because the data reflected where the Secret Service focused its efforts. For example, the GAO noted that in fiscal 1994 nearly 50 percent of the counterfeit currency detected overseas occurred in the six countries where the Secret Service maintained permanent staff; in other countries, detection statistics "tend to be more inconsistent."

In addition, the GAO suggested that the Secret Service was failing to detect much of the high-quality counterfeit currency in circulation, especially the superdollar. Much of that money, the GAO said, circulated outside of formal banking systems overseas and "therefore would not be reported to the Treasury if detected." The Treasury Department rejected that contention and insisted that the superdollar was being detected.

Whatever the true level of counterfeiting, the current impact on the U.S. economy was minimal, the GAO quoted government officials as saying. Treasury and State Department officials told the GAO that counterfeiting—while a serious problem—was economically insignificant. Further, the GAO quoted foreign banking officials as saying that counterfeiting had not weakened world confidence in U.S. currency, and there were few reports of dollars not being accepted overseas because of counterfeiting concerns.

In interviews with the GAO, overseas law enforcement officials tended to be more concerned about the level of counterfeiting of U.S. currency than did foreign banking officials. Some foreign bankers said they were more worried about credit card fraud or counterfeiting of their countries' currencies.

The GAO was unable to determine the extent to which counterfeiting was on the rise. The report quoted Secret Service figures showing a sharp increase in detections of counterfeit U.S. currency overseas, from $30 million in fiscal 1992 to $121 million a year later. However, the GAO said some of the increase might be the result of improved detection methods *and more aggressive work by the Secret Service. Detection figures for any given year might also be skewed by a few large seizures of counterfeit currency.*

Much of the GAO report dealt with efforts by the Secret Service to bolster its presence overseas. The GAO noted that the Secret Service had no law enforcement powers in foreign countries and was heavily dependent on cooperation from local agencies and financial institutions—some of which lacked skills or equipment for routine detection of counterfeit U.S. currency.

The GAO said the Secret Service had been trying to beef up its overseas presence but had encountered budgetary limits and bureaucratic obstacles. The agency had more than 2,000 agents in the United States but less than 20 overseas.

The "Superdollar"

The GAO report gingerly addressed the most controversial counterfeiting issue of the 1990s: an extremely sophisticated fake $100 bill known in media reports as the "superdollar." A report by a House Republican research committee alleged that the fake $100 bill was produced in the Middle East with the help of a government; it did not name the country but implied it was Iran. Several media reports had alleged that the Iranian government was producing the superdollar with printing equipment sold to the Shah before he was overthrown in 1978.

The Treasury Department insisted that the House Republican report contained no hard evidence to back up its allegations. Further, Treasury rejected reports that hundreds of millions and possibly billions worth of superdollars were in circulation. Government officials said detections showed that superdollars accounted for only a small amount of counterfeit currency.

While not directly disputing this statement, the GAO said it was impossible to determine how many superdollars had been produced. The GAO found that overseas law enforcement and financial officials had inconsistent or incomplete information on how to detect the superdollar, suggesting that detection rates might not be very high.

The GAO report did not speculate on where the superdollar was produced. However, it did quote an unidentified State Department official as saying that in May 1995 the United States asked officials of Middle Eastern countries to locate the printing plants and those responsible for printing the superdollars. The official said the countries involved were, at a minimum, tolerating the counterfeiting if not actually participating in it. The GAO also quoted law enforcement and financial officials as speculating that the dollar was circulated by terrorist organizations.

Law enforcement officials told the GAO that diplomatic efforts would be required to eliminate production of the superdollar because jurisdictional constraints made it difficult for them to prevent counterfeiting that was condoned or even sponsored by foreign governments. U.S. law enforcement agencies had no leverage in a country with which the United States had no diplomatic relations, such as Iran.

Currency Redesign

On March 25, U.S. officials unveiled a new $100 bill incorporating numerous security features to foil counterfeiters. The new design represented the most significant change to U.S. currency in nearly seventy years.

The most obvious change was an enlarged portrait of Benjamin Franklin (50 percent larger than before), which was moved off-center. The new bills also contain a watermark that is visible when the note is held against a light. Another feature is a polyester thread containing the words "USA 100" that can be seen when held against a light and that glows red when held under ultraviolet light.

Treasury Secretary Robert Rubin said a new $50 note would be introduced in the next year or two, to be followed by redesigned notes in the $20, $10, and $5 denominations. A decision on redesigning the $1 bill had not been made, he said.

Officials said the $100 bill was redesigned first because it was the most widely counterfeited U.S. note and had become a standard unit of currency in many countries with unstable currencies of their own, notably Russia. Rubin said the government did not recall the old $100 bills because of the expense involved and out of fear that a recall might undermine world confidence in U.S. currency. Instead, the Federal Reserve would take old $100 notes out of circulation as they were turned in.

Following are excerpts from the report, "Counterfeit U.S. Currency Abroad: Issues and U.S. Deterrence Efforts," issued by the General Accounting Office on February 26, 1996:

Background

The widespread use of U.S. currency abroad, together with the outdated security features of the currency, makes it a particularly vulnerable target for international counterfeiters. According to the Federal Reserve, the proportion of U.S. currency in circulation abroad has increased from 40 percent in 1970 to over 60 percent today.

High foreign inflation rates and the relative stability of the dollar have contributed to the increasing use of U.S. currency outside the United States. And, in fact, the United States benefits from this international use. When U.S. currency remains in circulation, it essentially represents an interest-free loan to the U.S. government. The Federal Reserve has estimated that the U.S. currency held abroad reduces the need for the government to borrow by approximately $10 billion a year.

Despite this benefit, its increasing international use has made U.S. currency a target for counterfeiting. Furthermore, with the exception of two changes introduced in 1990, the security features of the currency have not substantially changed since 1929, which has resulted in the U.S. dollar's becoming increasingly vulnerable to counterfeiting. . . .

Congressional groups and the media have continued to highlight their concerns that the counterfeiting of U.S. currency abroad is becoming an increasingly serious problem. Concerns about counterfeiting abroad were heightened in 1992 with the issuance of the first of two reports by the House Republican Research Committee's Task Force on Terrorism and Unconventional Warfare. These reports charged that a foreign government was producing a very high-quality counterfeit note, commonly referred to as the Superdollar, to support terrorist activities. In 1993, the House Appropriations Committee's Surveys and Investigations staff completed a report on the Secret Service's counterfeiting deterrence efforts and briefed the House Appropriations Committee. In the same year, a bill—the International Counterfeiting Deterrence Act—was introduced to address international counterfeiting and economic terrorism; however, it was not passed.

The Nature of Counterfeiting of U.S. Currency Abroad Is Diverse

The nature of counterfeiting of U.S. currency abroad is diverse, including various types of perpetrators, uses, and methods. The relative sophistication of the counterfeiter and method used results in counterfeit notes of differing quality. According to a National Research Council report requested by Treasury, the counterfeiting problem will increase as technologies improve and are made more accessible to the public. Already, the Secret Service has been troubled by some very high-quality counterfeits of U.S. currency identified as originating abroad.

Perpetrators include both the casual and the professional counterfeiter. The casual counterfeiter is a person who commits the crime because it is convenient or easy to do. For example, an office worker may use a copying machine to counterfeit U.S. currency. The number of casual counterfeiters is expected to increase with the greater accessibility of and improvements to modern photographic and printing devices, according to the National Research Council report. Conversely, the professional counterfeiter may be a member of a gang, criminal organization, or terrorist group. Foreign law enforcement and Secret Service officials that we interviewed told us of suspected links between counterfeiting and organized crime.

Counterfeit U.S. currency is used for economic gain and is sometimes linked to other crimes. According to foreign law enforcement and Secret Service officials, counterfeit U.S. currency is sometimes distributed in conjunction with drug trafficking, illicit arms deals, and other criminal and/or terrorist activities. Moreover, Secret Service and foreign law enforcement officials told us that counterfeit U.S. currency is now sometimes produced by counterfeiters in one country for export to another country. For example, in Milan, Italy, counterfeiting has become an industry in which counterfeit U.S. currency is produced for export, according to Italian law enforcement officials. They added that the counterfeits typically were exported to the former Soviet Union and Eastern Europe.

The methods used by counterfeiters of U.S. currency abroad are the same as those used within the United States, according to Secret Service officials. Common techniques include using black and white, monochromatic, or color photocopiers; cutting and taping or gluing numerals from high denomination notes to the corners of a note of lower denomination, also known as making "raised notes"; using sophisticated computers, scanners, and laser or ink jet printers; bleaching good notes and reprinting higher denominations on the genuine paper; and using photomechanical or "offset" methods to make a printing plate from a photographic negative of a genuine note. . . .

High-quality counterfeit notes are difficult for the general public to discern, but according to Federal Reserve officials, the notes can be detected by experienced bank tellers. . . .

[Extent of Problem Undetermined]

The criminal nature of the activity precludes determination of the actual extent to which U.S. currency is being counterfeited abroad. The best data available to reflect actual counterfeiting are Secret Service counterfeit-detection data. However, these data have limitations and thus provide only a limited measure of the extent of counterfeiting activities. Use of these data should be qualified to reflect these limitations so that conclusions reached using the data do not mislead. Overall, detected counterfeits have represented a minuscule amount of the currency in circulation. According to Secret Service officials, the data that they gathered was supplemented by intelligence information and field experience to demonstrate an increase in counterfeiting activity abroad. However, our analysis of the same counterfeit-detection data proved inconclusive. Moreover, foreign officials' views about the seriousness of the problem of counterfeit U.S. currency were mixed. Foreign financial organization and law enforcement officials that we interviewed reported no significant numbers of chargebacks and few reported instances of U.S. currency not being accepted abroad.

[Level of Counterfeiting Believed Insignificant]

On the basis of the number of Secret Service counterfeit-detections, Treasury officials concluded that counterfeiting of U.S. currency was economically insignificant and thus did not pose a threat to the U.S. monetary system. According to Secret Service and Treasury officials, detected counterfeits represented a minuscule portion of U.S. currency in circulation. Secret Service and Federal Reserve data showed that, in fiscal year 1994, of the $380 billion in circulation, $208.7 million had been identified as counterfeit notes, a figure which represented less than one one-thousandth of the currency in circulation. However, while Treasury and Secret Service officials agreed that, overall, counterfeiting was not economically significant, they considered any counterfeiting to be a serious problem.

[Counterfeiting Abroad Believed to Be Increasing]

The Secret Service reported that counterfeiting of U.S. currency abroad was increasing. It used counterfeit-detection data, supplemented with intelligence information and field experience, to support this claim. It also employed two counterfeit-detection data measures to illustrate the extent of counterfeiting abroad: (1) counterfeit-detections abroad and (2) domestic detections of counterfeits that were produced abroad. Counterfeits detected abroad are categorized as "appearing abroad," while counterfeits detected domestically are divided into two separate categories. Domestic detections of counterfeits not yet in circulation are called "seizures," and those counterfeits detected while in circulation are called "passes."

The Secret Service has reported a significant recent increase in detections of counterfeit U.S. currency abroad. In one analysis, it reported that the amount of counterfeit currency detected abroad increased 300 percent, from $30 million in fiscal year 1992 to $121 million in fiscal year 1993, thereby surpassing domestic detections in the same period. . . .

The Secret Service has also reported that, in recent years, a larger dollar amount of the notes detected as domestic passes has been produced outside the United States. Since 1991, the dollar amount of counterfeit U.S. notes detected while in circulation and produced abroad has exceeded the dollar amount of those produced domestically. . . . In fiscal year 1994, foreign-produced notes represented approximately 66 percent of total domestic passes detected. . . .

Additional U.S. Counterfeit Currency Deterrence Efforts

The U.S. government, primarily through the Treasury Department and its Secret Service and the Federal Reserve, has been increasing its counterfeiting deterrence efforts. These recent efforts include redesigning U.S. currency; increasing exchanges of information abroad; augmenting the Secret Service presence abroad; and undertaking efforts to stop production and distribution of counterfeit currency, including the Superdollar.

In an effort to combat counterfeiting both domestically and abroad, Treasury is redesigning U.S. currency to incorporate more security features intended to combat rapid advances in reprographic technology. This change, the most significant to the U.S. currency in over 50 years, is, according to some U.S. and foreign officials, a long overdue one. The redesigned currency is planned for introduction in 1996 starting with changes to the $100 note, with lower denominations to follow at 9- to 12-month intervals. According to Treasury officials, the currency redesign will continue, becoming an ongoing process, because no security features are counterfeit-proof over time. These officials also said that the old currency would not be recalled and would retain its full value. Moreover, Treasury is leading a worldwide publicity campaign to facilitate introduction of the redesigned currency, ensure awareness and use of the overt security features, and assure the public that the old currency will retain its full value. Through this campaign, the Federal Reserve hopes to encourage the public to turn in old currency for the redesigned notes. . . .

Further, the Secret Service has been attempting to increase its presence abroad, although it has encountered difficulties in obtaining approval. The Secret Service has over 2,000 agents stationed in the United States, but it has fewer than 20 permanent positions abroad. . . .

Additionally, the U.S. government has undertaken special efforts to eradicate the highest quality counterfeit note—the Superdollar. These efforts include the use of task forces and diplomatic efforts among senior policy-level officials of the U.S. and certain foreign governments. Due to the sensitivity and ongoing nature of this investigation, we were made generally aware of these efforts but not provided with specific information. . . .

EDUCATION SECRETARY ON
THE STATE OF EDUCATION
February 28, 1996

Improving how students read was the most fundamental and urgent challenge facing American schools at the end of the twentieth century, Education Secretary Richard W. Riley said in his third annual State of American Education address. Speaking at the Maplewood-Richmond Heights High School outside St. Louis, Riley said parents and teachers shared the responsibility of making sure students can read before they enter the job market or go on to college.

The status of public education was a campaign issue in 1996. President Bill Clinton's standard campaign litany of federal spending items that needed to be protected included education, Medicare, Medicaid, and the environment. Clinton's Republican challenger, Bob Dole, joined critics of public education, especially of teachers and their unions. In his speech accepting the Republican nomination in August, Dole said the country was among "the biggest education spenders and among the lowest education achievers among the leading industrialized nations."

Reports issued during the year by several prestigious groups gave mixed views on how well public education was performing. One bipartisan commission in September condemned as a "national shame" the training and treatment of teachers in most states. Another bipartisan group, the National Education Goals Panel, reported in November that the nation's schools had made little progress toward achieving a list of goals set by most of the fifty governors in 1989. On the other side, the National Science Foundation in April reported significant improvements in math and science education at the elementary through high school levels. The College Board said in August that it had encouraging evidence of improving scores on Scholastic Aptitude Tests, especially for math, among high school students.

Riley's Seven Challenges

In his annual speech, Riley offered a broad defense of American public education, acknowledging that it had many shortcomings and was under attack from several quarters. Without naming names, Riley challenged those who, he said, "believe that we can prepare for the future by cutting education today, who see little value in public education, and some who— quite literally—would like to abolish it as an institution." That view was wrong, he said, because it was "too narrow, too divisive, too fond of bashing teachers, too quick to tear down rather than build up."

In particular, Riley attacked proposals to use public tax dollars to provide vouchers for parents to use at private and parochial schools. Some of those who advocate such a system "seek nothing less than the dismemberment of public education," he said. As an alternative, Riley called for more public support for, and involvement with, the public schools. He praised those "who see the rebuilding and the expansion of public education as the very cornerstone of our nation's economic and democratic future."

Riley cited seven challenges facing public education, the most important of which was improving reading skills. Citing demands for well-educated workers in an increasingly technology-driven economy, Riley said: "To my way of thinking, improving America's literacy rate is just as important to this nation's future economic growth as balancing the budget."

To bolster his argument that the teaching of reading needs to be improved, Riley noted the final report of the 1994 National Assessment of Educational Progress, a broad barometer of how American students perform. It found that 41 percent of fourth grade students, 31 percent of eighth grade students, and 25 percent of high school seniors scored below level for basic reading skills. Further, the assessment found that average reading proficiency for high school seniors declined from 1992 to 1994. "This is just not good enough," Riley said.

Riley made an extraordinary appeal to American parents to become more involved with the schools and to take a more active role in helping their children. "Slow down your lives," Riley said to parents. "Talk to your children. Teach the difference between right and wrong. Make your children proud to be Americans."

Other Assessments of American Education

Several reports issued during 1996 offered ammunition both for those who said American public education was in decline and for those who saw rays of hope. Most of the reports came from groups that supported public education and advocated devoting more tax dollars to it.

One of the broadest measures of the schools was issued November 19 by the National Education Goals Panel, which had been created by the nation's governors to assess how much progress had been achieved toward meeting ambitious education targets for the year 2000. The National Governors' Association had set the targets at a 1989 meeting in Virginia that was attended by President George Bush. (Education goals report, Historic Documents of 1990, p. 153)

In its report, the panel said some states had made progress toward meeting the education goals, but schools nationally were lagging behind the tar-

gets for 2000. After nearly six years of work, "overall national performance is virtually static," it said.

The goals set by the governors included such standards as: at least 90 percent of all students will graduate from high school; American students will be the best in the world in mathematics and science; every American adult will be literate; and schools will be free of drugs, guns, and violence. The panel found little encouragement when it measured national progress toward those goals. For example, the panel noted a decline in reading scores among high school seniors and a drop in the number of high school teachers having degrees in their primary classroom assignments.

The report noted that thirty-two states had developed academic standards and means to measure whether students were meeting them; another fourteen states were developing such standards.

Another partisan committee found discouraging evidence when it examined qualifications, pay, working conditions, and other issues concerning the nation's public school teachers. The National Commission on Teaching and America's Future reported on September 12 that more than one-fourth of new teachers did not have proper credentials or teaching skills and that states and localities gave them little help to improve their skills.

The commission said the basic problem with American education was a nationwide failure to train, recruit, and support qualified teachers. It noted, for example, that more than forty states allow local districts to hire teachers who did not have basic education requirements. "States pay more attention to the qualification of veterinarians treating the nation's cats and dogs than to those of teachers educating the nation's children and youth," the report said.

The commission called for stricter professional standards for teachers, along with pay scales that reward teaching skills and knowledge. It also said schools should have more leeway to fire incompetent teachers.

In another report, released in December, the Educational Trust cited data showing a widening gap in educational achievement between white and minority students. Using data from the National Assessment of Educational Progress, the report noted that minorities had started to catch up with whites during the 1970s and 1980s, but the trend reversed in the early 1990s.

> *Following are excerpts from the third annual State of American Education address by Richard W. Riley, secretary of education, delivered February 28, 1996, at the Maplewood-Richmond Heights High School near St. Louis:*

I have come here to the heartland of America to talk about American education where it is happening. . . . I am here at a typical American high school, where the future of America is being created each and every day, to tell you that the era of "dumbing down" American education is over. That is my message today.

American education must reach for a new level of excellence, because of the most basic of reasons: our very prosperity as a nation—and the economic security and quality of each and every American family—depends on it.

Today, in many ways, we face the same challenges that confronted the pioneers who left St. Louis and headed West across the frontier. For we are crossing our own frontier defined by new knowledge, a new economic landscape, new ways of communicating.

We need to remember that the pioneers who crossed the Mississippi set out as a community, bound together with a common goal. They surely had their differences, but they came together for the common good. And that is a lesson we must heed now in 1996.

For there is a growing debate in America about how we educate our children. On one side are those who believe that we can prepare for the future by cutting education today, who see little value in public education, and some who—quite literally—would like to abolish it as an institution.

This view, to my mind, is wrong—a view too narrow, too divisive, too fond of bashing teachers, too quick to tear down rather than build up.

I disagree with that vision. The politics of blame and exploiting people's legitimate anxieties have never served America well, and it is so wrong when it comes to the education of our children. Sometimes, people can get so caught up listening to themselves debate that they live, die, and get buried and nothing ever gets done.

On the other side are those who are willing to roll up their sleeves and invest in our children, who see the rebuilding and the expansion of public education as the very cornerstone of our nation's economic and democratic future.

Yes, public education has its problems. We have to contend with too much violence, with too little accountability, and some schools are just beyond repair.

But for every problem, I have found many more successful school communities that have come together and found common purpose in getting about the business of helping their children learn. And that's the right way to go. . . .

We need to challenge ourselves to strive for the excellence of high standards and teach our young people real-life skills to get good jobs. And we must make sure that the doors to a college education are open wide to every deserving student who has worked hard to make the grade.

Becoming a Nation of Readers

Our very first challenge is to get America reading again. That big model of a computer behind me symbolizes that the American people "smell the future." They recognize the need to get computers into the classroom as quickly as possible.

But you can't cruise or use the Internet if you don't know how to read. And that, to my mind, is our most urgent task—teaching our children good reading habits—getting America serious about reading.

Our national math and science scores are up because we have invested more than ten years of hard work in that effort. We are turning the corner. This is a great success story for American education, and it tells me that we know how to get results.

Our national reading scores, however, are flat and they have been flat for far too long. Now, America does reasonably well on international comparisons when it comes to literacy. But too many of our young people are groping through school without having mastered this most essential and basic skill.

The 1994 NAEP [National Assessment of Educational Progress] report tells us that 41 percent of all 4th graders, 31 percent of all 8th graders, and 25 percent of all 12th graders scored below the basic reading level. This is just not good enough.

A young person who cannot read is placed at an extraordinary disadvantage. And, in far too many cases, these are the very young people who start down the road to truancy, giving up, and eventually dropping out.

Let us recognize what we are all about here. Reading is much more than just a skill. It allows us to learn the wisdom of the ages, to see beauty in a line of poetry, even as we test the new ideas of our times. To read Jefferson is to be engaged with the very spirit of our democracy. To read the poetry of Maya Angelou is to capture the surging spirit of a rising and hopeful America.

And, in our new complex economic environment, 89 percent of the jobs that are now being created require much higher levels of literacy and math. To my way of thinking, improving America's literacy rate is just as important to this nation's future economic growth as balancing the budget.

This is why I am announcing today the beginning of a long-term effort to improve America's literacy. We are creating a national reading and writing partnership of more than thirty-five diverse groups dedicated to the single goal of improving reading and writing in America.

Working with the American Library Association, the Center for the Book at the Library of Congress, the National Retired Teachers Association, Hadassah, AMC Theaters, Pizza Hut, the Girl Scouts of America, and the many members of our Family Partnership for Learning—we want to encourage Americans to open a book and read.

This is a new partnership which is going to put the spotlight on literacy. We are going to take our case to the American people and tell them that reading is where it all begins. We are going to lay out a strategy that gives parents "check points of progress" and encourages educators and state leaders to stay focused on helping our young people gain this most essential skill.

We can all make a positive contribution. I urge every family to follow the first rule of education and read to their children. Start early and keep at it. I encourage parents to find an extra thirty minutes in the day to help their children. If all parents in America made it their patriotic duty to find an extra thirty minutes to help their children learn more—each and every day—it would revolutionize American education.

All of our research tells us that this is so important. Read a book, read the sports page, read the comics or read R. L. Stine's "Goosebumps" and get scared together—it doesn't matter. Just read! . . .

The Challenge to Support the American Family

So, getting America reading again is our first challenge. Our second challenge is to give parents the power to help their children learn. Strong families make strong schools. When parents get involved in their children's education, good things start to happen. . . .

I urge parents to have a fierce commitment to the education of their children. Volunteer in school and stay connected to your children. Too often we live such busy lives that we disconnect from our children, and we don't even know it is happening. The time crunch can just about wear you down. But don't give up.

Slow down your lives. Talk to your children. Teach them the difference between right and wrong. Make your children proud to be Americans. Define your moral standards, and if that means turning off the television sometimes or using a "V" chip, then be strong and determined. And do it!

And here it is important to remind all Americans that our nation's public schools are not "religion-free" zones. Children do not have to leave their religious faith at the school house door. The First Amendment provides a broad mantle of religious freedom. At the same time it ensures every parent that school officials do not overstep their bounds and coerce students to violate their freedom of conscience.

I can report to you today that President Clinton's Guidelines on Religion have been well received. There has been a marked decline in the confusion and legal confrontation about the right of students to express their religious faith.

The Challenge to Make Our Schools Safe

Our third great challenge is to keep our schools safe, orderly and disciplined. That is a basic rule. No teacher should ever fear to walk into a classroom. And no child should ever stay home from school because he or she is afraid.

Alternative schools need to be seen as options for the most troublesome students. We cannot let a few bad apples ruin the school day for the majority of our young people. We need to get these young people out of the regular classroom but not give up on them. They need good, structured learning environments.

School districts need to keep a sharp eye on truancy as a first sign that young people are losing their way. Graduating from high school still remains a significant benchmark for keeping young people out of trouble and off welfare.

The President has gotten a great deal of mail lately from young people across the country regarding his comments in the State of the Union speech on uniforms. Last week, the President was in Long Beach, California and talked about it some more. His point about uniforms is well taken. If parents and teachers think that uniforms can help their children learn, then uniforms ought to be seen as one positive way to instill discipline and prevent violence.

I now want to speak very directly to the parents of middle school children. For four years in a row, drug use has gone up among 8th graders. This is a nationwide trend. It disturbs me. Our research tells us that many young people simply do not believe that drugs are harmful, life threatening or addictive. Parents need to help their children develop some strong inner fiber—good character—to make important decisions about their own personal lives.

Nothing will be accomplished unless the young people of America live their lives by a new code of conduct, an honor code that isn't written on paper but written in their hearts, because growing up really comes down to choices.

The choice not to cheat on a test or drive drunk; the courage to say no to peer pressure when it comes to smoking marijuana; the willingness of young men and women not to throw their lives away in a moment of passion, to wind up with a baby, and maybe even on the welfare line.

The Challenge to Achieve High Standards

Our fourth challenge is to recognize that we are smarter than we think. We will never help our young people to measure up—especially those living in poverty—if we lower their expectations, water down their curriculum, and write them off by categorizing and stigmatizing them.

I believe in the young people of America. They have the same capacity to achieve as the generation that won World War II, as the generation that sent man to the Moon, as the generation that set out to save the environment and as the generation that created the pentium chip.

To those who say America's effort to raise standards and increase accountability has lost its momentum—I assure you, the standards movement is alive and well. We have had our peaks and valleys, but we are moving forward. I can report to you today that work is underway all across America to develop high standards in core academic subjects. . . .

Now, setting standards is not easy. The new national standards for math, science, civics, geography and the arts have been well received. They are useful "road maps" for local and state educators who are defining their own high standards. But the history standards were unacceptable to me, and the effort to set English standards has run into difficulties as well.

But when you run into difficulties, you don't quit. You go back at it and try again. This is exactly what Missouri did with the new "Show Me" standards. And that is exactly what is being done now as a new panel of historians redrafts the national history standards.

I want to be very clear in saying that there is no one way to establish standards. Every state is going to have to decide what works best for its students. Look at the various model standards that are out there and use what works best for you. But please aim high.

President Clinton and I urge every community and state, each in its own way, to reach for new levels of excellence. We will continue to support the good work now being done in so many local communities through the Goals 2000 education quality initiative.

Now, Goals 2000 attracts a lot of heat, and there are some people who have some very strange notions about what it is. So I want to tell you how it works. Every principal in this country has a desk drawer full of good ideas. Most teachers do too. Too often those good ideas never see the light of day because our schools are always hard pressed just trying to make ends meet.

And that is where Goals 2000 makes the difference. Because Goals 2000 gives schools the extra money they never get to improve themselves. That is what it is. The energy to get better. Nothing more. I won't surrender this good idea to a few people who see ghosts under their bed every night—who never roll up their sleeves and make a positive contribution for the sake of our children by trying to improve our public schools.

I urge those committed to high standards to keep this effort as mainstream and bipartisan as possible. And I look forward to the new energy that the nation's governors and business leaders will bring to the issue at next month's education summit.

But aiming high is only half the battle. Teachers need to be able to teach to high standards and we need a greater sense of accountability in public education.

Let's remember that teaching is not just a job but a demanding and exacting profession. I'm tired of those who make a living out of bashing teachers. We will only win the battle for excellence if we have excellent teachers.

If we give our teachers the support they deserve, then we must also ask our public schools to be much more accountable. Graduating from high school has to mean more than getting to go to the senior prom. Many creative efforts need to be looked at to make this happen: testing at 4th, 8th and 12th grade, statewide exit exams, school "report cards," parent-teacher compacts, new demanding standards for initial certification and recertification of teachers and principals.

We need to find ways to keep the best teachers in the classroom, to weed out teachers who just can't cut it, and to have the good sense to counsel teachers to leave the profession when they have lost the excitement and the zeal to teach.

I encourage teachers and their professional organizations to help make this happen. Public trust grows stronger when there is public accountability and public trust is good for all who have dedicated their lives to quality education.

The Challenge to Innovate Effectively

As we seek to aim high and increase public accountability, we need to press on in our effort to open up public education to new ways of doing business.

Technology is very much at the heart of our national effort to bring America's schools up to date. We are making good progress. One year ago, only 35 percent of all of America's public schools were hooked up to the Internet. Today, that figure stands at 50 percent. And we now have a new telecommunications law that gives schools the opportunity to be the first in line to get on line and at a lower cost.

We cannot miss this opportunity. We need to "fast forward" our efforts and make sure teachers are trained well. This is our national mission. It is as important as sending men to the Moon. If we persevere we will achieve President Clinton's goal of making sure that every library, school and classroom in this nation is wired and on-line by the year 2000.

Getting computers into America's classrooms has to be seen as just one step in our growing effort to move American education into the future. Public school choice, schools-within-schools, and the expansion of the charter school movement are three other winning examples of American creativity.

Public school choice needs to be seen as an option. Some of our most successful schools are small schools that create a community of learning. Young people should not get lost in school and then be forgotten.

This is why President Clinton is a strong supporter of charter schools with public accountability. The President has asked the Congress in his new budget to create new "venture capital" to encourage the development of charter schools. I urge the Congress to respond with enthusiasm. I have visited charter schools, and I am particularly impressed by what charter schools are doing for disabled and under-achieving children.

Now, there are some who will tell you that private school vouchers are good for education as well. I believe they are dead wrong. Unlike charter schools, private school vouchers offer us no public accountability. They are a retreat from the democratic purposes of public education, a way to divert public tax dollars, and they will cost taxpayers a great deal of money. Moreover, receiving public tax dollars through the voucher threatens the very nature of private and parochial schools. It makes them less private and less parochial.

I am keenly sensitive to the fact that many parochial school supporters see vouchers as one way to support the good work that they do. I recognize their day-to-day financial struggle. This is why I shall encourage actively that the United States Supreme Court reconsider its ruling in *Aguilar v. Felton,* which continues to place an undue burden—both financial and educational—on many Catholic, Lutheran, Jewish and other religiously affiliated schools.

But, I am concerned that some private school voucher proponents have something else in mind when they talk about vouchers. I fear that they seek nothing less than the dismemberment of public education. It dismays me that some think-tank intellectuals are leading this assault on public education, and away from the democratic spirit that has always defined American public education at its best. You and I know what public education really needs. It needs hands-on leaders. Leaders like Governor Mel Carnahan here in Missouri who worries about class size, computers in the classroom and high standards. And leaders like Dr. J in Denver and the late Ernie Boyer and thousands like them who are making a difference every day.

114

The Challenge to Prepare Young People for Work

Our sixth great challenge is helping our young people to make something of themselves in these new economic times, to have an education relevant to real and good jobs.

Today, too many of our young people see no connection between what they learn in school and the skills they need to function in real life. And too many business leaders rightly complain that high school graduates come to them without the skills for today's jobs.

We need to redesign our schools for success, and place more attention on the forgotten middle—the average kids with untapped potential who are still looking for direction. Today's young people will be tomorrow's paramedics, emergency room nurses, Army helicopter pilots, and the skilled technicians who build the NASA rockets. There is no point in preparing our young people for jobs in a widget factory.

This is why I am a strong believer in rethinking the American high school by creating partnerships between high schools and business and community colleges. Our young people need career paths that fit the new economic times.

Apprenticeships, career academies, tech prep and other school-to-work opportunities represent concrete examples of how we can help young people prepare for good paying jobs. I urge young students to look at these new opportunities as real stepping-stones to go on to a local community college and to future job security.

Keeping the Doors to College Wide Open

Keeping the doors to college wide open is our seventh and final great challenge.

Today, our nation's system of colleges and universities represents the brightest gemstone in America's educational and economic crown. It is the envy of the world. For more than fifty years, we have made access to higher education part of the American Dream.

Yet today, the burden of paying for college is being placed more and more on students and their families. Students have taken on a larger share of the cost of their education. Four out of five students work today. And too many parents are struggling to make ends meet today, while trying to save for their children's college education in the future. I heard an interview on TV this morning. A young mother was asked what she would do with the money if she won the lottery. "I would be able to send all my children to college," she replied. That is a grand example of what parents are thinking about.

In the last twenty years, forty million Americans have used a federal student loan to pay for their college education. That is the American middle class!

Today, two-thirds of all student financial aid dollars in this country come from my department. I am pleased to tell you that we have cut the student loan default rate in half, and we are collecting on many more defaulted loans, saving taxpayers millions of dollars.

Yet despite this good progress, we face difficulties reaffirming this national commitment to opening the doors to higher education even wider.

I remain perplexed, just about baffled, by the thinking of some in the Congress who want to cut student loans—who don't seem to remember that they got their chance to go to college with the help of the American taxpayer. This is why we have spent the last year fighting to keep the new Congress from cutting $10 billion from our student loan program.

I also once again urge the Congress to preserve and expand our "direct lending program" which has the support of America's higher education community. This is no time to cave in to the special interests, who don't like the competition and who are up in arms because their profit margin is dwindling. Students will always win with healthy competition.

As we look to the future we need to create a new sense of shared responsibility in finding new ways to finance American higher education. This needs to be a broad effort working on many fronts.

Our elementary and secondary schools must do a much better job of preparing students for college level work. As standards go up, colleges will be able to shift resources away from remedial courses.

State leaders must look down the road. In nine out of the last ten years, state budgets have declined in their commitment to higher education. This year, I see new evidence that many Governors and state legislators are already thinking ahead.

They are increasing funding for higher education and supporting creative financing mechanisms, including: the creation of pre-paid college tuition programs; education IRAs; and tax credits for full-time students. I support these creative new initiatives.

I urge our colleges and universities to use their ingenuity to hold the line on the cost of going to college. We are already pricing too many young people—smart students, who are just poor—out of an education. And we have too many middle class families already stretched to the limit.

For our part, I want to speak directly to every high school student in America today and make this promise. If you do your share, we will do ours. Through a continuation of loans, grants, Americorps and work study, we will widen the opportunity to go to college.

We believe in rewarding excellence and hard work. This is why President Clinton has called for the creation of a new Presidential Honors Scholarship of $1,000 for the top 5 percent of all graduating students in every high school in America.

We also believe that the maximum Pell Grant program should go up during each of the next five years to ultimately reach $3,120. And it makes good sense to me to rapidly expand our college work-study program to help millions of young people get ahead in life.

I encourage Congress to enact into law President Clinton's tuition tax deduction, which would allow middle class families to deduct up to $10,000 a year for college tuition and other costs. This is a sensible proposal that will make an immediate difference for thousands of American families.

To those who say we cannot afford to help this generation of young people—I say look at our record of success and look down the road. We are on the brink of change—at the gateway of a new time. This is absolutely the wrong time to cut our investment in education at all levels—and it is the wrong time for Congress to be so out of touch with the American people.

The Challenge to Come Together as Americans

The story of America in this century is the story of giving each new generation the opportunity to advance themselves through education. We are a people who believe in education, who know its value. And this I know for sure: We did not become the world's greatest superpower, the most productive nation in the world, on a foundation of ignorance.

As we cross this new frontier of knowledge, we need to recognize that the success and freedom of being an American—in this day and age—is the freedom of excellence—the ability to be highly educated and highly trained—to negotiate a complex economic environment and become productive and responsible citizens.

I urge every citizen in this great country to remember that we are raising our children not as Republicans, Democrats or Independents, but as Americans—the future of our country. If we want to enlarge the civic life of this nation, let us re-invigorate our people's love of learning and put the "public" back into public education.

Public education is one of the great essential building blocks of our democracy—the public space where we teach our children good citizenship, and where we—as adults—often exercise our own citizenship by working with others for the good of our children.

E Pluribus Unum—out of many, one—doesn't come easy for America. But only America has done it well. Our task in these new times is not to retreat to our own separate racial, ethnic, cultural, or political interest group—but rather to do the opposite—to do the hard work of learning to come together for the good of all of our children.

Finding common ground is the urgent work of America in 1996. If we are not quite the melting pot that we want to be, we are—at the very least—a rich American stew, full of many flavors. We all can contribute to what is good for America.

We know how to create good schools and now is the time to get the job done. It is the right thing to do for our children and the right thing to do for America's future.

Thank you.

March

FEDERAL APPEALS COURT ON PHYSICIAN-ASSISTED SUICIDE
March 6, 1996

The emotion-laden question of whether the terminally ill have a constitutional right to physician-assisted suicide came to center stage in 1996 when two federal courts struck down state laws barring the practice. The U.S. Court of Appeals for the Ninth Circuit on March 6 overturned a Washington state law forbidding physician-assisted suicide, holding that it violated the Fourteenth Amendment's due process clause. Less than a month later another appeals court used different legal grounds to strike down a similar New York law.

The Supreme Court agreed October 1 to review the two cases, and arguments were scheduled for January 1997. The decision in that case could have an effect on society to rival that of Roe v. Wade, *the 1973 case in which the Court held that women had a constitutional right to abortion. According to Choice in Dying, an information organization based in New York, thirty-three states explicitly prohibited doctor-assisted suicides, ten other states and the District of Columbia banned them by case law, and the law was unclear in six other states. Oregon citizens voted in 1994 to permit the practice, but court challenges have kept the statute from taking effect.*

Extending the Right to Die

The question whether and under what circumstances a person has a right to a doctor's help in committing suicide is fraught with moral, ethical, and religious overtones. As the majority opinion in the Washington case said, its decision was opening "a controversy that may touch more people more profoundly than any other issue the courts will face in the foreseeable future."

Those arguing in behalf of the right to doctor-assisted suicide, including the majorities on the two appeals courts, said that mentally competent, terminally ill adults should be able to choose to end their lives in a humane and dignified way. "What interest can the state possibly have in requiring

121

the prolongation of a life that is all but ended?" a three-judge panel of the Second Circuit Court of Appeals wrote in the April 3 decision striking down the New York law. "And what business is it of the state to require the continuation of agony when the result is imminent and inevitable?"

Opponents of the practice, which included the Clinton administration, the American Medical Association (AMA), and the Roman Catholic Church, offered a range of arguments. Most centered on the potential for abuse and on ethical questions such as who will define what is meant by "terminally ill" and who will decide whether a person seeking a doctor's help to commit suicide is mentally competent or clinically depressed.

A Washington Post *telephone survey, conducted in March 1996, found that half of those surveyed thought assisted suicide should be legal; two-fifths thought it should not. According to various other polls, as many as one-quarter of all doctors have quietly acquiesced to the wishes of at least one terminally ill patient, generally by prescribing drugs—usually morphine—that would allow the patient to bring about his or her death. Among doctors who specialize in certain diseases, such as AIDS, the percentage was even higher.*

Until the federal appeals court rulings caught the public's attention, the best-known proponent of assisted suicide was Jack Kevorkian, a former pathologist from Michigan who by the end of 1996 had helped approximately forty people take their own lives. Kevorkian, known in the popular media as Dr. Death, was acquitted in May for the third time of charges of criminal wrongdoing. Many other doctors, including those who believe in physician-assisted suicide, strongly objected to Kevorkian's tactics, noting that he rarely knew his patients well and that some of them were not terminally ill and might have been helped by treatment for depression.

The national debate about physician-assisted suicide was the next step in a continuing controversy over the right to die. That debate has been before the public since at least 1976, when the New Jersey Supreme Court ruled that a comatose patient, Karen Ann Quinlan, could be removed from a respirator. More than forty states have since adopted "living will" statutes that permit competent adults to declare in advance that they do not want to be kept alive by medical treatment in the later stages of a terminal illness. Several states also permit competent adults to stipulate that they do not want medical treatment if they become permanently and irreversibly unconscious and to delegate decision-making power to a surrogate. (Quinlan decision, Historic Documents of 1976, p. 197)

In 1990 Congress required all hospitals receiving federal assistance to disclose to their patients the state's laws on their right to refuse or terminate medical treatment. That law was passed following the Supreme Court's only decision to date on the right to die. In the case of Cruzan v. Director, Missouri Department of Health, *the Court in 1990 enunciated a constitutional right to refuse medical attention. "The principle that a competent person has a constitutionally protected liberty interest in refusing unwanted medical treatment may be inferred from our earlier decisions,"*

Chief Justice William H. Rehnquist wrote for the five-justice majority.
(Supreme Court on right to die, Historic Documents of 1990, p. 373)

The Appeals Court Rulings

The 8–3 ruling of the Ninth Circuit Court of Appeals, with Chief District Judge Barbara J. Rothstein presiding, overturned an earlier decision by a three-judge panel of the same court upholding Washington's prohibition against doctor-assisted suicide. In its broad-based ruling, the majority found that there was "a constitutionally protected liberty interest in determining the time and manner of one's own death" implicit in the due process clause of the Fourteenth Amendment. The Supreme Court has ruled that similar "liberty interests" protect an individual's right to privacy in making personal decisions relating to marriage, bearing a child, and ending an unwanted pregnancy, the majority noted. "A common thread running through these cases is that they involve decisions that are highly personal and intimate as well as of great importance to the individual," wrote Judge Stephen Reinhardt for the majority. "Certainly, few decisions are more personal, intimate or important than the decision to end one's life, especially when the reason for doing so is to avoid excessive and protracted pain."

The question then was whether the state may constitutionally restrict that right. Acknowledging that the state had a legitimate interest both in preserving life and preventing suicide, the majority found that interest insufficient in this case. "One of the heartaches of suicide is the senseless loss of a life ended prematurely," Reinhardt wrote. "In the case of a terminally ill adult who ends his life in the final stages of an incurable and painful degenerative disease, in order to avoid debilitating pain and a humiliating death, the decision to commit suicide is not senseless, and death does not come too soon. . . . Not only is the state's interest in preventing such individuals from hastening their deaths of comparatively little weight, but its insistence on frustrating their wishes seems cruel indeed."

While the appeals court struck down the state's absolute ban on doctor-assisted suicide, it encouraged the state to adopt laws or regulations to guard against errors and abuse. For example, the court said, the state might require waiting periods; second medical opinions to confirm that an illness is terminal and that the patient has been receiving proper care, including comfort care; witnesses to ensure that the procedure is voluntary; and psychological examinations to ensure that the patient is not suffering from a treatable depression.

The three-judge panel of the Second Circuit Court of Appeals was unanimous in striking down New York's law, but its grounds for doing so were much narrower. It held that the law violated the equal protection clause of the Fourteenth Amendment in that terminally ill patients in New York had the right to hasten their own death by asking a physician to stop certain treatment but did not have the right to hasten death by asking a physician to provide certain treatments. If terminally ill patients can effectively commit suicide by refusing certain treatment, wrote Judge Roger J. Miner,

123

"they should be free to do so by requesting appropriate medication to terminate life during the final stages of terminal illness."

Opposition to the Rulings

Officials in Washington and New York appealed the circuit rulings to the Supreme Court, which agreed on October 1 to hear the cases. Among the many organizations that filed briefs with the Court in favor of the two states was the Clinton administration. "There is an important and common-sense distinction between withdrawing artificial supports so that a disease will progress to its inevitable end and providing chemicals to be used to kill someone," wrote Solicitor General Walter E. Dellinger III. Dellinger also argued that the interest of the states in protecting life overrode an individual liberty that might exist: "The difficulty that physicians have in determining whether requests for assisted suicide come from patients with treatable pain or depression, the vulnerability of terminally ill patients to subtle influences from physicians [and] family members . . . and the continuing possibility that someone can be misdiagnosed as terminally ill all support a state's decision to ban all assisted suicides."

The American Medical Association also filed a brief supporting the states. In June the AMA's governing body, the House of Delegates, reaffirmed its opposition to assisted suicide and called for greater efforts to prepare physicians to provide pain relief for their terminally ill patients. "Patients need to know that our goal in providing care will always be to relieve suffering and never to eliminate the sufferer," said the report adopted by the House of Delegates. The delegates rejected a proposal to adopt a "neutral position" on physician-assisted suicide.

The National Conference of Catholic Bishops said March 19 that the majority opinion in the Washington case "creates a 'right to die' that threatens to sweep away all meaningful limits or restrictions." The bishops also voiced what some have called the "slippery slope" argument, saying they feared the decision "sets the stage for physicians to give lethal injections to patients who never asked to be killed," such as the incompetent and the comatose.

Following are excerpts from the Ninth Circuit Court of Appeals's majority opinion, issued March 6, 1996, in the case of Compassion in Dying v. State of Washington, *in which the court ruled that a Washington state law barring physician-assisted suicide violated a mentally competent, terminally ill individual's constitutional right to choose the manner and timing of his or her own death:*

I.

This case raises an extraordinarily important and difficult issue. It compels us to address questions to which there are no easy or simple answers, at law or otherwise. It requires us to confront the most basic of human concerns—the mortality of self and loved ones—and to balance the interest in preserving human life against the desire to die peacefully and with dignity. People of good will can and do passionately disagree about the proper result, perhaps even more intensely than they part ways over the constitutionality of restricting a woman's right to have an abortion. Heated though the debate may be, we must determine whether and how the United States Constitution applies to the controversy before us, a controversy that may touch more people more profoundly than any other issue the courts will face in the foreseeable future.

Today, we are required to decide whether a person who is terminally ill has a constitutionally-protected liberty interest in hastening what might otherwise be a protracted, undignified, and extremely painful death. If such an interest exists, we must next decide whether or not the state of Washington may constitutionally restrict its exercise by banning a form of medical assistance that is frequently requested by terminally ill people who wish to die. We first conclude that there is a constitutionally-protected liberty interest in determining the time and manner of one's own death, an interest that must be weighed against the state's legitimate and countervailing interests, especially those that relate to the preservation of human life. After balancing the competing interests, we conclude by answering the narrow question before us: We hold that insofar as the Washington statute prohibits physicians from prescribing life-ending medication for use by terminally ill, competent adults who wish to hasten their own deaths, it violates the Due Process Clause of the Fourteenth Amendment.

[II and III omitted]

IV. Is There a Liberty Interest?

. . . In deciding right-to-die cases, we are guided by the Court's approach to the abortion cases. *[Planned Parenthood of Southeastern Pennsylvania v.] Casey* [1992] in particular provides a powerful precedent, for in that case the Court had the opportunity to evaluate its past decisions and to determine whether to adhere to its original judgment. Although *Casey* was influenced by the doctrine of stare decisis, the fundamental message of that case lies in its statements regarding the type of issue that confronts us here: "These matters, involving the most intimate and personal choices a person may make in a lifetime, choices central to personal dignity and autonomy, are central to the liberty protected by the Fourteenth Amendment." *Casey.*

[A Omitted]

B. The Legal Standard

There is no litmus test for courts to apply when deciding whether or not a liberty interest exists under the Due Process Clause. Our decisions involve difficult judgments regarding the conscience, traditions, and fundamental tenets of our nation. We must sometimes apply those basic principles in light of changing values based on shared experience. Other times we must apply them to new problems arising out of the development and use of new technologies. . . . In all cases, our analysis of the applicability of the protections of the Constitution must be made in light of existing circumstances as well as our historic traditions.

Historically, the Court has classified "fundamental rights" as those that are "implicit in the concept of ordered liberty." . . .

In recent years, the Court has spoken more frequently of substantive due process interests than of fundamental due process rights. . . . The Court has also recently expressed a strong reluctance to find new fundamental rights. . . .

The Court's evolving doctrinal approach to substantive due process claims is consistent with the basic truth enunciated by Justice Harlan and later endorsed by the Court in *Casey*: "the full scope of the liberty guaranteed by the Due Process Clause is a rational continuum which, broadly speaking, includes a freedom from all substantial arbitrary impositions and purposeless restraints . . . ." *Casey*, citing *Poe v. Ullman*, (1961) (Harlan, J., dissenting from dismissal on jurisdictional grounds). As Justice Harlan noted, some liberty interests are weightier than others. Under the Court's traditional jurisprudence, those classified as fundamental rights cannot be limited except to further a compelling and narrowly tailored state interest. . . . Other important interests, such as the liberty interest in refusing unwanted medical treatment, are subject to a balancing test that is less restrictive, but nonetheless requires the state to overcome a substantial hurdle in justifying any significant impairment.

Recent cases, including *Cruzan [v. Director, Missouri Department of Health (1990)]*, suggest that the Court may be heading towards the formal adoption of the continuum approach, along with a balancing test, in substantive due process cases generally. . . . However, we need not predict the Court's future course in order to decide the case before us. Here, as we have said, even under the Court's traditional mode of analysis, a balancing test is applicable. . . .

[C and D omitted]

E. Prior Court Decisions

Next we examine previous Court decisions that delineate the boundaries of substantive due process. We believe that a careful examination of these decisions demonstrates that there is a strong liberty interest in determining how and when one's life shall end, and that an explicit recognition of that interest follows naturally, indeed inevitably, from their reasoning.

The essence of the substantive component of the Due Process Clause is to limit the ability of the state to intrude into the most important matters of our lives, at least without substantial justification. In a long line of cases, the Court has carved out certain key moments and decisions in individuals' lives and placed them beyond the general prohibitory authority of the state. . . .

A common thread running through these cases is that they involve decisions that are highly personal and intimate, as well as of great importance to the individual. Certainly, few decisions are more personal, intimate or important than the decision to end one's life, especially when the reason for doing so is to avoid excessive and protracted pain. . . .

While the cases we have adverted to lend general support to our conclusion, we believe that two relatively recent decisions of the Court, *Casey* (1992) and *Cruzan* (1990), are fully persuasive, and leave little doubt as to the proper result.

F. Liberty Interest Under *Casey*

. . . Like the decision of whether or not to have an abortion, the decision how and when to die is one of "the most intimate and personal choices a person may make in a lifetime," a choice "central to personal dignity and autonomy." A competent terminally ill adult, having lived nearly the full measure of his life, has a strong liberty interest in choosing a dignified and humane death rather than being reduced at the end of his existence to a childlike state of helplessness, diapered, sedated, incontinent. How a person dies not only determines the nature of the final period of his existence, but in many cases, the enduring memories held by those who love him. . . .

Surely, a person's decision whether to endure or avoid such an existence constitutes one of the most, if not the most, "intimate and personal choices a person may make in a life-time," a choice that is "central to personal dignity and autonomy." *Casey*. Surely such a decision implicates a most vital liberty interest.

G. Liberty Interest under *Cruzan*

In *Cruzan*, the Court considered whether or not there is a constitutionally-protected, due process liberty interest in terminating unwanted medical treatment. The Court said that an affirmative answer followed almost inevitably from its prior decisions holding that patients have a liberty interest in refusing to submit to specific medical procedures. . . . Writing for a majority that included Justices O'Connor and Scalia, Chief Justice Rehnquist said that those cases helped answer the first critical question at issue in *Cruzan*, stating: "The principle that a competent person has a constitutionally protected liberty interest in refusing unwanted medical treatment may be inferred from our prior decisions." *Cruzan*. . . .

These passages make it clear that *Cruzan* stands for the proposition that there is a due process liberty interest in rejecting unwanted medical treatment, including the provision of food and water by artificial means. . . . Moreover, the Court majority clearly recognized that granting the request to remove the tubes through which Cruzan received artificial nutrition and hydration would lead inexorably to her death. *Cruzan*. Accordingly, we conclude that *Cruzan*, by recognizing a liberty interest that includes the refusal of artificial provision of life-sustaining food and water, necessarily recognizes a liberty interest in hastening one's own death. . . .

H. [Omitted]

V. Relevant Factors and Interests

1. Preserving Life

. . . Although the state's interest in preserving life may be unqualified, and may be asserted regardless of the quality of the life or lives at issue, that interest is not always controlling. Nor is it of the same strength in each case. To the contrary, its strength is dependent on relevant circumstances, including the medical condition and the wishes of the person whose life is at stake.

Most tellingly, the state of Washington has already decided that its interest in preserving life should ordinarily give way—at least in the case of competent, terminally ill adults who are dependent on medical treatment—to the wishes of the patients. In its Natural Death Act, Washington permits adults to have "life-sustaining treatment withheld or withdrawn in instances of a terminal condition or permanent unconsciousness." In adopting the statute, the Washington legislature necessarily determined that the state's interest in preserving life is not so weighty that it ought to thwart the informed desire of a terminally ill, competent adult to refuse medical treatment. . . .

As the laws in state after state demonstrate, even though the protection of life is one of the state's most important functions, the state's interest is dramatically diminished if the person it seeks to protect is terminally ill or permanently comatose and has expressed a wish that he be permitted to die without further medical treatment (or if a duly appointed representative has done so on his behalf). When patients are no longer able to pursue liberty or happiness and do not wish to pursue life, the state's interest in forcing them to remain alive is clearly less compelling. Thus, while the state may still seek to prolong the lives of terminally ill or comatose patients or, more likely, to enact regulations that will safeguard the manner in which decisions to hasten death are made, the strength of the state's interest is substantially reduced in such circumstances.

2. Preventing Suicide

a.

While the state's general commitment to the preservation of life clearly encompasses the prevention of suicide, the state has an even more particular interest in deterring the taking of one's own life. The fact that neither Washington nor any other state currently bans suicide, or attempted suicide, does not mean that the state does not have a valid and important interest in preventing or discouraging that act. . . .

While the state has a legitimate interest in preventing suicides in general, that interest, like the state's interest in preserving life, is substantially diminished in the case of terminally ill, competent adults who wish to die. One of the heartaches of suicide is the senseless loss of a life ended prematurely. In the case of a terminally ill adult who ends his life in the final stages of an incurable and painful degenerative disease, in order to avoid debilitating pain and a humiliating death, the decision to commit suicide is not senseless, and death does not come too early. . . . While some people who contemplate suicide can be restored to a state of physical and mental well-being, terminally ill adults who wish to die can only be maintained in a debilitated and deteriorating state, unable to enjoy the presence of family or friends. Not only is the state's interest in preventing such individuals from hastening their deaths of comparatively little weight, but its insistence on frustrating their wishes seems cruel indeed. . . .

b.

The state has explicitly recognized that its interests are frequently insufficient to override the wishes of competent, terminally ill adult patients who desire to bring their lives to an end with the assistance of a physician. Step by step, the state has acknowledged that terminally ill persons are entitled in a whole variety of circumstances to hasten their deaths, and that in such cases their physicians may assist in the process. Until relatively recently, while physicians routinely helped patients to hasten their deaths, they did so discreetly because almost all such assistance was illegal. However, beginning about twenty years ago a series of dramatic changes took place. Each provoked the type of division and debate that surrounds the issue before us today. Each time the state's interests were ultimately subordinated to the liberty interests of the individual, in part as a result of legal actions and in part as a result of a growing recognition by the medical community and society at large that a more enlightened approach was essential.

The first major breakthrough occurred when the terminally ill were permitted to reject medical treatment. The line was drawn initially at extraordinary medical treatment because the distinction between ordinary and extraordinary treatment appeared to some to offer the courts an objective, scientific standard that would enable them to recognize the right to refuse certain medical treatment without also recognizing a right to suicide or euthanasia. That distinction, however, quickly proved unworkable, and after a while, terminally ill patients were allowed to reject both extraordinary and ordinary treatment. For a while, rejection of treatment, often through "do not resuscitate" orders, was permitted, but termination was not. This dividing line, which rested on the illusory distinction between commission and omission (or active and passive), also appeared for a short time to offer a natural point of repose for doctors, patients and the law. However, it, too, quickly proved untenable, and ultimately patients were allowed both to refuse and to terminate medical treatment, ordinary as well as extraordinary. Today, many states also allow the terminally ill to order their physicians to discontinue not just traditional medical treatment but the artificial provision of life-sustaining food and water, thus permitting the patients to die by self-starvation. Equally important, today, doctors are generally permitted to administer death-inducing medication, as long as they can point to a concomitant pain-relieving purpose.

In light of these drastic changes regarding acceptable medical practices, opponents of physician-assisted suicide must now explain precisely what it is about the physician's conduct in assisted suicide cases that distinguishes it from the conduct that the state has explicitly authorized. The state responds by urging that physician-assisted suicide is different in kind, not degree, from the type of physician-life-ending conduct that is now authorized, for three separate reasons. It argues that "assisted suicide": 1) requires doctors to play an active role; 2) causes deaths that would not result from the patient's underlying disease; and 3) requires doctors to provide the causal agent of patients' deaths.

The distinctions suggested by the state do not individually or collectively serve to distinguish the medical practices society currently accepts. The first distinction—the line between commission and omission—is a distinction without a difference now that patients are permitted not only to decline all medical treatment, but to instruct their doctors to terminate whatever treatment, artificial or otherwise, they are receiving. In disconnecting a respirator, or authorizing its disconnection, a doctor is unquestionably committing an act; he is taking an active role in bringing about the patient's death. In fact, there can be no doubt that in such instances the doctor intends that, as the result of his action, the patient will die an earlier death than he otherwise would.

Similarly, drawing a distinction on the basis of whether the patient's death results from an underlying disease no longer has any legitimacy. While the distinction may once have seemed tenable, at least from a metaphysical standpoint, it was not based on a valid or practical legal foundation and was therefore quickly abandoned. When Nancy Cruzan's feeding and hydration tube was removed, she did not die of an underlying disease. Rather, she was allowed to starve to death. In fact, Ms. Cruzan was not even terminally ill at the time, but had a life expectancy of 30 years. The removal of the gastronomy tube, which was clearly the precipitating cause of her death, is not considered to be the legal cause only because a judicial judgment has been made that removing the feeding tube is permissible. Similarly, when a doctor provides a conscious patient with medication to ease his discomfort while he starves himself to death—a practice that is not only legal but has been urged as an alternative to assisted suicide—the patient does not die of any underlying ailment. To the contrary, the doctor is helping the patient end his life by providing medication that makes it possible for the patient to achieve suicide by starvation.

Nor is the state's third and final distinction valid. Contrary to the state's assertion, given current medical practices and current medical ethics, it is not possible to distinguish prohibited from permissible medical conduct on the basis of whether the medication provided by the doctor will cause the patient's death. As part of the tradition of administering comfort care, doctors have been supplying the causal agent of patients' deaths for decades. Physicians routinely and openly provide medication to terminally ill patients with the knowledge that it will have a "double effect"—reduce the patient's pain and hasten his death. . . . Such medical treatment is accepted by the medical profession as meeting its highest ethical standards. . . .

In the case of "double effect" we excuse the act or, to put it more accurately, we find the act acceptable, not because the doctors sugarcoat the facts in order to permit society to say that they couldn't really know the consequences of their action, but because the act is medically and ethically appropriate even though the result—the patient's death—is both foreseeable and intended. It commonly takes the form of putting a patient on an intravenous morphine drip, with full knowledge that, while such treatment will alleviate his pain, it will also indubitably hasten his death. Analgesics, most notably morphine, when applied in sufficient doses, will bring about a patient's death because they serve to repress respiration. There can be no doubt, therefore, that the actual cause of the patient's death is the drug administered by the physician or by a person acting under his supervision or direction. Thus, the causation argument is simply "another bridge crossed" in the journey to vindicate the liberty interests of the terminally ill, and the state's third distinction has no more force than the other two. . . .

VI. Application of the Balancing Test and Holding

Weighing and then balancing a constitutionally-protected interest against the state's countervailing interests, while bearing in mind the various consequences of the decision, is quintessentially a judicial role. . . . [I]n the end balancing entails the exercise of judicial judgment rather than the application of scientific or mathematical formulae. No legislative body can perform the task for us. Nor can any computer. In the end, mindful of our constitutional obligations, including the limitations imposed on us by that document, we must rely on our judgment, guided by the facts and the law as we perceive them.

As we have explained, in this case neither the liberty interest in choosing the time and manner of death nor the state's countervailing interests are static. The magnitude of each depends on objective circumstances and generally varies inversely with the other. The liberty interest in hastening death is at its strongest when the state's interest in protecting life and preventing suicide is at its weakest, and vice-versa.

The liberty interest at issue here is an important one and, in the case of the terminally ill, is at its peak. Conversely, the state interests, while equally important in the abstract, are for the most part at a low point here. We recognize that in the case of life and death decisions the state has a particularly strong interest in avoiding undue influence and other forms of abuse. Here, that concern is ameliorated in large measure because of the mandatory involvement in the decision-making process of physicians, who have a strong bias in favor of preserving life, and because the process itself can be carefully regulated and rigorous safeguards adopted. Under these circumstances, we believe that the possibility of abuse, even when considered along with the other state interests, does not outweigh the liberty interest at issue.

The state has chosen to pursue its interests by means of what for terminally ill patients is effectively a total prohibition, even though its most important interests could be adequately served by a far less burdensome measure. The consequences of rejecting the as-applied challenge would be disastrous for the terminally ill, while the adverse consequences for the state would be of a far lesser order. This, too, weighs in favor of upholding the liberty interest.

We consider the state's interests in preventing assisted suicide as being different only in degree and not in kind from its interests in prohibiting a number of other medical practices that lead directly to a terminally ill patient's death. Moreover, we do not consider those interests to be significantly greater in the case of assisted suicide than they are in the case of those other medical practices, if indeed they are greater at all. However, even if the difference were one of kind and not degree, our result would be no different. For no matter how much weight we could legitimately afford the state's interest in preventing suicide, that weight, when combined with the weight we give all the other state's interests, is insufficient to outweigh the terminally ill individual's interest in deciding whether to end his agony and suffering by hastening the time of his death with medication prescribed by his physician. The individual's interest in making that vital decision is compelling indeed, for no decision is more painful, delicate, personal, important, or final than the decision how and when one's life shall end. If broad general state policies can be used to deprive a terminally ill individual of the right to make that choice, it is hard to envision where the exercise of arbitrary and intrusive power by the state can be halted. In this case, the state has wide power to regulate, but it may not ban the exercise of the liberty interest, and that is the practical effect of the program before us. . . .

VII.

. . . There is one final point we must emphasize. Some argue strongly that decisions regarding matters affecting life or death should not be made by the courts. Essentially, we agree with that proposition. In this case, by permitting the individual to exercise the right to choose we are following the constitutional mandate to take such decisions out of the hands of the government, both state and federal, and to put them where they rightly belong, in the hands of the people. We are allowing individuals to make the decisions that so profoundly affect their very existence—and precluding the state from intruding excessively into that critical realm. The Constitution and the courts stand as a bulwark between individual freedom and arbitrary and intrusive governmental power. Under our constitutional system, neither the state nor the majority of the people in a state can impose its will upon the individual in a matter so highly "central to personal dignity and autonomy". . . . Those who believe strongly that death must come without physician assistance are free to follow that creed, be they doctors or patients. They are not free, however, to force their views, their religious convictions, or their philosophies on all the other members of a democratic society, and to compel those whose values differ with theirs to die painful, protracted, and agonizing deaths.

Affirmed

STATE DEPARTMENT ON
HUMAN RIGHTS IN CHINA
March 6, 1996

The State Department's annual report on human rights practices around the world during 1995 contained exceptionally harsh criticism of human rights abuses in China. The report, released March 6, documented widespread abuses of civil and political liberties in China, including the suppression of nearly all political dissent.

In an unusual move, the report also acknowledged that economic advances in China had not translated into a broader acceptance of internationally recognized human rights practices. A key sentence of the report said: "The experience in China in the past few years demonstrates that while economic growth, trade and social mobility create an improved standard of living, they cannot by themselves bring about greater respect for human rights in the absence of a willingness by political authorities to abide by the fundamental international norms."

For years, U.S. policy was based on the assumption that an improved economy and increased exposure to the outside world would encourage China's leaders to loosen their authoritarian grip on power. In the annual congressional debates over granting China most-favored-nation trading status, Clinton and his Republican predecessors argued that maintaining friendly diplomatic relations and close economic ties with China would help improve the Chinese political situation. The Clinton administration called this a "balanced approach" to winning concessions from Beijing.

Although it did not directly challenge that policy assumption, the State Department report provided strong ammunition for those who argued the opposite position: that Chinese leaders wanted the economic benefits of trade with the United States and other countries but were unwilling to make any political concessions in exchange.

Clinton, who came into office promising a tough stance on Chinese human rights issues, by 1994 had adopted a position essentially giving U.S.-China trade prominence over human rights in the making of U.S. policy. The president each year renewed most-favored-nation trading status for China, over the opposition of many in Congress who wanted to make U.S.-Chinese economic relations more dependent on Beijing's human rights practices.

Chinese leaders always had argued that all aspects of their country's political system—including human rights issues—were internal matters that were of no business to the rest of the world. China in April rebuffed an attempt by the United States and other Western countries to subject Beijing's human rights practices to the scrutiny of the United Nations Human Rights Commission. China won the support of many Third World nations during a UN meeting in Geneva to block a resolution that mildly criticized Beijing's human rights record and would have given the UN agency authority to review that record.

The State Department report reviewed human rights practices in 194 countries, focusing particular attention on nations without legal or institutional protection for their citizens. Among the nations cited for abuses were several U.S. allies, including Turkey, which continued to suppress the Kurdish minority; Egypt, which was charged with abusing police powers in its crackdown on Islamic fundamentalists; Saudi Arabia, which discriminated against the Shiite minority; and Israel, which denied equal rights to its Arab citizens.

Details of Chinese Human Rights Abuses

The report said China during 1995 "continued to commit widespread and well-documented human rights abuses, in violation of internationally accepted norms, stemming both from the authorities' intolerance of dissent and the inadequacy of legal safeguards for basic freedoms." Documenting a host of specific human rights and political abuses, the report concluded that China remained under the control of a harshly authoritarian regime that had no intention of allowing dissent, much less broadening the political system.

The government's crackdown on opposition forces was so severe, the report said, that by the end of 1995 "almost all public dissent against the central authorities was silenced." The government accomplished that, the report added, through "intimidation, exile or imposition of prison terms or administrative detention" of anyone bold enough to voice dissent.

China continued that crackdown in 1996. On October 30, a Chinese court sentenced Wang Dan, a leader of the 1989 Tiananmen Square democracy protests, to an eleven-year prison term. His crime: "plotting to subvert the government" through his political writings and association with other dissidents.

The report reviewed the general failure of China's legal system to protect rights of the accused. It noted, for example, that attorneys were rarely allowed to offer a serious defense of their clients and that most trials were little more than sentencing proceedings.

The lack of due process had "egregious consequences" when defendants received the death penalty, the report said, noting that China by 1995 allowed that penalty for sixty-five crimes. Chinese media reported approximately 1,100 executions in 1995, but the State Department said the real number of executions was "probably significantly higher."

Despite the litany of abuses, the report said the Chinese government did take some steps in 1995 raising "the possibility of positive developments" on the human rights front "over the long term." It cited, for example, the passage of legislation by the National Peoples' Congress making limited reforms in the political and legal systems. The report also noted that China hosted the United Nations Fourth World Conference on Women and a related forum of nongovernment organizations—even though China imposed restrictions on free speech and domestic news coverage of those events and harassed some of the participants. (UN conference on women, Historic Documents of 1995, p. 581)

Difficulties in U.S.-China Relations

The toughly worded State Department report came in the midst of a particularly sensitive period of relations between Washington and Beijing. The two countries had been at odds over a host of political and economic issues, and some U.S. diplomats had worried about the impact on bilateral relations of such a forthright challenge to China's human rights record. Major bilateral issues on the table during 1996 included weapons proliferation, Taiwan, Chinese pirating, and opening Chinese markets.

In May, after months of negotiations, Washington and Beijing settled a dispute over U.S. charges that in 1995 China had sold Pakistan equipment that could be used to help develop nuclear weapons. China never admitted selling the equipment—steel magnets for use in centrifuges that process highly enriched uranium, an essential component of nuclear devices. Under U.S. pressure and the threat of economic sanctions, Beijing promised that it would not sell nuclear weapons-related equipment to Pakistan and other countries that were trying to develop nuclear arsenals.

Beijing tried unsuccessfully to influence the first free presidential election in Taiwan, which China regarded as a breakaway province that should be incorporated under the control of the mainland. In the weeks before Taiwan's March 23 election, China conducted missile tests and threatening military maneuvers in the Taiwan Strait. Beijing's leaders apparently hoped to influence voters to elect a candidate who would take a conciliatory approach. The Chinese intimidation failed, as Taiwan reelected its president, Lee Teng-hui, who had worked to raise the island's international profile without necessarily declaring total independence from the mainland. The confrontation between China and Taiwan made all of Asia nervous. The United States, which had official diplomatic relations with Beijing but only informal ties with Taipei, stationed two aircraft carriers near the Taiwan Strait to demonstrate Washington's concern about the situation.

The Clinton administration in May threatened trade sanctions in retaliation for China's failure to halt pirating of American computer programs, movies, and music. The sanctions would have included $3 billion in puni-

tive tariffs on Chinese exports of consumer electronics and clothing to the United States. In return, China threatened its own sanctions against American imports, such as Boeing airplanes. The two sides resolved the dispute, at least for the time being, in June with an agreement in which China promised to crack down on pirating. The issue was a perennial one, and it was unclear whether China's promise to curtail pirating would have any more lasting effect than previous unkept promises along the same lines.

On a similar recurring matter, the administration pressed China to open its markets to American products, in effect giving American businesses free access to what is potentially the biggest market in the world. China had some of the world's toughest restrictions on imports, including regulations requiring all foreign trade to pass through state-controlled trade companies. In return for reducing those restraints, the Clinton administration offered to drop its opposition to Chinese membership in the World Trade Organization, a step that would give China easier access to world markets.

China resisted the U.S. pressure despite a personal appeal from President Clinton in a November meeting with Chinese president Jiang Zemin during an international conference in Manila. Specialists noted that China had much to lose in opening its markets to foreign competition, which might overwhelm the country's outmoded and inefficient state-controlled industries.

The issue of Chinese market access had great political and economic consequences for the United States, which was running an increasingly large trade deficit with China. That deficit was expected to approach $40 billion in 1996, the largest U.S. trading deficit with any country.

Following is the introduction to the State Department report on human rights practices in China, issued March 6, 1996:

The People's Republic of China (PRC) is an authoritarian state in which the Chinese Communist Party (CCP) is the paramount source of power. At the national and regional levels, party members hold almost all top civilian, police, and military positions. Retired senior leaders retain considerable power, but the top leadership announced in mid-1995 that ultimate authority had been passed to the younger generation of Communist Party leaders that makes up the 21–member Politburo. Economic decentralization has increased the authority of regional officials. Socialism continues to provide the ideological underpinning of Chinese politics, but Marxist ideology has given way to pragmatism in recent years. The party's authority rests primarily on the success of economic reform, its ability to maintain stability, appeals to patriotism, and control of the security apparatus.

The security apparatus comprises the Ministries of State Security and Public Security, the People's Armed Police, the People's Liberation Army, and the state judicial, procuratorial, and penal systems. The security forces were responsible for numerous human rights abuses.

China has a mixed economy that is robust and expanding rapidly. Economic reforms continue to raise living standards, encourage private entrepreneurial activity, diminish central control over the economy, and create new economic opportunities. Income disparities between coastal regions and the interior are significant and growing, but there has been a sharp drop in the number of Chinese living in absolute poverty in recent years.

During the year the Government continued to commit widespread and well-documented human rights abuses, in violation of internationally accepted norms, stemming both from the authorities' intolerance of dissent and the inadequacy of legal safeguards for basic freedoms. Abuses included arbitrary and lengthy incommunicado detention, forced confessions, torture, and mistreatment of prisoners. Prison conditions remained harsh. The Government continued severe restrictions on freedom of speech, the press, assembly, association, religion, privacy, movement, and worker rights.

Although the Government denies that it holds political prisoners, the number of persons detained or serving sentences for "counterrevolutionary crimes" or for criminal convictions for peaceful political or religious activities are believed to number in the hundreds—perhaps thousands. The Government still has not provided a comprehensive, credible public accounting of all those missing or detained in connection with the suppression of the 1989 demonstrations. Persons detained during 1995 included activists arrested after the issuance of pro-democracy petitions in March and May. Throughout the year, Chinese leaders moved swiftly to cut off organized expressions of protest or criticism and detained government critics, including those advocating worker rights. Discrimination against women, minorities, and the disabled, and violence against women and the abuse of children remain problems.

Although the Government permits local, competitive elections in villages inhabited by millions of rural Chinese, citizens have no ability peacefully to change either their leaders at higher levels of government or the form of government. The Constitution provides for fundamental human rights, but they are frequently ignored in practice, and challenges to the CCP's political authority are often dealt with harshly and arbitrarily. Legal safeguards for those detained or imprisoned are ignored or inconsistently implemented. The Government attaches higher priority to maintaining public order and suppressing political opposition than to enforcing legal norms. For example, the judicial system denies criminal defendants basic legal safeguards such as due process or adequate defense, as demonstrated by the 20-month incommunicado detention, abrupt formal arrest, and sentencing to 14 years' imprisonment of leading dissident Wei Jingsheng for the peaceful expression of his political beliefs.

Overall, in 1995 the authorities stepped up repression of dissent. By year's end, almost all public dissent against the central authorities was silenced by intimidation, exile, or imposition of prison terms or administrative detention. The Government's November decision to name a Panchen Lama without the Dalai Lama's concurrence was symptomatic of the politicization of this question and a broader tightening of strictures on some religious believers. Nonofficial Christian churches and some Muslim groups also experienced intensified repression in 1995. In similar fashion, the Government strengthened controls over disaffected ethnic groups in Tibet, Inner Mongolia, and Xinjiang.

During 1995 the Government also took some steps that raised the possibility of positive developments in the human rights situation in China over the long term. In August and September the Government hosted the U.N. Fourth World Conference on Women and an associated Nongovernmental Organizations Forum (NGO Forum) both of which discussed women's and universal human rights. Government restrictions on the free exercise of internationally recognized freedoms of speech and association hampered the discussion, however. The Government also moved forward with legislation designed to make political and judicial processes more transparent. In February the National Peoples' Congress (NPC) passed three new laws designed to hold judges, prosecutors, and policemen to higher standards; the new laws came into effect July 1. In October the Ministry of Justice promulgated implementing regulations for 1994 legislation that allows citizens to sue government agencies for malfeasance and to collect damages. The Government has also drafted a lawyer's law that would clarify the nature of the attorney-client relationship, improve professional standards, separate most lawyers from state employment, and improve the ability of citizens to defend their legal interests; the legislature had not passed this law by year's end.

In many respects, Chinese society continued to open up: greater disposable income, looser ideological controls, and freer access to outside sources of information have led to greater room for individual choice, more diversity in cultural life, and increased media reporting. Although the sale and use of satellite dishes are tightly regulated, satellite television broadcasts are widely available, particularly in coastal areas. Telephone and facsimile communication is also extensively used. In many cities, the introduction of commercial Internet service promoted access to international sources of information. At year's end, however, new government limits on Internet access threatened to halt the growth of Internet use. In addition, new controls on reporting economic information introduced doubts about the Government's commitment to freedom of information.

Government control of news media generally continues to depend on self-censorship to regulate political and social content, but the authorities also consistently penalize those who exceed the permissible. China continued a human rights dialog with some foreign interlocutors in the first half of 1995. Although no formal dialogs were held in the second half of the year, the Government agreed in late 1995 to schedule some bilateral dialogs in early 1996. The Government is increasingly willing to acknowledge openly certain human rights problems, especially official abuse of citizens' rights; some of these abuses are documented in the press.

GAO ON NUCLEAR MATERIAL IN THE FORMER SOVIET UNION
March 8, 1996

Russia and other successor states to the Soviet Union do not have adequate control over tons of weapons-grade nuclear material, according to a report issued March 8 by the General Accounting Office (GAO), the investigative arm of Congress. Much of the nuclear material could be vulnerable to theft or misuse by terrorist groups, organized crime syndicates, or rogue nations seeking to build their own nuclear weapons, the GAO said. Such a prospect represented a "primary national security concern" for the United States, the report stated.

In the early 1990s Washington began providing funding to the former Soviet states for programs to improve controls over highly enriched uranium and plutonium, which can be used to develop nuclear weapons. The GAO said the U.S.-funded programs were slow to get off the ground, and it warned that upgrading control of nuclear materials in Russia and the other states would take years to accomplish.

The GAO report came during a critical election year in Russia. President Boris Yeltsin, frail in health, was facing a serious challenge from a reinvigorated Communist Party, headed by Gennady Zyuganov. Yeltsin defeated Zyuganov in the final June balloting, but his victory failed to erase concerns in the West about political and economic stability in Russia.

The Washington Times *on October 22 printed portions of a classified CIA report, "Prospects for Unsanctioned Use of Russian Nuclear Weapons," which said that Russian control over nuclear weapons and materials was weakening. The report, later verified by CIA officials, nevertheless said there was only a "low" current danger of an unauthorized launch of a Russian nuclear weapon or the use of such a weapon for blackmail.*

The CIA report said the greatest danger for diversion of Russian nuclear weapons appeared to involve tactical weapons—such as short-range battlefield missiles and torpedoes. Russian safeguards over those weapons could be overcome "probably within weeks or days depending on the weapon involved," according to the version of the CIA report quoted by the newspaper.

The Soviet Nuclear Stockpile

The GAO report focused on the enormous quantity of weapons-grade nuclear material that had been produced by the Soviet Union before its collapse: 1,200 metric tons of highly enriched uranium and 200 metric tons of plutonium. These materials can be used without additional processing to make a nuclear explosive device. The GAO cited International Atomic Energy Agency estimates that a nuclear explosive device can be made with twenty-five kilograms of highly enriched uranium or eight kilograms of plutonium.

Much of the weapons-grade material produced by the Soviet Union was never put into weapons and remained in storage at eighty to one hundred civilian or military locations. Other quantities of weapons-grade material were being removed from weapons under U.S.-Russian arms control treaties. Most of this material was located in Russia, but large quantities remained at laboratories, military bases, and weapons complexes in Ukraine, Kazakstan, Georgia, Latvia, Belarus, and Uzbekistan. Between November 1994 and January 1996 GAO investigators interviewed officials in the United States, Russia, and other former Soviet states and visited several former Soviet nuclear facilities. The GAO prepared its report at the request of senior members of the House Armed Services Committee and the Permanent Subcommittee on Investigations of the Senate Governmental Affairs Committee.

The fundamental problem the GAO found was that authorities in Russia and the other states did not know exactly how much nuclear material they had. The GAO reported that the Soviet Union did not conduct complete and comprehensive inventories of the nuclear material it produced, and the successor states have not done so either. Some of the facilities the GAO visited "did not have a comprehensive inventory of their nuclear materials on hand," the report said. Without reliable records about the amount of nuclear material on hand, the former Soviet states would have trouble determining if and when any of it had been lost or stolen, the GAO said.

Further, the GAO found controls over nuclear material weakening in the former Soviet states. The Soviets never implemented the sophisticated control and accounting procedures that are common in the United States and other Western countries, the GAO said. Instead, the Soviets relied on intense secrecy and the heavy hand of the police state to prevent misuse of nuclear supplies. Russia and other successor states were not nearly as authoritarian as the Soviet regime, and so their controls over nuclear supplies were less reliable.

The weakness of state control was exacerbated by low pay and poor working conditions among civilian and military workers in installations where former Soviet nuclear weapons and materials were stored, the GAO said. The report quoted an official at a major Russian facility as saying that the threat of "insider" diversion of nuclear materials was growing because workers were frustrated by not having been paid in months.

In addition, the GAO noted that weapons-grade fissile material was vulnerable to theft because it was not very radioactive and was relatively safe to handle. The report said much of this material in the former Soviet Union was stored in containers that could be transported by one or two people.

The GAO cited several cases in which authorities in Russia and other countries seized small quantities of nuclear materials from unauthorized people. The most serious incident involved approximately six pounds of weapons-grade uranium seized by police in Prague in December 1994.

The GAO quoted U.S. officials as saying that there was no direct evidence that the seized material was destined for use in nuclear weapons. Even so, the agency said, these incidents were "troubling" because they showed that some people "are willing to take high risks" to deal in smuggled nuclear material, and the seized material was detected by chance rather than through systematic controls within the former Soviet Union.

Responses to the Problem

Under the leadership of Sens. Sam Nunn, D-Ga., and Richard Lugar, R-Ind., Congress in the early 1990s began providing money for various programs to help Russia and other former Soviet states dismantle their nuclear weapons and improve controls over stockpiles of nuclear materials. For example, the United States was providing computers and technical advice to help each of the countries determine how much nuclear material they owned.

The GAO report said those programs showed promise, but it expressed concern at delays in getting them under way. In several cases, Russian officials had been slow in giving U.S. agencies the access to facilities that was necessary to determine what needed to be done. In other cases, bureaucratic battling among Russian agencies delayed action.

The GAO also noted that congressional restrictions hampered some parts of the Nunn-Lugar program. For example, the Defense and Energy Departments were required to use U.S. materials and contractors to the maximum extent feasible—even when foreign suppliers might have been able to perform a job more quickly or for less money.

Other efforts to reduce the potential dangers of nuclear material were sidetracked by domestic political considerations in the former Soviet states. For example, Russian president Yeltsin agreed in 1994 to close three reactors in Siberia that produced weapons-grade plutonium. Yeltsin later reversed himself because alternative sources could not be found to provide heat and electricity to neighboring cities. Leaders in Russia and other former Soviet republics also have been reluctant to shut down nuclear reactors for safety reasons, even including those similar in design to the Chernobyl reactor, which was involved in the world's worst nuclear accident. (Chernobyl nuclear accident, Historic Documents of 1986, p. 383)

Following is the executive summary of the report, "Nuclear Non-proliferation: Status of U.S. Efforts to Improve Nuclear Material Controls in Newly Independent States," issued March 8, 1996, by the General Accounting Office:

Purpose

Safeguarding nuclear material that can be used directly in nuclear explosives has become a primary national security concern for the United States and the newly independent states of the former Soviet Union. Terrorists and countries seeking nuclear weapons could use as little as 25 kilograms of highly enriched uranium (HEU) or 8 kilograms of plutonium to build a nuclear explosive. The seizure of HEU and plutonium in Europe and Russia has prompted concerns about how the newly independent states control their direct-use materials. The Ranking Minority Member of the Permanent Subcommittee on Investigations, Senate Governmental Affairs Committee, and the Chairman and Ranking Minority Member of the House Committee on National Security requested that GAO review U.S. efforts to help the newly independent states strengthen their nuclear material controls.

GAO's report addresses (1) the nature and extent of problems with controlling direct-use nuclear materials in the newly independent states; (2) the status and future prospects of U.S. efforts to help strengthen controls in Russia, Ukraine, Kazakstan, and Belarus; and (3) the executive branch's consolidation of U.S. efforts in the Department of Energy (DOE). The scope of GAO's review included direct-use nuclear material controlled by civilian authorities in the newly independent states and direct-use material used for naval nuclear propulsion purposes. GAO did not review the protection, control, and accounting systems used for nuclear weapons in the possession of the Ministry of Defense in Russia. U.S. officials believe there to be relatively better controls over weapons in the custody of the Ministry of Defense than over material outside of weapons. GAO recently issued a report that addressed the safety of nuclear facilities in the newly independent states.

Background

"Direct-use nuclear material" consists of HEU and plutonium that is relatively easy to handle because it has not been exposed to radiation or has been separated from highly radioactive materials. Direct-use material presents a high proliferation risk because it can be used to manufacture a nuclear weapon without further enrichment or irradiation in a reactor. Many types of nuclear facilities routinely handle, process, or store such direct-use materials. Direct-use material can be found at research reactors, reactor fuel fabrication facilities, uranium enrichment plants, spent fuel reprocessing facilities, and nuclear material storage sites, as well as nuclear weapons production facilities. Material protection, control, and accounting (MPC&A) systems are used at such facilities to deter, detect, and respond to attempted thefts.

The United States is pursuing two different, but complementary strategies to achieve its goals of rapidly improving nuclear material controls over direct-use material in the newly independent states: a government-to-government program, and an initiative known as the lab-to-lab program. Under the government-to-government program, initially sponsored and funded by the Department of Defense Cooperative Threat Reduction (CTR) program, the United States agreed in 1993 to work directly with the governments of Russia, Ukraine, and Kazakstan to develop national MPC&A systems and improve controls over civilian nuclear material. The United States extended such assistance to Belarus in 1995. Although CTR funds were used, DOE was responsible for implementing the program. In April 1994, DOE initiated the lab-to-lab program to work directly with Russian nuclear facilities in improving their MPC&A systems. The program is limited to Russia and intended to rapidly improve controls at civilian research, naval nuclear propulsion, and civilian-controlled, nuclear weapons-related facilities. This program is funded jointly by DOE and the CTR program.

Results in Brief

The Soviet Union produced approximately 1,200 metric tons of HEU and 200 metric tons of plutonium. Much of this material is outside of nuclear weapons, is highly attractive to theft, and the newly independent states may not have accurate and complete inventories of the material they inherited. Social and economic changes in the newly independent states have increased the threat of theft and diversion of nuclear material, and with the breakdown of Soviet-era MPC&A systems, the newly independent states may not be as able to counter the increased threat. Nuclear facilities rely on antiquated accounting systems that cannot quickly detect and localize nuclear material losses. Many facilities lack modern equipment that can detect unauthorized attempts to remove nuclear material from facilities. While as yet there is no direct evidence that a black market for stolen or diverted nuclear material exists in the newly independent states, the seizures of direct-use material in Russia and Europe have increased concerns about theft and diversion.

U.S. efforts to help the newly independent states improve their MPC&A systems for direct-use material had a slow start, but are now gaining momentum. DOD's government-to-government CTR program obligated $59 million and spent about $4 million from fiscal years 1991 to 1995 for MPC&A improvements in Russia, Ukraine, Kazakstan, and Belarus. The program has provided working group meetings, site surveys, physical protection equipment, computers, and training for projects in Russia, Ukraine, Kazakstan, and Belarus. Initially, the program was slow because (1) until January 1995, the Russian Ministry of Atomic Energy (MINATOM) had refused access to Russian direct-use facilities and (2) CTR-sponsored projects at facilities with direct-use materials in Ukraine, Kazakstan, and Belarus were just getting underway. According to DOD officials, program requirements for using U.S. goods and services and for audits and examinations also delayed implementation. The program began to gain momentum in January 1995 when CTR program and MINATOM officials agreed to upgrade nuclear material controls at five high-priority facilities handling direct-use material. DOE and Russia's nuclear regulatory agency have also agreed to cooperate on the development of a national MPC&A regulatory infrastructure.

DOE's lab-to-lab program obligated $17 million and spent $14 million in fiscal years 1994 and 1995. This program has improved controls at two "zero-power" research reactors, and begun providing nuclear material monitors to several MINATOM defense facilities to help them detect unauthorized attempts to remove direct-use material. In fiscal year 1996, the program is implementing additional projects in MINATOM's nuclear defense complex.

In fiscal year 1996, the United States expanded the MPC&A assistance program to include all known facilities with direct-use material outside of weapons in the newly independent states. Management and funding for the expanded program were consolidated within DOE. DOE plans to request from Congress $400 million over 7 years for the program. However, the expanded program faces several inherent uncertainties involving its overall costs and U.S. ability to verify that assistance is being used as intended. DOE is responding to these uncertainties by developing a long-term plan and a centralized cost reporting system and by implementing a flexible audit and examination program.

Principal Findings

Nature and Extent of the Problem

Much of the 1,200 metric tons of highly enriched uranium and 200 metric tons of plutonium produced by the Soviet Union is outside of nuclear weapons; this stockpile of material is expected to grow rapidly as Russia proceeds to dismantle its nuclear weapons. According to DOE, this material is located at 80 to 100 civilian research, naval nuclear propulsion, and civilian controlled nuclear weapons-related facilities. It is considered to be highly attractive to theft because it is (1) not very radioactive and is therefore relatively safe to handle and (2) in forms that make it readily accessible to theft, such as items stored in containers that can easily be carried by one or two persons, or in components from dismantled weapons.

Nuclear materials in the newly independent states are more vulnerable to theft and diversion than in the past. Soviet-era control systems relied heavily on (1) keeping nuclear material in secret cities and facilities, (2) closely monitoring nuclear industry personnel, and (3) severely punishing control violations. Closed borders and the absence of a black market for nuclear material also lessened the threat of diversion. Without the secrecy and heavy security of the Soviet system, facilities in the newly independent states must now rely to a greater degree on other control systems such as manual, paper-based tracking systems—which cannot quickly locate and assess material losses—and on labor-intensive physical protection systems that lack monitors for detecting attempts to steal nuclear material from a facility. In addition, the newly independent states may not have complete and accurate inventories of their nuclear materials because the Soviet Union did not conduct complete and comprehensive physical inventories at their nuclear facilities. Some of the facilities GAO visited in March 1995 did not have a comprehensive inventory of their nuclear materials on hand.

Initial Efforts to Improve Control Systems in the Newly Independent States Had a Slow Start

Until January 1995, MINATOM refused to grant CTR technical experts access to direct-use facilities, limiting the program's efforts to a low-enriched uranium fuel fabrication line. This obstacle was removed in January 1995 when MINATOM agreed to allow access to five facilities with direct-use material. In July 1995, the CTR-sponsored program made progress in controlling direct-use material by installing physical protection equipment and providing training at a MINATOM facility that includes an HEU fuel fabrication line. The Kazakstani, Ukrainian, and Belarussian governments have been more willing to allow the United States to help upgrade MPC&A systems at their direct-use material facilities. However, CTR-sponsored projects in these countries are just beginning, and improvements to controls over their direct-use materials will not be completed until the middle of 1996 at the earliest.

Working directly with institutes and operating facilities, DOE's lab-to-lab program has completed the first phase of an MPC&A project at a MINATOM zero-power research reactor that will eventually computerize its inventory system for thousands of kilograms of direct-use material and upgrade its MPC&A systems. DOE's program has also upgraded controls at a zero-power research reactor in Moscow containing about 80 kilograms of direct-use material by (1) increasing physical protection for the reactor building, (2) implementing a computerized material accounting system, and (3) installing access control equipment. The lab-to-lab program has also deployed nuclear material monitors at three MINATOM nuclear weapons facilities and two civilian research facilities. Additional monitors were being shipped as GAO concluded its review.

United States Expands MPC&A Assistance

The executive branch has decided to consolidate MPC&A assistance in DOE. In September 1995, the President directed DOE to develop a long-range plan to improve MPC&A systems at all facilities in the newly independent states handling direct-use material by the year 2002. The President also transferred funding and management responsibilities for the CTR MPC&A program from DOD to DOE in fiscal year 1996. However, DOE faces several inherent uncertainties in managing an expanded assistance program over the next 7 years. For example, while DOE estimates that the program will require $400 million to upgrade 80 facilities with direct-use material, it faces uncertainties in both the number of facilities to be covered (which could range to more than 100) and the cost per facility (ranging from $5 million to $10 million per facility). Because of these uncertainties, program costs could range from $400 million to over $1 billion. In addition, DOE's ability to directly assess program progress and confirm that U.S. assistance is used for its intended purposes may be limited because the Russians may limit the measures that can be used for these purposes at highly sensitive facilities.

DOE Is Responding to Program Uncertainties

DOE is taking steps to ensure that the program is successful and that U.S. funds are well spent.

- DOE is developing a long-term plan for the expanded program that consolidates the program plans for the government-to-government and lab-to-lab programs. According to DOE, the plan establishes objectives, priorities, and timetables for implementing projects at the 80 to 100 facilities in the newly independent states. DOE has drafted the plan; however, the plan had not been issued at the time GAO concluded its review in January 1996.
- DOE is developing a consolidated centralized program cost-reporting system intended to provide DOE with current financial status for government-to-government and lab-to-lab projects. The information should be useful in responding to changing budgetary requirements for the program.
- DOE is implementing a flexible audit and program evaluation approach to provide some assurances that assistance is used only for its intended purposes. Under the approach, the United States will pay Russian laboratories for services and equipment upon completion of clearly defined delivered products and will use a series of direct and indirect measures to evaluate program progress and effectiveness. DOE expects to issue a report on assurances obtained by the lab-to-lab program in March 1996.

Recommendations

GAO is making no recommendations in this report.

Agency Comments

In commenting on this report, the Departments of Energy and State generally agreed with GAO's assessment of the U.S. effort to improve nuclear material controls in the newly independent states. The Department of State offered additional editorial comments that have been incorporated into the report where appropriate. DOD officials also agreed with the facts as presented in this report, but expressed concern about how the report portrays the relative success of the government-to-government and lab-to-lab programs. These officials stated that the programs are complementary approaches to achieving the goal of improving controls and accountability over direct-use nuclear material in the newly independent states. GAO agrees and has modified the report accordingly.

GAO ON DEFICIT REDUCTION
March 13, 1996

In contrast to the nasty battles that led to partial government shutdowns in 1995, the pressures of an election year somewhat reduced partisan squabbling over federal budget issues in 1996. But with a Democratic president facing off against a Republican-controlled Congress, it was certain that Washington once again would be gripped by conflicts over budget cutting.

The battling of 1995 produced a general consensus in Washington that the budget should be balanced by 2002. There was little agreement, however, on how that goal should be met. That was especially true in the case of entitlement programs, including Medicare and Medicaid. President Bill Clinton denounced Republicans for suggesting deep cuts in those programs, while he offered his own proposals for more limited cutbacks.

Another issue that was certain to arise again was the proposal for a constitutional amendment requiring a balanced budget. Such a proposal died in the Senate in 1995, falling one vote short of the two-thirds vote needed for approval of constitutional amendments. Voters in 1996 gave the Republicans two more Senate seats, increasing the likelihood that the constitutional amendment would prevail if brought to the floor in 1997. (1995 budget issues, Historic Documents of 1995, p. 737)

Long-Term Deficit Reduction

Even as Congress was sidestepping most long-term spending issues in 1996, it received a reminder that those issues could not be ignored for long. Testifying on March 13 before the House Budget Committee, a senior official of the General Accounting Office (GAO) presented long-term projections showing the impact of the federal budget deficit on the U.S. economy.

Paul L. Posner, the GAO's director of budget issues, noted that Congress and the president essentially agreed on the need to balance the budget. The key remaining questions involved when and how the budget deficit would be narrowed. The answers to those questions would affect the national economy for decades to come, he said.

Posner gave the Budget Committee computer simulations showing the effect by year 2025 of three scenarios: continuing the fiscal policies in effect as of late 1994, before there was consensus on eliminating the deficit; "muddling through," which was defined as assuming that annual federal budget deficits would average 3 percent of gross domestic product; and bringing the budget into balance by 2002 and keeping it there.

Under the first, or "no action," scenario, by 2025 the overall economy would grow only marginally and the federal debt (as opposed to the annual deficit) would stand at $60,200 per capita—more than four times its $13,500 per capita level as of 1994. The result, Posner said, would be "collapsing investment, declining capital stock, and, inevitably, a declining economy by 2025." Such a scenario was unlikely, he said, because the prospect of an economic decline would force the government to take action on the deficit.

Under the "muddling through" scenario, the economy would grow much faster, but the federal debt still would rise to $21,400 per capita. If the budget was brought into balance by 2002 and kept there, under the third scenario, the economy would grow faster still and the federal debt would decline sharply to about $4,800 per capita.

Posner told the committee that how the deficit was reduced was almost as important as whether and when it was reduced. Decision makers needed to remember the economic importance of federal investment in public infrastructure, education, and research and development. He added that curtailing the fastest growing parts of the budget—particularly health care programs—would have more impact on cutting the deficit than would cuts in slower growing programs. Beyond those generalities, the GAO report made no specific recommendations.

Fiscal 1996 Budget Fiasco

The fiscal 1996 budget had caused the most contentious and drawn out spending battle between Congress and a president in years. Congressional Republicans, especially House members led by Speaker Newt Gingrich, sought during 1995 to use the budget as a battering ram against the president. The standoff led to passage of a record-setting fourteen stopgap funding bills and two lengthy shutdowns of much of the federal government late in 1995. The Republican strategy backfired, as the public blamed Gingrich and his cohorts—rather than the president—for the costly government closures.

The Republicans dropped their confrontational approach early in 1996 and by April reached agreement with Clinton on an omnibus $163 billion measure incorporating five separate appropriations bills that had been held hostage for nearly seven months. Clinton said the battle showed that the public did not want "gridlock, stalemate, vetoes, government shutdown."

A Smoother Fiscal 1997 Budget Process

Stepping gingerly to stay out of the budget brier patch they got them-selves into in 1995, congressional Republicans during 1996 chose cooper-ation and negotiation over confrontation when it came to working on spending bills for the 1997 fiscal year, which began October 1.

Congress passed seven of the thirteen required fiscal 1997 appropria-tions bills with little trouble but saved six others for late session negotia-tion just before adjournment. The main issue was Clinton's demand that Congress boost spending on domestic programs, such as education and the environment, by $6.5 billion. Clinton eventually got nearly everything he wanted, and Congress finished all work on its appropriations bills before the midnight September 30 deadline—only the fourth time that had hap-pened in modern budget history.

Line-Item Veto

Congress in May took a major step toward shifting the balance of power on spending issues, passing a bill giving the president an effective line-item veto on appropriations bills. The new law (PL 104–130) was to take effect on January 1, 1997.

Republicans had begun a push, during the Reagan administration, for a line-item veto that would allow the president to block individual spend-ing items. The theory was that presidents—Republican presidents, GOP lawmakers hoped—would use this power to cut out "pork barrel" projects that lawmakers could not resist. The proposal languished until Republi-cans took control of Congress at the beginning of 1995. Even then, it encountered stiff opposition from some congressional leaders, including Republicans, who feared handing over so much power to a president, what-ever the political affiliation.

The two chambers passed conflicting versions of a line-item veto bill in 1995 but were unable to agree on a unified approach until early in the 1996 session, when the imperative was to demonstrate legislative accom-plishments for the Republican-led Congress. The version finally sent to the president on March 28 established a complex procedure called "enhanced rescissions." In essence, it allowed a president to propose cuts in appro-priations bills after they had become law. The president's cuts would take effect unless both chambers of Congress passed bills to overturn them; those bills would then have to survive a likely presidential veto.

Congress crafted this cumbersome formula in hopes of making the line-item veto withstand legal scrutiny on constitutional grounds. Several legal challenges were filed against the new law, however, and scholars were divided on whether the Supreme Court would uphold its constitu-tionality.

Following are excerpts from the report, "Budget Issues: Deficit Reduction and the Long Term," issued March 13, 1996, by the

*General Accounting Office. The report was presented during tes-
timony before the House Budget Committee by Paul L. Posner,
director of budget issues of the GAO's Accounting and Information Management Division:*

In 1992, we examined the role of fiscal policy in promoting or inhibiting
long-term economic growth and concluded that deficit reduction was key to
our nation's future economic health. We noted then that long-term economic growth and the requisite investment are central to almost all our major
concerns as a society. The surest way to increase the resources available for
investment is to increase national savings, and the surest way to increase
national savings is to reduce the federal deficit. We also noted that how the
deficit is reduced matters. Last year, we updated this work for you and [Sen-
ate Budget Committee] Chairman [Pete V.] Domenici [R-N.M.].

By now, the relationship of the deficit to the nation's long-term interest has
been more broadly recognized. Both the Congress and the President have
proposed plans to reverse previous fiscal trends and balance the budget. It
seems reasonable to conclude that the debate is no longer over whether to
balance the budget, but rather over when and how.

In my testimony today, I will first describe GAO simulations of the economic impact of different fiscal policies over the long term and then address
several issues related to the impact of deficit reduction specifically:

- the important and compelling benefits to be gained from successfully
  shifting to a new fiscal policy;
- the importance of how we reduce the deficit—by which I mean both the
  composition of federal spending and the need to deal with the drivers of
  the deficit; and
- the experience of other industrial nations.

Long-Term Simulations

Long-term simulations can be useful for comparing potential outcomes
of alternative policies within a common economic framework. Given the
broad range of uncertainty about future economic changes, however, any
simulations should not be interpreted as forecasts of the level of economic
activity 30 years in the future. Instead, simulation results provide illustra-
tions of the budget or economic outcomes associated with alternative policy paths.

In our most recent work, we used a long-term economic growth model to
simulate three of the many possible fiscal paths through the year 2025:

- a "no action" path that assumed the continuation of fiscal policies in
  effect at the end of fiscal year 1994;
- a "muddling through" path that assumed annual deficits of approximately 3 percent of gross domestic product (GDP); and
- a path that reaches balance in 2002 and sustains it.

To suggest some of the trade-offs facing policymakers in choosing among fiscal policies, we examined some long-term economic and fiscal outcomes of these paths. We also simulated how some types of early action on the deficit, including early action on health care spending, might affect the long-term deficit outlook. Finally, we examined the prospects for sustaining balance over the long term.

While we discuss the consequences of alternative fiscal paths, we do not suggest any particular course of action, since only the Congress can resolve the fundamental policy question of choosing the fiscal policy path and the composition of federal activity.

In our simulations we employed a model originally developed by economists at the Federal Reserve Bank of New York (FRBNY) that relates long-term GDP growth to economic and budget factors. Details of that model and its assumptions can be found in our reports.

The Compelling Case for Deficit Reduction

As we noted in 1992 and 1995, important and compelling benefits can be gained from shifting to a new fiscal policy path. . . . [C]hronic deficits have consumed an increasing share of a declining national savings pool, leaving that much less for private investment.

Lower investment will ultimately show up in lower economic growth. Future generations of taxpayers will pay a steep price for this lower economic growth in terms of lower personal incomes and a generally lower standard of living at a time when they will face the burden of supporting an unprecedented number of retirees as the baby boom generation reaches retirement.

The problem has been that the damage done by deficits is long-term, gradual, and cumulative in nature and may not be as visible as the short-term costs involved in reducing deficits. This has presented, and continues to present, a difficult challenge for public leaders who must mount a compelling case for deficit reduction—and for the steps required to achieve it—that can capture public support. The updated simulations we presented to you and Chairman Domenici last spring confirmed that the nation's current fiscal policy path is unsustainable over the longer term. Specifically, a fiscal policy of "no action" on the deficit through 2025 implies federal spending of nearly 44 percent of GDP, and . . . a deficit over 23 percent of GDP.

Let me explain these ominous trends. The increased spending is principally a function of escalating federal spending on health care and Social Security, which is driven by projected rising health care costs and the aging of our population. Spending on interest on our national debt also rises as annual deficits and accumulated public debt expand. Essentially, current commitments in these areas become progressively unaffordable for the nation over time. Without any significant changes in spending or revenues, such an expanding deficit would result in collapsing investment, declining capital stock, and, inevitably, a declining economy by 2025.

As emphasized in both our 1992 and 1995 reports, we do not believe that such a scenario would take place. Rather, we believe that the prospect of economic decline would prompt action before the end of our simulation period. Nevertheless, this "no action" scenario, by illustrating the future logic of existing commitments, powerfully makes the case that we have no choice but to take action on the deficit. The questions that remain are when and how.

Our 1995 simulations also confirm the long-term economic and fiscal benefits of deficit reduction. We assessed the long-term impacts of balancing the budget by 2002, as was contemplated in the fiscal year 1996 budget resolution and in the recent executive-congressional discussions over budget policy, and of sustaining such a posture through 2025. We also estimated the effects of following a path that we called "muddling through"—that is, running deficit of about 3 percent of GDP over the next 30 years. Although current policy is better than this in the near term, it is still a useful illustration.

A fiscal policy of balance would yield a stronger economy in the long term than either a policy of no action or of muddling through. [Government data show] that a budget balance reached in 2002 and sustained until 2025 would, over time, lead to increased investment, increased capital stock, a larger economy, and a much lower national debt than either of the other scenarios. This means that Americans could enjoy a higher standard of living than they might otherwise experience.

Reaching and sustaining balance would also shrink the share of federal spending required to pay interest costs, thereby reducing the long-term programmatic sacrifice necessary to attain deficit reduction targets. Even "muddling through" with deficits of 3 percent of GDP would exact a price through higher interest costs and thus require progressively harder fiscal choices as time progresses. Under the balance path, debt per capita would decline from $13,500 in 1994 to $4,800 in 1995 dollars by 2025; debt as a percentage of the economy would drop from about 52 percent to 13 percent. Because of this shrinkage in the debt, by 2025 a balance path could bring interest costs down from about 12 percent in 1994 to less than 5 percent of our budget, compared to about 18 percent under "muddling through" and almost a third of our budget with no action. . . .

Alarming as these model results may appear, they are probably understated. Our model incorporates conservative assumptions about the relationship between savings, investment and GDP growth that tend to understate the differences between the economic outcomes associated with alternative fiscal [policies]. Furthermore, budget projections for the near term and those assumed in our long-term model results may not tell the whole story. By convention, baseline budget projections do not include all the legitimate claims that may be made on the budget in the future. Rather, budget projections ignore many future claims and the costs of unmet needs unless they are the subject of policy proposals in the budget. Examples of such claims and needs would include the cost of cleaning up and restructuring the Department of Energy's (DOE) nuclear weapons production complex, the cost of hazardous waste pollution clean-up at military facilities, and cost overruns in weapons systems. In short, most of the risks to future budgets seem to be on the side of worse-than-expected, rather than better-than-expected outcomes. I make this observation not to create despair but to underline the need to continue efforts at deficit reduction.

The Type of Spending Reduction Matters

Not all spending cuts have the same impact over the long run. Decisions about how to reduce the deficit will reflect—among other considerations—judgments about the role of the federal government and the effectiveness of individual programs. I would like to call attention today to two significant considerations in deficit reduction: (1) the importance of federal invest-ment in infrastructure, human capital, and research and development (R&D), and (2) the importance of addressing the fast-growing programs in the budget.

Composition of Federal Spending: Investment

In our 1992 work, we drew particular attention to the importance of well-chosen federal investment in infrastructure, human capital, and R&D. A high-er level of national savings is essential to the achievement of a higher rate of economic growth but, by itself, is not sufficient to assure that result. Certain other ingredients are necessary—including the basic stability with which this nation has been blessed in its social, political, and economic environment. In addition, however, economic growth depends on an efficient public infra-structure, an educated work force, an expanding base of knowledge, and a continuing infusion of innovations.

In the past, the federal government, through its investments in these areas, has played an important role in providing an environment conducive to growth. Thus the composition of federal spending, as well as overall fiscal policy, can affect long-term economic growth in significant ways.

Dealing with the Deficit Drivers

The extent to which deficit reduction affects spending on fast-growing programs also matters. Although a dollar is a dollar in the first year it is cut—regardless of what programmatic changes it represents—cutbacks in the base of fast-growing programs generate greater savings in the future than those in slower-growing programs, assuming the specific cuts are not offset by increases in the growth rates of the programs.

[An illustration of this compares] the long-run effects of a $50 billion cut in health spending with those of the same dollar amount cut from unspeci-fied other programs. For both paths the cut occurs in 1996 and is assumed to be permanent but, after 1996, spending is assumed to continue at the same rates of growth as those shown in the "no action" simulation. We used the simple assumption that a reduction in either health or other programs would not alter the expected growth rates simply to illustrate the point that a cut in high-growth areas of spending will have a greater fiscal effect in the future than the same size cut in low-growth areas. A $50 billion cut in health spending in 1996 leads to a deficit in 2025 that is about 4 percent of GDP lower than would be the case from a $50 billion cut in a low-growth program.

Further, our simulations show that even if a balanced budget is achieved early in the next century, deficits would reappear if we fail to contain future growth in health, interest, and social security costs.

The Experience of Other Industrial Democracies

We conclude from these simulations that how and when deficit reduction occurs can have important long-term implications for the future economy and future budgets. As noted earlier, the benefits of deficit reduction in the long run may not seem as compelling as the short-term costs necessary to reduce the deficit. Nevertheless our work on the deficit reduction experiences in other nations shows that significant fiscal improvement is indeed possible in modern democracies, at least for a time.

To reach fiscal balance or surplus, the governments we studied instituted often painful measures while generating and maintaining political support. Spending control proved the dominant policy tool used to achieve fiscal goals, although few programs were actually eliminated. Notably, however, several countries restrained social benefit commitments in their quest for savings. Government leaders sought to gain support or at least defuse potential opposition by bringing key interest groups that would be affected into the decision-making process.

In addition, the design of the specific deficit-reducing strategies helped. Approaches such as reducing benefits instead of eliminating programs, targeting benefit cuts to higher-income beneficiaries, and deferring or shifting painful adjustments all helped maintain political support for spending reductions.

The deficit reduction brought about in these governments provided significant fiscal benefits by slowing or reversing the growth of public debt, thereby slowing or reversing the growth of government interest costs. As we simulated in our long-term growth model, what was once a "vicious" circle of rising deficits, debt, and interest, which can in turn increase deficits, became a "virtuous" circle of falling deficits or rising surpluses, accrued even though most governments we studied did not sustain fiscal balance or surplus, possibly in part because public support for austerity was frequently linked to relatively short-run concerns. Despite this return to deficit, the increases in savings and investment resulting from deficit reduction may have boosted economic prospects for the long-term future, as well as provided fiscal benefits in the short run.

Conclusion

Although the experiences of the nations in GAO's study suggest that resolving deficits is possible in advanced democracies, they also indicate that sustaining fiscal discipline over the longer term is difficult. Thus, deficit reduction strategies designed to promote long-term fiscal progress may help ensure that future budgets are better positioned to withstand future economic and political pressures.

For the United States, reaching budgetary balance in 2002 would indeed represent an achievement that by itself would bring about fiscal and economic benefits. Yet this achievement will not eliminate the need for future fiscal discipline. In fact, the needs of an aging society will be more easily met if fiscal balance—or even surplus—is both achieved and sustained for several years.

In conclusion, Mr. Chairman, I would repeat our view that current policy is unsustainable. The question, therefore, is not whether to reduce the deficit but when and how. We believe those choices matter. . . .

REPORT ON THE FEDERAL AIDS RESEARCH PROGRAM
March 14, 1996

Researchers were heartened in 1996 by significant breakthroughs in understanding and treating AIDS, the acquired immune deficiency syndrome that has no known cure, and HIV, the human immunodeficiency virus that causes the disease. Mounting evidence that a combination of drugs could reduce HIV infection to undetectable levels gave hope to those people who had already been diagnosed with the virus, while the discovery that the presence of two copies of a mutant gene can apparently immunize humans against the virus gave hope that a vaccine for the disease might someday be a reality.

A hard-hitting report from a panel of independent doctors, scientists, and representatives from pharmaceutical companies tempered some of that enthusiasm by concluding that the federal AIDS research effort was unfocused and uncoordinated, and that too much funding was devoted to "research that is only peripherally related to AIDS." The report, released March 14, advocated a shift in funding, allotting more money to investigator-initiated research, vaccine development, and human immune system research and less to drug development.

Also sobering was a United Nations report released in June that detailed the continuing and rapid spread of AIDS and HIV, particularly in parts of Asia and Southern Africa. In contrast, the numbers for the United States appear to have stabilized, at levels lower than were predicted ten years earlier.

Report on AIDS Research

AIDS research conducted and supported by the National Institutes of Health (NIH) received repeated praise from the NIH AIDS Research Evaluation Working Group, which was appointed in February 1995 by the Office of AIDS Research (OAR) to undertake the first review of the nation's AIDS research program since 1981 when research on the epidemic first began. Several drugs and a blood test that has kept the nation's blood sup-

ply virtually free of HIV were among the developments supported by NIH. But the panel minced few words in its recommendations for a clearer focus, better coordination, and more effective use of money. NIH spent about $1.4 billion in fiscal 1996 on AIDS-related research.

The working group, headed by Arnold J. Levine of Princeton University, recommended that NIH double the amount of money it now devotes to unsolicited research instigated by outside investigators. "There is no better way to enhance the diversity and productivity of research approaches," the panel said. The panel also called for improvements in the peer review process used to determine which research proposals to fund. The panel said there were "numerous instances" where "the most promising research projects" were not identified, primarily because the review group lacked the "breadth, depth, or expertise" to make the best decisions.

On other issues, the panel urged that NIH put more effort into developing a safe and effective vaccine against HIV. To that end it recommended that a committee headed by a nongovernment scientist be formed to oversee a vaccine development effort that spanned all of NIH. The panel also called on President Bill Clinton to create a National AIDS Vaccine Task Force to coordinate AIDS vaccine research throughout the government.

The panel said NIH should elevate the priority it gives to research on the human immune system, in part to help understand why attempts to find a vaccine against HIV have so far been unsuccessful. The report also noted that NIH should decrease the attention it gives to drug discovery efforts, in part because some of those efforts duplicate what the pharmaceutical industry is already doing and in part because vaccines and other preventive medicines and interventions are likely to have a greater long-term effect than drug therapies on reducing the global epidemic.

William Paul, director of the OAR, which was established by Congress with authority to plan, coordinate, evaluate, and distribute all AIDS research funds at NIH, told the New York Times he was pleased with the report. "The report has the potential, if implemented appropriately, to make a real difference in AIDS research," Paul said.

Heightened Hope from New Discoveries

Two important developments in AIDS research were highlighted at the eleventh international conference on AIDS, held in Vancouver in July. The first involved a new test, called "viral load," that measures the amount of HIV RNA, the infection's genetic information, circulating in a milliliter of blood. Viral load can thus help assess the intensity of the infection in a person; the greater the viral load, the more the infection is assaulting the patient's immune system.

The second breakthrough involved studies showing that certain combinations of drug therapies are capable of reducing the viral load to undetectable levels in AIDS patients. The combinations included two older drugs, AZT and 3TC, together with a newer drug. In two studies, the third *drug was a protease inhibitor (indinavir or ritonavir); in another the third drug was nevirapine.*

While the discoveries signify a potentially major advancement in treatment, scientists stressed that the drug combinations were not a cure for the disease. It was also unclear how long the three-drug combination would suppress the virus and whether the virus might eventually grow resistant to the combination. Furthermore, the drug treatment itself was not only expensive, but grueling, involving precisely timed medication regimens throughout the day and side effects that some patients cannot tolerate.

A breakthrough with even more promise was announced in September, this one involving a genetic mutation that appears to slow the progress of HIV infection or, in some people, prevent it altogether. Researchers, led by scientists at the National Cancer Institute, said their findings might lead to vaccines or medicines that mimic the effect of the mutated gene.

Humans carry two CKR5 genes that contain instructions for making a protein on the white blood cells; the protein acts as a receptor for the HIV infection. According to the study, about one in seven whites and about one in fifty-nine blacks in the United States inherit one CKR5 gene that is defective; the defect interferes with production of the protein receptor and thus prevents the HIV from invading the cell. Because these people still have one normal CKR5 gene, they can still be infected with HIV, but the disease appears to progress more slowly, taking longer to develop into AIDS.

About 1 percent of whites in the United States inherit two defective CKR5 genes, making them virtually immune to HIV infection. Noting that "people can live perfectly well without CKR5," David Baltimore, a molecular biologist at the Massachusetts Institute of Technology, said that "if you can develop a drug that blocks CKR5, it could block HIV without serious side effects."

Continuing Spread of the Disease

According to a report released in early July by the Centers for Disease Control (CDC) and the National Cancer Institute, the number of Americans infected with HIV has appeared to stabilize at 650,000 to 900,000, with 100,000 of those diagnosed with the life-threatening illnesses associated with AIDS. An estimated 450,000 people were infected with HIV in 1984 and between 550,000 and 650,000 in 1986. Although the 650,000 to 900,000 estimate was for the end of 1992, John M. Karon, a CDC statistician, said other studies "suggest very strongly that the estimates" are accurate for 1996 as well.

One reason that the number has stabilized is because the number of new infections each year is roughly equal to the number of deaths from AIDS. Although the number of women with HIV infection was growing faster than the number of men, the number of HIV-infected men was still much larger; about 1 of every 160 men had the virus in 1992, compared with 1 out of every 1,000 women. Gay and bisexual men accounted for about half the infections; drug users who inject their drugs accounted for one-quarter of the infections. Blacks suffered an infection rate six times that of whites and twice that of Hispanics.

"The fact that the total number of living HIV-infected individuals has leveled off is good news," Karon told the Washington Post. *"However, the epidemic has stabilized at a very high level. It's as if we were running in place, but it is a deadly place to run." On average, HIV infection developed into serious illness within ten years.*

Worldwide, some 21 million were infected with HIV, according to a report released June 6 by the United Nations Joint Program in HIV-AIDS. An estimated 980,000 people died of AIDS-related illnesses in 1995, and the number was projected to reach 1,120,000 in 1996.

The UN report said that HIV infection had appeared to stabilize in the United States, other industrialized countries, and in some developing countries like Uganda and Thailand, all of which had mounted extensive public awareness and education efforts. The disease was still prevalent in several of the Caribbean and African countries and was spreading rapidly in China, India, Vietnam, and several southern African countries. An estimated 10 percent of the adults in South Africa were infected, 17 percent in Zambia and Zimbabwe, and 18 percent in Botswana.

A series of new studies showing that HIV can be transmitted orally could require public awareness campaigns to shift their focus somewhat. The studies, which involved monkeys and thus were not directly equatable to humans, strongly suggested that an oral dose of semen from an HIV-infected man could infect another person through contact with tissue in the person's mouth. Kissing and sharing utensils was still not considered to pose any risk of transmission.

Following are excerpts from the "Report of the NIH AIDS Research Program Evaluation Working Group of the Office of AIDS Research Advisory Council" on the effectiveness of the National Institutes of Health AIDS research program, released March 14, 1996:

Introduction

Fifteen years of AIDS research have begun to yield new dramatic interventions that can prevent disease, prolong health, improve quality of life and extend survival. With the development of new, more powerful, anti-HIV drugs, we have the first real chance to transform HIV disease from an inexorably fatal condition to a chronic, manageable viral infection, and in the case of children born to HIV-infected women, actually prevent many HIV infections. Great strides have been made in understanding basic aspects of the biology of HIV, and these insights lay a strong foundation for the development of even more effective therapies to treat HIV infection and new intervention strategies to prevent infection.

The present challenge for the biomedical research community is to use our newly acquired knowledge expeditiously to develop new and better therapies, to derive effective vaccines and behavioral interventions, enabling us to stop the expanding devastation of AIDS, and to one day eradicate the disease entirely. To guide the National Institutes of Health (NIH) in these new directions, a unique process was undertaken. A group of scientific experts from outside the government was assembled and asked to evaluate each of the components of the current NIH AIDS research program. This review was unprecedented in its breadth and scope, due to the magnitude of the research program, which cuts across every NIH institute and center. The group was asked to take a broad view in assessing how these components fit together and determining whether the program as a whole is moving effectively and efficiently toward the goal of preventing and curing AIDS.

The United States funds 85 percent of the worldwide public sector investment in AIDS research. The driving force of this research effort is the NIH, whose portfolio of AIDS and AIDS-related research has grown from a several-million dollar investment during the early 1980s to a $1.4 billion effort today involving virtually all of the Institutes and Centers.

This report provides a blueprint for restructuring the NIH AIDS research program to streamline research, strengthen high-quality programs, eliminate inadequate programs, and ensure that the American people reap the full benefits of their substantial investment in AIDS research. . . .

Cross-Cutting Themes and Recommendations

While much of the NIH AIDS research portfolio is of the highest quality and relevance, the Area Review Panels and the Working Group were convinced that there is a need for improved focus and better coordination between ICD [Institutes, Centers, and Divisions, NIH] research programs. Many specific needs and recommendations were identified in the individual panel reports; however, a number of common themes emerged:

- The need for ongoing scientific oversight and review by non-government scientists. The Working Group commends NIH for sponsoring this evaluation, and urges it to increase the involvement of non-government scientists in review and oversight of all important NIH programs, including AIDS research.
- The need for better integration and coordination of AIDS research among the ICDs and between intramural and extramural researchers. This will require a strong and viable OAR [Office of AIDS Research, NIH].
- The need for intensified collaboration with the pharmaceutical and biotechnology industries to develop new classes of drugs as well as safe and effective vaccines.
- The need for a rededication to basic research initiatives. This will require a redistribution of funds and the recruitment of high caliber investigators to AIDS research. Specific initiatives should focus on HIV

pathogenesis, viral gene-coded products and their functions; novel interventions that interfere at various stages of the viral life cycle; the human immune system and its response to HIV infection; and basic biology and pathogenesis of opportunistic infections and malignancies.

- The need to intensify and integrate research to prevent HIV transmission, including its biomedical and its behavioral aspects.
- The need for continued and enhanced HIV community involvement in AIDS research. Among the unique features of NIH's AIDS research effort is that HIV community advocates are involved at all levels of the research infrastructure, including reviews such as this one. AIDS community representatives play a critical role in making research more accessible to communities affected by HIV and more responsive, relevant, and acceptable to target populations. The Working Group urges NIH to continue to support HIV community involvement in AIDS research programs.

Because the OAR has the authority to plan and coordinate NIH AIDS research, the Working Group charges the OAR to rapidly develop and implement an action plan to address the specific needs identified by this evaluation. We also call on the NIH Director, the OAR Director, and the ICD Directors to work with the research community in a collaborative spirit to expedite the implementation of the proposed recommendations.

I. Investigator-Initiated Research

Increase support for and improve peer-review of investigator-initiated research

The nurturing of novel research approaches, concepts, and directions is essential for progress against AIDS. Research innovation and productivity require adequate levels of funding for meritorious projects, stability of grant support for productive, experienced AIDS researchers and an ongoing infusion of new investigators to the AIDS field. The Working Group believes that the success of the NIH's AIDS research effort absolutely depends on high-quality, informed peer review of research proposals.

Support for Investigator-Initiated AIDS Research

The Working Group believes that there is no better way to enhance the diversity and productivity of research approaches than to actively encourage and support peer-reviewed, investigator-initiated and driven research. This principle holds true for all areas of AIDS research including the basic sciences, the clinical sciences, the epidemiological sciences, and the behavioral sciences. However, the pool of funds dedicated to support investigator-initiated AIDS research is proportionally less than those typically devoted to other NIH-sponsored research programs. Indeed, in 1994 only about 20 percent of NIH AIDS extramural research expenditures could be classified as unsolicited investigator-initiated research, as compared with approximately 50 percent for non-AIDS projects. Since the beginning of the AIDS epidemic, the ICDs have tended to manage AIDS research with more direct scientific control than other research portfolios. Requests for applications (RFAs), collaborative agreements, and contracts were heavily utilized as research support mechanisms. Earlier in the epidemic, when the available level of knowledge was less and the community of researchers involved in AIDS research was smaller, this was an effective approach to establish the infrastructure and preliminary knowledge base for nascent AIDS research efforts. However, given the maturation of the field and the nature of the contemporary research needs, the continuation of this approach represents an impediment to progress.

A primary consequence of the current distribution of funds is that the resources available for unsolicited investigator-initiated research are simply insufficient. Proposals that ultimately receive funding most often do so only after multiple submissions for review. Delays resulting from multiple review cycles inevitably slow progress that can be made against the disease. Another negative consequence of the intense competition for research dollars is that many investigators are reluctant to submit novel or innovative proposals. Furthermore, the tight competition for grants has led IRGs [initial review groups] to heavily favor applications containing extensive preliminary data. While this is an important criterion by which to evaluate the merit of grant applications, it represents a major barrier to attracting new investigators to the field of AIDS research.

To remedy this situation, the Working Group recommends a substantial increase in the support for investigator-initiated AIDS research across the NIH.

Recommendation

I. 1 The proportion of the NIH AIDS research budget allocated to support unsolicited investigator-initiated research should be approximately doubled.

. . . The Working Group has determined that there are funds allocated for AIDS research that are being used to support both intramural and extramural research that is only peripherally related to AIDS. Redirection of such funds will be required to implement this recommendation. The Working Group appreciates that such redirection of funds will require time and careful planning. . . .

Quality, Scope, and Flexibility of AIDS-Related IRGs

The peer review process is central to the success of the entire research endeavor. It must be of the highest quality. The paramount consideration in achieving expert peer review is the scientific expertise of the members of the IRGs. Scientific expertise can be defined through previous record of scientific accomplishment and knowledge of the field relevant to the review. The Working Group became aware of numerous instances where the IRG process unfortunately appears to have failed in the identification of the most promising research projects. The Working Group believes that these failures were primarily due to limitations in the breadth, depth, or expertise of the membership of certain AIDS-related IRGs. These limitations seem to be the result of a number of factors, including constraints placed on DRG [Division of Research Grants] with respect to choosing IRG members, the limited enthusiasm that many members of the extramural scientific community may feel for service on IRGs in an environment where so few grant applications are funded, and the absence of an aggressive campaign on the part of the NIH and DRG to recruit expert scientists to serve on IRGs. The Working Group strongly believes that these limitations must be remedied. . . .

Recruiting New Investigators to HIV/AIDS Research

It is critical that the NIH actively encourage exceptionally creative and productive individuals to devote at least a portion of their research effort to HIV/AIDS-related areas. A number of factors may have contributed to limited success in attracting many expert investigators to AIDS research in the past. These factors include concerns about working with infectious agents, unfamiliarity with the central scientific issues in AIDS, the perception that the field was insufficiently mature to support very focused investigations, the daunting complexity of the disease process, a lack of understanding of the human immune system and of tools to study it in detail, and the often public and contentious nature of the earlier AIDS research effort. Many of the barriers have lessened significantly over the past decade. Although provision of adequate funding to investigator-initiated research is, as discussed earlier, a necessary component of a program to attract new investigators to AIDS research, it is not the only remedy that is needed. . . .

In the current NIH funding environment, it is very difficult for researchers who are just beginning their independent scientific careers to compete against more established investigators for funding. As the financial constraints on universities and academic medical centers continue to mount, new investigators are under increasing pressure to rapidly gain independent support. Delays in obtaining research support or the inability of attracting sufficient levels of funding to establish an independent research program can result in either the loss of a junior investigator's position or redirection of his or her efforts to teaching, service or clinical responsibilities.

The NIH has been successful in recruiting investigators to understudied areas of science in some instances. The Working Group identified several features that are likely to be important to achieve such success in the area of AIDS research. Key among them are the quality and dedication of NIH staff involved in program initiation and oversight, and the involvement of the extramural scientific community in identifying research needs and opportunities. The Working Group recommends an active program to recruit outstanding new investigators to AIDS research. . . .

II. AIDS Vaccine Research

Establish a restructured trans-NIH vaccine research effort

The development of a safe and effective vaccine to prevent HIV infection is among the highest priorities for the AIDS research effort. Yet, vaccine research historically has received less funding and attention than other areas of AIDS research. Although this may have been justifiable in the past, the continued spread of the HIV epidemic and recent advances in our knowledge dictate a reassessment of priorities and a restructuring of the NIH vaccine initiative. . . .

Recommendation

II. 1 The entire AIDS vaccine research effort of the NIH should be restructured. A trans-NIH vaccine program should be established with leadership and oversight provided by distinguished, non-government scientists. . . .

Coordinated direction across ICDs and between intramural and extramural investigators is necessary to achieve effective planning and implementation of strategies to rapidly exploit new advances. In addition to facilitating the development and evaluation of HIV vaccines, this initiative should stimulate the integration of basic research advances in immunology and vaccine science that could energize the development of new vaccines for a wide range of infectious diseases, including microorganisms that cause opportunistic infections.

Recommendation

II. 2 A National AIDS Vaccine Task Force (NAVTF) should be established in the White House Office of the National AIDS Policy, chaired by the Director of OAR, with responsibility for coordinating all government-sponsored vaccine programs. . . .

III. Research on the Human Immune System
Augment research efforts to better understand the human immune system

There is a critical need for a greater understanding of the human immune system. Illumination of the intricacies of this system holds the keys to developing a successful vaccine to prevent HIV infection and for designing more effective therapies to limit immune system damage and to restore functional immune responses in HIV-infected persons. . . . The study of HIV/SIV [simian immunodeficiency virus] immunology in human and primate models is under-represented in the scientific portfolio of the NIH. Many of the most capable immunologists have not committed major efforts to AIDS research. Research on the immune systems of uninfected, and HIV-infected humans and SIV-infected primates must be established as a high priority for the NIH. To focus attention on HIV/SIV immunology and actively engage talented immunologists in AIDS research, the Working Group recommends:

Recommendations

III. 1 OAR should convene a series of workshops of expert immunologists to develop a plan to accelerate progress in understanding the following:

- The basic biology and development of human immunocompetent cells and of the unique aspects of the physiology of the human immune system.
- How HIV or SIV perturbs the human or primate immune system to impair the function of and destroy immunocompetent cells.
- Why normal replacement mechanisms are unable to restore a functional immune system in infected individuals.
- Why normal host defenses are unable to ultimately contain HIV infection. . . .

[IV and V omitted]

VI. Drug Discovery Research

Refocus and restructure the drug discovery research effort

. . . In considering NIH's AIDS drug discovery efforts, some members of the Working Group questioned whether having a program that replicates the functions of the pharmaceutical industry is the best use of NIH resources. For example, these members felt that NIH's proper scientific function is to support the development of mechanism-based screens rather than support a screening program per se. Certainly, research required to develop such screening assays is clearly a high priority for NIH. There may be unique drug development situations that require more extensive Federal support, particularly research on "orphan" diseases, such as treatment of certain AIDS-associated OIs [opportunistic infections], where there is limited or no commercial interest. The availability of NIH resources to support such drug discovery research is certainly warranted.

One large endeavor, the NCI [National Cancer Institute] drug discovery program, located within the Developmental Therapeutics Program (DTP), requires review and restructuring. The scope of the DTP effort essentially replicates that found in the pharmaceutical industry: resources are allocated for acquisition of natural and synthetic products, screening, medicinal chemistry, synthesis, characterization of mechanism of action, pharmacology and toxicology. Although this program identified active agents in the mid-1980s when its cell-based antiviral screen was the only assay available, DTP's continued dependence on this nonselective screen is no longer warranted. Since the screen is not aimed at specific molecular targets, compounds identified as active may have the same target as agents already well studied in the clinic, as has been the case for the non-nucleoside reverse transcriptase inhibitors identified by DTP. The few agents that have advanced to further study represent a restricted number of antiviral mechanisms, and no truly novel agent has reached the clinic. The overall program is rather diffuse, in spite of the fact that day-to-day management of its many component branches, laboratories, and contractors appears to be well integrated. As a result, the productivity of this program over the last 8 years has been limited. Although the basic research studies that have elucidated the mechanism of action of active compounds have been of good quality, these studies have not met the goal of discovering truly novel inhibitors of HIV.

The DTP program has a unique resource in its library of defined compounds and in its various acquisition contracts, particularly for natural products. The program also has substantial capabilities in medicinal chemistry, in the characterization of drug mechanisms, and in the assessment of toxicology and pharmacology sufficient to support the filing of an investigational new drug (IND) application with the FDA [Food and Drug Administration]. Because the pharmaceutical industry's continued active interest in drug discovery for HIV and its associated OIs and malignancies cannot be assured, maintenance of a drug discovery infrastructure supported by NIH may be justifiable. However, resources would be better utilized if the DTP's efforts were refocused on the development of novel mechanism-based screens with high through-put capacity that are derived from basic research advances. Moreover, the DTP should use its core resources to support NIH-wide antiretroviral and opportunistic disease drug discovery research efforts; it would not be cost-effective to reproduce the considerable DTP infrastructure in other ICDs.

Recommendation

VI.1 An external scientific advisory board, including a representative from OAR, should be constituted to provide guidance regarding appropriate goals for future DTP AIDS research activities. Future assessment of the DTP AIDS drug discovery program should include its ability to support the overall NIH drug discovery effort for HIV and for the anti-OI discovery efforts of other ICDs. NCI bears a particular responsibility for the development of novel treatments for AIDS-associated malignancies. To accomplish these goals, DTP management and structure require careful review, both to determine what can be eliminated from the AIDS drug discovery effort and to appropriately assign the funds allotted to AIDS-directed research. A substantial decrease in the size and funding of the DTP's current AIDS-related drug discovery effort is appropriate. . . .

HUD ON CRISIS IN
RENTAL HOUSING MARKET
March 14, 1996

The Clinton administration chided Congress for cutting back federal housing assistance at a time when the number of poor people needing that aid was growing. Continued federal housing aid was especially necessary for the elderly and the working poor, the administration said.

The Department of Housing and Urban Development (HUD) on March 14 sent Congress a report detailing trends among what it called the "worst case" housing needs categories: low-income families and individuals who pay more than 50 percent of their income for rent or who live in severely inadequate housing. None of those households received federal housing assistance, despite their desperate circumstances. The report said the number of households in that category (estimated at 5.3 million in 1993) was growing, but the supply of housing for them was declining.

HUD secretary Henry Cisneros called the report "a wake up call," alerting policymakers and the public that housing shortages for low income people were getting worse, not better. "None of us, no matter how cold we are in thinking about this, wants the grim scenario ahead for our country if these trends continue," he said at a press conference when the report was released.

The report came as Congress was considering legislation that would radically change many of the basic tenets of federal housing policy. Two months after the report was released, the House passed far-reaching legislation (HR 2406) that would have repealed the Housing Act of 1937—the foundation of public housing programs—and the Brooke Amendment of 1968, which generally required that public housing tenants pay no more than 30 percent of their incomes in rent. The Senate also approved a bill making less sweeping housing policy changes, but the two chambers never took the issue to a formal conference committee in 1996 and the legislation died at the end of the session.

During the year Congress continued to cut spending for federal housing programs, appropriating $18.2 billion for HUD housing efforts in fiscal

1997, more than $1 billion below the previous fiscal year and $1.9 billion below Clinton's request. In the fiscal 1997 appropriations bill for HUD and other agencies, Congress also mandated a consolidation of numerous HUD programs into three main and three smaller programs.

Responding to the HUD report, Rep. Jerry Lewis, R-Calif., noted that spending on HUD programs had increased substantially in previous years and that Congress was determined to curtail further growth. Lewis acknowledged that the government was not providing assistance to "all the people who could use help," but he charged that HUD programs were too "top heavy in Washington" and needed to be streamlined. Lewis chaired the House Appropriations subcommittee that handled funding for HUD.

The Census Bureau on September 26 released a report showing that household income for Americans, including low-income people, rose in 1995. The report showed that households living below the poverty level declined from 14.5 percent in 1994 to 13.8 percent in 1995, the sharpest decline in nearly three decades.

HUD Report

Mandated in 1990 by the Senate Appropriations Committee, the report was produced by HUD's Office of Policy Development and Research. It said the number of households falling into the "worst case" housing needs category was growing rapidly, reaching an all-time high of 5.3 million in 1993, the most recent year for which complete statistics were available for analysis. The figure of 5.3 million households translated into nearly 12.8 million people, representing 5.6 percent of the nation's population.

HUD said the number of households in that category had grown by nearly 400,000 in two years, despite the improving economy at the end of the 1989–1991 recession. The increase demonstrated that the growth of severe housing needs was "a persistent trend, and not a short-term manifestation of higher unemployment and income stagnation associated with economic downturns."

Most of the increase in the "worst case" category was among families with children, Hispanics, and those living in the western region of the country, HUD said. Many of those families were the working poor, subsisting on minimum wage jobs or part-time employment. The rapid growth of Hispanics in that category was especially worrisome, the report said, because that population was "disproportionately underserved" by federal housing programs.

The report identified a "serious mismatch" between the number of low-income households and the supply of rental units that would be affordable for them. It cited two statistics to bolster that claim: in 1993 there were 1.7 million fewer housing units available for poor households than the number of renters needing those units; and the number of privately owned low-rent units fell by 478,000 between 1985 and 1993, despite the increase in need.

Those figures demonstrated, the report said, that the private market was failing to serve the poorest people in the United States, leaving government programs as the only option. "If housing assistance does not expand, the gap between supply and demand will continue to widen and the number of households with acute needs is likely to grow," the report said.

HUD's two main policy recommendations ran counter to trends underway in Congress. One recommendation was that the federal government "must continue to expand rental assistance" because cutting back would "exacerbate worst case needs." Congress was instead curtailing the growth of that program.

The report's second main recommendation was that federal rental assistance programs should be "carefully targeted" to those with the greatest needs. Congress was considering proposals that would end preferences for lowest-income households and instead give local housing officials more flexibility in deciding what populations to serve.

GAO Report on HUD Reforms

In a related development, the General Accounting Office (GAO) reported to Congress on March 27 that HUD had made limited progress in reforming its management practices and financial controls. The report added that it would be years before the agency would be able to make all the changes needed to assure that its programs were efficiently run and its money was well spent. (Public housing issues, Historic Documents of 1995, p. 294)

The GAO, the investigative arm of Congress, in 1994 had designated HUD as a "high risk" agency, meaning that its programs were vulnerable to waste, fraud, and abuse. The GAO cited four serious problems at the agency: weak internal controls, an ineffective organizational structure, an insufficient mix of staff with the proper skills, and inadequate information and financial management systems. The GAO also reported that Congress and the administration had not resolved pressing issues over the direction and financing of public housing programs in general.

Testifying on March 27 to the House Appropriations subcommittee on Veterans Affairs, Housing and Urban Development, and Independent Agencies, GAO official Judy A. England-Joseph reported that HUD remained "an agency in limbo." England-Joseph was director of housing and community development issues for the GAO. The housing department had taken some positive steps, she reported, including beginning a major reorganization of field offices, implementing new management controls, and adopting a new management philosophy of balancing risks with results.

Even so, England-Joseph said, HUD still faced a monumental task of improving its management. The GAO also said that the agency would have only a limited capacity to reform itself until the administration and Congress agreed on an approach to revamping federal housing programs.

Following is the executive summary and chapter 3 of the report, "Rental Housing Assistance at a Crossroads: A Report to Congress on Worst Case Housing Needs," issued March 14, 1996, by the Office of Policy Development and Research of the U.S. Department of Housing and Urban Development:

Executive Summary

As momentous decisions on Federal housing assistance policy are being contemplated, this report tells a story important to every Member of Congress. It documents conditions and trends among very low-income families and individuals with worst case housing needs: those who pay over 50 percent of their income for rent or live in severely inadequate housing. The report presents newly available data and analysis that document:

1. A record—and growing—number of households and people who face worst case housing needs, particularly among families with children, Hispanics, and those living in the western part of the United States.
2. The concentration of those with acute housing needs at the very lowest income levels.
3. The persistence of acute housing needs among the elderly and persons with disabilities, despite successful efforts of housing policy to serve those populations.
4. The high proportion of working people currently assisted by Federal housing programs and among those who have acute housing needs but do not receive assistance.
5. The failure of private housing markets to supply housing at rents affordable to the most needy households without Federal rental assistance.

The introduction to the report (Chapter 1) explains the background and approach of this congressionally mandated report. Chapter 2 summarizes statistical data from the U.S. Department of Housing and Urban Development's (HUD) analyses of worst case needs and of rental housing supply, documenting these five major findings. Chapter 3 explores the important implications of those findings for current policy decisions. Following is a synopsis of those findings and policy implications.

Major Findings

Finding 1: Worst case housing needs reached an all-time high of 5.3 million households in 1993.

- After growing by 1.1 million between 1978 and 1991, the number of households with unmet worst case needs for housing assistance rose another 400,000 between 1991 and 1993 and reached an all-time high of 5.3 million households.
- The growth in worst case needs persisted between 1991 and 1993 despite steady economic expansion during the period. Both in recession and recovery, the increases in worst case needs resulted solely from

higher numbers of very low-income households paying more than half of their income for rent, not problems in housing quality. In 1993, almost 95 percent of those with worst case problems paid over half of their reported income for housing, while fewer than 9 percent lived in severely inadequate housing.

- Growth in worst case needs reflects declining incomes at the lowest income levels, especially among families with children.
- Acute housing needs have more than doubled among Hispanics since 1978 and rapid growth in worst case needs in the West has left the region relatively underserved by housing assistance. Hispanics now account for more than 18 percent of worst case households (950,000 worst case households), but only 12 percent of those receiving Federal rental assistance. Similarly, 26 percent of 1993 worst case needs households live in the West, while only 17 percent of assisted units are in the region.

Finding 2: Worst case housing needs are concentrated at the lowest income levels.

- Over three-fourths of households with worst case needs—and almost three-fourths of all renters with severe housing problems—have incomes below 30 percent of area median income.
- The likelihood of having severe housing problems declines sharply as incomes rise above 30 percent of median. Over 70 percent of unassisted renters with incomes below 30 percent of median have priority problems compared to only 23 percent of unassisted renters with incomes between 31 and 50 percent of median, and 5 percent of households in the 51–80 percent of median range.
- Increases in worst case needs reflect large shifts of renter households into the extremely low-income category. Worst case needs increased by 1.25 million between 1978 and 1993 for renters with incomes below 30 percent of median, but only by 250,000 for those with incomes between 31 and 50 percent of median. Severe housing problems actually fell for renters with incomes between 51 and 80 percent of median.
- Current Federal rental programs are well targeted to the income groups that are otherwise most likely to have acute housing needs. More than 7 of every 10 households assisted by public housing and Section 8 programs are occupied by households with incomes below 30 percent of area median.

Finding 3: Acute housing needs remain high among the elderly. Close to 1 million households with adults with disabilities have acute needs for rental assistance.

- Of the 5.3 million households with worst case housing needs, almost 1.2 million are headed by an elderly person. Almost half (49 percent) of unassisted elderly renters with very low incomes have acute housing needs. Federal housing assistance reaches over one-third of households headed by the eligible elderly, but another one-third have unmet acute needs for housing assistance. Over two-thirds of the elderly with acute housing needs have incomes below 30 percent of median.

- At least 550,000 households currently served by housing assistance programs have an adult member with a disability, yet almost 40 percent of unassisted very low-income households that include an adult member with a disability have worst case housing needs.

Finding 4: Almost 2 million of those with worst case needs are working, including many working poor families with children.

- Over two-thirds of unassisted working poor renters (1.2 million households) have acute needs for rental assistance. Very large portions of very low-income renters—including those with worst case needs—are working, even at income levels as low as 20 percent of median. In the income group between 31 and 50 percent of median, 9 out of 10 households with children report earnings of at least half-time work at the minimum wage. More than four out of five have earnings that exceed full-time work at minimum wage.

- Current rental assistance programs serve many of the working poor. Over 1 million households living in public housing or receiving Section 8 rental assistance have earnings as their primary source of income. Almost one-half of these working households have incomes below 30 percent of median. Moreover, only slightly over half of extremely low-income households with children report receiving any income from welfare or Supplemental Security Income (SSI), a proportion that has remained constant since the mid-1980s.

Finding 5: Despite large and growing demand, housing markets are not responding to the acute needs of the lowest income renters by producing units affordable for them.

- There is a serious mismatch between extremely low-income renters and rental units affordable for them. In 1993, there were 1.7 million fewer units affordable to households with incomes below 30 percent of area median than there were renters at that income level. The private market stock of extremely low-rent units fell by 478,000 units—or over one-fifth—between 1985 and 1993.

- Housing markets are not responding to the increasing demand for units at extremely low rents. Instead, numbers of extremely low-rent units are shrinking as rents "filter up" (i.e., rise).

- The market added 1.5 million units with rents affordable to households with incomes between 50 and 80 percent of median between 1985 and 1993. Because of the expansion of units with moderate rents, tenant-based rental housing assistance has become easier to use in most parts of the country.

Policy Implications

Federal housing assistance policy is at a crossroads as of early 1996. Congress is considering—or in some areas has already begun—to make profound changes in both the funding and structure of Federal rental assistance. Congress has already ended a 30-year record of funding annual increases in the number of renter households assisted through HUD programs. Congress is also considering loosening the income targeting of rental assistance, thus diverting current slots of rental assistance to higher income households with less serious housing needs.

The analysis of housing needs and housing markets summarized in this report raises questions about the prudence of such steps. The implications of this report's findings on worst case housing needs are:

- The Federal Government must continue to expand rental assistance. Ending annual increases in rental housing assistance will exacerbate worst case needs. Incremental assistance can be a critical tool for States and localities to use for assisting the working poor and helping families make the transition from welfare to work.
- Federal rental assistance must continue to have careful income targeting in order to serve households with worst case needs. While there is broad support for eliminating Federal preferences, such preferences should be replaced with income targeting that ensures that Federal assistance continues to serve extremely low-income renters with serious housing needs. Moreover, the objectives of deconcentrating poverty and achieving mixed-income housing do not require housing programs to bypass those with the most serious housing needs.
- Federal programs that supply affordable housing—the HOME Investment Partnership Program (HOME) and the Low Income Housing Tax Credit program—must be complemented by continued growth of tenant-based rental assistance to help relieve worst case housing needs. Without a tenant-based subsidy, extremely low-income households are not likely to be able to afford the housing created by these programs. . . .

Chapter 3

Policy Implications

Congress is on the brink of making fundamental changes in the Nation's housing policies for the poor. This report documents that the number of poor families with severe housing needs is at an all-time high and still growing. The report's findings have three clear implications for future policy directions. First, the number of households subsidized by the Federal Government must continue to grow. Second, Federal housing assistance should continue to be targeted to those with the most severe housing needs. Finally, tenant-based housing assistance is a critical complement to Federal housing supply programs in assisting renters with worst case needs.

At the start of 1996, the Administration and Congress are struggling with the challenge of balancing the Federal budget while maintaining the Nation's commitment to decent housing for all Americans. Congress has taken some troubling steps. It has ended the bipartisan commitment to expanding the number of households getting Federal housing assistance each year and it has directed housing authorities to delay the reissuance of tenant-based Section 8 assistance when households leave the program. Both of these changes lengthen the already-long period that families must spend on waiting lists for assisted housing.

Congress has also suspended Federal preferences that direct housing assistance to those with worst case needs *without substituting any additional income targeting for households with very low incomes or worst case needs*. This, too, leaves the neediest families, even those who are working, at risk of permanent exclusion from assisted housing.

Congress is considering additional fundamental changes in Federal housing assistance policy. Important new legislation intended to streamline public housing and tenant-based rental assistance is likely to be enacted in 1996.

In addition, the Nation continues to debate key elements of welfare reform. In this regard, there is a fundamental consensus that public assistance programs must reward family responsibility and help families make the transition from welfare to work.

The remainder of this chapter draws some key implications for the future of national housing policy.

Policy Implication 1: The Federal Government must continue to expand rental assistance.

Finding 1 showed that the number of renter households with worst case needs grew by 1.5 million between 1978 and 1993. This increase resulted from the rapid growth in the number of extremely low-income renters and the reduction in the number of private market units affordable to them.

Throughout this period, however, there was consistent bipartisan support for expanding rental assistance programs. From 1978 to 1993, the number of units added to the Federal rental assistance inventory averaged 82,000 each year. This increase in Federal housing assistance kept an even larger number of extremely low-income renters from swelling the numbers of those with worst case needs. In fact, the share of extremely low-income renters receiving Federal housing assistance increased—from one quarter to one third. The likelihood that any particular extremely low-income family had acute needs was actually lower in 1993 than in 1978.

Thus, a cornerstone of any effort to contain the growth in worst case housing needs must be the continued expansion of Federal rental assistance—or "incremental" assistance.

- **Without incremental housing assistance, worst case needs will undoubtedly grow even faster than they have in the past few years.** For the foreseeable future, it is unlikely that wages of the lowest paid workers or income supports for those who cannot work will increase to a level that makes most private rental housing affordable. Nor is there any reason to suggest that housing markets will begin to supply a large volume of housing at rents that poor households can afford. Incremental assistance makes the housing costs of even the poorest households affordable.

- **Without incremental assistance, States and localities will lose an important tool for assisting the working poor and helping families make the transition from welfare to work.** Struggling families are more likely to slip back into dependency if they are forced to move to avoid eviction, to settle for housing far from jobs or transportation, to move in with relatives, or to lose housing altogether and be forced into homelessness.
- **Without incremental assistance, demographic groups and regions now underserved by housing assistance—notably Hispanics and the western region of the United States—will never receive their fair share of housing assistance.**

To continue the growth of rental assistance, President Clinton has proposed 50,000 additional units of rental assistance per year, while adhering to the goal of a balanced budget in FY 2002. For FY 1997, this assistance would be used by States in direct support of their welfare reform experiments. States would partner with PHAs [Public Housing Authorities] and with organizations that help families link their housing choice to jobs, schools, and community supports. In combination with welfare reform efforts, rental assistance could be used as a powerful incentive and support for families with worst case needs who are taking responsibility for their future.

Policy Implication 2: Housing assistance must have careful income targeting.

Congress is currently considering legislation that would dramatically relax income targeting for both public housing and Section 8 rental assistance. Under some proposals, the basic income eligibility would be set at 80 percent of area median income. There is also broad consensus about eliminating the current Federal preferences for those with extreme rent burden or severely substandard housing that currently serve to direct housing aid to those with worst case needs. The relaxation of income targeting combined with the elimination of Federal preferences could result in rental assistance serving fewer households with worst case needs and a greater number of families with less pressing housing problems.

As shown in Finding 2, an income limit of 80 percent of median would put an additional 6.4 million households in competition for scarce Federal housing resources. These households, though by no means affluent, are much less likely to have severe housing problems than those with lower incomes. In fact, housing needs in the group between 51 and 80 percent of median are actually on the decline. Those with incomes above 60 percent of median are unlikely to have any housing problem at all—not even moderate rent burden or modest physical problems.

Some targeting of housing assistance to those with acute needs would be likely to occur even if there were no income limits. For example, the modest amenities and poor locations of many assisted housing projects would make them unattractive to households with incomes much above the poverty level. Even with very modest rents, many relatively higher income families would not be attracted to many public and assisted housing projects.

However, changes in the income targeting of the assisted housing could affect a large proportion of the 4.5 million currently assisted housing units. Three issues deserve serious consideration:

- **With relaxed income targeting, the best assisted housing will be unavailable for the lowest income families.** Units in stable communities, close to job opportunities, or in neighborhoods with good schools are most likely to be attractive to higher income households with less severe housing needs. There is a real danger that the most desirable assisted housing will become, not mixed-income housing, but housing that serves families with incomes well above the poverty level. Not only would extremely low-income households have to compete for a more limited amount of Federal assistance, they also could well be relegated to the least desirable projects in the poorest neighborhoods. Without substantial targeting of assistance to families with incomes below 30 percent of median, the best part of the assisted housing stock may not be available to help families make the transition from welfare to work and to help the working poor continue the climb out of poverty.

- **The objectives of deconcentrating poverty and achieving mixed-income housing do not require housing programs to ignore the most serious housing needs.** It is not necessary to raise income limits to 60, 70, or 80 percent of median to find working families to serve as role models for the children in assisted housing. Most families with incomes in the range of 31 to 50 percent of median are working. Between 51 and 60 percent of median, virtually all have the equivalent of a full-time worker.

- **Perhaps the greatest risk of removing Federal preferences without rigorous income targeting affects elderly households.** Over time, housing for the elderly could attract substantial numbers of elders with relatively high incomes, while acute housing needs among the elderly poor begin to grow—reversing one of the most significant accomplishments of Federal housing assistance.

There is no strong argument for transforming housing projects for the elderly into mixed-income housing. The social benefits of income diversity and poverty deconcentration do not apply to properties occupied only by the elderly. However, this housing very often has real potential for attracting households with incomes above 50 percent of median. Housing for the elderly is often in neighborhoods where competing, market-rate housing has quite high rents, and elderly projects rarely have physical or management problems that would discourage higher-income elders from moving in.

Policy Implication 3: Tenant-based assistance complements Federal supply programs to assist worst case needs.

Finding 5 shows that the private market alone does not provide housing to families with worst case housing needs. The overall supply of rental units affordable to families with the lowest incomes has been shrinking as a result of significant filtering up of rents and because significant numbers of these units left the rental inventory for nonresidential use.

These findings reinforce the idea that government should intervene on both the supply and demand side of the housing markets. Demand-side programs—tenant-based subsidies—allow households with the very lowest incomes to afford housing produced by the private housing market. Supply side programs, such as the HOME program and the Low Income Housing Tax Credit, produce housing affordable for unassisted low-income households and for very low income households receiving tenant-based assistance.

The Clinton Administration enthusiastically supports HOME and the Low Income Housing Tax Credit, programs that increase the supply of affordable rental housing. Since 1986, the tax credit has produced more than 400,000 units of rental housing; since 1990, HOME has added 63,000 units. These two production programs work quite effectively to address worst case needs in conjunction with HUD's tenant-based rental assistance.

Both HOME and the Low Income Housing Tax Credit produce housing that is priced at or near the FMRs [fair market rents] for tenant-based Section 8. These units generally charge rents higher than households with worst case housing needs can afford. Only 6 percent of the rental units produced by HOME are occupied by extremely low-income households at rents affordable without additional rental assistance. This is understandable, because HOME and the tax credit subsidize the capital costs of rental housing. Neither program funds ongoing operating expenses. Therefore, neither program can always hold rents down to extremely low levels.

Tenant-based assistance is thus a critical complement to HOME and the Low Income Housing Tax Credit in making the units produced under these two programs affordable to households with worst case needs. Without a tenant-based subsidy, extremely low-income households are not likely to be able to afford the housing created by these programs.

TASK FORCE ON EXTREMISTS
IN THE U.S. ARMY
March 21, 1996

A task force of senior military officials found "minimal" evidence of extremist activity within the United States Army, but it reported considerable confusion among the troops about army regulations governing participation in extremist organizations. The task force also found that army training programs did not adequately address the issue of extremist behavior and that officers frequently were unaware of what their troops were doing in off-duty hours.

The study of hate group activity in and around the army was prompted by the December 7, 1995, slaying of a black couple in Fayetteville, North Carolina, allegedly by three white soldiers based at nearby Fort Bragg. At the direction of Defense Secretary William Perry, Army Secretary Togo D. West Jr. appointed the task force of four officials from the army and one from the navy to determine the extent of extremist activity by army personnel and what could be done about it.

Nationwide concern about possible links between extremist groups and the military also arose following the 1995 bombing of the federal office building in Oklahoma City. Two former soldiers with ties to right-wing militia groups, Timothy J. McVeigh and Terry L. Nichols, were charged in that case. (Oklahoma City bombing, Historic Documents of 1995, p. 176)

Upon receiving the task force report, West ordered that army regulations be studied for possible changes governing participation in extremist groups. West also asked for Defense Department help in developing ways to screen applicants who participate in such groups.

Leaders of several civil rights groups praised the army for investigating the issue of extremist behavior. However, some civil rights leaders said the army should drop a policy that distinguished between "active" and "passive" participation in racist and extremist organizations. The army banned "active" roles, such as attending meetings or participating in demonstrations, but condoned "passive" activity, such as membership.

Joe Roy, director of the "Klanwatch" program at the Southern Poverty

Law Center, told the House National Security Committee on June 25 that "any kind of involvement with the white supremacist groups, including mere membership, should be grounds for discharge" from the army. Membership in such groups "involves an affirmative step," Roy testified, and should be subject to stricter policy because of the unique role of the military.

Task Force Findings

The task force was chaired by Major General Larry R. Jordan, deputy inspector general of the army, and included two other senior military personnel and two senior civilian Pentagon officials. West appointed the task force less than a week after the Fayetteville murders. During January and February 1996 task force members visited twenty-eight major army installations in the United States, Germany, and South Korea and reviewed the findings of a written survey of 17,080 soldiers and interviews with 7,638 soldiers.

In the personal interviews, forty persons (about .5 percent) said they knew of another soldier, army employee, or family member who they believed to be an active participant in an extremist group. Another seventy-two persons (less than 1 percent) reported coming into contact with extremist groups on or near army installations during the previous year.

In the written survey, however, substantially higher proportions of soldiers reported contact with extremist groups. In that survey, 3.5 percent said they had been approached to join an extremist organization after they entered the army, and 7.1 percent said they knew a soldier whom they believed to be a member of an extremist organization. Another 17.4 percent said they had come into contact with extremist or racist material, such as pamphlets, billboards, posters, graffiti, or electronic mail messages.

The task force determined that, for several technical reasons, the findings from personal interviews were more accurate than those from the broader written survey. Based on its interviews, the survey, and a review of investigative reports by military and civilian law enforcement agencies, the task force concluded that there was no evidence of "widespread or organized extremist activity" by army personnel. Further, the task force reported that the vast majority of soldiers said that extremism had no place in the army.

The task force found little active recruiting of soldiers by extremist organizations. It reported that some senior commanders believed that Special Operations Forces (such as the elite Green Berets) were targeted by right-wing militia groups, but the task force said it could not reach a conclusion on this.

The task force said hate groups were active in communities close to most major army installations, and many soldiers had reported contact with members of such groups at local bars, shopping areas, or other places. Many soldiers said they had heard about paramilitary militia groups, but the task force said it found only two soldiers confirmed to have affiliations with such groups.

Gangs were of greater concern to most soldiers because they were the most likely of all extremist groups to operate on military installations, the task force said. The task force noted that gangs generally were not considered an extremist group under the army's formal definition.

Task Force Recommendations

The task force made twelve recommendations, ranging from revising the army's definition of "extremism" to including a discussion of extremism issues in each level of army training programs. It recommended that several steps be taken to clear up confusion within the ranks on the army's policy toward extremist groups. Perhaps the most important proposal along this line was that the army drop the term "passive" in its definition of the types of extremist behavior that were acceptable, in favor of "more precisely defined language."

West initiated a review of the policy on the day the task force issued its report. "The fact is, we simply cannot have our soldiers out there clear on their values and unclear on army values," he told reporters. "That is unacceptable." He said the matter would require careful study by lawyers and other specialists because the military could not violate First Amendment protections in the Constitution, including the rights of free speech and association.

The task force also suggested giving army recruiters and investigative agents broader authority to check on the backgrounds of individuals applying for entrance into the army. For example, it said recruiters should be allowed to question applicants about previous extremist affiliations or activity.

West said the recruit issue was a "touchy" one because it involved the kinds of questions the army could ask of private citizens before they signed up for duty. He said the issue would be studied by the Defense Department because it involved all the services, not just the army.

Following are excerpts from the report, "Defending American Values," issued by the secretary of the army's Task Force on Extremist Activities, on March 21, 1996:

Executive Summary

For over 220 years the United States Army has been the defender of the Nation and the values embodied in our Constitution. That sacred bond of trust between the Army and the American people was brought into question on December 7, 1995, when soldiers allegedly committed two racially motivated murders in Fayetteville, North Carolina. The Army is a reflection of American society and has a 21% annual turnover of personnel. The Army cannot escape the growing impact of extremist and racist organizations in our society at large; but clearly, the Army must identify and address indications of extremist and racist attitudes among soldiers and appropriately deal with extremist behavior when it occurs. The Secretary of the Army formed this Task Force to determine the scope and impact of extremist activities within our ranks and to make recommendations.

The Task Force visited 28 major Army installations in the United States, Germany and Korea during January and February 1996. Task Force support teams interviewed soldiers, both individually and in groups stratified by race, ethnicity and rank; and checked a variety of military and local law enforcement records for evidence of extremist activity. During 7,638 interviews, less than one percent (0.52%) reported that a soldier or Army civilian was an active participant in an extremist group. Additionally, less than one percent (0.98%) reported coming into other types of contact with extremist groups on or near Army installations.

The Army Research Institute analyzed confidential written surveys of 17,080 soldiers administered at the 28 installations where interviews were conducted. In the survey 3.5% of the soldier participants reported they have been approached to join an extremist organization since joining the Army. Another 7.1% reported they knew another soldier whom they believed to be a member of an extremist organization. The Task Force concludes that interview findings are more accurate than survey findings due to the greater ability of personal interviews to corroborate reports and eliminate duplicative reporting. We also consulted with nationally recognized human rights organizations to ensure a full understanding of the challenges of extremism and racism in the Army.

The Task Force concludes that there is minimal evidence of extremist activity in the Army. However, other areas of concern were identified. While leaders and soldiers perceive that extremist activity is minimal in the Active Army, all soldiers agree that the Amy is no place for extremists. Extremist groups are visible and active in communities outside some Army installations; however, local law enforcement authorities state that extremist groups do not seem to be specifically targeting soldiers for recruitment. The Army regulation on participation in extremist organizations is misunderstood and confusing to soldiers and junior leaders. Existing Army training programs and assessment tools do not adequately address extremism. Gang-related activities appear to be more pervasive than extremist activities on and near Army installations and are becoming a significant security concern for many soldiers. Existing open installations combined with less regulated barracks policies have degraded the commander's knowledge about potential illegal activities after duty hours.

While assessing the extent of extremism in the Army, the Task Force found many contributing factors. Overt racism is suppressed by Army policy, however there is an undercurrent of subtle racism which reflects a similar undercurrent in contemporary American society. The impact of this undercurrent is aggravated by the high Operational Pace of units, a "zero defect" mentality, and inexperience among first-line supervisors. The Army's Equal Opportunity Program is not effectively educating soldiers in units and in

Army schools on extremism nor providing a tool for commanders to assess and improve the human relations environment in their units.

The Task Force makes twelve major recommendations:

- Clarify and expand the Army's regulation on extremist activity.
- Conduct separate assessments of extremist activity in the Reserve Components and Army civilian workforce.
- Develop a reporting process for timely and accurate information sharing on extremism among appropriate staff agencies.
- Ensure that all law enforcement and other relevant information on extremist activities is disseminated to battalion and lower levels.
- Develop a process to evaluate soldiers' behavior, adaptability and human relations sensitivity during recruitment and Initial Entry Training.
- Review soldier Initial Entry Training to ensure necessary discipline, motivation, team building, and inculcation of Army values.
- Review leadership and human relations training in all pre-commissioning and professional development training.
- Review the Army Equal Opportunity Program, including staffing, training and the complaint process, to ensure responsiveness to the contemporary needs of soldiers and leaders.
- Clarify Army policies and chain of command responsibilities for soldier quarters.
- Ensure that membership in fraternal, social or private organizations does not impact on the conduct of official Army duties.
- Request Department of Defense review DOD Directive 1325.6 and issue guidance on extremist organizations and activities.
- Develop a Department of the Army Pamphlet on extremist activity for use by leaders at all levels. . . .

Conclusions

- Most commanders, leaders, and soldiers perceive that extremist activity is minimal the Active Army.
- The vast majority of soldiers perceive extremist activity as incompatible with military service.
- Although there were relatively few extremists identified in the Army, leaders recognize that even a few extremists can have a pronounced dysfunctional impact on the Army's bond with the American people, institutional values, and unit cohesion.
- Extremist groups are visible and active in communities outside some Army installations. Local law enforcement authorities state that extremist groups do not seem to be specifically targeting soldiers for recruitment. The results of Task Force interviews and surveys tend to substantiate this conclusion.
- The current policy on participation in extremist organizations is confusing and complicates the commander's interpretation of extremist activity.

- Gang-related activities appear to be more pervasive than extremist activities as defined in Army Regulation 600–20. Gang-related activity, both off post and on post (i.e., billets, military housing areas, schools, and Morale, Welfare, and Recreation facilities), sometimes involves family members and young soldiers. Gangs are a significant security concern for many soldiers.
- Many soldiers and leaders were unfamiliar with the guidance contained in Army Regulation 600–20. Most soldiers believe no participation in extremist organizations, active or passive, should be tolerated. The vast majority of soldiers believe that membership should be prohibited.
- The sharing of criminal intelligence, to include extremist activity, by military and civilian law enforcement authorities occurs routinely.
- Existing open installations combined with less regulated barracks policies degrade the commander's knowledge about potential extremist activities after duty hours.

Contributing Factors

- The overall human relations environment in the Army generally reflects the degree of tolerance and intolerance in American society and impacts the degree of vulnerability of soldiers to extremism.
- The Army's annual recruitment of approximately 21% of its personnel strength ensures that it remains reflective of the nation's values. This turnover also continually exposes the Army to new soldiers who may hold extremist views and affiliations.
- Most majority and many minority soldiers believe overt racism and discrimination are suppressed by the Army's unequivocal Equal Opportunity policy and its firm enforcement. The human relations environment is best where the chain of command is clear in its policy, proactive, and both quick and unambiguous in its response to incidents or complaints.
- Many soldiers believe teamwork, racial and ethnic integration, and equitable treatment occur in the workplace, yet most minority and many majority soldiers believe that subtle racism exists. On an interpersonal level, junior soldiers report an undercurrent which focuses on racial, ethnic, and cultural differences, stereotyping, separatism, self-polarization, misperception, and individual racial animosity. Most report that off-duty socialization often polarizes along ethnic, cultural, or other lines, which is often viewed as natural and acceptable.
- Leaders and soldiers alike cited high Operational Pace, unpredictability, reorganization impacts, and financial hardship of junior soldiers as contributing to a stressful human relations environment.
- Many soldiers and leaders, especially junior noncommissioned officers and officers, perceive a "Zero Defect" environment. Many believe this concern with failure avoidance leads to shielding superiors from bad news and to not attacking the root cause of problems for fear of unwanted attention or criticism.

- In some instances, leadership at battalion or higher levels may have differing perceptions of the human relations environment from those of junior soldiers, due to "hierarchical insulation," generational differences, or preconceptions.
- Some new sergeants and staff sergeants are viewed as lacking the necessary experience and leadership training to effectively resolve human relations problems.
- The Army does not have a formal process to evaluate soldier extremist behaviors, adaptability, and sensitivity to human relations issues during the recruiting process or Initial Entry Training.
- Sexual harassment and sexism have received greater emphasis and attention from commanders than other human relations issues in the last two to three years. Based on their experience in the 1970s and 1980s, senior leaders in the field appeared to believe the Army's racial problems were being adequately addressed. Racism and extremism were perceived as lesser problems and were less likely to have been targeted for training or leadership focus.
- Equal Opportunity and other human relations training within many units appears to be conducted erratically or with varying degrees of effectiveness. Until recently, little has been included on the subject of extremism.
- Many junior soldiers expressed little confidence in the responsiveness of the Equal Opportunity complaint system. They also consider the unit-level Equal Opportunity Representatives ineffective. By contrast, the Equal Opportunity complaint system is often viewed by junior leaders and some other soldiers as being abused by minorities and females.
- Most leaders believe that the absence of an Army standard and confusing billets policies degrade commanders' ability to be aware of and influence after-duty activities. Single Soldier Initiatives (SSI) and Better Opportunities for Single Soldiers (BOSS) are widely misunderstood, confused with each other, and often misinterpreted as limiting the chain of command's authority/ability to manage the billets (establish policy, inspect, enforce standards).
- Most soldiers believe that open-post policies, coupled with either lax screening of patrons for eligibility at Morale, Welfare, and Recreation outlets and clubs, or unruly conduct by "guests" of authorized patrons, can contribute to disruptive activities and undesirable incidents.
- Alcohol abuse reduces individual inhibitions against unacceptable and illegal behavior, and when coupled with varying degrees of racial, ethnic, and cultural polarization, can degrade the general human relations environment in units.

Recommendations

- Revise Army Regulation 600–20, *Army Command Policy*, paragraph 4–12, to eliminate the confusion created by the distinctions between active and passive participation in organizations and activities; to specify more clearly when commanders will counsel and/or take adverse action against soldiers who are displaying extremist behavior, and to make the regulation punitive.

- Conduct separate in-depth reviews of the extent of extremist activity and the human relations environment in the Reserve Components and in the Army civilian workforce.
- Develop a reporting process for the timely and accurate sharing of information on extremism among appropriate staff agencies, e.g., Equal Opportunity, Military Police, and Judge Advocates.
- Ensure that all information on extremist activities is disseminated to leaders at battalion and lower levels.
- Develop a process to evaluate soldiers' behaviors, adaptability, and sensitivity to human relations issues during recruitment and initial entry training, and screen for extremist views and participation during recruitment and initial entry training.
- Review Initial Entry Training to determine whether it is properly structured, resourced, and conducted to instill necessary individual discipline and motivation, team building, and inculcation of Army values. Review sustainment training of Army Values after Initial Entry Training.
- Review officer pre-commissioning programs to determine the adequacy of leadership and human relations training with an eye toward adopting a comprehensive program like the United States Military Academy's *Consideration of Others'* program.
- Ensure that officer and noncommissioned officer professional development courses include sufficient instruction on leadership, human relations, and extremism.
- Review the Army Equal Opportunity Program, including the complaint process, training, reporting, and oversight to ensure responsiveness to the contemporary needs of soldiers.
- Improve Equal Opportunity training in Army schools and in units, conduct as required by regulation, and incorporate relevant portions on extremism.
- Fully staff Equal Opportunity Staff Officer, Advisor, and Representative positions with appropriately trained personnel who represent the racial and gender composition of the Army.
- Establish an Army policy and clarify guidance on Single Soldier Initiatives and the Better Opportunities for Single Soldiers programs. Clarify policies on acceptable standards of conduct in and appearance of soldier quarters and on the chain of command's role in enforcement.
- Clearly state policy and then ensure that membership in fraternal, social, or private organizations will in no way impact upon the conduct of official or on-duty activities.
- Implement the derailed recommendations concerning Policy, Training, Data Reporting, and Accessions contained in Part II. . . .

April

GAO ON RAILROAD SAFETY
April 1, 1996

A series of passenger train wrecks early in 1996 focused renewed public attention on safety lapses in the nation's railroad system, which carried some 350 million passengers annually. Experts and government agencies called for speeded up efforts to improve safety standards, but the railroad industry and the government's chief railway regulator—the Federal Railroad Administration—warned that many of the proposed improvements would be very expensive.

The most spectacular of the 1996 train wrecks occurred on February 16 in Silver Spring, Maryland, when a commuter train hit an Amtrak train, killing eleven people. Survivors said they were unable to locate emergency exits on the passenger car of the commuter train, which exploded into flames after it was drenched with fuel. Safety experts said several of those who died might have survived the crash if they had been able to get out of the car.

Three persons died on February 9 when two New Jersey Transit trains collided in Secaucus. On February 21 two people died when a freight train derailed in Colorado.

The General Accounting Office (GAO), the investigative arm of Congress, on April 1 issued the latest in a series of reports calling for improved safety standards. The report outlined numerous safety improvements and suggested that the Federal Railroad Administration (FRA) had been slow to implement changes proposed by experts and mandated by Congress.

Officials of the National Transportation Safety Board (NTSB) also said they had been calling for widescale railway safety improvements for years—only to have many of the most important proposals sidetracked or delayed by the railway industry and the FRA. James Hall, safety board chairman, told the Senate Commerce Committee on February 27 that some railroads were not using safety technology "that has been available since the 1920s."

Hall and other safety experts noted, for example, that less than 10 percent of railway track had automatic systems to stop a train or alert the

*engineer when it improperly ran through a signal—a technology the gov-
ernment required in 1922 but later allowed most railroads to dismantle.
The government also had no regulations requiring railway passenger cars
to meet minimum standards for crashworthiness or flammability. The
government required passenger cars to have emergency windows and
doors, but not until after the Silver Spring wreck did the government insist
that emergency exits be in working order and marked so passengers could
find them.*

*Despite the publicity generated by the 1996 accidents, railroad industry
officials insisted that rail travel remained much safer than travel on the
nation's highways. The* New York Times *on February 25 quoted statistics
showing that railway passenger deaths averaged ten a year during the previous decade; calculated in relation to passenger miles, that rate was about
one-tenth the death rate for automobile travel.*

*Safety experts noted, however, that the same standard meant that air
travel was about four times safer than rail travel. Airlines were subject to
tougher safety regulation than were railroads.*

*The Federal Railroad Administration, which received much public crit-
icism for failing to speed up safety rules, said it was overworked and
understaffed and was developing forty new regulations as quickly as possible. Administrator Jolene Molitoris also noted that her agency was
required to apply a stringent cost-benefit analysis to all proposed regulations; that requirement meant that some safety requirements might be too
expensive relative to the small number of lives that might be saved.*

GAO Recommendations

*The GAO had issued more than a dozen reports on railway safety issues
since 1987. On April 1, Phyllis F. Scheinberg, associate director of transportation and telecommunication issues for the GAO, provided an update
on those reports to the Subcommittee on Railroads of the House Transportation and Infrastructure Committee.*

*Scheinberg's testimony focused on three issues: improving safety at the
nation's 168,000 intersections of public highways and railways; improving safety on railway tracks; and improving the safety of railroad passenger cars. In each area, she said, the GAO for years had joined safety experts
in urging faster improvements.*

*Collisions between automobiles and trains at railway crossings repre-
sented the greatest railroad safety hazard, Scheinberg testified. She noted
that 501 people had been killed and 1,764 others injured in these types of
collisions in 1994. Most of the collisions could have been prevented, either
with better warning signals or with improved driver education and
stricter enforcement of traffic laws.*

*Scheinberg told the subcommittee that the Federal Railroad Adminis-
tration had made some recommended improvements in its program
to inspect the safety of railway track, but she noted that the agency still
had not revised track safety standards, as Congress had ordered it to do*

in 1980. Scheinberg raised concerns about the railroad industry's practice of exempting thousands of miles of track from federal safety standards.

The GAO testimony also reported that the FRA for years had not tightened its safety standards for railway passenger cars, as had been urged by the NTSB. Under a 1994 congressional mandate, the agency was planning to issue revised standards by November 1999.

Revised Safety Regulations

In response to the Maryland and New Jersey accidents, Transportation Secretary Federico Peña on February 20 announced several emergency regulations. He said the regulations were intended to deal with the problems that lead to those accidents.

One regulation required engineers, after their trains pass a signal, to call out to another crew member whether the signal was red or yellow. The regulation applied to trains exceeding thirty miles an hour that were not equipped with certain kinds of safety technology. Peña said this regulation was intended "to make sure that people are alert, and that the entire crew is taking responsibility for the safety of the train."

Another new regulation imposed a speed limit of forty miles an hour on trains after they let passengers off at a station, when the next signal was at a switching point where two tracks meet. Peña likened this regulation to "traveling on a yellow light every time you leave a station." Such a procedure might have prevented the Silver Spring crash, in which the Maryland commuter train was traveling at sixty-three miles an hour.

Peña also ordered that all emergency window exits on passenger trains be clearly marked, both inside and outside the car, and be in operating condition so they open as intended. Defective exits "must be replaced, period," he said. In addition, Peña ordered all commuter railroads to submit safety plans to the Federal Railroad Administration for review and comment.

Peña's emergency orders apparently did not satisfy the NTSB, which on April 30 called for emergency inspections of the nation's sixteen commuter rail lines. The board said inspections should determine whether emergency windows and doors worked properly and emergency signs were visible on passenger cars. The Federal Railroad Administration had relied on voluntary inspections by railroads.

Following are excerpts from the written testimony delivered April 1, 1996, by Phyllis F. Scheinberg, associate director for transportation and telecommunications issues at the General Accounting Office, before the Subcommittee on Railroads of the House Transportation and Infrastructure Committee:

Recent rail accidents at Cajon Pass, California; Silver Spring, Maryland; and Weyauwega, Wisconsin, have heightened concern about the safety of passenger and freight lines in the United States. Since 1987, GAO has issued many reports describing safety problems on the nation's rail lines. This statement is based on recent GAO reviews of safety at highway railroad crossings, the adequacy of track safety inspections and enforcement, and the safety of passenger cars operated by commuter railroads and Amtrak. In summary, we found the following:

• Accidents at railroad crossings are the leading cause of deaths associated with the railroad industry; almost half of all rail-related deaths in the United States are caused by collisions of trains and vehicles at public railroad crossings.

In 1994, these collisions killed 501 people and injured 1,764 others. Strategies to improve safety at railroad crossings include targeting funds to high-risk areas through revisions in the Department of Transportation's (DOT) formula for distributing railroad improvement funds to the states; closing more railroad crossings; installing new technologies, such as four-quadrant gates, at the most dangerous crossings; and developing education and enforcement programs that increase the public's awareness of the dangers of railroad crossings.

Although DOT has an action plan incorporating these strategies, the plan will be costly to implement and will require DOT to seek congressional approval to implement key proposals.

• The Federal Railroad Administration (FRA) has developed an overall strategy for inspecting and enforcing track safety standards. As we recommended in our 1994 report, to further strengthen the rail safety program, FRA needs to include site-specific data on volumes of passenger and hazardous materials traffic in its inspection plan and improve the reliability of its accident and injury data. Information on the numbers of passengers and amounts of hazardous materials transported is important, since train routes carrying these types of traffic must be adequately maintained to prevent accidents that will injure passengers or expose populated areas to chemical risks. Accurate and complete information on the numbers of accidents and injuries is equally important in identifying high-risk routes. However, FRA's database, derived from the industry's reports to FRA, is inaccurate and incomplete. Without reliable information on passenger and hazardous materials traffic, accidents, and injuries, FRA and its inspectors do not have the means to direct inspectors to the routes that have the highest potential for accidents.

• Although Amtrak and commuter railroads transport over 20 and 330 million passengers, respectively, each year, FRA has established few regulations concerning passenger car safety. FRA does not have minimum safety standards for mechanical components on passenger cars, as it does for freight cars and locomotives. In 1984, FRA informed the Congress that it planned to study the need for standards governing the condition of safety-critical passenger car components. The Congress subsequently directed FRA, in the Swift Rail Development Act of 1994, to complete rulemaking governing passenger car safety by 1999.

Improving Railroad Crossing Safety

On October 25, 1995, Americans were reminded of the dangers that drivers/passengers often face when they travel over railroad crossings in the United States. On that day, in Fox River Grove, Illinois, seven high school students were killed when a commuter train hit a school bus.

The potential for tragedies like the one at Fox River Grove is significant—the United States has over 168,000 public highway-railroad intersections. The types of warning for motorists at these crossings range from no visible devices to active devices, such as lights and gates. About 60 percent of all public crossings in the United States have only passive warning devices—typically, highway signs known as crossbucks. In 1994, this exposure resulted in motor vehicle accidents at crossings that killed 501 people and injured 1,764 others. Many of these deaths should have been avoided, since nearly one-half occurred at crossings where flashing lights and descended gates had warned motorists of the approaching danger.

In August 1995, we issued a comprehensive report on safety at railroad crossings. We reported that the federal investment in improving railroad crossing safety had noticeably reduced the number of deaths and injuries. Since the Rail-Highway Crossing Program—also known as the section 130 program—was established in 1974, the federal government has distributed about $5.5 billion (in 1996 constant dollars) to the states for railroad crossing improvements. This two-decade investment, combined with a reduction in the total number of crossings since 1974, has significantly lowered the accident and fatality rates—by 61 percent and 34 percent, respectively. However, most of this progress occurred during the first decade, and since 1985, the number of deaths has fluctuated between 466 and 682 each year. . . . Since 1977, the federal funding for railroad crossing improvements has also declined in real terms. Consequently, the question for future railroad crossing safety initiatives will be how best to target available resources to the most cost-effective approaches.

Our report discussed several strategies for targeting limited resources to address railroad crossing safety problems. The first strategy is to review DOT's current method of apportioning section 130 funds to the states. Our analysis of the 1995 section 130 apportionments found anomalies among the states in terms of how much funding they received in proportion to three key risk factors: accidents, fatalities, and total crossings. For example, California received 6.9 percent of the section 130 funds in 1995, but it had only 4.8 percent of the nation's railroad crossings, 5.3 percent of the fatalities, and 3.9 percent of the accidents. Senators [Richard] Lugar [R-Ind.] and [Daniel] Coats [R-Ind.] have proposed legislation to change the formula for allocating section 130 funds by linking the amounts of funding directly to the numbers of railroad crossings, fatalities, and accidents. Currently, section 130 funds are apportioned to each state as a 10-percent set-aside of its Surface Transportation Program funds.

The second means of targeting railroad crossing safety resources is to focus the available dollars on the strategies that have proved most effective in preventing accidents. These strategies include closing more crossings, using innovative technologies at dangerous crossings, and emphasizing education and enforcement. Clearly, the most effective way to improve railroad crossing safety is to close more crossings. The Secretary of Transportation has restated FRA's goal of closing 25 percent of the nation's railroad crossings, since many are unnecessary or redundant. For example, in 1994, the American Association of State Highway and Transportation Officials found that the nation had two railroad crossings for every mile of track and that in heavily congested areas, the average approached 10 crossings for every mile. However, local opposition and localities' unwillingness to provide a required 10-percent match in funds have made it difficult for the states to close as many crossings as they would like. When closing is not possible, the next alternative is to install traditional lights and gates. However, lights and gates provide only a warning, not positive protection at a crossing.

Hence, new technologies such as four-quadrant gates with vehicle detectors, although costing about $1 million per crossing, may be justified when accidents persist at signaled crossings. The Congress has funded research to develop innovative technologies for improving railroad crossing safety.

Although installing lights and gates can help to prevent accidents and fatalities, it will not preclude motorists from disregarding warning signals and driving around descended gates. Many states, particularly those with many railroad crossings, face a dilemma. While 35 percent of the railroad crossings in the United States have active warning devices, 50 percent of all crossing fatalities occurred at these locations. To modify drivers' behavior, DOT and the states are developing education and enforcement strategies. For example, Ohio—a state with an active education and enforcement program—cut the number of accidents at crossings with active warning devices from 377 in 1978 to 93 in 1993—a 75-percent reduction. Ohio has used mock train crashes as educational tools and has aggressively issued tickets to motorists going around descended crossing gates.

In addition, DOT has inaugurated a safety campaign entitled "Always Expect a Train," while Operation Lifesaver, Inc., provides support and referral services for state safety programs.

DOT's educational initiatives are part of a larger plan to improve railroad crossing safety. In June 1994, DOT issued a Grade Crossing Action Plan, and in October 1995, it established a Grade Crossing Safety Task Force. The action plan set a national goal of reducing the number of accidents and fatalities by 50 percent from 1994 to 2004. As we noted in our report, whether DOT attains the plan's goal will depend, in large part, on how well it coordinates the efforts of the states and railroads, whose contributions to implementing many of the proposals are critical. DOT does not have the authority to direct the states to implement many of the plan's proposals, regardless of how important they are to achieving DOT's goal.

Therefore, DOT must rely on either persuading the states that implementation is in their best interests or providing them with incentives for implementation. In addition, the success of five of the plan's proposals depends on whether DOT can obtain the required congressional approval to use existing funds in ways that are not allowable under current law.

The five proposals would (1) change the method used to apportion section 130 funds to the states, (2) use Surface Transportation Program funds to pay local governments a bonus to close crossings, (3) eliminate the requirement for localities to match a portion of the costs associated with closing crossings, (4) establish a $15 million program to encourage the states to improve rail corridors, and (5) use Surface Transportation Program funds to increase federal funding for Operation Lifesaver.

Finally, the action plan's proposals will cost more money. [Transportation] Secretary [Federico] Peña has announced a long-term goal of eliminating 2,250 crossings where the National Highway System intersects Principal Rail Lines. Both systems are vital to the nation's interstate commerce, and closing these crossings is generally not feasible. The alternative is to construct a grade separation—an overpass or underpass. This initiative alone could cost between $4.5 billion and $11.3 billion—a major infrastructure investment.

DOT established the Grade Crossing Safety Task Force in the aftermath of the Fox River Grove accident, intending to conduct a comprehensive national review of highway-railroad crossing design and construction measures. On March 1, 1996, the task force reported to the Secretary that "improved highway-rail grade crossing safety depends upon better cooperation, communication, and education among responsible parties if accidents and fatalities are to be reduced significantly."

The report provided 24 proposals for five problem areas it reviewed: (1) highway traffic signals that are supposed to be triggered by oncoming trains; (2) roadways where insufficient space is allotted for vehicles to stop between a road intersection and nearby railroad tracks; (3) junctions where railroad tracks are elevated above the surface of the roadway, exposing vehicles to the risk of getting hung on the tracks; (4) light rail transit crossings without standards for their design, warning devices, or traffic control measures; and (5) intersections where slowly moving vehicles, such as farm equipment, frequently cross the tracks.

Improving Track Safety

Under the Federal Railroad Safety Act of 1970, as amended, FRA is responsible for regulating all aspects of railroad safety. FRA's safety mission includes 1) establishing federal rail safety rules and standards; 2) inspecting railroads' track, signals, equipment, and operating practices; and 3) enforcing federal safety rules and standards. The railroads are primarily responsible for inspecting their own equipment and facilities to ensure compliance with federal safety regulations, while FRA monitors the railroads' actions.

We have issued many reports identifying weaknesses in FRA's railroad safety inspection and enforcement programs. For example, in July 1990, we reported on FRA's progress in meeting the requirements, set forth in the Federal Railroad Safety Authorization Act of 1980, that FRA submit to the Congress a system safety plan to carry out railroad safety laws. The act directed

FRA to (1) develop an inspection methodology that considered carriers' safety records, the location of population centers, and the volume and type of traffic using the track and (2) give priority to inspections of track and equipment used to transport passengers and hazardous materials. The House report accompanying the 1980 act stated that FRA should target safety inspections to high-risk track—track with a high incidence of accidents and injuries, located in populous urban areas, carrying passengers, or transporting hazardous materials.

In our 1990 report, we found that the inspection plan that FRA had developed did not include data on passenger and hazardous materials routes—two important risk factors. In an earlier report, issued in April 1989, we noted problems with another risk factor—accidents and injuries.

We found that the railroads had substantially underreported and inaccurately reported the number of accidents and injuries and their associated costs. As a result, FRA could not integrate inspection, accident, and injury data in its inspection plan to target high-risk locations.

In our 1994 report on FRA's track safety inspection program, we found that FRA had improved its track inspection program and that its strategy for correcting the weaknesses we had previously identified was sound. However, we pointed out that FRA still faced challenges stemming from these weaknesses. First, it had not obtained and incorporated into its inspection plan site-specific data on two critical risk factors—the volume of passenger and hazardous materials traffic. Second, it had not improved the reliability of another critical risk factor—the rail carriers' reporting of accidents and injuries nationwide. FRA published a notice of proposed rulemaking in August 1994 on methods to improve rail carriers' reporting. In February 1996, FRA reported that it intended to issue a final rule in June 1996.

To overcome these problems, we recommended that FRA focus on improving and gathering reliable data to establish rail safety goals. We specifically recommended that FRA establish a pilot program in one FRA region to gather data on the volume of passenger and hazardous materials traffic and correct the deficiencies in its accident/injury database. We recommended a pilot program in one FRA region, rather than a nationwide program, because FRA had expressed concern that a nationwide program would be too expensive. The House and Senate Appropriations Conference Committee echoed our concerns in its fiscal year 1995 report and directed the agency to report to the Committees by March 1995 on how it intended to implement our recommendations.

In its August 1995 response to the Committees, FRA indicated that the pilot program was not necessary, but it was taking actions to correct the deficiencies in the railroad accident/injury database. For example, FRA had allowed the railroads to update the database using magnetic media and audited the reporting procedures of all the large railroads.

We also identified in our 1994 report an emerging traffic safety problem—the industry's excessive labeling of track as exempt from federal safety standards. Since 1982, federal track safety standards have not applied to about

12,000 miles of track designated by the industry as "excepted"; travel on such track is limited to 10 miles per hour, no passenger service is allowed, and no train may carry more than five cars containing hazardous materials. We found in our 1994 report that the number of accidents on excepted track had increased from 22 in 1988 to 65 in 1992—a 195-percent increase.

Similarly, the number of track defects cited in FRA inspections increased from 3,229 in 1988 to 6,057 in 1992. However, with few exceptions, FRA cannot compel railroads to correct these defects. According to FRA, the railroads have applied the excepted track provision far more extensively than envisioned. For example, railroads have transported hazardous materials through residential areas on excepted track or intentionally designated track as excepted to avoid having to comply with minimum safety regulations. In November 1992, FRA announced a review of the excepted track provision with the intent of making changes. FRA viewed the regulations as inadequate because its inspectors could not write violations for excepted track and railroads were not required to correct defects on excepted track.

FRA stated that changes to the excepted track provision would occur as part of its rulemaking revising all track safety standards. In February 1996, FRA reported that the task of revising track safety regulations would be taken up by FRA's Railroad Safety Advisory Committee. FRA noted that this committee would begin its work in April 1996 but did not specify a date for completing the final rulemaking. The Congress had originally directed FRA to complete its rulemaking revising track safety standards by September 1994.

Improving Passenger Car Safety

In September 1993, we issued a report examining whether Amtrak had effective procedures for inspecting, repairing, and maintaining its passenger cars to ensure their safe operation and whether FRA had provided adequate oversight to ensure the safety of passenger cars.

We found that Amtrak had not consistently implemented its inspection and preventive maintenance programs and did not have clear criteria for determining when a passenger car should be removed from service for safety reasons. In addition, we found that Amtrak had disregarded some standards when parts were not available or there was insufficient time for repairs. For example, we observed that cars were routinely released for service without emergency equipment, such as fire extinguishers. As we recommended, Amtrak established a safety standard that identified a minimum threshold below which a passenger car may not be operated, and it implemented procedures to ensure that a car will not be operated unless it meets this safety standard.

In reviewing FRA's oversight of passenger car safety (for both Amtrak and commuter rail), we found that FRA had established few applicable regulations. As a result, its inspectors provided little oversight in this important safety area. For more than 20 years, the National Transportation Safety Board has recommended on numerous occasions that FRA expand its regulations for passenger cars, but FRA has not done so. As far back as 1984, FRA told the Congress that it planned to study the need for standards governing the condition of safety-critical passenger car components.

Between 1990 and 1994, train accidents on passenger rail lines ranged between 127 and 179 accidents each year. . . . In our 1993 report, we maintained that FRA's approach to overseeing passenger car safety was not adequate to ensure the safety of the over 330 million passengers who ride commuter railroads annually. We recommended that the Secretary of Transportation direct the FRA Administrator to study the need for establishing minimum criteria for the condition of safety-critical components on passenger cars. We noted that the Secretary should direct the FRA Administrator to establish any regulations for passenger car components that the study shows to be advisable, taking into account any internal safety standards developed by Amtrak or others that pertain to passenger car components. However, FRA officials told us at the time that the agency could not initiate the study because of limited resources.

Subsequently, the Swift Rail Development Act of 1994 required FRA to issue initial passenger safety standards within 3 years of the act's enactment and complete standards within 5 years. In 1995, FRA referred the issue to its Passenger Equipment Safety Working Group consisting of representatives from passenger railroads, operating employee organizations, mechanical employee organizations, and rail passengers. The working group held its first meeting in June 1995.

An advance notice of proposed rulemaking is expected in early 1996, and final regulations are to be issued in November 1999. Given the recent rail accidents, FRA could consider developing standards for such safety-critical components as emergency windows and doors and safety belts as well as the overall crashworthiness of passenger cars.

In conclusion, safety at highway-railroad crossings, the adequacy of track safety inspections and enforcement, and the safety of passenger cars operated by commuter railroads and Amtrak will remain important issues for Congress, FRA, the states, and the industry to address as the nation continues its efforts to prevent rail-related accidents and fatalities.

AGRICULTURE SECRETARY ON 1996 FARM BILL
April 4, 1996

President Bill Clinton on April 4 signed into law the most sweeping changes in federal farm policy since the Depression. The bill (HR 2854— PL 104–127) ended farm price supports that had been in effect since the New Deal, replacing them with fixed payments that would decline over seven years. The bill also ended most government controls over what farmers could plant and how much acreage they could use. Enactment of the bill marked a major political victory for House Republicans, who had seized the initiative on farm policy and wanted to reduce the federal government's role in agriculture.

Clinton signed the bill even though he disagreed with many of its provisions. Clinton said the replacement of price supports with fixed payments based on acreage would further endanger small family farms, which were nearing extinction. The president said he would send Congress proposals in 1997 to improve the farm "safety net."

Agriculture Secretary Dan Glickman said Clinton signed the bill "with reluctance" but pledged that the administration would begin carrying it out immediately. Glickman said his department faced a "monumental task" in making farmers aware of provisions in the new bill, including one that limited participation in the new commodity payment program to those who signed up between May and July of 1996.

Critics said Clinton exercised little influence over Congress as it wrote the bill because he feared political backlash from agricultural states heading into an election year. In an editorial on April 7, the Washington Post *said Clinton allowed a major policy change "to occur on his watch, largely without his touch." The new bill took effect with Clinton's signature. The previous farm bill had expired at the end of 1995.*

A New System of Federal Payments

The heart of the bill was a radical restructuring of federal price supports for wheat, feed grains, cotton, and rice. Under the old system, the govern-

ment set target prices for those crops. When actual market prices fell below the targets, the government paid the difference to farmers. At the same time, the government set limits on the amount of acreage farmers could plant and on the payments they could receive.

The 1996 bill established a system of fixed payments to farmers, not based on market prices, that would decline over the seven-year lifespan of the farm bill. In the first two years, many farmers actually would receive more money—altogether an estimated $5 billion—than under the old system.

Advocates, such as Rep. Pat Roberts, R-Kan., who chaired the House Agriculture Committee that drafted much of the bill, said the new system would increase U.S. farm production, especially for export markets.

Critics noted that many farmers would continue to receive sizable federal payments even though most agriculture prices were at an all-time high. Sen. Tom Harkin, D-Iowa, a chief opponent of the new measure, said the legislation "has it exactly backward."

The Congressional Budget Office estimated that the new system would cost about $36 billion over seven years, a savings of $2 billion from what previous price supports would have cost. However, the Agriculture Department and other analysts said the bill might actually cost several billion dollars more than the previous system.

Politically, one of the most sensitive issues addressed by Congress in the new bill was milk prices, largely because of the low profit margin on which many dairy farms operate. Rather than eliminate all dairy price supports, as some in Congress wanted, the bill created a compromise under which federal supports for butter, powdered milk, and cheese would be phased out over four years. A complex system of regional price supports for milk would remain in effect for three years, after which the Agriculture Department would establish a national milk pricing system.

To appease politically powerful members of Congress from southern states, the bill made only modest reductions in federal price supports for sugar and peanuts. It also did not touch the controversial tobacco subsidy, which was run under a separate program.

Reaction among farmers to the new program varied depending on region and the type of commodities they raised. Corn and soybean farmers in the Midwest stood to benefit the most from the new fixed payments and reduced government oversight. Other farmers who had benefited from the old system appeared to be more skeptical. Included in that category were rice and cotton growers and wheat farmers in drier regions, such as the Texas Panhandle and the Dakotas.

Conservation and Other Provisions

Conservation and environmental programs in recent years had become a major focus of federal farm legislation, but House Republicans had tried to keep those matters out of the 1996 bill. Senate Democrats, led by Patrick J. Leahy of Vermont, senior minority member of the Agriculture Commit-

tee, demanded environmental provisions as the price for Senate action on the bill, and they got them. Leahy said those provisions "will make a significant difference in the lives of all Americans by ensuring safer drinking water, cleaner rivers, and abundant wildlife."

The most significant step was retention of the conservation reserve program, which paid farmers for not planting some 36 million acres of environmentally sensitive land. Other provisions included: payments of nearly $1.4 billion over seven years to farmers and livestock producers to reduce water pollution; $200 million to buy farmland in the Florida Everglades that had been used for sugar production, along with authority for another $100 million for the same purpose through the sale or transfer of other federal land in the state; a $50 million program to improve habitat for wildlife; and $35 million to buy easements on farmland threatened by development. (Everglades restoration, p. 80)

At the insistence of Democrats, the bill also created a three-year, $300 million fund for economic development in rural areas, where the loss of family farms had been devastating for many years. This Fund for Rural America would be divided between research projects and rural development.

Following are excerpts from a statement by Secretary of Agriculture Dan Glickman on April 4, 1996, shortly after President Clinton signed into law a bill making sweeping changes in U.S. farm policies:

Now that the President has signed the bill, it is the time for us to begin immediate implementation. We hope to have this ready so that sign-up can begin sometime towards the middle of next month. We have to prepare a variety of rules changes and implementation guidelines so that our county offices around the country will be in a position to let people know, as clearly and unequivocally as possible, what the rules are.

It is also very late. Planting has begun in many parts of this country, so we are writing the rules and doing sign-up at a time when planting has already taken place all over this country. But that's the way it is. So, we don't want farmers to wait any longer than necessary.

This bill changes the way farmers have operated for 60 years. And by that, I mean program crop farmers—largely wheat, corn, cotton, and rice. But it will affect farmers all over the country.

We have a monumental task making farmers aware of the options in time for this planting season. We need your help in getting this information out.

A critical deadline is fast approaching. A one-time sign-up for commodity programs will run from late May, or mid-to-late May, through mid-July of this year. I repeat that: a one-time sign-up. That was in the statute.

With the exception of the Conservation Reserve Program, producers who do not sign up during this program cannot enroll at a later date.

So, this is, again, going to require us, as well as, frankly, the news media, to get that information out there so people will not be prejudiced by failure to sign up.

Many changes the Farm Bill brings are good. They are changes the Clinton administration proposed more than a year ago. The hallmark of the bill's commodity title is the planting flexibility provisions which we proposed. Farmers finally will be free to plant for the market, not for the government.

Again, I am hopeful that you can help us get this message out to people as they deal with the sign-up.

We wholeheartedly endorse the bill's conservation provisions. Congress has responded to the administration's proposal that conservation and environmental programs be expanded, made simpler, and made more workable for agriculture.

We have made tremendous gains in conserving highly erodable crop land and stemming wetlands losses. The bill's provisions safeguard these gains all over the country.

We are very pleased with the rural development title of the bill. Congress has accepted our principle that we must put more resources into research and into rural development to enable rural areas to participate and compete in the growing world market.

The administration proposed, and Congress accepted, the creation of a fund for rural America to address these needs and to provide additional resources for agricultural research, which is also very critical for us.

But while there are a lot of positive things that the administration fought for in this bill, and the Congress provided, the President did sign it with reluctance because the new legislation fails to provide an adequate safety net in the outyears to protect farmers when prices will inevitably fall.

Now, we hope they don't. We may be into a miracle world of increased economic growth in the Third World, and increased need for our product, and we won't see that happen. But I suspect that history does repeat itself, and we will see weaker prices down the road.

And so this bill does not provide a long-term safety net. It tends to over-finance the safety net in the early years. And so that is something that we are concerned about. And in this regard I would mention something the President said to me.

He said—Some people will need these transition payments to just survive—just to be able to stay alive. And those people will use that money to do so. Others probably don't need that money initially. And rather than spending it, it would be prudent to bank it, or reserve it in those later years, when in fact investments and/or operating expenses will be more serious. And there's nothing in the bill to do that.

But I would say that the President's admonition is one that I'm going to repeat, and talk with bankers and lenders all over the country to do my best to encourage farm groups, and lending institutions, and bankers, and others to work with farmers to come up with creative savings instruments, so that not all of these dollars are spent right away—that they are reserved for, perhaps, the times when nature calls in an unwilling way, or when prices go down.

We do not support severing the relationship we've had with farmers to share their risks, market their products, conserve their land, conduct the best research in the world, and provide economic opportunity in rural communities. That relationship, that sharing relationship has insured that Americans have the most abundant, affordable, safe food supply in the world. And this bill does break that relationship, going to an almost fully decoupled situation.

We are disappointed that Congress has rolled back an important reform of the Crop Insurance Program, enacted just 18 months ago. However, we do support development of new revenue insurance approaches, which will help farmers manage risks.

And one of our highest priorities is, within the next several months, to work aggressively with farmers, the private insurance industry, and other folks to develop creative alternative risk management systems that can perhaps form part of the safety net that will be removed as a result of this bill.

We are firmly committed to working with Congress to strengthen the safety net features of this bill. And we will fully utilize the tools provided in the legislation to help farmers manage risks, to create new economic opportunities for farmers and everyone in rural America, and to insure the sustainability of the agricultural system.

As agriculture continues to move away from restrictive government programs to more market-oriented government programs, which this bill does, what government does outside the traditional commodity programs will become increasingly important. And those are the tools of research, of rural development, of risk management, of trade. Those things the government has to be an aggressive partner with agriculture, since its role in stabilizing price has largely been neutered as a result of this bill.

And that was a decision that the Congress has made, and one that we have accepted, obviously, by signing this bill. But we still worry that one of the inevitable results will be the potential for increased volatility in prices.

And therefore farmers will have to have other tools, beyond the government, involved in a supply management scheme in order to help them. And that's why the tools of research, of rural development, and risk management improvements are tools that farmers will need to help them manage the risk in a modern world.

So, saying that, I would just say that we begin immediately the implementation of this bill. While we don't like all of it, we will implement it fully, and with vigor, and with enthusiasm—because the farmers need to know out there that the program is on-track and moving ahead expeditiously.

CLINTON ON DEATH OF
COMMERCE SECRETARY BROWN
April 6, 1996

*A U.S. military airplane slammed into the side of a hill near Dubrovnik,
Croatia, on April 3, 1996, killing Commerce Secretary Ronald H. Brown
and a delegation of government officials and business leaders who had
been looking into possible reconstruction projects in the former Yugoslavia.
A reporter for the* New York Times, *the plane's crew, and a Croatian inter-
preter and photographer were also killed.*

*Brown, a close friend of President Clinton, had been the first black
chairman of a major political party and was instrumental in Clinton's
1992 election to the White House. Clinton and his wife, Hillary Rodham
Clinton, lost not only a close friend but an able political strategist and one
of the president's most important links to the black business and political
community. Brown was fifty-four at the time of his death.*

*On April 12, Clinton named U.S. Trade Representative Mickey Kantor as
Brown's successor. Kantor, a Los Angeles attorney, was chairman of Clinton's 1992 presidential election campaign.*

*News of the crash sent much of official Washington into mourning.
Clinton, his wife, and Vice President Al Gore went to the Commerce
Department on the afternoon of April 4, where Clinton told about five hun-
dred employees that "Ron Brown walked and ran and flew through life. And
he was a magnificent life force." In addition to Brown, six other Commerce
Department officials died in the crash.*

*On April 6 Clinton, most of his Cabinet, and the families of the other
crash victims met at Dover Air Force Base in Delaware to receive the
remains of the thirty-three Americans. With the transport plane and several flag-draped hearses in the background, Clinton spoke movingly at the
brief memorial service. At the end of his eulogy, Clinton read the names,
in alphabetical order, of the dead. "Today, we bring their bodies back home
to America, but their souls are surely at home with God," he said.*

*Brown's funeral service was held at the National Cathedral in Washington
on April 10, a week after the crash. Once again Clinton gave the eulogy: "The*

Bible tells us, 'though we weep through the night, joy will come in the morning.' Ron Brown's incredible life force brought us all joy in the morning. No dark night could ever defeat him. And as we remember him, may we always be able to recover his joy. For this man loved life and all the things in it." Attesting to Brown's personal popularity, nearly five thousand people attended the service, including politicians, entertainers, and business people. A Newsweek *reporter described Brown as "that rare figure in public life who moved effortlessly across racial divides that are still all too wide."*

The Crash

The plane, an Air Force T-43A—a military version of the Boeing 737 commercial jet—was flying in extremely foul weather as it approached the Dubrovnik airport for landing. Dubrovnik airport does not have the sophisticated equipment for approaches and landing that most major airports do. Mountains near the runway made it a difficult landing in bad weather. Although five flights had landed in the hours just before Brown's plane was expected, Croatian Airlines had diverted some of its commercial flights from the airport because of fog, driving rain, and winds gusting to seventy miles an hour. Brown's plane was about a mile off course when it crashed into a mountain in the fog. Investigators said the pilots might not have realized until the last second that they were approaching the hillside.

Both Hillary Clinton and Defense Secretary William J. Perry had used the plane shortly before the Brown mission. Brown and his entourage had flown from Paris to Tuzla, Bosnia, where they visited with U.S. peacekeeping forces. The plane, based in Ramstein, Germany, had its last complete inspection in June 1995.

In a report made public June 8, air force investigators concluded that several factors contributed to the plane crash. One was pilot error. Fifteen minutes behind schedule, the pilots were flying too fast as they approached the airport and did not begin to slow the plane as soon as they should have. They also began their approach to the airport before they received clearance, and they were off course.

A second factor, according to the investigators, was an improperly designed approach for instrument landings at the airport. The Croatian government rejected this factor as a contributor to the accident.

The third factor was what the investigators called "a failure of command." The report said air force commanders were wrong to permit the plane to fly to Dubrovnik without first having completed a required safety inspection of the airport. An inspection would almost certainly have barred military planes from flying into the airport because of its inadequate electronic landing system. The report also criticized commanders for not providing sufficient training for pilots flying into airports lacking sophisticated navigational equipment.

Had any one of these three factors not been present, the report concluded, the accident would not have occurred. Weather was not a cause, the investigators said.

*On August 6 the air force announced that sixteen officers had been rep-
rimanded in connection with the crash. The most serious punishments
were given to Brig. Gen. William E. Stevens, commander of the 86th Airlift
Wing at Ramstein Air Base, and a deputy, Col. John E. Mazurowski, who
was in charge of flight operations. The two were charged with dereliction
of duty for failing to ensure that safety inspections had been performed at
the Dubrovnik airport. Both Stevens and Mazurowski had been relieved of
their commands in May, as had Col. Roger W. Hansen, the wing's vice commander. Hansen received a letter of reprimand, as did Maj. Gen. Jeffrey G.
Cliver, former director of operations for U.S. air forces in Europe. He was
cited for "failing to exercise effective oversight of Air Force flight direc-
tives." Twelve other officers received lesser punishments, but the air force
did not make their names public. The announcement brought the investigation to a close.*

*Even before the official investigation was concluded, Defense Secretary
Perry on April 9 ordered all military aircraft that carry passengers to be
equipped as soon as possible with voice and flight data recorders and with
the satellite-based Global Positioning system, which determines a plane's
precise position. None of this equipment was on Brown's air force plane,
and although there was no indication that lack of the equipment contributed to the crash, the air force was embarrassed by its absence. "We
have to prioritize where we spend our dollars," one air force brigadier general explained. On April 26 Pentagon officials announced that the air force
passenger fleet would be equipped with voice and flight data recorders by
1997, the navy fleet by 1998. Hand-held instruments to pinpoint position
within fifty feet were to be in planes by the fall.*

Brown's Record

*Many regarded Brown as exceptionally able at promoting American
interests in new markets overseas. Brown had made nearly twenty similar trade missions to all parts of the world, acting as a booster for American business, although some complained that the trips were little more
than junkets for corporate contributors to the Democratic party. Some of
those criticisms came from House Republicans who had been trying to
abolish the Commerce Department, which they said was a wasteful
bureaucracy that needlessly meddled in the marketplace. In the face of
strong objections from Clinton and Brown, that effort had not been successful.*

*Brown grew up in Harlem in the 1940s and 1950s, where his father
managed a hotel that catered to the black entertainers and politicians who
were not welcome at the white hotels downtown. He attended white prep
schools in Manhattan and was the only black in his class at Middlebury
College in Vermont. Brown worked in the civil rights movement in the late
1960s, where his mentors were Whitney Young and Vernon Jordan. In the
1970s he worked for the Urban League and then went to work on Ted
Kennedy's 1980 presidential campaign.*

From 1981 to 1992 Brown worked for the Washington law firm of Pat-
ton, Boggs & Blow as a lobbyist. He also served in a variety of Democratic
party jobs, including deputy chairman of the Democratic National Com-
mittee (DNC) from 1982 to 1985. In 1988 Brown served as Jesse Jackson's
convention manager and helped broker the agreement between Jackson and
the party's nominee, Gov. Michael S. Dukakis of Massachusetts, in which
Dukakis agreed to share the convention limelight with Jackson in exchange
for an endorsement. Early in 1989 Brown was elected chairman of the
DNC, where he proceeded to rebuild a badly demoralized political party.

Prior to his death, Brown had been under investigation for alleged
financial misdealings. An independent counsel, Daniel S. Pearson, was
looking into how Brown had made more than $300,000 by selling, to his
partner, his interest in a company that he had helped form but in which he
had never invested any money. Pearson was also investigating charges
that Brown had filed inaccurate financial disclosure reports and mislead-
ing statements on a mortgage application and that a natural gas company
in Oklahoma, seeking to curry favor in the Commerce Department, had
hired Brown's son Michael. The Internal Revenue Service was also looking
into whether Brown had violated federal tax laws. Brown insisted that the
investigation would clear his name, but White House aides were quoted as
saying that, given the charges, Brown would be doing well if he escaped
indictment and was not forced to resign his Cabinet position. As it was,
Clinton did not name Brown chairman of his reelection campaign,
although the secretary remained a trusted adviser.

> *Following is the text of President Bill Clinton's remarks April*
> *6, 1996, at Dover Air Force Base upon the return of the remains*
> *of Commerce Secretary Ronald H. Brown and thirty-two others*
> *killed in a crash of a military airplane April 3 near Dubrovnik,*
> *Croatia:*

My fellow Americans, today we come to a place that has seen too many
sad, silent homecomings. For this is where we in America bring home our
own—those who have given their lives in the service of their country.

The 33 fine Americans we meet today, on their last journey home, ended
their lives on a hard mountain a long way from home. But in a way they never
left America. On their mission of peace and hope, they carried with them
America's spirit, what our greatest martyr, Abraham Lincoln, called "the last,
best hope of earth."

Our loved ones and friends loved their country and they loved serving
their country. They believed that America, through their efforts, could help to
restore a broken land, help to heal a people of their hatreds, help to bring a
better tomorrow through honest work and shared enterprise. They knew
what their country had given them and they gave it back with a force, an
energy, an optimism that every one of us can be proud of.

They were outstanding business leaders who gave their employees and their customers their very best. They were brave members of our military, dedicated to preserving our freedom and advancing America's cause.

There was a brilliant correspondent, committed to helping Americans better understand this complicated new world we live in. And there were public servants, some of them still in the fresh springtime of their years, who gave nothing less than everything they had, because they believed in the nobility of public service.

And there was a noble Secretary of Commerce who never saw a mountain he couldn't climb or a river he couldn't build a bridge across.

All of them were so full of possibility. Even as we grieve for what their lives might have been, let us celebrate what their lives were, for their public achievements and their private victories of love and kindness and devotion are things that no one—no one—could do anything but treasure.

These 33 lives show us the best of America. They are a stern rebuke to the cynicism that is all too familiar today. For as family after family after family told the Vice President and Hillary and me today, their loved ones were proud of what they were doing, they believed in what they were doing, they believed in this country, they believed we could make a difference. How silly they make cynicism seem. And, more important, they were a glowing testimonial to the power of individuals who improved their own lives and elevate the lives of others and make a better future for others. These 33 people loved America enough to use what is best about it in their own lives, to try to help solve a problem a long, long way from home.

At the first of this interminable week, Ron Brown came to the White House to visit with me and the Vice President and a few others. And at the end of the visit he was bubbling with enthusiasm about this mission. And he went through all the people from the Commerce Department who were going. And then he went through every single business leader that was going. And he said, you know, I've taken so many of these missions to advance America's economic interest and to generate jobs for Americans; these business people are going on this mission because they want to use the power of the American economy to save the peace in the Balkans.

That is a noble thing. Nearly 5,000 miles from home, they went to help people build their own homes and roads, to turn on the lights in cities darkened by war, to restore the everyday interchange of people working and living together with something to look forward to and a dream to raise their own children by.

You know, we can say a lot of things, because these people were many things to those who loved them. But I say to all of you, to every American, they were all patriots, whether soldiers or civil servants or committed citizens, they were patriots.

In their memory and in their honor, let us rededicate our lives to our country and to our fellow citizens; in their memory and in their honor, let us resolve to continue their mission of peace and healing and progress. We must not let their mission fail. And we will not let their mission fail.

The sun is going down on this day. The next time it rises it will be Easter morning, a day that marks the passage from loss and despair to hope and redemption, a day that more than any other reminds us that life is more than what we know, life is more than what we can understand, life is more than, sometimes, even we can bear. But life is also eternal. For each of these 33 of our fellow Americans and the two fine Croatians that fell with them, their day on Earth was too short, but for our country men and women we must remember that what they did while the sun was out will last with us forever.

If I may now, I would like to read the names of all of them, in honor of their lives, their service and their families:

Staff Sergeant Gerald Aldrich

Ronald Brown

Duane Christian

Barry Conrad

Paul Cushman III

Adam Darling

Captain Ashley James Davis

Gail Dobert

Robert Donovan

Claudio Elia

Staff Sergeant Robert Farrington, Jr.

David Ford

Carol Hamilton

Kathryn Hoffman

Lee Jackson

Stephen Kaminski

Katherine Kellogg

Technical Sergeant Shelly Kelly

James Lewek

Frank Maier

Charles Meissner

William Morton

Walter Murphy

Nathaniel Nash

Lawrence Payne

Leonard Pieroni

Captain Timothy Schafer

John Scoville

I. Donald Terner

P. Stuart Tholan

Technical Sergeant Cheryl Ann Turnage

Naomi Warbasse

Robert Al Whittaker

Today we bring their bodies back home to America, but their souls are surely at home with God. We welcome them home. We miss them. We ask God to be with them and their families.

God bless you all, and God bless our beloved nation. Amen.

REPORT ON PROLIFERATION OF WEAPONS OF MASS DESTRUCTION
April 11, 1996

The Clinton administration sought during 1996 to draw public atten-tion to the threat posed by the worldwide proliferation of nuclear, chemi-cal, and biological weapons. The centerpiece of the administration's warn-ing was a report, "Proliferation: Threat and Response," issued by the Defense Department on April 11.

Defense Secretary William Perry called the report an updated counter-part to the Reagan administration's annual series, "Soviet Military Power," which warned of the military buildup in the Soviet Union. Perry said the new report showed that the proliferation of weapons of mass destruction posed as significant a threat to U.S. security as did the Soviet military during the cold war. "The proliferation of these horrific weapons presents a grave and urgent risk to the United States and our citizens, and troops abroad," Perry said in a preface to the report. "Reducing this risk is an absolute priority of the United States."

Perry and other administration officials said there had been some progress during the early 1990s in curtailing the proliferation of nuclear weapons. In particular, they noted arms control agreements that reduced the size of nuclear arsenals in the United States and the four states that inherit-ed Soviet weapons: Russia, Ukraine, Belarus, and Kazakstan. In 1995 sig-natory nations also extended indefinitely the Treaty on Non-Proliferation of Nuclear Weapons, which placed restrictions on how countries used nuclear materials and technology. However, Pentagon officials said Pakistan, India, and several other countries were continuing their nuclear weapons pro-grams, and a host of countries held or were developing chemical and biolog-ical weapons. (Nonproliferation Treaty, Historic Documents of 1995, p. 233)

The Pentagon report did not provide enough stimulus for the Senate to approve ratification of the Chemical Weapons Convention, an internation-al treaty banning most chemical weapons. Senate approval of the UN-nego-tiated treaty had been a priority for the Clinton administration. Despite bipartisan support, the treaty fell victim to presidential year politics.

Republican presidential candidate Bob Dole, apparently seeking to distance himself from President Clinton's foreign policy initiatives, on September 11 sent the Senate a letter urging that the treaty be delayed. Dole cited concerns about whether the United States could verify compliance by other countries. That letter from Dole, who in May had resigned as Senate majority leader, provided the ammunition that treaty critics needed to stall the measure until after the election.

The "New" Threat

The April 11 Pentagon report said the United States and its allies face a new threat posed by hostile nations and terrorist groups that owned or were trying to develop nuclear, chemical, and biological weapons.

"Hostile groups and nations have tried—or have been able—to obtain these weapons, the technology, and homegrown ability to make them or ballistic missiles that can deliver the massive annihilation, poison, and death of the weapons hundreds of miles away," Perry said in his preface. "For rogue nations, these weapons are a ticket to power, stature, and confidence in regional war."

The report discussed China's role in the spread of weapons technology and the continuing nuclear arms race between India and Pakistan. A brief section dealt with efforts by terrorist groups, insurgent factions, and organized crime syndicates to obtain weapons of mass destruction. Much of the report focused on the nations said to be the most active in trying to develop nuclear, chemical, or biological weapons: North Korea, Iran, Iraq, Libya, India, and Pakistan.

North Korea. *The report noted that during the previous ten years, North Korea had "significantly advanced" its programs to produce nuclear and chemical weapons, as well as ballistic missiles. These programs were part of a massive military buildup by the Pyongyang government—a buildup that was continuing despite the country's general economic collapse.*

Nuclear power facilities in North Korea had produced enough weapons-grade plutonium for several nuclear weapons, according to the report, which did not speculate on whether such weapons had been built. The report noted that in October 1994 North Korea signed an agreement with the United States pledging to allow international inspections of all its nuclear facilities. If North Korea adheres to that agreement, the report said, "its current nuclear program will phase out over time." (U.S.-North Korea agreement, Historic Documents of 1994, p. 602)

North Korea had developed a large arsenal of chemical weapons, the report said, including nerve and blister gas and chemical agents that attack victims' blood supplies. The report noted that North Korea had also organized military and civilian defense programs against chemical weapons, including chemical warfare drills among the civilian population.

The Pentagon report outlined an aggressive North Korean program to develop ballistic missiles, cruise missiles, and other means of delivering weapons of mass destruction. The country had several hundred Scud missiles with ranges of 300 to 500 kilometers and was developing new systems with ranges of up to 4,000 kilometers—an area that would encompass much of China, Russia, and South Asia. In addition, North Korea had sold hundreds of Scud missiles to Iran, Syria, and other Middle Eastern countries, and it was actively trying to sell copies of its new Nodong missile, which had an estimated range of 1,000 kilometers.

Iran. The Pentagon said Iran had placed a "high priority" on obtaining nuclear, chemical, and biological weapons since it lost the Iran-Iraq war in 1988. While Iran had made some progress in developing the technology to produce chemical and biological weapons and had acquired Scud ballistic missiles from North Korea and China, it had been thwarted in its efforts to obtain the technology and supplies necessary for a nuclear weapons program.

Iraq. Defeat in the Persian Gulf war had not quelled Iraqi leader Saddam Hussein's ambitions to obtain weapons of mass destruction as a means of dominating the Middle East, the Pentagon report said. The report charged that Iraqi officials had used "concealment, deceit, and intimidation" to avoid sanctions and inspections that were intended to block Iraq's resumption of nuclear, chemical, and biological weapons programs.

Much of Iraq's nuclear and chemical weapons programs had been destroyed during and after the Persian Gulf war, but the report added that Iraq probably could rebuild those programs if the United Nations dropped its inspections and if Iraq received significant assistance and supplies from other countries. Iraq's key facilities to produce biological weapons remained intact after the Gulf war, so production of those weapons could easily be resumed. In addition, the report said, Iraqi officials had refused to provide evidence for claims that they had destroyed all their biological weapons after the Gulf war.

Iraq retained some capability of producing ballistic missiles after the war, and the report suggested that Iraq still had a small number of mobile missile launchers and several dozen Scud missiles.

Libya. Like his counterparts in Iran and Iraq, Libyan leader Muammar al-Qaddafi sought to acquire weapons of mass destruction in hopes of intimidating his neighbors and establishing his country as a regional military power, the report noted. Several of Qaddafi's efforts had failed, and he was doggedly pursuing his objective while squandering his country's oil wealth. Libya had signed the nonproliferation treaty and submitted its limited nuclear facilities to international inspections, but the report said that Qaddafi remained determined to acquire nuclear weapons.

At the time of the report, Libya was nearing completion of a large underground chemical weapons complex at Tarhunah, about 60 kilometers southeast of Tripoli. However, the report said Libya had not succeeded in establishing a biological weapons program and probably would be unable to do so in the foreseeable future. Libya possessed only short-range Scud ballistic missiles with a range of 300 kilometers—posing no serious threat to its neighbors. International sanctions also made it difficult for Libya to acquire longer-range missiles, such as those made by North Korea, the report said.

India and Pakistan. *Spurred by mutual hostility and suspicion, India and Pakistan were each pursuing their programs to develop weapons of mass destruction, along with the missiles to carry them to enemy territory.*

India exploded a nuclear test device in 1974 and, the report said, had enough fissile material to enable it to assemble actual weapons "within a short time of deciding to do so." Pakistan also possessed all the material needed to build a nuclear device, including enough fissile material to assemble "a few" weapons, the report said. However, the Pentagon noted that Pakistan—unlike India—remained heavily dependent on foreign suppliers, especially China, for nuclear technology and equipment.

Both India and Pakistan had the infrastructure to produce chemical and biological weapons, but the report suggested that neither country had made much of an effort to do so. Both countries possessed short-range ballistic missiles, but only India had a program capable of developing longer-range missiles that could pose a regional threat.

U.S. Responses

A second section of the Pentagon report detailed U.S. responses to proliferation threats. Pentagon officials said those responses fell into three categories: preventing the proliferation of weapons of mass destruction; deterring the use of those weapons; and defending the United States and its vital interests against those weapons should they be used.

Ashton Carter, assistant secretary of defense for international security policy, told reporters that the Pentagon was spending about one-tenth of its budget, or $25 billion annually, on those counterproliferation efforts.

The Pentagon report cited several successes in preventing the spread of dangerous weapons, most notably with U.S. programs in Russia and other successor states to the Soviet Union. The report noted that the United States was actively engaged in helping the Russian military comply with nuclear arms control treaties and in destroying Russia's vast arsenal of chemical weapons. The other three states that inherited Soviet nuclear weapons— Belarus, Kazakhstan, and Ukraine—had declared their intention to give up those weapons and the United States was providing aid and technical advice.

Following are excerpts from the report, "Proliferation: Threat and Response," issued April 11, 1996, by the U.S. Department of Defense:

The New Threat from Nuclear, Biological, and Chemical Weapons

During the height of the Cold War, the Russian physicist Andre Sakharov said, "Reducing the risk of annihilating humanity in a nuclear war carries an absolute priority over all other considerations." The end of the Cold War has reduced the threat of global nuclear war, but today a new threat is rising from the global spread of nuclear, biological, and chemical weapons. Hostile groups and nations have tried—or have been able—to obtain these weapons, the technology, and homegrown ability to make them or ballistic missiles that can deliver the massive annihilation, poison, and death of these weapons hundreds of miles away. For rogue nations, these weapons are a ticket to power, stature, and confidence in regional war.

We received a wake-up call with Saddam Hussein's use of SCUD missiles during Operation Desert Storm and new information on his ambitious nuclear, biological, and chemical weapons programs. The proliferation of these horrific weapons presents a grave and urgent risk to the United States and our citizens, allies, and troops abroad. Reducing this risk is an absolute priority of the United States.

The way we reduce the risk from weapons of mass destruction has changed dramatically. During the Cold War, the United States and the Soviet Union lived under a doctrine known as Mutually Assured Destruction, commonly known as "MAD." MAD was essentially a balance of terror that assumed neither nuclear power would launch an attack and risk nuclear retaliation. This nuclear stand-off has ended. Instead, the United States and Russia are working together to reduce and dismantle our nuclear arsenals, and to prevent the export and sale of those weapons and related technology throughout the world.

Our progress is good news. The bad news is that in this era the simple threat of retaliation that worked during the Cold War may not be enough to deter terrorists or aggressive regimes from using nuclear, biological, and chemical weapons. Terrorists operate in a shadowy world in which they can detonate a device and disappear, as the poison gas attack in Tokyo illustrates. Rogue regimes may try to use these devastating weapons as blackmail, or as a relatively inexpensive way to sidestep the U.S. military's overwhelming conventional military superiority. Aggressors may also actually use these weapons in an attempt to gain a decisive edge in a regional war. The bottom line is, unlike during the Cold War, those who possess nuclear, biological, and chemical weapons may actually come to use them. The increase in the likelihood of regional war in today's world raises the risk.

This new danger requires some new thinking and new leadership on how to prevent, deter and, if necessary, respond to this threat. Through the Nunn-Lugar program, we have hastened dismantlement of Russia's nuclear weapon systems; denuclearized Ukraine, Kazakstan, and Belarus; strengthened the safety and security of nuclear weapons and fissile material; and removed 600 kilograms of highly enriched uranium from Kazakstan in the dramatic Project Sapphire. America's diplomatic leadership helped bring the nations of the world to extend—indefinitely—the Nuclear Non-Proliferation Treaty, which will serve to stem regional or even new global arms races. In one region in particular—the Korean peninsula—American diplomatic leadership helped bring North Korea to sign the Agreed Framework, which in effect froze its nuclear program. These successes demonstrate that U.S. diplomatic leadership in the world is critical to nonproliferation of nuclear, biological, and chemical weapons.

At the same time, America's defense leadership bolsters the diplomatic nonproliferation effort by helping to protect the United States and our citizens, allies, and military forces abroad from aggressors who may possess or obtain nuclear, biological, and chemical weapons. The Department of Defense (DoD) provides this leadership through a three-part strategy:

1. Reduce the threat, by leading the U.S. effort to help the former Soviet Union republics reduce, dismantle, safeguard, and even eliminate these weapons.
2. Deter against the threat, by maintaining strong conventional forces and a smaller but robust nuclear deterrent force.
3. Defend against the threat through the Defense Counterproliferation Initiative.

The DoD Counterproliferation Initiative involves a range of Department-wide activities that help to prevent, protect against, and even reverse the danger from spreading nuclear, biological, and chemical weapons; technology; and missiles that can deliver them. These efforts include developing systems that can intercept or destroy these weapons, providing vaccines and protective suits for our troops, keeping track of the movement of weapons and technology, and providing unique DoD support for various nonproliferation agreements.

This document details the proliferation phenomenon, the threat it poses to the United States, and the programs and policies DoD employs through the Defense Counterproliferation Initiative to counter this growing threat.

The Regional Proliferation Challenge

The quest for nuclear, biological, and chemical (NBC) weapons and the missiles to deliver them creates serious challenges to U.S. interests around the world. Many states have agreed voluntarily to terminate their weapon development programs, but others have not. This section discusses the threat from proliferation to regional stability, U.S. defense strategies, and other interests of the United States and its allies.

The United States faces several regional proliferation challenges. North Korea's decades-long threat to the security of Northeast Asia, and in particular to South Korea and Japan, has become more serious as the Democratic People's Republic of Korea has in recent years significantly advanced its nuclear, chemical, and ballistic missile programs. The United States is leading international efforts, through implementation of the October 1994 Agreed Framework, to bring North Korea into compliance with its nonproliferation obligations including the Nuclear Non-Proliferation Treaty (NPT), International Atomic Energy Agency (IAEA) safeguards, and the North-South denuclearization accord. In the Middle East/North Africa region, the United States remains concerned about the threat that Iran, Iraq, and Libya pose to the stability of the region and to the security of U.S. interests, allies, and friends. The United States continues efforts to prevent Iran and Libya from advancing and Iraq from reconstituting their weapon programs. In both regions, the Middle East/North Africa and Northeast Asia, where states are seeking to incorporate these weapons of mass destruction into their militaries, the Department of Defense is working to ensure that the United States retains the ability to defend its interests and to maintain the credibility of U.S. defense commitments to our allies and friends.

In the former Soviet Union, the vast amount of nuclear technology and material in the region presents an attractive target for determined proliferators, including terrorist and criminal groups. Maintaining control over the accountability of these capabilities and materials presents a daunting challenge to the United States, the new governments of the region, and the rest of the international community. Several bilateral and multilateral agreements with Russia and the other states of the former Soviet Union, such as those supported by the Defense Department's Cooperative Threat Reduction program, have significantly reduced the proliferation threat from that region.

In South Asia, the United States has important security interests in enhancing stability in the region and preventing another Indo-Pakistani war. The nuclear and ballistic missile programs of India and Pakistan threaten the stability of the region and could result in grave loss of life. The United States seeks first to cap and then reduce and, eventually, eliminate regional capabilities to produce NBC weapons and the missiles that deliver them.

In some areas, nonproliferation efforts have already greatly enhanced regional security. For example, the proliferation threat in sub-Saharan Africa has largely receded as South Africa has dismantled its nuclear weapons program, joined the NPT, and accepted full-scope safeguards on its nuclear facilities. Similarly, Argentina, Brazil, and Chile have accepted full-scope safeguards on their nuclear facilities and brought into force the Treaty of Tlatelolco, and Argentina and Chile have joined the NPT. In addition, the Treaty of Tlatelolco is approaching full implementation with the anticipated ratification by Cuba. All these steps have reduced the danger of nuclear rivalry in the Western Hemisphere.

Northeast Asia

Goals and Interests

Northeast Asia remains a region of vital importance to the United States, particularly in view of the growing prominence of the Pacific Rim nations as trading partners and as important players in the global economy. Security and stability in this region are essential if our economic relations are to continue to flourish. Our overarching long-term objective in the region remains the peaceful reunification of the Korean peninsula. The United States will continue to maintain forces on the peninsula to assure security for South Korea as long as the Republic of Korea Government wants them to stay.

Although the October 1994 Agreed Framework with North Korea over its nuclear facilities mitigated the immediate nuclear threat, Pyongyang still possesses an unnecessarily large conventional force, as well as militarily significant chemical weapons and the means to deliver them. Proliferation, particularly the broad-based NBC weapons and missile programs that North Korea has implemented, poses a significant challenge to U.S. security interests as well as to those of our allies and friends.

In the event of another war on the Korean peninsula, these weapons present a significant threat to our forces and the security of our allies. Should a conflict occur, North Korea likely will try to consolidate and control strategic areas of South Korea by striking quickly and attempting to destroy allied defenses before the United States can provide adequate reinforcements. Pyongyang hopes to do this with its large conventional force and its chemical weapons and ballistic missiles complement.

Strong bilateral relations with our allies and friends are the foundation of our Asia-Pacific strategy, and the North Korean NBC weapons and missile programs have the potential to complicate relationships within our bilateral alliances throughout the region. Should a proliferant go unchecked, calling U.S. capabilities and commitments into question, states may seek unilateral alternatives to ensure their security, thus stimulating proliferation. Nearly 100,000 soldiers, sailors, marines, and airmen of the U.S. Pacific Command maintain the strong forward presence that deters aggression, reassures our allies, and enhances stability throughout the region—a critical mission.

China, which has been a nuclear weapons state since 1964, remains a source of concern primarily because of the role of Chinese companies in supplying a wide range of materials, equipment, and technologies that could contribute to NBC weapons and missile programs in countries of proliferation concern. Beijing has signaled some willingness to adopt a more responsible supply policy by adhering to international nonproliferation norms such as the Nuclear Non-Proliferation Treaty (1992) and reaffirming to the United States its pledge to abide by the basic tenets of the Missile Technology Control Regime (MTCR). However, Chinese firms' continued willingness to engage in nuclear and missile cooperation with countries of serious proliferation concern, such as Pakistan and Iran, presents security concerns in many regions where the United States has defense commitments. Counterproliferation will continue to be a strong component of our regional strategy in Northeast Asia as long as our defense commitments and our forces are threatened by the spread of NBC weapons and missiles. . . .

The Middle East and North Africa

Goals and Interests

U.S. goals in the Middle East and North Africa include securing a just, lasting, and comprehensive peace between Israel and all Arab parties with which it is not yet at peace; maintaining our steadfast commitment to Israel's security and well-being; building and maintaining security arrangements that assure the stability of the Gulf region and unimpeded commercial access to its petroleum reserves, which are vital to our economic prosperity; ensuring fair access for American business to commercial opportunities in the region; combating terrorism; and promoting more open political and economic systems and respect for human rights and the rule of law. In this volatile region, the proliferation of NBC weapons and the means to deliver them poses a significant challenge to our ability to achieve these goals. Iran, Iraq, and Libya are aggressively seeking NBC weapons and missile capabilities, constituting the most pressing threats to regional stability. Iran and Iraq have demonstrated their intent to dominate the Persian Gulf and to control access to critical oil supplies.

Iran is actively attempting to acquire a full range of NBC weapons and missiles. The United States believes Iran is committed to acquiring nuclear weapons, either through indigenous development or by covertly acquiring enough fissile material to produce them. During its eight-year war with Iraq, Tehran initiated biological and chemical warfare programs, the latter in direct response to Iraq's use of chemical weapons. In addition, Iran is dedicated to expanding its ballistic missile programs.

Iraq has long had NBC warfare and missile efforts. The challenges these weapons pose in time of conflict became clear during the Persian Gulf War when U.S. and allied forces had to deal with real and potential complications posed by Iraq's arsenal of NBC weapons and missiles. Iraq entered the Gulf War with a known chemical warfare capability and a demonstrated willingness to use it (Iraq used chemical weapons against Iranian troops and its own Kurdish population during the 1980s); a known biological warfare capability; and a developing, complex nuclear weapons program (despite intense nonproliferation and export control efforts by the United States and the international community (for example, the IAEA)). During the Gulf War, Iraq attempted to weaken the cohesion and resolve of the U.S.-led coalition by using its ballistic missiles as weapons of terror against Saudi Arabia and Israel; however, Iraq did not use its SCUDs with chemical or biological warheads.

In their quests to establish regional hegemony, Iran and Iraq probably regard NBC weapons and missiles as necessary to guarantee their territorial integrity and national security. Possession of nuclear weapons would likely lead to increased intimidation of their Gulf neighbors, as well as increased willingness to confront the United States. The U.S. defense commitment, military presence, and demonstrated ability to defend U.S. and allied interests against such threats are vital to achieving our goals in the region.

Libya remains a significant proliferation concern. Libyan leader Muammar Qadhafi has shown that he is willing and capable of using chemical weapons and missiles against his enemies. Libya sees the United States as its primary external threat, owing especially to U.S. support for UN sanctions against Tripoli for its refusal to turn over suspects in the terrorist bombing of Pan Am 103. Although Libya's capabilities to use chemical agents and missiles are limited, Qadhafi could provide these weapons to states he supports and that support him in return.

The Proliferation Challenge: Regional Capabilities, Intentions, and Trends

Iran poses the greatest threat to the stability of the region and to U.S. interests; this will remain the case as long as the UN Security Commission on Iraq is able to maintain its intrusive inspection regime in neighboring Iraq. In the past, Iran has demonstrated both the will and the ability to use NBC to advance and defend national goals. Tehran used chemical weapons and ballistic missiles with conventional warheads during the Iran-Iraq war and has fired conventionally-armed cruise missiles at U.S.-flagged oil tankers.

In August 1995, Iraq admitted to a far more extensive NBC weapons and missile program than had been previously revealed. The Iraqis divulged to UN inspectors that prior to the Gulf War they had produced large quantities of biological warfare agents, had loaded them into missiles and bombs, had begun a crash program to build a nuclear weapon, and had produced engines for SCUD missiles.

In the future, the quality, scope, and staying power of the UN inspectors and on-site monitoring and verification processes will be central in determining whether the Iraqi weapon programs are dismantled, kept in check, or eventually succeed. However, Iraq's military production capabilities (not affected by UN sanctions and monitoring), past use of chemicals and missiles, and consistent efforts to deceive UN inspectors are strong indicators that Iraq will attempt to produce NBC weapons and missiles when outside constraints are absent.

In October 1994, the Iraqis repeated their oft-demonstrated willingness to threaten military action to attain their goals when they deployed Republican Guard forces to southern Iraq, thereby threatening Kuwait and its oil fields. With reconstructed conventional forces and NBC weapons and missile capabilities, Iraq could again threaten states in the region, oil fields and facilities, U.S. forces, and key logistics facilities. . . .

The Former Soviet Union:
Russia, Ukraine, Kazakstan, and Belarus

Goals and Interests

The fundamental interests of the United States regarding Russia and the independent states of the former Soviet Union, as articulated by President Clinton, are to reduce the nuclear threat, to support the development of these states as stable democracies, and to assist them to establish market economies.

Within these broad foreign policy goals, the United States has five primary national security interests in this region: implementing START I and II and all other arms control agreements, and safeguarding the enormous nuclear arsenal that is the legacy of the Cold War; deterring the use of nuclear weapons should a strategic reversal occur in the former Soviet Union and a regime emerge which is hostile to U.S. interests; preventing the proliferation of NBC weapons; maintaining regional stability in and among the nations of the former Warsaw Pact; and avoiding reestablishing an antagonistic global rivalry with Russia.

The Proliferation Challenge: Capabilities, Intentions, and Trends

From the former Soviet Union, Russia has inherited the largest stockpile of NBC weapons and delivery systems in the world. Although additional strategic weapons are still deployed in the new independent states of Ukraine and Belarus, these weapons are under Russian control. Russia's public statements and actions regarding the safety, security, and dismantlement of this massive inventory and commitment to cease all offensive BW [biological weapons] activities have been positive, although Moscow still needs to fully implement these commitments, and its adherence to some proliferation control norms has been uneven.

The magnitude of the numbers, the complexity of weapons systems to be moved, dismantled, or destroyed, and the vast distances involved have been and will continue to be daunting challenges to Russia and to U.S. interests for several years to come. In the face of serious economic and political challenges, most of Moscow's actions regarding its strategic programs—and the actions of Ukraine, Kazakstan, and Belarus—demonstrate a commitment to denuclearization and nonproliferation. Nonetheless, the United States continues to have concerns about Russian biological and chemical warfare programs, including about information provided by Russia regarding those programs.

Russia, Ukraine, Kazakstan, and Belarus have stated publicly that they consider proliferation to be a potential threat to their own security. Although compliance with the various nonproliferation norms varies, turbulent political, social, and economic conditions continue to complicate their nonproliferation efforts. Additionally, scientists and technicians may be enticed to emigrate by money from abroad, and could provide critical knowledge to develop such weapons to nations with emerging NBC weapons programs. Furthermore, crime and corruption are significant threats to the security of nuclear materials. The December 1994 Czech seizure of highly enriched uranium (HEU) is one of several cases involving smuggled nuclear material that serves as a stark example of the need to safeguard these materials. These and other factors could have an adverse effect on Western efforts to prevent proliferation.

As a result of the break-up of the Soviet Union, Russia assumed control over thousands of strategic weapons. Russia is a party to the START I Treaty and has signed the START II Treaty that will reduce significantly the size of its strategic forces. It is also removing nuclear weapons and delivery systems from Ukraine, Kazakstan, and Belarus, primarily for dismantlement.

In his February 1994 State of the Union Address, Russian President Boris Yeltsin described one of two priorities for Russia's national security as: "strengthening the arrangements governing the nonproliferation of mass destruction weapons and sophisticated technologies, and enhancing control over the international arms trade while watching over Russia's commercial interest in this sphere." Russia has continued to implement effective export controls on missile-related items, and in August 1995, Russia joined the MTCR.

Ukraine agreed in January 1994 to return the strategic nuclear warheads located on its territory to Russia for dismantlement in exchange for security assurances, compensation for the nuclear material in the warheads and expanded Western assistance. Ukraine has acted on its commitment by returning strategic nuclear weapons to Russia. In accompanying letters to the Lisbon Protocol, the former Republics of Ukraine, Kazakstan, and Belarus agreed to eliminate from their territory all former Soviet nuclear arms. In addition, Ukraine acceded to the NPT as a non-nuclear weapons state on December 5, 1994. This action fulfilled a Russian precondition for implementing START I, which entered into force on December 5, 1994. In May 1994, Ukraine signed a Memorandum of Understanding with the United States, committing itself to adhere to MTCR Guidelines.

Kazakstan also faces major challenges, but has demonstrated its commitment to denuclearization and nonproliferation in several important ways. It ratified START I and the Lisbon Protocol in 1992 and acceded to the NPT as a non-nuclear weapons state in 1993. Also, Kazakstan informed the United States about a vulnerable cache of approximately 600 kg of HEU and cooperated with a joint Department of Defense/Department of Energy team in removing the cache from Kazakstani soil for safe and secure storage in the United States.

Kazakstan had returned to Russia all the strategic nuclear warheads on its territory by April 1995. Kazakstan does not possess, nor can it afford to acquire, the infrastructure needed to maintain and operate a nuclear force.

Kazakstan inherited a small amount of the Soviet Union's defense industrial facilities. The outlook for Kazakstan's defense industry remains bleak. There is limited demand for weapons internally; few of the military systems are exportable; and most importantly, Russian orders have been drastically reduced. However, Russia and Kazakstan will retain close military ties through a series of military cooperation agreements, encompassing Moscow's 20-year lease of the Baikonur Cosmodrome (Tyuratam Space Missile Test Center), and various military test ranges.

Belarus is also committed to denuclearization. In February 1993, its parliament ratified the START Treaty and the Lisbon Protocol, and acceded to the NPT as a non-nuclear weapons state, thereby codifying Belarus' intent to become nuclear-free. Also, Belarus and Russia have agreed that the withdrawal—already underway—of nuclear weapons and support equipment located in Belarus will be completed by the end of 1996. Further, in an effort to provide evidence of its commitment to nonproliferation, Minsk is cooperating with the United States on improving the Belarus export control system. . . .

South Asia

Goals and Interests

The United States has important security interests in South Asia, including preventing another Indo-Pakistani war and enhancing regional stability. Our nonproliferation goal is to persuade India and Pakistan to first cap, then reduce, and eventually eliminate their capabilities to produce nuclear weapons and ballistic missiles. This approach supports our global objective to reduce and ultimately eliminate nuclear weapons. The consequences of a nuclear war between India and Pakistan would be catastrophic, both in terms of the loss of life and for potentially lowering the threshold for nuclear use in other parts of the world, particularly the adjacent Middle East/North Africa region.

Deployment of ballistic missiles would pose especially troubling security risks given the relatively short distances between major population centers in South Asia and the brief time required for missiles to travel such distances. This factor will compress decisionmaking cycles for national leaders and battlefield commanders, reducing stability during times of crisis.

In addition to the immediate risks to regional security, the development of NBC weapons in South Asia has the potential to undercut broader U.S. and international nonproliferation objectives. Both India and Pakistan, for different reasons, have refused to sign the NPT. Their nuclear programs, outside of this widely accepted international norm, serve as dangerous examples for nations in other regions.

The NBC weapons and missile infrastructures in South Asia also pose potential proliferation threats, as possible sources of supply. India and Pakistan's slowness to adopt export controls consistent with established international control regimes is reason for concern. As each nation continues its programs, the danger of transferring technology to states outside the region remains possible.

The Proliferation Challenge: Regional Capabilities, Intentions, and Trends

India and Pakistan

The bitter rivalry between India and Pakistan, which dates to the partitioning of the subcontinent in 1947, remains the impetus behind the proliferation of NBC weapons and missiles in the region. The security dynamics of the region are complicated further by India's perception of China as a threat. Pakistan's efforts to develop NBC weapons and missile systems are intended primarily to counter India's substantial conventional military advantage and its perception of India's nuclear threat.

India and Pakistan continue to cloak their NBC weapons programs in secrecy or deliberate ambiguity. Both continue to deny possessing nuclear weapons, while periodically issuing veiled threats alluding to their capability to employ these weapons if necessary. India and Pakistan deny possessing chemical and biological weapons, but point with pride to the progress of their indigenous missile development programs.

India's pursuit of nuclear weapons was first spurred by a 1962 border clash with China and by Beijing's 1964 nuclear test. New Delhi continues to view its northern neighbor as a long-term threat despite recently improved relations. It sees Pakistan's NBC weapons and missile capabilities as a more immediate threat. Nuclear rhetoric from Pakistani leaders and Islamabad's pursuit of a mobile SRBM [short range ballistic missile] capability reinforce India's perception that New Delhi continues to need a nuclear capability.

Pakistani leaders believe that a nuclear capability is essential to deter war with India, or failing that, to ensure the survival of the nation. Its nuclear program has widespread political and popular support. Missile procurement and development, initially to counter the Indian missile program which began in the mid-1980s, are driven by a desire to augment limited offensive air capabilities against India (which holds almost a 3:1 advantage in combat aircraft) and to field a more effective delivery system. . . .

The Transnational Threat: Dangers from Terrorism, Insurgencies, Civil Wars, and Organized Crime

Transnational groups of proliferation concern include terrorists, insurgents, opposing factions in civil wars, and members of organized criminal groups. Such groups are not generally bound by the same constraints and mores or motivated by the same factors as are nation-states, but pose significant threats to the interests of the United States and our allies and friends worldwide. Terrorist acts pose an especially potent threat to U.S. interests. When carried out by small, close-knit groups, these attacks are difficult to detect in advance, despite diligent intelligence efforts.

This category of proliferation threat is truly a global problem, cutting across all regions. The threat has been starkly demonstrated by the 1995 nerve gas attack in Japan, the bombing of the New York World Trade Center, and the increased involvement of criminal groups in the smuggling of nuclear materials. Furthermore, with numerous ongoing insurgencies and civil wars worldwide, there are additional dangers for escalation should NBC weapons or missiles be introduced to the conflict. Finally, there is an increased potential for leakage of NBC weapons or missile technology, or individuals with technological know-how. Such leakage would most likely occur between states that have reduced or dismantled their programs and states with programs under development.

Terrorist Groups

Terrorist groups that acquire NBC weapons and stridently oppose U.S. policies could pose significant potential dangers to U.S. interests. Terrorists armed with these weapons can gain leverage for their demands because of the weapons' nature.

Terrorists might wish to obtain NBC weapons for a variety of motives. Such groups might threaten using NBC weapons as "saber rattlers" to raise the ante in response to Western political or military actions or to achieve a specific objective, but would risk losing its base of support.

Most terrorist groups do not have the financial and technical resources necessary to acquire nuclear weapons, but could gather materials to make radiological dispersion devices and some biological and chemical agents. Some groups have state sponsors that possess or can obtain NBC weapons. Nations such as Iran and Libya have backed numerous groups over the years, but no sponsor has yet demonstrated a willingness to provide such groups with NBC weapons, perhaps a testament to the looming and certain threat of retaliation should the state be identified as the supplier.

Terrorist acts involving NBC weapons represent a particularly dangerous threat that must be countered. The ability of terrorists to take the initiative in the choice of targets and timing of attacks significantly complicates our ability to combat this threat. U.S. policy in countering terrorism is four-fold: make no concessions to terrorists, use political and economic instruments to pressure states that sponsor terrorism, exploit fully all available legal mechanisms to punish international terrorists, and help other governments improve their capabilities to combat terrorism.

Insurgents and Civil War Factions

Insurgent groups and separatist movements, should they acquire NBC weapons or missiles, pose another potential threat to U.S. interests. Presently, there are dozens of insurgencies ongoing throughout the world. Insurgent groups aim to overthrow existing governments, thus destabilizing regional balances of power. In some cases, such groups have kidnapped U.S. citizens or conducted economic retaliation against U.S. commercial interests abroad. For the most part, these groups operate with unsophisticated weapons, receive little financial backing, and lack an industrial base to develop or produce NBC weapons or missiles.

The primary proliferation concern about insurgent groups is that they might capture such weapons, acquire them from sympathizers in the government's forces, or purchase them, possibly from organized criminal groups. Insurgents might also attract sympathizers among knowledgeable scientists and technicians who might aid in developing weapons. Acquisition of such weapons could alter the regional balance of power and change the terms of conflict, if not its outcome, decisively.

Opposing factions in civil wars also could have access to NBC weapons and missiles. Such factions might be motivated to use these weapons as force multipliers to achieve quick and decisive victories. Factions could threaten or actually use the weapons against civilians for psychological and strategic effect. Tactically, the weapons might be used against a larger conventional force to disrupt staging or resupply efforts, thus prompting an evacuation of noncombatants.

Recently, opposing factions in two civil wars acquired and employed ballistic missiles with conventional warheads. After the Soviets withdrew from Afghanistan, Afghan rebel factions acquired a number of SCUD missiles, some of which the rebel groups fired at government forces in Kabul in January 1994. The second instance involved the Yemen civil war. During the spring of 1994, the southern faction launched SCUD missiles against civilians in the northern cities of Sana and Tai'z. None of the strikes in these two cases caused significant damage or casualties or affected the fighting significantly.

Organized Criminal Groups

The potential for international organized criminal groups to obtain, use, or sell NBC weapons has grown in the last few years. In the wake of the Cold War, some of these groups have emerged as a growing threat to U.S. interests. This situation is particularly critical in the former Soviet Union.

A careful distinction must be made, however, between material the criminal groups claim to offer for sale and what they can deliver. For example, numerous criminal elements throughout Europe have been implicated in scams involving the sale of what was advertised as weapons grade nuclear materials. To date, those materials seized by law enforcement officials have been well below enrichment or quantity levels suitable for weapons. Most appear to have come from research facilities rather than from weapons-related facilities.

Over the past several years, organized criminal groups and smugglers have become increasingly involved in trafficking illegal nuclear materials. The growing number and sophistication of groups attempting to acquire these materials or weapons is an increasingly crucial concern for international law enforcement.

Beginning in 1991, multiple incidents involving criminal activity and the theft of nuclear material surfaced in Europe. During a 1994 appearance before the Permanent Subcommittee on Investigations, the head of the German Federal Criminal Police (the Federal Bureau of Investigation's German counterpart) offered his insight into criminal trafficking of nuclear material. He reported that the number of incidents involving nuclear materials within Germany was increasing over time: from 41 in 1991, to 158 in 1992, to 241 in 1993, and to 267 in 1994. In late 1994, responding to the incidents involving nuclear material smuggled into Germany in August 1994, Moscow and Bonn agreed to new bilateral security measures.

Implications for Regional Security

Controlling or containing proliferation involving transnational groups is particularly difficult because these groups evade or defy recognized export controls or nonproliferation regimes. Should these groups acquire NBC weapons or missiles, they may be more inclined to employ them in order to achieve their goals than would a member in good standing of the international community of nations. Countering the transfer of these weapons and related technologies to or from these groups has become increasingly difficult. Furthermore, the sophistication of some of the groups—especially organized crime—involved in the smuggling of NBC-related materials has complicated the related problems of locating stolen materials and disabling weapons. In some cases, the difficulty is further complicated by the dual-use nature and availability of the raw materials associated with biological or chemical agents.

Of the transnational groups discussed above, the greatest dangers to U.S. interests stem from terrorists and, to a lesser extent, organized criminal groups. One of the most volatile and frightening scenarios for U.S. defense planning posits a terrorist group, whose actions are directed principally against the United States, with nuclear material or an actual NBC weapon. Though direct U.S. interests are always exposed to some risks, it is unlikely that attacks from insurgents or opposing sides in a civil war that involved such weapons would focus their main attacks on U.S. interests specifically.

Department of Defense Response

Introduction

The proliferation of weapons of mass destruction provokes regional instability and challenges to the interests of the United States. The United States is an international leader in developing and sustaining global norms against the proliferation of these weapons and missiles. The United States is actively engaged in dialogues with several states in regions around the world to persuade them not to acquire these capabilities or to eliminate capabilities they might have already developed. The United States also is working with states to combat proliferation by assisting them in gaining and assuring greater control over their dual-use equipment and technology. States that gain weapons of mass destruction are able to pose a significant military threat to the interests of the United States, our allies, and friends. The Department of Defense actively contributes to overall U.S. efforts to stem proliferation wherever it occurs and from whatever source, including through active and passive defenses, and maintaining the credibility of our security commitments against military threats, including from adversaries armed with nuclear, biological, or chemical weapons and the missiles to carry them. This section outlines the steps the Department is taking to respond to the challenge of proliferation, and DoD measures to respond to the military threats states pose with their NBC weapons, in support of overall U.S. government efforts to respond to this challenge.

Informed by lessons learned (and some unpleasant surprises) from the Gulf War against Iraq and by the systematic Bottom-Up Review that identified post-Cold War military requirements, DoD has developed the Defense Counterproliferation Initiative. As part of this initiative, the Secretary of Defense has directed that the Joint Chiefs of Staff (JCS), the operational Commanders in Chief (CINCs) responsible for the planning and conduct of military operations, and the military departments and their uniformed services give greater emphasis to counterproliferation requirements and considerations.

Specific objectives of the Defense Counterproliferation Initiative are to: (1) prevent the acquisition of NBC weapons and their delivery systems, (2) roll back proliferation where it has occurred, (3) deter the use of NBC weapons and their delivery systems, and (4) adapt U.S. military forces and planning to respond to regional contingencies in which U.S., allied, and coalition forces face NBC threats. The ordering of objectives is deliberate. In line with national policy, proliferation prevention is the top priority.

To achieve these objectives, the Department of Defense has requested $165.2 million in FY 1996 for counterproliferation. This effort would fund specific high priority acquisition activities to provide required military capabilities. DoD will also use these funds to modify and adapt other programs (totaling $3.8 billion) that are strongly related to the counterproliferation mission.

The Defense Department plays a role in support of all facets of national counterproliferation policy. This overview begins with proliferation protection, for which DoD has unique responsibilities, and then reviews contributions to proliferation prevention.

Protection

Overview

One of the core objectives in proliferation protection policy is to convince potential and actual proliferants that NBC weapons will be of no value because the United States and its coalition partners will have the capability to deny or limit the political and military utility of NBC weapons, and because the damage inflicted by U.S. and coalition forces in response will far outweigh any potential benefits of use.

There is no simple solution or single response to the threat posed by the proliferation of NBC weapons and their delivery systems. As is essential with all new initiatives, the right balance has to be struck between thorough, step-by-step planning and early action to remedy long identified shortfalls. A comprehensive review of the military missions and functions related to counterproliferation has been completed to ensure that all aspects of the issue are assessed. DoD assessments have been coordinated with congressionally mandated national reviews. Several acquisition programs already in the pipeline have been augmented to remedy identified shortfalls. Proliferation protection measures can be grouped into five areas of emphasis: policy, military planning and operations, acquisition, intelligence, and international cooperation initiatives. While much work is yet to be done to acquire the required capabilities, there have been significant achievements to date.

Policy

President Clinton's September 1993 policy statement to the United Nations General Assembly established the groundwork for building a new consensus within the United States and with our friends and allies abroad concerning counterproliferation objectives.

Early in his Administration, President Clinton issued guidance defining national nonproliferation policy objectives. Responding to this guidance, the

Secretary of Defense issued DoD implementation instructions. Counterproliferation objectives and capabilities are now routinely addressed in the Department's planning and programming processes, with prominent emphasis in the Defense Planning Guidance. Military planning, training, and exercises now give much more emphasis to proliferation when potential major regional contingencies are addressed.

The underlying objective of the Defense Counterproliferation Initiative is to make counterproliferation one of the matters that is routinely given consideration within the Department's activities. Counterproliferation is not of a unique nature requiring a stand-alone organizational structure. Rather, counterproliferation considerations have ramifications for virtually every aspect of the defense mission in this new security era and, therefore, should be embedded in the day-to-day operations. [Defense] Secretary [William] Perry has directed the establishment of a DoD Directive to fully reinforce implementation of counterproliferation policy. The Assistant Secretary of Defense for International Security Policy has been assigned responsibility for the development and implementation of DoD's counterproliferation policy.

Proliferation protection is based on the enhancement and utilization of existing resources. Proliferation protection requires a broad range of capabilities, including effective strategic and tactical intelligence; battlefield surveillance; counterforce; active defense; passive defense; and response to paramilitary, covert, and terrorist threats. . . .

Prevention

Overview

Proliferation prevention is the United States' primary objective. DoD contributions to proliferation prevention are part of a coordinated national effort involving multiple departments and agencies, allied states, and international organizations. Defense Department support includes the Nunn-Lugar Cooperative Threat Reduction (CTR) program, export control activities and DoD inspection, verification, and enforcement support for the treaties and arms control regimes that limit NBC weapons and associated delivery systems. The Defense Department also plays an important role in the four thrusts involved in proliferation prevention—denial, reassurance, dissuasion, and actions to reverse proliferation.

International norms and standards make an important contribution to proliferation prevention. In addition to creating an atmosphere of restraint, they may provide the preconditions, e.g., inspections, that impede proliferation. These international norms can be specifically agreed to in export control and arms control agreements or they can result from informal arrangements between states.

A great success in the area of norm establishment has been DoD support for the unconditional and indefinite extension of the Non-Proliferation Treaty (NPT). The NPT, which became effective in 1970, establishes obligations for both nuclear weapons and non-nuclear weapons states regarding the transfer, manufacture, or acquisition of nuclear weapons or other nuclear explosive devices. It allows all parties to participate in the fullest possible exchange of equipment, materials, and scientific and technological information for the peaceful uses of nuclear energy while at the same time prohibiting transfer and acquisition of nuclear weapon capabilities.

Cooperative Threat Reduction Program

The CTR program provides the services, tools, and technology required to help the New Independent States (NIS) with the elimination or reduction of weapons of mass destruction and to modernize and expand safeguards against proliferation within the NIS. The program consists currently of nearly 40 separate projects, grouped into three categories, reflecting the objectives established by Congress.

First, Destruction and Dismantlement activities help with the dismantlement and elimination of weapons of mass destruction and their launchers in the four eligible states where they remain (Russia, Belarus, Kazakstan, and Ukraine). The availability of U.S. assistance encourages these countries to undertake the dismantling of weapons, and then the CTR program provides the actual equipment, services, and training required to implement their dismantlement decisions. Specifically, CTR Dismantlement and Destruction activities are:

> Assisting Ukraine, Belarus, and Kazakstan in becoming non-nuclear weapons states.
> Assisting Russia in accelerating strategic arms reduction to START levels.
> Initiating and accelerating the destruction of Russian chemical weapons.

Projects in this area assist in the dismantlement or destruction of strategic nuclear missiles, silo launchers, liquid and solid rocket propellants, and Russian chemical weapons. Also included is assistance in the destruction of the launcher tubes in ballistic missile-firing submarines, the elimination of heavy bombers, and the elimination or conversion of the infrastructure (hardware and personnel) that supports these systems.

Second, through chain of custody activities, the CTR program decreases the dangers from the nuclear weapons and fissile materials that remain in the NIS, particularly Russia. During the difficult and uncertain period of transition in these states, the continued secure chain of custody of nuclear weapons and materials is vitally important to both the United States and the NIS. Chain of Custody activities enhance security, safety, and control of nuclear weapons and fissile material in Russia by assisting in centralizing fissile material in a limited number of storage areas and strengthening safety, security, and control during movement and interim storage. Projects provide assistance to enhance effective controls over nuclear weapons and the fissile materials removed from them throughout the drawdown and dismantlement of these weapons. This includes providing safe and secure transportation of nuclear weapons from operational sites and storage areas to dismantlement facilities; improved security and accountability for weapons in transit; safer and more secure storage and transport of fissile material removed from nuclear weapons by providing storage containers; and designing, equipping, and assisting in construction of centralized fissile material storage facilities.

Finally, CTR supports Demilitarization efforts. CTR Demilitarization activities are encouraging the demilitarization of Ukraine, Belarus, Kazakstan, and Russia by supporting conversion of NIS defense enterprises, expanding defense military contacts, and reemploying weapons scientists. These activities are decreasing the long-term threat by reducing the capacity and economic pressures in the NIS to continue to produce weapons of mass destruction.

CTR supported defense conversion industrial partnerships help to reduce the potential of a future nuclear threat at its source, as do international science and technology centers the United States and other countries have set up in Moscow and Kiev. Through these centers, former Soviet nuclear scientists and engineers are being reemployed in peaceful, civilian endeavors. These projects reduce the supply of weapons of mass destruction available for foreign sale, the incentives for relying on such sales for income, and provide job alternatives for weapons scientists who might otherwise be tempted to sell their nuclear expertise abroad. The defense conversion investments under CTR are win-win-win—they help reduce the threats from weapons of mass destruction; they help the NIS build peaceful, commercially viable market economies while reducing excess military capacity; and they provide opportunities for U.S. industry's entry into potentially large markets for civilian goods and services.

CTR Accomplishments

CTR has gone far to reduce the threat of proliferation within and outside the former Soviet Union in the three short years of its existence, and the bulk of the achievements have been in just the past year. The program has facilitated the return to Russia of over 1,700 warheads from Belarus, Kazakstan, and Ukraine; the removal to secure storage of over 2,800 warheads from missile and bomber bases; the deactivation of four regiments of SS-19 ICBMs in Ukraine; the removal of 750 missiles from their launchers; and the elimination of approximately 630 strategic launchers and 91 bombers throughout the NIS. CTR assistance also helped prompt Ukraine to begin early deactivation and shipment to Russia of SS-19 and SS-24 warheads and to accede to the Nuclear Non-Proliferation Treaty as a non-nuclear weapons state, thereby allowing the Start I treaty to enter into force—a key nonproliferation success.

CTR has contributed to other efforts to prevent proliferation. Over 5,000 former Soviet weapon scientists and engineers once engaged in nuclear weapons research are now or soon will be employed on peaceful, civilian research projects, thus reducing the threat of the transfer of their deadly expertise to potential proliferant states. The Project Sapphire mission in November 1994 to remove 600 kilograms of highly enriched uranium to the United States from Kazakstan was partially financed with CTR funds. . . .

CLINTON ON
ANTITERRORISM BILL
April 24, 1996

On April 18, one day before the first anniversary of the deadly bombing of the federal building in Oklahoma City, Congress sent. President Bill Clinton a bill (S 735—PL 104–132) giving the federal government new powers to fight domestic and international terrorism. Clinton signed the measure into law on April 24.

Although fighting terrorism might be seen as a politically popular thing to do, especially as an election approached, Congress had delayed action on the bill for months. Conservative Republicans in the House had opposed some of Clinton's appeals for greater authority for federal law enforcement officials. Liberals and civil libertarians were distressed by provisions restricting federal appeals by death row inmates and making it easier for the government to turn away aliens who claimed to be fleeing persecution.

Congress passed a second series of antiterrorism measures in September, following three incidents: the June 25 bombing of an apartment building in Dhahran, Saudi Arabia, killing nineteen U.S. service members; the July 17 unexplained crash off Long Island, N.Y., of TWA flight 800; and the July 27 bombing of Centennial Olympic Park in Atlanta during the summer Olympic games. (Saudi bombing, p. 672; Olympic Park bombing, p. 445)

Antiterrorism Law Enforcement Powers

The bill finally passed by Congress in April 1996 was a direct outgrowth of the April 19, 1995, bombing of the Alfred P. Murrah Federal Building in Oklahoma City. The truck bomb explosion killed 168 people, several of them children attending a daycare center in the building. (Oklahoma City bombing, Historic Documents of 1995, p. 176)

Shortly after the Oklahoma bombing, Clinton asked Congress for legislation giving federal law enforcement agencies new authority to combat both domestic and foreign terrorism. The Senate acted quickly, passing an antiterrorism bill (S 735) on June 7, 1995, by a vote of 91–8. But conser-

vative Republicans—many fearful of alleged misuse of powers by the FBI and other federal law enforcement agencies—prevented House leaders from taking the bill to the floor in 1995.

The House finally acted in March 1996, but only after Republicans succeeded in stripping from the bill many of the new investigative powers sought by Clinton and approved by the Senate. On a key vote in the House, a majority of Republicans were joined by some Democrats in deleting provisions that would have allowed the administration to bar fund raising in the United States by terrorist groups and that would have allowed authorities to use illegally obtained wiretap evidence in terrorism cases if they could demonstrate a "good faith" belief that the surveillance had been legal.

At the same time, House Republicans demanded inclusion of provisions not sought by the administration, including restrictions on repeated appeals by inmates facing death sentences. The House included these provisions as one way of getting action on controversial anticrime provisions in the Republican Contract with America. (Contract with America, Historic Documents of 1994, p. 374)

On April 13 Clinton sought to step up the pressure on Congress to finish work on the bill. In his weekly radio address, the president noted that congressional leaders had promised to send him an antiterrorism bill within six weeks of the Oklahoma City bombing but had failed to do so. "There is simply no excuse for this foot-dragging. This bill should have been law a long time ago," he said.

Clinton's prodding, coupled with the rapidly approaching anniversary of the bombing, finally forced Congress to act. House and Senate negotiators reached final agreement on the bill on April 15, and both chambers adopted the conference report by April 18—one day before the bombing anniversary.

The bill gave the president some of the expanded law enforcement powers he had requested. For example, it made participation in international terrorism activity within the United States a federal crime; it required the marking of plastic explosives with special "taggants" for easier detection by law enforcement authorities; and it allowed the government to deny visas to foreigners who belong to groups designated as engaged in or supporting terrorism.

To gain the votes of House conservatives, conferees had excluded several provisions they opposed, particularly those giving federal law enforcement officials expanded powers to wiretap the telephone calls of suspected terrorists. One major provision dropped for this reason would have allowed "roving wiretaps"—electronic surveillance of all the telephones used by a terrorism suspect.

The National Rifle Association and other elements of the gun lobby succeeded in narrowing the president's proposal to require manufacturers of explosives to include taggants to make the substance easier to trace. The final bill required these tracing elements only in plastic explosives. The Treasury Department was required to conduct a feasibility study of plac-

ing tracing elements in other forms of explosives, such as the fertilizer-based bomb used to demolish the Oklahoma City federal building. Treasury could mandate additional taggants if warranted by the study, but Congress would have ninety days to overturn that action.

Republicans in both chambers also succeeded in including in the bill controversial provisions limiting appeals by inmates on death row. This had been an important agenda item of conservatives for many years. As enacted, the bill set time limits for state prisoners to file appeals in the federal courts after they had exhausted their state appeals. The time limit for prisoners sentenced to death was six months, assuming that the state had provided a competent attorney. Federal courts would face deadlines for acting on these appeals.

Civil liberties organizations objected to the limits on appeals but had little political influence in the Republican-led Congress. These groups also opposed a procedure included in the bill called "summary exclusion," which made it easier for the government to deport foreigners who arrive without proper documentation and claim to be fleeing persecution.

Clinton signed the bill into law in a ceremony on the South Lawn of the White House on April 24. The ceremony was attended by leading members of Congress who had worked on the bill and by family members of some of those killed in the Oklahoma City bombing.

Antiterrorism Funding

The bombing of Olympic Park in Atlanta and the crash of TWA flight 800, both in July, offered yet another opportunity for the president and Congress to demonstrate an interest in combating terrorism. Clinton sent Congress another bill containing some of the provisions Congress had cut from the April antiterrorism legislation, such as authority for roving wiretaps of telephone calls by suspected terrorists. The House passed a version of a new bill in August, after deleting most of the president's proposals, but the Senate never acted on it.

Congress included $1.1 billion in new antiterrorism funding provisions in a catchall appropriations bill for fiscal year 1997 (HR 3610—PL 104–208), sent to the president on September 30. The biggest portion, $353.3 million, went to the Pentagon to study—and if necessary secure or move—overseas military installations and to improve overseas intelligence gathering techniques. These provisions were an outgrowth of the bombing in Saudi Arabia.

The bill also included funding to improve safety at U.S. diplomatic missions and to hire more FBI agents specializing in counterterrorism. The Department of Transportation also received $236 million for new equipment to detect bombs at airports.

Following are excerpts from the statement by President Bill Clinton upon signing an antiterrorism bill (S 735—PL 104–132) at the White House on April 24, 1996:

To Senator [Bob] Dole and Chairman [Orrin] Hatch and Chairman [Henry] Hyde, the other members of Congress who are here; Governor [Frank] Keating and the Attorneys General who are here and the others in law enforcement; to the members of the administration, and especially to the victims' families who are here.

I thank the families for coming today. I thank their advocates for coming. But I think we should all acknowledge that the importance of this event is embodied in no small measure by the fact that the families were willing to come here, knowing that it would in some measure force them to relive the pain that they have endured because of acts of terror. It took a lot of courage for them to endure that pain. So while this is a good day for America, we can't really say it is a happy day. Not all good days can be happy days, but every American is in debt to these families for standing up for the need for the changes that we have experienced. And I ask the rest of us to acknowledge that. And we thank you. [Applause.]

I also would point out that Presidents can advocate and the Executive Branch can enforce the laws, but this would not have happened but for the remarkable convergence of Republicans and Democrats in the Congress. The Vice President introduced those who were especially active in the leadership who are over here to my left who will come up in a moment when we sign the bill. But there are so many more members of Congress here, for the benefit of all of you, I would like to ask every member who is here and who worked so hard on this legislation to please stand and be recognized. Would the members of Congress please stand? [Applause.] Thank you very much.

This is a good day because our police officers are now going to be better prepared to stop terrorists, our prosecutors better prepared to punish them, our people being better protected from their designs. This legislation is more important today because of the very forces which have unlocked so much potential for progress—the new technologies, the instant communications, the open borders. These things have done so much good. But they have also made it easier for the organized forces of hatred and division to endanger the lives of innocent people. We have seen terrorism take its horrible toll all around the world, from Tokyo to London to Jerusalem, and, of course, in our own country.

When a terrorist car bomb took the lives of 241 American Marines in Beirut, we felt the shock waves here at home. When savage killers took the life of Leon Klinghoffer, countless Americans wept for him and for his family. When Pan Am 103 went down over Lockerbie, Scotland, killing 270 people including 189 Americans, we saw again that there are no borders or bounds on the forces of hatred. When the bomb exploded at the World Trade Center, as Mary Jo said, by the grace of God killing only six but injuring over 1000 people, we knew again that we had no place to hide. And, of course, five days ago we marked the first anniversary of the most terrible terrorist attack upon these shores in our history, reminding us that even the very young and the most innocent are not immune.

We also have to remember as we remember those who were lost that as painful as that loss is, their deaths and their destructions are not the terrorists' only goals, for each and every act of terrorism is also a means to another end. The unbelievable idea that it is all right to kill an innocent person to achieve a political goal, to stop us from living our lives in the light of liberty, to force us to cower in the dark grip of fear, to terrify us as targets into submission.

So let us honor those who lost their lives by resolving to hold fast against the forces of violence and division, by never allowing them to shake our resolve or break our spirit, to frighten us into sacrificing our sacred freedoms or surrendering a drop of precious American liberty. Rather we must guard against them, speak against them, and fight against them.

Fighting terrorism is and will for a long time to come be one of the top security priorities of the United States. On our own and with our allies, we have implemented strong sanctions against states that harbor terrorists and encourage them. We have intensified partnerships with other countries to stand together against terrorists around the world. We have increased our investment, our personnel, and our training for law enforcement efforts here at home.

I sent Congress antiterrorism legislation over a year ago, and after the Oklahoma City bombing I asked for additional measures. I applaud the great majority of Congress who stood up for the safety of the American people, worked through the policy debates, and made sure that in the end politics faltered and common sense prevailed. Democrats and Republicans, Republicans and Democrats, people who love their country as patriots came together, worked together, and got the job done.

The antiterrorism bill is grounded in common sense and steeled with force. Because of this bill, law enforcement will be better prepared than ever to stop terrorists before they strike and to bring them to justice when they do. From now on we can quickly expel foreigners who dare to come to America and support terrorist activities. From now on American prosecutors can wield new tools and expanded penalties against those who terrorize Americans at home or abroad. From now on we can stop terrorists from raising money in the United States to pay for their horrible crimes.

From now on criminals sentenced to death for their vicious crimes will no longer be able to use endless appeals to delay their sentences, and families of victims will no longer have to endure years of anguish and suffering.

We have new laws and better controls against chemical and biological weapons. We have agreed to put chemical markers in plastic explosives that will help us to detect explosives like those used to bring down Pan Am 103. We will be able to require chemical taggants in some other explosive materials as well. They will make it easier for police to trace bombs to the criminals who made them and bring those criminals to justice.

This legislation is a strong step forward for our security, but we mustn't stop there. I am directing the Secretary of the Treasury to complete the study of taggants required by Congress and propose appropriate regulations as quickly as possible. We must also address the problem of black and smokeless powders routinely used to make illegal smokeless devices like pipe bombs. I'm directing [Treasury] Secretary [Robert] Rubin to consult with industry representatives and the law enforcement community to report back with appropriate recommendations.

Finally, I believe we have to take additional steps. I believe we must do more to help police keep terrorists who are suspected terrorists under surveillance. I believe we should give law enforcement more time to investigate and prosecute terrorists who use machine guns, sawed-off shotguns and explosive devices. I agree with police officers that instead of creating a commission to study them, in the end we must ban cop-killer bullets.

Nonetheless, make no mistake about it: This bill strikes a mighty blow against terrorism, and it is fitting that this bill becomes law during National Crime Victims Rights Week, because it stands up for victims in so many important ways. There are a lot of victims' advocates and victims here, and I thank them for their presence today. This bill recognizes that victims have a compelling interest in the trials of those accused of committing crimes against them and requires closed-circuit television coverage when federal trials are moved far away, a provision we owe to the vigilance of the members of Congress from Oklahoma. And we thank you for it. [Applause.]

I'd like to close with a word to all of the family members of Americans slain by terrorists, and to the survivors of terrorism, to the children who lost their parents in Pan Am 103 and parents who lost their children in Israel, to all of you from Oklahoma City, to Andrew Kerr on my staff of the National Security Council whose father was murdered in Beirut, to each and every one of you with us today and those who are watching all across this great land of ours. Your endurance and your courage is a lesson to us all. Your vigilance has sharpened our vigilance.

And so I sign my name to this bill in your names. We renew our fight against those who seek to terrorize us in your names. We send a loud, clear message today all over the world in your names. America will never surrender to terror. America will never tolerate terrorism. America will never abide terrorists. Wherever they come from, wherever they go, we will go after them. We will not rest until we have brought them all to justice, and secured a future for our people, safe from the harm they would do—in your names.

Thank you. God bless you. And God bless America.

GAO TESTIMONY ON
THE FAA AND AIRLINE SAFETY
April 30, 1996

Two American commercial passenger planes crashed in 1996, at least momentarily unnerving the flying public and renewing questions about the capacity of the Federal Aviation Administration (FAA) to ensure the safety and security of American airlines and airports. A ValuJet DC-9 crashed May 11 in the Florida Everglades, killing all 110 passengers. The cause of the crash was traced to improperly packaged oxygen generators carried in the plane's cargo hold. TWA Flight 800 carrying 230 people from New York to Paris exploded in midair on July 17 just minutes after takeoff, killing all on board. Officials had not determined by the end of the year whether the explosion was caused by a bomb or by mechanical failure that triggered an explosion in one of the plane's fuel tanks. (Airline security, p. 662)

The FAA Under Scrutiny

The ValuJet crash raised nearly as many questions about the federal government's chief airline safety inspection agency as it did about the airline's safety. The FAA is charged with regulating the safety of all commercial and general aviation aircraft, aircraft repair facilities, schools for pilot training and maintenance, and pilots, as well as with promoting the airline industry. Immediately after the crash, FAA administrator David R. Hinson assured the public that ValuJet was safe, despite several accidents and incidents during the past two years involving ValuJet planes.

Several FAA inspectors, however, apparently thought otherwise. They had urged their superiors in February to ask the discount airline to address immediately "known safety-related issues." According to Newsweek *magazine, a draft report citing major safety problems with the airline—the result of a special investigation initiated in February—was in FAA hands on May 12, when Hinson declared the airline safe. Speculation began to mount that top officials at the FAA and the Department of Transportation (DOT) were reluctant to take any significant action against ValuJet, the most successful of the start-up airlines that the DOT had worked to promote.*

On June 17 the FAA announced it was shutting down the airline because an intense review had turned up "serious deficiencies" in its safety and maintenance procedures, according to Hinson. Asked why the FAA had not grounded the airline sooner, Hinson said the airline had been deemed to be safe "based upon the evidence that existed at that time." He said the intensive inspection begun after the crash "turned up a number of issues" that led to the grounding.

The next day, June 18, the government took steps to bolster public confidence in the FAA. Hinson announced several new rules designed to make maintenance contractors more accountable for their performance. He also announced that the FAA's top safety officer, Anthony J. Broderick, was retiring from his job. Since it was established in 1958, the FAA has been charged with both promoting and regulating the airlines, dual duties that many view as incompatible. Department of Transportation Secretary Federico F. Peña asked Congress to change the FAA's charter to make safety its primary mission. (Congress complied in October, in a bill authorizing funding for the agency.)

At a congressional hearing June 25, Hinson acknowledged that his agency should have acted sooner on the safety problems surrounding ValuJet. "It is apparent now that the extraordinarily rapid growth of this airline created problems that should have been more clearly recognized and dealt with sooner and more aggressively," he said.

The ValuJet Crash

One of the more successful new discount airlines, ValuJet was founded in 1993 and quickly grew from two aircraft to fifty-one in less than three years. The airline held down costs in part by buying old aircraft and hiring less experienced pilots than those flying for the major airlines; it also contracted much of its maintenance work to outside firms. It was this last practice that became central to the crash investigation.

Investigators for the National Transportation Safety Board looking for the cause of the May 11 crash quickly focused on mislabeled and improperly sealed oxygen generators. The generators, used to supply oxygen to a plane's oxygen masks in an emergency, were past their shelf life and had been removed from another ValuJet plane by the airline's maintenance contractor, Sabretech. The generators were not sealed with protective caps designed to prevent accidental ignition, were mistakenly marked "empty," packed loosely in cardboard boxes, and returned to the ValuJet terminal in Miami, where they were loaded aboard the DC-9. Investigators speculated that one of the generators burst into flames, igniting the others and other material in the cargo hold, including old tires, and destroying the aircraft controls.

The Department of Transportation on May 23 prohibited airlines from transporting such generators as cargo on passenger airlines. In November the FAA said it would seek a regulation to require fire detection and suppression systems in airline cargo holds. Newer planes already had such equipment, but about 2,800 older craft did not. The DOT also said it would seek a permanent ban prohibiting airliners from carrying oxidizing materials that feed a fire. The ban would cover oxygen generators like those involved in the ValuJet crash, as well as other chemicals such as hydrogen peroxide bleach.

The new rules the FAA announced June 18 focused almost entirely on ensuring that outside contractors meet safety standards. Under the new rules airlines would have to show that their contract maintenance and training programs complied with FAA safety regulations. Air carriers would have to certify that any maintenance or training contractor it hired would perform the work according to the carriers' FAA-approved program specifications, and the FAA would have to approve an air carrier's use of any new maintenance or training contractor.

On June 18 the FAA also released the list of safety-related incidents turned up in its post-crash investigation that led it to ground ValuJet. Among the findings: one DC-9 made seven flights with a broken windshield; another DC-9 had a malfunctioning weather radar that was reported thirty-one times before it was repaired; the airline failed to complete several fleetwide inspections the FAA had ordered after accidents on other airlines; and some ValuJet mechanics were not properly trained for their jobs. As serious as these problems may have been for the safe operations of ValuJet airplanes, they also raised questions about why FAA inspectors had not found these safety violations sooner, or if they had, why they had not done more to see that they were corrected.

On September 16 the DOT allowed ValuJet to resume service. The airline renewed operations with just nine aircraft and was permitted to increase that number to fifteen over thirty days. ValuJet would have to seek permission from the DOT to expand beyond that number. The airline also revamped much of its operations, including reducing the number of outside maintenance contractors it used, redesigning its cockpits so that they all conformed to a single design, and hiring additional maintenance and management personnel to increase safety and maintenance oversight.

Shortcomings in FAA Inspection Program

On April 30, just days before the ValuJet crash, the General Accounting Office (GAO), the investigative arm of Congress, told a Senate subcommittee about "persistent" problems with the FAA's safety inspection program, much of it attributable to overall decreases in the agency's budget. Inspectors did not always have needed technical training, the number of inspectors with aircraft-specific training was limited, and flight training for inspectors who conducted flight checks of pilots was cut back. Furthermore, the FAA had been slow to improve the data in a computer system intended to help the FAA target the areas of greatest potential risk, said Gerald L. Dillingham, associate director of the GAO. "Garbage in, garbage out," he told the Senate Government Operations Subcommittee on Government Management.

Another witness, speaking from behind a screen to protect his identity, said he was an aviation consultant who once worked for an airline. He said that many FAA inspectors were easily influenced by airlines' efforts to cover up problems. "The airline wings could be falling off, but as long as the paperwork is all right, they don't care," he said. "So we make the paperwork look right."

On May 14, three days after the ValuJet crash, the secretary of transportation outlined several steps to strengthen the FAA inspection system, including hiring additional inspectors; developing a strategy for upgrading the agency's computer data systems; and reviewing the FAA's inspection operations, including its training and work assignments. In addition, the agency undertook its own review and on September 26 issued a report listing more than thirty recommendations for improvement and strategies for implementing them. Among the recommendations were that the agency more closely inspect new airlines during their first five years of operation. In a report to Congress on October 17, the GAO said that these and other initiatives "taken together, have the potential to address several of FAA's long-standing problems."

> *Following are excerpts from testimony on "Targeting and Training of FAA's Safety Inspector Workforce," given April 30, 1996, to the Senate Governmental Affairs Subcommittee on Governmental Management by Gerald L. Dillingham, associate director for transportation and telecommunications issues at the General Accounting Office:*

We appreciate the opportunity to testify on the Federal Aviation Administration's (FAA) safety inspection program. Although the accident rates for air travel in this country are among the lowest in the world and aviation is one of the safest means of transportation, recent fatal accidents have raised concerns about the safety of air travel. FAA's Office of Flight Standards Service develops the federal aviation regulations that airlines must follow and prepares guidance on how FAA safety inspectors should perform inspections. This office also inspects commercial and general aviation aircraft, aircraft repair stations, schools for pilot training and maintenance, and pilots. These inspections serve as part of an early warning system to identify potential safety-related problems. . . .

In summary, we have found that

- FAA needs to target its inspection resources to the areas of greatest potential risk. Because of the magnitude of the inspectors' workload, targeting is essential because FAA may never have enough resources to inspect all pilots, aircraft, and facilities. Since 1991, FAA has been working to develop its Safety Performance Analysis System (SPAS) to target resources for aviation inspections. However, problems with the quality of the source data, such as data on the results of safety inspections, jeopardize the potential benefits of the $32-million SPAS system. We recommended in February 1995 that FAA develop a comprehensive strategy to improve the quality of these data. FAA officials planned to develop such a strategy by the end of 1995, but the strategy drafted by an FAA contractor has yet to receive agency approval.

- Over the last decade, we, the DOT IG [inspector general], and FAA have reported on problems related to the technical training for inspectors, including inspectors performing inspections for which they did not have appropriate or current credentials. Our work has shown persistent problems with FAA's training of inspectors. Specifically, inspectors have been unable to take courses that they believe are necessary to perform their inspection responsibilities. Additionally, FAA has limited aircraft-specific training and decreased the frequency of flight training for inspectors responsible for overseeing pilot proficiency. Decreases in FAA's overall budget have reduced the funding available for technical training by 42 percent from fiscal years 1993 through 1996. FAA estimates that it will have a shortfall of $20 million for technical training that FAA had identified as essential in its fiscal year 1996 training needs assessment process.

FAA Efforts to Develop an Inspector Targeting System

As early as 1987, we identified the need for FAA to develop criteria for targeting safety inspections to airlines with characteristics that may indicate safety problems and noted that targeting was important because FAA may never have enough resources to inspect all aircraft, facilities, and pilots. FAA employs about 2,500 aviation safety inspectors to oversee about 7,300 scheduled commercial aircraft, more than 11,100 charter aircraft, about 184,400 active general aviation aircraft, about 4,900 repair stations, slightly more than 600 schools for training pilots, almost 200 maintenance schools, and over 665,000 active pilots.

Although FAA has taken steps to better target its inspection resources to areas with the greatest safety risks, these efforts are still not complete. SPAS, which FAA began developing in 1991, is intended to analyze data from up to 25 existing databases that contain such information as the results of airline inspections and the number and the nature of aircraft accidents. This system is then expected to produce indicators of an airline's safety performance, which FAA will use to identify safety-related risks and to establish priorities for FAA's inspections. FAA completed development and installation of the initial SPAS prototype in 1993. As of April 1996, FAA had installed SPAS in 59 locations but is experiencing some logistical problems in installing SPAS hardware and software. Full deployment of the $32-million SPAS system to all remaining FAA locations nationwide is scheduled to be completed in 1998.

In February 1995, we reported that although FAA had done a credible job in analyzing and defining the system's user requirements, SPAS could potentially misdirect FAA resources away from the higher-risk aviation activities if the quality of its source data is not improved. SPAS program officials have acknowledged that the quality of information in the databases that are linked to SPAS poses a major risk to the system. To improve the quality of data to be used in SPAS analyses, we recommended that FAA develop and implement a comprehensive strategy to improve the quality of all data used in its source databases. FAA concurred with the need for this comprehensive strategy and planned to complete it by the end of 1995. As of April 1996, the strategy drafted by an FAA contractor had not been approved by agency management. Until FAA completes and implements its strategy, the extent and the impact of the problems with the quality of the system's data will remain unclear.

Although we have not determined the full extent of the problems, our recent audit work and recent work by the DOT IG have identified continuing problems with the quality of data entered into various source databases for SPAS. FAA's Program Tracking and Reporting Subsystem (PTRS), which contains the results of safety inspections, has had continuing problems with the accuracy and consistency of its data. Several FAA inspectors mentioned concerns about the reliability and consistency of data entered into PTRS. According to an inspector who serves on a work group to improve SPAS data inputs, reviews of inspectors' entries revealed some inaccurate entries and a lack of standardization in the comment section, where inspectors should report any rules, procedures, practices, or regulations that were not followed. He said inspectors continued to comment on things that were not violations while some actual violations went unreported. For example, during our ongoing work we recently found a PTRS entry indicating an inspection that never occurred on a type of aircraft that the carrier did not use. The DOT IG also concluded in a November 1995 report that FAA inspectors did not consistently and accurately report their inspection results in PTRS because reporting procedures were not interpreted and applied consistently by FAA inspectors, and management oversight did not identify reporting inconsistencies. The DOT IG recommended that FAA clarify PTRS reporting procedures to ensure consistent and accurate reporting of inspections and to establish controls to ensure supervisors review PTRS reports for reporting inconsistencies and errors. Such problems can jeopardize the reliability of SPAS to target inspector resources to airlines and aircraft that warrant more intensive oversight than others.

Adequacy of Inspector Training
Continues to Be a Concern

Over the last decade, we, the DOT IG, and internal FAA groups have repeatedly identified problems and concerns related to the technical training FAA has provided to its inspectors. For example, both we and the IG have reported that FAA inspectors were inspecting types of aircraft that they had not been trained to inspect or for which their training was not current. In the wake of these findings, FAA has revised its program to train inspectors by (1) developing a process to assess training needs for its inspector workforce,

(2) attempting to identify those inspections that require aircraft-specific training and limiting this training to the number of inspectors needed to perform these inspections, and (3) decreasing the requirements for recurrent flight training for some of its inspectors.

However, our interviews with 50 inspectors indicate that some inspectors continue to perform inspections for which they are not fully trained, and some inspectors do not believe they are receiving sufficient training. While we cannot determine the extent of these problems from our limited interviews, the training issues reflect persistent concerns on which we and others have reported for many years. For example, we reported in 1989 that airworthiness inspectors received about half of the training planned for them in fiscal year 1988. Furthermore, we reported in 1989 and the DOT IG reported again in 1992 that inspectors who did not have appropriate training or current qualifications were conducting flight checks of pilots. The Director of FAA's Office of Flight Standards Service acknowledged that the adequacy of inspector training remains a major concern of inspectors.

Some Inspectors Still Do Not Receive Needed Technical Training

Recognizing that some of its employees had received expensive training they did not need to do their jobs while others did not receive essential training, in 1992 FAA developed a centralized process to determine, prioritize, and fund its technical training needs. . . . To identify initial course sequences for new hires and time frames for their completion as well as some continuing development courses that are not aircraft-specific, FAA created profiles for the various types of inspectors.

Although each profile notes that additional specialized training may be required according to an inspector's assigned responsibilities and prior experience, the centralized process provides no guidance for analyzing individualized needs. According to several inspectors we interviewed who had completed initial training, they were not receiving the specific technical training needed for their assigned responsibilities. The inspectors said that the assessment process does not fully address their advanced training needs and that some inspectors were performing inspections for which they have not received training. For example, one maintenance inspector told us he was responsible for inspecting seven commuter airlines but had never attended maintenance training school for the types of aircraft he inspects. He said that he had requested needed training for 5 years with his supervisor's approval, but his requests were not ranked high enough in the prioritization process to receive funding. Instead, FAA sent the maintenance inspector to training on Boeing 727s and composite materials, which were not related to the aircraft he was responsible for. He said that he did not request these courses and assumed he was sent to fill available training slots. Another maintenance inspector said that although he was trained on modern, computerized Boeing 767s, he was assigned to carriers who fly 727s, 737s, and DC-9s with older mechanical systems.

While the Director of the Flight Standards Service said that inspectors could obtain some aircraft-specific training by attending classes given by the airlines they inspect, inspectors with whom we spoke said that supervisors have not allowed them to take courses offered by airlines or manufacturers because their participation could present a potential conflict of interest if the courses were taken for free. Some inspectors we interviewed said that when they could not obtain needed training through FAA they have audited an airline's classes while inspecting its training program. Although the inspectors might acquire some knowledge by auditing an airline's class, they stressed that learning to oversee the repair of complex mechanical and computerized systems and to detect possible safety-related problems requires concentration and hands-on learning, not merely auditing a class. The inspectors said that extensive familiarity with the aircraft and its repair and maintenance enhances their ability to perform thorough inspections and to detect safety-related problems.

While technical training is especially important when inspectors assume new responsibilities, other inspectors we interviewed said that they sometimes do not receive this training when needed. For example, although an operations inspector requested Airbus 320 training when a carrier he inspected began using that aircraft, he said that he did not receive the training until 2 years after that carrier went out of business. Similarly, several inspectors told us that despite their responsibility to approve global positioning system (GPS) receivers, a navigation system increasingly being used in aircraft, they have had no formal training on this equipment. Finally, a maintenance inspector, who was responsible for overseeing air carriers and repair stations that either operate or repair Boeing 737, 757, 767, and McDonnell Douglas MD-80 aircraft, said that the last course he received on maintenance and electronics was 5 years ago for the 737. Although the other three aircraft have replaced mechanical gauges with more sophisticated computer systems and digital displays, the inspector has not received training in these newer technologies. While acknowledging the desirability of updating training for new responsibilities, the Director of the Flight Standards Service said that prioritizing limited training resources may have defined essential training so narrowly that specialized training cannot always be funded. . . .

FAA Has Limited the Number of Inspectors Who Receive Aircraft-Specific Training

Because of resource constraints, FAA has reduced the number of inspections for which aircraft-specific training is considered essential and has limited such training to inspectors who perform those inspections. . . .

According to the Director of the Flight Standards Service and the Acting Manager of the Evaluations and Analysis Branch, identifying inspections that require aircraft-specific training and limiting training to those who perform such inspections has reduced the number of inspectors who need expensive aircraft-specific flight training. They said this policy also helps to ensure that inspections requiring a type rating are only conducted by inspectors who hold appropriate, current credentials. As we recommended in 1989, reevaluating the responsibilities of inspectors, identifying the number needed to perform flight checks, and providing them with flight training makes sense in an era of limited resources for technical training.

The DOT IG's ongoing work has found differences of opinion and confusion within FAA about which inspections require aircraft-specific training and type ratings. For example, while the Flight Standards Service training needs assessment manual lists 48 inspection activities for which operations inspectors need aircraft-specific training, during the DOT IG's ongoing audit the Acting Manager of the Evaluations and Analysis Branch listed only 15 inspection activities requiring current type ratings. Until FAA identifies the specific inspection activities that require aircraft-specific training or type ratings, it will remain unclear whether some inspections are being performed by inspectors without appropriate credentials. The DOT IG's ongoing study is evaluating this issue in more detail.

FAA Has Reduced Flight Training Requirements for Operations Inspectors

We and the DOT IG have previously reported that FAA inspectors making pilot flight checks either did not have the credentials (type ratings) or were not current in their aircraft qualifications in accordance with FAA requirements. Being current is important because some inspectors may actually have to fly an aircraft in an emergency situation. In May 1993, FAA decreased the frequency of inspector training and more narrowly defined those inspector activities requiring type ratings. Under FAA's previous policy, inspectors overseeing air carrier operations received actual flight training (aircraft or simulator flying time) every 6 months to maintain their qualifications to conduct flight checks on pilots. FAA now requires recurrent flight training every 12 months and limits this requirement to those inspectors who might actually have to assume the controls (flight crewmember, safety pilot, or airman certification) in aircraft requiring type ratings. Because inspectors who ride in the jump seat would not be in a position to assume control of an aircraft, they no longer need to remain current in their type ratings, whereas inspectors of smaller general aviation aircraft who might actually have to assume the controls are required to receive flight training. However, this annual requirement for general aviation inspectors has been changed to every 24 months.

Inspectors we interviewed opposed the change requiring less frequent flight training. An operations inspector for general aviation aircraft believed training every 2 years was inadequate for inspectors who have to be at the controls every time they conduct a check ride. Another inspector, who is type rated in an advanced transport category aircraft, said he has not received any aircraft flying time and only half the simulator time he needs.

According to the Acting Manager of the Evaluations and Analysis Branch, the decision to reduce the requirements for flight training was driven by budget constraints, and FAA has not studied the potential or actual impact of this reduction. Consequently, it is unknown whether the change in inspector flight training frequency is affecting aviation safety. The Director of the Flight Standards Service said that FAA has been placed in a position of having to meet the safety concerns of the aviation industry and the public at a time when air traffic is projected to continue increasing while resources are decreasing.

Funding for Technical Training Has Decreased Significantly

Between fiscal years 1993 and 1996, decreases in FAA's overall budget have significantly reduced the funding available for technical training. FAA's overall training budget has decreased 42 percent from $147 million to $85 million. FAA has taken a number of steps over the years to make its technical training program more efficient. For example, the prescreening of air traffic controller trainees has improved the percentage of students who successfully complete this training and decreased the number of FAA and contract classes needed. Additionally, in response to our recommendation, FAA has limited expensive flight training to inspectors who require current flight experience. FAA has also realized savings from the increased use of distance learning (e.g., computer-based instruction) and flight simulation in place of more expensive aircraft training time.

FAA's reduced funding for technical training has occurred at a time when it has received congressional direction to hire over 230 additional safety inspectors in fiscal year 1996. To achieve this staffing increase, FAA will have to hire about 400 inspectors to overcome attrition. New staff must be provided initial training at the FAA Academy to prepare them to assume their new duties effectively. The cost of this training, combined with overall training budget reductions, constrains FAA's ability to provide its existing inspectors with the training essential to effectively carry out FAA's safety mission.

For fiscal year 1996, FAA's training needs assessment process identified a need for $94 million to fund operationally essential technical training. However, due to overall budget reductions, FAA was allocated only $74 million for this purpose. For example, the budget for Regulation and Certification is $5.2 million short of the amount identified for operationally essential training. Specific effects of this shortfall include: delaying the training of fourth quarter inspector new hires until fiscal year 1997; cancellation of 164 flight training, airworthiness, and other classes planned to serve over 1,700 safety inspectors; and delay of recurrent and initial training for test pilots who certify the airworthiness of new aircraft. Based on the fiscal year 1997 request, the gap between FAA's request and the amount needed to fund operationally essential technical training will be even greater in fiscal year 1997, in part because of training postponed in fiscal year 1996. Regulation and Certification, for example, is projecting an $8.1-million shortfall in operationally essential training. . . .

Mr. Chairman, this concludes our statement. We would be pleased to respond to questions at this time.

May

NEW CONSTITUTION
FOR SOUTH AFRICA
May 8, 1996

South African president Nelson Mandela on December 10 signed into law a new constitution—a document firmly committing South Africa to a nonracial government and promising its citizens an extensive bill of rights. The new constitution was to take effect gradually over three years, leading to new elections in 1999 and the formation of a new parliament alongside a strong executive branch.

The interim parliament, elected in South Africa's first nonracial voting in 1994, had approved the new constitution on May 8. That document was the result of nearly two years of tough negotiating among the country's political leaders, and its approval represented a major step in the maturing of democracy in South Africa. Mandela said the country's leaders were able to resolve their disagreements because they were determined "to seek what was common to them, rather than stand on the smaller things that divided them."

The Constitutional Court ruled on September 6, however, that the May 8 constitution did not meet several criteria that had been established before the 1994 elections. Most of the court's objections were on technical grounds, but the ruling sent negotiators back to the bargaining table. Less than a month later they produced a new version, which the court found acceptable on December 5. Mandela's signature five days later made the new constitution formal.

The constitution created a federal system of government that would be headed by a strong president and a legislature consisting of two chambers: a National Assembly of up to 400 members elected by proportional representation, and a Council of Provinces (or Senate) composed of ten delegates from each of the nine provinces. The Council members were to be appointed by the parties of the provincial legislatures, in proportion to their strength.

The president would be elected by the National Assembly for a five-year term following the 1999 elections and would be limited to two terms in office. For at least the foreseeable future, this provision guaranteed that Mandela's African National Congress would dominate South African political life, since it was by far the country's biggest political party.

The judiciary was to be an independent branch of government, headed by a new Constitutional Court, which would be appointed by the president after consultation with other political leaders and a judicial review commission.

Negotiations Toward the Constitution

The interim parliament's landmark adoption of the constitution on May 8 came on an overwhelming vote: 421 to 2, with 10 abstentions. That margin disguised intense negotiations leading to the agreement. With political power reversed from the days of apartheid, white political leaders lobbied hard for guarantees of political and other rights for minorities. Much of the last-minute negotiating dealt with a demand by whites for the right to continue single-language schools, in other words schools where Afrikaans was spoken. White leaders also fought for protection of property rights, since some 75 percent of the country's property remained in the hands of white individuals and businesses.

Those matters ultimately were resolved with compromises that satisfied most white leaders. The National Party, which had created the apartheid policy and ruled South Africa for nearly forty years, supported the Constitution. Ten members of the far right Freedom Front abstained on the May 8 vote but still pledged to work within the political framework established by the new constitution.

Provincial powers, including the role of the Council of Provinces, also had been a major issue in the negotiations leading to the May 8 vote. The issue arose again in the Constitutional Court's deliberation on the May 8 version. Some provincial leaders—particularly the Inkatha Freedom party, based in KwaZulu province—had demanded a greater share of power and a more substantive role for the Council of Provinces. Inkatha representatives had walked out of the parliament in 1995 over disagreements with the African National Congress on this issue. The final document, as adopted in December, gave the Council slightly more power than did the early version.

Sweeping Bill of Rights

One of the most remarkable aspects of the new constitution was its Bill of Rights, which had one of the broadest range of guaranteed political and social rights of any constitutional document in the world. The constitution was clearly a reflection of lessons learned in South Africa during the apartheid years. The country's new leaders wanted to ensure that all citizens would be protected from the kinds of abuses of power that nonwhite citizens had suffered under white minority rule.

Many of the rights were similar to those contained in the U.S. Constitution, such as freedom of speech and religion and the guarantee of a speedy trial. Several other constitutional provisions went well beyond the guarantees found in most other national documents. For example, the constitution stated that everyone in South Africa had a right to adequate housing, food and water, education, and health care. It also prohibited discrimination based on race, gender, age, sexual orientation, pregnancy, or marital status.

In keeping with a 1995 ruling by the Constitutional Court, the constitution effectively banned the death penalty. It also contained provisions widely viewed as guaranteeing abortion rights. (South African death penalty ruling, Historic Documents of 1995, p. 283)

Most observers noted that the social guarantees—such as the rights to housing and health care—represented wishful thinking on the part of South African leaders. Even though it was the wealthiest country in sub-Saharan Africa, South Africa did not have the financial resources to provide full social services for all its 43 million citizens.

Advocates said the adoption of these rights was an important step because it meant the country was recognizing a national obligation to millions of people who had been repressed for generations. Enshrining such rights in the constitution would force the government to take them seriously, according to this argument.

National Party Enters Opposition

If adoption of the new constitution on May 8 represented a major step down South Africa's road of democracy, then an event the next day demonstrated the kinds of stresses that democracy would have to endure. The National Party, led by former president F. W. de Klerk, announced that it was pulling out of the coalition government that had led South Africa since the 1994 elections.

De Klerk, who had served as a deputy president to Mandela, clearly was chafing at his status as junior partner to the man he had freed from prison in 1990. While publicly putting up a united front, the two men had many disagreements and were no longer working together as a political team.

De Klerk said his party's resignation from the government would put it in the more "natural" role of an opposition party. "Our decision should be seen as an important step in the growing maturity and normalization of our young democracy," he said, adding that the action was not taken in "a negative spirit." Even so, the event created the impression of a crisis in the government and led to a temporary sell-off in the South African stock exchange.

> *Following are excerpts from the Preamble, Founding Provisions, and Bill of Rights of the new constitution of South Africa, as adopted May 8, 1996, by the National Assembly and revised for final approval December 11, 1996:*

Preamble

We, the people of South Africa,

Recognise the injustices of our past;

Honour those who suffered for justice and freedom in our land;

Respect those who have worked to build and develop our country; and

Believe that South Africa belongs to all who live in it, united in our diversity.

We therefore, through our freely elected representatives, adopt this Constitution as the supreme law of the Republic so as to—

Heal the divisions of the past and establish a society based on democratic values, social justice and fundamental human rights;

Lay the foundations for a democratic and open society in which government is based on the will of the people and every citizen is equally protected by law;

Improve the quality of life of all citizens and free the potential of each person; and

Build a united and democratic South Africa able to take its rightful place as a sovereign state in the family of nations.

May God protect our people.

Nkosi Sikelel' Afrika. Morena boloka setjhaba sa heso.

God seNn Suid-Afrika. God bless South Africa.

Mudzimu fhatutshedza Afurika. Hosi katekisa Afrika.

Founding Provisions—Republic of South Africa

1. The Republic of South Africa is one sovereign democratic state founded on the following values:

> (a) Human dignity, the achievement of equality and the advancement of human rights and freedoms.

> (b) Non-racialism and non-sexism.

> (c) Supremacy of the constitution and the rule of law.

> (d) Universal adult suffrage, a national common voters roll, regular elections and a multi-party system of democratic government, to ensure accountability, responsiveness and openness.

Supremacy of Constitution

2. This Constitution is the supreme law of the Republic; law or conduct inconsistent with it is invalid, and the obligations imposed by it must be fulfilled.

Citizenship

3. (1) There is a common South African citizenship.

> (2) All citizens are—

> (a) equally entitled to the rights, privileges and benefits of citizenship; and

> (b) equally subject to the duties and responsibilities of citizenship.

(3) National legislation must provide for the acquisition, loss and restoration of citizenship.

National anthem

4. The national anthem of the Republic is determined by the President by proclamation.

National flag

5. The national flag of the Republic is black, gold, green, white, red and blue, as described and sketched in Schedule 1.

Languages

6. (1) The official languages of the Republic are Sepedi, Sesotho, Setswana, siSwati, Tshivenda, Xitsonga, Afrikaans, English, isiNdebele, isiXhosa and isiZulu.

(2) Recognising the historically diminished use and status of the indigenous languages of our people, the state must take practical and positive measures to elevate the status and advance the use of these languages.

(3) (a) The national government and provincial governments may use any particular official languages for the purposes of government, taking into account usage, practicality, expense, regional circumstances and the balance of the needs and preferences of the population as a whole or in the province concerned; but the national government and each provincial government must use at least two official languages.

(b) Municipalities must take into account the language usage and preferences of their residents.

(4) The national government and provincial governments, by legislative and other measures, must regulate and monitor their use of official languages. Without detracting from the provisions of subsection (2), all official languages must enjoy parity of esteem and must be treated equitably.

(5) A Pan South African Language Board established by national legislation must—

(a) promote and create conditions for the development and use of—
(i) all official languages;
(ii) the Khoi, Nama and San languages; and
(iii) sign language; and

(b) promote and ensure respect for—
(i) all languages commonly used by communities in South Africa, including German, Greek, Gujarati, Hindi, Portuguese, Tamil, Telegu and Urdu; and

(ii) Arabic, Hebrew, Sanskrit and other languages used for religious purposes in South Africa.

Bill of Rights

Rights

7. (1) This Bill of Rights is a cornerstone of democracy in South Africa. It enshrines the rights of all people in our country and affirms the democratic values of human dignity, equality and freedom.

(2) The state must respect, protect, promote and fulfil the rights in the Bill of Rights.

(3) The rights in the Bill of Rights are subject to the limitations contained or referred to in section 36, or elsewhere in the Bill.

Application

8. (1) The Bill of Rights applies to all law, and binds the legislature, the executive, the judiciary and all organs of state.

(2) A provision of the Bill of Rights binds a natural or a juristic person if, and to the extent that, it is applicable, taking into account the nature of the right and the nature of any duty imposed by the right.

(3) When applying a provision of the Bill of Rights to a natural or juristic person in terms of subsection (2), a court—

(a) in order to give effect to a right in the Bill, must apply, or if necessary develop, the common law to the extent that legislation does not give effect to that right; and

(b) may develop rules of the common law to limit the right, provided that the limitation is in accordance with section 36(1).

(4) A juristic person is entitled to the rights in the Bill of Rights to the extent required by the nature of the rights and the nature of that juristic person.

Equality

9. (1) Everyone is equal before the law and has the right to equal protection and benefit of the law.

(2) Equality includes the full and equal enjoyment of all rights and freedoms. To promote the achievement of equality, legislative and other measures designed to protect or advance persons, or categories of persons, disadvantaged by unfair discrimination may be taken.

(3) The state may not unfairly discriminate directly or indirectly against anyone on one or more grounds, including race, gender, sex, pregnancy, marital status, ethnic or social origin, colour, sexual orientation, age, disability, religion, conscience, belief, culture, language and birth.

(4) No person may unfairly discriminate directly or indirectly against anyone on one or more grounds in terms of subsection (3). National legislation must be enacted to prevent or prohibit unfair discrimination.

(5) Discrimination on one or more of the grounds listed in subsection (3) is unfair unless it is established that the discrimination is fair.

Human dignity

10. Everyone has inherent dignity and the right to have their dignity respected and protected.

Life

11. Everyone has the right to life.

Freedom and security of the person

12. (1) Everyone has the right to freedom and security of the person, which includes the right—

(a) not to be deprived of freedom arbitrarily or without just cause;

(b) not to be detained without trial;

(c) to be free from all forms of violence from either public or private sources;

(d) not to be tortured in any way; and

(e) not to be treated or punished in a cruel, inhuman or degrading way.

(2) Everyone has the right to bodily and psychological integrity, which includes the right—

(a) to make decisions concerning reproduction;

(b) to security in and control over their body; and

(c) not to be subjected to medical or scientific experiments without their informed consent.

Slavery, servitude and forced labour

13. No one may be subjected to slavery, servitude or forced labour.

Privacy

14. Everyone has the right to privacy, which includes the right not to have—

(a) their person or home searched;

(b) their property searched;

(c) their possessions seized; or

(d) the privacy of their communications infringed.

Freedom of religion, belief and opinion

15. (1) Everyone has the right to freedom of conscience, religion, thought, belief and opinion.

(2) Religious observances may be conducted at state or state-aided institutions, provided that—

(a) those observances follow rules made by the appropriate public authorities;

(b) they are conducted on an equitable basis; and

(c) attendance at them is free and voluntary.

(3) (a) This section does not prevent legislation recognising—

(i) marriages concluded under any tradition, or a system of religious, personal or family law; or

(ii) systems of personal and family law under any tradition, or adhered to by persons professing a particular religion.

(b) Recognition in terms of paragraph (a) must be consistent with this section and the other provisions of the Constitution.

Freedom of expression

16. (1) Everyone has the right to freedom of expression, which includes—

(a) freedom of the press and other media;

(b) freedom to receive or impart information or ideas;

(c) freedom of artistic creativity; and

(d) academic freedom and freedom of scientific research.

(2) The right in subsection (1) does not extend to—

(a) propaganda for war;

(b) incitement of imminent violence; or

(c) advocacy of hatred that is based on race, ethnicity, gender or religion, and that constitutes incitement to cause harm.

Assembly, demonstration, picket and petition

17. Everyone has the right, peacefully and unarmed, to assemble, to demonstrate, to picket and to present petitions.

Freedom of association

18. Everyone has the right to freedom of association.

Political rights

19. (1) Every citizen is free to make political choices, which includes the right—

(a) to form a political party;

(b) to participate in the activities of, or recruit members for, a political party; and

(c) to campaign for a political party or cause.

(2) Every citizen has the right to free, fair and regular elections for any legislative body established in terms of the Constitution.

(3) Every adult citizen has the right—

(a) to vote in elections for any legislative body established in terms of the Constitution, and to do so in secret; and

(b) to stand for public office and, if elected, to hold office.

Citizenship

20. No citizen may be deprived of citizenship.

Freedom of movement and residence

21. (1) Everyone has the right to freedom of movement.

(2) Everyone has the right to leave the Republic.

(3) Every citizen has the right to enter, to remain in and to reside anywhere in, the Republic.

(4) Every citizen has the right to a passport.

Freedom of trade, occupation and profession

22. Every citizen has the right to choose their trade, occupation or profession freely. The practice of a trade, occupation or profession may be regulated by law.

Labour relations

23. (1) Everyone has the right to fair labour practices.

(2) Every worker has the right—

(a) to form and join a trade union;

(b) to participate in the activities and programmes of a trade union; and

(c) to strike.

(3) Every employer has the right—

(a) to form and join an employers' organisation; and

(b) to participate in the activities and programmes of an employers' organisation.

(4) Every trade union and every employers' organisation has the right—

(a) to determine its own administration, programmes and activities;

(b) to organise; and

(c) to form and join a federation.

(5) Every trade union, employers' organisation and employer has the right to engage in collective bargaining. National legislation may be enacted to regulate collective bargaining. To the extent that the legislation may limit a right in this Chapter, the limitation must comply with section 36(1).

(6) National legislation may recognise union security arrangements contained in collective agreements. To the extent that the legislation may limit a right in this Chapter, the limitation must comply with section 36(1).

Environment

24. Everyone has the right—

(a) to an environment that is not harmful to their health or well-being; and

(b) to have the environment protected, for the benefit of present and future generations, through reasonable legislative and other measures that—

(i) prevent pollution and ecological degradation;

(ii) promote conservation; and

(iii) secure ecologically sustainable development and use of natural resources while promoting justifiable economic and social development.

Property

25. (1) No one may be deprived of property except in terms of law of general application, and no law may permit arbitrary deprivation of property.

(2) Property may be expropriated only in terms of law of general application—

(a) for a public purpose, or in the public interest; and

(b) subject to compensation, the amount of which and the time and manner of payment of which have either been agreed to by those affected or decided or approved by a court.

(3) The amount of the compensation and the time and manner of payment must be just and equitable, reflecting an equitable balance between the public interest and the interests of those affected, having regard to all relevant circumstances, including—

(a) the current use of the property;

(b) the history of the acquisition and use of the property;

(c) the market value of the property;

(d) the extent of direct state investment and subsidy in the acquisition and beneficial capital improvement of the property; and

(e) the purpose of the expropriation.

(4) For the purposes of this section—

(a) the public interest includes the nation's commitment to land reform, and to reforms to bring about equitable access to all South Africa's natural resources; and

(b) property is not limited to land.

(5) The state must take reasonable legislative and other measures, within its available resources, to foster conditions which enable citizens to gain access to land on an equitable basis.

(6) A person or community whose tenure of land is legally insecure as a result of past racially discriminatory laws or practices is entitled, to the extent provided by an Act of Parliament, either to tenure which is legally secure or to comparable redress.

(7) A person or community dispossessed of property after 19 June 1913 as a result of past racially discriminatory laws or practices is entitled, to the extent provided by an Act of Parliament, either to restitution of that property or to equitable redress.

(8) No provision of this section may impede the state from taking legislative and other measures to achieve land, water and related reform, in order to redress the results of past racial discrimination, provided that any departure from the provisions of this section is in accordance with the provisions of section 36(1).

(9) Parliament must enact the legislation referred to in subsection (6).

Housing

26. (1) Everyone has the right to have access to adequate housing.

(2) The state must take reasonable legislative and other measures, within its available resources, to achieve the progressive realisation of this right.

(3) No one may be evicted from their home, or have their home demolished, without an order of court made after considering all the relevant circumstances. No legislation may permit arbitrary evictions.

Health care, food, water and social security

27. (1) Everyone has the right to have access to—

(a) health care services, including reproductive health care;

(b) sufficient food and water; and

(c) social security, including, if they are unable to support themselves and their dependants, appropriate social assistance.

(2) The state must take reasonable legislative and other measures, within its available resources, to achieve the progressive realisation of each of these rights.

(3) No one may be refused emergency medical treatment.

Children

28. (1) Every child has the right—

(a) to a name and a nationality from birth;

(b) to family care or parental care, or to appropriate alternative care when removed from the family environment;

(c) to basic nutrition, shelter, basic health care services and social services;

(d) to be protected from maltreatment, neglect, abuse or degradation;

(e) to be protected from exploitative labour practices;

(f) not to be required or permitted to perform work or provide services that—

(i) are inappropriate for a person of that child's age; or

(ii) place at risk the child's well-being, education, physical or mental health or spiritual, moral or social development;

(g) not to be detained except as a measure of last resort, in which case, in addition to the rights a child enjoys under sections 12 and 35, the child may be detained only for the shortest appropriate period of time, and has the right to be—

(i) kept separately from detained persons over the age of 18 years; and

(ii) treated in a manner, and kept in conditions, that take account of the child's age;

(h) to have a legal practitioner assigned to the child by the state, and at state expense, in civil proceedings affecting the child, if substantial injustice would otherwise result; and

(i) not to be used directly in armed conflict, and to be protected in times of armed conflict.

(2) A child's best interests are of paramount importance in every matter concerning the child.

(3) In this section "child" means a person under the age of 18 years.

Education

29. (1) Everyone has the right—

    (a) to a basic education, including adult basic education; and

    (b) to further education, which the state, through reasonable measures, must make progressively available and accessible.

(2) Everyone has the right to receive education in the official language or languages of their choice in public educational institutions where that education is reasonably practicable. In order to ensure the effective access to, and implementation of, this right, the state must consider all reasonable educational alternatives, including single medium institutions, taking into account—

    (a) equity;

    (b) practicability; and

    (c) the need to redress the results of past racially discriminatory laws and practices.

(3) Everyone has the right to establish and maintain, at their own expense, independent educational institutions that—

    (a) do not discriminate on the basis of race;

    (b) are registered with the state; and

    (c) maintain standards that are not inferior to standards at comparable public educational institutions.

(4) Subsection (3) does not preclude state subsidies for independent educational institutions.

Language and culture

30. Everyone has the right to use the language and to participate in the cultural life of their choice, but no one exercising these rights may do so in a manner inconsistent with any provision of the Bill of Rights.

Cultural, religious and linguistic communities

31. (1) Persons belonging to a cultural, religious or linguistic community may not be denied the right, with other members of that community—

    (a) to enjoy their culture, practise their religion and use their language; and

    (b) to form, join and maintain cultural, religious and linguistic associations and other organs of civil society.

(2) The rights in subsection (1) may not be exercised in a manner inconsistent with any provision of the Bill of Rights.

Access to information

32. (1) Everyone has the right of access to—

    (a) any information held by the state; and

(b) any information that is held by another person and that is required for the exercise or protection of any rights.

(2) National legislation must be enacted to give effect to this right, and may provide for reasonable measures to alleviate the administrative and financial burden on the state.

Just administrative action

33. (1) Everyone has the right to administrative action that is lawful, reasonable and procedurally fair.

(2) Everyone whose rights have been adversely affected by administrative action has the right to be given written reasons.

(3) National legislation must be enacted to give effect to these rights, and must—

(a) provide for the review of administrative action by a court or, where appropriate, an independent and impartial tribunal;

(b) impose a duty on the state to give effect to the rights in subsections (1) and (2); and

(c) promote an efficient administration.

Access to courts

34. Everyone has the right to have any dispute that can be resolved by the application of law decided in a fair public hearing before a court or, where appropriate, another independent and impartial tribunal or forum.

Arrested, detained and accused persons

35. (1) Everyone who is arrested for allegedly committing an offence has the right—

(a) to remain silent;

(b) to be informed promptly—

(i) of the right to remain silent; and

(ii) of the consequences of not remaining silent;

(c) not to be compelled to make any confession or admission that could be used in evidence against that person;

(d) to be brought before a court as soon as reasonably possible, but not later than—

(i) 48 hours after the arrest; or

(ii) the end of the first court day after the expiry of the 48 hours, if the 48 hours expire outside ordinary court hours or on a day which is not an ordinary court day;

(e) at the first court appearance after being arrested, to be charged or to be informed of the reason for the detention to continue, or to be released; and

(f) to be released from detention if the interests of justice permit, subject to reasonable conditions.

(2) Everyone who is detained, including every sentenced prisoner, has the right—

(a) to be informed promptly of the reason for being detained;

(b) to choose, and to consult with, a legal practitioner, and to be informed of this right promptly;

(c) to have a legal practitioner assigned to the detained person by the state and at state expense, if substantial injustice would otherwise result, and to be informed of this right promptly;

(d) to challenge the lawfulness of the detention in person before a court and, if the detention is unlawful, to be released;

(e) to conditions of detention that are consistent with human dignity, including at least exercise and the provision, at state expense, of adequate accommodation, nutrition, reading material and medical treatment; and

(f) to communicate with, and be visited by, that person's—

(i) spouse or partner;

(ii) next of kin;

(iii) chosen religious counsellor; and

(iv) chosen medical practitioner.

(3) Every accused person has a right to a fair trial, which includes the right—

(a) to be informed of the charge with sufficient detail to answer it;

(b) to have adequate time and facilities to prepare a defence;

(c) to a public trial before an ordinary court;

(d) to have their trial begin and conclude without unreasonable delay;

(e) to be present when being tried;

(f) to choose, and be represented by, a legal practitioner, and to be informed of this right promptly;

(g) to have a legal practitioner assigned to the accused person by the state and at state expense, if substantial injustice would otherwise result, and to be informed of this right promptly;

(h) to be presumed innocent, to remain silent, and not to testify during the proceedings;

(i) to adduce and challenge evidence;

(j) not to be compelled to give self-incriminating evidence;

(k) to be tried in a language that the accused person understands or, if that is not practicable, to have the proceedings interpreted in that language;

(l) not to be convicted for an act or omission that was not an offence under either national or international law at the time it was committed or omitted;

(m) not to be tried for an offence in respect of an act or omission for which that person has previously been either acquitted or convicted;

(n) to the benefit of the least severe of the prescribed punishments if the prescribed punishment for the offence has been changed between the time that the offence was committed and the time of sentencing; and

(o) of appeal to, or review by, a higher court.

(4) Whenever this section requires information to be given to a person, that information must be given in a language that the person understands.

(5) Evidence obtained in a manner that violates any right in the Bill of Rights must be excluded if the admission of that evidence would render the trial unfair or otherwise be detrimental to the administration of justice.

Limitation of rights

36. (1) The rights in the Bill of Rights may be limited only in terms of law of general application to the extent that the limitation is reasonable and justifiable in an open and democratic society based on human dignity, equality and freedom, taking into account all relevant factors, including—
　(a) the nature of the right;
　(b) the importance of the purpose of the limitation;
　(c) the nature and extent of the limitation;
　(d) the relation between the limitation and its purpose; and
　(e) less restrictive means to achieve the purpose.

(2) Except as provided in subsection (1) or in any other provision of the Constitution, no law may limit any right entrenched in the Bill of Rights.

States of emergency

37. (1) A state of emergency may be declared only in terms of an Act of Parliament, and only when—
　(a) the life of the nation is threatened by war, invasion, general insurrection, disorder, natural disaster or other public emergency; and
　(b) the declaration is necessary to restore peace and order.

(2) A declaration of a state of emergency, and any legislation enacted or other action taken in consequence of that declaration, may be effective only—
　(a) prospectively; and
　(b) for no more than 21 days from the date of the declaration, unless the National Assembly resolves to extend the declaration. The Assembly may extend a declaration of a state of emergency for no more than three months at a time. The first extension of the state of emergency must be by a resolution adopted with a supporting vote of a majority of the members of the Assembly. Any subsequent extension must be by a resolution adopted with a supporting vote of at least 60 per cent of the members of the Assembly. A resolution in terms of this paragraph may be adopted only following a public debate in the Assembly.

(3) Any competent court may decide on the validity of—
　(a) a declaration of a state of emergency;
　(b) any extension of a declaration of a state of emergency; or
　(c) any legislation enacted, or other action taken, in consequence of a declaration of a state of emergency.

(4) Any legislation enacted in consequence of a declaration of a state of emergency may derogate from the Bill of Rights only to the extent that—

(a) the derogation is strictly required by the emergency; and

(b) the legislation—

(i) is consistent with the Republic's obligations under international law applicable to states of emergency;

(ii) conforms to subsection (5); and

(iii) is published in the national Government Gazette as soon as reasonably possible after being enacted.

(5) No Act of Parliament that authorises a declaration of a state of emergency, and no legislation enacted or other action taken in consequence of a declaration, may permit or authorise—

(a) indemnifying the state, or any person, in respect of any unlawful act;

(b) any derogation from this section; or

(c) any derogation from a section mentioned in column 1 of the Table of Non-Derogable Rights, to the extent indicated opposite that section in column 3 of the Table. . . .

Interpretation of Bill of Rights

39. (1) When interpreting the Bill of Rights, a court, tribunal or forum—

(a) must promote the values that underlie an open and democratic society based on human dignity, equality and freedom;

(b) must consider international law; and

(c) may consider foreign law.

(2) When interpreting any legislation, and when developing the common law or customary law, every court, tribunal or forum must promote the spirit, purport and objects of the Bill of Rights.

(3) The Bill of Rights does not deny the existence of any other rights or freedoms that are recognised or conferred by common law, customary law or legislation, to the extent that they are consistent with the Bill. . . .

NASA ON NEW ESTIMATES
OF THE AGE OF THE UNIVERSE
May 9, 1996

Determining the age of the universe long has been one of the most tantalizing—and elusive—goals facing scientists. New data from the Hubble Space Telescope and other sources offered hopes during 1996 that astronomers might be nearing the best answer yet to that question.

The National Aeronautics and Space Administration (NASA) reported on May 9 that two competing teams of scientists were narrowing their differences on key factors used in calculating estimates of the age of the universe. One team estimated that the universe was between 9 billion and 12 billion years old; another used a range of 11 billion to 14 billion years. Previously, the estimates of the two camps were much farther apart. NASA said the new estimates showed that the views of the two teams were "converging," and it said both camps believed their differences would continue to narrow as the result of further observations and analysis. (Hubble findings, Historic Documents of 1994, p. 458; Historic Documents of 1995, p. 288)

While intriguing to those interested in such big-picture astronomical questions, the debate about the age of the universe was overshadowed during 1996 by a more sensational report: an Earth-bound meteor fragment might have come from Mars and might contain evidence of primitive forms of life on that planet. (Mars report, p. 471)

Measuring the Hubble Constant

The teams of astronomers investigating the age of the universe were led by scientists based at the Carnegie Observatories in Pasadena, California. Wendy L. Freedman headed the team that gave the lower range for the age of the universe. Allan R. Sandage headed the team using the higher age range.

At the center of the dispute between the two groups of scientists was a difference over measurements of the rate at which the universe is expanding. For more than half a century, most scientists have agreed that the universe is still growing as the consequence of a massive and incredibly rapid expansion of material that took place billions of years ago—popularly referred to as the "Big Bang" theory. ("Big Bang" theory, Historic Documents of 1992, p. 379)

Scientists want to know the rate at which the universe is expanding so that they can then work backward to determine how long ago the Big Bang happened. Their measurement of that expansion is called the Hubble Constant, after American astronomer Edwin P. Hubble (and the man after whom the orbiting Hubble Space Telescope is named).

Scientists have not been able to agree on a value for the Hubble Constant, and different groups of astronomers have used different means to produce a measurement for it. In recent years the two groups of astronomers led by Freedman and Sandage have produced sharply different figures for the Hubble Constant and thus have come to opposing conclusions about the age of the universe. The Hubble Constant is shown as the number of kilometers per second per megaparsec (3.26 million light years) that the universe is expanding.

Freedman's group created a stir in the scientific community in 1994, when it developed an estimate of the Hubble Constant that would mean the universe might be only 8 billion to 10 billion years old, roughly half the age previously accepted by many scientists. Perhaps more startling was the fact that other observations indicated that the oldest stars were 12 billion to 16 billion years old. This created an apparent contradiction: How could the universe be younger than some of its stars? Scientists have said that something must be wrong with one of the measurements or else there are other age-determining factors that are not yet apparent to observers on Earth.

Sandage said in March that his team had developed new calculations putting the age of the universe at 15 billion years and the age of its oldest stars at about 13 billion years. Another member of that team, Abhijit Saha of the Space Telescope Science Institute in Baltimore, said two months later that the group was using a range for the age of the universe of 11 billion to 15 billion years.

At a news conference arranged by NASA, Freedman on May 9 said her team had used new information to increase its estimate of the age of the universe to a range of 9 billion to 12 billion years. The views of the two sides were converging, she said, as her group upped its age estimate and the other team lowered its estimate.

Hubble Observations

The new calculations were made possible, in large part, by observations provided by the Hubble Space Telescope, which can peer about ten times deeper into space than any instrument based on Earth. The Hubble measures the amount of light produced by distant galaxies, and those measurements are used to determine how fast the galaxies are moving away from Earth—the value of the Hubble Constant.

On September 4, NASA announced that the Hubble had taken images that might show galaxies being formed. The images showed a group of eighteen gigantic clusters of stars in such close proximity that they might have merged into a few galaxies.

The stars are about 11 billion light-years from the Earth, so the images taken by the Hubble showed them in the general period when the universe itself was in formation. NASA said the images gave new weight to a theo-ry that galaxies begin as clusters of stars that eventually consolidate into larger formations such as the Milky Way, in which Earth is located.

> *Following is the text of an announcement May 9, 1996, by the National Aeronautics and Space Administration on the nar-rowing of differences between two scientific teams investigat-ing the age of the universe:*

Two international teams of astronomers, using NASA's Hubble Space Tele-scope [HST], are reporting major progress in converging on an accurate mea-surement of the Universe's rate of expansion—a value which has been debat-ed for over half a century.

These new results yield ranges for the age of the Universe from 9–12 bil-lion years, and 11–14 billion years, respectively. The goal of the project is to measure the Hubble Constant to ten percent accuracy.

The Hubble Space Telescope Key Project team, an international group of over 20 astronomers, is led by Wendy Freedman of Carnegie Observatories, Pasadena, CA, Robert Kennicutt, University of Arizona, Tucson, AZ, and Jere-my Mould, Mount Stromlo and Siding Springs Observatory, Australia. The group's interim results, presented today at a meeting held at the Space Tele-scope Science Institute (STScI) in Baltimore, MD, are consistent with their preliminary result, announced in 1994, of 80 kilometers per second per mega-parsec (km/sec/Mpc), based on observations of a galaxy in the Virgo cluster.

"We have five different ways of measuring the Hubble Constant with HST," said Dr. Freedman. "The results are coming in between 68 and 78 km/sec/-Mpc". (For example, at an expansion rate of 75 km/sec/Mpc, galaxies appear to be receding from us at a rate of 162,000 miles per hour for every 3.26 mil-lion light years farther out we look.)

Two months ago, a second team, led by Allan Sandage, also of the Carnegie Observatories, Abhijit Saha, STScI, Gustav Tammann and Lukas Labhardt, Astronomical Institute, University of Basel, Duccio Macchetto and Nino Panagia, STScI/European Space Agency, reported a slower expansion rate of 57 km/sec/Mpc.

The value of the Hubble Constant allows astronomers to calculate the expansion age of the Universe, the time elapsed since the Big Bang. Astronomers have been arguing recently whether the time since the Big Bang is consistent with the ages of the oldest stars.

The ages are calculated from combining the expansion rate with an esti-mate of how much matter is in space. The younger age values from each team assume the Universe is at a critical density where it contains just enough matter to expand indefinitely. The higher age estimates are calculated based on a low density of matter in space.

"A point of great interest is whether the age of the Universe arrived at this way is really older than the independently derived ages of the oldest stars," said Saha, an investigator on both Hubble teams.

"The numbers lean on the side that the stellar ages are a little lower, or that the hypothesis that we live in a critical density universe needs to be questioned," said Saha. "As further results accumulate over the next few years, we hope to tighten the constraints on these issues."

The Observations

The Key Project team is midway along in their three-year program to derive the expansion rate of the Universe based on precise distance measurements to galaxies. They have now measured Cepheid distances to a dozen galaxies, and are about halfway through their overall program.

The Key Project team also presented a preliminary estimate of the distance to the Fornax cluster of galaxies. The estimate was obtained through the detection and measurement with the Hubble Space Telescope of pulsating stars known as Cepheid variables found in the Fornax cluster. The Fornax cluster is measured to be approximately as far away as the Virgo cluster of galaxies—about 60 million light-years.

The Key Project team member who led this effort, Caltech astronomer Barry Madore said, "This cluster allows us to make independent estimates of the expansion rate of the Universe using a number of different techniques. All of these methods are now in excellent agreement. With Fornax we are now at a turning point in this field."

The team is measuring Cepheid distances to the Virgo and Fornax clusters of galaxies as a complementary test. Their strategy is to compare and contrast expansion numbers from a variety of distance indicators.

The Key Project team is systematically looking into a variety of methods for measuring distances. They are using Cepheids in a large sample to tie into five or six "secondary methods". One such secondary method relates the total luminosity of a galaxy to the rate at which the galaxy is spinning, the Tully-Fisher relation. Another secondary method makes use of a special class of exploding star known as a type Ia supernova. This phase of the Hubble Constant research will be completed within another two years.

In contrast, the Sandage team focused on a single secondary distance indicator, one of the same indicators also used by the Key Project team, the type Ia supernova. Sandage maintains that these stars are "standard bombs" according to theory. He suggests that when they explode they all reach exactly the same intrinsic brightness. This would make them extremely reliable "standard candles" (objects with a well-known intrinsic brightness) visible 1,000 times farther away than Cepheids. Since they are intrinsically brighter than any other standard candle, they offer the opportunity for an accurate measurement of the Universe's overall expansion by looking out the farthest.

Although both teams are still in disagreement over the precise rate at which the Universe is expanding and on how old it is, they are optimistic that their estimates will continue to converge with further observations and analysis.

The Space Telescope Science Institute is operated by the Association of Universities for Research in Astronomy, Inc. (AURA), for NASA, under contract with the Goddard Space Flight Center, Greenbelt, MD. The Hubble Space Telescope is a project of international cooperation between NASA and the European Space Agency (ESA).

DOLE ON RESIGNATION FROM THE SENATE
May 15, 1996

Hoping to energize his lackluster presidential campaign, Sen. Bob Dole, R-Kan., announced on May 15 that he would resign from the Senate—thereby relinquishing his post as Senate majority leader. Dole made his statement before a crowd of supporters and congressional colleagues in a room on the top floor of the Hart Senate Office Building, near the Capitol. At that point the presumptive Republican nominee, Dole told supporters he had "nowhere to go but the White House or home."

Dole's dramatic and unexpected step had the desired effect, at least momentarily. Dole had been lagging behind President Bill Clinton in the polls by as many as twenty points; polls in late May and early June showed him gaining on the president.

The resignation from the Senate was one of three risky steps Dole took during his campaign. Another was his embrace of a 15 percent tax cut proposal to spur the economy (a plan he had previously derided). The third was his selection of Jack Kemp as his vice presidential running mate (despite a history of antagonism between the two men).

But while these moves helped provide focus for the campaign and stirred enthusiasm among some Republican party loyalists, they ultimately were unsuccessful in warming the public to Bob Dole as a presidential candidate. Dole never came close to Clinton in the opinion polls. In the one poll that counted, on Election Day, he ended up eight points behind—better than the polls had predicted but not good enough. (Convention documents, pp. 478, 496; presidential debate documents, p. 707; election documents, p. 747)

Background to Dole's Move

The 1996 campaign was Dole's fourth national campaign and his third run for the White House. He was the Republican vice presidential candidate in 1976, and he unsuccessfully sought the Republican presidential nomination in 1980 and 1988.

In all his campaigns, Dole's main asset was experience: his widely acknowledged legislative skill in Congress, first as an influential leader of the Finance Committee, then as minority or majority leader of the Senate, depending on whether the Republican party was in power.

Never an ideologue, Dole was best known inside the Washington beltway for his ability to put together a political deal. Dole had the patience to sit through endless meetings with his Senate colleagues, waiting for just the right moment for a compromise. When the Clinton administration came into office in 1993, Dole's specialty became legislative gridlock—preventing the Democratic majority in Congress from enacting legislation wanted by the Democratic president.

After the Republicans captured control of the Senate in the 1994 elections, Dole seemed well-positioned as majority leader to run for president. His congressional stature made him the automatic front-runner, the candidate who could most easily capture public attention with his actions in Washington.

During the presidential primary season, Dole found his congressional role a double-edged sword. While it demonstrated his leadership abilities, the Senate position also meant Dole had to spend time attending to events on Capitol Hill. Increasingly, Dole was seen as a leader who was falling victim to the very legislative gridlock he had once used for his own purposes. Democrats were successfully blocking the Republican-led Senate from passing key elements of the Republican legislative program, most notably a constitutional amendment requiring a balanced budget. Democrats were also putting Dole on the defensive with an aggressive, and politically popular, move to increase the minimum wage.

Congress, never high in public esteem, was again becoming the subject of ridicule, this time with the Republicans in charge of both houses. Although he had little sympathy for the antigovernment agenda of Republican conservatives in the House, Dole could not entirely escape the backlash of growing public dissatisfaction with the contentious style of his House counterpart, Speaker Newt Gingrich. By resigning, Dole clearly was hoping to rise above the partisan squabbling in Congress and present himself as a leader with a national constituency. "He needs to be more than majority leader in a Senate that hasn't met public expectations," said Georgetown University political scientist Stephen Wayne.

Dole on the Stump

To symbolize his decision to leave his Washington power base, Dole flew to Chicago the day after his resignation announcement and campaigned wearing a suit, but without a tie. "Well, it's good to be out of Washington, D.C.," he told the crowd.

While Dole continued to campaign, he returned often to Washington, where he remained in the Senate until his resignation took effect on June 11. Senate Republicans the next day elected Trent Lott of Mississippi, who had been majority whip, to succeed Dole as majority leader. Lott easily defeated his fellow Mississippian, Thad Cochran.

Dole also abandoned the tieless, informal look he had sported in Chicago, apparently deciding it was better to be seen as presidential. Free of his Senate duties, Dole was able to spend all his time campaigning.

The shock effect of his resignation from the Senate soon wore off, however, and by the Republican convention in August Dole was once again struggling to explain to the public why he should be elected and Bill Clinton should be ousted from the White House. The backroom bargaining and cajoling skills that had made Dole an effective leader in the Senate were of little use in a national presidential campaign.

Ultimately, Dole's big gamble of leaving the Senate did not pay off. He could not credibly portray himself as an outsider who would bring fresh vision and ideas to Washington—a part Clinton had successfully played in 1992. Once he gave up his base of power and prestige on the floor of the Senate, Dole became just another politician desperately grabbing for the top rung of American politics.

Following is the text of the statement issued May 15, 1996, by Sen. Bob Dole, R-Kan., announcing that he would resign from the Senate to devote all his time to running for the presidency:

Let me say to many of my friends, and my wife, Elizabeth, and daughter, Robin, and others, we're very honored to have you here.

And I'd just say, ladies and gentlemen, one of the qualities of American politics that distinguishes us from other nations is that we judge our politicians as much by the manner in which they leave office as by the vigor with which they pursue it. You do not lay claim to the office you hold, it lays claim to you. Your obligation is to bring to it the gifts you can of labor and honesty and then to depart with grace. And my time to leave this office has come, and I will seek the presidency with nothing to fall back on but the judgment of the people, and nowhere to go but the White House or home. [Applause.]

Six times I've run for Republican leader of the United States Senate and six times my colleagues, giving me their trust, have elected me, and I'm proud of that.

So my campaign for the president is not merely about obtaining office. It's about fundamental things, consequential things, things that are real. My campaign is about telling the truth, it's about doing what is right, it's about electing a president who's not attracted to the glories of the office, but rather to its difficulties. It's about electing a president, who once he takes office, will keep his perspective and remain by his deepest nature and inclination one of the people.

Therefore, as the campaign for the president begins in earnest, it is my obligation to the Senate and to the people of America to leave behind all the trappings of power, all comfort and all security.

So today I announce that I will forego the privileges not only of the office of the majority leader but of the United States Senate itself, from which I resign effective on or before June 11th. And I will then stand before you without office or authority, a private citizen, a Kansan, an American, just a man. But I will be the same man I was when I walked into the room, the same man I was yesterday and the day before, and a long time ago when I arose from my hospital bed and was permitted by the grace of God to walk again in the world. And I trust in the hard way, for little has come to me except in the hard way, which is good because we have a hard task ahead of us.

We are gaining, but still behind in the polls. The press does not lean our way. And many Beltway pundits confidently dismiss my chances of victory. I do not find this disheartening and I do not find it discouraging, for this is where I touch the ground, and it is in touching the ground in moments of difficulty that I've always found my strength. I have been there before, I have done it the hard way, and I will do it the hard way once again. [Applause.]

For today I will begin to reconstitute our momentum until it is a great and agile force—clear in direction, irresistible in effect. Our campaign will leave Washington behind to look to America. As summer nears, I will seek the bright light and open spaces of this beautiful country and will ask for the wise counsel of its people, from the sea coasts of Maine and California to the old railroad towns in the Midwest to the verdant South, from the mountains of Colorado to the suburbs of Chicago, and in places in between known mainly to you who call them home.

I have absolute confidence in the victory that to some may seen unattainable; this is because I have seen victory and I have seen defeat and I know when one is set to give way to the other. And to concentrate upon the campaign, giving all and risking all, I must leave Congress that I have loved, and which I have been honored to serve—many of my friends here today. And some might find it surprising, given the view that Congress has been my life, but that is not so. With all due respect to Congress, America has been my life.

And the very least a presidential candidate owes America is his full attention—everything he can give, everything he has—and that is what America shall receive from me.

I am highly privileged to be my party's presidential nominee, and I am content that my fate and my story are for the American people to decide. For the American people have always known, through our long and trying history, that God has blessed the hard way. Because of this, as I say thank you and farewell to the Senate, as summer nears, and as the campaign begins, my heart is buoyant.

Thank you, and may God guide us to what is right. Thank you very much.

SUPREME COURT ON
PUNITIVE DAMAGES
May 20, 1996

*The Supreme Court waded into the debate on limits on punitive dam-
ages on May 20 when it struck down as "grossly excessive" an award of $2
million to an Alabama man who had bought a new BMW without being told
its paint had been retouched. On May 2 President Bill Clinton had vetoed
legislation that sought to place limits on the amount of money that could
be awarded to consumers who were injured by faulty products.*

*Congress has tried and failed several times to resolve the issue of limit-
ing the amounts that juries could award in consumer product liability
cases. Manufacturers have long sought uniform federal limits on liability,
arguing that an explosion of litigation and unpredictable jury awards
raise costs to manufacturers, discouraging innovation and keeping new
and helpful products from the market. Costly litigation also raises the price
of consumer goods. Consumers and trial lawyers counter that limits would
unfairly curb consumers' rights to seek legal remedy when they have been
injured. They also maintain that punitive damages are an incentive for
manufacturers to market safe products.*

The Court Decision

In finding the award in the case of BMW v. Gore *so excessive as to be a
violation of due process of law, the Court did not take sides in the debate,
but it did indicate its concern that liability awards not be arbitrary. "Elementary notions of fairness enshrined in our constitutional jurisprudence
dictate that a person receive fair notice not only of the conduct that will
subject him to punishment but also of the severity of the penalty that a
state may impose," Justice John Paul Stevens wrote for the five-justice
majority.*

*In the original trial, Ira Gore Jr., the owner of the repainted BMW,
argued that his repainted car was worth 10 percent less than a new car
that had not been touched up. He therefore sought and won $4 million in
punitive damages. That amount represented $4,000—10 percent of the*

purchase price of the car—multiplied by one thousand, the approximate number of repainted cars BMW had sold in the United States in the last ten years without disclosing the repair. On appeal, the Alabama Supreme Court said the trial jury had erred in taking BMW sales in other states into account, and it reduced the award to $2 million.

In determining that the $2 million award was still excessive, Stevens said the majority used three guideposts: "the degree of reprehensibility of the nondisclosure; the disparity between the harm or potential harm suffered by Dr. Gore and his punitive damages award; and the difference between this remedy and the civil penalties authorized or imposed in comparable cases." The majority found that BMW's conduct was not egregiously improper, that the ratio between Gore's economic loss and his award was a "breathtaking 500 to 1," and that the maximum civil penalty under Alabama law for a deceptive trade practice was $2,000.

In a dissent joined by Chief Justice William H. Rehnquist, Justice Ruth Bader Ginsburg said the majority "unnecessarily and unwisely ventures into territory traditionally within the States' domain, and does so in the face of reform measures recently adopted or currently under consideration" in several state legislatures. In a separate dissent Justice Antonin Scalia, joined by Justice Clarence Thomas, also objected to the Court's hearing the case, calling it "an unjustified incursion into the province of state governments." Scalia also rejected the Court's guideposts, saying "these criss-crossing platitudes" will "mark a road to nowhere; they provide no real guidance at all."

Clinton's Veto

The legislation that Clinton vetoed would have limited not only the amount of punitive damages a jury could award in a product liability case, but also the cases in which such awards could be made. To be awarded punitive damages, a plaintiff would have to show with "clear and convincing evidence" that the injury caused by a faulty product resulted from the manufacturer's conscious and flagrant indifference to safety. The cap on punitive damages for large manufacturers and municipalities would be the larger of $250,000 or two times compensatory damages, which is the sum of economic damages, such as lost wages and medical expenses, and noneconomic damages for pain and suffering. Damage awards for businesses and municipalities with fewer than twenty-five full-time employees and individuals with a net worth of less than $500,000 could not exceed the lesser of those two amounts. Judges would be allowed to increase a punitive damage award to punish egregious conduct in cases involving large companies or municipalities.

In his veto message, Clinton said the legislation went too far to protect manufacturers at the expense of consumers and that it interfered with the traditional role of the states in this area. "This bill inappropriately intrudes on State authority, and does so in a way that tilts the legal playing field against consumers," Clinton said. Sen. Bob Dole of Kansas, the leading Republican presidential challenger, was quick to charge that Clinton vetoed the legislation "because he believes what's good for the trial lawyers is also good for America." The American Trial Lawyers Association, a powerful lobbying force in Washington and strong supporter of the president's reelection bid, opposed the legislation.

House Republicans had passed an even broader product liability bill as one of the planks in their Contract with America. That version would have applied a stringent cap on all punitive damages in all civil cases and put special limits on medical malpractice awards.

Following are excerpts from the majority and dissenting opinions in BMW of North America, Inc. v. Ira Gore, Jr., *in which the Supreme Court ruled on May 20, 1996, that a punitive damages award of $2 million to the owner of a new car that had been repainted without the buyer's knowledge was "grossly excessive":*

No. 94–896

BMW of North America, Inc.,
Petitioner
v.
Ira Gore, Jr.

On writ of certiorari to the
Supreme Court of Alabama

[May 20, 1996]

JUSTICE STEVENS delivered the opinion of the Court.

The Due Process Clause of the Fourteenth Amendment prohibits a State from imposing a "'grossly excessive'" punishment on a tortfeasor. *TXO Production Corp.* v. *Alliance Resources Corp.* (1993). The wrongdoing involved in this case was the decision by a national distributor of automobiles not to advise its dealers, and hence their customers, of predelivery damage to new cars when the cost of repair amounted to less than 3 percent of the car's suggested retail price. The question presented is whether a $2 million punitive damages award to the purchaser of one of these cars exceeds the constitutional limit.

I

In January 1990, Dr. Ira Gore, Jr. (respondent), purchased a black BMW sports sedan for $40,750.88 from an authorized BMW dealer in Birmingham, Alabama. After driving the car for approximately nine months, and without noticing any flaws in its appearance, Dr. Gore took the car to "Slick Finish," an independent detailer, to make it look "'snazzier than it normally would appear.'" Mr. Slick, the proprietor, detected evidence that the car had been repainted. Convinced that he had been cheated, Dr. Gore brought suit against petitioner BMW of North America (BMW), the American distributor of BMW automobiles. Dr. Gore alleged, *inter alia*, that the failure to disclose that the car had been repainted constituted suppression of a material fact. The complaint prayed for $500,000 in compensatory and punitive damages, and costs.

At trial, BMW acknowledged that it had adopted a nationwide policy in 1983 concerning cars that were damaged in the course of manufacture or transportation. If the cost of repairing the damage exceeded 3 percent of the car's suggested retail price, the car was placed in company service for a period of time and then sold as used. If the repair cost did not exceed 3 percent of the suggested retail price, however, the car was sold as new without advising the dealer that any repairs had been made. Because the $601.37 cost of repainting Dr. Gore's car was only about 1.5 percent of its suggested retail price, BMW did not disclose the damage or repair to the Birmingham dealer.

Dr. Gore asserted that his repainted car was worth less than a car that had not been refinished. To prove his actual damages of $4,000, he relied on the testimony of a former BMW dealer, who estimated that the value of a repainted BMW was approximately 10 percent less than the value of a new car that had not been damaged and repaired. To support his claim for punitive damages, Dr. Gore introduced evidence that since 1983 BMW had sold 983 refinished cars as new, including 14 in Alabama, without disclosing that the cars had been repainted before sale at a cost of more than $300 per vehicle. Using the actual damage estimate of $4,000 per vehicle, Dr. Gore argued that a punitive award of $4 million would provide an appropriate penalty for selling approximately 1,000 cars for more than they were worth.

... BMW argued that it was under no obligation to disclose repairs of minor damage to new cars and that Dr. Gore's car was as good as a car with the original factory finish. It disputed Dr. Gore's assertion that the value of the car was impaired by the repainting and argued that this good-faith belief made a punitive award inappropriate. BMW also maintained that transactions in jurisdictions other than Alabama had no relevance to Dr. Gore's claim.

The jury returned a verdict finding BMW liable for compensatory damages of $4,000. In addition, the jury assessed $4 million in punitive damages, based on a determination that the nondisclosure policy constituted "gross, oppressive or malicious" fraud.

BMW filed a post-trial motion to set aside the punitive damages award. The company introduced evidence to establish that its nondisclosure policy was consistent with the laws of roughly 25 States .... The most stringent of these statutes required disclosure of repairs costing more than 3 percent of the suggested retail price; none mandated disclosure of less costly repairs. ... BMW contended that its conduct was lawful in these States and therefore could not provide the basis for an award of punitive damages.

BMW also drew the court's attention to the fact that its nondisclosure policy had never been adjudged unlawful before this action was filed. Just months before Dr. Gore's case went to trial, the jury in a similar lawsuit filed by another Alabama BMW purchaser found that BMW's failure to disclose paint repair constituted fraud. Before the judgment in this case, BMW changed its policy by taking steps to avoid the sale of any refinished vehicles in Alabama and two other States. When the $4 million verdict was returned in this case, BMW promptly instituted a nationwide policy of full disclosure of all repairs, no matter how minor.

In response to BMW's arguments, Dr. Gore asserted that the policy change demonstrated the efficacy of the punitive damages award. He noted that while no jury had held the policy unlawful, BMW had received a number of customer complaints relating to undisclosed repairs and had settled some lawsuits. Finally, he maintained that the disclosure statutes of other States were irrelevant because BMW had failed to offer any evidence that the disclosure statutes supplanted, rather than supplemented, existing causes of action for common-law fraud.

The trial judge denied BMW's post-trial motion, holding, *inter alia*, that the award was not excessive. On appeal, the Alabama Supreme Court also rejected BMW's claim that the award exceeded the constitutionally permissible amount. (1994). The court's excessiveness inquiry applied the factors articulated in *Green Oil Co.* v. *Hornsby* (Ala. 1989) and approved [by the U.S. Supreme Court] in *Pacific Mut. Life Ins. Co.* v. *Haslip* (1991). Based on its analysis, the court concluded that BMW's conduct was "reprehensible"; the nondisclosure was profitable for the company; the judgment "would not have a substantial impact upon [BMW's] financial position"; the litigation had been expensive; no criminal sanctions had been imposed on BMW for the same conduct; the award of no punitive damages in [the prior Alabama case] reflected "the inherent uncertainty of the trial process"; and the punitive award bore a "reasonable relationship" to "the harm that was likely to occur from [BMW's] conduct as well as . . . the harm that actually occurred."

The Alabama Supreme Court did, however, rule in BMW's favor on one critical point: The court found that the jury improperly computed the amount of punitive damages by multiplying Dr. Gore's compensatory damages by the number of similar sales in other jurisdictions. Having found the verdict tainted, the court held that "a constitutionally reasonable punitive damages award in this case is $2,000,000" and therefore ordered a remittitur in that amount. The court's discussion of the amount of its remitted award expressly disclaimed any reliance on "acts that occurred in other jurisdictions"; instead, the court explained that it had used a "comparative analysis" that considered Alabama cases, "along with cases from other jurisdictions, involving the sale of an automobile where the seller misrepresented the condition of the vehicle and the jury awarded punitive damages to the purchaser."

Because we believed that a review of this case would help to illuminate "the character of the standard that will identify constitutionally excessive awards" of punitive damages, see *Honda Motor Co.* v. *Oberg* (1994), we granted certiorari (1995).

[II omitted]

III

Elementary notions of fairness enshrined in our constitutional jurisprudence dictate that a person receive fair notice not only of the conduct that will subject him to punishment but also of the severity of the penalty that a State may impose. Three guideposts, each of which indicates that BMW did not receive adequate notice of the magnitude of the sanction that Alabama might impose for adhering to the nondisclosure policy adopted in 1983, lead us to the conclusion that the $2 million award against BMW is grossly excessive: the degree of reprehensibility of the nondisclosure; the disparity between the harm or potential harm suffered by Dr. Gore and his punitive damages award; and the difference between this remedy and the civil penalties authorized or imposed in comparable cases. We discuss these considerations in turn.

Degree of Reprehensibility

Perhaps the most important indicium of the reasonableness of a punitive damages award is the degree of reprehensibility of the defendant's conduct. . . . This principle reflects the accepted view that some wrongs are more blameworthy than others. . . .

In this case, none of the aggravating factors associated with particularly reprehensible conduct is present. The harm BMW inflicted on Dr. Gore was purely economic in nature. The presale refinishing of the car had no effect on its performance or safety features, or even its appearance for at least nine months after his purchase. BMW's conduct evinced no indifference to or reckless disregard for the health and safety of others. To be sure, infliction of economic injury, especially when done intentionally through affirmative acts of misconduct or when the target is financially vulnerable, can warrant a substantial penalty. But this observation does not convert all acts that cause economic harm into torts that are sufficiently reprehensible to justify a significant sanction in addition to compensatory damages.

Dr. Gore contends that BMW's conduct was particularly reprehensible because nondisclosure of the repairs to his car formed part of a nationwide pattern of tortious conduct. Certainly, evidence that a defendant has repeatedly engaged in prohibited conduct while knowing or suspecting that it was unlawful would provide relevant support for an argument that strong medicine is required to cure the defendant's disrespect for the law. . . .

. . . There is no evidence that BMW acted in bad faith when it sought to establish the appropriate line between presumptively minor damage and damage requiring disclosure to purchasers. . . .

Finally, the record in this case discloses no deliberate false statements, acts of affirmative misconduct, or concealment of evidence of improper motive. . . . We accept, of course, the jury's finding that BMW suppressed a material fact which Alabama law obligated it to communicate to prospective purchasers of repainted cars in that State. But the omission of a material fact may be less reprehensible than a deliberate false statement, particularly when there is a good-faith basis for believing that no duty to disclose exists.

. . . Because this case exhibits none of the circumstances ordinarily associated with egregiously improper conduct, we are persuaded that BMW's conduct was not sufficiently reprehensible to warrant imposition of a $2 million exemplary damages award.

Ratio

The second and perhaps most commonly cited indicium of an unreasonable or excessive punitive damages award is its ratio to the actual harm inflicted on the plaintiff. . . . Our decisions in both *Haslip* and *TXO* endorsed the proposition that a comparison between the compensatory award and the punitive award is significant.

In *Haslip* we concluded that even though a punitive damages award of "more than 4 times the amount of compensatory damages" might be "close to the line," it did not "cross the line into the area of constitutional impropriety." *TXO*, following dicta in *Haslip*, refined this analysis by confirming that the proper inquiry is "'whether there is a reasonable relationship between the punitive damages award and *the harm likely to result* from the defendant's conduct as well as the harm that actually has occurred.'" Thus, in upholding the $10 million award in *TXO*, we relied on the difference between that figure and the harm to the victim that would have ensued if the tortious plan had succeeded. That difference suggested that the relevant ratio was not more than 10 to 1.

The $2 million in punitive damages awarded to Dr. Gore by the Alabama Supreme Court is 500 times the amount of his actual harm as determined by the jury. Moreover, there is no suggestion that Dr. Gore or any other BMW purchaser was threatened with any additional potential harm by BMW's nondisclosure policy. The disparity in this case is thus dramatically greater than those considered in *Haslip* and *TXO*.

Of course, we have consistently rejected the notion that the constitutional line is marked by a simple mathematical formula, even one that compares actual and potential damages to the punitive award. Indeed, low awards of compensatory damages may properly support a higher ratio than high compensatory awards, if, for example, a particularly egregious act has resulted in only a small amount of economic damages. A higher ratio may also be justified in cases in which the injury is hard to detect or the monetary value of noneconomic harm might have been difficult to determine. It is appropriate, therefore, to reiterate our rejection of a categorical approach. Once again, "we return to what we said . . . in *Haslip:* 'We need not, and indeed we cannot, draw a mathematical bright line between the constitutionally acceptable and the constitutionally unacceptable that would fit every case. We can say, however, that [a] general concer[n] of reasonableness . . . properly enter[s] into the constitutional calculus.'" *TXO*. In most cases, the ratio will be within a constitutionally acceptable range, and remittitur will not be justified on this basis. When the ratio is a breathtaking 500 to 1, however, the award must surely "raise a suspicious judicial eyebrow." *TXO* (O'CONNOR, J., dissenting).

Sanctions for Comparable Misconduct

Comparing the punitive damages award and the civil or criminal penalties that could be imposed for comparable misconduct provides a third indicium of excessiveness. . . . In this case the $2 million economic sanction imposed on BMW is substantially greater than the statutory fines available in Alabama and elsewhere for similar malfeasance.

The maximum civil penalty authorized by the Alabama Legislature for a violation of its Deceptive Trade Practices Act is $2,000; other States authorize more severe sanctions, with the maxima ranging from $5,000 to $10,000. . . .

The sanction imposed in this case cannot be justified on the ground that it was necessary to deter future misconduct without considering whether less drastic remedies could be expected to achieve that goal. The fact that a multimillion dollar penalty prompted a change in policy sheds no light on the question whether a lesser deterrent would have adequately protected the interests of Alabama consumers. In the absence of a history of noncompliance with known statutory requirements, there is no basis for assuming that a more modest sanction would not have been sufficient to motivate full compliance with the disclosure requirement imposed by the Alabama Supreme Court in this case.

IV

The fact that BMW is a large corporation rather than an impecunious individual does not diminish its entitlement to fair notice of the demands that the several States impose on the conduct of its business. Indeed, its status as an active participant in the national economy implicates the federal interest in preventing individual States from imposing undue burdens on interstate commerce. While each State has ample power to protect its own consumers, none may use the punitive damages deterrent as a means of imposing its regulatory policies on the entire Nation.

As in *Haslip*, we are not prepared to draw a bright line marking the limits of a constitutionally acceptable punitive damages award. Unlike that case, however, we are fully convinced that the grossly excessive award imposed in this case transcends the constitutional limit. Whether the appropriate remedy requires a new trial or merely an independent determination by the Alabama Supreme Court of the award necessary to vindicate the economic interests of Alabama consumers is a matter that should be addressed by the state court in the first instance. The judgment is reversed, and the case is remanded for further proceedings not inconsistent with this opinion.

It is so ordered.

JUSTICE SCALIA, with whom JUSTICE THOMAS joins, dissenting.

Today we see the latest manifestation of this Court's recent and increasingly insistent "concern about punitive damages that 'run wild.'" *Pacific Mut.*

Life Ins. Co. v. *Haslip* (1991). Since the Constitution does not make that concern any of our business, the Court's activities in this area are an unjustified incursion into the province of state governments. . . .

[I and II omitted]

III

In Part III of its opinion, the Court identifies "[t]hree guideposts" that lead it to the conclusion that the award in this case is excessive: degree of reprehensibility, ratio between punitive award and plaintiff's actual harm, and legislative sanctions provided for comparable misconduct.

The legal significance of these "guideposts" is nowhere explored, but their necessary effect is to establish federal standards governing the hitherto exclusively state law of damages. Apparently . . . all three federal "guideposts" can be overridden if "necessary to deter future misconduct"—a loophole that will encourage state reviewing courts to uphold awards as necessary for the "adequat[e] protect[ion]" of state consumers. By effectively requiring state reviewing courts to concoct rationalizations—whether within the "guideposts" or through the loophole—to justify the intuitive punitive reactions of state juries, the Court accords neither category of institution the respect it deserves.

Of course it will not be easy for the States to comply with this new federal law of damages, no matter how willing they are to do so. In truth, the "guideposts" mark a road to nowhere; they provide no real guidance at all. As to "degree of reprehensibility" of the defendant's conduct, we learn that "'nonviolent crimes are less serious than crimes marked by violence or the threat of violence,'" and that "'trickery and deceit'" are "more reprehensible than negligence." As to the ratio of punitive to compensatory damages, we are told that a "'general concer[n] of reasonableness . . . enter[s] into the constitutional calculus,'"—though even "a breathtaking 500 to 1" will not necessarily do anything more than "'raise a suspicious judicial eyebrow.'" . . . And as to legislative sanctions provided for comparable misconduct, they should be accorded "'substantial deference.'" One expects the Court to conclude: "To thine own self be true."

These criss-crossing platitudes yield no real answers in no real cases. And it must be noted that the Court nowhere says that these three "guideposts" are the only guideposts; indeed, it makes very clear that they are not. . . . In other words, even these utter platitudes . . . may be overridden by other unnamed considerations. The Court has constructed a framework that does not genuinely constrain, that does not inform state legislatures and lower courts—that does nothing at all except confer an artificial air of doctrinal analysis upon its essentially ad hoc determination that this particular award of punitive damages was not "fair." . . .

For the foregoing reasons, I respectfully dissent.

JUSTICE GINSBURG, with whom THE CHIEF JUSTICE joins, dissenting.

The Court, I am convinced, unnecessarily and unwisely ventures into territory traditionally within the States' domain, and does so in the face of reform measures recently adopted or currently under consideration in legislative arenas. The Alabama Supreme Court, in this case, endeavored to follow this Court's prior instructions; and, more recently, Alabama's highest court has installed further controls on awards of punitive damages. I would therefore leave the state court's judgment undisturbed, and resist unnecessary intrusion into an area dominantly of state concern.

[I omitted]

II

A

Alabama's Supreme Court reports that it "thoroughly and painstakingly" reviewed the jury's award, according to principles set out in its own path-marking decisions and in this Court's opinions in *TXO* and *Pacific Mut. Life Ins. Co.* v. *Haslip* (1991). The Alabama court said it gave weight to several factors, including BMW's deliberate ("reprehensible") presentation of refinished cars as new and undamaged, without disclosing that the value of those cars had been reduced by an estimated 10%, the financial position of the defendant, and the costs of litigation. These standards, we previously held, "impos[e] a sufficiently definite and meaningful constraint on the discretion of Alabama factfinders in awarding punitive damages." Alabama's highest court could have displayed its labor pains more visibly, but its judgment is nonetheless entitled to a presumption of legitimacy. . . .

B

The Court finds Alabama's $2 million award not simply excessive, but grossly so, and therefore unconstitutional. The decision leads us further into territory traditionally within the States' domain, and commits the Court, now and again, to correct "misapplication of a properly stated rule of law." . . . The Court is not well equipped for this mission. Tellingly, the Court repeats that it brings to the task no "mathematical formula," no "categorical approach," no "bright line." It has only a vague concept of substantive due process, a "raised eyebrow" test, as its ultimate guide.

In contrast to habeas corpus review . . . , the Court will work at this business alone. It will not be aided by the federal district courts and courts of appeals. It will be the only federal court policing the area. The Court's readiness to superintend state court punitive damages awards is all the more puzzling in view of the Court's longstanding reluctance to countenance review, even by courts of appeals, of the size of verdicts returned by juries in federal district court proceedings. And the reexamination prominent in state courts and in legislative arenas serves to underscore why the Court's enterprise is undue.

For the reasons stated, I dissent from this Court's disturbance of the judgment the Alabama Supreme Court has made.

SUPREME COURT ON
DISCRIMINATION AGAINST GAYS
May 20, 1996

In a case that had come to symbolize the nationwide controversy over gay rights, the Supreme Court, on a 6–3 ruling May 20, overturned an amendment to Colorado's constitution that would have prevented any government efforts to protect homosexuals from discrimination. The amendment, wrote Justice Anthony M. Kennedy for the majority, "classifies homosexuals not to further a proper legislative end but to make them unequal to everyone else. This Colorado cannot do. A state cannot so deem a class of people a stranger to its laws."

The ruling in Romer v. Evans *was considered a significant victory for gay rights. Although it did not necessarily signal how the Court would rule in other gay rights cases likely to come before it—namely, the military's "don't ask, don't tell" policy toward homosexuals and same-sex marriages—gay rights activists were heartened by the majority's forceful opinion holding that antigay sentiment by a majority of a state's voters did not justify discrimination.* (Same-sex marriages, p. 687)

In a heated dissent, Justice Antonin Scalia said the majority's ruling "places the prestige of this institution behind the proposition that opposition to homosexuality is as reprehensible as racial or religious bias. Whether it is or not is precisely the cultural debate that gave rise" to the state constitutional amendment in the first place. "This Court has no business imposing upon all Americans the resolution favored by the elite class from which the Members of this institution are selected, pronouncing that 'animosity' toward homosexuality is evil."

The sharp polarization among the justices echoed that in Colorado and several other states where antigay measures were under consideration. The Colorado amendment, adopted in a statewide referendum in 1992 with 53 percent of the vote, barred any government entity in the state from adopting any policy that would entitle anyone of "homosexual, lesbian or bisexual orientation . . . to have or claim any minority status, quota preferences, protected status or claim of discrimination." Any change in policy

*toward homosexuals would have to be done through another state constitu-
tional amendment.*

*The amendment was adopted after several local governments, including
the city of Denver, had banned discrimination against gays in housing,
employment, education, public accommodations, and health and welfare
services. The campaign to put the amendment on the state ballot was initiated by Kevin Tebedo, executive director of Colorado for Family Values in
Colorado Springs, and was supported by conservative organizations
across the state.*

*Controversy over the amendment continued after its adoption in
November 1992, when gays and their supporters mounted a nationwide
boycott against the state. Meanwhile, the amendment was challenged in
court by several gays, who argued that the amendment deprived gays of
their federal constitutional right to equal protection of the laws because it
removed the ability of local governments to offer them specific protections
from discrimination similar to those that might be offered to the handi-
capped or other groups.*

*Reaction to the Supreme Court's ruling was also sharply divided. "There
is justice in America. We are jubilant," said Elizabeth Birch of the Human
Rights Campaign. "Moral people in Colorado" have been denied "the right
to set standards for their community," countered the Traditional Values
Coalition, which said it represented 31,000 churches.*

The last time the Court dealt with homosexual rights was in the case of
Bowers v. Hardwick *in 1986, when it upheld a Georgia statute prohibiting
sodomy. On a 5–4 vote, the Court said that the Constitution's guarantees of
personal liberty and privacy did not protect private homosexual conduct
between consenting adults. Since his retirement in 1987, Justice Lewis
Powell, who was part of the majority, has stated that he "probably made a
mistake" in voting to uphold the Georgia law.*

The Majority and Dissenting Opinions

*The Supreme Court majority rejected the state's argument that the
amendment did no more than revoke special rights for homosexuals. "We
find nothing special in the protections Amendment 2 withholds," Kennedy
wrote. "These are protections taken for granted by most people either
because they already have them or do not need them; these are protections
against exclusion from an almost limitless number of transactions and
endeavors that constitute ordinary civic life in a free society."*

*The majority said the state constitutional amendment failed even the
Court's lowest level of scrutiny, which permits a state to classify groups of
people so long as the classification has a rational basis suited to achieving
some legitimate end. The primary rationale the state offered, Kennedy
said, was respect for other citizens' freedom of association, particularly
those landlords or employers who object to homosexuality. However,
Kennedy said "the breadth of the Amendment is so far removed from these
particular justifications that we find it impossible to credit them. We can-*

not say that Amendment 2 is directed to any identifiable legitimate purpose or discrete objective. It is a status-based enactment divorced from any factual context from which we could discern a relationship to legitimate state interests; it is a classification of persons undertaken for its own sake, something the Equal Protection Clause does not permit." Justices John Paul Stevens, Sandra Day O'Connor, David H. Souter, Ruth Bader Ginsburg, and Stephen G. Breyer joined Kennedy's opinion.

In his dissent, which was joined by Chief Justice William H. Rehnquist and Justice Clarence Thomas, Scalia said the amendment was "not the manifestation of a 'bare . . . desire to harm' homosexuals, but is rather a modest attempt by seemingly tolerant Coloradans to preserve traditional sexual mores through use of the laws." Scalia also maintained that the state had a legitimate rational reason for barring special protections for homosexuals. "If it is constitutionally permissible for a State to make homosexual conduct criminal," he wrote, referring to the Court's ruling in Bowers, *"surely it is constitutionally permissible for a State to enact other laws merely disfavoring homosexual conduct."*

Reaction to the Ruling

Gay activists and their supporters were pleased not only with the decision, but also with its forcefulness and with the fact that the majority opinion was written by one of the more conservative justices. The Court's conclusion that "antidiscrimination protections are not special rights, they are equal rights, has enormous implications because the Court speaks not only to the parties in this case but to the entire country about what's right in a democratic society," said Matt Coles, director of the Lesbian and Gay Rights Project of the American Civil Liberties Union.

Supporters of the amendment disagreed. The decision came from "an out-of-control judiciary" and "should send chills down the back of anyone who cares whether the people of this nation any longer have the power of self-rule," said Gary L. Bauer, president of the Family Research Council. Rep. Charles T. Canady, R-Fla., said "American citizens should be outraged" by the ruling. "It is no small matter for the Court to invalidate a popularly adopted measure. . . . Quite apart from the particular context of the Colorado case, all Americans should be profoundly troubled by the effect of this decision on our democratic way of life."

> *Following are excerpts from the majority and minority opinions in the Supreme Court's ruling May 20, 1996, in* Romer v. Evans, *in which the Court declared unconstitutional a state constitutional amendment prohibiting any state government unit from enacting any measure to protect homosexuals from discrimination:*

No. 94–1039

Roy Romer, Governor of Colorado, et al., Petitioners
v.
Richard G. Evans et al.

On writ of certiorari to the Supreme Court of Colorado

[May 20, 1996]

JUSTICE KENNEDY delivered the opinion of the Court.

One century ago, the first Justice Harlan admonished this Court that the Constitution "neither knows nor tolerates classes among citizens." *Plessy* v. *Ferguson* (1896) (dissenting opinion). Unheeded then, those words now are understood to state a commitment to the law's neutrality where the rights of persons are at stake. The Equal Protection Clause enforces this principle and today requires us to hold invalid a provision of Colorado's Constitution.

I

The enactment challenged in this case is an amendment to the Constitution of the State of Colorado, adopted in a 1992 statewide referendum. The parties and the state courts refer to it as "Amendment 2," its designation when submitted to the voters. The impetus for the amendment and the contentious campaign that preceded its adoption came in large part from ordinances that had been passed in various Colorado municipalities. For example, the cities of Aspen and Boulder and the City and County of Denver each had enacted ordinances which banned discrimination in many transactions and activities, including housing, employment, education, public accommodations, and health and welfare services. What gave rise to the statewide controversy was the protection the ordinances afforded to persons discriminated against by reason of their sexual orientation. Amendment 2 repeals these ordinances to the extent they prohibit discrimination on the basis of "homosexual, lesbian or bisexual orientation, conduct, practices or relationships."

Yet Amendment 2, in explicit terms, does more than repeal or rescind these provisions. It prohibits all legislative, executive or judicial action at any level of state or local government designed to protect the named class, a class we shall refer to as homosexual persons or gays and lesbians. The amendment reads:

"No Protected Status Based on Homosexual, Lesbian, or Bisexual Orientation. Neither the State of Colorado, through any of its branches or departments, nor any of its agencies, political subdivisions, municipalities or school districts, shall enact, adopt or enforce any statute, regulation, ordinance or policy whereby homosexual, lesbian or bisexual orientation, conduct, practices or relationships shall constitute or otherwise be the basis of or entitle any person or class of persons to have or claim any minority status, quota preferences, protected status or claim of discrimination. This Section of the Constitution shall be in all respects self-executing."

Soon after Amendment 2 was adopted, this litigation to declare its invalidity and enjoin its enforcement was commenced in the District Court for the City and County of Denver. Among the plaintiffs (respondents here) were homosexual persons, some of them government employees. They alleged that enforcement of Amendment 2 would subject them to immediate and substantial risk of discrimination on the basis of their sexual orientation. Other plaintiffs (also respondents here) included the three municipalities whose ordinances we have cited and certain other governmental entities which had acted earlier to protect homosexuals from discrimination but would be prevented by Amendment 2 from continuing to do so. Although Governor Romer had been on record opposing the adoption of Amendment 2, he was named in his official capacity as a defendant, together with the Colorado Attorney General and the State of Colorado.

The trial court granted a preliminary injunction to stay enforcement of Amendment 2, and an appeal was taken to the Supreme Court of Colorado. Sustaining the interim injunction and remanding the case for further proceedings, the State Supreme Court held that Amendment 2 was subject to strict scrutiny under the Fourteenth Amendment because it infringed the fundamental right of gays and lesbians to participate in the political process. *Evans* v. *Romer* (1993) (*Evans I*). To reach this conclusion, the state court relied on our voting rights cases and on our precedents involving discriminatory restructuring of governmental decisionmaking. On remand, the State advanced various arguments in an effort to show that Amendment 2 was narrowly tailored to serve compelling interests, but the trial court found none sufficient. It enjoined enforcement of Amendment 2, and the Supreme Court of Colorado, in a second opinion, affirmed the ruling. *Evans* v. *Romer* (1994) (*Evans II*). We granted certiorari and now affirm the judgment, but on a rationale different from that adopted by the State Supreme Court.

II

The State's principal argument in defense of Amendment 2 is that it puts gays and lesbians in the same position as all other persons. So, the State says, the measure does no more than deny homosexuals special rights. This reading of the amendment's language is implausible. We rely not upon our own interpretation of the amendment but upon the authoritative construction of Colorado's Supreme Court. The state court, deeming it unnecessary to determine the full extent of the amendment's reach, found it invalid even on a modest reading of its implications. The critical discussion of the amendment, set out in *Evans I*, is as follows:

"The immediate objective of Amendment 2 is, at a minimum, to repeal existing statutes, regulations, ordinances, and policies of state and local entities that barred discrimination based on sexual orientation. . . .

"The 'ultimate effect' of Amendment 2 is to prohibit any governmental entity from adopting similar, or more protective statutes, regulations, ordinances, or policies in the future unless the state constitution is first amended to permit such measures."

Sweeping and comprehensive is the change in legal status effected by this law. . . . Homosexuals, by state decree, are put in a solitary class with respect to transactions and relations in both the private and governmental spheres. The amendment withdraws from homosexuals, but no others, specific legal protection from the injuries caused by discrimination, and it forbids reinstatement of these laws and policies. The change that Amendment 2 works in the legal status of gays and lesbians in the private sphere is far-reaching, both on its own terms and when considered in light of the structure and operation of modern anti-discrimination laws. . . .

Amendment 2 bars homosexuals from securing protection against the injuries that these public-accommodations laws address. That in itself is a severe consequence, but there is more. Amendment 2, in addition, nullifies specific legal protections for this targeted class in all transactions in housing, sale of real estate, insurance, health and welfare services, private education, and employment.

Not confined to the private sphere, Amendment 2 also operates to repeal and forbid all laws or policies providing specific protection for gays or lesbians from discrimination by every level of Colorado government. The State Supreme Court cited two examples of protections in the governmental sphere that are now rescinded and may not be reintroduced. The first is Colorado Executive Order D0035 (1990), which forbids employment discrimination against "'all state employees, classified and exempt' on the basis of sexual orientation." Also repealed, and now forbidden, are "various provisions prohibiting discrimination based on sexual orientation at state colleges." The repeal of these measures and the prohibition against their future reenactment demonstrates that Amendment 2 has the same force and effect in Colorado's governmental sector as it does elsewhere and that it applies to policies as well as ordinary legislation. . . .

. . . [E]ven if, as we doubt, homosexuals could find some safe harbor in laws of general application, we cannot accept the view that Amendment 2's prohibition on specific legal protections does no more than deprive homosexuals of special rights. To the contrary, the amendment imposes a special disability upon those persons alone. Homosexuals are forbidden the safeguards that others enjoy or may seek without constraint. They can obtain specific protection against discrimination only by enlisting the citizenry of Colorado to amend the state constitution or perhaps, on the State's view, by trying to pass helpful laws of general applicability. This is so no matter how local or discrete the harm, no matter how public and widespread the injury. We find nothing special in the protections Amendment 2 withholds. These are protections taken for granted by most people either because they already have them or do not need them; these are protections against exclusion from an almost limitless number of transactions and endeavors that constitute ordinary civic life in a free society.

III

The Fourteenth Amendment's promise that no person shall be denied the equal protection of the laws must co-exist with the practical necessity that most legislation classifies for one purpose or another, with resulting disadvantage to various groups or persons. We have attempted to reconcile the principle with the reality by stating that, if a law neither burdens a fundamental right nor targets a suspect class, we will uphold the legislative classification so long as it bears a rational relation to some legitimate end.

Amendment 2 fails, indeed defies, even this conventional inquiry. First, the amendment has the peculiar property of imposing a broad and undifferentiated disability on a single named group, an exceptional and, as we shall explain, invalid form of legislation. Second, its sheer breadth is so discontinuous with the reasons offered for it that the amendment seems inexplicable by anything but animus toward the class that it affects; it lacks a rational relationship to legitimate state interests.

Taking the first point, even in the ordinary equal protection case calling for the most deferential of standards, we insist on knowing the relation between the classification adopted and the object to be attained. The search for the link between classification and objective gives substance to the Equal Protection Clause; it provides guidance and discipline for the legislature, which is entitled to know what sorts of laws it can pass; and it marks the limits of our own authority. In the ordinary case, a law will be sustained if it can be said to advance a legitimate government interest, even if the law seems unwise or works to the disadvantage of a particular group, or if the rationale for it seems tenuous. . . .

Amendment 2 confounds this normal process of judicial review. It is at once too narrow and too broad. It identifies persons by a single trait and then denies them protection across the board. The resulting disqualification of a class of persons from the right to seek specific protection from the law is unprecedented in our jurisprudence. . . .

It is not within our constitutional tradition to enact laws of this sort. Central both to the idea of the rule of law and to our own Constitution's guarantee of equal protection is the principle that government and each of its parts remain open on impartial terms to all who seek its assistance. . . . Respect for this principle explains why laws singling out a certain class of citizens for disfavored legal status or general hardships are rare. A law declaring that in general it shall be more difficult for one group of citizens than for all others to seek aid from the government is itself a denial of equal protection of the laws in the most literal sense. . . .

A . . . related point is that laws of the kind now before us raise the inevitable inference that the disadvantage imposed is born of animosity toward the class of persons affected. . . . Even laws enacted for broad and ambitious purposes often can be explained by reference to legitimate public policies which justify the incidental disadvantages they impose on certain persons. Amendment 2, however, in making a general announcement that gays and lesbians shall not have any particular protections from the law, inflicts on them immediate, continuing, and real injuries that outrun and belie any legitimate justifications that may be claimed for it. We conclude that, in addition to the far-reaching deficiencies of Amendment 2 that we have noted, the principles it offends, in another sense, are conventional and venerable; a law must bear a rational relationship to a legitimate governmental purpose, and Amendment 2 does not.

The primary rationale the State offers for Amendment 2 is respect for other citizens' freedom of association, and in particular the liberties of landlords or employers who have personal or religious objections to homosexuality. Colorado also cites its interest in conserving resources to fight discrimination against other groups. The breadth of the Amendment is so far removed from these particular justifications that we find it impossible to credit them. We cannot say that Amendment 2 is directed to any identifiable legitimate purpose or discrete objective. It is a status-based enactment divorced from any factual context from which we could discern a relationship to legitimate state interests; it is a classification of persons undertaken for its own sake, something the Equal Protection Clause does not permit. "[C]lass legislation . . . [is] obnoxious to the prohibitions of the Fourteenth Amendment. . . . " *Civil Rights Cases.*

We must conclude that Amendment 2 classifies homosexuals not to further a proper legislative end but to make them unequal to everyone else. This Colorado cannot do. A State cannot so deem a class of persons a stranger to its laws. Amendment 2 violates the Equal Protection Clause, and the judgment of the Supreme Court of Colorado is affirmed.

It is so ordered.

JUSTICE SCALIA, with whom THE CHIEF JUSTICE and JUSTICE THOMAS join, dissenting.

The Court has mistaken a Kulturkampf for a fit of spite. The constitutional amendment before us here is not the manifestation of a "'bare . . . desire to harm'" homosexuals, but is rather a modest attempt by seemingly tolerant Coloradans to preserve traditional sexual mores against the efforts of a politically powerful minority to revise those mores through use of the laws. That objective, and the means chosen to achieve it, are not only unimpeachable under any constitutional doctrine hitherto pronounced (hence the opinion's heavy reliance upon principles of righteousness rather than judicial holdings); they have been specifically approved by the Congress of the United States and by this Court.

In holding that homosexuality cannot be singled out for disfavorable treatment, the Court contradicts a decision, unchallenged here, pronounced only 10 years ago, see *Bowers* v. *Hardwick* (1986), and places the prestige of this institution behind the proposition that opposition to homosexuality is as reprehensible as racial or religious bias. Whether it is or not is precisely the cultural debate that gave rise to the Colorado constitutional amendment (and to the preferential laws against which the amendment was directed). Since the Constitution of the United States says nothing about this subject, it is left to be resolved by normal democratic means, including the democratic adoption of provisions in state constitutions. This Court has no business imposing upon all Americans the resolution favored by the elite class from which the Members of this institution are selected, pronouncing that "animosity" toward homosexuality is evil. I vigorously dissent.

I

Let me first discuss Part II of the Court's opinion, its longest section, which is devoted to rejecting the State's arguments that Amendment 2 "puts gays and lesbians in the same position as all other persons," and "does no more than deny homosexuals special rights." The Court concludes that this reading of Amendment 2's language is "implausible" under the "authoritative construction" given Amendment 2 by the Supreme Court of Colorado.

In reaching this conclusion, the Court considers it unnecessary to decide the validity of the State's argument that Amendment 2 does not deprive homosexuals of the "protection [afforded by] general laws and policies that prohibit arbitrary discrimination in governmental and private settings." I agree that we need not resolve that dispute, because the Supreme Court of Colorado has resolved it for us. In *Evans* v. *Romer* (1994), the Colorado court stated:

> "[I]t is significant to note that Colorado law currently proscribes discrimination against persons who are not suspect classes, including discrimination based on age; marital or family status; veterans' status; and for any legal, off-duty conduct such as smoking tobacco. Of course Amendment 2 is not intended to have any effect on this legislation, but seeks only to prevent the adoption of anti-discrimination laws intended to protect gays, lesbians, and bisexuals."

The Court utterly fails to distinguish this portion of the Colorado court's opinion. Colorado Rev. Stat. §24–34–402.5, which this passage authoritatively declares not to be affected by Amendment 2, was respondents' primary example of a generally applicable law whose protections would be unavailable to homosexuals under Amendment 2. The clear import of the Colorado court's conclusion that it is not affected is that "general laws and policies that prohibit arbitrary discrimination" would continue to prohibit discrimination on the basis of homosexual conduct as well. This analysis . . . lays to rest such horribles, raised in the course of oral argument, as the prospect that assaults upon homosexuals could not be prosecuted. The amendment prohibits special treatment of homosexuals, and nothing more. . . .

Despite all of its hand-wringing about the potential effect of Amendment 2 on general antidiscrimination laws, the Court's opinion ultimately does not dispute all this, but assumes it to be true. The only denial of equal treatment it contends homosexuals have suffered is this: They may not obtain preferential treatment without amending the state constitution. . . .

The central thesis of the Court's reasoning is that any group is denied equal protection when, to obtain advantage (or, presumably, to avoid disadvantage), it must have recourse to a more general and hence more difficult level of political decisionmaking than others. The world has never heard of such a principle, which is why the Court's opinion is so long on emotive utterance and so short on relevant legal citation. And it seems to me most unlikely that any multilevel democracy can function under such a principle. For whenever a disadvantage is imposed, or conferral of a benefit is prohibited, at one of the higher levels of democratic decisionmaking (i.e., by the state legislature rather than local government, or by the people at large in the state constitution rather than the legislature), the affected group has (under this theory) been denied equal protection. . . . It is ridiculous to consider this a denial of equal protection, which is why the Court's theory is unheard-of. . . .

II

I turn next to whether there was a legitimate rational basis for the substance of the constitutional amendment—for the prohibition of special protection for homosexuals. It is unsurprising that the Court avoids discussion of this question, since the answer is so obviously yes. The case most relevant to the issue before us today is not even mentioned in the Court's opinion: In *Bowers* v. *Hardwick* [1986], we held that the Constitution does not prohibit what virtually all States had done from the founding of the Republic until very recent years—making homosexual conduct a crime. That holding is unassailable, except by those who think that the Constitution changes to suit current fashions. But in any event it is a given in the present case: Respondents' briefs did not urge overruling *Bowers*, and at oral argument respondents' counsel expressly disavowed any intent to seek such overruling. If it is constitutionally permissible for a State to make homosexual conduct criminal, surely it is constitutionally permissible for a State to enact other laws merely disfavoring homosexual conduct. . . . And a fortiori it is constitutionally permissible for a State to adopt a provision not even disfavoring homosexual conduct, but merely prohibiting all levels of state government from bestowing special protections upon homosexual conduct. . . .

III

The foregoing suffices to establish what the Court's failure to cite any case remotely in point would lead one to suspect: No principle set forth in the Constitution, nor even any imagined by this Court in the past 200 years, prohibits what Colorado has done here. But the case for Colorado is much stronger than that. What it has done is not only unprohibited, but eminently reasonable, with close, congressionally approved precedent in earlier constitutional practice.

First, as to its eminent reasonableness. The Court's opinion contains grim, disapproving hints that Coloradans have been guilty of "animus" or "animosity" toward homosexuality, as though that has been established as Unamerican. Of course it is our moral heritage that one should not hate any human being or class of human beings. But I had thought that one could consider certain conduct reprehensible—murder, for example, or polygamy, or cruelty to animals—and could exhibit even "animus" toward such conduct. Surely that is the only sort of "animus" at issue here: moral disapproval of homosexual conduct, the same sort of moral disapproval that produced the centuries-old criminal laws that we held constitutional in *Bowers*. . . .

But though Coloradans are, as I say, entitled to be hostile toward homosexual conduct, the fact is that the degree of hostility reflected by Amendment 2 is the smallest conceivable. The Court's portrayal of Coloradans as a society fallen victim to pointless, hate-filled "gay-bashing" is so false as to be comical. Colorado not only is one of the 25 States that have repealed their antisodomy laws, but was among the first to do so. But the society that eliminates criminal punishment for homosexual acts does not necessarily abandon the view that homosexuality is morally wrong and socially harmful; often, abolition simply reflects the view that enforcement of such criminal laws involves unseemly intrusion into the intimate lives of citizens. . . .

There is a problem, however, which arises when criminal sanction of homosexuality is eliminated but moral and social disapprobation of homosexuality is meant to be retained. The Court cannot be unaware of that problem; it is evident in many cities of the country, and occasionally bubbles to the surface of the news, in heated political disputes over such matters as the introduction into local schools of books teaching that homosexuality is an optional and fully acceptable "alternate life style." The problem . . . is that, because those who engage in homosexual conduct tend to reside in disproportionate numbers in certain communities, and of course care about homosexual-rights issues much more ardently than the public at large, they possess political power much greater than their numbers, both locally and statewide. Quite understandably, they devote this political power to achieving not merely a grudging social toleration, but full social acceptance, of homosexuality. . . .

By the time Coloradans were asked to vote on Amendment 2, their exposure to homosexuals' quest for social endorsement was not limited to newspaper accounts of happenings in places such as New York, Los Angeles, San Francisco, and Key West. Three Colorado cities—Aspen, Boulder, and Denver—had enacted ordinances that listed "sexual orientation" as an impermissible ground for discrimination, equating the moral disapproval of homosexual conduct with racial and religious bigotry. The phenomenon had even appeared statewide: the Governor of Colorado had signed an executive order pronouncing that "in the State of Colorado we recognize the diversity in our pluralistic society and strive to bring an end to discrimination in any form," and directing state agency-heads to "ensure non-discrimination" in hiring and promotion based on, among other things, "sexual orientation." I do not mean to be critical of these legislative successes; homosexuals are as entitled to use the legal system for reinforcement of their moral sentiments as are the rest of society. But they are subject to being countered by lawful, democratic countermeasures as well.

That is where Amendment 2 came in. It sought to counter both the geographic concentration and the disproportionate political power of homosexuals by resolving the controversy at the statewide level, and making the election a single-issue contest for both sides. It put directly, to all the citizens of the State, the question: Should homosexuality be given special protection? They answered no. The Court today asserts that this most democratic of procedures is unconstitutional. Lacking any cases to establish that facially absurd proposition, it simply asserts that it must be unconstitutional, because it has never happened before. . . .

. . . [T]his is proved false every time a state law prohibiting or disfavoring certain conduct is passed, because such a law prevents the adversely affected group—whether drug addicts, or smokers, or gun owners, or motorcyclists—from changing the policy thus established in "each of [the] parts" of the State. What the Court says is even demonstrably false at the constitutional level. The Eighteenth Amendment to the Federal Constitution, for example, deprived those who drank alcohol not only of the power to alter the policy of prohibition locally or through state legislation, but even of the power to alter it through state constitutional amendment or federal legislation. The Establishment Clause of the First Amendment prevents theocrats from having their way by converting their fellow citizens at the local, state, or federal statutory level; as does the Republican Form of Government Clause prevent monarchists.

But there is a much closer analogy, one that involves precisely the effort by the majority of citizens to preserve its view of sexual morality statewide, against the efforts of a geographically concentrated and politically powerful minority to undermine it. The constitutions of the States of Arizona, Idaho, New Mexico, Oklahoma, and Utah to this day contain provisions stating that polygamy is "forever prohibited." Polygamists, and those who have a polygamous "orientation," have been "singled out" by these provisions for much more severe treatment than merely denial of favored status; and that treatment can only be changed by achieving amendment of the state constitutions. The Court's disposition today suggests that these provisions are unconstitutional, and that polygamy must be permitted in these States on a state-legislated, or perhaps even local-option, basis—unless, of course, polygamists for some reason have fewer constitutional rights than homosexuals. . . .

IV

. . . Today's opinion has no foundation in American constitutional law, and barely pretends to. The people of Colorado have adopted an entirely reasonable provision which does not even disfavor homosexuals in any substantive sense, but merely denies them preferential treatment. Amendment 2 is designed to prevent piecemeal deterioration of the sexual morality favored by a majority of Coloradans, and is not only an appropriate means to that legitimate end, but a means that Americans have employed before. Striking it down is an act, not of judicial judgment, but of political will. I dissent.

CENSUS BUREAU ON
AGING OF U.S. POPULATION
May 20, 1996

The aging of the "baby boom" generation will dramatically increase the senior citizen portion of the U.S. population during the early decades of the twenty-first century, according to a special Census Bureau report issued May 20. The bureau said its report, entitled "65+ in the United States," was intended to give political leaders and policy makers plenty of advance notice that they will have to deal with the consequences of a huge population of elderly citizens.

By the year 2020, about one in six Americans will be sixty-five years of age or older, the report predicted. That "will place tremendous strain on the myriad specialized services and programs required of an elderly population," it added. "A window of opportunity now exists for planners and policymakers to prepare for the aging of the Baby Boom generation."

Many political leaders acknowledged, during the 1996 election campaign, that Social Security, Medicare, and other programs for senior citizens will come under tremendous pressure as baby boomers retire. There was little agreement on how to deal with the problem, in large part because both of the major parties seemed as interested in gaining political advantage from the issue as they were in confronting tough decisions.

Aging of the Boomers

The bulk of the Census Bureau's detailed report centered on what it called the "inevitability" of an expanding population of senior citizens when members of the baby boom generation start turning sixty-five. The report defined the generation as the 75 million Americans born between 1946 and 1964.

The report cited several ranges of population estimates, each depending on such variables as fertility rates, immigration trends, and life expectancy. For the most part, the report used a "middle" range of estimates that assumed modest changes in those variables during the first decades of the twenty-first century.

The bulk of the baby boomers will turn sixty-five between the years 2010 and 2020. By the latter year, there will be approximately 53 million senior citizens out of a total U.S. population of 325 million. That means that about one in six Americans will be sixty-five or older, compared with one in eight Americans as of 1990. By 2030, the United States will have about 75 million senior citizens—about one-fifth of the population.

The report noted several trends that will distinguish the aging of the baby boomers from all previous generations.

Education. Because millions of them went to college, baby boomers will be the best educated senior citizens ever. That may translate into a healthier generation of seniors, since people with more education tend to have healthier lifestyles.

Women. As with previous generations, baby boom women will live longer than men, but the relative proportions between the two sexes may be somewhat different as baby boom men live longer than before. One consequence: baby boom women will become widows later than did their mothers. These women also will be better educated than their mothers, and many more will have worked for a living, so they may be economically more independent. On the other hand, a higher proportion of baby boom women will be divorced, or will never have married, by the time they are ready for retirement.

Caring for parents. As they enter retirement years, many baby boomers will still be caring for very aged and frail parents or relatives. The report noted that the parents of baby boomers will live longer than any generation preceding them, in many cases well into their eighties and nineties. That will put a burden on baby boomers in their sixties and seventies.

Poverty. As the twentieth century neared its end, the elderly were relatively better off—economically speaking—than their parents were at the same stage of life. In 1959, according to the report, about 33 percent of elderly white persons and 62 percent of elderly black persons had incomes below the poverty level. By 1992 the comparable figures were 11 percent of elderly whites and 33 percent of elderly blacks. The main explanations were "catch-up" increases in pensions and other benefits and the indexing of Social Security payments to inflation. The report made no projections for poverty rates among the baby boom generation as they retire.

The "old old." Because of improvements in health care, millions of Americans can expect to live well into their late eighties or even nineties, a group the demographers call the "old old." The report projected that by 2020 nearly 7 million people will be eighty-five or older; that translates to 2 percent of the population, nearly twice the percentage as in 1990.

U.S. Racial Makeup

The Census Bureau on March 13 released another report projecting changes in the racial composition of the U.S. population into the twenty-first century. That report, "Population Projections of the United States by

Age, Sex, Race and Hispanic Origin: 1995 to 2050," estimated that the non-Hispanic white population would fall from about 74 percent of the total in 1995 to about 53 percent in 2050. At that point, whites will constitute less than one-half of those under age eighteen, probably guaranteeing that the United States eventually will have as a majority those now considered minorities.

Because of immigration and birth rates, Hispanics and Asians will continue to be the fastest growing segment of the population in the twenty-first century, the report said. Hispanics, who made up about 10 percent of the population in 1995, will comprise nearly 25 percent by 2050. Asians—a tiny minority of less than 2 percent as recently as 1980—will reach about 8 percent of the population by 2050. The black population will be much more stable, changing from about 12 percent of the population in 1995 to slightly under 14 percent in 2050.

Following is the "Highlights" section of the report, "65+ in the United States," by Frank B. Hobbs, with Bonnie L. Damon, issued May 20, 1996, by the U.S. Bureau of the Census:

Population Profile and Growth

Our Nation's population continues to age. In 1860, half the population was under age 20; in 1994, half were age 34 or older; by 2030, at least half could be 39 years or older.

In July 1994, there were 33.2 million elderly (aged 65 or older), one-eighth of the total population. Among the elderly, 18.7 million were aged 65 to 74, 11.0 million were aged 75 to 84, and 3.5 million were 85 or older.

The elderly population increased 11-fold from 1900 to 1994, compared with only a 3-fold increase for those under age 65. Elderly population growth rates for the 1990–2010 period will be modest, but during the 2010–30 period, elderly growth rates will increase dramatically as the Baby-Boom generation ages into the 65 and over group.

From 1960 to 1994, the oldest old population (persons aged 85 and over) increased by 274 percent, compared with 100 percent for the 65 and over, and 45 percent for the total population. The oldest old population in 1994 would more than double to 7 million in 2020 under middle series projections. The oldest old would reach 19 million by 2050, or as many as 27 million under the Census Bureau's "highest series" assumptions of future life expectancy and net immigration.

The number of centenarians, persons aged 100 years or older, has grown rapidly in recent years. This group has more than doubled since 1980. About 4 in 5 centenarians are women.

California had the largest number of persons aged 65 or older in 1993 (3.3 million), yet its proportion elderly ranked 46th among the States and the District of Columbia. Florida, Pennsylvania, and States in the Midwest are among the States with the highest proportions elderly. Florida had by far the largest proportion elderly (18.6 percent) in 1993.

Eight States would double their elderly population between 1993 and 2020. Seven of these States are in the West. The slowest-growing elderly population States are expected to be in the Midwest and Northeast.

The five States with the highest proportions of oldest old in 1993 were all in the Midwest: Iowa, North Dakota, South Dakota, Nebraska, and Kansas.

11 of the 12 States in the Midwest were net losers of elderly migrants between 1985 and 1990. Among the 25 States with net elderly inmigration, 22 were in the South and West.

The elderly represented 20 percent or more of the population in over 400 counties of the United States in 1991. The elderly were 30 percent or more of the population in 11 counties, 6 of which were in Florida.

The ratio of elderly persons to those of working age (20 to 64 years) for the nation will nearly double between 1990 and 2050.

357 million people in the world were aged 65 or older in 1994, about 6 percent of the world's total population.

Worldwide, the elderly grew by 2.8 percent during 1993–94, compared with only 1.6 percent for the world's total population. The rate of elderly population growth is more rapid in developing countries than in developed countries. Over half the world's elderly lived in developing nations in 1994, and nearly two-thirds of the world's elderly are projected to live in such countries by 2020.

Racial, Ethnic, and Gender Diversity and Change

Racial and ethnic diversity within the elderly population will continue to increase. The proportion of the elderly that is White, non-Hispanic is projected to decline from 87 percent in 1990 to 67 percent in 2050. Among the elderly in 2050, 10 percent would be Black, non-Hispanic; 7 percent Asian and Pacific Islander, non-Hispanic; less than 1 percent American Indian, Eskimo, and Aleut, non-Hispanic; and 16 percent Hispanic.

Among elderly Blacks and Hispanics, about 1 in 5 were 80 years or older in 1990. By 2050, these proportions could increase to 30 percent for elderly Blacks and 36 percent for elderly Hispanics. The proportion aged 80 years and over among elderly Whites would be even higher (40 percent).

In 1990, 12 percent of all elderly persons spoke some language other than English at home. Spanish speakers will become an increasing share of the elderly population that speaks a language other than English at home.

Income and poverty differences are significant for population subgroups. Elderly White men had higher median income in 1992 than other population subgroups of the elderly. The 1992 poverty rates were higher for elderly Blacks (33 percent) and Hispanics (22 percent) than for Whites (11 percent).

Gender and racial gaps in life expectancy at birth persist. Life expectancy at birth in 1991 was about 80 years for White females, 74 years for Black females, 73 years for White males, and 65 years for Black males.

In the United States, there were 3 elderly women to every 2 elderly men in 1994, and 5 oldest old women to every 2 oldest old men. Globally, there were

50 million more elderly women than men in 1994, and elderly women outnumbered men 4 to 3.

Elderly White men are more likely to commit suicide (44 per 100,000 population) than to die in a motor vehicle accident (31 per 100,000 population).

Elderly men are more likely to smoke, smoke heavily, drink, and drink heavily than elderly women. Elderly Black men are about twice as likely to smoke as elderly White men.

Elderly women are less likely than men to live in a family setting. After age 75, most women are widowed and live alone, while most men are married and live with their wives.

Women's share of the older labor force (55 years and over) increased from 23 percent in 1950 to 44 percent in 1993.

Elderly women (16 percent) were more likely to be poor in 1992 than elderly men (9 percent). Of the 2.3 million elderly poor who lived alone in 1992, 2.0 million were women.

Health, Social, and Economic Profile

Poor health is not as prevalent as many assume, especially among the young old. Among noninstitutionalized persons in 1992, three in four aged 65 to 74 consider their health to be good, very good, or excellent, as do about 2 in 3 aged 75 and over.

Noninstitutionalized elderly persons reporting the need for personal assistance with everyday activities in 1990–91 increased with age, from only 9 percent of persons aged 65 to 69 up to 50 percent of the oldest old.

In 1990, elderly with a selfcare or mobility limitation were more likely to be poor (20 percent) than elderly without such limitations (11 percent).

Eighty percent of newborns would survive to age 65 under the mortality conditions of 1991.

About 7 in 10 persons who died in 1991 were age 65 or older. Heart disease is still the leading cause of death among the elderly, even though heart disease death rates have declined from 1960 levels.

In 1990, 1.6 million elderly (or 5 percent of all elderly) lived in nursing homes. Ninety percent of all nursing home residents are elderly; 7 in 10 are female; and 1 in 3 is a woman aged 85 or over.

Of all oldest old persons, nearly one-fourth (24 percent) lived in a nursing home in 1990.

In 1992, 70 percent of elderly reported voting in the presidential election.

The share of older workers in the nations's labor force declined between 1950 and 1993.

Median income of the elderly in 1992 ($14,548 for men, $8,189 for women) more than doubled since 1957 (in constant 1992 dollars). Social Security benefits were the primary source of income for 63 percent of beneficiaries in 1992, and were the only source of income for 14 percent of beneficiaries.

The percentage of elderly living in poverty declined from 24.6 percent in 1970 to 12.9 percent in 1992, partly because of "catch-up" increases in Social Security benefits and the indexing of benefits to inflation rates.

Elderly not living with relatives or living alone were more likely to be poor (25 percent) in 1992 than elderly persons in married couple families (6 percent).

Most elderly householders (77 percent) owned their own homes in 1991, and their median net worth was more than 15 times that of households with a householder under age 35.

Future Implications

Tomorrow's elderly will have quite different social, demographic, health, and economic characteristics than today's elderly.

The sheer size and inevitable aging of the Baby-Boom generation will continue to drive public policy debate.

Research on genetic, biochemical, and physiological aspects of aging is certain to alter the future world of the elderly. Issues pertaining to ethics and aging are likely to receive increasing attention.

Educational attainment levels of the elderly population will increase in the coming decades, especially as relatively well-educated Baby Boom cohorts reach older age.

Baby-Boom women are likely to experience widowhood later in life than today's elderly women, and more may be divorced or never have married. Women will be increasingly likely to have been in the labor force long enough to have their own retirement income.

As average length of life continues to increase, issues regarding the quality of extended life (active life expectancy) are likely to assume greater importance.

WORLD HEALTH ORGANIZATION ON INFECTIOUS DISEASES
May 20, 1996

Infectious diseases were the leading cause of death in the world in 1995, killing more than seventeen million of the fifty-two million people that died that year, according to the World Health Organization (WHO). Many of those diseases could have been prevented or cured for as little as one dollar a person, but many others were diseases for which there is yet no known treatment or cure. Several diseases that once seemed under control, such as cholera and tuberculosis, were making a deadly comeback as the microbes that cause them grew resistant to antibiotics.

"We are standing on the brink of a global crisis in infectious diseases. No country is safe from them. No country can any longer afford to ignore their threat," said Hiroshi Nakajima, the director general of WHO, upon releasing the organization's annual report May 20. "The optimism of a relatively few years ago that many of these diseases could easily be brought under control has led to fatal complacency among the international community. This complacency is now costing millions of lives—lives that we have the knowledge and means to save, yet that we are allowing to trickle through our fingers."

The WHO report divided infectious diseases into three broad categories, each of which required a different kind of intervention. The "old diseases–old problems" category included diseases that were on the verge of being eradicated, such as polio and guinea-worm disease (dracunculiasis); those that were nearly eliminated as public health threats, such as leprosy, measles, and river blindness (onchocerciasis); and those that could be controlled, such as cholera and other diarrheal diseases, intestinal worms, hepatitis, and typhoid.

Cost-effective interventions for this latter class of disease were known, the report said; what was needed was "commitment and resources" to ensure delivery. Proven interventions included immunizing children against six common childhood diseases, which the report estimated would cost about sixty cents a child in low-income countries. Providing clean drinking water and basic sanitation facilities and setting up school pro-grams that treated worm infections and nutritional deficiencies were also cost-effective treatments, the report said.

The second category, termed "old diseases–new problems," included tuberculosis, malaria, dengue fever, and other vector-borne diseases (those transmitted by mosquito, fly, or some other insect). Treatments existed for these diseases, but resistance to the drugs that killed the microbes or to the pesticides used to kill the vectors was making those treatments less effec-tive, putting people at greater risk of dying, and prolonging epidemics. Two million people died of malaria in 1995; another three million died of tuberculosis. "A major cause of the antibiotic resistance crisis is the uncontrolled and inappropriate use of antibiotics globally," the health organization said in an accompanying press release. "They are used by too many people to treat the wrong kind of infections at the wrong dosage and for the wrong period of time."

The third category was labeled "new diseases–new pathogens" and cov-ered eighteen diseases identified since 1973. In addition to HIV, the human immunodeficiency virus that causes AIDS, the list included Legionnaires' disease, Ebola virus, Hantaan virus, and a newly discovered strain of E. coli bacteria. Because the history, mechanisms, and emergence of these diseases were not well understood, the report said, research was needed "on the disease agents, their evolution, the vectors of disease spread and methods of controlling them, and vaccines and drug development."

In a related development, public health officials in the United States and Europe announced in November that they had agreed to set up a global net-work to warn governments and the health community about budding epi-demics. The group said it would start by registering outbreaks of E. coli bacteria and other microbes that cause deadly food-borne diseases. Other governments would be encouraged to participate in the reporting process, in some instances by promises of aid to help fight epidemics. If the plan worked for food-borne diseases, the group planned to expand it to all other communicable diseases.

Infectious diseases were not the only threat to global health. A study con-ducted by the Harvard School of Public Health, the World Health Organiza-tion, the World Bank, and health officials from several countries found that noncommunicable diseases and accidents were a growing worldwide prob-lem. Heart disease and cancers have long been the leading causes of death in the industrialized world. With the aging of populations around the world, combined with accidents and the growing use of tobacco, such deaths were beginning to be felt in the developing world as well.

Five million deaths a year were attributable to accidents, the report said, both from unintentional injuries, such as car accidents, and inten-tional ones, such as murder or suicide. If disabilities were taken into account, the report said, injuries accounted for 15 percent of the global "disease burden." The report, published in September, was the last in a ten-volume project called the Global Burden of Disease and Injury Series.

Following are excerpts from the executive summary of World Health Report 1996: Fighting Disease, Fostering Development, *the annual report of the World Health Organization, released on May 20, 1996:*

The State of World Health

A Fatal Complacency

Until relatively recently, the long struggle for control over infectious diseases seemed almost over. Smallpox was eradicated and half a dozen other diseases were targeted for eradication or elimination. Vaccines protected about eight out of 10 of the world's children against six killer diseases. Antimicrobial drugs were effectively suppressing countless infections. However, in the path of these successes, cautious optimism has been overtaken by a fatal complacency that is costing millions of lives a year. Infectious diseases are the world's leading cause of death, killing at least 17 million people—most of them young children—every year. Up to half the 5,720 million people on earth are at risk of many endemic diseases.

Far from being over, the struggle to control infectious diseases has become increasingly difficult. Diseases that seemed to be subdued, such as tuberculosis and malaria, are fighting back with renewed ferocity. Some, such as cholera and yellow fever, are striking in regions once thought safe from them. Other infections are now so resistant to drugs that they are virtually untreatable. In addition, deadly new diseases such as Ebola haemorrhagic fever, for which there is no cure or vaccine, are emerging in many parts of the world. At the same time, the sinister role of hepatitis viruses and other infectious agents in the development of many types of cancer is becoming increasingly evident.

The result amounts to a global crisis: no country is safe from infectious diseases. The socioeconomic development of many countries is being crippled by the burden of these diseases. Much of the progress achieved in recent decades towards improving human health is now at risk. . . .

Breaking the Chains

Focusing on the ways in which diseases are transmitted, this report explains the present situation, and the interventions needed to achieve prevention or control. Breaking the chains of transmission is possible. A handful of diseases are within range of elimination or eradication in the next few years and others are under control. Poliomyelitis and guinea-worm disease, for example, could be eradicated by the end of the century. Leprosy could be eliminated as a public health danger. However, the eradication of a disease is an immensely difficult task, fully achieved only once, with the last reported case of smallpox in 1977, and global eradication announced in 1980. This success has not been repeated, due mainly to logistical problems and a series of events and developments, some natural and others man-made, that have occurred in recent years. Some are poverty-related, while others are the consequences of economic prosperity. . . .

The Global Situation—1995 Update

Population

In mid-1995, the global population was about 5,720 million people. It is projected to reach 7,900 million in 2020, and 9,800 million in 2050. By 2050 the least developed nations will have a population of about 1,700 million compared with about 589 million today. For the foreseeable future, the heaviest burdens of ill-health are therefore likely to continue to fall on the 80% of the world's population who live in developing countries, and especially in those countries whose populations are growing fastest and which are least able to sustain economic development.

Urbanization

By 1995, about 2,600 million people, or 45% of the world's population, were living in urban areas. About 200 million now live in cities with populations exceeding 10 million; the total is expected to be 450 million in the next 20 years, almost all of the increase taking place in the developing world, where already there is a proliferation of slums and squatter settlements with millions of people lacking safe and adequate drinking-water, sanitation and solid-waste disposal facilities. Consequently there are growing risks of water-borne and foodborne diseases.

Fertility

Women are having fewer babies: in 1970, they had an average of 4.7, and the average declined to 3.7 by 1980, to 3.2 by 1990, and is now 3. Increasing use of contraception is the main explanation. In 1995, about 140 million babies were born—16 million in the industrialized world, 25 million in the least developed countries, and 98 million in other developing countries.

Life Expectancy

Globally, average life expectancy at birth in 1995 was more than 65 years, an increase of more than three years since 1985. The life expectancy gap between the industrialized and the developing world has narrowed to 13.3 years in 1995 from 25 years in 1955. But the gap between least developed and other developing countries has widened from seven years to more than 13 years in the same period.

Mortality

About 52 million people died in 1995. The number is almost the same as it was 35 years ago, but the global population has almost doubled in that time. The developing world's death rate has declined sharply from 20 per 1,000 population in 1960 to about nine in 1995, due to mortality reduction particularly in the youngest age groups. The least developed countries lag about 25 years behind other developing nations in the decline in death rates. The rate is highest in Africa.

Child Mortality

Defined as the probability of dying by the age of five years, the global average in 1995 was 81.7 per 1,000 live births; 8.5 in the industrialized world, 90.6 in the developing world and 155.5 in the least developed nations. Of more than 11 million such deaths in the developing world, nine million have been attributed to infectious diseases, about 25% preventable by immunization.

Emerging diseases

Emerging infectious diseases are those whose incidence in humans has increased during the last two decades or which threatens to increase in the near future. The term includes newly-appearing infectious diseases or those spreading to new geographical areas. It also refers to those that were easily controlled by chemotherapy and antibiotics but have developed antimicrobial resistance.

The most dramatic example of a new disease is AIDS, caused by the human immunodeficiency virus (HIV), whose existence was unknown until 15 years ago. About 26.6 million adults could be living with HIV/AIDS by the year 2000.

A new breed of deadly haemorrhagic fevers, of which Ebola is the most notorious, have struck in Africa, Asia, Latin America and the United States. Ebola appeared for the first time in Zaire and Sudan in 1976 and has emerged several times since, most notably in Zaire in 1995, where it was fatal in about 80% of cases.

The United States has seen the emergence of hantavirus pulmonary syndrome with a case fatality rate of over 50%. Other hantaviruses have been recognized for many years in Asia.

Epidemics of foodborne and waterborne infections due to new organisms such as cryptosporidium or new strains of bacteria such as E. coli O157:H7 have hit industrialized as well as developing countries. A completely new strain of cholera, O139, appeared in south-east India in 1992 and has since spread to other areas of India and parts of South-East Asia.

Despite the emergence of some 29 new diseases in the last 20 years, there is still a lack of national and international political will and resources to develop and support the systems necessary to detect them and stop their spread. Without doubt, diseases as yet unknown but with the potential to be the AIDS of tomorrow, lurk in the shadows.

Antimicrobial Resistance

Resistance of diseases to antimicrobials has increased dramatically in the last decade, with a deadly impact on the control of diseases such as tuberculosis, malaria, cholera, dysentery and pneumonia. As a result people with infections are ill for longer periods and are at greater risk of dying, and epidemics are prolonged.

Resistant organisms have no natural barriers; aided by international air travel they can move quickly from remote locations to have a worldwide impact. As resistance spreads, the effective life span of drugs shrinks; as fewer new drugs appear, the gulf widens between infection and control. In the case of malaria there is a double threat: on the one hand the malaria parasites are resistant to antimalarial drugs, and on the other the malaria-carrying mosquitos are resistant to insecticides. Rapid development of malaria drug resistance has already occurred in most areas of the world.

Resistant strains of the tuberculosis bacilli are also widespread: there have been alarming outbreaks of tuberculosis caused by multidrug-resistant strains in the United States. Both of the organisms that cause pneumonia, a major cause of death in children, are becoming increasingly resistant to drugs. The same is true of salmonellae, a leading cause of foodborne infections, and enterococci bacteria, which cause a host of complications in hospital patients. Hospital infections are a huge problem worldwide and are responsible for 70,000 deaths a year in the United States alone.

Person-to-Person Transmission

The combination of population growth (especially in cities), international air travel, incessant migration and the ebb and flow of refugees means that the peoples of the world are more intermingled now than at any time in history. Thus human transmission could become the predominant way in which diseases are spread quickly, not just from person to person but from continent to continent—by airborne and droplet spread, sexual transmission, bloodborne transmission or direct contact.

In children, the major diseases disseminated by *airborne and droplet* spread are acute respiratory infections, particularly pneumonia, influenza, measles, pertussis (whooping cough), meningococcal meningitis and diphtheria, which together kill at least four million. *Direct contact diseases* in children include poliomyelitis and trachoma, a major cause of blindness in developing countries. Among adults, tuberculosis is the leading airborne disease, killing three million people and infecting almost nine million others every year. It is already the opportunistic infection that most frequently kills HIV-positive people: of an estimated one million AIDS-related deaths in 1995, about one-third may have been due to tuberculosis. Leprosy still affects 1.8 million people in 70 countries, but is steadily being eliminated as a public health problem. Influenza and pneumonia strike children and adults, especially the elderly.

Of all *sexually transmitted diseases*, HIV/AIDS continues to have the greatest global impact, with an estimated 20 million adults currently affected. In addition to HIV, at least 333 million new cases of other sexually transmitted diseases occurred in 1995.

Among *bloodborne infections*, hepatitis causes most concern. More than 2,000 million people alive today have been infected with hepatitis B; some 350 million are chronically infected and thus at risk of serious illness and death from liver cirrhosis and liver cancer. In addition, some 100 million are chronically infected with the hepatitis C virus. Unlike hepatitis B, there is no vaccine for hepatitis C.

Foodborne, Waterborne and Soilborne Diseases

Almost half the world's population suffers from diseases associated with insufficient or contaminated water and is at risk from waterborne and food-borne diseases, of which diarrhoeal diseases are the most deadly. They caused over three million deaths in 1995, 80% of them among children under age five. Typhoid fever causes about 16 million cases and over 600,000 deaths a year, about 80% of them in Asia. There are epidemics of cholera and dysentery, with cholera alone causing 120,000 deaths a year. Seventy-nine million people are estimated to be currently at risk of cholera infection in Africa. Worldwide, some 40 million people have intestinal trematode infections. However, dracunculiasis (guinea-worm disease) could be eradicated in the next few years; about 122,000 cases were reported in 1995 compared to 3.6 million in 1986.

Foodborne diseases have a major impact throughout the world. Estimates in the United States range from 6.5 million to 80 million cases a year. The leading foodborne bacteria worldwide are salmonellae, campylobacter, Escherichia coli and listeria. Foodborne viruses include hepatitis A, also common worldwide.

Soilborne infections affect several million people a year, intestinal worm infections being the most widespread. The most deadly soilborne disease is tetanus, which annually kills at least 450,000 newborn babies, and 50,000 mothers around the time of childbirth.

Insect-Borne Diseases

Of all disease-transmitting insects, the mosquito is the greatest menace, spreading malaria, dengue and yellow fever, which together are responsible for several million deaths and hundreds of millions of cases every year. Mosquitos also transmit lymphatic filariasis and Japanese encephalitis. Other insect species carry a variety of diseases. Sleeping sickness is spread by the tsetse fly, with 55 million people at risk. The leishmaniasis group of diseases is spread by sandflies, with 350 million people at risk. Another 100 million in Latin America are at risk of Chagas disease, spread by household bugs. Onchocerciasis, or river blindness, is carried by blackflies, and plague by fleas.

Malaria is endemic in 91 countries, with about 40% of the world's population at risk. By undermining the health and working capacity of hundreds of millions, it is closely linked to poverty and stunts social and economic development. Up to 500 million cases occur every year, 90% of them in Africa, and there are up to 2.7 million deaths annually.

Dengue is the world's most important mosquito-borne virus disease, with 2500 million people worldwide at risk of infection and 20 million cases a year in more than 100 countries. In 1995, the worst dengue epidemic in Latin America and the Caribbean for 15 years struck at least 14 countries, causing more than 200,000 cases of dengue fever and almost 6,000 cases of the more serious dengue haemorrhagic fever.

Many major cities of the world, especially in the Americas, are at risk of potentially devastating epidemics of yellow fever because they are infested with Aedes aegypti mosquitos which can transmit the disease. Lymphatic filariasis (elephantiasis) infects about 120 million people in tropical areas of Africa, India, South-East Asia, the Pacific Islands and South and Central America.

Among diseases spread by other insects, leishmaniasis occurs in 88 countries, and its spread is accelerated by road building, dam construction, mining and other development programmes that bring more people into contact with the sandflies that transmit the causative parasite. Sleeping sickness affects 36 countries of sub-Saharan Africa. Onchocerciasis affects some 17.6 million people in Africa, and a smaller number in Central and South America. At least 16 million people in Latin America are infected with Chagas disease. Plague continues to strike relatively small numbers of people in Africa, the Americas and Asia. . . .

Charting the Future

The situation described in the report—the emergence or re-emergence of certain infectious diseases and increasing resistance to antibiotic drugs—constitutes a serious crisis requiring immediate action. Some of the diseases can be controlled, eliminated or eradicated, for instance, by means of immunization, personal hygiene and/or public health and sanitation practices. The proper use of antimicrobial drugs and vector control methods have a part to play in the fight against certain diseases. All these measures can lead to a rapid reduction in infectious diseases and thus enhance overall development, provided that there is political and professional commitment to finance and sustain well-planned, cost-effective interventions.

The diseases concerned can be conveniently classified in three categories, each requiring a different type of intervention. First, there are what may be termed *"old diseases–old problems"*: those that can be eradicated (poliomyelitis, dracunculiasis), eliminated as public health problems (leprosy, neonatal tetanus, measles, Chagas disease, onchocerciasis) or controlled (cholera and other diarrhoeal diseases, intestinal worms, hepatitis, typhoid). What is needed is the commitment and resources to undertake the following cost-effective interventions (the per capita cost in low-income countries is indicated in most cases):

- (1) immunization of children against six vaccine-preventable diseases—diphtheria, pertussis, tetanus, poliomyelitis, measles and tuberculosis (US$ 0.50);
- (2) the integrated approach to the management of the sick child (US$ 1.60);
- (3) provision of adequate clean drinking-water and of basic sanitation facilities and collection of household garbage, as well as the simple

hygienic measures of washing hands after defecation and before preparing food;

- (4) school health programmes treating worm infections and micronutrient deficiencies and providing health education (US$ 0.50);
- (5) case management of conventional sexually transmitted diseases using simple algorithms to decide on the appropriate diagnosis and treatment in peripheral health facilities (US$ 11).

The second category of diseases—*"old diseases–new problems"*—are tuberculosis, malaria, dengue and other vector-borne diseases. Cost-effective interventions exist, but drug or pesticide resistance poses a problem, requiring the use of additional or more expensive or toxic drugs. The strategy for controlling these diseases includes such interventions as early diagnosis and prompt treatment, vector control measures and the prevention of epidemics, for malaria; as well as directly observed treatment, short-course (DOTS) therapy for tuberculosis; undertaking research on treatment regimens and improved diagnostics, drugs and vaccines; and above all, epidemiological and drug-resistance surveillance mechanisms and procedures with laboratory support for early detection, confirmation and communication.

The natural history and the reasons for the emergence of the third category—*"new diseases–new pathogens"*—such as Ebola and other viral haemorrhagic fevers, is not well understood. Research is therefore needed on the disease agents, their evolution, the vectors of disease spread and methods of controlling them, and vaccines and drug development. Much of this already applies to HIV/AIDS, one of the most serious diseases to emerge in recent decades. The strategy required includes improving surveillance systems and public health infrastructure, strengthening laboratory services, and responding rapidly to urgent threats to public health. WHO is developing a global surveillance programme to recognize and respond to emerging diseases, making maximum use of existing WHO collaborating centres. A further component is WHONET, the computer programme that is designed to facilitate management of the results of antibiotic susceptibility tests, for use by microbiology laboratories.

Epidemics of various infectious diseases have been occurring repeatedly in several countries. As a result, there is now an international consensus that priorities have to be set and activities initiated speedily. This favourable environment for action needs to be exploited, and in WHO's view there are three priorities for international action during the next five years.

The *first priority* is to complete unfinished business, namely to complete the eradication and elimination of diseases such as poliomyelitis, dracunculiasis, leprosy, measles, Chagas disease and onchocerciasis. This does not require a huge expenditure, and if the resources are not found, these diseases will return with a vengeance, and previous efforts will be wasted.

The *second priority* is to tackle old diseases such as tuberculosis and malaria which present new problems of drug and insecticide resistance. Here there is a need to remove infectious sources in the community and cure a high proportion of infectious cases, establish appropriate national and international epidemiological surveillance, and undertake research on treatment regimens and improved diagnostics, drugs and vaccines. Work is needed on developing new and improved vaccines against measles, neonatal tetanus, bacterial meningitis, tuberculosis and other diseases.

The *third priority* is to take short-term and long-term action to combat newly emerging diseases. A speedy response is needed to outbreaks of important new infections, wherever they occur. At the same time, there is a need for intensive research on the natural history of new diseases and on possibilities for preventing, treating and controlling them. A global surveillance programme is also essential. . . .

GAO ON THREATS TO PENTAGON COMPUTER SYSTEMS

May 22, 1996

The federal government's computer systems—including Pentagon computers containing huge quantities of sensitive national security information—were increasingly vulnerable to attacks and sabotage, according to reports issued in 1996. Officials said that computer "hackers" and others were posing a potentially serious threat to the United States. John M. Deutch, director of the Central Intelligence Agency, told a Senate subcommittee June 25 that he considered attacks on computer security the second most serious national security threat facing the country, after the worldwide proliferation of nuclear, chemical, and biological weapons.

According to investigative reports and congressional testimony, many government agencies were slow to recognize the dangers of inadequate computer security and were not doing enough to protect their computer systems or to train their personnel to deal with the problem. Deutch said faulty protection of computerized information was a problem for private business, as well. He warned that a sustained and coordinated attack by a foreign country or terrorists on computer systems in the United States could seriously damage the nation's economy.

In his testimony, Deutch acknowledged that federal agencies, including intelligence agencies, were not doing enough to protect themselves against attacks on their computer systems. He said those agencies were working on various plans to make their systems more secure.

President Bill Clinton on July 16 signed Executive Order 13–010 creating a presidential commission to propose policy recommendations on improving security for the nation's "critical information infrastructure," including both government and private computer systems. The commission was to make its recommendations in 1997.

Attacks on Government Computers

One of the most detailed reports on computer security was issued on May 22 by the General Accounting Office (GAO), the investigative arm of

Congress. That report reviewed computer security lapses at the Defense Department. It focused on the Pentagon because it had one of the largest computer systems in the world—with some two million users—and much of its information was vital to U.S. national security. In its report the GAO said Pentagon computers were increasingly vulnerable to attack through the Internet, which was originally developed by the Pentagon and which the military used extensively for worldwide communications.

The GAO cited an estimate by the Defense Information Systems Agency (DISA) that Pentagon computers were attacked approximately 250,000 times in 1995, that most of the attacks succeeded in gaining at least some access, and that the number of attacks was growing. From 1992 to early 1996, the DISA conducted 38,000 attacks of its own, via the Internet, to test Pentagon computer security; 65 percent of those attacks succeeded in gaining access to Pentagon computers. Of the successful attacks, only 4 percent were detected by the target Pentagon office and only 25 percent of the detected attacks were reported to the proper authorities.

Pentagon computers were coming under attack by three types of intruders, the GAO said. The least harmful were invasions by "hackers" looking for amusement or a challenge. Such raids were not intended to be malicious, but they often caused damage. Computer "vandals," by contrast, deliberately tried to cause harm to the systems they attacked. More dangerous still, the GAO said, were professional thieves and spies who gained entry to computer systems, copied information, and left, often without being detected.

Because personal computers were becoming increasingly sophisticated and affordable, the GAO warned, anyone with the right equipment and a modest amount of training could pose a threat to the Pentagon's information systems. The GAO noted, for example, that informal groups of hackers openly shared information on the Internet about how to break into computer systems.

The report reviewed several high-profile cases of successful raids on Pentagon computers, the most important of which was a 1994 attack on the Air Force's Rome Air Development Center, in Rome, New York. The center conducts highly sophisticated research on weapons systems. In that incident, at least two computer hackers, working through telephone switching devices in Chile and Colombia, entered and gained control of the center's computers for several days. The hackers copied information about weapons and research projects and used the Rome center's computers to attack computer systems at other government facilities, including NASA's Goddard Space Flight Center and the Jet Propulsion Lab, Wright-Patterson Air Force Base in Ohio, and at least two defense contractors.

British authorities arrested and filed charges against two people, one a 16-year-old, in the Rome case. The GAO quoted Air Force officials as saying the hackers "may have been working for a foreign country" that wanted information on U.S. military research. The officials did not name the country.

The GAO cited four other serious attacks on U.S. military systems since 1990, all apparently made through the Internet. While acknowledging the communications value of the Internet, the GAO said the Internet exposed computer systems to widespread attack. In December 1996 the Pentagon was forced to shut down its public sites on the Internet's World Wide Web for several days after a computer hacker damaged an air force site on the Web.

Security Weaknesses Cited

In its report, the GAO noted a number of weaknesses in the Pentagon's computer system that made it vulnerable to attack. Among those problems were: many of the Pentagon's systems to protect computer security were antiquated because they were developed in the days before computers were tied into networks; the Pentagon had no priorities for determining which systems were vulnerable, or for correcting vulnerabilities once they were discovered; there was no policy requiring individual units to report computer attacks or to assess the damage caused by attacks; and many Pentagon installations did not have trained computer security officers who could manage and update programs to protect information systems.

The GAO also said many Pentagon employees were unaware of the problems caused by computer lapses and lacked training to deal with them. For example, it cited one estimate that 80 percent of computer security lapses stemmed from inadequate passwords chosen by Pentagon employees.

Overall, the GAO found that many Pentagon managers, from the most senior levels on down to administrators of local computer networks, did not take security issues seriously enough. As a result, the GAO said, these officials did not allocate adequate resources to protecting their computer systems or training their employees. The report cited one example: few of the army's 4,000 computer systems administrators had received security training. The army was developing a training course for them but did not have the money in its budget to conduct the training.

A report by the staff of the Permanent Investigations Subcommittee of the Senate Governmental Affairs Committee found a similar situation within U.S. intelligence agencies. Sam Nunn, the subcommittee's ranking Democrat, said that report had concluded that the computer security issue "is not presently enough of a priority in our intelligence community."

After reviewing the GAO and other reports, Sen. William Cohen, R-Maine, said at a July 16 hearing that "government information security is in shambles, and we should address that issue as quickly as possible as our first priority. And we have to establish the public's confidence in the effectiveness of the federal government's security measures to protect not only national security data, but private data of its citizens as well." Cohen later was to have an opportunity to act on those sentiments; Clinton in December nominated him as secretary of defense, succeeding William Perry.

Following are excerpts from the executive summary and the body of the report, "Information Security: Computer Attacks at Department of Defense Pose Increasing Risks," issued May 22, 1996, by the General Accounting Office:

Purpose

Unknown and unauthorized individuals are increasingly attacking and gaining access to highly sensitive unclassified information on the Department of Defense's computer systems. Given the threats the attacks pose to military operations and national security, GAO was asked to report on the extent to which Defense systems are being attacked, the potential for further damage to information and systems, and the challenges Defense faces in securing sensitive information.

Results in Brief

Attacks on Defense computer systems are a serious and growing threat. The exact number of attacks cannot be readily determined because only a small portion are actually detected and reported. However, Defense Information Systems Agency (DISA) data implies that Defense may have experienced as many as 250,000 attacks last year. DISA information also shows that attacks are successful 65 percent of the time, and that the number of attacks is doubling each year, as Internet use increases along with the sophistication of "hackers" and their tools.

At a minimum, these attacks are a multimillion dollar nuisance to Defense. At worst, they are a serious threat to national security. Attackers have seized control of entire Defense systems, many of which support critical functions, such as weapons systems research and development, logistics, and finance. Attackers have also stolen, modified, and destroyed data and software. In a well-publicized attack on Rome Laboratory, the Air Force's premier command and control research facility, two hackers took control of laboratory support systems, established links to foreign Internet sites, and stole tactical and artificial intelligence research data.

The potential for catastrophic damage is great. Organized foreign nationals or terrorists could use "information warfare" techniques to disrupt military operations by harming command and control systems, the public switch network, and other systems or networks Defense relies on.

Defense is taking action to address this growing problem, but faces significant challenges in controlling unauthorized access to its computer systems. Currently, Defense is attempting to react to successful attacks as it learns of them, but it has no uniform policy for assessing risks, protecting its systems, responding to incidents, or assessing damage. Training of users and system and network administrators is inconsistent and constrained by limited resources. Technical solutions being developed, including firewalls, smart cards, and network monitoring systems, will improve protection of

Defense information. However, the success of these measures depends on whether Defense implements them in tandem with better policy and personnel solutions.

Principal Findings

Computer Attacks Are an Increasing Threat

In preventing computer attacks, Defense has to protect a vast and complex information infrastructure: currently, it has over 2.1 million computers, 10,000 local networks, and 100 long-distance networks. Defense also critically depends on information technology—it uses computers to help design weapons, identify and track enemy targets, pay soldiers, mobilize reservists, and manage supplies. Indeed, its very warfighting capability is dependent on computer-based telecommunications networks and information systems.

Defense's computer systems are particularly susceptible to attack through connections on the Internet, which Defense uses to enhance communication and information sharing. In turning to the Internet, Defense has increased its own exposure to attacks. More and more computer users—currently over 40 million worldwide—are connecting to the Internet. This increases the risks of unauthorized access to information and disruption of service by outsiders. Defense systems connected to outside networks contain information that, while unclassified, is nevertheless sensitive and warrants protection because of the role it plays in Defense missions.

Attacks Are Costly and Damaging

DISA estimates indicate that Defense may have been attacked as many as 250,000 times last year. However, the exact number is not known because, according to DISA, only about 1 in 150 attacks is actually detected and reported. In addition, in testing its systems, DISA attacks and successfully penetrates Defense systems 65 percent of the time. According to Defense officials, attackers have obtained and corrupted sensitive information—they have stolen, modified, and destroyed both data and software. They have installed unwanted files and "back doors" which circumvent normal system protection and allow attackers unauthorized access in the future. They have shut down and crashed entire systems and networks, denying service to users who depend on automated systems to help meet critical missions. Numerous Defense functions have been adversely affected, including weapons and supercomputer research, logistics, finance, procurement, personnel management, military health, and payroll.

In addition to the security breaches and service disruptions they cause, these attacks are expensive. The 1994 Rome Laboratory incident alone cost Defense over $500,000 to assess the damage to its systems, ensure the reliability of the information in the systems, patch the vulnerabilities in its networks and systems, and attempt to identify the attackers and their locations. Although Defense has not estimated the total cost of repairing damage caused by the thousands of attacks experienced each year, it believes they are costing tens or possibly even hundreds of millions of dollars.

Potential Threat to National Security

There is mounting evidence that attacks on Defense computer systems pose a serious threat to national security. Internet connections make it possible for enemies armed with less equipment and weapons to gain a competitive edge at a small price. As a result, this will become an increasingly attractive way for terrorist or adversaries to wage attacks against Defense. For example, major disruptions to military operations and readiness could threaten national security if attackers successfully corrupted sensitive information and systems or denied service from vital communications backbones or power systems.

The National Security Agency has acknowledged that potential adversaries are developing a body of knowledge about Defense's and other U.S. systems and about methods to attack these systems. According to Defense officials, these methods, which include sophisticated computer viruses and automated attack routines, allow adversaries to launch untraceable attacks from anywhere in the world. In some extreme scenarios, studies show that terrorists or other adversaries could seize control of Defense information systems and seriously degrade the nation's ability to deploy and sustain military forces. Official estimates show that more than 120 countries already have or are developing such computer attack capabilities.

Challenges in Countering Attacks

In guarding its information, Defense faces the same risks and challenges as other government and private sector organizations that rely heavily on information technology. The task of preventing unauthorized users from compromising the confidentiality, integrity, or availability of sensitive information, is increasingly difficult in the face of the growth in Internet use, the increasing skill levels of attackers themselves, and technological advances in their tools and methods of attack.

Defense is taking actions to strengthen information systems security and counter computer attacks, but increased resources, and management commitment are needed. Currently, many of Defense's policies relating to computer attacks are outdated and inconsistent. They do not set standards or mandate specific actions for important security activities such as vulnerability assessments, internal reporting of attacks, correction of vulnerabilities, and damage assessments. Many of Defense's policies were developed when computers were physically and electronically isolated and do not reflect today's "networked" environment. Computer users are often unaware of system vulnerabilities and weak security practices. The majority of system and network administrators are not adequately trained in security and do not have sufficient time to perform their duties. Technical solutions to security show promise, but these alone do not ensure security. While Defense is attempting to react to attacks as it becomes aware of them, it will not be in a strong position to deter them until it develops and implements more aggressive, proactive detection and reaction programs.

Recommendations

Chapter 4 of this report contains recommendations to the Secretary of Defense for ensuring that sufficient priority, resources, and top-management attention are committed to establishing a more effective information systems security program—one that includes (1) improving security policies and procedures, (2) increasing user awareness and accountability, (3) setting minimum standards for ensuring that system and network security personnel have sufficient time and training to properly do their jobs, (4) implementing more proactive technical protection and monitoring systems, and (5) evaluating Defense's incident response capability. It also includes a recommendation to the Secretary for assigning clear responsibility and accountability throughout the Department for the successful implementation of the security program.

Agency Comments

GAO provided Department of Defense officials a draft of this report and discussed it with them on May 15, 1996. These officials generally agreed with the findings, conclusions, and recommendations in this report. The Department's comments and our evaluation are discussed in chapter 4 and have been incorporated where appropriate. . . .

Attacks Have Caused Considerable Damage

According to Defense officials, attacks on Department computer systems have been costly and considerably damaging. Attackers have stolen, modified, and destroyed both data and software. They have installed unwanted files and "back doors" which circumvent normal system protection and allow attackers unauthorized access in the future. They have shut down entire systems and networks, thereby denying service to users who depend on automated systems to help meet critical missions. Numerous Defense functions have been adversely affected, including weapons and supercomputer research, logistics, finance, procurement, personnel management, military health, and payroll.

Following are examples of attacks to date. The first attack we highlight, on Rome Laboratory, New York, was well-documented by Defense and of particular concern to committees requesting this report because the attack shows how a small group of hackers can easily and quickly take control of Defense networks.

Rome Laboratory

Rome Laboratory, New York, is Air Force's premier command and control research facility. The facility's research projects include artificial intelligence systems, radar guidance systems, and target detection and tracking systems. The laboratory works cooperatively with academic institutions, commercial research facilities, and Defense contractors in conducting its research and relies heavily on the Internet in doing so.

During March and April 1994, more than 150 Internet intrusions were made on the Laboratory by a British hacker and an unidentified hacker. The attackers used trojan horses [a computer program] and sniffers to access and control Rome's operational network. . . . [T]hey also took measures to prevent a complete trace of their attack. Instead of accessing Rome Laboratory computers directly, they weaved their way through various phone switches in South America, through commercial sites on the east and west coast, and then to the Rome Laboratory.

The attackers were able to seize control of Rome's support systems for several days and establish links to foreign Internet sites. During this time, they copied and downloaded critical information such as air tasking order systems data. By masquerading as a trusted user at Rome Laboratory, they were also able to successfully attack systems at other government facilities, including the National Aeronautics and Space Administration's (NASA) Goddard Space Flight Center, Wright-Patterson Air Force Base, some Defense contractors, and other private sector organizations. . . .

Because the Air Force did not know it was attacked for at least 3 days, vast damage to Rome Laboratory systems and the information in those systems could potentially have occurred. As stated in the Air Force report on the incident, "We have only the intruders to thank for the fact that no lasting damage occurred. Had they decided, as a skilled attacker most certainly will, to bring down the network immediately after the initial intrusion, we would have been powerless to stop them." However, the Air Force really does not know whether or not any lasting damage occurred. Furthermore, because one of the attackers was never caught, investigators do not know what was done with the copied data.

The Air Force Information Warfare Center (AFIWC) estimated that the attacks cost the government over $500,000 at the Rome Laboratory alone. Their estimate included the time spent taking systems off the networks, verifying systems integrity, installing security patches, and restoring service, and costs incurred by the Air Force's Office of Special Investigations and Information Warfare Center. It also included estimates for time and money lost due to the Laboratory's research staff not being able to use their computer systems.

However, the Air Force did not include the cost of the damage at other facilities attacked from the Rome Laboratory or the value of the research data that was compromised, copied, and downloaded by the attacker. For example, Rome Laboratory officials said that over 3 years of research and $4 million were invested in the air tasking order research project compromised by the attackers, and that it would have cost that much to replace it if they had been unable to recover from damage caused by the attackers. Similarly, Rome laboratory officials told us that all of their research data is valuable but that they do not know how to estimate this value.

There also may have been some national security risks associated with the Rome incident. Air Force officials told us that at least one of the hackers may have been working for a foreign country interested in obtaining military research data or information on areas in which the Air Force was conducting advanced research. In addition, Air Force Information Warfare Center officials told us that the hackers may have intended to install malicious code in software which could be activated years later, possibly jeopardizing a weapons system's ability to perform safely and as intended, and even threatening the lives of the soldiers or pilots operating the system.

Other Attacks

• The U.S. Naval Academy's computer systems were penetrated by unknown attackers in December 1994. The intrusions originated from Great Britain, Finland, Canada, the University of Kansas, and the University of Alabama. During the attack, 24 servers were accessed and sniffer programs were installed on 8 of these. A main router was compromised, and a system's name and address were changed, making the system inaccessible to authorized users. In addition, one system back-up file and files from four other systems were deleted. Six other systems were corrupted, two encrypted password files were compromised, and over 12,000 passwords were changed. The Navy did not determine how much the attack cost and Navy investigators were unable to identify the attacker(s). At a minimum, however, the attack caused considerable disruptions to the Academy's ability to process and store sensitive information.

• Between April 1990 and May 1991, hackers from the Netherlands penetrated computer systems at 34 Defense sites. The hackers browsed directories and modified systems to obtain full privileges allowing them future access. They read e-mail, in some cases searching the messages for key words such as nuclear, weapons, missile, Desert Shield, and Desert Storm. In several instances, the hackers copied and stored military data on systems at major U.S. universities. After the attacks, the hackers modified systems logs to avoid detection and to remove traces of their activities. We testified on these attacks before the Subcommittee on Government Information and Regulation, Senate Committee on Governmental Affairs, on November 20, 1991.

• In 1995 and 1996, an attacker from Argentina used the Internet to access a U.S. university system, and from there broke into computer networks at the Naval Research Laboratory, other Defense installations, NASA, and Los Alamos National Laboratory. The systems at these sites contained sensitive research information, such as aircraft design, radar technology, and satellite engineering, that is ultimately used in weapons and command and control systems. The Navy could not determine what information was compromised and did not attempt to determine the cost of the incident.

• Unknown person(s) accessed two unclassified computer systems at the Army Missile Research Laboratory, White Sands Missile Range and installed a sniffer program. The intruder was detected entering the systems a second and third time, but the sniffer program was removed before the intruder could be identified. The missile range's computer systems contain sensitive data, including test results on the accuracy and reliability of sophisticated weaponry. As with the case above, the Army could not determine what data was compromised. However, such data could prove very valuable to foreign adversaries.

While these are specific examples, Defense officials say they reflect the thousands of attacks experienced every year. Although no one has attempted to determine the total cost of responding to these attacks, Defense officials agreed the cost of these incidents is significant and probably totals tens or even hundreds of millions of dollars per year. Such costs should include (1) detecting and reacting to attacks, repairing systems, and checking to ensure the integrity of information, (2) lost productivity due to computer shutdowns, (3) tracking, catching, and prosecuting attackers, and (4) the cost and value of information compromised. . . .

The task of precluding unauthorized users from compromising the confidentiality, integrity, or availability of information is increasingly difficult given the complexity of Defense's information infrastructure, growth of and reliance on outside networks including the Internet, and the increasing sophistication of the attackers and their tools. Absolute protection of Defense information is neither practical nor affordable. Instead, Defense must turn to risk management to ensure computer security. In doing so, however, it must make tradeoffs that consider the magnitude of the threat, the value and sensitivity of the information to be protected, and the cost of protecting it.

Elements of a Good Information Systems Security Program

In our review of key studies and security documents and discussions with Defense security experts, certain core elements emerged as critical to effective information system security. A good computer security program begins with top management's understanding of the risks associated with networked computers, and a commitment that computer security will be given a high priority. At Defense, management attention to computer security has been uneven. The Defense information infrastructure has evolved into a set of individual computer systems and interconnected networks, many of which were developed without sufficient attention to the entire infrastructure. While some local area networks and Defense installations have excellent security programs, others do not. However, the overall infrastructure is only as secure as the weakest link. Therefore, all components of the Defense infrastructure must be considered when making investment decisions.

In addition, policies and procedures must also reflect this philosophy and guide implementation of the Department's overall security program as well as the security plans for individual Defense installations. The policies should set minimum standards and requirements for key security activities and clearly assign responsibility and accountability for ensuring that they are carried out. Further, sufficient personnel, training, and resources must be provided to implement these policies.

While not intended to be a comprehensive list, following are security activities that all of the security studies and experts agreed were important:

(1) clear and consistent information security policies and procedures,

(2) vulnerability assessments to identify security weaknesses at individual Defense installations,

(3) mandatory correction of identified network/system security weaknesses,

(4) mandatory reporting of attacks to help better identify and communicate vulnerabilities and needed corrective actions,

(5) damage assessments to reestablish the integrity of the information compromised by an attacker,

(6) awareness training to ensure that computer users understand the security risks associated with networked computers and practice good security,

(7) assurance that network managers and system administrators have sufficient time and training to do their jobs,

(8) prudent use of firewalls, smart cards, and other technical solutions, and

(9) an incident response capability to aggressively detect and react to attacks and track and prosecute attackers.

Defense has recognized the importance of good computer security. The Assistant Secretary of Defense for Command, Control, Communications and Intelligence has stated, "The vulnerability to . . . systems and networks is increasing. . . . The ability of individuals to penetrate computer networks and deny, damage, or destroy data has been demonstrated on many occasions. . . . As our warfighters become more and more dependent on our information systems, the potential for disaster is obvious."

In addition, as part of its Federal Managers' Financial Integrity Act requirements, the Department identified information systems security as a system weakness in its *Fiscal Year 1995 Annual Statement of Assurance*, a report documenting high-risk areas requiring management attention. In its statement, Defense acknowledged a significant increase in attacks on its information systems and its dependence on these systems.

Also, Defense has implemented a formal defensive information warfare program. This program was started in December 1992 through Defense Directive 3600.1. The directive broadly states that measures will be taken as part of this program to "protect friendly information systems by preserving the availability, integrity, and confidentiality of the systems and the information contained within those systems." DISA, in cooperation with the military services and defense agencies, is responsible for implementing the program. The Department's December 1995 Defensive Information Warfare Management Plan defines a three-pronged approach to protect against, detect, and react to threats to the Defense information infrastructure. The plan states that Defense must monitor and detect intrusions or hostile actions as they occur, react quickly to isolate the systems under attack, correct the security breaches, restore service to authorized users, and improve security.

DISA has also taken a number of actions to implement its plan, the most significant being the establishment of its Global Control Center at DISA headquarters. The center provides the facilities, equipment, and personnel for directing the defensive information warfare program, including detecting and responding to computer attacks. DISA has also established its Automated Systems Security Incident Support Team (ASSIST) to provide a centrally coordinated around-the-clock Defense response to attacks. DISA also performs other services to help secure Defense's information infrastructure, including conducting assessments of Defense organizations' vulnerability to computer attacks. AFIWC has developed a computer emergency response capability and performs functions similar to DISA. The Navy and Army have just established similar capabilities through the Fleet Information Warfare Center (FIWC) and Land Information Warfare Activity (LIWA), respectively.

Defense is incorporating some of the elements we describe above as necessary for strengthening information systems security and countering computer attacks, but there are still areas where improvement is needed. Even though the technology environment has changed dramatically in recent years, and the risk of attacks has increased, top management at many organizations do not consider computer security to be a priority. As a result, when resources are allocated, funding for important protective measures, such as training or the purchase of protection technology, take a back seat.

As discussed in the remainder of this chapter, Defense needs to establish a more comprehensive information systems security program. A program which ensures that sufficient resources are directed at protecting information systems. Specifically, (1) Defense's policies for protecting, detecting, and reacting to computer attacks are outdated and incomplete, (2) computer users are often unaware of system vulnerabilities and weak security practices, (3) system and network administrators are not adequately trained and do not have sufficient time to perform their duties, (4) technical solutions to security problems show promise, but these alone cannot guarantee protection, and (5) while Defense's incident response capability is improving, it is not sufficient to handle the increasing threat. . . .

Conclusions

Networked computer systems offer tremendous potential for streamlining and improving the efficiency of Defense operations. However, they also greatly increase the risks that information systems supporting critical Defense functions will be attacked. The hundreds of thousands of attacks that Defense has already experienced demonstrate that (1) significant damage can be incurred by attackers and (2) attacks pose serious risks to national security. They also show that top management attention at all levels and clearly assigned accountability are needed to ensure that computer systems are better protected. The need for such attention and accountability is supported by the Joint Security Commission which considers the security of information systems and networks to be the major security challenge of this decade and possibly the next century. The Commission itself believes there is insufficient awareness of the grave risks Defense faces in this arena.

We recognize that no organization can anticipate all potential vulnerabilities, and even if one could, it may not be cost-effective to implement every measure available to ensure protection. However, Defense can take some basic steps to vastly improve its position against attackers. These steps include strengthening (1) computer security policies and procedures, (2) security training and staffing, and (3) detection and reaction programs. Since the level of protection varies from installation-to-installation, the need for corrective measures should be assessed on a case-by-case basis by comparing the value and sensitivity of information with the cost of protecting it and by considering the entire infrastructure.

Recommendations

To better focus management attention on the Department's increasing computer security threat and to ensure that a higher priority and sufficient resources are devoted to addressing this problem, we recommend that at a minimum the Secretary of Defense strengthen the Department's information systems security program by

- developing departmentwide policies for preventing, detecting, and responding to attacks on Defense information systems, including mandating that (1) all security incidents be reported within the Department, (2) risk assessments be performed routinely to determine vulnerability to attacks and intrusions, (3) vulnerabilities and deficiencies be expeditiously corrected as they are identified, and (4) damage from intrusions be expeditiously assessed to ensure the integrity of data and systems compromised;
- requiring the military services and Defense agencies to use training and other mechanisms to increase awareness and accountability among installation commanders and all personnel as to the security risks of computer systems connected to the Internet and their responsibility for securing their systems;
- requiring information system security officers at all installations and setting specific standards for ensuring that these as well as system and network managers are given sufficient time and training to perform their duties appropriately;
- continually developing and cost-effectively using departmentwide network monitoring and protection technologies; and
- evaluating the incident response capabilities within DISA, the military services, and the Defense agencies to ensure that they are sufficient to handle the projected threat.

The Secretary should also assign clear responsibility and accountability within the Office of the Secretary of Defense, the military services, and Defense agencies for ensuring the successful implementation of this computer security program. . . .

JUSTICE DEPARTMENT ON
LOCAL CURFEWS FOR JUVENILES
May 30, 1996

President Bill Clinton and his Republican challenger, Sen. Bob Dole, injected into the presidential race the issue of curfews for teenagers. Competing with each other to propose low-cost ways to combat crime, Clinton and Dole in late May endorsed curfews and suggested that local governments should enact more of them.

Just a day after Dole endorsed curfews during a speech in California, Clinton on May 30 used an appearance in New Orleans to draw attention to a tough curfew law in that city. Curfews, he said, are "designed to help people be better parents. They help keep our children out of harm's way. They give parents a tool to impart discipline, respect, and rules at an awkward and difficult time in children's lives."

To buttress his point, the president drew attention to a report, "Curfew: An Answer to Juvenile Delinquency and Victimization?" issued in April by the Justice Department's Office of Juvenile Justice and Delinquency Prevention. The report noted that as of 1995, many of the nation's largest cities had enacted some form of juvenile curfew. The report concluded that "comprehensive, community-based juvenile curfew programs are helping to reduce juvenile delinquency and victimization." Clinton ordered Attorney General Janet Reno to distribute the report to the nation's mayors. Clinton did not endorse a national policy on curfews, however.

New Popularity of Curfews

The Justice Department report reviewed the increasing use of curfews by local authorities as one tool to combat the rise of juvenile crime. It quoted one study showing a "dramatic surge in curfew legislation during the first half of the 1990s." According to that study, 93 of the nation's 200 largest cities had curfew laws in effect at the beginning of 1990; by the spring of 1995, an additional 53 cities had enacted curfews, putting the total at 146 cities, or 73 percent of the total.

Most of the curfews applied to youths under sixteen years of age, the report said, but some included sixteen- and seventeen-year-olds. Typically, curfews required juveniles to be off the streets (unless accompanied by an adult or attending supervised school or religious activities) between the hours of 11 p.m. and 6 a.m. on school nights and between midnight and 6 a.m. on weekends. Local jurisdictions enforced curfews in many ways, but most used recreation centers, churches, or other facilities staffed by social service professionals and volunteers to receive juveniles who were picked up by police for curfew violations. In most cases, fines or other penalties were levied only on repeat offenders and/or their families.

The report reviewed curfew ordinances and enforcement procedures in seven cities: Dallas, Phoenix, Chicago, New Orleans, Denver, North Little Rock, and Jacksonville. In each case, the report said, the curfew was part of a broader program "designed to protect both the community and the juvenile from victimization and to serve as a constructive intervention against developing patterns of delinquency." All the curfews cited in the report were carefully drawn in hopes of withstanding legal and constitutional challenges, the report said.

The New Orleans curfew cited by President Clinton was one of the most comprehensive programs reviewed in the report. That curfew required youths under age seventeen to be off the streets by 8 p.m. on weekdays when school was in session, by 9 p.m. on weekdays during the summer, and by 11 p.m. on weekends. The city established a Central Curfew Center, where police took youths who violated the curfew. At the center, professional and volunteer staff members screened the youths, contacted their parents, and counseled both the youths and the parents. Parents of repeat offenders were issued a court summons and risked being fined.

The city of New Orleans also stepped up funding for youth recreation programs, especially in the summer. In addition, the city created 1,300 new summer jobs for youth and received $1.8 million in federal funding for year-round employment of youth in education, park, and recreation programs.

The Justice Department report said the combination of the curfew and other programs helped produce a 27 percent reduction in juvenile crime during curfew hours in 1994, when compared with 1993. The most significant decreases were in armed robbery and auto theft. The report quoted New Orleans Sheriff Charles Foti praising the program as "a coordinated effort of unprecedented proportions" that had earned "unqualified support" in the community.

Objections to Curfews

Despite their popularity with politicians, law enforcement officials, and the general public, curfews were sharply criticized by civil liberties groups and some criminal justice experts. Some observers said the enthusiasm for curfews during the 1990s might be merely a temporary fad and that local officials would soon be discouraged by the high cost of enforcement.

The American Civil Liberties Union (ACLU) took the lead in opposing many curfew ordinances as violations of the constitutional rights of freedom of speech and assembly and the guarantee against unreasonable searches. The Washington Post on May 31 quoted Laura W. Murphy, director of the ACLU's Washington office, as saying "the only winners in this dirty war are the politicians. The losers are the law-abiding young people whose constitutional rights are being violated, and their parents who will be subject to fines and court summonses."

Several carefully drawn curfew laws have withstood legal challenge by the ACLU and other organizations, including an ordinance adopted by the city council in Dallas in 1991. The U.S. Court of Appeals for the Fifth Circuit upheld the Dallas law in 1993, and the Supreme Court in 1995 refused to hear an appeal of that ruling. The Justice Department report said curfews can withstand a constitutional challenge when local jurisdictions can demonstrate a "compelling state interest" in curbing juvenile crime and when they "narrowly tailor the means to achieve the law's objective."

In addition to constitutional issues, some experts on criminal justice questioned juvenile curfews on more practical grounds. First, they noted that curfews were expensive to enforce, often requiring a big city to dedicate dozens of police officers and other professionals to the task of rounding up wayward juveniles, transporting them to detention centers, and ensuring that parents take them home. In New Orleans, according to the Justice Department report, the sheriff's office assigned thirty deputies and several other staff members to the curfew center, and the police department had more than fifty police officers on the street and five or six officers at the curfew center.

Some criminal justice experts noted that a minority of juvenile crimes were committed during the hours when curfews were in effect. According to several studies, between one-half and three-fourths of juvenile crimes were committed during the daylight hours, when school was in session, or in the hours right after school, from 3 p.m. to 7 p.m. Some crimes committed by juveniles, especially violent ones such as murder and rape, tended to occur later at night, during curfew hours. Officials in several cities said they were having success with truancy-prevention programs aimed at keeping habitual offenders in school and off the streets.

Some experts also derided curfews as a simplistic approach to complex social and economic problems. The New York Times on June 3 quoted Alfred Blumstein, a criminologist at Carnegie-Mellon University in Pittsburgh, as saying that the public viewed curfews as a "cheap and easy" solution to juvenile crime. Blumstein and others said society should be more willing to address the fundamental causes of juvenile crime, such as poverty, an increasing lack of parental supervision and guidance, and inadequate inner city schools. According to some of these experts, the money spent to enforce curfews might be more effectively spent on youth recreation and employment programs and counseling for parents.

Following are excerpts from the report, "Curfew: An Answer to Juvenile Delinquency and Victimization?" released May 30, 1996, by the Justice Department's Office of Juvenile Justice and Delinquency:

Traditionally, the determination of a minor's curfew has been considered to be a family issue, within the parental purview, rather than a matter to be determined by government. Nevertheless, public curfews have been enacted and enforced throughout the Nation's history in reaction to increased juvenile delinquency, decreased parental supervision, and other social trends. Recent increases in juvenile crime and victimization have prompted local communities in many States to once again consider evening curfews (e.g., from 11 P.M. to 6 A.M. on school days and from midnight to 6 A.M. on non-school days) as a viable means to enhance the safety of the community and its children. Although most curfew ordinances apply to juveniles under 16 years of age, some include 16- and 17-year-olds. This Bulletin explores developments in curfew ordinances, legal issues related to curfews, how jurisdictions have responded to legal challenges, the elements of sound community-based curfew programs, and examples of a range of curfew programs and services from seven jurisdictions.

In a recent study of curfew ordinances in the 200 largest U.S. cities (population of 100,000 or greater in 1992), Ruefle and Reynolds found a dramatic surge in curfew legislation during the first half of the 1990's. Of the 200 cities surveyed, 93 (47 percent) had curfews in effect on January 1, 1990. Between January 1990 and the spring of 1995, an additional 53 of these 200 cities (27 percent) enacted juvenile curfew ordinances, bringing the total of those with curfew laws to 146 (73 percent). During the same period, 37 of the 93 cities with an existing curfew ordinance revised that legislation.

Legal Challenges

The question of curfews has raised a variety of legal issues and divided numerous communities, as the following sample of newspaper headlines illustrates: "The Trouble With Curfews," "Cities Deciding That It's Time for Teen Curfews," "Curfew Not a Good Idea," "Curfew Needs To Be Stronger," "Limiting Kids' Time on the Streets Elicits Both Relief and Resentment." Differences in opinion have led individuals and civil rights organizations in many communities to challenge the legality of juvenile curfew ordinances. The American Civil Liberties Union (ACLU), the most vocal opponent, has challenged the constitutionality of juvenile curfew ordinances in jurisdictions across the country, either directly or by providing assistance to individuals who wish to test such laws in court.

Legal challenges to the constitutionality of curfew ordinances are most often based on the 1st, 4th, 5th, 9th, and 14th amendments to the U.S. Constitution. The first amendment guarantees the right to freedom of speech, religion, and peaceful assembly. The fourth amendment protects persons against unreasonable searches and seizures and has been interpreted to include protection against unreasonable stopping and detainment of individuals. The fifth amendment guarantees citizens the right to due process under the law. The ninth amendment has been interpreted to include a right to privacy, including the right to family autonomy. The 14th amendment protects persons against the deprivation of their liberty without due process of law and includes the right to travel, which is embodied in the privileges and immunities clause.

In 1975, the first Federal case concerning the constitutionality of juvenile curfews was heard by the U.S. District Court for the Middle District of Pennsylvania. In *Bykofsky v. Borough of Middletown*, the court upheld a juvenile curfew that was challenged on the grounds that it violated juveniles' 1st and 14th amendment rights and encroached upon parents' rights to raise their children, which is embodied in the 9th amendment and in the due process and equal protection clauses of the 14th amendment. In its opinion, the court found that the regulations on juveniles' 14th amendment due process rights were "constitutionally permissible." The court further declared that the curfew ordinance did not suppress or impermissibly regulate juveniles' right to freedom of speech or parents' rights to raise their children as they saw fit. The court stated, "The parents' constitutionally protected interest . . . which the ordinance infringes only minimally, is outweighed by the Borough's interest in protecting immature minors. . . ."

Fourteen years later, in 1989, Simbi Waters challenged a juvenile curfew ordinance in the District of Columbia on the grounds that it violated her first, fourth, and fifth amendment rights. The U.S. District Court for the District of Columbia, in *Waters v. Barry*, found the juvenile curfew law to be unconstitutional on the grounds that it violated the first and fifth amendment rights of juveniles in the District: "The right to walk the streets, or to meet publicly with one's friends for a noble purpose or for no purpose at all—and to do so whenever one pleases is an integral component of life in a free and ordered society." However, the court did not find that the curfew violated the fourth amendment rights of District juveniles: "So long as the officer could reasonably have believed that the individual looked 'young,' the search, seizure or arrest would take place on the basis of probable cause and no Fourth Amendment violation would occur." Although the district court invalidated this particular curfew, in July 1995 the District of Columbia enacted another juvenile curfew ordinance modeled after one enacted in Dallas, Texas, that had survived constitutional scrutiny by the U.S. Court of Appeals for the Fifth Circuit in 1993.

The seminal issue of the State's authority to restrict the constitutional rights of minors is consistently raised in juvenile curfew cases. In the *Bykofsky* case cited above, the court held that "the conduct of minors may be constitutionally regulated to a greater extent than those of adults." The U.S. Court of Appeals for the Fifth Circuit, in upholding the Dallas curfew, applied the reasoning of the Supreme Court of the United States in *Hodgson v. Minnesota*, which held that a parental notification requirement of the State's abortion statute passed constitutional muster because States have ". . . a strong and legitimate interest in the welfare of [their] young citizens, whose immaturity, inexperience, and lack of judgment may sometimes impair their ability to exercise their rights wisely."

The Strict Scrutiny Test

In order to pass constitutional muster, laws that impinge on fundamental constitutional rights must pass a two-pronged strict scrutiny test that requires jurisdictions to (1) demonstrate that there is a compelling State interest and (2) narrowly tailor the means to achieve the law's objective. The Dallas curfew provides an excellent example of an ordinance that has been held by a Federal court to satisfy both prongs of the strict scrutiny test.

The Dallas City Council adopted its curfew ordinance in 1991 after hearings that included testimony on increased incidences of late-night juvenile violence. Challenged by the ACLU, Dallas' curfew ordinance was upheld in 1993 by the U.S. Court of Appeals for the Fifth Circuit in *Qutb v. Strauss*. The Fifth Circuit held that the Dallas curfew satisfied the strict scrutiny test because the city had demonstrated a compelling State interest in reducing juvenile crime and victimization and because the ordinance was properly aimed, that is, narrowly tailored to ". . . allow the city to meet its stated goals while respecting the rights of the affected minors." A subsequent appeal was refused by the Supreme Court of the United States without comment in May 1994. However, this ruling neither guarantees protection from future constitutional legal challenges to curfews in other circuits under the provisions of the U.S. Constitution or State constitutions, nor forecloses challenges based on nonconstitutional grounds.

Jurisdictions that seek to enact curfew laws may want to examine how Dallas laid the groundwork needed to pass the strict scrutiny test. Data on juvenile crime and victimization helped meet the compelling State interest test. The city provided the following statistical information:

- Juvenile delinquency increases proportionally with age between the ages of 10 and 16 years.
- In 1989, Dallas recorded 5,160 juvenile arrests, and in 1990, there were 5,425 juvenile arrests, including 40 murders, 91 sex offenses, 233 robberies, and 230 aggravated assaults. From January through April 1991, juveniles were arrested for 21 murders, 30 sex offenses, 128 robberies, 107 aggravated assaults, and an additional 1,042 crimes against property.
- The most likely time for the occurrence of murders by juveniles was between 10 P.M. and 1 A.M.; the most likely place was in apartments and apartment parking lots and on streets and highways.
- Aggravated assaults by juveniles were most likely to occur between 11 P.M. and 1 A.M.
- Rapes were most likely to occur between 1 A.M. and 3 A.M., and 16 percent of rapes occurred on public streets and highways.
- Thirty-one percent of robberies occurred on public streets and highways.

The Court relied on these data in holding that the City of Dallas provided sufficient evidence to establish that the ordinance was in keeping with the State's compelling interest in reducing juvenile crime and victimization.

Second, the Dallas legislation was narrowly tailored to address the specific needs enumerated by the jurisdiction by the least restrictive means possible. The Dallas curfew was applied to youth under the age of 17 and in effect from 11 P.M. through 6 A.M. Sunday through Thursday and from midnight to 6 a.m. Friday and Saturday. The statute exempted juveniles who were:

- Accompanied by an adult.
- Engaged in activities related to interstate commerce or protected by the first amendment.
- Traveling to or from work.
- Responding to an emergency.
- Married.
- Attending a supervised school, religious, or recreational activity.

The Fifth Circuit found, in *Qutb v. Strauss*, that the exemptions under the Dallas ordinance, which permitted juveniles to exercise their fundamental rights and remain in public, demonstrated that the ordinance was narrowly tailored to meet the city's legitimate objectives.

Other challenges to juvenile curfews have been based on the concepts of vagueness and overbreadth. A statute is void for vagueness if it is too general and its "... standards result in erratic and arbitrary application based on individual impressions and personal predilections." A statute that broadly restricts fundamental liberties when less restrictive means are available may be void on the grounds of overbreadth. Therefore, when constructing juvenile curfew ordinances, in addition to considering constitutional issues that involve fundamental rights, jurisdictions should ensure the legislation is both precise in its language and limited to necessary restrictions.

In addition to constitutional and structural challenges to juvenile curfews, jurisdictions enacting curfew laws should also bear in mind the core requirement of the Juvenile Justice and Delinquency Prevention (JJDP) Act of 1974, as amended, which addresses the deinstitutionalization of status offender and non-offender juveniles (DSO). In general, this JJDP Act core requirement prohibits a status offender (i.e., a juvenile who has committed an offense that would not be a crime if committed by an adult, such as truancy or curfew violations) or nonoffender (i.e., a dependent or neglected child) from being held in secure detention or confinement. However, Office of Juvenile Justice and Delinquency Prevention (OJJDP) regulations allow detention for brief periods in a juvenile detention facility—not to exceed 24 hours exclusive of weekends and holidays—necessary for pre- or postcourt appearance, processing, release to a parent or guardian, or transfer to court or an appropriate nonsecure facility. The statute also makes exceptions that allow the detention or confinement of status offenders who violate a valid court order or who violate State law provisions prohibiting the possession of a handgun. Status and nonoffender juveniles cannot be detained or confined in an adult

jail or lockup for any length of time. To comply with the DSO core requirement of the JJDP Act Formula Grants Program, and to reduce the burden on
police, Dallas and many other cities have established comprehensive, community-based curfew programs that provide local sites, such as community
and recreation centers, where police officers can bring curfew violators for
temporary detention pending release to their parents or other appropriate
disposition. These sites provide an atmosphere conducive to investigation,
processing, prerelease counseling, and planning for appropriate followup
services.

Representative Curfew Programs

Local governments have enacted juvenile curfews pursuant to their general police powers or State statutes specifically authorizing such ordinances.
The seven cities whose curfew programs are discussed below enacted their
ordinances pursuant to specific authorizing State legislation. Law enforcement professionals generally view a juvenile curfew ordinance as an effective means to combat late evening crime. However, curfews are also intended to protect youth from becoming victims of crime. The curfew ordinances
described below were enacted in the context of a comprehensive, community-based program designed to protect both the community and the juvenile
from victimization and to serve as a constructive intervention against developing patterns of delinquency.

Each of the jurisdictions . . . collected statistical data on juvenile crime
and victimization prior to passing a curfew ordinance. This activity also laid
a foundation for formulating a curfew ordinance that addressed the jurisdiction's unique juvenile crime and victimization problems. Although juvenile
crime is not restricted to evening hours, the data analysis done by these cities
demonstrated that their rates of juvenile crime and victimization were serious enough to warrant a carefully crafted evening curfew program.

Each of these seven cities has its own unique and innovative approach to
addressing the problem of juvenile crime and victimization through a curfew
ordinance. The approaches demonstrate a range of community partnerships
and nonpunitive strategies designed to promote early intervention to prevent
the development of delinquent behavior and to address the issues of parental
responsibility, discipline, and family dysfunction. The strategies have been
credited with helping to prevent juvenile crime and victimization and repeated curfew violations while providing protection and safety to the community.

While the comprehensive, community-based curfew programs implemented by the seven cities employ a variety of strategies, each program includes
one or more of the following common elements:

- Creation of a dedicated curfew center or use of recreation centers and
  churches to receive juveniles who have been picked up by the police for
  violating curfew.
- Staffing of curfew centers with social service professionals and community volunteers.

- Intervention, in the form of referrals to social service providers and counseling classes, for the juveniles and their families.
- Procedures for repeat offenders, including fines, counseling, or sentences to community service.
- Recreation and jobs programs.
- Antidrug and antigang programs.
- Hotlines for followup services and crisis intervention.

The cornerstone of each of the seven programs is creative community involvement that works to transform the juvenile curfew from a reactive, punitive response to a proactive intervention against the root causes of juvenile delinquency and victimization. . . .

Summary

Curfew ordinances are in effect in a majority of the Nation's largest cities. While curfews have been challenged in many jurisdictions on a variety of constitutional and other grounds, narrowly crafted ordinances designed to address specifically identified problems appear able to withstand such challenges. Statistical analyses of the impact of curfew ordinances on delinquency and juvenile victimization in many communities continue to be conducted. The information made available by the communities highlighted in this bulletin and by other communities where curfew programs have been implemented indicates that comprehensive, community-based juvenile curfew programs are helping to reduce juvenile delinquency and victimization. It is important for communities that are enforcing curfews or considering a curfew ordinance to keep abreast of legal developments, establish a firm foundation for the ordinance, and model the curfew program after community-based efforts in other jurisdictions.

The initial evidence offered by the seven communities profiled in this Bulletin is that community-based curfew programs that offer a range of services are more easily and effectively enforced, enjoy community support, and provide a greater benefit in preventing juvenile delinquency and victimization. In addition, several of the benefits of positive interventions that community-based curfew programs can provide may not be easily quantifiable—at least in the short term. Phoenix curfew staff have observed that many of the curfew violators brought into the recreation centers that function as curfew reception centers welcome the opportunity for social interaction with other youth and with program staff. Often these youth seek advice, assistance, and counsel from program staff. Parents sometimes bring their son or daughter to a curfew site to seek assistance and advice on the best approach for curfew compliance or to deal with other problem behaviors.

Communities that develop and implement curfew ordinances in conjunction with programs and services designed to assist youth and families to solve underlying individual or family problems have an opportunity to enhance positive youth development, prevent delinquency, and reduce the victimization of children.

June

NETANYAHU ON HIS ELECTION
AS PRIME MINISTER OF ISRAEL
June 2, 1996

A sharply divided Israeli electorate on May 29 narrowly elected Benjamin Netanyahu, leader of the rightist Likud faction, as prime minister. His election threw into question the future of the fragile "peace process" between Israel and its Arab foes, especially the Palestinians. Netanyahu owed his election primarily to doubts among Israeli Jews about the peace process, doubts that were enhanced in the weeks before the election by terrorist bombings that killed nearly sixty Israelis. Netanyahu defeated Shimon Peres, who had become prime minister after Yitzhak Rabin was assassinated in November 1995.

Despite his own harsh criticism of peace agreements negotiated by his predecessors, Netanyahu pledged to honor those accords. In a victory statement on June 2, Netanyahu called on Arab leaders to "come and join us" and "take the path of true peace together."

Within three months of his election, Netanyahu met for the first time with Palestinian leader Yasir Arafat, the man most reviled by the Israeli right, a man whom Netanyahu himself had repeatedly called a "terrorist." Arafat in 1996 won his own election as president of a new Palestinian authority for the West Bank and Gaza Strip. It was the first election by Palestinians under the terms of a peace agreement that Arafat signed in 1995 with Rabin. Rabin later was assassinated by an Israeli zealot. (Death of Prime Minister Rabin, Historic Documents of 1995, p. 689)

At year's end, Netanyahu and Arafat were engaged in tense negotiations over procedures for Israel's military withdrawal from the contested city of Hebron on the West Bank of the Jordan River. Under the 1995 peace agreement Israel was supposed to have withdrawn its troops from Hebron by mid-June 1996.

Arafat was pressing for commitments by Netanyahu to abide by all terms of the 1995 accord. Netanyahu's maneuvering room was limited by the refusal of some of his governing coalition partners to make any concessions to Palestinians. The difficulty of those talks raised serious ques-

tions about the prospect of negotiations between Israel and its Arab neigh-bors over broader and even more contentious issues, such as the status of Jerusalem and the Israeli-occupied Golan Heights overlooking Syria. (Israeli-Palestinian peace agreement, Historic Documents of 1993, p. 747; West Bank agreement, Historic Documents of 1995, p. 622)

Background to the Election

The year had begun on a relatively upbeat note for the Middle East peace process, as Israel began withdrawing from territories it had seized from Arabs in the 1967 war and as Palestinians prepared for their first-ever elections. These were two of the most important steps mandated by the 1995 peace agreement.

Considering the violence and upheaval that attended practically any event in the region, the peace process was off to a good start. The Israeli withdrawals went smoothly. By the time of the Israeli election, the Peres government had pulled troops from all major population centers in the ter-ritories except Hebron. Palestinians went to the polls in large numbers on January 20 to elect an eighty-eight-member parliament, called the Pales-tinian Authority, with Arafat as president.

Peres and his election chances were undermined by a series of suicide bombings by Palestinian extremists, starting February 25, that killed nearly sixty Israelis and infuriated the Israeli populace. Although the Peres government responded with a forceful crackdown on Palestinian areas, many Israelis held Peres and the peace process he supported respon-sible for the terrorist attacks.

On April 18, responding to rocket attacks from the Iranian-backed Hezbollah guerrillas based in southern Lebanon, Israel shelled a United Nations refugee camp in the area, killing nearly one hundred civilians. The incident gave Peres an opportunity to demonstrate his toughness against Arab radicals, but it brought widespread condemnation interna-tionally and threatened to derail further peace talks between Israel and Arabs. A UN report cast doubt on Israel's claim that the shelling of civilian refugees was accidental.

Intense diplomatic negotiating by the United States was necessary to produce a cease-fire agreement between Israel and Lebanon on April 27. That agreement essentially revived, in written form, a tacit understanding between Israel and the Hezbollah that neither side would attack civilian areas.

A Victory for the Right

The May 29 election was the first in which Israel's prime minister was elected directly by the voters. Netanyahu edged Peres by just 30,000 votes out of nearly 3 million cast—a margin of 50.4 percent to 49.5 percent. Polls showed that a strong majority of Israeli Jews voted for Netanyahu, while Peres carried nearly all of Israel's small Arab vote along with a minority of Jews. In voting for the parliament (the Knesset), narrowly based reli-

gious or nationalist parties won 54 of the 120 seats, undermining support for the two broad-based Labor and Likud parties, which had taken turns governing Israel since its founding in 1948.

Netanyahu's victory was greeted with rejoicing by conservative, religious, and nationalist factions, which had charged that the Labor government was undermining Israel's heritage and security by negotiating peace agreements with the Palestinians. Arafat was described by associates as being in a state of shock. The Clinton administration, which clearly had hoped for a Peres victory, reacted cautiously and called on Netanyahu to respect the peace process.

Unable to control the Knesset with just his own minority Likud party, Netanyahu was forced to assemble a coalition government dependent on the support of several small special interest factions, including two ultra-orthodox parties. The coalition had just 62 votes, ensuring that Netanyahu would have to conduct delicate balancing acts on all major issues to hold his government together.

The necessity of appeasing a broad range of interests affected all of Netanyahu's actions during his first months in office, especially those concerning the Palestinians. The issue of expanding Jewish settlements on the West Bank was a prime example. Religious and nationalist parties expected that a Likud government would order an immediate expansion of the size and number of Jewish settlements, a step that would have violated both the letter and spirit of the peace accord. Netanyahu's government did not expand the settlements, although in December the cabinet did take a controversial vote to restore government subsidies for 144 settlements on the West Bank and in the Gaza Strip.

The Hebron Talks

The negotiations over the Israeli military withdrawal from Hebron represented another case in which the Netanyahu government struggled to satisfy its rightist supporters while keeping the peace process on track. The prospect of a withdrawal from Hebron had been a key issue in the election because of security concerns for the 450 Jewish settlers who lived there among some 90,000 Palestinians. Peres had deferred a Hebron withdrawal until after the election; most leaders of Netanyahu's Likud coalition strongly opposed pulling Israeli troops from the city.

President Clinton in October stepped up pressure for agreement on the Hebron issue and dispatched his top Middle East negotiator, Dennis Ross, to Israel in hopes of resolving the impasse. Ross quickly reached agreement between Israel and the Palestinians on most technical issues, but he had trouble overcoming political resistance on both sides.

Arafat balked at signing an agreement on Hebron without receiving specific commitments in writing from Netanyahu that Israel would comply with requirements for three additional withdrawals from the West Bank by September 1997. Netanyahu reportedly was willing to offer assurances concerning the first withdrawal, due in March 1997, but he was worried about losing cabinet support for any pledges on further withdrawals. The two sides were haggling over the issue as 1996 ended.

Following is the text of a statement by Benjamin Netanyahu on June 2, 1996, as translated from Hebrew, following his election as prime minister of Israel:

Citizens of Israel, Friends.

The State of Israel is embarking on a new path today, a path of hope and of unity, a path of security and of peace. And the first and foremost peace we must make is peace at home, amongst ourselves.

This is our most important task because in recent years the polarization in Israeli society has deepened, the gaps have become larger, and the tension has increased.

Dear friends, I see my first task as prime minister to mend the rifts, to reduce the tensions and to strengthen the unity and the sense of partnership, which is the basis of our existence. And I want to tell you: the first peace is peace at home.

Israeli society is blessed with many shades and persuasions. Our unity is not based on blurring the uniqueness of each group. It is expressed by nurturing tolerance and mutual respect while maintaining the religious status quo.

I am talking about a coming together of all the sectors in Israeli society, while maintaining the delicate balance between differing world views. This is our way and we will pursue it.

These principles are enshrined in the Jewish heritage, which is the basis of our unity as a people, and from which we draw the principles of justice and equality for all of Israel's citizens, Jewish and non-Jewish alike.

I turn this evening to the non-Jewish citizens of Israel. I want to tell you something: I see you as full and equal partners in every field of endeavor in the country.

I turn to the entire Israeli public—those who voted for me and those who did not. I tell you that I intend to be the prime minister of you all, without exception. The peace we bring will not be peace for Likud or the national camp. It will be peace for all, with security for all, and with prosperity and welfare for all.

I say this because I believe it is my duty to be the prime minister of all Israel's citizens—secular and religious, Jews and non-Jews, new immigrants and veteran Israelis, residents of development towns and of established cities.

In the next four years we will work together for a better future, the future of our country, of our people.

Friends, I said peace begins at home. But we must also continue with peace abroad. We intend to advance the dialogue with our neighbors to reach a stable peace, a real peace, peace with security, for all people in the region.

"God shall give strength to his people, God will bless his people with peace." Strength, security, these are the basis for a real peace.

This evening I extend my hand in peace to all the Arab leaders and to our Palestinian neighbors. I am calling on you all: come and join us. Let us take the path of true peace together. Let us take the path of security for all of us, for all the nations of the region.

The government we will form in a few days, with God's help, will act to strengthen ties of peace which have already been forged with Jordan and Egypt. We will continue the negotiations with the Palestinians. And we will work to further peace accords and coexistence with other Arab countries. I call upon them too: join the circle of peace.

I see our friend, the United States of America, as a true partner in this process of making real peace. The relations between the U.S. and Israel are rock solid, and I am certain they will remain that way in the next four years. Our relations are built not only on common interest. They are founded on the shared values of democracy and human dignity.

I am committed to the values of freedom and democracy, just as I am committed to the eternal values of the Jewish people, and there is no contradiction between the two. I am committed to the rule of law in our country just as I am committed to our Jewish identity, and there is no contradiction between the two.

On the basis of these values we intend to make social and economic changes in the country. We believe that every citizen is entitled to equal opportunity to realize his full potential. We will finally introduce a truly free market in Israel. An economy which is not controlled by bureaucrats, an economy that does not stunt initiative. I am sure that in this way we will unleash our creativity, the genius laden in this people, so that the society and the economy will burst forth and take off, and will blossom and flourish.

I want to tell you another thing. Many times I hear it said that there is a social sphere and an economic sphere. I don't believe it. You can't separate between the economic and the social. Only if there is a strong economy can we take care of the weak—and we will take care of the weak.

We will close the poverty gap. We will take care of deprived neighborhoods and development towns, we will help the elderly and the elderly among the new immigrants, and the soldiers who finished their service.

And the most important tool for closing these gaps is education. A few days ago I was in Tamara, and I saw a cute little boy there. I put my hand on his shoulder and said: this boy deserves the same opportunity as my son, Yair. No difference between them. Only by getting the best possible education will he be able to compete in the world of tomorrow, and to succeed. I believe this with all my heart. I will act to implement this to the best of my ability.

Every child in Israel will receive the means to develop his or her abilities so he can be part of the world of tomorrow and succeed in it. There will not be here a First Israel, a Second Israel and a Third Israel. There will be here one Israel, with equal opportunity for all—in Julis, in Ramat Gan, in Kiryat Shmona and in Ramat Aviv. I believe in this with all my heart.

And I want to tell you another thing: a free economy, an open society, without obstacles, without bureaucracy, without arrogance, without patronage—this is the way to bring millions of immigrants to Israel. And we intend to do it because only in this way can we realize the Zionist dream of bringing here the vast majority of the Jewish People.

Friends, exactly a hundred years ago, in 1896, a Jewish visionary named Benjamin Zeev Herzl sat and wrote a dream called 'The Jewish State'. We realized this dream; we continue to realize it today. We will complete its achievement—to be a free people in our land.

This State was founded to bring back an ancient people to its historic homeland and restore its national and cultural life. Only thanks to our Jewish heritage were we able to keep that hope alive in the Diaspora. Because of our heritage, we came back to our land.

Our Jewish heritage, ladies and gentlemen, is not just part of our past. It is the basis for guaranteeing our future. It is also the only way to maintain our link with the Jewish Diaspora. There is no other basis, and so we will act together to strengthen and foster our heritage. We will work to deepen our ties to the Land of Israel. We will keep Jerusalem united under Israeli sovereignty. I declare this here tonight, in Jerusalem, the eternal capital of the Jewish People, the city which will never again be divided.

We will go together on this path, with faith, with unity, in peace and security.

For the first time, a prime minister in Israel has received the mandate in a new way—a direct mandate from the people. All of these things we will do together because I received from you, each one of you, a mandate to bring a new era to the State of Israel.

I know this will take some time for the public, which is perhaps concerned, to understand that everything we say here we mean. We are truly talking of a change, not pronouncements, and of justice, not injustice.

Thanks to all of you for the tremendous effort, the dedication, the trust. And a special thanks to my wife Sarah, who is my full partner in my path. Her wisdom helped me greatly and her partnership filled me with belief and gave me strength.

My friends, I want to send tonight additional thanks to a man who has done much for the State of Israel. I want to express appreciation to Mr. Shimon Peres. No my friends, the campaign is behind us. We are now in another era, an era of combining forces, and this means across the whole nation. I want to tell you something about Mr. Peres: we had differences of opinion, even sharp differences of opinion, but no one here will forget the importance of the contribution that Mr. Peres made to the State of Israel over fifty years. Mr. Peres, the nation of Israel owes you a debt of gratitude.

I want to say here before you what I told Mr. Peres when we spoke the day after the election: we have only one state. We have one country. We will protect it. We will protect it and will bring, with God's help, the security and peace, which is the heart's desire of us all.

God shall give strength to his People. God will bless his People with peace.

UNICEF REPORT ON MATERNAL DEATHS
June 11, 1996

An estimated 585,000 women die in pregnancy and childbirth each year, according to a report released June 11 by the United Nations Children's Fund (UNICEF). For every woman who dies, thirty more suffer infection, injury, and sometimes lifelong disability. "It is no exaggeration to say that this is one of the most neglected tragedies of our times, when 1,600 women—some in their teens—die every day during pregnancy or childbirth and many of these diseases are readily preventable," said Carol Bellamy, the executive director of UNICEF and former president of the New York City Council.

The figures, reported in the chapter on women in UNICEF's The Progress of Nations 1996, *were compiled by UNICEF, the World Health Organization, and Johns Hopkins University. These estimates are about 20 percent higher than those from previous, less comprehensive studies. The figures showed that about 1 woman in 13 died of maternal causes in sub-Saharan Africa, 1 in 35 in South Central Asia, 1 in 3,200 in Western Europe, 1 in 3,300 in the United States, and 1 in 7,300 in Canada.*

Hemorrhage killed about 140,000 women each year, the report said; sepsis, or blood-poisoning, 100,000; self-attempted abortion, 75,000; and obstructed labor, 40,000. Among the injuries and disabilities, the most distressing was fistula, a destruction of the tissues of the birth canal that leads to abscesses and the leakage of fluids; this condition developed in some 80,000 women a year. The report estimated that between 500,000 and 1 million women were living with this debilitating problem.

Unlike most such reports, this one was graphic in its presentation. "This is a story of unimaginable suffering," it began. "And it is a story that will be inadequately told. For no one who has not experienced what is meant by maternal mortality and morbidity can know its depths. And those who do know are usually silenced—by their early deaths, by their poverty, by their gender, and by the insulating layers of censorship and embarrassment that still surround the issues of sex, blood, and birth in most societies of the world."

To reduce these maternal mortality and morbidity rates, the report said, governments should make family planning services accessible to anyone who wants them; provide quality health care before, during, and after pregnancy; and make skilled obstetric care available. It was not necessary to build hundreds more hospitals and train thousands more obstetricians, the report said. "Fully trained and qualified midwives, working in modern health units with inexpensive equipment and reliable supplies of relatively inexpensive drugs, can usually cope" with most problems of pregnancy and delivery.

First, however, the report said, "What is needed now is a much wider and noisier demand for action in order to force this issue into public consciousness and onto the political agenda." Politicians, journalists, health professionals, women's groups, and nongovernmental organizations were all responsible for taking action "to break the mould of silence."

Maternal Deaths in the United States

Two studies of maternal deaths in the United States concluded that the number of women who died or sustained serious health problems from pregnancy or childbirth was underreported. A report published in the August issue of Obstetrics and Gynecology *said the pregnancy-related maternal mortality rate in the United States rose from 7.2 per 100,000 births in 1987 to 10 per 100,000 in 1990. Although the authors of the report, researchers at the U.S. Centers for Disease Control (CDC) in Atlanta, Georgia, attributed the increase primarily to better reporting and surveillance, they nonetheless concluded that "more than half" of such deaths "are probably still unreported."*

A report from the Department of Health and Human Services, commissioned by Rep. Patricia Schroeder, D-Colo., said that if the maternal mortality rate in the United States were the same as the rate in France and other European countries, where reporting was more comprehensive, it would be 23.5 per 100,000 births. "There is a myth that pregnancy is no problem and that the only reason someone would want to end it is for something trivial or selfish," Schroeder said July 30, releasing the Health and Human Services report. "We need to look at pregnancy as we do any other health condition, and we haven't looked at the serious problems of pregnancy since the 1920s."

According to the CDC researchers, hemorrhage, complications from blood clots, and pregnancy-induced high blood pressure were the leading causes of maternal death between 1987 and 1990. The incidence of infection and cardiomyopathy, a kind of heart failure, also rose. Moreover, for every one maternal death, there were an estimated 3,100 hospitalizations for pregnancy-related complications. "There are still women who die as a result of the complications of pregnancy," said Dr. Jeffrey C. King. "But people in the United States believe that . . . it's not a problem anymore. People treat pregnancy as just a state of life, not one that has a finite risk of mortality attached to it." King was vice chairman of the department of gynecology and obstetrics at Wright State University in Dayton and chairman of the Maternal Mortality Task Force of the American College of Obstetrics and Gynecology.

Following are excerpts from the chapter on women in UNICEF's
The Progress of Nations 1996, *released June 11, 1996. The chapter, entitled "A Failure of Imagination," was written by Peter Adamson, editor of the UNICEF report:*

This is a story of unimaginable suffering. And it is a story that will be inadequately told. For no one who has not experienced what is meant by maternal mortality and morbidity can know its depths. And those who do know are usually silenced—by their early deaths, by their poverty, by their gender, and by the insulating layers of censorship and embarrassment that still surround the issues of sex, blood, and birth in most societies of the world.

For a decade, the figure of 500,000 maternal deaths a year has been part of the statistical liturgy. In 1996, new estimates are showing that the number of women who die each year in pregnancy and childbirth is probably closer to 600,000.

But before the new estimates replace the old as a way of packaging up the problem, it should be said that a mistake has been made in allowing statistics such as these to slip into easy usage. For these are not deaths like other deaths, and death is only a part of the story they have to tell.

They die, these hundreds of thousands of women whose lives come to an end in their teens and twenties and thirties, in ways that set them apart from the normal run of human experience.

Over 140,000 die of haemorrhaging, violently pumping blood onto the floor of bus or bullock cart or blood-soaked stretcher as their families and friends search in vain for help.

About 75,000 more die from attempting to abort themselves. Some have taken drugs. Others have submitted to violent massage. Many more have inserted a sharp object—a straightened coat-hanger, a knitting-needle, or a sharpened stick—through the vagina into the uterus. Fifty thousand women and girls attempt such procedures every day. Most survive, though often with crippling discomfort, pelvic inflammatory disease, and a continuing foul discharge. But many do not survive: with punctured uterus, infected wound, and creeping sepsis, they die in pain and alone, bleeding and frightened and ashamed.

Perhaps 75,000 more die with brain and kidney damage in the convulsions of eclampsia, a condition that has been described by a survivor as "the worst feeling in the world that can possibly be imagined."

Another 100,000 die of sepsis, the bloodstream poisoned by a rising infection from an unhealed uterus or from retained pieces of placenta, bringing fever and hallucinations and appalling pain.

Smaller but still significant numbers die of an anaemia so severe that the muscles of the heart fail.

And as many as 40,000 a year die of obstructed labour—days of futile contractions repeatedly grinding down the skull of an already asphyxiated baby onto the soft tissues of a pelvis that is just too small.

In the 1990s so far, 3 million young women have died in one or more of these ways. And they continue to die at the rate of 1,600 every day, yesterday and today and tomorrow.

Ratio of Injuries

For the most part, these are the deaths not of the ill, or of the very old, or of the very young, but of healthy women in the prime of their lives upon whom both young and old may depend.

But the numbers of the dead alone do not reveal the full scale of this tragedy. For every woman who dies, approximately 30 more incur injuries, infections, and disabilities which are usually untreated and unspoken of, and which are often humiliating and painful, debilitating and lifelong.

It is part of the silence that has for so long surrounded the issue of maternal morbidity that there is so little research into its prevalence. But based on a few studies and many assumptions, the best estimate that can be made puts the ratio of injuries to deaths at about 30 to 1.

This means that at least 15 million women a year sustain the kind of damage in pregnancy and childbirth that will have a profound effect on their lives. And even allowing for the fact that some women will suffer such injuries more than once during their child-bearing years, the cumulative total of those affected can be conservatively estimated at some 300 million, or more than a quarter of the adult women now alive in the developing world.

It is therefore no exaggeration to say that the issue of maternal mortality and morbidity, fast in its conspiracy of silence, is in scale and severity the most neglected tragedy of our times.

Obvious Signs

Many of the injuries sustained during pregnancy and childbirth are distressingly obvious. Rupture of the uterus, prolapse, pelvic inflammatory disease, and lower genital tract injuries, make life miserable for millions.

Most obvious and distressing of all is fistula.

Fistula occurs when the tissues of the birth canal are deadened by prolonged labour and days of pressure from the baby's skull. In the days and weeks after the birth, the dead tissue falls away, leaving holes which allow leakage from the bladder and rectum, or both, into the vagina. Urine and faeces now bypass the muscles that normally control the flow. The woman is incontinent. And without an operation to repair the fistula, she will remain so all her life. Special clothing is not available. She must make do with cloths and rags which quickly become soaked and soiled. The constant leaking abrades the skin of the genital area and produces a permanent and painful rash. Washing is difficult. Frequent bathing is impossible.

Soon, the woman is excluded from her husband's bed, and then from his home. Living in an outhouse or animal shed, she cannot visit anyone or travel anywhere except by walking. Each year, unknown numbers decide that suicide is preferable to such a life.

The best available estimates suggest that perhaps 80,000 women develop fistula every year. Most cases go untreated, and somewhere between 500,000 and 1 million women are living with the problem at this moment.

Anaemia

Other conditions can be more successfully hidden, at least at first.

Most hidden of all are the long-term effects of the haemorrhages that are suffered by an estimated 14 million women every year.

Half of those women, it may be assumed, were already anaemic. But a haemorrhage in childbirth, or in repeated childbirths, can push women further and further down the anaemia road, slowly lowering the quality of life for uncounted millions, making every task an unwelcome effort, every day a day of drudgery, leaving no energy even for the common enjoyments of life.

For a smaller percentage of women, the trauma of haemorrhage brings something worse than anaemia.

Those who experience hypopituitarism, or Sheehan's syndrome, almost always assume that they are suffering only from temporary tiredness. But as the months pass, the tiredness becomes a chronic weakness, a listlessness stirred by alarm as other symptoms begin to appear—the cessation of monthly periods, the loss of pubic hair, an increasing confusion and forgetfulness. Without knowing what is wrong, such women grow old while still young. And eventually their alarm will give way to the cruellest symptom— the deepening apathy which makes it unlikely that treatment will ever be sought.

To the extent that Sheehan's syndrome is known at all, it is assumed to be a rare condition. For obvious reasons, definitions are shadowy and figures vague, but recent estimates suggest that Sheehan's overtakes the lives of 100,000 women a year, and may currently affect a total of over 3 million.

A Lifetime of Abuse

Further still into the realms of the unreported lies dyspareunia—the pain that some women suffer during sexual intercourse.

After childbirth, a woman is bruised and battered and needs time to recuperate. Many will also have suffered specific injuries, often including the tearing or the surgical cutting of the vagina. But in many societies, and in many millions of individual cases, women have no choice but to resume sexual relations within two or three days, regardless of the pain it causes.

Pain during intercourse may last for up to a year after a birth. It may also be so severe that a woman lives in dread of having sex. Few can count on sympathy or support, and many endure anger, rejection, and violence.

Once again, this problem of unknown extent is made worse by the silence that surrounds it. Yet the truth is that it is just one more abuse in a lifetime of abuses that are linked, in one way or another, to the different ways in which different societies make a woman suffer for her reproductive role. As a child, she may endure genital mutilation in order to contain sexuality and protect marriageability. As a menstruating girl, she may be set aside as unclean, polluting, and made to feel dirty and ashamed. As a teenager, she may be married to someone she does not know, and made pregnant before her own body is fully grown. As a woman unable to bear children, she may be abused and abandoned, even though it may be the husband who is infertile, or even if her infertility is caused by a sexually transmitted disease originally contracted by her partner. As a pregnant woman, she may be denied the basic consideration, the rest and the food and the antenatal care, to which she is entitled. As a woman in labour, she will run the risk of dying from the lack of obstetric care, and of sustaining injuries and disabilities for which she will not receive treatment. As a woman enduring a prolonged childbirth, she may be left to die alone and in agony, the baby asphyxiated inside her, in societies where men interpret obstructed labour as a sign of unfaithfulness. As a woman suffering from a childbirth injury, from a still-open artery or a ruptured uterus, she may die because her husband will not allow her to be seen by a male doctor. As the mother of a baby girl, she may be blamed and beaten despite the fact that it is the chromosomes of the male that determine the sex of the baby. As a wife, she may be forced to submit to sex within a few days of giving birth, or subjected to violence if she refuses. As a new mother, she may be expected to become pregnant again before her body has recovered. And finally, even if she has sustained an injury or infection that is serious and treatable, and even in those rare cases when health worker[s] seek her out knowing that she will not come to them, she may still not be allowed to go into a hospital because there will be no one to cook the meals.

Silence

How can such a heavy burden of death, disease and disability have continued for so long with so little outcry?

In part, the conspiracy of silence surrounding this issue is a reflection of the fact that women are conditioned not to complain but to cope. No matter the injuries or disabilities they labour under, they will usually continue to look after children, fetch and carry wood and water, go to market, and work long hours in the fields, while hoping that the pain will go away, that the wound will heal, that the discharge will stop, that they will soon be able to have sex without pain, and that they will one day recover their vitality. And for the most part they cope in silence. They neither ask nor receive a lesser workload, or medical care, or consideration for what they have suffered or the condition they are in.

Ultimately, therefore, little is either said or done about this problem because it is a "woman's problem", a problem that, by long tradition, most men and most governments do not wish to know about. As one midwife with 25 years' experience of developing countries has put it: "If hundreds of thousands of men were suffering and dying every year, alone and in fear and in agony, or if millions upon millions of men were being injured and disabled and humiliated, sustaining massive and untreated injuries and wounds to their genitalia, leaving them in constant pain, infertile and incontinent, and in dread of having sex, then we would all have heard about this issue long ago, and something would have been done."

What Can Be Done?

The first and most obvious step towards reducing the toll of maternal mortality and morbidity is to make high-quality family planning services available to all who need them. With today's knowledge, it is possible to do this in ways that are acceptable to all countries and cultures.

Meeting only the existing demand for family planning would reduce pregnancies in the developing world by up to a fifth, bringing at least an equivalent reduction in maternal deaths and injuries. Add in the many other benefits of family planning for all—fewer abortions, better health and nutrition of women and children, faster progress towards gender equality, slower population growth, reduced environmental pressures—and the costs are almost derisory. Yet family planning receives less than 2% of all government health spending in the developing world, and less than 2% of all international aid.

Beyond the preventing of unwanted pregnancies lies the greater challenge of reducing deaths and injuries in the great majority of cases where the pregnancy is wanted.

Some will always fall back on the idea that this must await economic development, and that only when women are healthier, better educated, and better nourished, will maternal risk be lowered.

But the historical record gives scant support to such complacency. In the United Kingdom, for example, there was almost no fall in maternal mortality rates during the century before 1930 when standards of health, nutrition, education, and hygiene were advancing rapidly. Only when skilled midwifery made deliveries cleaner and safer—and modern obstetric care began to cope with obstructed labour, haemorrhage, infection, and hypertensive disorders—did maternal deaths begin their sharp fall to today's levels. On a smaller scale, these same conclusions have been demonstrated by a study of a sect in the United States whose members were relatively prosperous, well nourished, and well educated, but who would not accept modern medical care. The study found that the maternal mortality rate was approximately 100 times higher than the average for the United States, and approximately the same as in rural India. . . .

Upgrading

Can obstetric care be afforded? Or is it still only long-term economic development that can make such services available to all who need them?

First of all, it should be said that no developing country is starting from scratch. Even in the largest and poorest nations, there are usually health units and district hospitals with the doctors, midwives, nurses, drugs, and equipment that can provide obstetric care when needed. If they cannot, then this usually reflects a lack of priority, or a lack of relatively small amounts of funds for basic training and equipment, rather than the inherent impossibility of the task. This is what Deborah Maine, who has done so much to draw attention to the importance of emergency obstetric care over the last decade, has to say on the subject:

> "You don't need five-star hospitals and expensive equipment. There are thousands of hospitals in the developing world that, with minimum upgrading, could provide adequate obstetric care in emergencies. But even in hospitals that are supposed to have obstetric operating rooms, many are unusable for the lack of $100 worth of maintenance—a repair to an anaesthesia machine, the installation of proper lighting. Many of those hospitals also have qualified surgeons who are not sufficiently trained and experienced in doing caesarean sections, which are needed in 5% of all deliveries and can save the life of mother and baby. In many others, doctors and surgeons do not have the few hundred dollars' worth of equipment needed to cope with emergency obstetric cases. In still more, the doctors are on site for only six hours a day, offering no night or emergency service, so that many women who do reach a hospital in time still die. People are too quick to say that maternal mortality is a complex problem involving all sorts of deeply rooted cultural issues, when it seems to me that, as there is so little that can be done to prevent complications, it is in fact one of the simpler problems: women get complications and they need treatment. . . ."

Fathers

Few figures are available on how many women have access to obstetric care, but in a country like India, informed estimates suggest that perhaps three quarters of the 150,000 women who die each year in childbirth live within a few miles of a health unit or district hospital where emergency care is or should be available. And there is usually enough time for a woman to be transferred to such a facility if danger signs are recognized in time. It would also help if it were widely accepted that fathers-to-be should make stand-by arrangements—knowing where to go and how to get there and by what means—in case a transfer is needed.

Action on this issue has been paralysed for too long by the idea that only the building of hundreds more hospitals and the training of thousands more obstetricians can make the right kind of care available to the 15% who need it. But the fact is that fully trained and qualified midwives, working in modern health units with inexpensive equipment and reliable supplies of relatively inexpensive drugs, can usually cope with haemorrhage, prevent shock, deal with a retained placenta, prevent sepsis, set up a drip, inject oxytocic drugs after delivery, give prophylactic antibiotics, use a manual vacuum pump to deal with an incomplete abortion, and know when to call in obstetricians if a caesarean section is necessary. A great deal of confusion has arisen because the terms "midwife", "traditional birth attendant" and "trained birth attendant" are frequently used interchangeably. In particular, much of the argument about what midwives can and cannot be expected to do is born of the failure to distinguish between a fully qualified midwife, working with the support of modern health services, and a minimally trained birth attendant unconnected to obstetric services. A great deal of training is required to give the kind of care that can prevent death and injury, but properly qualified midwives and health workers who are used to dealing with such problems will usually cope better than many doctors who may encounter such problems only a few times a year.

Priority

The task of improving health in the developing world is very largely a task of prevention and promotion—of breaking health care out of the clinics and hospitals and putting relatively inexpensive ways and means of preventing and treating disease at the disposal of communities. But the task of reducing maternal deaths and injuries is a task of a different kind. The opportunity must be there for every woman who becomes pregnant to be brought in to a health unit or hospital if and when complications occur.

Making sure that all families know when help is needed is a major undertaking. Making modern obstetric care more available is also no insignificant task. And building the bridge between the two—across a gap that may be as much social as financial or physical—will demand a different attitude from many health service providers. But the financial cost of all this would be only a very small proportion of the $85 billion a year that the governments of the developing world currently spend on their health services, or of the $5 billion a year in international aid that is allocated to those services.

Reducing maternal deaths and injuries is therefore not a matter of possibilities but of priorities.

The two greatest claims on health resources, by any standard that bears a relationship to the greatest good or the greatest number, are the control of the five conditions that account for two thirds of all child deaths in the world each year, and the making available of modern obstetric care for the many millions of women who now die or are injured and disabled in the process of giving birth.

The statistics alone would be enough to justify the claim to priority of a problem that has affected perhaps 25% of the women now alive and which causes some 585,000 deaths a year.

But there is also a dimension that statistics cannot capture. It is perhaps not possible to give a weighting to the pain and the fear, the undermining of confidence and self-esteem, or the nagging injuries and humiliations and anxieties that are the constant companions of so many women's lives. But the world at the close of the 20th century is guilty of a colossal failure of imagination if it remains deaf to the cries of so many women who daily live with the sadnesses and sufferings that travel under the name of maternal morbidity.

The strategies that work have been identified. And the resources will follow if priority lights the way. What is needed now is a much wider and noisier demand for action in order to force this issue into public consciousness and onto the political agenda. The first task is to break the mould of silence. And there is scarcely a politician, or health professional, or researcher, or journalist, or non-governmental organization, or women's group, or member of the public, that could not play some part in such a movement. In particular, the professional organizations of obstetricians and gynaecologists that exist in almost all countries could say more and do more about the issue. All of these voices are needed to press for government health budgets and international aid programmes that specifically confront the taboo tragedy of maternal deaths and injuries.

Failure to do so, in the face of an issue that has affected so many so severely and for so long, amounts to a tacit complicity with the forces of silence, an acquiescence in the long reign of the idea that these issues should not be spoken about too loudly because they are faintly embarrassing and because, after all, they affect mainly women and mainly the poor.

Aldous Huxley wrote of human suffering: "Screams of pain and fear go pulsing through the air at the rate of eleven hundred feet per second. After travelling for three seconds they are perfectly inaudible." It is time to amplify the screams.

FEDERAL COURT ON
INTERNET PORNOGRAPHY BAN
June 11, 1996

Congress in 1996 tried to ban pornography from the Internet, the fast-growing medium linking millions of computer users worldwide. That attempt sparked legal protests that would ultimately put the issue before the Supreme Court.

The high court on December 6 agreed to review a June 11 ruling by a special three-judge panel in Philadelphia that blocked enforcement of the Communications Decency Act of 1996. The act, which sought to regulate indecency on the Internet, was included in a massive revision of telecommunications law (PL 104–104) that had been signed into law by President Bill Clinton on February 8. Clinton had opposed the Decency Act provisions but signed the larger bill because it was one of his top legislative priorities, and his Justice Department defended the Decency Act in court.

Political Pressure for Pornography Ban

The rapid growth of the Internet and other interactive online computer services, such as America Online and CompuServe, made it all but inevitable that questions would arise about the types of information available on those services. The Internet was perhaps the most easily accessible medium of mass communication ever devised; anyone with a personal computer, modem, and telephone line could post messages that could be read by millions of people.

By the early 1990s people and businesses were using the Internet and related online services to sell all types of products and services. Among those joining the rush to display their wares on the Internet were numerous purveyors of pornography; advertisements for their sites were featured in mass circulation computer publications and sexually oriented magazines.

As the popularity of the Internet soared, members of Congress proposed legislation regulating the types of material that could appear on it. In 1995 Sen. Jim Exon, D-Neb., won Senate approval of an amendment to the

*telecommunications bill that banned indecent material from online com-
puter services. Both chambers included such provisions in the telecommunications bill; the provisions met with little resistance and only limited
debate. No public hearings were held on the issue in either chamber. Exon
called adoption of the provision in the final telecommunications bill "a victory for children and families."*

*As signed into law, the act made it a federal criminal offense to "make
available" indecent material on computer networks, where it might be seen
by minors. The ban defined indecency as "any comment, request, suggestion, proposal, image, or other communication that, in context, depicts or
describes, in terms patently offensive as measured by contemporary community standards, sexual or excretory activities or organs." This standard
for indecency was taken from federal regulations of commercial television
and radio broadcasting.*

*The provision applied to anyone displaying such material, as well as to
those who knowingly permitted their telecommunications facilities to be
used for such purposes. Penalties for violations included prison terms of
up to two years and fines of up to $250,000 for individuals or $500,000
for corporations.*

*The law provided some exceptions and legal defenses for online comput-
er service firms. For example, companies such as America Online that
simply provided a "gateway" to the Internet or other services not under
their control could not be prosecuted under the indecency provisions. Computer service companies could defend against a suit if they could demonstrate a good faith and "effective" effort to keep minors away from indecent
material, or if they had restricted access to such material, for example by
requiring users to give a credit card number.*

*A related provision of the telecommunications law also prohibited use of
interactive computer services to transmit material or information about
abortion. This provision extended to computer services the 1873 Comstock
law, which banned interstate commerce in drugs, medicine, and written
material related to abortions. Clinton said the Justice Department would
not enforce this provision because it was unconstitutional. A coalition of
abortion rights groups filed suit in U.S. District Court in Brooklyn, New
York, to overturn the provision.*

First Amendment Issues

*The Internet indecency provisions drew immediate fire from a broad
coalition, including the American Civil Liberties Union (ACLU), the
American Library Association (ALA), the American Booksellers Association, and major high-technology companies such as Microsoft and America Online. The ACLU took the lead in the fight against the provision, filing suit in Philadelphia the same day Clinton signed it into law. The ALA
filed a similar suit. A special three-judge panel combined the two suits
into one case, as the Decency Act had provided for expedited proceedings
in such cases.*

The ACLU, the ALA, and other organizations charged that the indecency provisions violated the First Amendment rights to free speech and free press. The high-tech companies also charged that the new law would stifle growth of the Internet by spreading confusion about acceptable limits for material on its services. Judith F. Krug, director of the ALA's Office for Intellectual Freedom, said it was "unconstitutional to force adults to limit the information they can see to a level suitable for children."

These groups also charged that the indecency standard for broadcasting was inappropriate for computer networks because a user must actively seek out Internet locations that displayed pornography, whereas finding pornography on television could simply be a matter of switching channels. Critics of the law also noted that a substantial portion of content on the Internet—at least 40 percent by some estimates—originated outside the United States and therefore would not be subject to U.S. criminal penalties.

Supporters defended the indecency provisions, saying they merely extended to cyberspace the same standards that the Supreme Court had endorsed for television. Among those endorsing this position were the Christian Coalition and the Family Research Council.

Acting on the combined suits brought by the ACLU, the ALA, and other organizations, the panel ruled on June 11 that the key antipornography clauses of the telecommunications law were "unconstitutional on their face." The judges issued a temporary restraining order barring the Justice Department from enforcing the law, including investigating violations of it.

Judges Dolores K. Sloviter, Stewart R. Dalzell, and Ronald L. Buckwalter ruled that the Internet indecency law violated the First Amendment protections of free speech and free press. The judges used much of their lengthy opinions to explain the inherently freewheeling aspect of the Internet and how it differed from previous communications mediums. The decision quoted testimony by an analyst for the Air Force Office of Special Investigation, who stated that the "odds are slim" that a user would accidentally encounter sexually explicit content on the Internet.

The judges acknowledged that much of the material on the Internet was objectionable. Judge Dalzell said some of it "surely tests the limits of conventional discourse." But, he added, "we should expect such speech to occur in a medium in which citizens from all walks of life have a voice. We should also protect the autonomy that such a medium confers to ordinary people as well as media magnates."

Groups opposed to the indecency provisions called the decision a major victory for free speech. Supporters of the law said they were dismayed that the decision struck down nearly all its key aspects.

The Justice Department immediately appealed the decision. The Supreme Court announced on December 6 that it would hear the case in its 1996–1997 term.

Following are excerpts from the opinions of district court judges Dolores K. Sloviter, Ronald L. Buckwalter, and Stewart R. Dalzell in American Civil Liberties Union, et al. v. Janet Reno, Attorney General of the United States *in which the court held unconstitutional key sections of the Communications Decency Act of 1996:*

[Sloviter, District Judge; I, II omitted]

III

[A through F omitted]

G. Preliminary Injunction

When Congress decided that material unsuitable for minors was available on the Internet, it could have chosen to assist and support the development of technology that would enable parents, schools, and libraries to screen such material from their end. It did not do so, and thus did not follow the example available in the print media where non-obscene but indecent and patently offensive books and magazines abound. Those responsible for minors undertake the primary obligation to prevent their exposure to such material. Instead, in the CDA [Communications Decency Act] Congress chose to place on the speakers the obligation of screening the material that would possibly offend some communities.

Whether Congress' decision was a wise one is not at issue here. It was unquestionably a decision that placed the CDA in serious conflict with our most cherished protection—the right to choose the material to which we would have access.

The government makes what I view as an extraordinary argument in its brief. It argues that blocking technology needed for effective parental control is not yet widespread but that it "will imminently be in place." . . . It then states that if we uphold the CDA, it "will likely unleash the 'creative genius' of the Internet community to find a myriad of possible solutions." I can imagine few arguments less likely to persuade a court to uphold a criminal statute than one that depends on future technology to cabin the reach of the statute within constitutional bounds.

The government makes yet another argument that troubles me. It suggests that the concerns expressed by the plaintiffs and the questions posed by the court reflect an exaggerated supposition of how it would apply the law, and that we should, in effect, trust the Department of Justice to limit the CDA's application in a reasonable fashion that would avoid prosecution for placing on the Internet works of serious literary or artistic merit. That would require a broad trust indeed from a generation of judges not far removed from the attacks on James Joyce's *Ulysses* as obscene. . . . Even if we were to place confidence in the reasonable judgment of the representatives of the Department of Justice who appeared before us, the Department is not a monolithic structure, and individual U.S. Attorneys in the various districts of the country have or appear to exercise some independence, as reflected by the Department's tolerance of duplicative challenges in this very case.

But the bottom line is that the First Amendment should not be interpreted to require us to entrust the protection it affords to the judgment of prosecutors. Prosecutors come and go. Even federal judges are limited to life tenure. The First Amendment remains to give protection to future generations as well. I have no hesitancy in concluding that it is likely that plaintiffs will prevail on the merits of their argument that the challenged provisions of the CDA are facially invalid under both the First and Fifth Amendments.

Buckwalter, District Judge

A.

. . . Essentially, my concerns are these: above all, I believe that the challenged provisions are so vague as to violate both the First and Fifth Amendments, and in particular that Congress' reliance on *Pacifica* [*FCC* v. *Pacifica Foundation* (1978)] is misplaced. In addition, I believe that technology as it currently exists—and it bears repeating that we are at the preliminary injunction phase only—cannot provide a safe harbor for most speakers on the Internet, thus rendering the statute unconstitutional under a strict scrutiny analysis. . . .

B.

. . . The fundamental constitutional principle that concerns me is one of simple fairness, and that is absent in the CDA. The Government initially argues that "indecent" in this statute is the same as "patently offensive." I do not agree that a facial reading of this statute supports that conclusion. The CDA does not define the term "indecent," and the FCC has not promulgated regulations defining indecency in the medium of cyberspace. If "indecent" and "patently offensive" were intended to have the same meaning, surely section (a) could have mirrored section (d)'s language. Indecent in this statute is an undefined word which, standing alone, offers no guidelines whatsoever as to its parameters. Interestingly, another federal crime gives a definition to indecent entirely different from that proposed in the present case. While not applicable here, this example shows the indeterminate nature of the word and the need for clear definition, particularly in a statute which infringes upon protected speech. . . .

The thrust of the Government's argument is that the court should trust prosecutors to prosecute only a small segment of those speakers subject to the CDA's restrictions, and whose works would reasonably be considered "patently offensive" in every community. Such unfettered discretion to prosecutors, however, is precisely what due process does not allow. . . .

Dalzell, District Judge

[A and B omitted]

C. Plaintiff's Likelihood of Prosecution Under the Act

. . . [E]ven though it is perhaps unlikely that the Carnegie Library will ever stand in the dock for putting its card catalogue online, or that the Government will hale the ACLU into court for its online quiz of the seven dirty words, we cannot ignore that the Act could reach these activities. The definition of indecency, like the definition of obscenity, is not a rigid formula. Rather, it confers a large degree of autonomy to individual communities to set the bounds of decency for themselves. This is as it should be, since this flexibility recognizes that ours is a country with diverse cultural and historical roots. . . .

D. A Media-Specific Analysis

The Internet is a new medium of mass communication. As such, the Supreme Court's First Amendment jurisprudence compels us to consider the special qualities of this new medium in determining whether the CDA is a constitutional exercise of governmental power. Relying on these special qualities, which we have described at length in our Findings of fact above, I conclude that the CDA is unconstitutional and that the First Amendment denies Congress the power to regulate protected speech on the Internet. . . .

. . . Four related characteristics of Internet communication have a transcendent importance to our shared holding that the CDA is unconstitutional on its face. . . . First, the Internet presents very low barriers to entry. Second, these barriers to entry are identical for both speakers and listeners. Third, as a result of these low barriers, astoundingly diverse content is available on the Internet. Fourth, the Internet provides significant access to all who wish to speak in the medium, and even creates a relative parity among speakers. . . .

After the CDA, however, the content of a user's speech will determine the extent of participation in the new medium. If a speaker's content is even arguably indecent in some communities, he must assess, inter alia, the risk of prosecution and the cost of compliance with the CDA. Because the creation and posting of a Web site allows users anywhere in the country to see that site, many speakers will no doubt censor their speech so that it is palatable in every community. Other speakers will decline to enter the medium at all. Unlike other media, there is no technologically feasible way for an Internet speaker to limit the geographical scope of his speech (even if he wanted to), or to "implement[] a system for screening the locale of incoming" requests. . . .

The CDA will, without doubt, undermine the substantive, speech-enhancing benefits that have flowed from the Internet. Barriers to entry to those speakers affected by the Act would skyrocket, especially for non-commercial and not-for-profit information providers. Such costs include those attributable to age or credit card verification (if possible), tagging (if tagging is even a defense under the Act), and monitoring or review of one's content.

The diversity of the content will necessarily diminish as a result. The economic costs associated with compliance with the Act will drive from the Internet speakers whose content falls within the zone of possible prosecution. Many Web sites, newsgroups, and chat rooms will shut down, since users cannot discern the age of other participants. In this respect, the Internet would ultimately come to mirror broadcasting and print, with messages tailored to a mainstream society from speakers who could be sure that their message was likely decent in every community in the country.

The CDA will also skew the relative parity among speakers that currently exists on the Internet. Commercial entities who can afford the costs of verification, or who would charge a user to enter their sites, or whose content has mass appeal, will remain unaffected by the Act. Other users, such as Critical Path or Stop Prisoner Rape, or even the ACLU, whose Web sites before the CDA were as equally accessible as the most popular Web sites, will be profoundly affected by the Act. This change would result in an Internet that mirrors broadcasting and print, where economic power has become relatively coterminous with influence.

Perversely, commercial pornographers would remain relatively unaffected by the Act, since we learned that most of them already use credit card or adult verification anyway. Commercial pornographers normally provide a few free pictures to entice a user into proceeding further into the Web site. To proceed beyond these teasers, users must provide a credit card number or adult verification number. The CDA will force these businesses to remove the teasers (or cover the most salacious content . . .), but the core, commercial product of these businesses will remain in place. . . .

It is no exaggeration to conclude that the Internet has achieved, and continues to achieve, the most participatory marketplace of mass speech that this country—and indeed the world—has yet seen. The plaintiffs in these actions correctly describe the "democratizing" effects of Internet communication: individual citizens of limited means can speak to a worldwide audience on issues of concern to them. Federalists and Anti-Federalists may debate the structure of their government nightly, but these debates occur in newsgroups or chat rooms rather than in pamphlets. Modern-day Luthers still post their theses, but to electronic bulletin boards rather than the door of the Wittenberg Schlosskirche. More mundane (but from a constitutional perspective, equally important) dialogue occurs between aspiring artists, or French cooks, or dog lovers, or fly fishermen.

Indeed, the Government's asserted "failure" of the Internet rests on the implicit premise that too much speech occurs in that medium, and that speech there is too available to the participants. This is exactly the benefit of Internet communication, however. The Government, therefore, implicitly asks this court to limit both the amount of speech on the Internet and the availability of that speech. This argument is profoundly repugnant to First Amendment principles.

My examination of the special characteristics of Internet communication, and review of the Supreme Court's medium-specific First Amendment jurisprudence, lead me to conclude that the Internet deserves the broadest possible protection from government-imposed, content-based regulation. . . .

The Internet is a far more speech-enhancing medium than print, the village green, or the mails. Because it would necessarily affect the Internet itself, the CDA would necessarily reduce the speech available for adults on the medium. This is a constitutionally intolerable result.

Some of the dialogue on the Internet surely tests the limits of conventional discourse. Speech on the Internet can be unfiltered, unpolished, and unconventional, even emotionally charged, sexually explicit, and vulgar—in a word, "indecent" in many communities. But we should expect such speech to occur in a medium in which citizens from all walks of life have a voice. We should also protect the autonomy that such a medium confers to ordinary people as well as media magnates.

Moreover, the CDA will almost certainly fail to accomplish the Government's interest in shielding children from pornography on the Internet. Nearly half of Internet communications originate outside the United States, and some percentage of that figure represents pornography. Pornography from, say, Amsterdam will be no less appealing to a child on the Internet than pornography from New York City, and residents of Amsterdam have little incentive to comply with the CDA.

My analysis does not deprive the Government of all means of protecting children from the dangers of Internet communication. The Government can continue to protect children from pornography on the Internet through vigorous enforcement of existing laws criminalizing obscenity and child pornography. As we learned at the hearing, there is also a compelling need for public education about the benefits and dangers of this new medium, and the Government can fill that role as well. In my view, our action today should only mean that the Government's permissible supervision of Internet content stops at the traditional line of unprotected speech.

Parents, too, have options available to them. As we learned at the hearing, parents can install blocking software on their home computers, or they can subscribe to commercial online services that provide parental controls. It is quite clear that powerful market forces are at work to expand parental options to deal with these legitimate concerns. More fundamentally, parents can supervise their children's use of the Internet or deny their children the opportunity to participate in the medium until they reach an appropriate age. . . .

E. Conclusion

Cutting through the acronyms and argot that littered the hearing testimony, the Internet may fairly be regarded as a never-ending worldwide conversation. The Government may not, through the CDA, interrupt that conversation. As the most participatory form of mass speech yet developed, the Internet deserves the highest protection from governmental intrusion.

True it is that many find some of the speech on the Internet to be offensive, and amid the din of cyberspace many hear discordant voices that they regard as indecent. The absence of governmental regulation of Internet content has unquestionably produced a kind of chaos, but as one of plaintiffs' experts put it with such resonance at the hearing:

> What achieved success was the very chaos that the Internet is. The strength of the Internet is that chaos.

Just as the strength of the Internet is chaos, so the strength of our liberty depends upon the chaos and cacophony of the unfettered speech the First Amendment protects.

For these reasons, I without hesitation hold that the CDA is unconstitutional on its face. . . .

FBI DIRECTOR ON THE
SURRENDER OF THE "FREEMEN"
June 13, 1996

The longest showdown in U.S. history between federal law enforcement officials and criminal suspects ended June 13 with the peaceful surrender of sixteen antigovernment "Freemen." For eighty-one days, FBI agents had surrounded the rebels on a complex of four ranches in the remote plains of eastern Montana.

Employing a new strategy for dealing with domestic rebels, the FBI essentially outwaited the Freemen, gradually stepping up pressure on them while negotiating through intermediaries. The strategy, while costly in terms of manpower, produced a successful and bloodless conclusion.

The ending was in sharp contrast to two highly publicized previous confrontations between federal authorities and antigovernment groups. In 1992 the FBI attacked the fortified home in Ruby Ridge, Idaho, of white separatist Randy Weaver, killing his wife and child. In 1993 a federal standoff with the Branch Davidian religious sect ended in tragedy when agents attacked the group's compound near Waco, Texas, and someone inside set the buildings on fire, killing some eighty persons. The FBI and other law enforcement agencies had come under harsh attack, especially from conservatives, for their handling of those two cases. (Waco incident, Historic Documents of 1993, pp. 293, 819)

Largely in response to such criticisms, the federal agencies in 1995 adopted new procedures for handling such crises. One of the main reforms was allowing more time, when possible, to negotiate an end to a standoff. After the surrender of the Freemen, FBI director Louis J. Freeh told reporters that the Montana standoff had "put those reforms to the test" and that the new procedures had worked.

The lengthy confrontation between the FBI and the Freemen also focused new public attention on the issue of paramilitary groups, or "militias," which refused to acknowledge the authority of the federal government. The number of such groups reportedly had grown rapidly during the 1980s and 1990s as disaffected white males, primarily in rural areas, came to believe that the federal government was giving preference to minorities and that the country was falling under the control of the United Nations and other world government forces.

The bombing of the federal office building in Oklahoma City in 1995 also drew national attention to the militia movement. It was reported that the two men charged in the case—Timothy McVeigh and Terry Nichols— had links with militia groups and may have drawn inspiration for the bombing from writings that were popular among such groups. (Oklahoma City bombing, Historic Documents of 1995, p. 176)

The Freemen Standoff

Many of the Freemen were farmers and ranchers whose businesses had failed, or had come close to failing, during the farm crises of the 1980s. According to most reports, the Freemen blamed the government for their inability to pay their debts and hold onto their farms—even though some had received large agricultural subsidies from the government.

The Freemen put together an organization claiming to be the legitimate government. They refused to pay taxes or obey any laws of the U.S. or state government; instead, they issued their own currency and established their own court system. They developed an elaborate financial scheme, using illegitimate checks and money orders, to extract money from financial institutions and other businesses. They put together a complex of ranches near Jordan, Montana, and threatened retaliation against local citizens or public officials who tried to take action against them.

A federal grand jury in 1995 indicted several of the Freemen on fifty-one counts, including bank fraud, mail fraud, weapons violations, and threatening public officials. On March 25, 1996, an FBI "sting" operation resulted in the arrest of two key Freemen leaders, LeRoy Schweitzer and Daniel Petersen Jr. At the same time, the FBI surrounded the Freemen ranch complex in hopes of forcing the remaining Freemen to surrender.

While conducting negotiations with the Freemen through forty-five intermediaries—including family members and some who shared their right-wing political views—the FBI gradually stepped up the pressure on the holdouts. Early in June the FBI cut off electricity to the ranches and surrounded them with armored vehicles. Those steps resulted in the surrender of five people, including the last three children remaining on the compound.

Finally, the FBI gave safe passage for one of the Freemen, Edwin Clark, to visit Schweitzer at his jail cell in Billings, Montana. Schweitzer reportedly agreed to the surrender of the remaining Freemen. The sixteen holdouts turned themselves over to the FBI early in the evening of June 13. Fourteen of the Freemen faced criminal charges; thirteen were ordered held without bail.

Hours later, Freeh told reporters that the FBI had "acted absolutely honorably" in its negotiations with the Freemen and had made "no deals" to drop or reduce legal charges in return for their surrender. The FBI "accomplished our mission" of arresting the Freemen without bloodshed, Freeh said.

Report on Militias

With few exceptions, right-wing militias operated in secrecy, often holding weekend encampments and shooting competitions at remote locations where they could feel free from government and public scrutiny. After the Oklahoma City bombing, news organizations stepped up their scrutiny of militias and government officials issued warnings about the growth of such groups.

One organization that had long paid attention to antigovernment militias was the Southern Poverty Law Center, a civil rights advocacy group based in Montgomery, Alabama. The center in 1979 established a "Klanwatch" program to monitor white supremacist groups; in 1994 it set up a Militia Task Force to examine the militias, many of which grew out of Ku Klux Klan-type organizations. In April 1996 the center issued a report, "False Patriots: The Threat of Antigovernment Extremists," which described the philosophy, goals, and methods of right-wing militia groups. The report listed 809 so-called antigovernment groups that were active around the country in 1994 and 1995. The report referred to these groups as "Patriots" because that was the one label they all accepted.

The report said the Patriot movement had no national organization or leadership. It consisted instead of "previously unrelated groups and individuals who have found a common cause in their deep distrust of the government and their eagerness to fight back."

Despite the lack of organization, Patriot groups and individuals were "connected like no rebel force has ever been," the report said. It noted that militia members used the Internet and fax machines to trade tips on how to avoid tax laws and fight government regulations.

In its report, the law center made fourteen recommendations for the rest of society to counter militia groups. On the government side, the report said states should prosecute those who violate antimilitia and antiparamilitary training laws; states that lacked such laws should adopt and enforce them. The report also called for a federal law banning private militias not specifically authorized by the states and suggested heightened monitoring of militia groups. Other recommendations were more general in nature, such as calling on news organizations to "balance" claims by militias that they have an unrestricted constitutional right to bear arms and suggesting that schools should do more to teach democratic ideals, including the values of tolerance and cooperation.

Following are excerpts from the statement by FBI director Louis J. Freeh on June 13, 1996, shortly after the peaceful surrender of sixteen antigovernment rebels, who called themselves the "Freemen":

Just to update you, all of the subjects as well as the non-subjects are safe, in custody, or accounted for on their way to Billings, Montana, to be arraigned. That is a trip which will take approximately 3½ hours.

They are accompanied, since they are in custody, by several FBI agents as well as Montana law enforcement officials.

From March 25th, when members of the FBI's hostage rescue team skillfully made the arrests of LeRoy Schweitzer and Daniel Petersen, our unwavering goal has been to peacefully resolve the standoff in Montana.

I am pleased to announce that today we have accomplished our mission. Everyone has left the ranch, and those wanted on criminal charges, as I said, have been taken into custody.

Let me say that I am deeply indebted to the attorney general, Janet Reno, for her leadership and steadfast support throughout the crisis. She has been with us and the Montana state law enforcement authorities since the beginning, giving us her leadership, full support and counsel to the men and women in Montana, and to the strategy of patient but resolute efforts to negotiate a peaceful end to the standoff.

Likewise, Deputy Attorney General Jamie Gorelick, and the United States attorney for Montana, Sherry Matteucci, have been superb throughout this ordeal.

I am extraordinarily proud of the men and women of the FBI and Montana law enforcement, whose great skill and perseverance brought this complex case to a successful conclusion. I am all the more proud and grateful to them for exposing themselves and their families to great risks and personal danger.

To achieve this peaceful resolution, the FBI acted absolutely honorably in all the negotiations. We made no deals to drop or lessen the federal charges against anyone. Our posture from the very beginning was to build solid federal criminal cases and arrest everyone charged with a federal crime whenever we could do so safely.

We never wavered from that position.

Last October, I testified before Congress about a series of reforms I made to the FBI's crisis response procedures.

The Freeman situation put those reforms to the test. I'm gratified that both the new procedures and FBI employees performed as I had expected they would.

In Montana, we followed the guiding principles that I established last year as part of those reforms. First, whenever the FBI reacts in a crisis situation, the reaction must be commensurate with the facts as we know them. In Montana, no shots had been fired, no subject was injured or threatened with injury and the two Freemen leaders had been arrested by the FBI without incident.

The charges against those who were on the ranch are not for committing violent acts.

I know some criticized us for waiting too long and not attempting a tactical solution. I understand their impatience.

But it was essential that we followed our established crisis management procedures. In my view, given the situation, the prudent thing was to put patience above the risk of bloodshed. The safety of the law enforcement personnel and the innocent people inside the Freemen-occupied property was paramount. There was no factor of violence forcing us to move in at the risk of loss of life.

Second, I intended that our negotiation drive our strategy. The situation permitted, it even called for it, and that's what we did. Our negotiators and tactical people sat equally at the table. In this instance, a strategy from day one of patient, honest and persistent attempts at negotiation ultimately prevailed.

Finally, last October, I testified that the FBI must never hesitate to go outside of government to seek other experts or other people who might help us peacefully resolve a crisis situation.

In Montana, we used a wide variety of experts and 45 different third-party intermediaries. I thank all who aided the quest for a peaceful solution. Both the FBI's deputy director, Weldon Kennedy, and I visited the scene to assess firsthand the application of these principles.

We both were convinced we had chosen the prudent course, the right strategy, given the circumstances. FBI Assistant Director Robert Bryant personally directed the crisis on-scene in Montana for several weeks.

I'd like the American people to know that the FBI's intention and purpose throughout this ordeal has been to enforce the law fairly, firmly and safely. It is our duty and responsibility to do so.

At the same time, as I said we would in October, we tried a fundamentally different approach in the first crisis situation to develop. That approach may not always work, but it worked here.

I think the American people can take great comfort in the fact that the law was enforced, as it should always be, and that it was done in a way that did not bring harm to anyone.

There are too many people to thank or name, but I would like to give some special recognition. First, to those members of Congress—both from the House and the Senate from both parties—who courageously offered to assist the FBI in a number of ways and gave personal support to me and the attorney general in all our efforts to peacefully resolve the situation.

The good and honest people of Montana who made us feel at home. Montana state officials and law enforcement personnel gave as much to the effort as we did. From here at FBI headquarters, Assistant Director Bryant, his deputy John Lewis, Section Chief Bob Blitzer, the FBI's general counsel, Howard Shapiro, and many others gave superb guidance, leadership, and support to the operation.

Many FBI leaders and crisis managers from the field were critically involved. Special agent in charge Tom Kubic from Salt Lake City, Robin Montgomery, the SAC in charge of the crisis incident response group, Roger Knisely, the head of our Hostage Rescue Team, who spent many weeks in the field on the very difficult and very dangerous conditions.

Finally, the FBI special agents and support personnel who were there during many difficult weeks. Likewise, the families of those fine people, who endured much hardship during that period.

We were deeply saddened by the untimely death of one of our agents, Special Agent Kevin Kramer, who was killed in Montana in an automobile accident on April 14th, 1996.

In my view, the greatest tribute we could pay to him, his lovely wife Heidi and their family, was to conclude this dangerous and very complicated case in the most professional and safe way possible.

The hundreds of FBI agents who served in Montana have, indeed, created a splendid monument to his memory. I was deeply touched by the roadside monument local ranchers erected, also in his memory, and offer our heartfelt thanks to those who gave that recognition.

Thank you very much. That completes my statement. . . .

SUPREME COURT ON
RACIAL GERRYMANDERING
June 13, 1996

For the third time in four years, the Supreme Court signaled its dislike of race-based redistricting, but the Court neither barred outright the consideration of race as a factor in drawing U.S. House districts nor set out firm guidelines stating the conditions under which race-conscious redistricting might be permissible. This left those congressional districts deliberately drawn to give majority status to blacks and other minorities open to continued legal challenge.

The Court action, which came June 13 on 5–4 votes in a pair of cases, invalidated three congressional districts in Texas and one in North Carolina. The issue in the North Carolina case, Shaw v. Hunt, *was straightforward, in part because it was the second time the Court had dealt with a challenge to two North Carolina districts by a group of white voters. In 1993, in the case of* Shaw v. Reno, *the Court held that two racially drawn districts with "highly irregular" shapes were suspect and directed the federal district court to subject them to the strictest judicial scrutiny. That standard required that any race-based classification by a state could be justified under the equal protection clause of the Fourteenth Amendment only if it was narrowly tailored to meet a compelling state interest. (Court on gerrymanders, Historic Documents of 1993, p. 459)*

On remand, the lower court upheld the two districts in question, saying that they were narrowly tailored to meet the state's compelling interest in complying with the 1965 Voting Rights Act and with eliminating the effects of racial segregation, which had kept any black from those districts from being elected to Congress for the first ninety years of the century.

It was that ruling as it pertained to the Twelfth District that the Court overturned in Shaw v. Hunt. *Complying with the Voting Rights Act might be a compelling state interest, Chief Justice William H. Rehnquist wrote for the majority, but the district itself was not narrowly tailored to achieve that interest. The Court dismissed the challenge to North Carolina's First District because none of the challengers actually lived in the district.*

The issue in the Texas case, Bush v. Vera, *presented a different question—whether race had been the predominant factor in drawing the three challenged districts. If it were the predominant factor, the district would be subject to strict scrutiny under the Court's 1995 ruling in the case of* Miller v. Johnson. *The state acknowledged that race was a factor in shaping the districts but insisted that more traditional—and legal—redistricting principles, such as the desire to protect incumbents, guided the drawing of the district boundaries.* (Court on race-based redistricting, Historic Documents of 1995, p. 369)

Writing a plurality opinion for herself, Rehnquist, and Justice Anthony M. Kennedy, Justice Sandra Day O'Connor rejected the argument that race had not been the predominant factor. "In some circumstances, incumbency protection might explain as well as, or better than, race a State's decision to depart from other traditional districting principles, such as compactness in the drawing of bizarre district lines," O'Connor wrote. She added that evidence presented at the trial court provided "ample bases on which to conclude both that racially motivated gerrymandering had a qualitatively greater influence on the drawing of district lines than politically motivated gerrymandering, and that political gerrymandering was accomplished in large part by the use of race as a proxy. . . ."

Because race was determined to be the predominant factor in the drawing of the disputed districts, strict scrutiny applied, O'Connor said, and under that standard, the districts failed the "narrow tailoring" requirement. "Significant deviations from traditional districting principles, such as the bizarre shape and noncompactness demonstrated . . . here, cause constitutional harm insofar as they convey the message that political identity is, or should be, predominantly racial," she wrote.

The majority in Bush v. Vera *was not speaking with a single voice. Justices Clarence Thomas and Antonin Scalia concurred with the judgment but not with the reasoning in the plurality opinion. "All racial classifications by government must be strictly scrutinized and, even in the sensitive area of state legislative redistricting, I would make no exceptions," Thomas wrote.*

In an unusual move, O'Connor wrote a separate concurring opinion to her own plurality opinion, in which she agreed with the dissenters that compliance with the Voting Rights Act could be a compelling state interest justifying the drawing of race-conscious districts. The other four justices in the majority had not taken a position on this question.

O'Connor, the swing vote in this group of cases, was clearly trying to carve out a middle ground between barring race-conscious districts altogether and permitting "excessive" use of racial considerations in drawing district boundaries, much as she did in affirmative action cases. "The Voting Rights Act requires the States and the courts to take action to remedy the reality of racial inequality in our political system, sometimes necessitating race-based action, while the Fourteenth Amendment requires us to look with suspicion on the excessive use of racial considerations by the

government," O'Connor wrote, acknowledging that the difficulty in recon-
ciling the two goals was "inevitable."

Justices John Paul Stevens, David H. Souter, Ruth Bader Ginsburg, and
Stephen G. Breyer dissented in both cases, urging the Court to abandon its
line of racial gerrymandering decisions that began with Shaw v. Reno.
Stevens, joined by Ginsburg and Breyer, said that the Court has "struck out
into a jurisprudential wilderness that lacks a definable constitutional core
and threatens to create harms more significant than any suffered by the
individual plaintiffs challenging these districts." Souter, joined by Ginsburg and Breyer, also decried the Court's inability to fashion a standard
for defining when race was a predominant factor. "The result of this failure to provide a practical standard for distinguishing between the lawful
and unlawful use of race has not only been inevitable confusion in state
houses and courthouses, but a consequent shift in responsibility for setting
district boundaries from the state legislatures, which are invested with
front-line authority by . . . the Constitution, to the courts, and truly to this
Court, which is left to superintend the drawing of every legislative district
in the land."

Unanswered Questions, Undefined Standards

Under the Voting Rights Act, the Justice Department must "preclear" districting maps in states with a history of discrimination. The department
has used that authority to push those states to adopt minority-dominant
districts, and many civil rights leaders feared that the Court's decisions on
racial gerrymandering had essentially gutted the Voting Rights Act. "Only
the shell still stands," said Theodore Shaw of the NAACP Legal Defense and
Educational Fund. "The Supreme Court has constitutionalized a double
standard," said Penda D. Hair, executive director of the fund's Washington
office, "because it is only African-Americans and Latinos that have to have
compact districts in order to achieve representation of their communities
of interest."

Several parties to the debate criticized the Court's failure to define the
compelling interests that would justify racial gerrymandering or to set
any standards for determining when racial considerations would be excessive. "We still have absolutely undefined standards here as to what counts
as a district that passes muster—that is race-conscious but not race-dri-
ven," said Abigail Thernstrom, a prominent critic of race-based districting. "How is a district just supposed to know what's in Justice O'Connor's
mind?" asked Pamela Karlan, a law professor at the University of Virginia
who supports race-conscious districting.

New Districts in Texas, North Carolina

The Court's action invalidating the four districts came after both parties
in North Carolina and Texas had already held their primaries to choose
nominees to run in the general elections. On July 30 a three-judge federal
panel set up to oversee the redrawing of North Carolina's congressional

districts ruled that it was too close to the election to allow for new lines to be drawn and new primaries to be held. The panel directed the state legislature to produce a new map by April 1, 1997. If it failed to do so, the judges said they would take over the task themselves.

A similar panel in Texas decided that it would redraw the lines in that state. On August 6 it announced that it had redrawn the lines for thirteen of the state's thirty U.S. House districts to meet the objections of the Supreme Court and that it was voiding the results of the earlier primary elections in those districts. House candidates in those thirteen districts ran in open primaries held November 5 along with the general election for other offices.

Ironically, the three incumbents in the districts that had been declared unconstitutional won election on November 5, but candidates in three of the other ten districts were forced into runoff elections on December 10. Rep. Ken Bentsen, a Democrat, held on to his seat, but a Republican, Rep. Steve Stockman, was unseated by Democrat Nick Lampson. Republican Kevin Brady won the third seat at stake, replacing a Republican, Jack Fields, who was retiring.

Following are excerpts from the plurality, concurring, and dissenting opinions in the case of Bush v. Vera, *decided by a 5–4 vote, in which the Supreme Court on June 13, 1996, struck down three congressional districts in Texas as unconstitutional racial gerrymanders:*

Nos. 94–805, 94–806 and 94–988

George W. Bush, Governor of
Texas, et al., Appellants
v.
Al Vera et al.

William Lawson, et al., Appellants
v.
Al Vera et al.

United States, Appellant
v.
Al Vera et al.

On appeals from the United States District Court for the Southern District of Texas

[June 13, 1996]

JUSTICE O'CONNOR announced the judgment of the Court and delivered an opinion, in which the CHIEF JUSTICE and JUSTICE KENNEDY join.

This is the latest in a series of appeals involving racial gerrymandering challenges to state redistricting efforts in the wake of the 1990 census. See *Shaw* v. *Hunt (Shaw II); United States* v. *Hays* (1995); *Miller* v. *Johnson* (1995); *Shaw* v. *Reno* (1993) *(Shaw I)*. That census revealed a population increase, largely in urban minority populations, that entitled Texas to three additional congressional seats. In response, and with a view to complying with the Voting Rights Act of 1965 (VRA), . . . the Texas Legislature promulgated a redistricting plan that, among other things: created District 30, a new majority-African-American district in Dallas County; created District 29, a new majority-Hispanic district in and around Houston in Harris County; and reconfigured District 18, which is adjacent to District 29, to make it a majority-African-American district. The Department of Justice precleared that plan under VRA §5 in 1991, and it was used in the 1992 congressional elections.

The plaintiffs, six Texas voters, challenged the plan, alleging that 24 of Texas' 30 congressional districts constitute racial gerrymanders in violation of the Fourteenth Amendment. The three-judge United States District Court for the Southern District of Texas held Districts 18, 29, and 30 unconstitutional. (1994). The Governor of Texas, private intervenors, and the United States (as intervenor) now appeal. Finding that, under this Court's decisions in *Shaw I* and *Miller*, the district lines at issue are subject to strict scrutiny, and that they are not narrowly tailored to serve a compelling state interest, we affirm.

[I omitted]
II

We must . . . determine whether those districts are subject to strict scrutiny. Our precedents have used a variety of formulations to describe the threshold for the application of strict scrutiny. Strict scrutiny applies where "redistricting legislation . . . is so extremely irregular on its face that it rationally can be viewed only as an effort to segregate the races for purposes of voting, without regard for traditional districting principles," *Shaw I*, or where "race for its own sake, and not other districting principles, was the legislature's dominant and controlling rationale in drawing its district lines," *Miller*, and "the legislature subordinated traditional race-neutral districting principles . . . to racial considerations," *id*. . . .

Strict scrutiny does not apply merely because redistricting is performed with consciousness of race. Nor does it apply to all cases of intentional creation of majority-minority districts. See *DeWitt* v. *Wilson* (ED Cal. 1994) (strict scrutiny did not apply to an intentionally created compact majority-minority district), summarily aff'd, (1995); *cf. Shaw I* (reserving this question). Electoral district lines are "facially race neutral," so a more searching inquiry is necessary before strict scrutiny can be found applicable in redistricting cases than in cases of "classifications based explicitly on race." For strict scrutiny to apply, the plaintiffs must prove that other, legitimate districting principles were "subordinated" to race. By that, we mean that race must be "the predominant factor motivating the legislature's [redistricting] decision." We thus differ from JUSTICE THOMAS, who would apparently hold that it suffices that racial considerations be a motivation for the drawing of a majority-minority district.

The present case is a mixed motive case. The appellants concede that one of Texas' goals in creating the three districts at issue was to produce majority-minority districts, but they also cite evidence that other goals, particularly incumbency protection (including protection of "functional incumbents," i.e., sitting members of the Texas Legislature who had declared an intention to run for open congressional seats), also played a role in the drawing of the district lines. . . .

[The District Court's] findings—that the State substantially neglected traditional districting criteria such as compactness, that it was committed from the outset to creating majority-minority districts, and that it manipulated district lines to exploit unprecedentedly detailed racial data—together weigh in favor of the application of strict scrutiny. We do not hold that any one of these factors is independently sufficient to require strict scrutiny. The Constitution does not mandate regularity of district shape, and the neglect of traditional districting criteria is merely necessary, not sufficient. For strict scrutiny to apply, traditional districting criteria must be *subordinated to race*. Nor, as we have emphasized, is the decision to create a majority-minority district objectionable in and of itself. The direct evidence of that decision is not, as JUSTICE STEVENS suggests, "the real key" to our decision; it is merely one of several essential ingredients. Nor do we "condemn state legislation merely because it was based on accurate information." The use of sophisticated technology and detailed information in the drawing of majority-minority districts is no more objectionable than it is in the drawing of majority-majority districts. But, as the District Court explained, the direct evidence of racial considerations, coupled with the fact that the computer program used was significantly *more* sophisticated with respect to race than with respect to other demographic data, provides substantial evidence that it was race that led to the neglect of traditional districting criteria here. We must therefore consider what role other factors played in order to determine whether race predominated.

Several factors other than race were at work in the drawing of the districts. Traditional districting criteria were not entirely neglected: Districts 18 and 29 maintain the integrity of county lines; each of the three districts takes its character from a principal city and the surrounding urban area; and none of the districts is as widely dispersed as the North Carolina district held unconstitutional in *Shaw* II. . . . More significantly, the District Court found that incumbency protection influenced the redistricting plan to an unprecedented extent. . . .

Strict scrutiny would not be appropriate if race-neutral, traditional districting considerations predominated over racial ones. We have not subjected political gerrymandering to strict scrutiny. See *Davis* v. *Bandemer* (1986). And we have recognized incumbency protection, at least in the limited form of "avoiding contests between incumbent[s]," as a legitimate state goal. [Citations omitted.] Because it is clear that race was not the only factor that motivated the legislature to draw irregular district lines, we must scrutinize each challenged district to determine whether the District Court's conclusion that race predominated over legitimate districting considerations, including incumbency, can be sustained.

A

The population of District 30 is 50% African-American and 17.1% Hispanic. Fifty percent of the district's population is located in a compact, albeit irregularly shaped, core in south Dallas, which is 69% African-American. But the remainder of the district consists of narrow and bizarrely shaped tentacles—the State identifies seven "segments"—extending primarily to the north and west. Over 98% of the district's population is within Dallas County, but it crosses two county lines at its western and northern extremities. Its western excursion into Tarrant County grabs a small community that is 61.9% African-American; its northern excursion into Collin County occupies a hook-like shape mapping exactly onto the only area in the southern half of that county with a combined African-American and Hispanic percentage population in excess of 50%. . . .

Appellants do not deny that District 30 shows substantial disregard for the traditional districting principles of compactness and regularity, or that the redistricters pursued unwaveringly the objective of creating a majority-African-American district. But they argue that its bizarre shape is explained by efforts . . . to protect incumbents. . . .

In some circumstances, incumbency protection might explain as well as, or better than, race a State's decision to depart from other traditional districting principles, such as compactness, in the drawing of bizarre district lines. And the fact that, "[a]s it happens, . . . many of the voters being fought over [by the neighboring Democratic incumbents] were African-American," would not, in and of itself, convert a political gerrymander into a racial gerrymander, no matter how conscious redistricters were of the correlation between race and party affiliation. . . .

If the State's goal is otherwise constitutional political gerrymandering, it is free to use the kind of political data on which JUSTICE STEVENS focuses—precinct general election voting patterns, precinct primary voting patterns, and legislators' experience—to achieve that goal regardless of its awareness of its racial implications and regardless of the fact that it does so in the context of a majority-minority district. To the extent that the District Court suggested the contrary, it erred. But to the extent that race is used as a proxy for political characteristics, a racial stereotype requiring strict scrutiny is in operation. . . .

Here, the District Court had ample bases on which to conclude both that racially motivated gerrymandering had a qualitatively greater influence on the drawing of district lines than politically motivated gerrymandering, and that political gerrymandering was accomplished in large part by the use of race as a proxy. . . .

B

In Harris County, centered on the city of Houston, Districts 18 and 29 interlock "like a jigsaw puzzle . . . in which it might be impossible to get the pieces apart." [Quoting *The Almanac of American Politics* (1996).] . . . According to the leading statistical study of relative district compactness and regularity, they are two of the three least regular districts in the country. . . .

Not only are the shapes of the districts bizarre; they also exhibit utter disregard of city limits, local election precincts, and voter tabulation district lines. This caused a severe disruption of traditional forms of political activity. Campaigners seeking to visit their constituents "had to carry a map to identify the district lines, because so often the borders would move from block to block"; voters "did not know the candidates running for office" because they did not know which district they lived in. In light of Texas' requirement that voting be arranged by precinct, with each precinct representing a community which shares local, state, and federal representatives, it also created administrative headaches for local election officials. . . .

As with District 30, appellants adduced evidence that incumbency protection played a role in determining the bizarre district lines. The District Court found that one constraint on the shape of District 29 was the rival ambitions of its two "functional incumbents," who distorted its boundaries in an effort to include larger areas of their existing state legislative constituencies. But the District Court's findings amply demonstrate that such influences were overwhelmed in the determination of the districts' bizarre shapes by the State's efforts to maximize racial divisions. The State's VRA §5 submission explains that the bizarre configuration of Districts 18 and 29 "result[s] in the maximization of minority voting strength" in Harris County, corroborating the District Court's finding that "[i]n the earliest stages of the Congressional redistricting process, state Democratic and Republican leaders rallied behind the idea of creating a new Hispanic safe seat in Harris County while preserving the safe African-American seat in District 18." . . . And, even more than in District 30, the intricacy of the lines drawn, separating Hispanic voters from African-American voters on a block-by-block basis, betrays the critical impact of the block-by-block racial data available. . . . The District Court's conclusion is, therefore, inescapable: "Because Districts 18 and 29 are formed in utter disregard for traditional redistricting criteria and because their shapes are ultimately unexplainable on grounds other than the racial quotas established for those districts, they are the product of [presumptively] unconstitutional racial gerrymandering."

III

Having concluded that strict scrutiny applies, we must determine whether the racial classifications embodied in any of the three districts are narrowly tailored to further a compelling state interest. Appellants point to three compelling interests: the interest in avoiding liability under the "results" test of VRA §2(b), the interest in remedying past and present racial discrimination, and the "nonretrogression" principle of VRA §5 (for District 18 only). We consider them in turn.

A

Section 2(a) of the VRA prohibits the imposition of any electoral practice or procedure that "results in a denial or abridgement of the right of any citizen . . . to vote on account of race or color." In 1982, Congress amended the VRA by changing the language of §2(a) and adding §2(b), which provides a "results" test for violation of §2(a). A violation exists if,

> "based on the totality of circumstances, it is shown that the political processes leading to nomination or election in the State or political subdivision are not equally open to participation by members of a class of citizens protected by subsection (a) of this section in that its members have less opportunity than other members of the electorate to participate in the political process and to elect representatives of their choice." 42 U.S.C. §1973(b).

Appellants contend that creation of each of the three majority-minority districts at issue was justified by Texas' compelling state interest in complying with this results test.

As we have done in each of our previous cases in which this argument has been raised as a defense to charges of racial gerrymandering, we assume without deciding that compliance with the results test, as interpreted by our precedents, can be a compelling state interest. We also reaffirm that the "narrow tailoring" requirement of strict scrutiny allows the States a limited degree of leeway in furthering such interests. If the State has a "strong basis in evidence," *Shaw I,* for concluding that creation of a majority-minority district is reasonably necessary to comply with §2, and the districting that is based on race "substantially addresses the §2 violation," *Shaw II,* it satisfies strict scrutiny. . . .

A §2 district that is reasonably compact and regular, taking into account traditional districting principles such as maintaining communities of interest and traditional boundaries, may pass strict scrutiny without having to defeat rival compact districts designed by plaintiffs' experts in endless "beauty contests." The dissenters misread us when they make the leap from our disagreement about the facts of this case to the conclusion that we are creating a "stalemate" by requiring the States to "get things just right" or to draw "the precise compact district that a court would impose in a successful §2 challenge." . . . [N]othing that we say today should be read as limiting "a State's discretion to apply traditional districting principles" in majority-minority, as in other, districts. The constitutional problem arises only from the subordination of those principles to race.

Strict scrutiny remains, nonetheless, strict. The State must have a "strong basis in evidence" for finding that the threshold conditions for §2 liability are present:

> "first, 'that [the minority group] is sufficiently large and geographically compact to constitute a majority in a single member district'; second, 'that it is politically cohesive'; and third, 'that the white majority votes sufficiently as a bloc to enable

it . . . usually to defeat the minority's preferred candidate.'" *Growe* [v. *Emison* (1993)], (emphasis added) (quoting *Thornburg* v. *Gingles* (1986)).

And, as we have noted above, the district drawn in order to satisfy §2 must not subordinate traditional districting principles to race substantially more than is "reasonably necessary" to avoid §2 liability. Districts 18, 29, and 30 fail to meet these requirements.

We assume, without deciding, that the State had a "strong basis in evidence" for finding the second and third threshold conditions for §2 liability to be present. We have, however, already found that all three districts are bizarrely shaped and far from compact, and that those characteristics are predominantly attributable to gerrymandering that was racially motivated and/or achieved by the use of race as a proxy. . . .

These characteristics defeat any claim that the districts are narrowly tailored to serve the State's interest in avoiding liability under §2, because §2 does not require a State to create, on predominantly racial lines, a district that is not "reasonably compact." If, because of the dispersion of the minority population, a reasonably compact majority-minority district cannot be created, §2 does not require a majority-minority district; if a reasonably compact district can be created, nothing in §2 requires the race-based creation of a district that is far from compact. Appellants argue that bizarre shaping and noncompactness do not raise narrow tailoring concerns. . . .

These arguments cannot save the districts before us. . . . [D]istrict shape is not irrelevant to the narrow tailoring inquiry. Our discussion in *Miller* served only to emphasize that the ultimate constitutional values at stake involve the harms caused by the use of unjustified racial classifications, and that bizarreness is not necessary to trigger strict scrutiny. Significant deviations from traditional districting principles, such as the bizarre shape and noncompactness demonstrated by the districts here, cause constitutional harm insofar as they convey the message that political identity is, or should be, predominantly racial. For example, the bizarre shaping of Districts 18 and 29, cutting across pre-existing precinct lines and other natural or traditional divisions, is not merely evidentially significant; it is part of the constitutional problem insofar as it disrupts nonracial bases of political identity and thus intensifies the emphasis on race.

B

The United States and the State next contend that the district lines at issue are justified by the State's compelling interest in "ameliorating the effects of racially polarized voting attributable to past and present racial discrimination." In support of that contention, they cite Texas' long history of discrimination against minorities in electoral processes, stretching from the Reconstruction to modern times, including violations of the Constitution and of the VRA. [Citations omitted.] Appellants attempt to link that history to evidence that in recent elections in majority-minority districts, "Anglos usually bloc voted against" Hispanic and African-American candidates. [Quoting district court opinion.]

A State's interest in remedying discrimination is compelling when two conditions are satisfied. First, the discrimination that the State seeks to remedy must be specific, "identified discrimination"; second, the State "must have had a 'strong basis in evidence' to conclude that remedial action was necessary, 'before it embarks on an affirmative action program.'" *Shaw II.* Here, the only current problem that appellants cite as in need of remediation is alleged vote dilution as a consequence of racial bloc voting, the same concern that underlies their VRA §2 compliance defense, which we have assumed to be valid for purposes of this opinion. We have indicated that such problems will not justify race-based districting unless "the State employ[s] sound districting principles, and . . . the affected racial group's residential patterns afford the opportunity of creating districts in which they will be in the majority." *Shaw I.* Once that standard is applied, our agreement with the District Court's finding that these districts are not narrowly tailored to comply with §2 forecloses this line of defense.

C

The final contention offered by the State and private appellants is that creation of District 18 (only) was justified by a compelling state interest in complying with VRA §5. We have made clear that §5 has a limited substantive goal: "'to insure that no voting-procedure changes would be made that would lead to a retrogression in the position of racial minorities with respect to their effective exercise of the electoral franchise.'" *Miller* (quoting *Beer* v. *United States* (1976)). Appellants contend that this "nonretrogression" principle is implicated because Harris County had, for two decades, contained a congressional district in which African-American voters had succeeded in selecting representatives of their choice, all of whom were African-Americans.

The problem with the State's argument is that it seeks to justify not maintenance, but substantial augmentation, of the African-American population percentage in District 18. At the previous redistricting, in 1980, District 18's population was 40.8% African-American. As a result of Hispanic population increases and African-American emigration from the district, its population had reached 35.1% African-American and 42.2% Hispanic at the time of the 1990 census. The State has shown no basis for concluding that the increase to a 50.9% African-American population in 1991 was necessary to insure nonretrogression. Nonretrogression is not a license for the State to do whatever it deems necessary to insure continued electoral success; it merely mandates that the minority's opportunity to elect representatives of its choice not be diminished, directly or indirectly, by the State's actions. . . . Applying that principle, it is clear that District 18 is not narrowly tailored to the avoidance of §5 liability.

IV

. . . This Court has now rendered decisions after plenary consideration in five cases applying the *Shaw I* doctrine (*Shaw I, Miller, Hays, Shaw II,* and this case). The dissenters would have us abandon those precedents, suggesting that fundamental concerns relating to the judicial role are at stake. While we agree that those concerns are implicated here, we believe they point the other way. Our legitimacy requires, above all, that we adhere to *stare decisis*, especially in such sensitive political contexts as the present, where partisan controversy abounds. Legislators and district courts nationwide have modified their practices—or, rather, reembraced the traditional districting practices that were almost universally followed before the 1990 census—in response to *Shaw I*. Those practices and our precedents, which acknowledge voters as more than mere racial statistics, play an important role in defining the political identity of the American voter. Our Fourteenth Amendment jurisprudence evinces a commitment to eliminate unnecessary and excessive governmental use and reinforcement of racial stereotypes. [Citations omitted.] We decline to retreat from that commitment today.

* * *

The judgment of the District Court is

Affirmed.

JUSTICE O'CONNOR, concurring.

I write separately to express my view on two points. First, compliance with the results test of §2 of the Voting Rights Act (VRA) is a compelling state interest. Second, that test can co-exist in principle and in practice with *Shaw* v. *Reno* (1993), and its progeny, as elaborated in today's opinions.

I

As stated in the plurality opinion, this Court has thus far assumed without deciding that compliance with the results test of VRA §2(b) is a compelling state interest. Although that assumption is not determinative of the Court's decisions today, I believe that States and lower courts are entitled to more definite guidance as they toil with the twin demands of the Fourteenth Amendment and the Voting Rights Act. [Quotation of §2(b) omitted; see plurality opinion, section III (A), above.]

In the 14 years since the enactment of §2(b), we have interpreted and enforced the obligations that it places on States in a succession of cases, assuming but never directly addressing its constitutionality. [Citation of cases omitted.] Meanwhile, lower courts have unanimously affirmed its constitutionality. [Citation of cases omitted.] . . .

In my view, therefore, the States have a compelling interest in complying with the results test as this Court has interpreted it.

II

Although I agree with the dissenters about §2's role as part of our national commitment to racial equality, I differ from them in my belief that that commitment can and must be reconciled with the complementary commitment of our Fourteenth Amendment jurisprudence to eliminate the unjustified use of racial stereotypes. At the same time that we combat the symptoms of racial polarization in politics, we must strive to eliminate unnecessary race-based state action that appears to endorse the disease.

Today's decisions, in conjunction with the recognition of the compelling state interest in compliance with the reasonably perceived requirements of §2, present a workable framework for the achievement of these twin goals. I would summarize that framework, and the rules governing the States' consideration of race in the districting process, as follows.

First, so long as they do not subordinate traditional districting criteria to the use of race for its own sake or as a proxy, States may intentionally create majority-minority districts, and may otherwise take race into consideration, without coming under strict scrutiny. Only if traditional districting criteria are neglected and that neglect is predominantly due to the misuse of race does strict scrutiny apply.

Second, where voting is racially polarized, §2 prohibits States from adopting districting schemes that would have the effect that minority voters "have less opportunity than other members of the electorate to . . . elect representatives of their choice." §2(b). That principle may require a State to create a majority-minority district where the three *Gingles* factors are present—viz., (i) the minority group "is sufficiently large and geographically compact to constitute a majority in a single-member district," (ii) "it is politically cohesive," and (iii) "the white majority votes sufficiently as a bloc to enable it . . . usually to defeat the minority's preferred candidate," *Thornburg* v. *Gingles* [1986].

Third, the state interest in avoiding liability under VRA §2 is compelling. If a State has a strong basis in evidence for concluding that the *Gingles* factors are present, it may create a majority-minority district without awaiting judicial findings. Its "strong basis in evidence" need not take any particular form, although it cannot simply rely on generalized assumptions about the prevalence of racial bloc voting.

Fourth, if a State pursues that compelling interest by creating a district that "substantially addresses" the potential liability and does not deviate substantially from a hypothetical court-drawn §2 district for predominantly racial reasons, its districting plan will be deemed narrowly tailored.

Finally, however, districts that are bizarrely shaped and non-compact, and that otherwise neglect traditional districting principles and deviate substantially from the hypothetical court-drawn district, for predominantly racial reasons, are unconstitutional. . . .

. . . [T]he application of the principles that I have outlined sometimes requires difficult exercises of judgment. That difficulty is inevitable. The Voting Rights Act requires the States and the courts to take action to remedy the reality of racial inequality in our political system, sometimes necessitating race-based action, while the Fourteenth Amendment requires us to look with suspicion on the excessive use of racial considerations by the government. But I believe that the States, playing a primary role, and the courts, in their secondary role, are capable of distinguishing the appropriate and reasonably necessary uses of race from its unjustified and excessive uses.

JUSTICE KENNEDY, concurring.

I join the plurality opinion, but the statements in Part II of the opinion that strict scrutiny would not apply to all cases of intentional creation of majority-minority districts require comment. Those statements are unnecessary to our decision, for strict scrutiny applies here. I do not consider these dicta to commit me to any position on the question whether race is predominant whenever a State, in redistricting, foreordains that one race be the majority in a certain number of districts or in a certain part of a State. In my view, we would no doubt apply strict scrutiny if a State decreed that certain districts had to be at least 50 percent white, and our analysis should be no different if the State so favors minority races. . . .

JUSTICE THOMAS, with whom JUSTICE SCALIA joins, concurring in the judgment.

In my view, application of strict scrutiny in this case was never a close question. I cannot agree with JUSTICE O'CONNOR's assertion that strict scrutiny is not invoked by the intentional creation of majority-minority districts. . . .

Strict scrutiny applies to all governmental classifications based on race, and we have expressly held that there is no exception for race-based redistricting. While we have recognized the evidentiary difficulty of proving that a redistricting plan is, in fact, a racial gerrymander, we have never suggested that a racial gerrymander is subject to anything less than strict scrutiny. . . .

We have said that impermissible racial classifications do not follow inevitably from a legislature's mere awareness of racial demographics. But the intentional creation of a majority-minority district certainly means more than mere awareness that application of traditional, race-neutral districting principles will result in the creation of a district in which a majority of the district's residents are members of a particular minority group. In my view, it means that the legislature affirmatively undertakes to create a majority-minority district that would not have existed but for the express use of racial classifications—in other words, that a majority-minority district is created "because of," and not merely "in spite of," racial demographics. When that occurs, traditional race-neutral districting principles are necessarily subordinated (and race necessarily predominates), and the legislature has classified persons on the basis of race. The resulting redistricting must be viewed as a racial gerrymander. . . .

JUSTICE STEVENS, with whom JUSTICE GINSBURG and JUSTICE BREYER join, dissenting.

The 1990 census revealed that Texas' population had grown, over the past decade, almost twice as fast as the population of the country as a whole. As a result, Texas was entitled to elect three additional Representatives to the United States Congress, enlarging its delegation from 27 to 30. Because Texas' growth was concentrated in South Texas and the cities of Dallas and Houston, the state legislature concluded that the new congressional districts should be carved out of existing districts in those areas. The consequences of the political battle that produced the new map are some of the most oddly shaped congressional districts in the United States.

Today, the Court strikes down three of Texas' majority-minority districts, concluding, *inter alia*, that their odd shapes reveal that the State impermissibly relied on predominantly racial reasons when it drew the districts as it did. For two reasons, I believe that the Court errs in striking down those districts.

First, I believe that the Court has misapplied its own tests for racial gerrymandering, both by applying strict scrutiny to all three of these districts, and then by concluding that none can meet that scrutiny. . . . [T]he Court improperly ignores the "complex interplay" of political and geographical considerations that went into the creation of Texas' new congressional districts and focuses exclusively on the role that race played in the State's decisions to adjust the shape of its districts. A quick comparison of the unconstitutional majority-minority districts with three equally bizarre majority-Anglo districts [Districts 3, 6, and 25] demonstrates that race was not necessarily the predominant factor contorting the district lines. [Appendix with maps of districts omitted.] I would follow the fair implications of the District Court's findings and conclude that Texas' entire map is a political, not a racial, gerrymander.

Even if strict scrutiny applies, I would find these districts constitutional, for each considers race only to the extent necessary to comply with the State's responsibilities under the Voting Rights Act while achieving other race-neutral political and geographical requirements. The plurality's finding to the contrary unnecessarily restricts the ability of States to conform their behavior to the Voting Rights Act while simultaneously complying with other race-neutral goals.

Second, even if I concluded that these districts failed an appropriate application of this still-developing law to appropriately read facts, I would not uphold the District Court decision. The decisions issued today serve merely to reinforce my conviction that the Court has, with its "analytically distinct" jurisprudence of racial gerrymandering, *Shaw* v. *Reno (Shaw I)*(1993), struck out into a jurisprudential wilderness that lacks a definable constitutional core and threatens to create harms more significant than any suffered by the individual plaintiffs challenging these districts. . . .

[I through VI omitted]

VII

The history of race relations in Texas and throughout the South demonstrates overt evidence of discriminatory voting practices lasting through the 1970's. Even in recent years, Texans have elected only two black candidates to statewide office; majority-white Texas districts have never elected a minority to either the State Senate or the United States Congress. One recent study suggests that majority-white districts throughout the South remain suspiciously unlikely to elect black representatives. And nationwide, fewer than 15 of the hundreds of legislators that have passed through Congress since 1950 have been black legislators elected from majority-white districts. In 1994, for example, 36 of the Nation's 39 black Representatives were elected from majority-minority districts, while only three were elected from majority-white districts.

Perhaps the state of race relations in Texas and, for that matter, the Nation, is more optimistic than might be expected in light of these facts. If so, it may be that the plurality's exercise in redistricting will be successful. Perhaps minority candidates, forced to run in majority-white districts, will be able to overcome the long history of stereotyping and discrimination that has heretofore led the vast majority of majority-white districts to reject minority candidacies. Perhaps not. I am certain only that bodies of elected federal and state officials are in a far better position than anyone on this Court to assess whether the Nation's long history of discrimination has been overcome, and that nothing in the Constitution requires this unnecessary intrusion into the ability of States to negotiate solutions to political differences while providing long-excluded groups the opportunity to participate effectively in the democratic process. I respectfully dissent.

JUSTICE SOUTER, with whom JUSTICE GINSBURG and JUSTICE BREYER join, dissenting.

When the Court devises a new cause of action to enforce a constitutional provision, it ought to identify an injury distinguishable from the consequences of concededly constitutional conduct, and it should describe the elements necessary and sufficient to make out such a claim. . . . Those principles of justification, fair notice, and guidance, have never been satisfied in the instance of the action announced three Terms ago in *Shaw* v. *Reno* (1993) (*Shaw I*), when a majority of this Court decided that a State violates the Fourteenth Amendment's Equal Protection Clause by excessive consideration of race in drawing the boundaries of voting districts, even when the resulting plan does not dilute the voting strength of any voters and so would not otherwise give rise to liability under the Fourteenth or Fifteenth Amendments, or under the Voting Rights Act.

. . . *Shaw I* addressed a putative harm subject to complaint by any voter objecting to an untoward consideration of race in the political process. Although the Court has repeatedly disclaimed any intent to go as far as to outlaw all conscious consideration of race in districting, after three rounds of appellate litigation seeking to describe the elements and define the contours of the *Shaw* cause of action, a helpful statement of a *Shaw* claim still eludes this Court. This is so for reasons that go to the conceptual bone.

The result of this failure to provide a practical standard for distinguishing between the lawful and unlawful use of race has not only been inevitable confusion in state houses and courthouses, but a consequent shift in responsibility for setting district boundaries from the state legislatures, which are invested with front-line authority by Article I of the Constitution, to the courts, and truly to this Court, which is left to superintend the drawing of every legislative district in the land.

Today's opinions do little to solve *Shaw*'s puzzles or return districting responsibility to the States. . . . [T]he combined plurality, minority, and Court opinions do not ultimately leave the law dealing with a *Shaw* claim appreciably clearer or more manageable than *Shaw I* itself did. And to the extent that some clarity follows from the knowledge that race may be considered when reasonably necessary to conform to the Voting Rights Act, today's opinions raise the specter that this ostensible progress may come with a heavy constitutional price. The price of *Shaw I*, indeed, may turn out to be the practical elimination of a State's discretion to apply traditional districting principles, widely accepted in States without racial districting issues as well as in States confronting them.

As the flaws of *Shaw I* persist, and as the burdens placed on the States and the courts by *Shaw* litigation loom larger with the approach of a new census and a new round of redistricting, the Court has to recognize that *Shaw*'s problems result from a basic misconception about the relation between race and districting principles, a mistake that no amount of case-by-case tinkering can eliminate. There is, therefore, no reason for confidence that the Court will eventually bring much order out of the confusion created by *Shaw I*, and because it has not, in any case, done so yet, I respectfully dissent.

I

. . . Article I of the Constitution places responsibility for drawing voting districts on the States in the first instance. The Court has nonetheless recognized limits on state districting autonomy when it could discern a strong constitutional justification and a reasonably definite standard for doing so, as, for example, in announcing the numerical requirement of one person, one vote, *Reynolds* v. *Sims* (1964). But the Court has never ignored the Constitution's commitment of districting responsibility to the political branches of the States and has accordingly assumed over the years that traditional districting principles widely accepted among States represented an informal baseline of acceptable districting practices. We have thus accorded substantial respect to such traditional principles (as those, for example, meant to preserve the integrity of neighborhood communities, to protect incumbents, to follow existing political boundaries, to recognize communities of interest, and to achieve compactness and contiguity); we have seen these objectives as entirely consistent with the Fourteenth and Fifteenth Amendments' demands. [Citation of cases omitted.] . . .

A

. . . [B]efore *Shaw I*, the Court required evidence of substantial harm to an identifiable group of voters to justify any judicial displacement of these traditional districting principles. . . .

Before *Shaw I*, we not only thus limited judicial interference with state districting efforts to cases of readily demonstrable harm to an identifiable class of voters, but we also confined our concern with districting to cases in which we were capable of providing a manageable standard for courts to apply and for legislators to follow. Within two years of holding in *Baker* v. *Carr* (1962) that malapportionment was a justiciable issue, "the Court recognized that its general equal protection jurisprudence was insufficient for the task and announced an increasingly rigid, simple to apply, voting-specific mandate of equipopulousity." [Quoting law review article.] Likewise, although it is quite true that the common definition of a racial vote-dilution injury ("less opportunity . . . to participate in the political process and to elect representatives . . . ," 42 U.S.C. §1973(b)) is no model of concrete description, the Court has identified categories of readily comprehensible evidence bearing on the likelihood of such an injury, including facts about size of minority population, quantifiable indications of political cohesiveness and bloc voting, historical patterns of success or failure of favored candidates, and so on. See, e.g., *Thornburg* v. *Gingles* (1986); *White* v. *Regester* [1973]. The particularity of this evidence goes far to separate victims of political "inequality" from those who just happened to support losing candidates.

B

Shaw I, however, broke abruptly with these standards, including the very understanding of equal protection as a practical guarantee against harm to some class singled out for disparate treatment. Whereas malapportionment measurably reduces the influence of voters in more populous districts, and vote dilution predestines members of a racial minority to perpetual frustration as political losers, what *Shaw I* spoke of as harm is not confined to any identifiable class singled out for disadvantage. . . .

C

The Court's failure to devise a concept of *Shaw* harm that distinguishes those who are injured from those who are not, or to differentiate violation from remedy, is matched by its inability to provide any manageable standard to distinguish forbidden districting conduct from the application of traditional state districting principles and the plans that they produce. This failure, while regrettable, need not have occurred, for when the Court spoke in *Shaw I* of a district shape so "bizarre" as to be an unequivocal indication that race had influenced the districting decision to an unreasonable degree, *Shaw I* could have been pointing to some workable criterion of shape translatable into objective standards. . . .

The Court, however, rejected this opportunity last Term in *Miller* v. *Johnson* [1995] when it declined to contain *Shaw* by any standard sufficiently quantifiable to guide the decisions of state legislators or to inform and limit review of districting decisions by the courts. The Court rejected shape as a sufficient condition for finding a *Shaw* violation, or even a necessary one. . . . Instead, it recharacterized the cause of action in terms devised in other cases addressing essentially different problems, by proscribing the consideration of race when it is the "predominant factor motivating the legislatur[e]," or when the use of race is "in substantial disregard of customary and tradition-al districting practices."

As a standard addressed to the untidy world of politics, neither "predomi-nant factor" nor "substantial disregard" inspires much hope. . . .

. . . It is not merely that the very nature of districting decisions makes it difficult to identify whether any particular consideration, racial or otherwise, was the "predominant motive," though that is certainly true. . . .

The reason that use of the predominant motive standard in reviewing a districting decision is bound to fail is more fundamental than that: in the political environment in which race can affect election results, many of these traditional districting principles cannot be applied without taking race into account and are thus, as a practical matter, inseparable from the supposedly illegitimate racial considerations. . . .

If, for example, a legislature may draw district lines to preserve the integri-ty of a given community, leaving it intact so that all of its members are served by one representative, this objective is inseparable from preserving the com-munity's racial identity when the community is characterized, or even self-defined, by the race of the majority of those who live there. This is an old truth, having been recognized every time the political process produced an Irish or Italian or Polish ward. . . .

Or take the traditional principle of providing protection for incumbents. The plurality seems to assume that incumbents may always be protected by drawing lines on the basis of data about political parties. But what if the incumbent has drawn support largely for racial reasons? What, indeed, if the incumbent was elected in a majority-minority district created to remedy vote dilution that resulted from racial bloc voting? It would be sheer fantasy to assume that consideration of race in these circumstances is somehow sepa-rable from application of the traditional principle of incumbency protection, and sheer incoherence to think that the consideration of race that is consti-tutionally required to remedy Fourteenth and Fifteenth Amendment vote dilution somehow becomes unconstitutional when aimed at protecting the incumbent the next time the census requires redistricting. . . .

[II and III omitted]

IV

. . . [T]here is presently no good reason that the Court's withdrawal from the presently untenable state of the law should not be complete. While I take the commands of *stare decisis* very seriously, the problems with *Shaw* and its progeny are themselves very serious. The Court has been unable to pro-vide workable standards, the chronic uncertainty has begotten no discernible reliance, and the costs of persisting doubt about the limits of state discretion and state responsibility are high.

There is, indeed, an added reason to admit *Shaw*'s failure in providing a manageable constitutional standard and to allow for some faith in the politi-cal process. That process not only evolved the very traditional districting principles that the Court has pledged to preserve, but has applied them in the past to deal with ethnicity in a way that should influence our thinking about the prospects for race. It is difficult to see how the consideration of race that *Shaw* condemns (but cannot avoid) is essentially different from the consideration of ethnicity that entered American politics from the moment that immigration began to temper regional homogeneity. Recognition of the ethnic character of neighborhoods and incumbents, through the application of just those districting principles we now view as traditional, allowed ethnically identified voters and their preferred candidates to enter the mainstream of American politics and to attain a level of political power in American democracy. The result has been not a state regime of ethnic apartheid, but ethnic participation and even a moderation of ethnicity's divisive effect in political practice. For although consciousness of ethnicity has not disappeared from the American electorate, its talismanic force does appear to have cooled over time. It took Boston Irish voters, for example, to elect Thomas Menino mayor in 1993.

There is, then, some reason to hope that if vote dilution is attacked at the same time that race is given the recognition that ethnicity has historically received in American politics, the force of race in politics will also moderate in time. There are even signs that such hope may be vindicated, even if the evidence is necessarily tentative as yet. . . . This possibility that racial politics, too, may grow wiser so long as minority votes are rescued from submergence should be considered in determining how far the Fourteenth and Fifteenth Amendments require us to devise constitutional common law to supplant the democratic process with litigation in federal courts. It counsels against accepting the profession that *Shaw* has yet evolved into a manageable constitutional standard, and from that case's invocation again today I respectfully dissent.

SUPREME COURT ON PRIVACY FOR PSYCHOLOGICAL TREATMENT
June 13, 1996

Psychiatrists, psychologists, and their patients won major victories in the Supreme Court and Congress in 1996. The Supreme Court June 13 held that federal courts could not compel mental health professionals to reveal patient records in court proceedings. By a vote of 7–2, the Court created a new evidentiary privilege for mental health professionals, including clinical social workers, similar to the confidentiality privilege long accorded lawyers and their clients and husbands and wives.

After killing a more ambitious proposal earlier in the year, Congress agreed to require group health insurance plans to set the same annual and lifetime limits on mental illnesses as they do on physical ailments. Currently, most health insurance plans that offer coverage for mental illnesses set lifetime limits on benefits for such diseases at $50,000, compared with up to $1 million for physical illnesses. Big business was opposed to the provision, claiming it would cost too much money.

The Court Ruling

The Court's ruling in the case of Jaffee v. Redmond *brought the federal courts into line with the fifty states, which all recognized some form of therapist-patient privilege. "The psychotherapist privilege serves the public interest by facilitating the provision of appropriate treatment for individuals suffering the effects of a mental or emotional problem. The mental health of our citizenry, no less than its physical health, is a public good of transcendent importance," Justice John Paul Stevens wrote for the majority.*

The case arose when a police officer and the clinical social worker she consulted after killing a man in the line of duty refused to make records of their sessions available during a federal civil rights case brought against the officer by the dead man's family. The trial judge ruled that the refusal was legally unjustified and that the jury could assume that the therapy records were incriminating. The Court of Appeals for the Seventh Circuit reversed, holding that "reason and experience" compelled recognition of a psychotherapist-patient confidentiality privilege.

In upholding the appeals court ruling, Stevens noted that "effective psychotherapy" depends on trust and confidence that the counseling will remain confidential. "Because of the sensitive nature of the problems for which individuals consult psychotherapists, disclosure of confidential communications made during counseling sessions may cause embarrassment or disgrace," Stevens wrote. "For this reason, the mere possibility of disclosure may impede development of the confidential relationship necessary for successful treatment."

The Court went beyond the appeals court ruling, however, in holding the privilege to be absolute, not a qualified one to be balanced by the need for disclosure, as the lower court had held. "Making the promise of confidentiality contingent upon a trial judge's later evaluation of the relative importance of the patient's interest in privacy and the evidentiary need for disclosure would eviscerate the effectiveness of the privilege," Stevens wrote. Stevens was joined by Justices Sandra Day O'Connor, David H. Souter, Anthony M. Kennedy, Ruth Bader Ginsburg, Clarence Thomas, and Stephen G. Breyer.

The majority extended the privilege to clinical social workers as well as to psychologists and psychiatrists, noting that these social workers provide "a significant amount" of counseling and that "their clients often include the poor and those of modest means" who might not be able to afford the services of either a psychologist or a psychiatrist.

In dissent, Justice Antonin Scalia said the Court was "creating a privilege that is new, vast, and ill-defined," one whose price would be "occasional injustice." Scalia questioned the public good to be had from psychotherapy and suggested that one might be better off consulting one's mother rather than a therapist. "Yet there is no mother-child privilege," he said. Chief Justice William H. Rehnquist joined a single part of Scalia's dissent objecting to extending the confidentiality privilege to clinical social workers.

The Congressional Provision

The mental health insurance provision was added to the fiscal 1997 appropriations bill for the Departments of Veterans' Affairs and Housing and Urban Development. The provision did not require group health insurance plans to offer mental health coverage, but if such coverage were offered, the plan had to set the same annual and lifetime limits for both mental illnesses and physical ailments. The mandate did not apply to companies with fifty or fewer employees and would be waived for companies if it caused their premiums to rise 1 percent or more. The requirement was scheduled to be in effect only from January 1, 1998, through September 30, 2001.

Sen. Pete V. Domenici, R-N.M., who had been seeking more equitable insurance treatment of the mentally ill for a decade, hailed passage of the provision. "Today we have a recognition that illnesses and diseases of the brain, when it comes to coverage, will no longer be discriminated against," he said on September 19 after House-Senate negotiators agreed to the provision. An estimated 40 million Americans have suffered from severe mental or emotional illness.

The provision was opposed by big business interests, who earlier in the year had killed a broader provision attached to legislation ensuring that workers' health insurance benefits were "portable." Although the Congressional Budget Office estimated that the provision would increase the cost of a typical fee-for-service plan by four-tenths of 1 percent, several companies said the costs were likely to be much higher. Helen Darling, manager of health programs at Xerox, said she feared "an explosion of costs."

The director of employee benefits at the accounting firm of KPMG Peat Marwick said that "some employers will look at these requirements and decide that it's too expensive for them to begin or continue providing health benefits." James A. Klein, the executive director of the Association of Private Pension and Welfare Plans, said employers were "likely to reduce other valuable benefits in order to accommodate the cost of the new mandates. If some specific benefits are required, different benefits valued by other workers will be sacrificed to pay for them."

Following are excerpts from the majority opinion, written by Justice John Paul Stevens, in the case of Jaffee v. Redmond, in which the Supreme Court ruled on June 13, 1996, that confidential consultations between psychiatrists, psychologists, clinical social workers, and their patients did not need to be disclosed in federal court proceedings:

No. 95-266

Carrie Jaffee, special administrator
for Ricky Allen, Sr., deceased,
Petitioner
v.
Mary Lu Redmond et al.

On writ of certiorari to the United
States Court of Appeals for the
Seventh Circuit

[June 13, 1996]

JUSTICE STEVENS delivered the opinion of the Court.

After a traumatic incident in which she shot and killed a man, a police officer received extensive counseling from a licensed clinical social worker. The question we address is whether statements the officer made to her therapist during the counseling sessions are protected from compelled disclosure in a federal civil action brought by the family of the deceased. Stated otherwise, the question is whether it is appropriate for federal courts to recognize a "psychotherapist privilege" under Rule 501 of the Federal Rules of Evidence.

I

Petitioner is the administrator of the estate of Ricky Allen. Respondents are Mary Lu Redmond, a former police officer, and the Village of Hoffman Estates, Illinois, her employer during the time that she served on the police force. Petitioner commenced this action against respondents after Redmond shot and killed Allen while on patrol duty.

On June 27, 1991, Redmond was the first officer to respond to a "fight in progress" call at an apartment complex. As she arrived at the scene, two of Allen's sisters ran toward her squad car, waving their arms and shouting that there had been a stabbing in one of the apartments. Redmond testified at trial that she relayed this information to her dispatcher and requested an ambulance. She then exited her car and walked toward the apartment building. Before Redmond reached the building, several men ran out, one waving a pipe. When the men ignored her order to get on the ground, Redmond drew her service revolver. Two other men then burst out of the building, one, Ricky Allen, chasing the other. According to Redmond, Allen was brandishing a butcher knife and disregarded her repeated commands to drop the weapon. Redmond shot Allen when she believed he was about to stab the man he was chasing. Allen died at the scene. Redmond testified that before other officers arrived to provide support, "people came pouring out of the buildings," . . . and a threatening confrontation between her and the crowd ensued.

Petitioner filed suit in Federal District Court alleging that Redmond had violated Allen's constitutional rights by using excessive force during the encounter at the apartment complex. . . . At trial, petitioner presented testimony from members of Allen's family that conflicted with Redmond's version of the incident in several important respects. They testified, for example, that Redmond drew her gun before exiting her squad car and that Allen was unarmed when he emerged from the apartment building.

During pretrial discovery petitioner learned that after the shooting Redmond had participated in about 50 counseling sessions with Karen Beyer, a clinical social worker licensed by the State of Illinois and employed at that time by the Village of Hoffman Estates. Petitioner sought access to Beyer's notes concerning the sessions for use in cross-examining Redmond. Respondents vigorously resisted the discovery. They asserted that the contents of the conversations between Beyer and Redmond were protected against involuntary disclosure by a psychotherapist-patient privilege. The district judge rejected this argument. Neither Beyer nor Redmond, however, complied with his order to disclose the contents of Beyer's notes. At depositions and on the witness stand both either refused to answer certain questions or professed an inability to recall details of their conversations.

In his instructions at the end of the trial, the judge advised the jury that the refusal to turn over Beyer's notes had no "legal justification" and that the jury could therefore presume that the contents of the notes would have been unfavorable to respondents. The jury awarded petitioner $45,000 on the federal claim and $500,000 on her state-law claim.

The Court of Appeals for the Seventh Circuit reversed and remanded for a new trial. Addressing the issue for the first time, the court concluded that "reason and experience," the touchstones for acceptance of a privilege under Rule 501 of the Federal Rules of Evidence, compelled recognition of a psychotherapist-patient privilege. . . . "Reason tells us that psychotherapists and patients share a unique relationship, in which the ability to communicate freely without the fear of public disclosure is the key to successful treatment." As to experience, the court observed that all 50 States have adopted some form of the psychotherapist-patient privilege. . . . The court attached particular significance to the fact that Illinois law expressly extends such a privilege to social workers like Karen Beyer. . . .

The Court of Appeals qualified its recognition of the privilege by stating that it would not apply if "in the interests of justice, the evidentiary need for the disclosure of the contents of a patient's counseling sessions outweighs that patient's privacy interests.". . . Balancing those conflicting interests, the court observed, on the one hand, that the evidentiary need for the contents of the confidential conversations was diminished in this case because there were numerous eyewitnesses to the shooting, and, on the other hand, that Officer Redmond's privacy interests were substantial. . . . Based on this assessment, the court concluded that the trial court had erred by refusing to afford protection to the confidential communications between Redmond and Beyer.

. . . Because of the conflict among the courts of appeals and the importance of the question, we granted certiorari. . . . We affirm.

II

. . . The common-law principles underlying the recognition of testimonial privileges can be stated simply. "'For more than three centuries it has now been recognized as a fundamental maxim that the public . . . has a right to every man's evidence. When we come to examine the various claims of exemption, we start with the primary assumption that there is a general duty to give what testimony one is capable of giving, and that any exemptions which may exist are distinctly exceptional, being so many derogations from a positive general rule.'" *United States* v. *Bryan* (1950). . . . Exceptions from the general rule disfavoring testimonial privileges may be justified, however, by a "'public good transcending the normally predominant principle of utilizing all rational means for ascertaining the truth.'" *Trammel* [v. *United States* (1950)], quoting *Elkins* v. *United States* (1960) (Frankfurter, J., dissenting).

Guided by these principles, the question we address today is whether a privilege protecting confidential communications between a psychotherapist and her patient "promotes sufficiently important interests to outweigh the need for probative evidence. . . ." [*Trammel*]. Both "reason and experience" persuade us that it does.

III

Like the spousal and attorney-client privileges, the psychotherapist-patient privilege is "rooted in the imperative need for confidence and trust." *Trammel.* Treatment by a physician for physical ailments can often proceed successfully on the basis of a physical examination, objective information supplied by the patient, and the results of diagnostic tests. Effective psychotherapy, by contrast, depends upon an atmosphere of confidence and trust in which the patient is willing to make a frank and complete disclosure of facts, emotions, memories, and fears. Because of the sensitive nature of the problems for which individuals consult psychotherapists, disclosure of confidential communications made during counseling sessions may cause embarrassment or disgrace. For this reason, the mere possibility of disclosure may impede development of the confidential relationship necessary for successful treatment. As the Judicial Conference Advisory Committee observed in 1972 when it recommended that Congress recognize a psychotherapist privilege as part of the Proposed Federal Rules of Evidence, a psychiatrist's ability to help her patients

> "is completely dependent upon [the patients'] willingness and ability to talk freely. This makes it difficult if not impossible for [a psychiatrist] to function without being able to assure . . . patients of confidentiality and, indeed, privileged communication. Where there may be exceptions to this general rule. . . , there is wide agreement that confidentiality is a sine qua non for successful psychiatric treatment." . . .

By protecting confidential communications between a psychotherapist and her patient from involuntary disclosure, the proposed privilege thus serves important private interests.

Our cases make clear that an asserted privilege must also "serv[e] public ends." *Upjohn Co.* v. *United States* (1981). Thus, the purpose of the attorney-client privilege is to "encourage full and frank communication between attorneys and their clients and thereby promote broader public interests in the observance of law and administration of justice." Ibid. And the spousal privilege, as modified in *Trammel*, is justified because it "furthers the important public interest in marital harmony". . . . The psychotherapist privilege serves the public interest by facilitating the provision of appropriate treatment for individuals suffering the effects of a mental or emotional problem. The mental health of our citizenry, no less than its physical health, is a public good of transcendent importance.

In contrast to the significant public and private interests supporting recognition of the privilege, the likely evidentiary benefit that would result from the denial of the privilege is modest. If the privilege were rejected, confidential conversations between psychotherapists and their patients would surely be chilled, particularly when it is obvious that the circumstances that give rise to the need for treatment will probably result in litigation. Without a privilege, much of the desirable evidence to which litigants such as petitioner seek access—for example, admissions against interest by a party—is unlikely to come into being. This unspoken "evidence" will therefore serve no greater truth-seeking function than if it had been spoken and privileged.

That it is appropriate for the federal courts to recognize a psychotherapist privilege under Rule 501 is confirmed by the fact that all 50 States and the District of Columbia have enacted into law some form of psychotherapist privilege. We have previously observed that the policy decisions of the States bear on the question whether federal courts should recognize a new privilege or amend the coverage of an existing one. . . . Because state legislatures are fully aware of the need to protect the integrity of the factfinding functions of their courts, the existence of a consensus among the States indicates that "reason and experience" support recognition of the privilege. In addition, given the importance of the patient's understanding that her communications with her therapist will not be publicly disclosed, any State's promise of confidentiality would have little value if the patient were aware that the privilege would not be honored in a federal court. Denial of the federal privilege therefore would frustrate the purposes of the state legislation that was enacted to foster these confidential communications. . . .

Because we agree with the judgment of the state legislatures and the Advisory Committee that a psychotherapist-patient privilege will serve a "public good transcending the normally predominant principle of utilizing all rational means for ascertaining truth," *Trammel*, we hold that confidential communications between a licensed psychotherapist and her patients in the course of diagnosis or treatment are protected from compelled disclosure under Rule 501 of the Federal Rules of Evidence.

IV

All agree that a psychotherapist privilege covers confidential communications made to licensed psychiatrists and psychologists. We have no hesitation in concluding in this case that the federal privilege should also extend to confidential communications made to licensed social workers in the course of psychotherapy. The reasons for recognizing a privilege for treatment by psychiatrists and psychologists apply with equal force to treatment by a clinical social worker such as Karen Beyer. Today, social workers provide a significant amount of mental health treatment. . . . Their clients often include the poor and those of modest means who could not afford the assistance of a psychiatrist or psychologist . . . but whose counseling sessions serve the same public goals. Perhaps in recognition of these circumstances, the vast majority of States explicitly extend a testimonial privilege to licensed social workers. We therefore agree with the Court of Appeals that "[d]rawing a distinction between the counseling provided by costly psychotherapists and the counseling provided by more readily accessible social workers serves no discernible public purpose."

We part company with the Court of Appeals on a separate point. We reject the balancing component of the privilege implemented by that court and a small number of States. Making the promise of confidentiality contingent upon a trial judge's later evaluation of the relative importance of the patient's interest in privacy and the evidentiary need for disclosure would eviscerate the effectiveness of the privilege. As we explained in *Upjohn*, if the purpose of the privilege is to be served, the participants in the confidential conversation "must be able to predict with some degree of certainty whether particular discussions will be protected. An uncertain privilege, or one which purports to be certain but results in widely varying applications by the courts, is little better than no privilege at all."

These considerations are all that is necessary for decision of this case. A rule that authorizes the recognition of new privileges on a case-by-case basis makes it appropriate to define the details of new privileges in a like manner. Because this is the first case in which we have recognized a psychotherapist privilege, it is neither necessary nor feasible to delineate its full contours in a way that would "govern all conceivable future questions in this area."

V

The conversations between Officer Redmond and Karen Beyer and the notes taken during their counseling sessions are protected from compelled disclosure under Rule 501 of the Federal Rules of Evidence. The judgment of the Court of Appeals is affirmed.

It is so ordered.

CENSUS BUREAU ON
INCOME INEQUALITY
June 19, 1996

The gap between the richest and poorest Americans was higher in 1994 than it has been since the end of World War II, according to a Census Bureau report released June 19. The report confirmed what everyone already seemed to know—the rich were getting richer, while the poor and the middle class were either getting poorer or just holding their own. Changes in the labor market and in family demographics were thought to be the primary causes of the growing gap.

The report, entitled "A Brief Look at Postwar U.S. Income Inequality," looked at five different indicators assessing the distribution of money income among American households. All five showed an increasing income gap between 1968 and 1994. The Census Bureau also reviewed several experimental measures of income that add the value of noncash income, such as food stamps and employers' contributions to health insurance, and subtract taxes. Although such measures indicate the distribution of income is more equal, income inequality still grew between 1979 and 1994.

The implications of an ever-widening gap were not entirely clear. Some analysts have argued that two troubling trends—political alienation, as indicated by a steady drop-off in voter turnout, and a slower-growing economy—are results of the income disparity. "There are enormous social, political, and even moral consequences from widening inequality," Secretary of Labor Robert Reich told a reporter for USA Today. "A two-tiered society divided sharply between winners and losers ultimately is an unstable society."

Other analysts do not share the same degree of concern. They point to data showing large increases in the standard of living since the 1960s. "More people are living better even though they have less than the guys in the top 5 percent," said sociologist Seymour Martin Lipset. "The Horatio Alger notion is probably more alive today than at any time."

The most commonly used measure of income inequality is known as the Gini index, which ranges from zero if there is perfect income equality (that is, everyone receives an equal share of the total income distribution) to one if there is perfect inequality (that is, one person receives all the income). By that measure, inequality of family incomes declined 7.4 percent between 1947 and 1968. Since then the gap in family incomes has been widening, increasing 16.1 percent from 1968 to 1992. The index showed a large jump in income inequality between 1992 and 1993, which the Census Bureau said was caused partly by changes in the survey method. Although the bureau could not say how much of the jump was caused by the change, "there was nonetheless a real increase in inequality between 1992 and 1993."

Daniel Weinberg, the author of the report, said the increase in the income gap was significant regardless of any changes caused by shifting the measurement methodology. "Whether it's gone up 15 percent or 20 percent, it's still gone up," he told the New York Times. *"That's the basic story, and I hope that people don't get misled by this apparent dramatic increase since 1992."*

A second indicator measures the shares of total aggregate money income received by households. Households are typically grouped together in quintiles—the 20 percent with the highest aggregate share, the 20 percent with the next highest aggregate share, and so on. According to this measure, the share of aggregate household income received by the quintile with the lowest income declined, from 4.2 percent in 1969 to 3.6 percent in 1994; the share for the highest quintile rose from 43.0 percent to 49.1 percent in the same period. Even more telling, the richest 5 percent of households controlled 21.2 percent of the aggregate income in 1994.

The report said that much of the widening income gap could be traced to changes in the labor market. The wage distribution was growing more unequal, with workers at the top end of the wage scale experiencing gains in real wages (wages in which inflation has been taken into account), while workers toward the bottom of the wage scale had suffered declines in real wages. That gap was caused by a variety of factors, including the shift away from manufacturing jobs that offered high-wage opportunities for relatively low-skilled workers toward service jobs that place a premium on highly educated, highly skilled workers. Even within industries, the demand is greater for high-skilled workers than for low-skilled workers. Other factors that were putting downward pressure on workers with comparatively low skills were global competition, the increasing use of temporary workers, the eroding value of the minimum wage, a continuing decline in union membership, and increasing demands for workers with computer skills.

Demographic changes were also responsible for some of the widening income gap. One of these was the trend away from married-couple households toward single-parent and nonfamily households, which typically have lower incomes. Moreover, men with higher-than-average incomes were increasingly tending to marry women who also had higher-than-average incomes, thereby increasing the gap between rich and poor households.

*In the past those women would have stayed home to raise their children or,
because of discrimination, would not have had the education or the highly
skilled jobs held by their present-day counterparts.*

*Following is the text of the report, "A Brief Look at Postwar U.S.
Income Inequality," written by Daniel H. Weinberg and released
by the Bureau of the Census on June 19, 1996:*

Are the rich getting richer and the poor getting poorer?

*Historical Census Bureau statistics on income can shed some light on
that debate. Although the Bureau has been measuring incomes for a half-
century and a large number of factors have been identified as contributing
to changes in inequality, the root causes are still not entirely understood.*

The Census Bureau has been studying the distribution of income since the
late 1940's. The first income inequality statistics were published for families
and came from the annual demographic supplement to the Current Population Survey (CPS). The most commonly used measure of income inequality,
the Gini index (also known as the index of income concentration), indicated
a decline in family income inequality of 7.4 percent from 1947 to 1968. Since
1968, there has been an increase in income inequality, reaching its 1947 level
in 1982 and increasing further since then. The increase was 16.1 percent from
1968 to 1992 and 22.4 percent from 1968 to 1994. . . .

Living conditions of Americans have changed considerably since the late
1940's. In particular, a smaller fraction of all persons live in families (two or
more persons living together related by blood or marriage). Therefore, starting in 1967, the Census Bureau began reporting on the income distribution of
households in addition to families. By coincidence, 1968 was the year in
which measured postwar income was at its most equal for families. The Gini
index for households indicates that there has been growing income inequality over the past quarter-century. Inequality grew slowly in the 1970's and
rapidly during the early 1980's. From about 1987 through 1992, the growth in
measured inequality seemed to taper off, reaching 11.9 percent above its 1968
level. This was followed by a large apparent jump in 1993, partly due to a
change in survey methodology. The Gini index for households in 1994 was
17.5 percent above its 1968 level.

Income inequality measures such as the Gini index or shares of aggregate
income are particularly sensitive to changes in data collection measures. A
change that may only affect a relatively small number of cases (especially
those in the upper end of the income distribution) can affect these measures,
while having virtually no effect on median income. We are unable to determine what fraction of the measured increase in income inequality between
1992 and 1993 was due to changes in survey administration between those
two years, though our analysis suggests there was nonetheless a real
increase in inequality between 1992 and 1993.

... [The] share of aggregate household money income received by the highest income quintile (households with incomes above $62,841 in 1994) [is increasing]—49.1 percent in 1994 and 46.9 percent in 1992, up from 42.8 percent in 1968—and the ... share for households in the middle 60 percent and those in the bottom quintile (incomes below $13,426) [is declining]. During that same period, the share received by households in the top 5 percent of the income distribution went from 16.6 percent in 1968 to 18.6 percent in 1992 and 21.2 percent in 1994.

Yet another way to look at the change in inequality involves the income at selected positions in the income distribution. [I]n 1994 dollars the household at the 95th percentile in 1994 had $109,821 in income, 8.2 times that of the household at the 20th percentile, which was $13,426 (the comparable 1992 ratio was 7.9). In contrast, in 1968, the household at the 95th percentile had but 6.0 times the income of the household at the 20th percentile.

A parallel way to look at this change examines the average (mean) household income in each quintile. . . . The average income of households in the top quintile grew from $73,754 in 1968 to $96,240 in 1992 and $105,945 in 1994. In percentage terms, this growth was 30 percent from 1968 to 1992 and 44 percent from 1968 to 1994. During the 1968–1994 period, the average income in the bottom quintile grew by only 8 percent, from $7,202 to $7,762 (7 percent from 1968 to 1992). Consequently, the ratio of the average income of the top 20 percent of households to the average income of the bottom 20 percent went from 10.2 in 1968 to 12.5 in 1992 and 13.6 in 1994.

Yet one more way to look at the income distribution corrects for family size changes over the period, by examining the change in the ratio of family income to its poverty threshold. Poverty thresholds vary by family size and composition reflecting consumption efficiencies achieved through economies of scale (i.e., families of two or more persons can share certain goods such as housing). A ratio of 1.00 thus indicates that the family has an income equal to the poverty threshold for its size and composition. The average ratio in the bottom quintile in 1968 was 1.04, while the average in the top quintile was 6.13. By 1994, these ratios were 0.92 and 9.22, respectively (and 0.89 and 8.39 in 1992), also indicating a widening income gap. . . . The ratio for the middle quintile also rose, from 2.80 in 1968 to 3.26 in both 1992 and 1994.

In sum, when money income is examined, each of these indicators shows increasing income inequality over the 1968–1994 period. But, are there other perspectives that change this story?

Since 1979, the Census Bureau has examined several experimental measures of income. These measures add the value of noncash benefits (such as food stamps and employer contributions to health insurance) to, and subtract taxes from, the official money income measure. The Bureau's research in this area has shown that the distribution of income is more equal under a broadened definition of income that takes account of the effects of taxes and noncash benefits. Further, government transfer benefits play a much more equalizing role on income than do taxes. Nonetheless, while the levels of inequality are lower, this alternative perspective does not change the picture of increasing income inequality over the 1979–1994 period.

Why are these changes in inequality happening?

The long-run increase in income inequality is related to changes in the Nation's labor market and its household composition. The wage distribution has become considerably more unequal with more highly skilled, trained, and educated workers at the top experiencing real wage gains and those at the bottom real wage losses. One factor is the shift in employment from those goods-producing industries that have disproportionately provided high-wage opportunities for low-skilled workers, towards services that disproportionately employ college graduates, and towards low-wage sectors such as retail trade. But within-industry shifts in labor demand away from less-educated workers are perhaps a more important explanation of eroding wages than the shift out of manufacturing. Also cited as factors putting downward pressure on the wages of less-educated workers are intensifying global competition and immigration, the decline of the proportion of workers belonging to unions, the decline in the real value of the minimum wage, the increasing need for computer skills, and the increasing use of temporary workers.

At the same time, long-run changes in living arrangements have taken place that tend to exacerbate differences in household incomes. For example, divorces and separations, births out of wedlock, and the increasing age at first marriage have led to a shift away from married-couple households and toward single-parent and nonfamily households, which typically have lower incomes. Also, the increasing tendency over the period for men with higher-than-average earnings to marry women with higher-than-average earnings has contributed to widening the gap between high-income and low-income households. . . .

July

GAO ON GULF WAR PERFORMANCE OF U.S. "SMART" WEAPONS
July 2, 1996

Many high-technology weapons did not perform as well during the Persian Gulf War as the Pentagon and weapons manufacturers claimed—and some of those weapons were no better than older versions. That assessment came from the General Accounting Office (GAO), the investigative arm of Congress, in a report issued on July 2. The report, "Operation Desert Storm: Evaluation of the Air War," used Pentagon figures to measure the relative effectiveness of various types of aircraft and munitions used by the air force during the forty-three-day air war against Iraq in January and February 1991.

The GAO said its report was the first to correlate the damage done to strategic targets in Iraq with the type of weapons used against those targets. The full 250-page GAO report was classified; the published unclassified version contained an overview of the report and its major conclusions. A GAO team worked on the report between July 1992 and December 1995.

The Pentagon accepted most of the GAO findings and said it had been taking steps to correct the shortcomings the GAO had found in the weapons. Even so, the report generated some controversy. The Washington Post, *in an editorial on July 15, said the report's analysis "appears weak on questions of content and comparison." The next day, the* Post *printed an op-ed column by Eliot Cohen, professor of strategic studies at Johns Hopkins University's School of Advanced International Studies, strongly attacking the GAO report as "not merely incorrect, but, if taken to heart, downright dangerous." Cohen, who had directed a study of the Persian Gulf air war for the air force from 1991 to 1993, said the GAO appeared to be suggesting that the United States take "a technological step backward, to the day of cheap fighter planes and unguided missiles."*

GAO Findings

The GAO report's fundamental conclusion was that expensive, high-technology airplanes and munitions—often called "smart" weapons—did not

403

necessarily perform better in the Gulf War than older, "dumb" weapons lacking the latest technological innovations. High-tech weapons faced many of the same limitations as the older weapons, and some of the newer weapons needed ideal conditions (such as good weather) to work at peak performance.

The GAO cited interviews with pilots who said that high-tech lasers and other sensors used to detect targets on the ground did not work well in clouds, rain, fog, smoke, and even high humidity—factors often present during war. In such conditions, pilots said they could not determine with their sensors "whether a presumed target was a tank or a truck and whether it had already been destroyed." Much of the GAO report also focused on the inability of military and intelligence agencies to provide commanders with accurate and timely assessments of the damage inflicted on Iraqi targets by the allied air campaign.

Pilots and their planes were safer when they flew at medium and high altitudes, but high-tech sensors did not work as well when they were further from their targets. The GAO also said that high-cost airplanes, in particular the F-117 "Stealth" fighter, did not necessarily out-perform older planes. In some cases, the GAO said, the more expensive planes had greater operating limitations.

Much of the media's attention during the Gulf War was focused on high-tech missiles and bombs, especially the Patriot surface-to-air missile and the Tomahawk guided cruise missile. The GAO report did not discuss the Patriot missile, which was shown by numerous reports after the war to have been much less effective than advertised in stopping Iraqi Scud missiles. The GAO said its study was unable to validate claims for the effectiveness of the Tomahawk and other guided or smart munitions.

The GAO noted that guided munitions were costly; in tonnage, they represented only 8 percent of all bombs and missiles used during the war but consumed 84 percent of the total cost. In addition, the costly guided munitions often needed "specific operating conditions to operate effectively," the GAO said, and such conditions were not always present during the Gulf War and cannot be assumed for any future conflict.

In summary, the GAO said, claims by the Pentagon and weapons makers about the performance of specific high-tech weapons "were overstated, misleading, inconsistent with the best available data, or unverifiable." The GAO said this assessment applied specifically to the Stealth fighter, the Tomahawk cruise missile, and laser-guided bombs.

GAO Recommendations

The GAO offered three main recommendations, each stemming from military shortcomings evident during the Gulf War. First, the GAO said the Pentagon should analyze the performance of target sensors—such as lasers—in varying weather conditions and at different altitudes. New or improved sensors also should be tested under "fully realistic" conditions at least as stressful as the ones that hurt the effectiveness of sensors during the Gulf War.

Second, the GAO said the Pentagon needed to work harder to resolve problems in determining the actual damage to targets caused by U.S. weapons. The timeliness and accuracy of bomb damage assessments must be improved, the GAO said, in part by cultivating intelligence sources.

In its most controversial recommendation, the GAO said the Pentagon should reconsider its increasing reliance on expensive guided munitions, such as cruise missiles and smart bombs. The Gulf War demonstrated that, under some circumstances, older unguided munitions "proved equally or more effective," the GAO said. This recommendation applied specifically to "asymmetrical warfare"—cases such as the Gulf War, where the United States has overwhelming military superiority against a military foe.

Following are excerpts from the unclassified version of the General Accounting Office report, "Operation Desert Storm: Evaluation of the Air War," issued July 2, 1996:

Background

Operation Desert Storm was primarily a sustained 43-day air campaign by the United States and its allies against Iraq between January 17, 1991, and February 28, 1991. It was the first large employment of U.S. air power since the Vietnam war, and by some measures (particularly the low number of U.S. casualties and the short duration of the campaign), it was perhaps the most successful war fought by the United States in the 20th century. The main ground campaign occupied only the final 100 hours of the war.

The air campaign involved nearly every type of fixed-wing aircraft in the U.S. inventory, flying about 40,000 air-to-ground and 50,000 support sorties. Approximately 1,600 U.S. combat aircraft were deployed by the end of the war. By historical standards, the intensity of the air campaign was substantial. The U.S. bomb tonnage dropped per day was equivalent to 85 percent of the average daily bomb tonnage dropped by the United States on Germany and Japan during the course of World War II.

Operation Desert Storm provided a valuable opportunity to assess the performance of U.S. combat aircraft and munitions systems under actual combat conditions. Unlike operational tests or small-scale hostilities, the air campaign involved a very large number of conventional systems from all four services used in tandem, which permits potentially meaningful cross-system comparisons. The combat data in this report can be seen as an extension of the performance data generated by DOD's operational test and evaluation programs that we have previously reviewed.

Objectives

To respond to your questions about the effectiveness of the air campaign; the performance of individual weapon systems; the accuracy of contractor claims, particularly in regard to stealth technology and the F-117; and the relationship between the cost of weapon systems and their performance and contributions to the success of the air campaign, we established the following report objectives:

1. Determine the use, performance, and effectiveness of individual weapon systems in pursuit of Desert Storm's objectives, and in particular, the extent to which the data from the conflict support the claims that DOD and weapon contractors have made about weapon system performance.
2. Describe the relationship between cost and performance for the weapon systems employed.
3. Identify the degree to which the goals of Desert Storm were achieved by air power.
4. Identify the key factors aiding or inhibiting the effectiveness of air power.
5. Identify the contributions and limitations of advanced technologies to the accomplishments of the air campaign.
6. Determine whether the unique conditions of Desert Storm limit the lessons learned.

Summary

Operation Desert Storm was a highly successful and decisive military operation. The air campaign, which incurred minimal casualties while effecting the collapse of the Iraqis' ability to resist, helped liberate Kuwait and elicit Iraqi compliance with U.N. resolutions. However, our analysis of the air campaign against strategic targets revealed several air power issues that require attention before the next campaign. First, the effectiveness of air power in Desert Storm was inhibited by the aircraft sensors' inherent limitations in identifying and acquiring targets and by DOD's failure to gather intelligence on the existence or location of certain critical targets and its inability to collect and disseminate timely battle damage assessments (BDA). Pilots noted that infrared, electro-optical, and laser systems were all seriously degraded by clouds, rain, fog, smoke, and even high humidity, and the pilots reported being unable to discern whether a presumed target was a tank or a truck and whether it had already been destroyed. The failure of intelligence to identify certain targets precluded any opportunity for the coalition to fully accomplish some of its objectives. And the reduced accuracies from medium and high altitudes and absence of timely BDA led to higher costs, reduced effectiveness, and increased risks from making unnecessary restrikes.

Second, U.S. commanders were able to favor medium- to high-altitude strike tactics that maximized aircraft and pilot survivability, rather than weapon system effectiveness. This was because of early and complete air superiority, a limited enemy response, and terrain and climate conditions generally conducive to air strikes. Low-altitude munitions deliveries had been emphasized in prewar training, but they were abandoned early. The subsequent deliveries from medium and high altitudes resulted in the use of sensors and weapon systems at distances from targets that were not optimal for their identification, acquisition, or accuracy. Medium- and high-altitude tactics also increased the exposure of aircraft sensors to man-made and natural impediments to visibility.

Third, the success of the sustained air campaign resulted from the availability of a mix of strike and support assets. Its substantial weight of effort was made possible, in significant part, by the variety and number of air-to-ground aircraft types from high-payload bombers, such as the B-52, to platforms capable of delivering guided munitions such as the stealthy F-117, to high-sortie-rate attack aircraft such as the A-10. A range of target types, threat conditions, and tactical and strategic objectives was best confronted with a mix of weapon systems and strike and support assets with a range of capabilities.

Fourth, despite often sharp contrasts in the unit cost of aircraft platforms, it is inappropriate, given aircraft use, performance, and effectiveness demonstrated in Desert Storm, to characterize higher cost aircraft as generally more capable than lower cost aircraft. In some cases, the higher cost systems had the greater operating limitations; in some other cases, the lower cost aircraft had the same general limitations but performed at least as well; and in still other cases, the data did not permit a differentiation.

Fifth, "one-target, one-bomb" efficiency was not achieved. The air campaign data did not validate the purported efficiency or effectiveness of guided munitions, without qualification. On average, more than 11 tons of guided and 44 tons of unguided munitions were delivered on targets assessed as successfully destroyed; still more tonnage of both was delivered against targets where objectives were not fully met. Large tonnages of munitions were used against targets not only because of inaccuracy from high altitudes but also because BDA data were lacking. Although the relative contribution of guided munitions in achieving target success is unknowable, they did account for the bulk of munitions costs. Only 8 percent of the delivered munitions tonnage was guided, but at a price that represented 84 percent of the total munitions cost. During Desert Storm, the ratio of guided-to-unguided munitions delivered did not vary, indicating that the relative preferences among these types of munitions did not change over the course of the campaign. More generally, Desert Storm demonstrated that many systems incorporating complex or advanced technologies require specific operating conditions to operate effectively. These conditions, however, were not consistently encountered in Desert Storm and cannot be assumed in future contingencies.

Lastly, many of DOD's and manufacturers' postwar claims about weapon system performance—particularly the F-117, TLAM, and laser-guided bombs—were overstated, misleading, inconsistent with the best available data, or unverifiable.

Scope and Methodology

Scope

In this report, we evaluate the aircraft and munitions that we deemed to have had a major role in the execution of the Desert Storm air campaign by virtue of their satisfying at least one (in most cases, two) of the following criteria. The system

- played a major role against strategic targets (broadly defined),
- was the focus of congressional interest,
- may be considered by DOD for future major procurement,
- appeared likely to play a role in future conflicts, or
- even if not slated currently for major procurement, either was used by allied forces in a manner or role different from its U.S. use or used new technologies likely to be employed in the future.

These criteria led us to assess the A-6E, A-10, B-52, F-111F, F-117A, F-15E, F-16, F/A-18, and British Tornado (GR-1). We examined both guided and unguided munitions, including laser-guided bombs, Maverick missiles, Tomahawk land-attack (cruise) missiles (TLAMs), and unguided "dumb" bombs.

We assess the effectiveness of various U.S. and allied air campaign aircraft and weapon systems in destroying ground targets, primarily those that fall into the category of "strategic" targets. We focused our analysis on strategic targets in part because they received the best documented BDA, although there was substantial variation from target to target and among target types in the quantity and quality of BDA. . . .

Historically, studies of air power have articulated differing points of view on the relative merits of focusing air attacks on targets deemed to be strategic (such as government leadership, military industry, and electrical generation) and focusing them on tactical targets (such as frontline armor and artillery). These contending points of view have been debated in many official and unofficial sources. In this study, we did not directly address this debate because data and other limitations (discussed below) did not permit a rigorous analysis of whether attacks against strategic targets contributed more to the success of Desert Storm than attacks against tactical targets.

Methodology

Data Sources

A primary goal of our work was to cross-validate the best available data on aircraft and weapon system performance, both qualitative and quantitative, to test for consistency, accuracy, and reliability. The data we analyzed in this report are the best information collected during the war. They were compiled for and used by the commanders who managed the air campaign. These data also provided the basis for postwar DOD and manufacturer assessments of aircraft and weapon system performance during Desert Storm. We balanced the limitations of the data, to the extent possible, against qualitative analyses of the systems. For example, we compared claims made for system performance and contributions to what was supportable given all the available data, both quantitative and qualitative.

We collected and analyzed data from a broad range of sources, including the major DOD databases that document the strike histories of the war and cumulative damage to targets; numerous after-action and lessons-learned reports from military units that participated in the war; intelligence reports; analyses performed by DOD contractors; historical accounts of the war from the media and other published literature; and interviews with participants, including more than 100 Desert Storm pilots and key individuals in the planning and execution of the war. We also interviewed key Desert Storm planners and analysts from a wide spectrum of organizations, both within and outside DOD.

After we collected and analyzed the air campaign information, we interviewed DOD, Joint Chiefs of Staff, and service representatives and reviewed plans for the acquisition and use of weapon systems in future campaigns to observe how the lessons learned from Desert Storm have been applied. Our analyses were also reviewed by several experts on either air power issues in general or the conduct of Operation Desert Storm in particular.

Data Analysis

To compare the nature and magnitude of the power that Operation Desert Storm employed against strategic targets to the nature of outcomes, we analyzed two databases—the "Missions" database generated by the Air Force's Gulf War Air Power Survey (GWAPS) research group (to assess inputs) and the Defense Intelligence Agency's (DIA's) phase III battle damage assessment reports (to assess outcomes). The Missions database represents a strike history of air-to-ground platforms and ordnance in the Persian Gulf war. There are data on 862 targets, with basic encyclopedia (or BE) numbers, that together comprise more than 1 million pieces of strike information. The phase III reports provided the best cumulative all-source functional BDA for each strategic target available to planners during the course of the war.

To determine the use of aircraft and munitions in achieving air campaign objectives, we used the Missions database to determine weight-of-effort (WOE) and type-of-effort (TOE) measures at two levels. First, we calculated WOE and TOE at the broad level of the target category for each of the 12 strategic target categories shown in appendix II. Second, we calculated WOE and TOE for each aircraft and TLAM across the 12 categories.

We used phase III reports on fixed strategic targets to determine the extent to which the functional capabilities of the target had been eliminated. To correlate outcomes on targets with the input to them, we matched phase III data with data in the Missions database. For strategic targets where both BDA and WOE/TOE data existed, we sought to assess the relationship between the WOE and TOE data representing campaign inputs with phase III BDA data representing campaign outcomes, at the target level. While this methodology has limitations, no other study of Desert Storm has produced the target-specific input-outcome database that can be derived from merging these sources.

Study Strengths and Limitations

This analysis of the campaign and aircraft and munitions use and effectiveness benefited from our use of the most comprehensive strike and BDA data produced from the Persian Gulf war, a previously untried methodology to match inputs and outputs on targets; additional qualitative and quantitative data obtained from Desert Storm veterans and after-action reports to corroborate information in the primary databases; and our utilization of the results of other Desert Storm analyses, such as the Gulf War Air Power Survey.

This study is the first to match available Desert Storm strike and BDA data by target and to attempt to assess the effectiveness of multiple weapon systems across target categories. Despite the data limitations discussed below, our methodology provided systematic information on how weapon systems were employed, what level and types of weapons were required to achieve success, and the relative cost-effectiveness of multiple platforms. The reliability and validity of these findings are strengthened by our use of interviews, after-action reports, and other Desert Storm analyses to better understand platform performance variables and place the results of our effectiveness analyses in the appropriate context.

Our analyses of campaign inputs (from the Missions database) and outcomes (from the phase III reports) against ground targets have limitations of both scope and reliability imposed by constraints in the primary Desert Storm databases. Systematically correlating munition inputs against targets to outcomes was made highly problematic by the fact that the phase III BDA reports did not provide a comprehensive compilation of BDA for all strategic targets and could not differentiate the effects of one system from another on the same target.

We sought to work around data limitations through qualitative analysis of systems, based on diverse sources. Claims made for system performance were assessed in light of the most rigorous evaluation that could be made with the *available* data. We have explicitly noted data insufficiencies and uncertainties. Overall, data gaps and inconsistencies made an across-the-board cost-effectiveness evaluation difficult. However, there were sufficient data either to assess all the major claims made by DOD for the performance of the major systems studied or to indicate where the data are lacking to support certain claims.

We conducted our work between July 1992 and December 1995 in accordance with generally accepted government auditing standards.

Conclusions

We reached the following conclusions from our review of the air campaign:

- DOD's future ability to conduct an efficient, effective, and comprehensive air campaign will depend partly on its ability to enhance sensor capabilities, particularly at medium altitudes and in adverse weather, in order to identify valid targets and collect, analyze, and disseminate timely BDA.
- A key parameter in future weapon systems design, operational testing and evaluation, training, and doctrine will be pilot and aircraft survivability.

- The scheduled retirement of strike and attack aircraft such as the A-6E, F-111F, and most A-10s will make Desert Storm's variety and number of aircraft unavailable by the year 2000.
- The cost of guided munitions (now estimated to be over $58 billion), their intelligence requirements, and the limitations on their effectiveness demonstrated in Desert Storm need to be considered by DOD and the services as they determine the optimal future mix of guided and unguided munitions.

DOD and associated agencies have undertaken initiatives since the war to address many, but not all, of the limitations of the air campaign that we identified in our summary and conclusions. We have not analyzed each of these initiatives in this report; however, we briefly describe those that apply to one or more of our conclusions below.

First, DOD officials told us that the most sophisticated targeting sensors used in Desert Storm (which were available only in limited quantities) have now been deployed on many more fighter aircraft, thereby giving them a capability to deliver guided munitions. However, the same limitations exhibited by these advanced sensor and targeting systems in Desert Storm—limited fields-of-view, insufficient resolution for target discrimination at medium altitudes, vulnerabilities to adverse weather, and limited traverse movement—remain today.

Second, DOD officials told us that to address the Desert Storm BDA analysis and dissemination shortcomings, they have created an organization to work out issues, consolidate national reporting, and provide leadership; developed DOD-wide doctrine, tactics, techniques, and procedures; established more rigorous and realistic BDA training and realistic exercises; and developed and deployed better means to disseminate BDA. However, DOD officials acknowledge that additional problems remain with improving BDA timeliness and accuracy, developing nonlethal BDA functional damage indicators (particularly for new weapons that produce nontraditional effects), and cultivating intelligence sources to identify and validate strategic targets. Moreover, as our analyses of the air campaign revealed, timely and accurate BDA is crucial for the efficient employment of high-cost guided munitions (that is, for avoiding unnecessary restrikes). Therefore, acquisition plans for guided munitions must take fully into account actual BDA collection and dissemination capabilities before a final determination can be made on how much to acquire.

Third, DOD officials told us that survivability is now being emphasized in pilot training, service and joint doctrine, and weapon system development. Pilot training was modified immediately after the air campaign to meet challenges such as medium-altitude deliveries in a high antiaircraft artillery and infrared surface-to-air missile threat environment. Service and joint doctrine now reflect the lessons learned from Desert Storm's asymmetrical conflict. Several fighter aircraft employment manuals specifically incorporate the tactics that emphasized survivability in the campaign. DOD and service procurement plans include new munitions with global positioning system guidance systems, justified in part by their abilities to minimize the medium-altitude shortcomings and adverse weather limitations of Desert Storm while maximizing pilot and aircraft survivability.

Fourth, DOD officials told us that although Desert Storm's successful aircraft mix will not be available for the next contingency, DOD and the services have made plans to maintain an inventory of aircraft that they believe will be more flexible and effective in the future. Flexibility will be anticipated partly from the modernization of existing multirole fighters to enable them to deliver guided munitions (the aircraft systems being retired are single-role platforms), and their effectiveness is expected to increase as new and more accurate guided munitions are put in the field. However, we believe that strike aircraft modernization and munition procurement plans that include increasing the number and variety of guided munitions and the number of platforms capable of delivering them require additional justification.

Recommendations

Desert Storm established a paradigm for asymmetrical post-cold war conflicts. The coalition possessed quantitative and qualitative superiority in aircraft, munitions, intelligence, personnel, support, and doctrine. It dictated when the conflict should start, where operations should be conducted, when the conflict should end, and how terms of the peace should read. This paradigm—conflict where the relative technological advantages for the U.S. forces are high and the acceptable level of risk or attrition for the U.S. forces is low—underlies the service modernization plans for strike aircraft and munitions. Actions on the following recommendations will help ensure that high-cost munitions can be employed more efficiently at lower risk to pilots and aircraft and that the future mix of guided and unguided munitions is appropriate and cost-effective given the threats, exigencies, and objectives of potential contingencies.

Specifically,

- In light of the shortcomings of the sensors in Desert Storm, we recommend that the Secretary of Defense analyze and identify DOD's need to enhance the capabilities of existing and planned sensors to effectively locate, discriminate, and acquire targets in varying weather conditions and at different altitudes. Furthermore, the Secretary should ensure that any new sensors or enhancements of existing ones are tested under fully realistic operational conditions that are at least as stressful as the conditions that impeded capabilities in Desert Storm.

- In light of the shortcomings in BDA exhibited during Desert Storm and BDA's importance to strike planning, the BDA problems that DOD officials acknowledge continue today despite DOD postwar initiatives need to be addressed. These problems include timeliness, accuracy, capacity, assessment of functional damage, and cultivating intelligence sources to identify and validate strategic targets. We recommend that the Secretary of Defense expand DOD's current efforts to include such activities so that BDA problems can be fully resolved.

- In light of the quantities and mix of guided and unguided munitions that proved successful in Desert Storm, the services' increasing reliance on guided munitions to conduct asymmetrical warfare may not be appropriate. The Secretary should reconsider DOD's proposed mix of guided and unguided munitions. A reevaluation is warranted based on Desert Storm experiences that demonstrated limitations in the effectiveness of guided munitions; survivability concerns for aircraft delivering these munitions; and circumstances where less complex, less constrained unguided munitions proved equally or more effective.

Agency Comments

The Department of Defense partially concurred with each of our three recommendations. In their response to a draft of our report, DOD did not dispute our conclusions; rather, they reported that several initiatives were underway that will rectify the shortcomings and limitations demonstrated in Desert Storm. Specifically, they cited (1) the acquisition of improved and new precision-guided munitions, (2) two studies in process—Deep Attack/Weapons Mix Study (DAWMS) and Precision Strike Architecture study, and (3) several proposed fiscal year 1997 Advanced Concept Technology Demonstrations (ACTDs) as programs capable of correcting Desert Storm shortcomings. In addition, DOD emphasized the importance of providing funds to retain the operational test and evaluation function to ensure the rigorous testing of our weapons and weapon systems.

We agree that the actions cited by DOD address the shortcomings in sensors, guided munitions, and battle damage assessment we report here. However, the degree to which these initiatives are effective can be determined only after rigorous operational test and evaluation of both new and existing munitions and after the recommendations resulting from the Deep Attack/Weapons Mix and Precision Strike Architecture studies have been implemented and evaluated. Moreover, we concur with the continuing need for operational test and evaluation and underscore the role of this function in rectifying the shortcomings cited in this report.

DOD also provided us with a list of recommended technical corrections. Where appropriate, we have addressed these comments in our report.

AGRICULTURE SECRETARY ON NEW MEAT INSPECTION RULES
July 6, 1996

The Clinton administration on July 6 announced the first major reform in nearly ninety years of federal regulations governing the safety of meat and poultry. The new regulations, which were to be phased in over three years, for the first time required scientific testing of meat and poultry to detect the bacteria responsible for most cases of food poisoning.

The government, the meat industry, and consumer advocacy groups had been debating meat inspection standards for more than a decade. That debate was spurred by a 1985 report by the National Academy of Sciences recommending the scientific testing of meat. Political pressure for action came after an outbreak of food poisoning in January 1993, when several hundred people became ill and three children died after eating undercooked hamburgers at a fast food chain.

Some elements of the meat industry had resisted new inspection standards, and congressional Republicans tried unsuccessfully in 1995 to prevent the Department of Agriculture from putting standards into effect. Agriculture Secretary Dan Glickman said the government made compromises to get industry support for the new standards. Following the July 6 announcement, several meat industry groups said they supported the reforms.

The federal government began inspecting meat in 1907, one year after the publication of Upton Sinclair's muckraking novel, The Jungle, *which exposed unsanitary conditions at slaughterhouses and meat packing plants. The government required basic sanitary standards in meat plants but its inspections involved no scientific testing for hidden bacteria; instead, Agriculture Department inspectors would examine and smell meat for obvious signs of decay or disease. The basic inspection standards had not changed from 1907 until the 1996 revision.*

New Standards

The new standards will not replace the old-fashioned "poke and sniff" meat inspections, Glickman said. They will put more emphasis on pre-

venting meat contamination than on catching it once it occurs. The new rules consisted of four major elements:

First, each of the 6,200 meat and poultry plants inspected by the federal government was required to establish a plan called Hazard Analysis and Critical Control Points (or HACCP, pronounced Has–ip). For each plant, the plan would identify the critical points at which meat can be contaminated, such as cutting and grinding, and show the steps taken to reduce the risk of contamination. Each plant must demonstrate to federal inspectors how its plan works, and inspectors can regularly spot check it. This requirement was to be phased in; large plants were required to have their plans in place within eighteen months and smaller plants were given thirty to forty-two months to comply. The Food and Drug Administration in December 1995 ordered seafood processors to adopt similar HACCP plans.

Second, every slaughterhouse was required to regularly test carcasses for the generic E. coli bacteria, which is considered the best indicator of fecal contamination that produces harmful bacteria. Testing was to begin in 1997.

Third, the Agriculture Department will regularly test for the presence of salmonella bacteria in meat at slaughterhouses and meat processing plants. Some salmonella is almost always present in meat, especially poultry; new Agriculture Department standards would determine acceptable levels in each type of meat. For example, salmonella could be present in up to 20 percent of the whole chickens and up to 49.9 percent of the ground turkey produced by any given plant. The Agriculture Department began its salmonella testing program in September 1996 and planned to reduce the acceptable levels of contamination by 1998.

Michael R. Taylor, acting undersecretary of agriculture for food safety, said this testing requirement represented a "major shift" in policy because, for the first time, meat plants would be legally required to reduce bacteria levels. A plant that did not meet the new standards would be ordered to comply and, if it failed to do so, could be ordered to shut down.

Fourth, every slaughterhouse and meat processing plant was required to adopt sanitary operating procedures to reduce meat contamination. Plants were required to have these procedures in effect in 1997.

Costs and Benefits of New Rules

The government estimated that the new standards would cost the meat industry an additional $100 million a year—a figure Taylor said represented about one-tenth of a cent per pound of meat produced in the United States. By reducing the risk of food poisoning, the standards could save consumers an estimated $1 billion to $4 billion a year in health costs, he said. The Agriculture Department estimated that as many as four thousand deaths and five million illnesses in the United States each year could be traced to consumption of contaminated meat.

Glickman said the new standards would not cost taxpayers more money because the Agriculture Department would implement the new program within its current budget by streamlining its operations. Glickman on July 26 announced a reorganization of the Food Safety and Inspection Service, including a consolidation of the bureau's management and field units. The service had 9,200 full-time employees, most of whom were plant inspectors.

Taylor acknowledged that some elements of the meat industry had resisted new federal regulation, but he said failure to enact new standards "will be costly to everybody" because of possible threats to public confidence in meat safety. Taylor noted that, after the outbreak of the "mad cow" disease in Great Britain, meat consumption in Germany—where there was no threat of the disease—dropped by 50 percent. "What we have to understand is that by increasing the public confidence that the system is testing for the things that need to be tested, the public's desire to buy meat and poultry will be significantly augmented, not reduced," he said.

Following is the text of the written announcement July 6, 1996, by Agriculture Secretary Dan Glickman of new federal standards for inspections of meat and poultry plants:

My most fundamental responsibility as Secretary of Agriculture is ensuring that American families have the safest meat and poultry possible. Since joining the President's Cabinet, I have been personally involved in and committed to putting the HACCP/Pathogen Reduction rulemaking into effect.

The reason I have been so committed is simple. We had to improve the safety of American meat and poultry. The current system had not been fundamentally changed for 90 years, and it had a critical gap: It did not focus on the most serious public health problem of pathogenic bacteria such as E. coli 0157:H7 and Salmonella, which cause thousands of deaths and millions of illnesses every year.

And the Hazard Analysis and Critical Control Point (HACCP)/Pathogen Reduction final rule we are releasing today will do just that: Improve the safety of American meat and poultry by directly targeting the reduction of the pathogens that cause foodborne illness. It is the most significant achievement I've seen since I came to the U.S. Department of Agriculture, and it will revolutionize the way we ensure the safety of American meat and poultry.

I wish I could take all the credit, but I have to share it with a whole lot of people—beginning with President Clinton. This rule is an example of how this Administration responds to the basic needs of individuals. And it is an example of how this Administration feels about keeping American families safe.

I have to thank all of the constituents, consumer groups, industry representatives, agricultural producers, and scientists who participated in our public meetings on the HACCP proposal. And I want to thank the families who lost loved ones to foodborne illnesses who forcefully—and rightfully—have demanded that USDA take action to improve the safety of our meat and poultry.

We learned a great deal from meeting with all these groups and from all of the comments we received during the rulemaking process. As a result, the final rule is better than the proposed rule. It will improve food safety—our primary objective—while costing less.

Our first obligation has always been to meet our public health and safety responsibilities. But we knew these policies had to be practical and had to make good common sense.

We have announced a new rule. And with it, we will start a new—a revolutionary—way of doing business. HACCP represents sweeping reform and a fundamental modernization of the food inspection system.

By incorporating science-based controls and microbiological testing directly targeted at preventing and reducing contamination of meat and poultry with harmful bacteria such as E. coli 0157:H7 and Salmonella, the HACCP/Pathogen Reduction rule will save lives and reduce foodborne illness.

In 1962, author Upton Sinclair said, "You don't have to be satisfied with America as you find it. You can change it." Fifty-six years earlier, he wrote *The Jungle*, an exposé of the nation's meat packing industry that led to the last fundamental modernization of our meat safety system. It is long past due the time to change America again.

We are bringing modern technology and sound science into the nation's food processing plants. The public has demanded nothing less, and we intend to deliver. If meat and poultry is stamped "USDA Inspected," consumers expect the product to be safe to eat. And it should be.

When I was sworn in as Secretary of Agriculture—after my mother expressed her pride—she gave one instruction: "Make sure the food is safe." I haven't been able to rest easy until I could assure my mother that I had done what she asked.

Even when this new system is implemented, American consumers still need to follow safe handling instructions and be careful how they handle raw meat and poultry, and make sure that meat is well-cooked before they eat it. Our meat and poultry is safe now, but the HACCP/Pathogen Reduction rule will make it even safer.

SURGEON GENERAL ON THE BENEFITS OF PHYSICAL EXERCISE
July 11, 1996

Most Americans could markedly lower their risk of premature death with only moderate amounts of physical activity, according to a report of the surgeon general released July 11. "You don't have to be training for the Boston Marathon to derive real health benefits from physical activity," Donna Shalala, secretary of health and human services, said in a message accompanying the report. "A regular, preferably daily regimen of at least 30–45 minutes of brisk walking, bicycling, or even working around the house or yard will reduce your risks of developing coronary heart disease, hypertension, colon cancer, and diabetes."

Although that might sound like a simple prescription to some, a majority of Americans could find it difficult medicine to swallow. According to the report, 60 percent of American adults did not engage in regular physical activity, and 25 percent of all adults were not physically active at all. The statistics for youngsters were even more worrisome. Nearly half of all adolescents aged twelve to twenty-one were not vigorously active on a regular basis. Studies found that physical activity declined dramatically during adolescence. Overall, an estimated 250,000 deaths in the United States each year—about 12 percent of the total—could be linked to a sedentary life style.

The 278-page report, entitled Physical Activity and Health, *was the first of the Surgeon General's annual reports to focus on the benefits of exercise. Prepared by the Centers for Disease Control and Prevention (CDC), the National Center for Chronic Disease Prevention and Health Promotion, and the President's Council on Physical Fitness and Sports, with help from several of the National Institutes of Health, it summarized results on a multitude of studies of physical activity. It was signed by acting Surgeon General Audrey F. Manley. The report's release was timed to coincide with public interest in the 1996 summer Olympic Games, which were scheduled to begin in Atlanta later in the month.*

The report's emphasis on moderate activity represented a change from the 1970s when many medical experts and organizations, such as the

American Heart Association, advised vigorous aerobic exercise of at least twenty minutes three times a week to reduce the risks of heart disease. More recently most of these groups and public health experts in the federal government had begun to publicize the benefits of moderate exercise. Numerous studies showed that regular exercise lowered overall risk of premature death. While estimates varied on the amount of exercise required, sedentary people appeared to be about twice as likely as active people to die prematurely. "People who go from a sedentary life style to moderate activity cut their heart disease mortality rate in half," said Steven N. Blair, director of epidemiology at the Cooper Institute for Aerobics Research in Dallas and the senior scientific editor of the surgeon general's report.

In addition to reducing the risk of coronary heart disease, colon cancer, high blood pressure, and diabetes, moderate physical exercise was necessary to maintain normal muscle and joint strength and to aid normal skeletal development, the report stated. It was unclear whether physical activity could reduce the loss of bone mass in postmenopausal women, a condition that leads to osteoporosis. Other benefits include reduced risk of depression and enhanced quality of life. "Becoming active has many long-term benefits in preventing and controlling numerous diseases, but there are also immediate benefits in improving the quality of daily life," said David Satcher, director of the CDC. "We know that people feel better, sleep better, and have a more positive outlook on life when they get regular physical exercise."

The report focused on endurance-type activity, such as walking or biking, because the health benefits of endurance activity had been studied extensively. It did not deal with resistance exercise, such as lifting weights, but said studies were finding that form of exercise to be a good way to preserve muscle strength, prevent falls, and improve mobility in the elderly. The report also focused on disease prevention but did not discuss the growing body of evidence on the benefits of exercise in treating or recovering from disease.

The report listed several examples of moderate physical activity that people could do at home, including stair walking for fifteen minutes, walking two miles in thirty minutes, gardening for thirty to forty-five minutes, or washing and waxing a car for forty-five minutes to an hour. This much exercise, pursued on most days of the week, would improve health, the report said. "People who can maintain a regular regimen of activity that is of longer duration or of more vigorous intensity are likely to derive greater benefit," the report added.

The report acknowledged that motivating sedentary Americans to change their habits would not be easy. Lack of physical activity was greater among women than men, among blacks and Hispanics than whites, among older than younger adults, and among the less affluent than the more affluent. The CDC, which spent about $10 million in fiscal 1997 to promote physical activity, was requesting $60 million for that purpose in fiscal 1998.

In a related development, a study published in the Journal of the American Medical Association *a week after the Surgeon General's report was released added dramatic new evidence in support of moderate physical activity. The report, prepared by the Cooper Institute, found that moderately fit male smokers with high blood pressure and high cholesterol had a 15 percent lower death rate than sedentary but otherwise healthy male nonsmokers. "It's the first study to show that low fitness is at the top with smoking" as a health risk, said Steven Blair, the report's lead author. "It's a more powerful risk factor than high blood pressure, high cholesterol, obesity, and family history." The report also found that the mortality rate for moderately fit nonsmoking men was 41 percent lower than the rate for nonsmoking men who were sedentary.*

Following are excerpts from Chapter 1 of the Executive Summary of Physical Activity and Health, *a report released July 11, 1996, by the surgeon general recommending that Americans engage in at least moderate amounts of physical activity on most days of the week to improve their health:*

Introduction

This is the first Surgeon General's report to address physical activity and health. The main message of this report is that Americans can substantially improve their health and quality of life by including moderate amounts of physical activity in their daily lives. Health benefits from physical activity are thus achievable for most Americans, including those who may dislike vigorous exercise and those who may have been previously discouraged by the difficulty of adhering to a program of vigorous exercise. For those who are already achieving regular moderate amounts of activity, additional benefits can be gained by further increases in activity level.

This report grew out of an emerging consensus among epidemiologists, experts in exercise science, and health professionals that physical activity need not be of vigorous intensity for it to improve health. Moreover, health benefits appear to be proportional to amount of activity; thus, every increase in activity adds some benefit. Emphasizing the amount rather than the intensity of physical activity offers more options for people to select from in incorporating physical activity into their daily lives. Thus, a moderate amount of activity can be obtained in a 30-minute brisk walk, 30 minutes of lawn mowing or raking leaves, a 15-minute run, or 45 minutes of playing volleyball, and these activities can be varied from day to day. It is hoped that this different emphasis on moderate amounts of activity, and the flexibility to vary activities according to personal preference and life circumstances, will encourage more people to make physical activity a regular and sustainable part of their lives.

The information in this report summarizes a diverse literature from the fields of epidemiology, exercise physiology, medicine, and the behavioral sciences. The report highlights what is known about physical activity and health, as well as what is being learned about promoting physical activity among adults and young people.

Development of the Report

In July 1994, the Office of the Surgeon General authorized the Centers for Disease Control and Prevention (CDC) to serve as lead agency for preparing the first Surgeon General's report on physical activity and health. The CDC was joined in this effort by the President's Council on Physical Fitness and Sports (PCPFS) as a collaborative partner representing the Office of the Surgeon General. Because of the wide interest in the health effects of physical activity, the report was planned collaboratively with representatives from the Office of the Surgeon General, the Office of Public Health and Science (Office of the Secretary), the Office of Disease Prevention (National Institutes of Health [NIH]), and the following institutes from the NIH: the National Heart, Lung, and Blood Institute; the National Institute of Child Health and Human Development; the National Institute of Diabetes and Digestive and Kidney Diseases; and the National Institute of Arthritis and Musculoskeletal and Skin Diseases. CDC's nonfederal partners—including the American Alliance for Health, Physical Education, Recreation, and Dance; the American College of Sports Medicine; and the American Heart Association—provided consultation throughout the development process.

The major purpose of this report is to summarize the existing literature on the role of physical activity in preventing disease and on the status of interventions to increase physical activity. . . . This report focuses on disease prevention and therefore does not include the considerable body of evidence on the benefits of physical activity for treatment or rehabilitation after disease has developed. This report concentrates on endurance-type physical activity (activity involving repeated use of large muscles, such as in walking or bicycling) because the health benefits of this type of activity have been extensively studied. The importance of resistance exercise (to increase muscle strength, such as by lifting weights) is increasingly being recognized as a means to preserve and enhance muscular strength and endurance and to prevent falls and improve mobility in the elderly. Some promising findings on resistance exercise are presented here, but a comprehensive review of resistance training is beyond the scope of this report. In addition, a review of the special concerns regarding physical activity for pregnant women and for people with disabilities is not undertaken here, although these important topics deserve more research and attention.

Finally, physical activity is only one of many everyday behaviors that affect health. In particular, nutritional habits are linked to some of the same aspects of health as physical activity, and the two may be related lifestyle characteristics. This report deals solely with physical activity; a Surgeon General's Report on Nutrition and Health was published in 1988.

Chapters 2 through 6 of this report address distinct areas of the current understanding of physical activity and health. Chapter 2 offers a historical perspective: after outlining the history of belief and knowledge about physical activity and health, the chapter reviews the evolution and content of physical activity recommendations. Chapter 3 describes the physiologic responses to physical activity—both the immediate effects of a single episode of activity and the long-term adaptations to a regular pattern of activity. The evidence that physical activity reduces the risk of cardiovascular and other diseases is presented in Chapter 4. Data on patterns and trends of physical activity in the U.S. population are the focus of Chapter 5. Lastly, Chapter 6 examines efforts to increase physical activity and reviews ideas currently being proposed for policy and environmental initiatives.

Major Conclusions

1. People of all ages, both male and female, benefit from regular physical activity.
2. Significant health benefits can be obtained by including a moderate amount of physical activity (e.g., 30 minutes of brisk walking or raking leaves, 15 minutes of running, or 45 minutes of playing volleyball) on most, if not all, days of the week. Through a modest increase in daily activity, most Americans can improve their health and quality of life.
3. Additional health benefits can be gained through greater amounts of physical activity. People who can maintain a regular regimen of activity that is of longer duration or of more vigorous intensity are likely to derive greater benefit.
4. Physical activity reduces the risk of premature mortality in general, and of coronary heart disease, hypertension, colon cancer, and diabetes mellitus in particular. Physical activity also improves mental health and is important for the health of muscles, bones, and joints.
5. More than 60 percent of American adults are not regularly physically active. In fact, 25 percent of all adults are not active at all.
6. Nearly half of American youths 12–21 years of age are not vigorously active on a regular basis. Moreover, physical activity declines dramatically during adolescence.
7. Daily enrollment in physical education classes has declined among high school students from 42 percent in 1991 to 25 percent in 1995.
8. Research on understanding and promoting physical activity is at an early stage, but some interventions to promote physical activity through schools, worksites, and health care settings have been evaluated and found to be successful.

Summary

The benefits of physical activity have been extolled throughout western history, but it was not until the second half of this century that scientific evidence supporting these beliefs began to accumulate. By the 1970s, enough information was available about the beneficial effects of vigorous exercise on cardiorespiratory fitness that the American College of Sports Medicine (ACSM), the American Heart Association (AHA), and other national organizations began issuing physical activity recommendations to the public. These recommendations generally focused on cardiorespiratory endurance and specified sustained periods of vigorous physical activity involving large muscle groups and lasting at least 20 minutes on 3 or more days per week. As understanding of the benefits of less vigorous activity grew, recommendations followed suit. During the past few years, the ACSM, the CDC, the AHA, the PCPFS, and the NIH have all recommended regular, moderate-intensity physical activity as an option for those who get little or no exercise. The Healthy People 2000 goals for the nation's health have recognized the importance of physical activity and have included physical activity goals. The 1995 Dietary Guidelines for Americans, the basis of the federal government's nutrition-related programs, included physical activity guidance to maintain and improve weight—30 minutes or more of moderate-intensity physical activity on all, or most, days of the week.

Underpinning such recommendations is a growing understanding of how physical activity affects physiologic function. The body responds to physical activity in ways that have important positive effects on musculoskeletal, cardiovascular, respiratory, and endocrine systems. These changes are consistent with a number of health benefits, including a reduced risk of premature mortality and reduced risks of coronary heart disease, hypertension, colon cancer, and diabetes mellitus. Regular participation in physical activity also appears to reduce depression and anxiety, improve mood, and enhance ability to perform daily tasks throughout the life span.

The risks associated with physical activity must also be considered. The most common health problems that have been associated with physical activity are musculoskeletal injuries, which can occur with excessive amounts of activity or with suddenly beginning an activity for which the body is not conditioned. Much more serious associated health problems (i.e., myocardial infarction, sudden death) are also much rarer, occurring primarily among sedentary people with advanced atherosclerotic disease who engage in strenuous activity to which they are unaccustomed. Sedentary people, especially those with preexisting health conditions, who wish to increase their physical activity should therefore gradually build up to the desired level of activity. Even among people who are regularly active, the risk of myocardial infarction or sudden death is somewhat increased during physical exertion, but their overall risk of these outcomes is lower than that among people who are sedentary.

Research on physical activity continues to evolve. This report includes both well-established findings and newer research results that await replication and amplification. Interest has been developing in ways to differentiate between the various characteristics of physical activity that improve health. It remains to be determined how the interrelated characteristics of amount, intensity, duration, frequency, type, and pattern of physical activity are related to specific health or disease outcomes.

Attention has been drawn recently to findings from three studies showing that cardiorespiratory fitness gains are similar when physical activity occurs in several short sessions (e.g., 10 minutes) as when the same total amount and intensity of activity occurs in one longer session (e.g., 30 minutes). Although, strictly speaking, the health benefits of such intermittent activity have not yet been demonstrated, it is reasonable to expect them to be similar to those of continuous activity. Moreover, for people who are unable to set aside 30 minutes for physical activity, shorter episodes are clearly better than none. Indeed, one study has shown greater adherence to a walking program among those walking several times per day than among those walking once per day, when the total amount of walking time was kept the same. Accumulating physical activity over the course of the day has been included in recent recommendations from the CDC and ACSM, as well as from the NIH Consensus Development Conference on Physical Activity and Cardiovascular Health.

Despite common knowledge that exercise is healthful, more than 60 percent of American adults are not regularly active, and 25 percent of the adult population are not active at all. Moreover, although many people have enthusiastically embarked on vigorous exercise programs at one time or another, most do not sustain their participation. Clearly, the processes of developing and maintaining healthier habits are as important to study as the health effects of these habits.

The effort to understand how to promote more active lifestyles is of great importance to the health of this nation. Although the study of physical activity determinants and interventions is at an early stage, effective programs to increase physical activity have been carried out in a variety of settings, such as schools, physicians' offices, and worksites. Determining the most effective and cost-effective intervention approaches is a challenge for the future. Fortunately, the United States has skilled leadership and institutions to support efforts to encourage and assist Americans to become more physically active. Schools, community agencies, parks, recreational facilities, and health clubs are available in most communities and can be more effectively used in these efforts.

School-based interventions for youth are particularly promising, not only for their potential scope—almost all young people between the ages of 6 and 16 years attend school—but also for their potential impact. Nearly half of young people 12–21 years of age are not vigorously active; moreover, physical activity sharply declines during adolescence. Childhood and adolescence may thus be pivotal times for preventing sedentary behavior among adults by maintaining the habit of physical activity throughout the school years. School-based interventions have been shown to be successful in increasing physical activity levels. With evidence that success in this arena is possible, every effort should be made to encourage schools to require daily physical education in each grade and to promote physical activities that can be enjoyed throughout life.

Outside the school, physical activity programs and initiatives face the challenge of a highly technological society that makes it increasingly convenient to remain sedentary and that discourages physical activity in both obvious and subtle ways. To increase physical activity in the general population, it may be necessary to go beyond traditional efforts. This report highlights some concepts from community initiatives that are being implemented around the country. It is hoped that these examples will spark new public policies and programs in other places as well. Special efforts will also be required to meet the needs of special populations, such as people with disabilities, racial and ethnic minorities, people with low income, and the elderly. Much more information about these important groups will be necessary to develop a truly comprehensive national initiative for better health through physical activity. Challenges for the future include identifying key determinants of physically active lifestyles among the diverse populations that characterize the United States (including special populations, women, and young people) and using this information to design and disseminate effective programs.

Chapter Conclusions

Chapter 2: Historical Background and Evolution of Physical Activity Recommendations

Nearly half of American youths 12–21 years of age are not vigorously active on a regular basis. Moreover, physical activity declines dramatically during adolescence.

1. Physical activity for better health and well-being has been an important theme throughout much of western history.
2. Public health recommendations have evolved from emphasizing vigorous activity for cardiorespiratory fitness to including the option of moderate levels of activity for numerous health benefits.
3. Recommendations from experts agree that for better health, physical activity should be performed regularly. The most recent recommendations advise people of all ages to include a minimum of 30 minutes of physical activity of moderate intensity (such as brisk walking) on most, if not all, days of the week. It is also acknowledged that for most people, greater health benefits can be obtained by engaging in physical activity of more vigorous intensity or of longer duration.
4. Experts advise previously sedentary people embarking on a physical activity program to start with short durations of moderate-intensity activity and gradually increase the duration or intensity until the goal is reached.
5. Experts advise consulting with a physician before beginning a new physical activity program for people with chronic diseases, such as cardiovascular disease and diabetes mellitus, or for those who are at high risk for these diseases. Experts also advise men over age 40 and women over age 50 to consult a physician before they begin a vigorous activity program.
6. Recent recommendations from experts also suggest that cardiorespiratory endurance activity should be supplemented with strength-developing exercises at least twice per week for adults, in order to improve

musculoskeletal health, maintain independence in performing the activities of daily life, and reduce the risk of falling.

7. Daily enrollment in physical education classes has declined among high school students from 42 percent in 1991 to 25 percent in 1995.

Chapter 3: Physiologic Responses and Long-Term Adaptations to Exercise

1. Physical activity has numerous beneficial physiologic effects. Most widely appreciated are its effects on the cardiovascular and musculoskeletal systems, but benefits on the functioning of metabolic, endocrine, and immune systems are also considerable.

2. Many of the beneficial effects of exercise training—from both endurance and resistance activities—diminish within 2 weeks if physical activity is substantially reduced, and effects disappear within 2 to 8 months if physical activity is not resumed.

3. People of all ages, both male and female, undergo beneficial physiologic adaptations to physical activity.

Chapter 4: The Effects of Physical Activity on Health and Disease

Overall Mortality

1. Higher levels of regular physical activity are associated with lower mortality rates for both older and younger adults.

2. Even those who are moderately active on a regular basis have lower mortality rates than those who are least active.

Cardiovascular Diseases

1. Regular physical activity or cardiorespiratory fitness decreases the risk of cardiovascular disease mortality in general and of coronary heart disease mortality in particular. Existing data are not conclusive regarding a relationship between physical activity and stroke.

2. The level of decreased risk of coronary heart disease attributable to regular physical activity is similar to that of other lifestyle factors, such as keeping free from cigarette smoking.

3. Regular physical activity prevents or delays the development of high blood pressure, and exercise reduces blood pressure in people with hypertension.

Cancer

1. Regular physical activity is associated with a decreased risk of colon cancer.

2. There is no association between physical activity and rectal cancer. Data are too sparse to draw conclusions regarding a relationship between physical activity and endometrial, ovarian, or testicular cancers.

3. Despite numerous studies on the subject, existing data are inconsistent regarding an association between physical activity and breast or prostate cancers.

Non-Insulin-Dependent Diabetes Mellitus

1. Regular physical activity lowers the risk of developing non-insulin-dependent diabetes mellitus.

Osteoarthritis

1. Regular physical activity is necessary for maintaining normal muscle strength, joint structure, and joint function. In the range recommended for health, physical activity is not associated with joint damage or development of osteoarthritis and may be beneficial for many people with arthritis.
2. Competitive athletics may be associated with the development of osteoarthritis later in life, but sports-related injuries are the likely cause.

Osteoporosis

1. Weight-bearing physical activity is essential for normal skeletal development during childhood and adolescence and for achieving and maintaining peak bone mass in young adults.
2. It is unclear whether resistance- or endurance-type physical activity can reduce the accelerated rate of bone loss in postmenopausal women in the absence of estrogen replacement therapy.

Falling

1. There is promising evidence that strength training and other forms of exercise in older adults preserve the ability to maintain independent living status and reduce the risk of falling.

Obesity

1. Low levels of activity, resulting in fewer kilocalories used than consumed, contribute to the high prevalence of obesity in the United States.
2. Physical activity may favorably affect body fat distribution.

Mental Health

1. Physical activity appears to relieve symptoms of depression and anxiety and improve mood.
2. Regular physical activity may reduce the risk of developing depression, although further research is needed on this topic.

Health-Related Quality of Life

1. Physical activity appears to improve health-related quality of life by enhancing psychological well-being and by improving physical functioning in persons compromised by poor health.

Adverse Effects

1. Most musculoskeletal injuries related to physical activity are believed to be preventable by gradually working up to a desired level of activity and by avoiding excessive amounts of activity.
2. Serious cardiovascular events can occur with physical exertion, but the net effect of regular physical activity is a lower risk of mortality from cardiovascular disease.

Chapter 5: Patterns and Trends in Physical Activity

Adults

1. Approximately 15 percent of U.S. adults engage regularly (3 times a week for at least 20 minutes) in vigorous physical activity during leisure time.
2. Approximately 22 percent of adults engage regularly (5 times a week for at least 30 minutes) in sustained physical activity of any intensity during leisure time.
3. About 25 percent of adults report no physical activity at all in their leisure time.
4. Physical inactivity is more prevalent among women than men, among blacks and Hispanics than whites, among older than younger adults, and among the less affluent than the more affluent.
5. The most popular leisure-time physical activities among adults are walking and gardening or yard work.

Adolescents and Young Adults

1. Only about one-half of U.S. young people (ages 12–21 years) regularly participate in vigorous physical activity. One-fourth report no vigorous physical activity.
2. Approximately one-fourth of young people walk or bicycle (i.e., engage in light to moderate activity) nearly every day.
3. About 14 percent of young people report no recent vigorous or light-to-moderate physical activity. This indicator of inactivity is higher among females than males and among black females than white females.
4. Males are more likely than females to participate in vigorous physical activity, strengthening activities, and walking or bicycling.
5. Participation in all types of physical activity declines strikingly as age or grade in school increases.
6. Among high school students, enrollment in physical education remained unchanged during the first half of the 1990s. However, daily attendance in physical education declined from approximately 42 percent to 25 percent.
7. The percentage of high school students who were enrolled in physical education and who reported being physically active for at least 20 min-

utes in physical education classes declined from approximately 81 percent to 70 percent during the first half of this decade.

8. Only 19 percent of all high school students report being physically active for 20 minutes or more in daily physical education classes.

Chapter 6: Understanding and Promoting Physical Activity

1. Consistent influences on physical activity patterns among adults and young people include confidence in one's ability to engage in regular physical activity (e.g., self-efficacy), enjoyment of physical activity, support from others, positive beliefs concerning the benefits of physical activity, and lack of perceived barriers to being physically active.

2. For adults, some interventions have been successful in increasing physical activity in communities, worksites, and health care settings, and at home.

3. Interventions targeting physical education in elementary school can substantially increase the amount of time students spend being physically active in physical education class.

YELTSIN'S VICTORY
IN RUSSIAN ELECTIONS
July 11, 1996

Russia's fragile democracy passed a crucial test in 1996, with the holding of a landmark presidential election. Although physically weak and politically vulnerable, President Boris Yeltsin defeated a challenge by a resurgent Communist party. Yeltsin pledged to continue economic reforms that were slowly and painfully moving Russia from communism to a free market.

On November 5, the sixty-five-year-old Yeltsin underwent a quintuple bypass heart operation, raising new questions about whether he would be able to serve out his new four-year term. That operation appeared to be a success, and Yeltsin was back at work on December 23. But at year's end Yeltsin was battling a case of pneumonia that again caused concerns about his health—and the future of Russian politics as well.

Despite the political turmoil, Yeltsin, his government, and a host of budding capitalists kept the economy moving toward a free market. Banks, retail businesses, services, and other private companies continued to spring up all over the country as many Russians pursued entrepreneurial opportunities. The International Monetary Fund responded to this progress with a $10 billion loan, the second biggest in the agency's fifty-year history.

No single action ensured the continuation of capitalism as much as a decree Yeltsin issued in March allowing people to buy and sell land for the first time since the 1917 Bolshevik revolution. The decree would take years to implement fully, but it had enormous potential to change the lives of average Russians. Yeltsin's decree gave millions of people the prospect of having a tangible stake in economic reform.

Throughout the tumultuous year, the Clinton administration stood by Yeltsin, offering him verbal support and his government financial aid. The administration resisted suggestions from some quarters that the United States should avoid overly committing itself to a Russian president who might not live out his four-year term in office and who had no obvious successor.

Deputy Secretary of State Strobe Talbott, the administration's key point man on Russian policy, said eight days after Yeltsin's reelection that the United States would continue to back Yeltsin and his government. The election was an affirmation, he said, of the administration's policy of "supportive engagement with Russian reform."

A Remarkable Comeback

Yeltsin was first elected Russian president in 1991, months before the attempted military coup against Soviet leader Mikhail Gorbachev that led to the collapse of the Soviet Union. Yeltsin then oversaw the transition of the Russian political and economic systems from communism to democracy and capitalism. (Gorbachev's resignation, Historic Documents of 1991, p. 527; Yeltsin on crises in Russia, Historic Documents of 1993, p. 769)

The transition was anything but smooth. Unskilled in the ways of democracy, Yeltsin and other Russian politicians engaged in rough-and-tumble antics that slowed real progress on the enormous economic and social issues confronting the country. Yeltsin missed several opportunities to consolidate the power of anticommunist forces; most notably, he never formed a real political party that could rally around a platform and establish a line of succession. He often seemed more interested in the gamesmanship of internal Kremlin politics than in governing the country. Yeltsin paid a political price: anti-Yeltsin nationalists finished first in parliamentary elections in 1993, and Communists took control of the lower house of parliament in 1995.

As 1996 began, most observers agreed that Yeltsin was too ill to govern and that he had little or no chance of winning the presidency again. But after announcing in February his intention to seek reelection, Yeltsin suddenly found the energy to campaign. In more than thirty trips around the country, Yeltsin promised pay raises, new pension benefits, and tax breaks—none of which the impoverished government could afford.

Although he had been president for nearly five years, Yeltsin campaigned as an outsider, railing against Moscow bureaucrats as responsible for the economic misery felt by millions of unemployed, underpaid, or unpaid Russians. He fired unpopular aides, including his closest adviser, Major General Aleksander V. Korzhakov, who had suggested postponing the elections. Gradually, Yeltsin overtook the presumed front-runner, Gennady Zyuganov, a former Communist functionary who rebuilt the party by fomenting public dissatisfaction with the painful transition to capitalism.

Yeltsin finished first and Zyuganov second in a crowded field in the first round of elections June 16. Two days later, Yeltsin practically assured his victory in the final round by naming Aleksander I. Lebed, a retired general who finished a strong third in the voting, as his national security adviser.

Apparently exhausted from the stress of the campaign, Yeltsin then disappeared from public view until the day of the runoff, July 3. Despite public concerns about his health, Yeltsin easily won the election with 55 per-

cent of the vote. Zyuganov captured 40 percent. Another 5 percent voted for "none of the above."

Most analysts said the election was not so much a victory for Yeltsin and his path of economic reform as a defeat for the discredited communist past. About 30 million Russians voted for the Communist party candidate, but many of those appeared to be more frustrated by the painful consequences of economic reform than anxious for a return to dictatorship and a command economy.

Yeltsin was inaugurated on August 9 in a brief Kremlin ceremony. He slurred his oath of office and failed to deliver any kind of inaugural speech indicating what he intended to do in his second term in office.

The end of the election campaign did not mean an end to political infighting in the Kremlin. Lebed, who had helped carry Yeltsin to victory, was unable to control his thirst for political power even while nominally serving as an adviser to the president. Lebed had worked in the Kremlin for less than four months when Yeltsin declared Lebed's self-promotional schemes to be intolerable and fired him.

The War in Chechnya

Before his ouster, Lebed performed one miracle on Yeltsin's behalf, brokering an end to the brutal war against the secessionist republic of Chechnya, in southern Russia. Chechen rebels had declared independence from Russia in 1991, and in 1994 Yeltsin sent some 40,000 Russian troops into the republic to put down the rebellion. The Chechens proved tough fighters, however, and the supposedly elite Russian army units often turned out to be ill-trained, badly led, and demoralized. The war dragged on for nearly two years, with the Chechen capital, Grozny, coming under the control of one side, then another, as it was reduced to rubble. By 1996 estimates of the war dead ranged from 30,000 to 80,000; whatever the actual figure, most of the dead were civilians caught in the fighting.

Most Russians, while despising the Chechens, were sick of the war as the election year came around. Hoping to capitalize on the yearning for peace, Yeltsin on March 31 ordered a unilateral cease-fire and said Russian troops would be withdrawn in phases. Despite that move, fighting continued until August, when Lebed arranged a peace agreement that finally ended the war but postponed a decision on Chechen independence until 2000.

Lebed's agreement enabled Yeltsin to remove the last Russian troops from Chechnya at the end of 1996. It also set the stage for elections in Chechnya in January 1997 that would give international legitimacy to the region's quest for independence.

> *Following are excerpts from a speech July 11, 1996, by Deputy Secretary of State Strobe Talbott to the U.S.-Russia Business Council in which he assessed the Russian elections held July 3, 1996:*

I can't imagine a more appropriate group to address on the subject of U.S.-Russian relations. The American government and the American private sector are, in a very real sense, partners in a joint enterprise to promote, participate in—and benefit from—reform in Russia. You have a business interest in seeing Russia succeed in its transition from Soviet Communism to democracy and market economics and to full integration with the rest of the world. We have a national-security interest in seeing the same thing. From our different vantage points and with our different resources, we are cooperating to support that transition.

Over the past several years, and particularly over the past several months, we've followed the ups and downs, the twists and turns, of Russian politics. Together, we've followed, with varying degrees of skepticism, the conventional wisdom about Russia—laced, as it has often been, with pessimism, even panic, and the counsel of despair. Just since January, we've listened to experts predict confidently—first, that Boris Yeltsin would lose the election; then that he would cancel it; then that he would steal it; then that he would not survive it. From the outset, and throughout this long period of suspense and tumult and controversy, President Clinton and Secretary Christopher made sure we were prepared for any outcome. But they also maintained an underlying confidence in democracy—and in the wisdom of active, patient engagement with a reforming Russia. In choosing that strategy and staying with it, they rejected advice from prophets of doom, who called, in effect, for a return to a Cold War policy of containment and confrontation.

Here is how we see what happened in Russia last week. For the Russian people, the election was a chance to express their hopes and fears on many subjects: from crime-and-corruption to Chechnya to privatization to social security and insecurity. But in the broadest and deepest sense it was a vote about whether to maintain the difficult course on which they've been embarked for the last five years, or whether to turn back the clock.

President Clinton framed the choice succinctly two and a half years ago. During his first visit to Moscow as President, in January 1994, he posed for the Russian people a fundamental question. "How will you define your role in the world as a great power?" he asked. "Will you define it in yesterday's terms, or tomorrow's?"

Last week a clear majority of the Russian people answered that question with a vote for reform, for the future and against a candidate representing a Party whose very name is a synonym for the past. And as they chose their head-of-state for the first time in their thousand year history, Russians also voted resoundingly for democracy itself. More than 72 million citizens, over sixty-seven percent of the eligible voters, turned out at 96,000 polling places from Kaliningrad to Vladivostok, across the Russian Federation's eleven time zones. Those figures are as impressive and significant as the 14-point margin of victory.

So Russian democracy and American support for Russian democracy have both come through an important test. But it was not, of course, a final test. Far from it. Reform is a difficult work in progress. It will take a generation or more. It is marked by imperfections and what Marxists—remember them?—might call "internal contradictions." Plenty of Russians still identify reform with hardship and peril. After all, forty percent of them did vote for Gennady Zyuganov. And not all those who voted for Boris Yeltsin are content with life today.

Nonetheless, as President Yeltsin begins his second administration, he will have an important new asset with which to meet the daunting challenges he faces. He now has a clear mandate from the Russian people to continue his program of reform. As he capitalizes on that mandate, he will be able to count on our continuing engagement. He can also count on our total candor about the terms of that engagement. Our support for Russia is not unconditional. It never has been. As President Eisenhower once said, "I have one yardstick by which I test every problem: Is it good for America?" President Clinton uses that same yardstick. Every time we face a new issue, or the recurrence of an old one, we take the measure of our own interests, and we calibrate our policy accordingly.

The first high-level chance we will have to engage the second-term Yeltsin Administration will come this weekend, when Vice President Al Gore goes to Russia for the seventh meeting of the Gore-Chernomyrdin Commission [GCC]. The Vice President will take with him [Defense] Secretary [William J.] Perry, Secretary [Mickey] Kantor [U.S. Trade Representative], [Energy] Secretary [Hazel R.] O'Leary, [Health and Human Services] Secretary [Donna E.] Shalala and a number of other senior officials. They include two colleagues well known to this group: Jim Collins and Dick Morningstar, who, by the grace of recent Senate actions are now to be addressed as Mr. Ambassador, or—if you prefer—Your Excellency. As you all know, the GCC, as we call it, has been an invaluable mechanism. The strong personal and professional ties that the Vice President has developed with the Prime Minister have been a force both for stability in U.S.-Russian relations and for progress in Russian reform.

We regard it as significant and encouraging that President Yeltsin began the process of forming his new government by asking Mr. Chernomyrdin to continue as his Prime Minister. Viktor Stepanovich has proved to be steadfast in his advocacy of reform and effective in its implementation. He has played a key role in dismantling an authoritarian, centrally controlled economy, privatizing the industrial sector, beating back the beast of inflation, developing capital markets, and giving Russians their first experience of private ownership. He has dealt effectively with the leadership of the IMF as well as with leading officials of our own government.

But much work remains to be done. In the months ahead, we will use the GCC and other forums to roll up our sleeves and get to work with the Russians. We will concentrate on three broad areas: security, regional cooperation, and economics and trade. Let me say a very brief word about each, but with particular emphasis on the third.

First, security—which really should come first, since it concerns the most fundamental of all issues: our safety, indeed our survival, as a nation. Over the past three and a half years, we have already reduced our two nuclear arsenals by 9,000 warheads. We're going to press ahead to cut another 5,000. We will continue to cooperate with the Russians to reduce weapons stockpiles, to end nuclear testing, and to prevent the spread of nuclear weapons and weapons of mass destruction throughout the world.

Second, we are, whenever and wherever possible, cooperating rather than competing in troubled regions of the world. The best example is Bosnia, where American and Russian troops are serving side-by-side. Secretary Perry will address issues of security and regional cooperation in his own talks in Moscow next week.

Let me turn now to the area of most direct and immediate concern to you. In a very real sense, the fate of Russian reform in general hinges upon what happens to Russian economic reform in particular. The increased security, stability, and prosperity that millions of Russians called for with their votes last week will remain out of reach if Russia does not succeed in the transition from a command system to the open market. The American business community has a crucial role to play in helping Russia complete that transition. You possess the necessary resources and expertise.

Boris Yeltsin knows this. When he and President Clinton spoke on the telephone last Friday, Mr. Yeltsin had one main message to convey. He urged that the United States help mobilize private investment on a massive scale. President Clinton replied that the United States will do everything it can to help Russia reach this goal. He mentioned two institutions in particular: first, the American government will work through the Gore-Chernomyrdin Commission, and second, as investment conditions improve, the American business community will intensify its engagement through many channels, including this one: the U.S.-Russia Business Council. Just to make sure Mr. Yeltsin understood, the President added that he was referring to Bob Strauss's outfit. Mr. Yeltsin responded not just with recognition, but with enthusiasm at the name of his old friend. Gene, please pass my report on this exchange along to Bob.

Now, all of us here today are, I'm sure, as realistic about remaining challenges as we are encouraged by recent developments. We in the government know that we've got our work cut out for us on a wide variety of very tough diplomatic and security issues. You in the business community are coping with obstacles that seem sometimes to be permanent fixtures on the Russian landscape. The Vice President will meet next week with representatives of the more than 600 American companies that have offices in Moscow. He knows that only about a third of them are engaged in trade and investment— and only half of those have made significant investments. And he knows why that is. While Russia has made impressive progress in removing the state from the management of the economy, it has yet to build the institutions and legal structures that will bring order and efficiency to its burgeoning free market.

The Vice President also knows that there are limits to what Prime Minister Chernomyrdin and his government can do to accelerate and guide that transformation. As my friend and colleague at the Treasury Department, Larry Summers, has said, "Setting up [a stable business climate that inspires investor confidence] requires not just top-down reforms, but bottom-up changes in the way Russia works. It's not just a question of writing new rules, but of knowing that they'll be applied, and who to turn to if they aren't."

Still, the climate in Russia is more conducive to that kind of bottom-up reform now than it was even ten days ago. In the immediate wake of the election, Russia's financial markets are already showing signs of new life. Stock prices are rising steadily and bond prices indicate greater confidence in government. President Yeltsin and Prime Minister Chernomyrdin are acutely aware that this trend must continue. They realize that investment capital must not just come home from abroad, where so much of it has fled; it must stay home and go to work creating jobs and raising the standard of living for the mainstream of society.

This is an issue of politics as well as economics. After all, only if the economy improves in ways that tangibly improve the lives of the Russian people can Russia's leaders be confident that the next time there's an election, there will be a decline, rather than an increase, in the number of Russians who vote against reform.

For much the same reason—that is, because it's an imperative of political survival as well as a matter of good government—President Yeltsin, Prime Minister Chernomyrdin and their colleagues must bring under control the epidemic of crime and corruption. Widespread lawlessness in Russia today constitutes a major threat to public confidence in government, a threat to reform, and a threat to the political fortunes of reformers. The strong showing of General Lebed in the first round of the election reflected this public concern. I need hardly add to this audience that crime and corruption are also a threat to the willingness and ability of firms like yours to do business there.

Let me summarize what we'll be doing on our end to deliver on President Clinton's commitment to help Russia move ahead with economic reform. Next week in Moscow, Vice President Gore will urge the Yeltsin-Chernomyrdin Administration to move ahead with the laws, rules, and institutions necessary to give investors confidence to expand their activities. He and the other members of the American delegation will focus on four issues of particular concern to international business.

The first is taxation. The current system is confusing, it lacks predictability, and is often excessive and unreasonable. Businesses will not invest in Russia if they can't make a profit, and they can't make a profit if earnings are going to be confiscated. That's why Russia must, in its own interest, move without delay toward a new tax code that encourages investment.

Second, the Vice President will urge that Russia adopt new laws and regulations for the energy sector. Right now there are too many conflicts in the existing legislation, and inadequate means of arbitration. A stable legal and tax framework would unblock the $50–60 billion in unrealized oil and gas investments.

Third, this seventh round of the GCC will be the first to address the growing concern over commercial crime. With the recent passage of a criminal code, the Russians have already made progress in this area. Yesterday, in a major speech promising that reform will continue, President Yeltsin vowed that, "fighting corruption at all levels will be a most important part of my work." Vice President Gore will encourage the Prime Minister to enact a criminal procedure code, laws on corruption and money laundering, and other key pieces of anti-crime legislation soon. After the GCC sessions in Moscow, we will continue to work with Russian law enforcement to insure that this new legislation will be vigorously enforced.

And finally, the Vice President will reaffirm our commitment to work closely with the IMF [International Monetary Fund] and multilateral development banks. Since 1993, when the U.S. led the effort to mobilize IFI [international financial institutions] support for reform throughout the former Soviet Union, these organizations have helped design and finance programs that are needed for both growth and stability. These include the daunting but essential task of stabilizing the currency and maintaining low inflation rates, as well as continuing structural reforms like privatization, banking reform, and easing the shock of industrial downsizing.

In conclusion, I would underscore that last week's election was a big step for Russia, a step very much in the right direction. It was also an affirmation—I'm tempted even to say a vindication—of our Administration's policy of supportive engagement with Russian reform. It was an incentive for us to stay the course with Russia as long as Russia itself keeps on course. And finally, it was a fresh incentive for the American government and the American private sector to redouble our own cooperation—our own joint venture—in helping Russia succeed, for its sake, and for ours.

UN REPORT ON
HUMAN DEVELOPMENT
July 16, 1996

The gap between rich and poor—both within most countries and between countries—widened during the 1990s, according to a report by the United Nations Development Programme (UNDP). Despite rapid economic growth in much of the world, eighty-nine countries, with one-quarter of the world's population, were worse off in the mid-1990s than they were a decade earlier. In 1990 the UNDP began issuing an annual report on human development to focus international attention on the world's disadvantaged populations. The 1996 report, released July 16 by UNDP administrator James Gustave Speth, concentrated on inequities in the distribution of wealth. The report argued that the greater the equitable distribution of wealth in any country, the more likely it will be that economic growth can be sustained over the long term. The report disputed a widely held belief that rapid economic growth and the equitable distribution of income cannot occur at the same time.

In a speech to the National Press Club in Washington, D.C., Speth said the report showed that promoting economic equity "is a necessary condition for sustained growth." Worsening disparities between the rich and the poor not only diminish human lives, he said, "they also compromise the prospects of sustained growth."

To bolster that contention, the report examined the rapid growth of countries such as China, Indonesia, South Korea, and Malaysia. In general, the report said, those countries had a more equitable distribution of land and credit and a greater emphasis on human development issues, such as education and health, than did other countries with less rapid growth. Equitable growth, Speth said, "is not only ideal in the abstract, it is possible in the real world."

Poor Countries Falling Behind

The UNDP report examined the relative standing over the past three decades of rich and poor nations, and rich and poor people, using the stan-

dard measurement of per capita income. By this measurement alone, it found that 89—more than half of the 174 members of the United Nations— were worse off than they were a decade before. Only 3 of those countries were considered "rich"—Canada, Finland, and Iceland—and the rest were developing countries, most in Africa, Asia, and Latin America.

In 70 of the countries that were falling behind, per capita income was below the levels of the 1960s or 1970s. In nineteen countries—such as Haiti, Ghana, Liberia, Nicaragua, Rwanda, and Venezuela—per capita income had fallen below the level of 1960. Speth said these figures showed that economic decline in much of the developing world "has lasted for longer and gone deeper than the Great Depression in the 1930s."

To contrast this trend, the report noted that the assets of the 358 known billionaires exceeded the combined annual incomes of 2.3 billion people, representing 45 percent of the world's population. In another measurement, the report showed the overall gap between the 20 percent of the world population with the highest per capita incomes and the 20 percent with the lowest incomes. In the mid-1960s, the gap was 30-to-1; by the mid 1990s, the gap had doubled to 61-to-1. Over the same thirty-year period, the world's poorest 20 percent saw their share of income fall from 2.3 percent to 1.4 percent.

The "Capability" Measurement of Poverty

The 1996 report introduced a new statistical measure of poverty, called the Capability Poverty Measure, which was intended to present a broader picture of the impact of poverty than typical measurements based solely on income. The statistic was supposed to find the percentage of people in each country who lacked "minimally essential human capabilities."

The statistic was an index of three items: the percentage of children under five years of age who were underweight (an indicator of nutrition and public health), the percentage of births unattended by trained health personnel (a measurement of healthy reproduction), and the rate of female illiteracy. The authors said the emphasis on women was due to their central role in families, and thus in society, no matter what the culture.

Under this broad capability index, 37 percent of the people in developing countries were considered to be in poverty; by comparison, the traditional income measurement found 21 percent in poverty. In terms of numbers, that meant that approximately 900 million people had poverty-level incomes, while 1.6 billion were "capability" poor. The overall lesson, the report said, was that "poverty cannot be eradicated merely by boosting income. It will also take a broad expansion of basic human capabilities and the productive use of those capabilities."

UNDP'S Policy Prescriptions

The UNDP report offered several suggestions for policies, at both the national and international levels, to encourage equitable economic growth. In general, most of the suggestions centered around policies that involved

devoting a greater share of public and private resources to basic social ser-
vices (such as education, health care, and housing) so that poor people
would be better prepared for productive work.

As an example of desirable policies, Speth cited the "20:20" compact
endorsed by delegates to an international social development summit in
Copenhagen in 1995. That proposal urged developing countries to devote
20 percent of their governmental budgets to basic social services and
industrial countries to put 20 percent of their foreign aid budgets into such
programs. (UN summit on poverty, Historic Documents of 1995, p. 134)

In his July 16 speech, Speth acknowledged that many nations were
reducing, rather than increasing, their spending on these types of services
for poor people and that industrialized countries were cutting their foreign
aid programs. He said these trends were ironic because the need for such
programs is growing and "we know so much more about what works and
does not work" in development programs.

> *Following are excerpts from a speech delivered at the National*
> *Press Club in Washington, D.C., on July 16, 1996, by James*
> *Gustave Speth, administrator of the United Nations Develop-*
> *ment Programme, in which he discussed the UNDP's* Human
> Development Report 1996*:*

I have come to think of the *Human Development Report* as a slayer of
dragons. The dragons it slays, like all dragons, are myths. This year the report
aims its lance at two myths, both very widespread and very dangerous.

The first myth is that most of the developing world is doing rather well, led
by some 15 rapidly growing developing economies and spurred by the opportunities of market globalization. As a result, the myth has it, the poor are
catching up, and we are seeing a convergence of rich and poor. As the report
amply documents, this is simply not the case. Unfortunately, we live in a
world that has in fact become more polarized economically, both between
countries and within them. If current trends continue, if they are not quickly
corrected, economic disparities will move from inequitable to inhuman—
from unacceptable to intolerable.

The second myth is that the early stage of economic growth is inevitably
associated with growing inequality within the country. Again, this report marshals convincing evidence that this need not be the case. Equitable growth is
not only ideal in the abstract, it is possible in the real world.

Indeed, the overall message of this year's report is that economic growth
and equitable human development must move together in the long run, if
both are to succeed. It maintains that neither economic growth nor advances
in human development are sustainable without the other over the longer
haul. The report's message is therefore not anti-growth. It is pro-growth.

But the report also concludes that there is no automatic link between economic growth and human development—a simple fact, often forgotten by

growth advocates. The links between overall growth and human betterment have failed in too many countries, for too many people. In most countries, growth has failed in recent decades, and, where it has occurred, it has more often than not been neither equitable nor balanced.

The report concludes that the links between economic growth and human development must be deliberately forged by governments and regularly fortified by skillful and intelligent policy management. New patterns of growth that translate the benefits of economic expansion into the lives of people must be sustained well into the 21st century. And new mechanisms must be found to integrate the weak and vulnerable into the expanding global economy.

The consequences of this failed growth are stunning. Polarization, increased inequality and profound poverty not only violate basic principles of justice and fairness, they breed alienation, despair and instability.

Today, we live on a planet which increasingly represents not 'one world', but 'two worlds'. The 'two worlds' result in part from the failure of growth in more than 100 countries. As the *Human Development Report 1996* indicates, these countries' per capita income is lower than it was 15 years ago, and, as a result, more than a quarter of humanity—1.6 billion people—are worse off today than they were 15 years ago.

In 70 developing countries, today's levels of income are less than those reached in the 1960s or 1970s. In 19, per capita income is less than it was in 1960 or before. Economic decline in much of the developing world has lasted for longer and gone deeper than the Great Depression of the 1930s.

There is another reason for our polarized world today. Not only has there been a failure of economic growth, but, as this year's report shows, the translation of economic growth into equitable human development has been very uneven.

You must be wondering by now whether there is any good news on the growth side. Yes, there is. The report documents that throughout much of the world there has been positive growth. In fact, three quarters of the world population live in countries that experienced economic growth over the last few decades—sometimes at a spectacular pace, as in China and the East Asia industrializing tigers. Though the proportion of people experiencing declines in per capita income between 1965–1980 and 1980–1993 more than tripled (from 5 per cent to 18 per cent), the proportion enjoying high rates of growth of more than 5 per cent a year more than doubled, from 12 per cent to 27 per cent. Growth rates of income in 15 countries have been spectacular by historical standards. In the early phases of the Industrial Revolution, it took Britain 60 years to achieve a doubling of income. China achieved this feat in 10 years only.

This economic growth came with mixed blessings. Too often it was associated with joblessness, widening income gaps and growing impoverishment. In recent years, the world has been witnessing a famine of jobs. The report contains an employment analysis of 69 countries over the last decade. Of the 46 countries with positive economic growth, only 27 saw employment also grow; 19 experienced jobless growth, including the large countries of South Asia.

Another problem is that many countries have not been translating growth into the development of human capabilities (as measured by a modified Human Development Index in the 1996 report). Notable exceptions include countries such as Malaysia, Korea, Indonesia, Botswana, Costa Rica, and China which have translated income growth into major progress in human development.

Poverty and income gaps have also grown amidst economic growth. World poverty is increasing about as fast as world population, which itself is growing in unprecedented number. The World Bank recently estimated that 1.3 billion people live—or don't live—on less than a dollar a day. Equally depressing, the number of people with incomes of less that $750 per year, hardly more than $2 per day, is about 3.3 billion people, or 60 per cent of humanity. We must face the fact that we live in a world where between 1960 and 1993 total global income increased by 6-fold to $23 trillion, and where average world per capita income tripled, but where three-fifths of humanity still lives in a prison of poverty. . . .

In countries like Brazil and Guatemala the richest 20 per cent earn more than 30 times the poorest, and even in the United States, the United Kingdom, Switzerland and Australia, the difference is about 10-fold. These trends cumulate into startling patterns of inequity and injustice. Consider these indicators.

During the last three decades, the ratio of the income share of the richest 20 per cent to that of the poorest 20 per cent has more than doubled from 30:1 to 61:1. The poorest 20 per cent saw their share of global income decline from 2.3 per cent to 1.4 per cent over the last 30 years.

Today, the net worth of the 358 richest people is equal to the combined income of the poorest 45 per cent of the world's population—2.3 billion people. . . .

The world, on many fronts, is divided—between rich and poor, between haves and have-nots, between wealthy and the dispossessed. It has become more polarized, both between countries and within countries. If present trends continue, the global economy will be gargantuan in its excesses and grotesque in its inequalities. Vast inequality would be the norm and instability and violence its accompaniment.

A house divided against itself cannot stand. We cannot tolerate such a situation. Equity needs to become a guiding principle for all our actions. Equity combines the ideas of justice and of equal opportunity, of people coming out of poverty to share in the world's bounty, of becoming integral members of society. Equity demands jobs for all, it demands an end to mass poverty in our rich world, it demands economic growth for all and full choices for all. It is essential if our increasingly interdependent and interconnected world is to work.

The defining concerns of international affairs in the next century will revolve around the struggle for equity—equity among nations; equity within nations; equity between the sexes; and equity for future generations.

With equity at the centre-stage of the economic growth-human development nexus, the *Human Development Report 1996* makes two important points, which also challenge traditional thinking.

First, economic growth and equitable human development must move together in the long run. Human development cannot be sustained without growth, nor growth without human development. . . .

Second, there is no inevitable trade-off between equity and economic growth. In fact, a more equitable distribution of assets, of productive resources and of growth itself can enhance both economic growth and human development. . . .

A new theory of growth is thus emerging that rejects the necessity of income inequalities for growth. In fact, the new theory is grounded on the belief that equity is a necessary condition for sustained growth. The powerful point made in this year's report is that worsening disparities are not only diminishing human lives, they also compromise the prospects of sustained growth.

What policies are needed to realize this new "growth with equity" model? These policies must place people at the centre-stage. Furthermore, actions are needed both at the national as well as at the international levels. The *Human Development Report 1996* offers a policy framework that has the following components:

At the national level:

- more attention and policy action on the structure and quality of growth to give priority to human development, poverty reduction, employment and long-term sustainability.
- formulation of an equity-based growth strategy—equity in enhancement of capabilities, access to opportunities, especially for women, and inter-generational equity in natural resource management.
- strengthening the links between economic growth and human development through household activities, government policies and action by various institutions of civil society.
- faster economic growth in three groups of countries—the low human development ones, especially those of sub-Saharan Africa and the LDCs [less developed countries], the CIS [Commonwealth of Independent States] countries and slow growing countries of Latin America, the Arab States and Asia.
- a political commitment to full employment, backed up by new approaches to expand and improve employment: labor intensive high-growth strategies, sustained investments in human capabilities, broader access to land and credit, and encouragement of the informal sector.

At the international level:

- a new framework for development cooperation, backed by reforms in development cooperation and a quick reversal of recent declines in official development assistance.
- urgent action on debt relief, especially for the poor and heavily indebted countries.

- aggressive support for key international support initiatives such as the United Nations System Conferences Action Plan, the Special Initiative for Africa, the LDC Programme of Action, the 20/20 Compact, and the new OECD [Organization for Economic Cooperation and Development] Development Assistance Committee goals, which are based on agreements reached at recent United Nations Conferences.
- an international commission to assess national policy options for full employment and to formulate supportive international measures.
- new mechanisms to help weak and vulnerable countries seize the opportunities of the global economy while protecting them from marginalization.

The challenges of today and the next century cannot be met without a revitalized commitment to an enlarged but reformed development cooperation. A new framework of development cooperation must recognize that economies exist for people, not people for economies. There should be a new motivation for aid, based on fighting the growing threat of global poverty rather than the receding threat of the cold war. A decisive improvement must be engineered in the quality and effectiveness of aid by linking it with commonly accepted global objectives. And to meet these challenges, our world today needs more development assistance, not less, whatever the trend might be. . . .

Let it not be said of our time that we, who had the power to do better, allowed the world to become further divided. We need cohesive globalization, not fractured globalization. Together, let us build a new World Wide Web—A World Wide Web of equity, hope and opportunity.

REOPENING OF OLYMPIC PARK FOLLOWING A BOMBING
July 30, 1996

A pipe bomb explosion, responsible for two deaths and more than one hundred injuries, briefly dampened the mood at the summer Olympic games in Atlanta, Georgia. The bomb exploded during a late-night rock concert at Centennial Olympic Park in downtown Atlanta.

The bombing was one of a handful of incidents in a two-year period that raised fears about whether the United States was becoming vulnerable to the types of terrorist actions that had long plagued most other parts of the world. The two most prominent cases were the April 1995 truck bomb explosion at a federal office building in Oklahoma City that killed 168 people and the explosion July 17 of TWA flight 800 from New York to Paris that killed all 230 people on board and created fears about terrorism against airlines. (Oklahoma City bombing, Historic Documents of 1995, p. 176; airline security, p. 662)

Within days of the bombing, speculation about a possible upsurge in terrorism was overtaken by the controversy surrounding Richard Jewell, a security guard at Centennial Olympic Park. As the man who found the bomb moments before it exploded, Jewell was first hailed as a hero. Three days later news reports identified him as the FBI's only suspect in the case. Jewell remained in limbo—identified in the media as a suspect but never formally accused of the crime—until October 26, when the Justice Department sent him a letter saying he was no longer considered a suspect.

The Bombing and Aftermath

The bomb that rocked Centennial Olympic Park was an unsophisticated device. Three pipe bombs containing explosive material had been taped together and placed in a plastic container filled with nails and screws. Wired to a timing device and detonator, the bomb was hidden in a green knapsack that was left next to a sound-and-light tower in the twenty-one-acre park.

A rock concert was under way at the park late on July 26. Shortly before 1 a.m., Jewell, who was working as a security guard under contract for

AT&T, reportedly noticed the suspicious knapsack and notified an agent of the Georgia Bureau of Investigation. After experts determined that the knapsack contained a bomb, Jewell helped police shoo people from the site. The bomb exploded at 1:25 a.m., spewing metal hundreds of feet. One person was killed by the explosion and about one hundred more were injured. A Turkish television cameraman died of a heart attack as he rushed to film the aftermath. Officials said that a male with no discernible accent had called the 911 emergency number shortly after 1 a.m. from a telephone booth near the park, warning that a bomb would explode at the park in thirty minutes.

Police closed Centennial Olympic Park after the explosion and spent two full days picking through debris at the site. The morning after the explosion, Olympic officials met and decided to continue the games. Canceling the games would represent a victory for the bomber, they said. Georgia governor Zell Miller agreed, saying that "we should not let a terrorist or a twisted personality hold us hostage."

Under pressure from Atlanta and Olympics officials, investigators allowed the park to reopen July 30. At a concert and ceremony at the site, Andrew Young, a former mayor of Atlanta and cochairman of the Atlanta Committee for the Olympic Games, called the games and the reopening of the park "a triumph of the human spirit."

Although some of the enthusiasm that had been generated by the games had been lost, the competition continued with no further incident. The games came to a close August 4, after sixteen days of competition and ceremony.

The Jewell Case

The case of Richard Jewell raised a host of questions concerning the FBI's investigative practices and journalistic ethics. Jewell and his attorneys insisted he had been wrongly accused by unnamed sources that had relied on flimsy circumstantial evidence. News executives debated their responsibilities to report breaking news developments versus the fairness of targeting a man who was never officially identified as a suspect.

Jewell was an unlikely figure to be at the center of such a controversy. The thirty-three-year-old Jewell had long wanted a career in law enforcement and had worked as a deputy sheriff and as a security guard at a college in northern Georgia. For several days, Jewell was honored as the hero who helped save lives.

Three days after the bombing, the Atlanta Journal-Constitution, *citing unnamed investigators, named Jewell as a suspect in the bombing. Other news organizations quickly followed the newspaper's lead.*

Some news organizations held back, in accordance with the traditional journalistic standard of not naming criminal suspects until they are formally charged. The magnitude of the bombing story quickly overwhelmed such ethical qualms, and nearly all news organizations carried reports about Jewell—if only as the man at the center of a controversy over whether he should have been identified as a suspect. The story was difficult for news organizations to ignore, especially as the FBI searched Jewell's apart-

ment, followed his movements, and showed his picture at stores where material for the bomb could have been purchased.

News reports then turned to the FBI's difficulty in obtaining hard evidence against Jewell or anyone else. Jewell's attorneys mounted a public campaign to pressure the Justice Department into clearing their client. That campaign included an interview with Jewell on the CBS news program 60 Minutes, in which he insisted he was innocent. The effort by Jewell's attorneys paid off on October 26 when U.S. Attorney Kent B. Alexander sent Jewell a one-paragraph letter saying he "is not considered a target" of the bombing investigation. The letter added: "Barring any newly discovered evidence, this status will not change."

Alexander also released a statement defending the FBI investigation of the case and insisting that the agency had not wanted to focus public attention on Jewell. The controversy over Jewell "interfered with the investigation," Alexander said. He noted that Jewell had never been charged with a crime.

Jack Martin, one of Jewell's attorneys, said the letter amounted to a vindication of his client, but some legal experts noted that Alexander's letter left open the possibility that Jewell could once again become a suspect if additional evidence surfaced.

Jewell held a press conference on October 28 and described his three-month ordeal as a "nightmare" during which "I felt like a hunted animal, followed constantly, waiting to be killed." Despite his ordeal, Jewell said he still wanted a career in law enforcement. He was unemployed at the time, although he had received local job offers.

That same day, acting under a court order, officials released a ten-page affidavit the FBI had used to obtain warrants to search Jewell's property. The affidavit contained no hard evidence against Jewell but did include a psychological profile describing him as someone seeking glory.

Jewell on November 6 sent the Atlanta paper a letter demanding a retraction of its stories naming him as a suspect. The newspaper stood by its coverage. On December 9 Jewell reached a cash settlement with the NBC television network; he had complained that news anchor Tom Brokaw all but declared him guilty of the bombing. The Wall Street Journal later reported that the settlement exceeded $500,000—a report that neither side would confirm or deny.

Also on December 9 the FBI posted a $500,000 reward for information leading to a conviction in the bombing case. The agency released a recording of the call to the 911 dispatcher warning about the bomb at Centennial Olympic Park.

> Following are remarks made July 30, 1996, at a ceremony for the reopening of Centennial Olympic Park in Atlanta, Georgia, by Billy Payne and Andrew Young, cochairmen of the Atlanta Committee for the Olympic Games:

PAYNE'S REMARKS

Hello everybody, I'm Billy Payne. And I'm honored, thank you. I am honored and delighted to welcome you back to Centennial Olympic Park.

The welcome that we extend today is the welcome of a partnership representing the great Olympic family as well as the state of Georgia and the city of Atlanta. It's my pleasure to recognize and to salute the governor of the state of Georgia, Governor Zell Miller.

The worldwide head of the Olympic family is Juan Antonio Samaranch, president of the International Olympic Committee. And the honorable and wonderful mayor of the city of Atlanta, Mr. Bill Campbell.

On behalf of all of these wonderful gentlemen, it's my honor and pleasure to welcome you and to thank you for attending this special program of remembrance and of revival.

I would also like to recognize Olympic champion Janet Evans, who is here today representing the athletes of the world.

I would like to thank AT&T Vice President George Burnett for making this wonderful facility available to us this morning.

And finally I would like to especially welcome the family members and friends of the victims that we remember here today.

It is now my pleasure to introduce the co-chairman of the Atlanta Committee for the Olympic Games, the honorable Andrew Young.

YOUNG'S REMARKS

We are here to proclaim a victory. We are here not to wallow in tragedy but to celebrate a triumph, a triumph of the human spirit. We are here to remember the lives of Alice Hawthorne and Melih Uzunyol. Two wonderful citizens one from America and one from Turkey, who sought to come here to celebrate with 197 nations of the world—the possibilities of this planet living together into the 21st century, with a new measure of peace and prosperity.

We are here because the 111 victims of a tragic and ruthless incident lay in the hospital. And as Jesse Jackson and I visited with them on yesterday, we did not find a single proclamation of despair. We didn't see a single incident of resentment. If there ever was a triumph of the human spirit it was in the young people from Georgia, from Connecticut, from Kentucky, from England, from all over the world who were the victims of this incident. Who were only looking forward to getting on with their lives, and many of them hoping to get out of the hospital in time to get back to the games.

We are here because the athletes said that they had not come—except to compete peacefully on the fields of athletic endeavor. And indeed we have seen some remarkable triumphs, from young and old, from one part of the world and the other, seeking to celebrate their triumph over their own minds and bodies and spirits, representing the best that their nations and this planet can put forward.

So we are here on what will be a memorable occasion. Indeed, it will be an unforgettable occasion. It's unfortunate that our lives are too often defined by the tragedies and suffering that we experience. And yet it's because those tragedies and those sufferings have often been the incidents which bring us to our senses and remind us who we really are.

Yes, we enjoy the frivolity; we loved this park. We still love this park. We will love this park on into the future.

This has been in every sense of the word a people's park. You didn't have to have a ticket to come here. You could meet with all of the people from all over the world. And all of the people from all over the world came to this park. And more than a million people enjoyed this park in the days that it was open. And we didn't have a single incident, a single fight, people didn't even get too drunk.

We learned to celebrate the joy of humanity. And we learned that we were brothers and sisters regardless of our race, regardless of our religion, regardless of our national origin.

And unfortunately, some people felt like they didn't belong. Like they weren't invited, but the whole world was welcome here. And the whole world remains welcome here, and we want everybody to know that there's no need in being alienated from that loving community.

There is nothing that keeps you out except an unwillingness to open your heart, and open your mind to the love and fellowship that this planet offers to all of its citizens.

Unfortunately, had it not been for the tragedy of Saturday morning, we—all of us—might have taken this joy for granted.

We are the privileged of the world. We are the brightest and best of all of the nations on the face of the earth. And we come together in peace because we know an enormous level of prosperity.

And we might not have taken account and given thanks for all of our blessings; we may have taken them for granted had it not been for this, what we felt to be needless, certainly unearned suffering. But Martin Luther King Jr. reminded us that unearned suffering is always redemption.

There is no religion on the face of the earth that doesn't give recognition to the power of the suffering servant. To the need for renunciation of the things of this world. That you might be lifted up into a new power of the human spirit of a divine spirit that really is the basis of our unity.

And so we say to those who suffered here, that we assure you that your suffering is not in vain. We assure you that we the children of the world will learn new lessons from this experience. And we are sure that the 21st century will remember the joy, the wonderful, the celebration, vitality of the people of the earth gathered in this park. And that we will define the future, not hatred, not bitterness, not alienation, but joy, happiness.

The celebration that we see here this morning, we have been wonderfully blessed by our presence together. I don't know what the future holds. But I know you represent the future. You are the people of the future. The people of the planet can solve all of the problems of the planet together and we have no need for hatred and violence.

We love you. We thank you. God bless you.

CLINTON AND REPUBLICANS
ON WELFARE OVERHAUL BILL
July 31, 1996

Bowing to election-year pressures, and wanting to keep his 1992 campaign promise to "end welfare as we know it," President Bill Clinton on July 31 said he would sign Republican-written legislation overhauling the nation's welfare system. The bill, which Clinton signed into law on August 22 (PL 104–193), ended the sixty-one-year guarantee of federal welfare aid to all eligible families with dependent children.

The bill transferred most welfare responsibilities to state and local governments. The federal government would give the states block grants for welfare programs, along with substantial freedom to use the money as they saw fit. One major restriction was among the most controversial: adult welfare recipients would have to begin working within two years of receiving aid, with no adult receiving federally funded welfare for more than five years. Over Clinton's objections, the bill sharply reduced the federal food stamp program and denied most federal benefits to immigrants, even those in the country legally.

A Political Issue

Welfare had been a hot-button political issue for more than two decades, as Republicans from Ronald Reagan to Newt Gingrich accused the system of perpetuating dependence on the "welfare state" at the expense of middle-class taxpayers. In his 1992 campaign for president, Clinton jumped on the antiwelfare bandwagon, pledging to end the complex system and replace it with one less costly and more efficient.

During his first two years in office, when Democrats controlled Congress, Clinton forfeited the opportunity to craft a new system to his liking by failing to send a welfare reform proposal to Congress. When Republicans took control of Congress in 1995, welfare was high on their political agenda. The Republicans twice sent Clinton legislation abolishing the welfare system and replacing it with federal block grants; Clinton vetoed both measures as extreme and unfair to poor people.

450

As the 1996 elections approached, the tenor of the debate began to change. Both Clinton and Republican congressional leaders saw the advantage of reaching agreement on a welfare overhaul bill that could be signed into law: Clinton so he could keep his campaign promise, Republicans so they could claim credit for a major piece of legislation easing the burden on taxpayers.

One of the key political events came in July, when the Republicans dropped their insistence on linking a welfare bill with an overhaul of the Medicaid system, which provides federal health aid for low-income people. Clinton had said he would veto any legislation undermining Medicaid. Linking reform of the two programs had been a demand of Sen. Bob Dole, R-Kan., when he was majority leader. After Dole resigned from the Senate to shore up his lagging presidential campaign, his fellow Republican leaders on Capitol Hill decided to take seriously Clinton's threat to veto legislation cutting Medicaid; in early July they separated the two issues. As enacted, the final bill guaranteed that Medicaid would remain available to anyone who met the eligibility requirements in effect in 1996. Protecting Medicaid made it easier for some Democrats to support welfare overhaul legislation.

The bill that emerged from a House-Senate conference committee made limited concessions to Democrats and moderate Republicans who wanted to preserve some features of the federal government's social "safety net." The measure generally was the product of conservative Republicans in both chambers who regularly had denounced nearly every facet of the welfare system.

Among the most controversial items in the final legislative bargaining were two of the biggest money-savers: a strict time limit on food stamps for most able-bodied adults and a ban on most federal aid to immigrants, regardless of their legal status. These two items accounted for most of the $54.1 billion in savings that Republicans said the bill would net through fiscal year 2002.

As Congress readied for its closing debate on the bill in late July, Clinton agonized over whether to sign it. The decision was perhaps the most important one he had yet faced in his presidency on domestic policy. Clinton met with his key advisers on the morning of July 31, the day the House was to take up the bill. Some advisers, including Vice President Al Gore, urged Clinton to sign the bill; others, including Chief of Staff Leon E. Panetta, urged a veto. After a two-and-a-half hour session with a broad group of advisers, and then fifteen minutes with just Gore and Panetta, Clinton decided to sign the bill.

Members of Congress from both parties watched on television as Clinton made a dramatic midafternoon announcement of his decision. Recalling his pledge to end the welfare system and his vetoes of two previous Republican bills, Clinton said the measure pending in Congress was flawed but still was "the best chance in a long, long time" to make needed changes in welfare.

Following Clinton's announcement, the House approved the bill 328–101. All but two Republicans voted for it and Democrats split evenly,

98–98. The Senate vote on August 1 was 78–21, with all the no votes coming from Democrats.

Republicans exulted in their success: "This is a Republican victory," said House Majority Leader Dick Armey of Texas. Some Democrats, reflecting the mood of advocates for the poor who were protesting outside the White House and the Capitol, warned that the bill would hurt millions of people, especially children, who were unable to help themselves. Sen. Daniel Patrick Moynihan, D-N.Y., a leading congressional expert on welfare, said the bill was premised on the belief that "the behavior of certain adults can be changed by making the lives of their children as wretched as possible. This is a fearsome assumption."

Transforming Welfare

The centerpiece of the bill was its elimination of the six-decade-old program called Aid to Families with Dependent Children, which provided cash grants to low-income mothers and their children. This program, along with several related programs, would be replaced with a block grant called Temporary Assistance for Needy Families. Funding for the program was set at $16.4 billion annually through fiscal year 2001. States were required to convert to the new block grant program, with its new eligibility requirements, by July 1, 1997, although they could do so earlier.

Adults receiving welfare benefits would be required to begin working within two years. States could exempt from this requirement parents of children under age one, but a parent could be exempted for no more than twelve months. States could not use federal aid to provide welfare for an adult for more than five years, although local and state funds could extend this period. The bill also allowed, but did not require, states to deny aid under certain circumstances, such as children born to welfare recipients or unwed parents under age eighteen.

The bill placed restrictions on two other major aid programs for the needy. A new definition of disability would sharply limit the number of children eligible under Supplementary Security Income (SSI), a cash program for low-income blind, aged, and disabled individuals. The food stamp program was curtailed by reducing individual allotments and by imposing a new work requirement. Able-bodied adults between the ages of eighteen and fifty without dependent children would have to work an average of twenty hours a week. Otherwise, they would not be eligible to receive food stamps for more than three months out of every three years, plus an additional three months if they were laid off work.

Republicans also used the welfare bill to block federal aid to immigrants, whether they were in the country legally or illegally. Illegal immigrants and legal nonimmigrants (such as travelers and students) would be denied nearly all federal benefits. Legal immigrants would be denied benefits under the SSI program and food stamps until they became citizens or had worked in the United Sates for at least ten years. States could also deny them welfare, Medicaid, and other social service aid. Noncitizens who arrived in

*the United States after the bill became law would be denied most aid pro-
grams for five years, including SSI, food stamps, welfare, and Medicaid.*

*In announcing July 31 that he would sign the welfare bill, Clinton
strongly objected to the cutbacks in the food stamp program and the limits
on aid to legal immigrants. The latter provision, he said, will hurt "people
who work hard for their families, pay taxes, serve in our military. This
provision has nothing to do with welfare reform. It is simply a budget-saving measure, and it is not right."*

*Clinton said he would work with Congress in the future to reverse some
of the food stamp cuts and the ban on aid to legal immigrants. The reelection of Republican majorities in both chambers in November appeared to
make it unlikely that he would have much success, however.*

*Following are excerpts from President Bill Clinton's announce-
ment at the White House July 31, 1996, that he would sign a welfare overhaul bill pending in Congress, followed by excerpts
from statements the same day by House Republican leaders—
Speaker Newt Gingrich, Budget Committee Chairman John
Kasich, Susan Molinari, and E. Clay Shaw Jr.:*

CLINTON'S REMARKS

Good afternoon. When I ran for president four years ago, I pledged to end
welfare as we know it. I have worked very hard for four years to do just that.
Today, the Congress will vote on legislation that gives us a chance to live up
to that promise—to transform a broken system that traps too many people in
a cycle of dependence to one that emphasizes work and independence; to
give people on welfare a chance to draw a paycheck, not a welfare check.

It gives us a better chance to give those on welfare what we want for all
families in America, the opportunity to succeed at home and at work. For
those reasons I will sign it into law.

The legislation is, however, far from perfect. There are parts of it that are
wrong, and I will address those parts in a moment.

But, on balance, this bill is a real step forward for our country, our values
and for people who are on welfare. For 15 years I have worked on this problem, as governor and as a president. I've spent time in welfare offices, I have
talked to mothers on welfare who desperately want the chance to work and
support their families independently. A long time ago I concluded that the
current welfare system undermines the basic values of work, responsibility
and family, trapping generation after generation in dependency and hurting
the very people it was designed to help.

[Historic Opportunity]

Today we have an historic opportunity to make welfare what it was meant
to be—a second chance, not a way of life. And even though the bill has seri-

ous flaws that are unrelated to welfare reform, I believe we have a duty to seize the opportunity it gives us to end welfare as we know it.

Over the past 3½ years I have done everything in my power as president to promote work and responsibility, working with 41 states to give them 69 welfare reform experiments. We have also required teen mothers to stay in school, required federal employees to pay their child support, cracked down on people who owe child support and crossed state lines.

As a result, child support collections are up 40 percent, to $11 billion, and there are 1.3 million fewer people on welfare today than there were when I took office. From the outset, however, I have also worked with members of both parties in Congress to achieve a national welfare reform bill that will make work and responsibility the law of the land. I made my principles for real welfare reform very clear from the beginning.

First and foremost, it should be about moving people from welfare to work. It should impose time limits on welfare. It should give people the child care and the health care they need to move from welfare to work without hurting their children. It should crack down on child support enforcement, and it should protect our children.

This legislation meets these principles. It gives us a chance we haven't had before—to break the cycle of dependency that has existed for millions and millions of our fellow citizens, exiling them from the world of work that gives structure, meaning, and dignity to most of our lives.

[Different Priorities]

We've come a long way in this debate. It's important to remember that not so very long ago, at the beginning of this very Congress, some wanted to put poor children in orphanages and take away all help for mothers simply because they were poor, young and unmarried. Last year the Republican majority in Congress sent me legislation that had its priorities backward. It was soft on work and tough on children. It failed to provide child care and health care. It imposed deep and unacceptable cuts in school lunches, child welfare and help for disabled children. The bill came to me twice and I vetoed it twice.

The bipartisan legislation before the Congress today is significantly better than the bills I vetoed. Many of the worst elements I objected to are out of it. And many of the improvements I asked for are included. First, the new bill is strong on work. It provides $4 billion more for child care so that mothers can move from welfare to work and protects their children by maintaining health and safety standards for day care. These things are very important. You cannot ask somebody on welfare to go to work if they're going to neglect their children in doing it.

It gives states powerful performance incentives to place people in jobs. It requires states to hold up their end of the bargain by maintaining their own spending on welfare. And it gives states the capacity to create jobs by taking money now used for welfare checks and giving it to employers as income subsidies as an incentive to hire people or to create community service jobs.

Second, this new bill is better for children than the two I vetoed. It keeps the national nutritional safety net intact by eliminating the food stamp cap and the optional block grant. It drops the deep cuts and devastating changes in school lunch, child welfare and help for disabled children. It allows states to use federal money to provide vouchers for children whose parents can't find work after the time limits expire. And it preserves the national guarantee of health care for poor children, the disabled, pregnant women, the elderly and people on welfare.

Just as important, this bill continues to include the child support enforcement measures I proposed two years ago, the most sweeping crackdown on deadbeat parents in history. If every parent paid the child support they should, we could move 800,000 women and children off welfare immediately. With this bill we say to parents, if you don't pay the child support you owe, we will garnish your wages, take away your driver's license, track you across state lines and, as necessary, make you work off what you owe. It is a very important advance that could only be achieved in legislation. I did not have the executive authority to do this without a bill.

So I will sign this bill. First and foremost because the current system is broken. Second, because Congress has made many of the changes I sought. And, third, because even though serious problems remain in the non-welfare reform provisions of the bill, this is the best chance we will have for a long, long time to complete the work of ending welfare as we know it by moving people from welfare to work, demanding responsibility and doing better by children.

However, I want to be very clear. Some parts of this bill still go too far. And I am determined to see that those areas are corrected.

[Nutrition Cuts]

First, I am concerned that although we have made great strides to maintain the national nutritional safety net, this bill still cuts deeper than it should in nutritional assistance, mostly for working families with children. In the budget talks, we reached a tentative agreement on $21 billion in food stamp savings over the next several years. They are included in this bill.

However, the congressional majority insisted on another cut we did not agree to, repealing a reform adopted four years ago in Congress, which was to go into effect next year. It's called the Excess Shelter Reduction, which helps some of our hardest pressed working families. Finally, we were going to treat working families with children the same way we treat senior citizens who draw food stamps today.

Now, blocking this change, I believe—I know—will make it harder for some of our hardest pressed working families with children. This provision is a mistake, and I will work to correct it.

[Effect on Immigrants]

Second, I am deeply disappointed that the congressional leadership insisted on attaching to this extraordinarily important bill a provision that will hurt legal immigrants in America, people who work hard for their families, pay taxes, serve in our military. This provision has nothing to do with welfare reform. It is simply a budget-saving measure, and it is not right.

These immigrant families with children who fall on hard times through no fault of their own—for example because they face the same risks the rest of us do from accidents, from criminal assaults, from serious illnesses—they should be eligible for medical and other help when they need it.

The Republican majority could never have passed such a provision standing alone. You see that in the debate in the immigration bill, for example, over the Gallegly amendment and the question of education of undocumented and illegal immigrant children.

This provision will cause great stress for states, for localities, for medical facilities that have to serve large numbers of legal immigrants. It is just wrong to say to people, we'll let you work here, you're helping our country, you'll pay taxes, you serve in our military, you may get killed defending America—but if somebody mugs you on a street corner or you get cancer or you get hit by a car or the same thing happens to your children, we're not going to give you assistance any more.

I am convinced this would never have passed alone, and I am convinced when we send legislation to Congress to correct it, it will be corrected.

In the meantime, let me also say that I intend to take further executive action directing the INS to continue to work to remove the bureaucratic roadblocks to citizenship to all eligible, legal immigrants. I will do everything in my power, in other words, to make sure that this bill lifts people up and does not become an excuse for anyone to turn their backs on this problem or on people who are generally in need through no fault of their own.

This bill must also not let anyone off the hook. The states asked for this responsibility, now they have to shoulder it and not run away from it. We have to make sure that in the coming years reform and change actually result in moving people from welfare to work.

The business community must provide greater private sector jobs that people on welfare need to build good lives and strong families. I challenge every state to adopt the reforms that Wisconsin, Oregon, Missouri and other states are proposing to do, to take the money that used to be available for welfare checks and offer it to the private sector as wage subsidies to begin to hire these people, to give them a chance to build their families and build their lives.

All of us have to rise to this challenge and see this reform, not as a chance to demonize or demean anyone, but instead as an opportunity to bring everyone fully into the mainstream of American life, to give them a chance to share in the prosperity and the promise that most of our people are enjoying today.

And we here in Washington must continue to do everything in our power to reward work and to expand opportunity for all people. The earned-income tax credit [EITC], which we expanded in 1993 dramatically, is now rewarding the work of 15 million working families.

I am pleased that congressional efforts to gut this tax cut for the hardest pressed working people have been blocked. This legislation preserves the

EITC and its benefits for working families. Now we must increase the minimum wage, which also will benefit millions of working people with families and help them to offset the impact of some of the nutritional cuts in this bill.

Through these efforts, we all have to recognize, as I said in 1992, the best anti-poverty program is still a job. I want to congratulate the members of Congress in both parties who worked together on this welfare reform legislation. I want to challenge them to put politics aside and continue to work together to meet our other challenges and to correct the problems that are still there with this legislation.

I am convinced that it does present an historic opportunity to finish the work of ending welfare as we know it, and that is why I have decided to sign it.

[Effect on Children]

Q: Mr. President, some civil rights groups and children's advocacy groups still say that they believe that this is going to hurt children. I wonder what your response is to that. And, also, it took you a little while to decide whether you would go along with this bill or not. Can you give us some sense of what you and your advisers kind of talked about and the mood in the White House over this?

P: Sure. Well, first of all, the conference was not completed until late last evening, and there were changes being made in the bill right up to the very end. So when I went to bed last night, I didn't know what the bill said. And this was supposed to be a day off for me, and when I got up and I realized that the conference had completed its work late last night and that the bill was scheduled for a vote late this afternoon, after I did a little work around the house this morning, I came in and we went to work I think about 11:00.

And we simply—we got everybody in who had an interest in this and we went through every provision of the bill, line by line, so that I made sure that I understood exactly what had come out of the conference. And then I gave everybody in the administration who was there a chance to voice their opinion on it and to explore what their views were and what our options were. And as soon as we finished the meeting, I went in and had a brief talk with the vice president and with [White House Chief of Staff Leon E.] Panetta, and I told them that I had decided that, on balance, I should sign the bill. And then we called this press conference.

Q: And what about the civil rights groups. . . .

P: I would say to them that there are some groups who basically have never agreed with me on this, who never agreed that we should do anything to give the states much greater flexibility on this if it meant doing away with the individual entitlement to the welfare check. And that is still, I think, the central objection to most of the groups.

My view about that is that for a very long time it's hard to say that we've had anything that approaches a uniform AFDC [Aid to Families with Dependent Children] system when the benefits range from a low of $187 a month to a high of $655 a month for a family of three or four. And I think that the system we have is not working. It works for half the people who just use it for a little while and get off. It will continue to work for them. I think the states will continue to provide for them.

For the other half of the people who are trapped on it, it is not working. And I believe that the child support provisions here, the child care provisions here, the protection of the medical benefits—indeed, the expansion of the medical guarantee now from 1998 to 2002, mean that on balance these families will be better off. I think the problems in this bill are in the non-welfare reform provisions, in the nutritional provisions that I mentioned and especially in the legal immigrant provisions that I mentioned.

[Credit or Blame]

Q: Mr. President, it seems likely there will be a kind of political contest to see who gets the credit or the blame on this measure. Sen. Dole is out with a statement calling—saying that you've been brought along to sign his bill. Are you concerned at all that you will be seen as having been kind of dragged into going along with something that you originally promised to do and that this will look like you signing onto a Republican initiative?

P: No. First of all, because I don't—you know, if we're doing the right thing there will be enough credit to go around. And if we're doing the wrong thing there will be enough blame to go around. I'm not worried about that. I've always wanted to work with Senator Dole and others. And before he left the Senate, I asked him not to leave the budget negotiations. So I'm not worried about that.

But that's a pretty hard case to make, since I vetoed their previous bills twice and since while they were talking about it we were doing it. It's now generally accepted by everybody who has looked at the evidence that we effected what the *New York Times* called a quiet revolution in welfare. There are 1.3 million fewer people on welfare today than there were when I took office.

But there are limits to what we can do with these waivers. We couldn't get the child support enforcement. We couldn't get the extra child care. Those are two things that we had to have legislation to do. And the third thing is we needed to put all the states in a position where they had to move right now to try to create more jobs. So far—I know that we had Wisconsin and earlier, Oregon, and I believe Missouri. And I think those are the only three states, for example, that had taken up the challenge that I gave to the governors in Vermont a couple of years ago to start taking the welfare payments and use it for wage subsidies to the private sector to actually create jobs. You can't tell people to go to work if there is no job out there.

So now they all have the power and they have financial incentives to create jobs, plus we've got the child care locked in and the medical care locked in and the child support enforcement locked in. None of this could have happened without legislation. That's why I thought this legislation was important.

Q: Mr. President, some of the critics of this bill say that the flaws will be very hard to fix because that will involve adding to the budget, and, in the current political climate, adding to the expenditures is politically impossible. How would you respond to that?

P: Well, it just depends on what your priorities are. For one thing, it will be somewhat easier to balance the budget now in the time period because the deficit this year is $23 billion less than it was the last time we did our budget calculations. So we've lowered that base $23 billion this year. Now, in the out years it still comes up, but there's some savings there that we could turn around and put back into this.

Next, if you look at—my budget corrects it right now. I had $42 billion in savings, this bill has about $57 billion in savings. You could correct all these problems that I mentioned with money to spare in the gap there. So when we get down to the budget negotiations, either at the end of this year or at the beginning of next year, I think the American people will say we can stand marginally smaller tax cuts, for example, or cut somewhere else to cure this problem of immigrants and children, to cure the nutritional problems. We're not talking about vast amounts of money over a six year period. It's not a big budget number, and I think it can easily be fixed, given where we are in the budget negotiations.

Q: The last couple days in these meetings among your staff and this morning, would you say there was no disagreement among people in the administration about what you should do? Some disagreement? A lot of disagreement?

P: No, I would say that there was—first of all, I have rarely been as impressed with the people who work in this administration on any issue as I have been on this. There was significant disagreement among my advisers about whether this bill should be signed or vetoed, but 100 percent of them recognized the power of the arguments on the other side. It was a very moving thing. Today the conversation was almost 100 percent about the merits of the bill and not the political implications of it. Because I think those things are very hard to calculate anyway. I think they're virtually impossible.

I have tried to thank all of them personally, including those who are here in the room and those who are not here, because they did have differences of opinion about whether we should sign or veto, but each side recognized the power of the arguments on the other side. And 100 percent of them, just like 100 percent of the Congress, recognized that we needed to change fundamentally the framework within which welfare operates in this country. The only question was whether the problems in the non-welfare reform provisions were so great that they would justify a veto and giving up what might be, what I'm convinced is, our last best chance to fundamentally change the system.

[Democratic Legacy]

Q: Mr. President, even in spite of all the details of this, you as a Democrat are actually helping to dismantle something that was put in place by Democrats 60 years ago. Did that give you pause, that overarching question?

P: No. No, because it was put in place 60 years ago when the poverty population of America was fundamentally different than it is now. As Sen. Moynihan [D-N.Y.]—you know, Sen. Moynihan strongly disagrees with me on this— but as he has pointed out repeatedly, when welfare was created, the typical welfare recipient was a miner's widow with no education, small children, husband dies in the mine, no expectation that there was a job for the widow to do or that she ever could do it, very few out-of-wedlock pregnancies and births. The whole dynamics were different then.

So I have always thought that the Democratic Party should be on the side of creating opportunity and promoting empowerment and responsibility for people, and a system that was in place 60 years ago that worked for the poverty population then is not the one we need now. But that's why I have worked so hard too to veto previous bills. That does not mean, I think, we can walk away from the guarantee that our party gave on Medicaid, the guarantee our party gave on nutrition, the guarantee our party gave in school lunches, because that has not changed. But the nature of the poverty population is so different now that I am convinced we have got to be willing to experiment, to try to work to find ways to break the cycle of dependency that keeps dragging folks down.

And I think the states are going to find out pretty quickly that they're going to have to be willing to invest something in these people to make sure that they can go to work in the ways that I suggested.

Yes, one last question.

Q: Mr. President, you have mentioned Senator Moynihan. Have you spoken to him or other congressional leaders, especially congressional Democrats? And what was the conversation and reaction to your indication?

P: Well, I talked to him as recently, I think, as about a week ago. When we went up to meet with the TWA families, we talked about it again. And, you know, I have an enormous amount of respect for him. And he has been a powerful and cogent critic of this whole move. I'll just have to hope that in this one case I'm right and he's wrong—because I have an enormous regard for him. And I've spoken to a number of other Democrats, and some think I'm right and some don't.

This is a case where, you know, I have been working with this issue for such a long time—a long time before it became—to go back to Mr. Hume's question—a long time before it became a cause célèbre in Washington or anyone tried to make it a partisan political issue. It wasn't much of a political hot potato when I first started working on it. I just was concerned that the system didn't seem to be working. And I was most concerned about those who were trapped on it and their children and the prospect that their children would be trapped on it.

I think we all have to admit here—we all need a certain level of humility today. We are trying to continue a process that I've been pushing for three and a half years. We're trying to get the legal changes we need in federal law that will work to move these folks to a position of independence where they can support their children, and their lives as workers and in families will be stronger.

But if this were an easy question, we wouldn't have had the two and a half hour discussion with my advisers today and we'd all have a lot more answers than we do. But I'm convinced that we're moving in the right direction. I'm convinced it's an opportunity we should seize. I'm convinced that we have to change the two problems in this bill that are not related to welfare reform, that were just sort of put under the big shade of the tree here, that are part of this budget strategy with which I disagree. And I'm convinced when we bring those things out into the light of day we will be able to do it. And I think some Republicans will agree with us, and we'll be able to get what we need to do to change it.

GINGRICH'S REMARKS

Let me just say, first of all, I am delighted by what seems to be the president's decision to sign this bill. I think welfare reform is very important. I think it's particularly important for children who are currently trapped in poverty. I believe this bill will dramatically help young Americans have a chance to rise and to do better.

I think that by establishing the work experience and by creating the natural expectation that people will be busy working it is a very big step. I also believe the additional money that was put in for child care is very, very important and the fact is I think we have about $1 billion more in for child care than the president asked for.

So, this is a bill which both provides for child care and provides for collecting child support. And it provides for a work requirement. It returns power to the states. And I thought that his commitment to sign it was, frankly, very, very important.

In one or two places—and I hope Clay Shaw will address one of them—where he was, I think, factually wrong. But I think that we have to recognize this is a historic moment, when we are working together to do something very good for America and something which is very, very important. . . .

KASICH'S REMARKS

Let me just say that this is a great victory for the sense of fairness for all Americans. The American people feel fundamentally that if somebody's disabled, we're going to help them. But if somebody's able bodied and can work, then they need to go to work.

America has been crying for this bill now for a generation. They're sick of generational dependency and, frankly, they wanted a fundamental change.

I'm glad the president is going to sign the bill. And I want to compliment him for that. But, at a sense of fair play, this Republican Congress committed to doing this nearly two years ago.

This has been a very difficult road. We have had two vetoes. But we stayed committed to our principles. And our principles are a reflection of the principles of, not just Republicans, but hard-working Democrats as well.

And because we stuck to our principles, and because we believed that the American people needed to be listened to in this Congress, we were able to pass a welfare bill and were able to convince the president that this bill is a bill that America wants and America needs.

This is a great day for this United States Congress. It's a great day for the American people. And this is one of those successes that when we get old and we're all in our rocking chairs, we're going to look back and say, thank God we were able to make America a little bit better.

MOLINARI'S REMARKS

I come from a city where, up until recently—and a lot of the initiatives that we've just adopted are or about to adopt on a national level had been adopted on a city level—and prior to that, one out of eight New Yorkers was on welfare.

So, we are a city where our taxpayers know that this is a system that desperately needs to be changed, as do the people who are recipients.

Let me just add to all that's been said. I think those of you who are standing down here heard a tremendous sigh of relief which came from the House of Representatives, particularly the Republican side, just a few moments ago when President Clinton announced, finally, that he would sign this welfare bill.

And we are relieved for all the reasons stated by our prior speakers and for all the people you'll talk to from throughout our communities.

There's a relief that finally there will be a sense of order and responsibility established, that a system that has been broken for so very long will finally be fixed, that the people who need help in getting up through welfare and off welfare to find real opportunities in their community will really get that chance, and that there will be some fairness and order to the taxpayers, who see a system that will reward them.

Let me just again conclude by echoing what the speaker said. This is a bill that is a compassionate bill. It helps those people who need help and it forces those people who need a little help to get to work to do just that.

And lastly, it is a tremendous bill when it comes to the concerns of women, (A) from a child care component that always was over and above funded prior years' commitments, and past what the president had requested, and above what the Senate had given us.

And of course, extremely important to people throughout this nation is very tough national child support enforcement mechanisms that will finally find the sense and the fairness of the national government behind those parents who find themselves out and alone, oftentimes without any additional assistance in trying to find the support that they need from a paying—an often-absent parent.

So again, we all breathed a huge sigh of relief about 10 minutes ago when President Clinton told us that he was going to join with us in reforming this system.

And as John Kasich said, this is a great day for the people on welfare and for American taxpayers.

SHAW'S REMARKS

This is—when the Senate passed with a good bipartisan vote, with half the Democrats joining the Republicans on the welfare bill, at that time I began to think for the first time that, indeed, the president would sign this bill. But I have to confess that the realization of his speech is still sinking in.

This is an incredible day in the history of this country. July 31 has got to go down as Independence Day for those who have been trapped in a system that has been left dormant and left to allow people to actually decay on layers of intergenerational welfare, which has corrupted their souls and stolen their future.

We're going to have to work together. And I would, today, reach out to my Democrat colleagues who don't agree with us that this is real welfare reform, and say let's be patient with each other. And let's work together over the next few years to be sure this works.

Whether they agree or disagree with welfare reform, we are in this together, and together it's going to be very important for us to be sure that this does work, because I don't really believe—even those that do not believe that it's going to work and would vote against it today—I don't believe that any of them would really want it to fail because if it fails, we fail.

So it's going to take a lot of work.

We're not through with welfare reform. We're going to be coming back with bills that are going to adjust it and fine tune it.

The Congress of the United States is not going to walk away from this. This is a responsibility that we have taken on, and for the first time this Congress has said we are unsatisfied with the status quo and we're going to reach out for those that are less fortunate than we are and we're going to do what's necessary to bring the jobs to them to see that this system does actually work.

It will work. The states have provided great laboratories. And I think that this is going to be a great day for all Americans.

I would like to correct one thing that the president said. I praise him for his courage in going on television and endorsing the bill. He did say though—and he made reference twice in his speech that I detected—that non-citizen veterans were not covered. Non-citizen veterans are covered by welfare.

That's one of the exceptions, where the vast majority of non-citizens are no longer going to be getting welfare, but those that served in our armed forces certainly will. . . .

August

CLINTON ON PESTICIDE
REGULATION REFORM
August 3, 1996

Pressured into action by court decisions that threatened to eliminate some of the most important pesticides used by farmers, Congress in 1996 rushed through the most sweeping changes in pesticide regulations in nearly two decades. Regulating pesticides had been so contentious that Congress had been unable to adopt major legislation on the issue since 1978. A sudden willingness to compromise by farmers, consumer groups, and environmentalists enabled Congress to pass a bill in July without a single dissenting vote. President Bill Clinton signed the pesticide bill into law (PL 104–170) on August 3, saying it would "revolutionize the way we protect food from harmful pesticides. It proves we don't have to choose between a healthy environment and a healthy economy."

The bill was one of two major actions taken by the federal government in 1996 to revamp its regulation of food safety. The other was a new set of procedures announced by the Agriculture Department on July 6 for inspection of meat and poultry. (Meat inspection regulations, p. 414)

Revising the Delaney Clause

The central issue before Congress was how to revise the so-called Delaney Clause (named after its sponsor, Rep. James J. Delaney, D-N.Y.), which had been enacted in 1958 as part of the Federal Food, Drug, and Cosmetic Act. It barred processed foods from containing even minute traces of cancer-causing chemicals. (Carcinogens in the diet, p. 71)

Recent advances in scientific methods meant that some carcinogens could be detected in amounts as low as parts per trillion—levels that in most cases were unlikely to cause significant health problems. Federal court decisions in 1992 and 1995 forced the Environmental Protection Agency (EPA), which regulated the use of pesticides in food, to take steps under the Delaney Clause toward banning as many as fifty common agricultural chemicals. Farm groups said such a ban would cause serious disruptions in the nation's food supply.

The American Farm Bureau Federation and other industry groups pressured Congress to intervene by relaxing the provisions of the Delaney Clause. At the same time, organizations representing consumers and environmentalists saw an opportunity to advance some proposals of their own, such as increasing consumer awareness of pesticide dangers and tightening regulations governing pesticides used on fresh fruit and other foods that children consume in large quantities. Children were found to be particularly susceptible to illnesses caused by ingestion of pesticides.

In mid-July, aides to key members of the House Commerce Committee hammered out a compromise that satisfied the competing interests on the pesticide issue. Once that agreement was reached, nearly two decades of political squabbling were swept aside in an amazingly short time. The Commerce Committee approved the compromise bill unanimously on July 17. The full House—using a "suspension of the rules" procedure normally employed for minor legislation—endorsed it unanimously on July 23, and the Senate cleared it for the president the next day by voice vote.

Members of Congress on both sides of the aisle expressed astonishment that a bill dealing with such a politically charged issue as pesticides in food could sail through a Congress that was so bitterly divided on partisan grounds. "It just shows that we can get something done if we just work together and compromise and forget that there is an election . . . which I know is very difficult to do these days," said Rep. Bill Richardson, D-N.M.

The Bill's Major Provisions

The pesticide bill, formally called the Food Quality Protection Act, replaced the Delaney Clause with a requirement for the EPA to establish a new tolerance level ensuring that people who eat both raw and processed foods would have a "reasonable certainty of no harm" from pesticide and other chemical residues. This was generally interpreted to mean that there could be no more than a one-in-a-million chance that the residue would cause cancer. The EPA was required to review all the tolerance levels within ten years.

At the urging of consumer and environmental groups, the bill also required the EPA to set tougher standards for pesticides and chemicals that were known to severely affect children and that were applied to foods (such as apples) eaten in large quantities by children. In these cases, the EPA would heighten the health standard by as much as tenfold; in other words, there could be no more than a one-in-ten-million chance that the pesticide or chemical residue could cause cancer in children.

The bill gave the EPA limited discretion to relax these standards if they threatened a significant disruption of the domestic food supply or if a public health problem would result from not using a certain pesticide. Even so, the annual risk of relaxing a regulation could not be more than ten times the standard level of safety, and the lifetime risk to individuals could not be more than twice the standard level.

At the request of business groups, the bill generally prohibited states from imposing tighter pesticide standards than those adopted by the federal government. A state could impose a tougher standard only if it petitioned the EPA to do so, and the EPA did not object.

The bill also included a "consumers right-to-know" provision that was sought by consumer groups and environmentalists and opposed by business interests. That provision required the EPA, in consultation with the Agriculture Department and the Food and Drug Administration, to publish pamphlets for display in grocery stores. The pamphlets would summarize the risks and benefits of pesticides and alert consumers to foods having a higher pesticide residue than the one-in-a-million standard.

Following are excerpts of remarks by President Bill Clinton at a White House ceremony August 3, 1996, for the signing of the Food Quality Protection Act, which revised standards for the presence of pesticides in foods:

. . . Ladies and gentlemen, we are here today in celebration and we should be immensely proud of the Food Quality Protection Act that will revolutionize the way we protect food from harmful pesticides. It proves we don't have to choose between a healthy environment and a healthy economy. It shows when we come together across party lines and do the right thing for the American people we can get real results. This is important, not only for what was done, but for how it was done; and I want to thank everyone here who has been a part of it.

From the day I took office I have worked hard to meet what I think is a fundamental promise that we should make to our people. People should know that the food they eat and the water they drink will not make them sick. We strengthened and expanded the Community Right to Know law, which requires industries to tell our citizens what substances are being released into the world around us. Last year we put in place strong new protections to ensure that seafood is safe. Last month we announced steps to revamp our meat and poultry inspection system for the first time in 90 years.

Today we add the cornerstone to this solid foundation with the Food Quality Protection Act. I like to think of it as the "peace of mind" act, because it'll give parents the peace of mind that comes from knowing that the fruits, the vegetables, the grains that they put down in front of their children are safe. It's long overdue. The old safeguards that protected our food from pesticides were written with the best of intentions, but they weren't up to the job. And as you can see from the vast array of support here across every sector of American life, nobody liked them very much and no one thought that they really worked as they were supposed to. Bad pesticides stayed on the market too long, good alternatives were kept out. In this new provision we deal with the problem of existing law, which is that there are strong protections against cancer, but not against other health dangers. There is simply no uniform standard for what's safe.

These weaknesses in the present law cause real problems for everyone involved in producing and distributing our food, and for, most of all, the people who consume it—especially our children. According to the National Academy of Sciences, infants and young people are especially vulnerable to pesticides—chemicals can go a long way in a small body.

This Act puts the safety of our children first. It sets a clear, consistent standard for all pesticide use on all foods for all health risks. It sets a standard high—if a pesticide poses a danger to our children, it won't be in our food, period. The Act will reform the regulatory process for pesticides so that new and safer substitutes will be approved faster, and this is also very important. The sooner they get on the market, the sooner farmers will be able to use them to replace older pesticides that may pose greater health risks. The pesticides will be reviewed regularly using the best science available.

. . . [T]his legislation will see to it that consumers get the information they need. Supermarkets will be required to provide health information to shoppers about the pesticides used on food they're buying. A family ought to be able to gather for a summer dinner knowing that the food before them will provide nothing more than nourishment and joy. Americans have enough on their minds without having to worry about that. With this legislation, Americans will continue to know that the world's most bountiful food supply is also its safest.

And as I said before, to me, almost as important as what the law does is how it was done. This Act comes to our desk—to my desk and to our administration—with the support of farmers and environmentalists, consumer groups and agribusiness and the medical community. After more than a decade of work, these groups have come together to say with this bill, we do not have to choose between a clean environment and a safe food supply and a strong economy. If we do it right, we can have both. It comes with the unanimous backing of every member of Congress in both parties. And I must say, I am gratified to see this, because I see this effort to preserve the environment in a way that will permit us to grow the economy as an essential component of our national security in the 21st century.

Last year, we were fighting about efforts to weaken our most basic safeguards for clean air, clean water, safe food. Now, we see a bipartisan public commitment to the public health. This is an area where we stand on common ground. And as a people, we should continue to stand on common ground.

I want to compliment the Congress for the work that was done in this last week—moving people from welfare to work, raising the minimum wage, helping small businesses, passing health care reform, making this effort to safeguard our food. Last night Congress passed strong legislation to help keep our drinking water safe. This has been a very good season of progress. Turning away from extremism toward common ground, around opportunity, responsibility and community. I am very pleased. I thank the members of Congress here for their leadership. And I thank the American people, and especially those here represented, for making this day happen.

470

NASA STATEMENTS ON EVIDENCE OF POSSIBLE LIFE ON MARS
August 6–7, 1996

One of mankind's most treasured suppositions—that there might be life on other planets—received an important dose of scientific backing on August 6 when the National Aeronautics and Space Administration (NASA) said a 4.2 pound, potato-size meteor contained "evidence of primitive life on early Mars." NASA's announcement caused a worldwide sensation and revived public interest in the ancient question of whether Earth is the only home to living creatures.

Announcing the discovery in response to news media reports, NASA administrator Daniel S. Goldin stressed that "we are not talking about 'little green men.' These are extremely small, single-cell structures that somewhat resemble bacteria on Earth. There is no evidence or suggestion that any higher life form ever existed on Mars." At a news conference on August 7, an excited Goldin said: "This day may well go down in history." NASA scientists published a detailed report of their findings in the August 16 issue of the journal Science.

The finding gave new impetus for a long-planned NASA project: an unmanned landing on Mars that would gather rock samples for up to two years before returning to Earth. NASA had planned such a mission for no earlier than 2005, but Goldin said the finding might justify speeding up that project.

President Bill Clinton gave general backing to this project, saying: "I am determined that the American space program will put its full intellectual power and technological powers behind the search for further evidence of life on Mars."

Skeptics immediately raised questions about the validity of NASA's research and conclusions. Among their most important questions: Was the meteor really from Mars? Even if the rock came from Mars, was it possible that the bacteria-like material it contained originated on Earth? Were the structures in the meteor really organic fossils or something of nonbiological origin? Goldin said NASA welcomed such questions and would

*make samples of the meteor available to qualified researchers for indepen-
dent analysis.*

*At least one independent study of meteor samples later in 1996 raised
significant questions about whether the material really was biological in
nature. An international geochemistry journal,* Geochimica et Cosmochim-
ica Acta, *in December published findings by one team of scientists whose
examination of the material convinced them it was not "of biogenic origin."*

The Meteorite

*NASA scientists said the meteorite was formed about 4.5 billion years
ago—indicating that it came from among the most ancient terrain on
Mars. The possibly organic material found in the meteor was formed
between 3.6 billion and 4 billion years ago, they said.*

*The scientists concluded that the meteor probably was "ejected" from the
Martian surface about 16 million years ago when a comet or asteroid hit
the planet, spewing tons of rock into space. After its space travels (probably circling the sun), the meteor hit the Earth about 13,000 years ago. The
meteor was found in Antarctica in 1984. In a statement released August
12, Nadine G. Barlow, a planetary scientist at the University of Central
Florida, reported identifying two craters on Mars that matched the characteristics of the area from which the meteor may have come.*

*When the meteor left Mars, NASA scientists said, the planet almost cer-
tainly was much wetter and warmer than it is today. Under such conditions, they said, it was reasonable to conclude that very primitive forms of
life may have developed on Mars but never evolved to a higher level.*

*At the August 7 news conference, NASA scientists David S. McKay and
Everett K. Gibson showed images taken by high-powered electron micro-
scopes of tiny tube-shaped and egg-shaped structures within the Martian
meteor. The structures were much smaller than the smallest organisms
found on Earth—in some cases by a factor of 100. The scientists said they
believed these structures were fossils of organisms that existed on Mars at
the time the meteor was ejected. McKay and Gibson were members of a
team of scientists who analyzed the meteor for two-and-a-half years at the
Johnson Space Center in Texas; the team members agreed on the findings,
they said.*

*The NASA news conference also included a presentation by William
Schopf, a paleobiologist at the University of California–Los Angeles, who
expressed some skepticism about the findings. Schopf said he wanted to see
more hard evidence about the age of the meteor, its origin, and the source
of the microscopic material found in it. Schopf said he was particularly
anxious to learn whether the material contained cells, the basic structures
of living organisms on Earth.*

Water on the Moon?

*If the announcement about possible life on Mars held out hope of con-
firming age-old speculations, another announcement in 1996 appeared to*

refute another ancient belief: that the Earth's moon is totally dry. At a Pentagon news conference on December 3, scientists said a U.S. satellite had picked up radar signals suggesting the presence of ice on the dark side of the moon's south pole.

Paul Spudis, a geologist with the Lunar and Planetary Institute of Rice University in Houston, said: "We're not positive, but we see signals consistent with ice, and we think it's there." Spudis and other scientists said the Pentagon's Clementine satellite appeared to have detected a lake of frozen water and dirt, covering about thirty-eight square miles on the moon. The findings were reported in the November 29 issue of Science *magazine.*

If the finding is confirmed, NASA officials said the presence of ice on the moon might offer logistical support for future lunar explorations. Astronauts might be able to use it for drinking water or convert it to hydrogen and oxygen for fuel.

Other Space Findings

In August scientists at the Jet Propulsion Laboratory in Pasadena, California, announced findings that suggested the presence of an ocean of ice on Europa, one of the planet Jupiter's sixteen moons. Scientists had long considered that moon one of the most likely homes in the solar system for living beings.

Also during 1996, astronomers continued to detect planets circling stars in distant constellations. Scientists at the University of California–Berkeley and San Francisco State University reported in April finding a large planet in orbit around a star that appears in the constellation Cancer. Astronomers at the University of Texas announced in October the discovery of a planet in the constellation Cygnus. That brought to eight the number of planets circling Sun-like stars that had been discovered since late 1995.

Following is the text of a statement issued August 6, 1996, by NASA administrator Daniel S. Goldin, in which he announced the discovery of possible life-forms in a meteor thought to be from Mars, followed by an August 7, 1996, statement by NASA providing additional details on the discovery:

STATEMENT BY NASA ADMINISTRATOR

NASA has made a startling discovery that points to the possibility that a primitive form of microscopic life may have existed on Mars more than three billion years ago. The research is based on a sophisticated examination of an ancient Martian meteorite that landed on Earth some 13,000 years ago.

The evidence is exciting, even compelling, but not conclusive. It is a discovery that demands further scientific investigation. NASA is ready to assist the process of rigorous scientific investigation and lively scientific debate that will follow this discovery.

I want everyone to understand that we are not talking about 'little green men.' These are extremely small, single-cell structures that somewhat resemble bacteria on Earth. There is no evidence or suggestion that any higher life form ever existed on Mars.

The NASA scientists and researchers who made this discovery will be available at a news conference tomorrow to discuss their findings. They will outline the step-by-step "detective story" that explains how the meteorite arrived here from Mars, and how they set about looking for evidence of long-ago life in this ancient rock. They will also release some fascinating images documenting their research.

NASA STATEMENT

A NASA research team of scientists at the Johnson Space Center (JSC), Houston, TX, and at Stanford University, Palo Alto, CA, has found evidence that strongly suggests primitive life may have existed on Mars more than 3.6 billion years ago.

The NASA-funded team found the first organic molecules thought to be of Martian origin; several mineral features characteristic of biological activity; and possible microscopic fossils of primitive, bacteria-like organisms inside of an ancient Martian rock that fell to Earth as a meteorite. This array of indirect evidence of past life will be reported in the August 16 issue of the journal *Science*, presenting the investigation to the scientific community at large for further study.

The two-year investigation was co-led by JSC planetary scientists Dr. David McKay, Dr. Everett Gibson and Kathie Thomas-Keprta of Lockheed-Martin, with the major collaboration of a Stanford team headed by Professor of Chemistry Dr. Richard Zare, as well as six other NASA and university research partners.

"There is not any one finding that leads us to believe that this is evidence of past life on Mars. Rather, it is a combination of many things that we have found," McKay said. "They include Stanford's detection of an apparently unique pattern of organic molecules, carbon compounds that are the basis of life. We also found several unusual mineral phases that are known products of primitive microscopic organisms on Earth. Structures that could be microscopic fossils seem to support all of this. The relationship of all of these things in terms of location—within a few hundred thousandths of an inch of one another—is the most compelling evidence."

"It is very difficult to prove life existed 3.6 billion years ago on Earth, let alone on Mars," Zare said. "The existing standard of proof, which we think we have met, includes having an accurately dated sample that contains native microfossils, mineralogical features characteristic of life, and evidence of complex organic chemistry."

474

"For two years, we have applied state-of-the-art technology to perform these analyses, and we believe we have found quite reasonable evidence of past life on Mars," Gibson added. "We don't claim that we have conclusively proven it. We are putting this evidence out to the scientific community for other investigators to verify, enhance, attack—disprove if they can—as part of the scientific process. Then, within a year or two, we hope to resolve the question one way or the other."

"What we have found to be the most reasonable interpretation is of such radical nature that it will only be accepted or rejected after other groups either confirm our findings or overturn them," McKay added.

The igneous rock in the 4.2–pound, potato-sized meteorite has been age-dated to about 4.5 billion years, the period when the planet Mars formed. The rock is believed to have originated underneath the Martian surface and to have been extensively fractured by impacts as meteorites bombarded the planets in the early inner solar system. Between 3.6 billion and 4 billion years ago, a time when it is generally thought that the planet was warmer and wetter, water is believed to have penetrated fractures in the subsurface rock, possibly forming an underground water system.

Since the water was saturated with carbon dioxide from the Martian atmosphere, carbonate minerals were deposited in the fractures. The team's findings indicate living organisms also may have assisted in the formation of the carbonate, and some remains of the microscopic organisms may have become fossilized, in a fashion similar to the formation of fossils in limestone on Earth. Then, 16 million years ago, a huge comet or asteroid struck Mars, ejecting a piece of the rock from its subsurface location with enough force to escape the planet. For millions of years, the chunk of rock floated through space. It encountered Earth's atmosphere 13,000 years ago and fell in Antarctica as a meteorite.

It is in the tiny globs of carbonate that the researchers found a number of features that can be interpreted as suggesting past life. Stanford researchers found easily detectable amounts of organic molecules called polycyclic aromatic hydrocarbons (PAHs) concentrated in the vicinity of the carbonate. Researchers at JSC found mineral compounds commonly associated with microscopic organisms and the possible microscopic fossil structures.

The largest of the possible fossils are less than 1/100 the diameter of a human hair, and most are about 1/1000 the diameter of a human hair—small enough that it would take about a thousand laid end-to-end to span the dot at the end of this sentence. Some are egg-shaped while others are tubular. In appearance and size, the structures are strikingly similar to microscopic fossils of the tiniest bacteria found on Earth.

The meteorite, called ALH84001, was found in 1984 in Allan Hills ice field, Antarctica, by an annual expedition of the National Science Foundation's Antarctic Meteorite Program. It was preserved for study in JSC's Meteorite Processing Laboratory and its possible Martian origin was not recognized until 1993. It is one of only 12 meteorites identified so far that match the unique Martian chemistry measured by the Viking spacecraft that landed on

Mars in 1976. ALH84001 is by far the oldest of the 12 Martian meteorites, more than three times as old as any other.

Many of the team's findings were made possible only because of very recent technological advances in high-resolution scanning electron microscopy and laser mass spectrometry. Only a few years ago, many of the features that they report were undetectable. Although past studies of this meteorite and others of Martian origin failed to detect evidence of past life, they were generally performed using lower levels of magnification, without the benefit of the technology used in this research. The recent discovery of extremely small bacteria on Earth, called nanobacteria, prompted the team to perform this work at a much finer scale than past efforts.

The nine authors of the *Science* report include McKay, Gibson and Thomas-Keprta of JSC; Christopher Romanek, formerly a National Research Council post-doctoral fellow at JSC who is now a staff scientist at the Savannah River Ecology Laboratory at the University of Georgia; Hojatollah Vali, a National Research Council post-doctoral fellow at JSC and a staff scientist at McGill University, Montreal, Quebec, Canada; and Zare, graduate students Simon J. Clemett and Claude R. Maechling and post-doctoral student Xavier Chillier of the Stanford University Department of Chemistry.

The team of researchers includes a wide variety of expertise, including microbiology, mineralogy, analytical techniques, geochemistry and organic chemistry, and the analysis crossed all of these disciplines. Further details on the findings presented in the *Science* article include:

• Researchers at Stanford University used a dual laser mass spectrometer—the most sensitive instrument of its type in the world—to look for the presence of the common family of organic molecules called PAHs. When microorganisms die, the complex organic molecules that they contain frequently degrade into PAHs. PAHs are often associated with ancient sedimentary rocks, coals and petroleum on Earth and can be common air pollutants. Not only did the scientists find PAHs in easily detectable amounts in ALH84001, but they found that these molecules were concentrated in the vicinity of the carbonate globules. This finding appears consistent with the proposition that they are a result of the fossilization process. In addition, the unique composition of the meteorite's PAHs is consistent with what the scientists expect from the fossilization of very primitive microorganisms. On Earth, PAHs virtually always occur in thousands of forms, but, in the meteorite, they are dominated by only about a half-dozen different compounds. The simplicity of this mixture, combined with the lack of light-weight PAHs like napthalene, also differs substantially from that of PAHs previously measured in non-Martian meteorites.

• The team found unusual compounds—iron sulfides and magnetite—that can be produced by anaerobic bacteria and other microscopic organisms on Earth. The compounds were found in locations directly associated with the fossil-like structures and carbonate globules in the meteorite. Extreme conditions—conditions very unlikely to have been encountered by the meteorite—would have been required to produce these compounds in close proximity to one another if life were not involved. The carbonate also contained tiny grains of magnetite that are almost identical to magnetic fossil remnants often left by certain bacteria found on Earth. Other minerals commonly associated with biological activity on Earth were found in the carbonate as well.

- The formation of the carbonate or fossils by living organisms while the meteorite was in the Antarctic was deemed unlikely for several reasons. The carbonate was age dated using a parent-daughter isotope method and found to be 3.6 billion years old, and the organic molecules were first detected well within the ancient carbonate. In addition, the team analyzed representative samples of other meteorites from Antarctica and found no evidence of fossil-like structures, organic molecules or possible biologically produced compounds and minerals similar to those in the ALH84001 meteorite. The composition and location of PAH organic molecules found in the meteorite also appeared to confirm that the possible evidence of life was extraterrestrial. No PAHs were found in the meteorite's exterior crust, but the concentration of PAHs increased in the meteorite's interior to levels higher than ever found in Antarctica. Higher concentrations of PAHs would have likely been found on the exterior of the meteorite, decreasing toward the interior, if the organic molecules are the result of contamination of the meteorite on Earth.

REPUBLICAN NATIONAL CONVENTION AND SPEECHES
August 12–15, 1996

The Republican candidates for president and vice president accepted their nominations, at the close of the Republican National Convention on August 15, with speeches intended to broaden the party's appeal beyond its conservative core. Former senator Bob Dole, who closed out a long career of public service with his run for the presidency, told delegates that the party is "broad and inclusive. It represents many streams of opinion and many points of view." Dole and his running mate, Jack F. Kemp, both reminded their audiences in the convention hall and at home watching television that Republicans were "the party of Lincoln."

The acceptance speeches wound up a Republican convention at which party leaders made every effort to submerge the internal conflicts the party has faced since the retirement of former president Ronald Reagan, its most popular leader in recent times. Religious conservatives, who controlled the party's machinery at the grass-roots level in many states, used the 1996 nominating process, the party platform, and the convention to enforce their uncompromising views on abortion and other politically charged social issues. The party's remaining moderate leaders, including Dole and several key governors, sought to soften the conservative wing's hard edge with inclusionary rhetoric. (Republican platform, p. 496)

Some of the party's most controversial figures—including House Speaker Newt Gingrich—were excluded from prime-time speaking engagements at the convention. Unsuccessful presidential candidate Patrick Buchanan, whose hard-right views reflected those of many convention delegates, was not permitted to speak from the convention podium at all.

In its prime-time events, the Republicans attempted to showcase their party as a broad-based, inclusionary political force. The highlight of that effort was a twenty-minute speech on the opening night of the convention by retired general Colin L. Powell.

Powell said the party "must always be the party of inclusion," and he was straightforward in his references to abortion and affirmative action, two of the most controversial issues before the party and, indeed, the country. "You all know that I believe in a woman's right to choose, and I strongly support affirmative action," he told the convention.

The next night, the keynote speech was delivered by Rep. Susan Molinari of New York, who demonstrated that the party's criticism of Clinton was not limited to its far-right wing. Party operatives gave the coveted keynote speechmaking role to Molinari, a supporter of abortion rights, to signal moderates that they were welcome in the party.

Another star performer for the party was Dole's wife, Elizabeth, who on the third night hosted a "This Is Your Life" style tribute to her husband. Strolling among delegates on the convention floor, microphone in hand, she introduced people who had been important to her husband, including a woman who had been a nurse at a hospital where Dole recovered from his World War II wounds. Sen. John McCain of Arizona delivered the nominating speech for Dole, calling his former Senate colleague "a modest, good man."

Dole on Dole, Clinton, and Values

Dole's acceptance speech offered him one of the best opportunities of the campaign to sell himself to the American people and to explain why they should retire Bill Clinton from the White House, but he faced several problems. Dole had always been reluctant to discuss a personal philosophy or to beat his own drum, usually referring to himself in the third person and often in a wry, self-deprecating manner. Sharpening his anti-Clinton rhetoric would remind voters how he earned his reputation, during the 1976 race when he was Gerald Ford's vice presidential candidate, as a dour attack dog. His acceptance speech, initially drafted by novelist Mark Helprin, overcame those difficulties with a careful balance. Dole first offered warm memories of his childhood in Russell, Kansas, recalled his service in World War II, and spoke of bedrock values such as God, family, and country—then he sternly denounced Clinton's failures.

At the close of his speech, after he had warned of the rising crime rate, a tide of illegal immigrants, and continuing threats to American interests worldwide, Dole said his life had made him "the most optimistic man in America." He acknowledged his reputation for abrasiveness, saying that "if I am combative, it is for love of country. It is to uphold a standard that I was born and bred to defend."

At age seventy-three, Dole could, and in his speech did, claim a measure of wisdom from his years of public service. He had to face the fact that many Americans were reluctant to hand the presidency to a man that old, so he took on the question directly. "I was born in 1923, and facts are better than dreams, and good presidents and good candidates do not run from the facts," he said. "Age has its advantages. Let me be a bridge to an America that only the unknowing call myth. Let me be a bridge to a time of tranquillity, faith, and confidence in action. And to those who say it was never so, that America's not been better, I say you're wrong. And I know because I was there. And I have seen it. And I remember."

Dole heaped scorn on Clinton and the youthful White House advisers who were prominent in the first two years of his administration. Dole said they were elitists who "don't have faith in people" but in government. "It is demeaning to the nation that within the Clinton administration a corps of the elite who never grew up, never did anything real, never sacrificed, never suffered, and never learned, should have the power to fund with your earnings their dubious and self-serving schemes," he said.

Testing a message that was to dominate his rhetoric in the latter stages of the campaign, Dole indirectly challenged Clinton's character. For too long, he said, "we have had a leadership that has been unwilling to risk the truth, to speak without calculation, to sacrifice itself."

Kemp Reaches Out

Vice presidential nominee Jack Kemp brought several positive attributes to the ticket: boundless energy, a genuine interest in ideas for their own sake, and a long record of trying to make the Republican party a more welcome home for minorities and the disadvantaged. But as the convention got underway, Kemp appeared to undermine his record on this last count by giving into demands by conservatives that he embrace the party platform's positions against affirmative action and federal welfare assistance to children of illegal aliens.

In his exuberant, although sometimes mangled, acceptance speech, Kemp played the role for which Dole selected him: As one of the party's most dynamic figures, a leader of conservatives who might be able to broaden the party's base of support. Kemp opened his speech with a reference to Lincoln, and he wasted no time in appealing to those outside the party.

"I am putting our opponents on notice. We will be asking for the support of every single American," he said. "The appeal of opportunity crosses every boundary of geography and race. We may not get every vote, but we will speak to every heart. In word and action, we will demonstrate that we intend to represent the entire American family."

Kemp indirectly acknowledged that he and Dole had been on the opposite sides of a long debate within the Republican party about whether it was more important to reduce the deficit (Dole's long-time priority) or to cut taxes (Kemp's primary theme). Now, he said, "we stand united to say that the answer is that they must come together—and Bob Dole and I will do it."

Following are excerpts of speeches at the Republican National Convention in San Diego, California, as delivered by Jack F. Kemp and Robert J. Dole, accepting the party's nomination for vice president and president, respectively, on August 15, 1996:

KEMP ACCEPTANCE SPEECH

Before I speak, may I say a few words? J. C. Watts [R-Okla.] told us the other night that the greatest title a man can have is "Dad." Now you know why. Thank you, Jeffrey.

It was a little too short, but. . . . Abraham Lincoln believed you serve your party best by serving our country first. Ladies and gentlemen, I cannot think of a better way of serving our nation than by electing Bob Dole the next president of the United States of America.

And by the way, this time let's re-elect a Republican Congress to help Bob Dole restore the American dream.

That's what is important in 1996. It's just that we need to re-elect our Republican Congress.

Tonight, here in San Diego, Bob Dole and I begin this campaign to take our message of growth, hope, leadership and cultural renewal to all Americans.

As I said in Russell, Kansas, Bob Dole's home town, last Saturday. . . . We're going to take our cause from the boroughs of New York to the barrios of California. We're not going to leave anyone out of this cause and this campaign.

We're going to carry the word to every man, woman and child of every color and background that today, on the eve of the new American century, it's time to renew the American promise and to recapture the American dream, and to give our nation a new birth of freedom with liberty, equality and justice for all. That's what it means to be a Republican.

Tonight, I'm putting our opponents on notice. We're going to ask for the support of every single American. Our appeal of boundless opportunity crosses every barrier of geography, race and belief in America. We're not going to leave anybody out of this opportunistic society. . . .

We may not get every vote. Now, listen to me for a moment. We may not get every vote, but we'll speak to every heart. In word and action, we will represent the entire American family. That's what we must be all about.

And so, in the spirit of Mr. Lincoln, who believed that the purpose of a great party was not to defeat the other party. The purpose of a truly great party is to provide superior ideas, principled leadership and a compelling cause, and in that spirit, I accept your nomination for the vice presidency of the United States of America. [Applause]

Thank you. OK, I accept, I accept, I accept.

I had to say it.

Our convention is not just the meeting of a political party; our convention is a celebration of ideas. Our goal is not just to win, but to be worthy of winning.

This is a great nation with a great mission, and last night we nominated a leader whose stature is equal to that calling, a man whose words convey a quiet strength, who knows what it means to sacrifice for others, to sacrifice for his country, and to demonstrate courage under fire; who brings together all parties and backgrounds in a common cause.

In recent years it has been a presidential practice when delivering the State of the Union address to introduce heroes in the balcony. Next year, when Bob Dole delivers the State of the Union address there'll be a hero at the podium.

There is another hero with us tonight. He's here in our hearts, he's here in our spirit. He's here in our minds. He brought America back and restored America's spirit. He gave us a decade of prosperity and expanding horizons. Make no mistake about it, communism came down, not because it fell, but because he pushed it.

Thank you, Ronald Reagan. The Gipper.

Our campaign—for just a moment, let me talk about this campaign, this cause—is dedicated to completing that revolution. I'm sure he's watching us. So let me just say to him, on behalf of all of us who love him, thanks to the Gipper.

And tonight is the party of Abraham Lincoln and Ronald Reagan and Bob Dole, and all the great Republicans who precede us and upon whose shoulders we stand, we begin our campaign to restore the adventure of the American dream.

With the end of the Cold War, all the "isms" of the 20th century—Fascism, Nazism, Communism, Socialism, and the evil of Apartheidism—have failed, except one. Only democracy has shown itself true to the hopes of all mankind. We must be that party.

You see, democratic capitalism is not just the hope of wealth, but it's the hope of justice. When we look into the face of poverty, we see the pain, the despair and need of human beings. But above all, in every face of every child, we must see the image of God.

You see, the Creator of All has planted the seed of creativity in every single one of us, the desire within every child of God to work and build and improve our lot in life, and that of our families and those we love.

And in our work, and in the act of creating that is part of all labor, we discover that part within ourselves that is divine. I believe the ultimate imperative for growth and opportunity is to advance human dignity.

Dr. Martin Luther King believed that we must see a sleeping hero in every soul. I believe America must establish policies that summon those heroes and call forth their boundless potential and that of the human spirit. But our fullest potential will never be achieved by following leaders who call us to timid tasks, diminished dreams and some era of limits.

[Hope or Despair]

You see, every generation faces choices: hope or despair—to plan for scarcity or to embrace the possibilities. Societies throughout history believed they had reached the frontiers of human accomplishment. But in every age, those who trusted that divine spark of imagination discovered that vastly greater horizons still lay ahead.

You see, Americans do not accept limits. We transcended those limits. We do not settle for things as they are. We are intent on succeeding.

I learned this as a lesson as a young boy growing up in the street in Los Angeles, California. My dad was a truck driver. My daddy was a truck driver. He and my uncle bought the truck, started a trucking company, put four boys through college. From them and my mom, a teacher, I learned to never to give up. Now I want you to know tonight, from the bottom of my heart, to me, and my children and my family, faith, freedom and family, as well as life, are the greatest gifts of God to all humanity. It is precious and we need to be that party.

Today America is on the threshold of the greatest period of economic activity, technological development and entrepreneurial adventure in the history of the world. We have before us tomorrows that are even more thrilling than our more glorious of our yesterdays.

And yet the genius of the American people is being stifled. Our economy is growing at the slowest pace in any recovery in this century. The income of working men and woman in America is dropping or stagnant. And there's kind of a gnawing feeling throughout our nation that—in some way, for some reason—there is just something wrong.

[Elitists]

Our friends in the other party say the economy is great. It's moving forward. It's moving, like a ship dragging an anchor, the anchor of taxes, and excessive regulations and big government and bureaucracy.

They say it's the best we do and the best we can hope for. But that's because they have put their entire trust in government rather than people.

They want a government that runs our lives, runs our businesses, runs our schools.

You see, they just don't believe in the unlimited possibilities that freedom can bring.

Today, the Democratic Party is not democratic. They are elitist.

They don't have faith in people. They have in government.

They trust government more than markets. And that's why they raised taxes on middle income families. That's why they tried to nationalize health care. That's why that today they say they are "unalterably opposed" to cutting taxes on the American family.

That's the problem with elitists—they think they know better than the people. But the truth is, there's a wisdom, there's an intelligence in ordinary women and men far superior to the greatest so-called experts that have ever lived.

That's what our party must be all about.

The Democratic Party is the party of the status quo. And as of tonight, with Bob Dole as our leader, we are the party of change.

Our first step will be to balance the budget with a strategy that combines economy in government with the type of tax cuts designed to liberate the productive genius of the American people.

Now, of course, the naysayers in the Clinton White House say it can't be done. They've got to say that. They don't know Bob Dole and they don't know Jack Kemp.

As Bob and I have said before. . . . As Bob and I have said before and will continue to say throughout this campaign, with a pro-growth Republican Congress, balancing the budget while cutting taxes is just a matter of presidential will. If you have it, you can do it. Bob Dole has it. And Bob Dole will do it.

You can count on it.

And guess what? And guess what? And guess what?

All the critics aside, I'm going to be with him, at his side, every step of the way.

And so will you, so will you.

But this is just the beginning. But this is just the beginning. This is the first step.

We're going to scrap the whole fatally flawed tax code of America, and replace it with a flatter, fairer, simpler, pro-family, pro-growth tax code for the 21st century. We can do it.

And guess what? Guess what? Guess what? That's rhetorical. You don't have to answer.

We're going to end the IRS and its intrusiveness as we have known it these past 83 years.

We're going to start with a 15 percent across-the-board tax rate cut. There's going to be tax relief and a $500 per child tax credit. We're going to cut the capital gains tax in half, and not apologize for it.

We're going to take the side of the worker, the side of the saver, the entrepreneur, the family. The American people can use their money more wisely than can government. It's time they had more of a chance, and we're going to give them that opportunity, that chance.

That's what this is all about.

[Two Earners, One Pay]

Here we are, on the eve of the 21st century, in the middle of that technological revolution that is transforming the world in which we live. But how can it be that so many families find themselves struggling just to keep even, or just to get by?

And I want to say this from the heart—that as long as it takes two earners to do what one earner used to do, how can anybody say this economy is good enough for the American people?

Our tax cut will mean that parents will have more time to spend with their children—and with each other.

It means that a working parent can afford to take a job that lets them maybe be home when the kids come home from school.

It means that the struggling, single mother in the inner city of America will find it easier to get out of poverty and to work off the welfare system which is a drag on her hopes and aspirations.

We cannot forget, my friends, that a single mom and her children in this country cannot be left out of our great revolution for this country.

The American society as a whole can never achieve the outer reaches of its potential so long as it tolerates the inner cities of despair. And I can tell you that Bob Dole and Jack Kemp will not tolerate that despair in our nation's cities.

I read the account by a reporter—I read the report—when I was at Housing and Urban Development, I read the account of a reporter of his conversation with a 10-year-old child at Henry Horner public housing in Chicago, which I had had the honor of visiting.

The reporter told in his book that he asked the little boy what he wanted to be when he grew up. The little boy said, "If I grow up, I'd like to be a bus driver."

He said, "If I grow up." He said "If"—not when. At the age of 10 he wasn't sure he'd even make it to adulthood.

Think how much poorer our nation is, and deprived of, not allowing that child to reach his or her potential. And those like him. Think how much richer our nation will be when every single child is able to grow up to reach for his or her God-given potential—including those who come to America. Including those who are willing to risk everything to come to this nation.

My friends, we are a nation of immigrants. And as the former president of Notre Dame University, Father Theodore Hesburgh, said, the reason we have to close the back door of illegal immigration is so that we can keep open the front door of legal immigration.

That is what it means to be in America.

[Our Goal]

You see, our goal. . . . You see, our goal is not just a more prosperous America, but a better America. An America that recognizes the infinite worthwhile of every individual and, like the Good Shepherd, leaves the 99 to find the one stray lamb.

An America that honors all its institutions—the values that moms and dads want to pass on to their children.

An America that makes the ideal of equality a daily reality—equality of opportunity, equality in human dignity, equality before the laws of mankind as well as in the eyes of God.

An America that transcends the boundaries between the races with the revolutionary power of the simple, yet profound idea to love our neighbors as ourselves.

We must remember all that is at stake in America's cultural renewal—not just the wealth of our nation but the meaning as well.

Today, more than ever before, America's ideals and ideas grip the imaginations of women and men in every corner of the globe. And isn't it exciting—isn't it exciting to think, that it's 1776—only this time all over the world?

You know, President Reagan spoke of America as a shining city on a hill, a light unto nations. And in decades past, so many of those who looked for that light did so from behind a wall and barbed wire, and tyrannical regimes.

Now, because the American people stood strong, those people are free.

Freedom is not free. It's never guaranteed. Our nation and its president must be strong enough to stand up for freedom against all who would challenge it.

A world of peace. A world of hope. That's what America's economic and cultural renewal means at home and around the globe.

This is what our cause is all about. This is why we'll elect Bob Dole the next president. This is why we need a Republican Congress.

And I want you to know, the other night I was honored, I was so honored to be part of that tribute, but so meaningfully to President Reagan. Afterwards. Mrs. Reagan said she was touched by my calling Ronald Reagan the last lion of the 20th century. Well, I said history will record that.

I believe America is fortunate that last night you, and you, and you nominated a leader worthy of succeeding President Reagan—a man with the strength, the determination and the vision to do the job that lies ahead.

And I want you to know tonight from the bottom of my heart, I believe Bob Dole will be the first lion of the 21st century.

Thank you.

DOLE ACCEPTANCE SPEECH

This is a big night for me, and I'm ready. We're ready to go.

Thank you, California.

And thank you, San Diego, for hosting the greatest Republican convention of them all. The greatest of them all.

Thank you, President Ford and President Bush. And God bless you, Nancy Reagan, for your moving tribute to President Reagan.

By the way, I spoke to President Reagan this afternoon, and I made him a promise that we would win one more for the Gipper. Are you ready? Thank you. And he appreciated it very much.

Ladies and gentlemen, delegates to the convention, and fellow citizens, I cannot say it more clearly than in plain speaking. I accept your nomination to lead our party once again to the presidency of the United States.

CROWD: Go, Bob, Go! Go, Bob, Go! Go, Bob, Go! Go, Bob, Go!

DOLE: Thank you. I will.

And I am profoundly moved by your confidence and trust, and I look forward to leading America into the next century. But this moment. . . .

But this is not my moment, it is yours. It is yours, Elizabeth. It is yours, Robin. It is yours, Jack and Joanne Kemp.

And do not think I have forgotten whose moment this is above all. It is for the people of America that I stand here tonight, and by their generous leave. And as my voice echoes across darkness and desert, as it is heard over car radios on coastal roads, and as it travels above farmland and suburb, deep into the heart of cities that, from space, look tonight like strings of sparkling diamonds, I can tell you that I know whose moment this is: It is yours. It is yours entirely.

[Man of the Plains]

And who am I that stands before you tonight?

I was born in Russell, Kansas, a small town in the middle of the prairie surrounded by wheat and oil wells. As my neighbors and friends from Russell, who tonight sit in front of this hall, know well, Russell, though not the West, looks out upon the West.

And like most small towns on the plains, it is a place where no one grows up without an intimate knowledge of distance. And the first thing you learn on the prairie is the relative size of a man compared to the lay of the land. And under the immense sky where I was born and raised, a man is very small, and if he thinks otherwise, he is wrong.

I come from good people, very good people, and I'm proud of it. My father's name was Doran and my mother's name was Bina. I loved them and there's no moment when my memory of them and my love for them does not overshadow anything I do—even this, even here—and there is no height to which I have risen that is high enough to allow me to forget them—to allow me to forget where I came from, and where I stand and how I stand—with my feet on the ground, just a man at the mercy of God.

And this perspective has been strengthened and solidified by a certain wisdom that I owe not to any achievement of my own, but to the gracious compensations of age.

Now I know that in some quarters I may not—may be expected to run from this, the truth of this, but I was born in 1923, and facts are better than dreams and good presidents and good candidates don't run from the truth.

I do not need. . . . I do not need the presidency to make or refresh my soul. That false hope I will gladly leave to others. For greatness lies not in what office you hold, but on how honest you are in how you face adversity and in your willingness to stand fast in hard places.

Age has its advantages . . . has its advantages. Let me be the bridge to an America that only the unknowing call myth. Let me be the bridge to a time of tranquillity, faith and confidence in action.

And to those who say it was never so, that America's not been better, I say you're wrong. And I know because I was there. And I have seen it. And I remember.

And our nation, though wounded and scathed, has outlasted revolutions, civil war, world war, racial oppression and economic catastrophe. We have fought and prevailed on almost every continent. And in almost every sea.

We have even lost. But we have lasted, and we have always come through.

And what enabled us to accomplish this has little to do with the values of the present. After decades of assault upon what made America great, upon supposedly obsolete values, what have we reaped? What have we created? What do we have?

What we have in the opinions of millions of Americans is crime and drugs, illegitimacy, abortion, the abdication of duty, and the abandonment of children.

And after the virtual devastation of the American family, the rock upon which this country was founded, we are told that it takes a village, that is collective, and thus the state, to raise a child.

The state is now more involved than it ever has been in the raising of children. And children are now more neglected, more abused and more mistreated than they have been in our time.

This is not a coincidence. This is not a coincidence. And with all due respect, I am here to tell you it does not take a village to raise a child. It takes a family to raise a child.

If I could by magic . . . could by magic. . . . If I could by magic restore to every child who lacks a father or a mother that father or that mother, I would.

And though I cannot, I would never turn my back on them. And I shall as president vote measures that keep families whole.

[Honor and Liberty]

And I'm here to tell you that permissive and destructive behavior must be opposed.

That honor and liberty must be restored and that individual accountability must replace collective excuse.

And I'm here to say. . . . I am here to say to America, do not abandon the great traditions that stretch to the dawn of our history. Do not topple the pillars of those beliefs—God, family, honor, duty, country—that have brought us through time, and time, and time, and time again.

And to those who believe that I am too combative, I say if I am combative, it is for love of country.

It is to uphold a standard that I was . . . I was born and bred to defend. And to those who believe that I live and breathe compromise, I say that in politics honorable compromise is no sin. It is what protects us from absolutism and intolerance . . . absolutism and intolerance.

But one must never compromise in regard to God and family and honor and duty and country. And I'm here to set a marker, that all may know that it is possible to rise in politics, with these things firmly in mind, not compromised and never abandoned, never abandoned. . . .

[Economic Liberty]

It is not as was said by the victors four years ago, "the economy, stupid." It's a kind of nation we are. It's whether we still possess the wit and determination to deal with many questions including economic questions, but certainly not limited to them. All things do not flow from wealth or poverty.

I know this firsthand and so do you. All things flow from doing what is right.

The cry of this nation lies not in its material wealth but in courage, and sacrifice and honor. We tend to forget when leaders forget. And we tend to remember it when they remember it.

The high office of the presidency requires not a continuous four-year campaign for re-election, but rather broad oversight and attention to three essential areas: the material, the moral and the nation's survival in that ascending order of importance . . . order of importance.

And in the last presidential election. . . . In the last presidential election, you the people were gravely insulted. You were told that the material was not only the most important of these three, but in fact, really the only one that mattered.

I don't hold to that for a moment. No one can deny the importance of material well-being. And in this regard, it is time to recognize we have surrendered too much of our economic liberty. I do not appreciate the value of economic liberty nearly as much for what it has done in keeping us fed, as to what it's done in keeping us free.

The freedom of the marketplace is not merely the best guarantor of our prosperity. It is the chief guarantor of our rights, and a government that seizes control of the economy for the good of the people ends up seizing control of the people for the good of the economy.

And our opponents portray the right to enjoy the fruits of one's own time and labor as a kind of selfishness against which they must fight for the good of the nation. But they are deeply mistaken, for when they gather to themselves the authority to take the earnings and direct the activities of the people, they are fighting not for our sake but for the power to tell us what to do.

And you now work from the first of January to May just to pay your taxes so that the party of government can satisfy its priorities with the sweat of your brow because they think that what you would do with your own money would be morally and practically less admirable than what they would do with it.

And that simply has got to stop. It's got to stop in America.

It is demeaning. . . . It is demeaning to the nation that within the Clinton administration, a core of the elite who never grew up, never did anything real, never sacrificed, never suffered, and never learned, should have the power to fund with your earnings their dubious and self-serving schemes. . . .

And make no mistake about it, my economic program is the right policy for America and for the future, and for the next century . . . the next century.

Here's what it will mean to you. Here's what it will mean to you. It means you will have a president who will urge Congress to pass and send to the states for ratification a balanced-budget amendment to the Constitution.

It means you will have a president and a Congress who have the will to balance the budget by the year 2002.

It means you will have a president who will reduce taxes 15 percent across-the-board for every taxpayer in America.

And it will include a $500-per-child tax credit for lower and middle-income families in America.

Taxes for a family of four making $35,000 a year would be reduced by more than half—56 percent to be exact. And that's a big, big reduction.

It means you will have a president who will help small businesses, the businesses that create most new jobs, by reducing the capital gains tax rate by 50 percent. Cut it in half.

It means you will have a president who will end the IRS as we know it.

It means you will have a president who will expand individual retirement accounts, repeal President Clinton's Social Security tax increase, provide estate tax relief, reduce government regulations, reform our civil justice system, provide educational opportunity scholarships and a host of other proposals that will create more opportunity for all Americans and all across America . . . all across America.

And I will not stop there. Working with Jack Kemp and a Republican Congress, I will not be satisfied until we have reformed our entire tax code and made it fairer and flatter and simpler for the American people.

The principle involved here is time-honored and true, and that is—it's your money.

You shouldn't have to apologize for wanting to keep what you earn. To the contrary, the government should apologize for taking too much of it.

The Clinton administration—the Clinton administration just doesn't get it. And that's why they have got to go.

The president—the president's content with the way things are. I am not. We must commit ourselves to a far more ambitious path that puts growth, expanding opportunities, rising incomes and soaring prosperity at the heart of national policy . . . of national policy.

We must also commit ourselves to a trade policy that does not suppress pay and threaten American jobs. And by any measure, the trade policies of the Clinton administration has been a disaster. Trade deficits are skyrocketing and middle-income families are paying the price.

My administration will fully enforce our trade laws and not let our national sovereignty be infringed by the World Trade Organization . . . or any other international body.

Jack Kemp and I will restore the promise of America and get the economy moving again, and we'll do so without leaving anybody behind.

[Social Policy]

And I have learned in my own life, from my own experience that not every man, woman or child can make it on their own. And that in time of need, the bridge between failure and success can be the government itself. And given all that I have experienced, I shall always remember those in need. That is why I helped to save Social Security in 1983 and that is why I will be, I will be the president who preserves and strengthens and protects Medicare for America's senior citizens.

For I will never forget the man who rode on a train from Kansas to Michigan to see his son who was thought to be dying in an Army hospital.

When he arrived, his feet were swollen and he could hardly walk because he had to make the trip from Kansas to Michigan standing up most of the way. Who was that man? He was my father. My father was poor and I love my father. Do you imagine for one minute that as I sign the bills that will set the economy free, I will not be faithful to Americans in need? You can be certain that I will . . . that I will.

For to do otherwise would be to betray those whom I love and honor most. And I will betray nothing.

Let me speak about immigration. Yes. Let me speak about immigration. The right and obligation of a sovereign nation to control its borders is beyond debate. We should not have here a single illegal immigrant.

But the question of immigration is broader than that, and let me be specific. A family from Mexico that arrives this morning legally has as much right to the American Dream as the direct descents of the Founding Fathers.

The Republican Party is broad and inclusive. It represents—the Republican Party is broad and inclusive. It represents many streams of opinion and many points of view.

But if there's anyone who has mistakenly attached themselves to our party in the belief that we are not open to citizens of every race and religion, then let me remind you, tonight this hall belongs to the Party of Lincoln. And the exits which are clearly marked are for you to walk out of as I stand this ground without compromise.

And though, I can only look up—and though I can look up, and at a very steep angle, to Washington and Lincoln, let me remind you of their concern for the sometimes delicate unity of the people . . . of the people.

The notion that we are and should be one people rather than "peoples" of the United States seems so self-evident and obvious that it's hard for me to imagine that I must defend it. When I was growing up in Russell, Kansas, it was clear to me that my pride and my home were in America, not in any faction, and not in any division. . . .

Must we give in to the senseless drive to break apart that which is beautiful and whole and good? . . . whole and good?

And so tonight I call on every American to rise above all that may divide us, and to defend the unity of the nation for the honor of generations past, and the sake of those to come.

The Constitution of the United States mandates equal protection under the law. This is not code language for racism.

It is plain speaking against it.

And the guiding light in my administration will be that in this country, we have no rank order by birth, no claim to favoritism by race, no expectation of judgment other than it be even-handed. And we cannot guarantee the outcome, but we shall guarantee the opportunity in America.

I will speak plainly—I will speak plainly on another subject of importance. We're not educating all of our children.

Too many are being forced to absorb the fads of the moment.

Not for the nothing are we the biggest education spenders and among the lowest education achievers among the leading industrial nations.

The teachers unions nominated Bill Clinton in 1992. They're funding his re-election now. And they, his most reliable supporters, know he will maintain the status quo.

And I say this—I say this not to the teachers, but to their unions.

I say this, if education were a war, you would be losing it. If it were a business, you would be driving it into bankruptcy. If it were a patient, it would be dying.

And to the teachers union, I say, when I am president, I will disregard your political power for the sake of the parents, the children, the schools and the nation . . . and the nation.

I plan to enrich your vocabulary with those words you fear—school choice and competition and opportunity scholarships.

All this for low- and middle-income families so that you will join the rest of us in accountability, while others compete with you for the commendable privilege of giving our children a real education.

There is no reason why those who live on any street in America should not have the same right as the person who lives at 1600 Pennsylvania Avenue— the right to send your child to the school of your choice.

[Crime and the Judiciary]

And if we want to reduce crime—if we want to reduce crime and drug use and teen pregnancies, let's start by giving all our children a first-class education.

And I also want these children to inherit a country that is far safer than it is at present. I seek for our children and grandchildren a world more open and with more opportunity than ever before.

But in wanting these young Americans to be able to make the best of this, I want first and foremost for them to be safe. I want to remove the shadow that darkens opportunities for every man, woman and child in America . . . child in America.

We are a nation paralyzed by crime. And it's time to end that in America. And to do so . . . to do so, I mean to attack the root cause of crime—criminals, criminals, violent criminals.

And as our many and voracious criminals go to bed tonight, at say, 6:00 in the morning, they had better pray that I lose this election. Because if I win, the lives of violent criminals are going to be hell.

During the Reagan administration—during the Reagan administration we abolished parole at the federal level. In the Dole administration we will work with the nation's governors to abolish parole for violent criminals all across America.

And with my national instant check initiative, we will keep all guns out of the hands of criminals.

And I have been asked if I have a litmus test for judges. I do. My litmus test for judges is that they be intolerant of outrage; that their passion is not to amend, but to interpret the Constitution . . . that they are restrained in regard to those who live within the law, and strict with those who break it.

And for those who say that I should not make President Clinton's liberal judicial appointments an issue in this campaign, I have a simple response. I have heard your argument.

The motion is denied . . . motion is denied.

I save my respect for the Constitution, not for those who would ignore it, violate it or replace it with conceptions of their own fancy.

My administration will zealously protect civil and constitutional rights while never forgetting that our primary duty is protecting law-abiding citizens, everybody in this hall.

I have no intention of ignoring violent—I said violent criminals, understanding them or buying them off. A nation that cannot defend itself from outrage does not deserve to survive. And a president who cannot lead itself against those who prey upon it does not deserve to be president of the United States of America.

[National Security]

I am prepared to risk more political capital in defense of domestic tranquillity than any president you have ever known.

The time for such risk is long overdue.

And in defending our nation from external threats, the requirements of survival cannot merely be finessed. There is no room for margin of error. On this subject perhaps more than any other, a president must level with the people and be prepared to take political risks. And I would rather do what is called for in this regard and be unappreciated, than fail to do so and win universal acclaim.

And it must be said because of misguided priorities, there have been massive cuts in funding for our national security. I believe President Clinton has failed to adequately provide for our defense. And for whatever reason the neglect, it is irresponsible. It is irresponsible.

I ask that you consider these crystal-clear differences. He believes that it is acceptable to ask our military forces to do more with less. I do not.

He defends giving a green light to a terrorist state, Iran, to expand its influence in Europe. And he relies on the United Nations to punish Libyan terrorists who murdered American citizens. I will not.

He believes that defending our people and our territory from missile attack is unnecessary. I do not.

And on my first day in office, I will put America on a course that will end our vulnerability to missile attack and rebuild our armed forces.

It is a course President Clinton has refused to take. And on my first day in office, I will put terrorists on notice. If you harm one American, you harm all Americans.

And America will pursue you to the ends of the earth.

In short, don't mess with us if you're not prepared to suffer the consequences. . . .

And I am content and always will be content to see my own story subsumed in great events, the greatest of which is the simple onward procession of the American people. What a high privilege it is to be at the center in these times—and this I owe to you, the American people.

I owe everything to you. And to make things right, and to close the circle, I will return to you as much as I possibly can. It is incumbent upon me to do so. It is my duty and my deepest desire.

[Trust]

And so tonight. . . . I respectfully ask for your blessing and your support.

The election will not be decided—the election will not be decided by the polls or by the opinion-makers or by the pundits . . . by the pundits.

It will be decided by you. It will be decided by you.

And I ask for your vote so that I may bring you an administration that is able, honest, and trusts in you.

For the fundamental issue is not of policy, but of trust—not merely whether the people trust the president, but whether the president and his party trust the people, trust in their goodness and their genius for recovery.

That's what the election is all about.

For the government cannot direct the people, the people must direct the government.

This is not the outlook of my opponent—and he is my opponent, not my enemy.

And though he has tried of late to be a good Republican . . . and I expect him here tonight . . . there are certain distinctions that even he cannot blur. There are distinctions between the two great parties that will be debated and must be debated in the next 82 days.

He and his party brought us the biggest tax increase in the history of America. And we are the party of lower taxes—we are the party of lower taxes and greater opportunity.

We are the party whose resolve did not flag as the Cold War dragged on. We did not tremble before a Soviet giant that was just about to fall, and we did not have to be begged to take up arms against Saddam Hussein.

We are not the party, as drug use has soared and doubled among the young, hears no evil, sees no evil, and just cannot say, "Just say no. Just say no."

We are the party that trusts in the people. I trust in the people. That is the heart of all I have tried to say tonight.

My friends, a presidential campaign is more than a contest of candidates, more than a clash of opposing philosophies.

It is a mirror held up to America. It is a measurement of who we are, where we come from, and where we are going. For as much inspiration as we may draw from a glorious past, we recognize American pre-eminently as a country of tomorrow. For we were placed here for a purpose, by a higher power. There's no doubt about it.

Every soldier in uniform, every school child who recites the Pledge of Allegiance, every citizen who places her hand on her heart when the flag goes by, recognizes and responds to our American destiny.

Optimism is in our blood. I know this as few others can. There once was a time when I doubted the future. But I have learned as many of you have learned that obstacles can be overcome.

And I have unlimited confidence in the wisdom of our people and the future of our country.

Tonight, I stand before you tested by adversity, made sensitive by hardship, a fighter by principle, and the most optimistic man in America.

My life is proof that America is a land without limits. And with my feet on the ground and my heart filled with hope, I put my faith in you and in the God who loves us all. For I am convinced that America's best days are yet to come.

May God bless you. And may God bless America. Thank you very much.

REPUBLICAN
PARTY PLATFORM
August 12, 1996

The Republican National Convention on August 12 adopted a platform crafted by the party's conservative majority. It called for a half-dozen amendments to the Constitution, including a total ban on abortion and a denial of automatic citizenship for children born in the United States to illegal immigrants.

Both Bob Dole, the party's presidential nominee, and Haley Barbour, the party chairman, said they had not read the document. Dole, who had tried unsuccessfully to moderate the tough antiabortion language, said he would not be bound by the platform provisions. The Dole campaign, which was trying to position the party for an uphill battle against Bill Clinton, the incumbent Democratic president, worked to divert attention from the platform and its controversial positions on some of the most important issues facing the country.

The platform reflected the continuing dominance of the Republican party, most clearly at the state and local level, by conservatives, including the Christian Coalition and other religious forces who sought to put a moral stamp on public policy. But they, and the candidate many of them favored in 1996, commentator Patrick Buchanan, were shut out of leadership roles at the convention. Buchanan, who had challenged Dole for the presidential nomination, was not even allowed to address the full convention. Although they won a victory on the platform, antiabortion activists were distressed that their issue received little attention from major convention speakers, including Dole.

The Abortion Fight

Dole and his allies lost the only significant battle over a platform plank, and that concerned abortion, perhaps the single most contentious issue dividing Republicans. The Dole forces had wanted to insert what came to be known as a "tolerance plank." That proposal would have acknowledged that some Republicans "have deeply held and sometimes differing views of issues of personal conscience like abortion and capital punishment." When he first suggested such a plank on June 10, Dole said: "It's not negotiable. If you want to make it clear to the people out there that we are tolerant . . . it ought to be right up there where people can see it."

The tolerance plank did not directly undermine the platform's otherwise strongly worded positions, but it would have given at least a nod to party moderates who dissented on those matters. Some critics outside the party said Dole's plank was a blatant appeal for the votes of women whose right to choose abortion would be taken away if the Republican platform became law.

Antiabortion forces within the party were infuriated by Dole's proposed plank, arguing that abortion was an unambiguous moral question that should not be considered a matter of "personal conscience." The dispute dominated discussions within the platform committee in late June and early July—and news coverage of the issue undermined Dole's hopes of playing down the religious right's growing influence within the party. Interest in the issue was heightened by the threat by two leading party moderates—California governor Pete Wilson and Massachusetts governor William F. Weld—to fight the antiabortion platform on the convention floor.

After a month of controversy, Dole on July 12 retreated in the face of a likely rejection of his proposal on the convention floor. He accepted a compromise eliminating the "tolerance" language from the section of the platform dealing with abortion. Instead, the platform referred generally to the party's "historic principles and ideals" and acknowledged that "members of our party have deeply held and sometimes differing views."

Dole's aides claimed that language represented a victory for their "tolerance" position, and they hoped it would remove the party's dispute over abortion from the headlines. With this, Wilson and Weld withdrew their threat of a convention floor flight, but it was widely agreed that antiabortion forces had demonstrated their clout by rebuffing the party's presidential candidate on one of the most sensitive issues of the day.

Meeting in San Diego a week before the convention was to open, the platform subcommittee dealing with abortion and other social issues rejected, 20–4, a motion by Vermont state senator Walter Freed to remove antiabortion language from the platform. That language called for a "human life" constitutional amendment banning abortion, along with legislation that would extend citizenship and its constitutional protections under the Fourteenth Amendment to unborn children.

Other Issues

Other portions of the platform catalogued the conservative wing of the party's views on a host of social, economic, and general governmental issues. It called for the abolition of several federal agencies (starting with the Departments of Commerce, Education, Energy, and Housing and Urban Development) and proposed several constitutional amendments.

The most controversial of the suggested constitutional amendments was a bar to automatic citizenship for children born in the United States to "alien parents who are not long-term residents." Sponsors said this was needed to curb unwanted immigration, but critics called it mean-spirited. After initially taking an ambiguous position on that issue, Dole on August 23 told a group of African-American journalists that he opposed the proposal. That statement came nearly two weeks after the platform was adopted.

On other controversial issues, the platform:

- *Opposed discrimination but rejected the use of civil rights laws to "cover sexual preferences." The platform also opposed most affirmative action programs by saying equal rights should be achieved "without quotas or other forms of preferential treatment."*
- *Called for abolition of the Education Department and all "federal meddling in our schools." The party said it would promote "family choice at all levels of learning," a reference to proposals for taxpayer-funded voucher programs allowing parents to choose between public and private schools.*
- *Supported Dole's campaign proposal for an across-the-board 15 percent tax cut, along with a $500 per child tax credit. The party also backed a 50 percent cut in the top tax rate on capital gains.*
- *Chastised what it called the "Clintonite view" that nationhood is obsolete and that "all states will recognize a single authority," presumably the United Nations. The platform opposed the commitment of U.S. troops to UN peacekeeping forces under foreign commanders and pledged that "we will never compel American servicemen to wear foreign uniforms or insignia."*
- *Called for other constitutional amendments requiring a balanced budget, banning desecration of the U.S. flag, establishing certain rights for victims of crime, and setting strict term limits for members of Congress.*

Following is the excerpted text of the platform adopted August 12, 1996, by delegates to the Republican National Convention at its meeting in San Diego:

Preamble

We meet to nominate a candidate and pass a platform at a moment of measureless national opportunity. A new century beckons, and Americans are more than equal to its challenges. But there is a problem. The Clinton administration has proven unequal to the heritage of our past, the promise of our times, and the character of the American people. They require more and demand better. With them, we raise our voices and raise our sights.

We are the heirs of world leadership that was earned by bravery and sacrifice on half a thousand battlefields. We will soon nominate for the presidency a man who knew battle and so loves peace, a man who lives bravely and so walks humbly with his God and his fellow citizens. We walk with him now as he joins one more battle, every bit as crucial for our country's future as was the crusade in which he served.

Just when America should be leading the world, we have an administration squandering the international respect it did not earn and does not value. Just when America should be demonstrating anew the dynamic power of economic freedom, we have an administration working against both history and public opinion to expand the reach and burden of government. Just when Americans are reasserting their deepest values, we have an administration locked into the counterculture battles of its youth.

Americans are right to say we are on the wrong track. Our prestige in the world is declining. Economic growth here at home is anemic. Our society grows more violent and less decent. The only way the Clinton administration can magnify its questionable accomplishments is to lower our expectations. Those who lead the Democrat party call America to smaller tasks and downsized dreams.

That is not the calling of an American president.

Today's Democrat leaders do not understand leadership. They reduce principles to tactics. They talk endlessly and confront nothing. They offer, not convictions, but alibis. They are paralyzed by indecision, weakened by scandal and guided only by the perpetuation of their own power.

We asked for change. We worked for reform. We offered cooperation and consensus. Now, the asking is over. The Clinton administration cannot be reinvented, it must be replaced.

Republicans do not duplicate or fabricate or counterfeit a vision for the land we love. With our fellow citizens, we assert the present power of timeless truths.

This is what we want for America: real prosperity that reaches beyond the stock market to every family, small business and worker. An economy expanding as fast as American enterprise and creativity will carry it, free from unnecessary taxes, regulation and litigation.

This is what we want for America: the restoration of self-government by breaking Washington's monopoly on power. The American people want their country back. We will help them to regain it.

This too we want for America: moral clarity in our culture and ethical leadership in the White House. We offer America, not a harsh moralism, but our sincere conviction that the values we hold in our hearts determine the success of our lives and the shape of our society. It matters greatly that our leaders reflect and communicate those values, not undermine or mock them.

The diversity of our nation is reflected in this platform. We ask for the support and participation of all who substantially share our agenda. In one way or another, every Republican is a dissenter. At the same time, we are not morally indifferent. In this, as in many things, Lincoln is our model. At a time of great crisis, he spoke both words of healing and words of conviction. We do likewise, not for the peace of a political party, but because we citizens are bound together in a great enterprise for our children's future.

The platform that follows marshals these principles and sends them into action. We aim at nothing less than an economy of dynamic growth; a renewal of community, self-government and citizenship; and a national reaffirmation of the enduring principles on which America's greatness depends. We will count our victories, not in elections won or in economic numbers on a chart, but in the everyday achievements of the American dream: when a man or woman discovers the dignity and confidence of a job; when a child rejects drugs and embraces life; when an entrepreneur turns an idea into an industry; when a family once again feels the security of its savings and has control over the education of its children.

None of the extraordinary things about our country are gifts of government. They are the accomplishments of free people in a free society. They are achievements, not entitlements—and are sweeter for that fact. They result when men and women live in obedience to their conscience, not to the state. All our efforts as Republicans are guided by the fixed star of this single principle: that freedom always exceeds our highest expectations.

This is the greatest task before the Republican Party: to raise the bar of American expectations. Of the potential of our economy. Of the order and civility of our culture. Of what a president can be, and what the presidency must be again.

There is a continuing revolution in the yellowed parchment and faded ink of the American creed . . . a revolution that will long outlive us. It can carry the weight of all our hopes. It can reward every dreamer. It is the reason that America's finest hour is never a memory and always a goal.

With trust in God and in fidelity to generations past and generations to come, we respectfully submit this platform to the American people.

Principles of the 1996 Republican Platform

Introduction

Because Americans are a diverse and tolerant people, they have differences of opinion on many issues. But as a people, we share a common dream and common goals:

- A strong America that protects its citizens and champions their democratic ideals throughout the world,
- An America with a vibrant and growing economy that improves the standard of living for all,
- An America with a smaller, more effective and less intrusive government that trusts its people to decide what is best for them,
- An America whose people feel safe and secure in their homes, on their streets, and in their communities,
- An America where our children receive the best education in the world and learn the values like decency and responsibility that made this country great,
- And an America with the compassion to care for those who cannot care for themselves.

Principles

1. Because the American Dream fulfills the promise of liberty, we believe it should be attainable by all through more and secure jobs, home ownership, personal security, and education that meets the challenges of the century ahead.

2. Because a dynamic and growing economy is the best way to create more and better paying jobs, with greater security in the work place, we believe in lower taxes within a simpler tax system, in tandem with fair and open trade and a balanced federal budget.

3. Because wasteful government spending and over-regulation, fueled by higher taxes, are the greatest obstacles to job creation and economic growth, we believe in a Balanced Budget Amendment to the Constitution and a common-sense approach to government rules and red tape.

4. Because we recognize our obligation to foster hope and opportunity for those unable to care for themselves, we believe in welfare reform that eliminates waste, fraud and abuse; requires work from those who are capable; limits time on public assistance; discourages illegitimacy; and reduces the burden on the taxpayers.

5. Because all Americans have the right to be safe in their homes, on their streets, and in their communities, we believe in tough law enforcement, especially against juvenile crime and the drug traffic, with stiff penalties, no loopholes, and judges who respect the rights of law-abiding Americans.

6. Because institutions like the family are the backbone of a healthy society, we believe government must support the rights of the family; and recognizing within our own ranks different approaches toward our common goal, we reaffirm respect for the sanctity of human life.

7. Because our children need and are entitled to the best education in the world, we believe in parental involvement and family choice in schooling, teacher authority and accountability, more control to local school boards, and emphasis upon the basics of learning in safe classrooms.

8. Because older Americans have built our past and direct us, in wisdom and experience, toward the future, we believe we must meet our nation's commitments to them by preserving and protecting Medicare and Social Security.

9. Because a good society rests on an ethical foundation, we believe families, communities, and religious institutions can best teach the American values of honesty, responsibility, hard work, compassion, and mutual respect.

10. Because our country's greatest strength is its people, not its government, we believe today's government is too large and intrusive and does too many things the people could do better for themselves.

11. Because we trust our fellow Americans, rather than centralized government, we believe the people, acting through their State and local elected officials, should have control over programs like education

and welfare—thereby pushing power away from official Washington and returning it to the people in their communities and states.

12. Because we view the careful development of our country's natural resources as stewardship of creation, we believe property rights must be honored in our efforts to restore, protect, and enhance the environment for the generations to come.

13. Because we are all one America, we oppose discrimination. We believe in the equality of all people before the law and that individuals should be judged by their ability rather than their race, creed, or disability.

14. Because this is a difficult and dangerous world, we believe that peace can be assured only through strength, that a strong national defense is necessary to protect America at home and secure its interests abroad, and that we must restore leadership and character to the presidency as the best way to restore America's leadership and credibility throughout the world.

Building A Better America

"This is no time for diminished expectations. This is no time to sell America's potential short. This is a time to let go of the 20th Century and embrace the 21st—to seize the promise of the new era by liberating the genius of the American people."

—*Bob Dole, September 5, 1995, in Chicago, Illinois*

Improving the Standard of Living

We are the party of America's earners, savers, and taxpayers—the people who work hard, take risks and build a better future for our families and our communities. Our party believes that we can best improve the standard of living in America by empowering the American people to act in their own behalf by:

- Cutting the near-record tax burden on Americans;
- Reducing government spending and its size, while balancing the budget;
- Creating jobs;
- Using the benefits of science, technology and innovations to improve both our lives and our competitiveness in the global economy;
- Dramatically increasing the number of families who can own their own home; and
- Unleashing the competitiveness and will to win of individual Americans on the world trade scene with free but fair trade.

That's not wishful thinking; it's what we, the American people, used to take for granted before the growth of big government began to shadow our days and smother our hopes. In the 1980s—when we cut taxes, restrained regulation, and reduced government spending as a share of the nation's econ-

502

omy—prosperity made a comeback. Jobs were created, incomes rose and poverty fell for seven straight years. Then the Democrat-controlled Congress forced the tax hikes of 1990 and jammed through Bill Clinton's tax bill of 1993.

Since then, Clintonomics has produced an economy that is squeezing the middle class between high taxes and low growth. The astounding fact is that we were growing 50% faster in 1992, when Bill Clinton described the economy as the worst in five decades. We've managed to avoid a recession only because the Republican Congress put the brakes on Bill Clinton's rush to ruin by substantially reducing government spending over the last two years. But we cannot go on like this. For millions of families, the American Dream is fading. Our goal is to revive it, renew it, and extend it to all who reach for it.

Our formula for growth, opportunity, and a better family life is simple: Trust the people, cut their taxes, scale back the size and scope of government, foster job creation, and get out of the way. We've done it before, we can do it again.

Tax Relief for Economic Growth

American families are suffering from the twin burdens of stagnant incomes and near-record taxes. This is the key cause of middle-class anxiety. It is why people feel they are working harder, but falling further behind; why they fear the current generation will not be as successful as the last generation; why they believe their children will be worse off; and why they feel so anxious about their own economic future.

After averaging 1.7 percent growth annually during the expansion following the 1981 tax cut, family incomes have failed to grow at all under Bill Clinton. Since 1990, families have actually lost much of the ground they gained during the low-tax, high-growth 1980s.

Anemic economic growth under Bill Clinton is largely responsible for this lost ground. The current economic expansion has not only failed to compare to the growth seen in the decade preceding his administration, it is the slowest recovery in the last 100 years. Since 1992, the economy has grown by only 2.4 percent per year, compared to 3.2 percent in the previous 10 years and 3.9 percent between 1983 and 1989.

Bill Clinton has demonstrated that he fails to understand the role excessive tax burdens play on the economy and family incomes. In the first year of his administration, he pushed through the largest tax increase in history, raising taxes on families, senior citizens, and small businesses. Confronted with Republican attempts to cut family and business taxes, he vetoed the 1995 Balanced Budget Act which included the $500 per child tax credit as well as incentives to increase savings, economic growth and job creation.

The Clinton tax increase has produced the second-highest tax burden in American history. Federal tax collections now consume more than one-fifth of our total economic output. Federal, state, and local taxes take more than 38 cents out of every dollar the American family earns. The federal tax burden alone is now approaching a record 25 percent of family income.

American families deserve better. They should be allowed to keep more of their hard-earned money so they can spend on their priorities, as opposed to sending ever-increasing amounts to Washington to be spent on the priorities of federal bureaucrats.

In response to this unprecedented burden confronting America, we support an across-the-board, 15-percent tax cut to marginal tax rates. Fifteen percent represents the total increase in the federal tax burden since Bill Clinton took office, and we believe such a cut should be the first step towards reducing overall tax burdens while promoting the economic growth that will raise family incomes and our overall standard of living.

Another drag on family finances has been government's failure to maintain the personal and dependent exemption at historic levels. If the personal and dependent exemption that was $600 in 1950 had kept pace with inflation, it would be $3,800 rather than the current $2,500. That is why Republicans have made the $500-per-child family tax credit one of the primary features of our tax cut package.

Job creation and increasing family incomes depend on economic growth, and a precondition for economic growth is a healthy rate of saving and investment. Nevertheless, Bill Clinton vetoed Republican bills to provide these incentives, including expanded and more generous IRAs—and new spousal IRAs—which could be used for health care, education, and home-buying. As a result, today's personal savings rate is less than half what it was two decades ago. Republicans support expansion of IRAs and the establishment of spousal IRAs to encourage savings and investment.

Bill Clinton also vetoed provisions to reduce the capital gains tax rate. Excessive taxes on investment cripple the American economy and kill American jobs by increasing the cost of capital, locking in resources, and stifling small business growth and entrepreneurial activity. Largely because of these excessive taxes, American businesses face a competitive disadvantage with respect to our major trading partners, hurting their ability to export products abroad and create jobs. To remove impediments to job creation and economic growth, we support reducing the top tax rate on capital gains by 50 percent.

In 1993, Bill Clinton raised taxes on millions of middle-class retirees by dramatically increasing the income tax on Social Security benefits. This targeted attack on the economic security of our elderly was unfair and misguided. Republicans believe that this Clinton initiative must be repealed.

These proposals making the current tax code fairer and less burdensome should be viewed as an interim step towards comprehensive tax reform. The current tax code is ridiculously complex and unfair. It is also an unnecessary drag on the economy. At a time when business investment plans are greatly diminished and savings rates are unacceptably low, we must reform our tax system to remove existing artificial, government-induced bias against saving and investment.

To that end, we firmly commit to a tax code for the 21st century that will raise revenue sufficient for a smaller, more effective and less wasteful government without increasing the national debt. That new tax system must be flatter, fairer, and simpler, with a minimum of exclusions from its coverage, and one set of rules applying to all. It must be simple enough to be understood by all and enforced by few, with a low-cost of compliance which replaces the current stack of endless forms with a calculation which can be performed on the back of a postcard.

It must expand the economy and increase opportunity by rewarding initiative and hard work. It must foster job creation and end bias against saving. It must promote personal freedom and innovation. It must do all this in order to boost wages and raise living standards for all of America's working families.

A simple, fair tax system that is pro-growth and pro-family will not need today's burdensome IRS. That agency has become a nightmare for law-abiding taxpayers. It must be dramatically downsized—with resources going to more important efforts like drug enforcement— and made less intrusive.

To protect the American people from those who would undo their forthcoming victory over big government, we support legislation requiring a super-majority vote in both houses of Congress to raise taxes.

We also support a government that keeps its word. Retroactive taxation, like Bill Clinton's infamous 1993 tax hike, breaks that word. We pledge a legislative or constitutional remedy to prohibit its repetition. Because of their vital role in fostering charity and patriotism, we oppose taxing religious and fraternal benefit societies. We will not tolerate attempts to impose taxes by federal judges.

Balancing the Budget and Reducing Spending

"We didn't dig ourselves into a $5 trillion debt because the American people are undertaxed. We got that $5 trillion debt because government overspends."

"The budget deficit is a 'stealth tax' that pushes up interest rates and costs the typical family $36,000 on an average home mortgage, $1,400 on an ordinary student loan, and $700 on a car loan."

—Bob Dole

Raising tax rates is the wrong way to balance the budget. It enables the Clinton tax addicts to wastefully spend the public's money. Republicans support a Balanced Budget Amendment to the Constitution, phased in over a short period and with appropriate safeguards for national emergencies. We passed it in the House of Representatives, but Bill Clinton and his allies— especially the Senate's somersault six, who switched their long-standing position on the issue—blocked it by a single vote. As president, Bob Dole will lead the fight for that amendment, and in the States, Republicans will finish the fight for its speedy ratification.

Once and for all, we declare:

- The budget deficit and high taxes are two halves of the vise that is producing the Clinton middle class squeeze;

- A balanced budget and lower taxes go hand in hand, not in separate directions;
- Reducing the budget deficit by shrinking government produces a fiscal dividend in stronger growth and lower interest rates;
- Ending that deficit will make possible a dramatic return of resources to the American people;
- Tax relief is the only way to return the economy to the growth rates our country enjoyed from World War II to the coming of Bill Clinton; and
- We will not mortgage our children's future by incurring deficits.

A president should be Commander-in-Chief in the nation's budget battle as well as in military conflicts. Bill Clinton has been AWOL —Absent Without Leadership. Congressional Republicans had to fight his Senate allies for over a year just to give him a line-item veto for appropriation bills. Instead of helping us strengthen the presidency in this way, he set an historic precedent: vetoing whole appropriation bills because they spent too little money! His vetoes essentially shut down much of the government.

We make this promise: A Republican president will veto money bills that spend too much, not too little, and will use the line-item veto to lead the charge against wasteful spending. A Republican president will build on the achievements of our Republican Congress which has cut spending in excess of $53 billion over the last two years.

The Clinton Administration's tactic of using irresponsible monetary policy to hide the effects of their bad fiscal policies leads to:

- Higher inflation;
- Lower growth;
- Fewer jobs; and
- Scarcity of capital to fund small businesses.

This is not only bad economics; it is a hidden tax against both income and savings. We pledge a non-political monetary policy to keep prices stable and maintain public confidence in the value of the dollar.

Creating Jobs for Americans

Our goal is to empower the American people by expanding employment and entrepreneurial opportunities. Fundamentally, jobs are created in the private sector.

Small businesses are the engines of growth and job creation. They generate 75 percent of new jobs and 55 percent of our gross domestic product. The Republican Party is committed to the survival, the revival, and the resurgence of small business. In addition to our overall program of lower taxes, regulatory reform, and less spending, we will:

- Allow small businesses to deduct the costs of their health insurance;
- Restore the fair home-office deduction so important to start-up businesses;

- Assure that no one who inherits a small business or farm has to sell it to pay inheritance taxes;
- Make the IRS stop its discrimination against independent contractors;
- Enact both legal reform and product liability legislation to shield small businesses and protect jobs from the threat of unfair litigation; and
- Transfer from the public sector services that can be provided by the private sector more efficiently and cost effectively.

Small business is a force for enormous progress, socially, politically, and economically. This is both an economic and a civil rights agenda. Small businesses owned by women now employ more people than all the Fortune 500 companies combined.

Republican-created enterprise zones will offer dramatic opportunities to workers employed by small businesses, particularly minorities and the "Forgotten Workers." Republicans support the creation of jobs in all areas of the country, from the inner city to rural America.

We must create the workplace of the future so that it becomes a vehicle for personal liberation for those who seek a foothold on the opportunity ladder. We advocate increased access to capital for businesses to expand, export, and bring new products and technologies to market. We propose to consolidate federal training programs and to transfer their administration to the States and local governments.

Restraining the size and spending of government is only part of the job. We must transform official policies and attitudes toward productive Americans. Many of our labor laws and job training programs are out of date and out of touch with the needs of today's workers. Both the Davis-Bacon Act and the Service Contract Act, for example, have come to restrict opportunity, increase costs, and inhibit innovation.

Congressional Republicans have already launched a fight against the union bosses' ban on flex-time and comp-time in private industry. Those innovations are especially important to families with children. Government has no business forbidding America's workers to arrange their schedules to suit the needs of their own families.

In the same spirit, we will enact the TEAM Act to empower employers and employees to act as a team, rather than as adversaries, to advance their common interests. (It is opposed only by those who profit from labor conflict, for whom Bill Clinton has vetoed the bill.) Another way to replace conflict with concerted action is to transform OSHA [Occupational Safety and Health Administration] from an adversarial agency into a pioneering advocate of safer productivity. We will mesh its activities with the work of councils formed under the TEAM Act to advance worker protection from the ground up.

In contrast, the Clinton Administration has produced no regulatory reform, no tax relief, no product liability reform, and no legal reform.

Our vision is that everyone who seeks a job will have a job. We will break the "job lock" and bring employment opportunities to all Americans.

Science, Technology, and Innovation in the 21st Century

Our goal is to empower the American people by using the benefits of advanced science to improve their quality of life without undue restraint from government. Our bottom line is more jobs, better jobs, and a higher standard of living for the families of America.

As we prepare for the dawn of a new century, it is essential that our public policies keep pace with an evolving economy. Increased productivity is essential to expand the economy and improve the standard of living of all Americans. A recent report by the Office of Technology Assessment attributes at least half of all economic growth in the United States to advances in technology.

America is expanding its leadership role as a country that fosters innovation and technological advances, the essential ingredients of increased productivity. Leading these efforts are the men and women —and high technology businesses—that foster creative solutions to world problems. We must create policies that enable these thoughtful leaders to continue to invest in research and development. U.S. research and development (R&D) investment has increased significantly over the past two decades and currently accounts for about 2.6 percent of the nation's gross domestic product. The private sector has been the main engine behind this growth, contributing over 60 percent of the national R&D investment. Such investment has led to increased employment and high-quality jobs. Businesses that invest heavily in R&D tend to create more jobs, and to employ high-skilled workers in those new jobs at above average wage levels.

Research and development is our commitment to the future. It is our investment in the future. We must design tax and regulatory policies that encourage private sector research and experimentation, while lowering the cost of such investments.

We believe the marketplace, not bureaucrats, can determine which technologies and entrepreneurs best meet the needs of the public. American companies must use the most advanced production technologies, telecommunications, and information management systems. Technological advance means economic growth, higher productivity, and more security. We therefore support private-sector funding of applied research, especially in emerging technologies, and improved education in science and engineering. American workers must have the knowledge and training to effectively utilize the capabilities of those new systems.

Federal science programs must emphasize basic research. The tax code must foster research and development. These policies will increase the pace of technological developments by de-emphasizing the role of government and strengthening the role of the private sector. We will advance the innovative ideas and pioneering spirit that make possible the impossible.

New discoveries to bolster America's international competitiveness are essential. The fruits of federally funded research led to the creation of the biotechnology industry through the Bayh-Dole Act. This is an example of innovation and risk-taking, creating 2,000 biotechnology companies employing thousands of employees and selling billions of dollars of products to keep us first and foremost in the global marketplace.

The communications revolution empowers individuals, enhances health care, opens up opportunity for rural areas, and strengthens families and institutions. A Dole-led Congress passed the Telecommunications Act of 1996 to promote the full and open competition and freedom of choice in the telecommunications marketplace. In contrast, the Clinton-Gore Administration repeatedly defended big-government regulation. This micromanagement of the Information Age is an impediment to the development of America's information superhighway.

We support the broadest access to telecommunications networks and services, based upon marketplace capabilities. The Internet today is the most staggering example of how the Information Age can and will enhance the lives of Americans everywhere. To further this explosion of new-found freedoms and opportunities, privacy, through secured communications, has never been more important. Bob Dole and the Republican Party will promote policies that ensure that the U.S. remains the world leader in science, technology, and innovation.

Homeownership

Homeownership is central to the American Dream. It is a commitment to a safe and stable community. It is not something government gives to the people, but rather something they can attain for themselves in a non-inflationary, growing economy. For most Americans, our home is our primary asset. Mortgage interest should remain deductible from the income tax.

We applaud Republican congressional efforts to pursue federal budget policies that will result in lower interest rates. Lower interest rates will open up more housing opportunities for more Americans than any program Washington could devise.

Republicans support regulatory reform efforts that make buying a house easy, understandable, and affordable.

We affirm our commitment to open housing, without quotas or controls, and we condemn the Clinton Administration's abuse of fair housing laws to harass citizens exercising their First Amendment rights.

In addition, we support transforming public housing into private housing, converting low-income families into proud homeowners. Resident management of public housing is a first step toward that goal, which includes eliminating the Department of Housing and Urban Development (HUD). HUD's core functions will be turned over to the States. Its civil rights component will be administered by the appropriate federal agency while enforcement will remain with the Department of Justice.

With the housing sector representing such a significant segment of the Nation's economy, housing policy is and should continue to be a priority. We believe in a federal role which supplements, not directs or competes with, States and localities. We believe in federal programs which augment, not displace, private sector capital and resources.

The Federal Government should not impose prescriptive solutions on State and local governments. Republicans believe that States and localities should have maximum flexibility to design programs which meet the individual needs of their communities. Washington must abandon the "one size fits all" approach and concentrate on adding value to the efforts of States, localities, private and faith-based organizations and individuals. Republicans believe we can and will accomplish this without disrupting services to the elderly, disabled and families with children.

Promoting Trade and International Prosperity

Republicans believe that the United States, as the sole superpower in the world today, has a responsibility to lead— economically, militarily, diplomatically, and morally—so that we have a peaceful and prosperous world.

Republicans support free and fair trade. In the American Century ahead, our country will lead in international trade. American workers will be the winners in any fair competition, and American technology will drive a prosperity revolution around the world. Exports already fuel our economy; their continuing expansion is essential for full employment and long-term prosperity. That is possible only within the context of expanding trade, and we can do it better without a Department of Commerce.

Our country's merchandise trade deficit exploded to $175 billion in 1995 and will likely set an all-time record in 1996, siphoning American wealth into the hands of foreigners. Trade deficits with all our major trading partners were worse in 1995 than in 1992. With China alone, the deficit more than doubled to $35 billion in the last three and a half years. With Japan, Bill Clinton announced a series of hollow agreements that have done little to improve market access. With Russia, he approved a $1 billion Export-Import Bank loan to foster competition with the American aircraft industry. With Canada, he tolerates discrimination against the United States beverage industry and focused on our lumber crisis too late to help closed logging mills. With Mexico, he ignored injury to American agriculture from massive surges in imports.

We should vigorously implement the North American Free Trade Agreement, while carefully monitoring its progress, to guarantee that its promised benefits and protections are realized by all American workers and consumers.

Republicans are for vigorous enforcement of the trade agreements we already have on the books, unlike the Clinton Administration that uses United States trade policy as a bargaining chip and as a vehicle for pursuing a host of other social agenda items. Republicans will enforce United States trade laws, including our antidumping laws, and will use the Super 301 investigations that give the President authority to challenge foreign barriers to our exports. And we will use the Export Enhancement Program to boost American farm exports. To advance economic freedom, we insist that United States foreign aid, whether bilateral or through the World Bank and International Monetary Fund, promote market reforms, limit regulation, and encourage free trade. Republicans will stop subsidizing socialism in the less developed nations. Republicans will not allow the World Trade Organization to undermine United States sovereignty and will support a World Trade Organization oversight commission.

Free market capitalism is the right model for economic development throughout the world. The Soviet model of a state-controlled economy has been discredited, and neither stage of development nor geographic location can justify economic authoritarianism. Human nature and aspirations are the same everywhere, and everywhere the family is the building block of economic and social progress. We therefore will protect the rights of families in international programs and will not fund organizations involved in abortion. The cost of turning our back on the global marketplace is the loss of opportunity and millions of jobs for United States citizens.

Changing Washington from the Ground Up

"On November 8, 1994, the American people sent a message to Washington. . . . Their message is my mandate: To rein in government and reconnect it to the values of the American people. That means making government a whole lot smaller, a lot less arrogant, and getting it out of matters best left to the states, cities, and families across America."
—*Bob Dole, March 10, 1995, in Washington, D.C.*

We are the party of small, responsible and efficient government, joining our neighbors in cities and counties, rather than distant bureaucrats, to build a just society and caring communities. We therefore assert the power of the American people over government, rather than the other way around. Our agenda for change, profound and permanent change in the way government behaves, is based on the Tenth Amendment to the Constitution:

The powers not delegated to the United States by the Constitution, nor prohibited by it to the States, are reserved to the States respectively, or to the people.

For more than half a century, that solemn compact has been scorned by liberal Democrats and the judicial activism of the judges they have appointed. We will restore the force of the Tenth Amendment and, in the process, renew the trust and respect which hold together a free society. As its first initiative enacted into law, the new Republican majority on Capitol Hill launched that effort early in 1995 by forbidding the imposition of new unfunded mandates upon State and local taxpayers. From now on, if official Washington promises benefits, official Washington must pay for them. We will apply that same principle to the ill-conceived Motor-Voter Act, the Democrats' costly invitation to ballot fraud.

To permanently restore balance in the federal system, States must have the proper tools to act as a counterforce to the Federal Government. Our country's founders attempted to carefully balance power between the two levels. The Tenth Amendment, as well as the ability of State legislatures to initiate constitutional amendments, and other constitutional tools given to States to protect their role in the system have now been either eroded away, given away, or rendered impossible to use. Thus, States lack the tools necessary to do their job as a counterbalance to the national government.

We call upon Congress, governors, State legislators and local leaders to adopt structural reforms that will permanently restore balance in our federal system. In this Information Era of uncertainty and rapid change, it is government close to home, controlled by neighborhood and community leaders, that can best respond to the needs and values of all citizens.

As a first step in reforming government, we support elimination of the Departments of Commerce, Housing and Urban Development, Education, and Energy, and the elimination, defunding or privatization of agencies which are obsolete, redundant, of limited value, or too regional in focus. Examples of agencies we seek to defund or to privatize are the National Endowment for the Arts, the National Endowment for the Humanities, the Corporation for Public Broadcasting, and the Legal Services Corporation.

In addition, we support Republican-sponsored legislation that would require the original sponsor of proposed federal legislation to cite specific constitutional authority for the measure. . . .

Cleaning Up Government

In 1992, Bill Clinton promised "the most ethical Administration in the history of the Republic." Instead, the Clinton Administration has been rife with scandal. An unprecedented four Independent Counsels have been appointed since the Clinton Inauguration to investigate various allegations of wrongdoing by members of this Administration. The Clinton White House has abused executive power in both the White House Travel Office firings situation and in the FBI files matter. The FBI Director said there have been "egregious violations of privacy" in the gathering of FBI files of officials who worked in the White House under Republican administrations. We believe that misuse of law enforcement authorities for partisan political ends is no trivial matter. Such abuses strike at the heart of the relationship between citizen and government and undermine the rule of law and confidence in our leaders.

Scandals in government are not limited to possible criminal violations. The public trust is violated when taxpayers money is treated as a slush fund for special interest groups who oppose urgently needed reforms. For example, the Democrats have denied school vouchers for poor children in the nation's capital at the demand of special interest unions. They have blocked urgently needed legal reforms at the command of the trial lawyers, now the biggest source of revenue for the Democrat party. They have rejected reforms to improve the workplace to please union bosses who committed $35 million to aid the Clinton reelection effort.

It is time to restore honor and integrity to government. We propose to:

- revoke pension rights of public officials who have been convicted of crimes;
- strengthen citizen privacy laws and reform the FBI to guard against the politicization of law enforcement that we have seen by the Clinton White House;

- refuse to allow special interest groups to block innovative solutions for the poor or to block workplace or legal reforms that would help all working Americans; and
- recruit for public service, at all levels, men and women of integrity and high ethical standards.

We will end welfare for lobbyists. Every year, the federal government gives away billions of dollars in grants. Much of that money goes to interest groups which engage in political activity and issue advocacy at the taxpayers' expense. This is an intolerable abuse of the public's money. A Republican Congress will enact legislation, currently blocked by Bill Clinton's congressional allies, to make groups choose between grants and lobbying.

We will establish Truth in Testimony, requiring organizations which receive government funds and testify before Congress to disclose those funds. Our "Let America Know" legislation will force public disclosure of all taxpayer subsidies and lobbying by groups seeking grants. We will permit "private attorney general" lawsuits against federal grantees to ensure better enforcement of anti-lobbying restrictions. A Republican administration will impose accountability on grantees, to reveal what the public is getting for its money, and will end the process of automatic grant renewal. We will halt the funding of frivolous and politicized research grants.

Streamlining Government

Republicans believe we can streamline government and make it more effective through competition and privatization. We applaud the Republican Congress and Republican officials across the country for initiatives to expand the use of competition and privatization in government. It is greater competition—not unchallenged government bureaucracies—that will cut the cost of government, improve the delivery of services, and ensure wise investment in infrastructure. A Dole administration will make competition a centerpiece of government, eliminating duplication and increasing efficiency.

Honest Budgets and Real Numbers

We have a moral responsibility not to leave our children a legacy of monstrous debt. Spending $1.6 trillion a year should be more than an accounting exercise. Restraining government spending, discussed elsewhere in this platform, is part of the solution. Reforming the entire budget process is the rest of it.

Our goal is clarity, simplicity, and accountability in the nation's budget. The keystone of that agenda is the enactment of a constitutional amendment to require a balanced budget which a majority of congressional Democrats have vigorously opposed. We do not take that step lightly; but then, a $5 trillion debt is no laughing matter for tomorrow's taxpayers. We vow to offer that amendment again and again, until Congress sends it to the States for ratification.

In addition, we must eliminate all built-in biases toward spending. For example, the "current service baseline" builds in automatic budget increases for inflation and other factors and works like this: If the Democrats want a $1 billion program to grow to $2 billion, they then count an increase to $1.5 billion as a half-billion dollar cut—and the media dutifully reports it as such. This is a deceptive and reprehensible shell game that must be stopped.

A Republican president will fight wasteful spending with the line-item veto which was finally enacted by congressional Republicans this year over bitter Democrat opposition, 120 years after President Grant first proposed it.

Even more important, we will stop the runaway growth of entitlement spending—the programs which automatically grow without any action required by Congress or the President. This spending has jumped 11-fold since 1970 and consumes more than half the federal budget. We will take entitlements off automatic pilot and make Congress accountable for their funding. To end outdated and wasteful programs, we will make the Government Performance and Results Act an integral part of our budget process.

Regulatory Reform

Regulatory reform is needed more than ever. Bill Clinton promised to "reinvent government," but he returned to the old mindset of controls and red tape. To make matters worse, he vetoed a comprehensive regulatory reform bill crafted by Republicans in the House and Senate. That measure will become law when Bob Dole is President.

We commend House Speaker Newt Gingrich and congressional Republicans in their innovative efforts to rescind, overturn and zero-out absurd bureaucratic red tape and rules through the process known as "Corrections Day."

A Republican administration will require periodic review of existing regulations to ensure they are effective and do away with obsolete and conflicting rules. We will encourage civil servants to find ways to reduce regulatory burdens on the public and will require federal agencies to disclose the costs of new regulations on individuals and small businesses. A new regulatory budget will reveal the total cost of regulations on the American people.

We will target resources on the most serious risks to health, safety, and the environment, rather than on politically inspired causes, and will require peer-reviewed risk assessments based on sound science. We will require agencies to conduct cost-benefit analyses of their regulations and pursue alternatives to the outdated Clinton command-and-control approach. These common-sense reforms will restore fairness and predictability to government rules and, even more important, will enable us to achieve equal or superior levels of protection for the public at lower cost.

Just as important, we recognize that all too often, in its ever-present zeal to expand into every aspect of our daily lives, the federal government intrudes into the private economy by establishing new services in direct competition with already existing private firms. We oppose the use of taxpayer funds to provide a competitive advantage for government agencies seeking to compete with private firms in the free market.

Restoring Justice to the Courts

"When I am president, only conservative judges need apply."
—*Bob Dole, May 28, 1996, in Aurora, Colorado*

The American people have lost faith in their courts, and for good reason. Some members of the federal judiciary threaten the safety, the values, and the freedom of law-abiding citizens. They make up laws and invent new rights as they go along, arrogating to themselves powers King George III never dared to exercise. They free vicious criminals, pamper felons in prison, frivolously overturn State laws enacted by citizen referenda, and abdicate the responsibility of providing meaningful review of administrative decisions.

The delicate balance of power between the respective branches of our national government and the governments of the 50 states has been eroded. The notion of judicial review has in some cases come to resemble judicial supremacy, affecting all segments of public and private endeavor. Make no mistake, the separation of powers doctrine, complete and unabridged, is the linchpin of a government of laws. A Republican Congress and president will restore true separation of powers and guarantee the American people a government of law.

The federal judiciary, including the U.S. Supreme Court, has overstepped its authority under the Constitution. It has usurped the right of citizen legislators and popularly elected executives to make law by declaring duly enacted laws to be "unconstitutional" through the misapplication of the principle of judicial review. Any other role for the judiciary, especially when personal preferences masquerade as interpreting the law, is fundamentally at odds with our system of government in which the people and their representatives decide issues great and small.

No systemic reform of the judiciary can substitute for the wise exercise of power of appointment vested in the president of the United States. A Republican president will ensure that a process is established to select for the federal judiciary nominees who understand that their task is first and foremost to be faithful to the Constitution and to the intent of those who framed it. In that process, the American Bar Association will no longer have the right to meddle in a way that distorts a nominee's credentials and advances the liberal agenda of litigious lawyers and their allies.

Justice is mocked by some of today's litigation practices, which hinder our country's competitiveness, and drain billions of dollars away from productive Americans. While we fully support the role of the judiciary in vindicating the constitutional and statutory rights of individuals and organizations, we believe the proliferation of litigation hits the consumer with higher prices and cripples the practice of medicine. Despite bipartisan congressional efforts to enact legal reforms, Bill Clinton vetoed such legislation at the behest of his financial friends: the trial lawyers. A Republican president will sign that bill, and more. We encourage State governments to adopt reforms similar to those we propose to restore fairness to the federal system:

- Strengthen judicial sanctions for lawsuits that are substantially without merit, thereby hitting unethical lawyers in their pocketbooks;
- Apply the Racketeer Influenced and Corrupt Organizations law (RICO) as originally intended, to criminal proceedings, not civil litigation;
- Award punitive damages on a fair and reasonable basis after clear proof of wrongdoing, with limits that discourage opportunistic litigation. Since punitive damages are intended to punish egregious wrongdoing, a substantial portion of the amount awarded should go to a crime-victim compensation fund or similar program;
- Restore limited liability to non-profit organizations—churches, civic and community groups, and the volunteers who sustain them—to provide protection against profit-seeking lawsuits and to encourage volunteerism;
- Increase sanctions for abuses of the discovery process used to intimidate opponents and drive up the costs of litigation;
- Reform medical malpractice to reduce health care costs and keep doctors practicing in critical areas like obstetrics;
- Eliminate the use of "junk science" by opportunistic attorneys by requiring courts to verify that the science of those called as expert witnesses is reasonably acceptable within the scientific community, and forbid the practice of making their fees conditional upon a favorable verdict. This action will reduce the practice of so-called hired-gun "experts" who make up theories to fit the facts of the case in which they are testifying;
- Eliminate joint and several liability in order to ensure that responsible parties pay their "fair share" in proportion to their degree of fault; and
- Guard against non-meritorious lawsuits that are designed to have a chilling effect on First Amendment rights.

A federal products liability law goes hand in hand with legal reform. Its absence not only penalizes consumers with higher costs and keeps needed products off the market, but also gives foreign nations a competitive edge over American workers. Bill Clinton doesn't mind that. He vetoed Republican reforms that would have saved the public tens of billions of dollars.

Bill Clinton even vetoed the Securities Litigation Reform Act, a Republican initiative to protect shareholders against avaricious litigation. That obstructionism was too much for even the Democrats in Congress, many of whom joined in overriding his veto. A Republican president will work with Congress to restore justice to the nation's courts and fair play to the practice of law. . . .

Individual Rights and Personal Safety

"We are discovering as a nation that many of our deepest social problems are problems of character and belief. We will never solve those problems until the hearts of parents are turned toward their children; until respect is restored for life and property; until a commitment is renewed to love and serve our neighbor. The common good requires that goodness be common."

—*Bob Dole, May 23, 1996, in Philadelphia*

Upholding the Rights of All

This section of our platform deals with rights and responsibilities. But it deals also with something larger: the common good, our shared sense of what makes a society decent and noble. That takes us beyond government policies and programs to what we are as a people, and what we want to be.

We are the party of the open door. As we approach the start of a new century, the Republican Party is more dedicated than ever to strengthening the social, cultural, and political ties that bind us together as a free people, the greatest force for good the world has ever seen. While our party remains steadfast in its commitment to advancing its historic principles and ideals, we also recognize that members of our party have deeply held and sometimes differing views. We view this diversity of views as a source of strength, not as a sign of weakness, and we welcome into our ranks all Americans who may hold differing positions. We are committed to resolving our differences in a spirit of civility, hope, and mutual respect.

Americans do not want to be afraid of those they pass on the street, suspicious of strangers, fearful for their children. They do not want to have to fight a constant battle against brutality and degradation in what passes for entertainment. We oppose sexual harassment in the workplace, and must ensure that no one in America is forced to choose between a job and submitting to unwelcome advances. We also oppose indoctrination in the classroom. Americans should not have to tolerate the decline of ethical standards and the collapse of behavioral norms. Most important, they should not have to doubt the truthfulness of their elected leaders.

Reversing those trends won't be easy, but our homes and our children are worth the effort. Government has a small, but vital, role. But most of the burden must be ours: as parents, as consumers, as citizens whose right of free speech empowers us to stand up for the weak and vulnerable—and speak out against the profiteers of violence and moral decay.

That needs to be done, both in our house and in the White House. Bill Clinton can't—or won't—do it. So we will do it without him, and with new national leadership of character and conscience.

We are the party of individual Americans, whose rights we protect and defend as the foundation for opportunity and security for all. Today, as at our founding in the day of Lincoln, we insist no one's rights are negotiable.

As we strive to forge a national consensus on the divisive issues of our time, we call on all Republicans and all Americans to reject the forces of hatred and bigotry. Accordingly, we denounce all who practice or promote racism, anti-Semitism, ethnic prejudice, and religious intolerance. We condemn attempts by the EEOC [Equal Employment Opportunity Commission] or any other arm of government to regulate or ban religious symbols from the work place, and we assert the right of religious leaders to speak out on public issues. We condemn the desecration of places of worship and are proud that congressional Republicans led the fight against church arsons. We believe religious institutions and schools should not be taxed. When government funds privately operated social, welfare, or educational programs, it must not discriminate against religious institutions, whose record in providing services to those in need far exceeds that of the public sector.

The sole source of equal opportunity for all is equality before the law. Therefore, we oppose discrimination based on sex, race, age, creed, or national origin and will vigorously enforce anti-discrimination statutes. We reject the distortion of those laws to cover sexual preference, and we endorse the Defense of Marriage Act to prevent states from being forced to recognize same-sex unions. Because we believe rights inhere in individuals, not in groups, we will attain our nation's goal of equal rights without quotas or other forms of preferential treatment. We scorn Bill Clinton's notion that any person should be denied a job, promotion, contract or a chance at higher education because of their race or gender. Instead, we endorse the Dole-Canady Equal Opportunity Act to end discrimination by the federal government. We likewise endorse this year's Proposition 209, the California Civil Rights Initiative, to restore to law the original meaning of civil rights.

We renew our historic Republican commitment to equal opportunity for women. In the early days of the suffragist movement, we pioneered the women's right to vote. We take pride in this year's remarkable array of Republican women serving in and running for office and their role in leadership positions in our party, in Congress, and in the states. Two women serve in our House Leadership—a record untouched by the Democrats during their 40 years in power. The full exercise of legal rights depends upon opportunity, and economic growth is the key to continuing progress for women in all fields of endeavor. Public policy must respect and accommodate women whether they are full-time homemakers or pursue a career.

Under Senator Dole's sponsorship, the Americans with Disabilities Act was enacted to ensure full participation by disabled citizens in our country's life. Republicans emphasize community integration and inclusion of persons with disabilities, both by personal example and by practical enforcement of the Individuals with Disabilities Education Act, the Air Carriers Access Act, and other laws. We will safeguard the interests of disabled persons in Medicare and Medicaid, as well as in federal work force programs. Under a Republican renewal, the abilities of all will be needed in an expanding economy, which alone can carry forward the assistive technology that offers personal progress for everyone. We support full access to the polls, and the entire political process, by disabled citizens. We oppose the non-consensual withholding of health care or treatment because of handicap, age, or infirmity, just as we oppose euthanasia and assisted suicide, which, especially for the poor and those on the margins of society, threaten the sanctity of human life.

The unborn child has a fundamental individual right to life which cannot be infringed. We support a human life amendment to the Constitution and we endorse legislation to make clear that the Fourteenth Amendment's protections apply to unborn children. Our purpose is to have legislative and judicial protection of that right against those who perform abortions. We oppose using public revenues for abortion and will not fund organizations which advocate it. We support the appointment of judges who respect traditional family values and the sanctity of innocent human life.

Our goal is to ensure that women with problem pregnancies have the kind of support, material and otherwise, they need for themselves and for their babies, not to be punitive towards those for whose difficult situation we have only compassion. We oppose abortion, but our pro-life agenda does not include punitive action against women who have an abortion. We salute those who provide alternatives to abortion and offer adoption services. Republicans in Congress took the lead in expanding assistance both for the costs of adoption and for the continuing care of adoptive children with special needs. Bill Clinton vetoed our adoption tax credit the first time around—and opposed our efforts to remove racial barriers to adoption—before joining in this long overdue measure of support for adoptive families.

Worse than that, he vetoed the ban on partial-birth abortions, a procedure denounced by a committee of the American Medical Association and rightly branded as four-fifths infanticide. We applaud Bob Dole's commitment to revoke the Clinton executive orders concerning abortion and to sign into law an end to partial-birth abortions.

We reaffirm the promise of the Fifth Amendment: "nor shall private property be taken for public use, without just compensation." This Takings Clause protects the homes and livelihood of Americans against the governmental greed and abuse of power that characterizes the Clinton Administration; we will strictly enforce it.

We defend the constitutional right to keep and bear arms. We will promote training in the safe usage of firearms, especially in programs for women and the elderly. We strongly support Bob Dole's National Instant Check Initiative, which will help keep all guns out of the hands of convicted felons. The point-of-purchase instant check has worked well in many states and now it is time to extend this system all across America. We applaud Bob Dole's commitment to have the national instant check system operational by the end of 1997. In one of the strangest actions of his tenure, Bill Clinton abolished Operation Triggerlock, the Republican initiative to jail any felon caught with a gun. We will restore that effort and will set by law minimum mandatory penalties for the use of guns in committing a crime: 5 years for possession, 10 years for brandishing, and 20 for discharge.

We affirm the right of individuals to participate in labor organizations and to bargain collectively, consistent with State laws. Because that participation should always be voluntary. we support the right of States to enact Right-to-Work laws. We will restore the original scope of the Hobbs Act, barring union officials from extortion and violence. We will vigorously implement the Supreme Court's Beck decision to ensure that workers are not compelled to subsidize political activity, like the $35 million slush fund extorted this year from rank and file members by Washington-based labor leaders. We will reverse Bill Clinton's unconscionable Executive Order that deprived workers of their right to know how their union dues are spent.

A Sensible Immigration Policy

As a nation of immigrants, we welcome those who follow our laws and come to our land to seek a better life. New Americans strengthen our economy, enrich our culture, and defend the nation in war and in peace. At the same time, we are determined to reform the system by which we welcome them to the American family. We must set immigration at manageable levels, balance the competing goals of uniting families of our citizens and admitting specially talented persons, and end asylum abuses through expedited exclusion of false claimants.

Bill Clinton's immigration record does not match his rhetoric. While talking tough on illegal immigration, he has proposed a reduction in the number of border patrol agents authorized by the Republicans in Congress, has opposed the most successful border control program in decades (Operation Hold the Line in Texas), has opposed Proposition 187 in California which 60 percent of Californians supported, and has opposed Republican efforts to ensure that non-citizens do not take advantage of expensive welfare programs. Unlike Bill Clinton, we stand with the American people on immigration policy and will continue to reform and enforce our immigration laws to ensure that they reflect America's national interest.

We also support efforts to secure our borders from the threat of illegal immigration. Illegal immigration has reached crisis proportions, with more than four million illegal aliens now present in the United States. That number, growing by 300,000 each year, burdens taxpayers, strains public services, takes jobs, and increases crime. Republicans in both the House and Senate have passed bills that tighten border enforcement, speed up deportation of criminal aliens, toughen penalties for overstaying visas, and streamline the Immigration and Naturalization Service.

Illegal aliens should not receive public benefits other than emergency aid, and those who become parents while illegally in the United States should not be qualified to claim benefits for their offspring. Legal immigrants should depend for assistance on their sponsors, who are legally responsible for their financial well-being, not the American taxpayers. Just as we require "deadbeat dads" to provide for the children they bring into the world, we should require "deadbeat sponsors" to provide for the immigrants they bring into the country. We support a constitutional amendment or constitutionally-valid legislation declaring that children born in the United States of parents who are not legally present in the United States or who are not long-term residents are not automatically citizens.

We endorse the Dole/Coverdell proposal to make crimes of domestic violence, stalking, child abuse, child neglect and child abandonment committed by aliens residing in this country deportable offenses under our immigration laws.

We call for harsh penalties against exploiters who smuggle illegal aliens and for those who profit from the production of false documents. Republicans believe that by eliminating the magnet for illegal immigration, increasing border security, enforcing our immigration laws, and producing counter-

feit-proof documents, we will finally put an end to the illegal immigration crisis. We oppose the creation of any national ID card.

From Many, One

America's ethnic diversity within a shared national culture is one of our
country's greatest strengths. While we benefit from our differences, we must
also strengthen the ties that bind us to one another. Foremost among those
is the flag. Its deliberate desecration is not "free speech," but an assault
against our history and our hopes. We support a constitutional amendment
that will restore to the people, through their elected representatives, their
right to safeguard Old Glory. We condemn Bill Clinton's refusal, once again,
to protect and preserve the most precious symbol of our Republic.

English, our common language, provides a shared foundation which has
allowed people from every corner of the world to come together to build the
American nation. The use of English is indispensable to all who wish to participate fully in our society and realize the American dream. As Bob Dole has
said: "For more than two centuries now, English has been a force for unity,
indispensable to the process of transforming untold millions of immigrants
from all parts of the globe into citizens of the most open and free society the
world has ever seen." For newcomers, learning the English language has
always been the fastest route to the mainstream of American life. That
should be the goal of bilingual education programs. We support the official
recognition of English as the nation's common language. We advocate foreign
language training in our schools and retention of heritage languages in homes
and cultural institutions. Foreign language fluency is also an essential component of America's competitiveness in the world market.

We will strengthen Native Americans' self-determination by respecting
tribal sovereignty, encouraging a pro-business and pro-development climate
on reservations. We uphold the unique government-to-government relationship between the tribes and the United States, and we honor our nation's
trust obligations to them. In fulfillment thereof, we will ensure that the
resources, financial and otherwise, which the United States holds in trust are
well-managed, audited, and protected. We second Bob Dole's call for legislation authorizing tribal governments to reorganize the Bureau of Indian
Affairs and the Indian Health Service. We endorse efforts to ensure equitable
participation in federal programs by Native Americans, Native Alaskans and
Native Hawaiians and to preserve their culture and languages.

Getting Tough on Crime

> "Women in America know better than anyone about the randomness and ruth-
> lessness of crime. It is a shameful, national disgrace that nightfall has become
> synonymous with fear for so many of America's women."
> —*Bob Dole, May 28, 1996, in Aurora, Colorado*

During Bill Clinton's tenure, America has become a more fearful place,
especially for the elderly and for women and children. Violent crime has

turned our homes into prisons, our streets and schoolyards into battle-grounds. It devours half a trillion dollars every year. Unfortunately, far worse could be coming in the near future. While we acknowledge the extraordinary efforts of single parents, we recognize that a generation of fatherless boys raises the prospect of soaring juvenile crime.

This is, in part, the legacy of liberalism—in the old Democrat Congress, in the Clinton Department of Justice, and in the courts, where judges appointed by Democrat presidents continue their assault against the rights of law-abiding Americans. For too long government policy has been controlled by criminals and their defense lawyers. Democrat Congresses cared more about rights of criminals than safety for Americans. Bill Clinton arbitrarily closed off Pennsylvania Avenue, the nation's Main Street, for his protection, while his policies left the public unprotected against vicious criminals. As a symbol of our determination to restore the rule of law—in the White House as well as in our streets—we will reopen Pennsylvania Avenue.

After the elections of 1994, the new Republican majorities in the House and Senate fought back with legislation that ends frivolous, costly, and unnecessarily lengthy death-row appeals, requires criminals to pay restitution to their victims, speeds the removal of criminal aliens, and steps up the fight against terrorism. Congressional Republicans put into law a truth-in-sentencing prison grant program to provide incentives to states which enact laws requiring violent felons to serve at least 85% of their sentences and replaced a myriad of Democrat "Washington knows best" prevention programs with block grants to cities and counties to use to fight crime as they see fit. They put an end to federal court early-release orders for prison overcrowding and made it much harder for prisoners to file frivolous lawsuits about prison conditions.

There's more to do, once Bill Clinton's veto threats no longer block the way. We will establish no-frills prisons where prisoners are required to work productively and make the threat of jail a real deterrent to crime. Prisons should not be places of rest and relaxation. We will reform the Supreme Court's fanciful exclusionary rule, which has allowed a generation of criminals to get off on technicalities.

Juvenile crime is one of the most difficult challenges facing our nation. The juvenile justice system is broken. It fails to punish the minor crimes that lead to larger offenses, and lacks early intervention to keep delinquency from turning into violent crime. Truancy laws are not enforced, positive role models are lacking, and parental responsibility is overlooked. We will stress accountability at every step in the system and require adult trials for juveniles who commit adult crimes.

In addition, not only is juvenile crime on the rise, but unsupervised juveniles (especially at night) are most often the victims of abuse in our society. Recognizing that local jurisdictions have a clear and concise understanding of their problems, we encourage them to develop and enact innovative programs to address juvenile crime. We also encourage them to consider juvenile nocturnal curfews as an effective law enforcement tool in helping reduce juvenile crime and juvenile victimization.

Juvenile criminal proceedings should be open to victims and the public. Juvenile conviction records should not be sealed but made available to law enforcement agencies, the courts, and those who hire for sensitive work in schools and day-care centers.

Because liberal jurists keep expanding the rights of the accused, Republicans propose a Constitutional amendment to protect victims' rights: audio and visual testimony of victims kept on file for future hearings, full restitution, protection from intimidation or violence by the offender, notification of court proceedings, a chance to be heard in plea bargains, the right to remain in court during trials and hearings concerning the crimes committed against them, a voice in the sentencing proceedings, notice of the release or escape of offenders. Bill Clinton hypocritically endorsed our Victim's Rights Amendment while naming judges who opposed capital punishment, turned felons loose, and even excused murder as a form of social protest. Bob Dole, the next Republican president, will end that nonsense and make our courts once again an instrument of justice.

While the federal government's role is essential, most law enforcement must remain in the hands of local communities, directed by State and local officials who are closely answerable to the people whose lives are affected by crime. In that regard, we support community policing; nothing inhibits local crime like an officer in the neighborhood. Bill Clinton promised 100,000 more police officers on the beat but, according to his own Attorney General, delivered no more than 17,000. He ignored local law enforcers by tying the program in knots of red tape and high costs. Now he is diverting millions of its dollars, appropriated by congressional Republicans to fight street crime, to state parks and environmental projects. It's time to return those anti-crime resources to communities and let them decide what works best to keep their homes, schools, and workplaces safe. This would result in far more new police officers than Bill Clinton's program and give communities additional crime fighting resources they need.

We will work with local authorities to prevent prison inmates from receiving disability or other government entitlements while incarcerated. We support efforts to allow peace officers, including qualified retirees, to assist their colleagues and protect their communities even when they are out of their home jurisdictions to the extent this is consistent with applicable state and local law. We will amend the Fair Labor Standards Act so that corrections officers can volunteer to assist local law enforcement.

Crimes against women and children demand an emphatic response. Under Bob Dole and Dick Zimmer's leadership, Republicans in Congress pushed through Megan's Law—the requirement that local communities be notified when sex offenders and kidnappers are released—in response to the growing number of violent sexual assaults and murders like the brutal murder of a little girl in New Jersey. We call for special penalties against thugs who assault or batter pregnant women and harm them or their unborn children. We endorse Bob Dole's call to bring federal penalties for child pornography in line with far tougher State penalties: ten years for a first offense, fifteen for the second, and life for a third. We believe it is time to revisit the Supreme Court's arbitrary decision of 1977 that protects even the most vicious rapists from the death penalty. Bob Dole authored a tough federal statute which provides for the admissibility of prior similar criminal acts of defendants in sexual assault cases. This important law enforcement tool should serve as a model for the states. We continue our strong support of capital punishment for those who commit heinous federal crimes; including the kingpins of the narcotics trade.

We wish to express our support and sympathy for all victims of terrorism and their families. Acts of terrorism against Americans and American interests must be stopped and those who commit them must be brought to justice. We recommend a presidentially appointed "blue ribbon" commission to study more effective methods of prosecuting terrorists.

Only Republican resolve can prepare our nation to deal with the four deadly threats facing us in the early years of the 21st Century: violent crime, drugs, terrorism, and international organized crime. Those perils are interlocked—and all are escalating. This is no time for excuses. It's time for a change.

Solving the Drug Crisis

The verdict is in on Bill Clinton's moral leadership: after 11 years of steady decline, the use of marijuana among teens doubled in the two years after 1992. At the same time, the use of cocaine and methamphetamines dramatically increased.

That shocks but should not surprise. For in the war on drugs—an essential component of the fight against crime—today's Democratic Party has been a conscientious objector. Nowhere is the discrepancy between Bill Clinton's rhetoric and his actions more apparent. Mr. Clinton's personal record has been a betrayal of the nation's trust, sending the worst possible signal to the nation's youth. At the urging of the Secret Service, the White House had to institute a drug-testing program for Clinton staffers who were known to be recent users of illegal narcotics. At the same time, he drastically cut funding for drug interdiction. The Office of National Drug Control Policy was cut by 80 percent, and federal drug prosecutions dropped 25 percent. His Attorney General proposed to reduce mandatory minimum sentences for drug trafficking and related crimes, and his Surgeon General advocated legalization of narcotics. Hundreds of suspected drug smugglers have been allowed to go free at the border. Simultaneously, the use of marijuana, cocaine, and heroin has increased, especially among young people. Now narcotics are again fueling the acceleration of crime rates, putting the nation on a collision course with the future.

Bill Clinton's weakness in international affairs has worsened the situation here at home. One case in point: He certified that Mexico has cooperated with our drug interdiction effort when 70 percent of drugs smuggled into the U. S. come across our southern border—and when the Mexican government ignored 165 extradition orders for drug criminals. Discredited at home and abroad, he lacks both the stature and the credibility to lead us toward a drug-free America.

A war against drugs requires moral leadership now lacking in the White House. Throughout the 1980s, the Republican approach—no legalization, no tolerance, no excuses—turned the tide against drug abuse. We can do it again by emphasizing prevention, interdiction, a tough international approach, and a crack-down on users. That requires reversing one of Bill Clinton's most offensive actions: his shocking purge of every U. S. Attorney in the country shortly after he took office. This unprecedented firing destroyed our first line of defense against drug traffickers and other career criminals. Our country's most experienced and dedicated prosecutors were replaced with Clintonite liberals, some of whom have refused to prosecute major drug dealers, foreign narcotics smugglers, and child pornographers.

In a Dole Administration, U. S. Attorneys will prosecute and jail those who prey upon the innocent. We support upgrading our interdiction effort by establishing a Deputy Commissioner for Drug Enforcement within the Customs Service. We will intensify our intelligence efforts against international drug traffickers and use whatever means necessary to destroy their operations and seize their personal accounts.

We support strong penalties, including mandatory minimum sentences, for drug trafficking, distribution and drug-related crimes. Drug use is closely related to crime and recidivism. Drug testing should be made a routine feature of the criminal justice process at every stage, including the juvenile justice system. Test results should be used in deciding pretrial release, sentencing, and probation revocation.

A safer America must include highways without drunk or drug-impaired drivers. We support the toughest possible State laws to deal with drivers impaired by substance abuse and advocate federal cooperation, not compulsion, toward that end.

The Bottom Line: From the Top Down

Making America safe again will be a tremendous undertaking, in its own way as heroic as was the liberation of Europe from a different kind of criminal half a century ago. At the grassroots, that crusade already has enlisted the men and women of local law enforcement. Now they need a leader worthy of their cause—someone whose life reflects respect for the law, not evasion of it. Bill Clinton need not apply.

Bob Dole will be a president committed to the protection and safety of all Americans. However, his strength is diminished without a court system supportive of the national fight against violent crime. That is the bottom line of this year's presidential election: Who should chart the course of law enforcement for the next generation by naming as many as an additional 30 percent of our federal judges and the next several justices to the U. S. Supreme Court? Bill Clinton, the master of excuse and evasion? Or Bob Dole, whose life has been an exercise in honor and duty?

Families and Society

"The alternative to cold bureaucracy is not indifference. It is the warmth of families and neighborhoods, charities, churches, synagogues and communities. These value-shaping institutions have the tools to reclaim lives—individual responsibility, tough love, and spiritual renewal. They do more than care for the body; they restore the spirit."

—Bob Dole, May 23, 1996, in Philadelphia

Stronger Families

We are the party of the American family, educating children, caring for the sick, learning from the elderly, and helping the less fortunate. We believe that strengthening family life is the best way to improve the quality of life for everyone.

Families foster the virtues that make a free society strong. We rely on the home and its supportive institutions to instill honesty, self-discipline, mutual respect and the other virtues that sustain democracy. Our goal is to promote those values by respecting the rights of families and by assisting, where appropriate, the institutions which mediate between government and the home. While recognizing a role for government in dealing with social ills, we look to mediating institutions—religious and community groups, private associations of all kinds—to take the lead in tackling the social ills that some government programs have only worsened.

This is the clearest distinction between Republicans and Clinton Democrats: We believe the family is the core institution of our society. Bill Clinton thinks government should hold that place. It's little wonder, then, that today's families feel under siege. They seem to work harder with less reward for their labor. They can no longer expect that life will be better for their children than it was for them.

Their problem starts in the White House. Bill Clinton has hit families with higher taxes, vetoed their tax relief, and given their money to special interest groups. He has meddled in their schools, fought family choice in education, and promoted lifestyles inimical to their values. He repeatedly vetoed pro-family welfare reforms before surrendering to the demands of the American people. He tried to impose a ruinous government takeover of health care; led a scare campaign against Republican efforts to preserve, protect, and strengthen Medicare; and appointed to major positions in his administration social theorists whose bizarre views are alien to those of most Americans.

Republicans want to get our society back on track—toward good schools with great teachers, welfare that really helps, and health care responsive to the needs of people, not government. We want to make sure our most important programs—like Social Security and Medicare—are there when people need them. In all those cases, we start with the family as the building block of a safe and caring society.

Our agenda for more secure families runs throughout this platform. Here we take special notice of the way congressional Republicans have advanced adoption assistance, promoted foster care reform, and fought the marriage penalty in the tax code. They have worked to let parents have flex-time and comp-time in private industry, and have safeguarded family choice in child care against the Democrats' attempts to control it. They passed the Defense of Marriage Act, which defines "marriage" for purposes of federal law as the legal union of one man and one woman and prevents federal judges and bureaucrats from forcing states to recognize other living arrangements as "marriages." Further, they have advanced the Family Rights and Privacy Act—a bill of rights against the intrusions of big government and its grantees.

In the House and Senate, Republicans have championed the economic rights of the family and made a $500 per child tax credit the centerpiece of their reform agenda. But that overdue measure of relief for households with children was vetoed.

We salute parents working at the State level to ensure constitutional protection for the rights of the family. We urge State legislators to review divorce laws to foster the stability of the home and protect the economic rights of the innocent spouse and children.

Improving Education

"At the center of all that afflicts our schools is a denial of free choice. Our public schools are in trouble because they are no longer run by the public. Instead, they're controlled by narrow special interest groups who regard public education not as a public trust, but as political territory to be guarded at all costs."
—*Bob Dole, July 17, 1996, in Minneapolis*

The American people know that something is terribly wrong with our education system. The evidence is everywhere: children who cannot read, graduates who cannot reason, danger in schoolyards, indoctrination in classrooms.

To this crisis in our schools, Bill Clinton responds with the same liberal dogmas that created the mess: more federal control and more spending on all the wrong things. He opposes family rights in education and opportunity scholarships for poor children. When it comes to saving our schools, he flunks.

Americans should have the best education in the world. We spend more per pupil than any other nation, and the great majority of our teachers are dedicated and skilled educators, whose interests are ignored by political union bosses. Our goal is nothing less than a renaissance in American education, begun by returning its control to parents, teachers, local school boards and, through them, to communities and local taxpayers.

Our formula is as simple as it is sweeping: the federal government has no constitutional authority to be involved in school curricula or to control jobs in the work place. That is why we will abolish the Department of Education, end federal meddling in our schools, and promote family choice at all levels of learning. We therefore call for prompt repeal of the Goals 2000 program and the School-To-Work Act of 1994, which put new federal controls, as well as unfunded mandates, on the States. We further urge that federal attempts to impose outcome- or performance-based education on local schools be ended.

We know what works in education, and it isn't the liberal fads of the last thirty years. It's discipline, parental involvement, emphasis on basics including computer technology, phonics instead of look-say reading, and dedicated teaching.

Abstinence education in the home will lead to less need for birth control services and fewer abortions. We support educational initiatives to promote chastity until marriage as the expected standard of behavior. This education initiative is the best preventive measure to avoid the emotional trauma of sexually-transmitted diseases and teen pregnancies that are serious problems among our young people. While recognizing that something must be done to help children when parental consent or supervision is not possible, we oppose school-based clinics, which provide referrals, counseling, and related services for contraception and abortion.

We encourage a reform agenda on the local level and urge State legislators to ensure quality education for all through programs of parental choice among public, private, and religious schools. That includes the option of home schooling, and Republicans will defend the right of families to make that choice. We support and vigorously work for mechanisms, such as opportunity scholarships, block grants, school rebates, charter schools, and vouchers, to make parental choice in education a reality for all parents.

On the federal level, we endorse legislation—like the Watts-Talent Low-Income Educational Opportunity Act, which is part of the Community Renewal Act of 1996, and the Coats-Kasich Educational Choice and Equity Act—to set up model programs for empowering the families who need good schooling the most.

We will continue to work for the return of voluntary prayer to our schools and will strongly enforce the Republican legislation that guarantees equal access to school facilities by student religious groups. We encourage State legislatures to pass statutes which prohibit local school boards from adopting policies of denial regarding voluntary school prayer. . . .

To reinforce our American heritage, we believe our nation's Governors, State legislators, and local school boards should support requiring our public schools to dedicate one full day each year solely to studying the Declaration of Independence and the Constitution.

America's families find themselves on a college treadmill: the more they work to pay tuition, the faster it seems to increase. Tuition has escalated far in excess of inflation, in defiance of market factors, and shows no sign of slowing down. Billions of dollars are wasted on regulations, paperwork, and "political correctness," which impedes the ability of the faculty to teach. We call for a national reassessment of the economics of higher education, to stop the treadmill and restore fiscal accountability to higher education. Congressional Republicans budgeted a 50 percent increase in student loans while fighting Bill Clinton's intrusion of Big Government into their financing. Heed-ing the outcry from the nation's campuses, we will end the Clinton Administration's perverse direct lending program. We support proposals to assist families to prepare for the financial strains of higher education, like the American Dream Savings Account, passed by congressional Republicans but vetoed.

To protect the nation's colleges and universities against intolerance, we will work with independent educators to create alternatives to ideological accrediting bodies. We believe meeting the higher education needs of America will require new, public and private institutions that are flexible, able to apply new technologies, willing to provide access to all those who need it, cost-effective and that place no burden on the American taxpayer.

Improving America's Health Care

Our goal is to maintain the quality of America's health care—the best in the world, bar none—while making health care and health insurance more accessible and more affordable. That means allowing health care providers to respond to consumer demand through consumer choice. . . .

But the Clinton Democrats are still blocking Republican efforts to preserve, protect, and strengthen Medicare. Until Medicare is financially secure again, our job is not finished. More than 38 million people depend on Medicare, which is rushing toward bankruptcy even more quickly than predicted. Bill Clinton doesn't seem to mind. Despite repeated Republican efforts to work with his administration to save Medicare, his response has been a barrage of propaganda. We proposed Medisave; he indulged in Mediscare. We say this with solemn deliberation: Bill Clinton lied about the condition of Medicare and lied about our attempts to save it.

We reaffirm our determination to protect Medicare. We will ensure a significant annual expansion in Medicare. That isn't "cutting Medicare." It's a projected average annual rate of growth of 7.1 percent a year—more than twice the rate of inflation—to ensure coverage for those who need it now and those who will need it in the future. We propose to allow unprecedented patient choice in Medicare, so that older Americans can select health care arrangements that work best for them, including provider-sponsored organizations offering quality care with strong consumer protections.

Our commitment is to protect the most vulnerable of our people: children, the elderly, the disabled. That is why we are determined to restructure Medicaid, the federal-State program of health care for the poor. Rife with fraud, poorly administered, with no incentives for patient or provider savings, Medicaid has mushroomed into the nation's biggest welfare program. Its staggering rate of growth threatens to overwhelm State budgets, while thwarting congressional progress towards a federal balanced budget. Bill Clinton's response has been to ignore the problem—and attack Republicans for trying to solve it.

We must find better ways to ensure quality health care for the poor. Medicaid should be turned over to State management with leeway for restructuring and reform. Low-income persons should have access to managed care programs and Medical Savings Accounts, just as other persons do, and State officials should have authority to weed out substandard providers and to eliminate excess costs. We endorse Republican legislation extending federal tort claim coverage to health care professionals who provide free medical services to persons who cannot afford them.

Preventive care is key to both wellness and lower medical bills, and strong families are the most powerful form of preventive care. Responsible families mean less child abuse, lower infant mortality, fewer unvaccinated youngsters, fewer teen pregnancies, and less involvement with drugs, alcohol, and tobacco. To help low-income families toward those goals, we will unify scattered federal resources into block grants.

We reaffirm our traditional support for generous funding of medical research, especially through the National Institutes of Health, and for continuing federal support for teaching hospitals and medical schools. We remain committed to, and place a high priority on, finding a cure for HIV disease. We support increased funding for research targeted at conditions that touch the families of most Americans, like Alzheimer's, breast cancer, prostate cancer, and diabetes. We call for an increased emphasis on prevention of diseases that threaten the lives of women. This requires dramatic expansion of outreach and education to expand public awareness. We call for fetal protection in biomedical research and will enforce the rights of human subjects in all federally funded studies.

The value of medical research and preventive care to wellness and lower health care spending can be highlighted by the example of diabetes. Approximately 16 million people in the U.S. have diabetes, and 50 percent of people above age 65 are at risk for developing some form of the disease. Diabetes is a leading cause of adult blindness, kidney disease, heart disease, stroke and amputations, and reduces life expectancy by up to 30 percent. As much as 25 percent of Medicare expenditures are incurred in the treatment of diabetes-related complications. Scientific discoveries, made possible by federal funding of medical research, have led to new efforts to prevent diabetes, as well as new treatment strategies to forestall the development of its debilitating and life-threatening complications. Today, people stricken with diabetes can, in concert with their health care providers, delay or prevent the serious and deadly complications of the disease. In other words, we now have the opportunity to reduce the burden of diabetes.

Renewing Hope and Opportunity

"Thirty years ago, the 'Great Society' was liberalism's greatest hope, its greatest boast. Today, it stands as its greatest shame, a grand failure that has crushed the spirit, destroyed the families, and decimated the culture of those who have become enmeshed in its web."
                                    —*Bob Dole, May 21, 1996, in Fond du Lac, Wisconsin*

Within a few weeks, Bill Clinton will sign into law a Republican reform of welfare. With a straight face, after twice vetoing similar legislation, he will attempt to take credit for what we have accomplished.

So be it. Our cause is justice for both the taxpayers and for the poor. Our purpose in welfare reform is not to save money but to bring into the mainstream of American life those who now are on the margins of our society and our economy. We will, in the words of the Speaker of the House of Representatives Newt Gingrich, replace the welfare state with an opportunity society for all. The Clinton administration's "Reinventing Government" program to reform the welfare state bureaucracy has failed. In fact, management reforms of the Reagan years were repealed and new labor-management councils that diluted efficient management were added as additional bureaucracy and red tape. We will revoke these Clinton administration policies and oppose the liberal philosophy that bureaucracy can reform welfare.

The current welfare system has spent $5 trillion in the last thirty years and has been a catastrophic failure. Despite this massive effort, conditions in our nation's poor communities have grown measurably worse. Poverty used to be an economic problem; now it is a social pathology.

The key to welfare reform is restoring personal responsibility and encouraging two-parent households. The path to that goal lies outside of official Washington. In the hands of State and local officials, and under the eye of local taxpayers, welfare can again become a hand up instead of a handout. All able-bodied adults must be required to work, either in private sector jobs or in community work projects. Illegal aliens must be ineligible for all but emergency benefits. And a firm time limit for receipt of welfare must be enforced.

Because illegitimacy is the most serious cause of child poverty, we will encourage States to stop cash payments to unmarried teens and set a family cap on payments for additional children. When benefits of any kind are extended to teen mothers, they must be conditioned upon their attendance at school and their living at home with a parent, adult relative, or guardian. About half the children of today's teen welfare mothers were fathered in statutory rape. We echo Bob Dole's call to our nation's governors to toughen and enforce State laws in this regard, as well as those concerning enforcement of child support.

Restoring common sense to welfare programs is only one side of the Republican equation for hope and opportunity. The other side is giving low-income households the tools with which they can build their own future. We propose to do this along the lines of the American Community Renewal Act, a Republican congressional initiative that would establish throughout the nation up to 100 renewal communities where residents, businesses, and investors would have unprecedented economic freedom and incentives to create prosperity. School choice for low-income families is an integral part of that initiative.

We call for the removal of structural impediments which liberals throw in the path of poor people: over-regulation of start-up enterprises, excessive licensing requirements, needless restrictions on formation of schools and child-care centers catering to poor families, restrictions on providing public services in fields like transport and sanitation, and rigged franchises that close the opportunity door to all but a favored few.

Not everyone can make it on their own. Government at various levels has a role—and some aid programs do work well—and so do private individuals and charitable and faith-based organizations, whose record of success far outshines that of any public welfare program. To promote personal involvement with anti-poverty efforts, we call for a Charity Tax Credit that will be consistent with the fundamental changes we propose in the nation's system of taxation. To ensure that religiously affiliated institutions can fulfill their helping mission, we endorse Republican legislation to stop discrimination against them in government programs.

Older Americans

Our commitment to older Americans runs throughout this platform. It strengthens our call for tax fairness, shows in our action agenda against violent crime, and motivates our crusade to preserve, protect, and strengthen Medicare.

The Republican Party has always opposed the earnings limitation for Social Security benefits, a confiscatory tax that discourages older Americans from active engagement in all walks of life. While Bill Clinton imposed his new tax on Social Security benefits, he also initially vetoed our legislation to reform the earnings limitation, just as he vetoed our estate tax reform.

The Social Security system remains the cornerstone of personal security for millions of the elderly. In 1983, a Republican president, working with the Republican Chairman of the Senate Finance Committee—Bob Dole—saved the Social Security system from fiscal disaster. We have a legal and moral responsibility to America's seniors and will continue to do everything in our power to ensure that government honors our commitment to Social Security beneficiaries, now and in the future. We will keep it financially sound and keep politics out of its administration. We will work to ensure the integrity and solvency of the Social Security trust funds.

Those who are not older Americans now will one day be so. Our common goal is a secure economic future. To that end, public policy should encourage cooperative efforts by businesses and employees alike to expand the availability of savings vehicles for all. We want to expand retirement options so that individual choice, not government fiat, steers the decision-making process. We must increase both the amount and the portability of personal savings, especially in today's rapidly changing and unpredictable economy. We salute congressional Republicans for their landmark legislation simplifying pension law, cutting away the red tape that prevented many businesses from offering pension plans, and establishing a new pension system designed to meet the needs of workers in small businesses.

We also salute Congressional Republicans for making long-term care more affordable and more available to those who need it. Too many seniors live in fear that they one day will incur long-term care costs that will wipe out their life savings and burden their children. The Republican Congress has passed legislation giving long-term care insurance policies the same tax-preferred treatment that health insurance policies now receive. Over the years, this legislation will give millions of Americans peace of mind and the financial wherewithal to obtain nursing home care of the highest quality.

A Cleaner, Safer, Healthier America

"Those of us who grew up in rural America grew up with a common set of values, a code of living that stays with us all our lives. Love of God and country and family. Commitment to honesty, decency and personal responsibility. Self-reliance tempered by a sense of community. . . . Those values made us the greatest country on earth. And the secret to getting our country back on track is simply to return to them as a matter of national policy."
—*Bob Dole, August 19, 1995, in Ames, Iowa*

We are the party of America's farmers, ranchers, foresters, and all who hold the earth in stewardship with the Creator. Republican leadership established the Land Grant College System under Abraham Lincoln, the National Park System under Ulysses Grant, the National Wildlife Refuge System under Teddy Roosevelt, and today's legal protections for clean air and water in more recent decades. We reaffirm our commitment to agricultural progress, environmental improvement, and the prudent development of our natural resources.

Our goal is to continue the progress we have made to achieve a cleaner, safer, healthier environment for all Americans—and to pass on to our children and grandchildren a better environment than we have today. We must recognize the unique role our States, localities, and private sector have in improving our environment. The States and communities are the laboratories of environmental innovation. Inflexible requirements hurt the environment, add unnecessary costs, and reduce technology development. While we have made substantial environmental progress, we must reject failed approaches created by fearmongering and centralized control which will not serve our environment well in the century ahead.

The Superfund program to clean up abandoned toxic waste sites is a classic case in point. More than half of the $30 billion already spent on Superfund has gone for litigation and administration. In other words, trial lawyers have profited from the current flawed and unfair liability scheme, while toxic waste sites wait to be cleaned up. Without the opposition of Bill Clinton, we will fix the broken Superfund law. We will direct resources to clean-up sites where there are real risks, and cooperate with citizens, States, and localities who want to help, rather than harassing them with unwarranted lawsuits.

The States have been leaders in returning contaminated sites to productive use under "brownfields" programs. These programs tailor clean-up standards appropriate for expected future use, thus enabling environmental cleanup and economic development. Accordingly, as an essential component of our comprehensive Superfund reform, we will remove disincentives in current Federal law in order to allow States to expand their innovative "brownfields" programs.

Inconsistent Federal policies have created a nightmare for our Nation's ports at a critical time of growth and change in international trade. We must protect the environment while recognizing the unique situation of each port. There must be a coordination of State, local, and Federal roles in encouraging our ports to expand to meet current and future needs.

Republicans trust Americans to honor their shared desire to live and raise their children in a clean and healthy environment. For all environmental problems, we propose a common sense approach based on flexibility and consensus, that builds a better future on free enterprise, local control, sound science, and technology development. This is our positive and proactive agenda:

- Assure that the air and water are clean and safe for our children and future generations;
- Assure that everyone has access to public outdoor recreation areas; and that historic and environmentally significant wilderness and wetlands areas will be protected without compromising our commitment to the rights of property owners;
- Set reasonable standards for environmental improvement that incorporate flexibility, acknowledge geographic differences, and create incentives for development of new technologies;
- Base all government environmental decisions on the best peer-reviewed scientific evidence, while encouraging advancements in research;
- Achieve progress, as much as possible, through incentives rather than compulsion, and improve compliance by letting States and localities play a greater role in setting and maintaining standards. Many States have enacted environmental education and "voluntary self-audit" laws to encourage people to find and correct pollution; the Congress should remove disincentives for States to achieve these goals; and
- Assure private property owners of due process to protect their rights, and make environmental decisions in concert with those whose homes, businesses, and communities are directly affected. Our commitment to an improved environment is best embodied in the recently enacted amendments to the Safe Drinking Water Act. This Republican initiative will guarantee all Americans a safe and clean source of drinking water and will grant local communities the flexibility to avoid unnecessary requirements. . . .

Republicans have always advocated conserving our animal and plant resources, but we recognize the current Endangered Species Act [ESA] is seriously flawed and, indeed, is often counterproductive because of its reliance on Federal command-and-control measures. The adherence of Clinton Democrats to these discredited ESA provisions has devastated the environment they pretend to protect by virtually encouraging landowners to remove habitat for marginal species to avoid government seizure of their property. We will improve the ESA by implementing an incentive-based program in cooperation with State, local, and tribal governments and private individuals to recognize the critical relationship between a healthy environment and a healthy economy founded on private property rights and responsibilities.

Securing Property Rights

Republicans consider private property rights the cornerstone of environmental progress. That lesson has been confirmed in the tragic environmental record of Communist rule and of socialist regimes in the less developed world. By safeguarding those rights— by enforcing the Takings Clause of the Fifth Amendment and by providing compensation—we not only stand true to the Constitution but advance sound environmentalism as well. Republicans, led by Senator Dole, have spearheaded efforts in Congress to protect private property rights.

Improving Public Lands

The nation's public lands—half the territory in the West—must be administered both for today's multiple uses and for tomorrow's generations. We support multiple use conducted in an environmentally and economically sustainable manner. We will preserve priority wilderness and wetlands—real wetlands of environmental significance, not the damp grounds of a bureaucrat's imagination.

We support a thorough review of the lands owned by the federal government with a goal of transferring lands that can best be managed by State, county, or municipal governments. This review should ensure that the federal government retains ownership to unique property worthy of national oversight. Properties transferred from federal control must recognize existing property and mineral rights, including water, mining claims, grazing permits, rights of access, hunting, fishing, and contracts.

We recognize the historic use of public lands for livestock production in compliance with legal requirements. Our renewable rangeland should continue to be available under conditions that ensure both expanded production of livestock and protection of the rangeland environment. We condemn the Clinton Administration's range war against this pillar of the western economy.

We recognize the need to keep our National Park System healthy and accessible to all. Our National Parks have a backlog of more than four billion dollars in maintenance and infrastructure repair projects. The nation's natural crown jewels are losing some of their luster, tarnished by neglect and indifference. Our park system needs to be rebuilt, restructured, and reinvigorated to ensure that all Americans can enjoy and be proud of their parks.

We stand for sustainable forestry to stabilize and provide continuity for our timber industry and to improve the health of the country's public forests. This requires active management practices, such as the responsible salvage harvesting of dead and diseased trees. The Democrats' hands-off approach has made our great forests vulnerable to ravaging fires, insects, and disease.

The Democrats' policies have devastated the economy of timber-dependent communities across the Pacific Northwest and in the Tongass National Forest, the Nation's largest and most productive, to please elite special interests. We join families and communities in rural America who rely on public forests for their livelihood in calling for the federal government to carefully evaluate the socioeconomic impacts of its actions and to live up to its commitments to provide an adequate timber supply to dependent communities through sustainable forest management.

We reaffirm the traditional deference by the federal government to the States in the allocation and appropriation of water. We deplore the Clinton Administration's disregard for State primacy through attempts to preempt State law with respect to water usage and watershed protection. We also recognize the need to protect adequate supplies of water for agriculture without unreasonable government mandates.

We support the original intent of the Mining Law of 1872: to provide the certainty and land tenure necessary for miners to risk tremendous capital investment on federal lands, thus preserving jobs—indeed, whole industries—and bolstering our domestic economy. We support appropriate changes to the law to ensure the taxpayer will receive a reasonable return for the value of extracted minerals. We oppose extremist attempts to shut down American mining in favor of our international competitors.

Power for Progress

Our goal is an energy supply available to all—competitively priced, secure, and clean—produced by healthy industries operating in an environmentally responsible manner using domestically available resources to the greatest extent practicable.

No one should take that for granted. Today's energy boom was hard won by Republican reforms in the 1980s, ending more than three decades of ruinous Federal meddling that drove up prices and drove down supplies. Now that progress is under attack from the same quarters that brought us energy crises, gas rationing, and dangerous dependence on unreliable supplies of foreign oil. That dependency is 50 percent today, and will be two-thirds in only a few short years. . . .

We support elimination of the Department of Energy to emphasize the need for greater privatization and to reduce the size of the federal government. The Department of Energy's defense concerns should be transferred to an independent agency under the Defense Department. Other necessary programs should be farmed out to other departments and offices.

We support environmentally responsible energy extraction from public and private lands. We will not tolerate poor reclamation or pollution from mining or drilling. We advocate environmentally sound oil production in the largest known onshore or offshore petroleum reserve in the Nation—the small coastal plain portion of the 19-million acre Arctic National Wildlife Refuge [ANWR]. Oil produced there, traveling through an existing pipeline, will bring billions of dollars in revenues to reduce the federal budget deficit. On the other hand, without ANWR coastal plain development, we will lose hundreds of thousands of potential jobs and untold billions of American dollars will be paid to foreign governments for the oil not produced from our home reserves.

We continue to support and encourage the development of our domestic natural gas industry. Natural gas is a clean, abundant, and domestically available resource, which can be provided, transported, and consumed in an environmentally responsible manner.

We will delegate management and collection of federal oil and gas royalties to the States, thereby increasing receipts both to the States and to the federal Treasury. This action will reduce bureaucratic involvement and administrative costs to the federal government. We urge the federal government to expedite and streamline the exploration, leasing, and permitting process for the domestic oil and gas industry.

The coal industry now supplies more than half of all electric generation and is vital for our entire economy. We encourage research for cleaner coal combustion technologies and will require that objective, peer-reviewed science be the basis for environmental decisions that increase costs for electric rate payers.

Because no single source of energy can reliably supply the needs of the American people, we believe in fostering alternative and renewable energy sources to assist in reducing dependence on unreliable foreign oil supplies. We anticipate the continuing development of energy from coal, oil, natural gas, agricultural products such as ethanol and biodiesel, nuclear, and hydro sources and . . . from wind, solar, and geothermal power.

The United States should continue its commitment to addressing global climate change in a prudent and effective manner that does not punish the U.S. economy. Despite scientific uncertainty about the role of human activity in climate change, the Clinton Administration has leapfrogged over reasoned scientific inquiry and now favors misdirected measures, such as binding targets and timetables, imposed only on the United States and certain other developed countries, to further reduce greenhouse gas emissions. Republicans deplore the arbitrary and premature abandonment of the previous policy of voluntary reductions of greenhouse gas emissions. We further deplore ceding U.S. sovereignty on environmental issues to international bureaucrats and our foreign economic competitors.

Energy policy and transportation policy go hand in hand. To prepare the National Highway System and the National Aviation System for the 21st Century, we will maintain the integrity of the Federal transportation trust funds and respect the call by Republican governors to ensure those funds are returned to the States with a minimum of federal red tape. Trusting the people, congressional Republicans passed the National Highway System Designation Act of 1995, returning to the States decisions about highway safety. We support reasonable speed limits, reflecting local needs and geography, and prudent personal safety measures, but we oppose Washington's one-size-fits-all approach to the mobility of the American people.

Agriculture in the 21st Century

The moral strength abundant on America's farms and rural communities has been the foundation and source of strength for our Nation since its earliest days. America's settlers built their farming communities on values like faith, hard work, dedication, and self-sacrifice.

Republicans see a very bright future for agriculture and rural America. Our program to strengthen rural America will benefit every sector of the economy and every part of the Nation. First and foremost, we will reduce the tax burden—both the estate tax and the capital gains levy—on those who produce America's food and fiber. This is essential to preserve production agriculture. Just like urban small businesses, rural producers need full deductibility of health insurance premiums and an overall tax structure that is simpler and fairer.

Deficit spending by government is death by strangulation for agriculture. Our farms are major users of capital, with over $150 billion in current borrowing. Interest payments are one of their heaviest burdens. The Republican balanced budget of last year, vetoed by Bill Clinton, would have saved farmers more than $15 billion in interest costs by the year 2002. We stand with the American farmer in demanding an end to the spending excesses in official Washington.

The elections of 1994 were a resounding victory for American agriculture. The first Republican majorities in both the House and Senate in 40 years won an historic breakthrough with the "Freedom to Farm" act. For the first time in six decades, Federal policy will allow individual farmers to grow what makes sense on their own land, not what a bureaucrat wants grown there. "Freedom to Farm" will permit them to respond to world trade opportunities for value-added exports that bring new jobs and broader prosperity to rural America.

Moreover, the Republican "Freedom to Farm" act is the most pro-environment farm bill ever. By liberating high-tech, high-yield U.S. agriculture to pursue ever greater levels of efficiency, it will enable growers to produce more from less land, saving wildlife habitat and fragile soils from the plow. The new law allows farmers to rotate crops, thereby reducing use of pesticides, herbicides, and fertilizer. It continues the Conservation and Wetland Reserve Programs and creates a new Environmental Quality Incentive Program to help farmers do what they do best—conserve the land and pass it on, enriched and enhanced, to future generations. . . .

Restoring American World Leadership

"It's time to restore American leadership throughout the world. Our future security depends on American leadership that is respected, American leadership that is trusted, and when necessary, American leadership that is feared."

—Bob Dole

We are the party of peace through strength. Republicans put the interests of our country over those of other nations—and of the United Nations. We believe the safety and prosperity of the American home and workplace depend upon ensuring our national security in a dangerous world. This principle was proven in our long struggle against Communism, and—as recent events have tragically shown—it is still true today. The gains we made for democracy around the world under two Republican presidents are now imperiled by a rudderless foreign policy. We vigorously support restoring the promotion of democracy worldwide as a cornerstone of U.S. foreign policy. Democracy is the best guarantor of peace and will ensure greater respect for fundamental human rights and the rule of law.

The international situation—and our country's security against the purveyors of evil—has worsened over the last three and a half years. Today, Russia's democratic future is more uncertain than at any time since the hammer and sickle was torn from the Kremlin towers. With impunity, Fidel Castro has shot American citizens out of the skies over international waters. North Korea has won unprecedented concessions regarding its nuclear capability from the Clinton Administration. Much of Africa has dissolved in tragedy— Somalia, Rwanda, Burundi, Liberia. The Clinton Administration objected to lifting the arms embargo on Bosnia while it facilitated the flow of Iranian weapons to that country. Bill Clinton made tough campaign pledges on China but subsequently failed in his attempt to bluff the Chinese government— diminishing American prestige while not addressing the serious issues of human rights, regional stability, and nuclear proliferation. Bill Clinton's weakness, indecision, and double-talk, have undermined America's role as leader of the free world.

In 1996, the nation's choice is clear: either we return responsible leadership to the White House, or Bill Clinton's lack of international purpose results in catastrophe. We must keep our country strong and sovereign, and assert the interests and values of the United States in the international arena.

The Atlantic Alliance and Europe

"Let us begin by reaffirming that Europe's security is indispensable to the security of the United States, and that American leadership is absolutely indispensable to the security of Europe."

—Bob Dole, June 25, 1996

The Atlantic Alliance: Our relations with the nations of Europe must continue to be based on the NATO alliance, which remains the world's strongest bulwark of freedom and international stability. Our policy will strive to consolidate our Cold War victory in Europe and to build a firm foundation for a new century of peace. In the same spirit that Ronald Reagan called for the integration of Spain into the NATO alliance, we call for the immediate expansion of the framework for peace to include those countries of Central Europe which demonstrate the strongest commitment to the democratic ideals NATO was created to protect.

With the people of Poland, the Czech Republic, and Hungary we have special bonds. These nations—and others—are rightfully part of the future of Europe. As Bob Dole said, "It is an outrage that the patriots who threw off the chains of Soviet bondage have been told by Bill Clinton that they must wait to join the NATO alliance." We strongly endorse Bob Dole's call for Poland, the Czech Republic, and Hungary to enter NATO by 1998.

Bosnia: We support America's men and women in uniform who are serving in Bosnia and Herzegovina. However, we did not support the ill-conceived and inconsistent policies that led to their deployment. In 1992, candidate Bill Clinton pledged to lift the arms embargo on Bosnia, but once in office he ignored his promises. For three years, Bill Clinton upheld the illegal and unjust arms embargo on Bosnia and allowed genocidal aggression to go virtually unchallenged, while Bob Dole successfully led the effort in the Congress to lift the U.S. arms embargo. Once again, Bill Clinton subordinated American national interests to the United Nations in vetoing bipartisan legislation that would have lifted the U.S. arms embargo and rendered the deployment of American forces unnecessary. At the same time Bill Clinton was opposing congressional efforts to lift the arms embargo, he made a secret decision to allow the terrorist Iranian regime to supply arms to Bosnia. This duplicitous policy has endangered U.S. and Allied forces and given Iran a foothold in Europe.

We look forward to a timely withdrawal of U.S. forces from Bosnia and recognize that providing the Bosnian Federation with adequate weapons and training is the only realistic exit strategy. We support the democratic process in Bosnia and, when conditions exist, the conduct of free and fair elections. We support bringing indicted war criminals to justice. We encourage the peoples of the region—and in particular those of Croatia, Bosnia and Herzegovina, and Serbia and Montenegro—to play a constructive role in fostering peace and stability there. We note with concern that repression and human rights abuses are escalating in Kosova and support the appointment of a U.S. special envoy to help resolve the situation there.

Russia: We salute the people of Russia in their quest for democracy and a free market economy. During this crucial period, the Clinton Administration has pursued an accommodationist and misguided policy toward Moscow. Bill Clinton's comparison of Russia's extreme brutality in Chechnya to the American Civil War is offensive. The Clinton Administration's passivity in the face of Russia's intimidation and economic blackmail against countries of the former Soviet Union has encouraged the rise of extreme nationalist and undemocratic forces. Its willingness to accept Russian changes to already agreed-to arms control treaties has undermined security. Its complacency over Russia's sale of nuclear technology to Iran and Cuba has contributed to the threat of nuclear proliferation.

Our foreign policy toward Russia should put American interests first and consolidate our Cold War victory in Europe. We have a national interest in a security relationship with a democratic Russia. Specifically, we will encourage Russia to respect the sovereignty and independence of its neighbors; support a special security arrangement between Russia and NATO—but not Moscow's veto over NATO enlargement; support Russian entry to the G-7 after its reforms have been achieved; and link U.S. assistance to Russian adherence to international treaty obligations.

Newly Independent States: We reaffirm our party's historic commitment to the independence of all former Captive Nations still recovering from the long night of Soviet Communism, especially Latvia, Lithuania, Estonia, Armenia, and Ukraine. We endorse Republican legislation to establish in Washington, D. C., funded by private contributions, an international memorial to the one hundred million victims of Communism.

Ireland: We support efforts to establish peace with justice in Northern Ireland through a peace process inclusive of all parties who reject violence. During this difficult period in Irish history, we encourage private U. S. investment in the North, fully consistent with the MacBride principles for fair employment, in order to address the systemic discriminatory practices that still exist, especially against Catholics, in the workplace and elsewhere. We call on all parties to renounce terrorism in the Northern Ireland conflict.

Cyprus: We encourage a peaceful settlement for Cyprus and respect by all parties for the wishes of the Cypriot people. Concerned about continuing tension in the Aegean Sea, we will maintain close ties to both Greece and Turkey and urge all parties to refrain from precipitous actions and assertions contrary to legally established territorial arrangements.

Defending America Against Missile Attack

We face two scandalous situations. First, most Americans do not realize our country has no defense against long-range missile attack. Second, the current occupant of the Oval Office refuses to tell them of that danger. So we will.

This is the frightening truth: The United States provided the technology to Israel to protect it from Iraqi missile attacks during the Persian Gulf War, but President Clinton refuses to provide the technology—technology that is readily available—to the American people to protect our country from the growing threat posed by long-range ballistic missiles. The Strategic Defense Initiative (SDI) of the last two Republican administrations has been dismantled by Bill Clinton, who—contrary to the national security interests of the United States—clings to the obsolete Cold War ABM [Antiballistic Missile] Treaty. Clinton slashed the funding budgeted by past presidents for missile defense and even violates the law by slowing down critical theater missile defenses. He has pursued negotiations to actually expand the outdated ABM Treaty, further tying America's hands, and hobbling our self-defense. He now seeks new limitations that will hinder the United States from developing and deploying even theater ballistic missile defenses to protect our troops abroad. . . .

The Republican Party is committed to the protection of all Americans—including our two million citizens in Alaska and Hawaii—against missile attack. We are determined to deploy land-based and sea-based theater missile defenses as soon as possible, and a national system thereafter. We will not permit the mistakes of past diplomacy, based on the immoral concept of Mutual Assured Destruction, to imperil the safety of our nation, our Armed Forces abroad, and our allies. Arms control will be a means to enhance American national security, not an end in itself. We therefore endorse the Defend America Act of 1996, introduced by Senator Bob Dole, which calls for a national missile defense system for all fifty States by the year 2003.

To cope with the threat of the proliferation of weapons of mass destruction, the United States will have to deter the threat or use of weapons of mass destruction by rogue states. This in turn will require the continuing maintenance and development of nuclear weapons and their periodic testing. The Clinton Administration's proposed Comprehensive Test Ban Treaty (CTBT) is inconsistent with American security interests.

Rebuilding America's Strength

Republicans are committed to ensuring the status of the United States as the world's preeminent military power. We must reverse the decline in what our nation spends for defense. In just three and a half years, an amateur approach to military matters and dramatic reductions in defense spending under the Clinton Administration have had a serious negative impact on the readiness and capabilities of our armed forces. . . .

We recognize that today's military research and development, as well as procurement, is tomorrow's readiness. We are committed to readiness not just today, but also tomorrow. Bill Clinton has decimated our research and development effort, and slashed procurement for our armed forces. Not since 1950 have we spent so little on new weapons for our military. Fortunately, the Republican Congress has restored some of the funding Bill Clinton sought to cut for research and development and for procurement. Only a Commander-in-Chief who fully understands and respects the military can rebuild America's defense capabilities. . . .

Money alone is not the answer. It must be spent the right way, with long-term efficiencies in mind. We call for reductions in the overhead and infrastructure of the Defense Department and successful demonstrations of weapons and equipment prior to full scale purchases. Budgetary decisions must be made with an eye to preserving the nation's defense industrial base, accelerating procurement of key military and dual-use technologies, incorporating emerging technologies into military operations, and maintaining an adequate, safe and reliable capability in nuclear weapons.

Only a Republican president and a Republican Congress can fulfill these duties.

Protecting American Interests

We scorn the Clintonite view that soon "nationhood as we know it will be obsolete; all states will recognize a single global authority." This is nonsense, but it explains why the Democrat Administration has lurched from one foreign policy fiasco to the next—and why Bill Clinton vetoed the first legislative restructuring of America's diplomatic institutions in a half century. A Republican president will reform the Department of State to ensure that America's interests always come first.

Republicans will not subordinate United States sovereignty to any international authority. We oppose the commitment of American troops to U.N. "peacekeeping" operations under foreign commanders and will never compel American servicemen to wear foreign uniforms or insignia. We will insist on

542

an end to waste, mismanagement, and fraud at the United Nations. We will ensure American interests are pursued and defended at the United Nations, will not tolerate any international taxation by the organization, nor will we permit any international court to seize, try, or punish American citizens. Before his departure from the Senate, Bob Dole introduced legislation prohibiting U.S. payments to the United Nations and any of its agencies if they attempt to implement global taxes. We support the passage of the Prohibition on United Nations Taxation Act of 1996 to preserve America's sovereignty and the American taxpayer's right to taxation with representation.

A Republican president will withdraw from Senate consideration any pending international conventions or treaties that erode the constitutional foundations of our Republic and will neither negotiate nor submit such agreements in the future. We will ensure that our future relations with international organizations not infringe upon either the sovereignty of the United States or the earnings of the American taxpayer.

American citizens must retain ownership of their private property, and must maintain full control of our national and state parks, without international interference.

International Terrorism

. . . A Republican president will forcefully lead the world community to isolate and punish state sponsors of terrorism. It is vital to our security that we actively work to reverse the threat posed by these regimes—through imposition and enforcement of sanctions, banning investment, and leading our allies in effective policies. The governments of North Korea, Iran, Syria, Iraq, Libya, Sudan, and Cuba must know that America's first line of defense is not our shoreline, but their own borders. We will be proactive, not reactive, to strike the hand of terrorism before it can be raised against Americans.

We denounce terrorist attacks made on American citizens at home or abroad. We must take all legitimate steps to swiftly apprehend and severely punish persons committing terrorist acts. However, we must also denounce any attempts to deprive law-abiding citizens of their God-given, constitutionally-protected rights while fighting terrorism. To take away the liberty of the American people while fighting terrorism is repugnant to the history and character of our nation. We firmly oppose any legislation that would infringe upon the rights of American citizens to freedom of religion, speech, press, and assembly; the right to keep and bear arms; and the right to judicial due process.

Africa

We support those U. S. aid programs to Africa which have proven records of success, especially the Child Survival Program of vitamins, immunizations, sanitation, and oral rehydration. We hail the social and economic progress of those nations which have used the free market to liberate the talent and striving of their people. They deserve our attention, but our outreach must be on a case-by-case basis. Our hope for the future of South Africa, for example, stands in contrast with the military rule now imposed on Nigeria, the continent's most populous country.

The Republican Party's commitment to freedom and human rights in Africa is as old as the establishment of the Republic of Liberia. Today, the tragic fate of that small nation symbolizes the larger tragedy that has befallen much of the continent. The Clinton Administration's dismal performance in Somalia, resulting in needless American deaths, set the stage for international passivity in the face of genocide in Rwanda and Burundi. The Clinton Administration has even failed to rally the world against the slave trade sponsored by the government of the Sudan, whose persecution of Sudanese Christians and others is nothing short of genocide. A Republican president will not tolerate this unconscionable treatment of children and women.

Asia

Bill Clinton's foreign policy failures loom large in Asia. Four years ago, most of that continent was rushing toward democratic reform. Today it threatens to slip backwards into conflict and repression. A Republican Administration will keep the mutual security treaties with Japan and with the Republic of Korea as the foundation of our role in the region. We will halt Bill Clinton's efforts to appease North Korea by rewarding treaty-breaking with American taxpayer-financed oil and nuclear reactors. We will make further improvement of relations with Vietnam and North Korea contingent upon their cooperation in achieving a full and complete accounting of our POW's and MIA's from those Asian conflicts.

China and Taiwan: We support the aspiration of the Chinese people for both economic and political liberty, which includes respect for the human rights of the people of Tibet. Our relationship with the Chinese government will be based on vigilance with regard to its military potential, proliferation activities, and its attitude toward human rights, especially in Hong Kong. The Taiwan Relations Act must remain the basis for our relations with the Republic of China on Taiwan. We reaffirm our commitment to Taiwan's security and will regard any threat to alter its status by force as a threat to our own security interests. We will make available to Taiwan the material it needs for self-defense, particularly theater missile defense and coastal patrol submarines. In recognition of its growing importance in the global economy, we support a larger role for Taiwan in international organizations.

Philippines: We reaffirm our historic friendship with the Philippine people, which has endured through changing circumstances.

The Middle East

Peace through strength continues to be central in the Middle East. Saddam Hussein reminded us just five years ago of the potential for aggression by radical states in this region. Republicans understand the importance of maintaining a robust U.S. military capability in the Eastern Mediterranean and the Persian Gulf, cooperating with our allies to ensure regional stability. Republicans also understand the need to be willing to use force to deter aggression and, where deterrence fails, to defeat it. That is why Republicans were the bedrock of support for the congressional vote to authorize the use of force against Iraq's aggression in 1991, while most Democrats voted against Operation Desert Storm.

The Middle East remains a region vital to American security. Our enduring goals there are to promote freedom and stability, secure access to oil resources, and maintain the security of Israel, our one democratic ally in the region with whom we share moral bonds and common strategic interests. Most of the world's oil exports flow from the Middle East, and thus its strategic significance remains. But it is still the most volatile region in the world. Islamic radicalism, increasing terrorism, and rogue states like Iran, Iraq, Syria, and Libya threaten regional and international stability. . . .

We reaffirm that Republican commitment to maintain Israel's qualitative military advantage over any adversary or group of adversaries. While we fully support Israel's efforts to find peace and security with its neighbors, we will judge the peace process by the security it generates both for Israel and for the United States. In that context, we support Israel's right to make its own decisions regarding security and boundaries. We strongly oppose the Clinton Administration's attempts to interfere in Israel's democratic process.

We applaud the Republican Congress for enacting legislation to recognize Jerusalem as the undivided capital of Israel. A Republican administration will ensure that the U.S. Embassy is moved to Jerusalem by May 1999. . . .

Western Hemisphere

The U.S. commitment to democratic institutions and market economies in the Western Hemisphere has paralleled our enduring interest in the security of the region, as laid out in the Monroe Doctrine. The success of Republican national security policies in the 1980s halted Soviet imperialism and promoted the process of economic and political reform in Latin America—defeating totalitarianism of the right and of the left. During the last decade and a half, Latin American countries have made enormous progress developing democratic institutions. We applaud their progress and offer our assistance to further expand and deepen democratic conditions in the region.

Hemispheric progress toward free and democratic societies has stalled during the Clinton Administration. A government bought and paid for by drug traffickers holds power in Colombia. Mexico—with whom we share hundreds of miles of border—is increasingly tainted by narcotics-related corruption at all levels of society. Similarly, there are signs of backsliding on democracy in Latin America, most notably in Paraguay, where a coup was narrowly averted earlier this year. . . .

Bill Clinton's outreach to Castro has only delayed the emergence of "Cuba Libre," extending the duration of Communist tyranny. The Republican Party has not wavered and will not waver in its goal of a democratic Cuba. We affirm our policy of isolating the Castro regime, including full implementation of the Helms-Burton Act to penalize foreign firms which do business there.

Bill Clinton's awkward and misguided intervention in Haiti has cost American taxpayers some $3 billion and risked the lives of American military personnel for a less than vital interest. We reject Clinton administration claims of "success" in its military intervention in Haiti. Human rights abuses by government forces go unpunished, promised economic reforms have not been made, and the democratic process is deeply flawed.

Security and Foreign Assistance

America is and must remain the leader of the world. We did not win the Cold War without allies and friends, and we hope to face future challenges with them. Our country should not bear world burdens alone. Providing friendly nations with access to U.S. defense equipment can protect American security interests abroad and reduce the likelihood that American forces will have to be directly engaged in military conflict. The Clinton Administration has been blind to that wisdom.

We have seen the result in Bosnia, where American ground forces have been deployed because the Clinton Administration denied Bosnia the opportunity to acquire defense equipment in the United States.

The Clinton administration has diverted aid from our friends to support U.N. operations and social welfare spending in the Third World. Congressional Republicans have done all they could to resist this folly. Only a Republican president can put an end to it.

The Clinton administration's failure to couple American interests abroad with foreign aid has produced wasteful spending and has presented an impediment to achieving a balanced budget. A Republican administration will ensure foreign aid is cost-effective and based on its important role in directly promoting American national interests. . . .

The Men and Women of Defense

As Commander-in-Chief, Bill Clinton has been out of touch with the needs of the troops under his command. Bob Dole has served in the military and will protect military families against inflation, restore appropriate funding levels for billets and family housing, and ensure an environment where promotions and awards are made on the basis of military merit. A Republican president who has been on active duty will not casually disrupt military family life by sending troops on non-military missions around the world.

We have a solemn obligation to those who fight for America. Our military personnel should not be denied a cost of living increase, as Bill Clinton proposed in his first year in office. A Republican president will ensure a high priority for the quality of life of our military personnel and their families.

We will maintain the All-Volunteer force and will resist attempts to bring back the draft, whether directly or through Democrat schemes for compulsory national service. We will maintain our Armed Forces as a meritocracy, a model for the rest of our society, without special preferences or double standards for any group.

We salute the men and women of the National Guard and Reserve, citizen soldiers who have been—and must continue to be—a tradition in America. They perform important military functions as an integral part of our warfighting capability, and provide a critical link between our national security efforts and every community in the country. Our National Guard and Reserve forces must not be treated as an afterthought.

We oppose Bill Clinton's assault on the culture and traditions of the Armed Forces, especially his attempt to lift the ban on homosexuals in the military. We affirm that homosexuality is incompatible with military service.

We support the advancement of women in the military. We reaffirm our support for the exemption of women from ground combat units and are concerned about the current policy of involuntarily assigning women to combat or near-combat units. A Republican president will continue to reevaluate and revise, as necessary, current policies in light of evidence with regard to the effect on military morale, discipline, and overall readiness. We will not tolerate sexual harassment or misconduct toward anyone in the uniform, but we oppose politically motivated witch-hunts that smear the innocent and destroy honorable careers. To promote the dignity of all members of the Armed Forces and their families, we endorse the efforts of congressional Republicans to halt the sale, in military facilities, of pornographic materials.

We deplore Bill Clinton's shameless attempt to use protections afforded active duty military personnel under the Soldiers' and Sailors' Civil Relief Act of 1940 to protect himself from a sexual harassment lawsuit. We will amend the Soldiers' and Sailors' Civil Relief Act of 1940 to make clear that its protection against civil suits while on active duty does not extend to the occupant of the Oval Office.

The Republican Party has always been the advocate of the nation's veterans and remains unequivocally committed to the faithful fulfillment of America's obligations to them. We have no greater duty than providing for the courageous men and women who have risked their lives in defense of our country, a major reason why we defeated Bill Clinton's plan to replace veterans' health care with socialized medicine. We will continue to meet the nation's promises to those who make the military their career. That is why Republicans proposed and created a separate Department of Veterans Affairs, support veterans' preference in federal employment education and retraining programs, and pledge sufficient funding for veterans' hospitals, medical care, and employment programs.

Intelligence

The intelligence community should be our first line of defense against terrorism, drug trafficking, nuclear proliferation, and foreign espionage. Bill Clinton's neglect of our country's intelligence service is one of his most serious sins of omission. He has underfunded, misutilized, and marginalized critical intelligence missions and capabilities. No wonder his first appointee as Director of Central Intelligence has endorsed Bob Dole. The nation's security—and the personal safety of our citizens—cannot be placed at risk.

Effective intelligence can be expensive. But what it costs is measured in dollars rather than lives—an important lesson of the Gulf War. A Republican Administration will reverse the decline in funding for intelligence personnel and operations while better managing the development of futuristic capabilities. We will not constrain U.S. intelligence personnel with "politically correct" standards that impede their ability to collect and act on intelligence information. We will conduct whatever intelligence operations are necessary to safeguard American lives against the terrorists who bomb our airplanes and buildings.

Space

The Republican Party led America into space and remains committed to its exploration and mastery. We consider space travel and space science a national priority with virtually unlimited benefits, in areas ranging from medicine to micro-machinery, for those on earth. Development of space will give us a growing economic resource and a source of new scientific discoveries. We look toward our country's return to the moon and to completion of the International Space Station, not just as a unique orbiting laboratory but also a framework for world cooperation in pursuit of expanding human knowledge.

Those and other ventures require leadership now lacking at the White House. The Democrat Party approaches space issues with a confined vision and misplaced appropriations, encouraging inefficient investments and pork barrel spending. Bill Clinton gives lip service to our space program but denies it crucial resources. A Republican president and a Republican Congress will work together to make space an American frontier again. We will develop the Reusable Launch Vehicle, promote markets for commercial space launch services, and push technology to its creative limits. Commercial space development holds the key to expanding our aerospace industry and strengthening our technology base, but it can be promoted only by removing unnecessary and artificial regulatory, legal, and tax barriers.

Space exploration and exploitation are a matter of national security. Our Armed Forces already rely on space assets to support their operations on earth, and space technology will rapidly become more critical to successful military operations. Space is the ocean of tomorrow, and we cannot allow its domination by another power. We must ensure that America can work and prosper there, securely and without outside influence. A new Republican team will secure the high frontier for peace on earth and for unlimited human opportunity. . . .

Conclusion

As we begin a new era and a new millennium, we deem it essential to reaffirm the truths of the Declaration of Independence:

- That all men are created equal;
- That they are endowed by their Creator with certain unalienable rights, among these are life, liberty, and the pursuit of happiness;

- That government derives its just powers only from the consent of the governed.

We close this platform with the wisdom of our forefathers who had the courage to set their names to the Declaration of Independence as they too began a new era. Like them, we appeal to the Supreme Judge of the world for the rectitude of our intentions. With a firm reliance on the protection of Divine Providence, we pledge to each other and to the American people an unfaltering commitment to restore to America a deep respect for the values of human freedom.

PEROT ON REFORM PARTY'S PRESIDENTIAL NOMINATION
August 18, 1996

Ross Perot, the Texas billionaire who in 1992 made the second-best showing of any third-party or independent candidate for president in U.S. history, found the going much tougher in 1996. Running as the presidential nominee of the Reform party, which he helped found after the 1992 election, Perot won just 8 percent of the vote in the 1996 race, compared with 19 percent four years earlier.

As his vote total suggested, Perot did not play as major a role in the 1996 presidential elections as he had four years earlier. In 1992, according to most analysts, Perot's candidacy helped Democrat Bill Clinton defeat the incumbent Republican president, George Bush, by splitting the anti-Democratic vote and drawing voters who otherwise would likely have supported the Republican ticket. In 1996 Perot's candidacy was not the novelty it was in 1992, and he was shut out of some public forums that had done much to boost his visibility in 1992. He was not permitted to participate in the presidential debates in 1996, as he had in 1992, and the major commercial television networks frustrated his efforts to buy prime time to air his infomercials. Perot in 1996 was also a victim of his own success in 1992. During that campaign he pressed the importance of reducing the deficit, reforming campaign finance and lobbying laws, and enacting term limits—all issues that the two major political parties effectively co-opted after the 1992 elections.

Reform Party Convention

On September 25, 1995, Perot returned to one of his favorite forums, CNN's Larry King Live, to announce that he was launching a new third party. The announcement came as a surprise—Perot had long resisted calls to begin a third party—and some saw his announcement as a self-serving attempt to regain a share of the political spotlight. Perot insisted that the new Reform party was "not about me running for president." Referring to a recent poll that showed that 62 percent of American voters *favored the formation of a new party, Perot said, "This is a party for that 62 percent."*

The Reform party immediately began to take steps to qualify its eventual presidential nominee for a place on the 1996 general election ballot in all fifty states. For several months Perot was coy about his plans. Former Democratic governor Richard D. Lamm of Colorado announced July 9, 1996, that he would seek the new party's presidential nomination; Perot's announcement that he would enter the race followed on July 11.

The Reform party held a two-phase convention. The first phase took place August 11 in Long Beach, California, and featured speeches from Perot and Lamm. The second phase occurred in Valley Forge, Pennsylvania, on August 18. In the intervening week, Reform party members voted for their choice by mail, electronic mail, or telephone. To no one's great surprise, Perot won nearly two-thirds of the vote, although the number of actual ballots was only a small fraction of the party's announced membership.

Accepting the party's nomination at the Valley Forge meeting, Perot credited himself and his supporters for setting the agenda for the 1996 presidential campaign. "Isn't it terrific that in just four years [the two major parties have] repented and reformed and you are setting the agenda for '96," he told the delegates. He chastised the Democrats and Republicans for failing to follow through on their promise to reform campaign finance laws. "The bad news is, they never did it. They just shook hands," Perot said. "Where I come from. . . , a handshake was worth more than a written contract."

As he had during the 1992 campaign, Perot pushed for debt reduction, opposed recent regional and international trade agreements, and urged parents to become more involved in their children's schooling. He also urged that schooling begin earlier in children's lives. A child "learns to learn how to learn . . . by the time he's three. The words a child hears before the child is two impacts the total capacity of the child's vocabulary. . . ," Perot said. "With this knowledge it's obvious that traditional concepts regarding public education must be radically altered. . . ."

Before Perot spoke, Lamm addressed the delegates, congratulating Perot for winning the nomination, but declining to endorse him. Lamm spent much of his speech on the key theme in his campaign, controlling immigration. "There is no essential difference in my mind," he said, "between exporting a job and importing a new worker."

Frustrations of the Fall Campaign

Although Perot had criticized public financing of presidential campaigns, he decided to accept the nearly $30 million in public matching funds that he qualified for in 1996 as a result of his strong showing in the 1992 election. In that campaign Perot spent more than $60 million of his own money. Acceptance of federal funding meant Perot was limited to spending $50,000 of his own money, although he could raise more from other contributors under the legal limits. Perot had hoped to win 25 per-

cent of the vote in 1996, the amount needed for his party to achieve public financing in the next presidential election equal to that of the two major parties.

Perot seldom was able to rise above single digits in the polls. He was frustrated in his attempts to buy prime network time to air his half-hour infomercials, a format that had worked well for him in 1992. His choice for a running mate, Pat Choate, an economist, consultant, and writer in Washington, D.C., did little to boost Perot's popularity. Coauthor with Perot of a book opposing the North American Free Trade Agreement, Choate had little name recognition outside Washington.

Perhaps the most devastating blow to his campaign was his failure to be included in the presidential debates in October. It was Perot's performance in the presidential debates of 1992 that had boosted his standing in the polls then, and he was hoping for a similar effect from the 1996 debates. On September 17 the bipartisan Commission on Presidential Debates recommended that Perot be excluded on grounds that he did not have a "realistic chance to win" the election. The decision was considered a victory for the Republican nominee, former Senate majority leader Bob Dole, who did not want Perot in the debates; Dole and his advisers believed that Perot's candidacy would hurt the Republican more than it would hurt Clinton. (1996 debates, p. 707; 1992 debates, Historic Documents of 1992, p. 907)

Dole actually gave Perot a last-minute lift in the opinion polls at the end of October when he urged the third-party candidate to abandon the race and support Dole. Perot, who had strongly criticized Dole for pushing a tax cut in the face of a continuing budget deficit, declined the request, but the publicity surrounding the incident pushed Perot's standing above 10 percent in several polls. That uptick had dissipated by the general election on November 5, however.

Perot did not come close to winning a single state. His best showings were 14 percent in Maine (where he had won 30 percent in 1992) and Montana. But by capturing 8 percent of the general election votes, his Reform party would qualify for public matching funds in the election in 2000 if it chose to run a presidential candidate.

Following are excerpts from Ross Perot's speech August 18, 1996, in Valley Forge, Pennsylvania, in which he accepted the presidential nomination of the Reform party:

Thank you for creating the Reform Party. It's an historic event. It only happens once every hundred years in this country. You're great. Thank you.

I am honored and I am humbled that you have chosen me as your candidate to be president.

And you have my solemn promise that I will only act in the best interest of our country.

This is your country. I will be your servant.

I will only belong to you, the people.

And I am absolutely committed—irrevocably committed to passing on a better world to our children and grandchildren.

After watching this introduction, surely you will agree that I have literally lived the American Dream.

I want to make sure that some other kid who's a nobody from nowhere has that same opportunity.

I'm here today because I'm absolutely determined to keep the dream alive. And we will pass on a better, stronger country to the next generation.

I would like to compliment Gov. Lamm on his speech and thank him for his participation. Thank you, Dick.

Have you listened to the messages from the other parties during the last few weeks?

Do their promises for 1996 sound familiar?

Who first brought these issues to the American people? You did!

Isn't it terrific that in just four years, they've repented, been reborn. And you are setting the agenda for '96. God bless you.

Now, here is the question for everybody in the good old U.S.A. Do you think they will keep those promises?

Remember Lech Walesa's message to our Congress when he said words are plentiful, but deeds are precious. We are here in Valley Forge tonight to remind everybody that the people who created this country made incredible sacrifices. That's why we have the convention here. . . .

[Big Government]

In 1995 the elected leaders from both of the parties publicly shook hands on national television and agreed to form a task force on campaign finance reform and lobbying. Remember that?

God bless them, they were going to hit the line and do it because they knew they had to do it to get your vote. The bad news is they never did it. They just shook hands.

Where I come from—as a boy, particularly—a handshake was worth more than a written contract is today.

And a handshake at that level ought to be worth that for now.

So after sending us that feel-good message, they went out and spent the year raising money for 1996 from the special interests. And as we sit here tonight, there is a big party at the Waldorf Astoria, and I know the room.

It may hold about 800 people. And I heard over television today that they're going to raise $8 million. I'll let you figure out what they're charging per plate for that.

Isn't this a compelling argument that the people who own this country should have their own political party with no special interests controlling it?

Now, we've got to keep rolling.

That's what. . . . We've got to face problems and solve them. And step one is identify the problems. Let's review them to see what we have to do to pass on a better, stronger country to our children in the 21st century, and make it the greatest in our country's history.

Our country's major problems are caused by huge social programs that were never designed to work properly, and have generated major cost over-runs. These major cost overruns have created a massive debt.

In addition, we have seriously damaged our job base with very poorly negotiated trade agreements. And that has caused our tax base to deteriorate.

You see, it all fits together like pieces in a puzzle. They just look at the problems individually. You've got to look at them all at once.

Today, the two political parties have created—here's the good news—America's No. 1 growth industry—and I want to give them full credit for that.

It's up there. You can see it. I can't.

The U.S. government makes our other major industries look insignificant. But as practical business people, you're saying, what product do they make, Ross? They don't make one.

Well, then where do they get the money for this great new industry? From you.

Well, how do the customers feel about this giant new industry?

Only 19 percent of the American people trust this giant new industry. That's how they feel.

OK. But now—look. We've got this huge thing going. We've got this big thing going. Right?

Does it make a profit? No. Does it lose money?

Yes. How much money does it have in the bank? None. Does it have any debt? Yes. And you know it's $5 trillion, right?

Well, there's business people out there working hard all day trying to make a living. You say, well, how does it avoid going bankrupt?

Let's look on page 18 of the president's 1997 budget. And here is the record. We have assets of $2.3 trillion. We have liabilities of $5.2 trillion. We have a negative net worth in the federal government of $2.9 trillion. And guess who's going to have to pick up all of that?

We are. You see, you're the only source of money. Well—but they left something out. They left out $17 trillion worth of guarantees.

So, that negative net worth is almost $20 trillion. So, that's where we are today.

[Straight Talk]

Now, do you get this kind of blunt, straight talk from the other political parties?

Would you rather hear this kind of talk from me or do you want me to get tears in my eyes, lean into the audience, and say, "I feel your pain?"

Do you want a president who led the fight to get GATT [General Agreement on Tariffs and Trade] and NAFTA [North American Free Trade Agreement] passed and then stood up in public over national television and said he was against both of them last week?

You remember that one, don't you? You remember that song—we had a movie a few years ago with Dolly Parton in it, *The Best Little "you know what" in Texas.*

And the sheriff—the sheriff had this song. It said, "Ooh, I love to do the little sidestep."

"Now you see me, now you don't, and here I go."

Keep that in mind when you watch these guys.

Can we count on the two political parties? Can we count on the two political parties to solve these problems? They are the problem, right?

Now, if you got a friend that's drinking too much, the first thing he's got to do is admit it, right?

They won't admit we have a problem, and therefore they cannot come up with real solutions. Instead of giving you advice, they hire professional speech writers and seek help from Hollywood's finest to manipulate you into casting an emotional vote.

And boy, has it been working. But you and I are going to get the facts out to the American people, and we're going to kill that little snake this time, right?

But wait a minute. Wait a minute. Wait a minute. Hang on.

But surely the president's huge tax increase in 1993 will balance the budget, and we'll live happily ever after? No.

Look at this slide, and you will see that it's a little trick. The deficit kind of floats in there through the year 2000. That's two terms in the White House, right? And then it takes off like a rocket.

And you say, Ross, where'd you get those numbers? Those are official government numbers.

Next, let's go to page 25 if you're still not convinced we have to act. And you will find—of the president's 1995 budget—and you will find that he predicts that the next generation to be born—a little baby born tonight, your children and grandchildren—will pay an 82 percent tax rate.

That is the end of the American Dream. It's now up to 84 percent. But you don't give the people any negative information, so they quit printing it in the budget.

Now, can we agree that if nothing else will motivate you on a bad day, that will?

OK. Are we going to pass this burden on to our children and grandchildren?

The Office of Management and Budget forecasts after the big tax increase that the national debt in the year 2020 will be increasing at the rate every year of $1.4 trillion a year. It's just $5 trillion now. It will be going up $1.4 trillion.

You say, well, what about out in 2030? By then, it's gone up to $4.1 trillion a year or four-fifths of the $5 trillion today.

Has all of this debt benefited the people? We should be in Utopia, right?

Here are the facts. Since 1980, the standard of living is down for four out of five working Americans. Manufacturing workers who were making $440 a week are now making $270 a week if they have a job.

After taxes, two paychecks today—with a man and a wife both working to give the children a middle-class life—are worth about the purchasing power of a single paycheck 25 years ago.

Conclusion. Over the last 35 years we tried big government. It didn't work. We can't keep on this route. . . .

[Trade Deficit]

We all know about the budget deficit, but we've got two deficits. We never talk about the other one because they really have worked hard—the special interests demanded it in return for their campaign money. And the boys in Washington delivered it.

And that is the trade deficit.

Now, the U.S. merchandise trade deficit last year was $174 billion. That's the largest of any nation in the history of man. In 1950, 90 percent of the goods sold in this country were made in the U.S.A. Today, less than 50 percent of the goods sold in this country are made in the U.S.A.

Two million manufacturing jobs have gone to Asia. Five hundred thousand jobs have gone to Mexico—the cumulative NAFTA trade deficit.

NAFTA was supposed to be a money-maker, right?

No wonder the guys who voted for it are now telling you they're against it because the accumulative NAFTA trade deficit is $52 billion and growing like a weed. Did NAFTA cause a giant sucking sound?

OK. Do you remember how we were ridiculed and derided?

Somebody said I'd rather be right than president. In this situation, we've got to be right and president to clean up this mess.

Thank you.

Now, in the last 10 years, if you add up our cumulative trade deficit for the last 10 years, it exceeds $1 trillion. Study history, study what all the economists say—we cannot exist with that.

We're the biggest market in the world for goods and services. Everybody wants to sell to us. Europe doesn't make dumb trade deals with Japan. We're the only industrialized nation in the world with a trade deficit with China.

We better find somebody that knows how to horse trade, don't you think?

Well, God bless my dad. He taught me as a boy. Thank him.

OK, now, since this is just imploding our job base and our tax base, which would give us the ability to balance our budget and pay our debt, why did both parties—and I mean they were bound at the hip on this one—pass these stupid trade—I'm for fair, free trade.

I'm against stupid trade. This is stupid trade.

Well, you know the answer, and I want to make sure that all the American people know the answer—the special interests who paid for their campaigns and all that glitz you saw last week and you'll see next week.

Our conventions cost about $800,000 together. They spent over $30 million on theirs. I think ours are better than theirs.

Don't you think if we had that kind of plain thinking in Washington, if we can do—keep in mind I remember last—in '92, they had spent $20 million, $30 million a piece. We had spent $1.5 million getting petitions signed.

[Medicare and Medicaid]

I think we've made the point that we're more cost effective than they are. But now, everywhere I go people ask me: "Ross, what's the problem with Medicare and Medicaid?". . .

The annual cost of Medicare and Medicaid today is at $250 billion a year. The two parties let this happen.

Why? And they let it keep on happening. The special interests who fund their campaigns are making huge amounts of money at your expense. We'll stop it.

I encourage you to read a book we published on this subject. The title of the book is *Intensive Care: We Must Save Medicare and Medicaid Now*. The devil is in the details, and the details are in the book.

Our government forecast that the cost of Medicare, Medicaid and Social Security in the year 2030 will be $3.9 trillion. That's more than twice as much money as we spend each year to operate our whole country today.

Once you see something like that coming you stop it quick, and we will after '96.

Then the next. . . . What's the problem with Social Security? What's the problem with Social Security?

Everybody thinks it's a pension fund. No. It's pay-as-you-go. The money comes in this week; it goes out next week to retired people. Then how did it ever work?

In 1945 we had 42 people that worked for every person retired. By 1950 that number dropped to 16 people that worked for every person retired. But we raised rates, expanded benefits, kept on working.

But today we only have 3.3 people at work for every person retired. And we're headed for two people at work, for every person retired in the year 2020.

We must transition Social Security from a pay-as-you-go fund to a true pension fund. And nobody in the Reform Party would ever tolerate taking Social Security away from retired people. Let me make that point. . . .

Now, all the political experts across the country who are watching this program will be shocked and are shocked already that I am talking about real problems and the fact that we have to face them and solve them in an acceptance speech.

This is supposed to be morning in America. You're supposed to leave feeling giddy and good because I just whistled good news all night.

That's not what we're about. We're about getting the facts, taking action, producing results.

I want you all to know the only reason I do this and the only reason I asked my family to go through all this unpleasantness, unfortunately, that goes with politics, is that I am absolutely devoted to solving these problems. . . .

[A New Tax System]

Get the facts. And we must have a new tax system. We know that.

The first step in solving any problem is to define the problem. Watch my lips, Washington.

If you want to solve a problem carefully, thoughtfully and rationally define it. Well, one of the things to do is look at history. You ain't going to believe this one.

Before our nation was formed, the total cost to run our government was 67 cents per person a year. Then, after our nation was formed, it went up to a dollar a year. Then 120 years later, in 1910, it was up to $6.75 per person a year. Now we're getting to be a pretty big nation, right?—$6.75 a year.

Then we passed the income tax law—amendment in 1913. And 16 years later it had gone from $6.75 to $29 per person a year.

Now strap in your seat belt and don't eject because you can't. Today it's $5,700 a year per person.

I hope I've made the point that when you've got a tax law that Congress can raise, it will.

See, it's the percent that's killing you, right?

Forty percent of your paycheck now goes to taxes. Back in 1910, it was 10 percent.

Now—and we know we're not getting our money's worth. Today we pay more in taxes to our nation than we pay for food, clothing, and shelter combined. Now the new tax system's got to be fair. It's got to be paperless. It's got to raise the necessary revenues.

I will not run up and down the streets of America promising you hope, opportunity, and growth, flat tax, flat tax, flat tax.

If that is the best tax, that's the one we'll do. But we're going to look at all of them carefully, thoughtfully and rationally. We're going to use the computer as our wind tunnel.

We'll nail it, give it you and then move on to our next problem.

But I am sick and tired of having a government where the benefits of our congressmen and the retirement plans of our congressmen and the people in the White House are better than those of the ordinary American citizen.

They are your servants.

Now, if you want them to feel your pain, let them have retirement and health insurance like yours, right?

Yes. Here on taxes—and this is my favorite—any new tax program, whatever it is, must have a provision that Congress cannot raise taxes without putting it on the ballot in the next federal election and having the voters approve it.

Now, imagine asking the voters to approve a tax increase. The whole House is running. A third of the Senate's running. The president's running. They won't even bring it up unless they really need it. And if they really need it, we'll make the sacrifice.

But now we've got discipline on spending. We put the cork in the bottle, right?

And everybody gets upset in Washington about that. And I said, wait a minute. If I'm going broke in business, I can't force my stockholders to give me more money. Just because you mismanage our economy, why should you be able to force us to pay you more money?

Why, in a free society that has a government with an unbroken record of undisciplined spending, should the owners of the country, the people, not make the final decision to pay more taxes? They should. A fundamental flaw.

As we approach the 1996 election, they've proposed solving these financial problems with a big tax cut. Since we cannot pay our bills, wouldn't it make a lot more sense to have a big spending cut first?

Now, what if you come to me—you come to me and say, Ross, I'm hopelessly in debt. I can't pay my bills. Can you get me some good advice?

Well, if I were these guys that proposed a tax cut, I'd look at you and smile, say, "God bless you, have them cut your salary."

And you would say, well, Ross, I can't pay my bills with my current salary. If I cut my salary, how can I pay my bills?

I'd say, let's change the subject, right?

Now, we have tried this supply-side economics in the '80s. It gave us the biggest increase in the deficit we ever had in our country's history. Even the people in the party that created it called it voodoo economics.

I said in 1992 if we ever do this again, we'll be in deep voodoo.

And there we are.

[Public Schools]

I've got to talk to you about our public schools. It's brains and wits time as we approach the 21st century. We've got to have the greatest public schools in the world. The intellectual ability and the creative abilities of the American people will determine our future.

In order to have a growing, expanding job base and a growing, expanding tax base and a growing, expanding middle class, we have to have the world's best educated work force, period.

This is the greatest legacy we can leave our children, no question. The greatest legacy we can leave our children. In 1960, we had the finest schools in the world.

Then the government took over, and 36 years later after spending $456 billion of federal money, our public schools rank at the bottom of the industrialized world. What happened? The federal government, ran by the two political parties, got involved.

Again, step one is to define the problem. We have the largest number of functional illiterates in the industrialized world. At the 12th grade level, I'm sad to report that 66 percent can't meet the reading and writing standards, 73 percent can't meet the geography standards, 84 percent can't meet the mathematics standards, and 89 percent can't meet the history standards.

The major discipline problems in our school in the 1940s were talking, chewing gum, making noise, running in the halls, getting out of line, wearing improper clothing, and not putting paper in the waste baskets.

I can live with those, right?

Here are our major discipline problems today: children carrying guns to school, drug abuse, pregnancy, suicide, rape, robbery, and assault. Isn't that sad?

Learning cannot occur in that environment. More importantly, why do parents allow their children to act this way? In a free society, isn't it our job as parents to teach our children to behave and keep our children under control?

When I was bad in school, what they did to me there wasn't nearly as significant as what they did to me when I got home. My parents never read my Miranda rights.

And if we want our children to be competitive we've got to have the finest schools in the world. That simple. This will have to come from us, the people.

We've got to restore local control over the schools. The schools must again become places of learning, not of play. We have to create small neighborhood schools near the child's home, especially in the primary grades.

We have to put great emphasis on teachers. Today we get preoccupied with building fancy buildings.

We will not have great schools without extensive parental control and involvement. This is an overwhelming argument for having the school near the home.

[A Child's Development]

We now know a great deal about how a child's brain develops. Now, all the political experts are saying, he's not going to talk about how a child's brain develops, is he?

Yes, I am. Because that will drive what the schools should be. This knowledge should be a major force in planning our schools. This is the kind of thinking we'll bring to Washington.

The human brain develops billions of cells before the baby is born. Each cell has its own circuit in the brain. When a baby comes into the world, the brain is a jumble of disconnected circuits waiting to be connected.

Some of these circuits are connected that allow the heart to beat, allow the baby to breathe and so on and so forth. But a thousand trillion circuits, literally, are unwired. That's the only number I've ever seen that's bigger than the national debt.

The love and attention a small child receives determines whether or not the child will tap his or her full intellectual capacity.

I can't tell you how important it is to love them and hug them. My greatest concern used to be that my grandchildren would never learn to walk. Nobody ever put them down.

Having read this, I'm thrilled. Babies either learn how to learn, or fail to learn how to learn by the time they're three. If you blindfold a baby for six months the baby will be blind for life; the circuits can't be wired.

A baby's six-months-old brain weighs 20 percent of what it will weigh as an adult—50 percent, excuse—of what it will weigh as an adult, even though the body weight is 20 percent.

But then the brain grows quickly by the time the child is a few years old to half of its adult weight. When a child is six years old, the brain has grown to 90 percent of its adult weight and begins to shut down the unused circuits.

Isn't that a paradox that that's when we start school, after the circuits are shutting down?

These circuits that represent sounds that form words are wired by the age of one year. A child learns to think well or poorly of himself by the time he's 18 months.

He learns to learn how to learn, or fail to learn how to learn by the time he's three. The words a child hears before the child is two impact the total capacity of the child's vocabulary. Isn't this fascinating?

Math and logic wiring takes place from birth to four years. The learning window for music is three to 10 years. With this knowledge it's obvious that traditional concepts regarding public education must be radically altered—and please listen carefully to this—particularly for disadvantaged children who don't get all that early attention.

[Preparing for 40 Years]

We can, we will and we must solve these problems. That's the reason I want to be your president. I didn't know it, but I've been preparing to do this for 40 years. I grew up having to manage money carefully.

I grew up being taught not to waste money and to pay cash for everything and to keep money in the bank. I was fortunate enough to be put into an industry where I had to learn to design, engineer and make work very complex systems and make them work in a cost-effective manner.

Isn't this what our problem is?

The only reason I am here tonight is I want to solve those problems for the great people in this country.

Thank you. Ordinary people in this country are capable of extraordinary achievements. You know that, and I do. There's nothing we can't do.

Keep in mind it's going to be tough for the next few months, but the same blow that shatters glass hardens steel. You've been here. You've been through the fight. And you are hard as steel. And boy, am I proud of you.

The other parties have a fortune to spend from now on. They have almost $100 million under the federal election laws. We only get $29 million.

I've got to go to the men and women across this country and ask them for their support. I particularly go to the people who own the 6 million small businesses and the 80 million people who work for them and ask them to send in small contributions.

I go to all of you and say, if this is worth fighting, you will have to contribute so that we can get a semi-level playing field so that we can compete from now until November.

If you want to send in a contribution, just send it to Perot '96, Post Office Box 96, Dallas, Texas. You don't even have to write that down, right? Fine.

As we work together, I ask all of you to remember it is better to light a candle than to curse the darkness. The shadows will fall behind you if you walk into the light. All the darkness in the world cannot put out the light of one little candle.

Millions of good, decent people like you must light these candles that will lead us to victory in the light in 1996. You are the wind beneath the Reform Party's wings. It would be nothing without you.

As we march forward together we will need the Spirit of '76 in '96. And in the middle of the effort, when things get tougher and tougher—and they will—just remember this, a bell is no bell until you ring it.

Think of the Liberty Bell.

And a song is no song until you sing it.

Think of the Star-Spangled Banner.

Love in your heart isn't put there to stay. Think of your children and grandchildren. Love isn't love until you give it away. Think of the millions of people you can help. God bless you all. Thank you very much.

A privilege to be with you. Thank you.

CLINTON'S REMARKS ON RAISING THE MINIMUM WAGE
August 20, 1996

Democrats won a significant—and unexpected—political and legislative victory in August when Congress passed legislation that would raise the minimum wage from $4.25 to $5.15 an hour, in two steps. It was the first time since 1991 that the minimum wage had been increased; about twelve million people who currently made less than $5.15 were expected to benefit from the increase.

The legislation was a major political embarrassment for the Republican leadership in both the House and Senate, where moderate GOP legislators broke with their leadership to provide Democrats with the majority they needed to pass the measure. House Majority Leader Dick Armey had vowed to fight a minimum wage increase "with every fiber of my being." Senate Majority Leader Bob Dole had been forced to pull major legislation off the floor after Democrats threatened to tie it up with an amendment to raise the minimum wage. The Democratic moves frustrated Dole, the leading contender for the Republican presidential nomination, who had sought to use his leadership post in the Senate to showcase his ability to lead the nation.

The minimum wage has been a defining issue between Democrats and Republicans since 1938 when it was first established, with Democrats and their union allies arguing that working Americans should be guaranteed some minimum level of pay and Republicans and their business allies responding that increases in the minimum wage unfairly burdened businesses, especially small retail businesses, and lead to the loss of jobs for the low-wage earners the measure is intended to help.

Although President Bill Clinton proposed a hike in the minimum wage in his 1995 State of the Union message and Democrats in the Senate pushed for a vote on the issue in 1995, little concerted congressional action occurred until 1996, when Democrats saw an opportunity to turn the minimum wage into a campaign issue. Ironically, they were aided by Patrick J. Buchanan, the conservative GOP presidential candidate whose brief campaign in the Republican primaries focused on the widespread economic insecurities and wage stagnation experienced by Americans of both political parties. Economic anxieties "provided the kindling for the issue, and voters in the Republican primaries lit the match," said Sen. Edward M. Kennedy, D-Mass., a leader in pushing for the increase.

Pros and Cons of a Minimum Wage Hike

Inflation had whittled down the $4.25 minimum wage by 12.2 percent since 1991, when it was last raised. To get its purchasing power back to the 1991 level, the wage would have to go up to $5.04. To reach the purchasing power of the minimum wage in 1968, its historic high, it would have to be raised to $6.65. Even at $5.15 an hour, a full-time minimum wage worker would earn less than $11,000 a year, nearly $5,000 less than the official poverty line for a family of four.

Opponents of an increase argued that labor-intensive companies such as restaurants and food services would have to cut jobs to absorb the increases in their labor costs. One standard projection forecast that an increase of seventy-five cents would cost 60,000 entry-level jobs. Traditionally, most economists agreed with Republicans that a raise in the minimum wage discouraged hiring, but in recent years some had begun to reject that notion. "The evidence of job loss is weak, and the fact that the evidence is weak suggests that the impact on jobs is small," said Robert M. Solow, a 1995 Nobel laureate in economics at the Massachusetts Institute of Technology.

Opponents of an increase also argued that the minimum wage primarily benefits younger and single workers, many of whom are students working part-time, often in fast-food restaurants, who still receive support from their families. Data from the Department of Labor showed that more than 30 percent of the minimum wage earners were teenagers, but that only 7 percent were teenage students from families whose incomes were above average; that 40 percent of all minimum wage workers were food service workers; and that more than 60 percent worked part-time.

According to the Labor Department, about 39 percent of those paid the minimum wage were the sole earners in their households; according to the Employment Policies Institute, an industry group that opposed the wage hike, that number was inflated because it included single people living alone who might receive substantial help from their parents. The institute estimated that only 8.5 percent of all minimum wage recipients were the sole breadwinners in their families. According to two Princeton economists, David Card and Alan B. Krueger, about 30 percent of minimum-wage workers were from families whose incomes were in the lowest fifth of the income range, while 37 percent came from families in the top half. The statistics that were most influential with legislators, however, were the national polls, which uniformly showed overwhelming support for an increase in the minimum wage.

An Unanticipated Democratic Success

The opinion polls left little doubt that a minimum wage increase would pass on a straight up-or-down vote in Congress, and that gave Democrats their wedge. Together with strong support from organized labor, the Democrats began to push for a vote on the issue. In late March Senate Democrats forced Dole to pull a public lands bill from the Senate floor to avoid a vote on a minimum wage amendment; the same thing happened on April 16, when Dole was forced to shelve an immigration bill.

The first crack in the GOP front came in the House, however, when twenty Republican moderates introduced a bill on April 17 to raise the minimum wage by one dollar. As it became evident that there might not be a way to avoid a vote on the minimum wage, the Republican leadership began to explore options. "We're looking at maybe some way we can formulate an increase in the minimum wage plus some other features of the amendment the Democrats might not be so crazy about," Dole said on a national news program.

The first vote came in the House on May 23, when 93 Republicans joined 187 Democrats to raise the wage to $5.15 an hour in two stages, but only after the increase was tied to a Republican package of amendments designed to ease the burden on small businesses. That package contained a provision long opposed by Democrats that would allow employers to pay teenage workers a subminimum wage for their first ninety days of employment. An even more controversial amendment that would have exempted small businesses from paying the minimum wage and overtime was defeated by a 229–196 vote.

The Senate did not act on the legislation until July, after Dole had resigned his seat in the Senate to run for president. The July 9 vote was 74–24. The final version of the legislation passed August 3 by even wider margins: 354–72 in the House; 76–22 in the Senate. The final measure raised the minimum wage to $4.75 on October 1, 1996, and to $5.15 on September 1, 1997. It also allowed employers to pay teenagers a "training" wage of $4.25 an hour for their first ninety days. (Dole resignation, p. 270)

"This bill says to the working people of America: If you're willing to take responsibility and go to work, your work will be honored," Clinton said, signing the bill on August 20. The ceremony on the South Lawn of the White House, complete with marching bands and crowded with low-income families, union leaders, and Democratic legislators, seemed designed to blunt some of the criticism Clinton was receiving from liberals in his own party for his decision to sign the Republican welfare reform bill into law. (Welfare reform, p. 450)

Even Republicans acknowledged the Democratic triumph on the minimum wage legislation. "I would say to my friends, the Democratic Party, you won a great victory," House Speaker Newt Gingrich conceded in his September 28 speech closing the Congress. "Some of us swallowed more than we wanted to, yet it was clearly the American people's will."

Other provisions of the Small Business Job Protection Act of 1996 bene-
fited not only small businesses, but families and some large businesses.
These tax provisions were expected to cost the federal government $20 bil-
lion over ten years. These tax provisions:

- *gradually increased the amount of equipment purchases that small*
  businesses could expense on their taxes from $17,000 to $25,000 in
  2003.
- *made several changes in federal pension laws, including one that*
  would allow employees of small businesses (those with fewer than one
  hundred employees) to contribute up to $6,000 a year to an Individ-
  ual Retirement Account or other tax-deferred pension plans. Employ-
  ers would have to match the contribution up to 3 percent of the work-
  er's salary.
- *extended through May 31, 1997, the tax exclusion of up to $5,250 for*
  workers who receive employer-provided tuition assistance.
- *extended through May 31, 1997, the duty-free treatment of certain*
  products, particularly handicrafts from developing countries.
- *allowed a $5,000 tax credit to offset the costs of domestic and foreign*
  adoptions. The credit would expire on December 31, 2001. A $6,000
  credit for families who adopted hard-to-adopt domestic children, such
  as disabled children, was to be permanent.

Following are excerpts of remarks by President Bill Clinton dur-
ing a White House ceremony August 20, 1996, signing into law
legislation (PL 104–188) raising the minimum wage to $5.15
an hour by September 1, 1997:

Thank you very much. . . . [L]et me just begin by saying this is a truly
remarkable piece of legislation. It is pro-work, pro-business and pro-family;
it raises the minimum wage; it helps small businesses in a number of ways
that I will explain in a moment, including retirement and incentive to invest;
and it promotes adoption in two very sweeping ways that have long needed
to be done in the United States. This is a cause for celebration for all Americans of all parties, all walks of life, all faiths. This bill represents the very best
in our country.

It will give 10 million Americans . . . a chance to raise stronger families and
build better futures. By coming together across lines that have too often
divided us and finding common ground, we have made this a real season of
achievement for the people of America.

At its heart, this bill does reaffirm our most profoundly American values—
offering opportunity to all, demanding responsibility from all, and coming
together as a community to do the right thing. This bill says to the working
people of America: If you're willing to take responsibility and go to work,
your work will be honored. We're going to honor your commitment to your

family, we're going to recognize that $4.25 an hour is not enough to raise a family.

It's harder and harder to raise children today and harder and harder for people to succeed at home and at work. And I have said repeatedly, over and over again to the American people: We must not force our families to make a choice. Most parents have to work. We have a national interest in seeing that our people can succeed at home where it counts the most in raising their children, and succeed at work so they'll have enough income to be able to succeed at home. We must do both, and this bill helps us achieve that goal. . . .

[T]his bill ensures that a parent working full-time at the minimum wage can lift himself or herself and their children out of poverty. Nobody who works full-time with kids in the home should be in poverty. If we want to really revolutionize America's welfare system and move people from welfare to work and reward work, that is the first, ultimate test we all have to meet. If you get up every day and you go to work, and you put in your time and you have kids in your home, you and your children will not be in poverty.

We have some hard working minimum wage people here today. . . . Let me tell you about them. Seventy percent of them are adults, six of 10 are working women, and for them, work is about more than a paycheck, it's about pride. They want a wage they can raise their families on. By raising the minimum wage by 90 cents, this bill, over two years, will give those families an additional $1,800 a year in income—enough to buy seven months of groceries, several months of rent, or child care. Or . . . to pay all of the bills from the utilities in the same month.

For many, this bill will make the difference between their ability to keep their families together and their failure to do so. These people reflect America's values, and it's a lot harder for them than it is for most of us to go around living what they say they believe in. It's about time they got a reward and, today, they'll get it.

I would also like to say a very special word of thanks to the business owners, especially the small business owners who supported this bill. Many of the minimum wage employers I talk to wanted to pay their employees more than $4.25 an hour and would be happy to do so as long as they can do it without hurting their businesses, and that means their competitors have to do the same thing. This bill will allow them to compete and win, to have happier, more productive employees, and to know they're doing the right thing. For all of those small businesses, I am very, very appreciative.

I would also like to say that this bill does a remarkable number of things for small businesses. In each of the last three years, our nation has set a new record in each succeeding year in the number of new businesses started. And we know that most of the new jobs in America are being created by small- and medium-sized businesses. In 1993, I proposed a $15,000 increase in the amount of capital a small business can expense, to spark the kind of investment that they need to create jobs. Well, in 1993 we only won half that increase, but today I'll get to sign the second half into law, and I thank the Congress for passing that, as well.

As the Vice President said, this bill also includes a Work Opportunity Tax Credit to provide jobs for the most economically disadvantaged working Americans, including people who want to move from welfare to work. Now, there will be a tightly drawn economic incentive for people to hire those folks and give them a chance to enter the workforce, as well. It extends the research tax credit to help businesses stay competitive in the global economy. It extends a tax incentive for businesses to train and educate their employees. That's good news for people who need those skills, and it's good news for America because we have to have the best educated workforce in the world in the 21st century.

This legislation does even more to strengthen small business by strengthening the families that make them up. It helps millions of more Americans to save for their own retirement. It makes it much easier for small businesses to offer pension plans by creating a new small business 401(k) plan. It also lets more Americans keep their pensions when they change jobs without having to wait a year before they can start saving at their new jobs. As many as 10 million Americans without pensions today could now earn them as a result of this bill.

I'm delighted we are joined today, among others, by Shawn Marcell, the CEO of Prima Facie, a fast-growing video monitoring company in Pennsylvania, which now has just 17 employees—but that's a lot more than he started with. He stood with me in April and promised that if we kept our word and made pensions easier and cheaper for small businesses like his, he'd give pensions to all of his employees. Today, he has told us he's making good on that pledge. I'd like him to stand up, and say I predict that thousands more will follow Shawn's lead. Thank you, Shawn. Please stand up. Let's give him a hand. God bless you, sir. Thank you. [Applause.]

I'd also like to say a special word of thanks to our SBA Administrator, Phil Lader, and to the White House Conference on Small Business. When the White House Conference on Small Business met, they said one of their top priorities was increasing the availability and the security of pensions for small business owners in America. This is a good thing. It is also pro-work, pro-family and pro-business.

Finally, this bill does something else that is especially important to me and to Hillary—and I'm glad she's here with us today. It breaks down the financial and bureaucratic barriers to adoption, giving more children what every child needs and deserves—loving parents and a strong, stable home.

Two weeks ago, we had a celebration for the American athletes who made us so proud in Atlanta at the Centennial Olympics. Millions of Americans now know that one of them—the Decathlon Gold medalist, Dan O'Brien—speaks movingly about having been an adopted child and how much the support of his family meant in his life. Right now, there are tens of thousands of children waiting for the kind of family that helped to make Dan O'Brien an Olympic champion. At the same time, there are thousands of middle class families that want to bring children into their homes but cannot afford it. We're offering a $5,000 tax credit to help bring them together. It gives even more help to families that will adopt children with disabilities or take in two siblings, rather than seeing them split up.

And, lastly, this bill ends the long-standing bias against interracial adoption which has too often meant an endless, needless wait for America's children. You know, as much as we talk about strong, loving families, it's not every day that we here in Washington get to enact a law that literally creates them or helps them stay together. This is such a day. . . .

Beside me, or in front of me now, is the desk used by Frances Perkins—Franklin Roosevelt's labor secretary and the very first woman ever to serve in the Cabinet. She was one of our greatest labor secretaries. It was from her desk that many of America's pioneering wage, hour and workplace laws originated—including the very first 25 cent an hour minimum wage signed into law by President Roosevelt in 1938. Secretary Perkins understood that a living wage was about more than feeding a family or shelter from a storm. A living wage makes it possible to participate in what she called the culture of community—to take part in the family, the community, the religious life we all cherish. Confident in our ability to provide for ourselves and for our children, secure in the knowledge that hard work does pay. A minimum wage increase, portable health care, pension security, welfare to work opportunities—that's a plan that's putting America on the right track.

Now, we have to press forward, giving tax cuts for education and child-rearing and child care, buying a first home, finishing that job of balancing the budget without violating our obligations to our parents and our children and the disabled and health care, to education and the environment and to our future. That's a plan that will keep America on the right track, building strong families and strong futures by working together.

For everyone here who played a role in this happy day, I thank you, America thanks you, and our country is better because of your endeavors. God bless you. Thank you.

FEDERAL SURVEY
ON DRUG USE
August 20, 1996

An annual national survey, released August 20, showed that the proportion of adolescents using illegal drugs had more than doubled since 1992 to nearly 11 percent. The findings, which confirmed earlier surveys showing an upward trend in teenage drug abuse, quickly became the subject of intense election year politicking, with Republicans claiming that a large part of the increase was attributable to what they viewed as the permissiveness of the Clinton administration.

The survey findings were "nothing short of a national tragedy," Republican presidential nominee Bob Dole said at a campaign stop in Louisville, Kentucky, after the survey results were released. Drug abuse "is a bipartisan issue," countered Donna E. Shalala, secretary of health and human services, at a news conference announcing the results of the survey. "These are all of our children."

The National Household Survey on Drug Abuse (NHSDA) found that after declining steadily since 1979, drug use among young teenagers had begun to climb again, moving from a low of 5.3 percent in 1992, to 8.2 percent in 1994, and to 10.9 percent in 1995. Overall, an estimated 12.8 million Americans, or 6.1 percent of the population twelve years old or older, had used an illegal drug in the month before the survey. That was down from a high of 25.4 million (14.1 percent) in 1979, and only slightly above the low of 12 million (5.8 percent) recorded in 1992. The NHSDA had been conducted every year since 1971; since 1992 the survey had been directed by the Substance Abuse and Mental Health Services Administration within the Health and Human Services Department.

An increase in marijuana accounted for most of the rise in drug use among twelve- to seventeen-year-olds, although the numbers using cocaine and hallucinogens also rose. Cocaine use among young teenagers rose from 0.3 percent in 1994 to 0.8 percent in 1995; current use of hallucinogens went up from 1.1 percent to 1.7 percent. Some 4.5 million adolescents smoked in 1995, more than in 1994 but not a statistically significant increase. According to the survey, however, adolescent smokers were about eight times more likely to use illegal drugs and eleven times more likely to drink heavily than were nonsmoking adolescents. (Heavy drinking was defined as five or more drinks on the same occasion on at least five different days in the month before answering the survey.) The Clinton administration cited these data on August 23 in support of its new restrictions on the sale and marketing of tobacco products to teenagers. (Smoking regulations, p. 589)

Causes in the Rise of Teenage Drug Abuse

Although drug use among adolescents was still well below its high point of 16.3 percent in 1979, its steady upward climb was troubling. "The slope of the curve is a very bad slope: it shows an accelerating curve," one drug specialist observed. Drug experts attributed the surge in teenage drug use to several factors. Following the success of the antidrug campaigns in the 1970s and 1980s that saw drug usage cut in half, national and community leaders in the late 1980s and early 1990s turned their attention to other pressing issues. At the same time, drugs once again began to be glorified in movies, TV shows, and song lyrics. Efforts to decriminalize marijuana and to allow its use to relieve pain in the terminally ill may also have sent a subtle message that the drug was not harmful. (Marijuana initiative, p. 755)

As early as 1990, surveys began to show changes in teenage attitudes toward illegal drugs—particularly marijuana. The proportions of students who viewed drugs as dangerous and of those who disapproved of them both began to decline; a year later drug use among adolescents began to rise. This trend in perceptions was continuing in 1996, according to a survey released in February by the Partnership for a Drug-Free America. "Today's teens are less likely to consider drug use harmful and risky, more likely to believe that drug use is widespread and tolerated, and feel more pressure to try illegal drugs than teens did just two years ago," the survey concluded.

Lloyd D. Johnston, a social psychologist at the University of Michigan's Institute for Social Research and the chief researcher on the Monitoring the Future project, which has surveyed drug use among adolescents for years, has suggested that many of these causal factors are facets of what he called "inter-generational forgetting." Drug use declined so swiftly between 1985 and 1990, Johnston said, that "this generation doesn't know about the dangers of drugs the way the last one did."

"Each new generation needs to learn the same lessons about drugs if they're going to be protected from them," Johnston told the New York Times *in February. "Unless we do an effective job of educating the newer generations, they're going to be more susceptible to using drugs and have their own epidemic. And I think that's what is happening now."*

In their news conference, both Shalala and Clinton's drug czar, retired Gen. Barry R. McCaffrey, emphasized the importance of educating children and teenagers about the dangers of drug abuse. "None of us can afford to forget that youth substance abuse is an American problem—not a gov-

ernment problem," Shalala said, "and it is going to take the leadership" of citizens, communities, and especially parents "to save our children."

McCaffrey acknowledged that the administration had "done an inadequate job" of "explaining the centrality" of drug education and prevention. "It is not enough to have an annual antidrug day for high school seniors," he said. "There has to be a consistent message from kindergarten onward" that use of illegal drugs is dangerous. To that end, Shalala said, the Clinton administration was taking several steps to increase education efforts, including working with parent-teacher organizations, the entertainment industry, the Weekly Reader, *and* Scholastic Magazine *to get antidrug materials into schools and to parents. "The message must be clear," she said. "Drugs are illegal, they're dangerous, and they're wrong."*

Drug Abuse as a Campaign Issue

The Dole campaign immediately seized on the survey findings as evidence that the Clinton administration was soft on drugs. "We shouldn't be surprised that Clinton is losing the war on drugs," said Haley Barbour, chairman of the Republican National Committee, in a statement issued August 20 after the survey was released. "From the beginning he has treated illegal drug use with a wink and nod in his policies, appointments, and the attitude of his administration."

Dole had already been chiding the president as permissive, citing Clinton's admission during the 1992 presidential campaign that he had tried marijuana as a student and allegations that several young members of the Clinton White House staff had previously used drugs. Dole also pointed to Clinton's sizable reduction of the White House drug control policy staff shortly after taking office in 1993 as evidence that the president was neglecting the drug issue. Another four years of inattention, Dole said, would lead to "staggering" increases in teenage drug use. Dole promised voters that if he were elected, he would ensure enough staff and funding to get the job done.

Clinton was not particularly outspoken on the drug issue in his first years in office, but as the presidential election neared, he began to take action. Early in 1996 he restored the drug control policy staff to its full strength, named McCaffrey to head the office, and gave the post Cabinet status; McCaffrey had been running the government's drug interdiction efforts in Latin America. Clinton also sought a record $13.8 billion for federal antidrug programs in fiscal 1996, and he promised to make federal aid for building prisons conditional on states setting up comprehensive testing and treatment programs for inmates and parolees, a high proportion of whom abuse drugs.

When Dole began his attacks on Clinton's antidrug record, the president's campaign was quick to point out that the Republican-controlled Congress had drastically reduced funding for drug prevention and treatment programs in 1995 and that Senate appropriators had tried to kill the White House drug control policy office altogether.

Experts in drug policy were pleased with the attention the presidential campaign was giving to drug abuse problems, but cautioned that more than rhetoric was needed. "We're very happy that the politicians are on this issue, as long as it goes beyond finger-pointing," one spokesman for a coalition of community organizations combating illegal drug use told the New York Times.

Following are excerpts from the "Preliminary Estimates from the 1995 National Household Survey of Drug Abuse," released August 20, 1996, by the Office of Applied Studies in the Substance Abuse and Mental Health Services Administration:

Any Illicit Drug Use

• In 1995, an estimated 12.8 million Americans were current illicit drug users, meaning they had used an illicit drug in the month prior to interview. This represents 6.1 percent of the population 12 years old and older.

• Marijuana is the most commonly used illicit drug, used by 77 percent of current illicit drug users. . . . Approximately 57 percent of current illicit drug users used marijuana only, 20 percent used marijuana and another illicit drug, and the remaining 23 percent used only an illicit drug other than marijuana in the past month. An estimated 5.6 million Americans (2.6 percent of the population) were current users of illicit drugs other than marijuana and hashish.

• The number of current illicit drug users did not change between 1994 and 1995 (12.6 and 12.8 million, respectively). The number of current illicit drug users was at its highest level in 1979 (25.4 million, 14.1 percent), declined until 1992 (12.0 million, 5.8 percent), and has remained at approximately the same level since then. . . .

Age

• Rates of drug use show substantial variation by age. Among youths age 12–13, 4.5 percent were current illicit drug users. The highest rates were found among young people age 16–17 (15.6 percent) and age 18–20 (18.0 percent). Rates of use were lower in each successive age group, with only about one percent of persons age 50 and older reporting current illicit use. . . .

• Nearly half of young adults age 21–25 had tried illicit drugs at least once in their lifetime, and 12 percent were current users. More than half of adults age 26–44 had tried illicit drugs, but rates of current use were only 8.3 percent for those age 26–34 and 5.6 percent for those age 35–44.

• In 1995, 27.1 percent of current illicit drug users were age 35 and older. This percentage increased from 1979, when 10.3 percent of illicit drug users were age 35 and older, until 1990, when the percentage was 26.1 percent.

• The percentage of adolescents (12–17 years old) using drugs increased between 1994 and 1995, continuing a trend that began in 1993. In 1992, the rate of past month use among youth age 12–17 reached a low of 5.3 percent, the result of a decline from 16.3 percent in 1979. By 1994 the rate had climbed back up to 8.2 percent, and in 1995 it increased again to 10.9 percent. . . .

• Between 1994 and 1995, the percentage of adults reporting past month illicit drug use remained about the same. In 1995 the rates were 14.2 percent for persons age 18–25, 8.3 percent for those age 26–34, and 2.8 percent for those age 35 and older. . . .

• In 1979, the peak year for illicit drug use, rates were 38.0 percent for those age 18–25, 20.8 percent for those age 26–34, and 2.8 percent for persons age 35 and older. . . .

• In general, the aging of people in the heavy drug using cohorts of the late 1970s, many of whom continue to use illicit drugs, has diminished any observable reductions in use among the 35+ group and has resulted in an overall shift in the age distribution of the population of illicit drug users. This shift in the age composition of drug users is also reflected in data from the Drug Abuse Warning Network (DAWN), which shows that visits by patients age 35 and older to hospital emergency rooms for drug related problems have increased in recent years. . . . For example, in 1985, 19 percent of cocaine-related episodes involved persons age 35 and older. By 1995, this percentage had increased to 43 percent.

Race/Ethnicity

• The rate of current illicit drug use for blacks (7.9 percent) remained somewhat higher than for whites (6.0 percent) and Hispanics (5.1 percent) in 1995. However, among youths the rates of use are about the same for the three groups.

• The rate of current illicit drug use for youths in "other" race/ethnicity groups increased from 2.7 percent to 11.2 percent between 1994 and 1995. This result should be viewed with caution, however, as the NHSDA [National-al Household Survey on Drug Abuse] sample size is small for this group. This racial/ethnic group is comprised mainly of Asian Americans, Pacific Islanders, and Native Americans.

• Most current illicit drug users were white. There were an estimated 9.6 million whites (75 percent of all users), 1.9 million blacks (15 percent), and 1.0 million Hispanics (8 percent) that were current illicit drug users in 1995.

• There were no significant changes in rates between 1994 and 1995 for any of the racial/ethnic groups. However, the recent (between 1992 and 1995) increase in illicit drug use among youths has occurred among white, black and Hispanic youths.

Gender

• As in 1994, men continued to have a higher rate of current illicit drug use than women (7.8 percent vs. 4.5 percent) in 1995.

Region/Urbanicity

• The current illicit drug use rate ranged from 7.8 percent in the West region to 4.9 percent in the Northeast.

- There was little difference in rates of use in large metropolitan areas, small metropolitan areas, and nonmetropolitan areas.

Education

- Illicit drug use rates remain highly correlated with educational status. Among young adults age 18–34 years old in 1995, those who had not completed high school had the highest rate of use (15.4 percent), while college graduates had the lowest rate of use (5.9 percent). This is despite the fact that young adults at different educational levels are equally as likely to have tried illicit drugs in their lifetime (50 percent of those not completing high school and 52 percent of college graduates).

Employment

- Current employment status is also highly correlated with rates of illicit drug use, as 14.3 percent of unemployed adults (age 18 and older) were current illicit drug users in 1995, compared with 5.5 percent of full-time employed adults. The rate for full-time employed adults decreased significantly between 1994 (6.7 percent) and 1995 (5.5 percent). . . .
- Seventy-one percent of all current illicit drug users age 18 and older (7.4 million adults) were employed, including 5.4 million full-time workers and 1.9 million part-time workers.

Marijuana and Hashish Use

- In 1995, an estimated 9.8 million Americans were current (past month) marijuana or hashish users. This represents 4.7 percent of the population aged 12 and older.
- Marijuana is by far the most prevalent drug used by illicit drug users since approximately three quarters (77 percent) of current illicit drug users were marijuana or hashish users in 1995. Because of this, trends and demographic differences are generally similar for any illicit use and marijuana/hashish use.
- Between 1994 and 1995 the rate of marijuana use among youths age 12–17 increased from 6.0 percent to 8.2 percent, continuing a trend that began during 1992–93. Since 1992, the rate of use among youth has more than doubled. Similar trends are evident among both boys and girls; among whites, blacks, and Hispanics; in all four geographic regions; and in metropolitan and nonmetropolitan areas. . . .
- Frequent use of marijuana, defined as use on at least 51 days during the past year, remained unchanged from 1994 to 1995 at just over 5 million users (5.3 million, 2.5 percent of the population in 1995) but was significantly lower than in 1985, when there were an estimated 8.4 million frequent users (4.4 percent of the population).

Cocaine Use

- In 1995, an estimated 1.5 million Americans were current cocaine users. This represents 0.7 percent of the population aged 12 and older.

- The number of cocaine users did not change between 1994 and 1995 (1.4 million in 1994). It had declined from 5.7 million in 1985 (3.0 percent of the population) to 1.4 million (0.7 percent of the population) in 1992.
- There were an estimated 582,000 (0.3 percent of the population) frequent cocaine users in 1995. Frequent use, defined as use on 51 or more days during the past year, was not significantly different than in 1994, when there were an estimated 734,000 frequent cocaine users. Since this measure of frequent cocaine use was first estimated in 1985, no significant increases or decreases have been detected. It should be noted that these estimates are subject to large sampling error and potentially large nonsampling error.
- The estimated number of occasional cocaine users (people who used in the past year but on fewer than 12 days) was 2.5 million in 1995, similar to what it had been in 1994. The number of users was down significantly from 1985 when it was 7.1 million.
- The estimated number of current crack users was about 400,000 in 1995, and there have been no statistically significant changes since 1988.

Age

- As in the past, the rate of current cocaine use in 1995 was highest among those age 18–25 years old (1.3 percent) and age 26–34 years old (1.2 percent). Rates were 0.8 percent for youths age 12–17 years and 0.4 percent for adults age 35 and older. Except for youths, all of these rates were similar to rates in 1994.
- The past month cocaine use prevalence rate for the 12–17 year old age group increased from 0.3 percent in 1994 to 0.8 percent in 1995. Prior to 1994, the rate among youth had declined from 1.9 percent in 1982. . . .

Other Illicit Drug Use

Prevalence rates for other illicit drugs are smaller and consequently more difficult to accurately measure. There were no major changes in the prevalence of the use of inhalants, heroin or non-medical use of psychotherapeutics between 1994 and 1995. However, a significant increase in hallucinogen use was seen, particularly among youths age 12–17, and a significant increase in the lifetime rate of heroin smoking was evident for the population 12 and older.

- Estimates of heroin use from the NHSDA are considered very conservative due to the probable undercoverage of the population of heroin users. Estimates of lifetime heroin prevalence have generally remained at around 2 million since 1979, and no significant changes in past year or past month prevalence have been detected. While the estimated number of current heroin users was 117,000 in 1994 and 196,000 in 1995, this is not a statistically significant change.
- The 1995 NHSDA estimated that 1.4 million people had smoked heroin in their lifetime. This estimate was about twice as large as the 1994 estimate. Although the change was statistically significant only for the 35-and-older age group, estimates for other age groups were also higher in 1995 than in 1994, including youths age 12–17.

• The rate of current use of hallucinogens increased between 1994 and 1995 (0.5 percent in 1994 and 0.7 percent in 1995). Among youth age 12–17, the rate increased from 1.1 percent to 1.7 percent.

• For inhalants, the overall rate of past month use was 0.4 percent in both 1994 and 1995.

• The estimated prevalence rate of nonmedical use of psychotherapeutics (tranquilizers, sedatives, analgesics, or stimulants) in the past month was 1.2 percent in both 1994 and 1995.

• The estimated number of persons who have tried methamphetamine in their lifetime was 4.7 million (2.2 percent of the population) in 1995. In 1994, the estimate had been 3.8 million (1.8 percent). However, this change was not statistically significant.

Alcohol Use

Estimates of the prevalence of alcohol use are presented primarily for three levels of use, defined for this report as follows:

Current—At least one drink in the past month (includes binge and heavy use).

Binge use—Five or more drinks on the same occasion at least once in the past month (includes heavy use).

Heavy use—Five or more drinks on the same occasion on at least five different days in the past month.

• In 1995, approximately 111 million persons age 12 and over were current alcohol users, which was about 52 percent of the total population age 12 and older. About 32 million persons (15.8 percent) engaged in binge drinking, and about 11 million Americans (5.5 percent of the population) were heavy drinkers.

• About 10 million current drinkers were under age 21 in 1995. Of these, 4.4 million were binge drinkers, including 1.7 million heavy drinkers.

• Alcohol usage rates were not significantly different between 1994 and 1995. This was true for all three measures of drinking.

• The level of alcohol use was strongly associated with illicit drug use in 1995, as in prior years. Of the 11.3 million heavy drinkers, 25 percent (2.8 million people) were current illicit drug users. Among binge (but not heavy) drinkers, 18 percent (3.8 million) were illicit drug users. Other drinkers (i.e., past month but not binge) had a rate of 5.5 percent (3.9 million) for illicit drug use, while only 1.9 percent (1.9 million) of nondrinkers were illicit drug users. . . .

Age

• Rates of current alcohol use were above 60 percent for age groups 21–25, 26–29, 30–34, 35–39, and 40–44 in 1995. For younger and older age groups rates were lower. Young adult (18–25 years old) drinkers were the most likely to binge or drink heavily. About half of the drinkers in this age group were binge drinkers and about one in five were heavy drinkers. . . .

Race/Ethnicity

• In 1995, whites continued to have the highest rate of alcohol use at 56 percent. Rates for Hispanics and blacks were 45 percent and 41 percent, respectively. The rates of binge use were lower among blacks (11.2 percent) than among whites (16.6 percent) and Hispanics (17.2 percent). Heavy use showed no statistically significant differences by race/ethnicity (5.7 percent for whites, 6.3 percent for Hispanics, and 4.6 percent for blacks).

Gender

• Sixty percent of men were past month alcohol users, compared with 45 percent of women. Men were much more likely than women to be binge drinkers (23.8 percent and 8.5 percent, respectively) and heavy drinkers (9.4 and 2.0 percent, respectively). . . .

Education

• In contrast to the pattern for illicit drugs, the higher the level of educational attainment, the more likely was the current use of alcohol. In 1995, 68 percent of adults with college degrees were current drinkers, compared with only 42 percent of those having less than a high school education. Binge alcohol use rates were similar across different levels of education. However, the rate of heavy alcohol use was 3.7 percent among adults who had completed college and 7.1 percent among adults who had not completed high school.

Tobacco Use

• An estimated 61 million Americans were current smokers in 1995. This represents a smoking rate of 29 percent for the population age 12 and older. There was no change between 1994 and 1995 overall.

• Current smokers were more likely to be heavy drinkers and illicit drug users. Among smokers, the rate of heavy alcohol use (five or more drinks on five or more days in the past month) was 12.6 percent and the rate of current illicit drug use was 13.6 percent. Among nonsmokers, only 2.7 percent were heavy drinkers and 3.0 percent were illicit drug users.

• An estimated 6.9 million Americans (3.3 percent of the population) were current users of smokeless tobacco in 1995.

Age

• Approximately 4.5 million youths age 12–17 were current smokers in 1995. The rate of smoking among youths age 12–17 was 20 percent. The rate was 18.9 percent in 1994, but this does not represent a statistically significant change.

• Youths age 12–17 who smoked were about 8 times as likely to use illicit drugs and 11 times as likely to drink heavily as nonsmoking youths. . . .

Trends in Initiation of Drug Use

Estimates of drug use incidence, or initiation, provide another measure of the Nation's drug problem. They can suggest emerging patterns of use among young people. In the past, increases and decreases in incidence have usually been followed by corresponding changes in the prevalence of use. . . .

The incidence estimates are based on retrospective reports of age at first drug use by survey respondents interviewed during 1994–95, and may therefore be subject to several biases. . . . Thus, estimates for these recent years (i.e., 1992–94) may be less stable than other estimates, and should be interpreted with caution.

Marijuana

- An estimated 2.3 million Americans used marijuana for the first time in 1994. The number has been increasing since 1991, after a long-term decrease that had been occurring since 1975. It is interesting to note that the decrease in prevalence of marijuana use that occurred in the 1980s did not begin to occur until several years after the peak in incidence estimates. This suggests that unless there are changes in the factors that influence drug use behaviors, we should not expect decreases in prevalence to occur soon, since incidence was still rising in 1994. The rising incidence seems to be fueled largely by the increasing rate of new use among youths age 12–17 years (from 38 per 1,000 person years in 1991 to 74 per 1,000 person years in 1994). This is in contrast with the epidemic of the late 1960s and early 1970s, which involved increases among youths and young adults. . . .

Cocaine and Crack Cocaine

- The annual number of new cocaine users remained stable from 1990 to 1994, but at a lower level than during the early 1980's. In 1994 there were an estimated 530,000 new users, while during 1980–1984 there had been about 1.3 million cocaine initiates per year. . . .

GAO ON DETERIORATING
CONDITIONS AT NATIONAL PARKS
August 23, 1996

Budget cutbacks and problems stemming from overuse forced some of the nation's most famous national parks to curtail their services to visitors in 1996. Yellowstone, Yosemite, and other popular parks closed campgrounds and hiking trails, and National Park Service officials considered more drastic long-term steps, such as limiting the number of visitors or curbing automobile traffic at some parks.

The General Accounting Office (GAO), the investigative arm of Congress, said in an August 23 report that many of the 369 national parks and related facilities faced serious "internal threats," including overuse and vandalism. The GAO said that the National Park Service, which administers the parks, did not have enough information about those threats to set priorities for dealing with them.

As summer visitors flooded into the parks, news media reports focused on specific problems at some of the most famous sites. The Washington Post, *in an August 21 report, noted a failing water supply system at the Grand Canyon and serious water damage to the Washington Monument. The* Post *cited park service figures showing a maintenance backlog at the parks totaling $4 billion. The park service also estimated that deferred but necessary maintenance at the 23,000 historic structures under its supervision totaled about $1 billion.*

The National Park Service said it had also been forced to cut back on routine operations, such as patrolling backcountry locations at some of the big national parks. At Yosemite, for example, nineteen rangers once patrolled the farther reaches of the park; in 1996 three rangers were left for this patrol. Systemwide, the park service left nearly nine hundred ranger positions unfilled in 1996.

Until the summer of 1996, most cutbacks were not apparent to casual visitors. Starting in 1996, several big parks reduced their services to visitors and closed sections to the public. The Great Smoky National Park in North Carolina and Tennessee closed 20 percent of its campgrounds, a move that effectively reduced overall visitation to the park. Yellowstone closed some of its museums and the Norris campground, one of its largest.

The park service said its overall annual budget increased from $1.1 billion in fiscal 1983 to $1.5 billion in fiscal 1996. Taking inflation into account, the service said its real budget declined by about $200 million. During the same period, the number of visitors to the parks went from 207 million annually to 270 million—an increase of about one-third.

Some park service officials said long-term solutions might have to include limiting the number of visitors allowed at any given time in the most popular parks. At some parks, including Yosemite, officials were dusting off old proposals to ban or sharply cutback automobile traffic.

New Parks Added

Even while existing parks were forced to trim their budgets and curtail services, new parks and national monuments were added to the system. A major parks bill cleared by Congress on October 3 gave park status to the Presidio (a former military base on 1,400 acres of valuable real estate in San Francisco) and authorized a federal purchase of the privately owned Sterling Forest in northern New Jersey and southern New York.

President Bill Clinton on September 18 added a huge tract of land to the park system: the Grand Staircase-Escalante National Monument, consisting of 1.7 million acres of red rock canyonlands in southern Utah. Clinton used the same authority—which did not require congressional approval— that Theodore Roosevelt invoked to protect the Grand Canyon in 1908. Four other national parks in Utah originally were designated as national monuments and later upgraded to park status.

Clinton acted, over the objections of business interests and most Utah officials, to protect the area from coal mining and other development. The area, most of which was already owned by the Bureau of Land Management, became the largest national monument in the country.

GAO Report

In response to a request from Rep. Bill Richardson, D-N.M., the General Accounting Office on August 23 released a report documenting what it called "internal threats" to the national park system. The GAO report covered a sampling of the types of units within the park service: four national parks, one historical park, one military park, one lakeshore park, and one national recreation area. The report quoted officials at those facilities as identifying 127 internal threats, including such problems as overuse, commercial development within the parks, vandalism and looting, and the growth of "nonnative plant or animal species that degrade the park's resources."

Park managers told the GAO that most of the problems had become more severe during the previous decade, including those related to the growing number of visitors to the parks. The park service had acted to mitigate some of the problems, but the steps were limited, such as closing hiking trails that were deteriorating from overuse. In many cases, the individual parks had neither the authority nor the resources to implement permanent solutions to overuse and other problems.

One obstacle the park service faced, according to the GAO, was a lack of systemwide information about threats to its facilities. Because it could not identify those threats, the GAO said, the park service "is not fully equipped to meet its mission of preserving and protecting these resources." Among other things, the park service needed to be able to set priorities "so that the greatest threats can be addressed first," the GAO said.

The GAO report quoted park service officials as saying they did have enough information on which to make decisions. The GAO said park service officials insisted they were trying to improve the amount and quality of that information.

Corporate Sponsorship and Fee Increases

Congress in 1996 considered, but did not approve, a proposal allowing corporate "sponsorship" of the national parks. Under the proposal, about ten corporations each year would be allowed to become official sponsors of the park system, in return for contributions of $10 million each to a park fund. The corporations could advertise their sponsorship but could not offer products or services related to that sponsorship within the parks.

Although park officials and supporters were eager for the additional funding, many were concerned about the potential for commercial exploitation of the parks. "Hopefully, you won't have Bridal Veil Falls brought to you by Fuji," Dave Mihalic, superintendent of Glacier National Park in Montana, told the New York Times. *"We have to ask ourselves: What are we selling? There's a value to corporations and to us, but these are international treasures."*

Some environmental groups opposed the sponsorship provision on grounds that it would lead to unseemly commercialization of the parks. They pointed to the widespread corporate sponsorship of American participation in the Olympics as an example of how such a system could get out of hand. The proposal had administration support, but several Democratic senators managed to block it in the closing weeks of the session.

In its fiscal 1997 appropriations bill for the Interior Department and other agencies (PL 104–208), Congress gave the park service limited authorization to raise fees in some facilities. The service for years had been barred from increasing park fees; in some parks, fees were the same in 1996 as when the parks were founded fifty or seventy years earlier.

Following are excerpts from the report, "National Park Service: Activities Within Park Borders Have Caused Damage to Resources," issued August 23, 1996, by the General Accounting Office, in which the GAO assessed internal threats to eight parks and other facilities:

Results in Brief

While the Park Service does not have a national inventory of the threats to the parks' resources, individual park units may have resource management and other databases that contain information on the threats. Specific information on the number and types of threats facing the parks is not generally consolidated in the parks or nationally. Without systemwide data on the threats to the parks' resources, the agency is not fully equipped to meet its mission of preserving and protecting these resources.

Park managers have, however, acquired knowledge of the threats to individual parks through their professional training and experience. Cultural and natural resource managers at the eight parks we studied identified 127 internal threats that directly affected the parks' resources. Most of these threats fell into one of five categories: the impact of private inholdings or commercial development within the parks, the impact of nonnative wildlife or plants on native species or other resources of the parks, the damage caused by illegal activities such as poaching, the routine wear and tear on the parks' resources stemming from visitors' daily use of the parks, and the unintended adverse effects of the agency's or park managers' actions (e.g., the accumulation of undergrowth because of past decisions to suppress naturally caused fires, which could result in a more serious fire). Overall, the park managers said that the most serious threats facing the parks were shortages in three areas—staffing, funding, and resource knowledge. While the managers emphasized these as threats, we classified them as indirect ones because, according to the managers, the insufficiencies in these areas caused many of the conditions now directly threatening the parks' resources. This report focuses on the conditions that directly threaten resources.

In the eight parks we reviewed, the managers said that more than 80 percent of the 127 direct threats have already caused more than minor damage to the parks' resources. The relative severity of the damage caused by various types of threats ranged from temporary to permanent. For example, cultural resources such as historic rock art or other archeological resources have suffered more permanent damage than natural resources in many areas. While much of the damage to cultural resources is irreversible, the damage to natural resources, such as native vegetation or wildlife, is not as likely to be permanent, according to the park managers.

The majority (77 of 127) of the direct internal threats to resources, such as the impact of increased visitation and the threat of more serious fires, have worsened over the past decade, according to the park managers. About one-fourth (34) of the threats remained about the same, and most of the rest have diminished. The managers said, however, that their ability to accurately judge trends in severity was limited because they lack baseline data on the condition of the parks' resources.

The managers at the eight parks we studied reported that some action has been taken to mitigate 104 of the 127 direct internal threats to resources. Many parks have studied the threats to develop ways to address them. Mitigation measures implemented have generally been limited to such actions as closing trails to reduce erosion, installing more rugged equipment to reduce vandalism, and posting signs to inform visitors of the damage resulting from inappropriate activities.

Background

In the 124 years since the first national park, Yellowstone, was created, the national park system has grown to include 369 park units. In all, these units cover more than 80 million acres of land, an area larger than the state of Colorado. The mix of park units is highly diverse and includes more than 20 types; these range from natural resource preserves encompassing vast tracts of wilderness to historic sites and buildings in large urban areas.

The Park Service's mission is twofold: to provide for the public's enjoyment of these parks and to protect the resources so that they will remain unimpaired for the enjoyment of future generations.

The Park Service's 1980 survey of threats found not only that the parks' resources were being harmed but also that improvements were needed in determining what cultural and natural resources existed in each park, what their condition was, and how and to what extent they were being threatened. In response, the Park Service called for the development of resource management plans to identify the condition of each park's resources and the problems with managing them, including significant threats. Three times since 1987, we have reported that the Park Service has made limited progress in meeting the information and monitoring needs it had identified in 1980. Our findings included incomplete, out-of-date, or missing resource management plans and an incomplete inventory of threats, their sources, or mitigating actions.

In 1994, after examining the external threats to the parks, we recommended that the Park Service revise its resource management planning system to identify, inventory, categorize, and assign priorities to these threats; describe the actions that could be taken to mitigate them; and monitor the status of the actions that had been taken. Such an inventory has not been implemented, according to Park Service headquarters officials, because of funding and hiring freezes that have prevented the completion of needed changes to the planning system's guidelines and software. In commenting on a draft of this report, the Park Service said that implementing this recommendation is no longer appropriate. . . .

Internal Threats to Park Resources
Are a Continuing Problem

For internal, as for external threats, the Park Service has limited systemwide information. It does not have a national inventory of internal threats that integrates information it already has, and many of its individual units do not have a readily available database on the extent and severity of the threats arising within their borders.

However, in commenting on this report, Park Service officials told us that headquarters has the systemwide information it needs to make decisions and that many decisions are made at the park level, where the superintendents decide what information is needed. They added that rather than developing a database of threats to resources, they need better data on the condition of resources to allow park managers to identify those that are the most threatened.

According to headquarters officials, the Park Service has developed systems focused on particular categories of resources. Park managers and headquarters staff use these systems to identify, track, or assess problems, resource conditions, or threats. . . .

Although the Park Service's guidance requires the parks to develop resource management plans, it does not require the plans to include specific information on the internal and external threats facing the parks. Such information would assist managers of the national park system in identifying the major threats facing parks on a systemwide basis, and it would give the managers of individual parks an objective basis for management decisions.

Threats Identified by Managers at the Eight Parks We Reviewed

At the eight parks studied, the managers identified 127 internal threats that directly affected natural and cultural resources. Most of these threats fell into one of five broad categories: the impact of private inholdings or commercial development within the parks, the results of encroachment by nonnative wildlife or plants, the damage caused by illegal activities, the adverse effects of normal visits to the parks, and the unintended adverse effects of the agency's or park managers' actions. The majority of the threats affected natural resources, such as plants and wildlife, while the remainder threatened cultural resources, such as artifacts, historic sites, or historic buildings.

Overall, the park managers we visited said that the most serious threats facing the parks were shortages in staffing, funding, and resource knowledge. The managers identified 48 additional threats in these categories. We classified these as indirect threats to cultural and natural resources because, according to the managers, the shortages in these areas were responsible for many of the conditions that directly threaten park resources. In addition, the managers identified other threats in such categories as laws or regulations, agency policies, and park boundaries. After reviewing the information about these threats provided by park managers in documents and interviews, we decided that the threats were indirect and should not be listed among the direct threats. In gathering data for each park, we also identified threats to services for visitors.

Our analysis showed that many of these threats also appeared as threats to cultural and natural resources. We did not compile a list of threats to services for visitors because this report focuses on cultural and natural resources.

Private inholdings and commercial development within park boundaries accounted for the largest number of specific threats. The managers of seven of the eight parks we reviewed identified at least one threat in this category. For example, at Olympic National Park in Washington State, the managers said that the homes situated on inholdings along two of the park's largest lakes threatened groundwater systems and the lake's water quality. At Lake Meredith National Recreation Area in Texas, the managers were concerned about the impact of the frequent repair and production problems at about 170 active oil and gas sites and the development of additional sites.

At the Minute Man National Historical Park, the long, linear park is bisected by roads serving approximately 20,000 cars per day. The traffic affects cultural resources, such as nearby historic structures; natural resources, such as populations of small terrestrial vertebrates (e.g., the spotted salamander and spotted turtle); and visitors' enjoyment of the park. . . .

Encroachment by nonnative wildlife and plants—such as mountain goats, trout introduced into parks' lakes and streams, and nonnative grasses and other plants—accounted for the second largest number of reported threats. The managers at all of the parks we reviewed identified at least one threat in this category. . . .

Illegal activities, such as poaching, constituted the third main category of threats. The managers at the eight parks reported that such activities threatened resources. For example, at Crater Lake National Park in Oregon, the managers believe that poaching is a serious threat to the park's wildlife. Species known to be taken include elk, deer, and black bear. . . .

About 30 percent of the internal threats identified by park managers fell into two categories—the adverse effects of (1) people's visits to the parks and (2) the Park Service's own management actions. The number of recreational visits to the Park Service's 369 units rose by about 5 percent over the past 5 years to about 270 million visits in 1995. Park managers cited the effects of visitation, such as traffic congestion, the deterioration of vegetation off established trails, and trail erosion.

The threats created unintentionally by the Park Service's own management decisions at the national or the park level included poor coordination among park operations, policies calling for the suppression of naturally caused fires that do not threaten human life or property, and changes in funding or funding priorities that do not allow certain internal threats to parks' resources to be addressed. For example, at Gettysburg National Military Park, none of the park's 105 historic buildings have internal fire suppression systems or access to external hydrants because of higher-priority funding needs.

Threats Have Damaged Cultural Resources More Permanently Than Natural Resources

Park managers estimated that about 82 percent of the direct threats they identified in the eight parks we reviewed have caused more than minor damage to the parks' resources. We found evidence of such damage at each of the eight parks. According to the managers, permanent damage to cultural resources has occurred, for example, at Indiana Dunes National Lakeshore in

Indiana and at Arches National Park in Utah. Such damage has included looting at archeological sites, bullets fired at historic rock art, the deterioration of historic structures, and vandalism at historic cemeteries. At both of these parks, the managers also cited damage to natural resources, including damage to vegetation and highly fragile desert soil from visitors venturing off established trails and damage to native plants from the illegal use of off-road vehicles. . . .

Managers Generally Saw Threats Increasing in Severity

At all eight parks, internal threats are more of a problem than they were 10 years ago, according to the park managers. They believed that about 61 percent of the threats had worsened during the past decade, 27 percent were about the same, and only 11 percent had grown less severe.

At seven of the eight parks, the managers emphasized that one of the trends that concerned them most was the increase in visitation. They said the increasing numbers of visitors, combined with the increased concentration of visitors in certain areas of many parks, had resulted in increased off-trail hiking, severe wear at campgrounds, and more law enforcement problems. At Arches National Park, for example, where visitation has increased more than 130 percent since 1985, greater wear and tear poses particular problems for the cryptobiotic soil. This soil may take as long as 250 years to recover after being trampled by hikers straying off established trails, according to park managers.

Another increasing threat noted by managers from parks having large natural areas (such as Crater Lake, Olympic, and Lake Meredith) is the possibility that undergrowth, which has built up under the Park Service's protection, may cause more serious fires. According to the managers, the Park Service's long-standing policy of suppressing all park fires—rather than allowing naturally occurring fires to burn—has been the cause of this threat.

Although the park managers believed that most threats were increasing in severity, they acknowledged that a lack of specific information hindered their ability to assess trends reliably. The lack of baseline data on resource conditions is a common and significant problem limiting park managers' ability to document and assess trends. They said that such data are needed to monitor trends in resource conditions as well as threats to those resources.

Mitigation Has Been Limited Primarily to Studies

Park managers said that they believed some action had been taken in response to about 82 percent of the direct threats identified. However, the Park Service does not monitor the parks' progress in mitigating internal threats. Various actions had been taken, but many were limited to studying what might be done. Only two actions to mitigate an identified threat have been completed in the eight parks, according to the managers. However, they noted that in many cases, steps have been taken toward mitigation, but completing these steps was often hampered by insufficient funding and staffing.

At Arches National Park, actions ranged from taking steps to remediate some threats to studying how to deal with others. To reduce erosion and other damage to sensitive soils, park managers installed rails and ropes along some hiking trails and erected signs along others explaining what damage would result from off-trail walking. Managers are also studying ways to establish a "carrying capacity" for some of the frequently visited attractions. This initiative by the Park Service stemmed from visitors' comments about the need to preserve the relative solitude at the Delicate Arch. According to park managers, about 600 visitors each day take the 1½-mile trail to reach the arch. . . .

Conclusions

The natural and cultural resources of our national parks are being threatened not only by sources external to the parks but also by activities originating within the parks' borders. Without systemwide data on these threats to the parks' resources, the Park Service is not fully equipped to meet its mission of preserving and protecting these resources. In times of austere budgets and multibillion-dollar needs, it is critical for the agency to have this information in order to identify and inventory the threats and set priorities for mitigating them so that the greatest threats can be addressed first. . . .

Agency Comments and Our Evaluation

We provided a draft of this report to the Department of the Interior for its review and comment. We met with Park Service officials—including the Associate Director for Budget and Administration, the Deputy Associate Director for Natural Resources Stewardship and Science, and the Chief Archeologist—to obtain their comments. The officials generally agreed with the factual content of the report and provided several technical corrections to it, which have been incorporated as appropriate. . . .

Park Service officials stated that obtaining an inventory of and information on the condition of the parks' resources was a greater priority for the agency than tracking the number and types of threats to the parks' resources, as our previous report recommended. They said that headquarters has the necessary systemwide information to make decisions but added that better data on the condition of resources are needed to allow the park managers to better identify the most threatened resources. They stated that the Park Service is trying to develop a better inventory and monitor the condition of resources as staffing and funding allow. . . .

FDA REGULATIONS TO CURB THE SALE OF TOBACCO TO CHILDREN
August 23, 1996

Calling smoking "the most significant public health problem facing our people," President Bill Clinton on August 23 announced final regulations restricting the sale and marketing of cigarettes and other tobacco products to children under age eighteen. "Today we are taking direct action to protect our children from tobacco and especially the advertising that hooks children on a product," the president said on the eve of the Democratic National Convention.

The regulations were issued amid numerous reports and surveys showing that smoking among teenagers was on the rise and that people who do not smoke as adolescents are unlikely to begin as adults. A survey from the federal Centers for Disease Control (CDC), for example, reported on May 24 that the proportion of high school students under age eighteen who had smoked in the month before the survey had increased from 27.5 percent in 1991 to 34.8 percent in 1995. An estimated 4.5 million children and adolescents smoked in the United States, and another million used smokeless tobacco. Each year another million youngsters become regular smokers, the survey showed. The CDC estimated the health care costs associated with smoking at $50 billion a year. If the regulations achieved their goal of cutting tobacco use among adolescents in half in seven years, the Food and Drug Administration (FDA) projected that eventually between $28 billion to $43 billion in health care costs could be saved each year.

To reach that goal, the controversial regulations not only tightened restrictions on access to tobacco products by children and adolescents but also sharply curbed tobacco advertising that especially appealed to teenagers. "Children are bombarded daily by massive marketing campaigns that play on their vulnerabilities, their insecurities, their longings to be something in the world," Clinton said. "Joe Camel promises that smoking will make you cool. Virginia Slims models whisper that smoking will help you stay thin."

Under the new regulations, which would be administered by the FDA, cigarette ads on billboards and in publications that adolescents were likely to read had to be in black-and-white text with no pictures. Cigarette makers were barred from advertising their brand products on T-shirts, sporting goods, baseball caps, or other promotional items. While tobacco companies could sponsor events in their corporate name, they were not allowed to sponsor any sporting, cultural, or other event in the brand name, logo, or colors that would associate the event with a particular brand of cigarettes or smokeless tobacco.

Cigarette manufacturers, advertisers, distributors, and retailers opposed the regulations, arguing that the FDA did not have the legal authority to regulate tobacco products and that the restrictions on advertising were an unconstitutional infringement on their rights of free speech. All four groups had filed legal challenges to the regulations when the FDA first proposed them in August 1995. Those suits had been on hold in a federal district court in North Carolina, awaiting publication of the final regulations. Many Republicans also voiced opposition to the new rules. (Proposed cigarette regulations, Historic Documents of 1995, p. 670)

The Regulations

Although the FDA received more than 700,000 pieces of mail commenting on its proposed regulations, the final regulations did not differ substantially from those originally proposed. The rules made it a federal violation to sell tobacco products to anyone under eighteen; all fifty states already prohibited sales to minors, but surveys showed that most minors had little trouble buying cigarettes. Retailers were required to check ID cards for anyone who looked twenty-six or younger. The rules banned the distribution of free samples and prohibited the sale or distribution of the so-called kiddie packs—single cigarettes and packages with fewer than twenty cigarettes. The rules also banned vending machines and self-service displays except in places that served only adults, such as night clubs.

The regulations aimed at reducing the appeal of tobacco products to adolescents were much more controversial than those limiting access. The rules banned outdoor advertising within one thousand feet of schools and public playgrounds. All other outdoor advertising, including signs on buses and in stores, had to be in black-and-white text only. Use of color and imagery was prohibited. The same restriction applied to advertising in any publication with "significant" readership under age eighteen; significant was defined as more than 15 percent or more than two million readers. Magazines such as Rolling Stone *and* Sports Illustrated *would have to follow the ad restrictions;* Time *and* Newsweek *would not.*

Cigarette makers were also barred from selling or giving away promotional products such as caps and gym bags that carried the brand name or logo of any cigarette or smokeless tobacco. Manufacturers could no longer use their brand names or logos in sponsoring sporting or entertainment events. The final regulations extended these prohibitions to auto racing and rodeos, which had not been covered in the proposed rules. To give companies time to meet the sponsorship requirements, this part of the regulation would not take effect until August 1998. Most of the other regulations would take effect in August 1997, but the requirement to check ID cards to ensure no sales to minors was scheduled to go into effect in February 1997.

The final regulations dropped a proposal to require cigarette makers to set up a $150 million fund to educate youngsters about the dangers of smoking. Instead, the FDA said it would seek to require the six tobacco companies that it said had attracted the largest numbers of underage smokers to run a campaign, including television spots, warning youngsters about these dangers.

The Legal Challenges

It was unclear whether the restrictions on advertising would survive a constitutional challenge that was filed by a coalition of advertising agencies and publishers even before the final regulations were announced. In May the Supreme Court struck down state restrictions on liquor advertising, although that case (44 Liquormart, Inc. v. Rhode Island) involved a ban on advertising directed at adults, while the FDA regulations sought to restrict ads aimed at children.

The Supreme Court has generally said that commercial speech such as advertising is protected by the First Amendment unless the government shows a substantive reason for restricting it and demonstrates that the restrictions are narrowly drawn to achieve that purpose. The FDA argued that its rules were narrowly drawn to achieve a substantial government interest—protecting the health of children and young adolescents. Cigarette manufacturers are still free to market their products to adults, the FDA said, noting that the regulations do not affect the content of the advertising, only its appearance.

The advertisers disagreed, saying that the regulations would make most cigarette advertising ineffective. "Ads which contain no color and no pictures amount to no advertisements at all," said a spokesman for the Freedom to Advertise Coalition. Hal Shoup of the American Association of Advertising Agencies said August 23 that the coalition's "quarrel is with the violation of the right to speak truthfully about legal products. These regulations are clearly unconstitutional, they are unauthorized, and they will be ineffective. They make good headlines but they make lousy policy."

The other major legal issue was whether the FDA had authority to regulate cigarettes. Under the Federal Food, Drug, and Cosmetic Act, the FDA has jurisdiction over drugs or devices "intended to affect the structure or any function of the body." Asserting that cigarettes and smokeless tobacco were delivery devices for nicotine, which was widely recognized to be an addictive drug, the FDA said that by the design of its products, the tobacco industry "intended" its customers to become addicted to nicotine.

The manufacturers argued that Congress never gave the FDA the authority to regulate tobacco. "Our position on this issue is clear: kids should not *smoke, nor should they have access to tobacco products," Steven Parrish, senior vice president for corporate affairs for Philip Morris Companies, said in a statement released August 23. But, he continued, "We are equally committed to defending our right to manufacture and sell cigarettes and the rights of adult smokers to purchase and smoke those cigarettes. . . . [W]e will continue to vigorously oppose the FDA's illegal seizure of jurisdiction over tobacco products."*

The Political Reaction

Republicans, especially those from tobacco states, were quick to denounce the regulations. "The president is in effect declaring war on 76,000 North Carolinians who gain their livelihood in one form or another from tobacco," said North Carolina's senior senator, Jesse Helms.

Republican presidential nominee Bob Dole did not attack the regulations directly, in part because they were popular with voters, both smokers and nonsmokers, and in part because Dole had suffered a great deal of negative publicity earlier in the campaign when he suggested that nicotine might not be addictive. Various spokespeople in his campaign charged that Clinton's announcement was timed to draw attention away from a report released three days earlier showing that drug use among adolescents was going up. Elizabeth Dole, wife of the Republican nominee, said the rules were simply "an election-year gimmick." Dole's campaign press secretary said the announcement "was designed to distract attention from Bill Clinton's abject failure in the war on drugs." In response, Clinton's campaign secretary said that Dole faced "a big decision. Protect children or protect the tobacco lobby." (Survey on teenage drug use, p. 570)

> *Following are excerpts from the executive summary of "The Regulations Restricting the Sale and Distribution of Cigarettes and Smokeless Tobacco to Protect Children and Adolescents," issued August 23, 1996, by the Food and Drug Administration, and the text of a response to those regulations issued the same day by Steven Parrish, senior vice president of corporate affairs for the Philip Morris Companies, Inc.:*

EXECUTIVE SUMMARY

I. Introduction

With the August 1996 publication of a final rule on tobacco in the Federal Register, the Food and Drug Administration (FDA) will regulate the sale and distribution of cigarettes and smokeless tobacco to children and adolescents. The action results from the agency's assertion of jurisdiction over tobacco products. This was based on an intensive FDA investigation of the tobacco industry, tobacco use and its health consequences. The rule will prohibit the sale of cigarettes and smokeless tobacco to those under 18 while leaving them on the market for adults.

Tobacco use is the single leading preventable cause of death in the United States. It kills more than 400,000 Americans each year—more people each year than AIDS, car accidents, alcohol, homicides, illegal drugs, suicides, and fires, combined.

The use of tobacco products, and the resulting nicotine addiction, begins predominantly in children and adolescents and is, consequently, a pediatric disease. Approximately 3 million American adolescents currently smoke, and an additional 1 million adolescent males use smokeless tobacco. Each year, another 1 million young people become regular smokers. Approximately one out of every three of these young people will die prematurely as a result.

Studies suggest that anyone who does not begin to use tobacco as a child or adolescent is unlikely to start as an adult. Eighty-two percent of adults who ever smoked had their first cigarette before age 18, and more than half of them had already become regular smokers by that age. Among smokers ages 12 to 17 years, 70 percent already regret their decision to smoke and 66 percent say that they want to quit.

Furthermore, studies show that children and adolescents are starting to smoke at earlier and earlier ages. Data reported in December 1995 showed that the proportion of 8th- and 10th-graders who reported smoking in the 30 days before the survey had risen by one-third since 1991, to about 19 percent and 28 percent respectively.

Similar problems exist with underage use of smokeless tobacco. School-based surveys in 1991 estimated that 19.2 percent of 9th- to 12th-grade boys use smokeless tobacco.

Finally, studies show that young people do not fully understand the serious health risks of these products, or believe that those risks do not apply to them. They are also very impressionable and therefore vulnerable to the sophisticated marketing techniques employed by the tobacco industry, techniques that associate the use of tobacco products with excitement, glamour, and independence.

The wealth of information assembled by the agency about nicotine's addictive properties led FDA to conclude that it has jurisdiction over tobacco products. The age of onset of nicotine addiction, and its well-known consequences, suggested the best way for the agency to regulate tobacco to protect the public health.

Of the fifty million people who smoke cigarettes, 77–92 percent are addicted. Because an outright ban of tobacco products could have profound health consequences for these tens of millions of addicted smokers, FDA has chosen instead to focus on preventing children and adolescents from becoming addicted to these products in the first place. Evidence in the administrative record (the collection of documents gathered by FDA during its investigation and made publicly available) demonstrates that the most effective way to achieve this goal is to limit the access to, and appeal of, cigarettes and smokeless tobacco to children and adolescents.

Specifically, the rule makes the sale of cigarettes and smokeless tobacco to children and adolescents, anyone younger than 18 years of age, a federal violation. In addition, the rule requires manufacturers, distributors, and retailers to comply with certain conditions regarding the sale, distribution and promotion of tobacco products. It prohibits all free samples and limits retail sales in most circumstances to face-to-face transactions. As a result, vending machines and self-service displays are prohibited, except in facilities where the retailer or operator ensures that no person younger than 18 is present or is permitted to enter at any time.

The rule limits advertising generally to a black-and-white, text-only format to ensure that advertising is not used to create demand for these products among young people and thus undermine the restrictions on access. Billboards and other outdoor advertising are prohibited within 1,000 feet of schools and public playgrounds. The sale and distribution of non-tobacco items, such as hats and tee shirts that carry cigarette logos, such as Joe Camel, are prohibited, and sponsorship of sporting and other events is limited to the corporate name only.

[Part II omitted]

III. Overview of Statutory and Constitutional Authority

The federal Food and Drug Administration's authority to carry out its mission to protect the public health derives primarily from the federal Food, Drug, and Cosmetic Act (the act). This statute provides the agency authority to regulate a wide array of consumer products, including drugs and devices.

In order to assert jurisdiction over cigarettes and smokeless tobacco, these products must meet at least one of the definitions of a regulated product. As discussed thoroughly in the 1996 Jurisdictional Determination, FDA has concluded: (1) that cigarettes are "combination products," having both a drug component, including nicotine, and device components, namely processed tobacco, the ventilation system, and filters; and (2) that smokeless tobacco is a combination product that consists of a drug component, nicotine, and device components, specifically processed tobacco, and for some products, a porous pouch.

Congress gave the agency considerable latitude to decide whether to regulate drug/device combination products using the act's drug authorities, device authorities, or both. FDA has determined that tobacco products are most appropriately regulated under the device provisions of the act, including the restricted device authority in section 520(e) of the act, which allows the agency to impose restrictions on the sale, distribution, and use of a product.

During the public comment period, some opponents challenged FDA's legal authority to impose the proposed restrictions, arguing that the agency's action would violate various laws and parts of the Constitution, including the Separation of Powers and Nondelegation doctrines, and the First, Fifth, Ninth and Tenth Amendments. After carefully considering these arguments, the agency has concluded that the statutory and constitutional bases of FDA's jurisdiction and regulation are sound.

IV. The Rule

The provisions of the rule are based on the agency's investigation of tobacco products and nicotine's addictiveness, the evidence in the public administrative record, and the review and consideration of the comments received on the proposed rule. In some instances, that review strengthened FDA's original position; in others, it caused the agency to either eliminate or modify some provisions.

1. Restricting Access to Children and Adolescents

The rule makes the sale of cigarettes and smokeless tobacco products to children and adolescents younger than age 18 a violation of federal law. Currently, young people purchase an estimated $1.26 billion of tobacco products annually. Despite laws in all 50 states that prohibit sales to minors, numerous studies show that adolescents have little difficulty purchasing tobacco products. . . .

2. Reducing Appeal of Advertising to Children and Adolescents

In August 1995, FDA announced its proposal to restrict cigarette and smokeless tobacco advertising in ways that would reduce the appeal of such ads to children and adolescents. FDA's purpose in proposing the advertising restrictions was to ensure that the access restrictions are not undermined by advertising that heightens the appeal of cigarettes and smokeless tobacco to young people. The proposed rule included a range of restrictions that attempted to preserve the components of advertising and labeling which can provide product information for adult smokers, while eliminating the imagery and color that make advertising appealing to children and adolescents.

Briefly, the final regulation generally limits tobacco advertising in all existing media forms to a black-and-white, text-only format. Outdoor advertising is prohibited within 1,000 feet of public playgrounds, elementary schools or secondary schools. Advertisements in publications read primarily by adults and advertisements placed in adult-only locations are exempt from any advertising restrictions.

Tobacco companies will not be permitted to sell or distribute promotional items such as tee shirts, caps, and sporting goods identified with tobacco products, for example through use of a brand name or logo. Similarly, logos, brand names, and other identifiers of tobacco products cannot be used in sponsorship of musical, cultural, and other events or on teams and entries. However, sponsored events and entries in the name of a tobacco company may continue.

Tobacco products are among the most heavily advertised in this country, accounting for advertising and promotional expenditures of more than $6 billion in 1993. Studies show that tobacco advertising significantly influences children and adolescents in their decision to start smoking or using smokeless tobacco, and it must be considered in any serious effort to reduce tobacco use among youth.

This aspect of FDA's proposal produced substantial comment that either praised the proposed restrictions as critical to reducing the numbers of children and adolescents who begin using tobacco or attacked the advertising provisions as unwise and unconstitutional. Based on its review of the comments, studies, surveys and expert opinion, the agency has refined some of the advertising restrictions to ensure that they are narrowly tailored to achieve FDA's public health objectives.

a. Impact of Advertising

FDA relied heavily on two reports that summarized the evidence concerning the effect of advertising on young people's tobacco use. One came from the Institute of Medicine, and the other was the 1994 Surgeon General's Report. Both reports concluded that advertising was an important factor in young people's tobacco use, and that restrictions on advertising must be part of any meaningful approach to reducing smoking and smokeless tobacco use among young people.

In reviewing the literature, FDA found hundreds of studies examining psychological and social factors affecting tobacco use. These studies were conducted by noted researchers in the fields of medicine, psychology, marketing, public health, and other disciplines, and were published in respected, peer-reviewed scientific journals. Overall, the research provides strong evidence that restrictions on the advertising of cigarettes and smokeless tobacco will serve to protect the health of children and adolescents.

Collectively, the studies show that children and adolescents are widely exposed to, aware of, respond favorably to, and are influenced by cigarette advertising. One study found that 30 percent of 3 year olds and 91 percent of 6 year olds identified Joe Camel as a symbol for smoking. Other studies have shown that young people's exposure to cigarette advertising is positively related to smoking behavior and their intention to smoke. Still others have suggested that cigarette advertising helps young people to decide what is normal or socially acceptable behavior, and that those who overestimate the prevalence of smoking seem to be more likely to begin smoking and progress to regular smoking. Finally, brand advertising appears to be particularly effective with children and adolescents. The three most heavily advertised brands are smoked by 86 percent of young people who smoke; by contrast, adults are far more likely to choose one of the "generic" brands, which are advertised less.

The tobacco and advertising industries were critical of FDA's proposed regulation, focusing their criticism on the failure of the evidence to establish empirically that advertising causes young people to use tobacco, or on whether each proposed restriction would substantially reduce young people's smoking and use of smokeless tobacco. Moreover, they argued that FDA should not eliminate imagery and color since these are essential elements of effective advertising to adults.

In contrast, a comment from the nation's largest psychological association contended imagery and color in advertisements should be eliminated because of their effectiveness in appealing to children. The comment maintained that children generally have less information-processing ability than adults, are less able or less willing to heed the factual information in advertisements, and are less motivated to carefully consider information such as tar and nicotine content or the Surgeon General's warnings in cigarette and smokeless tobacco advertising.

In the final regulation, FDA narrowed the advertising restrictions as much as possible to retain the informational value that advertising has for adults. Information regarding price, tar and nicotine levels, and taste, information typically important to adults who smoke, can be communicated effectively to adults through words alone.

b. The First Amendment

Those opposed to the regulation criticized the proposed rule for violating the First Amendment and understating the protection that commercial speech is afforded. In support of this contention, their comments not only relied on traditional First Amendment jurisprudence, but cited as well to two recent cases, *Rubin v. Coors*, 115 S. Ct. 1585, and *44 Liquormart, Inc. v. Rhode Island*, 116 S. Ct. 1495 (May 13, 1996). FDA in no way underestimates the protection afforded commercial speech, and did weigh its proposal against the Supreme Court's recent rulings in deciding on the provisions of the final rule.

Other comments maintained that tobacco advertising concerns unlawful activity and that therefore it is not protected by the First Amendment. These comments pointed out that it is unlawful in all 50 states to sell tobacco to children under the age of 18. Opponents argued that it is lawful for adults to buy tobacco, and therefore the advertising for those products cannot be considered to be unlawful. Based on its consideration of these arguments, FDA found that a credible basis exists on which to conclude that, at least to the extent that tobacco advertising is related to sale of these products to children under 18, it is not speech protected by the First Amendment.

However, the agency did not rest its regulation solely on this rationale, but considered whether the rule meets the standards for regulating commercial speech under the three-prong test established in *Central Hudson Gas and Electric Corp. v. Public Service Commission of New York*. The agency's analysis under each prong is provided below.

(1) Is the government's interest substantial? Tobacco use is the leading cause of preventable death in the United States. More than 400,000 people die each year from tobacco-related illnesses. Most people who become addicted to cigarettes begin smoking before they reach the age of 18. Of the one million young people who become regular smokers each year, a third will die prematurely as a result from tobacco use. Even those who opposed the reg-

ulation did not seriously contest that the government had a substantial interest in protecting the health of individuals under 18 years of age.

(2) Do the regulations directly advance the government's interest? Some comments asserted that the agency needs to prove conclusively by empirical evidence that the restrictions that it enacts will completely solve the problem of youth tobacco use. The agency found, based on the available evidence, expert opinion, surveys, and studies, that advertising plays a material role in children's tobacco use, and that the regulation will contribute to a reduction in young people's use of tobacco.

(3) Are the provisions of the regulation narrowly drawn? Comments opposing the proposed restrictions asserted that to meet this requirement, the restrictions must be the "least restrictive means" available. In contrast, a number of comments said that to satisfy this requirement, the restrictions must accomplish a "reasonable fit" between the regulation and the governmental interest to be served. The agency agreed with the latter interpretation, and found that its regulation meets this requirement by restricting only those elements of advertising and promotion that affect young people, while preserving those aspects of advertising that provide information to adults. . . .

RESPONSE BY PHILIP MORRIS

The President's goal of reducing underage tobacco use is shared by Philip Morris. Our position on this issue is clear: kids should not smoke, nor should they have access to tobacco products.

President Clinton has said repeatedly that he would prefer a legislative solution to the very real problem of underage tobacco use. We remain committed and willing to work with the President, the Congress and others for the swift enactment of comprehensive federal legislation with tough enforcement to address the issue of youth smoking.

Our opposition to the FDA's rule rests not with its stated goal of reducing underage tobacco use but with the FDA's specious and arbitrary interpretation of federal law. The rule opens a Pandora's box of regulation that tramples on the Constitution and the rights of millions of adult Americans. We will stand by those adults who choose to smoke.

The FDA's rule sets the stage for restrictions that could lead the agency to do even more to deprive adults of their rights by unilaterally forcing the prohibition of cigarettes. Commissioner [David] Kessler continues to evade questions as to whether the FDA would effectively ban cigarettes. According to an August 4 interview in the *New York Times Magazine*, Commissioner Kessler 'won't say what measures he would take' if the FDA's rule does not reduce youth smoking. However, the agency does claim that it possesses the right to impose a ban by regulatory fiat.

The law and Congressional intent are crystal clear: only Congress can change the law to give FDA the authority to regulate tobacco. The FDA, however, has chosen to ignore the law and Congress by imposing a regulation that is unprecedented, unauthorized, unrealistic and unlawful. This it cannot do.

Congress has amended the Food, Drug, and Cosmetic Act more than 70 times, and has never granted FDA the jurisdiction the agency now claims. Moreover, on more than 20 occasions Congress has rejected specific legislation to do so. And in 1994, prior to the Congressional elections, Commissioner Kessler testified before Congress that he needed Congressional direction before he could assert regulatory jurisdiction over tobacco. He has never received this direction.

Philip Morris U.S.A. is committed to keeping cigarettes away from kids. We have proven our commitment through our recently announced federal legislative proposal to restrict youth access to tobacco products, as well as our Action Against Access initiative.

As committed as Philip Morris U.S.A. is to preventing kids from having access to tobacco products, we are equally committed to defending our right to manufacture and sell cigarettes and the rights of adult smokers to purchase and smoke those cigarettes. On behalf of these individuals—as well as our employees, customers, business partners, tobacco growers and shareholders—we will continue to vigorously oppose the FDA's illegal seizure of jurisdiction over tobacco products.

The company will amend its complaint of its August 10, 1995 lawsuit in the U.S. District Court for the Middle District of North Carolina in order to stop the FDA from proceeding on its illegal course of action, and will continue to support a legislative solution in the Congress to solve underage tobacco use.

DEMOCRATIC NATIONAL CONVENTION AND SPEECHES
August 26–29, 1996

For Bill Clinton, his appearance at the Democratic National Convention August 29 to accept his party's nomination for a second term must have been sweet indeed. In November 1994, midway through his first term in office, Clinton's presidency was in disarray, and the Republicans had seized control of both chambers of Congress for the first time in forty years. A year and a half later, Clinton became the first Democratic incumbent since Lyndon B. Johnson in 1964 to win an uncontested nomination to a second term in office.

The various factions of the often divided Democratic party seemed prepared to put aside their differences, at least until after the November 5 election, and focus their energies on returning Clinton and Vice President Al Gore to the White House and perhaps regaining control of Congress. Unity and centrism were the themes that dominated the convention, held August 26–29 in Chicago's aptly named United Center. Even the party platform was adopted virtually without dissent. (Democratic party platform, p. 623)

The proceedings were in sharp contrast with the last Democratic convention held in Chicago. That was in 1968, when opposition to the Vietnam War tore apart the party and led to riots between antiwar protesters and Chicago police in the streets outside the convention hall.

With no wars imminent and a growing economy, the Clinton administration could set a forward-looking agenda. Throughout the week, in speech after speech, Democrats declared that they were the party of the twenty-first century—and that the Republican nominee, former Senate majority leader Bob Dole, was the candidate of the past.

All the normal convention hoopla was carefully orchestrated to showcase on prime time television the message and achievements of the Clinton administration. From time to time images were beamed into the convention center from the campaign train carrying Clinton from Washington to Chicago through the Midwest. The train, dubbed the "21st Century

Express," began in Huntington, West Virginia, on August 25 and ended in Michigan City, Indiana, on the evening of August 28. From there Clinton flew by helicopter to Chicago in time to watch his nomination from his hotel room.

The only sour note sounded during the convention occurred on the last day, when Clinton's chief campaign strategist, Dick Morris, resigned after a tabloid paper reported his liaison with a prostitute. Republicans seized the incident, saying that it reintroduced the "sleaze factor" in a White House that had been buffeted by several ethics dilemmas. Dole took a different position, arguing that without Morris, Clinton would veer to the left politically. Morris had been the chief architect of the strategy to reposition Clinton as a centrist after the 1994 elections. With Morris's departure, Dole suggested, Clinton's campaign would take on liberal tones.

Carefully Orchestrated Festivities

Like their Republican counterparts, Democratic officials went to great lengths to turn their convention into a tightly scripted television show designed to entertain. Like the Republicans, the Democrats were not entirely successful. Ratings for the three major networks' broadcasts of both conventions were off sharply from four years earlier. Still, as at the Republican convention in San Diego earlier in the month, traditional political speeches were deemed to be less important than scripted moments designed to arouse the public's emotions.

At the opening session on August 26, politicians shared the podium with "real people," such as actor Christopher Reeve, who had been paralyzed from a horse-riding accident in 1995. Speaking from a wheelchair in a strained and sometimes barely audible voice, Reeve called for increased research funding for diseases such as multiple sclerosis, Parkinson's disease, spinal cord injuries, and AIDS.

The symbolic highlight of the evening was an appearance by a pair of lifelong Republicans—James S. Brady, the former press secretary who was grievously wounded in an assassination attempt on Ronald Reagan in 1981, and his wife Sarah. After the shooting, Brady, who remained partly paralyzed, and his wife led a campaign to impose a national seven-day waiting period on people seeking to buy a handgun. Pro-gun rights legislators kept the "Brady bill" bottled up during the Reagan and Bush presidencies; it was not until 1993, after Clinton made it a top legislative priority, that the measure became law. (Clinton on signing Brady bill, Historic Documents of 1993, p. 965)

Two of the Democrats' most liberal and most skilled orators, civil rights leader Jesse Jackson and former New York governor Mario M. Cuomo, fired up the convention delegates on the second day of the convention. Jackson and Cuomo were not totally uncritical of the president, particularly on his signing of welfare reform legislation that was strongly opposed by many in the party's liberal wing. Both men gave rousing endorsements of Clin-

ton's reelection, describing it as a bulwark against what they called the "extremist" policies of the Republican congressional majority. "They are the real threat," Cuomo said.

Jackson and Cuomo were followed to the podium by Hillary Rodham Clinton, who offered a passionate explanation of her view of family values and a refutation of Republican efforts to portray negatively her activist approach to her role as first lady. A native of suburban Chicago, Clinton received a foot-stamping welcome that lasted several minutes. Her family-centered remarks blended the personal and the professional. She spoke about her husband and their experiences raising their daughter and then applied these anecdotes to societal concerns and family-related programs, such as the Family and Medical Leave Act, which the Clinton administration has embraced. The final speaker of the evening was Indiana governor Evan Bayh, widely regarded as a rising Democratic star. Like other speakers of the evening, his keynote address was centered on family issues, such as education.

Gore Speech

The highlight of the third evening was Vice President Gore's speech, which was moved forward one night from its traditional place on the last evening of the convention. Gore first delighted the delegates with jokes about his reputation for stiffness, rallied them with sharp jabs at Dole, and then brought many of them to tears with an emotional recounting of his sister's painful death from lung cancer after a lifetime of cigarette smoking. Only days before, Clinton had approved final federal regulations designed to reduce teenage smoking. (Smoking regulations, p. 589)

Gore began by lauding the Clinton administration's record on domestic and foreign policy. He then turned to the Republican challenger, first giving a tip of the cap to Dole as "a good and decent man" before dismissing him as a political anachronism. "In his [acceptance] speech from San Diego, Sen. Dole offered himself as a bridge to the past," said Gore. "Tonight, Bill Clinton and I offer ourselves as a bridge to the future."

Clinton Nomination and Acceptance Speech

The actual nominations of Clinton and Gore, which followed Gore's speech, seemed almost anticlimactic. Clinton's name was placed in nomination by Sen. Christopher J. Dodd of Connecticut, who hailed the president for leading the nation into an era of prosperity and thanked Dole for the personal sacrifices he had made for his country. Nonetheless, Dodd said, Dole was the wrong choice for president. "It is not Bob Dole's reputation that I question. It is his agenda for America. Sometimes a fine person has flawed ideas. This is such a time," Dodd said. After the formal roll-call of the states, Clinton was declared the party's nominee by unanimous vote.

Capping the final night of the convention August 29, President Clinton promised to "build a bridge to the 21st century" and appealed to Americans for a second term by offering a host of new policy initiatives aimed at help-

ing working Americans and their families. Constrained by his promises to balance the budget and reduce the size of government, most of the initiatives were modest in scope. Clinton's crowning day was clouded by Morris's resignation, but the president did not let the incident knock him off stride.

In his sixty-six minute acceptance speech, Clinton ticked off his administration's achievements, including the creation of ten million new jobs, a substantial reduction in the federal deficit, and the passage of anticrime legislation, which aimed to put 100,000 new police on the nation's streets. He also took pride in the 1.8 million people who moved from the welfare rolls into work.

Among Clinton's proposals were a series of targeted tax cuts, such as tax credits and deductions for college tuition and tax breaks for first-time home buyers. He criticized Dole's plan for a 15 percent cut in income taxes, arguing that it would balloon the federal deficit and require deep cuts in popular government programs.

Clinton contrasted his agenda with the one Dole offered at the Republican convention, where the GOP nominee attempted to offset the issue of his age by saying that he could serve as a bridge to an earlier time in America of "tranquillity, faith, and confidence in action." "With all due respect," Clinton countered, "we do not need to build a bridge to the past. We need to build a bridge to the future."

Following are the text of an address at the Democratic National Convention in Chicago as delivered by Vice President Al Gore on August 28, 1996, and the text of the speech August 29, 1996, by President Bill Clinton accepting his party's nomination for president:

GORE ACCEPTANCE SPEECH

Thank you very much, ladies and gentlemen. Thank you very much.

Four years ago—four years ago, you gave me your nomination to be vice president. Tonight, I want to say from the bottom of my heart, thank you for the opportunity to serve our country and for the privilege of working beside a president who has done so much to lift the lives of America's families.

Tradition holds that this speech be delivered tomorrow night. But President Clinton asked me to speak tonight. And you can probably guess the reason why—my reputation for excitement.

This is some crowd. I've been watching you doing that "macarena" on television. And if I could have your silence, I would like to demonstrate for you the Al Gore version of the macarena.

Would you like to see it again?

Four years ago, America faced a set of problems that our leaders had lost the courage to confront. Our nation was not creating jobs. Our jobs were not increasing pay. Our people were running in place. Our nation was falling behind.

Four years later we meet in this great city of Chicago, the place Carl Sandberg called "the city of the Big Shoulders . . . with lifted head so proud to be alive . . . and strong."

Four years later, Democrats are proud. Our hopes are alive. And America is strong.

Bill Clinton's leadership is paying off. How can you tell?

By what the American people have achieved themselves. Just look at what all of us have created together these last four years.

Ten million new jobs. A deficit cut in half. A smaller, leaner reinvented government working better and costing less. Unemployment and inflation both down. Record exports. Wages on the rise. An economy moving forward.

Empowerment zones bringing neighborhoods back to life. Classrooms being connected to the information superhighway.

Communities given the right to know about environmental dangers. Toxic wastes being cleaned up. Rivers and lakes reclaimed and thriving. An America not just better off, but better.

And our strength at home has led to renewed respect abroad. Nuclear missiles no longer targeted at our cities. Democracy replacing tyranny in Haiti. Peace replacing war in Bosnia. Leadership toward reconciliation in Northern Ireland and the Middle East.

While our nation has made great progress, we have much more to do. And we are here to declare that the man who can help us fashion this better future is President Bill Clinton.

The President's opponent, Senator Bob Dole, is a good and decent man. We honor his service to America and his personal courage in fighting back from injuries sustained in battle.

Though we disagree with his ideas, only the unknowing would deny him the respect he deserves.

But make no mistake: There is a profound difference in outlook between the President and the man who seeks his office. In his speech from San Diego, Senator Dole offered himself as a bridge to the past.

Tonight Bill Clinton and I offer ourselves as a bridge to the future.

[The Party of Hope]

Ralph Waldo Emerson once said, "Humanity is divided between the past and the future . . . between memory and hope."

It is easy to understand the nostalgic appeal of the party of memory and the men who lead it. But let there be no doubt.

The future lies with the party of hope—and the man from Hope who leads it.

We Americans write our own history. And the chapters of which we're proudest are the ones where we had the courage to change.

Time and again, Americans have seen the need for change and have taken the initiative to bring that change to life, but always with a struggle. Always there were opponents.

Senator Dole was there. We remember. We remember that he voted against the creation of Medicare, against the creation of Medicaid, against the Clean Air Act, against Head Start, against the Peace Corps in the '60s, and AmeriCorps in the '90s.

He even voted against the funds to send a man to the moon.

If he's the most optimistic man in America, I'd hate to see the pessimists.

That pessimistic view of America is very different from ours.

And we saw, in the budget that Senator Dole and Speaker Gingrich tried to slip past the American people last fall. Their budget doubled Medicare premiums while slashing benefits, wiped out nursing home care for seniors, ended the guarantee of medical care to disabled children, rolled back protections for our air and water, increased the cost of college while making student loans harder to get, terminated anti-drug programs for our schools, and raised taxes on the hardest-hit working families.

They passed their reckless plan and then demanded that President Clinton sign it. They shut the government down—twice because they thought Bill Clinton would buckle under the pressure, wither in the face of their attacks, cave in to their demands.

But they did not know the true measure of this man.

He never flinched or wavered. He never stooped to their level. And of course, he never attacked his opponent's wife.

Let me tell you what Bill Clinton did do. President Clinton took Speaker Newt Gingrich and Senator Bob Dole into the Oval Office. I was there, I remember. And he said—President Clinton said, "As long as I occupy this office, you will never enact this plan because as long as I am president, I won't let you."

That's why they want to replace Bill Clinton. But we won't let them.

They want someone in that Oval Office who will rubber-stamp their plan. That's why they want to replace Bill Clinton. But we won't let them.

They want a president who will appoint the next three justices of the Supreme Court so they can control all three branches of government and take away a woman's right to choose. That's why they want to replace Bill Clinton. But we won't let them.

They want to give health insurance rip-off artists a license to change Medicare, to let this program for our seniors wither on the vine. That's why they want to replace Bill Clinton. But we won't let them.

They want to outlaw all affirmative action and many other measures to reach out to those who want to reach up. That's why they want to replace Bill Clinton. But we won't let them.

They want to cut education and undermine our schools, put down teachers instead of lifting up students. That's why they want to replace Bill Clinton. But we won't let them.

They want to give free rein to lobbyists for the biggest polluters in America to rewrite our environmental laws, allowing more poison in our air and water, and then auction off our natural wonders piece by piece. That's why they want to replace Bill Clinton. But we won't let them.

We will not, we cannot, we must not let them.

And you know what? We can make Bill Clinton's job a lot easier by making [House Minority Leader] Dick Gephardt [D-Mo.] Speaker of the House and [Senate Minority Leader] Tom Daschle [D-S.D.] Senate majority leader.

You can judge a president by the enemies he is willing to make. You know, someone who's been attacked as much as Bill Clinton is doing something right.

America has never changed without a president willing to confront the status quo and take on the forces of greed and indifference. It has changed only when we have had a president with the vision to tackle the real problems that really matter to our families. That's what this president has done, because families don't eat or breathe political slogans. They thrive or fail according to how they handle each day's challenges.

[Family Issues]

When your alarm goes off in the morning, if your family is like mine, everybody starts rushing around getting ready for school and work.

When one of your children reaches for cereal and fruit, you shouldn't have to worry about whether the food is safe. That's why just this month President Clinton brought farmers and environmentalists together and signed a historic law to keep dangerous pesticides off our fruits and vegetables.

When you pour a glass of water for each member of the family at the table you shouldn't have to wonder, "Should I buy bottled water? We really can't afford it."

That's why President Clinton signed the Safe Drinking Water Act to give, to give families more peace of mind that their water will be pure and safe.

When you notice your child staring at a television set and watching violent and explicit images he or she is not old enough to handle, you shouldn't be forced to choose between throwing the TV out of the house and monitoring every second that child watches. That is why last month the president persuaded the broadcasters to agree to air three hours of quality children's educational programming every single week.

And that's why we're giving parents a new tool, the v-chip, to keep violent and explicit programming out of their homes and away from their children. When our children turn on the TV, let them learn how to read and add and spell and think, not how to kill.

If one of your children has an operation, or some other serious health problem, you shouldn't have to choose between taking care of that child or keeping your job. That is why Bill Clinton fought to pass the Family and Medical Leave Act, so parents can get time off work to care for a sick child, bond with a newborn, or tend to an aging relative.

When your children do well in school and head toward graduation, they shouldn't have to wonder about whether their family can afford to send them to college. That is why President Clinton expanded scholarships, student loans and Pell Grants.

And that's why he wants to give a tax credit to pay $1,500 per year for tuition to make college more affordable for every single American family.

If the business where you work is changing in ways that cause you to think about getting a different kind of job, you ought to be able to get the training and education you need to learn new skills and plan for the future. That's why President Clinton is proposing a tax credit so if you go to a community college, you can take every single dollar you pay right off your taxes. If you take responsibility, President Clinton will give you the opportunity to learn.

And if you see an opportunity to move to a better job, you shouldn't feel forced to stay in your old job just because that's the only way you can keep your health insurance.

Even if you have some pre-existing condition, you ought to be able to change jobs and not lose your coverage. That's why President Clinton signed the Kennedy-Kassebaum law.

Americans shouldn't have to feel imprisoned in their homes because of crime. We have a right to streets and neighborhoods that are safe. That's why President Clinton fought for the Brady Bill and the assault weapons ban, and that's why he's putting 100,000 new community police officers on our streets and sidewalks.

These problems are real, and they must be addressed. It's been a long time since we've had a president so in tune with the issues that touch the real lives of America's families. It's been a long time since we've had a president willing to fight the powerful forces that often seem to stand in the way.

Some of the most powerful forces that do the most harm are often hard to see and even harder to understand.

[Loss of a Sister]

When I was a child, my family was attacked by an invisible force that was then considered harmless. My sister Nancy was older than me. There were only the two of us, and I loved her more than life itself.

She started smoking when she was 13 years old.

The connection between smoking and lung cancer had not yet been established, but years later, the cigarettes had taken their toll. It hurt very badly to watch her savaged by that terrible disease.

Her husband, Frank, and all of us who loved her so much tried to get her to stop smoking. Of course, she should have. But she couldn't.

When she was 45, she had a lung removed. A year later, the disease had come back, and she returned to the hospital. We all took turns staying with her.

One day, I was called to come quickly because things had taken a turn for the worse. By then, her pain was nearly unbearable, and as a result, they used very powerful painkillers. Eventually, it got so bad they had to use such heavy doses that she could barely retain consciousness.

We sometimes didn't know if she could hear what we were saying or recognize us.

But when I responded to that call and walked into the hospital room that day, as soon as I turned the corner, someone said, "Al's here."

She looked up and from out of that haze, her eyes focused tensely right at me. She couldn't speak, but I felt clearly I knew she was forming a question.

Do you bring me hope?

All of us have tried to find whatever new treatment or new approach might help. But all I could do was to say back to her, with all the gentleness in my heart, "I love you."

And then I knelt by her bed and held her hand. And in a very short time, her breathing became labored and then she breathed her last breath.

Tomorrow morning, another 13-year-old girl will start smoking. I love her too.

Three thousand young people in America will start smoking tomorrow. One thousand of them will die a death not unlike my sister's. And that is why until I draw my last breath, I will pour my heart and soul into the cause of protecting our children from the dangers of smoking.

And that is also why I was intensely proud last week when President Clinton stood up for American families by standing up to tobacco advertising aimed at getting our children addicted.

He proposed—he proposed the first-ever comprehensive plan to protect children from smoking, to ban tobacco advertising aimed at our children and to ban it for good.

It took courage for Bill Clinton to take on the tobacco companies. I promise you it is no accident that no president has ever been willing to do it before.

But coming from him, that's no surprise. I've seen him get up day after day and make the toughest decisions, and always by asking what is right for the American people.

As a result, with Bill Clinton's leadership, our nation is moving forward with confidence. Americans don't believe our best days are behind us. We see better days ahead because we have the courage to meet our challenges and protect our values. And now, once again, in pursuit of the American Dream, we are crossing the bridge to the future.

Thirty-three years ago this very day, one American told us about his dream. Martin Luther King Jr. stood in the shadow of the Lincoln Memorial on that August afternoon and described the America that he saw in his mind's eye. He called on our nation "to open the doors of opportunity to all of God's children."

How do we build an America worthy of this dream? Is it with brick and mortar? Is it with second-hand smoke and rear-view mirrors? Or do we build it in the nearest well-raised child?

By shepherding, guiding and protecting our children's souls we build a better America. The American spirit lives within that child. The child grows up to believe in it, to add new vision to it. It's not a vision of a distant future, nor of a remote past, but a constant accumulation of our best instincts and our noblest aspirations.

From the spirit of our Founding Fathers to the courage of today's families it is one vision. It is an American vision. It is the vision of President Bill Clinton.

Thank you, God bless you, and God bless America.

CLINTON ACCEPTANCE SPEECH

Mr. Chairman, Mr. Vice President, my fellow Democrats, and my fellow Americans, thank you for your nomination. I don't know if I can find a fancy way to say this, but I accept.

Thank you.

So many—so many have contributed to the record we have made for the American people, but one above all: My partner, my friend, and the best vice president in our history—Al Gore.

Tonight, I thank the city of Chicago, its great mayor and its wonderful people for this magnificent convention.

I love Chicago for many reasons—for your powerful spirit, your sports teams, your lively politics, but most of all for the love and light of my life—Chicago's daughter, Hillary.

I love you.

You and I set forth on a journey to bring our vision to our country, to keep the American dream alive for all who are willing to work for it, to make our American community stronger, to keep America the world's strongest force for peace and freedom and prosperity.

Four years ago, with high unemployment, stagnant wages, crime, welfare and the deficit on the rise, with a host of unmet challenges and a rising tide of cynicism, I told you about a place I was born, and I told you I still believed in a place called Hope.

Well, for four years now, to realize our vision, we have pursued a simple but profound strategy—opportunity for all, responsibility from all, a strong united American community.

Four days ago as you were making your way here, I began a train ride to make my way to Chicago through America's heartland.

I wanted to see the faces, I wanted to hear the voices of the people for whom I have worked and fought these last four years. And did I ever see them.

I met an ingenious businesswoman who was once on welfare in West Virginia; a brave police officer shot and paralyzed, now a civic leader in Kentucky.

An auto worker in Ohio, once unemployed, now proud to be working in the oldest auto plant in America to help make America No. 1 in auto production again for the first time in 20 years.

I met a grandmother fighting for her grandson's environment in Michigan.

And I stood with two wonderful little children proudly reading from their favorite book, *The Little Engine That Could.*

At every stop, large and exuberant crowds greeted me and, maybe more important, when we just rolled through little towns there were always schoolchildren there waving their American flags, all of them believing in America and its future.

I would not have missed that trip for all the world. For that trip showed me that hope is back in America. We are on the right track to the 21st century.

[Economic Accomplishments]

Look at the facts. Just look at the facts: 4.4 million Americans now living in a home of their own for the first time. Hundreds of thousands of women have started their own new businesses.

More minorities own businesses than ever before. Record numbers of new small businesses and exports.

Look at what's happened. We have the lowest combined rates of unemployment, inflation and home mortgages in 28 years.

Look at what happened. Ten million new jobs, over half of them high-wage jobs. Ten million workers getting the raise they deserve with the minimum-wage law.

Twenty-five million people now having protection in their health insurance because the Kennedy-Kassebaum bill says you can't lose your insurance anymore when you change jobs, even if somebody in your family's been sick.

Forty million Americans with more pension security, a tax cut for 15 million of our hardest working, hardest pressed Americans and all small businesses. Twelve million Americans—12 million of them taking advantage of the Family and Medical Leave Law so they could be good parents and good workers.

Ten million students have saved money on their college loans.

We are making our democracy work.

We have also passed political reform, the line-item veto bill, the motor voter bill, tougher registration laws for lobbyists, making Congress live under the laws they impose on the private sector, stopping unfunded mandates to state and local government.

We've come a long way. We've got one more thing to do. Will you help me get campaign finance reform in the next four years?

We have increased our investments in research and technology.

We have increased investments in breast cancer research dramatically. We are developing a supercomputer, a supercomputer that will do more calculating in a second than a person with a hand-held calculator can do in 30,000 years.

More rapid development of drugs to deal with HIV and AIDS and moving them to the market quicker have almost doubled life expectancy in only four years, and we are looking at no limit in sight to that.

We'll keep going until normal life is returned to people who deal with this.

Our country is still the strongest force for peace and freedom on earth. On issues that once before tore us apart, we have changed the old politics of Washington. For too long, leaders in Washington asked, "Who's to blame?"

But we asked, "What are we going to do?"

On crime, we're putting 100,000 police on the streets.

We made three-strikes-and-you're-out the law of the land. We stopped 60,000 felons, fugitives and stalkers from getting handguns under the Brady Bill.

We banned assault rifles.

We supported tougher punishment and prevention programs to keep our children from drugs and gangs and violence.

Four years now—for four years now, the crime rate in America has gone down.

On welfare, we worked with states to launch a quiet revolution. Today, there are 1.8 million fewer people on welfare than there were the day I took the oath of office.

We are moving people from welfare to work.

We have increased child support collections by 40 percent. The federal work force is the smallest it's been since John Kennedy. And the deficit has come down for four years in a row for the first time since before the Civil War—down 60 percent, on the way to zero.

We will do it.

We are on the right track to the 21st century. We are on the right track, but our work is not finished.

What should we do? First, let us consider how to proceed. Again, I say the question is no longer, "Who's to blame?" but "What to do?"

I believe that Bob Dole and Jack Kemp and Ross Perot love our country. And they have worked hard to serve it.

It is legitimate, even necessary, to compare our record with theirs, our proposals for the future with theirs. And I expect them to make a vigorous effort to do the same.

But I will not attack. I will not attack them personally, or permit others to do it in this party if I can prevent it.

My fellow Americans, this must be. . . . This must be a campaign of ideas, not a campaign of insults. The American people deserve it.

Now, here's the main idea. I love and revere the rich and proud history of America. And I am determined to take our best traditions into the future. But with all respect, we do not need to build a bridge to the past. We need to build a bridge to the future.

And that is what I commit to you to do.

So tonight, let us resolve to build that bridge to the 21st century, to meet our challenges and protect our values.

Let us build a bridge to help our parents raise their children, to help young people and adults to get the education and training they need, to make our streets safer, to help Americans succeed at home and at work, to break the cycle of poverty and dependence, to protect our environment for generations to come, and to maintain our world leadership for peace and freedom.

Let us resolve to build that bridge.

Tonight, my fellow Americans, I ask all of our fellow citizens to join me and to join you in building that bridge to the 21st century.

Four years now—from now—just four years from now—think of it. We begin a new century full of enormous possibilities. We have to give the American people the tools they need to make the most of their God-given potential. We must make the basic bargain of opportunity and responsibility available to all Americans, not just a few. That is the promise of the Democratic Party, that is the promise of America.

I want to build a bridge to the 21st century in which we expand opportunity through education. Where computers are as much a part of the classroom as blackboards. Where highly trained teachers demand peak performance from their students. Where every 8-year-old can point to a book and say, "I can read it myself."

By the year 2000 the single most critical thing we can do is to give every single American who wants it the chance to go to college.

We must make two years of college just as universal in four years as a high school education is today. And we can do it.

We can do it, and we should cut taxes to do it.

I propose a $1,500-a-year tuition tax credit for Americans, a Hope Scholarship for the first two years of college to make the typical community college education available to every American.

I believe every working family ought also to be able to deduct up to $10,000 in college tuition costs per year for education after that.

I believe the families of this country ought to be able to save money for college in a tax-free IRA, save it year in and year out and withdraw it for a college education without penalty.

We should not tax middle-income Americans for the money they spend on college. We'll get the money back down the road many times over.

I want to say here, before I go further, that these tax cuts and every other one I mention tonight are all fully paid for in my balanced-budget plan, line by line, dime by dime, and they focus on education.

Now, one thing so many of our fellow Americans are learning is that education no longer stops on graduation day. I have proposed a new GI Bill for American workers—a $2,600 grant for unemployed and underemployed Americans so that they can get the training and the skills they need to go back to work at better-paying jobs, good high-skill jobs for a good future.

But we must demand excellence at every level of education. We must insist that our students learn the old basics we learned and the new basics they have to know for the next century.

Tonight let us set a clear national goal. All children should be able to read on their own by the third grade.

[An Army of Tutors]

When 40 percent of our 8-year-olds cannot read as well as they should, we have to do something. I want to send 30,000 reading specialists and National Service Corps members to mobilize a volunteer army of one million reading tutors for third graders all across America.

They will teach our young children to read.

Let me say to our parents: You have to lead the way. Every tired night you spend reading a book to your child will be worth it many times over. I know that Hillary and I still talk about the books we read to Chelsea when we were so tired we could hardly stay awake. We still remember them. And, more important, so does she.

But we're going to help the parents of this country make every child able to read for himself or herself by the age of 8, by the third grade. Do you believe we can do that? Will you help us do that?

We must give parents, all parents, the right to choose which public school their children will attend and to let teachers form new charter schools with a charter they can keep only if they do a good job. We must keep our schools open late so that young people have some place to go and something to say yes to and stay off the street.

We must require that our students pass tough tests to keep moving up in school. A diploma has to mean something when they get out.

We should reward teachers that are doing a good job, remove those who don't measure up. But, in every case, never forget that none of us would be here tonight if it weren't for our teachers. I know I wouldn't. We ought to lift them up, not tear them down.

We need schools that will take our children into the next century. We need schools that are rebuilt and modernized with an unprecedented commitment from the national government to increase school construction, and with every single library and classroom in America connected to the information superhighway by the year 2000.

Now folks, if we do these things, every 8-year-old will be able to read, every 12-year-old will be able to log in on the Internet, every 18-year-old will be able to go to college and all Americans will have the knowledge they need to cross that bridge to the 21st century.

I want to build a bridge to the 21st century in which we create a strong and growing economy to preserve the legacy of opportunity for the next generation by balancing our budget in a way that protects our values and ensuring that every family will be able to own and protect the value of their most important asset, their home.

Tonight, let us proclaim to the American people we will balance the budget, and let us also proclaim we will do it in a way that preserves Medicare, Medicaid, education, the environment, the integrity of our pensions, the strength of our people.

Now, last year—last year when the Republican Congress sent me a budget that violated those values and principles, I vetoed it, and I would do it again tomorrow.

I could never allow cuts that devastate education for our children, that pollute our environment, that end the guarantee of health care for those who are served under Medicaid, that end our duty or violate our duty to our parents through Medicare. I just couldn't do that.

As long as I'm president, I'll never let it happen.

And it doesn't matter—it doesn't matter if they try again, as they did before, to use the blackmail threat of a shutdown of the federal government to force these things on the American people. We didn't let it happen before. We won't let it happen again.

Of course, there is a better answer to this dilemma. We could have the right kind of balanced budget with a new Congress.

A Democratic Congress.

I want to balance the budget with real cuts in government and waste. I want a plan that invests in education as mine does, in technology and yes, in research—as Christopher Reeve so powerfully reminded us we must do.

And my plan gives Americans tax cuts that will help our economy to grow. I want to expand IRAs so that young people can save tax free to buy a first home. Tonight I propose a new tax cut for home ownership that says to every middle-income working family in this country, if you sell your home you will not have to pay a capital gains tax on it ever, not ever.

I want every American to be able to hear those beautiful words: Welcome Home.

Let me say again: Every tax cut I call for tonight is targeted, it's responsible and it is paid for within my balanced-budget plan. My tax cuts will not undermine our economy. They will speed economic growth. We should cut taxes for the family sending a child to college, for the worker returning to college, for the family saving to buy a home or for long-term health care, and a $500-per-child credit for middle income families raising their children who need help with child care and what the children will do after school. That is the right way to cut taxes: Pro-family, pro-education, pro-economic growth.

Now, our opponents have put forward a very different plan—a risky $550 billion tax scheme that will force them to ask for even bigger cuts in Medicare, Medicaid, education and the environment than they passed and I vetoed last year.

But even then, they will not cover the cost of their scheme. So that even then this plan will explode the deficit, which will increase interest rates—by 2 percent according to their own estimates last year.

It will require huge cuts in the very investments we need to grow and to grow together, and at the same time, slow down the economy. You know what higher interest rates mean. To you it means a higher mortgage payment, a higher car payment, a higher credit card payment. To our economy it means businesspeople will not borrow as much money, invest as much money, create as many new jobs, create as much wealth, raise as many raises.

Do we really want to make that same mistake all over again?

Do we really want to stop economic growth again?

Do we really want to start piling up another mountain of debt?

Do we want to bring back the recession of 1991 and '92?

Do we want to weaken our bridge to the 21st century?

Of course we don't.

We have an obligation, you and I, to leave our children a legacy of opportunity, not a legacy of debt. Our budget would be balanced today—we would have a surplus today—if we didn't have to make the interest payments on the debt run up in the 12 years before the Clinton-Gore administration took office.

Thank you.

Let me say—This is one of those areas in which I respectfully disagree with my opponent.

I don't believe we should bet the farm, and I certainly don't believe we should bet the country. We should stay on the right track to the 21st century.

Opportunity alone is not enough. I want to build an America in the 21st century in which all Americans take personal responsibility for themselves, their families, their communities and their country.

I want our nation to take responsibility to make sure that every single child can look out the window in the morning and see a whole community getting up and going to work.

We want these young people to know the thrill of the first paycheck, the challenge of starting that first business, the pride in following in a parent's footsteps.

The welfare reform law I signed last week gives America a chance, but not a guarantee, to have that kind of new beginning.

To have a new social bargain with the poor, guaranteeing health care, child care and nutrition for the children, but requiring able-bodied parents to work for the income.

Now I say to all of you, whether you supported the law or opposed it—but especially to those who supported it—we have a responsibility, we have a moral obligation to make sure the people who are being required to work have the opportunity to work.

We must make sure the jobs are there.

There should be one million new jobs for welfare recipients by the year 2000. States under this law can now take the money that was spent on the welfare check and use it to help businesses provide paychecks.

I challenge every state to do it soon. I propose also to give businesses a tax credit for every person hired off welfare and kept employed.

I propose to offer private job placement firms a bonus for every welfare recipient they place in a job who stays in it.

And, more important, I want to help communities put welfare recipients to work right now, without delay, repairing schools, making their neighborhoods clean and safe, making them shine again.

There's lots of work to be done out there. Our cities can find ways to put people to work and bring dignity and strength back to these families.

My fellow Americans, I have spent an enormous amount of time, with our dear friend, the late [Commerce Secretary] Ron Brown, and with [Acting Commerce] Secretary Kantor and others, opening markets for America around the world.

And I'm proud of every one we opened.

[Untapped U.S. Markets]

But let us never forget the greatest untapped market for American enterprise is right here in America, in the inner cities, in the rural areas, who have not felt this recovery.

With investment and business and jobs they can become our partners in the future. And it's a great opportunity we ought not to pass up.

I propose more empowerment zones, like the one we have right here in Chicago, to draw business into poor neighborhoods.

I propose more community development banks, like the Southshore Bank right here in Chicago to help people in those neighborhoods start their own small businesses—more jobs, more incomes, new markets for America, right here at home making welfare reform a reality.

Now, folks, you cheered and I thank you. But the government can only do so much.

The private sector has to provide most of these jobs. So I want to say again, tonight I challenge every business person in America who has ever complained about the failure of the welfare system to try to hire somebody off welfare.

And try hard.

Thank you.

After all, the welfare system you used to complain about is not here anymore. There is no more "Who's to blame?" on welfare.

Now the only question is what to do. And we all have a responsibility, especially those who have criticized what was passed and who have asked for a change and who have the ability to give the poor a chance to grow and support their families.

I want to build a bridge to the 21st century that ends the permanent underclass, that lifts up the poor and ends their isolation, their exile, and they are not forgotten anymore.

Thank you.

I want to build a bridge to the 21st century where our children are not killing other children anymore. Where children's lives are not shattered by violence at home or in the schoolyard. Where a generation of young people are not left to raise themselves on the streets.

With more police and punishment and prevention the crime rate has dropped for four years in a row, now. But we cannot rest, because we know it's still too high. We cannot rest until crime is a shocking exception to our daily lives, not news as usual. Will you stay with me until we reach that good day?

My fellow Americans, we all owe a great debt to Sarah and Jim Brady, and I'm glad they took their wrong turn and wound up in Chicago. I was glad to see them.

It is to them we owe the good news that 60,000 felons, fugitives and stalkers couldn't get handguns because of the Brady bill.

But not a single hunter in Arkansas or New Hampshire or Illinois or anyplace else missed a hunting season.

But now I say we should extend the Brady bill because anyone who has committed an act of domestic violence against a spouse or a child should not buy a gun.

And we must ban—we must ban those cop-killer bullets. They are designed for one reason only: to kill police officers.

We ask the police to keep us safe. We owe it to them to help keep them safe while they do their job for us.

We should pass a victims' rights constitutional amendment because victims deserve to be heard. They need to know when an assailant is released. They need to know these things, and the only way to guarantee them is through a constitutional amendment.

We have made a great deal of progress. Even the crime rate among young people is finally coming down. So it is very, very painful to me that drug use among young people is up.

Drugs nearly killed my brother when he was a young man, and I hate them.

He fought back. He's here tonight with his wife. His little boy is here. And I'm really proud of him.

But I learned something, I learned something in going through that long nightmare with our family. And I can tell you, something has happened to some of our young people. They simply don't think these drugs are dangerous anymore.

Or they think the risk is acceptable.

So beginning with our parents and without regard to our party, we have to renew our energy to teach this generation of young people the hard, cold truth.

Drugs are deadly. Drugs are wrong. Drugs can cost you your life.

General Barry McCaffrey, the four-star general who led our fight against drugs in Latin America, now leads our crusade against drugs at home—stopping more drugs at our borders, cracking down on those who sell them, and most important of all, pursuing a national anti-drug strategy whose primary aim is to turn our children away from drugs.

I call on Congress to give him every cent of funding we have requested for this strategy and to do it now.

There is more we will do. We should say to parolees, we will test you for drugs. If you go back on them, we will send you back to jail. We will say to gangs we will break with the same anti-racketeering law we used to put mob bosses in jail: You're not going to kill our kids anymore or turn them into murderers before they're teenagers.

My fellow Americans, if we're going to build that bridge to the 21st century, we have to make our children free—free of the vise-grip of guns and gangs and drugs; free to build lives of hope.

I want to build a bridge to the 21st century with a strong American community beginning with strong families. An America where all children are cherished and protected from destructive forces, where parents can succeed at home and at work.

Everywhere I've gone in America, people come up and talk to me about their struggle with the demands of work and their desire to do a better job with their children.

The very first person I ever saw fight that battle was here with me four years ago. And tonight, I miss her very, very much. My irrepressible, hardworking, always optimistic mother did the best she could for her brother and me, often against very stiff odds.

I learned from her just how much love and determination can overcome.

But from her and from our life, I also learned that no parent can do it alone. And no parent should have to.

She had the kind of help every parent deserves from our neighbors, our friends, our teachers, our pastors, our doctors and so many more.

You know, when I started out in public life with a lot of my friends from the Arkansas delegation down here there used to be a saying we'd hear from time to time, that every man who runs for public office will claim that he was born in a log cabin he built with his own hands.

Well, my mother knew better. And she made sure I did too. Long before she even met Hillary my mother knew it takes a village. And she was grateful for the support she got.

As Tipper Gore and Hillary said on Tuesday, we have, all of us in our administration, worked hard to support families in raising their children and succeeding at work. But we must do more. We should extend the Family and Medical Leave Law to give parents some time off to take their children to regular doctor's appointments or attend those parent-teacher conferences at school. That is a key determination of their success.

We should pass a flex-time law that allows employees to take their overtime pay in money, or in time off, depending on what's better for their family.

The FDA has adopted new measures to reduce advertising and sales of cigarettes to children.

The vice president spoke so movingly of it last night.

But let me remind you, my fellow Americans, that is very much an issue in this election, because that battle is far from over and the two candidates have different views.

I pledge to America's parents that I will see this effort all the way through.

Working with the entertainment industry, we're giving parents the "v-chip." TV shows are being rated for content so parents will be able to make a judgment about whether their small children should see them. And three hours of quality children's programming every week on every network are on the way.

The Kennedy-Kassebaum law says every American can keep his or her health insurance if they have to change jobs, even if someone in their family's been sick. That is a very important thing. But tonight, we should spell out the next steps.

The first thing we ought to do is to extend the benefits of health care to people who are unemployed. I propose in my balanced-budget plan, paid for, to help unemployed families keep their health insurance for up to six months.

A parent may be without a job, but no child should be without a doctor. And let me say again as the first lady did on Tuesday, we should protect mothers and newborn babies from being forced out of the hospital in less than 48 hours.

We respect the individual conscience of every American on the painful issue of abortion, but believe as a matter of law that this decision should be left to a woman, her conscience, her doctor and her God.

But abortion should not only be—abortion should not only be safe and legal, it should be rare. That's why I helped to establish and support a national effort to reduce out-of-wedlock teen pregnancy, and that is why we must promote adoption.

Last week, the minimum wage bill I signed contained a $5,000 credit to families who adopt children—even more, if the children have disabilities.

It put an end to racial discrimination in the adoption process.

It was a good thing for America.

My fellow Americans, already there are tens of thousands of children out there who need a good home with loving parents. I hope more of them will find it now.

[Environmental Protection]

I want to build a bridge to the 21st century with a clean and safe environment. We are making our food safer from pesticides. We're protecting our drinking water and our air from poisons. We saved Yellowstone from mining. We established the largest national park south of Alaska in the Mojave Desert in California.

We are working to save the precious Florida Everglades.

And when the leaders of this Congress—when the leaders of this Congress invited the polluters into the back room to roll back 25 years of environmental protections that both parties had always supported, I said no.

But we must do more.

Today 10 million children live within just four miles of a toxic waste dump. We've cleaned up 197 of those dumps in the last three years, more than in the previous 12 years combined.

In the next four years, we propose to clean up 500 more—two- thirds of all that are left and the most dangerous ones.

Our children should grow up next to parks, not poison.

We should make it a crime even to attempt to pollute. We should freeze the serious polluter's property until they clean up the problems they create.

We should make it easier for families to find out about toxic chemicals in their neighborhoods so they can do more to protect their own children. These are the things that we must do to build that bridge to the 21st century.

My fellow Americans, I want to build a bridge to the 21st century that makes sure we are still the nation with the world's strongest defense, that our foreign policy still advances the values of our American community in the community of nations.

Our bridge to the future must include bridges to other nations, because we remain the world's indispensable nation to advance prosperity, peace and freedom and to keep our own children safe from the dangers of terror and weapons of mass destruction.

We have helped to bring democracy to Haiti and peace to Bosnia. Now, the peace signed on the White House lawn between the Israelis and the Palestinians must embrace more of Israel's neighbors.

The deep desire for peace that Hillary and I felt when we walked the streets of Belfast and Derry must become real for all the people of Northern Ireland, and Cuba must finally join the community of democracies.

Nothing in our lifetimes has been more heartening than when people of the former Soviet Union and Central Europe broke the grip of communism.

We have aided their progress and I am proud of it. And I will continue our strong partnership with a democratic Russia.

And we will bring some of Central Europe's new democracies into NATO so that they will never question their own freedom in the future.

Our American exports are at record levels. In the next four years, we have to break down even more barriers to them, reaching out to Latin America, to Africa, to other countries in Asia, making sure that our workers and our products—the world's finest—have the benefit of free and fair trade.

In the last four years, we have frozen North Korea's nuclear weapons program. And I'm proud to say that tonight there is not a single Russian nuclear missile pointed at an American child.

Now, now we must enforce and ratify without delay measures that further reduce nuclear arsenals, banish poison gas and ban nuclear tests once and for all.

We have made investments, new investments in our most important defense asset: our magnificent men and women in uniform.

By the year 2000 we also will have increased funding to modernize our weapons systems by 40 percent. These commitments will make sure that our military remains the best-trained, best-equipped fighting force in the entire world.

We are developing a sensible national missile defense, but we must not, not now, not by the year 2000, squander $60 billion on an unproved, ineffective Star Wars program that could be obsolete tomorrow.

We are fighting terrorism on all fronts with a three-pronged strategy. First, we are working to rally a world coalition with zero-tolerance for terrorism. Just this month I signed a law imposing harsh sanctions on foreign companies that invest in key sectors of the Iranian and Libyan economies.

As long as Iran trains, supports and protects terrorists, as long as Libya refuses to give up the people who blew up Pan Am 103, they will pay a price from the United States.

Second, we must give law enforcement the tools they need to take the fight to terrorists. We need new laws to crack down on money laundering and to prosecute and punish those who commit violent acts against American citizens abroad; to add chemical markers or taggants to gunpowder used in bombs so we can track the bombmakers.

To extend the same power police now have against organized crime to save lives by tapping all the phones that terrorists use. Terrorists are as big a threat to our future, perhaps bigger, than organized crime. Why should we have two different standards for a common threat to the safety of America and our children?

We need, in short, the laws that Congress refused to pass. And I ask them again—please, as an American, not a partisan matter, pass these laws now.

Third, we will improve airport and air travel security. I have asked the vice president to establish a commission and report back to me on ways to do this. But now we will install the most sophisticated bomb detection equipment in all our major airports. We will search every airplane flying to or from America from another nation—every flight, every cargo hold, every cabin, every time.

[Foreign Policy]

My fellow Democrats and my fellow Americans, I know that in most election seasons, foreign policy is not a matter of great interest in the debates in the barbershops and the cafes of America, on the plant floors and at the bowling alleys.

But there are times—there are times when only America can make the difference between war and peace, between freedom and repression, between life and death.

We cannot save all the world's children, but we can save many of them. We cannot become the world's policeman, but where our values and our interests are at stake, and where we can make a difference, we must act and we must lead.

That is our job and we are better, stronger and safer because we are doing it.

My fellow Americans, let me say one last time. We can only build our bridge to the 21st century if we build it together, and if we're willing to walk arm-in-arm across that bridge together.

I have spent so much of your time that you gave me these last four years to be your president worrying about the problems of Bosnia, the Middle East, Northern Ireland, Rwanda, Burundi. What do these places have in common?

People are killing each other and butchering children because they are different from one another. They share the same piece of land, but they are different from one another. They hate their race, their tribe, their ethnic group, their religion.

We have seen the terrible, terrible price that people pay when they insist on fighting and killing their neighbors over their differences.

In our own country, we have seen America pay a terrible price for any form of discrimination. And we have seen us grow stronger as we have steadily let more and more of our hatreds and our fears go, as we have given more and more of our people the chance to live their dreams.

That is why the flame of our Statue of Liberty, like the Olympic flame carried all across America by thousands of citizen heroes, will always, always burn brighter than the fires that burn our churches, our synagogues, our mosques, always.

Look around this hall tonight. And there are fellow Americans watching on television. You look around this hall tonight. There is every conceivable difference here among the people who are gathered.

If we want to build that bridge to the 21st century, we have to be willing to say loud and clear: If you believe in the values of the Constitution, the Bill of

Rights, the Declaration of Independence, if you're willing to work hard and play by the rules, you are part of our family. And we're proud to be with you.

You cheer now because you know this is true. You know this is true. When you walk out of this hall, think about it. Live by it.

We still have too many Americans who give in to their fears of those who are different from them. Not so long ago, swastikas were painted on the doors of some African-American members of our Special Forces at Fort Bragg.

Folks, for those of you who don't know what they do, the Special Forces are just what the name says. They are special forces. If I walk off this stage tonight and call them on the telephone and tell them to go halfway around the world and risk their lives for you and be there by tomorrow at noon, they will do it.

They do not deserve to have swastikas on their doors.

Look around here. Look around here. Old or young, healthy as a horse or a person with a disability that hadn't kept you down, man or woman, Native American, native born, immigrant, straight or gay—whatever—the test ought to be I believe in the Constitution, the Bill of Rights, and the Declaration of Independence.

I believe in religious liberty. I believe in freedom of speech. I believe in working hard and playing by the rules. I'm showing up for work tomorrow. I'm building that bridge to the 21st century.

That ought to be the test.

My fellow Americans, 68 nights from tonight the American people will face once again a critical moment of decision. We're going to choose the last president of the 20th century and the first president of the 21st century.

But the real choice is not that. The real choice is whether we will build a bridge to the future or a bridge to the past; about whether we believe our best days are still out there or our best days are behind us; about whether we want a country of people all working together, or one where you're on your own.

Let us commit ourselves this night to rise up and build the bridge we know we ought to build all the way to the 21st century.

Let us have faith. . . . And let us have faith, faith, American faith, American faith that we are not leaving our greatness behind. We're going to carry it right on with us into that new century. A century of new challenge and unlimited promise.

Let us, in short, do the work that is before us, so that when our time here is over we will all watch the sun go down as we all must, and say truly, we have prepared our children for the dawn.

My fellow Americans, after these four good, hard years I still believe in the place called Hope—a place called America.

Thank you.

God bless you.

And good night.

DEMOCRATIC PARTY PLATFORM
August 27, 1996

Unlike many previous conventions, when arguments over the platform badly split the party, the 1996 Democratic party platform was adopted on August 27 with hardly a voice raised in opposition. Instead, Democrats agreed to unite behind President Bill Clinton's reelection and Democratic efforts to regain control of Congress. For a party whose past conventions had seen bitter displays of deeply held differences on Vietnam, civil rights, and other issues, the lack of dissent, as one delegate said, was "scary."

In contrast, the passage of a strong civil rights plank in the Democratic platform of 1948 caused the entire Mississippi delegation and a segment of the Alabama delegation to walk out of the convention. Some of the disgruntled southerners then went on to form their own States' Rights Democratic Party, which nominated Strom Thurmond, then governor of South Carolina, for president. In 1968 sharp divisions over platform language on the Vietnam War intensified a rift in the Democratic party that further undermined the already beleaguered presidential candidate, Hubert H. Humphrey.

None of that dissension afflicted the Democrats in 1996. From the first formal drafting session in Kansas City, Missouri, on July 10–11, party leaders sought a "moderate, achievable" agenda that reflected both unity and a broad appeal to the full spectrum of the party membership. The language, generated by the Clinton campaign, the Democratic National Committee (DNC), and the congressional Democratic leadership, owed much to the party's 1992 platform, which the Clinton campaign had dominated. That year, the platform embraced themes of economic growth, personal responsibility, family vitality, law and order, the need to limit welfare benefits, and preparation to use military force abroad if necessary. All those themes were again emphasized in the 1996 version. (1992 Democratic Platform, Historic Documents of 1992, p. 685)

The Abortion Issue

Unlike the Republicans, who tied themselves up in knots over the abortion issue, and unlike earlier Democratic conventions, the Democrats were able to avoid much discussion of the abortion issue, both in drafting sessions and at the convention itself. In Kansas City, the seventeen-member drafting committee, chaired by Georgia governor Zell Miller, retained language strongly supporting a woman's right to abortion, while adding language respecting differences of opinion on the issue. The "conscience clause," as some called it, read: "The Democratic Party is a party of inclusion. We respect the individual conscience of each American on this difficult issue, and we welcome all our members to participate at every level." Similar language was included in the plank supporting the death penalty for certain crimes.

The clause on abortion had been sought by a group of Democrats headed by Rep. Tony P. Hall of Ohio, who oppose abortion. "I am pleased with the conscience clause . . . and I think most pro-life Democrats will accept it," Hall said in a statement. "I hope that we have put this potentially divisive issue behind us so that all Democrats can get behind reelecting President Clinton in the fall."

Hall credited DNC chairman Donald Fowler with the compromise, which was also accepted by abortion rights activists who had been skeptical of any language alterations. "This party will remain a pro-choice party," Fowler told the drafting committee. But, he added, "we want [the antiabortion Democrats] to feel they are Democrats in the full sense of the word."

The Kansas City meeting was followed by an equally smooth meeting of the 186-member platform committee, held in Pittsburgh on August 5. That session took just three-and-a-half hours. Few amendments were debated and few changes made to the platform as it had been drafted in Kansas City. The only amendment to generate much heat was eventually defeated; it dealt with a plank that called for procedures for firing school teachers who fail to meet standards. Two protesters spoke out against President Clinton's decision to sign the Republican-led legislation overhauling the welfare system, but they were removed from the meeting, and no formal debate or vote was held on the issue.

"Today's Democratic Party"

The platform adopted August 27 blended traditional Democratic themes, such as support for the minimum wage, with more contemporary themes, such as calls for gay rights and reductions in greenhouse gas emissions. Liberally sprinkled throughout the document were references to "today's Democratic Party," as if trying to distance itself from the more ideological statements of the past. Indeed, the platform was colored by the centrist themes that Clinton had espoused as president. Declaring that the "American people do not want big government solutions" nor "empty promises," the platform said that "today's Democratic Party" offered "the end of the era of big government and a final rejection of the misguided call to leave our citizens to fend for themselves—and bold leadership into the future. . . ." Throughout, the platform characterized the Republican party and its pres-

idential nominee, former Senate Majority Leader Bob Dole, as mean-spirited, pro-big business, and insensitive to the needs of workers and the poor. (1996 Republican party platform, p. 496)

The section on responsibility praised the administration's efforts to put 100,000 more police officers on the streets and Clinton's signing of the Brady handgun control bill. At the same time, it said that when "young people commit serious violent crimes, they should be prosecuted like adults." It called for an end to illegal immigration but said Democrats deplored "those who blame [legal] immigrants for economic and social problems" and "those who use the need to stop illegal immigration as a pretext for discrimination." The party pledged to fix those parts of the welfare reform bill that need fixing, but it also said that "the new welfare plan gives America an historic chance: to break the cycle of dependency for millions of Americans...."

Although the platform focused primarily on domestic policy, the section on security said the party was committed to strengthening the military, reducing the threat of weapons of mass destruction, and meeting the challenges presented by terrorism and drug trafficking. It also quietly stressed the role of diplomacy in promoting peace and democracy.

The final section of the platform called for "putting families first," the theme emphasized in the Democratic campaign to wrest Congress from the control of Republicans. Blaming Republicans for twelve years of "all family-values-talk and no family-values-action," the platform said Democrats supported the "Families First Agenda—promoting paycheck, health care, retirements, and personal security; creating greater educational and economic opportunity; and requiring greater responsibility from individuals, businesses, and government." This section also called for the rebuilding of America's inner cities, protections for the environment, religious freedom, and a continued fight against discrimination. "Americans will always have differences, and when we reach across those differences, we are stronger for it," the platform said, echoing a familiar theme of the president's.

Following is the excerpted text of the draft platform presented to and adopted, with minor changes, August 27, 1996, by delegates to the Democratic National Convention at its meeting in Chicago:

In 1996, America will choose the President who will lead us from the millennium which saw the birth of our nation, and into a future that has all the potential to be even greater than our magnificent past. Today's Democratic Party is ready for that future. Our vision is simple. We want an America that gives all Americans the chance to live out their dreams and achieve their God-given potential. We want an America that is still the world's strongest force for peace and freedom. And we want an America that is coming together around our enduring values, instead of drifting apart.

Today's Democratic Party is determined to renew America's most basic bargain: Opportunity to every American, and responsibility from every American. And today's Democratic Party is determined to reawaken the great sense of American community.

Opportunity. Responsibility. Community. These are the values that made America strong. These are the values of the Democratic Party. These are the values that must guide us into the future.

Today, America is moving forward with the strong Presidential leadership it deserves. The economy is stronger, the deficit is lower, and government is smaller. Education is better, our environment is cleaner, families are healthier, and our streets are safer. There is more opportunity in America, more responsibility in our homes, and more peace in the world.

Today's Democratic Party stands proudly on the record of the last four years. We are living in an age of enormous possibility, and we are working to make sure that all Americans can make the most of it. America is moving in the right direction.

Now we must move forward, and we know the course we must follow. We need a smaller, more effective, more efficient, less bureaucratic government that reflects our time-honored values. The American people do not want big government solutions and they do not want empty promises. They want a government that is for them, not against them; that doesn't interfere with their lives but enhances their quality of life. They want a course that is reasonable, help that is realistic, and solutions that can be delivered—a moderate, achievable, common-sense agenda that will improve people's daily lives and not increase the size of government.

That is what today's Democratic Party offers: the end of the era of big government and a final rejection of the misguided call to leave our citizens to fend for themselves—and bold leadership into the future: To meet America's challenges, protect America's values, and fulfill American dreams.

Opportunity

For 220 years, America has been defined by a single ideal: Opportunity for all who take the responsibility to seize it. President Andrew Jackson put it best: We believe in equal opportunity for all, and special privileges for none. The mission of the Democratic Party in 1996 is to ensure that the great American Dream of opportunity for all is within reach for all, and that it travels with us, whole and intact, as we walk together into tomorrow.

Economic Growth

Since Bill Clinton became President, America has seen an explosion of job growth, economic renewal, and opportunity. The American people have created more than 10 million new jobs. After trailing Japan for 14 years, America once again became the world's leading manufacturer of automobiles in 1994, and remained number one last year. The combined rate of inflation, unemployment, and mortgage interest rates is the lowest in three decades. Now, 3.7 million more Americans own their own home, and Americans have started a record number of new small businesses in each of the last three years.

In the 12 years before President Clinton took office, Republicans in the White House allowed the deficit to spiral out of control, and ignored the economic interests of ordinary Americans. Bill Clinton was determined to turn things around and move America in a new direction. With his leadership, we put in place a comprehensive strategy for economic growth. Today's Democratic Party knows that the private sector is the engine of economic growth, and we fought to put America's economic house in order so private business could prosper. We worked to tap the full potential of a new global economy through open and fair trade. We fought to invest in the American people so they would have the capacity to meet the demands of the new economy. And we have invested in the roads, bridges, and highways that are the lifelines of American commerce.

Democrats in Congress supported this course and America is better off because they did. Republicans opposed our economic plan; America's economic growth over the last four years makes it clear that they were wrong. Our strategy is in place, and it is working. We are proud of our economic record over the last four years—and we know that our record is a record to build on, not to rest on. We have to move forward, to make sure that every American willing to work hard has the opportunity to build a good life and share in the benefits of economic success.

In the last four years we worked to get the American economy going: cutting the deficit, expanding trade, and investing in our people. In the next four years we have to make the new economy work for all Americans: balancing the budget, creating more jobs, making sure all families can count on good health care and a secure retirement, and, most of all, expanding educational opportunities so all Americans can learn the skills they need to build the best possible future.

Balancing the budget. For 12 years, Republicans hid behind rosy scenarios while quadrupling the national debt. We knew this had to stop. In 1992, we promised to cut the deficit in half over four years. We did. Our 1993 economic plan cut spending by over a quarter trillion dollars in five years. The only deficit left today is interest payments on the debt run up over the 12 Republican years before fiscal responsibility returned to the White House. President Clinton is the first President to cut the deficit four years in a row since before the Civil War.

Now the Democratic Party is determined to finish the job and balance the budget. President Clinton has put forward a plan to balance the budget by 2002 while living up to our commitments to our elderly and our children and maintaining strong economic growth. The Republican Congress' own economists admit the President's plan will balance the budget by 2002. It cuts hundreds of wasteful and outdated programs, but it preserves Medicare and Medicaid, it protects education and the environment, and it defends working families. The President's plan reflects America's values. The Republican plan does not.

Today's Democratic Party believes we have a duty to care for our parents, so they can live their lives in dignity. That duty includes securing Medicare and Medicaid, finding savings without reducing quality or benefits, and protecting Social Security for future generations. The Republican agenda rests on massive Medicare cuts, three times bigger than the largest Medicare cuts in history, including new premium increases on seniors, and drastic changes to Medicaid that will jeopardize the health care of children and seniors.

Today's Democratic Party believes that all children should have the opportunity and the education to make the most of their own lives. We believe that schools should be run by teachers and principals, not by Washington. The Republican agenda slashes college scholarships and college loans, cuts Head Start, and cuts funds to reduce class size and improve teacher standards.

Today's Democratic Party believes we have a duty to preserve God's earth and American quality of life for future generations. We are committed to reform, so we protect our environment but we do not trap business in a tangle of red tape. The Republican budget guts environmental protection.

Today's Democratic Party believes that working people should not be taxed into poverty. The Republican budget raises taxes on millions of working families.

Today's Democratic Party believes that America must put our families first. The Republican budget tried to take Big Bird away from 5-year-olds, school lunches away from 10-year-olds, summer jobs away from 15-year-olds, and college loans away from 20-year-olds.

Today's Democratic Party believes in a government that works better and costs less. We know that government workers are good people trapped in bad systems, and we are committed to reinventing government to reform those systems. The Republican budget cuts government where it is needed to protect our values, and they were even willing to shut down the government altogether to force their budget on the American people.

Tax relief for working families and small businesses. President Clinton and Democrats in Congress expanded the Earned Income Tax Credit, cutting taxes to help 40 million Americans in 15 million working families—without a single Republican vote. The Dole-Gingrich budget was designed to give a massive tax break to the wealthiest Americans, and pay for it by raising taxes on ordinary Americans and slashing health care for the elderly. America cannot afford to return to the era of something-for-nothing tax cuts and smoke-and-mirrors accounting that produced a decade of exploding deficits. Today's Democratic Party is committed to targeted tax cuts that help working Americans invest in their future, and we insist that any tax cuts are completely paid for, because we are determined to balance the budget.

We want to strengthen middle-class families by providing a $500 tax cut for children. We want to cut taxes to help families pay for education after high school and to guarantee the first two years of college. We want people to be able to use their IRA's to buy a first home, deal with a medical emergency, or provide for education. We want to cut taxes for small businesses that invest in the future and set up pensions for their workers. And we want to cut taxes for people who are self-employed and self-insured so their health care is more affordable.

Technology. We know investments in technology drive economic growth, generate new knowledge, create new high-wage jobs, build new industries, and improve our quality of life. In the face of Republican efforts to undermine America's dedication to innovation, President Clinton and the Democratic Party have fought to maintain vital investments in science and technology. We remember that government investment in technology is responsible for the computer, for jet aircraft, and for the Internet—no investments have ever paid off better, in jobs, in opportunity, or in growth.

We support government policies that encourage private sector investment and innovation to create a pro-growth economic climate, like a permanent research and development tax credit. . . .

Creating jobs through trade. We believe that if we want the American economy to continue strong growth, we must continue to expand trade, and not retreat from the world. . . .

In the last four years, the Clinton-Gore Administration has signed over 200 trade agreements, including NAFTA [North American Free Trade Agreement] and GATT [General Agreement on Tariffs and Trade], to open markets around the world to American products, and create more jobs for the people who make them here at home. We have put in place the most sweeping agreements to lower foreign trade barriers of any administration in modern American history, including over 20 such agreements with Japan alone—and American exports to Japan in the sectors covered by those agreements have increased by 85 percent. All over the world, barriers to American products have come down, exports are at an all time high—and we have created over one million high-paying export-related jobs.

In the next four years, we must continue to work to lower foreign trade barriers; insist that foreign companies play by fair rules at home and abroad; strengthen rules that protect the global economy from fraud and dangerous instability; advance American commercial interests abroad; and ensure that the new global economy is directly beneficial to American working families. As we work to open new markets, we must negotiate to guarantee that all trade agreements include standards to protect children, workers, public safety, and the environment. We must ensure adequate trade adjustment assistance and education and training programs to help working families compete and win in the global economy.

Education

Today's Democratic Party knows that education is the key to opportunity. In the new global economy, it is more important than ever before. Today, education is the fault line that separates those who will prosper from those who cannot. President Clinton and Democrats in Congress have spared no effort over the last four years to improve the quality of American education and expand the opportunity for all Americans to get the education they need to succeed.

Every step of the way, we have been opposed by Republicans intent on cutting education. Now, they want to cut education from Head Start through college scholarships. They want to undermine our public schools and make borrowing for college more difficult for millions of students.

Today's Democratic Party will stand firmly against the Republican assault on education. . . .

In the next four years, we must do even more to make sure America has the best public schools on earth. If we want to be the best, we should expect the best: We must hold students, teachers, and schools to the highest standards. Every child should be able to read by the end of the third grade. Students should be required to demonstrate competency and achievement for promotion or graduation. Teachers should be required to meet high standards for professional performance and be rewarded for the good jobs they do—and there should be a fair, timely, cost-effective process to remove those who do not measure up. And we should get rid of the barriers that discourage talented young people from becoming teachers in the first place. We should not bash teachers. We should applaud them, and find ways to keep the best teachers in the classroom. Schools should be held accountable for results. We should redesign or overhaul schools that fail. We should expand public school choice, but we should not take American tax dollars from public schools and give them to private schools. We should promote public charter schools that are held to the highest standards of accountability and access. And we should continue to ensure that America provides quality education to children with disabilities, because high-quality public education is the key to opportunity for *all* children. . . .

Technology in the classroom. We must bring the 21st century into every classroom in America. There is a vast realm of knowledge waiting for our children to tap into. Computers are powerful tools to teach students to read better, write better, and understand math. President Clinton and Vice President Gore understand that technological literacy is essential to success in the new economy. The only way to achieve that for every student is to give them all access to a computer, good software, trained teachers, and the Internet—and President Clinton and Vice President Gore have launched a partnership with high-tech companies, schools, state, and local governments to wire every classroom and library to the Information Superhighway by the year 2000. . . .

Higher education for all Americans. Finally, we must make sure that every American has the opportunity to go to college. Higher education is the key to a successful future in the 21st century. The typical worker with a college education earns 73 percent more than one without. America has the best higher education in the world. We do not need to change it—we need to make it available for all Americans. Our goal must be nothing less than to make the 13th and 14th years of education as universal as the first 12. . . .

Tax cuts for college. Over the next four years, we want to go even further: We should expand work-study so one million students a year can work their way through college by the year 2000. We should allow people to use money from their IRA to help pay for college. We should give a $1,000 honor scholarship for the top 5 percent of graduates in every high school. And we must make 14 years of education the standard for every American. The Democratic Party wants to create a $10,000 tax deduction for families to help pay for education after high school. And we want to create a $1,500 tax cut for Americans, modeled after Georgia's successful HOPE scholarships, to guarantee the first year of tuition at a typical community college, and the second year if individuals earn it by maintaining a B average. No tax cut will do more to raise American incomes than a tax cut to pay for college.

Economic Security for American Families in the 21st Century

In the old economy, most workers could count on one job for life. They knew that hard work was rewarded with raises and steady jobs; they were confident the company would take care of them, their families, their health, and their retirement. Success was tied to the success of their employer: sacrifice when times were tough and a share in the wealth when times were good. In the new economy, the rules have changed. We need to find new ways to help working families find economic security: better training to help workers learn skills to get new and better jobs; the security of good health care and safe pensions so they can take care of themselves and their families. This is a challenge that American workers and managers are ready to face, and the Democratic Party will continue to tackle.

Rewarding work. We honor work in America. Americans work hard, and they have a right to expect that work will pay. We want to continue reversing the trend of the eighties, so all Americans benefit from continued economic growth and rising wages. The President and Democrats in Congress raised the minimum wage to $5.15 an hour, after defeating fierce Republican opposition led by Senator Dole and Speaker Gingrich. We believe the minimum wage should be a wage you can live on. President Clinton and Congressional Democrats fought for and won the largest expansion of the Earned Income Tax Credit in history, a tax cut for 15 million working families, because no parent who takes the responsibility to work full time should have to raise children in poverty. We want to strengthen families, and we challenge the private sector to help their workers earn enough to support a family.

Health care. The Democratic Party is committed to ensuring that Americans have access to affordable, high-quality health care. Because of President Clinton's determined leadership and the tireless efforts of Democrats in Congress, we passed the Kennedy-Kassebaum health reform bill to stop insurance companies from denying coverage to families where one member has a preexisting condition, and to make sure that people can take their health insurance with them when they change jobs. No more Americans should have to turn down a better job because they would lose their health care if they took it. We have expanded the Women, Infants, and Children program that provides prenatal and early childhood nutrition, so that all eligible women, infants, and children will have access to the health and nutrition services they need. We established a comprehensive effort to immunize children, after defeating Republican opposition led by Senator Dole. Last year, the percentage of two-year-olds in America who were fully immunized reached an historic high. . . .

In the next four years, we must take further steps to ensure that Americans have access to quality, affordable health care. We should start by making sure that people get help paying premiums so they do not lose health care while they're looking for a new job. We support expanded coverage of home care, hospice, and community-based services, so the elderly and people with disabilities of all ages can live in their own communities and as independently as possible. We are disappointed Congress walked away from bipartisan efforts to provide mental health parity; we believe health insurance coverage for mental health care is vitally important and we support parity for mental health care.

Retirement. Over the last four years, President Clinton took strong steps to protect the pensions of more than 40 million workers and retirees by fixing the federal pension insurance system and demanding that companies fund their retirement plans fully. We established a nationwide retirement protection program to protect workers' 401(k) retirement savings from fraud and abuse. We recognize the unique concerns of women when it comes to preparing for retirement and have worked to protect women's pension rights.

Over the next four years, we want to take further steps to make sure that Americans who have worked hard for their whole lives can enjoy retirement in the dignity and security they have earned. We want to make sure people can carry their pensions with them when they change jobs, protect pensions even further, and expand the number of workers with pension coverage. Democrats created Social Security, we oppose efforts to dismantle it, and we will fight to save it. We must ensure that it is on firm financial footing well into the next century. We call on Republicans to put politics aside and join us in a serious bipartisan effort to make sure that Social Security will continue to provide true security for future generations, as it has done for millions of older Americans for decades.

Training. We must do more to make sure all Americans have the skills they need to compete. We want a G.I. Bill for Workers to transform the confusing tangle of federal training programs into a simple job-training skill grant that will go directly to unemployed workers so they will be able to get the training that is right for them. We want to strengthen training opportunities for people with disabilities, so they can learn the skills they need to live independent, productive lives.

Standing up for working Americans. We nearly doubled funding for the dislocated worker program and launched special projects to help workers displaced by base closures, natural disasters, and mass layoffs. We are reforming OSHA so it can do a better job to protect worker safety with less red tape, and we continue to oppose Republican efforts to gut it. We beat back efforts to undermine workers' rights to form and join unions and to dismantle the enforcement powers of the National Labor Relations Board. We vigorously oppose Republican efforts to pass Right-to-Work legislation, and we are proud the President vetoed efforts to undermine collective bargaining through the TEAM Act. We are working to eradicate sweatshops in the U.S. apparel industry by stepping up enforcement and public education. We oppose the hiring of permanent workers to replace lawful economic strikers; we support the President's action to stop the government from procuring goods and services from companies that do so; and we support legislation to prohibit the permanent replacement of lawfully striking workers. We believe in equal pay for equal work and pay equity.

Promoting economic growth and opportunity for all Americans. We know that it is good for America when small, minority, and women-owned businesses have the opportunity to grow and prosper. These business-owners create new jobs, expand opportunities, and serve as powerful role models for young people. Over the last four years, the President has transformed the Small Business Administration to eliminate burdensome paperwork and deliver real assistance to entrepreneurs as they work to start or expand their businesses. At the same time, since Bill Clinton became President, we have more than doubled the number of loans to small businesses, nearly tripled loans to minority businesses, and quadrupled loans to women-owned businesses. The President ordered all federal agencies to comply with laws designed to ensure that small, minority, and women-owned businesses can compete for their fair share of procurement dollars. We are committed to continued efforts to expand opportunity for small, minority, and women business owners.

Corporate citizenship. Employers have a responsibility to do their part as well. President Clinton and the Democratic Party stand on the side of working families. We believe that values like loyalty, fairness, and responsibility are not inconsistent with the bottom line. We call on our corporate leaders to invest in the long-term, by providing workers with good wages and benefits, education and training, and opportunities for greater involvement in company decision making and ownership. As workers increase their productivity, employers should make sure they share in the benefits of the good years, as well as the burdens of the bad ones. Employers should respect the commitment of workers to their families, and should work to provide good pensions and health care. When CEOs put their workers and long-term success ahead of short-term gain, their workers will do better and so will they.

Responsibility

Today's Democratic Party knows that the era of big government is over. Big bureaucracies and Washington solutions are not the real answers to today's challenges. We need a smaller government . . . and we must have a larger national spirit. Government's job should be to give people the tools they need to make the most of their own lives. Americans must take the responsibility to use them, to build good lives for themselves and their families. Personal responsibility is the most powerful force we have to meet our challenges and shape the future we want for ourselves, for our children, and for America.

Fighting Crime

Today's Democratic Party believes the first responsibility of government is law and order. Four years ago, crime in America seemed intractable. The violent crime rate and the murder rate had climbed for seven straight years. Drugs seemed to flow freely across our borders and into our neighborhoods. Convicted felons could walk into any gun shop in the country and buy a handgun. Military-style assault weapons were sold freely. Our people didn't feel safe in their homes, walking their streets, or even sending their children to school. Under the thumb of special interests like the gun lobby, Republicans talked tough about crime but did nothing to fight it.

Bill Clinton promised to turn things around, and that is exactly what he did. After a long hard fight, President Clinton beat back fierce Republican opposition, led by Senator Dole and Speaker Gingrich, to answer the call of America's police officers and pass the toughest Crime Bill in history. The Democratic Party under President Clinton is putting more police on the streets and tougher penalties on the books; we are taking guns off the streets and working to steer young people away from crime and gangs and drugs in the first place. And it is making a difference. In city after city and town after town, crime rates are finally coming down.

Community policing. Nothing is more effective in the fight against crime than police officers on the beat, engaged in community policing. The Crime Bill is putting 100,000 new police officers on the street. We deplore cynical Republican attempts to undermine our promise to America to put 100,000 new police officers on the street. We pledge to stand up for our communities and stand with our police officers by opposing any attempt to repeal or weaken this effort. But we know that community policing only works when the community works with the police. We echo the President's challenge to Americans: If 50 citizens joined each of America's 20,000 neighborhood watch groups, we would have a citizen force of one million strong to give our police forces the backup they need.

Protecting our children, our neighborhoods, and our police from criminals with guns. Bob Dole, Newt Gingrich, and George Bush were able to hold the Brady Bill hostage for the gun lobby until Bill Clinton became President. With his leadership, we made the Brady Bill the law of the land. And because we did, more than 60,000 felons, fugitives, and stalkers have been stopped from buying guns. President Clinton led the fight to ban 19 deadly assault weapons, designed for one purpose only—to kill human beings. We oppose efforts to restrict weapons used for legitimate sporting purposes, and we are proud that not one hunter or sportsman was forced to change guns because of the assault weapons ban. But we know that the military-style guns we banned have no place on America's streets, and we are proud of the courageous Democrats who defied the gun lobby and sacrificed their seats in Congress to make America safer.

Today's Democratic Party stands with America's police officers. We are proud to tell them that as long as Bill Clinton and Al Gore are in the White

House, any attempt to repeal the Brady Bill or assault weapons ban will be met with a veto. We must do everything we can to stand behind our police officers, and the first thing we should do is pass a ban on cop-killer bullets. Any bullet that can rip through a bulletproof vest should be against the law; that is the least we can do to protect the brave police officers who risk their lives to protect us.

Tough punishment. We believe that people who break the law should be punished, and people who commit violent crimes should be punished severely. President Clinton made three-strikes-you're-out the law of the land, to ensure that the most dangerous criminals go to jail for life, with no chance of parole. We established the death penalty for nearly 60 violent crimes, including murder of a law enforcement officer, and we signed a law to limit appeals. The Democratic Party is a party of inclusion, and we respect the conscience of all Americans on this issue.

We provided almost $8 billion in new funding to help states build new prison cells so violent offenders serve their full sentences. We call on the states to meet the President's challenge and guarantee that serious violent criminals serve at least 85 percent of their sentence. The American people deserve a criminal justice system in which criminals are caught, the guilty are convicted, and the convicted serve their time.

Fighting youth violence and preventing youth crime. Nothing we do to fight crime is more important than fighting the crime and violence that threatens our children. We have to protect them from criminals who prey on them—and we have to teach them good values and give them something to say yes to, so they stay away from crime and trouble in the first place.

The Democratic Party understands what the police have been saying for years: The best way to fight crime is to prevent it. That is why we fought for drug-education and gang-prevention programs in our schools. We support well thought out, well organized, highly supervised youth programs to provide young people with a safe and healthy alternative to hanging out on the streets. We made it a federal crime for any person under the age of 18 to carry a handgun except when supervised by an adult. Democrats fought to pass, and President Clinton ordered states to impose, zero tolerance for guns in school, requiring schools to expel for one year any student who brings a gun to school.

At the same time, when young people cross the line, they must be punished. When young people commit serious violent crimes, they should be prosecuted like adults. We established boot camps for young non-violent offenders. . . .

Battling illegal drugs. We must keep drugs off our streets and out of our schools. President Clinton and the Democratic Party have waged an aggressive war on drugs. . . . We are making progress. Overall drug use in America is dropping; the number of Americans who use cocaine has dropped 30 percent since 1992. Unfortunately casual drug use by young people continues to climb. We must redouble our efforts against drug abuse everywhere, especially among our children.

Earlier this year, the President appointed General Barry McCaffrey to lead the nation's war on drugs. General McCaffrey is implementing an aggressive four part strategy to reach young children and prevent drug use in the first place; to catch and punish drug users and dealers; to provide treatment to those who need help; and to cut drugs off at the source before they cross the border and pollute our neighborhoods. But every adult in America must take responsibility to set a good example, and to teach children that drugs are wrong, they are illegal and they are deadly.

Ending domestic violence. When it strikes, nothing is a more dangerous threat to the safety of our families than domestic violence, because it is a threat from within. Unfortunately, violence against women is no stranger to America, but a dangerous intruder we must work together to drive from our homes. We know that domestic violence is not a "family problem" or a "women's problem." It is *America's* problem, and we must all fight it. The Violence Against Women Act in the 1994 Crime Bill helps police officers, prosecutors, and judges to understand domestic violence, recognize it when they see it, and know how to deal with it. In February, the President launched a 24 hour, seven-day, toll-free hotline so women in trouble can find out how to get emergency help, find shelter, and report abuse to the authorities. The number is 1-800-799-SAFE. Everyone who knows it should pass it on to anyone who might need it. Every American must take the responsibility to stop this terrible scourge. As we fight it, we must remember that the victims are not to blame. This is a crime to be punished, not a secret to be concealed.

We must do everything we can to make sure that the victims of violent crime are treated with the respect and the dignity they deserve. We support the President's call for a constitutional amendment to protect the rights of victims. We believe that when a plea bargain is entered in public, a criminal is sentenced, or a defendant is let out on bail, the victims ought to know about it, and have a say. A constitutional amendment is the only way to protect those rights in every courtroom in America.

Immigration

Democrats remember that we are a nation of immigrants. We recognize the extraordinary contribution of immigrants to America throughout our history. We welcome legal immigrants to America. We support a legal immigration policy that is pro-family, pro-work, pro-responsibility, and pro-citizenship, and we deplore those who blame immigrants for economic and social problems. . . .

Today's Democratic Party also believes we must remain a nation of laws. We cannot tolerate illegal immigration and we must stop it. . . .

However, as we work to stop illegal immigration, we call on all Americans to avoid the temptation to use this issue to divide people from each other. We deplore those who use the need to stop illegal immigration as a pretext for discrimination. And we applaud the wisdom of Republicans like [New York City] Mayor [Rudolph] Giuliani and Senator [Pete] Domenici [N.M.] who oppose the mean-spirited and shortsighted effort of Republicans in Congress to bar the children of illegal immigrants from schools—it is wrong, and forcing children onto the streets is an invitation for them to join gangs and turn to crime. Democrats want to protect American jobs by increasing criminal and civil sanctions against employers who hire illegal workers, but Republicans continue to favor inflammatory rhetoric over real action. We will continue to enforce labor standards to protect workers in vulnerable industries. We continue to firmly oppose welfare benefits for illegal immigrants. We believe family members who sponsor immigrants into this country should take financial responsibility for them, and be held legally responsible for supporting them.

Welfare Reform

Today's Democratic Party knows there is no greater gap between mainstream American values and modern American government than our failed welfare system. When Bill Clinton became President, the welfare system undermined the very values—work, family, and personal responsibility—that it should promote. The welfare system should reflect those values: we want to help people who want to help themselves and their children.

Over the past four years, President Clinton has dramatically transformed the welfare system. He has freed 41 states from federal rules and regulations so they can reform their welfare systems. The Clinton Administration has granted 69 waivers—more than twice as many waivers as granted in the Reagan-Bush years. For 75 percent of all Americans on welfare, the rules have changed for good already, and welfare is becoming what it should be: a second chance, not a way of life. Welfare rolls are finally coming down—there are 1.3 million fewer people on welfare today than there were when President Clinton took office in January 1993.

Now, because of the President's leadership and with the support of a majority of the Democrats in Congress, national welfare reform is going to make work and responsibility the law of the land. Thanks to President Clinton and the Democrats, the new welfare bill includes the health care and child care people need so they can go to work confident their children will be cared for. Thanks to President Clinton and the Democrats, the new welfare bill imposes time limits and real work requirements—so anyone who can work, does work, and so that no one who can work can stay on welfare forever. Thanks to President Clinton and the Democrats, the new welfare bill cracks down on deadbeat parents and requires minor mothers to live at home with their parents or with another responsible adult. . . .

We know the new bill passed by Congress is far from perfect—parts of it should be fixed because they go too far and have nothing to do with welfare reform. First, Republicans cut too far into nutritional assistance for working families with children; we are committed to correcting that. Second, Republicans insisted on using welfare reform as a vehicle to cut off help to legal immigrants. That was wrong. Legal immigrants work hard, pay their taxes, and serve America. It is wrong to single them out for punishment just because they are immigrants. We pledge to make sure that legal immigrant families with children who fall on hard times through no fault of their own can get help when they need it. And we are committed to continuing the President's efforts to make it easier for legal immigrants who are prepared to accept the responsibilities of citizenship to do so.

But the new welfare plan gives America an historic chance: to break the cycle of dependency for millions of Americans, and give them a real chance for an independent future. It reflects the principles the President has insisted upon since he started the process that led to welfare reform. Our job now is to make sure this welfare reform plan succeeds, transforming a broken system that holds people down into a working system that lifts people up and gives them a real chance to build a better life.

States asked for this responsibility—now we have to make sure they shoulder it. We must make sure as many people as possible move from welfare to work. We must make sure that children are protected. In addition to health care and nutritional assistance, states should provide in-kind vouchers to children whose parents have reached the time limit. We challenge states to exempt battered women from time limits and other restrictions. We challenge the business community to provide more of the private sector jobs people on welfare need to build good lives and strong families. We know that passing legislation is not enough; we must make sure people get the skills they need to get jobs, and that there are jobs for them to go to so they leave welfare and stay off. We want to make sure welfare reform will put more people to work and move them into the economic mainstream, not take jobs away from working families.

We call on all Americans to make the most of this opportunity—never to use welfare reform as an excuse to demonize or demean people, but rather as a chance to bring all our people fully into the economic mainstream, to have a chance to share in the prosperity and the promise of American life.

Child support. Nobody has the right to walk away from the responsibility to care for his or her children. If you owe child support, paying it fully and promptly is just the first step in living up to your responsibility as a parent. The Clinton Administration has made a determined effort to crack down on deadbeat parents, collecting a record $11 billion in 1995 through tough enforcement—almost a 40 percent increase over 1992. President Clinton issued an Executive Order to track down federal workers who fail to pay child support, and force them to pay. The Clinton Administration is working to put wanted lists of parents who owe child support in the post office and on the Internet. President Clinton and Democrats in Congress insisted that the toughest possible child support enforcement be part of the new welfare reform plan—including the President's plan to deny drivers licenses and professional licenses to people who do not pay their child support. We are telling deadbeats: If you neglect your responsibility to your children, we will suspend your license, garnish your wages, track you down, and make you pay.

Teen pregnancy. For the first time in years, the teen pregnancy rate has leveled off and begun to drop. But we all know it is still far too high. Government alone cannot solve this problem. That is why President Clinton challenged community, business, and religious leaders together to form a national campaign to keep the teen pregnancy rate going down. And he expanded support for community-based prevention programs that teach abstinence and demand responsibility. We must send the strongest possible signal to young people that it is wrong to get pregnant or father a child until they are married and ready to support that child and raise that child.

We also know that half of all underage mothers were made pregnant by a man in his twenties, or even older. Statutory rape is a crime, but unfortunately the laws that protect young women from it are almost never enforced. We echo the President's call to America's prosecutors: Enforce the statutory rape laws vigorously against men who prey on underage women.

Choice

The Democratic Party stands behind the right of every woman to choose, consistent with *Roe v. Wade*, and regardless of ability to pay. President Clinton took executive action to make sure that the right to make such decisions is protected for all Americans. Over the last four years, we have taken action to end the gag rule and ensure safety at family planning and women's health clinics. We believe it is a fundamental constitutional liberty that individual Americans—not government—can best take responsibility for making the most difficult and intensely personal decisions regarding reproduction.

The Democratic Party is a party of inclusion. We respect the individual conscience of each American on this difficult issue, and we welcome all our members to participate at every level of our party.

Our goal is to make abortion less necessary and more rare, not more difficult and more dangerous. We support contraceptive research, family planning, comprehensive family life education, and policies that support healthy childbearing. For four years in a row, we have increased support for family planning. The abortion rate is dropping. Now we must continue to support efforts to reduce unintended pregnancies, and we call on all Americans to take personal responsibility to meet this important goal.

Reinventing Government

The American people have a right to demand that responsibility is the order of the day in Washington. The mission of today's Democratic Party is to expand opportunity, not bureaucracy. We have worked hard over the last four years to rein in big government, slash burdensome regulations, eliminate wasteful programs, and shift problem-solving out of Washington and back to people and communities who understand their situations best.

In the last four years, President Clinton, working with the National Performance Review chaired by Vice President Gore, has cut the federal government by almost 240,000 positions, making the smallest federal government in 30 years. We did it the right way, treating workers with respect. The federal government is eliminating 16,000 pages of outdated and unnecessary regulations, has abolished 179 programs and projects, and saved taxpayers billions of dollars. . . .

. . . Democrats are bringing responsibility back to Washington. In the last two years, Republicans under Senator Dole and Speaker Gingrich shut the federal government down in an irresponsible attempt at partisan blackmail. Democrats under President Clinton said, and America agreed: Partisan threats are no way to run a government. Nobody should ever shut down the government again. The Republican shutdown cost the taxpayers $1.4 billion. Democrats believe government should work better and cost less—not work less and cost more.

The Republican shutdown was an affront to the hardworking public servants in our cities, towns, states, and nation who devote their lives to improving life in our country. Thanks to them our streets are safer, our water is cleaner, and our nation is secure. We condemn Republican tactics to sow cynicism and mistrust by scapegoating those government workers. Front-line federal workers committed to providing quality services have joined the President's efforts to make government work better for the American people. With their help, we are saving money for the taxpayers and improving services for our people. Those workers who are doing more with less deserve our respect and admiration. . . .

Political Reform

Today's Democratic Party knows we have a responsibility to make our democracy work better for America, by limiting the influence of special interests and expanding the influence of the American people. Special interests have too much power in the halls of government. They often operate in secret and have special privileges ordinary Americans do not even know exist. Elections have become so expensive that big money can sometimes drown out the voices of ordinary voters—who should always speak the loudest.

Shortly after Bill Clinton took office, he implemented the toughest ethics code on executive officials in history: Senior appointees are barred from lobbying their own agencies for five years after they leave, and they can never lobby for foreign governments. After years of Republican delay, Democrats passed and the President signed the Motor Voter Bill to make it easier for people to participate in our democracy and exercise their civic responsibility in the voting booth. The President led the fight to repeal the tax loophole that let lobbyists deduct the cost of their activities, and prevailed. In 1995, after a Republican filibuster, Congress finally answered the President's call to stop taking gifts, meals, and trips from lobbyists; to bring lobbyists out from dark rooms and into the bright light of public scrutiny by requiring full disclosure; and to apply to itself the laws that apply to the rest of the country.

But we must take further strong action. The President and the Democratic Party support the bipartisan McCain-Feingold campaign finance reform bill. It will limit campaign spending, curb the influence of PACs and lobbyists, and end the soft money system. Perhaps most important of all, this bill provides free TV time for candidates, so they can talk directly to citizens about real issues and real ideas. Unfortunately, Republicans in Congress will not even let this bill come up for a vote. We call on them to stop stonewalling. It is time to take the reins of democracy away from big money and put them back in the hands of the American people, where they belong. We applaud efforts by broadcasters and private citizens alike, to increase candidates' direct access to voters through free TV. . . .

Security, Freedom and Peace

The firm, sustained use of American might and diplomacy helped win the greatest victory for freedom in this half of the century—the end of the Cold War. But to meet the challenges of this new era of promise and peril, America needed leadership that was able to see the contours of the new world— and willing to act with steadiness, strength, and flexibility in the face of change to make the most of it.

President Clinton and Vice President Gore have seized the opportunities of the post Cold War era. Over the past four years, their leadership has made America safer, more prosperous, and more engaged in solving the challenges of a new era.

Four years ago, thousands of Russian nuclear weapons were aimed at American cities. Today, not a single Russian missile points at our children, and through the START treaties we will cut American and Russian nuclear arsenals by two-thirds from their Cold War height.

Four years ago, the forces of reform in the former Soviet Union were embattled. Today, U.S. initiatives are helping democracy and free markets take root throughout the region, Russian troops are out of the Baltics, and democracy has triumphed in Russia's elections.

Four years ago, the Middle East process had not moved beyond a set of principles, and there were no signs of peace in Northern Ireland. Today, in the Middle East we have seen real agreements toward peace, and handshakes of history, and the people of Northern Ireland have seen a 17 month cease-fire and historic negotiations among the parties.

Four years ago, the North Koreans were operating a dangerous nuclear program. Today, that program is frozen, under international inspection, and slated to be dismantled.

Four years ago, the North Atlantic Treaty Organization—the bulwark of Western security during the Cold War—was losing direction and support. Today, NATO is keeping the peace in Bosnia with its Partnership for Peace allies and, as a result of American leadership, preparing to welcome new members from Central Europe.

Four years ago, America stood aloof as war and genocide spread through the former Yugoslavia. Today, thanks to NATO airstrikes, American diplomacy and the deployment of troops from the U.S. and other nations, the war has stopped and Bosnia has its first real chance for a lasting peace.

Four years ago, dictators ruled in Haiti, abusing human rights and leaving thousands of its citizens desperate to flee to our shores. Today, the dictators are gone, democracy has been restored, and Haiti's mass-exodus has stopped.

Four years ago, South Africa was struggling under political violence associated with apartheid. Now, following the 1994 elections—which the United

States strongly supported—there is a national unity government and South Africa is free and democratic.

Four years ago, there was good reason to worry that the world was dividing into separate, isolated, regional trading blocks. Today, thanks to Clinton Administration efforts to find new markets for American products and strengthen our existing ties, America's relations with our trading parties around the world are stronger than ever. We applaud efforts like the Summit of the Americas, the Asian Pacific Economic Cooperation meetings, and, especially, the extraordinary leadership of Commerce Secretary Ron Brown on behalf of American industry and workers everywhere. Ron Brown will always be remembered with great pride and the deepest gratitude by the Democratic Party and by all Americans.

The Clinton-Gore Administration's record of leadership has deterred America's adversaries and earned respect from our allies and partners. The Dole-Gingrich Congress and the Republican Party have a different approach to America's security. Too often they would force America to go it alone—or not at all. Their shortsighted approach has cut resources for diplomacy that could strengthen our security, and reflects an inadequate understanding of the threats and opportunities of this new era.

Today's Democratic Party is unwilling to surrender to the voices of retreat and indifference. We believe the only way to ensure America's security and prosperity over the long run is to continue exerting American leadership across a range of military, diplomatic, and humanitarian challenges around the world. Led by President Clinton and Vice President Gore, today's Democratic Party has set a far reaching agenda to strengthen our security, and promote peace and freedom.

Strengthening Our Security

The highest imperative for our security is the protection of our people, our territory, and our key interests abroad. While both parties share a commitment to strong security, there is a real difference. The Republican desire to spend more money on defense than the Pentagon requests cannot obscure their inability to recognize the challenges of a new era and build the balanced defenses we need to meet them.

Today's Democratic Party is committed to strengthening our military and adapting it to new challenges; reducing the threat of weapons of mass destruction; and meeting new challenges to our security such as terrorism, international crime, and drug trafficking.

Strengthening our military. Over the past four years, the Administration has undertaken the most successful restructuring of our military forces in history. Even as the size of our forces has decreased, their capabilities, readiness and qualitative edge have increased. The Administration has ensured that America is prepared to fight alongside others when we can, and alone when we must. We have defeated attempts to cut our defense budget irresponsibly. Three times in three years, President Clinton has increased our defense spending plans—a total of almost $50 billion—for readiness, force modernization, and quality of life improvements. We will continue our work to ensure that the men and women who wear American uniforms receive adequate pay and support, including: childcare, education, housing, access to quality health care for themselves and their families, and protection against discrimination and sexual harassment. The Administration defense plan reverses the downward trend in procurement with a 40 percent real increase for weapons modernization by 2001. At the same time, as part of its reinventing government program, the Administration has fundamentally reformed government procurement rules in order to get the most for our money. We should also work to increase our efforts to convert unnecessary or obsolete military facilities to serve important economic needs of local communities. . . .

Reducing the threat of weapons of mass destruction. Strengthening our security also requires an aggressive effort against weapons of mass destruction—nuclear, chemical, and biological—and their means of delivery. . . .

The Democratic Party supports efforts to sign a Comprehensive Test Ban Treaty this year and to bring it into force as soon as possible. We support immediate ratification of the Chemical Weapons Convention—delayed too long by the Dole Senate. We support full funding of the Nunn-Lugar Cooperative Threat Reduction program to eliminate former Soviet nuclear and chemical weapons and support funds to ensure that nuclear materials in the former Soviet Union are secure and do not fall into the wrong hands. We support vigilant efforts, in cooperation with the Republic of Korea, Japan, and others, to ensure North Korea fully abides by its agreements to dismantle its nuclear program, and we support the Administration's vigorous efforts to prevent Iraq, Iran, and other dangerous states from acquiring or developing weapons of mass destruction.

The Democratic Party is committed to a strong and balanced National Missile Defense (NMD) program. The Administration is spending $3 billion a year on six different systems to protect our troops in the field and our allies from short and medium range missiles. To prepare for the possibility of a long range missile attack on American soil by a rogue state the Clinton Administration is committed to developing by the year 2000 a defensive system that could be deployed by 2003, well before the threat becomes real. The Democratic Party opposes the Republican NMD plan—spending up to $60 billion on a revival of the Star Wars program that would force us to choose a costly system today that could be obsolete tomorrow. The Republican plan would waste money, weaken America's defenses and violate existing arms control agreements that make us more secure. It is the wrong way to defend America.

Meeting new challenges. Today's Democratic Party knows that stronger security requires vigorous efforts to address the new dangers of this era. Chief among these are the interwoven threats of terrorism, drug trafficking, and international crime. . . .

Today's Democratic Party is determined to keep the war on global terrorism, narcotics, and crime at the center of our security agenda. We will seek increased cooperation from our allies and friends abroad in fighting these threats. We will continue to work aggressively to shut off foreign drug flows, eradicate foreign drug crops, and assist countries that demonstrate active cooperation.

Promoting Peace and Democracy

Today's Democratic Party knows that peace and democracy are products of decisive strength and active diplomacy. That diplomacy must protect our interests while also projecting our values. The Republican Party too often has neglected diplomatic opportunities, slashed the budgets necessary for diplomatic successes, and overlooked the importance to our own security of democracy and human rights abroad. At its core, the Republican Party is locked in a Cold War mentality, and lacks a coherent strategy to nurture and strengthen the global progress toward peace and democracy. . . .

Europe and the former Soviet Union. Today's Democratic Party knows that the security of Europe remains a vital American interest, and that we must remain engaged in Europe, a region in which we have fought the two world wars and the Cold War this century. It is our vision to see, one day, a community of free, democratic, and peaceful nations, bound by political, security, cultural, and economic ties, spanning across North America and Europe. We applaud the Clinton-Gore Administration's efforts to foster a peaceful, democratic and undivided Europe—including expanded support for reform in former communist states; dramatically increased assistance to Ukraine; the Partnership for Peace program of military cooperation with Europe's new democracies; its steady, determined work to add new Central European members to NATO in the near future; and its efforts to resolve regional disputes such as between Greece and Turkey. We support continued efforts to secure a just and lasting peace in Bosnia, Northern Ireland and Cyprus. We are committed to the success of independence in Ukraine and the Baltics. And we support the continuing evolution of a prosperous and peaceful Russia. And as part of our effort to support we will pursue a relationship in which we seek cooperation when we can, and frankly express disagreements where they exist, such as on Chechnya.

Asia. We know that many of America's most pressing security challenges and most promising commercial opportunities lie in the Asia Pacific region. The Democratic Party applauds the important new security charter with Japan, the Administration's close cooperation with the Republic of Korea toward the goal of a unified and non-nuclear peninsula, and the deployment of an American naval task force to the Taiwan Straits to ensure that China's military exercises did not imperil the security of the region. The Party supports the Administration's policy of steady engagement to encourage a stable, secure, open and prosperous China—a China that respects human rights throughout its land and in Tibet, that joins international efforts against weapons proliferation, and that plays by the rules of free and fair trade. Today's Democratic Party strongly supports continued American troop presence in East Asia and efforts to promote increased regional security. And we are committed to building long-term relationships with India, Pakistan, and others in South Asia in order to advance America's diverse interests in that region, from democracy and commerce to nuclear non-proliferation.

The Middle East. President Clinton has overseen a remarkable record of achievement toward peace and security in the Middle East—the Israeli-Palestinian accords; the peace agreement between Israel and Jordan; new regional security and investment summits; Israel's increased acceptance throughout the Middle East and the world; the dual containment of Iraq and Iran. The Democratic Party is committed to help build on this record, knowing that peace and security are indivisible, and supports the efforts by the Clinton-Gore Administration to achieve a comprehensive and lasting peace among Israel and all its neighbors, including Lebanon and Syria. The Democratic Party remains committed to America's long-standing special relationship with Israel, based on shared values, a mutual commitment to democracy and a strategic alliance that benefits both nations. The United States should continue to help Israel maintain its qualitative edge. Jerusalem is the capital of Israel and should remain an undivided city accessible to people of all faiths. We are also committed to working with our Arab partners for peace to build a brighter, more secure and prosperous future for all the people of the Middle East. To that end, we seek to further and enhance our close ties with states and peoples in the Arab and Islamic world committed to non-aggression and willing to take risks for peace.

Latin America and the Caribbean. The Clinton-Gore Administration forged an historic partnership with the democracies of the Western Hemisphere, as reflected in the 1994 Summit of the Americas. Today, every country in the Hemisphere is a democracy except Cuba. Because democratic stability and prosperity in the countries to our south are in our interest and theirs, President Clinton took bold steps to bolster Mexico's economy when it was threatened by crisis; worked to resolve internal and border conflicts in the Hemisphere; joined with regional planners to combat narcotics trafficking; and tightened the tough embargo against Cuba while reaching out to its people. The Democratic Party is committed to further consolidating democracy, stability, and open markets throughout the Hemisphere.

Africa. The Clinton Administration championed South Africa's democratic transition; supported Africa's many emerging democracies and led international efforts to speed the return of democracy in Nigeria; helped save countless lives in Somalia, Rwanda, and elsewhere through conflict resolution, removal of landmines, and humanitarian relief; and took steps to help sub-Saharan Africa's 700 million people develop strong economies and markets. The Democratic Party believes that continuing to help the people of Africa nurture their continent's extraordinary potential and address its serious problems is both the right thing to do and profoundly in America's interest. . . .

Resources for diplomacy. There is a price to be paid for America's security and its leadership in world affairs—and the Republican Party now refuses to pay that price. Even though less than one percent of the federal budget goes to foreign policy spending, the Republican Party has savaged our diplomatic readiness, defaulted on treaty obligations to pay dues to the United Nations, slashed assistance to the poorest and most vulnerable populations on earth, and pushed the United States to dead last among developed nations in the global fight against starvation, infant mortality, natural disasters and environmental degradation and other worldwide problems. The Democratic Party understands that these efforts strengthen our security and express our values, and strongly supports the Clinton-Gore Administration's work to ensure adequate resources for American foreign policy.

Community

Across America, in far too many places, the bonds of community that tie us together and remind us that we rise or fall together, have too often frayed. Today's Democratic Party believes we must reawaken the strong sense of community that has helped America to prosper for 220 years. America is uniquely suited to lead the world into the 21st century because of our great diversity and our shared values. We must never let our differences divide us from each other; instead we must come together on a new common ground, based on the enduring values we share. When Americans work together—in our homes, our schools, our houses of worship, our civic groups, our businesses, labor unions and professional associations—we can meet any challenge, and realize every dream.

Putting Families First

The first and most sacred responsibility of every parent is to cherish our children and strengthen our families. The family is the foundation of American life. After 12 years of all family-values-talk and no family-values-action by the Republicans, President Clinton took office determined to put families first. We support the fundamental themes of the Families First Agenda—promoting paycheck, health care, retirement, and personal security; creating greater educational and economic opportunity; and requiring greater responsibility from individuals, businesses, and government.

Standing up for parents. In the first month of Bill Clinton's Presidency, the Democratic Party ended eight years of Republican gridlock and enacted the Family and Medical Leave Act. Americans blessed with a new child or troubled by a family health crisis can no longer be forced to choose between their families and their jobs. A bipartisan panel reported that 12 million workers have already been able to live up to their family obligations without risking their jobs. And almost 90 percent of businesses found that complying with this law cost them little or nothing. Despite how important this is to American families, Senator Dole led Republican opposition to it and still insists it was wrong. This law is good for families, it is good for America, and it would not be the law today without the Democratic Party. President Clinton fought for and secured tax credits to encourage adoption, because every child deserves a mother and father who will love them and raise them.

Now we want to take the next step. We believe parents should be able to take unpaid leave from work and choose flex time so they can do their job as parents: to do things like go to parent-teacher conferences or take a child to the doctor. . . .

Tobacco. Cigarette smoking is rapidly becoming the single greatest threat to the health of our children. We know that 3,000 young people start smoking every day, and 1,000 of them will lead shorter lives because of it. Despite that, Senator Dole and other Republicans continue to ignore volumes of medical research to make baffling claims that cigarettes are not addictive. They even argue with distinguished Republican experts like President Reagan's Surgeon General C. Everett Koop. President Clinton and Vice President Gore understand that we have a responsibility to protect our children's future by cracking down on illegal sales of tobacco to minors and by curbing sophisticated advertising campaigns designed to entice kids to start smoking before they are old enough to make an informed decision. The President has proposed measures to cut off children's access to cigarettes, crack down on those who sell tobacco to minors illegally, and curtail advertising designed to appeal to children. Tobacco companies may market to adults if they wish, but they must take the responsibility to draw the line on children.

Parents' responsibility. Today's Democratic Party knows that governments do not raise children, parents do. That is why President Clinton and Vice President Gore took action to order all federal agencies to make sure everything government does for children promotes responsibility from all parents, fathers as well as mothers. Now we challenge every parent to put their children first: to help them with their homework, to read to them, to know their teachers, and above all, to teach their children right from wrong and set the best example.

Community Empowerment and Cities

Today's Democratic Party understands that we cannot rebuild our poorest communities by imposing cookie-cutter solutions from Washington. We have to give communities the tools they need to create opportunity. Citizens, local government, the private sector, and civic groups must come together and take the responsibility to rebuild their communities from the bottom up.

Encouraging private sector investment, and community-based solutions. After over a decade of sustained Republican neglect and empty Republican promises, President Clinton and Democrats in Congress launched a comprehensive strategy to unleash economic growth and restore opportunity to our distressed neighborhoods. Without a single Republican vote, we created 105 Empowerment Zones and Enterprise Communities. This effort, chaired by Vice President Gore, is bringing jobs and businesses to our poorest urban and rural areas. Thousands of new businesses have already moved into these areas, or expanded existing operations, bringing new hope and new jobs to these neighborhoods. We reformed the Community Reinvestment Act to shift the focus from process toward results; we implemented low income mortgage purchase requirements on Fannie Mae and Freddie Mac; and we created a Community Development Financial Institutions Fund. Together, these efforts are unleashing billions of dollars in new private sector lending and investment for housing and economic development in our inner cities and poorest rural areas. The President and Vice President have created a brownfields initiative to bring life back to abandoned and contaminated property by reforming outdated regulations and providing incentives for cleanup.

Over the next four years, we want a second round of Empowerment Zones to bring economic growth to more American communities; a significant expansion of the Community Development Financial Institutions Fund to spur more private sector investment in local economies; and a new tax incentive to encourage further cleanup and redevelopment of brownfields. Today's Democratic Party knows that the best way to bring jobs and growth back to our poorest neighborhoods is to harness the job-creating power of the private sector. . . .

Agriculture and the Rural Community

America has the most abundant agricultural economy on earth, and it must be preserved and strengthened as we enter a new century. President Clinton and the Democrats have worked hard to promote economic growth in rural areas, protect the family farm, and ensure that farmers get a fair return for their labor and investment and consumers can continue to count on safe and nutritious foods. In the face of Republican efforts to gut food safety, the Clinton Administration has revolutionized meat inspection and set a new standard of consumer protection. President Clinton has reinvented the Agriculture Department, reducing regulations and bureaucracy and improving service. The Clinton Administration has cracked down on food stamp fraud, and approved experiments in state after state to reform the food stamp program. President Clinton and Democrats in Congress supported new voluntary conservation programs and saved economic development programs for rural areas through the 1996 Farm Bill. We are committed to expanding agricultural exports by reducing unfair subsidies and trade barriers around the world and protecting our farmers from predatory trade practices.

Protecting Our Environment

Today's Democratic Party wants all Americans to be able to enjoy America's magnificent natural heritage—and we want our people to know that the air they breathe is pure, the water they drink is clean, and the land they live on is safe from hazard. We understand we have a sacred obligation to protect God's earth and preserve our quality of life for our children and our children's children. For the 12 Republican years before Bill Clinton and Al Gore took office, protecting the environment was far from a priority. And in the last two years, 25 years of bipartisan environmental progress—started by a Democratic Congress under a Republican President—have come under attack from the far right. Time and again, President Clinton and the Democratic Party have stood firm against this onslaught.

The Republican Congress, under Senator Dole and Speaker Gingrich, voted to cut environmental enforcement resources by 25 percent. President Clinton and Democrats in Congress said no. We believe government has a responsibility to enforce the laws that help keep toxic chemicals from our water, pesticides from our food, and smog from our air.

The Republican Congress, under Senator Dole and Speaker Gingrich, let lobbyists for the polluters write their own loopholes into bills to weaken laws that protect the health and safety of our children. President Clinton and Democrats in Congress said no. We believe America's elected officials have a responsibility to protect America's families from threats to their health, and that trust must never be abdicated—especially not by placing control of environmental safeguards in the hands of the very polluters those safeguards are meant to keep in line.

The Republican Congress, under Senator Dole and Speaker Gingrich, tried to make taxpayers pick up the tab for toxic wastes, and let polluters who caused the problem and can afford to fix it off the hook. President Clinton and Democrats in Congress said no. We believe America should insist that toxic waste cleanup is paid for by those responsible for it in the first place—and not foisted off on the taxpayers.

In the last four years, President Clinton and Vice President Gore have taken strong action to make our air and water cleaner. They reformed the Superfund program—in each of the last two years nearly as many toxic dumps were cleaned as in the previous decade. They dramatically strengthened Community Right-to-Know efforts, because Americans should be informed about toxic chemicals being released into the air and water so they can take steps to protect themselves and their families. They took measures to cut toxic air pollution from chemical plants by 90 percent, and after years of Republican neglect they cleaned up hundreds of nuclear weapons sites and are committed to finishing the job.

Today's Democratic Party knows that we can protect the environment *and* expand the economy. We believe we can create more jobs over the long run by cleaning the environment. We want to challenge businesses and communities to take more initiative in protecting the environment, and we want to make it easier for them to do it. President Clinton and Vice President Gore launched Project XL which tells businesses: If you can find a cheaper, more efficient way than government regulations require to meet even tougher pollution goals, do it—as long as you do it right. This new approach offers business flexibility, incentives, and accountability.

Environmental protection should include more education on compliance for small and medium sized business, more strategies to increase compliance for all businesses, and tough enforcement—including criminal prosecution—for those who put human health and the environment at risk.

We are committed to protecting the majestic legacy of our National Parks and enhancing recreational opportunities. We are determined to continue working to restore the Florida Everglades, to preserve our wildlife refuges, and to fight any effort to open the Arctic National Wildlife Refuge to oil and gas drilling. We will be good stewards of our old-growth forests, oppose new offshore oil drilling and mineral exploration and production in our nation's many environmentally critical areas, and protect our oceans from oil spills and the dumping of toxic and radioactive waste.

The President and Vice President announced an historic partnership with the Big Three American automakers to develop the technology to produce cars up to three times more fuel efficient than those made today—cleaner cars for a cleaner environment. We will continue to support responsible recycling, and encourage energy efficiency that makes our economy more efficient and less reliant on foreign oil. We believe that adequate investments in better mass transit, cleaner cars, and renewable energy sources are good for the environment and good for the economy.

After years in which Republicans neglected the global environment, the Clinton Administration has made America a leader in the fight to meet environmental challenges that transcend national borders and require global cooperation. The Clinton-Gore Administration led the world in calling for a global ban on ocean-dumping of low-level radioactive waste and for a legally binding treaty to phase out persistent organic pollutants such as DDT and PCBs. We will seek a strong international agreement to further reduce greenhouse gas emissions worldwide and protect our global climate. We are committed to preserving the planet's biodiversity, repairing the depleted ozone layer, and working with other nations to stabilize population growth.

Democrats recognize that sustainable development is the key to protecting the environment and promoting economic growth. That is why the Clinton-Gore Administration has reformed our foreign aid programs to focus on sustainable development. At home, Democrats know that sound economic development means sound environmental protection.

The American Community

Today's Democratic Party knows that when America is divided we will likely fail, but when America is united we will always prevail. Americans will always have differences, and when we reach across those differences, we are stronger for it. And we share an abiding set of values that define us as Americans. Our task is to draw strength from both—from our great diversity and our constant values—to fashion the future we want for our children.

Fighting discrimination and protecting civil rights. Today's Democratic Party knows we must renew our efforts to stamp out discrimination and hatred of every kind, wherever and whenever we see it. We deplore the recent wave of burnings that has targeted African-American churches in the South, as well as other houses of worship across the country, and we have established a special task force to help local communities catch and prosecute those responsible, prevent further arsons, and rebuild their churches. We believe everyone in America should learn English so they can fully share in our daily life, but we strongly oppose divisive efforts like English-only legislation, designed to erect barriers between us and force people away from the culture and heritage of which they are rightly proud. We must remember we do not have an American to waste. We continue to lead the fight to end discrimination on the basis of race, gender, religion, age, ethnicity, disability, and sexual orientation. The Democratic Party has always supported the Equal Rights Amendment, and we are committed to ensuring full equality for women and to vigorously enforce the Americans with Disabilities Act. We support continued efforts, like the Employment Non-Discrimination Act, to end discrimination against gay men and lesbians and further their full inclusion in the life of the nation.

Over the last four years, President Clinton and the Democrats have worked aggressively to enforce the letter and spirit of civil rights law. The President and Vice President remain committed to an Administration that looks like America, and we are proud of the Administration's extraordinary judicial appointments—they are both more diverse and more qualified than any previous Administration. We know there is still more we can do to ensure equal opportunity for all Americans, so all people willing to work hard can build a strong future. President Clinton is leading the way to reform affirmative action so that it works, it is improved, and promotes opportunity, but does not accidentally hold others back in the process. Senator Dole has promised to end affirmative action. He's wrong, and the President is right. When it comes to affirmative action, we should mend it, not end it.

Religious freedom. Today's Democratic Party understands that all Americans have a right to express their faith. The Constitution prohibits the state establishment of religion, and it protects the free exercise of religion. The President fought for and signed the Religious Freedom Restoration Act, to reaffirm the great protection the Constitution gives to religious expression, and to recognize the historic role people of faith have played in America. Americans have a right to express their love of God in public, and we applaud the President's work to ensure that children are not denied private religious expression in school. Whenever the religious rights of our children—or any American—are threatened, we will stand against it.

Responsibility to our community and our country. Today's Democratic Party believes every American has a duty and a responsibility to give something back to their community and their country. In the past three years, 45,000 Americans have performed national service as part of the AmeriCorps program President Clinton and the Democrats fought so hard to create—and we applaud those Republicans who joined a bipartisan effort to preserve AmeriCorps when Speaker Gingrich's House tried to kill it.

We applaud the American spirit of voluntarism and charity. As we balance the budget, we must work even harder in our own lives to live up to the duties we owe one another. We must shrink the government, but we cannot shrink from our challenges. We believe every school and college in America should make service a part of its basic ethic, and we want to expand national service by helping communities give scholarships to high school students for community service. We challenge Americans in all walks of life to make a new commitment to taking responsibility for themselves, their families, their communities, and their country.

If we do our job, we will make the next American century as great as each one that has come before it. We will enter the 21st century with the American Dream alive for all, with America still the world's strongest force for peace and freedom, and with the American community coming together, enriched by our diversity and stronger than ever.

America's best days lie ahead, as we renew our historic pledge to uphold and advance the promise of America—One nation, under God, indivisible, with liberty and justice for all.

September

SECRETARY OF STATE
ON EXPANSION OF NATO
September 6, 1996

A long-discussed plan to expand the North Atlantic Treaty Organization (NATO) to include some former Warsaw Pact nations was kept on track during 1996 despite Russian fears that a bigger NATO alliance—closer to Russian borders—posed a potential threat to Moscow's security interests. NATO took several actions during the year to make expansion a reality, including inviting Moscow to negotiate a formal "charter" outlining its security relations with the alliance.

NATO was expected to invite at least three, and possibly more, Eastern European nations to join the alliance during the annual summit meeting scheduled for July 1997. It was widely assumed that Poland, Hungary, and the Czech Republic would be the first nations invited to join. Other nations with a serious chance of entering NATO on the first or second rounds of expansion were Romania and Slovenia.

President Bill Clinton said on October 22 that the first group of invited countries would become full NATO members in 1999. That would be the year of the alliance's fiftieth anniversary and the tenth anniversary of the fall of the Berlin Wall.

Christopher on NATO Expansion

U.S. Secretary of State Warren Christopher articulated the rationale for an expanded NATO—and for a formal security relationship with Russia—in a speech in Stuttgart, Germany, on September 6. Christopher spoke in the same auditorium where, exactly fifty years before, Secretary of State James Byrnes pledged continued American involvement in Europe, including aid for the reconstruction of countries devastated by World War II. Byrnes's speech, one of the landmark statements on an activist postwar American foreign policy, has been known as the "speech of hope."

In his address, Christopher formally announced the plans for NATO expansion, an event he said "will happen." When the first new members "pass through NATO's open door, that door will stay open for all of those who demonstrated that they are willing and able to shoulder the responsibilities of membership," he said.

At the same time, he called for negotiation of a "charter" covering security issues between NATO and Russia. "NATO and Russia need a charter because we share an interest in preventing armed conflict," he said. "We are equally threatened by proliferation, nuclear smuggling, and the specter of disasters like Chernobyl [the 1986 accident at a nuclear power plant in Ukraine]."

Under the charter, Christopher said, NATO and Russia could establish procedures for jointly responding to crises. The charter also could provide for regular cooperation on security matters, such as joint training for combined military operations. As an example of how such an arrangement might work, Christopher pointed to the United Nations peacekeeping mission in Bosnia, where Russian and NATO forces divided the task of keeping that nation's warring factions separated. (Peacekeeping mission in Bosnia, Historic Documents of 1995, p. 717)

Trying to Calm Russian Fears

The key concern raised by the Russians was the prospect of NATO nuclear weapons being deployed in Eastern Europe. Some Russian officials said they would view such a development in the same way the United States reacted to the Soviet Union's 1962 deployment of nuclear missiles in Cuba—as a hostile act.

Hoping to calm Russian fears on that score, NATO foreign ministers, meeting in Brussels on December 10, issued a statement saying the alliance had "no intention, no plan, and no reason to deploy nuclear weapons on the territory of new members." The statement stopped short of pledging that there never would be such a deployment, but it was the most direct statement on the issue the alliance had yet made. The statement came on the same day the NATO ministers formally ratified the plan to invite new members into the alliance in 1997.

The next day, after meeting with the NATO ministers, Russian foreign minister Yevgeny Primakov implicitly acknowledged the inevitability of NATO expansion. He agreed to negotiations with NATO toward the charter Christopher had proposed governing security relations between the alliance and Russia. Moscow previously had refused to discuss such issues until NATO abandoned its plans for expansion.

Primakov continued to insist that expanding NATO could lead to "a new division of Europe." Even so, he said, Russians were "pragmatists" on the issue. U.S. officials interpreted Primakov's remarks as indicating that the Russians realized they could not stop NATO expansion and might as well try to have some involvement in the process. NATO officials said they hoped to have agreement on a charter outlining security relations between NATO and Russia in time for the July 1997 summit meeting when the first Eastern European nations would be invited to join the alliance.

"I think that over time, the Russian fears can be resolved," Christopher said after the NATO meeting with Primakov. "There is no need to have the enlargement divide Europe."

Christopher's warm words did not put an end to public expressions of Russian anxiety, however. A week later, on December 18, Russian defense minister Igor Rodionov paid his first visit to NATO headquarters but denounced NATO expansion as a step that would "upset the strategic balance on the continent and restore a Cold War situation in Europe that would force Russia to take counter-measures." He did not specify what those measures might be.

Giving Europe a Bigger Role

Even while pushing eastward, NATO took steps during 1996 to give European countries the flexibility to respond to regional crises without necessarily calling on U.S. ground forces. NATO leaders in January 1994 had approved a concept called "joint task forces," under which a limited number of member nations could dispatch military forces to deal with a regional crisis. It took more than two years to work out the details of this task force proposal. NATO foreign ministers approved the detailed plan during a meeting in Berlin on June 3.

Under the task force arrangement, two or more member nations could respond to a military crisis and if necessary borrow units from other NATO countries. To do so, they would need the unanimous approval of NATO's governing body, the North Atlantic Council, and would have to coordinate military operations through the Western European Union, which in the past had been a shell organization that had little responsibility.

The primary purpose of the joint task force concept was to give European countries a means of responding to a crisis—such as the outbreak of civil war in Bosnia—without massive U.S. intervention. Under standard NATO procedures, the United States would almost always provide the bulk of the personnel and equipment for any mission.

Explaining the rationale for the joint task force proposal, German foreign minister Klaus Kinkel said: "In the long run, it is neither in the American nor the European interest that we have to call our American friends each time something flares up somewhere." Even so, U.S. officials said some American forces probably would be involved in any NATO deployment because the United States provided most of the equipment and logistical support for NATO units, and because Washington considered all of Europe as vital to its own security interests.

Interest in European-led NATO missions grew in the early 1990s because of Europe's embarrassing failure to take any direct action to stop the brutal war in Bosnia. Some officials argued that the joint task force concept might make it easier for European countries to respond to similar crises in the future.

Following are excerpts from a speech delivered September 6,
1996, in Stuttgart, Germany, by Secretary of State Warren
Christopher, in which he outlined a vision of an expanded
NATO and security cooperation between NATO and Russia:

As you know, I've come to commemorate with you the "speech of hope," which my predecessor, Secretary of State James Byrnes, gave here in Stuttgart fifty years ago on this very day, in this very auditorium. I have come to recall the half-century of progress we've achieved together since that speech, and to discuss how we can assure a thriving partnership into the next century. . . .

Of course, all of Europe listened intently, for its future hung in the balance. The United States had joined with our Allies to win the war because we knew America could not be free if Europe was not. But in 1946, we had not yet won the peace. . . .

Secretary Byrnes' address came to be known as the "speech of hope" because it put America firmly on the side of those who believed in a better future for Germany and Europe. The principles he expressed in the speech laid the foundation for our successful post-war partnership. They formed the basis for what became a bipartisan American strategy, symbolized by Republican Senator Arthur Vandenberg, who was present at Secretary Byrnes' speech, and you could see him in the newsreel that they showed at the beginning of these proceedings. The principles shaping our approach to Europe to this very day are the ones laid down by Secretary Byrnes.

First, Byrnes pledged that America would remain a political and military power in Europe. After World War I, we had withdrawn from European affairs and paid a terrible price. "We will not again make that mistake," Byrnes said. "We are staying here."

Second, Byrnes asserted that our support for democracy was the key to lasting peace and recovery in Germany and in Europe. "The American people want to return the government of Germany to the German people," he said. We were confident that a democratic Germany could emerge as our partner.

Finally, Byrnes expressed America's commitment to Germany's political and economic unity. The United States believed that Germany had to be united, democratic and free if Europe as a whole was to achieve stability and integration.

Byrnes' far-sighted approach set the stage for George Marshall, Konrad Adenauer, Jean Monnet and the remarkable generation that led the recovery of Europe and gave us 50 years of peace and prosperity. Thanks to them, we realized the promise of the speech of hope. America maintained its engagement and its armed forces in Europe. The German people chose freedom and achieved unification. And together, we stayed the course of the Cold War. . . .

Yet for all the progress that we've made, we still have challenges to meet here in Europe. The end of the Cold War did not bring an end to armed conflict on this continent. And while the division that resulted from the Cold

War is fading, it has not been fully overcome. That division is still visible in the economic gulf between east and west. It is perceptible in the pollution that shortens lives from Ukraine to Silesia. Above all, it is tangible in the desire for greater security felt by citizens from the Baltic to the Black Sea, across a region where our century's two great wars as well as the Cold War began. . . .

At the January 1994 NATO summit, President Clinton proposed and our Allies embraced a comprehensive strategy for European security. President Clinton believes that another summit is needed to complete the implementation of this comprehensive strategy. I would expect that our leaders will meet in the spring or early summer of 1997 at an extremely important summit. Their objective should be to agree on NATO's internal reforms, launch enlargement negotiations for NATO, and deepen NATO's partnership with Russia and other European states.

The purpose of NATO reform is to ensure that NATO can meet new challenges in a Europe where no power poses a threat to any other. . . .

NATO enlargement, too, is on track and it will happen. Right now, NATO is engaged in an intensive dialogue with interested countries to determine what they must do, and what NATO must do, to prepare for their accession to NATO. Based upon these discussions, at the 1997 summit we should invite several partners to begin accession negotiations. When the first new members pass through NATO's open door, that door will stay open for all of those who demonstrated that they are willing and able to shoulder the responsibilities of membership. NATO should enter a new phase of intensified dialogue with all those who continue to seek membership after the first candidates are invited to join.

Enlargement will ensure that NATO's benefits do not stop at a line that lost its relevance when the Berlin Wall fell. The steps our partners are taking to prepare for membership—steps like strengthening democracy and building trust with their neighbors—these steps have already given central Europe greater stability than it has seen this century. Indeed, no alliance has ever been more effective in preventing conflict than NATO. That is why we created it. That is why our partners in the Partnership for Peace wish to join it. And that is why NATO is at the heart of our European strategy.

Of course, all of Europe's new democracies, whether they join NATO sooner, later, or not at all, deserve a full opportunity to help shape Europe's future. For this reason, we must expand the scope of NATO's Partnership for Peace.

Thanks to the Partnership for Peace, we can now form the first truly European-wide military coalitions, in which soldiers from Russia and America, Poland and Ukraine, Germany and Lithuania train side by side, ready to deploy at a moment's notice to protect our security. To this end, we should expand the Partnership's mandate beyond its current missions. We should involve our partners in the Partnership for Peace in the planning as well as the execution of NATO's missions. We should give them a stronger voice by forming an Atlantic Partnership Council. In all of these ways, NATO gives us a foundation to build our New Atlantic Community—one in which all of Europe and North America work together to build lasting security. . . .

The vision I have outlined here today for the new Atlantic Community can succeed only if we recognize Russia's vital role in the New Atlantic Community. For most of this century, fear, tyranny and self-isolation kept Russia from the European mainstream. But now, new patterns of trust and cooperation are taking hold. The Russian people are building a new society on a foundation of democratic and free market ideals. Though their struggle is far from complete, as the assault on Chechnya has demonstrated, the Russian people have rejected a return to the past and vindicated our confidence in democracy—the same kind of confidence that Secretary Byrnes expressed from this platform 50 years ago. Now, an integrated, democratic Russia can participate in the construction of an integrated, democratic Europe.

Today, I want to say this to the Russian people: We welcome you as our full partners in building a new Europe that is free of tyranny, division and war. We want to work with you to bring Russia into the family of market democracies. We want you to have a stake and a role in the institutions of European security and economic cooperation. That is why we seek a fundamentally new relationship between Russia and the new NATO. Such a relationship, I am confident, is possible. It is important to all of us. And we are determined to make it happen.

Russia's cooperation with NATO should be expressed in a formal Charter. This Charter should create standing arrangements for consultation and joint action between Russia and the Alliance.

NATO and Russia need a charter because we share an interest in preventing armed conflict. We are equally threatened by proliferation, nuclear smuggling, and the specter of disasters like Chernobyl. The Charter we seek should give us a permanent mechanism for crisis management so we can respond together immediately as these challenges arise. Our troops should train together for joint operations. The potential of our partnership is already on display in Bosnia, where our troops are shouldering common burdens and sharing common achievements. Let us, with Russia, take the next logical step.

Our efforts in Bosnia have demonstrated both the possibilities and the urgency of building a New Atlantic Community. In many ways, Bosnia today stands where Europe stood in 1946. Its city parks have been turned into cemeteries. Its children have known terror and hunger and they have seen the destructive power of hatred. Yet it also stands on the threshold of a better future. The war is over and the way forward is clear: It depends on democracy, justice and integration. Last month, I was in Sarajevo and I saw the tremendous progress made since the Dayton Accord opened the way to peace. Germany's diplomacy, its economic aid, and its military contributions have all been vital in providing that new possibility for Bosnia and for all the people of that tragic country. . . .

Our second challenge in building a New Atlantic Community is to promote prosperity among our nations and to extend it globally. The United States and Europe have built the largest economic relationship in the world. It supports over 14 million jobs on both sides of the Atlantic.

We must move toward a free and open Transatlantic Marketplace, as the United States and the EU [European Union] foreshadowed in their summit meeting last December. As barriers fall and momentum builds, the boundaries of what seems feasible will certainly expand. We are already at a stage when we can realistically discuss the true integration of the economies of Europe and North America. We should now pursue practical steps toward even more visionary goals, such as reducing regulatory barriers.

Our vision for open trade and investment in the New Atlantic Community must be as broad as our vision of that community itself. In other words, it must extend to central Europe and the New Independent States, including Russia. . . .

Our New Atlantic Community will only be secure if we also work together to meet the threats that transcend our frontiers—threats like terrorism, nuclear proliferation, crime, drugs, disease and damage to the environment. The danger posed by these threats is as great as any that we faced during the Cold War. Meeting these threats is our third challenge for the waning years of this century, and I want to discuss today just two elements of it, that is: terrorism and the environment.

We must be united in confronting terrorism wherever it occurs. From the clubs of Berlin to the metros of Paris, from the sidewalks of London to the office towers of New York, lawless predators have turned our citizens into targets of opportunity and our public places into stalking grounds. . . .

Environmental threats also respect no borders. They harm our economies and the health of our people. That is why President Clinton and I have acted to place environmental issues in the mainstream of American foreign policy.

Here in Europe, our most urgent environmental challenge is to repair the ravages done by decades of communist misrule. From the abandoned villages around Chernobyl, to the depleted forests in Siberia, to the rusted hulks of factories in central Europe, environmental damage is among the most devastating legacies that Europe's new democracies must overcome. . . .

All the steps that I have suggested today will require our governments to work more closely together. . . .

All this began right here, amidst the rubble and despair of 1946. And if our hopes are high today, it is because of what Germany has achieved with its partners since then. Because of what we have done together, my country can look forward to a future partnership with a new Germany in a new Europe: a Europe where frontiers unite rather than divide; a Europe with horizons wider than its borders.

We struggled with you to build this new Europe. And now, as my predecessor did 50 years ago, let me say on behalf of America: We are staying here. We can meet the challenges I have outlined. We can build a free, united and prosperous new Atlantic Community. And when we do, people around the world will be inspired by the example that Europe and America have set, just as we have been inspired by the example that Germany has set. Thank you very much.

GAO ON AVIATION
SECURITY REQUIREMENTS
September 11, 1996

The crash of TWA flight 800 on July 17, killing all 230 on board, renewed concerns about terrorist threats to the U.S. aviation industry. Government investigators initially believed a bomb caused the explosion that destroyed the plane over Long Island Sound, but after months of research investigators appeared to have concluded that a mechanical failure was the more likely explanation.

Following the crash, President Bill Clinton took several steps to beef up security procedures at U.S. airports. He also appointed a commission, headed by Vice President Al Gore, to make long-term recommendations to guard against terrorism and similar threats to the aviation industry. Over the years, the government had periodically bolstered aviation security measures in the wake of specific incidents, such as the 1988 terrorist bombing of Pan American World Airways Flight 103 over Lockerbie, Scotland, and the Persian Gulf War in 1991. (Pan Am flight 103, Historic Documents of 1990, p. 301)

Congress supported most of the measures that Clinton implemented on his own authority or suggested as legislative remedies. Over the longer term, however, it was uncertain whether Congress would be willing to spend the kind of money some experts were recommending for tougher aviation security measures. One federal advisory committee, for example, suggested spending an additional $1 billion annually, which would be appropriated from general tax revenues.

The General Accounting Office (GAO), the investigative arm of Congress, on September 11 reported to a House subcommittee that protecting civil aviation against terrorism was an "urgent national issue" requiring greater attention and funding than it had received. The GAO said the domestic and international aviation system had "serious vulnerabilities," such as the limited ability of conventional X-ray screening devices to detect even a "moderately sophisticated explosive device," and the tendency of those devices to give false alarms. Further, the GAO said it would take years to develop some of the technology needed to detect bombs in luggage and cargo with reasonable certainty.

Clinton's Response to the Crash

Eight days after the TWA flight 800 explosion, President Clinton met in New York with families of crash victims and announced several steps to tighten airport security. The president pledged a thorough government investigation of the disaster and apologized for delays in notifying the victims' families.

Clinton's measures included increased hand searches of passenger baggage and cargo; mandatory preflight inspections of the passenger cabins and cargo areas of all planes flying within, to, or from the United States; and bans on curb-side check-in of luggage for international flights or airport check-ins of luggage by hotels for any flights, whether domestic or international.

The president also announced the formation of the Gore Commission, which he asked to come up with long-term recommendations for aviation safety. That commission made an interim report to the president on September 9, and he accepted its recommendations. The panel was to make a final report early in 1997.

"We know we can't make the world risk-free, but we can reduce the risks we face, and we have to take the fight to the terrorists," Clinton said at a White House ceremony at which Gore presented the initial findings.

In general, the commission called for a greatly expanded federal role in safeguarding security at airports—well beyond the government's previous primary role of monitoring the performance of airports and airlines. The president said he would ask Congress for $430 million in additional funds for a variety of airport security programs. The single most expensive item ($129 million) was for installing sophisticated equipment at key airports to detect bombs in carry-on and checked baggage. Other major requests and their projected costs were: expanded screening of cargo on international flights ($31 million); giving the U.S. Customs Service additional authority and manpower for security efforts ($27 million); doubling the budget of the Federal Aviation Administration (FAA) for research on safety measures ($20 million); and doubling the FAA's force of security agents to 1,200 ($18 million).

Other commission recommendations approved by the president included requiring background checks on all airport workers with access to secure areas, establishing a computer system enabling airlines to compare information about passengers (such as names and addresses) with government criminal records and "profiles" of persons with suspicious travel patterns, and creating a test program to match luggage and passengers on domestic flights (similar to what was being done on international flights).

Civil liberties groups raised constitutional concerns about some of these measures, particularly the proposal to match information about passengers with government criminal records. Acknowledging these concerns,

Gore set up a subcommittee to find ways of matching records while mini-mizing violations of passenger privacy.

FAA Authorization Bill

Congress in October approved some of Clinton's proposals, along with other aviation safety provisions, in a bill (PL 104–264) providing funding author-ity for the FAA. Among the administration recommendations, the bill autho-rized so-called passenger profiling, under which airlines could compare information about their passengers with government lists of suspected ter-rorists; required criminal background checks on employees who operate air-port metal detectors; mandated that airlines share information on applicants for pilot positions; and designated the National Transportation Safety Board as the primary agency to contact families of victims of air disasters. The last provision was in response to complaints by some victims' families that var-ious federal agencies did not coordinate their response to air disasters.

The bill also authorized funding for stepped up security measures at airports. These included doubling the number of FAA security agents over three years and acquiring additional baggage screeners to detect explosives and additional dog teams to sniff luggage for explosives.

Accepting a related administration recommendation, the bill ended the FAA's dual mandate to both regulate and promote civil aviation—a man-date some critics said compromised the agency's objectivity on safety-related issues. The bill made safety the FAA's primary mission. This rec-ommendation stemmed from controversy over the FAA's monitoring of the ValuJet airline; a ValuJet plane crashed in the Florida Everglades on May 11, killing 110 people. (Airline safety issues, p. 237)

FAA's Aviation Security Advisory Committee

An even more ambitious set of proposals came on December 12 from the Aviation Security Advisory Committee, created by the FAA on the day of the TWA explosion. That panel consisted of experts from inside and outside the government. That panel made some of the same recommendations as the Gore Commission, but went much further. Its proposals, estimated to cost about $1 billion annually above current spending levels, included such steps as requiring licenses for airport security workers (similar to the way airline mechanics were licensed) and screening all carry-on baggage for explosives (existing screening procedures generally were able to detect only weapons such as guns and knives).

The committee also recommended stationing FBI agents full-time at major airports and beefing up government spending on research and development programs for airport security. In addition, the committee proposed shifting the focus of FAA airport and airline inspections from locating specific security lapses to focusing on how regulations could be improved. In connection with this latter recommendation, the panel sug-gested penalties for journalists and others who conducted "unauthorized testing" of airport security. News organizations had found serious lapses in security procedures at numerous airports—embarrassing the FAA and the aviation industry generally.

The security committee suggested that most of the improvements be financed with general tax revenues, rather than through user fees such as additional taxes on ticket prices. The committee argued that bolstering aviation security and thwarting terrorism were national concerns that taxpayers should finance.

DOT Inspector General

In September the Transportation Department's inspector general released a report highly critical of FAA oversight of airport security. One section of the report, based on a 1995 audit of FAA inspections at twenty-eight airports, found that some FAA agents had reported the results of inspections in a manner that put airport security in a more favorable light than was warranted. The report also evaluated the FAA's inspections of airline security procedures and found that in some cases FAA agents failed to use realistic testing measures and attempted to give the airline "every opportunity to pass" the inspections. The report praised the work of other FAA inspectors as professional and objective.

Agents for the inspector general conducted their own security checks at airports by trying to pass guns, knives, and even fake bombs through metal detectors and onto airplanes. The results of these tests were not given in the published version of the report. However, the New York Times quoted officials familiar with the report as saying 40 percent of these efforts succeeded—a drop from a 75 percent success rate in a 1993 study. The Times cited evidence that the Transportation Department withheld the inspector general's report until after the summer Olympics in Atlanta because of fears that publication might unnerve travelers planning to attend the event.

> *Following are excerpts from testimony on "urgent issues" in aviation security, given September 11, 1996, by Keith O. Fulz, assistant comptroller general of the General Accounting Office's Resources, Community, and Economic Development Division, before the Subcommittee on Aviation of the House Committee on Transportation and Infrastructure:*

Protecting civil aviation from a terrorist attack is an urgent national issue. We appreciate the opportunity to testify before this Committee on the serious vulnerabilities that exist within the nation's air transportation system and ways to address them. Experts on terrorism within the government intelligence agencies believe that the threat to civil aviation is increasing. The threat from concealed explosive devices remains a high concern. The 1988 terrorist bombing of Pan Am flight 103, which killed 270 people, and the more recent, but as yet unexplained, explosion of TWA flight 800 have shaken the public's confidence in the safety and security of air travel. . . .

The following is our summary:

- The threat of terrorism against the United States has increased. Aviation is and will remain an attractive target for terrorists.
- The Federal Aviation Administration (FAA) has mandated additional security procedures as the threat has increased. Currently, aviation security relies on a mix of procedures and technology. However, the domestic and international aviation system has serious vulnerabilities. For example, conventional X-ray screening of checked baggage has performance limitations and offers little protection against a moderately sophisticated explosive device.
- Explosives detection devices that could improve security are commercially available for checked and carry-on baggage, but all of the devices have some limitations. Some of these devices are being tested domestically and are already in use at overseas locations. The Gore Commission has recommended that the federal government purchase some of this equipment for use in airports. Other devices are under development and may be available in a few years for screening baggage and passengers, but technologies for screening cargo and mail at airports are not as far along. Other security methods that could be expanded upon—and that have been recommended by the Gore Commission—include matching passengers with their bags and identifying passengers for additional security screening (profiling). A mix of technology and procedures will likely be needed to improve security.
- To improve aviation security, the Congress, the administration—specifically FAA and the intelligence community, among others—and the aviation industry need to agree and take action on what needs to be done to meet the threat of terrorism and who will pay for it. Several initiatives are under way to address this issue; they include two presidential commissions and an FAA working group. We have made recommendations to strengthen these initiatives. The Gore Commission's report provides opportunities for agreement on steps that could be taken in the short term; however, the issue of how to finance security over the long term still needs to be addressed. Given the urgent need to improve aviation security and FAA's problems in addressing long-standing safety and security concerns, once steps are agreed upon, it will be important for the Congress to monitor their implementation. Therefore, we believe that the Congress should establish goals and performance measures and require periodic reports from FAA and other federal agencies on the progress and effectiveness of efforts to improve aviation security.

The Threat of Terrorists' Attacks on U.S. Civil Aviation Has Increased

. . . Until the early 1990s, the threat of terrorism was considered far greater overseas than in the United States. However, the threat of international terrorism within the United States has increased. Events such as the World

Trade Center bombing have revealed that the terrorists' threat in the United States is more serious and extensive than previously believed.

Terrorists' activities are continually evolving and present unique challenges to FAA and law enforcement agencies. We reported in March 1996 that the bombing of Philippine Airlines flight 434 in December 1994 illustrated the potential extent of terrorists' motivation and capabilities as well as the attractiveness of aviation as a target for terrorists. According to information that was accidentally uncovered in January 1995, this bombing was a rehearsal for multiple attacks on specific U.S. flights in Asia.

Aviation Security System and Its Vulnerabilities

Even though FAA has increased security procedures as the threat has increased, the domestic and international aviation system continues to have numerous vulnerabilities. According to information provided by the intelligence community, FAA makes judgments about the threat and decides which procedures would best address the threat. The airlines and airports are responsible for implementing the procedures and paying for them. For example, the airlines are responsible for screening passengers and property, and the airports are responsible for the security of the airport environment. FAA and the aviation community rely on a multifaceted approach that includes information from various intelligence and law enforcement agencies, contingency plans to meet a variety of threat levels, and the use of screening equipment, such as conventional X-ray devices and metal detectors.

For flights within the United States, basic security measures include the use of walk-through metal detectors for passengers and X-ray screening of carry-on baggage—measures that were primarily designed to avert hijackings during the 1970s and 1980s, as opposed to the more current threat of attacks by terrorists that involve explosive devices. These measures are augmented by additional procedures that are based on an assessment of risk. Among these procedures are passenger profiling and passenger-bag matching.

Because the threat of terrorism had previously been considered greater overseas, FAA mandated more stringent security measures for international flights. Currently, for all international flights, FAA requires U.S. carriers, at a minimum, to implement the International Civil Aviation Organization's standards that include the inspection of carry-on bags and passenger-bag matching. FAA also requires additional, more stringent measures—including interviewing passengers that meet certain criteria, screening every checked bag, and screening carry-on baggage—at all airports in Europe and the Middle East and many airports elsewhere.

In the aftermath of the 1988 bombing of Pan Am flight 103, a Presidential Commission on Aviation Security and Terrorism was established to examine the nation's aviation security system. This commission reported that the system was seriously flawed and failed to provide the flying public with adequate protection. FAA's security reviews, audits prepared by the Department of Transportation's Office of the Inspector General, and work we have conducted show that the system continues to be flawed.

Providing effective security is a complex problem because of the size of the U.S. aviation system, the differences among airlines and airports, and the unpredictable nature of terrorism. In our previous reports and testimonies on aviation security, we highlighted a number of vulnerabilities in the overall security system, such as checked and carry-on baggage, mail, and cargo. We also raised concerns about unauthorized individuals gaining access to critical parts of an airport and the potential use of sophisticated weapons, such as surface-to-air missiles, against commercial aircraft. According to FAA officials, more recent concerns include smuggling bombs aboard aircraft in carry-on bags and on passengers themselves.

Specific information on the vulnerabilities of the nation's aviation security system is classified and cannot be detailed here, but we can provide you with unclassified information. Nearly every major aspect of the system—ranging from the screening of passengers, checked and carry-on baggage, mail, and cargo as well as access to secured areas within airports and aircraft—has weaknesses that terrorists could exploit. FAA believes that the greatest threat to aviation is explosives placed in checked baggage. For those bags that are screened, we reported in March 1996 that conventional X-ray screening systems (comprising the machine and operator who interprets the image on the X-ray screen) have performance limitations and offer little protection against a moderately sophisticated explosive device. In our August 1996 classified report, we provided details on the detection rates of current systems as measured by numerous FAA tests that have been conducted over the last several years.

In 1993, the Department of Transportation's Office of the Inspector General also reported weaknesses in security measures dealing with (1) access to restricted airport areas by unauthorized persons and (2) carry-on baggage. A follow-on review in 1996 indicated that these weaknesses continue to persist and have not significantly improved.

Explosives Detection Technology Has Limitations in Meeting the Increased Threat

New explosives detection technology will play an important part in improving security, but it is not a panacea. In response to the Aviation Security Improvement Act of 1990, FAA accelerated its efforts to develop explosives detection technology. A number of devices are now commercially available to address some vulnerabilities. Since fiscal year 1991, FAA has invested over $150 million in developing technologies specifically designed to detect concealed explosives. FAA relies primarily on contracts and grants with private companies and research institutions to develop these technologies and engages in some limited in-house research. The act specifically directed FAA to develop and deploy explosives detection systems by November 1993. However, this goal has not been met.

Since fiscal year 1991, these expenditures have funded approximately 85 projects for developing new explosives detection technology. Currently, FAA has 40 active development projects. Of these, 19 projects are developing explosives detection prototype systems. The remaining 21 projects are conducting basic research or developing components for use in explosives detection systems.

In September 1993, FAA published a certification standard that explosives detection systems for checked bags must meet before they are deployed. The standard is classified and sets certain minimum performance criteria. To minimize human error, the standard also requires that the devices automatically sound an alarm when explosives are suspected; this feature is in contrast to currently used conventional X-ray devices, whereby the operator has to look at the X-ray screen for each bag to determine whether it contains a threat. In 1994, we reported that FAA had made little progress in meeting the law's requirement for deploying explosives detection systems because of technical problems, such as slow baggage processing. As of today, one system has passed FAA's certification standard and is being operationally tested by U.S. airlines at two U.S. airports and one foreign location.

Explosives detection devices can substantially improve the airlines' ability to detect concealed explosives before they are brought aboard aircraft. While most of these technologies are still in development, a number of devices are now commercially available. However, none of the commercially available devices are without limitations. On the basis of our analysis, we have three overall observations on detection technologies.

- First, these devices vary in their ability to detect the types, quantities, and shapes of explosives.
- Second, explosives detection devices typically produce a number of false alarms that must be resolved either by human intervention or technical means. These false alarms occur because the devices use various technologies to identify characteristics, such as shapes, densities, and other properties, to indicate a potential explosive. Given the huge volume of passengers, bags, and cargo processed by the average major U.S. airport, even relatively modest false alarm rates could cause several hundreds, even thousands, of items per day to need additional scrutiny.
- Third, and most important, these devices ultimately depend upon human beings to resolve alarms. This activity can range from closer inspection of a computer image and a judgment call to a hand search of the item in question. The ultimate detection of explosives depends on extra steps being taken by security personnel—or their arriving at the correct judgment—to determine whether an explosive is present. Because many of the devices' alarms signify only the potential for explosives being present, the true detection of explosives requires human intervention. The higher the false alarm rate, the greater is the system's need to rely on human judgment. As we noted in our previous reports, this reliance could be a weak link in the explosives detection process. In addition, relying on human judgments has implications for the selection and training of operators for new equipment.

Despite the limitations of the currently available technology, some countries have already deployed some explosives detection equipment because of differences in their perception of the threat and their approaches to counter the threat. The Gore Commission recommends that $161 million in federal funds be used to deploy some of these devices. It has also recommended that decisions about deploying equipment be based on vulnerability assessments of the nation's 450 largest airports. . . .

Other Methods to Improve Aviation Security

In addition to technology-based security, FAA has other methods that it uses, and can expand upon, to augment domestic aviation security or use in combination with technology to reduce the workload required by detection devices. The Gore Commission has recommended expanded use of bomb-sniffing dogs, profiling passengers to identify those needing additional attention, and matching passengers with their bags.

Dogs are considered a unique type of trace detector because they can be trained to respond in specific ways to the smell of explosives. Dogs are currently being used at a number of U.S. airports. The Gore Commission has recommended that 114 additional teams of dogs and their handlers be deployed at a cost of about $9 million.

On July 25, 1996, the President announced additional measures for international and domestic flights that include, among other things, stricter controls over checked baggage and cargo as well as additional inspections of aircraft. Two procedures that are routinely used on many international flights are passenger profiling and passenger-bag matching. FAA officials have said that profiling can reduce the number of passengers and bags that require additional security measures by as much as 80 percent. The Gore Commission has recommended several initiatives to promote an automated profiling system. In addition, to determine the best way to implement systemwide matching of passengers with their bags, the Gore Commission has recommended testing techniques at selected airports.

Profiling and bag matching are unable to address certain types of threats. However, in the absence of sufficient or effective technology, these procedures are a valuable part of the overall security system. FAA has estimated that incorporating bag matching in everyday security measures could cost up to $2 billion in start-up costs and lost revenue. The direct costs to airlines include, among other things, equipment, staffing, and training. The airlines' revenues and operations could be affected differently because the airlines currently have different capabilities to implement bag matching, different route structures, and different periods of time allotted between connecting flights.

Initiatives to Address Vulnerabilities
Should Be Coordinated

Addressing the vulnerabilities in the nation's aviation security system is an urgent national issue. Although the Gore Commission made recommendations on September 9, no agreement currently exists among all the key players, namely, the Congress, the administration—specifically FAA and the intelligence community, among others—and the aviation industry, on the steps necessary to improve security in the short and long term to meet the threat. In addition, who will be responsible in the long term for paying for new security initiatives has not been addressed. While FAA has increased security at domestic airports on a temporary basis, FAA and Department of Transportation officials believe that more permanent changes are needed. Furthermore, the cost of these changes will be significant, may require changes in how airlines and airports operate, and will likely have an impact on the flying public. To achieve these permanent changes, three initiatives that are under way may assist in developing a consensus among all interested parties on the appropriate direction and response to meet the ever-increasing threat. . . .

In our August 1, 1996, testimony before the Senate Committee on Commerce, Science, and Transportation, we emphasized the importance of informing the American public of and involving them in this effort. Furthermore, we recommended that the following steps be taken immediately:

- Conduct a comprehensive review of the safety and security of all major domestic and international airports and airlines to identify the strengths and weaknesses of their procedures to protect the traveling public.
- Identify vulnerabilities in the system.
- Establish priorities to address the system's identified vulnerabilities.
- Develop a short-term approach with immediate actions to correct significant security weaknesses.
- Develop a long-term and comprehensive national strategy that combines new technology, procedures, and better training for security personnel. . . .

PENTAGON REPORT ON TERRORIST BOMBING IN SAUDI ARABIA
September 16, 1996

A tanker truck filled with explosives and parked outside an apartment building housing U.S. Air Force personnel in Dhahran, Saudi Arabia, blew up on the night of June 25, killing nineteen servicemen and wounding about five hundred others. It was the second bombing in less than a year involving U.S. military personnel in Saudi Arabia. Five Americans and two Indians were killed when a car bomb exploded at a Saudi National Guard facility in Riyadh on November 13, 1995.

As of the end of 1996, those responsible for the June bombing had not been captured. U.S. officials said they assumed the bombing was part of a terrorist campaign to force American military units out of Saudi Arabia, where they had been based to enforce United Nations resolutions isolating Iraq since the end of the Persian Gulf War in 1991.

A high-level investigation of the June bombing, ordered by President Bill Clinton, criticized virtually every aspect of the military's defense against terrorism in Saudi Arabia. In particular, it found numerous security lapses that made the Dhahran apartment building vulnerable to terrorist attack. The strongly worded report held the military chain of command—including the local commander, Air Force Brigadier General Terryl Schwalier—responsible for failing to take adequate steps to thwart such an attack.

The results of that investigation were released on September 16. Two days later, Defense Secretary William J. Perry told a House committee: "To the extent that this tragedy resulted from the failure of leadership, that responsibility is mine and mine alone."

In December a follow-up investigation ordered by the air force determined that no U.S. officials, including Schwalier, should be punished as a result of the bombing. According to air force officials, the second investigation determined that Schwalier and his superiors did what could reasonably be expected to protect their troops.

The air force had not released the text of the follow-up report as of the end of 1996. Officials said the findings would be reviewed by the new defense secretary, William Cohen, when he took office in January 1997. In the meantime, Schwalier's promotion to major general—which had been approved by the Senate before the bombing—appeared to be in limbo.

Some Pentagon officials insisted the two sets of findings were not as contradictory as they appeared because the investigations had different purposes. The first probe, headed by retired army major general Wayne Downing, was intended to find out what went wrong and recommend to the Pentagon ways of preventing future terrorist attacks. The aim of the second investigation, headed by air force lieutenant general James F. Record, was to determine whether Schwalier or anyone else should be held legally accountable.

Other officials said there was a widespread feeling in the upper echelons of the air force that it was unfair to single out Schwalier for criticism because the entire U.S. military and intelligence establishments were unprepared for the June 25 bombing. According to this view, Schwalier did not have adequate information on which to base the decisions he made in the months before the attack. In addition, some air force officials reportedly believed that punishing Schwalier, and none of his superiors, would have a demoralizing effect on field commanders.

The Bombing and Warnings About It

The November 1995 car bombing in Riyadh heightened concerns among U.S. military officials in Saudi Arabia about the threat of terrorism. After that incident, the military improved security measures at all U.S. installations in the country—including at the giant Khobar Towers apartment complex in Dhahran, where about three thousand air force personnel lived.

Early in 1996 U.S. intelligence agencies picked up numerous warnings about renewed terrorist attacks, and the agencies specifically cited the Khobar Towers complex as a vulnerable "soft target." By the time of the June 25 bombing, the Downing team's report said, Schwalier was aware of "a considerable body of information" about possible threats to the complex.

The Downing Investigation

The Downing team lodged a number of charges against Schwalier. They noted that, although he was warned of several types of threats to Khobar Towers, Schwalier "concentrated almost exclusively" on preventing a car bomb from entering the apartment compound. The truck bomb that did the damage was parked outside the gate of the compound, about eighty feet from buildings where U.S. airmen lived.

The report added that Schwalier failed to press Saudi officials to correct security weaknesses that were under their control, such as the location and maintenance of the fence surrounding the apartments. In addition, he failed to raise security issues with his superiors in the United States and he failed to ask for additional security personnel to ease the workload on his staff. Guards at the apartment compound often worked twelve-hour shifts six or seven days a week.

Despite two air force reports showing how Khobar Towers was vulnerable to attack, Schwalier failed to take some steps that were recommended to him and that might have reduced the damage caused by a bomb, such as ordering installation of a shatter-resistant film on windows. Most of the deaths and injuries on June 25 resulted from flying glass. The report also said Schwalier could have moved servicemen out of the apartment units that were most vulnerable to a bomb attack.

The Record Investigation

Air Force officials familiar with the follow-up investigation headed by General Record said Schwalier clearly did not do enough to protect his troops. But, they said, he was not negligent because he had taken numerous steps to upgrade security and he did the best he could based on the information available to him.

In particular, the Record investigation noted that Schwalier was never told of the one warning that might have been most useful. In April an air force investigations officer described local security measures as "outstanding," but he warned about precisely the kind of attack that was to occur: "[I]f a truck parks close to the fence line and the driver makes a quick getaway, I think the building should be cleared immediately." That message was sent to the officer's unit headquarters in Washington, D.C., and never passed to Schwalier or his aides.

Both the Downing and Record teams said this incident demonstrated the weakness of the military's "stovepipe" reporting system, under which officials often pass information up through their units' chain of command, bypassing officials in other units who might need that information. However, neither investigation found a general failure of U.S. intelligence-gathering in the Khobar Towers bombing.

Reaction to the Reports

President Clinton, who ordered the Downing investigation, praised its report as "unvarnished, blunt, straightforward" and said he had directed the Pentagon to "aggressively implement" its findings. Defense Secretary Perry on September 15 sent Clinton a detailed summary of the report and his proposals to correct the deficiencies found by the Downing team. For example, Perry said he was ordering that local commanders be given increased authority over security measures to protect their troops.

Members of Congress praised the Downing report and said they would support its recommendations. The Senate Intelligence Committee earlier in September issued its own report on the bombing, bolstering the case that the Pentagon failed to heed intelligence warnings about terrorist threats to U.S. forces in Saudi Arabia.

General Record's investigation clearing Schwalier of legal culpability drew praise from many air force officers, but several members of Congress said they were angered by the air force's apparent decision not to punish anyone. Sen. Arlen Specter, R-Pa., chairman of the Intelligence Committee, called the finding "completely unacceptable." Rep. Floyd Spence, R-S.C., chairman of the House National Security Committee, said the conclusions of the Record probe raised the possibility "of no one within the military chain of command being held accountable for the Khobar Towers tragedy."

Following are excerpts of the executive summary and the central findings on accountability from the report, "Assessment of the Khobar Towers Bombing," written by a Defense Department task force chaired by retired army general Wayne Downing and released September 16, 1996, by the Defense Department:

Executive Summary

On June 25, 1996, a terrorist truck bomb estimated to contain the equivalent of 3,000 to 8,000 pounds of TNT exploded outside the northern perimeter of Khobar Towers, Dhahran, Saudi Arabia, a facility housing U.S. and allied forces supporting the coalition air operation over Iraq, Operation SOUTHERN WATCH. There were 19 fatalities and approximately 500 wounded. The perpetrators escaped.

This bomb attack marked the second terrorist strike at U.S. forces in Saudi Arabia within eight months. On November 13, 1995, a 220-pound car bomb exploded in a parking lot adjacent to an office building housing the Office of the Program Manager, Saudi Arabian National Guard in Riyadh, causing five U.S. and two Indian fatalities. A Department of State Accountability Review Board investigated this attack and made recommendations to improve U.S. security in the region. The DoD also conducted a Department-wide review of antiterrorism readiness following the November 1995 bombing. The Antiterrorism Task Force report made recommendations concerning enhancements to the security posture of deployed forces, education and training, intelligence sharing, and interagency coordination. The Department of State recommendations were being addressed, and the DoD actions were approved and being implemented at the time of the second bombing.

The United States has strategic interests in maintaining a force presence in Saudi Arabia and the Gulf region and in conducting coalition military operations to contain regional aggression. Consequently, the security of U.S. Central Command forces is paramount. On June 28, 1996, the Secretary of Defense directed an assessment of both the facts and circumstances surrounding the attack on Khobar Towers and the security of U.S. forces in the Kingdom of Saudi Arabia and the remainder of southwest Asia. . . .

Major Findings and Recommendations of the Downing Assessment Task Force

. . . A Comprehensive Approach to Force Protection Is Required. The Assessment Task Force recommended that the Department of Defense take a range of actions to deter, prevent, or mitigate the effects of future terrorist attacks on servicemen and women overseas. None will—in and of themselves—provide an environment secure from all potential threats. However, the Task Force strongly believes that to assure an acceptable level of security for U.S. forces worldwide, commanders must aggressively pursue an integrated systems approach to force protection that combines awareness and training, physical security measures, advanced technology systems, and specific protection measures tailored to each location. A comprehensive approach using common guidance, standards, and procedures will correct the inconsistent force protection practices observed in the theater. The Task Force believes that the designation of a single Department of Defense element responsible for force protection, to include antiterrorism and counterterrorism, is required. This entity would have policy, resource, and research and development responsibilities, as well as a capability to assist commanders in the field with implementation of force protection measures.

DoD Must Establish Force Protection Standards. The Department of Defense must establish realistic standards for force protection that provide commanders and staff guidance for construction and hardening of facilities and other overseas sites against the terrorist threat. Basically, the Department of Defense uses State Department standards for physical security. For the threat level, Building 131 at Khobar Towers required no stand-off distance from the perimeter according to State Department standards. Actionable standards will allow commanders to plan and program for the appropriate resources to protect troops and installations. While all U.S. commanders in the Gulf thought they had sufficient resources for force protection, they were not knowledgeable of technologies to enhance protection or how to develop an integrated systems approach to security. Consequently, they underestimated true requirements.

U.S. Central Command Requires an Empowered Chain of Command in the Region. The joint chain of command must have the authority to execute force protection measures. The command relationships in the Gulf were designed to support a short term contingency operation, Operation SOUTHERN WATCH, and enhance the transition of U.S. Central Command to war. The retention of operational control of forces in the theater by service component headquarters located over 7,000 miles away and the assignment of tactical control and oversight to a small, functional Joint Task Force headquarters located in the theater did not support the intensive, day-to-day command attention required to ensure force protection of service members assigned to the Command. The issue of inadequate organization and structure of Joint Task Force Headquarters for peacetime command and control was addressed in the assessment of the Joint Task Force-PROVIDE COMFORT following the shoot-down of two U.S. Army helicopters by U.S. Air Force F-15s in April 1994. The DoD must clarify command relationships in U.S. Central Command to ensure that all commanders have the requisite authority to accomplish their assigned responsibilities. Further, review of temporary Joint Task Force organization and structure must occur frequently to allow adaptation to changing threats and missions.

Command Emphasis on and Involvement in Force Protection Are Crucial. While committees at all levels in the theater and in the United States were active in discussing force protection policies and practices, this did not contribute materially to the security of military people and facilities. Committees are not effective without the emphasis and personal attention of commanders. In part, the inconsistent, and sometimes inadequate, force protection practices among service forces, joint headquarters, and different countries resulted from insufficient command involvement.

The Intelligence Community Provided Warning of the Potential for a Terrorist Attack. U.S. intelligence did not predict the precise attack on Khobar Towers. Commanders did have warning that the terrorist threat to U.S. service members and facilities was increasing. DoD elements in the theater had the authority, but were not exploiting all potential sources of information. Human intelligence (HUMINT) is probably the only source of information that can provide tactical details of a terrorist attack. The U.S. intelligence community must have the requisite authorities and invest more time, people, and funds into developing HUMINT against the terrorist threat.

The Chain of Command Was Responsible for Protecting the Forces at Khobar Towers. The chain of command of the 4404th Wing (Provisional) did not take all measures possible to protect the forces at Khobar Towers. The command relationships established in the region did not support unity of effort in force protection. There were no force protection or training standards provided by U.S. Central Command to forces assigned or deploying to the theater. The rotation and manning policies established by the U.S. Air Force did not support complete, cohesive units, especially Security Police, who were capable of coping with a viable terrorist threat. The Commander, 4404th Wing (Provisional) focused the force protection efforts of the command on preventing a bomb from penetrating the compound at Khobar Towers. Other vulnerabilities were not addressed adequately. Intelligence indicated that Khobar Towers was a potential terrorist target, and incidents from April through June 1996 reflected possible surveillance of the facility. Combined with the November 1995 attack in Riyadh, this should have triggered enhanced force protection measures, regardless of their impact on workload or quality of life. The 4404th Wing commander was ill-served by the intelligence arrangement within his command which focused almost exclusively on the air threat for Operation SOUTHERN WATCH. His senior headquarters, U.S. Air Forces Central Command and U.S. Central Command, did not provide sufficient guidance, assistance, and oversight to the 4404th Wing (Provisional) to avert or mitigate the attack on Khobar Towers. Their location 7,000 miles away contributed to this shortcoming. Placing all forces in Saudi Arabia and the Gulf region under the command of a single commander in the theater will help resolve the force protection problems identified during the Task Force assessment.

Host Nations Share in the Responsibility for Force Protection. Host nations have responsibility for the security of U.S. service members and installations in their country. The option of locating forces in isolated areas may not always exist. U.S. commanders and staffs must appreciate the importance of positive, working relationships with their host nation counterparts for force protection. Through these relationships, they can influence selection of locations of installations, allocation of host nation guard forces and priorities, and enhancement of host nation security as threat conditions escalate.

Department of State/Department of Defense Division of Responsibility Does Not Provide U.S. Forces Adequate Force Protection. The division of responsibility for force protection in the Department of State and the Department of Defense Memorandum of Understanding does not adequately support U.S. forces in countries with a large military presence. In Saudi Arabia, the Chief of Mission did not have sufficient resources to fully execute the force protection mission. Further, not all forces were under the Chief of Mission or combatant commander, creating a seam where certain units did not benefit from active oversight. The Secretary of Defense has the authority to assign forces to the combatant commander to redress this shortfall.

During its visits, the Task Force was impressed with the magnificent work being performed by Americans throughout the region. The 4404th Wing (Provisional) was especially notable. The reaction of these men and women to the bombing on the night of June 25th saved many lives. The care accorded to the more than 500 injured by both their comrades and U.S. and Saudi medical teams was remarkable. The Wing reconstituted and began flying combat missions over Iraq within 48 hours of the tragedy, a testament to the professionalism and fortitude we observed throughout the command. This same quality and professionalism were evident in the men and women of all services everywhere we visited in southwest Asia. . . .

Part III: Facts and Circumstances Surrounding the Bombing Attack on Khobar Towers

The Chain of Command

Finding 19: The chain of command did not provide adequate guidance and support to the Commander, 4404th Wing (Provisional).

The Assessment Task Force has been directed to "Examine the facts and circumstances surrounding the June 25, 1996 bomb attack against Khobar Towers in Dhahran, Saudi Arabia, and assess whether the extent to which the casualties and damage sustained was the result of inadequate security infrastructures, policies, or systems. . . ." The Task Force determined that conditions and circumstances created at all levels of the chain of command caused vulnerabilities that were exploited in the actual attack. . . .

U.S. Air Forces Central Command. U.S. Air Forces Central Command had operational control of the 4404th Wing (Provisional) under the command relationships established by the Commander-in-Chief, U.S. Central Command. Commander, U.S. Air Forces Central Command, did not provide sufficient guidance and assistance to adequately protect the 4404th Wing (Provisional). Headquarters, U.S. Air Forces Central Command was not organized or structured to execute its full responsibilities for the security of forces in the Area of Responsibility. It relied upon Headquarters, U.S. Air Combat Command for some critical functions, like Inspector General inspections. This reliance on Air Combat Command did not, however, relieve U.S. Air Forces Central Command of its command responsibilities. . . .

Recommendation: That the Secretary of Defense take action, as appropriate.

Responsibility for the Security of Khobar Towers

Finding 20: The Commander, 4404th Wing (Provisional) did not adequately protect his forces from a terrorist attack.

Actions and Omissions by the Commander, 4404th Wing (Provisional)

Brigadier General Schwalier had both command responsibility and command authority for force protection matters in the 4404th Wing (Provisional). Therefore, he could take appropriate measures to protect his force and had the responsibility to notify his superiors when he was unable to do so. . . .

Summation. Brigadier General Schwalier was advised that a viable terrorist threat existed and was kept informed that his facility was a terrorist target. It was described as a "soft target," "critical target," and a "specific site of concern." Brigadier General Schwalier was informed of a number of vulnerabilities, but he concentrated almost exclusively on preventing a penetrating bomb attack. Knowing that some vulnerabilities were beyond his capability to correct, he failed to coordinate with his host nation counterpart to address these areas. He accepted the adequacy of host nation security measures in the area outside the fence. Additionally, he failed to raise any force protection issues to his superiors. Without notice and located 7,000 miles away, Brigadier General Schwalier's superiors were unable to assist him. Finally, he did not take those actions which would have mitigated the effects of clearly described vulnerabilities within his power to correct.

Recommendation: Refer to the Chain of Command for action, as appropriate.

CIA DIRECTOR ON
SITUATION IN IRAQ
September 19, 1996

The United States launched missile strikes on September 3 and 4 against Iraqi antiaircraft batteries and expanded the "no fly zone" in the southern part of Iraq. The U.S. moves were in response to the Iraqi military occupation on August 31 of much of the Kurdish "safe haven" region in the northern part of Iraq, which had been under United Nations protection since the 1991 Persian Gulf War. Iraqi leader Saddam Hussein intervened on behalf of one Kurdish faction, which had asked for his help in its ongoing battle with another Kurdish faction backed by Iran.

President Bill Clinton said he ordered the strikes against Iraq to demonstrate that Saddam would pay "a price" whenever he took military action in the region or threatened his neighbors. Saddam immediately withdrew his military from the Kurdish region, but before they left his troops reportedly imprisoned or killed many local opposition leaders.

The U.S.-Iraq confrontation was the latest in a series of low-level skirmishes since a U.S.-led coalition ejected the Iraqi army from Kuwait in 1991. In each case, Washington had taken limited military action in response to provocations by Saddam. In 1993, for example, the United States struck twice at Iraq, once in retaliation for a reported Iraqi assassination attempt against former president George Bush and the second time when an Iraqi antiaircraft battery fired on a U.S. plane enforcing the no-fly zone in northern Iraq. (Persian Gulf War, Historic Documents of 1991, p. 97)

Saddam and the Kurds

Saddam brought on the 1996 confrontation when he agreed to take sides in a complex civil war that had been raging for years between two major Kurdish factions in the northern part of the country. The faction that sought Saddam's help was the Kurdish Democratic Party, headed by Massoud Barzani, who previously had close ties with Washington. The opposing faction was the Patriotic Union of Kurdistan, headed by Jalal Talabani, which received most of its support from Iran.

680

Since the end of the war, the United States and its allies had been providing humanitarian aid and limited military protection to both factions, while trying to contain the civil war between them. In the weeks before the Iraqi invasion, U.S. diplomats tried unsuccessfully to broker a peace agreement between the factions.

When Barzani sought Iraqi military help against his foes, Saddam apparently did not hesitate. Intervening gave him a chance to reassert some authority over the Kurdish region from which his army had been expelled during the war. With a force estimated by U.S. officials at 30,000 to 40,000 troops, the Iraqi army moved into the region on August 31 and quickly occupied the city of Irbil, which had been Talabani's headquarters.

The United States responded with a warning to Saddam to pull his forces out. When Iraq refused to heed that warning, Clinton ordered an attack by Tomahawk cruise missiles on antiaircraft batteries in southern Iraq. Officials said the attacks were made in the south, rather than in the north, to avoid a direct U.S. intervention in the fighting among the Kurds.

Clinton also ordered a significant expansion of the no-fly zone that the United States and its allies had enforced against Iraq since the war. Allied planes routinely patrolled the no-fly zone. Previously, the zone extended from Iraq's southern borders with Kuwait and Saudi Arabia to the 32nd parallel—an area covering the southern one-third of Iraq. Clinton in September ordered the zone extended northward to the 33rd parallel. The expanded zone reached to within about thirty miles of Baghdad, Iraq's capital, and covered an area where many of Iraq's warplanes and antiaircraft missiles had been based.

In a statement from the White House on September 3, Clinton offered this general rationale for his military moves against Iraq: "We must make it clear that reckless acts have consequences, or those acts will increase. We must reduce Iraq's ability to strike out at its neighbors and we must increase America's ability to contain Iraq over the long run." Clinton also said he was warning Saddam Hussein that "when you abuse your own people or threaten your neighbors, you must pay a price."

Clinton and his aides gave several specific objectives. The president said the missile strikes were intended to protect U.S. and allied aircraft enforcing the no-fly zone. Administration officials said that if Saddam had been allowed to get away with the total suppression of his Kurdish foes, he could then have withdrawn the bulk of his military forces from the area, thus freeing his hand to cause trouble elsewhere in the region. White House press secretary Michael McCurry said the attacks were designed to "further restrict Saddam's use of his air power in the region and, quite frankly, to humiliate him in front of his own military."

There were several points of irony in the situation. For starters, Saddam had come to the aid of a Kurdish faction that his forces had repeatedly attacked over the years, even to the extent of using chemical weapons in

*1988. That faction, headed by Barzani, also had been a principal benefi-
ciary of direct U.S. aid since the war. Just two weeks after the U.S.-Iraq
confrontation, officials in Washington said Barzani was again asking for
U.S. support—this time to keep him from being overwhelmed by Saddam's
force. The opposing Kurdish faction headed by Talabani had been getting
most of its help from Iran; by attacking Iraqi forces once they moved into
the Kurdish region, the United States was, in effect, intervening on the
same side as Tehran.*

A Stronger Saddam?

*In the weeks after the U.S.-Iraq tussle, a partisan tussle broke out in the
United States over the question of whether Saddam had been strengthened
or weakened militarily and politically as a consequence of U.S. actions.
Clinton's Republican challengers insisted that Saddam was in a stronger
position than at any point since the Gulf War—and they said Clinton was
to blame. One of the main advocates of this viewpoint was Sen. John
McCain of Arizona, a key foreign policy adviser to Republican presidential
nominee Bob Dole.*

*The Republicans received a modest bit of support for their argument
from CIA director John Deutch. Testifying before the Senate Intelligence
Committee on September 16, Deutch said in response to questions that
Saddam probably was stronger politically than he had been six weeks previously—in other words, before his move into the Kurdish region. Deutch
explained that Saddam had been able to win some sympathy from other
Arab countries in the region. Even so, Deutch insisted that Saddam's military forces were "getting weaker" and were "significantly" less capable
than they had been just four years previously.*

UN-Iraq Aid Agreement

*The U.S.-Iraqi confrontation temporarily delayed a pending agreement
under which the United Nations would allow Iraq to sell oil on the international market to earn cash to pay for food and medical supplies. UN
sanctions, in effect since the war, had prohibited Iraq from selling oil, its
main foreign trade commodity.*

*International concern about deteriorating conditions inside Iraq led
the UN Security Council in 1995 to suggest allowing Iraq to sell limited
amounts of oil so it could buy food and medicine. The UN and Iraq argued
over the details for more than a year, reaching a final agreement on
December 9.*

*Under the agreement, Iraq was allowed to sell $2 billion worth of oil dur-
ing an initial six-month period, with all the proceeds earmarked for
humanitarian relief. Iraq was required to provide at least $130 million
worth of aid to the Kurds, all to be distributed by international relief agencies. About one-third of the total proceeds were to go to a compensation
fund for victims of Iraq's 1990 invasion of Kuwait. The remainder was to
be spent for food, medicine, and other humanitarian assistance to Iraqi*

civilians; that aid would be distributed by the Iraqi government, under UN supervision.

Following are excerpts from testimony to the Senate Intelligence Committee on September 19, 1996, by John M. Deutch, director of central intelligence, in which he reviewed the recent confrontation between Iraq and the United States:

Mr. Chairman, if I may, I would like to make some remarks about Iraq and put for you—just as you asked—in context what I believe from our intelligence sources an analysis what the situation is in Iraq and how we got there.

Let me go back and make a few remarks about internal developments in Iraq since 1990, give you a sense of how that country has changed. Today the per-capita income in Iraq is about $950 per year. In 1989 it was $2,300 per year.

Oil production in 1989 was 3.1 million barrels of oil per day. Today oil production is down to less than 600,000 barrels per day.

Give you a sense of what the social fabric is like in that country. Kurdish, Shi'a and Sunni rivalries continue. The regime continues to be dominated by the Tikriti family of Saddam Hussein, and Sunni areas are better supported, more prosperous and better fed.

Even though there is no embargo on food or medicine, public health has seriously declined since the Gulf War. As a result, infant mortality has risen to 140 deaths out of 1,000 births, compared to 29 deaths out of 1,000 births in 1991. Ten percent of the entire population of Iraq is dependent upon humanitarian assistance.

Corruption remains rampant in the government. Saddam Hussein's family profits from covert sales of Iraqi oil and dominance of the black market where money donated for medicines and food often end up.

Baghdad has begun construction on 48 new palaces and today Saddam Hussein and the VIP leadership have the choice of up to 78 different palaces and estates throughout Iraq.

Of course, there is no press freedom and brutal suppression continues. Baghdad continues to immediately stop any nascent political opposition. Saddam Hussein's security apparatus has systematically destroyed all groups that have formed inside the country. People are arrested and killed.

He continues to drain the marshes of southeastern Iraq to deny haven for the Shi'a Iraqi families who live there and change the entire circumstances of living.

In sum, the situation inside Iraq has become more brutal, less able for the Iraqi people to survive. In the meantime, there have been several changes in external factors bearing on Iraq and Saddam Hussein's position.

Let me say that in general I believe that Saddam Hussein's position has been strengthened in the region recently. Why?

First, six years of containment and sanctions have failed to dislodge Saddam Hussein from leadership. Secondly, Saddam Hussein still has the possibility of threatening his neighbors Kuwait, Saudi Arabia and Jordan.

These countries want to see Saddam Hussein overthrown, but they have other interests as well. They want to assure that there will be stability in the region, they want to assure that Iraqis' territorial integrity is maintained and they want to assure that there are better conditions for the Iraqi people.

Third, there is also perception of weakened determination of the coalition to meet Iraqi aggression. Initial sentiment in the region led to no support for U.S. air strikes for the first time, drowning out criticism of Iraqi aggression.

France temporarily stopped enforcing the extended no-fly zone. Russia criticized U.S. strikes and led a fight to kill a United Kingdom-sponsored draft resolution condemning Iraq's military operations against the Kurds.

Fourth, Turkey's apparent willingness to deal more directly with Saddam is driven by a number of new factors. The new Welfare Party is interested in addressing domestic energy concerns and strengthening trade relationships with Iraq.

The Turkish general staff remains focused on the problem of eradicating the PKK [Kurdistan Workers' Party]-led insurgency which is based in Iraq, Iran and Syria.

Finally, Saddam Hussein has cleverly parlayed concerns about relief to U.N. Resolution 986, which will permit Saddam to export oil for humanitarian goods in hopes to gain a collapse of the sanctions' regime.

All of these factors contribute to, today, a strengthened position for Saddam Hussein in the region.

Now, Saddam has several times in the past confronted the coalition on several occasions since the end of the Gulf War, approximately 10. Six confrontations involved challenges to the United States' inspection of Iraqi weapons of mass destruction. On one occasion, our response led to a cruise missile attack on nuclear weapons facilities near Baghdad in 1993.

In October of 1994, Iraq moved two Republican Guard divisions to the Kuwaiti border in an effort to threaten Kuwait and pressure the U.N. into relieving sanctions. Heavy reinforcements by the United States caused Saddam Hussein to back down.

In June of 1993, the United States struck the headquarters of the Iraqi intelligence service in retaliation for an Iraqi assassination attempt on the life of former President Bush in April of that year.

The most recent set of confrontations is the third time that Iraq has challenged the no-fly zone in the north and in the south. In August of 1993, a coalition aircraft struck a surface-to-air missile site in northern Iraq that fired on one of our aircraft.

In December of 1992, an Iraqi air force airplane was shot down as it penetrated the southern no-fly zone. The Iraqis followed by moving surface-to-air missile systems into the zone in January of 1993.

How did the current crisis emerge? Iraq's aggression against the Kurds was a catalyst of the most recent crisis. On August 31, the Iraqis, in conjunction with the KDP, the Kurdish Democratic Party, invaded the north and took the Kurdish-held city of Irbil.

Let me give you a sense of the extent of this military enterprise. Between 30 and 40 thousand Iraqi troops were engaged. Over 350 tanks were deployed. Three-hundred artillery pieces were deployed in the region for the sweep of the Iraqi motorized and armored divisions into the north.

In the wake of the attack, the Kurdish Democratic Party, led by Massoud Barzani is now in control of most of the Kurdish-held northern Iraq, with only isolated pockets of the opposition Kurdish Party, the PUK [Patriotic Union for Kurdistan]. Barzani asked for Iraqi military assistance after the KDP experienced defeats in northern Iraq, at the hands of the . . . PUK.

Barzani saw Iranian sponsorship of the PUK as upsetting the delicate balance between the Kurdish factions. And you will recall that in July of this year, the Iranians did intervene in Northern Iraq on behalf of the PUK and attacks.

Let me say that Barzani is playing an enormously dangerous game. First of all, in 1991, Saddam showed no reluctance to massacre Kurds and members of Barzani's family. While no Iraqi military units remain in Kurdish-held territory at the time, it is clear that there are Iraqi intelligence and security personnel in the region.

Several hundred Kurds and Turkomans have been executed by the Iraqis, according to Iraqi opposition sources, but we cannot verify a precise number. And finally, we estimate that there are roughly 40,000 Kurdish refugees, either in Iran or on the Iranian border.

After tactical alliance against the PUK, and after taking of Irbil, Mr. Barzani is now approaching the coalition for protection in an effort to hold Saddam Hussein at arm's length while Saddam Hussein is putting increasing pressure on Barzani to negotiate a framework for autonomy under Baghdad's overall control.

Iran has shown no intention of interfering yet. Tehran may be preoccupied by the refugee situation, certainly backs PUK guerrillas, along the border region and continues to show an interest of maintaining its influence in the region.

As a result of the United States response, which was to first of all strike at the SAM [surface-to-air missile] defense units in the South, and to extend the no-fly zone from 32 north, to 33 north, Iraq challenged our activities in the no-fly zone.

Iraq responded by reconstituting damaged sites, and deploying additional mobile SAM systems from central Iraq.

Iraqi air defense units fired missiles, and air defense artillery fired at our coalition aircraft in both the southern and the northern zone.

Today, for the last few days, Iraqi air defense units are standing down in the wake of the U.S. military buildup. Iraq ceased to fire—make any fire against coalition aircraft since 13, September. The mobile SAM systems deployed in the no-fly zone are returning to their garrisons in central Iraq.

What are the overall implications of this story that I've outlined to you?

First, we should anticipate that Saddam will continue to challenge the coalition. In contrast to the past, he has been clever at taking advantage of an opportunity in northern Iraq created by differences among the Kurds and changed Turkish attitudes.

Second, there will be no stability in the region or improved circumstances for the Iraqi people until Saddam Hussein and his regime is replaced.

Third, for all of these reasons, Iraq will continue to be and has been at the top of our intelligence priorities for both our collection and analytic effort. . . .

CLINTON ON LEGISLATION BARRING SAME-SEX MARRIAGES
September 20, 1996

In a move seemingly timed for maximum election-year appeal, conservatives in Congress pushed through legislation discouraging same-sex marriages. The measure, which pitted gay rights against traditional notions of marriage and family, put President Bill Clinton in a tight political spot. The president, who had openly courted the gay vote in his 1992 campaign, signed the legislation on September 20, late at night without ceremony, upon returning from a campaign trip.

The two-part legislation stipulated that no state need recognize the validity of another state's law allowing same-sex marriages. Under the Constitution, states generally give "full faith and credit" to the laws of other states.

Although no state had put forth legislation to sanction gay marriages, some members of Congress urged Congress to act because a pending court case in Hawaii could legalize same-sex marriages, which other states might then be forced to acknowledge. The second part of the legislation defined legal marriage in federal law as a union between a man and a woman, which would deny federal benefits, such as Social Security, to gay or lesbian couples, even if states were to recognize the legitimacy of such unions.

In his statement, Clinton said he was signing the bill because he had "long opposed governmental recognition of same-gender marriages," but he urged Congress to extend job discrimination protections to homosexuals. An amendment offered in the Senate to ban job discrimination against homosexuals lost by a single vote, 49–50.

Some gay rights advocates criticized Clinton for signing the bill, but the Republican effort to create a rift between the Democratic president and his gay and civil rights supporters did not appear to have much effect. "The president is first and foremost a politician," said Patricia Ireland, president of the National Organization for Women. "A lot of people are willing to give him a pass."

Moral Survival or Political Intolerance?

The controversial legislation represented an unusual intervention by federal lawmakers into an area of domestic law that was traditionally left to the states. Republican supporters said it was necessary to act quickly because a court case challenging a ban on same-sex marriages in Hawaii was about to be retried. In 1993 the Hawaiian supreme court ruled that the ban appeared to be illegal and sent the case back to a lower state court, ordering the state to show that it had a compelling interest in maintaining the ban. That trial began September 10.

Social conservatives feared that if Hawaii permitted same-sex marriages, the rest of the country would be compelled to recognize those marriages. "What is at stake in this controversy," said Rep. Charles T. Canady, R-Fla., during House Judiciary Committee consideration of the legislation June 12, "is nothing less than our collective moral understanding . . . of the essential nature of the family."

Many Democrats disagreed, saying that Congress had no authority to regulate which marriages states were required to recognize and no business writing a definition of marriage into federal law. They also disputed the need for hasty congressional action, pointing out that a final resolution of the Hawaii case was probably not likely for years. "We all know what is going on here," Sen. Edward M. Kennedy, D-Mass., said during Senate floor debate on the measure September 10. "I regard this bill as a mean-spirited form of Republican legislative gay-bashing cynically calculated to try to inflame the public eight weeks before the . . . elections."

Democrats also scoffed at the bill's title, "The Defense of Marriage Act." "How does the fact that I love another man . . . threaten your marriage?" asked Rep. Barney Frank of Massachusetts during House floor debate July 11–12. Frank was gay and lived with a male partner. Rep. Steve Gunderson, a Republican from Wisconsin who was also gay, was almost the only Republican to criticize the bill on the House floor. Gunderson said he was willing to affirm marriage as a heterosexual union but thought that same-sex couples should be able to qualify for certain legal rights, such as hospital visitation and health benefits. When his Republican colleagues refused even to add language calling for a study of such issues, Gunderson said he had decided the bill was an exercise in political intolerance.

The House passed the measure July 12 on a vote of 342–67. In the Senate the legislation barring federal recognition of same-sex marriages was passed by a vote of 85–14. A companion bill, offered by Kennedy, to bar job discrimination against gays and lesbians fell short by a single vote. Kennedy's bill was drawn to appeal to moderates: it exempted the military, businesses with fewer than fifteen employees, and nonprofit religious organizations. It specifically barred quotas and preferential treatment designed to help homosexuals get and retain jobs. By considering the two measures together, senators could take an election-year stand against gay marriages but then show their tolerance for gays in the workplace.

Reaction and Aftermath

Despite the legislative defeats, most of the gay political community was buoyed by the closeness of the Senate vote on antidiscrimination and vowed to push for passage in the 105th Congress. "We have witnessed gay civil rights in the 1990s completely embraced by the civil rights community in general," said Elizabeth Birch of the Human Rights Campaign, a gay rights group. "We have firmly established that it is no longer a question of whether Congress will pass the employment nondiscrimination act for gay Americans. It's a question of when." In May gays had won another significant victory, when the Supreme Court overturned an amendment to Colorado's constitution that would have prevented any state efforts to protect homosexuals from discrimination. (Supreme Court on discrimination against gays, p. 284)

Gay rights groups were also heartened by IBM's announcement on September 10 that the computer company would extend health care coverage and other benefits to the partners of its homosexual employees. With 110,000 workers, IBM was the sixth largest employer in the country; it became the largest company in the United States to adopt such a policy. "This is like having a small-sized city make the decision to fully value its gay citizens. . . . It sends a strong message to a lot of other companies," said Birch of the Human Rights Campaign.

An IBM spokesma n said the company's decision was driven by business factors. Several of IBM's competitors, including Apple Computer, Hewlett-Packard Co., Microsoft Corp., and Xerox Corp., already offered such benefits to their workers, and IBM did not want to lose valuable employees to those companies. The IBM plan covered only same-sex partners who signed an affidavit that they were in a long-term relationship and shared the same household. The plan did not extend to unmarried heterosexual couples, the company said, because they had the option to marry. Estimates of the number of companies that extend employee benefits to partners of their homosexual employees varied widely, but the number was still small. Other major companies that had adopted similar polices were American Express, Eastman Kodak, and Walt Disney.

In a related development, the trial court judge in the Hawaii case ruled on December 3 that the state had failed to show any compelling interest in barring same-sex marriages. He then stayed the ruling, pending an appeal to the Hawaiian supreme court. The federal judiciary does not have any jurisdiction over the matter, so the ruling by the state supreme court will be final. The lower court ruling thus moved Hawaii one step away from becoming the first state to recognize same-sex marriages.

If the Hawaiian supreme court were to rule against the ban—and it had already announced its skepticism of its constitutionality—the constitutionality of the provision of the federal law permitting states not to recognize gay marriages from other states could be called into question. Supporters of the federal legislation said the measure was necessary to over-

come a section of the U.S. Constitution, which states: "Full Faith and Cred-it shall be given in each State to the public Acts, Records, and judicial Pro-ceedings of every other State." The federal government had the authority to act under the second sentence in that section, which states: "And the Con-gress may by general Laws prescribe the Manner in which such Acts, Records, and Proceedings shall be proved, and the Effect thereof."

Several constitutional scholars questioned whether Congress could legit-imately pass legislation limiting the applicability of one state's laws to another state. "A good deal of the entire federal system could be undone," University of Chicago law professor Cass Sustein told the Senate Judicia-ry Committee on July 11. "Under the proponents' interpretation, Congress could simply say that any law Congress dislikes is of no effect in other states."

> *Following is the text of the statement by President Bill Clinton on September 20, 1996, upon signing legislation (PL 104–199) permitting states to refuse to recognize laws of other states allowing same-sex marriages and defining marriage, for pur-poses of federal law, as the union of a man and a woman:*

Throughout my life I have strenuously opposed discrimination of any kind, including discrimination against gay and lesbian Americans. I am sign-ing into law H.R. 3396, a bill relating to same-gender marriage, but it is impor-tant to note what this legislation does and does not do.

I have long opposed governmental recognition of same-gender marriages and this legislation is consistent with that position. The Act confirms the right of each state to determine its own policy with respect to same-gender marriage and clarifies for purposes of federal law the operative meaning of the terms "marriage" and "spouse."

This legislation does not reach beyond those two provisions. It has no effect on any current federal, state or local anti-discrimination law and does not constrain the right of Congress or any state or locality to enact anti-dis-crimination laws. I therefore would take this opportunity to urge Congress to pass the Employment Non-Discrimination Act, an act which would extend employment discrimination protections to gays and lesbians in the work-place. This year the Senate considered this legislation contemporaneously with the Act I sign today and failed to pass it by a single vote. I hope that in its next Session Congress will pass it expeditiously.

I also want to make clear to all that the enactment of this legislation should not, despite the fierce and at times divisive rhetoric surrounding it, be understood to provide an excuse for discrimination, violence or intimidation against any person on the basis of sexual orientation. Discrimination, vio-lence and intimidation for that reason, as well as others, violate the principle of equal protection under the law and have no place in American society.

CLINTON AND LUCID ON HER RETURN FROM SPACE
September 26, 1996

"I just had a great time," astronaut Shannon W. Lucid told President Bill Clinton via telephone on September 26, just a few hours after completing a 188-day mission in space. Lucid's stay set a space endurance record for Americans and a world record for women. The record for the longest stay in space was held by a Russian physician-cosmonaut, who spent 438 days in space in 1994–1995. Lucid's endurance record had not been planned—she spent seven weeks longer on the Russian Mir *space station than scheduled. Her return had been delayed by mechanical problems with the space shuttle* Atlantis *and foul weather.*

Atlantis *was finally launched on its "rescue" mission on September 16, docked with* Mir *on September 18, and remained docked for five days while the astronauts moved equipment, food, and fresh water to the space station and hardware and scientific samples to the shuttle for a return to Earth. The shuttle also brought Lucid's replacement, John E. Blaha, a retired air force colonel, to the* Mir. *Blaha was to spend four months at the space station.*

Lucid remained in good humor throughout her extended stay, although she said she missed hot showers, potato chips, and gooey desserts—as well as her husband and three grown children. As she left the Mir, *she said she was "really happy and I also feel just a little sad. This has been my home for six months, and I've had a great time here. But obviously I'm very, very anxious to go back to my real home back in Houston, Texas, with my family."*

At a press conference on October 24, a month after her return, the fifty-three-year-old Lucid told reporters that she felt fine physically and had not shown any major ill effects from spending six months in weightlessness. She experienced some calcium loss, which was expected, but she had exercised rigorously while in space, using a treadmill for an hour or two every day she was aboard the space station. That helped her maintain her weight and allowed her to walk off the space shuttle under her own power, albeit a bit wobbly, upon her return to Earth. Lucid's health would be monitored closely for several years, as scientists tried to determine the effects of prolonged weightlessness on the human body.

Lucid was the second of seven astronauts scheduled to spend a total of two and a half years aboard the Mir in preparation for constructing and operating a large international space shuttle. That project was expected to begin in late 1997. The first astronaut to stay on the Mir was Norman Thagard, who spent 112 days there in 1995. In addition to preparing for a future space station, the missions were designed to give the American astronauts experience with long-duration flights. (Thagard mission, Historic Documents of 1995, p. 419)

Women in Space

In his phone conversation with Lucid, Clinton told her that she was "a terrific inspiration for young women around the country and all around the world. . . . [I]t's a wonderful thing for these young girls that may have nontraditional aspirations to see someone like you up there doing that." With her Mir mission, which began with liftoff from the Kennedy Space Center in Cape Canaveral, Florida, on March 22, Lucid, a biochemist and a pilot, had completed five space flights, making her the senior American astronaut. She was one of the first six women that the National Aeronautics and Space Administration (NASA) selected for training. That class of 1978 included Sally Ride, who was the first American woman in space in 1983, and Kathy Sullivan, who became the first American woman to walk in space in 1984. Also in that class was Judith Resnick, who was killed in 1986 when the shuttle Challenger *exploded on takeoff.* (Challenger accident, Historic Documents of 1986, p. 39)

The first woman in space was Valentina Tereshkov, a Russian cosmonaut, who spent three days in space in 1963. Nineteen years would pass before another woman, also a Russian, would fly into space.

Lucid, who was born in China to missionary parents, always dreamed of being an explorer. "When I was a little girl I was very interested in being a pioneer like in the American West," until she realized that she was "born in the wrong time." Lucid said she had worried that all the Earth would be explored by the time she grew up, but then she discovered stories about Robert Goddard, the father of rocketry, and decided that she would explore space.

Lucid's Mission

Colleagues reported that upon her return to Earth, Lucid talked most about her scientific work aboard Mir. She ran several experiments, including one that documented how quail embryos developed in zero gravity. Lucid was likely to be best remembered for her grit and good humor, especially when she learned that her mission was going to be extended. She was supposed to come home in early August, but that was delayed when NASA discovered problems with the shuttle's boosters. The shuttle's departure was further delayed by a hurricane.

During the extra seven weeks in space, Lucid's original Russian crew-mates returned to Earth and a new cosmonaut crew was brought to the Mir. *In her conversation with Clinton and again in her October 24 news conference, Lucid praised her Russian colleagues, saying that despite the close quarters and differences in culture, language, and gender, there were few tensions. In her news conference she related a conversation in which the two Russian cosmonauts admitted that as children they had been afraid of the United States. "Here we were," Lucid said, "three people who had grown up . . . mortally afraid of each other, and here we were sitting in an outpost in space together, working together."*

Lucid said she maintained her spirit by exchanging almost daily e-mail messages with her family, reading, and exercising. She also had her own sleeping room and lavatory on the Mir, *which ensured her privacy. As the delays dragged on, Lucid began to tell NASA officials at the Houston control center that in addition to missing her family, she was longing for a hot shower (she had been restricted to sponge baths on the* Mir), *junk food, and sweets. She also worried that she would run out of M&M's. When she left the* Atlantis, *she was presented with a large box of M&M's wrapped in gold foil and stamped with the presidential seal. "It was about the size of two or three shoe boxes, so I think she'll be in M&M's for awhile," said NASA administrator Daniel Goldin.*

Following is the text of the telephone conversation between President Bill Clinton and astronaut Shannon W. Lucid, which took place a few hours after Lucid completed the longest stay in space of any American and of any woman:

Clinton: Welcome home.

Lucid: Why, thank you so much. It's so kind of you to call.

Clinton: Well, we're all so proud of you. We've been watching you, and I couldn't believe you walked off the shuttle.

Lucid: Well, I'm just really proud to be an American, and I'm just really proud to be part of this cooperative program that we have going with the Russians. It was just a great mission. And I just had a great time.

Clinton: Well, it was wonderful. And as I said, the whole country followed you, but I appreciate what you said about the cooperation with Russia, too. It really sets the stage for the work on the international space station. And it's very, very important. And I believe the way you captured the public imagination will also help us to build long-term support for the space program.

Lucid: Well, I think so. Of course, I don't know from a political standpoint or from the big boss standpoint, but I just know from the people that are actually working, you know, like the cosmonauts and the astronauts working together, that this works out just great. They were just wonderful people to work with.

Clinton: Yes, they are good people, and we're making real progress in working with them, I think.

Lucid: I think so. And it couldn't have been a better experience. And I just thoroughly enjoyed working with the cosmonauts.

Clinton: The other thing that I wanted to say was that on behalf of my wife and daughter, is that you have been a terrific inspiration for young women around the country and all around the world. And I know as you get out and around and people get to congratulate you, you'll see that. But it's a wonderful thing for these young girls that may have nontraditional aspirations to see someone like you up there doing that.

Lucid: Well, thank you, sir. Yes, I just didn't really give a thought to that. It was just something that I'd always wanted to do. And I was just very glad that it worked out.

Clinton: Did you have a good reunion with your kids?

Lucid: I sure did. [Laughter.] And they're here nagging me already.

Clinton: Did you get your M&M's I sent you?

Lucid: Oh, I sure did. I wanted to thank you first thing. That was so nice. They're already into them.

Clinton: That's good.

Lucid: That was so nice and so thoughtful of you. I really, really appreciate that.

Clinton: Thanks. I'm going down to Texas tomorrow and I just got a note that said you might be there at the time I land in Houston. If so, I hope I get to see you.

Lucid: Oh, well, that would be very nice. I hope that works out. That would just be great.

Clinton: Me, too. Well, congratulations. I know you want to go back to your family, but I just wanted to say hello. You've given us all a great deal to be proud of and a lot of thrills and we're glad you're home safe and sound.

Lucid: Thank you very much, Mr. President. And it was very nice of you to call. I really appreciate that. Thank you so much. . . .

CONGRESSIONAL LEADERS ON THE CLOSE OF THE 104TH CONGRESS
September 27, 1996, and October 3, 1996

The 104th Congress, in session during 1995 and 1996, was one of the most remarkable of the twentieth century. The first Congress in four decades in which both houses were controlled by Republicans, it was one of the most bitterly partisan Congresses in recent memory, particularly during 1995. When judged by the number of bills passed, it was also one of the least productive Congresses in decades; in terms of changes made in federal policy, it was one of the most revolutionary of modern times. It was also a Congress that produced a record number of retirements from both chambers, with many members of both parties saying they were fed up with the partisanship and harsh personal attacks that seemed increasingly to dominate life on Capitol Hill.

In closing statements, as Congress prepared to shut down just one month before elections, Republican leaders claimed to have effected a revolution by reversing or diminishing five decades of programs and policies implemented by Democrats since the New Deal. House Republicans claimed success for their Contract with America, which promised sweeping changes in the federal government.

Democrats acknowledged the Republican political success but rejected as "extreme" much of the legislation the Republicans had enacted or had tried to enact. The Democrats said they, along with President Bill Clinton and his veto power, had prevented the Republicans from carrying out key parts of their agenda—most notably a constitutional amendment requiring a balanced budget. (Congress's first one hundred days, Historic Documents of 1995, p. 165)

In the November elections, the voters appeared to indicate that they liked the results of divided government during the previous two years, but they sent mixed messages. While returning Bill Clinton to the presidency, they gave Republicans continued control of Congress. They narrowed the Republican margin of majority in the House but added two Republican seats in the Senate. (Elections, p. 747)

The Republican Impact

With Speaker Newt Gingrich of Georgia providing the intellectual guidance and partisan prodding, the House led the way to the Republican revolution in 1995. The House quickly passed most of the ten items on a Republican Contract with America, a laundry list of conservative causes, such as the balanced-budget amendment, reduced government regulations, term limits on members of Congress, and various reforms of congressional procedures. (Contract with America, Historic Documents of 1994, p. 374)

Only two of the most controversial items on the contract agenda made it through the Senate and were signed into law: a sweeping revision of welfare policy and a version of a presidential line-item veto. The handful of remaining contract items that became law never generated significant controversy, such as reducing federal paperwork requirements and limiting suits by investors against companies.

Two of the most important pieces of legislation cleared by the 104th Congress had not appeared in the House Contract with America. One was a telecommunications bill that reflected sweeping changes in the industry and opened local telephone service to competition. The other was a top-to-bottom overhaul of federal farm policy, replacing price supports for most crops with a new system of fixed but declining federal payments to farmers. (Farm bill, p. 199)

Many of the big-ticket items from the contract—the core of conservative political philosophy—fell by the wayside as Republicans discovered the limits to how far they could push for change in Washington. The most important victim was the balanced budget constitutional amendment, which fell just one vote short of the two-thirds majority needed in the Senate in 1995. Republican leaders viewed the amendment as the engine that ultimately would drive down the size of the federal government; they said its rigid spending limits would force Congress to make politically painful cuts in social programs and government services. There were enough questions about the amendment's potential impact to thwart its adoption in the 104th Congress.

Despite the failure of the amendment, Republicans scored a tactical victory on the balanced-budget issue in 1996, when Clinton agreed to the goal of balancing the budget by 2002. That victory came only after the Republicans paid a high political price, however. House Republicans in late 1995 had forced two lengthy shutdowns of much of the federal government, angering the public and giving Clinton ammunition for his charge of GOP extremism. After this political beating, the Republicans backed down early in 1996 and negotiated a budget compromise with Clinton—the very kind of compromise that some Republicans previously had scorned. (Budget issues, p. 147)

Republicans also failed to enact a limit on the number of terms members of Congress could serve. Expressing a generalized anger at politicians, vot-

ers had been imposing term limits at the state level for nearly a decade, but proposals for congressional term limits encountered both active and passive resistance on Capitol Hill. A proposed constitutional amendment mandating term limits died in the Senate and was given little chance of resurrection in the 105th Congress.

Democrats, thrown into disarray in 1995 with their new minority status, by 1996 had discovered ways to hamper the Republican majority— and they even won some victories of their own. The most notable was enactment of an increase in the minimum wage, an issue on which the Democrats skillfully maneuvered the Republicans into appearing hard-hearted during an election season. (Minimum wage, p. 563)

In many ways, the real impact of Republican control of Congress was felt in the day-to-day operations of the government. Republicans succeeded in trimming spending for, and imposing policy limits on, hundreds of government programs. The Clinton administration, hoping to beat Republicans to the punch, shifted scores of government policies rightward, on issues ranging from tearing down blighted public housing units to scaling back research on alternative fuels.

One of the ironies of the Republican-led Congress was its use of the federal government and federal policies to implement conservative ideological goals. When the government produced the policies they wanted, the Republicans fought to turn responsibility for programs over to the states, as in the welfare overhaul and the elimination of federal highway speed limits. In other cases, the Republicans sought to impose federal solutions on the states. The 104th Congress, for example, established national criteria for state-issued drivers licenses, ended state registration of mutual funds, created national food safety standards, nullified state laws restricting telecommunications competition, and extended federal criminal penalties to cover certain violent crimes.

Learning to Compromise

For some Republican leaders—especially combative House Speaker Gingrich—the 104th Congress provided a rude awakening to the limits of power. Gingrich had risen through the ranks of House Republicans with his blunt attacks on Democrats and their alleged abuses of power. Once he took control of the House, and imposed tighter party discipline than any Democrat had exercised in generations, Gingrich found that being in the majority does not necessarily translate into getting your way all the time.

The Republicans discovered that Clinton retained considerable leverage with his veto pen. As the 1996 elections approached, Clinton regained much of the political vigor he had lost after the humiliation of the Republican electoral victories in 1994.

The Republicans were not unanimous in their approach to some key issues, most notably the 1995 budget confrontation with Clinton. Senate Republican leaders were horrified by the brinkmanship of their House counterparts; that split guaranteed a Clinton victory on the issue.

In the end, the Republicans learned what a closer study of history might have shown: that the American political system in general—Congress in particular—is designed for incremental change and trying to force the pace of change can backfire. James A. Thurber, a congressional scholar at American University in Washington, D.C., put it this way: "I think this Congress will be known as one in which the majority came in as revolutionaries and left as pragmatists."

Following are excerpts from news conference statements concerning the close of the 104th Congress, made September 27, 1996, by Senate Minority Leader Tom Daschle, D-S.D., and House Minority Leader Richard A. Gephardt, D-Mo., and October 3, 1996, by Senate Majority Leader Trent Lott, R-Miss.:

DASCHLE'S REMARKS

We're here to look back and take measure at the 104th Congress, to put in its proper context and to draw the lessons learned in the past 21 months. We believe that the choices facing the American people in November are enormous in consequence, and that nothing can better inform their judgment about those choices than a fair assessment from you of what really happened.

The battles on this front are about to cease. It is now largely up to you to provide the country an accurate accounting of the 104th Congress. That is why we have chosen to address today the facts instead of the fanfare. Unlike our Republican colleagues, Democrats are prepared to stand on our record, not run from it.

Republicans want to hide behind slogans. Democrats are eager to talk substance. You can stand on the Capitol steps and hire a brass band and blow up a lot of balloons. But you still can't make a full scale retreat look like a full dress parade.

No amount of crepe paper and bunting can cover up the truth about a failed agenda and flawed priorities. The last couple of weeks, Republicans around here have needed name tags because I don't recognize them anymore. Contract? They never heard of it. Shutdown? Never happened. Cut education? Who, me?

If the Contract with America marked the beginning of Newt Gingrich's revolution, then the period during the government shutdown can certainly be described as the beginning of the end. It was that white-hot scrutiny that exposed Republican leaders as irrational and irresponsible. It was that conflict that brought the fight over priorities into sharp focus to the American people.

Newt Gingrich and his followers promised a train wreck, and they delivered. Way back in June of '95, the Speaker boasted about his blackmail strategy. Quote: "We could last 60 days, 80 days, 120 days, five years, a century.

There's a lot of stuff we don't care if it's never funded."

They lasted 27 days. Cost taxpayers $1.4 billion. Disrupted hundreds of thousands of lives during the holidays. Veterans disability claims backlogged. Child enforcement ceased. Superfund cleanups stopped. Prison guards and VA nurses worked without pay. Small business contractors were put out of work.

But more than that, it was the stuff they don't care about that disturbed people most of all. Their plans for all that so-called stuff included a doubling a Medicare premiums; denied over a million children the extra help they need to get math and reading; crippling environment protection initiatives; raising taxes on working families for those making less than $30,000; and deep draconian cuts in Medicare to finance huge tax breaks for the affluent.

It was the refusal of Democrats to abandon our priorities that changed the direction of the 104th Congress. It was the resolve of the president to stand up to their pressure tactics that exposed the extreme nature of Republican demands. From that point on, the only time the Republican Congress worked is when they let Democrats lead.

That's why the minimum wage will be raised on October 1. That's why workers will now have greater health care security. That's why mothers and babies can no longer be bounced from the hospital before they are ready. That's why our environmental laws remain intact. That's why their cuts in education were never achieved. That's why their Medicare cuts never resurfaced.

And although Democrats were successful in stopping the worst things the Republican revolution produced, the threats they proposed to Medicare and education and the environment remain. Republicans may be in an election season retreat but they will retrench. Democrats will defend those priorities in the 105th Congress if we must. We prefer progress.

Our Family's First agenda will move past the divisiveness of the Republican Congress and offer the American people a program for paycheck security and educational opportunity and government responsibility in 1997.

The co-architect and the co-leader in this whole effort, someone that I have admired immensely and had the good fortune to work with closely now for two years, our leader in the House, Dick Gephardt, will complete our opening remarks.

GEPHARDT'S REMARKS

It surely has been a pleasure and very satisfying opportunity for all of us in the House to work with our Senate colleagues. The relationship between the two bodies and the Democratic party has never been closer or more constructive than it is today and that's largely due to the leadership of Tom Daschle in the United States Senate. He's done an absolutely marvelous job.

The 104th Congress is likely to be remembered for what Democrats were able to stop the Republicans from doing to hurt the American people. Democrats led the fight to prevent the Republicans from cutting Medicare, school loans and student loans and school lunches. Democrats stood in their path as the Republicans tried to gut environmental protections and the Head Start program.

Democrats fought them tooth and nail to prevent Republicans from letting corporations raid their workers' pensions. But it is the pictures that really tell the story of what happened under Newt Gingrich's leadership of this Congress. The images of this Congress tell the story of a defiant Democratic minority and an angry American electorate who together fought back against the Gingrich Congress' march on the issues that matter most to America's families.

This Congress will be remembered by the pictures of the children and parents who turned out to protest the cuts in school lunch. By the seniors who were arrested and taken away in handcuffs because they demanded a say before the Republicans cut their Medicare to pay for a tax break for the wealthiest Americans. This Congress will be remembered for the hearings that we held but had to hold on the lawn of the Capitol because the Republicans refused to spend more than a single day talking about their cuts in Medicare and Medicaid.

We'll remember the college students, Republicans and Democrats alike, who protested their cuts in the student loan program. I will never ever forget the head of the Young Republicans from Georgetown who stood with us in a demonstration on the lawn and who told us afterwards that even though he supported Newt Gingrich and he supported the Republican party that he was astounded that the Republicans would take on a program that is accepted and supported by virtually every person in the American society.

And can we ever forget the series of endless, phony, photo-ops at zoos with Republican leaders and in attempt to cover up their undoing of 25 years of bipartisan protections of the environment.

What the American people may remember most will be the closed signs that you saw in the movie at the nation's parks and Social Security offices and veterans' offices during the long weeks when the Republicans shut down the government in order to force the president to make their cuts in Medicare, in education, in the environment.

When Newt Gingrich and his humbled revolutionaries met earlier today to commemorate their ascendancy to a majority, there was little talk about the Contract with America, which Republicans—many Republicans—now disavow. There wasn't bragging about the government shutdown or cutting Medicare and student loans.

Instead, they unveiled another slogan in another campaign to con the American voters into thinking banner. The Republicans will try to reinvent themselves as the common sense Congress. But we believe the people have too much sense to buy it.

I believe that the Republicans missed a historic opportunity. I've said many times if they had been reasonable and moderate and sensible, as they now say they want to be, they would have reached that opportunity.

Another year under Republican rule would be the Dole plan, which would be doubling the cuts in Medicare and school lunch and student loan. If you didn't like the last two years, you sure wouldn't like the next two years under Republican rule. They will revert to form. They will do exactly what they've tried to do these last two years, only they'll do it double.

They want a bigger tax cut for the wealthy and they'll take double the cuts in Medicare and education and the environment to pay for it. The American people will not be fooled again, and I believe they will opt for Families First, for common sense, for moderation, for modesty, for practicality and for realism.

And it has been a great thrill this year to work with Tom Daschle on that agenda, and I look forward to the opportunity to work with him in the majority next year to enact it.

LOTT'S REMARKS

... I do think we have had what clearly should be described as an historic Congress, one that has produced really very good results substantively. When you look at the bills that we have passed, it is a long list of accomplishments in a variety of areas, including regaining, you know, freedom from big government in a number of ways, including some of the tax relief that we passed. We took actions to try to restore fiscal integrity, much of which was vetoed by the president. But we also took action on crime and drugs at home and abroad. . . .

I do think that three of the very biggest ones we've passed in the past couple of months. Welfare reform, I think will be known as the most important bill that we have done in the 104th Congress and maybe one of the most important or historic bills that has been done in many, many years.

I was very pleased with what we did on health insurance reform. It was a bipartisan effort. But it included some things that we felt very strongly about, including the Medical Savings Accounts and the increase in the deductibility for self-employed, and, of course, the illegal immigration reform, I think was a major accomplishment.

Illegal immigration is a great big problem in this country and we had to deal with it.

Also the fact that we came to an agreement on the Omnibus Bill. You know all that we went through on that. I had hoped that we could have done all 13 appropriations bills free standing.

But as we got into September, it was obvious to me, after the experience on the Postal Service, Treasury-Postal Service bill and then the Interior Appropriations bill, that the Democratic leadership had made up their minds that they were just going to use it as a political tool.

They were going to advance their political agenda. And we even got off the Internet their agenda with the amendments, who would sponsor the amendments would accomplish specific things. And when I saw that I said, I'm not going to allow that.

So, we had to drop the individual appropriations bills and do the final six in the Omnibus bill, which made it a big bill. It made it more difficult. But we got it done. We got it done without a Continuing Resolution of a day or three extensions or threats or shutdowns. And I'm proud of that.

While the Democrats can say that they got some things they wanted in that, I acknowledge that. But I think that we did what was right for the country once again with that legislation. And I was pleased. . . .

Question: Senator, Senator Daschle said earlier today he thought you'd done quite well considering the. . . . Well, some people expected you to be more conservative and push a harder agenda than you have.

Lott: I don't think there's any doubt that I have a conservative philosophy. I still feel that way, and I think most of what we did reflected that philosophy.

But when I came in as majority leader, it was in the middle of the year, the middle of the session, middle of a presidential election. It was a tough situation to be in. And I was dealt a lot of cards that I didn't draw. I just had to play them.

And so I dealt with the agenda as it had come into my hands. And I said, when I stood in this spot the day I was elected, that the torch had been passed but the agenda was the same.

And I went forward with that.

In the legislative process, you have to be prepared to have some give and take. Compromise is required.

My goal was to get the big issues done, and I think we did that. I'm—you know, I wish we'd have gotten the broad economic growth for middle class Americans completed. We didn't get it done, first because the president vetoed and the likelihood of us being able to have a second budget resolution this year just was not feasible.

So I went forward with that idea. I was going to complete the agenda. We had things we wanted to get done, and I was going to do what was necessary to get those done, and I was going to get us out of here on time so we could go to the American people and talk about genuine tax reform.

So I've always—you know, my approach to life is one I think of moderation. My relationship with people—I mean, I really—I really do like people. I like dealing with a Bill Bradley. I like dealing with people on both sides of the aisle.

And I think if any—anytime you're willing to talk to people and hear them out—one of the things I learned is that many times over the past two months, we've reached intractable situations where no solution was apparent.

And yet what my approach was, all right, get in a room, let's get the key players in both parties, all philosophies, let's get them to sit down and see if there's an agreement possible. And in almost every case we found an agreement.

Was it the one I would write out in longhand? No.

Was it one that the representatives we put in that room to work out a solution could live with? Yes. And so that's the approach I've used.

I think it—I hope it worked pretty well. It may not be the same one I'll use next year. . . .

Question: Senator Lott, after two years of Republican control of Congress, the growth of government and government spending are both up. What do you say to voters who say I voted for Republicans, because their pledge, one of their bedrock foundations is to cut the growth of government, to reduce it.

What happened there? What do you say to that?

Lott: Well, first of all, we did cut the growth and the non- defense appropriated accounts by $53 billion over the two-year period. We had a plan to control the entitlement increases also. It was vetoed. You know, it, we need a Republican Congress and a Republican president to actually control spending the way that it should be done and also to give tax relief and tax cuts that the American people want.

So, the fact of the matter is we cut the appropriations accounts and we had a balanced-budget proposal that would have been achieved by the year 2002 that included entitlement reforms. So, we did what we said we were going to do, there is this little problem.

Bill Clinton down at the White House vetoed it.

Question: Yes, but taxpayers don't differentiate between Defense and discretionary domestic spending when they look at the growth of government. I mean, you didn't do what you said you were going to do.

Lott: We would have done if we'd had a president who would have cooperated with us and signed the bills that we sent to him instead of vetoing it.

There was, in the bill we sent to the president, that he vetoed over this seven year period, clearly there was going to be controls on spending that would have led us to a balanced budget. And we kept our commitment. But he vetoed what was sent to him.

October

PRESIDENTIAL AND
VICE PRESIDENTIAL DEBATES
October 6, 9, and 16, 1996

In the closing weeks of the 1996 campaign, conventional wisdom held that the debates between the Democratic and Republican presidential and vice presidential nominees would have little effect on the election outcome. For once, conventional wisdom was right. Republican Bob Dole entered the two presidential debates far behind President Bill Clinton in the public opinion polls. Dole was still behind when it really counted, on election day, although by a narrower margin than the polls had predicted.

The two debates between Dole and Clinton offered virtually no drama and shed no new light on the views or personalities of the two candidates. As a result, they did little to spur public interest in a campaign that, according to the polls, much of the public was ignoring. All that was bad news for Dole, who needed to generate controversy about the president's stewardship of power. As the incumbent leading in the polls, Clinton needed only to avoid new controversy.

In the weeks before the first debate, perhaps the most interesting question was whether Reform party candidate Ross Perot would be allowed to participate. Perot's debate presence in 1992 had raised his standing in the polls; based on his comparatively low ratings in the fall of 1996, it was clear that his showing on election day would depend on whether he debated Clinton and Dole. (Perot candidacy, p. 550)

After interviewing journalists and political science experts, the non-partisan Commission on Presidential Debates ruled on September 17 that Perot had no "realistic chance to win" the election and therefore should be excluded from the debates. Perot and Natural Law party candidate John Hagelin both filed suit against the commission, but their suit was dismissed on October 1 by U.S. District Judge Thomas P. Hogan.

Dole's Dilemma

In both debates, Dole faced a dilemma. On the one hand, his own principal obstacle to overcome was his attack-dog reputation—that he was a politician who got ahead by bringing down others. On the other hand, Dole's only chance for winning the presidency rested on his ability to foster public doubts about Clinton's character.

During the first debate, which was held in Hartford, Connecticut, Dole opted for a strategy of softening his own image. He smiled a lot, cracked a few jokes, and generally tried to portray himself as a friendly and wise statesman. Dole stepped back from a direct attack on the president, saying at one point: "I don't like to get into personal matters."

In the vice presidential debate on October 9 in St. Petersburg, Florida, Dole's running mate, Jack F. Kemp, reinforced the impression that the Republicans were avoiding a direct attack on Clinton. Kemp said: "[I]n my opinion, it is beneath Bob Dole to go after anyone personally."

After those debates, Dole and his aides engaged in a public discussion about whether to sharpen the attacks on Clinton. News media reports chronicled how some aides urged Dole to refer directly in the second debate to several ethical issues surrounding the president, ranging from Clinton's questionable investment in the failed Whitewater development project to reports of improper donations to Clinton's campaign by foreign nationals.

By October 16, the day of the second debate, there was widespread expectation that Dole would take the offensive. The debate took place in San Diego, following a town-hall format in which the questions were posed by undecided voters. Dole was more aggressive in the second debate than he had been in the first. Responding to the first question, about political partisanship, Dole challenged Clinton to promise that he would not pardon any of his former associates who had been convicted in the Whitewater case. "The president ought to say tonight . . . he's not going to pardon anybody he was involved in business with who might implicate him later."

Clinton ignored that challenge, and none of the questioners followed Dole's lead on that issue. Dole had to content himself with references to Clinton administration ethical problems, such as campaign donations from foreign nationals and a controversy over alleged White House misuse of FBI files.

Clinton shied away from one personal matter that had dogged Dole throughout the campaign: his age, seventy-three. When a college student asked Dole, in the San Diego debate, about the "age issue," Dole responded that "wisdom comes with age, experience and intelligence." In his follow-up answer, Clinton said: "I don't think Senator Dole is too old to be president. It is the age of his ideas that I question."

Taxes and Spending

Clinton and Dole both used the debates as sounding boards for their principal campaign themes. Clinton promised to protect four areas of the federal budget against what he said were Republican attacks: Medicare, Medicaid, education, and the environment. Those programs were threatened, Clinton said, by Dole's proposal for a 15 percent across-the-board cut *in federal income taxes. Dole's proposal represented a "$550 billion tax scheme that will blow a hole in the deficit," Clinton said.*

Dole defended his tax-cut plan, insisting in the second debate that it would "cut taxes and balance the budget" while allowing for growth in both Medicare and Social Security spending.

Vice Presidential Debate

The October 9 vice presidential debate had to be satisfying for those who claimed to be interested in the substance of issues, rather than personalities. Vice President Al Gore and Kemp, his Republican challenger, were both known as men intensely interested in ideas and policy issues. Both could talk at great length and in minute detail about the issues of particular interest to them—for Gore, the environment and technology; for Kemp, taxes and economic growth.

In responding to the first question, Kemp acknowledged his reputation for talking too much. Asked by moderator Jim Lehrer to keep his response to ninety seconds, Kemp said: "Wow, in ninety seconds? I can't clear my throat in ninety seconds, Jim."

While disagreeing on the issues, Gore and Kemp respected each other, and that cordiality came across in the debate. At the end of the debate, Gore said he had "enormous respect for Jack Kemp and Bob Dole. They're good men."

On the issues, Kemp focused on his principal theme that the federal government taxes and regulates its citizens too much, thus stifling individual initiative and economic growth. The result, he said, was that many frustrated citizens became "enemies of the U.S. government." Gore concentrated on specific differences between the two parties on issues such as the environment and affirmative action. Gore also noted past disagreements between Kemp and Dole on tax and spending issues.

> *Following are excerpts from the first presidential debate, held October 6, 1996, between President Bill Clinton and Republican nominee Bob Dole; the vice presidential debate, held October 9, 1996, between Vice President Al Gore and Republican nominee Jack F. Kemp; and the second presidential debate, held October 16, 1996, between Clinton and Dole. All three debates were moderated by Jim Lehrer:*

FIRST PRESIDENTIAL DEBATE

Lehrer: . . . Mr. President, first question. There is a major difference in your view of the role of the Federal government and that of Senator Dole. How would you define the difference?

Clinton: Well, Jim, I believe that the Federal government should give people the tools and try to establish the conditions in which they can make the most of their own lives. That, to me, is the key. And that leads me to some different conclusions from Senator Dole.

For example, we have reduced the size of the Federal government to its smallest size in 30 years. We reduced more regulations, eliminated more programs than my two Republican predecessors. But I have worked hard for things like the Family and Medical Leave Law, the Brady Bill, the assault weapons ban, the program to put 100,000 police on the street. All of these are programs that Senator Dole opposed that I supported, because I felt they were a legitimate effort to help people make the most of their own lives. I've worked hard to help families impart values to their own children. I supported the V-chip so that parents would be able to control what their kids watch on television when they're young, along with the ratings systems for television and educational television. I supported strong action against the tobacco companies to stop the marketing, advertising, and sale of tobacco to young people. I supported a big increase in the safe and drug-free schools program. These were areas on which Senator Dole and I differed, but I believed they were the right areas for America to be acting together as one country to help individuals and families make the most of their own lives and raise their kids with good values and a good future.

Lehrer: Senator Dole, one minute.

Dole: I think the basic difference is, and I have had some experience in this, I think the basic difference, I trust the people. The President trusts the government. We go back and look at the healthcare plan that he wanted to impose on the American people. One seventh the total economy, 17 new taxes, price controls, 35 to 50 new bureaucracies that cost $1.5 trillion. Don't forget that, that happened in 1993. A tax increase, a tax on everybody in America. Not just the rich. If you made $25,000 as the original proposal, you got your Social Security taxes increased. We had a BTU tax we turned into a $35 million gas tax, a $265 billion tax increase.

I guess I rely more on the individual. I carry a little card in my pocket called the Tenth Amendment. Where possible, I want to give power back to the states and back to the people. That's my difference with the President. We'll have specific differences later. He noted a few, but there are others.

Lehrer: Mr. President, 30 seconds.

Clinton: I trust the people. We've done a lot to give the people more powers to make their own decisions over their own lives. But I do think we are right when we try to, for example, give mothers and newborns 48 hours before they can be kicked out of the hospital, ending these drive-by deliveries.

I think we were right to pass the Kassebaum-Kennedy bill, which says you can't lose your health insurance just because you change jobs or because someone in your family's been sick. Our government is smaller and less bureaucratic and has given more authority to the states than its two predecessors under Republican presidents. But I do believe we have to help our people get ready to succeed in the 21st Century.

Lehrer: Senator Dole, the President said in his opening statement we are better off today than we were four years ago. Do you agree?

Dole: Well, he's better off than he was four years ago.

Clinton: I agree with that. That's right.

Dole: And I may be better off four years from now, but I don't know. I looked at the slowest growth in the century. He inherited a growth of 4.7, 4.8 percent, now it's down to about 2.4 percent. We're going to pass a million bankruptcies this year for the first time in history. We've got stagnant wages. In fact, women's wages have dropped 2.2 percent. Men's wages haven't gone up, gone down. So we have stagnation.

We have the highest foreign debt in history. And it seems to me that if you take a look, are you better off? Well, I guess some may be better off. Saddam Hussein is probably better off than he was four years ago. Renee Proval is probably better off than he was four years ago. But are the American people? They're working harder and higher and harder paying more taxes. For the first time in history, you pay about 40 percent of what you earn. More than you spend for food, clothing and shelter combined for taxes under this administration. So some may be better off.

They talk about family income being up. That's not true in Connecticut, family income is down. And it's up in some cases because both parents are working. One works for the family, and one works to pay taxes for the government. We're going to give them tax cuts so they can spend more time with their children, maybe even take a vacation. That's what America is all about.

Lehrer: One minute, Mr. President.

Clinton: Well, let me say, first of all, in February Senator Dole acknowledged that the American economy was in the best shape it's been in in 30 years. We have ten and a half million more jobs, a faster job growth rate than under any Republican administration since the 1920s. Wages are going up for the first time in a decade. We have record numbers of new small businesses. We have the biggest drop in the number of people in poverty in 27 years. All groups of people are growing. We had the biggest drop in income inequality in 27 years in 1995.

The average family's income has gone up over $1,600 just since our economic plan passed. So I think it's clear that we're better off than we were four years ago. Now we need to focus on what do we need to do to be better off still. How can we help people as we are to get their retirements when they work for small businesses, to be able to afford health insurance, to be able to educate their children. That's what I want to focus on. But we are clearly better off than we were four years ago, as Senator Dole acknowledged this year.

Lehrer: Senator Dole.

Dole: I doubt that I acknowledged that this year. But in any event, I think we just look at the facts. We ask the people that are viewing tonight, are you better off than you were in '94? Four years ago. It's not whether we're better off, it's whether they're better off.

Are you working harder to put food on the table, feed your children? Are your children getting a better education? Drug use has doubled the past 44 months all across America. Crime has gone down but it's because the mayors like Rudy Giuliani where one-third of the drop happened in one city, New York City.

So, yes, some may be better off. But of the people listening tonight, the working families who will benefit from economic packages, they'll be better off when Bob Dole is president and Jack Kemp is vice president.

Lehrer: Mr. President, Senator Dole has come pretty close in the last few days to accusing you of lying about his position on Medicare reform. Have you done so?

Clinton: Absolutely not. Let's look at the position. First of all, remember that in this campaign season, since Senator Dole's been a candidate, he has bragged about the fact that he voted against Medicare in the beginning, in 1965, one of only 12 members. He said he did the right thing then, he knew it wouldn't work at the time. That's what he said.

Then his budget that he passed along with Speaker [Newt] Gingrich [R-Ga.] cut Medicare $270 billion, more than was necessary to repair the Medicare trust fund. It would have charged seniors more for out-of-pocket costs as well as more in premiums because doctors could have charged them more. The American Medical, Hospital Association, the Nurses Association, the Catholic Hospital Association all said hundreds of hospitals could close and people would be hurt badly under the Dole-Gingrich Medicare plan that I vetoed.

And now with this risky $550 billion tax scheme of Senator Dole's, even his own friends, his campaign co-chair, Senator [Alfonse] D'Amato [R-N.Y.], says that they can't possibly pay for it without cutting Medicare more and cutting Social Security as well, according to him.

Now, my balanced budget plan adds ten years to the life of the Medicare trust fund, ten years. And we'll have time to deal with the long-term problems of the baby boomers. But it was simply wrong to finance their last scheme to cut Medicare $270 billion to run the risk of it withering on the vine. We always had to reform it over the years, but we need somebody who believes in it to reform it.

Lehrer: Senator Dole.

Dole: Well, I must say, I look back at the vote on Medicare in 1965, we had a program called Eldercare that also provided drugs and means tests to people who needed medical attention received it. I thought it was a good program. But I've supported Medicare ever since.

In fact, I used to go home, my mother would tell me, Bob, all I've got is my Social Security and my Medicare, don't cut it. I wouldn't violate anything my mother said. In fact, we had a conversation about our mothers one day, a very poignant conversation in the White House. I'm concerned about healthcare. I've had the best healthcare from government hospitals, Army hospitals and I know its importance, but we've got to fix it. It's his trustees, the President's trustees, not mine, who says it's going to go broke. He doesn't fix it for ten years. We ought to appoint a commission, just as we did in Social Security in 1983, when we rescued Social Security, and I was proud to be on that commission, along with Claude Pepper, the champion of senior citizens in Florida. And we can do it again, if we take politics out of it. Stop scaring the seniors, Mr. President. You've already spent $45 million scaring seniors and tearing me apart. I think it's time to have a truce.

Lehrer: Mr. President.

Clinton: Well, let me say, first of all, I'd be happy to have a commission deal with this and I appreciate what Senator Dole did on the '83 Social Security commission. But it won't be possible to do, if his tax scheme passes because even his own campaign co-chair, Senator D'Amato, says he'll have to cut Medicare even more than was cut in the bill that I vetoed. I vetoed that bill because it cut more Medicare and basically ran the risk of breaking up the system. My balanced budget plan puts ten years on the Medicare. We ought to do that, then we can have a commission. But Senator Dole's plans are not good for the country.

Lehrer: Senator Dole, speaking of your tax plan, do you still think that's a good idea, the 15 percent across the board tax cut?

Dole: Oh, yes. And you'll be eligible.

Clinton: Me too?

Dole: And so will the former President, yes.

Clinton: I need it.

Dole: Well, the people need it, that's the point. This is not a Wall Street tax cut. This is a family tax cut. This is a Main Street tax cut, 15 percent across— let's take a family making $30,000 a year, that's $1261. Now, may be some in this Bushnell Memorial that it's not a lot of money, but people watching tonight with a couple of kids, a working family, that's four or five months of day care, maybe a personal computer; it's maybe three or four months of mortgage payments. This economic package is about families but it's a six-point package. First of all, it's a balanced budget amendment to the Constitution which President Clinton defeated. He twisted arms and got six Democrats to vote the other way, but we lost by one vote. It's balancing a budget by the year 2002. It's a tax cut, cutting capital gains 50 percent. So you can go out and create more jobs and more opportunities. It's a state tax relief. It's a $500 per child tax credit. It's about litigation reforms.

Now that the President gets millions of dollars from the trial lawyers, he probably doesn't like this provision. In fact, when I fell off the podium in Chico, before I lit the ground, hit the ground I had a call on my cell phone from a trial lawyer saying I think we've got a case here. And it's also regulatory reform. It's a good package, Mr. President. We'd like to have your support.

Lehrer: Mr. President.

Clinton: Well, here's the problem with it: It sounds very good, but there's a reason that 500 economists, including seven Nobel prize winners and business periodicals like *Business Week*, and even Senator Dole's friends, Senator Warren Rudman, former Republican senator from New Hampshire, says it's not a practical program. It's a $550 billion tax scheme that will cause a big hole in the deficit which will raise interest rates and slow down the economy and cause people to pay more for home mortgages, car payments, credit card payments, college loans, and small business loans. It's not good to raise the deficit. We worked too hard to lower it. It will actually raise taxes on nine million people and, in addition to that, it will force bigger cuts in Medicare, Medicaid, education and the environment than the ones that he and Mr. Gingrich passed that I vetoed last year. So it sounds great, but our targeted tax cut for education, child rearing, healthcare and home buying, which is paid for in my balanced budget plan, something that he has not done, certified by the Congressional budget office, that's the right way to go.

Dole: The President wants to increase spending 20 percent over the next six years. I want to increase spending 14 percent, that's how simple it is. I want the government to pinch pennies for a change instead of the American families. We're talking about six percentage points over six years, and with that money you give it back to the working people. You also provide opportunity scholarships so low income parents will have the same choice that others have in sending their children to better schools. It will work, and when it does work, Mr. President, I know you'll congratulate me. . . .

Lehrer: Mr. President, Senator Dole said the other day that you practiced a photo-op foreign policy that has lessened the credibility of the United States throughout the world. Is he wrong about that?

Clinton: If he, that's what he said, he's not right about that. Look at where we are today. The United States is still the indispensable nation in the aftermath of the Cold War and on the brink of the 21st Century. I have worked to support our country as the world's strongest force for peace and freedom, prosperity and security.

We have done the following things: Number one, we've managed the aftermath of the Cold War, supporting a big drop in nuclear weapons in Russia. The removal of Russian troops from the Baltics. The integration of Central and Eastern European democracies into a new partnership with NATO. And, I might add, with the democratic Russia.

There are no nuclear missiles pointed at the children of the United States tonight and have not been in our administration for the first time since the dawn of the nuclear age.

We have worked hard for peace and freedom. When I took office, Haiti was governed by a dictator that had defied the United States. When I took office, the worst war in Europe was waging in Bosnia. Now there is a democratically elected president in Haiti. Peace in Bosnia. We just had the election there. We've made progress in Northern Ireland, in the Middle East. We've also stood up to the new threats of terrorism. The proliferation of weapons of mass destruction, organized crime, and we have worked hard to expand America's economic presence around the world with the biggest increase in trade with the largest new number of trade agreements in history. And that's one of the reasons America is number one in auto production again.

Lehrer: Senator.

Dole: Well, I have a different view. Again, I supported the President on Bosnia, and I think we were told the troops would be out in a year. Now I understand it's been extended until some time next year. But, let's start with

Somalia, where they dragged Americans through the streets, and where 18 Americans were killed one day, because they didn't have, they were pinned down for eight hours, the rangers. They didn't have the weapons, they didn't have the tanks. They asked for tanks. They didn't get the tanks from this administration because we were nation building. It's called mission creep. We turn it over to the United Nations. The President didn't have much to do about it. You look at Haiti, where we spend about $3 billion and we got an alarm call there about two weeks ago. You got to send down some more people, because the president's found out there are death squads on his own property. So we need more protection from America. Bosnia, Northern Ireland. There's no cease-fire in Bosnia. I think there are still a lot of problems in Bosnia. We agreed to train and arm the Muslims so they could defend themselves, the policy you had when you ran in 1992. We haven't done that. We're way behind, which means Americans can't come home. Americans shouldn't have gone there in the first place, had we let them defend themselves, as they have a right to do under Article 57 of the United Nations charter.

Lehrer: Mr. President.

Clinton: First of all, I take full responsibility for what happened in Somalia, but the American people must remember that those soldiers were under an American commander when that happened. I believe they did the best they could under the circumstances, and let's not forget that hundreds of thousands of lives were saved there.

Secondly, in Haiti, political violence is much, much smaller than it was. Thirdly, in Bosnia it's a virtual miracle that there has been no return to war and at least there has now been an election. And institutions are beginning to function.

In Northern Ireland, in the Middle East we are better off than we were four years ago. There will always be problems in this whole world. But if we're moving in the right direction and America is leading, we're better off.

Lehrer: Senator Dole, if elected president, what criteria would you use to decide when to send U.S. troops into harm's way.

Dole: Well it, after World War I, we had, you know, a policy of disengagement. Then from World War I to World War II we had sort of a compulsory engagement policy. Now I think we have a selective engagement policy. We have to determine when our interests are involved, not the United Nations' interests. And many of the things the President talked about, he turned over to the United Nations. They decided.

He's deployed more troops than any president in history around the world. It's cost us billions and billions of dollars for peace-keeping operations. Look these are facts. And it seems to me that when you make a decision, the decision is made by the President of the United States, by the Commander-in-Chief. He makes that decision when he commits young men or young women who are going to go round and defend our liberty and our freedom. That would be my position. . . .

But the bottom line is, we are the strongest nation in the world. We provide the leadership and we're going to have to continue to provide the leadership, but let's do it on our terms when our interests are involved and not when somebody blows the whistle at the United Nations.

Clinton: Our military is the strongest military in the world. It is the strongest, best prepared, best equipped it has ever been. There is very little difference in the budget that I proposed and the Republican budget over the next six-year period. We are spending a lot of money to modernize our weapons system. I have proposed a lot of new investments to improve the quality of life for our soldiers, for our men and women in uniform, for their families, for their training. That is my solemn obligation.

You ask when do you decide to deploy them. The interests of the American people must be at stake. Our values must be at stake. We have to be able to make a difference. And frankly we have to consider what the risks are to our young men and women in uniform. But I believe the evidence is that our deployments have been successful, in Haiti, in Bosnia, when we moved to Kuwait to repel Saddam Hussein's threatened invasion of Kuwait. When I have sent the fleet into the Taiwan straits. When we've worked hard to end the Northern Korean nuclear threat.

I believe the United States is at peace tonight in part because of the disciplined, careful, effective deployment of our military resources. . . .

Lehrer: Senator Dole, if you could single out one thing that you would like for the voters to have in their mind about President Clinton on a policy matter or a personal matter, what would it be? Something to know about him, understand it and appreciate it.

Dole: See, if I say anything it's going to be misconstrued. I don't think there is even a race between the two, it's about our vision for America.

I happen to like President Clinton personally. I'm addressing him all evening as Mr. President. I said in 1992 he didn't extend that courtesy to President Bush. But I respect the presidency. I've served under a number of presidents. They all have their strengths and they all have their weaknesses. So I'd rather talk about my strengths. And I think I have my strengths and I think the best thing going for Bob Dole is that Bob Dole keeps his word. It's a question between trust and fear, and I would say, I think, Mr. President, about all you've got going in this campaign is fear.

You're spending millions and millions of dollars in negative ads frightening senior citizens. I know this to be a fact because I had one tell me last week, Senator don't cut my Medicare. I'm trying to save your Medicare, just as I rescued Social Security with a bipartisan commission. I have relatives on Medicare. I used to sign welfare checks for my grandparents. I know all about poverty and all about need and all about taking care of people, and that's been my career in the United States Senate.

And I'll keep my word on the economic package. If I couldn't cut taxes and balance the budget the same time, I wouldn't look at you in the eye in your living room or wherever you might be and say that this is good for America. People will tell you who served with Bob Dole, agree or disagree, he kept his word. That's what this race is all about.

Clinton: I'd like the American people to know that I have worked very hard to be on their side. And to move this country forward and we're better off than we were four years ago. But the most important thing is my plan for the 21st Century is a better plan. A targeted tax cut, a real commitment to educational reform. A deep commitment to making welfare reform work with incentives to the private sector to move people from welfare to work. Now we have to create those jobs, now that we're requiring people to go to work.

A commitment to continuing step-by-step healthcare reform with the next step helping people who are between jobs to access healthcare and not lose it just because they are out of work for a while. A commitment to grow the economy while protecting the environment. That's what I'd like them to know about me; that I've gotten up every day and worked for the American people and worked so that their children could have their dreams come true. And I believe we've got the results to show we're on the right track. The most important thing is, I believe we've got the right ideas for the future. And I like, I like Senator Dole, you can probably tell we like each other. We just see the world in different ways. And you folks out there are going to have to choose who you think is right. . . .

Lehrer: . . . Let's go now to the closing statements. Mr. President. . . .

Clinton: Well, first, Jim, let me thank you and thank you, Senator Dole, and thank you, ladies and gentlemen, all of you listening tonight for the chance you've given us to appear.

I want to say in the beginning that I am profoundly grateful for the chance that you have given me to serve as president for the last four years. I never could have dreamed anything like this would come my way in life, and I've done my best to be faithful to the charge you've given me.

I'm proud of the fact that America is stronger and more prosperous and more secure than we were four years ago. And I'm glad we're going in the right direction. And I've done my best tonight to lay out my plans for going forward to an even better future in the next century. I'd like to leave you with the thought that the things I do as president are basically driven by the people whose lives I have seen affected by what does or doesn't happen in this country. The auto worker in Toledo who was unemployed when I was elected and now has a great job because we're number one in auto production again. All the people I've met who used to be on welfare who are now working and raising their children. And I think what others could do for our country and themselves if we did the welfare reform thing in the proper way. I think of the man who grabbed me by the shoulder once with tears in his eyes and said his daughter was dying of cancer and he thanked me for giving him a chance to spend some time with her without losing his job because of the Family and Medical Leave Act. I think of all the people I grew up with and went to school with and who I stay in touch with and who never let me forget how what we do in Washington affects all of you in America. Folks, we can build that bridge to the 21st Century, big enough and strong enough for all of us to walk across, and I hope you will help me build it.

Lehrer: Senator Dole, your closing statement, sir.

Dole: Thank you, Jim; thank you, Mr. President; thank everyone for watching and listening.

I want to address my remarks to the young people of America, because they're the ones that are going to spend most of their life in the 21st Century. They're the ones who have the challenges and they are people out there making predictions that it's not going to be the same. You're not going to have the opportunities; there are going to be more deficits, more drugs, more crime, and less confidence in the American people. And that's what you're faced with, the parents are faced with, and the grandparents are faced with. It's important, it's their future. And I would say to those I know there are more young people experimenting with drugs today than ever before; drug use has gone up. And if you care about the future of America, if you care about your future, just don't do it. And I know that I'm someone older than you. But I've had my anxious moments in my life. I've learned to feed myself and to walk and to dress. I'm standing here as proof that in America the possibilities are unlimited. I know who I am, and I know where I'm from, and I know where I want to take America. We are the greatest country on the face of the earth. We do more good things for more people in our communities, our neighborhoods, than anywhere that I know of. This is important business. This election is important. I ask for your support, I ask for your help. And if you really want to get involved, just tap into my home page, WWW.DoleKemp96.ORG. Thank you. God bless America.

VICE PRESIDENTIAL DEBATE

Lehrer: . . . Mr. Vice President, what do you see as the political philosophy differences in a general way between you and President Clinton on the one hand, Mr. Kemp and Senator Dole on the other?

Gore: The differences are very clear. We have a positive plan based on three principles. We want to provide opportunity for all Americans. We insist on responsibility being accepted in turn by everyone, and we want to strengthen our communities and their ability to support families and individuals in our common effort to create a bright future. Here's how we plan to do that: We have a balanced budget plan that has targeted tax cuts for middle-income families. We've already given tax cuts to 15 million of the hardest pressed working families in America. Our plan for the next four years features a $1,500 tax credit, called a Hope Scholarship, for tuition at community college, junior college or college. A $10,000 tax deduction for college tuition for those who go further, so that, in essence, no American family will ever be taxed on the money they spend for college tuition. Also, tax relief for first-time home buyers, tax encouragement for savings and help in paying health care expenses, and a tax break, actually, the elimination of capital gains taxes on the—on the profits from the sale of a home. All of this is within a balanced budget plan, which protects Medicare, Medicaid, education and the environment.

Kemp: Jim, this economy is overtaxed, overregulated, too many people suing each other, there's too much litigation. Our education is not up to the standards that the American family and the American people want for their children. And, clearly, the welfare system is a disgrace to our Judeo-Christian principles. It is not the values of the poor that should be called into question, it is the values of the welfare system from Washington and that prevent people from climbing out of poverty. Our biggest debate with this administration on domestic policy is that they think we're at our fullest capacity, reached our potential and 2.5 is enough growth for America. Frankly, that is not good enough for this country. We can not just run the clock out on the 20th Century. It, clearly, we need to lower the tax rate across the board on working and saving and investing. I know my friend, Al, will suggest that is trickle-down economics. Well, Al, if it's trickle-down economics, ask Van Woods, a young entrepreneur who owns a restaurant in Harlem, if it's trickle down. He said he would hire 60 more people if we cut the Capital Gains Tax. . . .

Lehrer: Mr. Kemp, back to the philosophy question. Do you think there's a basic philosophy difference between these two tickets, or is it about specifics, which both of you have talked about?

Kemp: Well, this is a perfect example. Bob Dole and I want to cut the tax rates across the board on each and every American, working, saving, investing and taking risks in America. All wealth is created, and all growth is generated by risk-taking entrepreneurs. The tax rate on capital in America is way too high. It's too high on the family and it's particularly too high on working men and women. The average family in America, at median level of income, probably is spending 25 to 26 percent of their income sent to the federal government. That's more than shelter, food, clothing, and energy. That's just not right. When I was growing up in Los Angeles, my parents were a one working family, one breadwinner per family was all that was necessary. Now if a woman wants to go to work or a man wants to go to work, it ought to be their choice, not the choice of the Washington, D.C. establishment. Bill Clinton, the President, and Al Gore, suggest that they'll give us a tax cut, but only if we do exactly what they want us to do. That isn't America. That's social engineering. The tax code should reflect our values in a Judeo-Christian sense, that work, honesty and integrity and contracts and property and investment and savings should be rewarded, and Bob Dole and Jack Kemp are not only going to cut the tax rates across the board and lower the Capital Gain Tax. I'll be glad to talk about it a little later, there's not enough time, but we are going to repeal the 83-year-old code and replace the seven and a half million words with a flatter, fairer, simpler code that will take this country roaring in the 21st Century.

Gore: This risky tax scheme would blow a hole in the deficit. You don't have to take my word for it. *Time, Newsweek, U.S. News & World Report, Business Week,* 83 percent of hundreds of economists in a random survey just recently all said it would blow a hole in the deficit. There's another feature I would like to hear Mr. Kemp speak about. Just before he joined Senator Dole on the ticket, he said that the plan—the part of the plan that raises taxes on 9 million of the hardest working families in America was uncon-scionable, that means it's wrong and it shouldn't happen. I agree, it is still part of the plan. We believe that taxes should not be increased on those families. We have a plan to cut taxes on middle income families within a balanced bud-get plan, eliminating the deficit and protecting Medicare, Medicaid, educa-tion and the environment. . . .

Lehrer: Mr. Kemp, do we have a serious race problem in the United States right now?

Kemp: Yeah, we really do. Um, this country has yet to deal with the type of exclusionary policies. It is so very important for Americans, white and black, Jew and Christian, immigrant and native-born, to sit down and talk and listen and begin to understand what it's like to come from that different perspective. Our country is as the Kerner Commission Report suggested a number of years ago was being split, but they said between white and black. I think it's being split, Jim, not so much between white and black, although that's still a very serious problem. We really have two economies. Our gener-al economy, our national economy, our mainstream economy is democratic, is based on incentives, a small "d" Al, it's capitalism and incentives for work-ing and saving and investing and producing, and families and the things that really lead to progress up that ladder that we call "The American Dream," but is what is really universal. But unfortunately, in urban America, and I was glad to hear the Vice President talk a little bit about it, uh there—they have abandoned the inner cities. There's a socialist economy. There's no private housing. There's mostly public housing. You're told where to go to school, you're told what to buy with food stamps. It is a welfare system that is more like a third-world socialist country than what we would expect from the world's greatest democratic free-enterprise system. That must change, and it will under Bob Dole and Jack Kemp.

Gore: Remember what I said just a moment ago. If it were not so, he would have told you. The problems between races in America must be addressed. The good news is we're making progress. We've seen 10.5 million new jobs created in the last four years. We've seen the unemployment rate come down dramatically. We've seen the African-American unemployment rate go below double digits for the first time in 25 years and stayed below for 25 months in a row. We have empowerment zones and enterprise communi-ties, 105 of them in communities all across the United States of America. Let me tell you a story about Joann Crowder in Detroit. She was on welfare for eight years until the empowerment zone was created there. She just got a job in the new business that—that launched its enterprise right in that empow-erment zone. We want to do that for millions more all across the country. . . .

Lehrer: Mr. Kemp, is it really possible to balance the budget without reforming drastically the entitlement programs, including Social Security and Medicare?

Kemp: Before I answer that, Jim, let me just say it is disgraceful, the cam-paign being waged to scare the American senior citizens, in this state and my home state of, well, New York and California, about Medicare.

Gore: One other one in there, isn't there?

Kemp: About Medicare. Yeah, Maryland now. The amount of money being spent to try to mislead the American people is demagoguery, and only in the Clinton White House and in Al Gore's mind could an increase in spending per capita on a senior citizen from $4,100 in 1996 to $7,200 over the next five years be considered a cut. Does anybody think that Bob Dole, who almost gave his life for his country, who has served in the Senate, who helped save Social Security, crawled out of a fox hole on Riva Ridge in Northern Italy in 1945 to save a wounded radioman? Does anybody think in this country that he could possibly want to move our country ahead and leave anybody behind? Of course, we can balance the budget. Of course, we have to hold down the growth in entitlement spending. But clearly, you cannot balance the budget, Jim, without growing this economy. It's only growing at about two-and-a-half percent. We should double the rate of growth and double the size of American economy. This means more jobs, more wealth, more income and more capital, particularly for our nation's poor and those left behind.

Gore: Mr. Lehrer, our balanced budget plan extends the Medicare Trust Fund ten years into the future. A commission is fine, but a commission would not do any good if we adopted this risky $550-billion tax scheme. The word "scary" has been used. A couple of days ago I went with Governor Lawton Chiles [D-Fla.], who was here, to Sarasota to the Friendship Senior Center. I talked with a woman there named Dorothy Wornell and she said, "You know, we may not be as sophisticated as some of those people in Washington, but we can add and subtract." Here are the numbers she's adding and subtracting. Bob Dole's plan would have already imposed an extra $268 on the average Medicare receiving couple, and his plan would have doubled deductibles. It would have cost an extra $1,700 over the lifetime of his plan and eliminated nursing home standards and guarantees of nursing home care for seniors. Bill Clinton prevented it from happening. We will never allow that to happen. . . .

Lehrer: Mr. Kemp, what, if anything, would a Dole/Kemp administration do to change the current legal status of abortion in this country?

Kemp: . . . [W]e recognize there's no consensus in America. This country is split between those who call themselves pro-choice, and I'm sure, very sincerely, and those of us who call ourselves pro-life, this is a very emotional issue. I'm sure it is for a woman. It certainly is for those of us like my wife and myself who have three adopted grandchildren. We thank God every night of our life that a young woman was given a choice, was given the opportunity to choose life. This country should not be torn asunder over this debate; it has to be carried out with civility and respect, and Bob and I believe it can be. But we should recognize that every human life is precious and there should be all of the protection that we can give for an unborn human being. And to think that in this country, for every three births, there is one abortion. But even worse than that, as ugly as that might be—and I know it's a tragedy to many people both on the pro-choice and pro-life position—we have a President who vetoed a congressional ban on the ugly and gruesome practice of snatching life away from a child just moments before he or she enters the world. That is unacceptable.

Lehrer: Mr. Vice President?

Gore: President Clinton has made it clear that he will sign legislation outlawing procedures such as this if there is a—an exception to protect the health of the mother where serious health consequences, such as the inability to have any further children, are involved and her doctor advises her so. What is really at stake here is whether or not women will have the right to choose. The platform on which Mr. Kemp and Senator Dole are running pledges a constitutional amendment to take away a woman's right to choose and to have the government come in and order that woman to do what the government says, no matter what the circumstances. Mr. Kemp has voted 47 out of 47 times to have such an amendment and to restrict this completely, no matter what the circumstances, even where rape and incest are involved. We will never allow a woman's right to choose to be taken away. . . .

Lehrer: Mr. Kemp, uh some are saying these days that something's gone terribly wrong with the American soul, that we've become too mean, too selfish, too uncaring and the spitting incident, how it was handled, the baseball players used as a recent example. What do you think about that?

Kemp: Civility, responsibility, racial reconciliation, healing the wounds of our country has to be one of the greatest, most singularly important goals for this country here on the edge of the 21st Century. How in the name of American democracy can we say to eastern Europe that democratic capitalism will work there if we can't make it work in East L.A. or East Harlem or East Palo Alto, California? How can we tell South Africa and the new Mandela government that democracy and private property and limited government and the rule of law and civility will work there if it's not working in our own backyard here at home or the South Bronx? How can America go into the next century and leave so many people behind? *USA Today*, just a few weeks ago, did a study. They said the affluent are doing very well in America, the haves, the have-nots and the poor are being left behind. It is a giant, in my opinion, zero sum game. Kind of like musical chairs when we were young boys and girls growing up. And it seemed like when the music stopped the big guy elbowed out the little guy from that last chair; that's not America folks. We need more chairs, we need a bigger table, we need a greater banquet. We need to create more wealth. We need to create more jobs and more access to credit and capital and educational choice and opportunity for any man or woman and child to be what God meant them to be, not what Washington, D.C. wants them to be.

Gore: I think Mr. Lehrer, that throughout most of his career, Jack Kemp has been a powerful and needed voice against the kind of coarseness and incivility that you refer to in the question. I think it's an extremely valuable service to have a voice within the Republican party who says we ought to be one nation. We ought to cross all of the racial and ethnic and cultural barriers. I think that is a very important message to deliver. And we ought to speak out against these violations of civility when they do occur. You asked about the incident involving Roberto Alomar. I won't hesitate to tell you what I think. I think he should have been severely disciplined, suspended perhaps, immediately. I don't understand why that action was not taken, but the same could be said of so many incidents in all kinds of institutions in our society, but I compliment Mr. Kemp for the leadership he has shown in moving us away from that kind of attitude.

Kemp: Well, I thank you, Al. I mean that very, very sincerely, but I'm trying to make a bigger point. That civility cannot return to our country unless every person feels that they have an equal shot at the American dream. That if you're born in this country to be a mezzo-soprano or a master carpenter or a school teacher, like my daughter, or a professional football quarterback, nothing should be in your way. And removing those barriers is what Bob Dole is all about, moving our country forward and leaving no one behind. . . .

Lehrer: . . . [N]ow we go to the closing statements. There will be three minutes each and Mr. Kemp, you are first.

Kemp: Thank you, Jim and thanks to the people of St. Petersburg for a fantastic hospitality and my friend, Al Gore, for a vigorous debate. I think this is the most exciting time in the history of the world to be alive. We have lived through what Jeane Kirkpatrick called the bloodiest century in mankind's history. We have defeated in this system of ours fascism, Nazism, communism, socialism is defunct or debunked around the world, the evil of apartheid has ended. There is only one last question remaining for the next century, indeed the next millennium. Can we, in America, make the world's greatest liberal democracy, this democratic experiment in private property, limited government, the rule of law, respect for families and traditional Judeo-Christian values work, so it can be a blessing to our country and a blessing to the rest of the world? With all due respect to this administration, they've got a foreign policy in disarray. They have a lack of credibility around the world. Weakness, I said earlier, is provocative and clearly, this economy is not performing up to the standards that we would expect from this great nation going into the most exciting global economy the world has ever known. There's something amiss. Our culture seems to be weakening all around us. Families are under tremendous pressure. People do not—do not feel safe in their homes. A mother doesn't feel safe sending her child to school. Our schools are not educating. It's not the problem of the teachers. They are overworked and my daughter will tell you, they are underpaid and we know that, they need to be empowered. We need to reform education. We need to reform welfare. We need to reform litigation and regulation. And we certainly need to reform this tax code that is a product of this terrible century of war and recession and inflations. It can be done. We need somebody who understands the potential of the American people, who are not just doing well for ourselves, we need to do well for the rest of the world, because they're looking at us. And we need to make it work in every neighborhood and community in America and for every family, so that no one as Bob Dole said in his San Diego acceptance speech is left behind. Bob Dole, as I said earlier, is a man of courage, a man of principles, a man who crawled out of a fox hole on Riva Ridge in 1945 to save a wounded brethren. The Bible says no greater love hath a man than he gave his life. Well, Bob Dole did, just about, he'd been through the valley of the shadow and he as Commander-in-Chief can take this country with the courage of Churchill. The principles of Lincoln and the indefatigable optimism and spirit that this nation expects from its Commander-in-Chief and the next President of the United States, Bob Dole.

Lehrer: Mr. Vice President?

Gore: Thank you very much, Mr. Lehrer. Thanks again to the people of St. Petersburg and thanks again to Jack Kemp. I have enormous respect for Jack Kemp and for Bob Dole. They're good men. I don't agree with their plan. I've tried to make that clear tonight. And one reason I've tried to make it clear is that in just 27 days, the United States of America has an important choice to make. Between two approaches to the future of this country. We have a plan that will create millions more jobs, bring the deficits down further and balance the budget, while protecting Medicare, protecting Medicaid, protecting and preserving the environment, our air, our water, the Everglades, the Tongas, the Mojave Desert in California, the Utah-Red Rocks area, all of which have been protected by President Bill Clinton. We also have a plan to expand access to education. There's a family in the audience tonight, the McNeil family, who lives right here in St. Petersburg. Both parents are teachers, they're not rich in money, but they have strong values and they value education. Their oldest son is a freshman at St. Petersburg Junior High—Junior College. Their younger son, Roderick, is a sophomore in the same high school that Don McNeil teaches at. Roderick is concerned that he may not be able to get the tuition he needs to go to college when the time comes. Our plan gives a $1500 tax credit to make that junior college essentially free. And a $10,000 tax deduction to make it so that no American family, or almost no family, will have to pay taxes on the money they pay for college tuition. This plan also gives tax breaks on the sale of a home, up to $500,000 in profit tax free. It gives the new break for first-time home buyers, and, again, all in the context of a balanced budget. We have seen progress during the last four years because policies like these have been working. This risky scheme that I've described tonight has been said by many objective observers to not add up, it would be a serious risk. Our plan, by contrast, has been working and will work more. We want to build a bridge to the 21st Century and we want it to be strong enough and broad enough for all families to cross and we want it to lead to a brighter future for America, 'cause our best days are ahead.

Lehrer: Thank you.

SECOND PRESIDENTIAL DEBATE

Lehrer: . . . We will follow a town-hall type format tonight. The questions over the next minutes will come from citizens of the greater San Diego area. . . .

Ms. McAfee: My name is Shannon McAfee. I'm a beginning educator in this country, and I really think it's important what children have to say. They're still very idealistic. And they—everything they say comes from the heart. I have a quote for you from "If I Were President," compiled by Peggy Gavin. A sixth grader says, "If I were president, I would think about Abraham Lincoln and George Washington and what they did to make our country great. We should unite the white and black people and people of all cultures. Democrats and Republicans should unite also. We should all come together and think of the best ways to solve the economic problems of our country. "I believe that when we are able to come together and stop fighting amongst yourself we will get along a lot better." These are the ideals and morals that we are teach—we are trying to teach our children in these days. Yet we don't seem to be practicing them in our government, in anything. If you are president, how will you begin to practice what we are preaching to our children, the future of our nation?

Dole: Well, I would say first of all, I think, it's a very good question. I appreciate the quote from the young man. There's no doubt about it that many American people have lost their faith in government. They see scandals almost on a daily basis. They see ethical problems in the White House today. They see 900 FBI files, private person, being gathered up by somebody in the White House. Nobody knows who hired this man. So there's a great deal of cynicism out there. But I've always tried in whatever I've done to bring people together. I said in my acceptance speech in San Diego about two months ago that the exits are clearly marked. If you think the Republican party is some place for you to come if you're narrow minded or bigoted or don't like certain people in America, the exits are clearly marked for you to walk out of as I stand here without compromise, because this is the party of Lincoln. I think we have a real obligation, obviously public officials. I'm no longer a public official. I left public life on June the 11th of this year. But it is very important. Young people are looking to us. They're looking to us for leadership. They're watching what we do, what we say, what we promise and what we finally deliver. And I would think, it seems to me that there are opportunities here. When I'm President of the United States, I will keep my word. My word is my bond.

Lehrer: Mr. President.

Clinton: One of the reasons that I ran for president, Sandy, is because not just children, a lot of grownups felt that way. And if you remember four years ago, we had not only rising unemployment, but a lot of rising cynicism. I had never worked in Washington as an elected official. It seemed to me that most of the arguments were partisan, Republican, Democrat, left, right, liberal, conservative. That's why I said tonight I'm for opportunity, responsibility and community. And we've gotten some real progress in the last four years. I've also done everything I could at every moment of division in this country, after Oklahoma City, when these churches were burned, to bring people together and remind people that we are stronger because of our diversity. We have to respect one another. You mentioned Washington and Lincoln. They were presidents at historic times. This is an historic time. It's important we go beyond those old partisan arguments and focus on people and their future. When we do that, instead of shutting the government down over a partisan fight over the budget, we're a better country and that's why we're making progress now. . . .

Mr. Fleck: President Clinton, my name is Jack Fleck. I'm a retired Air Force pilot. Sir, it's officially forecast that our annual Medicare and Social Security deficits are measured in the trillions of dollars next century. Depending on who you listen to, Social Security will be bankrupted. . . . I feel this is grossly unfair, especially to our younger generation who are losing faith in the system. My question is this: Assuming you agree that our entitlement programs are on an unsustainable course, what specific reforms do you propose?

Clinton: First of all, there are two different things. Social Security and Medicare are entirely different in terms of the financial stabilities. Let's talk about them separately. Social Security is stable until, as you pointed out, at least the third decade of the next century. But we'd like to have a Social Security fund that has about 70 years of life instead of about 30 years of life. What we have to do is simply to make some adjustments to take account of the fact that the baby boomers, people like me, are bigger in number than the people that went just before us and the people that come just after us. And I think what we'll plainly do is what we did in 1983 when Senator Dole served, and this is something I think he did a good job on when he served on the Social Security commission and they made some modest changes in Social Security to make sure that it would be alive and well into the 21st century. And we will do that. It's obvious that there are certain things that have to be done and there are 50 or 60 different options, and a bipartisan commission to take it out of politics, will make recommendations and build support for the people. Medicare is different. Medicare needs help now. I have proposed a budget which would put ten years on the life of the Medicare trust fund. That's more than it's had a lot of the time in the last years. It would save a lot of money through more managed care, but giving more options, more preventative care and lowering the inflation rate and the prices we're paying providers without having the kind of big premium increases and out-of-pocket costs that the budget I vetoed would provide. Then that would give us ten years to do with Medicare what we're going to do with Social Security; have a bipartisan group look at what we have to do to save it when the baby boomers retire. But now we can, we ought to pass this budget now and put ten years on it right away so no one has to worry about it.

Dole: Well again, if you're somebody thinking about the future, I think it's fair to say that it'll be—we'll work it out. This is a political year, and the President is playing politics with Medicare. After this year is over, we'll resolve it just as we did with Social Security in '83. It's a nonpartisan commission. Ronald Reagan got together with Tip O'Neill and Howard Baker, two Republicans and one Democrat. They appointed a commission; I was on that commission. We resolved, we rescued Social Security. We suggested—I think it has been over a year ago now—we do the same with Medicare, and the White House called it a gimmick. Now last week I guess it was Donna Shalala said well we'll cut Medicare a hundred billion and appoint a commission. It will probably have to be done by a commission. Take it out of politics. I think if I were a senior citizen I would be a little fed up with all these ads scaring seniors, scaring veterans and scaring students about education. When you don't have any ideas, you don't have any agenda, and all you have is fear, that's all you can use. We have ideas in the Dole-Kemp campaign and we will rescue Medicare as we did Social Security. . . .

Ms. Naudin: My name is Melissa Naudin. I'm a third-year student at UC, San Diego. I just want to say it's a great honor representing the voices of America. My voice, my question is concerning you, Mr. Dole. All the controversy regarding your age. How do you feel you can respond to young voices of America today and tomorrow?

Dole: Well, I think age is very—you know, wisdom comes from age, experience and intelligence. And if you have some of each—and I have some age, some experience and some intelligence—that adds up to wisdom. I think it also is a strength. It's an advantage. And I have a lot of young people work in my office, work in my campaign. This is about America. This is about, somebody said earlier, one of the first questions, we're together. It's one America, one nation. I'm looking at our economic plan because I'm concerned about the future for young people. I'm looking about drugs. The president has been AWOL for four years. I'm looking about crime. He'll claim credit now for crime going down, but it happens because mayors and governors and others have brought crime down. Rudy Giuliani, Mayor of New York, brought crime down 25 percent just in New York City. Of course the president will take credit for that. My view is we want to find jobs and opportunities and education. This year the Republican Congress, as far as student loans went from $24 billion to $36 billion over the next six years. A 50 percent increase. The highest appropriation. $6 billion for Pell Grants, very, very important. We also raised the amount of each Pell Grant. In our economic plan, the $500 child credit can be used for young people, rolled over and over and over, you, of course not this age, but if you have a child two years old, 7 percent interest would be worth about $18,000 by the time that child was ready for college.

Clinton: I can only tell you that I don't think Senator Dole is too old to be president. It's the age of his ideas that I question. You're almost not old enough to remember this. But we tried this before, promising people an election year tax cut that's not paid for.

Dole: You tried it last time you ran.

Clinton: Tell him you can have everything you got. And so let me just say this. Did you hear him say that Congress just voted to increase student loans and scholarships? They did after he left. The last budget he led cut Pell Grants, cut student loans. I vetoed it when they shut the government down. My plan would give students a dollar-for-dollar reduction for the cost of a typical community college tuition. A $10,000 deduction a year for the cost of college tuition. We let families save in an IRA, withdraw tax free to pay for the cost of education and it's all paid for. My whole administration is about your future. It's about what the 21st century is going to be like for you. I hope you will look at the ideas in it. Thank you.

Dole: When you don't have any ideas, I guess you say the other person's ideas are old. As I said earlier, they don't have any ideas. Their idea is to raise taxes and spend more money. That's the liberal philosophy. That's what you like, you've got a perfect candidate. President Clinton came to California in 1992. He said the centerpiece in my first four years is going to be a middle class tax cut. Now all you got that tax cut, congratulations. Because you got a big tax increase. You got a $265 billion tax increase. And he stands here and says politicians who make promises like that ought to be ignored. Well he made the promise. I keep my word, and you will have a tax cut. It will help you in whatever you're going to do in the next few years. Thank you. . . .

Ms. Sanders: Hello. My name is Tressia Sanders. And my question is, do you feel that America has grown enough and has educated itself enough to totally cut out Affirmative Action?

Clinton: No, ma'am, I don't. I am against quotas. I'm against giving anybody any kind of preference for something they're not qualified for. But because I still believe that there is some discrimination and that not everybody has an opportunity to prove they're qualified, I favor the right kind of Affirmative Action. I've done more to eliminate Affirmative Action programs I didn't think were fair and tighten others up than my predecessors have, since affirmative action's been around. But I have also worked hard to give people a chance to prove that they are qualified. Let me just give you some examples. We've doubled the number of loans from the Small Business Administration, tripled the number of loans to women business people, no one unqualified, everybody had to meet the standards. We've opened 260,000 new jobs in the military to women since I've been president. But the joint chiefs say we're stronger and more confident and solid than ever. Let me give you another example of what I mean. To me, Affirmative Action is making that extra effort. It's sort of like what Senator Dole did when he sponsored the Americans with Disabilities Act and said to certain stores, okay, you have to make it accessible to people in wheelchairs. We weren't guaranteeing anything, anybody anything except the chance to prove they were qualified, the chance to prove that they could do it. And that's why I must say I agree with General Colin Powell that we're not there yet. We ought to keep making those extra effort Affirmative Action programs, the law and the policy of the land.

Lehrer: Senator Dole.

Dole: Well, we may not be there yet but we're not going to get there by giving preferences and quotas. I supported that route for some time and again I think it gets back to experience. A little experience, a little age, a little intelligence. And I noted that nobody was really benefiting except a very small group at the top. The average person wasn't benefiting. People who had the money were benefiting. People who got all the jobs were benefiting. It seems to me that we ought to support the California civil rights initiative. It ought to be not based on gender or ethnicity or color. Or disability. I'm disabled. I shouldn't have a preference. I would like to have one in this race, come to think of it, but I don't get one. Maybe we can work that out. I get a 10-point spot. This is America. No discrimination. Discrimination ought to be punished but there ought to be equal opportunity. We ought to reach out, make certain everybody has a chance to participate. Equal opportunity. But we cannot guarantee equal results in America. That's not how America became the greatest country on the face of the earth. . . .

Mr. David: My name's Tim David. I'm a mechanical engineer. Senator Dole, how do you reduce taxes and balance the budget?

Dole: . . . I'm glad you asked, because you look like the type that might be able to benefit from a 15 percent across-the-board tax cut and $500-per-child tax credit, or—you know, estate tax relief which you're not interested in right now, but capital gains rate reduction. If you're taking care of an elderly parent, you get a $1,000 deduction. We think that's very important because a lot of people take care of their parents. How do we pay for it? You can have a constitutional amendment to balance the budget, which the President opposed and defeated. He twisted arms and got six Democrats to vote with him and lost by one vote. We're going to balance the budget, by the year 2000; the President wants to spend 20 percent more in the next six years, and I want to spend 14 percent more and give that 6 percent back to the people. Remember, it's your money; it's not his money. And it's not my money. It's your money. And you shouldn't have to apologize for wanting to keep all you can of it. But he ought to apologize for wanting to take more and more. He wants to give you sort of a government tax cut, which really doesn't mean anything.

Clinton: You know, one of the responsibilities of growing older, it seems to me, is being able to tell people something they may not want to hear just because it's true. When they had a $250 billion tax scheme, that is half the size of this one. This one is 550. They passed the budget. They have $270 billion in Medicare cuts, the first education cuts in history, cut environmental enforcement by 25 percent, took away the guarantee of quality standards in nursing homes, took away the guarantee of health care for folks with disabilities. Don't take my word for this. The *Economist* magazine polled lots of economists, seven Nobel prize winners, who said if this tax scheme passes, it will require huge cuts, 40 percent, in the environment and law enforcement and education. It will require bigger cuts in Medicare than I vetoed last time. My targeted tax cut is for child-rearing, buying a first-time home, paying for health care costs. And it's paid for, and I'll tell you how I'll pay for it. He won't tell you because he can't. . . .

Mr. Smith: Good evening. I'm Michael Smith. I'm an electronics technician in the Navy. My question was how you plan to deal with the trade deficit with Japan.

Clinton: Let me tell you what we have done. We have concluded with Japan 21—about to be 22—trade agreements now. And since we did that, in the areas where we concluded, trade agreements or exports to Japan have gone up by 85 percent in the last four years and our trade deficit with Japan has gone down. Until about five months ago the Japanese economy was in a deep recession. It's coming back now, so they can buy even more American products, and I think it will go down more. But I'm very—that's one of the real success stories here of the work we've done. We're selling Japanese rice from California for the first time. I visited a Chrysler dealership in Tokyo. I visited a Jeep plant, a plant in Toledo, Ohio, where they're going to export 41,000 right hand drive Jeeps this year, and they've got 700 new jobs because of it. There's no easy way to do this when you're dealing with an economy that's traditionally been more closed than one that's traditionally been more open. You have to gut it out, issue by issue by issue. We agreed in principle on an insurance agreement, and we're working on three or four other areas now, but the way you have to do it is make sure you're competitive. We're the most competitive country in the world now, and then just fight to open those markets and go try to make the sale, and that's what our trade ambassador, our commerce secretary and all the other people in our administration are trying to do.

Dole: Well, the bottom line is we have to stop exporting jobs here. There are 357,000 good jobs—manufacturing jobs, which are lost. And I assume some of those are because of our trading partners. We didn't have access to their markets. We ought to insist on access. If we don't have access to their markets the same way they've access to our markets, we ought to say, "Wait, that's enough. Time out. When you give us access, we'll give you access." It's very hard to get into the Japan market, as everybody knows. They want to get into our market. They sell a lot of automobiles here, create a lot of jobs— those who sell exports. And that's very important to the economy, but I think we want to make certain. I supported the President's trade policy. But we got to be more aggressive. Once you have a policy, then you have to go out and be aggressive and enforce that policy. There are American jobs that are being lost. This is what Ross Perot complains about. And I'd say to the Reform party, take a look at the Republican party. We're the reform party, and we're going to make things better, and one of the things we're going to do is stop exporting jobs in America. . . .

Lehrer: All right. Now we go to the closing statement. Senator Dole, you're first. Two minutes, sir.

Dole: Well, let me thank everybody here at the University and, Jim, thank you. All the people who may still be watching or viewing. This is what it's all about. It's not about me. It's not about President Clinton. It's about the process. It's about selecting a president of the United States. So we have our differences. We should have our differences. Mentioned other parties. They have their differences. We all agreed it would be a pretty dull place. We should have more debates. Maybe we will have another debate on the economy. But I would just say this. This is the highest honor that I have ever had in my life, to think that somebody from Russell, Kansas, somebody who grew up living in a basement apartment, someone whose parents didn't finish high school, somebody who spent about 39 months in hospitals after World War II, someone who uses a buttonhook every day to get dressed. Somebody who understands that there're real Americans out there with real problems, whether soccer moms, or the single parents, the families or the seniors, or people with disabilities, whoever it may be. There are some very fundamental differences in this campaign. President Clinton opposes term limits, opposes a constitutional amendment to balance the budget. President Clinton opposes the voluntary prayer amendment. Opposes an amendment to protect the flag of the United States of America. People give their lives. Couple of servicemen here. They sacrifice, give everything for America. We ought to protect the American flag with a constitutional amendment. But beyond that we need to address the economy. I will just say my time is running out here. It's a very proud moment for me. What I want the voters to do is to make a decision. And I want them to be proud of their vote in the years ahead. Proud that they voted for the right candidate. Proud that they voted hopefully for me. And I'll just make you one promise, my word is good. Democrats and Republicans said Bob Dole's word is good. I keep my word. I promise you the economy is going to get better. We're going to have a good economic plan. We're going into the next century a better America. Thank you.

Clinton: Thank you, Jim. And thank you, ladies and gentlemen, and all the people who are watching. One thing I would like to say is I agree with what Senator Dole said. It's a remarkable thing in a country like ours, a man who grew up in Russell, Kansas, and one who was born to a widowed mother in Hope, Arkansas, could wind up running for president. Could have a chance to serve as president. First thing I want to say is thank you for giving me the chance to be president. This election is about two different visions about how we should go into the 21st Century. Would we be better off as I believe, working together to give each other the tools we need to make the most of our God-given potential, or are we better off saying, you're on your own? Would we be better off building that bridge to the future together so we can all walk across it or saying you can get across yourself? If you don't agree—leave this room with anything else tonight and if the people watching us don't leave with anything else, I hope you will leave with this. This is a real important election. The world is changing dramatically in how we work and how we live, how we relate to each other, huge changes. And the decisions we make will have enormous practical consequences. So we've talked about our responsibility tonight. I want to talk about your responsibility, and your responsibility. Your responsibility is to show up on November the 5th. Because you're going to decide whether we're going to balance the budget now, but protect Medicare, Medicaid, education and the environment. You will decide whether we're going to keep fighting crime with a Brady Bill, assault weapons and finish putting those 100,000 police. Whether we're going to move a million people from welfare to work. Whether we're going to give our families more protection for their kids against drugs and tobacco and gangs and guns. Whether we're going to give our children a world-class education. Where every eight-year-old can read. Every 12-year-old can log in on the Internet. Every 18-year-old can go to college. If we do those things we will build that bridge to the 21st Century and the greatest country in history will be even greater. Thank you.

FBI REPORT ON CRIME
October 13, 1996

Crime in the United States continued its downward trend in 1995, according to the annual report of the Federal Bureau of Investigation, released October 13. The overall incidence of crime fell for the fourth straight year and the crime rate—the number of crimes committed per 100,000 population—dropped to its lowest level since 1985. Experts continued to predict, however, that crime levels might turn upward again as the 39 million children currently under age ten reach their teenage and young adult years, typically the most crime-prone ages.

Overall, according to the FBI's annual report, "Crime in the United States" (also known as the Uniform Crime Report), the number of crimes fell 1 percent, to 13.9 million, from 1994 to 1995. Southern states recorded more than one-third of the offenses, 38 percent, in 1995, while the incidence of crime was lowest in the Northeast (16 percent). (1994 report on crime, Historic Documents of 1995, p. 710)

The crime rate in 1995, 5,278 per 100,000 population, was down 2 percent from 1994 and was at its lowest level since 1985. The rate of violent crimes—murder, forcible rape, robbery, and aggravated assault—fell to its lowest level since 1989—685 violent crimes for every 100,000 people. The murder rate fell the most, a total of 7 percent from 1994; 21,597 people were murdered in 1995, for a rate of 8 per 100,000. The number of forcible rapes and aggravated assaults also dropped in 1995. The proportion of violent crimes committed with firearms remained about the same between 1994 and 1995, at 30 percent.

All crimes against property decreased in 1995 except larceny-theft, which accounted for 66 percent of all property crimes and which increased 2 percent over 1994. It was the increase in this category, a crime that is frequently committed by teenagers and young adults, that caused concerns among crime experts. "This is the first glimmer of the impact of the next generation," Alfred Blumstein, a noted criminologist at Carnegie-Mellon University, said in May when the FBI released its preliminary crime figures for 1995. "[L]arceny—such as bicycle theft, stealing auto parts, and shoplifting—is the crime with the youngest criminals. The peak age for larcenists is fifteen or sixteen."

Violent crime among juveniles might be falling, however, according to a report released by the Justice Department in August. The nationwide rate for juvenile crime was down slightly from its 1994 levels, the first overall decline in that category in more than a decade. The rate of juvenile murders was down for the second year in a row. It was a sharp rise in the juvenile crime rate that had led to the jump in crime in the late 1980s.

The Uniform Crime Report is based on data reported to the FBI by more than 16,000 state and local law enforcement agencies covering 95 percent of the population. A second annual survey, this one of victims of crimes that may not have been officially reported, was conducted by the Justice Department's Bureau of Justice Statistics. Its preliminary report, released on September 17, confirmed the downward trend in violent crime. An estimated 9.9 million violent crimes were committed in 1995, according to this survey, compared with 10.9 million in 1994. Rapes decreased 18 percent, robbery fell 14 percent, aggravated assault was down 19 percent, and purse snatchings and pocket-picking declined 18 percent. The bureau estimated that 63 percent of all crimes were never officially reported.

Firearm Use Declining

Yet another heartening study showed that the use of firearms to commit crimes was declining. According to a study by the Center to Prevent Handgun Violence, based on data in the Uniform Crime Report, the number of murders fell 7.4 percent between 1994 and 1995, while the number of murders committed with a gun dropped 11.6 percent. Gun use appeared to be down in robberies and aggravated assaults as well. "These data provide more compelling evidence that the Brady Law is working," said Sarah Brady, the chairwoman of the center and wife of former White House press secretary James Brady, whose shooting in a 1981 assassination attempt on President Ronald Reagan eventually led to passage of federal legislation controlling the purchase of handguns.

Control of handguns and a recent federal law barring assault weapons were two of several factors accounting for the decline in the crime rate. Law enforcement officials and crime experts cited other factors as well, although the contribution of each was hard to measure. The factors included the aging of the baby boom generation past the prime years for committing crimes; longer sentences for criminals; more police; new police strategies for preventing crime; and better police-community relations. Declining unemployment and a growing public intolerance for crime may also be factors. Better emergency care for gunshot victims may also be helping to lower the murder rate. A separate FBI report found that 92 percent of all gunshot victims who were hospitalized survived.

Related Developments

The Bureau of Juvenile Justice and the Office of Juvenile Justice and Delinquency Prevention released a report in March showing that nearly 20 percent of violent offenders serving time in state prisons in 1991 had victimized a child under age eighteen. More than 50 percent of the crimes were committed against children under age thirteen. Seventy percent of these offenders reported they were in prison for rape or sexual assault; more than 30 percent said they had victimized their own children. According to the report, entitled "Child Victimizers: Violent Offenders and Their Victims," these child abusers tended to be older than inmates who had committed violent crimes against adults. Nearly all were men; a high proportion were white. These inmates were "substantially" more likely than victimizers of adults to have been physically or sexually abused as children, but the majority of violent offenders, regardless of age of victim, did not have such a history.

Another report, released in April 1996, attempted to put a price tag on the cost of violence in the United States, estimating that crime cost at least $450 billion a year. The report, by the Justice Department's National Institute of Justice, calculated tangible costs, such as property damage; medical care, including mental health care; legal fees; police and fire services; services for victims, including abused children and battered wives; and wages and benefits that victims might have lost from being unable to work. The study also computed a valuation for intangible losses, such as pain and suffering and a reduced quality of life. The study did not include the costs of the nation's federal, state, and local prison systems, which would add another $40 billion to the annual cost of the bill.

The report, "Victim Costs and Consequences: A New Look," was the most comprehensive study of the costs of crime to date. Some experts questioned the accuracy of both its methodology and its results. Blumstein, for example, told the New York Times *that he thought the $450 billion estimate was inflated because the report gave too much weight to intangible losses.*

Following is a press release issued by the Federal Bureau of Investigation on October 13, 1996, which accompanied release of the FBI's annual report, "Crime in the United States," and summarized the data for 1995:

Final 1995 crime statistics released today by the FBI showed that 13.9 million Crime Index offenses were reported to law enforcement across the Nation. The 1995 total represents a rate of 5,278 offenses for every 100,000 United States inhabitants. The number of crimes was down 1 percent from 1994, while the crime rate declined 2 percent. The number of violent crimes dropped 3 percent, while the rate of violent crimes dropped 4 percent. In the eight U.S. cities with more than one million population, the decrease in the number of violent crimes was 8 percent. In the 64 largest cities, with populations over 250,000, Crime Index totals dropped 3 percent.

These statistics are based on a Crime Index of selected violent and property offenses reported to the FBI's Uniform Crime Reporting Program by over 16,000 law enforcement agencies, covering 95 percent of the Nation's population. Estimates are included for non-reporting areas. The 1995 data appear in Crime in the United States, the FBI's annual publication which was released today.

Highlights from the 1995 edition include:

Crime Volume

- In 1995, the Crime Index total of 13.9 million offenses, 1 percent lower than the 1994 total and 7 percent lower than the 1991 total, represented the fourth consecutive annual decline. A comparison with 1986 figures, however, showed a 5-percent increase over the last 10-year period.
- By region, the Southern States recorded 38 percent of all Crime Index offenses reported to law enforcement. The lowest volume was reported in the Northeastern States, accounting for 16 percent of the total. All regions except the West showed Crime Index decreases compared to 1994 figures.
- Property valued at $15.6 billion was stolen in connection with all Crime Index offenses.

Crime Rate

- The 1995 Crime Index rate, 5,278 per 100,000 population, was 2 percent lower than in 1994. For 5- and 10-year trend increments, the 1995 rate, the lowest since 1985, was 11 percent lower than the 1991 rate and 4 percent lower than 1986.
- Geographically, the total Crime Index rates ranged from 6,083 in the West to 4,180 in the Northeast. All regions recorded rate declines, 1994 versus 1995.
- The Crime Index rate was 5,761 per 100,000 inhabitants in the Nation's Metropolitan Statistical Areas (MSAs) and 5,315 per 100,000 for cities outside MSAs. The lowest rate was registered by the collective rural counties at 2,083 per 100,000 inhabitants.

Violent Crime

- Violent crimes (murder, forcible rape, robbery, and aggravated assault) reported to the country's law enforcement agencies during 1995 dropped below 1.8 million offenses resulting in the lowest violent crime rate since 1989; 685 violent crimes for every 100,000 inhabitants.
- From 1994 to 1995, the violent crimes collectively decreased by 3 percent. The 1995 total was 6 percent below the 1991 figure, but 21 percent above the 1986 figure.
- Data collected on weapons used in connection with murder, robbery, and aggravated assault showed that personal weapons (hands, fists,

feet, etc.) were used in 31 percent of the offenses and that firearms were used in 30 percent. The proportion of violent crimes committed with firearms remained relatively stable from 1994 to 1995.
- Aggravated assaults accounted for 61 percent and robberies for 32 percent of all violent crimes reported to law enforcement in 1995.
- A special study focusing on the use of weapons in violent crimes is included in this year's publication.

Property Crime

- The estimated property crime total in 1995 decreased 1 percent to 12.1 million offenses, the lowest level since 1987. The 1995 property crime rate was 4,593 offenses per 100,000 population, 1 percent lower than the 1994 figure and 11 percent lower than the 1991 figure.
- Larceny-theft, which comprised 66 percent of property crimes reported, increased 2 percent from 1994 to 1995. All other property crimes declined. Burglary accounted for 22 percent of property crime totals and motor vehicle theft for 12 percent.
- The value of property stolen in connection with property crimes was estimated at $15.1 billion for 1995, an average of $1,251 per offense reported.

Crime Clearances

- Law enforcement agencies nationwide recorded a 21-percent Crime Index clearance rate in 1995. The clearance rate for violent crimes was 45 percent; for property crimes, 18 percent.
- Among the Crime Index offenses, the clearance rate was highest for murder, 65 percent, and lowest for burglary, 13 percent.
- Offenses involving only offenders under 18 years of age accounted for 22 percent of the overall Crime Index clearances, 14 percent of the violent crime clearances, and 25 percent of the property crime clearances.

Arrests

- During the year, law enforcement agencies made an estimated 15.1 million arrests for all criminal infractions excluding traffic violations. The highest arrest counts were for larceny-theft and drug abuse violations, each at 1.5 million. Arrests for driving under the influence and simple assaults followed at 1.4 and 1.3 million arrests, respectively. Relating the number of arrests to the total U.S. population, the rate was 5,807 arrests per 100,000 population.
- The total number of arrests for all offenses except traffic violations increased 1 percent from 1994 to 1995.
- Of all persons arrested in 1995, 44 percent were under the age of 25, 80 percent were male, and 67 percent were white.
- Larceny-theft was the offense resulting in the most arrests of females and of persons under the age of 18. Adults were most often arrested for driving under the influence, and males most frequently for drug abuse violations.

Murder

- The murder count for 1995 totaled 21,597, a total 7 percent lower than 1994 and 13 percent lower than 1991. The murder rate was 8 per 100,000 inhabitants.
- Based on supplemental data received, 77 percent of murder victims in 1995 were males, and 88 percent were persons 18 years or older. By race, 49 percent of victims were black and 48 percent were white.
- Data based on a total of 22,434 murder offenders showed that 91 percent of the assailants were males, and 85 percent were 18 years of age or older. Fifty-three percent of the offenders were black and 45 percent were white.
- Fifty-five percent of murder victims were slain by strangers or persons unknown. Among all female murder victims in 1995, 26 percent were slain by husbands or boyfriends, while 3 percent of the male victims were slain by wives or girlfriends.
- By circumstance, 28 percent of the murders resulted from arguments and 18 percent from felonious activities such as robbery, arson, etc.
- In approximately 7 out of every 10 murders reported during 1995, firearms were the weapons used.

Forcible Rape

- The total of 97,464 forcible rapes reported to law enforcement during 1995 was the lowest total since 1989. The 1995 count was 5 percent lower than in 1994.
- In the Uniform Crime Reporting Program, the victims of forcible rape are always female, and in 1995 an estimated 72 of every 100,000 females in the country were reported rape victims.

Robbery

- In 1995, law enforcement agencies recorded 580,545 robberies, for a crime rate of 221 robberies per 100,000 population nationwide. The volume of robbery was down 6 percent from the 1994 total; and from 1994 to 1995 robbery rates per 100,000 inhabitants declined in all regions.
- Monetary loss attributed to property stolen in connection with this offense was estimated at $507 million. Bank robberies resulted in the highest average losses, $4,015 per offense; convenience store robberies the lowest, $400.
- Robberies on streets or highways accounted for more than half (54 percent) of the offenses in this category.
- In 1995, robberies committed with firearms accounted for 41 percent of the total, an 8-percent decrease from 1994; robberies committed through the use of strong-arm tactics also accounted for 41 percent of the total, a 3-percent decrease from 1994.

Aggravated Assault

- For the second consecutive year, aggravated assaults dropped over 1 percent in 1995 to an estimated total of 1,099,179. Aggravated assaults comprised 61 percent of the violent crimes in 1995.
- There were 418 victims of aggravated assault for every 100,000 people nationwide in 1995, the lowest rate since 1989.
- In 1995, 33 percent of the aggravated assaults were committed with blunt objects or other dangerous weapons. Personal weapons such as hands, fists, and feet were used in 26 percent; firearms in 23 percent; and knives or cutting instruments in the remainder.

Burglary

- Lower than in any other year of the past two decades, the estimated burglary total was 2.6 million, and the rate was 988 per 100,000 inhabitants.
- Two out of every 3 burglaries were residential in nature. Sixty-seven percent of all burglaries involved forcible entry, and over half (52 percent) occurred during the daylight hours.
- The value of property stolen during burglaries was estimated at $3.3 billion in 1995.

Larceny-theft

- Larceny-theft, with an estimated total of 8 million offenses, comprised 58 percent of the Crime Index total.
- The total dollar loss to victims nationwide was nearly $4.3 billion during 1995. The average value of property stolen was up from the 1994 figure, $505, to $535 per incident.
- Thefts of motor vehicle parts, accessories, and contents made up the largest portion of reported larcenies, 36 percent.

Motor Vehicle Theft

- In 1995, slightly under 1.5 million thefts of motor vehicles, the lowest total since 1989, were reported.
- Seventy-eight percent of all motor vehicles stolen in 1995 were automobiles.
- The estimated value of motor vehicles stolen nationwide was nearly $7.6 billion, for an average of $5,129 per vehicle.

Arson

- A total of 94,926 arson offenses was reported in 1995.
- As in previous years, structures were the most frequent targets of arsonists in 1995, comprising 53 percent of the reported incidents. Residential property was involved in 60 percent of the structural arsons during the year; 43 percent of the arsons were directed at single-family dwellings.
- In 1995, the monetary value of property damaged due to reported arson averaged $11,151 per offense.

- Of the arsons cleared during the year, 47 percent involved only young people under the age of 18, a higher percentage of juvenile involvement than for any other Index Crime.

Law Enforcement Employees

- A total of 13,052 city, county, and state police agencies submitting Uniform Crime Reporting data reported collectively employing 586,756 officers and 226,780 civilians in 1995.
- The average rate of 2.4 full-time officers for every 1,000 inhabitants across the country in 1995 showed a slight increase from the 1994 figure, 2.3 per 1,000 inhabitants.
- Geographically, the highest rate of officers to population was recorded in the Northeastern States where there were 2.7 officers per 1,000 inhabitants.

UN SECRETARY GENERAL ON
CHEMICAL WEAPONS TREATY
October 31, 1996

An international treaty banning chemical weapons reached a critical milestone toward becoming law—but without having been ratified by the United States and Russia, the superpowers that possessed the world's largest stockpiles of chemical weapons. Boutros Boutros-Ghali, the secretary general of the United Nations, announced on October 31 that sixty-five nations had ratified the treaty, the number required to start a 180-day clock that would put the treaty into legal force on April 29, 1997. Hungary was the sixty-fifth nation.

Officially known as the Convention on the Prohibition of the Development, Production, Stockpiling and Use of Chemical Weapons and on Their Destruction, the treaty was negotiated over a period of nearly twenty-five years and opened for signature in January 1993. (Chemical weapons treaty, Historic Documents of 1993, p. 71)

As its title stated, the treaty outlawed any possession or use of chemical weapons. It established an Organization for the Prohibition of Chemical Weapons, headquartered at The Hague, Netherlands, to monitor compliance. That organization had the right to inspect declared chemical weapons facilities as well as industrial operations with a significant potential for producing the weapons.

Boutros-Ghali noted that the treaty was the first international agreement banning an entire category of weapons of mass destruction. With it, he said, "the world has taken a significant step towards the complete eradication of chemical weapons."

Chemical weapons have not been widely used on the battlefield since World War I, and in recent decades there have been only isolated reports of the use of chemical weapons. In 1988 Iraq allegedly killed some 5,000 Kurds with poison gas. Iraq's action stimulated international concern about chemical weapons, as did the efforts of several countries, including Libya and North Korea, to develop large arsenals of them. (Iran-Iraq truce, Historic Documents of 1988, p. 529)

U.S. officials estimated in 1996 that about twenty countries had chemical weapons or were trying to develop them. Chemical weapons were often called the "poor nation's nuclear weapons" because they were relatively easy to produce. Any nation able to produce fertilizer could also develop crude chemical weapons.

The Reagan administration had spurred international interest in the issue when it began producing "binary" chemical weapons. These weapons, based on two inert chemicals that became harmful to humans when mixed, were much more sophisticated and safer to store and handle than previous chemical weapons in the U.S. arsenal.

The Push for U.S. Ratification in 1996

President George Bush signed the treaty for the United States as one of his last official acts before leaving the White House, leaving the job of securing Senate approval up to President Bill Clinton. Clinton did not make a concerted effort on behalf of the treaty during his first three years in office, concentrating instead on winning Senate approval of the START II treaty, which mandated reductions in the U.S. and Russian nuclear arsenals. The Senate approved the treaty in January 1996.

The administration then began its push for the chemical weapons treaty, assuming that election-year pressures would help get it through the Senate. The administration recruited an impressive line-up of supporters for the treaty, among them former president Bush, most recent secretaries of state and defense and former national security advisers, and the current top U.S. military officials. On August 29, fifty-three top executives of U.S. chemical companies sent the Senate a letter endorsing the treaty. Supporters inside the Senate included some of the most respected voices on defense and foreign affairs matters, in particular Sam Nunn, D-Ga., and Richard Lugar, R-Ind.

A vocal corps of opponents denounced the treaty and worked to delay Senate action on it. Outside the Senate, opposition was led by Frank J. Gaffney Jr., a conservative Republican defense expert who had served as a deputy assistant secretary of defense in the Reagan administration. Leading Senate opponents were Jesse Helms, R-N.C., chairman of the Foreign Relations Committee, and Jon Kyl, R-Ariz. The opponents received key support, late in 1996, from Richard Cheney, who had served as defense secretary under Bush.

Opponents raised three principal arguments against the treaty. First, they noted that some of the most likely users of chemical weapons—including Iran and Syria—had not signed the treaty and so would not legally be bound by it. Second, they insisted that the UN's monitoring organization could not verify compliance with the treaty if a country made a serious effort to hide its chemical weapons production and storage facilities. Finally, opponents argued that the treaty would subject thousands of U.S. companies to intrusive inspections by UN monitors; those inspections would be costly to the companies and might put valuable trade secrets at risk.

Administration officials and other treaty supporters rejected those arguments and said the treaty met U.S. national security interests. Secretary of State Warren Christopher, testifying before the Foreign Relations Committee on March 28, noted that existing U.S. law required the destruction of nearly all of this country's chemical weapons stockpile by 2004. An international ban on those weapons, he said, "puts all other states capable of deploying chemical weapons—including Russia—on the same footing as we are." U.S. ratification of the treaty would spur other countries, such as China, to do the same, he said.

Banning the international trade in chemicals that could be used to create such weapons "will make it much harder" for countries that had not ratified the treaty to develop those weapons, Christopher said. Countries that violated the ban would be subject to penalties and UN sanctions.

The administration also disputed the charge that the treaty would impose an undue burden on U.S. industry. Noting the letter from the fifty-three executives of major chemical companies, administration officials said there was no evidence that UN inspections would cause hardships for American industry. The only substantial business opposition to the treaty came from the National Federation of Independent Business, a lobby for small businesses, which included no major chemical producers.

In addition, administration officials noted that the United States would have no say over enforcement unless it ratified the treaty. To be represented at the UN monitoring organization and to have access to information developed by the inspections, a nation would have to ratify the treaty.

Bob Dole Intervenes

The Clinton administration's drive for Senate approval of the treaty seemed close to success early in September, when a climactic vote was scheduled. But on September 11, former Senate majority leader Bob Dole, the Republican presidential candidate, sent a letter to his successor, Sen. Trent Lott, R-Miss., echoing the criticisms of treaty opponents. Dole had not publicly opposed the treaty when he was in the Senate. In his letter, Dole said he supported the goal of eliminating chemical weapons, but he said he could support an international treaty on the issue only if all countries were covered and if it was "effectively verifiable."

Based on Dole's letter, Senators Kyl and Lott wrote a proposed amendment to the treaty providing that the United States would comply with it only if all other countries ratified it and if the CIA certified that it could be highly confident of catching any cheaters. Because some countries had said they would not sign the treaty and the CIA had admitted its inability to catch all cheaters, the amendment would have rendered the Senate's approval of the treaty meaningless.

Opposing the Kyl-Lott amendment, but also fearing that rejection of it would endanger the two-thirds vote the treaty needed for approval, backers of the treaty decided to put off action on it during 1996. Nunn said the

Clinton administration had not worked hard enough to counter the campaign against the treaty by "the Republican right-wing."

Following is the text of a statement issued October 31, 1996, by UN Secretary General Boutros Boutros-Ghali on the treaty banning production, possession, and use of chemical weapons:

The 31 October is a special day for the United Nations in our continuing efforts to further the cause of global disarmament. Today, I received the sixty-fifth instrument of ratification of the Convention on the Prohibition of the Development, Production, Stockpiling and Use of Chemical Weapons and on Their Destruction, the Chemical Weapons Convention.

With the deposit of this instrument, the requirements for the entry into force of the Convention are now fulfilled. It will enter into force 180 days from today. The Chemical Weapons Convention is the first disarmament agreement negotiated within a multilateral framework that provides for the elimination of an entire category of weapons of mass destruction. The world has taken a significant step towards the complete eradication of chemical weapons. The United Nations welcomes the efforts of Member States to outlaw the barbaric and indiscriminate horror of chemical warfare.

Under the terms of the Convention, each State party will undertake to destroy chemical weapons and production facilities. Specifically, the Convention prohibits State parties from engaging in the development, production or acquisition, stockpiling and retention of chemical weapons. The Convention establishes a tough and comprehensive verification system within the framework of the Organization for the Prohibition of Chemical Weapons in The Hague. Full compliance with the Convention will require vigilance, patience and political will.

The Chemical Weapons Convention was opened for signature in Paris on 13 January 1993, and its entry into force represents a remarkable achievement. Above all, the Convention emphasizes the importance of global cooperation and offers lasting hope for a more stable and peaceful future. I urge all States that have not yet ratified this Convention, and particularly those with significant chemical-weapon stockpiles, to join those that have already done so, and to give full meaning to this historic agreement.

November

POSTELECTION STATEMENTS OF DOLE AND CLINTON
November 5 and 6, 1996

President Bill Clinton won a second term as president on November 5, solidly defeating his Republican opponent, former Senate majority leader Bob Dole. Clinton carried thirty-one states and won 379 electoral votes to become the first Democrat since Franklin Delano Roosevelt to be elected to a second term in the White House. It was also the first time since 1960 and 1964 that the Democrats had won two consecutive presidential elections. Third-party candidate H. Ross Perot won only 8 percent of the vote, far below the 19 percent he had tallied four years earlier.

American voters also maintained the status quo in Congress, reinstalling a Republican majority in the U.S. Senate and the House of Representatives. The GOP had taken over both chambers of Congress in 1994 for the first time in forty years. In 1996 Senate Republicans increased their majority by two seats, to 55–45, while the majority for House Republicans narrowed to 227–207 (with 1 independent). Republicans had a thirty-eight seat edge immediately before the election. Given the new line-up, the Senate was likely to be a bit more conservative in the 105th Congress than it had been in the 104th, while the House was expected to be a little less so.

The Numbers

Tempering the results for both parties was a clear display of voter disinterest. Turnout fell below 50 percent of the voting age population for the first time in a presidential election year since women were extended the right to vote in the early 1920s. Altogether nearly ten million fewer votes were cast in 1996 than in 1992. Even though Perot received less than half as many votes as he did in 1992, he and an array of other minor party candidates collectively won nearly 10 percent of the vote. That made the third-party tally in 1992 and 1996 the largest in back-to-back presidential elections since 1856 and 1860, a politically volatile period that gave birth to the Republican party on the eve of the Civil War.

While Republicans lost their second straight presidential election after winning five of the previous six, Dole's dogged effort—which climaxed with a frenetic, four-day, round-the-clock campaign—helped to rally the Republican base. Dole and his running mate, Jack Kemp, finished with 41 percent of the vote, well above their average standing in the popular opinion polls in the months before the election. Despite a stumbling campaign that led many voters to dismiss him as too old and inarticulate for the television age, Dole managed to win a disproportionate share of voters who made up their minds in the final days of the campaign.

Clinton's share of the popular vote went up from 43 percent in 1992 to 49 percent in 1996, yet his eight-percentage-point margin of victory over Dole was less than half the lead he had enjoyed in public opinion surveys just a week or two before the election.

The Campaign

While the campaign lacked much drama, Clinton's comeback after the 1994 elections was indeed dramatic. In 1992 Clinton arrived in the White House vowing to erase the legacy of Ronald Reagan, remake the nation's health care system, and lead a government of "bold, persistent experimentation." His first two years were plagued with failures and missteps, the worst of which was the demise of his health care plan. In retaliation, the voters elected a Republican Congress, leaving Clinton to defend the "relevancy" of his own presidency.

Aided by savvy political strategists, helped by Republican mistakes, and blessed with tenacity and some good luck, Clinton staged one of the most remarkable comebacks in recent political history. Shaking off his image as a classic, big-spending liberal Democrat, Clinton moved to the political center, championing themes popular with middle-class families. During the campaign Clinton stressed programs to help more children read, to make higher education more affordable, to reduce crime rates, and to clean up the environment. He declared the era of big government to be over and he promised to balance the budget by the year 2002.

At the same time, Clinton and the Democrats relentlessly attacked Dole and the Republicans for being against Medicare, Medicaid, education, and the environment.

Unlike Clinton, who ran unopposed on the Democratic side, Dole faced a crowded field of Republican challengers intent on portraying him as a tax-increasing Washington insider. Despite his rapid succession of primary victories in March, his resignation from the Senate to concentrate on his presidential campaign, and the unveiling of his proposal to cut taxes by 15 percent, Dole never captured the imagination of the voters. Dole's efforts were not helped by the Republican Congress, whose demands to reverse forty years of Democratic programs went too far in the minds of many voters. There was widespread public dismay at the end of 1995 and the beginning of 1996 when Republicans, led by House Speaker Newt Gingrich of Georgia, allowed the government to shut down twice in an effort to force Clinton to concede to their budget demands. (Budget impasse, Historic Documents of 1995, p. 737)

Dole could not turn the economy to his advantage, as the Democrats had done so successfully in 1992. Although many Americans were still worried about job security and stagnating wages, inflation remained low, the stock market was high, and unemployment was at its lowest point in years.

The one weakness Dole was able to exploit to some degree was Clinton's character. Both Dole and Perot directed pointed attacks at Clinton, his wife Hillary Rodham Clinton, and members of the Clinton administration for their alleged roles in a series of scandals, including misuse of FBI files and allegations of improper conduct in the Whitewater land investment deal. In the days leading up to the election, Clinton's ethics were further challenged by stories about Democratic fundraising improprieties.

A Modest Agenda

In his election-night victory speech, Clinton called on Americans to work with him to build a bridge to the twenty-first century. Given the drive toward the political center and tight budget constraints, that bridge was likely to be one of modest proportions. The first priority for both the president and Congress was likely to be an attempt to agree on a plan for balancing the budget by the year 2002, as both parties had promised they would do.

Clinton called for bipartisanship in his second term. "The challenges we face—they're not Democratic or Republican challenges. They're American challenges," he told his supporters in Little Rock, Arkansas, after being declared the victor early on November 6. "What we have achieved as Americans of lasting good, we have achieved by working together." A chastened Speaker Gingrich also sounded less partisan the day after the elections. "I think you'll see us try to reach out and find a common ground with President Clinton," he said in an interview on CBS.

Whether either the president or the Speaker would be successful was anyone's conjecture. Like its predecessor, the new Congress was split along partisan and ideological lines, and some bitterness lingered over both the election campaign and some of the bruising legislative battles of 1995 and 1996.

Following are excerpts of the victory statement of President Bill Clinton in Little Rock, Arkansas, on November 6, 1996, and the concession speech given by former Senate majority leader Bob Dole in Washington, D.C., on November 5, 1996:

CLINTON'S REMARKS

My fellow Americans . . . thank you for being here.

Just four years from now, we will enter a new century of great challenge and unlimited possibility. Now, we've got a bridge to build, and I'm ready if you are.

Today the American people have spoken. They have affirmed our course. They have told us to go forward.

America has told every one of us—Democrats, Republicans and independents—loud and clear: It is time to put politics aside, join together and get the job done for America's future.

In the last four years, we've made remarkable progress. But in our schools, our families, our workplaces and our communities, our journey is not done.

My fellow Americans, we have work to do, and that's what this election was all about.

I want to say to all of you here and to all of the American people—no words can convey the gratitude I feel tonight for the honor that has been given to me.

It is an honor that belongs to many. First to my family, to my wonderful wife of 21 years, who from the day I first met her began teaching me that it does take a village to raise our children and build our future.

To our daughter Chelsea for understanding the work we have done together, the burdens it has imposed. . . .

Because of Al Gore, we have a stronger and more secure relationship with the democratic Russia. We are exploring the wonders of new technologies for the benefit of America. We are protecting our environment, and we have reinvented America's government so that it does more with less, thanks to his leadership. It is a legacy unique in the history of this republic. . . .

I would like to say a special word of thanks to Senator Dole, and I ask you to join me in applause for his lifetime of service to the United States.

And I thank Jack Kemp for his service to America and his devotion to the proposition that this is a country in which everyone should have a chance to live free and equal and to have a chance at success.

Let me say . . . I had a good visit with Senator Dole not too long before he went out to speak. I thanked him for his love of our country, for his years of service.

I applauded the campaign that he fought so bravely to the very last minute. I thanked him for the work we did together to advance the common cause of America. And on behalf of all Americans, I wish him well and Godspeed.

[Four Years Ago]

Four years ago, on these very steps, we set forth on a journey to change the course of America for the better, to keep the American dream alive for everyone willing to work for it, to keep America the world's strongest force for peace and freedom and prosperity, to come together as one American community.

The time was one of widespread frustration and doubt about our economic and social problems, about our ability to deal with the vast sweep of change that was all around us. The scope and pace of those changes were threatening to many, and our values seemed to be under attack on all sides.

But, together, you and I vowed to turn our country around, with a strategy to meet our challenges and protect our values, opportunity for all, responsibility from all, an American community of all Americans.

We have worked hard to end the politics of "who's to blame?" and instead to ask, "What are we going to do to make America better?"

Tonight, we proclaim that the vital American center is alive and well. It is a common ground on which we have made our progress. Today, our economy is stronger, our streets are safer, our environment is cleaner, the world is more secure and, thank God, our nation is more united.

To all the men and women across this country who have created our jobs, taught our children, patrolled our streets and kept America safe throughout our world, I say, America's success is your success. This victory is your victory. I thank you from the bottom of my heart.

Now, my fellow Americans, a vast new century lies before us. It will be a time more full of opportunity for people to live out their dreams than any in human history.

We have committed this night to continuing our journey, to doing the hard work that will build our bridge to the 21st century, to give the young people—here and those all across America—the America they deserve, and their children and their children's children.

["We Have Work to Do"]

But we have work to do. We have work to do to keep our economy growing steady and strong, by balancing the budget, while we honor our duties to our families, our parents and our children and our duty to pass on to our children the earth God gave us.

We have work to do to give all of our children the gift of an education, to make sure every 8-year-old can read, every 12-year-old can log on to the Internet and, yes, every single 18-year-old in this country willing to work for it can have a college education.

We have work to do to make the permanent underclass in the country a thing of the past, to lift our fellow citizens who are poor from the degradation of welfare dependency to the pride and dignity of work.

We have work to do to strengthen our families; to help our parents succeed at home and at work; to keep our children safe from harm in their schools, their streets, their homes and their communities; to clean up our environment so that our children grow up next to parks not poison; to tell them that drugs are wrong and illegal and they can kill them; to teach them right from wrong.

My fellow Americans, I will do all I can to advance these causes. But all our citizens must do their part to continue the upsurge of personal responsibility that in the last four years has brought crime to a 10-year low, child support collections to an all-time high, and reduced the welfare rolls.

Will you help me do that? We must do it together.

We must make our democracy stronger by enacting real, bipartisan campaign finance reform. Talk is no longer enough. We must act and act now. And the American people will be watching the leaders of both parties to see who is willing not just to talk but to act. I am willing to act, and I ask others to join me.

And we must keep America the world's indispensable nation. Finishing the unfinished business of the Cold War, meeting the new threats to our security through terrorism and the proliferation of dangerous weapons, and seizing these extraordinary opportunities to extend our values of peace and democracy and prosperity.

Every American here tonight and every American within the sound of my voice can take pride in the fact that in these last few years for the first time in all of human history, a majority of the human beings living on this globe live under democracies where the people rule.

The challenges we face, they're not Democratic or Republican challenges. They're American challenges. What we know from the budget battles of the last two years and from the remarkable success of the last few weeks of this Congress is the lesson we have learned for the last 220 years—what we have achieved as Americans of lasting good, we have achieved by working together. So let me say to the leaders of my Democratic Party and the leaders of the Republican Party, it is time to put country ahead of party.

We do not know the final outcome of the congressional elections but we know this: The races are close. The American people have been closely divided. The Congress, whatever happens, will be closely divided.

They are sending us a message: Work together. Meet our challenges. Put aside the politics of division and build America's community, together. . . .

Let me say that, as all of you here from my native state know, I believe this and I have tried to live by it because there is no person in America who has been given more gifts than I have. There is no person in America tonight who feels more humble in the face of this victory than I do.

Fifty years ago, when I was born in a summer storm to a widowed mother in a small town in the southwest part of our state, it was unimaginable that someone like me could have ever become president of the greatest country in human history.

It has been, for me, a remarkable journey, not free of failure, but full of adventure and wonder and grace. I have worked hard to serve but I did not get here on my own.

Every step along the way for these last 23 years and long before, there was a teacher, a doctor, a neighbor, a parent, a friend, a wife, a daughter, who always had time to care, who always tried to give me instruction and encouragement and who never gave up.

I got here tonight, my fellow Americans, because America gave me a chance. That is what all the children of America deserve. Our people have to give them the tools to give them not a guarantee, but that real chance to live up to their God-given potential.

And I ask you to join me in that commitment. Every child deserves the main chance that I was given. . . .

For the 53rd time in our history, our people have made their quiet and deliberate decision. They have come together with their powerful voice and expressed their will.

Tonight we celebrate the miracle of America. Tomorrow we greet the dawn and begin our work anew. I am more grateful than I can say. You have given me an opportunity and a responsibility that comes to few people.

I will do my best, and together we will—we will build that bridge to the 21st century. Thank you. Good night, and God bless America. Thank you.

DOLE'S REMARKS

Thank you very much. You know I was . . . I was just thinking on the way down . . . tomorrow will be the first time in my life I don't have anything to do.

But I wanted to come down and thank all of you. You've done a great job and I'm very proud of Trent [Lott, the Senate majority leader]. We're going to keep the Senate. We're going to keep the House. . . .

Let me say that I've talked to President Clinton. We had a good visit, and I congratulated him.

No, wait a minute. Wait a minute. No, I've said repeatedly—I've said repeatedly in this campaign that the president was my opponent and not my enemy. And I wish him well, and I pledge my support in whatever advances the cause of a better America, because that's what the race was about in the first place, a better America as we go into the next century.

And I'm very proud also of my teammate, Jack Kemp. I've talked to Jack, and I thank Jack Kemp. And I want to thank not only Jack, but his wife, Joanne, who did an outstanding job and all the Kemp family for the work they did in this campaign.

And obviously, I want to thank two outstanding women—my daughter, Robin, who did a great job . . . and of course, my wife, Elizabeth, who's traveled this country from one end to the other.

In fact, they've both been with me in this 96-hour marathon. And we had a great time; we had great crowds and a lot of enthusiasm. At 3:00 this morning, I guess it was, we were in Independence, Mo., and I never saw so many people in one place so excited about the Republican Party.

And let me say a special word—let me say a special word to all the young Americans and the young people who were involved in my campaign. You have been a constant source of inspiration for Elizabeth and myself. . . .

And I would say to the young people and all the others involved, it's a lot more fun winning. It hurts to lose an election. But stay involved and keep fighting the good fight because you are the ones who will make the 21st century the next American century.

And I don't want anybody, I don't want anybody to pass out here, but I also want to thank all the media that traveled with me on the plane and all my friends . . . and we have many friends in the media. They were there every day, every night, every day and every night as we flew around this country. And we met hundreds and thousands and thousands of good people all across America who want a better America and will continue to work for a better America.

And as I looked around tonight as I came in, I saw a lot of very special people who have been helping me for the last 10, 15, 20, 25 years and I say thank you for all you've done because I know your support . . . because I know that because of your support, I am still the most optimistic man in America.

And I know that thousands of you, thousands of you have worked day and night, and millions of you trusted Jack Kemp and me with your vote, and for that we will always be grateful. And I say thank you very much.

And I would say Haley [Barbour, chairman of the Republican National Committee], you've done an outstanding job. We appreciate it very much.

And we've had our co-chairman flying around with us. You've done a great job. We appreciated your being with us.

And I want to say to my campaign staff, to Scott and to Jill and to Joanne and everyone else; I could not have had a better, more faithful, more loyal team. And I want to thank everybody, and we'll have an opportunity to do that if. . . .

It's been a long time since I entered politics way back in 1951, and a lot of things have happened since that time. But some things never change.

A few days after I took my seat in the state Legislature, a reporter asked me what I had on my agenda. I said, well, I'm going to sit back and watch for a few days, and then I'll stand up for what I think is right. And any of you who wonder what my plans may be in the future: I'm going to sit back for a few days, then I'm going to start standing up for what I think is right for America and right for you.

So, I leave you all tonight with a full heart and a fervent prayer that we will meet again, and we will meet often in this land where miracles are always happening, where every day is a new beginning and every life a blessing from God.

So I want to say thanks to each one of you here. Thank you for all you've done and all you will do in the future for America. Thank you very much, and God bless America.

CALIFORNIA PROPOSITION 215
ON MEDICAL USE OF MARIJUANA
November 5, 1996

Voters in California and Arizona on November 5 approved initiatives legalizing the use of marijuana for medical reasons. Adoption of the initiatives surprised federal officials, who had to scramble to develop a policy for dealing with the resulting conflict between laws of those states and federal law, which prohibited growing, possession, or use of marijuana for any purpose.

The Clinton administration considered filing suit to block the measures but decided in December not to do so. Instead, the administration opted to try to prosecute doctors and dealers who helped supply drugs that were illegal under federal law for alleged medical purposes. The administration also adopted a stepped-up public relations effort to warn the public of the health dangers of marijuana and other drugs.

The controversy over the state initiatives came during a year in which the use of illegal drugs was an election issue. While drug use overall continued to decline, research studies showed increasing use of marijuana by teenagers. Republicans, including presidential candidate Bob Dole, claimed that trend resulted from what they insisted was a lax attitude toward narcotics by the Clinton administration. (Drug use, p. 570)

State Initiatives Approved

The initiatives approved in California and Arizona were similar in general intent but different in scope. The California initiative—known as Proposition 215—allowed persons in the state to grow, possess, and use marijuana when it had been recommended by a physician for a medical purpose. The use of marijuana would be permitted for treatment of cancer, anorexia, AIDS, chronic pain, spasticity, glaucoma, arthritis, migraine, or "any other illness for which marijuana provides relief." The physician's recommendation could be oral or written, and there was no requirement for a prescription or other record-keeping. Caregivers could grow and possess marijuana for a person for whom the drug was recommended, and doctors could not be prosecuted under state law for recommending its use.

The broader Arizona initiative allowed the use of most illegal drugs—not just marijuana—for medical purposes, if it had been prescribed by two doctors. For example, the initiative would allow the use of such drugs as heroin and LSD for medical purposes. Another controversial provision stipulated that anyone convicted in Arizona, on a first offense, of possessing illegal drugs would be given probation and treatment—not a jail sentence.

The initiatives were approved by comfortable margins, despite opposition from most law enforcement officials and established medical associations in both states. The California measure passed by a 56–44 margin; in Arizona the margin was even larger, 65–35.

Proponents argued that marijuana was effective in relieving pain and nausea and stimulating appetite for many patients with diseases such as cancer and AIDS. The Food and Drug Administration in 1985 approved prescription use in oral doses of a synthetic form of marijuana's major active ingredient, known as THC, for such treatment. Some patients said they received more relief when they smoked marijuana than when they took the oral doses of THC.

Clinton Administration Response

After an intense interagency review that took more than six weeks after the November 5 votes, the Clinton administration on December 30 denounced the Arizona and California initiatives. Barry McCaffrey, director of the Office of National Drug Control Policy, and key cabinet officials said at a news conference that the administration would continue to enforce federal laws banning the possession or use of marijuana and other narcotic drugs.

The state initiatives were "hoax initiatives, stealth initiatives," said McCaffrey. Both were really aimed at legalizing drugs, under the guise of providing "compassionate care of the terminally ill," he said.

Attorney General Janet Reno noted that "federal law still applies, and federal officials will continue to apply the law, as it always has done on a case-by-case basis." She noted that state and law local enforcement agencies always had handled the bulk of cases involving small amounts of marijuana and said that would continue to be the case. The federal government would take over prosecutions involving large amounts of drugs or cases that local officials in the two states could not handle because of the new conflict between state and federal law.

Reno said the Drug Enforcement Agency would review cases in Arizona and California "to determine whether to revoke the registration of any physician who recommends or prescribes" illegal narcotics. Revoking a license to issue prescriptions would hamper a physician's ability to practice medicine.

Administration officials said they were most concerned about the public relations aspect of the Arizona and California initiatives. Donna Sha-

lala, secretary of health and human services, said at the December 30 news conference that voters in those states "sent very confusing messages to the teenagers in those states, and to young people all across the country. And let me be very clear: this administration is opposed to the legalization of marijuana."

Shalala said that "all available research" indicated that marijuana was dangerous to health. "Marijuana harms the brain, the heart, the lungs, our immune system," she said. "Marijuana limits learning and memory perception and judgment and our ability to drive a car. And marijuana smoke typically contains over four hundred compounds, some of which are carcinogenic." Shalala said the administration would continue to conduct research on any possible health benefits from marijuana use that supporters of the two initiatives claimed. Even if benefits were found, she said, any permitted use of the drug "would be under very limited circumstances and where available medications have failed to provide relief to individual patients."

Alan Leshner, director of the National Institute on Drug Abuse, said existing research did not support the contention that smoked marijuana "is a viable effective medication." He noted that "the scientific community gave up the study of marijuana" as a medicine in the 1980s.

Following is the text of Proposition 215, adopted by the voters of California on November 5, 1996, amending the state constitution to allow the possession and use of marijuana for medical reasons when recommended by a physician:

SECTION 1. Section 1.1362.5 is added to the Health and Safety Code, to read:

11362.5. (a) This section shall be known and may be cited as the Compassionate Use Act of 1996.

(b)(1) The people of the State of California hereby find and declare that the purposes of the Compassionate Use Act of 1996 are as follows:

(A) To ensure that seriously ill Californians have the right to obtain and use marijuana for medical purposes where that medical use is deemed appropriate and has been recommended by a physician who has determined that the person's health would benefit from the use of marijuana in the treatment of cancer, anorexia, AIDS, chronic pain, spasticity, glaucoma, arthritis, migraine, or any other illness for which marijuana provides relief.

(B) To ensure that patients and their primary caregivers who obtain and use marijuana for medical purposes upon the recommendation of a physician are not subject to criminal prosecution or sanction.

(C) To encourage the federal and state governments to implement a plan to provide for the safe and affordable distribution of marijuana to all patients in medical need of marijuana.

(2) Nothing in this section shall be construed to supersede legislation prohibiting persons from engaging in conduct that endangers others, nor to condone the diversion of marijuana for nonmedical purposes.

(c) Notwithstanding any other provision of law, no physician in this state shall be punished, or denied any right or privilege, for having recommended marijuana to a patient for medical purposes.

(d) Section 11357, relating to the possession of marijuana, and Section 11358, relating to the cultivation of marijuana, shall not apply to a patient, or to a patient's primary caregiver, who possesses or cultivates marijuana for the personal medical purposes of the patient upon the written or oral recommendation or approval of a physician.

(e) For the purposes of this section, "primary caregiver" means the individual designated by the person exempted under this section who has consistently assumed responsibility for the housing, health, or safety of that person.

SEC. 2. If any provision of this measure or the application thereof to any person or circumstance is held invalid, that invalidity shall not affect other provisions or applications of the measure that can be given effect without the invalid provision or application, and to this end the provisions of this measure are severable.

CALIFORNIA VOTERS ON
AFFIRMATIVE ACTION
November 5, 1996

*State-sponsored affirmative action programs came under severe chal-
lenge in 1996 when voters in California, the nation's most populous state,
adopted an amendment to the state constitution effectively barring the
state from using affirmative action in public hiring, contracting, and university admissions. Fifty-four percent of those who went to the state polls
on November 5 apparently agreed with Republican governor Pete Wilson,
one of the amendment's key supporters, that state programs seeking to
equalize opportunity for minorities and women were themselves discriminatory and therefore unjust. "Government must judge all people equally,
without discrimination," Wilson and other supporters wrote.*

*Not everyone identified with the amendment was victorious. In the
waning days of the campaign, Republican presidential nominee Bob Dole
sought to win votes in the state by aligning himself with the amendment,
better known as Proposition 209. Dole contrasted his support for the
amendment with President Bill Clinton's opposition to it and said the
issue required two votes—"one for the measure itself and one for an American president who will not undermine it." His strategy failed; only 38
percent of California's voters cast their ballots for Dole.*

*Supporters' elation over adoption of the amendment was soon deflated.
Opponents of Proposition 209 immediately challenged it in federal district
court in San Francisco, where Judge Thelton E. Henderson issued an order
temporarily barring state officials from enforcing the amendment. Henderson said there was a "strong probability" that the amendment would be
found unconstitutional and permanently struck down.*

*Most observers thought the matter would eventually go to the U.S.
Supreme Court, which had not issued a clear line of rulings on affirmative action. Earlier in the year, the Court let stand an appeals court ruling
striking down an affirmative action plan the University of Texas used to
ensure racial diversity among its students. In the landmark case of*
Regents of the University of California v. Bakke, *decided in 1978, the Court*

had allowed the consideration of race as one of many factors in admissions for the purpose of achieving diversity. In recent cases, however, the Court had narrowed the circumstances under which it approved preferences based on race. (Bakke case, Historic Documents of 1978, p. 467)

Politics and Affirmative Action

Affirmative action programs had been used since the 1960s to equalize opportunity for minorities and women who, as groups, had been victims of discrimination. Some programs were voluntary; others were court-imposed. The federal government and most state governments had affirmative action programs covering their own hiring and promotion practices, as well as public contracting and public education. Many corporations also had adopted affirmative action programs. At a minimum the state programs involved outreach efforts to expand the participation of women and minorities. More ambitious programs reserved for women and minorities a specific number or percentage of public contracts or admissions to a public university.

Taken together, the programs had largely been successful in ensuring that women and racial minorities had access to opportunities formerly foreclosed to them. Some preference programs, especially those that set aside places for women and minorities, meant that sometimes more qualified applicants, often white men, were rejected, resulting in charges of reverse discrimination. The economic downturn of the early 1990s and continuing job anxieties exacerbated anti-affirmative action sentiment; that sentiment was thought to have played a major role propelling Republicans into control of Congress in the 1994 elections.

The results of the 1994 election were not lost on either party. Republican leaders immediately seized on the issue as one that had the potential to split the coalition of middle-class males, blacks, and women who had traditionally supported the Democratic party. Senate Majority Leader Bob Dole and several other contenders for the 1996 Republican presidential nomination promised to end affirmative action if elected. One of these contenders was Pete Wilson, who previously had supported affirmative action but now embraced a drive to place Proposition 209 on the 1996 state ballot.

For his part, President Clinton endorsed the concept of affirmative action in a major speech delivered in July 1995, after several months of weighing the issue. He also ordered a review of federal affirmative action programs in the wake of a Supreme Court ruling holding such programs to the highest level of judicial scrutiny. Acknowledging that affirmative action had "not always been perfect," Clinton declared that the need for such plans nonetheless remained. "Mend it, but don't end it," the president said. (Clinton endorsement of affirmative action, Historic Documents of 1995, p. 483; Court on affirmative action, Historic Documents of 1995, p. 307)

Affirmative action did not figure visibly in the presidential campaign. Although Dole told audiences he was opposed to the policy, Clinton seldom mentioned it until the final week of the campaign. That left national atten-tion focused on Proposition 209 and California voters.

Proposition 209

The California ballot initiative was brief, stating that the "state shall not discriminate against, or grant preferential treatment to, any individual or group on the basis of race, sex, color, ethnicity, or national origin in the operation of public employment, public education, or public contracting."

The leader of the drive to put Proposition 209 on the ballot was Ward Connerly, a black businessman from Sacramento who also was a regent of the University of California. In 1995 the regents voted to end all consider-ations of race and gender in admissions. It was time, Connerly said, to end reverse discrimination. In a campaign document, Connerly, Wilson, and Pamela A. Lewis, co-chair of the initiative effort, argued that it was "just plain wrong and unjust" for government to discriminate, either against or in favor of someone because of race or gender. Adoption of the amendment would "stop the terrible programs which are dividing our peo-ple and tearing us apart," the three said, adding that the state should no longer "perpetuate the myth that 'minorities' and women cannot compete without special preferences."

Opponents said the amendment would jeopardize the gains made by minorities and blacks and perpetuate the discrimination that has not yet been eliminated. Affirmative action was about "giving people a chance to prove that they are qualified"; Proposition 209 would eliminate the oppor-tunities for them to do that, Clinton said in a campaign speech in Oakland October 31. A Los Angeles Times *editorial called the amendment a "fraud," saying it would not end discrimination against minorities and women in public education, hiring, and contracting but would only make it harder for them. According to the* Times, *38 percent of all businesses in California were owned by women and 25 percent were owned by Latinos, Asian-Americans, and blacks. Yet in Los Angeles those companies were awarded six cents or less of every public construction contract dollar.*

According to the state's nonpartisan office of legislative analysis, the amendment could affect state programs where gender, race, and ethnicity were preferential factors in hiring, promotion, recruitment, and training. It would eliminate programs that gave preference on public contracts to businesses owned by women and minorities. Race and gender would be eliminated as factors in admissions at California State University (CSU) and tutoring, scholarship, and counseling programs at both CSU and the University of California. The amendment was also likely to eliminate vol-untary desegregation programs, such as magnet schools, run by the state's public school districts. The legislative analysis office estimated that the programs likely to be affected cost the state $125 million a year, although the amendment was unlikely to save that much.

The suit challenging the constitutionality of Proposition 209 was filed on November 6 by the American Civil Liberties Union of Southern Cali-

fornia on behalf of a minority business and contracting group and several labor and civil rights organizations. In issuing a temporary restraining order on November 27 against enforcement of the amendment, Judge Henderson said the key question was whether it forced women and minorities to "surmount a higher political hurdle" than other groups seeking relief from discrimination.

On December 23 Henderson issued a preliminary injunction against enforcement of the amendment, pending the outcome of trial or a successful appeal of his ruling. The groups that brought the lawsuit "have demonstrated a probability of success on their claim that Proposition 209 violates the Fourteenth Amendment's equal protection guarantee to full participation in the political life of the community." Three days earlier the Justice Department had announced that it believed the state amendment to be unconstitutional and that it would "intervene in the case at the appropriate time," according to a spokesperson. Attorneys in the Justice Department and the White House feared that the amendment could undermine federal civil rights policy and encourage other states to adopt similar amendments. The Justice Department had not decided whether to file a friend-of-the-court brief in the case or to become a direct participant in the litigation.

Governor Wilson called the announcement "absolutely Orwellian." The Clinton administration, he said, "now has the distinction of being the first administration since the enactment of the 1964 Civil Rights Act to contend that a state cannot enact a law prohibiting all racial- and gender-based discrimination."

The Texas Case

The challenge to the University of Texas affirmative action program was brought by four whites whose applications to the law school were rejected even though their test scores and grades were higher than those of some black and Hispanic applicants who were accepted. In defense of its admissions policy, the university said its admissions preferences were designed to achieve racial diversity.

In its unanimous ruling, the three-judge appeals court panel said that the white applicants had been discriminated against because "any consideration of race or ethnicity by the law school for the purpose of achieving a diverse student body is not a compelling interest under the Fourteenth Amendment." The Constitution, the court said, does not allow the university "to continue to elevate some races over others, even for the wholesome practice of correcting perceived racial imbalance in the student body."

The appeals court acknowledged that the Supreme Court in Bakke *had said that racial diversity was a compelling interest that could justify race-based preferences. But, it continued, since then, the Court's rulings have suggested that the only permissible use of race-based preferences is to remedy past discrimination.*

As is customary, the Supreme Court gave no reason for declining to review the Texas case, called Hopwood v. Texas. *The appeals court ruling applied only to public universities in the three states under its jurisdiction—Texas, Louisiana, and Mississippi. Until the Supreme Court ruled definitively on the matter, the* Bakke *ruling would continue as law in the rest of the nation. But the* Hopwood *rulings, together with the adoption of Proposition 209 in California, left public universities and other public institutions throughout the United States uncertain about the constitutionality of affirmative action programs.*

Following is the text of Proposition 209, an amendment to the constitution of California that barred state-sponsored affirmative action programs, as adopted November 5, 1996:

Proposed Amendment to Article I

Section 31 is added to Article I of the California Constitution as follows:

SEC. 31. (a) The state shall not discriminate against, or grant preferential treatment to, any individual or group on the basis of race, sex, color, ethnicity, or national origin in the operation of public employment, public education, or public contracting.

(b) This section shall apply only to action taken after the section's effective date.

(c) Nothing in this section shall be interpreted as prohibiting bona fide qualifications based on sex which are reasonably necessary to the normal operation of public employment, public education, or public contracting.

(d) Nothing in this section shall be interpreted as invalidating any court order or consent decree which is in force as of the effective date of this section.

(e) Nothing in this section shall be interpreted as prohibiting action which must be taken to establish or maintain eligibility for any federal program, where ineligibility would result in a loss of federal funds to the state.

(f) For the purposes of this section, "state" shall include, but not necessarily be limited to, the state itself, any city, county, city and county, public university system, including the University of California, community college district, school district, special district, or any other political subdivision or governmental instrumentality of or within the state.

(g) The remedies available for violations of this section shall be the same, regardless of the injured party's race, sex, color, ethnicity, or national origin, as are otherwise available for violations of then-existing California antidiscrimination law.

(h) This section shall be self-executing. If any part or parts of this section are found to be in conflict with federal law or the United States Constitution, the section shall be implemented to the maximum extent that federal law and the United States Constitution permit. Any provision held invalid shall be severable from the remaining portions of this section.

TEXACO CHAIRMAN ON ALLEGED RACIAL SLURS BY EXECUTIVES
November 6, 1996

Texaco Inc. announced November 15 that it had agreed to settle a lawsuit brought by a group of African-American employees; if approved by the court, the settlement would be the largest ever reached in a racial discrimination suit. The agreement came eleven days after the New York Times *made public a conversation, taped in 1994, in which two top officials in the company were heard to refer to African-American employees as "niggers" and "black jelly beans" as they discussed destroying documents that were being sought as evidence in the lawsuit. The class-action suit, involving about 1,400 current and former employees of Texaco, had been pending since 1994.*

The revelations were a significant embarrassment to the oil giant, which had 27,000 employees and $35.6 billion in sales in 1995. Texaco's stock price dropped, at least one institutional investor found the alleged comments "grossly offensive," and civil rights organizations and individual consumers threatened to boycott Texaco products and cut up their Texaco credit cards. A federal grand jury was investigating the allegations that evidence wanted in the lawsuit had been hidden or destroyed.

The company moved quickly to stem the damage, deploring the incident, punishing the officials involved, and eventually reaching agreement in the lawsuit. Texaco officials and others acknowledged that racist attitudes still existed within the corporate world. They urged companies to examine their workplaces and employment practices to uncover signs of discrimination against women and minorities and to take the steps necessary to eliminate bias from the workplace.

Evidence of Racial Bias

The alleged racial slurs were contained in a recorded conversation between Robert W. Ulrich, Texaco's former treasurer, and Richard Lundwall, a former personnel services officer in the company's finance department. Ulrich was quoted as saying: "We're going to purge the [expletive] out of those books," apparently referring to documents concerning employment practices that were relevant to the discrimination lawsuit. "I'm still having trouble with Hanukkah," Ulrich reportedly said. "Now we have Kwanzaa. These [expletive] niggers, they [expletive] all over us with this," he said referring to the lawsuit; Kwanzaa was a December holiday based on African harvest celebrations. Lundwall, who was responsible for keeping minutes at meetings held by personnel officials, had secretly taped the meeting. After the company laid off Lundwall in August, he turned the tapes over to attorneys for the employees who were suing Texaco.

Following the publication of the contents of the tapes on November 4 by the New York Times, *Peter I. Bijur, chairman and chief executive officer of Texaco, immediately sent a message to all employees saying that the company had hired outside counsel to investigate the truth of the allegations and declaring that such conduct would not be tolerated. On November 6 Bijur told a news conference that he had been shocked and angered upon hearing the tapes for the first time earlier that morning. "They are statements that represent attitudes we hoped and wished had long ago disappeared entirely from the landscape of our country—and certainly from our company," Bijur said. He said that Texaco was withdrawing its pension benefits from Ulrich and Lundwall and suspending two current employees who had also attended the taped meeting.*

Bijur further announced that Judge A. Leon Higgenbotham, chief judge emeritus of the U.S. Court of Appeals for the Third Circuit, would work with Texaco executives to ensure that the company's employment practices and policies were nondiscriminatory. He disclosed that the company was setting up a special committee of its board of directors to review Texaco's diversity programs. The committee was to be headed by John Brademas, former president of New York University and a former member of Congress.

Michael Hausfeld, an attorney for the employees involved in the lawsuit, said Bijur's steps were "late. They've been on notice that they have had the problem for years. They ignored it. And worse, they belittled it. . . . Bigotry has no place in business."

Civil rights leaders, including the Rev. Jesse Jackson and NAACP president Kweisi Mfume, threatened to call a boycott of Texaco stock and credit cards. In a letter to Bijur, New York State comptroller H. Carl McCall, who is African-American, said it was "imperative . . . that you take steps to strengthen Texaco's commitment to tolerance and inclusion." Texaco is headquartered in White Plains, New York; the New York state retirement fund owned 1.2 million shares of Texaco stock, worth about $114 million.

On November 11 Bijur announced that an expert had analyzed the tape and found that Ulrich and Lundwall had not, in fact, used racial slurs. In the conversation about December holidays, what sounded like "nigger" was in fact "Saint Nicholas," the expert said. The reference to jelly beans could have derived from a lecture on diversity Ulrich had attended in which the lecturer, R. Roosevelt Thomas Jr., used jars of jelly beans of many colors to illustrate his points. Nonetheless, Bijur said, the findings "do not change the categorically unacceptable context and tone of these conversations."

Bias Suit Settlement

On November 15, Bijur announced that Texaco had reached agreement on a settlement with its African-American employees, in which it agreed to pay $115 million to about 1,400 current and former employees and to give African-American employees a pay raise of about 11 percent, starting on January 1, 1997. Texaco also planned to spend $35 million on an independent task force that would develop company-wide diversity, mentoring, and sensitivity programs; broaden promotion efforts; and monitor the company's performance under the settlement agreement. The task force would operate for five years and have its own staff; its decisions on the company's human resources programs could be overturned only by a court.

In addition, Bijur said, the company promised to increase the amount of business it did with minority companies, including advertising, legal, banking, investment management, and accounting firms. He said Texaco would "actively work" to increase the number of Texaco stations owned by women and minorities. "I have committed myself—and the entire management team of this company—to the elimination of any trace of discrimination in Texaco," Bijur said. The objective, he added, was "zero tolerance of bigotry and scrupulously fair treatment for every individual."

Attorney Hausfeld said that he thought the creation of the independent task force was the most important aspect of the settlement and that the amount of authority it would have had been a major sticking point during the settlement negotiations, which began after the public revelations of the secret tapes.

Jackson and Mfume both welcomed the settlement as a good first step, but said it was only a first step. "The NAACP is in this process for the long haul," Mfume said. If Texaco did not follow through on its commitment, the NAACP would be prepared to call on African-Americans to sell their Texaco stock, he said. Mfume and others said that the Texaco settlement could serve as a precedent in other bias cases. "We hope that we are able to structure a model for other corporate entities to emulate," Mfume said.

On December 18, Texaco announced more specific plans for diversifying its work force. Its goal was to increase the percentage of all minorities working at the company from 23 percent to 29 percent by the end of the year 2000, the percentage of African-Americans from 9 percent to 13 percent, and the percentage of women from 32 percent to 35 percent. The company hoped to increase the percentage of female managers from 11.7 percent to 25 percent and the number of African-American managers from 4.3 percent to 6.6 percent. Texaco also said it would increase its spending on outside contracts with women and minority firms to $200 million a year, from $135 million; that it would increase deposits in minority- and women-owned banks and investment firms to $200 million, from $32 mil-

lion; and that it would seek to triple the number of independent retail out-
lets owned by African-Americans.

"The numbers sound good," said Robert L. Johnson, chairman and chief
executive of the Black Entertainment Television Network. But, Johnson
added, "all of this is meaningless if the soul of Texaco doesn't change."

> *Following is the text of a statement made at a news conference*
> *November 6, 1996, by Peter I. Bijur, chairman and chief execu-*
> *tive officer of Texaco, deploring the racial slurs made by com-*
> *pany officials and announcing steps the company had taken to*
> *ensure such conduct would not be repeated:*

Good afternoon. My name is Peter Bijur, and I am chairman and chief executive officer of Texaco. I have a brief statement for you, after which I will take your questions.

You are all aware of alleged misconduct, first reported by the *New York Times* on Monday, which referred to statements made by several current and former Texaco employees in 1994. As soon as we heard about these allegations, we immediately hired Michael Armstrong [of Kirkpatrick and Lockhart] as outside counsel to conduct an independent investigation to determine whether the allegations were true.

At the same time, I spoke and wrote to all of Texaco's employees, denouncing the alleged behavior in the strongest possible terms.

Until this morning, we did not have audible versions of the tapes. I have just today listened to them myself. I can tell you that the statements on the tapes arouse a deep sense of shock and anger among all the members of the Texaco family and decent people everywhere.

They are statements that represent attitudes we hoped and wished had long ago disappeared entirely from the landscape of our country—and certainly from our company.

They are statements that represent a profound contempt not only for the law, not only for Texaco's explicitly clear values and policies, but, even more importantly, for the most fundamental standards of fairness, of mutual respect, and of human decency.

We are now moving quickly to begin righting these wrongs. The first step in that process is to say, on behalf of all of the people of Texaco, that we believe unequivocally it is utterly reprehensible to deny another human of his or her self-respect and dignity because of race, color, religion or sex.

And it is absolutely deplorable and intolerable to evade the laws of this land.

These beliefs go beyond an understanding of our legal obligations; they are grounded in a recognition of our moral obligations.

Texaco's statement of our core values is very clear. It says, "Each person deserves to be treated with respect and dignity in appropriate work environments without regard to race, religion, sex, national origin, disability or position in the company. Each employee has the responsibility to demonstrate respect for others."

Our corporate conduct guidelines are also clear and state that "it is the obligation of all employees to report known or suspected violations of the law or company policies to their supervisor" or other appropriate corporate officials.

These are not empty words. They enunciate the immutable principles to which we adhere—to which every person in our company has agreed—and which must form the basis of every act and utterance of all Texaco people in the course of our duties. Every employee signs our guidelines each year acknowledging that they have read them, understood them, and are in compliance with them.

Our review of the tapes has made it clear to us that these values and policies have been violated.

With regard to the four individuals involved in the allegations before us, two are active employees. They are both being suspended today pending completion of the investigation, which will be accomplished promptly.

As to the two retired employees, we believe there is sufficient cause to withdraw benefits. Pending the outcome of the independent outside investigation, further financial or other penalties may be imposed.

As I told our employees on Monday, my personal commitment is to intensify our efforts to eliminate forever this kind of behavior from our workplace. To that end, I am also announcing the following steps:

One—senior executives from Texaco will visit every major company location in the U.S. to meet with our people. Their mission will be to apologize to them for the embarrassment and humiliation this has created. We want them to understand both our personal embarrassment and our firm resolve to ensure that nothing like this ever happens again at Texaco.

Two—we will gather employees together immediately to refocus on our core values and on what we each need to do to create a workplace free of intolerance. It will be a time of reflection and a time for taking personal accountability for actions and attitudes.

Three—we are expanding our diversity learning experience to include all employees, in addition to our managers and supervisors. This two-day seminar, in which I have already participated, along with the senior officers of the company, focuses on both the intent and the impact of personal behavior on peers, teams and the organization overall.

Four—we will reemphasize the critical importance of our confidential Ethics Hotline as a vital tool for reporting any behavior—any behavior—that violates our core values, policies or the law. Calls may be made anonymously, 24 hours a day, seven days a week. We are extending this service to a broader list of countries outside of the U.S.

Fifth—I have today asked Judge A. Leon Higgenbotham of the New York law firm of Paul, Weiss, Rifkind, Wharton & Garrison to work side by side with us to assure that the company's human relationship policies and practices are consistent with the highest standards of respect for the individual and to assure that the company treats all its employees with fundamental fairness.

Judge Higgenbotham is Chief Judge Emeritus of the United States Court of Appeals for the Third Circuit and Public Service Professor of Jurisprudence at Harvard University. The Judge is the recipient of numerous honors, including the Presidential Medal of Freedom, the nation's highest civilian honor, and the National Human Relations Award of the National Conference of Christians and Jews. He is the author of IN THE MATTER OF COLOR—Race and the American Legal Process. I am grateful that he will be assisting us.

Sixth—we are also creating a special committee of our Board of Directors, to be headed by John Brademas, President Emeritus of New York University. This committee will be charged with reviewing our company's diversity programs in their entirety—at every level within our company.

Fundamentally, we don't believe the statements and actions on the tapes are representative of Texaco; but we also recognize that we have more to learn—further to go. Our goal is to become a model company in providing opportunities for women and minorities, and in ensuring respect for every individual.

Let me leave you on a personal note, but one in which I know the people of Texaco join me. I want to offer an apology—to our fellow employees who were rightly offended by these statements; to men and women of all races, creeds and religions in this country; and to people throughout America and elsewhere around the world: I am sorry for this incident; I pledge to you that we will do everything in our power to heal the painful wounds that the reckless behavior of those involved have inflicted on all of us; and I look forward to the day we are all striving for when the attitudes in question are consigned to a sorrowful chapter of our past—and that we have created for our future, within the very soul of Texaco, a company of limitless opportunity and utmost respect for every man and woman amongst us.

DISTILLED SPIRITS COUNCIL AND CLINTON ON LIQUOR ADS
November 7 and 9, 1996

Distillers and distributors of whisky, bourbon, gin, and other "hard" liquors announced November 7 that they were ending their decades-old voluntary ban on advertising their products on radio and television. In his weekly radio address two days later, President Bill Clinton said the distillers were being "irresponsible."

Fred A. Meister, president and chief executive officer of the Distilled Spirits Council of the United States (DISCUS), said the distillers wanted to level the marketing field between alcoholic spirits and beer and wine. "For decades, beer and wine have been advertised on television and radio while the distilled spirits industry has upheld its own voluntary ban. . . . There is no difference in the alcohol in spirits, beer, and wine—alcohol is alcohol is alcohol. There is simply no justifiable social, political, or scientific basis for treating spirits differently than other beverage alcohol," Meister said.

It was unclear exactly what effect the announcement would have. The voluntary ban had been in place for radio since 1936 and for television since 1948. After Meister's announcement, the four major television networks—ABC, CBS, Fox, and NBC—said that they had policies in place against accepting liquor ads and had no plans to change those policies. That seemed to imply that, at least for the moment, distillers would have to rely on local television and radio stations and regional cable systems to air their ads.

In his weekly radio address to the nation, Clinton expressed disappointment that the distillers had decided to rescind their ban. Clinton, who had been elected to a second term as president just two days before the DISCUS announcement, had made families—particularly the protection of children—a centerpiece of his reelection campaign. In August the president had signed regulations curbing teenage access to cigarettes and sharply restricting cigarette advertising that might appeal to teenagers. "For a half-century now liquor companies have agreed not to advertise their products on television and radio for the simple reason that it was the right thing to do," the president said of the DISCUS announcement. Now the industry will be "exposing our children to such ads before they know how to handle alcohol or are legally allowed to do so. That is simply irresponsible," he said. (Smoking regulations, p. 589)

Decision to Lift the Ban

The DISCUS decision came about six months after one distiller, Seagram, broke ranks and placed ads in some local and regional television markets around the country. "We have felt for some time the ban was obsolete," said Arthur Shapiro, executive vice president for marketing and strategy for the Seagram America unit.

Some advertising agencies, broadcasters, and cable officials agreed. "The liquor industry is within its rights to advertise. But it's up to the industry to make sure the advertising is placed in a responsible manner," said O. Burtch Drake, president and chief executive of the American Association of Advertising Agencies. "Liquor is a legal product, and one that is no [more] damaging to society than wine or beer," Robert L. Johnson, chairman and chief executive of the Black Entertainment Television Network, told the Washington Post. *"For some reason there's been this historical attitude toward demon rum. It's something people frown on. But I see no reason why liquor ads, during the right time slots, aren't appropriate for television."*

In his announcement, Meister said that liquor ads would continue to follow the DISCUS Code of Good Practice and "be responsible, dignified and tasteful messages for adults. . . ." Meister said the ads would not be targeted on adolescents.

DISCUS may have been encouraged by a Supreme Court decision, announced on May 13, that struck down a Rhode Island law banning the advertisement of liquor prices. The decision was unanimous, but the justices were divided on their reasons for concluding that the ban violated the First Amendment's free speech protections. Rhode Island had argued that the advertising ban was meant to keep alcohol consumption down by making it difficult for consumers to go bargain-hunting.

"The First Amendment directs us to be especially skeptical of regulations that seek to keep people in the dark for what the government perceives to be their own good," Justice John Paul Stevens wrote, in an opinion that was joined by Anthony M. Kennedy, Clarence Thomas, and Ruth Bader Ginsburg. "[A] state legislature does not have the broad discretion to suppress truthful, nonmisleading information for paternalistic purposes," Stevens wrote. In a separate opinion, joined by Chief Justice William H. Rehnquist and Justices David H. Souter and Stephen G. Breyer, Sandra Day O'Connor said the state could have achieved the same purpose through more narrowly tailored means, such as raising the sales tax on liquor or setting minimum prices.

Most court watchers said the ruling in the case of 44 Liquormart v. Rhode Island *advanced the protections the Court had been giving to com-*

mercial speech since 1970. Because a majority did not support a single line of reasoning, it was difficult to extrapolate what the Court might do in other commercial speech cases involving legal products harmful to some consumers' health. The Clinton administration, for example, was careful to aim its curbs on cigarette advertising to ads likely to appeal to children under age eighteen. The courts would have to determine whether curbing cigarette smoking among underage children was a compelling government interest warranting restrictions on commercial speech and, if so, whether the restrictions were narrowly enough drawn to achieve that purpose without infringing on free speech.

Distillers flatly denied allegations that they had lifted their advertising ban in a ploy to get all ads for all alcoholic beverages off television and radio. Some observers, including a number of beer and wine makers, had suggested that the distillers hoped that the prospect of liquor ads on television would so anger antidrinking organizations, regulators, and lawmakers that advertising for all types of alcohol products would be banned. "It is absolutely, unequivocally not in our interest to see wine and beer off the air," Seagram's Shapiro said, "because they are legal products that have a right to promote themselves. We want the same access they have."

Between 1980 and 1995, according to one organization that studied the effect of advertising on sales, the estimated consumption of distilled spirits fell 29.2 percent; at the same time wine consumption fell 2.9 percent and beer consumption went up 4.4 percent. In 1995 breweries and wineries spent $682.4 million to advertise their products on television and radio. Distillers spent $227.6 million to advertise in newspapers, magazines, and billboards.

Reaction

Negative reaction to the announcement was swift. "I think this is a big mistake," said Senate Majority Leader Trent Lott, R-Miss., on November 10. After Seagram began its advertising earlier in the year, Rep. Joseph Kennedy, D-Mass., had introduced legislation to bar liquor ads from television. After the November DISCUS announcement, a group of lawmakers asked the Federal Communications Commission (FCC) to look into the matter. Immediately after the announcement, commission chairman Reed E. Hundt raised the possibility that the FCC might consider broadcast regulations of some sort if liquor ads were aired on television and radio. "Many steps can be taken, the government has many options, but it is not necessary that these options be explored if broadcasters say no to airing the liquor ads," Hundt said.

The Federal Trade Commission (FTC), however, was pursuing investigations of the Stroh Brewery Company's television ads for its Schlitz Malt Liquor to determine if the company was trying to lure underage adolescents to its products. The FTC, which was responsible for regulating truth in advertising, was reportedly looking both at the content of the ads and the time slots in which they ran. The commission was conducting a similar investigation of some ads run by Seagram America.

Following are the text of the press release issued on November 7, 1996, by the Distilled Spirits Council of the United States announcing that it was lifting its voluntary ban on advertising distilled spirits on television and radio, and excerpts from President Bill Clinton's radio address of November 9, 1996, in which he called that decision "irresponsible":

PRESS RELEASE

In a move to end discrimination against distilled spirits products, The Distilled Spirits Council of the United States (DISCUS) updated its Code of Good Practice for Distilled Spirits Advertising and Marketing today to include television and radio advertising.

"For decades, beer and wine have been advertised on television and radio while the distilled spirits industry has upheld its own voluntary ban," said DISCUS President and CEO Fred A. Meister. "The absence of spirits from television and radio has contributed to the mistaken perception that spirits are somehow 'harder' or worse than beer or wine and thus deserving of harsher social, political and legal treatment. Recently introduced federal legislation and regulatory initiatives have inappropriately sought to use the DISCUS Code as the basis for discrimination against distilled spirits advertising. For these reasons we have now amended our Code of Good Practice."

A cocktail (1.5 ounces spirits), a glass of wine (5 ounces) and a can of beer (12 ounces) all contain equivalent amounts of alcohol, a basic fact recognized by federal, state and local governments and prominent public health groups. Examples are Mothers Against Drunk Driving, the National Council on Alcoholism and Drug Dependence and the U.S. Department of Health and Human Services.

"There is no difference in the alcohol in spirits, beer, and wine—alcohol is alcohol is alcohol," said Meister. "There is simply no justifiable social, political, or scientific basis for treating spirits differently than other beverage alcohol."

"A decision to advertise on television or radio does not diminish the industry's proven commitment to the fundamental principles of the Code," said Meister. "Distilled spirits advertisements will continue to be responsible, dignified and tasteful messages for adults and will avoid targeting those under the legal purchase age, regardless of the medium."

The Code, first adopted in 1934, has been updated to include television and radio advertising while underscoring the industry's continued commitment to effective self-regulation and social responsibility. By adhering to the voluntary guidelines in the Code of Good Practice, the spirits industry holds itself to a higher standard than required by any laws or regulations that apply to beverage alcohol advertisements.

For more than half a century, distilled spirits products have been advertised in the print media. In recent years, the media landscape has changed dramatically blurring the lines among print, broadcast, cable and computer communications.

"The extensive growth and proliferation of cable, computer and broadcast communications continues to fragment audiences," said Meister. "Audience fragmentation enables the distilled spirits industry to direct its messages more precisely to adult audiences than would have been possible when we first voluntarily decided not to advertise on radio or television. At that time there were only a few channels."

Advertising on electronic media by DISCUS member companies will now be permitted under the same comprehensive voluntary guidelines which apply to all other media provisions in the Code. The DISCUS Code of Good Practice contains more than 20 separate provisions concerning responsible content and responsible placement of distilled spirits advertising and marketing.

CLINTON'S STATEMENT

Good morning. Today I want to talk with you about what we can do as a nation to help parents as they try to raise their children. . . .

We will continue to strengthen families by helping parents to protect their children from bad influences that come from outside the home. American parents are working overtime to set good examples, only to have the full force of popular culture make their work harder. That's why we gave parents the v-chip and a television system so they can keep televised violence and explicit sexuality out of their young children's lives. And that's why we'll continue our efforts to help parents protect their children from the corrosive dangerous influences of tobacco and alcohol. . . .

We also have a duty to protect our families from the consequences of alcohol abuse. In the last year alone, 2,200 young people between the ages of 15 and 20 died in alcohol-related car crashes. We've worked hard to keep our children away from alcohol. Just last month I issued a rule telling the states they could lose some of their federal highway funds if they did not make it illegal for anyone under 21 to drive with alcohol in their blood—zero tolerance.

Now the American Liquor Industry has made a decision that will make this hard work even harder. For a half-century now liquor companies have agreed not to advertise their products on television and radio for the simple reason that it was the right thing to do. This week, however, the liquor industry announced it would break its ban and put liquor ads on the air, exposing our children to such ads before they know how to handle alcohol or are legally allowed to do so. That is simply irresponsible.

I commend the four major broadcast networks for saying they will continue to honor the ban and keep liquor ads off the air. I urge all other broadcasters to follow that example. Parents have a hard enough time raising good kids these days, and all of us have a responsibility to help them to make those jobs easier, not harder.

To tobacco companies we should all say, sell your products to adults, but draw the line on kids. And to liquor companies we should say, you were right for the last 50 years when you didn't advertise on television; you're wrong to change your policy now. This is no time to turn back. Get back on the ban. That's the best way to protect all our families.

Our goal must be to help parents pass on their values to their children, help our children act responsibly, and teach them to take charge of their own lives. If we do this, America's days—best days are still ahead.

Thanks for listening.

LABOR ORGANIZATION REPORT ON CHILD LABOR
November 12, 1996

Some 250 million children between the ages of five and fourteen were working in developing countries, according to a report released November 12 by the International Labor Organization (ILO), an affiliate of the United Nations. This was nearly double the number of previous estimates. Of these, the ILO said, 120 million worked full-time; previous estimates had put the number of full-time child workers at 73 million.

Child slavery and forced child labor still existed in many countries of the world, as did child prostitution, the ILO said. Many other children worked in extremely hazardous conditions, performing work that endangered their development and health. Many girls worked as domestic servants, where the incidence of sexual abuse was believed to be high. "We all know that child labour is one of the faces of poverty and that many efforts over many years will be required to eliminate it completely," ILO director-general Michel Hansenne said. "But, there are some forms of child labour today which are intolerable by any standard. These deserve to be identified, exposed and eradicated without further delay."

Two other reports concerning children were also released in 1996. A UNICEF report focused on children victimized by war and other armed conflicts. In the United States, the Department of Health and Human Services released a survey estimating that the number of abused and neglected children had doubled between 1986 and 1993.

Child Workers

According to the ILO report, three-fifths of all child workers were in Asia, nearly one-third were in Africa, and most of the rest were in Latin America. Evidence of child labor was also reported in industrialized countries, including the United States. The minimum age for work recommended by the ILO was fifteen.

Commercial sexual exploitation of children was increasing, the ILO said, and organized networks were increasingly buying and selling chil-

dren across national borders; some of these children were sold into the United States. The report said that 1 million children in Asia were victims of the sex trade; customers assumed their youth meant they were free of the viruses that cause AIDS and other venereal diseases. The report also said surveys in many countries revealed "alarming evidence of physical, mental, and sexual abuse of adolescents and young girls in domestic service."

Children were also employed in a variety of dangerous industries, including mining, glass-making, match and fireworks production, where they were exposed to high temperatures, hazardous chemicals, and other materials that could cause serious diseases and retard growth and development. In deep-sea fishing, for example, young boys were made to dive without any protective gear and to spend hours every day in cold water. Children were also commonly employed in agricultural work, where they might be exposed to highly toxic and perhaps carcinogenic fertilizers, pesticides, and herbicides. In Sri Lanka, the report said, mortality among child farm workers from pesticide poisoning was higher than from a combination of such childhood diseases as malaria, diphtheria, and polio.

Urging immediate action to curb child labor, the ILO recommended concentrating available human and material resources on combating the most intolerable forms of child labor, such as prostitution and hazardous work.

UNICEF Report

In 1946 the United Nations International Children's Emergency Fund (UNICEF) was created to help children. In 1996 the organization marked the fiftieth anniversary of its founding with a renewed call to protect children from the carnage of war. In the past decade, according to the UNICEF report, The State of the World's Children 1996, *wars and conflicts around the world had left some 2 million children dead, 4 million to 5 million disabled, 12 million homeless, more than 1 million orphaned or separated from their parents, and some 10 million psychologically traumatized by their experiences.*

An increasing number of children were the victims of war and conflict for several reasons, the report said. Children were, for the most part, civilians; as technology advanced the reach of weaponry, more and more civilians fell victim. In World War II, 70 percent of all war victims were civilians, killed primarily in aerial bombardments. By 1990 that proportion had reached 90 percent, as wars occurred not between one nation and another but within them. Many of those were ethnic conflicts, where the factions viewed any member of the opposing faction, including children, as the enemy.

The report also said that more and more children were being recruited as soldiers, sometimes forcibly. In 1988 alone it was estimated that as many as 200,000 children under the age of sixteen had fought in wars. One reason for the increase: light weapons, such as AK-47 rifles, that children could handle. In some ways, the report said, children made better soldiers than adults: "They are easier to intimidate and they do as they are told.

They are also less likely than adults to run away and they do not demand salaries."

Rape, the danger of land mines, starvation, lack of medical supplies, displacement, and separation from their parents were some of the other conditions of war that children suffered. A survey of children in 1995 in Angola, where civil war had raged for years, found that 66 percent had seen people murdered, 91 percent had seen dead bodies, and 67 percent had seen people being tortured or beaten. "Millions of children have been present at events far beyond the worst nightmares of most adults," the report said. It was not surprising that many children who survived later suffered psychological and social problems, ranging from nightmares to a general sense of fear and insecurity.

UNICEF set out an agenda for action that called for a ban on land mines, systematic reporting of war crimes against women and children, an increase in the age at which children can be drafted into armed forces, and promotion of the principle of "children as zones of peace." This concept involved negotiating temporary cease-fires to allow children in war zones to be vaccinated, for example, or to allow food and medical supplies to pass through enemy lines. The principle was first used in El Salvador in 1985 and was later used in disputes in Lebanon, the Sudan, and Uganda.

HHS Report

Closer to home, the incidence of child abuse and neglect doubled between 1986 and 1993, according to a survey released September 18 by the Department of Health and Human Services. Data from the third National Incidence Study of Child Abuse and Neglect *indicated that the number of abused and neglected children rose from 1.4 million in 1986 to 2.8 million in 1993. During the same period the number of children who were seriously injured quadrupled, from about 143,000 to nearly 570,000.*

These estimates were higher than officially reported cases; state child protective services reported slightly more than 1 million cases of confirmed maltreatment in 1993, up from about 737,000 cases in 1986. The national incidence survey numbers were larger because the survey took into account information from more than 5,600 community service professionals as well as the officially reported cases.

The survey also found that while state child protective agencies were investigating the same number of reported incidents of child abuse and neglect as they had in the past, the proportion of reported cases that went uninvestigated was going up because the number of cases was going up. "It is shameful and startling to see that so many more children are in danger and that proportionately fewer incidents are investigated," said Donna Shalala, the secretary of health and human services.

Following is the text of a press release issued November 12, 1996, by the International Labor Organization, summarizing the findings of a report entitled "Child Labour: Targeting the

Intolerable," in which the agency called for immediate action to curb child labor in developing countries around the world:

Some 250 million children between the ages of 5 and 14 are working in developing countries, nearly double previous estimates, the International Labour Office (ILO) says in a new report. Of this total, some 120 million children are working full-time, and 130 million work part-time, says the ILO report, *Child Labour: Targeting the Intolerable.*

"We all know that child labour is one of the faces of poverty and that many efforts over many years will be required to eliminate it completely," says Michel Hansenne, Director-General of the ILO. "But, there are some forms of child labour today which are intolerable by any standard. These deserve to be identified, exposed and eradicated without further delay."

The ILO says that because the problem of child labour is so enormous and the need for action is urgent, choices must be made about where to concentrate available human and material resources.

"The most humane strategy must therefore be to focus scarce resources first on the most intolerable forms of child labour such as slavery, debt bondage, child prostitution and work in hazardous occupations and industries, and the very young, especially girls," the ILO report says.

Some 61 percent of child workers, or nearly 153 million, are found in Asia; 32 percent, or 80 million, are in Africa and 7 percent, or 17.5 million, live in Latin America.

There is evidence that child labour also exists in many industrialized countries, including Italy, Portugal, the United Kingdom and the United States. The problem is also emerging in many East European and Asian countries that are in transition to a market economy.

The results of an ILO survey published earlier this year showed that some 73 million children between the ages of 10 and 14 years were working full time in some 100 countries. The latest estimates are based on a new and more accurate methodology recently tested by the ILO in Ghana, India, Indonesia, Pakistan, Senegal and Turkey. This takes account of part-time as well as full-time work and covers all working children between the ages of 5 and 14.

Children may be crippled physically by being forced to work too early in life. For example, a large-scale ILO survey in the Philippines found that more than 60 percent of working children were exposed to chemical and biological hazards, and that 40 percent experience serious injuries or illnesses.

In addition, a comparative study carried out over a period of 17 years in India on both children who attend school and children who instead work in agriculture, industry or the service sector showed that working children grow up shorter and weigh less than school children.

In studies carried out in Bombay, the health of children working in hotels, restaurants, construction and elsewhere was found to be considerably inferior to that of a control group of non-working school children. Working children exhibited symptoms of constant muscular, chest and abdominal pain, headaches, dizziness, respiratory infections, diarrhoea and worm infection.

Sexual Differences

Girls more often work in domestic labour; boys work in construction, fields and factories, leading to sexual differences in exposure to hazards.

Girls, because of their employment in households, work longer hours than boys each day. This is one important reason why girls receive less schooling than boys. Girls are also more vulnerable than boys to sexual abuse and its consequences, such as social rejection, psychological trauma and unwanted motherhood. Boys, on the other hand, tend to suffer more injuries resulting from carrying weights too heavy for their age and stage of physical development.

The ILO survey focuses on unsafe and abusive working situations for children. Some of these examples include:

Slavery and forced child labour. Of all working children, those bound in slavery and forced child labour are the most imperiled.

These practices are often underground, but the ILO report points out that children are still being sold outright for a sum of money. Other times, landlords buy child workers from their tenants, or labour "contractors" pay rural families in advance in order to take their children away to work in carpet-weaving, glass manufacturing or prostitution. Child slavery of this type has long been reported in South Asia, South-East Asia and West Africa, despite vigorous official denial of its existence.

Prostitution and trafficking of children. The commercial sexual exploitation of children is on the rise, even though the subject has in recent years become an issue of global concern, says the ILO report.

Children are increasingly being bought and sold across national borders by organized networks. The ILO report states that at least five such international networks trafficking in children exist: from Latin America to Europe and the Middle East; from South and South-East Asia to northern Europe and the Middle East; a European regional market; an associated Arab regional market; and a West Africa export market in girls.

In Eastern Europe, girls from Belarus, Russia and Ukraine are being transported to Hungary, Poland and the Baltic states, or to Western European capitals.

Several well-defined child trafficking routes have been identified in South-East Asia—Myanmar to Thailand; internally within Thailand; from Thailand and other countries to China, Japan, Malaysia and the United States; and other routes.

Some one million children in Asia alone are victims of the sex trade, with reports showing the trafficking in young girls on the rise in Thailand and other countries. In Latin America, a large number of children work and live on the streets, where they become easy victims of commercial sexual exploitation. A number of African countries, including Burkina Faso, Côte d'Ivoire, Ghana, Kenya, Zambia and Zimbabwe are faced with rising child prostitution.

Agriculture. Children work in agriculture throughout the world and often face hazards through exposure to biological and chemical agents. Children can be found mixing, loading and applying pesticides, fertilizers or herbicides, some of which are highly toxic and potentially carcinogenic. Pesticides exposure poses a considerably higher risk to children than to adults, and has been linked to an increased risk of cancer, neuropathy, neuro-behavioral effects and immune system abnormalities.

Mortality among Sri Lanka children farm workers from pesticides poisoning is greater than from a combination of childhood diseases such as malaria, tetanus, diphtheria, polio and whooping cough.

The operation of farm machinery by children also leads to many accidents that kill and maim.

Mining. Child labour is used in small-scale mines in many countries in Africa, Asia and Latin America. Child miners work long hours without adequate protective equipment, clothing or training. They are also exposed to high humidity levels and extreme temperatures.

Mining hazards include exposure to harmful dusts, gases and fumes that cause respiratory diseases that can develop into silicosis, pulmonary fibrosis, asbestosis and emphysema after some years of exposure. Child miners also suffer from physical strain, fatigue and musculoskeletal disorders, as well as serious injuries from falling objects. Children working in gold mines are endangered by mercury poisoning.

Ceramics and glass factory work. Child labour in these industries is common in Asia but also can be found in other regions. Children often must carry molten loads of glass dragged from tank furnaces at a temperature of 1500—1800 degrees Centigrade. They also work long hours in rooms with poor lighting and little or no ventilation. The temperature inside these factories, some of which operate only at night, ranges from 40 to 45 degrees C. Floors are covered with broken glass and in many cases electric wires are exposed. The noise level from glass-pressing machines can be as high as 100 decibels or more, causing hearing impairment.

The main hazards in this industry are exposure to high temperatures leading to heat stress, cataracts, burns and lacerations; injuries from broken glass and flying glass particles; hearing impairment from noise; eye injuries and eye strain from poor lighting; and exposure to silica dust, lead and toxic fumes such as carbon monoxide and sulphur dioxide.

Matches and fireworks industry. Match production normally takes place in small cottage units or in small-scale village factories where the risk of fire and explosion is present at all time. Children as young as 3 years of age are reported to work in match factories in unventilated rooms where they are exposed to dust, fumes, vapours and airborne concentrations of hazardous substances—asbestos, potassium chlorate, antimony trisulphide, amorphous red phosphorous mixed with sand or powdered glass, tetraphosphorous trisulphide. Intoxication and dermatitis from these substances are frequent.

Deep-sea fishing. In many Asian countries, especially Myanmar (Burma), Indonesia, the Philippines and Thailand, children work in muro-ami fishing, which involves deep-sea diving without the use of protective equipment. Children are used to bang on coral reefs to scare the fish into nets.

Each fishing ship employs up to 300 boys between 10 and 15 years old recruited from poor neighbourhoods. Divers reset the nets several times a day, so that the children are often in the water for up to 12 hours. Dozens of children are killed or injured each year from drowning or from decompression illness or other fatal accidents from exposure to high atmospheric pressure. Predatory fish such as sharks, barracudas, needle-fish and poisonous sea snakes also attack the children.

Child domestic workers. Child domestic service is a widespread practice in many developing countries, with employers in cities often recruiting children from rural villages through family, friends and contacts. Violence and sexual abuse are among the most serious and frightening hazards facing children at work, especially those in domestic service. Such abuse leads to permanent psychological and emotional damage.

There are no estimates on how many children are employed in domestic service because of the "hidden" nature of the work, but the practice, especially in the case of girls, is certainly extensive. For example, studies in Indonesia estimate that there are around 400,000 child domestic workers in Jakarta and up to 5 million in the country as a whole. In Brazil, 22 percent of all working children are in domestic service, and in Venezuela, 60 percent of all working girls between 10 and 14 years are in domestic service.

The majority of child domestic workers tend to be between 12 and 17 years old, but some surveys have identified children as young as 5 or 6 years old. For example, a Bangladesh survey of child domestic workers found that 38 percent were 11 to 13 years old, and nearly 24 percent were 5 to 10 years old. Other surveys found that 11 percent of child domestic workers were 10 years old in Kenya; 16 percent were 10 years old or less in Togo; and 26 percent were less than 10 years old in Venezuela.

Hours for domestic child workers are very long. In Zimbabwe, the work day is 10-15 hours long; in Morocco, a survey found that 72 percent of such children start their working day before 7 a.m. and 65 percent could not get to bed before 11 p.m. Surveys in many countries uncovered alarming evidence of physical, mental and sexual abuse of adolescents and young girls in domestic service.

Construction. Children undertaking heavy work, carrying massive loads and maintaining awkward body positions for a long time can develop deformation of the spinal column. Sometimes, the pelvis can also be deformed, because of excessive stress being placed on the bones before the epiphysis has fused. Children working in construction and other fields are exposed to other toxic and carcinogenic substances, including asbestos, one of the best known of human carcinogens.

Priorities for Action

The ILO wants to focus attention on the "invisibility" of endangered children. "One reason why modern societies and governments have not been more active in curbing the most harmful forms of child labour is that working children are often not readily visible. It is a matter of 'out of sight, out of mind,'" the ILO report says.

One of the most important tools available to the ILO for improving the legislation and practice of its member States in the fight against child labour is the adoption and supervision of international labour Conventions and Recommendations. The ILO adopted its first Convention of child labour in 1919, the year of its foundation, and several more over the decades.

The ILO is now calling for a new Convention that would add specificity and focus on the worst forms and most hazardous types of child labour, including slavery, servitude, forced labour, bonded labour and serfdom, and the measures taken to eradicate them.

ILO action against child labour also includes a technical cooperation programme, the International Programme for the Elimination of Child Labour (IPEC) now active in 25 countries on three continents.

FINANCIAL CRISIS IN THE SCHOOLS OF THE DISTRICT OF COLUMBIA
November 12, 1996

A federally mandated financial control board on November 15 took over the troubled public school system in the District of Columbia. The school superintendent was fired and the elected school board was supplanted with an appointed board of trustees. The action came just three days after the control board issued a scathing report denouncing the "deplorable record" of the school system in the nation's capital. The report said the school board and its superintendent, Franklin L. Smith, had wasted millions of dollars and deprived the system's eighty thousand students of educational opportunity.

Congress created the control board—officially known as the District of Columbia Financial Responsibility and Management Assistance Authority—in 1995 when the city was approaching bankruptcy. Appointed by President Bill Clinton, the board had vast power to bring the city's spending under control and improve city services, including the schools. (D.C. financial crisis, Historic Documents of 1995, p. 497)

The board and its chief financial officer, Anthony A. Williams, had so much power over the city budget and policies that the elected mayor, Marion Barry, and city council essentially were reduced to the status of figureheads. In one major test of its power, the board in June forced Barry to fire the director of the city's Department of Human Services, Vernon E. Hawkins, a twenty-five-year veteran of District government. Andrew F. Brimmer, chairman of the Control Board, said Hawkins had mismanaged the agency and shortchanged the city's disadvantaged residents. Barry initially objected to the board's demand, saying it reminded him of Nazi Germany. That comment brought reprimands from House Speaker Newt Gingrich and others, and Barry ultimately relented and removed Hawkins from the post.

School System Shake-Up

The control board's action on November 15 amounted to a general takeover of the school system by appointed officials who had nearly unlim-

ited power to make decisions as they saw fit. The board negotiated a buy-out of Smith's superintendent contract and replaced him with Julius W. Becton Jr., a retired U.S. Army lieutenant general. The control board also suspended the duties of the district's elected school board—some members of which had been elected just the week before—and named in its place an eight-member "board of trustees" headed by Bruce K. McLaury, the recently retired president of the Brookings Institution, a think tank in Washington, D.C. Karen H. Shook, the former president of the school board, was given a seat on the new board.

Reaction to the control board's action was mixed, both among city officials and in the community. City Council Chairman David Clarke and four school board members praised the move as necessary to clean up what they said was a mess in the school system, but nine school board members tried unsuccessfully to block the control board action in court. Their motion for a restraining order against the board was dismissed by U.S. District Judge Gladys Kessler, who ruled that Congress had given the control board wide powers to take actions to "benefit the interests of the children of the District of Columbia."

Officials appointed by the control board moved swiftly to take charge of daily affairs in the school system. On December 4 Williams fired eleven budget officials, saying they lacked either the skills or the commitment to bring the system's spending under control.

A Damning Report

The control board's November 12 report on the school system obviously was intended to pave the way for the tough actions the board was to take. In blunt, unsparing language, it described the D.C. school system as a top-to-bottom failure. The report said schools were plagued by violence, students were given neither the proper environment nor adequate tools for learning, too much money was spent on management and not enough on classroom instruction, and morale among school employees was at rock-bottom.

The report devoted much attention to management failures, many of which it blamed on the superintendent, who had been in office for five years. Some of the system's most basic failures stemmed from an inability to keep track of what was happening in the schools and the executive offices, the report said. It noted, for example, that Smith's managers could not provide an exact count of how many students were in the city schools or even of how many teachers and other employees were on the system's payroll. Numerous employees were listed on the payroll under the wrong categories or at the wrong locations. The report noted that all but one of the system's top twenty-five executives, including the superintendent, were listed in improper payroll categories. The report called the school system's leadership "dysfunctional."

In comparison with similar systems around the country, the report found that the District school system was top-heavy with management per-

sonnel. The report said Smith's office budget totaled nearly $6 million, substantially more than in other urban districts (for example, this figure was three times that of the central office budget of the much larger Chicago school system). District schools also had an exceptionally low teacher-to-administrator ratio of 16-to-1, the report said. According to the report's figures, comparable urban districts around the country had a 41-to-1 ratio.

Even more serious than management failures, according to the report, was the system's inability to carry out its basic function of educating children. The report noted that children in the District's schools "score significantly lower on standardized academic achievement tests than their peers in comparable districts around the nation." In perhaps its most damning statement, the report said that "on average, for each additional year that students stay in [the District schools], the less likely they are to succeed, not because they are unable to succeed, but because the system does not prepare them to succeed."

> *Following is the executive summary of the report, "Children in Crisis," issued on November 12, 1996, by the District of Columbia Financial Responsibility and Management Assistance Authority:*

The District of Columbia Financial Responsibility and Management Assistance Authority (the "Authority") was created by the U.S. Congress in 1995 to repair the District of Columbia's (the District's) failing financial condition and to improve the management effectiveness of government agencies. The deplorable record of the District's public schools by every important educational and management measure has left one of the city's most important public responsibilities in a state of crisis, creating an emergency which can no longer be ignored or excused. The District of Columbia Public Schools (DCPS) is failing in its mission to educate the children of the District of Columbia. In virtually every area, and for every grade level, the system has failed to provide our children with a quality education and safe environment in which to learn. This report:

- Details the failures of the current education system
- Highlights the lack of accountability of its leadership
- Examines alternative approaches used by other local governments to revitalize deficient schools

The Authority recognizes the following fundamental principles:

- A safe, effective learning environment and a competitive education for our children is integral to the future of the District and its residents. The current system has failed to provide this fundamental need.
- The public schools' crisis did not occur overnight, nor will it be fixed quickly. Reform will take time but it must begin immediately. The

786

Authority will take steps to improve the District's public education system immediately and permanently. The status quo condemns our children to an inferior education and contributes to the further deterioration of the city while residents, concerned about their children's education, continue to leave the District for the suburbs. Although our efforts are immediate, it will take time to permanently change the face of the District's public schools.

- The leadership is dysfunctional. At the heart of most of the problems in the school system is the lack of leadership from the District's elected Board of Education and the Superintendent of Schools. With persistent educational and managerial problems year after year, the public school leadership—tragically—has abdicated its responsibilities, to the city and to its children, for providing a quality education in a safe environment. More than 80,000 of the city's children suffer daily due to the absence of leadership and the resulting inability to reform a dysfunctional organization.
- The District's public schools are not the first to face an educational crisis. Other school systems in major urban centers have grappled with challenges such as socioeconomic factors, resource constraints, and decaying infrastructures. The Authority recognizes that much of the environment in which the public school system must operate is beyond their ability to control. It also recognizes that many talented professionals and children achieve tremendous results in the District's public schools despite daunting obstacles. Nevertheless, the Authority notes that many urban school systems with comparable problems have moved faster and more decisively to resolve similar issues. It is these schools—and their success in helping children learn—that have provided some guidance in our approach to saving our schools and better educating our students.

The Failures

The Authority's full report details the major failures of the DCPS. This summary highlights the unacceptable conditions that children face every day:

- Education outcomes are well below the national norm. District students consistently lag behind the national averages and the averages of comparable urban school districts on the major exams that test competency and student achievement.
- Education inequity persists. Students' test scores in wards 7 and 8, the predominantly poorer areas of the city, have declined substantially while the more affluent wards of the District have remained stable.
- Mismanagement undermines learning. The inability of DCPS to effectively implement long-term education and operational plans leaves students without teachers or classrooms, textbooks unordered or lost in warehouses, teachers untrained and uncertified, and students who are

disabled without access. Additionally, poor resource allocation distorts priorities, ensuring that educational needs go unmet even when funds are available.

- Unsafe environments disrupt learning. The much publicized case of schools failing to open on schedule last September, due to fire code violations, highlights the collapsing infrastructure of the public schools. The alarming condition of facilities leaves students exposed to discomfort and even to potential harm—boilers burst, roofs leak, firedoors stick, bathrooms crumble, and poor security permits unauthorized individuals to gain access, threatening the safety of students. Such conditions make it almost impossible to focus on the primary mission of educating the children.

- Unacceptable service provision affects students. Poor contract management in the public schools has left an indelible mark on our children—who, among other things, have been forced to eat cold cereal for lunch and have been subjected to unqualified individuals operating school facilities, such as at the Kedar School.

Accountability

By law, the Board of Education and Superintendent are responsible and accountable for the performance of our public schools. Because the authority for overseeing DCPS has been delegated throughout the system, identifying who is responsible for its mismanagement is often difficult. Ultimately, no one is held accountable.

Radical change is necessary to implement an organizational structure within the public school system that holds its leadership accountable for educational quality, academic achievement, financial and personnel management, and procurement.

Alternative Approaches

In committing itself to reform, the Authority has examined alternative approaches now being used in other urban jurisdictions which faced similar crises. In most cases, including Chicago and Newark, the existing leadership structures were suspended, subsumed, or abolished. They were replaced by structures more accountable for public education performance, less bureaucratic, and less sensitive to the politics that can impede the education process. The goal of these reforms is to not only improve management efficiency, but also, more importantly, educational effectiveness. The mission of any school system is to educate students; failing in this mission provides a compelling basis for intervention.

Change is positive, and both Chicago and Newark have realized the benefits of effective reform. In its first year, for instance, the Chicago School Reform Board of Trustees:

- Eliminated the District's $1.3 billion deficit
- Restored its credit rating

- Eliminated the unwritten policy of social promotion
- Required summer school for thousands of students in order to advance to the next grade
- Created new educational programs for all grade levels
- Eliminated millions of dollars in waste
- Downsized the public school system
- Created enhanced educational opportunities
- Refurbished decaying facilities

Newark Public Schools in its first year:

- Revamped educational priorities
- Removed for cause nearly one-quarter of its school principals
- Recruited large numbers of volunteers to work in the schools
- Improved the condition of school facilities
- Reorganized the educational structure to better meet the needs of students

In both instances, there were almost immediate improvements in the day-to-day operations because of the changes in management. Although it is still too early to judge students' test score improvements, officials in these jurisdictions expect that their education and management improvements will quickly lead to better student performance.

Protecting Our Children

While individuals may differ over the form that restructuring might take, there should be no question that effective change must occur—now. The Authority believes that democratic institutions must be protected in our communities. Also, like other responsible officials in an increasing number of urban centers faced with failed education systems, we are determined to also protect the children in our communities. In the final analysis, the schools' primary function is to educate children in an optimal learning environment.

The Authority is convinced that only fundamental change will reverse the deplorable neglect of students' educational and environmental needs. The Authority is committed to instituting a structure for the public schools that puts students first, links performance and accountability for education results, and provides a safe environment in which learning can occur. Achieving this objective requires that the District's parents and children, its teachers, and other school system employees recognize that the status quo is harmful to the goals of a quality public education and therefore is unacceptable. . . .

NATIONAL CANCER INSTITUTE ON THE DECLINE IN CANCER DEATHS
November 14, 1996

Two separate studies released within days of each other reported that the rate of deaths from cancer had declined in the early 1990s. It was the first decline since nationwide records began to be collected and tabulated systematically in the 1930s. "This is the news we've been waiting for," said Richard Klausner, director of the National Cancer Institute (NCI), which issued one of the reports, on November 14. "The 1990s will be remembered as the decade when we measurably turned the tide against cancer." If the downward trends held, some experts predicted that overall cancer death rates could fall by 15 to 50 percent during the next twenty years.

Scientists attributed much of the decline in the cancer death rates to a decrease in smoking, but a reduction in consumption of alcoholic beverages, less exposure to the sun, and less exposure to carcinogenic substances in the workplace also contributed to the lower death rates. On the medical side, earlier detection of cancers and advances in treatment were also significant.

The institute's report showed that the cancer death rate had fallen by 2.6 percent between 1991 and 1995. The report was based on mortality data collected by the National Center for Health Statistics of the Centers for Disease Control and Prevention. A second analysis used the same mortality data as well as Vital Statistics of the United States *and mortality information from a broad-based national surveillance program conducted by NCI. That analysis, conducted by Philip Cole and Brad Rodu of the University of Alabama at Birmingham, concluded that the overall cancer death rate had declined by 3.1 percent during the same time period. From a high of 135 deaths per year per 100,000 population in 1990, Cole and Rodu said, the death rate had fallen to 130.8 per 100,000 in 1995. Cole and Rodu's findings were published in the November 15 issue of the journal* Cancer.

Cancer death rates declined most among blacks, but rates of death from cancer were still about 40 percent higher for black men than for white men and about 20 percent higher for black women than for white women. Over-all death rates among blacks went down 5.6 percent, compared with 1.7 percent for whites. From 1971 to 1990, the rate had increased 18.3 percent.

Smoking trends played the most significant role in the death rate trends. In 1955 nearly 60 percent of all men smoked, according to the NCI report. By 1994 that percentage had dropped to 28 percent of white men and 34 percent of black men. Between 1991 and 1995 lung cancer deaths for all men fell 6.7 percent; among black men they fell 10 percent. The story was different for women, however. Cigarette smoking patterns for women had risen through the 1960s before beginning to decline. In 1994 25 percent of white women and 22 percent of black women smoked. Between 1991 and 1995 lung cancer rates among women of all ages increased 6.4 percent (although lung cancer mortality among women under age sixty-five fell 4 percent).

Significant death rate declines also occurred in colorectal and prostate cancers among men and in breast, colorectal, and gynecologic cancers in women. Colorectal cancer has been declining for some years, due to early detection and treatment and possibly to dietary changes. The reasons both for an increase in deaths from prostate cancer that began in the early 1970s and the decrease that began in 1991 were unclear, the NCI report said, although earlier detection and advances in treatment are thought to have contributed to the decline. (Diet and cancer, p. 71)

Breast cancer mortality fell 6.3 percent among women, with mammography screening and treatment advances contributing to the decline. Widespread use of Pap smear tests to detect cervical cancer, as well as better reading of the tests and better follow-up of suspicious tests, contributed to a 9.7 percent decrease in the death rate for that form of cancer.

The statistics were not all positive. The declining death rates did not mean that the numbers of people succumbing to cancer were likely to decrease in the near future. That was because the U.S. population was increasing and because the elderly, who were more susceptible to cancers than younger people, were making up an ever-growing proportion of the population. Rates for deaths from other cancers, such as Hodgkin's disease, non-Hodgkin's lymphoma, and multiple myeloma, were increasing. Still, Harmon J. Eyre, chief medical officer of the American Cancer Society, noted that because of the decline in the overall death rate, at least 12,000 people survived cancer in 1996 who would have died if the 1990 rate had not changed.

NCI said its scientists expected to release a more detailed analysis of the cancer mortality trends in 1997.

Following is an excerpt from a press release issued by the National Cancer Institute on November 14, 1996, announcing that the overall death rate from cancer had declined steadily between 1991 and 1995:

The National Cancer Institute (NCI) announced today that the cancer death rate in the United States fell by nearly 3 percent between 1991 and 1995, the first sustained decline since national record-keeping was instituted in the 1930s.

The rates reported by NCI are based on mortality data collected by the National Center for Health Statistics of the Centers for Disease Control and Prevention. For 1995, preliminary data were used, so the precise numbers could change slightly once final data are available. But officials said they are confident that the trend is real.

"The recent drop in the cancer death rate marks a turning point from the steady increase we have seen throughout much of the century," said NCI Director Richard Klausner, M.D. "The 1990s will be remembered as the decade when we measurably turned the tide against cancer."

Klausner added that thousands of scientists, doctors, nurses, patients, volunteers, and others have devoted themselves to conquering this disease, and "this is the news we've been waiting for. We are on the eve of the 25th anniversary of the National Cancer Act, the legislation that made cancer research a high national priority. Now our nation's investment is paying off by saving lives. We are immensely gratified."

The overall cancer death rate is a composite of rates for many different types of cancer. The mortality trends for major cancers in men and women provide a more detailed picture of the relative success that has been achieved against each disease so far.

Most of the overall drop in the death rate is due to declines in lung, colorectal, and prostate cancer deaths in men, and breast, colorectal, and gynecologic cancer deaths in women. Some of these trends have been noted previously; for example, the breast cancer death rate has been falling since 1989, and the colorectal cancer rates have been falling for about 10 years in men and several decades in women. Other trends, such as the decline in prostate cancer mortality, have only now become apparent.

"The decline in mortality reveals the strides we have made in prevention through tobacco control, in early detection, and in treatment," said Brenda K. Edwards, Ph.D., associate director for NCI's Cancer Control Research Program. "The knowledge that has flowed from years of research, combined with a massive effort to apply that knowledge for the benefit of people, has made the difference."

The decline in mortality has been greater among men than women, although the absolute rate remains substantially higher in men. From 1991 to 1995 the rate declined 4.3 percent in men and 1.1 percent in women. By contrast, from 1971 to 1990, the rate rose 7.8 percent in men and 6.9 percent in women. The gender discrepancy in recent trends is largely a result of changes in lung cancer rates, which in turn are strongly influenced by smoking patterns. Lung cancer mortality fell 6.7 percent in men in the five-year period while rising 6.4 percent in women.

The decline in cancer mortality has been greater among African Americans than white Americans, although rates are still about 40 percent higher in black men than in white men. For blacks the overall rate declined 5.6 percent, while for whites the rate declined 1.7 percent. The decline in cancer mortality among blacks is largely due to trends in lung cancer in men and colorectal cancer in men and women.

The breast cancer death rate in women declined 6.3 percent between 1991 and 1995, with a larger decline in women under 65 (9.3 percent) compared with women 65 and older (2.8 percent). These gains reflect the success of both early detection and treatment advances. Cervical cancer deaths fell 9.7 percent, reflecting the continued widespread use of Pap screening. Ovarian cancer deaths fell 4.8 percent, nearly all of the decline due to the trend in women under age 65.

Prostate cancer mortality declined 6.3 percent. The rate for men under age 75 fell 7.4 percent, while the rate for men 75 and older fell 3.8 percent. White men had a greater decline in prostate cancer mortality than black men. Causes of the prostate cancer trend are largely unclear, and additional time will be required to determine whether the decline continues.

Colorectal cancer mortality continued to decline for both men and women, a trend that likely reflects the success of early detection, better treatment, and possibly changes in diet and other risk factors.

Mortality from non-Hodgkin's lymphoma continues to increase among both men and women. The causes of this lymphatic cancer are poorly understood and are under study.

NCI scientists plan to publish a detailed analysis of the trends in 1997. . . .

CIA-FBI STATEMENT ON
NICHOLSON ESPIONAGE CASE
November 18, 1996

New evidence emerged in 1996 debunking a public perception that the end of the cold war meant an end to espionage between Washington and Moscow. In two separate cases, senior CIA and FBI agents were indicted on charges of selling secrets to Russian intelligence agencies. The cases of the two agents were the most sensational spy revelations since 1994, when CIA agent Aldrich H. Ames pleaded guilty to charges of spying for Moscow for nearly nine years. (Ames espionage case, Historic Documents of 1994, p. 475)

On November 18, Harold James Nicholson, a branch chief in the CIA's counterterrorism center, was arraigned in federal court in Alexandria, Virginia, on a charge of conspiring to commit espionage. Nicholson was the most senior CIA official ever accused of espionage. He pleaded not guilty. A federal grand jury on December 19 indicted Nicholson on three counts of espionage.

On December 18, a senior FBI agent, Earl Edwin Pitts, was arrested on espionage charges. Pitts was only the second FBI agent in the bureau's history to be charged with espionage. Pitts also was indicted on December 19, on twelve counts of espionage.

Both men were accused of selling U.S. national security secrets to agents from Moscow. Nicholson allegedly passed secrets to Russia from 1994 to 1996, receiving cash payments totaling about $120,000. The FBI said Pitts began selling secrets to Soviet agents in 1987, receiving at least $224,000 for his efforts.

Senior U.S. officials said the cases demonstrated that Russian intelligence services continued to target the United States. After Nicholson's arrest, FBI director Louis J. Freeh told reporters that his agency had seen "no reduction" in Russian intelligence efforts against the United States. The FBI was responsible for U.S. efforts to counter foreign intelligence. CIA director John M. Deutch told CNN on November 20 that Nicholson's alleged espionage had damaged morale at the agency and had compromised the careers of numerous agents. Deutch said Nicholson had been one of the agency's "leading officers."

Two Men, Spying for Money

U.S. investigators said it appeared that both Nicholson and Pitts spied against their countries for money—not for ideological or other reasons. Nicholson reportedly faced pressing financial demands for taking care of his three children after a divorce in 1994, and Pitts may have wanted money to maintain a comfortable lifestyle.

Both men had access to a wide range of U.S. secrets. Nicholson served in several overseas assignments for the CIA from 1982 to 1994, most recently as station chief in Romania starting in 1990 and as deputy station chief in Malaysia two years later. From 1994 to mid-1996 Nicholson trained CIA agents in the techniques of overseas covert operations. In July 1996 he was made a branch chief of the CIA's headquarters operation combating terrorism. FBI officials said Nicholson sold the Russians information about many of the CIA agents he had helped train and had provided information about U.S. businessmen who traveled to Russia and voluntarily reported their impressions to the CIA.

At least in the early stages of the investigation into the Nicholson case, there was no evidence that any U.S. overseas agents were killed as a result of the information he handed over to Russia. Investigators had linked the deaths of ten U.S. intelligence sources to information that Ames had provided.

A joint FBI-CIA statement said Nicholson's responses to a routine polygraph test in October 1995 raised "unresolved questions about unauthorized contacts with foreign intelligence services." In April 1996 Nicholson asked at CIA headquarters for information about terrorism by Chechen rebels who had been battling Russia for independence. Nicholson reportedly said he needed the information for a training exercise, but his request aroused suspicions because the agency had no plans for such an exercise.

After he began his new counterterrorism job at CIA headquarters in July, Nicholson searched agency databases for information that was not necessary for his assignment. Court-authorized searches starting in August found that Nicholson possessed secret documents not related to his official duties. Shortly before his arrest, surveillance cameras in his office caught him taking photographs of CIA documents after removing the classification markings from them. He was arrested at Dulles International Airport, outside Washington, as he was preparing to board a shuttle flight to New York, where he had booked a seat on a plane to Switzerland.

The FBI said that Nicholson apparently used the money he earned from espionage to buy a car for an eighteen-year-old son, to pay off a loan and credit card bills, and for a vacation in southeast Asia with a woman he planned to marry.

The FBI arrested Pitts, a senior agent, after a sixteen-month undercover "sting" operation that included the cooperation of his wife. According to the agency, Pitts began spying for the Soviet Union in 1987 when he was assigned to the FBI counterintelligence office in New York. He continued to spy for the Russians after he was promoted in 1989 to a mid-level post managing documents at FBI headquarters in Washington. In 1992 he headed internal security investigations of FBI personnel, a position that gave him access to substantial amounts of information about the bureau's employees. About that time, however, he stopped spying actively for the Russians, the FBI said.

Acting on tips from a Russian informant and others, the FBI in 1993 began investigating its counterintelligence operations; that probe raised suspicions about Pitts but apparently no hard evidence. The FBI received new information about Pitts in 1995 that led to an undercover operation, in which his wife Mary participated. During the next sixteen months, FBI agents posing as Russian spies paid Pitts $65,000 for information from the bureau's files. At one point, Pitts found a surveillance device in his office, but he continued to provide documents to his "Russian" contacts anyway.

Security officials said Pitts may have caused great damage to U.S. intelligence operations because, at one point or another, he had access to substantial quantities of information about FBI personnel and U.S. secret operations.

Overhaul of Intelligence Agencies

Congress in 1996 mandated limited changes in the organizational set-up of the nation's intelligence agencies. The changes were part of the fiscal 1997 authorization bill for the intelligence agencies, cleared by Congress on September 25.

The bill gave the CIA director—who also serves as the director of central intelligence—additional resources for his role of coordinating operations by all fourteen government agencies with intelligence-gathering functions. A bipartisan commission appointed jointly by Congress and President Bill Clinton recommended expanded authority for the director of central intelligence, including personnel issues. The commission, headed by former defense secretary Harold Brown, also suggested turning day-to-day management of the CIA over to a deputy intelligence director appointed for a term of at least six years.

The Republican chairmen of the two congressional intelligence committees, Rep. Larry Combest of Texas and Sen. Arlen Specter of Pennsylvania, proposed legislation in 1996 that would greatly expand the authority of the central intelligence director. The Pentagon, which controlled the bulk of the government's intelligence budget and personnel, successfully fought that proposal, as did other agencies with intelligence components.

The final legislation gave the intelligence director more help for his coordinating role, including a new deputy director of management of the intelligence community and three assistant directors to oversee the areas of intelligence collection, analysis, and administration. The bill also required the defense secretary to consult with the intelligence director about the budgets for Pentagon-related intelligence services, but the Pentagon retained ultimate control.

Congress also killed a proposal to disclose the total amount of U.S. spending on intelligence agencies. President Clinton had said he supported the idea, and the Senate approved the proposal in its version of the authorization bill. House negotiators disagreed and managed in conference committee to kill a disclosure provision. Total spending on the intelligence agencies was generally assumed to be close to $30 billion annually.

Following is the text of a joint CIA-FBI statement issued November 18, 1996, on the arrest of CIA official Harold James Nicholson on a charge of conspiracy to commit espionage:

An employee of the Central Intelligence Agency was arrested November 16 for spying on behalf of Russia.

Attorney General Janet Reno, Director of Central Intelligence John Deutch, Federal Bureau of Investigation Louis J. Freeh, and US Attorney for the Eastern District of Virginia Helen Fahey today announced that Harold James Nicholson of Burke, Virginia, age 46, was arrested Saturday and charged this morning under Title 18, US Code, Section 794, with espionage and conspiracy to commit espionage by passing classified CIA documents to agents of the Russian Federation Foreign Intelligence Service (SVRR), the Russian successor to the KGB. Affidavits unsealed in the US District Court in Alexandria today include allegations that Nicholson made $120,000 in unexplained deposits to his bank account following trips abroad (including an unauthorized meeting with SVRR intelligence officers) and that federal authorities intercepted postcards mailed to his handlers, recovered classified information from his laptop computer, observed him photographing classified documents, and that a search of his office revealed numerous classified materials concerning Russia that were not related to his CIA duties.

DCI [Director of Central Intelligence] Deutch said, "The arrest of Nicholson is the direct result of an unprecedented level of cooperation between the CIA and the FBI. We are now able to demonstrate quite conclusively that the post-Ames reforms work as designed. Clearly the post-Ames analysis and detection mechanisms the CIA and FBI put in place succeeded in the identification of Nicholson and his alleged espionage activities on behalf of the Russian intelligence service."

Attorney General Janet Reno said, "I am extraordinarily proud of the men and women of all the agencies that worked together so diligently to make this possible. Cooperation among our US Attorneys' offices, the Department of Justice, the FBI, and the CIA is essential to preventing, detecting, and punishing espionage."

FBI Director Freeh said, "The announcement today starkly demonstrates the continuing threat to our national security by foreign intelligence services. The

Ames case demonstrated that the level of vigilance against espionage cannot be lessened without risking great harm to our national security. The most formidable weapon against this grave crime is a close partnership between the FBI and the CIA. It is that partnership that made today's announcement possible."

Deutch, Freeh, and Reno praised the many employees of the FBI and the CIA both here and abroad who worked so diligently on this investigation. Freeh especially praised the superb work done on this investigation by the Agents and employees of the FBI's Washington Field Office, those employees out on the front line who must delicately collect the pieces of evidence required to make these cases. Both Deutch and Freeh acknowledged that these extraordinarily complex and sensitive investigations require extreme professionalism and dedication if the United States is to prevent or solve these crimes, which are so repugnant to our system of government.

Both Deutch and Freeh also expressed grave concern, noting that the unauthorized disclosure of the type of information Nicholson had access to could irreparably damage the national security of the United States.

The complaint and supporting affidavit charge that Nicholson possessed documents containing the names and biographical data and assignment of CIA case officers and the identity of a CIA employee scheduled for a sensitive overseas assignment. Nicholson's position as a staff instructor gave him access to biographical information and the assignments of every new CIA officer trained at his location during his tenure. Nicholson also possessed classified reports by access agents, people who voluntarily provide information to the CIA, often at great risk to themselves.

The CIA and FBI have implemented a number of reforms and new procedures at the CIA that are designed to detect the slightest of early warning signs of espionage. As a direct result of these reforms, anomalies were detected that ultimately led to the identification of Nicholson and his alleged espionage activities. These reforms include:

- The Chief of CIA's Counterespionage Group is a senior FBI official who has full access to CIA's most sensitive counterintelligence data and is thus in a position to fully coordinate the joint efforts of both organizations.
- The Chief of CIA's Counterespionage Group is assisted by deputies from both the security and operational disciplines at CIA and has at least one FBI Special Agent on the Counterespionage Group staff full-time.
- Section 811 of the Fiscal Year 1995 Intelligence Authorization Act requires immediate notification to the FBI whenever there are indications that classified information may have been disclosed without authorization to a foreign power.
- The position of Associate Deputy Director of Operations/Counterintelligence was created to ensure high-level focus on the Agency's counterintelligence and counterespionage effort. The Associate Deputy Director of Operations/Counterintelligence's duties include full-time coordination with the FBI, currently including weekly meetings with senior FBI officials in the FBI's National Security Division.

- New training initiatives to enhance and improve counterespionage efforts have been undertaken.
- Congress has provided increased resources for joint counterespionage efforts.

Nicholson was a 16-year employee of the CIA. He held "Top Secret" and "Sensitive Compartmentalized Information" security clearances. He had access to information, the unauthorized disclosure of which could irreparably damage the national security of the United States or provide an advantage to a foreign national. It is a criminal violation to make an unauthorized disclosure of classified information and, as part of his employment with the CIA, Nicholson had pledged and agreed never to improperly divulge classified information. Nicholson is charged with providing highly classified information to the Russian intelligence service in return for substantial payments of money. The Criminal Complaint charges that:

- On or about October 16, 1995 and thereafter, Nicholson underwent a series of polygraph examinations administered by the CIA as part of a routine security update. An analysis of those polygraphs raised unresolved questions about unauthorized contacts with foreign intelligence services.
- An analysis of CIA records, as well as personal travel and financial records of Nicholson, uncovered a pattern of foreign travel followed by unexplained financial transactions.
- While stationed in Kuala Lumpur, Malaysia, Nicholson had authorized meetings with members of the Russian intelligence service (SVRR). On June 30, 1994, one day after his last meeting, financial records indicate Nicholson wired $12,000 into his savings account in the United States. No legitimate source of the funds could be identified.
- In December 1994, Nicholson left the United States on personal travel to London, New Delhi, Bangkok, and Kuala Lumpur. While in Kuala Lumpur, he wired $9,000 to his savings account and made a $6,000 cash payment to a credit card account. After returning, Nicholson used 130 $100 bills to pay off debts. No legitimate source of the funds could be identified.
- In June and July 1995, Nicholson again traveled while on annual leave to Kuala Lumpur. While there and shortly thereafter, he made financial transactions totaling $23,815.21. No legitimate source of the funds could be identified.
- In December 1995, Nicholson left the United States on personal travel to Bangkok and Phuket, Thailand. Financial records show $26,900 in financial transactions during and after the trip. No legitimate source of the funds could be identified.
- In March 1996, an SVRR liaison officer officially requested information about Chechnyan terrorism from the FBI. In April 1996, Nicholson went to CIA Headquarters and requested information about Chechnya for a training exercise. No such CIA training about Chechnya was planned.
- In June 1996, Nicholson went to Singapore on personal travel. Two known SVRR intelligence officers from Moscow were in Singapore

while Nicholson was there. While in Singapore, Nicholson used his counter-surveillance techniques before meeting with Russian intelligence officers at a remote location. Nicholson was not authorized to make the contact. After the contact, Nicholson made several large cash transactions involving approximately $20,000.

- On or about July 16, 1996, Nicholson reported to his new position at CIA Headquarters in the Counterterrorism Center. CIA computer records reveal he conducted a number of computer searches using key words "Russia[n]" and "Chechnya." Nicholson had no need for the information in his new assignment. Nicholson attempted access to other CIA databases.

- On two occasions, FBI surveillance detected Nicholson mailing envelopes containing post cards using a false return name and address to a post office box in a foreign country. The messages on the post cards pertained to his assignment at CIA Headquarters and expected travel to Switzerland on November 23–24, 1996.

- A court-authorized search conducted on or about August 11, 1996, of a notebook computer belonging to Nicholson revealed numerous classified CIA documents and fragments of documents relating to Russia. These document files had been deleted from program directories. The documents included information about the planned assignment of a CIA officer to Moscow, biographical data and assignment information about CIA employees, Russian recruitment pitches to CIA officers in the field, and reports regarding Chechnya. Also included was information about the CIA station in Moscow, a summary of a debriefing of Aldrich Ames, and extensive personal observations including information about Nicholson's polygraph tests. A computer diskette was also located that contained seven summary reports concerning CIA human assets and their confidential reporting on a number of topics. The human assets were identified by code names and positions.

- A court-authorized search of Nicholson's office on or about November 3, 1996 revealed Nicholson possessed a number of highly classified CIA documents concerning Russian military preparedness, Russian intelligence capabilities, and other matters that did not appear germane to his assignment at the CIA.

- Court-authorized electronic surveillance of Nicholson's office at CIA Headquarters revealed Nicholson photographing CIA documents after removing the classification markings on the documents.

Based on this information, Nicholson was charged with conspiracy to commit espionage.

In furtherance of the investigation, FBI Agents over the last three days also searched Nicholson's residence in Burke, Virginia, his office at CIA Headquarters, his vehicle, and his safe deposit box.

The charge against Nicholson carries a possible sentence of life imprisonment without parole or, if certain statutory conditions set out in Title 18, US Code, Section 794 are met, the death penalty. At this time, based on the state of the investigation to date, those statutory conditions have not been met.

PROPOSED REGULATIONS FOR AIR BAGS
November 22, 1996

The Clinton administration took steps in 1996 to reduce the potential dangers of automobile air bags. The administration proposed allowing car owners to have air bags deactivated, and all new cars would be required to have highly visible labels telling consumers about potential dangers of air bags. The administration also announced its intention to require automakers to install "smart" air bags in cars starting with the 1999 model year.

The administration's actions resulted from consumer complaints and research studies showing that air bags could cause injury and even death, particularly for children and small adults. The National Highway Traffic Safety Administration said air bags had saved about 1,500 lives since 1986 but had been responsible for the deaths of at least 50 children and adults.

Administration officials emphasized the overall safety of air bags, especially when passengers wear seat belts. Most cases of air bag injuries and deaths happened when passengers were not wearing seat belts.

Announcing the proposed regulations on November 22, Ricardo Martinez, administrator of the highway safety agency, said air bags had reduced driver fatalities by 11 percent since their introduction in 1986. "Because air bag technology is saving lives and [is] estimated to save over 3000 lives a year when all cars have air bags, we are committed to air bags and are working to improve them," Martinez said.

Congress in 1991 mandated air bags for all cars made after September 1997 and for all light trucks made the following year. Consumer demand for air bags motivated automakers to install the devices in cars earlier than required; by 1996, the agency said, virtually all new cars and trucks came equipped with air bags on both the driver and passenger sides.

Administration Proposals

The administration on August 1 announced tentative plans encouraging the introduction of safer air bag systems. On November 22 the highway safety administration outlined the following steps:

- *Automakers would be required to apply clearly visible labels warning about potential dangers from air bags. The labels were to be affixed to both sides of sun visors and on the center of the dashboard. Labels also were to be placed on child safety seats, warning parents of the danger of putting the seats in the front seat of the car. The agency required compliance with this rule by February 25, 1997. The requirement for labels would remain in effect until the smart air bags became available.*
- *Car owners would be given the option of having their air bags deactivated by a dealer or mechanic if they had "reasonable concerns" about the potential danger. A dealer would have to give the owner information about the benefits and dangers of deactivating an air bag system. Previously, the government allowed deactivation in only a few cases. This rule was to take effect early in 1997.*
- *The safety agency said it would extend an existing policy allowing automakers to install manual switches to deactivate air bags in cars and trucks without rear seats, or with rear seats that were too small to install a child safety seat.*
- *The agency planned to order automakers to "depower" or reduce the force of air bags by a factor of 20 to 35 percent. Martinez said this step should "dramatically reduce" the potential for air bag injuries to children and small adults, especially those not wearing seat belts. Standard air bags explode at a rate of about 200 miles per hour. This rule was to take effect early in 1997.*

Smart Air Bags

As a long-term solution, the traffic safety agency said it planned to require automakers to install sophisticated smart air bags by the fall of 1998 for the 1999 model year. These bags would be activated by sensors that would determine the size and weight of each occupant and the type of crash impact. For example, sensors would determine whether the front passenger seat was occupied by a child and, if so, would reduce the rate of speed at which the air bag deployed in a crash—or might even prevent a bag from inflating under some circumstances. Similarly, sensors could automatically tighten a car's seat belts in the event of a crash.

Martinez said he anticipated that development of the technology required for these systems would result from "intense competition in the air bag and automobile industries." Representatives of the auto industry said the new devices probably would add several hundred dollars to the cost of each new car.

As of the end of 1996, the safety agency had taken no formal steps to put this regulation into effect. However, officials said the agency planned to propose in 1997 several possible standards for smart bags, along with a specific timetable for requiring installation of them in new cars.

Following is the text of a statement on November 22, 1996, by Ricardo Martinez, administrator of the National Highway Traf-

fic Safety Administration, in which he announced proposed
regulations to reduce the dangers posed by automobile air bags:

The top priority of the National Highway Traffic Safety Administration [NHTSA] is the safety of the motoring public. Safety has been and always will be our chief concern, our motivation and our responsibility to the American people.

Since the introduction of air bags into the marketplace ten years ago, air bags have saved more than 1,500 lives and significantly reduced the number of serious head and chest injuries. They are responsible for an 11 percent reduction in driver fatalities in passenger cars and provide drivers with a 30 percent decrease in fatal injury in head-on crashes. In 1995 alone, air bags saved more than 460 lives.

Air bags are saving lives every day. Today, in this audience, we have individuals—parents, spouses, family members—who have been saved by air bag technology in potentially fatal crashes. One in particular, Kathryn Jones, is with us today—her crash pictured—after surviving a high-speed head-on collision. Hers and others' stories continue to accumulate as air bags become more common in crashes. I invite you to meet with them after this news conference.

Because airbag technology is saving lives and are estimated to save over 3000 lives a year when all cars have air bags, we are committed to air bags and are working to improve them.

As the number of air bags, and more particularly, passenger side air bags, has increased in the fleet, NHTSA has identified unacceptable problems and continues to take actions to reduce them. To date, with a fleet containing more than 70 million air bags, we have identified 19 adults killed by the driver side air bag, and 31 children by the passenger side air bag. Most of these adults and children were unrestrained. Nine of these children were in rear-facing infant seats.

In 1991 before the first air bag-related child fatality, NHTSA warned the public of the dangers of placing a rear-facing infant seat in front of a passenger side air bag. In 1993, NHTSA issued rules for warning labels on vehicles and child seats. In 1994, cut-off switches were permitted for passenger air bags in vehicles without a rear-seat.

Since passenger side air bags were increasingly coming into the marketplace for the 1996 model year cars. As Administrator, I formed a NHTSA task force in the Summer of 1995 to identify and investigate adverse effects and injuries so that we could take corrective action. In October, 1995, NHTSA issued another warning about the dangers of air bags to children, and cautioned that children should be placed in the back seat. We repeated our warning about the dangers of rear-facing infant seats and passenger side air bags. A month later in November, we issued a Request for Comments that opened the door to improving the federal standard. We requested information and comment on the risks of air bags and possible solutions. In January, 1996, we issued a "Call to Action" and brought together a large coalition of safety, medical, auto industry, insurance, and children's groups to get out the word on air bag safety and children. This led to the formation of the Air Bag Safety Campaign in May, which raised more than $10 million for public education and information, improved seat belt laws, and enhanced enforcement of existing seat belt laws.

Three months ago, in August, we released proposals to improve warning labels, extend the use of cut-off switches in vehicles without a back seat, and encouraged the introduction of new "smart" air bag technology into vehicles.

We also embarked on an intense research program to identify the exact cause of air bag injury and find possible solutions. That program continues. But the time necessary for acquiring in-depth knowledge must be weighed against the time delay in making good decisions and taking action. We are now at the point where we believe that a correct course of action is apparent and validated by our existing research.

There is much discussion about air bags and the public understandably is much concerned and confused about air bags. There is no silver bullet—no single solution that on its own solves this complex problem. Solving the problems while preserving the benefits was the fundamental maxim that guided all of our deliberations to make current and future air bags safer. Today, I will clearly lay out for you a comprehensive strategy to address the issues of today . . . and improve auto safety for the future.

First, we will propose setting a phase-in schedule for "smart" air bags to begin in model year 1999. Much of the problem today stems from the challenge of having an air bag provide protection to a wide range of occupants. A "smart" air bag's deployment can be tailored to the size of the occupant and the circumstances of a crash. This is the next quantum leap in frontal crash protection and it is within reach in the near future because of unprecedented growth and intense competition in the air bag and automobile industries. We will continue to do everything we can to encourage the rapid development and design flexibility of this new generation of air bags.

Having addressed future vehicles, we will make the following changes for vehicles produced in the near term until the introduction of smart air bag-equipped vehicles—depowering of air bags and enhanced warning labels. We will propose a new rule to bring depowered airbags quickly into the fleet.

Our research shows that depowering air bags by 20–35% will dramatically reduce the hazard air bags pose to belted children and at-risk adults, while still providing protection for unbelted adults. At the same time, the level of depowering to be will likely enhance, the safety benefits for those who are using a seat belt. Our intent is to bring depowering to all current production vehicles within one year.

Today, we are issuing a final rule requiring new, highly visible warning labels which will be required for all new cars and light trucks sold beginning in 90 days. The labels will be required for both sides of the sun visor. Another warning, which may only be removed by the owner after delivery, will be affixed to the dash board. A warning label will also be required for all automobile child safety seats beginning within 180 days. This requirement for labels will remain in effect until "smart" bags come on line.

In the meantime, we are also extending the current policy of permitting automakers to install manual cut-off switches in vehicles without back seats. Until "smart" bags are available, it is vitally important that owners of vehicles without rear seats be able to protect infants in car seats, children and at-risk adults.

For existing cars, some 50 million already on the road, we believe that education and information, some changes in driving habits, and legal disconnect remedy work together to minimize risk and enhance air bag safety.

We will propose a streamlined Notice of Proposed Rulemaking to permit auto dealers to deactivate the air bags of any owner who requests it. This deactivation policy, as opposed to our current case-by-case approval, is intended to provide those with children with medical conditions requiring monitoring, families that need to car pool children, short stature individuals unable to move back from the steering wheel, and others who are concerned about air bag risks, with a legal avenue to turn them off. Existing federal law prohibits dealers from rendering any safety equipment inoperative.

However, we strongly believe that very few people should take this action because the benefits for most occupants will vastly outweigh the potential hazard. Instead of deactivating the air bag, a few simple rules do work: keep belted and sit back from the air bag; never put children under 12 years old or a rear-facing infant seat in front of an air bag. We will work with automobile dealers and provide them with guidance so that they can help their customers make an informed decision on whether to deactivate an air bag, alert occupants as to the status of the air bag, and safeguard future car owners' use of the air bag. We want people to have the right to make an informed decision, not a panicked one.

We will increase our public awareness activities through all means, including our coordination with the national Air Bag Safety campaign, automakers, insurers, medical providers, health care organizations, and safety groups. We will build upon that success as we reach out to educate all drivers through a national distribution of information about air bags, and copies of the warning labels. We will use state motor vehicle offices, fast food chains, convenience stores and other distribution outlets. And, we are using our popular public service characters "Vince and Larry" to help convey information about air bag safety. But most of all, we need professionals like you in the media to keep the public informed about what they should and can do today and to help them have a perspective from which to make decisions.

We asked the auto manufacturers to send a letter to owners of air bag cars to warn them of known risks and what to do to enhance safety. They have agreed to do so, and I applaud them for taking this important step to communicate one-on-one with their customers. Along with enhanced warning labels, this was a priority of the victims.

In summing up, I want to underscore that—central to all of these actions—there are things that you should and can do today. Parents who own passenger air bag-equipped vehicles must make sure that children age 12 and under should always ride buckled up in the back seat. Rear-facing infant seats must never be placed in front of a passenger-side air bag. The changes we are announcing today will make tomorrow's air bags safer for children, but in the interim parents must take responsibility for their children's safety. And, drivers must drive back from the steering wheel hub where the air bag is located.

Here at NHTSA, where the safety of the motoring public is our top priority, we cannot overemphasize this responsibility. At the same time, we pledge to parents that we will make an unprecedented effort to provide you all the information you need about auto and air bag safety.

I want to thank the dedicated NHTSA staff that has worked hard on these measures. They are a first rate team. Now I want to introduce deputy administrator Phil Recht who has played a key role in the development of these actions, and he will address some additional details. . . .

December

STATE DEPARTMENT ON REFUGEE CRISIS IN CENTRAL AFRICA
December 4, 1996

A refugee crisis in central Africa—leading to the most massive and rapid migration of refugees in modern times—once again threatened stability in one of the most troubled regions of the world. The crisis brought a confused and uncertain response from Western nations and international aid agencies. Between the outbreak of fighting in eastern Zaire in October and the end of the year, more than 1 million people were forced out of refugee camps, where many of them had lived for more than two years, and returned to their homelands in neighboring Rwanda and Burundi. Hundreds of thousands more refugees were trapped by fighting in eastern Zaire.

The vast majority of the refugees were Hutu people who had fled Rwanda after their longtime enemies, the Tutsi, overthrew a Hutu-led government in 1994. During the 1994 fighting, Hutu militia massacred an estimated 500,000 people, most of them Tutsis. The huge refugee camps in eastern Zaire and western Tanzania were supplied by United Nations and other Western aid agencies, but they were largely under the control of Hutu militia, who used the camps as bases for guerrilla strikes into Rwanda and prevented their fellow Hutu from returning home.

The 1996 refugee crisis raised a host of questions about the future of the region, and also about the international community's obligations. The fighting destabilized Zaire, one of Africa's largest and most troubled countries. It was also one of the most important because it bordered nine other countries. At several points, much of Central Africa seemed on the verge of being drawn into a gigantic, bloody battle between ethnic groups.

The UN and Western nations, which had done virtually nothing in 1994 to prevent conflict between the Tutsi and Hutu peoples, once again were divided and uncertain how to respond. Canada proposed, and the UN Security Council endorsed, assembling an international military force to protect aid shipments to the refugees, but more than 500,000 refugees left Zaire before that mission could get under way, and the idea was dropped.

The crisis posed enormous logistical problems for the United Nations Office of the High Commissioner for Refugees (UNHCR), which since 1994 had supervised relief for the nearly 2 million Rwandan refugees who had fled into Zaire and Tanzania. After the outbreak of fighting, the UN agency found itself unable to get aid to hundreds of thousands of refugees. When many of them fled into Rwanda, the UNHCR applauded; the UN even helped force thousands of refugees out of camps so they would have to return home. The UN agency said it had no choice under the circumstances, but some critics said the UN was violating the long-held principle that refugees should never be forced back into situations where they had a reasonable fear of persecution.

The refugee crisis also exacerbated tensions among the Western powers, especially between France and the United States, which accused each other of worsening the situation.

Rebellion in Eastern Zaire

A low-level rebellion in eastern Zaire quickly expanded in late September and early October, shortly after the government announced that it was stripping Zaire's Tutsi population of citizenship. At about the same time, Zaire's longtime president, Mobutu Sese Seko, left the country for treatment in France of prostate cancer.

On October 13 a Tutsi rebel force, known as the Banyamulenge, attacked the disorganized and poorly led Zairian army. Taking advantage of the situation, a coalition of anti-Mobutu forces formed the Alliance of Democratic Forces for the Liberation of Congo-Zaire, which attacked refugee camps and drove the Zairian army from the area. The alliance's leader, Laurent Kabila, said the ultimate goal was to march west to Kinshasa, the capital of Zaire, and overthrow the Mobutu regime.

The rebel forces received support from the Rwandan army, which in early November shelled the key Zairian border city of Goma, the supply base for many of the region's refugee camps. By November the rebels controlled Goma and several other towns along a 300-mile swath of territory in the vicinity of Zaire's borders with Uganda, Rwanda, and Burundi.

The fighting set off the mass exodus of refugees, in several waves. After fighting became intense in October, guerrillas forced hundreds of thousands out of camps, many heading into forested wilderness and others crowding into already overcrowded camps and towns along the border. This exodus overwhelmed international aid agencies, several of which lost tons of supplies to looters.

As the fighting in eastern Zaire intensified, a second wave of refugees began leaving the camps, starting on November 15. Within a four-day period, an estimated 500,000 Rwandan refugees fled across the border from Zaire back into Rwanda; another 60,000 followed later in November and early December. This movement of refugees had the active encouragement of Western aid donors and the UNHCR, which supervised the camps. The UN position always had been that the refugees should return to their homeland as soon as possible.

In early December the United Nations estimated that another 250,000 refugees were still in the hills of eastern Zaire. Western officials said some of those refugees may have been members of the Hutu militia who committed atrocities in 1994 and who feared retaliation if they returned to Rwanda.

In mid-December the Tanzanian military and the United Nations precipitated another massive flow of refugees, this time from camps in western Tanzania. The Tanzanian army broke the grip of Hutu militants who had dominated refugee camps in that country; with the help of the UN refugee agency, the military expelled most of the 500,000 Rwandans who had been there. The UN had been trying to close the camps, which were costing Western governments and aid agencies about $2 million a day. Most of the refugees headed back to Rwanda, but others tried to cross east into Kenya and Malawi, insisting they feared they would be killed if they returned to Rwanda.

The Western Response

At the outbreak of fighting in Zaire, the United States had proposed an African Crisis Response Force, composed of troops from African nations but with financing, training, and logistical support from Western nations. That proposal aroused suspicion and opposition from key African leaders, so Washington dropped it.

As the refugee crisis worsened, Canada suggested assembling an international military force to open safe corridors for Rwandan refugees to return home. Opposition from Washington doomed the plan, which failed in the UN Security Council. The Clinton administration said it feared sending thousands of Western troops into a volatile region with no clear mission. The concept later developed into a plan to air drop humanitarian aid shipments. Aid agencies also asked for military protection of their operations, which were subject to frequent raids by one side or another.

Western nations faced two problems: the logistical difficulties of dealing with a rapidly changing refugee crisis caused by civil wars, and the sticky political issues of intervening in cases where it often was unclear who was fighting whom and who was supported by whom. Another difficulty was that not all the refugees were innocent victims of war. Thousands of the refugees had participated in massacres during recent civil wars in the region, and it was virtually impossible for outsiders to know who they were.

Before the West could settle its unanswered questions, most of the refugees returned to Rwanda. Many officials in the West said the crisis had solved itself and that international military intervention was no longer needed or even desirable. But fighting continued in eastern Zaire, raising the prospect that central Africa's ethnic and political turmoil could continue for years to come.

Following is an excerpt from testimony December 4, 1996, by Phyllis E. Oakley, assistant secretary of state for population, refugees, and migration, to the subcommittee on International Operations and Human Rights of the House International Relations Committee, in which she reviewed the refugee crisis in the "great lakes" region of central Africa:

We have been working together on a broad range of global issues in population, refugees, and migration. Few are as challenging as the refugee situation in the Great Lakes region of Africa; and so, we welcome the opportunity to review with you the current information on the status of the several refugee populations and the international response.

As you know, Rwanda and Burundi in particular have been plagued in recent decades with periodic rounds of ethnic massacres and consequent refugee flows. Each has been burdened with refugees from the other as have nearly all of their neighbors. Refugees from Zaire and Uganda have added to the regional mix over time. One of my first acts as Assistant Secretary of State for Population, Refugees, and Migration, just over three years ago, was to meet with the new president of Burundi, Melchior Ndadaye. We were discussing plans for the voluntary return of Burundi refugees who had fled the country in the early 1970s—as indeed had President Ndadaye himself—and reflecting on the civil war peace talks in neighboring Rwanda that were underway and that promised to make it possible for longtime Rwandan refugees to return home. Two weeks later, in October 1993, President Ndadaye was assassinated and the international community was coping with the exodus of over 600,000 Burundi fleeing the ethnic massacres that the president's killing unleashed. All here present know well the tragedy of genocide that took place in Rwanda some six months after that, leading to refugee outflows that shattered all previous records for magnitude and rapidity.

In mid-October of this year, we entered yet another phase in what seems to some to be an unending cycle of conflict in the Great Lakes region. Goaded by government announcements that they would be stripped of their Zairian citizenship Zairian Tutsis mounted an armed insurgency in eastern Zaire. Joining forces with other Zairian opposition elements and backed by the present Rwandan government, they have taken control of a swath of Zairian territory along the Rwandan and Burundi borders. They attacked and dispersed all of the forty-some refugee camps in eastern Zaire that housed some 1.2 million refugees from Rwanda and Burundi. In the ensuing chaos, many of the Rwandan refugees were able to break free of the former Rwandan government/former Rwandan army forces that had been intimidating them into remaining as refugees in Zaire. To date, some 600,000 have returned to Rwanda, most in massive movements between November 15 and 20. Almost all of these have now returned to their home areas (local administrative units known as communes) where they are being registered and receiving a settling in package of assistance that includes two months worth of food. Remarkably, given the still very fresh pains of the genocide, human rights monitors have seen almost no cases of retribution. As squatters whose own homes had been destroyed in the earlier war and genocide or who had recently returned from long-term exile are required to vacate the homes of the newly returning refugees, there are bound to be some tensions. To help calm the situation, the Government of Rwanda has temporarily suspended new arrests for genocide except in cases of egregious perpetrators.

We are delighted that so many of the Rwandan refugees in Zaire have returned home, while mourning what we assume to be thousands of deaths that resulted from the attacks on the camps. As you know, the situation of Rwandan refugees in Zaire had presented the entire international community with an acute moral dilemma—how to separate effectively and humanely the legitimate refugees from armed elements of the former regime and from those who would not be entitled to refugee status given their role in the 1994 genocide. In all of our attempts to accelerate voluntary repatriation of refugees to Rwanda, we have focused on three areas—creating a safe context inside Rwanda for repatriation; ensuring that international assistance programs were conducive to achieving repatriation; and stopping the intimidation of refugees by convincing the intimidators to accept return. Our relative success in the first two areas was overshadowed by our collective failure in the third. The attacks by the Zairian rebels broke the intimidators' hold for a large share of the refugees.

There remain, we believe, between 200,000 and 400,000 refugees who had been registered in the Zairian camps unaccounted for. You are no doubt aware of the shrill debate over numbers. Some claim that original refugee counts and recent re-counts were flawed and that most if not all Rwandans have now gone home. Some estimate that several hundred thousand people were guilty of genocide and therefore have no legitimate claim to refugee status. Others who had worked in the camps maintain that the numbers of beneficiaries were quite accurate. Interviews with returning refugees indicate that many are still stranded in Zaire, but good numbers are hard to come by. At this point, we simply do not know how many dispersed refugees and displaced Zairians there are or in what condition they may be. Aerial surveillance—and we must recognize all of its limitations when cloud cover is heavy and/or when dispersed refugees may be hiding out—has indicated that there are concentrations of people in eastern Zaire adding up to over 200,000. It is obviously critical that the international community have ground access in order to assess numbers and needs. It is equally obvious that under current conditions where there is active fighting in eastern Zaire, that such ground-truthing will be difficult. We are very encouraged, nevertheless, by recent international access that located some 40,000 people between the Goma and Bukavu sectors and has arranged to get them repatriated to Rwanda.

Another hotly debated topic is whether a multinational military force to carry out humanitarian operations in eastern Zaire as was authorized by the United Nations Security Council in November is still needed. Both the mission and the implications of introducing another force into the already very militarized and volatile eastern Zaire must be handled astutely. Military planners are working with the humanitarian community to explore the prospects for air dropping food supplies to those stranded refugees and displaced persons who may be in need of emergency rations. Everyone is well aware of the potential difficulties in getting supplies safely to the intended beneficiaries. UNHCR [United Nations Office of the High Commissioner for Refugees] has stressed that airdrops should only be considered as a last resort.

Some 62,000 of the 143,000 Burundi refugees in Zaire have returned to Burundi since mid-October, in many instances to a very uncertain welcome as Burundi itself continues to be convulsed by ethnic violence. We were particularly troubled by the reported massacre of up to 400 returnees who had sought shelter around a church. The Special Representative of the United Nations High Commissioner for Refugees to the Great Lakes region is urgently looking into the issue of safe return areas for Burundi refugees who at present cannot remain in Zaire.

I would also like to call your attention to the situation in Tanzania where there are currently over 700,000 refugees from Rwanda, Burundi, and Zaire. The numbers of new refugees from the fighting in Burundi continue to grow, potentially straining the response capacity of relief agencies in Tanzania. UNHCR has increased its emergency planning figure from 100,000 to 200,000 new arrivals. At the same time, it should be possible for the over 500,000 Rwandan refugees to contemplate orderly voluntary return to Rwanda. The Government of Rwanda is anxious to bring all of its refugees home in the coming weeks. Doubling the massive returns to Rwanda would of course create additional strains in absorptive capacity; but, there is little reason for people to languish as refugees any longer than need be.

We have at least five humanitarian objectives for the coming weeks and months. We want to assist the Rwandans in meeting the challenge of welcoming and reintegrating the 600,000 who have returned in recent weeks. We want to locate and assist those refugees stranded in Zaire. We want to assure that displaced Zairians receive the aid they need. We want to work for a rapid but orderly voluntary return from Tanzania to Rwanda. And we want to assure that Burundi who need it can find safe asylum.

In recent days, the U.S. Government has programmed an additional $145 million in humanitarian and development assistance. This brings our humanitarian contributions since 1994 to about one billion dollars. We are directing the greatest share of the new funding to the challenges of rapid reintegration, recovery, and reconciliation inside Rwanda. There will be a particular focus on the needs of women, both because there are so many female-headed households in the aftermath of Rwanda's upheaval, but also because we believe that is a fruitful path toward the kind of genuine reconciliation that Rwanda will need.

Finally, Mr. Chairman, I would like to briefly address the importance we attach to the full integration of reproductive health services into primary health care programs for refugees. These services include safe motherhood and child survival programs, prevention and management of the consequences of sexual violence, and protection against sexually transmitted diseases and HIV/AIDS.

The incidence of sexual violence, including rape, is very high in refugee crises—as was widely publicized in Bosnia. The number of women raped during the 1994 Great Lakes crisis is reported to be in the tens of thousands, with the result being thousands of unwanted pregnancies. For refugees, even the most optimal living conditions often barely meet minimum health standards. Overburdened health care resources and susceptibility to disease— especially sexually transmitted diseases and HIV/AIDS—compound a refugee woman's reproductive health risks. Furthermore, the breakdown of traditional social structures combined with decreased resources for refugee women to provide for their families too often lead to increased risk-taking behavior, such as prostitution.

Reproductive health services should be based on expressed need and sensitive to people's cultural, ethical, and religious values and must be responsive to refugee conditions. PRM [Bureau of Population, Refugees and Migration] has funded reproductive health activities within the broader component of primary health care programs for over a decade. This assistance has focused primarily on health education and maternal and child health programs. We will continue to support UNHCR and NGO [nongovernmental organization] efforts to incorporate reproductive health services as part of broader primary health care programs to refugees and internally displaced persons worldwide. I feel I would be negligent in my responsibilities if this total health package were not provided. . . .

LONDON CONFERENCE REPORT ON PROGRESS IN BOSNIA
December 4–5, 1996

After three years of the most devastating war in Europe since World War II, Bosnia-Herzegovina was at peace in 1996. According to the United Nations, not a single Bosnian died as a result of military conflict during the year. Moreover, some 2 million people participated in an election that chose a new national government in which the country's Muslim, Croatian, and Serbian populations had a share. Bosnia began the daunting process of rebuilding itself, with an infusion of outside aid. NATO agreed at year's end to extend until mid-1998 the mandate of a peacekeeping force, which was to have been withdrawn at the end of 1996.

The first year of peace in Bosnia was not an unqualified success. The election was deeply flawed, and the winners were the same nationalist parties that drove Bosnia to war in 1992. Foreign aid lagged behind promises, and so the reconstruction of Bosnia was painfully slow. An international report said that only 250,000 of the country's 2.1 million refugees were able to return to their homes. Human rights abuses continued, including restrictions on freedom of movement and the expulsion of people from their homes for ethnic reasons. Most of those indicted by an international tribunal for war crimes were still at large.

Assessing the Bosnia situation, an international conference attended by representatives of nearly fifty nations and international organizations meeting in London on December 4–5 concluded that financial aid represented the most important leverage for the outside world to secure more rapid progress by the various factions in Bosnia. While noting that the authorities and citizens in Bosnia "must progressively take charge of their own affairs," the conference of aid donors said their willingness to provide aid depended on Bosnia's commitment to carry out the 1995 Dayton peace agreement. The Dayton agreement provided for an end to Bosnia's civil war, supervised by an international peacekeeping force, and the reconstruction of the country with Bosnian, Croatian, and Serbian factions sharing power. (Dayton agreement, Historic Documents of 1995, p. 717)

Elections

Under the Dayton accord, Bosnia was to have two major regions: a Muslim-Croat federation and a Serbian republic. Both regions were to participate in an internationally supervised election for a new national government. A new constitution included in the Dayton agreement established a shared national presidency, with each of the three ethnic factions electing one representative. A national House of Representatives, with forty-two seats, was to unite all three factions with proportionate representation; a fifteen-member upper chamber, the House of Peoples, was to be equally divided among the three factions.

Even if they disliked the idea of cooperating with each other, all three factions had two important economic incentives to participate in the election. First, the United States and major European powers made it clear that their aid to rebuild Bosnia depended on an elected government being in place. Second, United Nations economic sanctions against the Bosnian Serbs and their allies in the former Yugoslavia—which had been suspended after the war—could be reimposed if the Serbs tried to disrupt the election.

During the year numerous observers expressed doubt that elections could be held in the fall as scheduled or, even if held, that they would be free and fair. A major obstacle to the election was the continued presence of the hard-line Serbian leader, Radovan Karadzic, who had been indicted by the international war crimes tribunal for his role in fashioning the Serbian policy of "ethnic cleansing"—forcing Muslims and Croats out of areas the Serbs wished to occupy and killing thousands in the process.

Even though he was indicted as a war criminal, Karadzic remained at large and resisted Western pressure to give up power as leader of the Bosnian Serbs. The NATO-led peacekeeping force made no move to arrest him, partly because Western military leaders opposed turning their troops into policemen.

Under intense diplomatic pressure from the United States, Russia, Britain, and other powers, Karadzic agreed on July 19 to resign as president of the Bosnian Serb republic and as leader of his Serbian political party. But Karadzic refused to leave Bosnia or to turn himself over to the war crimes tribunal, and it was clear that he would remain a major behind-the-scenes factor. Momcilo Krajisnik, president of the Bosnian Serb parliament and a longtime aide to Karadzic, became the de facto leader of the Bosnian Serbs and ran as the faction's candidate for the presidency.

The elections, held September 14, went surprisingly smoothly, given the remaining antagonisms in the country and the turmoil of displaced populations. Despite the presence of international monitors, there were numerous charges of fraud. The total number of votes tallied—2,431,554—exceeded some estimates of the number of eligible voters.

To no one's surprise, the winners were the same nationalist parties that had led Bosnia's three factions during the three-year war: the Muslim Party of Democratic Action, led by Bosnia's former president Alija Izetbe-

govic; the Croatian Democratic Union, led by Kresimir Zubak; and the Serb Democratic Party, headed by Krajisnik. Izetbegovic finished first in the balloting for the three-man presidency and so he became chairman for a two-year term.

For nearly a week after the election, diplomats and international observers debated whether to certify to the United Nations that the voting was free and fair. Some argued that the electoral process was too flawed to merit an international endorsement, but political realism won in the end. The Organization of Security and Cooperation in Europe, asked by the UN to determine the validity of the election, chose to argue that a peaceful, if flawed election, was better than none at all. That organization certified the election results on September 29, and Bosnia's three-man presidency held its first meeting the next day in a motel on the outskirts of the country's war-damaged capital, Sarajevo.

New Peacekeeping Force

With a new Bosnian government in place, Western leaders turned to the thorny question of how to continue ensuring peace in the country. In December 1995 the United States, other NATO countries, and Russia had sent a 60,000-member peacekeeping force into Bosnia to separate the warring parties and to monitor their compliance with the Dayton accord. The United States contribution was the largest, peaking at 18,400. In sending the troops, President Bill Clinton had said the American military presence in Bosnia would last just one year.

By most accounts, that mission was successful in keeping the Muslim, Croat, and Serbian military forces in their barracks and out of harm's way. There were no reports of serious armed clashes between the factions during 1996 or attacks on the peacekeepers.

As the year progressed, it became increasingly clear that Bosnia remained an unstable place and that the three armed factions probably would resume the war if the international peacekeepers left. A report prepared by the Defense Intelligence Agency for the Senate Intelligence Committee, dated February 22, 1996, offered a grim assessment of the prospects for long-term peace in Bosnia. The report said a huge international aid program—one exceeding anything forthcoming so far—would be necessary to rebuild the country's devastated economy. The report also said the ethnic factions still held the same strategic goals that led them into war, and so might resume fighting once the peacekeepers left.

The Clinton administration hinted during the year that the Bosnia peacekeeping force would have to be extended past the initial one-year period the president had promised. On November 15, ten days after the presidential election, Clinton announced that he had agreed to keep a smaller NATO-led peacekeeping force in Bosnia until June 1998. The new force would total 31,000 troops—roughly half the size of the original force—and would include 8,500 Americans—about half as many as before.

Clinton said the original peacekeeping force had "plowed the field in which the seeds of peace have been planted. The new mission will provide the time for them to take root."

Defense Secretary William J. Perry, who a year before had contended that the peacekeeping mission could stabilize Bosnia in twelve months, acknowledged that he had miscalculated. "It was right in the sense that all of the specific tasks spelled out we did do in twelve months," he told reporters. "It was wrong in the sense that those tasks were enough to allow us to safely leave the country." Some Republican lawmakers complained that Clinton had waited until after the election to acknowledge that troops would remain in Bosnia. It seemed unlikely, however, that there would be a serious move in Congress to force the president to bring the troops home.

Following are excerpts from the text of the "Summary of Conclusions," issued by an international conference on the implementation of the Bosnia peace agreement. The conference, attended by representatives of nearly fifty nations and international organizations such as the United Nations, was held in London on December 4–5, 1996:

Bosnia and Herzegovina 1997:
Making Peace Work

1. The future of Bosnia and Herzegovina is as an independent and democratic state within internationally recognised borders, with guaranteed human rights and fundamental freedoms for all, and with a restructured market-oriented economy, a commitment to free trade, strong economic and political relations with its neighbours, and developing links with the European Union. Meeting in London on 4 and 5 December 1996, the Peace Implementation Council [PIC] reaffirms its commitment to these objectives, to be achieved through full implementation of the General Framework Agreement for Peace in Bosnia and Herzegovina and its Annexes (the 'Peace Agreement'). It recalls the conclusions of the PIC Review Conference in Florence on 14 June 1996 and of the Ministerial Meeting of the Steering Board with the Presidency of Bosnia and Herzegovina in Paris on 14 November 1996, and welcomes the substantial progress made in the past year. In particular:

- peace has taken root: in 1996, no Bosnian has died in military conflict;
- elections have been held, with the participation of 2.4 million citizens;
- barriers to freedom of movement have begun to be dismantled;
- the establishment of the new multi-ethnic common institutions, most recently the setting up of the Council of Ministers, has begun;
- reconstruction is underway.

2. The next stage is to build upon the achievements of the past twelve months: to consolidate peace; to encourage reconciliation and economic,

political and social regeneration; to take the radical steps necessary to restore a multi-ethnic Bosnia and Herzegovina to economic health and prosperity and to enable it to take its place in the region and in Europe.

3. These objectives require the full commitment of all the leaders of Bosnia and Herzegovina and its two Entities (Federation of Bosnia and Herzegovina and Republika Srpska). There are important areas of the Peace Agreement where little progress has been made. Of the 2.1 million citizens who have been displaced or become refugees, only 250,000 have returned. Human rights abuses continue: people are still being expelled from their home areas for ethnic reasons and homes are still being destroyed. People are still being harassed when exercising their right to move freely around the country. Progress in reconstruction has been hampered by the failure of the authorities in Bosnia and Herzegovina to provide all the necessary mechanisms and structures to maximise the effectiveness of the international community's efforts. Some of the new common institutions have not yet been constituted. Persons indicted for war crimes by the International Criminal Tribunal for the Former Yugoslavia have not been surrendered to stand trial in The Hague. Agreed weapons reductions have still not been implemented. Mines have not been cleared.

4. While the Peace Implementation Council is committed to the peace process, responsibility for reconciliation lies with the authorities and citizens of Bosnia and Herzegovina, who must progressively take charge of their own affairs. The Council's willingness to devote human and financial resources is dependent upon a strengthened commitment from the authorities in Bosnia and Herzegovina to implementation of the Peace Agreement. Specific criteria for this conditionality are set out in the texts following this summary. The Republic of Croatia and the Federal Republic of Yugoslavia, as parties to the Peace Agreement and immediate neighbours, must continue to work for a peaceful, united and stable Bosnia and Herzegovina and for a normal and constructive relationship between themselves and with Bosnia and Herzegovina, including the early establishment of diplomatic relations. In particular the Council expects full cooperation from them on regional stabilisation, human rights, indicted persons and refugee return.

5. Following the development in Paris on 14 November 1996 of guiding principles for the two-year civilian consolidation plan, the Peace Implementation Council has approved at this conference the following Action Plan for the coming twelve-month period:

- **regional stabilisation:** continuing substantial progress in the implementation of confidence and security-building measures (Article II Agreement) and ensuring full implementation of the Agreement on sub-regional arms control (Article IV) by the agreed deadlines, including full implementation of the baseline validation inspections, correct reporting, proper application of counting rules and completion of first phase reductions by 31 December 1996 and second phase reductions by 31 October 1997, in close cooperation with the Personal Representatives of the OSCE [Organization of Security and Cooperation in Europe] Chairman-in-Office for both Agreements;

- **human rights:** respecting the highest level of internationally recognised human rights and fundamental freedoms and ensuring that the authorities in Bosnia and Herzegovina cooperate fully with the Ombudsman and the Human Rights Chamber and implement their conclusions and decisions;
- **war crimes:** ensuring that all states and Entities concerned execute arrest warrants against indictees and surrender them to the Tribunal without further delay; injecting extra resources into the Tribunal to improve its investigative capacity; insisting on full cooperation with Tribunal investigations and requests for information; insisting on full compliance with the 'Rules of the Road' agreed in Rome on 18 February 1996;
- **democratisation:** setting up effective institutions without delay; amending laws inconsistent with the Constitution; creating the conditions for a viable and democratic civil society;
- **refugees and displaced persons:** creating and maintaining conditions to encourage the return of refugees and displaced persons to places of their choice in either of the two Entities;
- **freedom of movement:** creating urgently an integrated strategy and a task force to secure full compliance with the freedom of movement requirements of the Peace Agreement; encouraging full respect for the 'rules of the road'; elimination of laws and regulations which inhibit free movement; establishment of a national number-plate system; extension of cross-Entity road and rail services; agreement on a linked telecommunications system and a commonly-administered airspace for Bosnia and Herzegovina;
- **elections:** holding municipal elections by summer 1997, supervised by the OSCE; promoting a politically open electoral environment, including full participation by opposition parties and equitable access to mass media;
- **policing:** improving the effectiveness of the International Police Task Force (IPTF) by allowing it to investigate or assist with investigations into allegations of misconduct by police and to propose the sanctioning of offenders; ensuring police reform and providing material and financial support conditional upon implementation of democratic policing principles and cooperation with the IPTF; obtaining additional resources from the international community;
- **market economy:** constructing a market economy based on respect for free market and open trading principles; instituting a legal framework including passage of central and Entity budgets; agreeing on an IMF [International Monetary Fund] stabilisation programme;
- **reconstruction:** insisting on continued linkage between the provision of reconstruction assistance and the authorities' commitment to implementation of the Peace Agreement; giving high priority to those recon-

struction projects which link and integrate the Entities, foster refugee return and create jobs; ensuring action by the authorities to enable early agreement on an IMF stabilisation programme which will encourage both substantial debt relief by the Paris and London Clubs and a positive response from the international community and the international financial institutions at the 1997 donors' conference; the distribution of aid on an equitable basis consistent with real needs throughout Bosnia and Herzegovina, conditional upon support for implementation of the Peace Agreement; recognition of the need for quicker disbursement, including disbursement of the vast majority of 1996 pledges by June 1997, and rapid commitment of 1997 pledges with disbursement of a significant percentage of these by the end of 1997, provided the authorities of Bosnia and Herzegovina cooperate;

- **Central Bank:** ensuring that the Central Bank is operational by early 1997; adoption of legislation and agreement on the practical arrangements for the new currency;
- **mine removal:** ensuring that the authorities in Bosnia and Herzegovina commit resources, waive taxation on humanitarian assistance and cooperate by providing complete information to the United Nations Mine Action Centre; implementing as soon as possible in 1997 an effective and extensive civilian mine clearing operation;
- **reconciliation:** adoption of legislation and other measures to encourage tolerance and equality and to secure basic rights; adoption of a Bosnia and Herzegovina flag and symbols; agreement on all Ambassadors representing Bosnia and Herzegovina;
- **media:** developing a media regulatory framework consistent with OSCE standards; providing the necessary licences and facilities to enable the Open Broadcast Network, TV-IN, as well as other independent broadcasters, to operate free of arbitrary interference;
- **education:** the restoration of educational systems and their transformation into systems which are open and non-discriminatory, teach democratic values and respect for human rights and recognise and respect the cultural heritage of all the peoples of Bosnia and Herzegovina;
- **Brcko Area:** re-commitment of the authorities in Bosnia and Herzegovina to unequivocal support for the arbitration of the Brcko Area and the Tribunal process, and to full implementation of the arbitration decision;
- **customs:** adoption of a customs law and a customs tariff law, coordination of customs procedures and administration between the Entities and removal of internal barriers to trade; facilitation of external trade through establishment of border crossing points along the entire state border line where appropriate.

6. The authorities in Bosnia and Herzegovina acknowledge their individual responsibilities to fulfil their obligations, and accept that any failure to do so by another party does not release them from these obligations.

7. The Peace Implementation Council, recognising Bosnia and Herzegovina's wish for a close relationship with the European Union, welcomes the European Commission's intention to consider proposing a contractual relationship between the European Union and Bosnia and Herzegovina.

8. The Council also confirms the continuation of the mandate of the High Representative, with reinforced co-ordination structures, including in the field of reconstruction. . . .

10. Recognising the fundamental importance of a secure environment to the task of civilian implementation during 1997, the Council, including the authorities in Bosnia and Herzegovina, welcomes the decision made in principle by NATO members, in cooperation with other states participating in IFOR [implementation force], to provide a smaller multinational stabilisation force (SFOR) in 1997 under the same robust rules of engagement as IFOR. By contributing to a secure environment for the Action Plan set out in these Conclusions, SFOR will make a vital contribution to the peace process in Bosnia and Herzegovina.

CLINTON AND BOUTROS-GHALI ON NEW UN SECRETARY GENERAL
December 13 and 17, 1996

Domestic American politics in an election year played a significant role in the dumping of the United Nations secretary general and the selection of his replacement. The Clinton administration prevented the UN from renewing the contract of Secretary General Boutros Boutros-Ghali and maneuvered the selection of a longtime UN official, Kofi Annan, to succeed him.

The Security Council approved Annan's appointment December 13, after nearly a month of backroom negotiations among the UN major powers. The General Assembly ratified the appointment December 18. Annan, who for nearly three years had been UN undersecretary general for peacekeeping, took over the top post on January 1, 1997. Annan became the first black man to head the UN, and the first from sub-Saharan Africa.

Booting Boutros-Ghali

Boutros-Ghali, a former deputy prime minister and minister of foreign affairs in Egypt, served one five-year term as the senior manager of the UN's vast and unwieldy bureaucracy. As the first secretary general from the African continent, he won high marks in some quarters for calling the world's attention to the plight of the underprivileged and for promoting the UN as a peacemaker in ethnic and ideological conflicts.

Boutros-Ghali never was able to make much of an impression in Washington, the largest single source of funding for the UN and the most important constituency for the UN. His reserved demeanor and intellectual approach to problem solving did not play well in the rough-and-tumble of Washington politics. Boutros-Ghali also headed the UN at a time when many Americans were becoming increasingly disenchanted with the world body, especially its handling of controversial peacekeeping missions in Somalia and Bosnia.

The Clinton administration chose to focus on another issue: the slow pace of organizational reform in the UN. Ever since the Reagan adminis-

tration, the United States had been pressing the UN to trim its bloated bureaucracy and eliminate duplicated services. Boutros-Ghali insisted he was moving as quickly as possible, given his limited authority and the fact that all major changes had to be approved by member-nations. The pace did not satisfy the Clinton administration, which decided in the fall to try to block reappointment of Boutros-Ghali to a second term.

The administration's decision put it in conflict with several allies, especially France, which championed Boutros-Ghali, in large part because he had studied at the Sorbonne in Paris and was a fluent French speaker. France insisted on putting Boutros-Ghali's name before the Security Council, provoking a U.S. veto on November 18. That action set off a furious round of diplomatic maneuvering, with the focus on candidates from Africa, at the insistence of third world countries. When the United States and some of its allies settled on Annan, France objected, reportedly in retaliation against the U.S. veto of Boutros-Ghali.

The deadlock was broken on December 13 when three candidates backed by France and other countries withdrew, leaving Annan as the consensus choice. Boutros-Ghali, who had not given up his quest for reappointment despite the determined U.S. opposition, issued a statement congratulating Annan and saying he was "especially gratified" that his successor was from Africa.

Praising the UN action, President Bill Clinton issued a statement acknowledging that his demand for a new secretary general was "controversial" and calling Boutros-Ghali "an honorable man who has had a great career." Most observers said Madeleine Albright, the United States ambassador to the United Nations, had led the fight to deny Boutros-Ghali's reappointment and to select Annan. Albright's success in that diplomatic battle helped win her a promotion to be secretary of state in Clinton's second term, the first woman to hold the top Cabinet post.

Annan's Rise Through the UN

Born in the Gold Coast—now Ghana—in 1938 to a prominent family, Annan was educated in the United States and Switzerland. He entered the UN system while studying in Geneva, taking a job with the World Health Organization. Except for a two-year stint heading the tourism department in Ghana, Annan worked for the UN his entire career.

Annan served in increasingly responsible management posts for various UN agencies in New York, Europe, and Africa, among them the posts of budget director and director of human resources. He won wide praise in 1990, after Iraq's invasion of Kuwait, when he successfully negotiated the release of hostages and safe passage out of Kuwait for Asian workers who had been trapped there.

On March 1, 1993, he was named to one of the UN's most important and visible positions: undersecretary general for peacekeeping operations. His department was engaged at the time in two controversial and unsuccessful operations: protecting deliveries of humanitarian aid to both Somalia and

Bosnia. Annan appealed for international intervention to stop ethnic war-
fare in 1994 between the Tutsi and Hutu factions in Rwanda, but the West
ignored that plea; an estimated 500,000 people died in the fighting there.
He negotiated the terms of the UN's departure from Somalia, and he won
praise for leading the transition in December 1995 of peacekeeping forces
in Bosnia from UN control to NATO supervision.

On the latter occasion, Annan gave a memorable speech in Sarajevo
recounting how the rest of the world stood by as Bosnia's ethnic factions
tore each other apart. "In looking back, we should all recall how we respond-
ed to the escalating horrors of the last four years," he said. "And, as we do,
there are questions which each of us must ask: What did I do? Could I have
done more? Did I let my prejudice, or my fear, overwhelm my reasoning?
And, above all, how would I react next time?"

Following is the text of a statement by President Bill Clinton on
December 13, 1996, commenting on the selection of Kofi Annan
as the new secretary general of the United Nations, followed by
excerpts from the farewell address December 17, 1996, to the Gen-
eral Assembly by Secretary General Boutros Boutros-Ghali:

CLINTON'S STATEMENT

I'm delighted by today's vote in the United Nations Security Council, selecting Kofi Annan of Ghana to be the new UN Secretary General. We are hopeful that the General Assembly will concur with the Security Council early next week.

Through his decades of work at the United Nations and in the international arena, Kofi Annan has established excellent working relations with many countries, including the United States. Over the last four years as UN Undersecretary for Peacekeeping, and throughout his impressive career, he has proven himself an able and energetic manager—professional, impartial, well-versed in the issues at hand, and a true proponent of reform. We are confident he will take concrete steps to inspire the world to support the UN, inspire the UN to live up to its ideals, and transform those ideals into action.

Since its founding more than half a century ago, the United Nations has been a vehicle for peace and progress that has served the interests of America and the world. Since taking office, I have worked hard with Congress to sustain America's support for the United Nations.

Precisely because we believe in the United Nations, my Administration has also led the fight for far-reaching UN reform. To meet the challenges of the 21st century, the UN must keep pace with the times—achieving its work with fewer people and resources, reducing waste and rationalizing priorities, and producing better results at lower costs. The world community needs a United Nations that spends less on overhead and outdated agencies and more on services that directly benefit people's daily lives.

I believe the United Nations must have a leader who is committed to these goals. That is why I decided we needed a new Secretary General. I knew this would be a controversial decision, but it was the right thing to do.

The outgoing UN Secretary General, Boutros Boutros-Ghali, is an honorable man who has had a great career—from the breakthrough for Middle East peace at Camp David to his leadership of the United Nations as it celebrated its 50th anniversary. Now, we must prepare the United Nations for the demands of the next 50 years. I am confident Kofi Annan will rise to this task with conviction.

I am committed to work closely with the Congress to meet America's obligations to the United Nations and to make good on our arrears. And I am sure that my nominee for our UN Ambassador, Bill Richardson, will work effectively with the new Secretary General to renew and revitalize this historic organization to take on the challenges of the future.

BOUTROS-GHALI'S STATEMENT

Five years ago, responsibility for the Office of Secretary-General was placed in my hands. I am grateful to have had the privilege of serving the Peoples of the United Nations during this time. Today I am proud of the way the United Nations has responded to the challenges of these difficult years. I have had the difficult task to guide the United Nations during the post-cold war period. The next century has already begun. Great transformations do not wait for the calendar. The past five years opened with optimism and enthusiasm. Member States called the United Nations to take action on an unprecedented scale: for peace, development, democratization and reform.

My first act for peace as Secretary-General was to sign at Chapultepec on 16 January 1992, the agreement on peace for El Salvador, a great achievement of my distinguished predecessor. The first ever Summit Meeting of the Security Council took place on 31 January 1992. My report issued in May 1992, "An Agenda for Peace", launched an international debate on preventive diplomacy, peacemaking, peace-keeping and the new concept of post-conflict peace-building. From El Salvador to Cambodia, to Angola and Mozambique, the United Nations adapted United Nations peace-keeping to unprecedented forms of conflict.

Development also was given a new opportunity. The easing of ideological tensions and the expected "peace dividend" raised hopes for development cooperation. The landmark Earth Summit in Rio in June 1992 brought the first ever global plan—Agenda 21—for a new and equitable partnership to achieve sustainable development.

Democratization became a new feature of the work of the United Nations. Member States, new and old, turned to the United Nations for support in democratization. The United Nations quickly developed its capacity to provide electoral assistance.

As I entered the Office of Secretary-General, it was clear to me that the United Nations would have to undergo comprehensive change. I simplified

Secretariat structures and began a process of managerial reform. This, in turn, stimulated more demand for reform. Throughout the period leading up to the fiftieth anniversary of the United Nations, reform was the issue of the day. In Governments, universities and foundations, proposals for restructuring and re-organization were drawn up.

But the middle years of this half-decade were deeply troubled. Disillusion set in. Where peace-keepers were asked to deal with warfare, serious setbacks occurred. The first came in Somalia, and weakened the will of the world community to act against genocide in Rwanda. In Bosnia too hard choices were avoided. The concept of peace-keeping was turned on its head, and worsened by the serious gap between mandates and resources.

The volume of assistance to developing countries was not only failing to grow, it was in fact declining. Resources for long-term development were being diverted to emergency efforts. Africa was hit hardest. Despite high hopes for democratization, a counter-trend emerged. Human rights atrocities reached unprecedented levels. The horror of ethnic cleansing emerged. In some countries, democratization proved more difficult than expected, creating political instability, social disarray and economic disappointment. Democratization in some cases slowed or was even eroded.

And it emerged that the conditions for major reform of the United Nations did not yet exist. The decisions required far exceeded the authority of any Secretary-General. Extensive reform of the United Nations can only emerge from a consensus among Member States on the goals of reform. Until such a consensus exists, and until the political will emerges to take hard decisions, and to reform inter-governmental machinery along with Secretariat structures, major institutional reform is impossible. And throughout this time of disillusion, the Organization's financial crisis continued to pose a serious obstacle to reform.

The United Nations is emerging from the mood of disillusion. The fiftieth anniversary brought an impressive recommitment by Member States to their world Organization. A new sense of maturity seems possible. We have begun to restore the logic of United Nations peace-keeping, and to clarify our approach to the range of instruments contained in the Charter. The division of labour between the United Nations and regional organizations continues to improve. . . .

For democratization, a more comprehensive and effective United Nations approach is taking shape. Beyond help in holding free and fair elections, the United Nations today offers a range of assistance, from support for a culture of democratization to institution-building. To succeed over time, democratization within a nation must be supported by a process of democratization among nations. The democratization of the international system is one of the greatest tasks ahead.

The past few years have brought a new and wide recognition—that reform is well under way. The path forward can now be seen. Roles and responsibilities are more clearly understood. Key issues of intergovernmental reform—relating to the Security Council, assessments, and peace-keeping debts—are seen to be linked. Proposals are being put forward by Member States for the settlement of arrears. Most important, there is a new recognition that reform is not an end in itself. Reform which seeks to turn the United Nations away from its fundamental responsibilities under the Charter can be legitimately opposed. The test of true reform will be whether it will improve the capacity of the United Nations to meet those responsibilities and to advance the common objectives of the Peoples of the United Nations and its Member States.

The downward trend has been broken. What is emerging is a United Nations more mature in outlook and stronger in achievement. A United Nations aware not only of its potentialities but also of its limits. Enthusiasm. Disillusion. Realism. This has been the history of the United Nations over the past five years. Now, let us look to the future.

Some old problems appear to be solved. But new problems—and old problems in new forms—have emerged. For some, the world seems more secure. But for many others, devastation, death and despair have become more common. For some, economic progress races forward. But for vast numbers of others, stark poverty crushes hope in every dimension of personal and community life. What use the world makes of the United Nations over the next few years can affect the course of world affairs for generations to come.

Most immediately there remains the financial crisis. Just as my distinguished predecessor said to this Assembly in his last address, I too must state that I have been unable to resolve the financial crisis. It is a threat to the future of the United Nations that began over a decade ago. We know what causes it and what is needed to end it. It is not the result of mismanagement. It is the refusal to fulfil a treaty obligation. Now that a new Secretary-General is being appointed, all arrears should be paid at once, as has been promised so often in the past few months.

In saying farewell to this great Assembly, I want to stress that nothing is more precious to the United Nations than its reputation. That reputation rests on four pillars: impartiality, equity, efficiency and achievement. A fifth principle is independence. If one word above all is to characterize the role of the Secretary-General, it is independence. The holder of this office must never be seen as acting out of fear of, or in an attempt to curry favour with, one State or group of States. Should that happen, all prospects for the United Nations would be lost. The Secretary-General's loyalty must be international and nothing but international, and the international civil service must be a real civil service.

Throughout the past five years, the first thing I thought of when I awoke in the morning were my responsibilities as Secretary-General to the ideal of the Charter and independence and credibility of the Organization.

By way of conclusion, my thoughts go to all the men and women of goodwill with whom I have worked over these past years to confront the difficulties that we have all faced together. I have appreciated their competence, their devotion and their self-denial. Sometimes I have also had to pay tribute to their sacrifices.

All those men and women who are devoted to the general interests of the international community are the real wealth—the real future—of this world Organization. I assure them today of my highest consideration and deepest gratitude.

In particular, I should like to congratulate the new Secretary-General of the United Nations, Kofi Annan, who has served this institution for many years with tenacity, competence and great energy. I am convinced that his varied experience will be useful in resolving problems that he will confront and in defending the interests of the Secretariat and of the entire staff of this world Organization.

Finally, I would like to thank the General Assembly for having entrusted to me five years ago this high post, in which I have continued the work that I have been conducting for so long now in the service of peace, development and human rights.

You can count on me to continue to place my energies in the service of the great ideals of the Charter. You can count on me to continue to defend the United Nations.

BROADCASTERS ON NEW TELEVISION RATING SYSTEM
December 19, 1996

Television broadcasters on December 19 unveiled a system for rating programs to give parents help in deciding what their children should be allowed to watch. Based on the type of content appropriate for various age groups, the system was similar to one the motion picture industry had used for nearly three decades.

Network executives adopted the rating system as a result of political pressure from Washington. Politicians for years had criticized the amount of violence and sexual content aired on television, even during the 8 p.m. to 9 p.m. "family hour." Broadcasters had opposed anything having to do with regulating the content of shows or warning viewers about that content. They had lobbied unsuccessfully in Congress against legislation requiring television sets built after 1998 to have a "V-chip" capable of screening out programs with objectionable content.

Even after agreeing to the voluntary ratings, the industry said it would fight any government attempt to impose a different set of standards. Jack Valenti, who chaired a committee that developed the system, warned that broadcasters would turn to "very expensive" lawyers to fight government regulation on First Amendment grounds. Valenti was president of the Motion Picture Association of America.

Political leaders from both parties took credit for finally getting television executives to agree to a rating system. President Bill Clinton appeared to have gotten the most political mileage on the issue. It was during a February 29 meeting at the White House that top television executives formally agreed to develop a rating system.

The rating system had plenty of critics, including numerous organizations that lobbied on behalf of children. They insisted the system would not give parents adequate information on which to base judgments about which programs their children should be allowed to watch. They advocated a content-based system under which programs would be rated by the amount of violence, foul language, or sexually-oriented situations they contained.

Some observers saw the battle over the rating system as one item in the broader question of who would deliver and control the content appearing on the next generation of machines that would combine televisions and computers. Given the rapid growth of the Internet as a source of both serious information and entertainment, many broadcasters were concerned about losing much of their audience. Adopting a rating system was one way for broadcasters to demonstrate that they were listening to public concerns about the content on television.

The Rating System

The system adopted by television broadcasters, to be put in effect at the beginning of 1997, contained six ratings that were to be applied to all programs except news and sports. Each rating would appear in the upper left corner of the television screen for the first fifteen seconds of a program. Valenti said newspapers and publications such as TV Guide *would be asked to carry the ratings with their television listings.*

Two of the ratings were for programs intended specifically for children: TV-Y designated programs considered appropriate for all children and TV-Y7 designated programs appropriate for children age seven and above.

TV-G designated programs that most parents would find suitable for all ages; TV-PG (for "parental guidance") designated programs containing material that parents might consider unsuitable for young children. Finally, TV-14 designated programs containing material that parents might find unsuitable for children under fourteen and TV-M designated programs that should be viewed by adults and therefore might be unsuitable for children under seventeen.

Valenti said the broadcasters adopted the system because it met three criteria: it was "simple to use, easy to understand, unconfusing"; it gave both suggested age categories and an indication of the type of content in a program; and it was simple enough that newspapers probably would be willing to carry the ratings in their television listings.

Producers of television shows would apply ratings to their own shows. Valenti said this was the only realistic way to apply the ratings to the estimated two thousand hours of programming aired on television in the United States each day. In comparison, he noted that the movie rating system grades an average of only two movies daily.

A nineteen-member board, chaired by Valenti, would monitor the system and handle any controversy about ratings of specific programs. The other members included six representatives each from the cable television industry, the creators of television programs, and television broadcasters.

Valenti said the system would be compatible with the V-chip when it became available. Manufacturers would ensure that V-chips conformed with the rating system, and parents could then program their individual sets to block out programs with certain ratings.

Months before the broadcasters unveiled their system, critics began challenging the direction in which the television industry was headed. Most of the criticism came from educators, religious leaders, pediatricians, and groups advocating higher quality programming for children. Their principal argument was that the broadcasters' system was too simple and did not give parents enough information to make informed judgments about whether to allow their children to watch certain programs.

Some of these groups advocated a more complex system using the symbols "V" for violence, "L" for language, and "S" for sexual situations. Each program would be rated on a scale of 0 to 5 or 0 to 10 for each symbol. For example, a show filled with violent scenes but little sex could be rated V-5 and S-1. Advocates said this system would give parents more detailed information about program content.

Rep. Edward J. Markey, D-Mass., who sponsored the legislation requiring installation of television V-chips, said the broadcast industry should try both rating systems to determine which one was more effective. President Clinton, on the other hand, said the system adopted by the broadcasters should be tried for a year and then reviewed.

The Telecommunications Act of 1996, which contained the V-chip requirement, also directed the Federal Communications Commission (FCC) to devise a television rating system if the broadcast industry did not do so on its own. The FCC was expected to review the broadcasters' system in 1997.

Children's Programming

On a related issue, President Clinton negotiated an agreement with broadcasters under which stations would be required to air three hours each week of "educational" shows for children. Announced at the White House on July 29, the agreement applied to programs "specifically designed to meet the educational and information needs" of children age sixteen and younger.

The agreement applied to commercial and public broadcasters but not to cable systems, which are licensed at the local and state levels. The FCC would determine which kinds of programs met the required standard. The FCC on August 9 made that agreement an official rule. Under the FCC's rule, stations were required to broadcast three hours each week of shows designed specifically for children. As an alternative, stations could attempt to satisfy the FCC that they offered other programming or public service activities that would qualify as meeting the educational and informational needs of children.

Following are excerpts from a statement, "Parental Guidelines for America's Television Programming," issued by the National Association of Broadcasters, describing the rating system announced by the television industry December 19, 1996:

Advance TV Information for Parents

On February 29, 1996, all segments of the television industry joined together and voluntarily pledged that within one year they would create television program guidelines to give parents additional information to more effectively supervise the TV viewing of their young children.

The industry said the guidelines would resemble but not duplicate the Motion Picture Ratings System, to which America's parents give high approval marks. It also said the guidelines would be applied by the industry in order to handle the huge amount of programming—some 2,000 hours a day—that must be reviewed. By contrast, the movie ratings system rates two-to-three movies each day.

On December 19, 1996, the industry fulfilled its commitment by announcing the TV Parental Guidelines, which offer parents content- and age-based advance, cautionary information about TV shows. TV Parental Guidelines' objective is to be simple to use, easy to understand and handy to find.

A Comprehensive Effort To Hear All Points of View

To develop the new guidelines system, the industry formed an Implementation Group under the leadership of Motion Picture Association of America (MPAA) President Jack Valenti, the creator of the movie ratings system.

The Implementation Group represented all segments of the television industry: the national broadcast networks; affiliated, independent and public television stations nationwide; cable programmers; producers and distributors of cable programming; entertainment companies; movie studios; and members of the creative guilds representing writers, directors, producers and actors.

The Implementation Group met and consulted with scores of parental, medical, religious, child advocacy and educational groups to get their views on how the parental guidelines system should be structured.

The TV Parental Guidelines

The guidelines that emerged from this process contain both content- and age-based information designed to communicate clear and consistent guidance about the vast amount of programming to America's parents, and to aid them in deciding what is appropriate for their young children to watch on television.

The guidelines are modeled after the movie ratings system, which the parents of America have known and trusted since 1968. The movie ratings categories are familiar to virtually all adults in the United States, and in annual surveys conducted since 1969, America's parents have given the system high marks. Currently, 79 percent of parents with children under age 13 say that the movie ratings are useful in helping them make decisions about the movie going of their children.

America's parents are also supportive of the new TV Parental Guidelines, according to a national survey conducted by Peter D. Hart Research Associates and Public Opinion Strategies, two highly-respected research firms. A poll of 1,207 parents with children under age 18 found that large majorities had positive attitudes about specific elements of the guideline system, with 90 percent of parents expressing an overall favorable attitude toward the guidelines.

More than four out of five parents (83 percent) said a television rating system similar to the movie system would be helpful to them, and after hearing the details of the TV Parental Guidelines, 90 percent said they favor the new system—58 percent "strongly" in favor and 32 percent "somewhat" in favor.

The TV Parental Guidelines follow:

The following categories apply to programs designed for children:

TV-Y: All Children. This program is designed to be appropriate for all children. Whether animated or live-action, *the themes and elements in this program are specifically designed for a very young audience, including children from ages 2–6.* This program is not expected to frighten younger children.

TV-Y7: Directed to Older Children. This program is designed for children age 7 and above. It may be more appropriate for children who have acquired the developmental skills needed to distinguish between make-believe and reality. *Themes and elements in this program may include mild physical or comedic violence, or may frighten children under the age of 7.* Therefore, parents may wish to consider the suitability of this program for their very young children.

The following categories apply to programs designed for the entire audience:

TV-G: General Audience. Most parents would find this program suitable for all ages. Although this rating does not signify a program designed specifically for children, most parents may let younger children watch this program unattended. *It contains little or no violence, no strong language and little or no sexual dialogue or situations.*

TV-PG: Parental Guidance Suggested. *This program may contain some material that some parents would find unsuitable for younger children. Many parents may want to watch it with their younger children. The theme itself may call for parental guidance.* The program may contain infrequent coarse language, limited violence, some suggestive sexual dialogue and situations.

TV-14: Parents Strongly Cautioned. *This program may contain some material that many parents would find unsuitable for children under 14 years of age. Parents are strongly urged to exercise greater care in monitoring this program and are cautioned against letting children under the age of 14 watch unattended.* This program may contain sophisticated themes, sexual content, strong language and more intense violence.

TV-M: Mature Audience Only. *This program is specifically designed to be viewed by adults and therefore may be unsuitable for children under 17.* This program may contain mature themes, profane language, graphic violence and explicit sexual content.

Separate Categories for Children's Programs

The Implementation Group was advised to pay special attention to the needs of young children. That advice was taken very seriously.

The children's guidelines divide at age 7 to separate programs that are designed for children of all ages from those that parents may not want their youngest children to see. According to child development experts, young children often cannot separate, or have difficulty in separating, make-believe from reality; and they are easily influenced and frightened by sights and sounds. By age 7, the cognitive abilities of children have advanced to the point where they can distinguish between the real world and the world of make-believe.

What Programs Will Receive Guidelines

The guidelines will apply to all television shows, including mini-series, specials, movies and other formats. In the case of television series, each weekly episode will be rated. Sports and news shows will not carry guidelines.

Who Rates the Programs—National and Local Responsibility

With 2,000 hours of programming to be reviewed each day, television networks, producers and distributors will apply guidelines to their shows. Logistically, it is the only rational way to deal with such a vast volume of programming. The final say in assigning program guidelines will, of course, rest with local television stations. All distributors will use and encode the common rating system of TV Parental Guidelines for use with V-chip technology, but some broadcast and cable networks may supplement the common system with additional information. HBO and Showtime will continue to offer additional information about their programming.

Displaying the Guidelines

Broadcasters and cable networks have agreed to certain standards regarding the display of the ratings. The guidelines will be shown at the beginning of each program, and will be found at the upper left-hand corner of television screens. The guidelines of many programs will begin to be displayed in January 1997.

Newspapers around the country will be asked to include the parental guidelines information in their television listings, as will *TV Guide*, on-screen cable listings and cable guides. The Newspaper Association of America, whose 1,500 members represent 87 percent of daily newspaper circulation in the U.S., has stated that because of space limitations in America's newspapers, "brevity and simplicity will tend to promote printing [the guideline icons] in newspapers." Different publications will have different timetables for beginning to provide the parental guidelines, but newspapers in the U.S. are expected to begin publishing the guidelines in early 1997.

Overseeing the TV Parental Guidelines Process

An Oversight Monitoring Board has been created to review the guidelines on a regular basis and make sure that the uniformity and consistency of the guidelines will be maintained to the greatest extent that is possible. Jack

Valenti will serve as the Board's first chairman. In addition to Mr. Valenti, there will be 18 members of the Board, including six each from the broadcast, cable and creative communities. Inquiries regarding the guidelines should be directed to: TV Parental Guidelines, P.O. Box 14097, Washington, D.C. 20004, (202) 879-9364.

The Oversight Monitoring Board will regularly hear the views of America's parents through an ongoing effort that will explore attitudes about the guideline system and the way in which the guidelines are being applied to programming. The Board has retained Peter D. Hart Research Associates and Public Opinion Strategies to conduct discussion sessions and quantitative studies throughout the coming year to determine whether the system is achieving its objective of informing America's parents. Rather than simply rely on anecdotal evidence or the views of interest groups, the Board will use the research to maintain a dialogue with parents, learn how the guidelines are being used and track how attitudes toward the system evolve over time.

Public Awareness Effort

In an effort to build public awareness of the guidelines, broadcast and cable networks will show public service announcements in both English and Spanish introducing the guidelines. Toll-free numbers have been established for people to obtain a free brochure—also in both English and Spanish—explaining the guidelines. Additional information is available on the World Wide Web. The TV Parental Guidelines home page address is *http://www.tvguidelines.org.* . . .

HOUSE ETHICS COMMITTEE ON RULES VIOLATION BY GINGRICH
December 21, 1996

Newt Gingrich, the highly partisan Republican who masterminded his party's takeover of the House of Representatives in the 1994 elections and then became the first Republican Speaker in four decades, discovered in 1996 just how tenuous political power can be. Battered by a public backlash against his use in 1995 of two partial shutdowns of the federal government to conduct a budget battle with President Bill Clinton, Gingrich spent much of 1996 out of public view. At the insistence of the party's presidential nominee, former senator Bob Dole, Gingrich was barely visible at the 1996 Republican National Convention.

Gingrich also faced serious ethical questions about his conduct. At the close of the year, a subcommittee of the House Committee on Standards of Official Conduct, commonly known as the House ethics committee, found that Gingrich had violated House rules—and brought discredit on the House—in a case involving his use of tax-exempt charities to further his political cause. The case had been pending for nearly two years. The bipartisan panel December 21 filed a "Statement of Alleged Violation," the equivalent of an indictment, which said Gingrich had not taken proper steps to ensure that his use of the charities would not bring them into conflict with federal tax law. More seriously, the committee said Gingrich had provided false and misleading information during its investigation of the matter.

The four-member subcommittee, equally divided between Republicans and Democrats, adopted the findings on a unanimous vote. Technically, the vote was 3–0, since one member, Nancy Pelosi, D-Calif., participated in the final decision making by telephone and could not vote under House rules requiring that she be present.

A humbled Gingrich accepted the subcommittee findings and admitted that his actions had "brought down on the people's house a controversy which could weaken the faith people have in their government." Because Gingrich admitted to the subcommittee's findings, the full ethics committee did not have to vote on the substance of the charges against him. The full House was to take up the question, in 1997, of whether and how Gingrich should be punished for his violation.

Another case against Gingrich was still pending before the ethics committee. It involved a complaint, filed on January 31 by House Democratic Whip David Bonior and several colleagues. That complaint alleged Gingrich received improper gifts, support, and contributions from GOPAC, a political action committee he once chaired. The committee said in September that it was reviewing the case and had not reached any conclusions about it.

Gingrich was only the second Speaker found guilty of violating House rules. The first was Jim Wright, D-Texas, who in 1989 resigned as Speaker and later resigned from the House after the ethics committee determined he had repeatedly violated rules on gifts and outside income. Ironically, it was Gingrich who doggedly pursued the case that led to Wright's downfall. (Ethics committee on Wright, Historic Documents of 1989, p. 239)

Whitewater and Campaign Finance

The finding against Gingrich came in a year during which the issue of political ethics was almost constantly before the public eye. Republicans used numerous opportunities during the year to remind voters that President Clinton, his wife Hillary Rodham Clinton, and members of the administration were under investigation by an independent counsel for their roles in the so-called Whitewater land investment deal that took place in Arkansas during the 1980s. Both the president and Mrs. Clinton gave sworn testimony in a case involving former business associates. Despite their testimony, an Arkansas jury on May 28 convicted Arkansas governor Jim Guy Tucker and President Clinton's former business partners, James B. and Susan McDougal, on bank fraud charges.

A Senate investigating committee on June 18 issued a detailed report denouncing Hillary Clinton's conduct and accusing senior White House officials of abuse of power. Democrats denounced the report as a partisan diatribe, and key Republicans—including Special Whitewater Committee Chairman Alfonse M. D'Amato of New York—later backed away from the Whitewater issue when it became clear the public was not aroused by it.

Toward the end of the election campaign, Republicans found another issue to use against Clinton and the Democrats: campaign finance. It was an issue that in previous years Democrats often used to clobber Republicans. In October Dole challenged campaign contributions that Democrats had solicited and received from foreign nationals; these contributions were politically questionable and possibly illegal. Dole was not deterred by the fact that he was one of many Republicans who had received similar contributions.

After the election, Democratic National Committee Chairman Donald L. Fowler conceded serious flaws in the party's fund-raising apparatus. The party began returning hundreds of thousands of dollars in donations that later proved suspect. On November 21 the Justice Department rejected a request by Sen. John McCain, R-Ariz., a close adviser to Dole, for an independent counsel investigation into disputed Democratic campaign donations. The department said it had the independence to investigate the issue on its own.

The Gingrich Case

Former representative Ben Jones, who unsuccessfully sought to defeat Gingrich in the 1994 elections, filed ethics complaints against him on September 7, 1994, and January 26, 1995. Jones's complaints to the ethics committee charged that Gingrich violated federal tax law by using tax-exempt charities to finance two projects of his that had partisan political agendas.

One project involved two televised "town hall" meetings—hosted by Gingrich—that were funded by the Abraham Lincoln Opportunity Foundation, a tax-exempt organization with the stated goal of helping inner-city youth. The broadcasts, called the American Opportunity Workshop, aired on July 21, 1990, and September 29, 1990. They were conceived by Gingrich and developed by GOPAC, the political action committee he chaired from 1986 to 1995. Both broadcasts contained overtly partisan content.

The ethics committee noted that the Abraham Lincoln foundation operated out of GOPAC offices, and the two organizations shared the same employees and officers. The foundation spent about $260,000 on the programs, the committee said.

The second project questioned by Jones involved a college course Gingrich taught at Kennesaw State College, in his district, during the fall of 1993, and at Reinhardt College in Georgia during the winters of 1994 and 1995. The course was called "Renewing American Civilization," and in it Gingrich expounded on one of his favorite themes: the need to replace what he called "the welfare state" with an "opportunity society." A central aspect of this theme was that liberal Democrats were responsible for a decline in America during the last half of the twentieth century and that only a Republican majority in Congress could reverse that decline.

In various letters and memos cited by the committee, Gingrich had said his course was a central element of a political movement. Describing the course to supporters, he said: "To the degree Democrats agree with our goals we will work with them but our emphasis is on the Republican Party as the primary vehicle for renewing American civilization."

The committee noted that GOPAC played a significant role in developing the course; indeed, GOPAC's executive director and two of Gingrich's assistants resigned from their positions in June 1993 to work on the course, but GOPAC continued to pay half their salaries for the next four months.

Gingrich's lectures—totaling twenty hours for each year's course—were widely distributed as videotapes and satellite broadcasts. The committee said this distribution was handled by the Kennesaw State College Foundation and the Progress and Freedom Foundation, both tax-exempt organi-

zations. Total expenditures on the course were about $300,000 in 1993 and $450,000 each in 1994 and 1995.

In both cases—the town hall broadcasts and the college courses—Gingrich should have, but did not, seek expert advice from a tax lawyer about using tax-exempt entities to support a partisan political campaign, the committee said. The committee noted that, under the federal tax code, tax-exempt organizations are prohibited "from providing any support to a political action committee."

The ethics committee hired a tax lawyer who found that the organizations used by Gingrich violated their tax-exempt status by aiding a political cause. The lawyer determined that the college courses "were intended to confer more than insubstantial benefits on Mr. Gingrich, GOPAC, and other Republican entities and candidates," the committee said.

A tax lawyer hired by Gingrich disagreed with the contention that the foundations violated their tax-exempt status. However, each of the tax lawyers told the committee that—had Gingrich sought his advice beforehand—he would have recommended that Gingrich not use the tax-exempt organizations to finance his projects.

Gingrich's False Statements

A second aspect of the case against Gingrich involved the information he provided to the ethics committee during its investigation. Some of that information later turned out to be false or misleading, the committee said.

A letter to the ethics committee dated December 8, 1994, which the committee said was prepared by Gingrich's attorney, Jan Barran, but signed by Gingrich himself, argued that GOPAC was not involved in the Renewing American Civilization course. Barran sent a more detailed letter, dated March 27, 1995, insisting, among other things, that "GOPAC has had absolutely no role in funding, promoting or administering Renewing American Civilization."

The committee said Gingrich reviewed his attorney's letters before they were submitted and was responsible for the content. It found therefore that Gingrich had provided the committee with information that he "should have known, was inaccurate, incomplete and unreliable."

The committee found that Gingrich violated House Rule 43(1), which states that: "A Member . . . shall conduct himself at all times in a manner which shall reflect creditably on the House of Representatives."

Following are excerpts from the Statement of Alleged Violation, issued December 21, 1997, by a special investigative subcommittee of the Committee on Standards of Official Conduct of the House of Representatives, in which the panel found that Speaker Newt Gingrich had violated House Rule 43(1); followed by a statement by Gingrich, in which he admitted to the violation:

COMMITTEE STATEMENT OF VIOLATION

... 6. In early 1990 GOPAC developed and carried out a project called American Opportunities Workshop ("AOW").

It consisted of producing and broadcasting a television program centered on a citizens' movement to reform government. The movement was based on three tenants [sic]:

1. Basic American Values;
2. Entrepreneurial Free Enterprise; and
3. Technological Progress.

The project also involved the recruitment of activists to set up local workshops around the broadcast in order to recruit people to the movement. The project was Mr. Gingrich's idea and he had a high level of involvement in it.

7. While AOW was described as being non-partisan, mailings sent by GOPAC to its supporters described AOW as having partisan, political goals. One letter sent over Mr. Gingrich's name stated the following:

> [W]e'll be reaching voters with our message, and helping drive down to the state and local level our politics of realignment.
>   Through the use of satellite hook-ups, not only can we reach new groups of voters not traditionally associated with our Party, but we'll be able to give them our message straight, without it being filtered and misinterpreted by liberal elements in the media.

The letter ended with the following:

> I truly believe that our Party and our President stand on the verge of a tremendous success this year, and that this workshop can be a great election year boost to us.

8. AOW consumed a large portion of GOPAC's financial resources during 1990. After one program the funding and operation of the project was transferred, with Mr. Gingrich's knowledge and approval, to the Abraham Lincoln Opportunity Foundation ("ALOF"), a corporation with a tax-exempt status under section 501(c)(3) of the Internal Revenue Code. ALOF operated out of GOPAC's offices. Its officers consisted of Howard Callaway, the Chairman of GOPAC, and Kay Riddle, Executive Director of GOPAC. In addition, the people who were listed as working for ALOF were GOPAC employees or consultants. ALOF raised and expended tax-deductible charitable contributions to carry out the project.

9. At ALOF the project was called American Citizens' Television ("ACTV") and had the same goals as AOW. . . .

10. ACTV broadcast three programs in 1990 and Mr. Gingrich continued his involvement in the project. The first two were produced by ALOF. They aired on July 21, 1990, and September 29, 1990, and were hosted by Mr. Gingrich. The last program was produced by the Council for Citizens Against

Government Waste, a 501(c)(4) organization, and did not include Mr. Gingrich. ALOF expended approximately $260,000 in regard to these programs.

11. Under the Internal Revenue Code, an organization which is exempt from taxation under section 501(c)(3) must be operated exclusively for exempt purposes. The presence of a single non-exempt purpose, if more than insubstantial in nature, will destroy the exemption regardless of the number or importance of truly exempt purposes. Conferring a benefit on private interests is a non-exempt purpose. Under the Internal Revenue Code, an organization which is exempt from taxation under section 501(c)(3) is also prohibited from providing any support to a political action committee. These prohibitions reflect Congressional concerns that tax-payer funds not be used to subsidize political activity.

12. Mr. Gingrich did not seek specific legal advice concerning the application of section 501(c)(3) of the Internal Revenue Code in regard to the facts described in paragraphs 2 through 10 and did not take affirmative steps to ensure that such legal advice was obtained by others. . . .

13. During the Preliminary Inquiry the Investigative Subcommittee ("Subcommittee") consulted with an expert in the law of tax-exempt organizations. Mr. Gingrich's activities on behalf of ALOF and the activities of others on behalf of ALOF with Mr. Gingrich's knowledge and approval were reviewed by the expert. The expert concluded that those activities violated ALOF's status under section 501(c)(3) of the Internal Revenue Code in that, among other things, those activities:

> a. were intended to confer more than insubstantial benefits on
>   GOPAC and Republican entities and candidates; and
> b. provided support to GOPAC.

14. The Subcommitee also heard from tax counsel retained by Mr. Gingrich for the purposes of this Preliminary Inquiry. According to Mr. Gingrich's tax counsel, this type of activity would not violate ALOF's status under section 501(c)(3) of the Internal Revenue Code.

15. Both the Subcommittee's expert and Mr. Gingrich's tax counsel agree that had they been consulted about this type of activity prior to its taking place, they would have advised that it not be conducted under the auspices of an organization exempt from taxation under section 501(c)(3) of the Internal Revenue Code.

16. If the legal advice described in paragraph 15 had been sought and followed, most, if not all, of the tax-deductible charitable contributions would not have been used for the activities described in paragraphs 2 through 10. As a result, the public controversy involving the legality of a Member's involvement with an organization exempt from taxation under section 501 (c)(3) of the Internal Revenue Code concerning activities described in paragraphs 2 through 10 would not have occurred.

17. In December 1992, Mr. Gingrich began to develop a movement which became known as Renewing American Civilization. The goal of this movement was the replacement of the "welfare state" with an "opportunity society." . . .

19. It was intended that a Republican majority would be part of the movement.

20. One aspect of the movement was to "professionalize" the House Republicans. One method for doing this was to use the movement's message to attract voters, resources, and candidates.

21. GOPAC was one of the institutions that was instrumental in developing and disseminating the message of the movement. In early 1993 Mr. Gingrich, as GOPAC's General Chairman, was instrumental in determining that virtually the entire political program for GOPAC in 1993 and 1994 would be centered on developing, disseminating, and using the message of Renewing American Civilization. . . .

23. In or about late 1992 or early 1993, Mr. Gingrich decided to teach a course. It was also entitled Renewing American Civilization. The course lasted ten weeks and devoted a separate session to each of the "five pillars" and each of the three substantive areas.

24. GOPAC had a number of roles in regard to the course. They included:

   a. Starting in or about February 1993, employees and consultants for GOPAC were involved in developing the course. As of June 1, 1993, Jeffrey Eisenach, GOPAC's Executive Director, and two of his assistants, resigned from their positions at GOPAC to manage the operations of the course. They did, however, maintain a consulting contract under which GOPAC paid one-half of their salaries through September 30, 1993. . . .

   d. GOPAC employees took part in fundraising for the course.

   e. GOPAC was involved in the promotion of the course. . . .

   f. In letters sent by GOPAC, a partisan, political role for the course was described. . . .

25. The course was taught at Kennesaw State College in the fall of 1993 and was taught at Reinhardt College in the winters of 1994 and 1995.

26. Each year the course consisted of forty hours of lectures. Mr. Gingrich presented twenty hours of lecture and a co-professor from each of the respective colleges was responsible for the other twenty hours of the course.

27. Each year the course was taught, it was also broadcast throughout the United States via satellite and local cable channels, and distributed via videotape and audiotape. The broadcasts and tapes only encompassed the twenty hours of lectures presented by Mr. Gingrich. Kennesaw State College Foundation and the Progress and Freedom Foundation were responsible for this dissemination of the course; Reinhardt College was not.

28. The money raised and expended for the course was used primarily for the dissemination of the course as described in paragraph 27. In 1993 course expenditures amounted to approximately $300,000, in 1994 course expenditures amounted to approximately $450,000, and in 1995 course expenditures amounted to approximately $450,000.

29. The main message of the course and the main message of the movement was renewing American civilization by replacing the welfare state with

an opportunity society. "Renewing American Civilization" was also the main message of GOPAC and the main message of virtually every political and campaign speech made by Mr. Gingrich in 1993 and 1994. The course was, among other things, the primary means for developing and disseminating this message. . . .

35. From in or about June 1993 through in or about December 1993, the course was funded and operated with tax-exempt funds under the auspices of the Kennesaw State College Foundation, an organization exempt from taxation under section 501(c)(3) of the Internal Revenue Code. From in or about December 1993 through in or about July 1995, the course was funded and operated under the auspices of the Progress and Freedom Foundation, an organization exempt from taxation under section 501(c)(3) of the Internal Revenue Code. In 1994 and 1995 the course was taught at Reinhardt College, an organization exempt from taxation under section 501(c)(3) of the Internal Revenue Code.

36. Under the Internal Revenue Code, an organization which is exempt from taxation under section 501(c)(3) must be operated exclusively for exempt purposes. The presence of a single non-exempt purpose, if more than insubstantial in nature, will destroy the exemption regardless of the number or importance of truly exempt purposes. Conferring a benefit on private interests is a non-exempt purpose. Under the Internal Revenue Code, an organization which is exempt from taxation under section 501(c)(3) is also prohibited from any participation in a political campaign or from providing any support to a political action committee. These prohibitions reflect Congressional concerns that tax-payer funds not be used to subsidize political activity.

37. Although Mr. Gingrich consulted with the House Committee on Standards of Official Conduct ("Committee") prior to teaching the course, he did not seek specific legal advice concerning the application of section 501(c)(3) of the Internal Revenue Code in regard to the facts described in paragraphs 17 through 35 from an appropriate source and did not take affirmative steps to ensure that such legal advice was obtained by others from an appropriate source.

38. During the Preliminary Inquiry the Subcommittee consulted with an expert in the law of tax-exempt organizations. Mr. Gingrich's activities on behalf of the Kennesaw State College Foundation, the Progress and Freedom Foundation, and Reinhardt College in regard to the course entitled "Renewing American Civilization" and the activities of others on behalf of those organizations with Mr. Gingrich's knowledge and approval were reviewed by the expert. The expert concluded that those activities violated Kennesaw State College Foundation's status under section 501(c)(3) of the Internal Revenue Code, the Progress and Freedom Foundation's status under section 501(c)(3) of the Internal Revenue Code, and Reinhardt College's status under section 501(c)(3) of the Internal Revenue Code in that, among other things, those activities were intended to confer more than insubstantial benefits on Mr. Gingrich, GOPAC, and other Republican entities and candidates.

39. The Subcommittee also heard from tax counsel retained by Mr. Gingrich for the purposes of this Preliminary Inquiry. According to Mr. Gingrich's tax counsel, this type of activity would not violate the status of the Kennesaw State College Foundation, the Progress and Freedom Foundation, or Reinhardt College under section 501(c)(3) of the Internal Revenue Code.

40. Both the Subcommittee's expert and Mr. Gingrich's tax counsel agree that had they been consulted about this type of activity prior to its taking place, they would have advised that it not be conducted under the auspices of an organization exempt from taxation under section 501(c)(3) of the Internal Revenue Code.

41. If the legal advice described in paragraph 40 had been sought and followed, most, if not all, of the tax-deductible charitable contributions would not have been used for the activities described in paragraphs 17 through 35. As a result, the public controversy involving the legality of a Member's involvement with organizations exempt from taxation under section 501(c)(3) of the Internal Revenue Code concerning activities described in paragraphs 17 through 35 would not have occurred.

42. On or about September 7, 1994, a complaint was filed against Mr. Gingrich with the Committee. The complaint centered on the course entitled "Renewing American Civilization." Among other things, it alleged that Mr. Gingrich had used his congressional staff to work on the course and that he had misused organizations that were exempt from taxation under section 501(c)(3) of the Internal Revenue Code because the course was a partisan, political project, with significant involvement by GOPAC, and was not a permissible activity for a section 501(c)(3) organization.

43. On or about October 4, 1994, Mr. Gingrich wrote the Committee in response to the complaint and primarily addressed the issues concerning the use of congressional staff for the course. In doing so he stated:

> I would like to make it abundantly clear that those who were paid for course preparation were paid by either the Kennesaw State Foundation, [sic] the Progress and Freedom Foundation or GOPAC. . . . Those persons paid by one of the aforementioned groups include: Dr. Jeffrey Eisenach, Mike DuGally, Lana Rogers, Patty Stechschultez [sic], Parnla Prochnow, Dr. Steve Hanser, Joe Gaylord and Nancy Desmond.

44. On or about October 31, 1994, the Committee sent Mr. Gingrich a letter asking for additional information concerning the allegations of misuse of tax-exempt organizations in regard to the course. The Committee also asked for information relating to the involvement of GOPAC in various aspects of the course.

45. Whether any aspects of the course were political or partisan in their motivation, application, or design was material to the Committee's deliberations in regard to the complaint. Whether GOPAC had any involvement with the course was also material to the Committee's deliberations in regard to the complaint.

46. In November 1994, Mr. Gingrich retained counsel to represent him in connection with the Committee's investigation. According to Mr. Gingrich, he then relied on counsel to respond to and otherwise address issues and concerns raised by the Committee. Mr. Gingrich, however, remained ultimately responsible for fully, fairly, and accurately responding to the Committee.

47. Between on or about December 8, 1994, and on or about December 15, 1994, Mr. Gingrich delivered or caused to be delivered to the Committee a letter dated December 8, 1994, signed by Mr. Gingrich in response to the Committee's letter described in paragraph 44.

According to testimony before the Subcommittee, the six-page December 8, 1994 letter was prepared by Mr. Gingrich's attorney and submitted to Mr. Gingrich for review during the transition following the 1994 election. In the December 8, 1994 letter Mr. Gingrich made the following statements:

> [The course] was, by design and application, completely nonpartisan. It was and remains about ideas, not politics. (Page 2).
>
> The idea to teach "Renewing American Civilization" arose wholly independent of GOPAC, because the course, unlike the committee, is non-partisan and apolitical. My motivation for teaching these ideas arose not as a politician, but rather as a former educator and concerned American citizen . . . . (Page 4).
>
> The fact is, "Renewing American Civilization" and GOPAC have never had any official relationship. (Page 4).
>
> GOPAC . . . is a political organization whose interests are not directly advanced by this non-partisan educational endeavor. (Page 5).
>
> As a political action committee, GOPAC never participated in the administration of "Renewing American Civilization." (Page 4).
>
> Where employees of GOPAC simultaneously assisted the project, they did so as private, civic-minded individuals contributing time and effort to a 501(c)(3) organization. (Page 4).
>
> Anticipating media or political attempts to link the Course to [GOPAC], "Renewing American Civilization" organizers went out of their way to avoid even the appearances of improper association with GOPAC. Before we had raised the first dollar or sent out the first brochure, Course Project Director Jeff Eisenach resigned his position at GOPAC. (Page 4).

48. On or about January 26, 1995, an amended complaint against Mr. Gingrich was filed with the Committee. The amended complaint encompassed the same allegations as the complaint described in paragraph 42, as well as additional allegations.

49. On or about March 27, 1995, Mr. Gingrich's attorney prepared, signed, and caused a fifty-two page letter dated March 27, 1995, with 31 exhibits to be delivered to the Committee responding to the amended complaint. The March 27, 1995 letter was submitted to Mr. Gingrich shortly before it was filed with the Committee.

50. Prior to the letter from Mr. Gingrich's attorney being delivered to the Committee, Mr. Gingrich reviewed it and approved its submission to the Committee. The ultimate responsibility for the accuracy of information submitted to the Committee remained with Mr. Gingrich.

51. The March 27, 1995 letter contains the following statements:

> As Ex. 13 demonstrates, the course solicitation . . . materials are completely non-partisan. (Page 19, footnote 1).
> GOPAC did not become involved in the Speaker's academic affairs because it is a political organization whose interests are not advanced by this non-partisan educational endeavor. (Page 35).
> The Renewing American Civilization course and GOPAC have never had any relationship, official or otherwise. (Page 35).
> As noted previously, GOPAC has had absolutely no role in funding, promoting, or administering Renewing American Civilization. (Pages 34-35).
> GOPAC has not been involved in course fundraising and has never contributed any money or services to the course. (Page 28).
> Anticipating media or political attempts to link the course to GOPAC, course organizers went out of their way to avoid even the appearance of associating with GOPAC. Prior to becoming Course Project Director, Jeffrey Eisenach resigned his position at GOPAC and has not returned. (Page 36).

52. Mr. Gingrich engaged in conduct that did not reflect creditably on the House of Representatives in that: regardless of the resolution of whether the activities described in paragraphs 2 through 41 constitute a violation of section 501(c)(3) of the Internal Revenue Code, by failing to seek and follow the legal advice described in paragraphs 15 and 40, Mr. Gingrich failed to take appropriate steps to ensure that the activities described in paragraphs 2 through 41 were in accordance with section 501(c)(3) of the Internal Revenue Code; and on or about March 27, 1995, and on or about December 8, 1994, information was transmitted to the Committee by and on behalf of Mr. Gingrich that was material to matters under consideration by the Committee, which information, as Mr. Gingrich should have known, was inaccurate, incomplete, and unreliable.

53. The conduct described in this Statement of Alleged Violation constitutes a violation of Rule 43(1) of the Rules of the United States House of Representatives.

GINGRICH'S STATEMENT

The investigative subcommittee of the Committee on Standards of Official Conduct has issued a statement of alleged violation. With great sadness, I have filed an answer which admits to that violation. I would like to comment on the statement as follows:

When I was elected to the House by my district in Georgia, I was dedicated to big ideas. I was and am in love with this country and convinced of its unlimited promise. At heart I'm a college professor, so I believed—and still do believe—that the theory of America is what makes us special in history. Our government exists to serve and protect a free people, born in equality with rights granted by God. It is the truths that define America that will save us: our problems can be eased by government, but only the American people can solve them.

This resounding belief was why I ran for office. Every time I make my way to the House chamber down the great marble halls of the Capitol, it fills me with excitement. And it has from the very first day. From the first day I was full of plans for organization and initiatives that I hoped would help light a fire under people. I wanted to inspire the American people to take control of their destiny.

I was overconfident, and in some way, naive. With deep sadness, I agree. I did not seek legal counsel when I should have in order to ensure clear compliance with all applicable laws, and that was wrong. Because I did not, I brought down on the people's house a controversy which could weaken the faith people have in their government. In responding to complaints in this matter, I did not manage the effort intensely enough to thoroughly direct or review information being submitted to the committee on my behalf. In my name and over my signature, inaccurate, incomplete and unreliable statements were given to the committee, but I did not intend to mislead the committee.

I accept responsibility for this, and I deeply regret it.

I did not seek personal gain, but my actions did not reflect creditably on the House of Representatives.

Clearly, I wish this had not happened. I appreciate the subcommittee's commitment of time, energy and integrity to correct it.

The ethics process is important, and the integrity of the people's house is central to honest self-government. I remain committed to supporting the ethics process and to ensuring that the public can look to our Capitol with pride.

In the future, I will aggressively seek to ensure that every activity is well within the rules and to the credit to the House.

Since this remains a pending matter, there will be no further comment.

PEACE AGREEMENT ENDING THE CIVIL WAR IN GUATEMALA
December 29, 1996

Guatemala's civil war—the longest-running and bloodiest conflict in Central America and one of the most intractable conflicts anywhere in the world—came to an end December 29. In a ceremony in Guatemala City, leaders of the Guatemalan government and a leftist rebel force signed the final two of twelve peace agreements negotiated since 1994. The peace ceremony, witnessed by United Nations Secretary General Boutros Boutros-Ghali and other world leaders, formally ended a war that began in 1961 and was responsible for the deaths or disappearances of an estimated 140,000 people.

In signing the final peace accord on behalf of the UN, Boutros-Ghali praised both sides for having the political will to "leave confrontation behind and turn their energies to peace development and reconciliation." The UN had mediated the Guatemala negotiations for two years.

The War and Its Toll

The Guatemalan conflict had its roots in the cold war, the sharp cleavages between economic classes and races in the country, and Washington's desire to make Central America a safe place for U.S. business. Most analysts dated the true beginnings of the war as 1954, when the CIA engineered a coup d'etat that ousted President Jacobo Arbenz Guzman, who had been democratically elected. Arbenz had angered the United Fruit Company, which appealed to the Eisenhower administration for intervention to protect its operations in Guatemala. The CIA installed a military-backed regime in power, the first in a long line of regimes controlled by the military either openly or behind the scenes.

In 1961 a small group of military officers launched a rebellion, which in a few years blossomed into a full-scale civil war led by leftist guerrillas based in mountain villages in the northeastern part of the country. The rebellion prompted a right-wing reaction from the wealthy elite who controlled the economy and the military.

In 1982 President Efrain Rios Montt, an army general, launched a attack on the Mayan Indian villages where the rebels were assumed to be based. Rios Montt's campaign, called "beans or bullets," destroyed more than four hundred villages and resulted in the deaths of tens of thousands of civilians, most of them impoverished Indians. The military campaign succeeded in weakening the guerrillas, who were driven into hiding in the remote mountains and were never again a significant threat to the government. The military also targeted intellectuals, human rights activists, labor leaders, students, and others believed to sympathize with the guerrillas. Some of these people were assassinated; others simply "disappeared" and were presumed to have been killed by the military or paramilitary death squads.

Horrified by the military's brutality, the U.S. Congress in 1983 cut off military aid to Guatemala, one of several actions that helped persuade the military to allow a return to nominal civilian government in 1985. Even so, the country's civilian presidents remained under the ultimate control of the military.

Efforts Toward Peace

Several attempts to negotiate an end to the war failed until the United Nations stepped in as mediator in 1994 and secured agreements on a timetable for negotiations, respect for human rights, and the rights of the Indian population. Even after the talks were on track, it was unclear how far the military would allow the civilian governments to go in negotiating peace.

The turning point was the election of a new president in January 1996. Alvaro Arzu, who campaigned on a promise to deliver peace within a year, moved quickly to take control of the military by sacking more than half its generals and ordering an end to the military's counterinsurgency campaign. Arzu replaced the fired generals with younger officers who saw the need for reform, including civilian control of the military.

Renewed talks between the government and the guerrillas produced a substantive agreement in May on social and economic reform issues, including a more equitable distribution of land ownership. Another landmark agreement signed in Mexico City on September 19 called for sharp reductions in the size and role of the military. Both sides said that agreement marked the de facto end to the civil war.

Negotiations toward final agreements on outstanding issues nearly broke down in late October, when Arzu denounced a guerrilla commander for kidnapping the eighty-four-year-old wife of a prominent businessman. After the guerrillas apologized, saying the commander had acted without authorization, the peace talks resumed. The two sides agreed to a formal cease-fire on December 4 and three days later signed an agreement on constitutional and electoral reforms intended to broaden political participation.

The way to final agreement was cleared by one of the most controversial actions of the peace process: enactment of a comprehensive amnesty. With the backing of the guerrillas and the military, Arzu on December 18 pushed through the National Assembly a bill giving amnesty for crimes committed during the course of the war. Excluded from the amnesty were the crimes of genocide, torture, and forced disappearance.

Arzu, his political allies, and rebel leaders said the amnesty was necessary to close the wounds of the war. Human rights advocates denounced the measure, saying it would allow military officials and rebels who had committed despicable crimes to go unpunished. "The attitude is one of erasing the page and starting all over again, and that is simply unacceptable because we cannot tolerate impunity," the New York Times *quoted Guatemalan human rights lawyer Karen Fischer as saying.*

Despite the anger generated by the amnesty, the signing of the final peace agreement, on December 29, was a time of joyful celebration for Guatemalans, many of whom had not been alive when the war started and only dimly understood what the fighting was about. The four top commanders of the rebel force returned from their base in Mexico City and participated in a ceremony witnessed by Mexican president Ernesto Zedillo and the presidents from the four other Central American countries. Thousands of Indians crowded into Guatemala City's central square, where the government had installed a permanent, gas-fired Flame of Peace.

Following is the text of the Agreement on a Firm and Lasting Peace, signed in Guatemala City on December 29, 1996, by representatives of the Guatemalan government and the rebel force, the Unidad Revolucionaria Nacional Guatemalteca (Guatemalan National Revolutionary Unity), and witnessed by UN Secretary General Boutros Boutros-Ghali:

Whereas:

The signing of this Agreement puts an end to more than three decades of armed conflict in Guatemala and thus to a painful era in our history,

In recent years, the search for a political solution to the armed conflict has created new opportunities for dialogue and understanding within Guatemalan society,

The country now faces the task, in which all Guatemalans must share, of preserving and consolidating peace,

To this end, the Peace Agreements provide the country with a comprehensive agenda for overcoming the root causes of the conflict and laying the foundations for a new kind of development,

Compliance with these Agreements is an historic, unavoidable commitment,

Present and future generations must be made aware of the full implications of the peace commitments,

The Government of the Republic of Guatemala and the Unidad Revolucionaria Nacional Guatemalteca (URNG) have agreed as follows:

I. Concepts

1. The Peace Agreements reflect a national consensus. They have been endorsed by the various sectors represented in the Assembly of Civil Society and outside it. Their progressive implementation must fulfil the legitimate aspirations of Guatemalans and, at the same time, unite the efforts of all behind these common objectives.

2. The Government of the Republic reaffirms its adherence to the principles and norms aimed at guaranteeing and protecting full respect for human rights, and its political determination to enforce them.

3. Population groups uprooted by the armed conflict have the right to reside and live freely in Guatemalan territory. The Government of the Republic undertakes to ensure their return and resettlement in conditions of dignity and security.

4. The Guatemalan people are entitled to know the full truth about the human rights violations and acts of violence that occurred in the context of the internal armed conflict. Shedding light objectively and impartially on what happened will contribute to the process of national reconciliation and democratization in the country.

5. Recognition of the identity and rights of indigenous peoples is essential for building a multi-ethnic, multicultural and multilingual country of national unity. Respect for and the exercise of the political, cultural, economic and spiritual rights of all Guatemalans is the foundation for a new coexistence reflecting the diversity of their nation.

6. Firm and lasting peace must be based on participatory socio-economic development that is geared to the common good and to the needs of the entire population. Such development requires social justice, as one of the cornerstones of national unity and solidarity, and sustainable economic growth as a prerequisite for meeting the population's social demands.

7. The genuine participation of citizens—both men and women—from all sectors of society is essential for achieving social justice and economic growth. The State must broaden these opportunities for participation and strengthen its own role as guiding force of national development, lawmaker, source of public investment, provider of basic services and promoter of social consensus and settlement of disputes. To that end, it must raise fiscal revenues and, as a matter of priority, channel public spending towards social investment.

8. In the search for growth, economic policy must be directed towards preventing processes of economic exclusion, such as unemployment and impoverishment, and towards optimizing the benefits of economic growth for all Guatemalans. Raising the standard of living and ensuring health care, education, social security and training for Guatemalans are preconditions for achieving sustainable development in Guatemala.

9. The State and organized sectors of society must join forces to find a solution to agrarian problems and promote rural development, both of which are the key to improving the situation of the majority of the population living

in rural areas—the population group most seriously affected by poverty, inequity and the weakness of State institutions.

10. The strengthening of civilian power is an essential prerequisite for the existence of a democratic regime. The ending of the armed conflict affords an historic opportunity to renew the country's institutions so that, working in coordination, they can guarantee Guatemalans the rights to life, liberty, justice, security, peace and the full development of the individual. The Guatemalan armed forces must adjust their functions to the new era of peace and democracy.

11. The legal integration of URNG, in conditions of security and dignity, is in the national interest and is directly related to the objective of reconciliation and the consolidation of a democratic system open to all.

12. The constitutional reforms set out in the Peace Agreements provide the fundamental substantive basis for the reconciliation of Guatemalan society within the framework of the rule of law, democratic coexistence and the full observance of and strict respect for human rights.

13. Elections are essential for Guatemala's current transition to a functional, participatory democracy. Improving the electoral regime will help to strengthen the legitimacy of public authority and facilitate the country's democratic transformation.

14. The implementation of the national agenda arising out of the Peace Agreements is a complex, long-term undertaking requiring the determination to fulfil the commitments made and the involvement of State bodies and of the country's various social and political forces. This undertaking calls for a strategy that sets realistic priorities for the gradual fulfilment of commitments, thereby ushering in a new chapter in Guatemala's history—one of development and democratic coexistence.

II. Entry into Force of the Peace Agreements

15. All agreements signed on the basis of the Framework Agreement on Democratization in the Search for Peace by Political Means, signed at Querétaro, Mexico, on 25 July 1991, and those concluded since the Framework Agreement for the Resumption of the Negotiating Process, signed at Mexico City on 10 January 1994, are hereby incorporated into this Agreement on a Firm and Lasting Peace.

Those agreements are:

(a) The Comprehensive Agreement on Human Rights, signed at Mexico City on 19 March 1994;

(b) The Agreement on Resettlement of the Population Groups Uprooted by the Armed Conflict, signed at Oslo on 17 June 1994;

(c) The Agreement on the Establishment of the Commission to Clarify Past Human Rights Violations and Acts of Violence that Have Caused the Guatemalan Population to Suffer, signed at Oslo on 23 June 1994;

(d) The Agreement on Identity and Rights of Indigenous Peoples, signed at Mexico City on 31 March 1995;

(e) The Agreement on Social and Economic Aspects and the Agrarian Situation, signed at Mexico City on 6 May 1996;

(f) The Agreement on the Strengthening of Civilian Power and on the Role of the Armed Forces in a Democratic Society, signed at Mexico City on 19 September 1996;

(g) The Agreement on the Definitive Ceasefire, signed at Oslo on 4 December 1996;

(h) The Agreement on Constitutional Reforms and the Electoral Regime, signed at Stockholm on 7 December 1996;

(i) The Agreement on the Basis for the Legal Integration of URNG, signed at Madrid on 12 December 1996;

(j) The Agreement on the Implementation, Compliance and Verification Timetable for the Peace Agreements, signed at Guatemala City on 29 December 1996.

16. With the exception of the Comprehensive Agreement on Human Rights, which has been in force since it was signed, all the agreements incorporated into the Agreement on a Firm and Lasting Peace shall enter into force formally and in full when the present Agreement is signed.

III. Expression of Gratitude

17. Upon completion of the historic negotiating process in the search for peace by political means, the Government of Guatemala and the Unidad Revolucionaria Nacional Guatemalteca wish to place on record their gratitude for the national and international efforts that have contributed to the conclusion of the Agreement on a Firm and Lasting Peace. They emphasize the role played by the National Reconciliation Commission, the Conciliation, the Assembly of Civil Society and United Nations Moderation. They also express appreciation for the support provided by the Group of Friends of the Guatemalan Peace Process, consisting of the Republic of Colombia, the United Mexican States, the Kingdom of Norway, the Kingdom of Spain, the United States of America and the Republic of Venezuela.

IV. Final Provisions

First. The Agreement on a Firm and Lasting Peace shall enter into force when it is signed.

Second. This Agreement shall be widely publicized, especially through formal education programmes.

Guatemala City, 29 December 1996.

For the Government of Guatemala:
(Signed) Gustavo PORRAS CASTEJN
(Signed) Otto PÉREZ-MOLINA, Brigadier General
(Signed) Raquel ZELAYA ROSALES
(Signed) Richard AITKENHEAD CASTILLO

For the Unidad Revolucionaria Nacional Guatemalteca:
(Signed) Ricardo RAM REZ DE LEN (Commander Rolando MORAN)
(Signed) Jorge Ismael SOTO GARCIA (Commander Pablo MONSANTO)
(Signed) Ricardo ROSALES ROMAN (Carlos GONZALES)
(Signed) Jorge Edilberto ROSAL MELÉNDEZ

For the United Nations:
(Signed) Boutros BOUTROS-GHALI

CUMULATIVE INDEX, 1992–1996

A

N

P